Images courtesy of Apple.

Don't have an iPod? Content can be viewed on any computer! Visit the text website for directions.

Want to see iPod in action?
Visit **www.mhhe.com/ipod** to view a demonstration of our iPod® content.

Website includes:

- Lecture presentations
    Audio and video
    Audio only
    Video only
- Demonstration problems[+]
- Interactive self quizzes
- Accounting videos[+]

+Available with some textbooks

McGraw-Hill's
HOMEWORK MANAGER PLUS™ online

THE COMPLETE SOLUTION

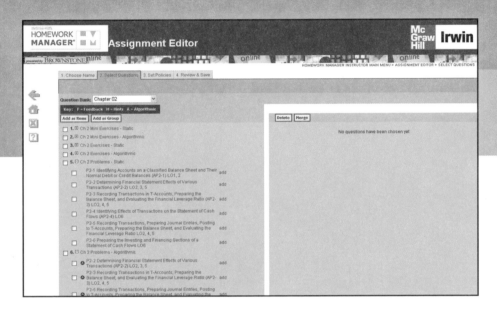

McGraw-Hill's
Homework Manager®

™ This online homework management solution contains this textbook's end-of-chapter material. Now you have the option to build assignments from static and algorithmic versions of the text problems and exercises or to build self-graded quizzes from the additional questions provided in the online test bank.

Features:

- Assigns book-specific problems/exercises to students
- Provides integrated test bank questions for quizzes and tests
- Automatically grades assignments and quizzes, storing results in one grade book
- Dispenses immediate feedback to students regarding their work

McGraw-Hill's
HOMEWORK MANAGER PLUS HM
THE COMPLETE SOLUTION

Spiceland/Sepe/Nelson/
Tomassini
Intermediate Accounting, 5/e
978-0-07-332445-6

INTERMEDIATE ACCOUNTING
FIFTH EDITION

2 TERM

Interactive Online Version
of this Textbook

In addition to the textbook, students can rely on this online version of the text for a convenient way to study. The interactive content is fully *integrated* with McGraw-Hill's Homework Manager® system to give students quick access to relevant content as they work through problems, exercises, and practice quizzes.

Features:
- Online version of the text *integrated* with McGraw-Hill's Homework Manager

- Students referred to appropriate sections of the online book as they complete an assignment or take a practice quiz

- Direct link to related material that corresponds with the learning objective within the text

McGraw-Hill's Homework Manager PLUS™ system combines the power of McGraw-Hill's Homework Manager® with the latest interactive learning technology to create a comprehensive, fully integrated online study package. Students working on assignments in McGraw-Hill's Homework Manager system can click a simple hotlink and instantly review the appropriate material in the Interactive Online Textbook.

By including McGraw-Hill's Homework Manager PLUS with your textbook adoption, you're giving your students a vital edge as they progress through the course and ensuring that the help they need is never more than a mouse click away. Contact your McGraw-Hill representative or visit the book's Web site to learn how to add McGraw-Hill's Homework Manager PLUS system to your adoption.

McGraw-Hill's
HM PLUS™

Imagine being able to create and access your test anywhere, at any time without installing the testing software. Now with **McGraw-Hill's EZ Test Online**, instructors can select questions from multiple McGraw-Hill test banks, author their own and then either print the test for paper distribution or give it online.

Use our EZ Test Online to help your students prepare to succeed with Apple® iPod® iQuiz.

Using our EZ Test Online you can make test and quiz content available for a student's Apple iPod.

Students must purchase the iQuiz game application from Apple for 99¢ in order to use the iQuiz content. It works on the iPod fifth generation iPods and better.

Instructors only need EZ Test Online to produce iQuiz ready content. Instructors take their existing tests and quizzes and export them to a file that can then be made available to the student to take as a self-quiz on their iPods. It's as simple as that.

Intermediate Accounting

Volume I

Intermediate Accounting

FIFTH EDITION

J. DAVID SPICELAND
University of Memphis

JAMES F. SEPE
Santa Clara University

MARK W. NELSON
Cornell University

LAWRENCE A. TOMASSINI
The Ohio State University

 McGraw-Hill Irwin

Boston   Burr Ridge, IL   Dubuque, IA   New York   San Francisco   St. Louis
Bangkok   Bogotá   Caracas   Kuala Lumpur   Lisbon   London   Madrid   Mexico City
Milan   Montreal   New Delhi   Santiago   Seoul   Singapore   Sydney   Taipei   Toronto

McGraw-Hill
Irwin

1 2 3 4 5 6 7 8 9 0 DOW/DOW 0 9 8

ISBN-13: 978-0-07-332465-4 (volume I)
ISBN-10: 0-07-332465-5 (volume I)

Editorial director: *Stewart Mattson*
Publisher: *Tim Vertovec*
Developmental editor II: *Daryl Horrocks*
Marketing manager: *Scott S. Bishop*
Lead project manager: *Pat Frederickson*
Production supervisor: *Gina Hangos*
Interior designer: *Laurie Entringer*
Senior photo research coordinator: *Jeremy Cheshareck*
Photo researcher: *Teri Stratford*
Senior media project manager: *Kerry Bowler*
Cover design: *Laurie Entringer*
Cover credit: *© Gerolf Kalt/zefa/Corbis*
Typeface: *10.5/12 Times Lt Std-Roman*
Compositor: *Laserwords Private Limited*
Printer: *R. R. Donnelley*

The Library of Congress has cataloged the single volume edition of this work as follows.

Library of Congress Cataloging-in-Publication Data

Intermediate accounting / J. David Spiceland ... [et al.].—5th ed.
    p. cm.
    Rev. ed. of: Intermediate accounting / J. David Spiceland, James F. Sepe, Lawrence A. Tomassini. 4th ed.
    Includes index.
    ISBN-13: 978-0-07-352687-4 (combined edition : alk. paper)
    ISBN-10: 0-07-352687-8 (combined edition : alk. paper)
    ISBN-13: 978-0-07-332465-4 (volume I : alk. paper)
    ISBN-10: 0-07-332465-5 (volume I : alk. paper)
    [etc.]
    1. Accounting. I. Spiceland, J. David, 1949- Intermediate accounting.
HF5635.S7838 2009
657'.044—dc22
                                        2008019272

About the Authors

DAVID SPICELAND

David Spiceland is professor of accounting at the University of Memphis, where he teaches intermediate accounting and other financial accounting courses at the undergraduate and master's levels. He received his BS degree in finance from the University of Tennessee, his MBA from Southern Illinois University, and his PhD in accounting from the University of Arkansas.

Professor Spiceland's primary research interests are in earnings management and educational research. He has published articles in a variety of journals including *The Accounting Review, Accounting and Business Research, Journal of Financial Research,* and *Journal of Accounting Education.* David has received university and college awards and recognition for his teaching, research, and technological innovations in the classroom.

JIM SEPE

Jim Sepe is an associate professor of accounting at Santa Clara University where he teaches primarily intermediate accounting in both the undergraduate and graduate programs. He previously taught at California Poly State University–San Luis Obispo and the University of Washington and has visited at Stanford University and the Rome campus of Loyola University of Chicago.

Professor Sepe received his BS from Santa Clara University, MBA from the University of California–Berkeley, and PhD from the University of Washington. His research interests concern financial reporting issues and the use of financial information by capital markets. He has published in *The Accounting Review,* the *Journal of Business Finance and Accounting, Financial Management,* the *Journal of Forensic Accounting,* the *Journal of Applied Business Research,* and the *Journal of Accounting Education.* He is a past recipient of the American Accounting Association's Competitive Manuscript Award and has served as a member of the editorial board of *The Accounting Review.*

Jim has received numerous awards for his teaching excellence and innovations in the classroom, including Santa Clara University's Brutocao Award for Excellence in Curriculum Innovation.

MARK NELSON

Mark Nelson is the Eleanora and George Landew Professor of Accounting at Cornell University's Johnson Graduate School of Management, where he teaches intermediate accounting at the MBA level. He received his BBA degree from Iowa State University and his MA and PhD degrees from Ohio State University. Professor Nelson has won teaching awards at Ohio State and Cornell, including three of the Johnson School's Apple Award for Teaching Excellence.

Professor Nelson's research is focused on decision making in financial accounting and auditing. His research has been published in *The Accounting Review,* the *Journal of Accounting Research, Contemporary Accounting Research, Accounting Organizations and Society, Auditing: A Journal of Practice and Theory,* and several other journals. He has won the American Accounting Association's Notable Contribution to Accounting Literature Award, and also the AAA's Wildman Medal for work judged to make the most significant contribution to the advancement of the public practice of accountancy. He has served three times as an editor or associate editor of *The Accounting Review,* and serves on the editorial boards of several journals. Professor Nelson also served for four years on the FASB's Financial Accounting Standards Advisory Council.

LARRY TOMASSINI

Larry Tomassini is professor of accounting and MIS and director of the undergraduate accounting program at The Ohio State University. He has held several endowed chair positions during his academic career, including the Ernst and Young Distinguished Professor at the University of Illinois and the Peat Marwick Mitchell Centennial Professorship in Accounting at the University of Texas.

His research has been widely published in scholarly journals, including *The Accounting Review, Accounting Horizons, Journal of Accounting Research and Contemporary Accounting Research.*

He teaches a variety of accounting courses at the undergraduate and master's levels. Recently, he was director of the Ohio State Master of Accounting Program and Vice President for Publications of the American Accounting Association.

Larry has been a pioneer in the use of Internet technology to support the teaching of accounting courses, and he has developed online versions of introductory financial and managerial accounting courses at Ohio State.

Your Vehicle to Success

"I am very impressed with this textbook and its supplements. The authors have carefully developed the book to meet the needs of a wide range of student learners. It is clearly written in understandable terms. There are many features available to provide your students with the best chance to master this material."

- Robert Gruber, University of Wisconsin—Whitewater

"SSNT have put together a comprehensive and complete intermediate accounting textbook and e-Learning system."

- Florence Atiase, University of Texas

"After reviewing this text, I would describe this text to our colleagues as an outstanding learning package and outstanding textbook."

- Habib El-Yazeed, Minnesota State University

As your students embark on their professional careers, they will be challenged to think critically and make good decisions. This new edition of *Intermediate Accounting* has been designed to ensure that your students' careers soar to the greatest heights—to be their vehicle to success!

Intermediate Accounting is the work not just of its talented authors but of the more than 130 faculty reviewers who shared their insights, experience, and opinions with us. Our reviewers helped us to build *Intermediate Accounting* into the vehicle that can propel your students to success in their accounting course, and we have the research to prove it: Spiceland was ranked #1 in improved student performance over a previous textbook, #1 in readability, and tied for #1 in overall professor satisfaction.*

Our development process began in the spring of 2006, when we received the first of what would become more than 130 in-depth reviews of *Intermediate Accounting*. A blend of Spiceland users and non-users, these reviewers explained how they use textbooks in their teaching, and many answered detailed questions about every one of Spiceland's 21 chapters. And the work of improving *Intermediate Accounting* is ongoing—even now, we're scheduling new symposia and reviewers' conferences to collect even more opinions from faculty.

Intermediate Accounting was designed from the start to be not simply a textbook, but a complete learning system, encompassing the textbook, key ancillaries, and online content, all of which are written by authors Spiceland, Sepe, Nelson, and Tomassini. The *Intermediate Accounting* learning system is built around five key attributes:

*Results from an independent market survey of intermediate accounting professors July–September 2002 by Professional Research Group, LLC.

in Intermediate Accounting

① **Clarity:** Reviewers, instructors, and students all have hailed *Intermediate Accounting*'s ability to explain both simple and complex topics in language that is clear and approachable. Its highly acclaimed conversational writing style establishes a friendly dialogue between the text and each individual student. So readable is Spiceland that we've even received letters from students who bought the book themselves—despite their instructors using competing books in the course! No surprise that Spiceland was found to be the most readable intermediate accounting textbook in independent research.*

② **A Decision-Making Perspective:** Recent events have focused public attention on the key role of accounting in providing information useful to decision makers. The CPA exam, too, is redirecting its focus to emphasize the professional skills needed to critically evaluate accounting method alternatives. *Intermediate Accounting* provides a decision maker's perspective to emphasize the professional judgment and critical thinking skills required of accountants today.

③ **Flexible Technology:** Today's accounting students have come of age in a digital world, and Spiceland's Learning System reflects that trend through its comprehensive technology package. The Coach tutorial software provides a browser-based, text-integrated multimedia environment in which to review concepts and take practice quizzes, while McGraw-Hill's Homework Manager™ system offers infinite algorithmically generated practice problems in an online environment students can access whenever they want. Feedback in McGraw-Hill's Homework Manager™ system is immediate, giving students an instant snapshot of their progress in mastering the material.

④ **Consistent Quality:** The *Intermediate Accounting* author team ensures seamless compatibility throughout the Spiceland learning package by writing every major supplement themselves: Coach, Study Guide, Instructor's Resource Manual, Solutions Manual, Testbank, and website content are all created by authors Spiceland, Sepe, Nelson, and Tomassini. The end-of-chapter material, too, is written by the author team and tested in their classrooms before being included in *Intermediate Accounting.* That dedication makes Spiceland users among the most satisfied of any intermediate accounting text.*

⑤ **A Commitment to Currency:** Few disciplines see the rapid change that accounting experiences, and the Spiceland team is committed to keeping your course up to date. The fifth edition fully integrates the latest FASB standards, including *SFAS 162*, "The Hierarchy of Generally Accepted Accounting Principles"; *SFAS 161*, "Disclosures about Derivative Instruments and Hedging Activities"; *SFAS 160*, "Noncontrolling Interests in Consolidated Financial Statements—An Amendment of ARB No. 51"; *SFAS 141(R)*, "Business Combination"; *SFAS 159* "The Fair Value Option for Financial Assets and Financial Liabilities"; *FIN 48*, "Accounting for Uncertainty in Income Taxes"; and *SFAS 158*, "Employers' Accounting for Defined Benefit Pension and Other Postretirement Plans".

*Results from an independent market survey of intermediate accounting professors July–September 2002 by Professional Research Group, LLC.

"The best available text for the intermediate accounting courses at both the graduate and undergraduate level."

- Gerard M. Engeholm, Pace University

"It is an excellent intermediate text with real-world examples and practical current commentary."

- Simon Pearlman, California State University—Long Beach

"When someone other than the authors prepares the [end-of-chapter material] they generally do not mirror the material that is presented in the chapters and they contain quite a few errors."

- Gloria Worthy, Southwest Tennessee Community College

"Overall, I find the Spiceland end-of-chapter material far superior to that in Kieso in terms of quantity, especially as it relates to the diversity of the problem material."

- Chula King, University of West Florida

What Stands Out in the Fifth Edition?

New Coauthor Mark Nelson

A new coauthor, Mark Nelson of Cornell University, has joined the Spiceland author team for the fifth edition. Mark is an award-winning full professor at Cornell University, where he has been teaching out of Spiceland for several years. Mark is an active and well-known instructor of financial accounting, while also serving as an editor of *The Accounting Review* and member of the Financial Accounting Standards Advisory Council.

> **"The Star Problems are challenging—a good way to illustrate the more difficult concepts and calculations."**
>
> *- Kenneth R. Henry,*
> *Florida International University*

Star Problems

Star problems are a new feature in the fifth edition. These are problems (more than one-third new) in each chapter that are designated by a ✯ to indicate that they are particularly challenging, requiring students to combine multiple concepts or requiring judgment beyond explicit explanation in chapter discussions.

Fair Value Option

New coverage of *SFAS No. 159* ("The Fair Value Option for Financial Assets and Financial Liabilities") and *SFAS No. 157* ("Fair Value Measurements") has been added to chapters 1, 12 and 14. Extensive assignment materials related to the fair value option have also been added.

Option to Report Liabilities at Fair Value

● LO3

SFAS No. 159 gives a company the option to value financial assets and liabilities at fair value.

Companies are not required to, but have the option to, value some or all of their financial assets and liabilities at fair value. This choice is permitted by *SFAS No. 159*, "The Fair Value Option for Financial Assets and Financial Liabilities." In Chapter 12, we saw examples of the option being applied to financial assets—specifically, companies reporting their investments in securities at fair value. Now, we see how liabilities, too, can be reported at fair value.

How does a liability's fair value change? Remember that there are two sides to every investment. For example, if a company has an investment in **General Motors'** bonds, that investment is an asset to the investor, and the same bonds are a liability to General Motors. So, the same market forces that influence the fair value of an investment in debt securities (interest rates, economic conditions, risk, etc.) influence the fair value of liabilities. For bank loans or other de~~~~at aren't t~~~~on a market ~~~~change, the mi~ of factor~ ~ill diff~

> **"A significant improvement over KWW in terms of thoroughness for schools wanting a rigorous textbook."**
>
> *- Mark Dawkins,*
> *University of Georgia*

P 2–11
Accrual accounting; financial statements

● LO4 LO6 LO8

McGuire Corporation began operations in 2009. The company purchases computer equipment from manufacturers and then sells to retail stores. During 2009, the bookkeeper used a check register to record all receipts and cash disbursements. No other journals were used. The following is a recap of the cash receipts a disbursements made during the year.

Cash receipts:
Sale of common stock	$ 50,000
Collections from customers	320,000
Borrowed from local bank on April 1, note signed requiring principal and interest at 12% to be paid on March 31, 2010	40,000

Revising a book as successful as Intermediate Accounting takes judiciousness and a strong vision of what a textbook should be. New features aren't piled on for their own sake; only when our users consistently point out an opportunity for improvement does the Spiceland team take action. The result is a book that never loses its original strengths as it gains in usefulness and flexibility with each revision.

New Coverage of International Financial Reporting Standards

The United States is moving rapidly toward converging U.S. GAAP with the **International Financial Reporting Standards (IFRS)** that are followed by most of the rest of the world. An extensive discussion has been added to Chapter 1 that provides an overview of the background and current status of the convergence process. Separate IFRS boxes within chapters highlight emerging issues and key differences between U.S. and international GAAP in the context of the chapter topics. End-of-chapter assignment material has been added to reinforce students' understanding of these differences.

INTERNATIONAL FINANCIAL REPORTING STANDARDS

Lease Classification. We discussed four classification criteria used under U.S. GAAP to determine whether a lease is a capital lease. Under IFRS, a lease is a capital lease (called a finance lease under *IAS No. 17*, "Leases"), if substantially all risks and rewards of ownership are transferred. Judgment is made based on a number of "indicators" including some similar to the specific criteria of U.S. GAAP. More judgment, less specificity, is applied.

CPA and CMA Review Questions

A new **CPA and CMA Review Questions** section has been added to the end-of-chapter material between the Exercises and Problems. The CPA questions are multiple choice questions used in the Kaplan CPA Review Course and focus on the key topics within each chapter, permitting quick and efficient reinforcement of those topics as well as conveying a sense of the way the topics are covered in the CPA exam. The CMA questions are adapted from questions that previously appeared on Certified Management Accountant (CMA) exams.

CPA AND CMA REVIEW QUESTIONS

CPA Exam Questions

KAPLAN
SCHWESER
● LO3

The following questions are used in the Kaplan CPA Review Course examination. Determine the response that best completes the stateme
1. A company leases the following asset:
- Fair value of $200,000.
- Useful life of 5 years with no salvage value.
- Lease term is 4 years.
- Annual lease payment is $30,000 and the lease rate is 11%.
- The company's overall borrowing rate is 9.5%.
- The firm can p_____ equipment____

"Intermediate Accounting is current, complete, well written, and highly detailed. It belongs in the library of anyone who is preparing for the CPA exam."

- Barbara K. Parks, American Intercontinental University – Online

Market-Leading Technology

iPod Content

Harness the power of one of the most popular technology tools students use today—the Apple iPod®. Our innovative approach allows students to download audio and video presentations right into their iPod and take learning materials with them wherever they go.

Students just need to visit the Online Learning Center at **www.mhhe .com/spiceland5e** to download our iPod content. For each chapter of the book, they will be able to download audio narrated lecture presentations, slideshows and even self-quizzes designed for use on various versions of iPods.

It makes review and study time as easy as putting on headphones.

> **"SSNT's _Intermediate Accounting_ is a very comprehensive, well-written text, that includes extensive EOC assignment material and student supplements. It achieves an effective balance of both preparer and user perspectives throughout the text."**
>
> _- Michael G. Welker,_
> _Drexel University_

> **"We encourage our students to sit for the exam, and it would prepare them for the testing mode and environment they will encounter when taking the exam."**
>
> _- Ronald Kilgore,_
> _University of Tennessee_

CPA Simulations

Students sitting for the new computerized CPA exam will confront an interface unlike any they've encountered before; from finding information in a research database to entering data into a spreadsheet, the CPA exam doesn't look or act like any other software program. Kaplan CPA Exam Simulations allow students to practice intermediate accounting concepts in a web-based environment identical to that used in the actual CPA exam. There'll be no hesitation or confusion when your students sit for the real exam: they'll know exactly what they need to do.

KAPLAN

SCHWESER

There's more to making a book better than adding new features. Organizing and updating the content is one of the foremost challenges a textbook faces, and **Intermediate Accounting** undergoes continual refinement to ensure that the content is as fresh and as easy to present and teach as possible.

Major Content Changes

A great many events have impacted accounting over the past few years, and *Intermediate Accounting* integrates every important development just where it belongs. A few examples of key updates for 5e:

- The **Testbank** is a key component of our Learning System and has been an area of major emphasis in the authors' development of the fifth edition. An extensive review process was undertaken to ensure the most complete, accurate, and flexible Testbank available. It been revised for all the changes and additions to the text. Greater variety has been added at each level of rigor. The fifth edition Testbank has over 800 new test items and more extensive explanations of solutions.
- The **financial statements** and **disclosure notes** of Google now are packaged with the textbook as well as available through a link at the text website. These replace the FedEx statements previously in a text appendix. The statements and notes are the basis for text references and cases in most chapters.
- For Chapter 5, the sections dealing with long-term contracts and profitability analysis have been rewritten for clarity. More end-of-chapter material has been added for these areas as well.
- Chapter 1, 12, and 14 have been revised to incorporate the latest fair value standards.
- Chapter 17 was extensively revised to incorporate *SFAS No. 158*, "Employers' Accounting for Defined Benefit Pension and Other Postretirement Plans." Since the publication of the Revised Fourth Edition, additional edits have been made for clarity.
- Chapter 12 has been rewritten to more clearly cover accounting for investments when the investor lacks significant influence. This section has been reordered to cover held-to-maturity investments, then trading securities, and then available-for-sale securities.
- For selected chapters, instructions are now included in the margin for using financial calculators.

> **"SSNT5e is a strong competitor to Kieso, and meets or exceeds Kieso in most areas. I prefer its organization to Kieso."**
>
> *- Derek Oler, Indiana University*

> **"An excellent intermediate text that presents the material in a well-organized manner. Readability, crisp graphics and layout make it the number once choice of students."**
>
> *- Denise de la Rosa, Grand Valley State University*

What Keeps **Spiceland** Users Coming Back?

Financial Reporting Cases

Each chapter opens with a Financial Reporting Case that places the student in the role of the decision maker, engaging the student in an interesting situation related to the accounting issues to come. Then, the cases pose questions of the student in the role of decision maker. Marginal notations throughout the chapter point out locations where each question is addressed. Finally, the questions are answered at the end of the chapter.

Decision Makers' Perspective

These sections appear throughout the text to illustrate how accounting information is put to work in today's firms. With the CPA exam placing greater focus on application of skills in realistic work settings, these discussions help your students gain an edge that will remain with them as they enter the workplace.

Earnings Management

With 86 percent of intermediate accounting faculty teaching earnings management in their courses,* Spiceland's integrated coverage of this key topic throughout the book is especially helpful.

FINANCIAL REPORTING CASE SOLUTION

1. **How can a compensation package such as this serve as an incentive to Ms. Veres?** *(p. xxx)* Stock-based plans like the restricted stock and stock options that Ms. Veres is receiving are designed to motivate recipients. If the shares awarded are restricted so that Ms. Veres is not free to sell the shares during the restriction period, she has an incentive to remain with the company until rights to the shares vest. Likewise, stock options can be made exercisable only after a specified period of employment. An additional incentive of stock-based plans is that the recipient will be motivated to take actions that will maximize the value of the shares.

2. **Ms. Veres received a "grant of restricted stock." How should NEV account for the grant?** *(p. xxx)* The compensation as...

> "The case at the beginning of each chapter is very captivating. After I read the case, I wanted to get paper and pencil and answer the questions."
>
> *- Carol Shaver,*
> *Louisiana Tech University*

DECISION MAKERS' PERSPECTIVE

Cash often is referred to as a *nonearning* asset because it earn... managers invest idle cash in either cash equivalents or short-ter... provide a return. Management's goal is to hold the minimum... conduct normal business operations, meet its obligations, and... ties. Too much cash reduces profits through lost returns, while... This tradeoff between risk and return is an ongoing choice m... ers. Whether the choice made is appropriate is an ongoing asse... creditors.

A company must have cash available for the compensating... previous section as well as for planned disbursements related... ing, and financing cash flows. However, because cash inflows... planned amounts, a company need... an additional cash cushion as a precaution against that... contingency...

> "This is an excellent feature of the book. It is so important to know why and how informatio... is used and not just memorizin... the "right" answers."
>
> *- Jeff Mankin, Lipscomb Universi...*

Real World Case 5–1
Chainsaw Al; revenue recognition and earnings management

● LO1

In May 2001, the Securities and Excha... the group with financial reporting fraud... is a recognized designer, manufacturer... Eastpak, First Alert, Grillmaster, Mixm... Sunbeam needed help: its profits had de... 50% from its high. To the rescue: Alb... ruthless executive known for his ability... ing jobs.

The strategy appeared to work. In 19... the brokerage firm of **Paine Webber** do... Webber had noticed unusually high acc...

> "I think that this discussion, an... others like it in the text, is exc... lent. Being a former CFO, I spe... a fair amount of time talking w... students about how earnings c... be managed, in the hands of a... biased (unethical?) CFO."
>
> *- Ron Tilden,*
> *University of Washington, Bothel...*

In talking to so many intermediate accounting faculty, we heard more than how to improve the book—there was much, much more that both users and nonusers insisted we keep exactly as it was. Here are some of the features that have made Spiceland such a phenomenal success in its previous editions.

ADDITIONAL CONSIDERATION

Some lessors use what's called the "gross method" [of a] lease. By this method, the lessor debits lease [payments] payments and credits *unearned interest revenue* [for the difference between] payments and the present value of the payment [...] be recorded as interest revenue over the term [...] entry by the gross method at the inception of th[e lease]

Lease receivable ($100,000 × 6) ....
    Unearned interest revenue (difference) .....
    Inventory of equipment (lessor's cost) ....

The same ultimate result is achieved either way [...] to more easily demonstrate the lessee's entries and the lessor's entries being "two sides of the same coin." Whichever method is used, both the lessee and the lessor must report in the disclosure notes both the net and gross amounts of the lease.

"This is a good technique that I actually use in my class and its good to see it in a book!"

- Ramesh Narasimhan, Montclair State University

ETHICAL DILEMMA

"I know we had discussed that they'r[e ...] option becomes exercisable," Ferris i[...] Jenkins, you know how fast computers [...] be worth only $10,000 in three years."

The computers to which Ferris ref[...] of the criteria for classification as a ca[pital lease ...] purchase option. Under the lease opti[...] three years.

"We could avoid running up our de[bt ...]

How could debt be avoided?

Do you perceive an ethical problem[...]

"Having ethical dilemma boxes in every chapter is much more significant than having a separate chapter devoted to ethics. Students can relate to the importance of being ethical in every aspect of business dealings."

- Gloria Worthy, Southwest Tennessee Community College

Additional Consideration Boxes

These are "on the spot" considerations of important, but incidental or infrequent aspects of the primary topics to which they relate. Their parenthetical nature, highlighted by enclosure in Additional Consideration boxes, helps maintain an appropriate level of rigor of topic coverage without sacrificing clarity of explanation.

Ethical Dilemmas

Because ethical ramifications of business decisions impact so many individuals as well as the core of our economy, Ethical Dilemmas are incorporated within the context of accounting issues as they are discussed. These features lend themselves very well to impromptu class discussions and debates.

Broaden Your Perspective Cases

Finish each chapter with these powerful and effective cases, a great way to reinforce and expand concepts learned in the chapter.

BROADEN YOUR PERSPECTIVE

Apply your critical-thinking ability to the knowledge you've gained. These cases will provide you an opportunity to develop your research, analysis, judgment, and communication skills. You will also work with other students, integrate what you've learned, apply it in real-world situations, and consider its global and ethical ramifications. This practice will broaden your knowledge and further develop your decision-making abilities.

Judgment Case 1–1
The development of accounting standards

● LO3

In 1934, Congress created the Securities and Exchange Commission (SEC) and gave the commission both the power and responsibility for setting acc[ounting standards...]
Required:
1. Explain the relationship between the [... has,] over time, been delegated the respon[sibility...]
2. Can you think of any reasons why th[...]

Research Case 1–2
Accessing SEC information

Internet access to the World Wide Web [...] ers. Many chapters in this text contain R[esearch...] ing issue. The purpose of this case is to [...] Commission (SEC) and its EDGA[R...]

"I think students would benefit tremendously from the cases."

- Joyce Njoroge, Drake University

*Results from an independent market survey of intermediate accounting professors July–September 2002 by Professional Research Group, LLC.

What's New in the Fifth Edition?

Chapter 1
ENVIRONMENT AND THEORETICAL STRUCTURE OF FINANCIAL ACCOUNTING

- Revised the section on our global marketplace to reflect the most recent developments in the move toward global accounting standards.
- Enhanced the coverage of the Sarbanes-Oxley Act to include information about the cost of compliance.
- Revised the section on the elements of financial statements to provide a more concise presentation of the material.
- Added a section on the evolution of accounting principles that includes discussions of the move to the asset/liability approach and the move toward fair value in standard setting. The fair value discussion includes information on two new, important FASB standards, SFAS No. 157 and SFAS No. 159.
- Moved the section on ethics in accounting to earlier in the chapter to provide a better flow of material.

Chapter 2
REVIEW OF THE ACCOUNTING PROCESS

- Enhanced the section on the conversion of cash basis to accrual basis to provide a more thorough analysis of the process and added additional end-of-chapter material on this topic.

Chapter 3
THE BALANCE SHEET AND FINANCIAL DISCLOSURES

- The introductory material on financial disclosures and disclosure notes has been enhanced to provide more thorough coverage of the topic.

Chapter 4
THE INCOME STATEMENT AND STATEMENT OF CASH FLOWS

- The section on comprehensive income has been moved from the beginning of Part A to the end. It will be easier for students to grasp this difficult topic after first covering the content and structure of the income statement.
- In the discussion of changes in accounting principles, a section has been added that addresses the accounting treatment of mandated changes in principles.

- The statement of cash flows illustration in Part B of the chapter has been expanded to include additional transactions. Presentation of cash flows from investing and financing activities also has been added to the illustration.

Chapter 5
INCOME MEASUREMENT AND PROFITABILITY ANALYSIS

- The section dealing with long-term contracts has been rewritten to clarify the similarities and differences between the percentage-of-completion and completed contract methods. Discussion has been added that clarifies the intuition underlying those approaches.
- Added discussion of multiple-deliverable revenue-recognition arrangements to cover the accounting approach indicated by EITF 00-21.
- Rewrote Part B of the chapter (Profitability Analysis) to organize it around the DuPont framework, adding discussion of leverage and using a peer analysis to illustrate the framework, and added end-of-chapter assignment material on this topic.

Chapter 6
TIME VALUE OF MONEY CONCEPTS

- Added discussion and illustration of how to use Excel and a calculator to determine present value and future value.

Chapter 7
CASH AND RECEIVABLES

- Enhanced the discussion of the valuation of noninterest-bearing notes including a computation aid for determining present value with Excel and with a calculator.

Chapter 8
INVENTORIES: MEASUREMENT

- Added information in the updated chapter-opening financial reporting case on LIFO liquidations.
- Added end-of-chapter material on physical quantities included in inventory, LIFO liquidations, and dollar-value LIFO.

Chapter 9
INVENTORIES: ADDITIONAL ISSUES

- Added a graphic to help students in their understanding of the lower-of-cost-or-market approach to valuing inventory.

Chapter 10
OPERATIONAL ASSETS: ACQUISITION AND DISPOSITION

- Updated material where necessary to reflect the issuance of SFAS No. 141(R), primarily the additional consideration that discusses negative goodwill and the section on purchased research and development.
- Revised the section on nonmonetary exchanges to provide more thorough coverage of the topic.

Chapter 11
OPERATIONAL ASSETS: UTILIZATION AND IMPAIRMENT

- The journal entry to record impairment losses has been added to impairment illustrations.

Chapter 12
INVESTMENTS

- Rewrote Part A (which covers accounting for investments when the investor lacks significant influence). This section has been reordered to cover held-to-maturity investments, then trading securities, and then available-for-sale securities. The same set of investments illustrate each approach, and a summary table compares and contrasts accounting under the three approaches to highlight similarities and differences among alternative approaches.
- Added coverage of SFAS No. 157 and determining fair value. Tied investor accounting for held-to-maturity investments to the debt issuer's accounting discussed under long-term liabilities in Chapter 14.
- Simplified the explanation of fair-value adjustments at period end for both trading securities and available-for-sale securities by using the same basic journal-entry structure for both, while highlighting the effects on net income and other comprehensive income.
- Enhanced Part B (which covers the equity method) by illustrating equity-method accounting for one of the investments discussed in Part A.
- Added a summary table that compares and contrasts accounting under the fair-value and equity-method approaches to help students understand similarities and differences between these approaches.
- Added a new learning objective for the fair value option to correspond with new discussion of SFAS No. 159 and the fair value option in both Parts A and Parts B. Also added end-of-chapter assignment material on this topic.

We received an incredible amount of feedback prior to writing the fifth edition of **Intermediate Accounting**. The following list of changes and improvements is a testament to our users and their commitment to making **Intermediate Accounting** the best book of its kind.

- Rewrote the decision-maker perspective to highlight the effects of alternative accounting approaches on income recognition and gains and losses and to emphasize the potential for earnings management.

Chapter
13
CURRENT LIABILITIES AND CONTINGENCIES

- Added discussion of accounting for contingent liabilities that a company acquires when it purchases another company under *SFAS No. 141(R)*, "Business Combinations."
- Revised coverage of contingencies for tax uncertainties that according to *FIN 48*, "Accounting for Uncertainty in Income Taxes" are no longer considered loss contingencies and added end-of-chapter assignment material on this topic

Chapter
14
BONDS AND LONG-TERM NOTES

- Since it's rare to have a delay in issuing bonds that causes them to be issued between interest dates, discussion of this infrequent event is moved to an appendix to the chapter.
- *SFAS No. 159*, "The Fair Value Option for Financial Assets and Financial Liabilities," gives companies the option to value some or all of their financial assets and liabilities at fair value. Discussion of how the fair value option is applied to liabilities has been added to the chapter, and extensive assignment materials related to the fair value option have been added.
- Added computation aids for determining present values with Excel and with a calculator.

Chapter
15
LEASES

- In an important pedagogical improvement, lessor accounting for nonoperating leases has been changed from the "gross method" of recording the lease receivable to the net method. Instruction is greatly simplified

as students now immediately see that the lessee's entries and the lessor's entries are "two sides of the same coin." End-of-chapter assignment materials have been revised accordingly.
- Added computation aids for determining present values with Excel and with a calculator.

Chapter
16
ACCOUNTING FOR INCOME TAXES

- Added a new section, "Coping with Uncertainty in Income Taxes," and related end-of-chapter assignment materials in response to *FIN 48*, "Accounting for Uncertainty in Income Taxes."
- Enhanced the deferred tax accounting illustrations.

Chapter
17
PENSIONS AND OTHER POSTRETIREMENT BENEFIT PLANS

- Enhanced and simplified the illustrations of recording the expense, gains and losses, and prior service cost for both pensions and other postretirement benefit plans prescribed by *SFAS No. 158*.
- Improved the format of the pension spreadsheet.

Chapter
18
SHAREHOLDERS' EQUITY

- Simplified and modernized the discussion of stock issuance by eliminating coverage of share purchase contracts.

Chapter
19
SHARE-BASED COMPENSATION AND EARNINGS PER SHARE

- Enhanced the discussion of incentive and nonqualified plans and their tax treatment.
- Restricted stock awards are quickly replacing stock options as the share-based compensation plan of choice. In response, the

discussion of EPS calculation is expanded to include the effect of these stock award plans as well as stock option plans that are not fully vested. Coverage is presented in a way that allows flexibility in the extent to which it is included in lesson plans and assignments.
- Coverage of SARs is moved to an appendix to the chapter. SARs along with options are becoming less popular. Their decline in popularity and their relatively complexity cause many to choose not to cover this topic.

Chapter
20
ACCOUNTING CHANGES AND ERROR CORRECTIONS

- Some changes in reporting entity are a result of changes in accounting rules, but the more frequent change in entity occurs when one company acquires another one. Discussion has been added to describe the disclosure required in these situations as prescribed by *SFAS No. 141(R)*.

Chapter
21
STATEMENT OF CASH FLOWS REVISITED

- This chapter continues to be devoted entirely to in-depth coverage of the statement of cash flows to complement and extend the more fundamental presentation of the statement in Chapter 4.

How Does Spiceland Help My Students Improve Their Performance?

Online Learning Center (OLC)

www.mhhe.com/spiceland5e

Today's students are every bit as comfortable using a web browser as they are reading a printed book. That's why we offer an Online Learning Center (OLC) that follows **Intermediate Accounting** chapter by chapter. It doesn't require any building or maintenance on your part, and is ready to go the moment you and your students type in the URL.

As your students study, they can refer to the OLC website for such benefits as:

iPod content	Check figures
Self-grading quizzes	Practice exams
Electronic flash cards	FASB pronouncements,
Audio narrated PowerPoints	summaries and updates
Alternate exercises and	Text updates
problems	

A secured Instructor Resource Center stores your essential course materials to save you prep time before class. The Instructor's Resource Manual, Solutions Manual, PowerPoint, and sample syllabi are now just a couple of clicks away. You will also find useful packaging information and transition notes.

The OLC website also serves as a doorway to other technology solutions such as PageOut, which is free to *Intermediate Accounting* adopters.

Coach

Coach is our award-winning tutorial software designed to help students understand critical accounting concepts. First, Coach actually provides spoken, narrated feedback as it helps students work through problems, rather than acting as just a reservoir of content that couldn't fit in the text. Second, the concept, content, and execution of Coach have been driven by and are part of the philosophy of the text authors.

Coach helps students master challenging material through a clear, step-by-step model. **Coaching Illustrations** are animated illustrations and examples similar to those found in the text that walk students through difficult concepts in a step-by-step manner. Look for the Coach icon in the text to identify these illustrations. **Show the Coach What You Know** provides students with a fun and interactive way to quiz themselves on key terminology and concepts.

> **"It is wonderful. I have my students evaluate each course I teach and rate the resources used. Time after time, students rate Coach as their number one choice. They love the interaction."**
>
> *- Janice Stoudemire, Midlands Technical College*

Intermediate Accounting's digital learning tools provide a comprehensive and cutting-edge environment for your students to practice in—and all digital content is prepared by the authors themselves.

McGraw-Hill's Homework Manager system is a Web-based supplement that duplicates problems directly from the textbook end-of-chapter material, using algorithms to provide a limitless supply of online self-graded practice for students, or assignments and tests with unique versions of every problem. Say goodbye to cheating in your classroom; say hello to the power and flexibility you've been waiting for in creating assignments.

The enhanced version of McGraw-Hill's Homework Manager system integrates all of Spiceland's online and multimedia assets to allow your students to brush up on a topic before doing their homework. You now have the option to give your students pre-populated hints and feedback. The Testbank has been added to McGraw-Hill's Homework Manager system so you can create online quizzes and exams and have them autograded and recorded in the same gradebook as your homework assignments. The enhanced version provides you with the option of incorporating the complete online version of the textbook, so your students can easily reference the chapter material as they do their homework assignment, even when their textbook is far away.

HOMEWORK MANAGER **PLUS**

McGraw-Hill's Homework Manager system is also a useful grading tool. All assignments can be delivered over the Web and are graded automatically, with the results stored in your private gradebook. Detailed results let you see at a glance how each student does on an assignment or an individual problem—you can even see how many tries it took them to solve it.

Students receive full access to McGraw-Hill's Homework Manager system when they purchase Homework Manager Plus® software, or you can have McGraw-Hill's Homework Manager system pass codes shrinkwrapped with the textbook. Students can also purchase access to McGraw-Hill's Homework Manager software directly from your class home page.

McGraw-Hill's Homework Manager Plus™ combines the power of McGraw-Hill's Homework Manager system with the latest interactive learning technology to create a comprehensive, fully integrated online study package.

Students using McGraw-Hill's Homework Manager Plus system can access not only McGraw-Hill's Homework Manager® software itself, but the interactive online textbook as well. For more than a textbook on a screen, this resource is completely integrated into McGraw-Hill's Homework Manager software, allowing students working on assignments to click a hotlink and instantly review the appropriate material in the textbook.

By including McGraw-Hill's Homework Manager Plus system with your textbook adoption, you're giving your students a vital edge as they progress through the course and ensuring that the help they need is never more than a mouse click away.

How Does Spiceland Help Me Build a Better Course?

> "The two [technology assets] that I find most exciting are Homework Manager and ALEKS. These alone are powerful reasons to choose this textbook."
>
> - Chula King,
> University of West Florida

ALEKS for the Accounting Cycle uses innovative adaptive learning technology to provide individualized guided learning to each and every student. ALEKS defines the key concepts, offers explanations and opportunities to practice, analyzes and corrects errors, and moves on to new topics when the student is ready.

When a student completes an initial assessment with ALEKS, the system analyzes the student's responses and determines an individual knowledge state for that student with great efficiency. From then on, ALEKS sets an appropriate learning path for the student by carefully analyzing his or her responses and determining what material is ready to be learned next.

You'll see increased motivation and confidence in your students after they use ALEKS. You'll see improved performance in courses where ALEKS is deployed, as well as fewer drops. And you'll see it all with minimal effort on your part—that's how easy it is to integrate ALEKS into your course.

What are the benefits of ALEKS for the Accounting Cycle?

- Intermediate accounting students can use ALEKS for a review of the accounting cycle. Since ALEKS is self-guided, you can reduce the time spent in your intermediate course reviewing material from financial accounting.

- ALEKS can be used as the curriculum for a bridge course between financial accounting and intermediate accounting.

- MBA students can use ALEKS for a self-guided review of accounting to prepare for their MBA program. Since it is online, students can do their work from anywhere in the world.

Contact your McGraw-Hill representative today and learn more about ALEKS, or email **aleks@mcgraw-hill.com.**

From innovative self-guided assessment and guidance to complete online course solutions, McGraw-Hill/Irwin lets you take full advantage of everything the digital age has to offer.

Flexible Online Course Content

No matter what platform you use, McGraw-Hill is committed to making your online course a success. We provide free, WebCT- and Blackboard-compatible course cartridges containing all the content you need.

> **"The course I will use this text for is a 'blended' course . . . partially online and partially on campus. This will be very useful."**
>
> *- Kathy Simons, Bryant College*

PageOut—McGraw-Hill's Course Management System

PageOut is the easiest way to create a Website for your accounting course.

There's no need for HTML coding, graphic design, or a thick how-to book. Just fill in a series of boxes with simple English and click on one of our professional designs. In no time, your course is online with a Website that contains your syllabus!

Should you need assistance in preparing your Website, we can help. Our team of product specialists is ready to take your course materials and build a custom Website to your specifications. You simply need to call a McGraw-Hill/Irwin PageOut specialist to start the process. Best of all, PageOut is free when you adopt *Intermediate Accounting*! To learn more, please visit **www.pageout.net.**

To see how these platforms can assist your online course, visit **www.mhhe.com**

A GREAT LEARNING SYSTEM DOESN'T STOP WITH THE BOOK.

INSTRUCTOR SUPPLEMENTS

> **"Very readable, impressive web-based supplements, excellent topic coverage."**
>
> - *Karen Foust, Tulane University*

ASSURANCE OF LEARNING READY

Many educational institutions today are focused on the notion of assurance of learning, an important element of some accreditation standards. *Intermediate Accounting* is designed specifically to support your assurance of learning initiatives with a simple, yet powerful, solution.

Each Testbank question for *Intermediate Accounting* maps to a specific chapter learning outcome/objective listed in the text. You can use our Testbank software, *EZ Test*, to easily query for learning outcomes/objectives that directly relate to the learning objectives for your course. You can then use the reporting features of *EZ Test* to aggregate student results in similar fashion, making the collection and presentation of assurance of learning data simple and easy. You can also use our Algorithmic-Diploma Testbank to do this.

AACSB STATEMENT

McGraw-Hill Companies is a proud corporate member of AACSB International. Recognizing the importance and value of AACSB accreditation, we have sought to recognize the curricula guidelines detailed in AACSB standards for business accreditation by connecting selected Testbank questions in *Intermediate Accounting* to the general knowledge and skill guidelines found in the AACSB standards.

The statements contained in *Intermediate Accounting* are provided only as a guide for the users of this text. The AACSB leaves content coverage and assessment clearly within the realm and control of individual schools, the mission of the school, and the faculty. The AACSB also charges schools with the obligation of doing assessment against their own content and learning goals. While *Intermediate Accounting* and its teaching package make no claim of any specific AACSB qualification or evaluation, we have labeled questions according to the six general knowledge and skills areas.

INSTRUCTOR'S RESOURCE MANUAL

This manual provides for each chapter: (a) a chapter overview; (b) a comprehensive lecture outline; (c) extensive teaching transparency masters that can be modified to suit an instructor's particular needs or preferences; (d) a variety of suggested class activities (real world,

ethics, Google, professional development activities including research, analysis, communication and judgment, and others); and (e) an assignment chart indicating topic, learning objective, and estimated completion time for every question, exercise, problem, and case.

SOLUTIONS MANUAL

The Solutions Manual includes detailed solutions for every question, exercise, problem, and case in the text.

INSTRUCTOR'S CD-ROM
ISBN-13: 9780073324494 (ISBN-10: 0073324493)

This all-in-one resource contains the Instructor's Resource Manual, Solutions Manual, Testbank Word files, Computerized, Testbank, and PowerPoint® slides.

TESTBANK

Written by the authors, this comprehensive Testbank contains over 3,700 problems and true/false, multiple-choice, matching, and essay questions.

COMPUTERIZED TESTBANK WITH ALGORITHMIC PROBLEM GENERATOR
ISBN-13: 9780073324333 (ISBN-10: 0073324337)

The Computerized Testbank is an algorithmic problem generator enabling instructors to create similarly structured problems with different values, allowing every student to be assigned a unique quiz or test. The user-friendly interface allows faculty to easily create different versions of the same test, change the answer order, edit or add questions, and even conduct online testing.

AUDIO POWERPOINT SLIDES

The Audio PowerPoint slides are created by Jon Booker and Charles Caldwell of Tennessee Technological University and Susan Galbreath of David Lipscomb University. The slides include an accompanying audio lecture with notes and are available on the Online Learning Center (OLC).

Online Learning Center (OLC): www.mhhe.com/spiceland5e

Intermediate Accounting authors Spiceland, Sepe, Nelson and Tomassini know from their years of teaching experience what separates a great textbook from a merely adequate one. Every component of the learning package must be imbued with the same style and approach, and that's why the **Intermediate Accounting** authors write every major ancillary themselves, whether printed or online. It's one more thing that sets **Intermediate Accounting** far above the competition.

STUDENT SUPPLEMENTS

STUDY GUIDE

Volume 1: ISBN-13: 9780073324593 (ISBN-10: 0073324590)
Volume 2: ISBN-13: 9780073324609 (ISBN-10: 0073324604)

The Study Guide, written by the text authors, provides chapter summaries, detailed illustrations, and a wide variety of self-study questions, exercises, and multiple-choice problems (with solutions).

WORKING PAPERS

ISBN-13: 9780073324630 (ISBN-10: 0073324639)

Working Papers provide students with formatted templates to aid them in doing homework assignments.

EXCEL TEMPLATES

Selected end-of-chapter exercises and problems, marked in the text with an icon, can be solved using these Microsoft Excel templates, located on the OLC.

UNDERSTANDING CORPORATE ANNUAL REPORTS

Seventh Edition, by William R. Pasewark

ISBN-13: 9780073526935 (ISBN-10: 0073526932)

This project provides students with instruction for obtaining an annual report from a publicly traded corporation and for making an industry or competitor comparison.

> **"This is a well-written text, with good integration. It has a full range of computerized and other support materials; and the authors personally write and check the practice questions, examples, and text items."**
>
> *- Elaine Henry, University of Miami*

ALTERNATE EXERCISES AND PROBLEMS

This online manual includes additional exercises and problems for each chapter in the text. Available on the OLC.

COACH

This step-by-step, tutorial software is available on the OLC and integrated throughout the text to help students better understand intermediate accounting topics.

PRACTICE SETS

Student ISBN-13: 9780073324449 (ISBN-10: 0073324442)

Grady Wholesale Practice Set: Review of the Accounting Cycle

> **"The text is a well written, easy to read intermediate accounting text with lots of graphics and color."**
>
> *- Patty Lobingier,*
> *Virginia Polytechnic Institute*

Acknowledgments

Fifth Edition Reviewers

Habib Abo-El-Yazeed, *Minnesota State University—Mankato*

Noel Addy, *Mississippi State University*

Pervaiz Alam, *Kent State University*

Joseph W. Antenucci, *Youngstown State University*

Marie Archambault, *Marshall University*

Jack Aschkenazi, *American Intercontinental University*

Florence Atiase, *University of Texas*

Joyce Barden, *DeVry University—Phoenix*

John Bildersee, *New York University*

Robert Bloom, *John Carroll University*

William J. Bradberry, *Bluefield State College*

Russell Briner, *University of Texas*

Nat R. Briscoe, *Northwestern State University*

R. Eugene Bryson, *University of Alabama—Huntsville*

Gary Burkette, *East Tennessee State University*

Al Case, *Southern Oregon University*

Jack M. Cathey, *University North Carolina—Charlotte*

Teresa Conover, *University of North Texas*

Cheryl Corke, *Genesee Community College*

Charles D'Alessandro, *SUNY—Suffolk*

Mark Dawkins, *University of Georgia*

Denise De La Rosa, *Grand Valley State University*

Susan A. Dehner, *Delaware Tech Community College—Dover*

Larry A. Deppe, *Weber State University*

Wendy Duffy, *Illinois State University*

Gerard M. Engeholm, *Pace University*

Kathryn K. Epps, *Kennesaw State University*

Patricia A. Fedje, *Minot State University*

Anita Feller, *University of Illinois—Champaign*

Karen Foust, *Tulane University*

Jeanne Gerard, *Franklin Pierce College*

Aloke Ghosh, *Bernard M. Baruch College*

Lori Grady, *Bucks County Community College*

Julia Grant, *Case Western Reserve University*

Mary Halford, *Prince Georges Community College*

John M. Hassell, *Indiana University–Purdue University Indianapolis*

Kenneth Henry, *Florida International University—Miami*

Paula Irwin, *Muhlenberg College*

Marianne James, *California State University—Los Angeles*

Cynthia Jeffrey, *Iowa State University*

Ronald Kilgore, *University of Tennessee—Martin*

Gordon Klein, *University of California—Los Angeles*

Philip Lee, *Nashville State Tech Community College*

Tim M. Lindquist, *University of Northern Iowa*

Danny S. Litt, *University of California—Los Angeles*

Patty Lobingier, *Virginia Polytechnic Institute*

Susan Logorda, *Lehigh Carbon Community College*

Jeff Mankin, *Lipscomb University*

Josephine Mathias, *Mercer County Community College*

Robert W. McGee, *Barry University*

Anita Morgan, *CTU Online*

Barbara Muller, *Arizona State University*

Ramesh Narasimhan, *Montclair University*

Siva Nathan, *Georgia State University*

Joyce Njoroge, *Drake University*

George Nogler, *University of Massachusetts—Lowell*

Derek Oler, *Indiana University*

Mitchell Oler, *Virginia Tech*

William A. Padley, *Madison Area Technical College—Truax*

Hong Pak, *California State Poly University—Pomona*

Barbara K. Parks, *American Intercontinental University*

Keith Patterson, *Brigham Young University*

Simon Pearlman, *California State University—Long Beach*

Anthony R. Piltz, *Rocky Mountain College*

Terence Pitre, *University of South Carolina*

David Plumlee, *University of Utah*

Grace Pownall, *Emory University*

Angela Sandberg, *Jacksonville State University*

Alex Sannella, *Rutgers University*

Paul Schloemer, *Ashland University*

Kathy Sevigny, *Bridgewater State College*

Carol Shaver, *Louisiana Tech University*

Ronald Singleton, *Western Washington University*

Kenneth Smith, *Salisbury University*

Katherene P. Terrell, *University of Central Oklahoma*

As you know if you've read this far, **Intermediate Accounting** would not be what it is without the passionate feedback of our colleagues. Through your time and effort, we were able to create a learning system that truly responds to the needs of the market, and for that, we sincerely thank each of you.

Michael Tyler, *Barry University*

Michael G. Welker, *Drexel University*

Gloria Worthy, *Southwest Tennessee University*

Jing-Wen Yang, *California State University—East Bay*

Fifth Edition Reviewers' Conference Attendees

Reviewers' conferences give our authors a valuable opportunity to interact with textbook users face to face, hearing firsthand their successes and difficulties in the classroom. That feedback was particularly valuable in crafting the fifth edition of *Intermediate Accounting,* and the Spiceland team extends special thanks to all those who participated:

Matilda Abavana, *Essex County College*

Noel D. Addy, Jr., *Mississippi State University*

Matthew Anderson, *Michigan State University*

Florence Atiase, *University of Texas*

Yoel Beniluz, *Rutgers University*

Lila Bergman, *Hunter College*

Russell Briner, *University of Texas*

Al Case, *Southern Oregon University*

Lanny Chasteen, *Oklahoma State University*

C. S. Agnes Cheng, *University of Houston*

Stanley Chu, *Bernard M. Baruch College*

Kwang Chung, *Pace University*

Edwin Cohen, *DePaul University*

Teresa Conover, *University of North Texas*

John Corless, *California State University—Sacramento*

Bobbie W. Daniels, *Jackson State University*

Mark Dawkins, *University of Georgia*

Gerard M. Engeholm, *Pace University*

Kathryn K. Epps, *Kennesaw State University*

Ehsan H. Feroz, *University of Washington—Tacoma*

Gail E. Fraser, *Kean University*

Frank Heflin, *Florida State University—Tallahassee*

Kenneth Henry, *Florida International University—Miami*

Agatha Jeffers, *Montclair State University*

Keith Jones, *George Mason University*

Khondkar Karim, *Rochester Institute of Technology*

Lisa Koonce, *University of Texas—Austin*

Cynthia L. Krom, *Marist College*

Joan Lacher, *Nassau Community College*

Janice Lawrence, *University of Nebraska—Lincoln*

Kevin Lightner, *San Diego State University*

Heidemarie Lundblad, *California State University—Northridge*

Robert W. McGee, *Barry University*

Mike Metzcar, *Indiana Wesleyan University*

Charles Miller, *California Polytechnic State University*

Sia Nassiripour, *William Paterson University*

Emeka Ofobike, *University of Akron*

Hong S. Pak, *California State Poly University—Pomona*

Rachel Pernia, *Essex County College*

Joann Pinto, *Montclair State University*

Frederick M. Richardson, *Virginia Polytech Institute*

Michael Riordan, *James Madison University*

Byung Ro, *Purdue University—West Lafayette*

Pamela Roush, *University of Central Florida*

Huldah A. Ryan, *Iona College*

Anwar Salimi, *California State Poly University—Pomona*

Gerald Savage, *Essex County College*

Gary Schader, *Kean University*

Nancy Snow, *University of Toledo*

Paulette Tandy, *University of Nevada—Las Vegas*

Katherene P. Terrell, *University of Central Oklahoma*

Robert Terrell, *University of Central Oklahoma*

Karen Turner, *University of Northern Colorado*

Michael L. Werner, *University of Miami—Coral Gables*

Previous Edition Reviewers and Focus Group Attendees

The Spiceland team also extends sincere thanks to the reviewers of our previous editions, without whose input we could not have made *Intermediate Accounting* the extraordinary success it has been.

Charlene Abendroth, *California State University—Hayward*

Marie Archambault, *Marshall University*

Peter Aghimien, *Indiana University—South Bend*

Tony Amoruso, *West Virginia University*

James Anderson, *St. Cloud Tech College*

Matt Anderson, *Michigan State University*

Florence Atiase, *University of Texas at Austin*

Craig Bain, *Northern Arizona University*

James Bannister, *University of Hartford*

Katherine Barker, *Lander University*

Acknowledgments

Homer Bates, *University of North Florida*

Daniel Bayak, *Lehigh University*

Jan Bell, *California State University—Northridge*

Whit Broome, *University of Virginia—Charlottesville*

Kevin Brown, *Drexel University*

John Brozovsky, *Virginia Tech*

Eddy Burks, *Athens State University*

Ronald Campbell, *North Carolina A&T University*

Al Case, *Southern Oregon University*

John Cezair, *Fayetteville State University*

Nandini Chandar, *Rutgers University*

Gyan Chandra, *Miami University, Oxford, Ohio**

Otto Chang, *California State University—Santa Barbara*

Kim Charland, *Kansas State University*

Betty Chavis, *California State University—Fullerton*

Alan Cherry, *Loyola Marymount University*

Steve Christian, *Jackson Community College*

Bryan Church, *Georgia Institute of Technology*

Marilyn G. Ciolino, *Delgado Community College*

Lynn Clements, *Florida Southern College*

Bob Cluskey, *State University of West Georgia*

Christie L. Comunale, *Long Island University—C.W. Post Campus*

Betty Conner, *University of Colorado at Denver*

Ellen Cook, *University of Louisiana at Lafayette*

Araya Debessay, *University of Delaware*

Marinus Debruine, *Grand Valley State University*

Larry Deppe, *Weber State University*

Judi Doing, *University of Arizona*

Orapin Duangploy, *University of Houston Downtown*

Wendy Duffy, *Illinois State University*

Tim Eaton, *Marquette University*

Jerry Engeholm, *Pace University*

Kathleen Fitzpatrick, *University of Toledo Community Tech College*

Sandra Fleak, *Truman State University*

Dick Fleischman, *John Carroll University*

Karen Foust, *Tulane University*

Clyde Galbraith, *West Chester University of Pennsylvania*

Susan Galbreath, *David Lipscomb University*

John Garlick, *Fayetteville State University*

Jennifer Gaver, *University of Georgia*

Nashwa George, *Montclair State University*

John Gillett, *Bradley University*

Sid Glandon, *University of Texas at El Paso*

Geoffrey Goldsmith, *Belhaven College*

Janet Greenlee, *University of Dayton*

Robert Gruber, *University of Wisconsin—Whitewater*

Amy Haas, *Kingsborough Community College*

Seth Hammer, *Towson University*

Coby Harmon, *University of California—Santa Barbara*

Charles Harter, *North Dakota State University—Fargo*

Robert Hatanaka, *University of Hawaii at Manoa*

Roger Hehman, *University of Cincinnati—Blue Ash*

Lyle Hicks, *Danville Area Community College*

Steve Hunt, *Western Illinois University*

Eliot Kamlet, *Binghamton University*

Ronald Kilgore, *University of Tennessee—Martin*

Chula King, *University of West Florida*

Gordon Klein, *University of California Los Angeles*

Larry Klein, *Bentley College*

David Knight, *Boro of Manhattan Community College*

Mary-Jo Kranacher, *York College, CUNY*

Jerry Krueze, *Western Michigan University**

Linda Kuechler, *Daemen College*

Tara Laken, *Joliet Junior College*

Jerry Lehman, *Madison Area Technical College—Truax*

Barbara Lippincott, *University of Tampa*

Susan Lynn, *University of Baltimore*

Mostafa Maksy, *Northeastern Illinois University*

Danny Matthews, *Midwestern State University*

Kevin McNelis, *New Mexico State University*

Wilda Meixner, *Texas State University—San Marcos*

Cathy Miller, *University of Michigan—Flint*

Bonnie Moe, *University of Illinois—Springfield*

Kathy Moffeit, *State University of West Georgia*

Jackie Moffitt, *Louisiana State University*

Louella Moore, *Arkansas State University*

Joe Moran, *College of DuPage*

Joe Morris, *Southeastern Louisiana University*

Barbara Muller, *Arizona State University—West*

Emeka Ofobike, *University of Akron*

Steven Onaitis, *University of Pittsburgh—Pittsburgh*

Janet C. Papiernik, *Indiana University—Purdue University—Fort Wayne*

Patricia Parker, *Columbus State Community College*

Sy Pearlman, *California State University—Long Beach*

Gary Pieroni, *University of California Berkeley*

Joanne Pinto, *Montclair State University*

Marion Posey, *Pace University*

Mike Prockton, *Finger Lakes Community College*

Judy Ramage, *Christian Bros University*

Donald Raux, *Siena College*

Sara Reiter, *SUNY—Bingham*

Randall Rentfro, *Florida Atlantic University—Fort Lauderdale*

David Roberts, *Texas A & M University International*

Luther Ross, *Central Piedmont Community College*

Eric Rothenburg, *Kingsborough Community College*

Marc Rubin, *Miami University, Oxford, Ohio*

John Rude, *Bloomsburg University of Pennsylvania*

Robert W. Rutledge, *Texas State University*

Maria Sanchez, *Rider University*

Angela Sandberg, *Jacksonville State University*

Alex Sannella, *Rutgers University—Newark*

Stanley Sauber, *Brooklyn College*

Gary Schader, *Kean University*

Carol G. Schaver, *Louisiana Tech University*

Paul Schloemer, *Ashland University*

Barbara Scofield, *University of Texas—Permian Basin*

Jerry Scott, *Ivy Tech State College*

Michael Serif, *Dowling College*

Rebecca Shortridge, *Ball State University*

Kathy Simons, *Bryant College*

Lorraine Stern, *York College, CUNY*

Doug Stevens, *Syracuse University*

Janice Stoudemire, *Midlands Technical College*

Lynn Suberly, *Valdosta State University**

John Surdick, *Xavier University*

Debbie Tanju, *University of Alabama at Birmingham*

Peter Theuri, *Northern Kentucky University*

Ron Tilden, *University of Washington, Bothell*

Michael Toerner, *Southern University—Baton Rouge*

Michael Trebesh, *Alma College*

Richard A. Turpen, *University of Alabama at Birmingham*

Michael Tyler, *Barry University*

Irwin Uhr, *Hunter College*

Frank Urbancic, *University of Southern Alabama*

Herbert Vessel, *Southern University—Baton Rouge*

James Voss, *Pennsylvania State Behrend-Erie*

Larry Walther, *University of Texas—Arlington**

Weiman Wang, *Tulane University*

Scott White, *Lindenwood University*

Gloria Worthy, *Southwest Tennessee Community College—Macon Campus*

Suzanne Wright, *Pennsylvania State University-University Park*

Robert Wyatt, *Drury University*

Thomas Yandow, *Norwich University*

George Young, *Florida Atlantic University—Fort Lauderdale*

Kay Zekany, *Ohio Northern University*

Mary Zenner, *College of Lake County*

We Are Grateful

We would like to acknowledge Barbara Muller, Arizona State University, for her detailed accuracy check of the Testbank; also, Patty Lobingier (Virginia Polytechnic Iusricure), Marianne James (California State, Los Angeles), and Jing-Wen Yang (California State University—East Bay) completed helpful reviews of the Testbank before we started revisions. Bill Padley of Madison Area Technical College contributed greatly to the production of the Working Papers. In addition, we thank Jon A. Booker and Charles W. Caldwell of Tennessee Technological University and Susan C. Galbreath of David Lipscomb University for crafting the PowerPoint Slides; and Jack E. Terry, ComSource Associates, for developing the Excel Templates.

Ilene Persoff, CW Post Campus/Long Island University and Beth Woods, Accuracy Counts, made significant contributions to the accuracy of the text, end-of-chapter material, and solutions manual. In addition, we appreciate the help and guidance received from Teresa Conover from North Texas University, for her insights regarding the International Financial Reporting Standards. A big thank you to Jerry Kreuze of Western Michigan University for his detailed analysis of the end-of-chapter material. We appreciate the assistance of James Lynch at KPMG, who provided us with valuable feedback on various difficult issues.

We appreciate the excellent Homework Manager accuracy checking work completed by Mark McCarthy, East Carolina University; Angela Sandberg, Jacksonville State University; Ilene Persoff, CW Post Campus/Long Island University; Lisa N. Bostick, The University of Tampa; Patty Lobingier, Virginia Polytechnic Institute; Marc A. Giullian, Montana State University; Barbara Muller, Arizona State University; Lori Grady, Bucks County Community College; and William Padley, Madison Area Technical College.

We are most grateful for the talented assistance and support from the many people at McGraw-Hill/Irwin. We would particularly like to thank Brent Gordon, editor in chief; Stewart Mattson, editorial director; Tim Vertovec, publisher; Daryl Horrocks, developmental editor; Scott Bishop, marketing manager; Greg Patterson, regional sales manager; Pat Frederickson, lead project manager; Gina Hangos, production supervisor; Laurie Entringer, designer; Jeremy Cheshareck, photo research coordinator; and Kerry Bowler, media project manager.

Finally, we extend our thanks to Kaplan CPA Review for their assistance developing simulations for our inclusion in the end-of-chapter material, as well as Google for allowing us to use its Annual Report throughout the text. We also acknowledge permission from the AICPA to adapt material from the Uniform CPA Examination, the IMA for permission to adapt material from the CMA Examination, and Dow Jones & Co., Inc., for permission to excerpt material from *The Wall Street Journal.*

David Spiceland   Jim Sepe
Mark Nelson   Larry Tomassini

Contents in Brief

1
SECTION

2
SECTION

3
SECTION

Contents

6 CHAPTER
Time Value of Money Concepts, 288

2 SECTION
Economic Resources

7 CHAPTER
Cash and Receivables, 326

11 CHAPTER
Operational Assets: Utilization and Impairment, 532

3 SECTION
Financial Instruments and Liabilities

12 CHAPTER
Investments, 586

Environment and Theoretical Structure of Financial Accounting

/// OVERVIEW

The primary function of financial accounting is to provide relevant and reliable financial information to users external to the business enterprise. The focus of financial accounting is on the information needs of investors and creditors. These users make critical resource allocation decisions that affect the nation's economy. The primary means of conveying financial information to external users is through financial statements and related notes.

In this chapter you explore important topics such as the FASB's conceptual framework that serve as a foundation for a more detailed study of financial statements, the way the statement elements are measured, and the concepts underlying these measurements and related disclosures.

LEARNING OBJECTIVES

After studying this chapter, you should be able to:

- **LO1** Describe the function and primary focus of financial accounting.
- **LO2** Explain the difference between cash and accrual accounting.
- **LO3** Define generally accepted accounting principles (GAAP) and discuss the historical development of accounting standards.
- **LO4** Explain why the establishment of accounting standards is characterized as a political process.
- **LO5** Explain the purpose of the FASB's conceptual framework.
- **LO6** Identify the objectives of financial reporting, the qualitative characteristics of accounting information, and the elements of financial statements.
- **LO7** Describe the four basic assumptions underlying GAAP.
- **LO8** Describe the four broad accounting principles that guide accounting practice.

FINANCIAL REPORTING CASE

Misguided Marketing Major

During a class break in your investments class, a marketing major tells the following story to you and some friends:

The chief financial officer (CFO) of a large company is interviewing three candidates for the top accounting position with his firm. He asks each the same question:

CFO:	What is two plus two?
First candidate:	Four.
CFO:	What is two plus two?
Second candidate:	Four.
CFO:	What is two plus two?
Third candidate:	What would you like it to be?
CFO:	You're hired.

After you take some good-natured ribbing from the nonaccounting majors, your friend says, "Seriously, though, there must be ways the accounting profession prevents that kind of behavior. Aren't there some laws, or rules, or something? Are they based on some sort of theory, or are they just arbitrary?"

By the time you finish this chapter, you should be able to respond appropriately to the questions posed in this case. Compare your response to the solution provided at the end of the chapter.

QUESTIONS ///

1. What should you tell your friend about the presence of accounting standards in the United States? Who has the authority for standard setting? Who has the responsibility? (page 9)

2. What is the economic and political environment in which standard setting occurs? (page 12)

3. What is the relationship among management, auditors, investors, and creditors that tends to preclude the "What would you like it to be?" attitude? (page 15)

4. In general, what is the conceptual framework that underlies accounting principles? (page 20)

PART A   FINANCIAL ACCOUNTING ENVIRONMENT

Have you ever envisioned yourself designing a blockbuster video game or creating the next great high-technology innovation that would make you rich and famous? Sergey Brin and Larry Page had such a vision. In 1998 in the rented garage of a home in Menlo Park, California, these two Stanford University computer science graduate students saw their vision become a reality by creating an Internet search engine that would revolutionize the industry and the way people use the Internet.

> "Not since Gutenberg invented the modern printing press more than 500 years ago, making books and scientific tomes affordable and widely available to the masses, has any new invention empowered individuals or transformed access to information as profoundly as Google."[1]

Brin and Page called their new search engine BackRub, named for its unique ability to analyze the "back links" pointing to a given website. They named their company **Google,** a play on the word "googol," which refers to a number represented by the number one followed by 100 zeroes. The use of the term relates to the company's mission to organize the infinite amount of information available on the Internet. During their first summer, the search engine served 10,000 queries per day; humble beginnings for a company that would become an Internet giant with daily search queries reaching 366 million by 2006.[2] Company profits for the 2007 fiscal year exceeded $4 billion and revenue topped $16 billion. Early in 2007, the combined value of Brin and Page's Google stock exceeded $26 billion.

Many factors contributed to the success of Google. The company's founders were visionary in terms of their search engine. A key factor contributing to the growth and success of Google was its access to external capital (resources). At various times in the company's brief history, the ability to raise external capital from investors and creditors was critical to its phenomenal growth. For example, Brin and Page raised initial capital by convincing family, friends, and acquaintances to invest almost $1 million in their new company, and in 2004 an initial public offering of the company's stock provided over $1.6 billion in equity financing.

Investors and creditors use information to assess risk and return.

Investors and creditors use many different kinds of information before supplying capital to business enterprises like Google. The information is used to assess the future risk and return of their potential investments in the enterprise.[3] For example, information about the enterprise's products and its management is of vital importance to this assessment. In addition, various kinds of financial information are extremely important to investors and creditors.

● **LO1**

The primary focus of financial accounting is on the information needs of investors and creditors.

You might think of accounting as a special "language" used to communicate financial information about a business to those who wish to use the information to make decisions. Financial accounting, in particular, is concerned with providing relevant financial information to various *external* users. The chart in Graphic 1–1 illustrates a number of financial information supplier groups as well as several external user groups. Of these groups, the primary focus of financial accounting is on the financial information provided by *profit-oriented companies to their present and potential investors and creditors.* The reason for this focus is discussed in a later section of this chapter. One external user group, often referred to as *financial intermediaries,* includes financial analysts, stockbrokers, mutual fund managers, and credit rating organizations. These users provide advice to investors and creditors and/or make investment-credit decisions on their behalf. The collapse of **Enron Corporation** in 2001 and other high profile accounting failures made immensely clear the importance of reporting reliable financial information.

On the other hand, managerial accounting deals with the concepts and methods used to provide information to an organization's *internal* users, that is, its managers. You study managerial accounting elsewhere in your curriculum.

Financial statements convey financial information to external users.

The primary means of conveying financial information to investors, creditors, and other external users is through financial statements and related disclosure notes. The financial statements most frequently provided are (1) the balance sheet or statement of financial

---

[1]David Vise, "The Google Story: An Excerpt," *washingtonpost.com* (December 16, 2005).
[2]Ryan Blitstein, "Google Garage," *San Jose Mercury News* (October 3, 2006), p. 1C.
[3]Risk refers to the variability of possible outcomes from an investment. Return is the amount received over and above the investment and usually is expressed as a percentage.

**PROVIDERS OF
FINANCIAL INFORMATION**

- Profit-oriented companies

- Not-for-profit entities
  (e.g., government entities,
  charitable organizations,
  schools)

- Households

EXTERNAL USER GROUPS

- Investors
- Creditors (banks,
  bondholders, other lenders)
- Employees
- Labor unions
- Customers
- Suppliers
- Government regulatory agencies
  (e.g., Internal Revenue Service,
  Securities and Exchange
  Commission)
- Financial intermediaries
  (e.g., financial analysts,
  stockbrokers, mutual fund
  managers, credit-rating
  organizations)

position, (2) the income statement or statement of operations, (3) the statement of cash flows, and (4) the statement of shareholders' equity. As you progress through this text, you will review and expand your knowledge of the information in these financial statements, the way the elements in these statements are measured, and the concepts underlying these measurements and related disclosures. We use the term financial reporting to refer to the process of providing this information to external users. Keep in mind, though, that external users receive important financial information in a variety of other formats as well, including news releases and management forecasts, prospectuses, reports filed with regulatory agencies, and the president's letter.

A copy of **Google Inc.**'s 2007 financial statements and related disclosure notes art provided with all new copies of the text. You also can locate the 2007 statements and notes online at **www.google.com**. To provide context for our discussions throughout the text, we occasionally refer to these statements and notes. Also, as new topics are introduced in later chapters, you might want to refer to the information to see how Google reported the items being discussed.

The Economic Environment and Financial Reporting

In the United States, we have a highly developed free-enterprise economy with the majority of productive resources privately owned rather than government owned. It's important in this type of system that a mechanism exists to allocate the scarce resources of our society, both natural resources and labor, in an efficient manner. Resources should be allocated to private enterprises that will use them best to provide goods and services desired by society and not to enterprises that will waste them. The mechanisms that foster this efficient allocation of resources are the capital markets. We can think of the capital markets simply as a composite of all investors and creditors.

The three primary forms of business organization are the sole proprietorship, the partnership, and the corporation. In the United States, sole proprietorships and partnerships outnumber corporations. However, the dominant form of business organization, in terms of the ownership of productive resources, is the corporation. The corporate form makes it easier for an enterprise to acquire resources through the capital markets. Investors provide resources, usually cash, to a corporation in exchange for evidence of ownership interest, that is, shares of stock. Creditors such as banks lend cash to the corporation. Also, creditors can

The *capital markets* provide a mechanism to help our economy allocate resources efficiently.

Corporations acquire capital from investors in exchange for ownership interest and from creditors by borrowing.

lend the corporation cash through the medium of bonds. Stocks and bonds usually are traded on organized security markets such as the New York Stock Exchange and the American Stock Exchange. The advantages and disadvantages of the corporate form are discussed at greater length in Chapter 18.

The transfers of these stocks and bonds among individuals and institutions are referred to as secondary market transactions. Corporations receive no new cash from secondary market transactions. New cash is provided in *primary* market transactions in which the shares or bonds are sold by the corporation to the initial owners. Nevertheless, secondary market transactions are extremely important to the efficient allocation of resources in our economy. These transactions help establish market prices for additional shares and for bonds that corporations may wish to issue in the future to acquire additional capital. Also, many shareholders and bondholders might be unwilling to initially provide resources to corporations if there were no available mechanism for the future sale of their stocks and bonds to others.

What information do investors and creditors need to decide which companies will be provided capital? We explore that question next.

The Investment-Credit Decision—A Cash Flow Perspective

While the decisions made by investors and by creditors are somewhat different, they are similar in at least one important way. They both are concerned with providing resources to companies, usually cash, with the expectation of receiving more cash in return at some time in the future. A corporation's shareholders will receive cash from their investment through the ultimate sale of the ownership shares of stock. In addition, many corporations distribute cash to their shareholders in the form of periodic dividends. For example, if an investor provides a company with $10,000 cash (that is, purchases ownership shares) at the end of 2008, receives $400 in dividends from the company during 2009, and sells the ownership interest (shares) at the end of 2009 for $10,600 ($600 share price appreciation), the investment would have generated a rate of return of 10% for 2009, calculated as follows:

$$\frac{\$400 \text{ dividends} + \$600 \text{ share price appreciation}}{\$10,000 \text{ initial investment}} = 10\%$$

Investors always are faced with more than one investment opportunity. There are many factors to consider before one of these opportunities is chosen. Two extremely important variables are the *expected rate of return* from each investment option, and the *uncertainty,* or *risk,* of that expected return. For example, consider the following two investment options:

1. Invest $10,000 in a savings account insured by the U.S. government that will generate a 5% rate of return.
2. Invest $10,000 in a profit-oriented company.

While the rate of return from option 1 is known with virtual certainty, the return from option 2 is uncertain. The amount and timing of the cash to be received in the future from option 2 are unknown. Investors require information about the company that will help them estimate the unknown return.

In the long run, a company will be able to provide investors with a return only if it can generate a profit. That is, it must be able to use the resources provided by investors and creditors to generate cash receipts from selling a product or service that exceed the cash disbursements necessary to provide that product or service. If this excess can be generated, the marketplace is implicitly saying that society's resources have been efficiently allocated. The marketplace is assigning a value to the product or service that exceeds the value assigned to the resources used to produce that product or service.

In summary, the primary objective of financial accounting is to provide investors and creditors with information that will help them make investment and credit decisions. More specifically, the information should help investors and creditors evaluate the *amounts, timing,* and *uncertainty* of the enterprise's future cash receipts and disbursements. The better this information is, the more efficient will be investor and creditor resource allocation decisions. Financial accounting, in providing key elements of the information set used by capital

---

Secondary market transactions provide for the transfer of stocks and bonds among individuals and institutions.

Investors and creditors both are interested in earning a fair return on the resources provided.

The expected *rate of return* and uncertainty, or risk, of that return are key variables in the investment decision.

A company will be able to provide a return to investors and creditors only if it can generate a profit from selling its products or services.

The objective of financial accounting is to provide investors and creditors with useful information for decision making.

market participants, plays a vital societal role in the resource allocation process. The importance of this role to society explains why the primary focus of financial accounting is on the information needs of investors and creditors.

The Financial Accounting Standards Board, the current private sector body responsible for setting accounting standards in the United States, has published a conceptual framework for financial reporting (discussed later in this chapter). The first concept statement of the framework describes the specific objectives of external financial reporting. These objectives affirm the importance of the cash flow information needs of investors and creditors.

Throughout this text, you will be reminded of this cash flow perspective. For example, Chapter 4 describes certain events that are reported separately in the income statement due to the fact that these historical events have implications for future cash flows that are different from the normal operating activities. Separation of these events from normal operating activities provides financial statement users with information to more easily predict an enterprise's future cash flows.

Cash versus Accrual Accounting

Even though predicting future cash flows is the primary objective, the model best able to achieve that objective is the accrual accounting model. A competing model is cash basis accounting. Each model produces a periodic measure of performance that could be used by investors and creditors for predicting future cash flows.

● LO2

CASH BASIS ACCOUNTING. Cash basis accounting produces a measure called net operating cash flow. This measure is the difference between cash receipts and cash disbursements during a reporting period from transactions related to providing goods and services to customers.

Net operating cash flow is the difference between cash receipts and cash disbursements from providing goods and services.

Net operating cash flow is very easy to understand and all information required to measure it is factual. Also, it certainly relates to a variable of critical interest to investors and creditors. What could be better in helping to predict future cash flows from selling products and services than current cash flows from these activities? Remember, a company will be able to provide a return to investors and creditors only if it can use the capital provided to generate a positive net operating cash flow. However, there is a major drawback to using the current period's operating cash flow to predict future operating cash flows. Over the life of the company, net operating cash flow definitely is the variable of concern. However, over short periods of time, *operating cash flows may not be indicative of the company's long-run cash-generating ability* (that is, its ability to generate positive net operating cash flows in the future).

To demonstrate this, consider the following example. In Illustration 1–1 net operating cash flows are determined for the Carter Company during its first three years of operations.

Over the three-year period, Carter generated a positive net operating cash flow of $60,000. At the end of this three-year period, Carter has no outstanding debts. Because total sales and cash receipts over the three-year period were each $300,000, nothing is owed to Carter by customers. Also, at the beginning of the first year, Carter prepaid $60,000 for three years' rent on the facilities. There are no uncompleted transactions at the end of the three-year period. In that sense, we can view this three-year period as a micro version of the entire life of a company.

	Year 1	Year 2	Year 3	Total
Sales (on credit)	$100,000	$100,000	$100,000	$300,000
Net Operating Cash Flows				
Cash receipts from customers	$ 50,000	$125,000	$125,000	$300,000
Cash disbursements:				
Prepayment of three years' rent	(60,000)	–0–	–0–	(60,000)
Salaries to employees	(50,000)	(50,000)	(50,000)	(150,000)
Utilities	(5,000)	(15,000)	(10,000)	(30,000)
Net operating cash flow	$ (65,000)	$ 60,000	$ 65,000	$ 60,000

ILLUSTRATION 1–1
Cash Basis Accounting

The company incurred utility costs of $10,000 per year over the period. However, during the first year only $5,000 actually was paid, with the remainder being paid the second year. Employee salary costs of $50,000 were paid in full each year.

Is net operating cash flow for year 1 (negative $65,000) an accurate indicator of future cash-generating ability?[4] Obviously, it is not a good predictor of the positive net cash flows that occur in the next two years. Is the three-year pattern of net operating cash flows indicative of the company's year-by-year performance? No. But, if we measure the same activities by the accrual accounting model, we get a more accurate prediction of future operating cash flows and a more reasonable portrayal of the balanced operating performance of the company over the three years.

Over short periods of time, operating cash flow may not be an accurate predictor of future operating cash flows.

Net income is the difference between revenues and expenses.

ACCRUAL ACCOUNTING. The accrual accounting model measures the entity's accomplishments and resource sacrifices during the period, regardless of when cash is received or paid. The accrual accounting model's measure of periodic accomplishments is called *revenues,* and the periodic measure of resource sacrifices is called *expenses.* The difference between revenues and expenses is *net income,* or net loss if expenses are greater than revenues.[5]

How would we measure revenues and expenses in this very simplistic situation? Illustration 1–2 offers a possible solution.

ILLUSTRATION 1–2 Accrual Accounting	CARTER COMPANY Income Statements			
		Year 1	Year 2	Year 3	Total

The accrual accounting model provides a measure of periodic performance called net income, the difference between revenues and expenses.		Year 1	Year 2	Year 3	Total
	Revenues	$100,000	$100,000	$100,000	$300,000
	Expenses:				
	Rent	20,000	20,000	20,000	60,000
	Salaries	50,000	50,000	50,000	150,000
	Utilities	10,000	10,000	10,000	30,000
	Total expenses	80,000	80,000	80,000	240,000
	Net Income	$ 20,000	$ 20,000	$ 20,000	$ 60,000

Net income is considered a better indicator of future operating cash flows than is current net operating cash flow.

Net income of $20,000 for year 1 appears to be a reasonable predictor of the company's cash-generating ability as total net operating cash flow for the three-year period is a positive $60,000. Also, compare the three-year pattern of net operating cash flows in Illustration 1–1 to the three-year pattern of net income in Illustration 1–2. The net income pattern is more representative of the steady operating performance over the three-year period.[6]

While this example is somewhat simplistic, it allows us to see the motivation for using the accrual accounting model. Accrual income attempts to measure the accomplishments and sacrifices that occurred during the year, which may not correspond to cash inflows and outflows. For example, revenue for year 1 is the $100,000 in sales. This is a better measure of the company's accomplishments during year 1 than the $50,000 cash collected from customers.

Does this mean that information about cash flows from operating activities is not useful? No. Indeed, when combined with information about cash flows from investing and financing activities, this information provides valuable input into decisions made by investors and creditors. In fact, collectively, this cash flow information constitutes the statement of cash flows—one of the basic financial statements.[7]

---

[4]A negative cash flow is possible only if invested capital (i.e., owners contributed cash to the company in exchange for ownership interest) is sufficient to cover the cash deficiency. Otherwise, the company would have to either raise additional external funds or go bankrupt.
[5]Net income also includes gains and losses, which are discussed later in the chapter.
[6]Empirical evidence that accrual accounting provides a better measure of short-term performance than cash flows is provided by Patricia DeChow, "Accounting Earnings and Cash Flows as Measures of Firm Performance: The Role of Accrual Accounting," *Journal of Accounting and Economics* 18 (1994), pp. 3–42.
[7]The statement of cash flows is discussed in detail in Chapters 4 and 21.

The Development of Financial Accounting and Reporting Standards

Accrual accounting is the financial reporting model used by the majority of profit-oriented companies and by many not-for-profit companies. The fact that companies use the same model is important to financial statement users. Investors and creditors use financial information to make their resource allocation decisions. It's critical that they be able to *compare* financial information among companies. To facilitate these comparisons, financial accounting employs a body of standards known as generally accepted accounting principles, often abbreviated as GAAP (and pronounced *gap*). GAAP are a dynamic set of both broad and specific guidelines that companies should follow when measuring and reporting the information in their financial statements and related notes. The more important broad principles or standards are discussed in a subsequent section of this chapter and revisited throughout the text in the context of accounting applications for which they provide conceptual support.[8] More specific standards, such as how to measure and report a lease transaction, receive more focused attention in subsequent chapters.

● LO3

FINANCIAL Reporting Case

Q1, p. 3

Historical Perspective and Standards

Pressures on the accounting profession to establish uniform accounting standards began to surface after the stock market crash of 1929. Some feel that insufficient and misleading financial statement information led to inflated stock prices and that this contributed to the stock market crash and the subsequent depression.

The 1933 Securities Act and the 1934 Securities Exchange Act were designed to restore investor confidence. The 1933 act sets forth accounting and disclosure requirements for initial offerings of securities (stocks and bonds). The 1934 act applies to secondary market transactions and mandates reporting requirements for companies whose securities are publicly traded on either organized stock exchanges or in over-the-counter markets.[9] The 1934 act also created the Securities and Exchange Commission (SEC).

The *Securities and Exchange Commission (SEC)* was created by Congress with the 1934 Securities Exchange Act.

In the 1934 act, *Congress gave the SEC the authority to set accounting and reporting standards for companies whose securities are publicly traded.* However, the SEC, a government appointed body, has delegated the task of setting accounting standards to the private sector. It is important to understand that the power still lies with the SEC. If the SEC does not agree with a particular standard issued by the private sector, it can force a change in the standard. In fact, it has done so in the past.

The SEC has the authority to set accounting standards for companies, but has delegated the task to the private sector.

The SEC does issue its own accounting standards in the form of *Financial Reporting Releases (FRRs),* which regulate what must be reported by companies to the SEC itself. These standards usually agree with those previously issued by the private sector. To learn more about the SEC, consult its Internet site at **www.sec.gov**.[10]

EARLY STANDARD SETTING.   The first private sector body to assume the task of setting accounting standards was the Committee on Accounting Procedure (CAP). The CAP was a committee of the American Institute of Accountants (AIA). The AIA, which was renamed the American Institute of Certified Public Accountants (AICPA) in 1957, is the national organization of certified professional public accountants. From 1938 to 1959, the CAP issued 51 *Accounting Research Bulletins (ARBs)* which dealt with specific accounting and reporting problems. No theoretical framework for financial accounting was established. This approach of dealing with individual issues without a framework led to stern criticism of the accounting profession.

In 1959 the Accounting Principles Board (APB) replaced the CAP. Members of the APB also belonged to the AICPA. The APB operated from 1959 through 1973 and issued 31

The *Accounting Principles Board (APB)* followed the CAP.

---

[8]The terms *standards* and *principles* sometimes are used interchangeably.
[9]Reporting requirements for SEC registrants include Form 10-K, the annual report form, and Form 10-Q, the report that must be filed for the first three quarters of each fiscal year.
[10]In 2000, the SEC issued regulation FD (Fair Disclosure) which redefined how companies interact with analysts and the public in disclosing material information. Prior to regulation FD, companies often disclosed important information to a select group of analysts before disseminating the information to the general public. Now, this type of selective disclosure is prohibited. The initial disclosure of market-sensitive information must be made available to the general public.

Accounting Principles Board Opinions (APBOs), various *Interpretations,* and four *Statements.* The *Opinions* also dealt with specific accounting and reporting problems. Many *ARBs* and *APBOs* have not been superseded and still represent authoritative GAAP.

The APB's main effort to establish a theoretical framework for financial accounting and reporting was *APB Statement No. 4,* "Basic Concepts and Accounting Principles Underlying Financial Statements of Business Enterprises." Unfortunately, the effort was not successful.

The APB was composed of members of the accounting profession and was supported by their professional organization. Members participated in the activities of the board on a voluntary, part-time basis. The APB was criticized by industry and government for its inability to establish an underlying framework for financial accounting and reporting and for its inability to act quickly enough to keep up with financial reporting issues as they developed. Perhaps the most important flaw of the APB was a perceived lack of independence. Composed almost entirely of certified public accountants, the board was subject to the criticism that the clients of the represented public accounting firms were exerting self-interested pressure on the board and influencing their decisions. Other interest groups were underrepresented in the standard-setting process.

CURRENT STANDARD SETTING. Criticism of the APB led to the creation in 1973 of the Financial Accounting Standards Board (FASB) and its supporting structure. The FASB differs from its predecessor in many ways. There are seven full-time members of the FASB, compared to 18–21 part-time members of the APB. While all of the APB members belonged to the AICPA, FASB members represent various constituencies concerned with accounting standards. Members have included representatives from the accounting profession, profit-oriented companies, accounting educators, and government. The APB was supported financially by the AICPA, while the FASB is supported by its parent organization, the Financial Accounting Foundation (FAF). The FAF is responsible for selecting the members of the FASB and its Advisory Council, ensuring adequate funding of FASB activities, and exercising general oversight of the FASB's activities.[11] The FASB is, therefore, an independent, private sector body whose members represent a broad constituency of interest groups.[12]

In 1984, the FASB's Emerging Issues Task Force (EITF) was formed to provide more timely responses to emerging financial reporting issues. The EITF membership includes 15 individuals from public accounting and private industry, along with a representative from the FASB and an SEC observer. The membership of the task force is designed to include individuals who are in a position to be aware of emerging financial reporting issues. The task force considers these emerging issues and attempts to reach a consensus on how to account for them. If consensus can be reached, generally no FASB action is required. The task force disseminates its rulings in the form of *EITF Issues.* These pronouncements are considered part of generally accepted accounting principles.

If a consensus can't be reached, FASB involvement may be necessary. The EITF plays an important role in the standard-setting process by identifying potential problem areas and then acting as a filter for the FASB. This speeds up the standard-setting process and allows the FASB to focus on pervasive long-term problems.

One of the FASB's most important activities has been the formulation of a conceptual framework. The conceptual framework project, discussed in more depth later in this chapter, deals with theoretical and conceptual issues and provides an underlying structure for current and future accounting and reporting standards. The FASB has issued seven *Statements of Financial Accounting Concepts (SFACs)* to describe its conceptual framework. The board also has issued over 160 specific accounting standards, called *Statements of Financial Accounting Standards (SFASs),* as well as numerous FASB *Interpretations Staff Positions* and *Technical Bulletins.*[13]

The *FASB* currently sets accounting standards.

The *Emerging Issues Task Force (EITF)* identifies financial reporting issues and attempts to resolve them without involving the FASB.

In addition to issuing specific accounting standards, the FASB has formulated a *conceptual framework* to provide an underlying theoretical and conceptual structure for accounting standards.

---

[11]The FAF's primary sources of funding are contributions and the sales of the FASB's publications. The FAF is governed by trustees, the majority of whom are appointed from the membership of eight sponsoring organizations. These organizations represent important constituencies involved with the financial reporting process. For example, one of the founding organizations is the Association of Investment Management and Research (formerly known as the Financial Analysts Federation) which represents financial information *users,* and another is the Financial Executives International which represents financial information *preparers.* The FAF also raises funds to support the activities of the Government Accounting Standards Board (GASB).

[12]The FASB organization also includes the **Financial Accounting Standards Advisory Council** (FASAC). The major responsibility of the FASAC is to advise the FASB on the priorities of its projects, including the suitability of new projects that might be added to its agenda.

[13]For more information, go to the FASB's Internet site at **www.fasb.org**.

HIERARCHY OF STANDARD-SETTING AUTHORITY

GRAPHIC 1–2

Accounting Standard
Setting

Graphics 1–2 and 1–3 summarize this discussion on accounting standards. Graphic 1–2 shows the hierarchy of accounting standards in order of authority. Congress gave the SEC the authority to set accounting standards, specifically for companies whose securities are publicly traded. However, the SEC has delegated the task to various private sector bodies (currently the FASB) while retaining its legislated authority.

Graphic 1–3 summarizes the framework for selecting the principles to be used in preparing financial statements in conformity with generally accepted accounting principles. The GAAP hierarchy includes the authoritative pronouncements and interpretations of the SEC, CAP, APB, and FASB, as well as AICPA industry guides, bulletins, and interpretations. The FASB has categorized these various sources in descending order (A through D) of authority. Previously, this formalization of a hierarchy existed only in the auditing literature.[14]

If the accounting treatment for a transaction is not specified by a category A pronouncement, then a source from categories B through D should be used. If there are multiple pronouncements that address a transaction, then the source from the highest category should be used.

GRAPHIC 1–3   Hierarchy of GAAP

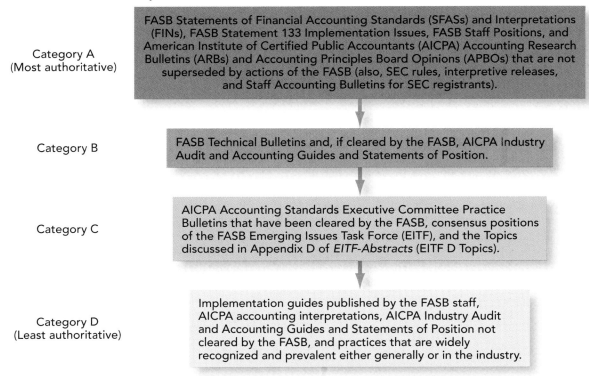

[14]"The Hierarchy of Generally Accepted Accounting Principles," *Statement of Financial Accounting Standards No. 162* (Norwalk, Conn.: FASB, 2008). The FASB's Concept Statements are not included in the hierarchy. They don't constitute GAAP, but instead provide a structure for evaluating current standards and for issuing new standards.

ADDITIONAL CONSIDERATION

Accounting standards and the standard-setting process discussed above relate to standards governing the measurement and reporting of information for profit-oriented organizations. In 1984, the Government Accounting Standards Board (GASB) was created to develop accounting standards for governmental units such as states and cities. The GASB operates under the oversight of the Financial Accounting Foundation and the Governmental Accounting Standards Advisory Council.

The Accounting Standards Codification will become the only level of authoritative U.S. GAAP.

In October 2007, the FASB announced its plan for the release of an *Accounting Standards Codification*. The codification will integrate and topically organize all relevant accounting pronouncements issued by the various U.S. standard setters listed in Graphic 1–3. After approval, expected in 2009, the codification will effectively eliminate the hierarchy above and become the only level of authoritative U.S. GAAP. All other literature will be nonauthoritative.[15]

The Establishment of Accounting Standards—A Political Process

● **LO4**

The setting of accounting and reporting standards often has been characterized as a *political process*. Standards, particularly changes in standards, can have significant differential effects on companies, investors and creditors, and other interest groups. A change in an accounting standard or the introduction of a new standard can result in a substantial redistribution of wealth within our economy.

FINANCIAL Reporting Case

Q2, p. 3

The FASB must consider potential economic consequences of a change in an accounting standard or the introduction of a new standard.

The role of the FASB in setting accounting standards is a complex one. Sound accounting principles can provide significant guidance in determining the appropriate method to measure and report an economic transaction. However, the FASB must gauge the potential economic consequences of a change in a standard to the various interest groups as well as to society as a whole. One obvious desired consequence is that the new standard will provide a better set of information to external users and thus improve the resource allocation process.

An example of the effect of economic consequences on standard setting was the highly controversial debate surrounding accounting for employee stock options. Employees often are given the option to buy shares in the future at a preset price as an integral part of their total compensation package. The accounting objective for any form of compensation is to report compensation expense during the period of service for which the compensation is given. At issue is the amount of compensation to be recognized as expense for stock options.

Historically, options were measured at their intrinsic value, which is the simple difference between the market price of the shares and the option price at which they could be acquired. For instance, an option that permits an employee to buy $60 stock for $42 has an intrinsic value of $18. The problem is that options for which the exercise price equals the market value of the underlying stock at the date of grant (which describes most plans) have no intrinsic value and thus result in zero compensation when measured this way, even though the fair value of the options can be quite substantial. To the FASB and many others, it seemed counterintuitive to not record any compensation expense for arrangements that routinely provide a large part of the total compensation of executives.

Public pressure sometimes prevails over conceptual merit in the standard-setting arena.

In 1995, after lengthy debate, the FASB bowed to public pressure and consented to encourage, rather than require, companies to expense the fair value of employee stock options. Nearly a decade later, the contentious issue resurfaced, and the FASB issued a standard requiring companies to measure options at their fair values and to expense that amount over an appropriate service period. This issue is discussed at greater length in Chapter 19.

The most recent example of the political process at work in standard setting is the heated debate that occurred on the issue of accounting for business combinations. Back in 1996, the FASB added to its agenda a project to consider a possible revision in the practice of

---

[15]"Codification and Retrieval," *Proposal for New Agenda Project,* (Norwalk, Conn.: FASB, 2004). A project update was provided by the FASB on November 16, 2007.

allowing two separate and distinct methods of accounting for business combinations, the pooling of interests method and the purchase method. A thorough explanation of the differences between these methods is beyond the scope of this text. For our discussion here, just note that a key issue in the debate related to goodwill, an intangible asset that arises only in business combinations accounted for using the purchase method. Under the then-existing standards, goodwill, like any other intangible asset, was amortized (expensed) over its estimated useful life thus reducing reported net income for several years following the acquisition. It was that negative impact on earnings that motivated many companies involved in a business combination to take whatever steps necessary to structure the transaction as a pooling of interests, thereby avoiding goodwill, its amortization to expense, and the resulting reduction in earnings.

DENNIS POWELL—CISCO SYSTEMS, INC. VP
Clearly the FASB listened and responded to extensive comments from the public and the financial community to make the purchase method of accounting more effective and realistic.[16]

As you might guess, when the FASB initially proposed eliminating the pooling method, many companies that were actively engaged in business acquisitions vigorously opposed the elimination of this means of avoiding goodwill. To support their opposition these companies argued that if they were required to use purchase accounting, many business combinations important to economic growth would prove unattractive due to the negative impact on earnings caused by goodwill amortization and would not be undertaken.

To satisfy opposition to its proposal, the FASB suggested several modifications over the years, but it wasn't until the year 2000 that a satisfactory compromise was reached. Specifically, under the new accounting standards issued in 2001[17], only the purchase method, now called the acquisition method, is acceptable, but to soften the impact, the resulting goodwill is *not* amortized. We discuss goodwill and its measurement in Chapters 10 and 11.

The FASB's dilemma is to balance accounting considerations and political considerations resulting from perceived possible adverse economic consequences. To help solve this dilemma, the board undertakes a series of elaborate information-gathering steps before issuing a substantive accounting standard involving alternative accounting treatments for an economic transaction. These steps include open hearings, deliberations, and requests for written comments from interested parties. Graphic 1–4 outlines the FASB's standard-setting process.

The FASB undertakes a series of information-gathering steps before issuing a substantive accounting standard.

These steps are the FASB's attempt to acquire consensus as to the preferred method of accounting, as well as to anticipate adverse economic consequences. The board's process is similar to that of an elected political representative, a U.S. congresswoman for example, trying to determine consensus among her constituency before voting on a bill on the floor of the House of Representatives. For this reason, accounting standard setting is a political process.

Our Global Marketplace

Advances in communication and transportation systems continue to expand the marketplace in which companies operate. The world economy is more integrated than ever, and many of the larger U.S. corporations are truly multinational in nature. These multinational corporations have their home in the United States but operate and perhaps raise capital in other countries. For example, **Coca-Cola, IBM, Colgate-Palmolive, Intel,** and many other companies generate more than 50% of their revenue from foreign sales. It is not uncommon for even relatively small companies to transact business in many different countries.

Many U.S. and foreign companies operate and raise capital in more than one country.

Of course, many foreign corporations operate in the United States as well. In fact, companies such as **Columbia Records** and **Bridgestone Americas Holding** are owned by companies that reside in other countries. The financial marketplace also has taken on a global dimension, with many companies crossing geographic boundaries to raise capital. For example, approximately 500 foreign companies are listed on the New York Stock Exchange

---

[16]Jonathan Weil, "FASB Backs Down on Goodwill-Accounting Rules," *The Wall Street Journal* (December 7, 2000).
[17]"Business Combinations," *Statement of Financial Accounting Standards No. 141* (Norwalk, Conn.: FASB, 2001), and "Goodwill and Other Intangible Assets," *Statement of Financial Accounting Standards No. 142* (Norwalk, Conn.: FASB, 2001).

GRAPHIC 1–4

The FASB's Standard-Setting Process

Step	Explanation
1. Identification of problem	A measurement or reporting issue is identified by the Emerging Issues Task Force and placed on the FASB's agenda.
2. The task force	A task force of approximately 15 knowledgeable persons is appointed to advise the Board on various matters.
3. Research and analysis	The FASB's technical staff investigates the issue.
4. *Discussion memorandum (DM)*	The DM, a detailed analysis of the problem along with alternative solutions, is prepared and disseminated to interested parties.
5. Public response	Public hearings are held to discuss the issue and letters of response are sent to the FASB which then analyzes this feedback.
6. *Exposure draft (ED)*	A preliminary draft of a proposed statement, called an exposure draft, is issued. The ED details the proposed treatment for the problem.
7. Public response	Written responses to the ED are accepted and analyzed. The ED is revised, if necessary, depending on the board's analysis.
8. *Statement* issued	An *SFAS* is issued if four of the seven FASB members support the revised ED.

and 400 foreign companies are listed on the London Stock Exchange. This expanded market place requires that company management understand the laws, customs, regulations, *and* accounting and reporting standards of many different countries.

TOWARD GLOBAL ACCOUNTING STANDARDS. Most industrialized countries have organizations responsible for determining accounting and reporting standards. In some countries, the United Kingdom for instance, the responsible organization is a private sector body similar to the FASB in the United States. In other countries, such as France, the organization is a governmental body.

Accounting standards prescribed by these various groups are not the same. Standards differ from country to country for many reasons, including different legal systems, levels of inflation, culture, degrees of sophistication and use of capital markets, and political and economic ties with other countries. These differences can cause problems for multinational corporations. A company doing business in more than one country may find it difficult to comply with more than one set of accounting standards if there are important differences among the sets. These differences also cause problems for investors who must struggle to compare companies whose financial statements are prepared under different standards. It has been argued that different national accounting standards impair the ability of companies to raise capital in international markets.

The *International Accounting Standards Board (IASB)* is dedicated to developing a single set of global accounting standards.

In response to this problem, the International Accounting Standards Committee (IASC) was formed in 1973 to develop global accounting standards. The IASC reorganized itself in 2001 and created a new standard-setting body called the International Accounting Standards Board (IASB). The IASC now acts as an umbrella organization similar to the Financial Accounting Foundation (FAF) in the United States. This new global standard-setting structure is consistent with an FASB vision report aimed at identifying an optimal standard-setting environment.[18] The IASB's objectives are (1) to develop a single set of high-quality, understandable, and enforceable global accounting standards that require transparent and comparable information in general purpose financial statements, and (2) to cooperate with national accounting standard-setters to achieve convergence in accounting standards around the world.

[18]*International Accounting Standard Setting: A Vision for the Future* (Norwalk. Conn.: FASB. 1998).

The IASC issued 41 International Accounting Standards (IASs). The IASB endorsed these standards when it was formed in 2001. Since then, the IASB has revised many of them and has issued eight standards of its own, called International Financial Reporting Standards (IFRSs). Compliance with these standards is voluntary, since the IASB has no enforcement authority. However, more and more countries are basing their national accounting standards on international accounting standards. The International Organization of Securities Commissions (IOSCO) approved a resolution permitting its members to use these standards to prepare their financial statements for cross-border offerings and listings. By late 2007, over 100 jurisdictions, including Hong Kong, Australia, and the countries in the European Union (EU), either require or permit the use of IFRS or a local variant of IFRS.[19] Some 7,000 listed EU companies are affected. In 2007, China began requiring its 1,400 listed companies to report under IFRS-aligned standards.

International Financial Reporting Standards are gaining support around the globe.

In the United States, the move toward convergence of accounting standards began in earnest with the cooperation of the FASB and the IASC in 1994 that led to a common EPS standard for both IFRS and U.S. GAAP. Chapter 19 describes this standard.

ROBERT HERZ—FASB CHAIRMAN
We believe now is the appropriate time to develop a plan for moving all U.S. public companies to an improved version of IFRS and to consider any actions needed to strengthen the IASB as the global accounting standard setter. (From his testimony before Congress, October 2007.)

In 2002, the FASB and IASB signed the so-called Norwalk Agreement, formalizing their commitment to convergence of U.S. GAAP and IFRS. Under this agreement, the boards pledged to remove existing differences between their standards and to coordinate their future standard-setting agendas so that major issues are worked on together. Recent standards issued by the FASB that you will encounter in our later discussions on share-based compensation, nonmonetary exchanges, inventory costs, and the fair value option are examples of this commitment to convergence. In the spring of 2008, the FASB and IASB outlined their plan to accelerate the convergence of U.S. GAAP and IFRS to enable U.S. companies to move to international standards by 2013. "It is a new world and we're going to have to figure out how to play in that," said Robert Herz, chairman of the FASB.[20] In the "new world" to which Herz refers, the financial statements in all major capital markets are based on a single set of standards.

The commitment to narrowing differences between U.S. GAAP and international standards has influenced many FASB Standards.

Although many argue that a single set of global standards will improve comparability of financial reporting and facilitate access to capital, others argue that U.S. standards should remain customized to fit the stringent legal and regulatory requirements of the U.S. business environment. There also is concern that differences in implementation and enforcement from country to country will make accounting appear more uniform than actually is the case. Another argument is that competition between alternative standard-setting regimes is healthy and can lead to improved standards.

At the time this textbook is being written, U.S. standards and IFRS have not fully converged, but in 2007 the SEC eliminated the requirement for foreign companies that issue stock in the United States to include in their financial statements a reconciliation of IFRS to U.S. GAAP. There also is serious discussion of allowing U.S. companies to choose whether to prepare their financial statements according to U.S. GAAP or IFRS.

International Financial Reporting Standards Boxes are included throughout the text that describe the important differences that still remain between U.S. GAAP and IFRS. In addition, your instructor may assign end-of-chapter IFRS exercises and IFRS cases that explore these differences.

The Role of the Auditor

FINANCIAL Reporting Case

It is the responsibility of management to apply accounting standards when communicating with investors and creditors through financial statements. Another group, auditors, serves as an independent intermediary to help ensure that management has in fact appropriately

Q3, p. 3

---

[19]See www.iasplus.com/country/useias.htm.
[20]"FASB, IASB speed up plan for convergence," *Reuters,* May 1, 2008.

Auditors express an opinion on the compliance of financial statements with GAAP.

Google

Auditors offer credibility to financial statements.

Certified public accountants (CPAs) are licensed by states to provide audit services.

Sarbanes-Oxley

applied GAAP in preparing the company's financial statements. Auditors examine (audit) financial statements to express a professional, independent opinion. The opinion reflects the auditors' assessment of the statements' "fairness," which is determined by the extent to which they are prepared in compliance with GAAP.

The report of the independent auditors of **Google Inc.**'s financial statements is in the annual report information included with the text. The first two paragraphs explain the scope of the audit, and the third states the auditors' opinion. After conducting its audit, the accounting firm of **Ernst & Young LLP** stated that "in our opinion, the financial statements referred to above present fairly, . . . , in conformity with U.S. generally accepted accounting principles." This is known as a clean opinion. Had there been any material departures from GAAP or other problems that caused the auditors to question the fairness of the statements, the report would have been modified to inform readers. The fourth paragraph in the report provides the auditors' opinion on the effectiveness of the company's internal control over financial reporting. We discuss this second opinion in the next section.

The auditor adds credibility to the financial statements, increasing the confidence of capital market participants who rely on the information. Auditors, therefore, play an important role in the resource allocation process.

In most states, only individuals licensed as certified public accountants (CPAs) in the state can represent that the financial statements have been audited in accordance with generally accepted auditing standards. Requirements to be licensed as a CPA vary from state to state, but all states specify education, testing, and experience requirements. The testing requirement is to pass the Uniform CPA Examination.

Financial Reporting Reform

The dramatic collapse of **Enron** in 2001 and the dismantling of the international public accounting firm of **Arthur Andersen** in 2002 severely shook U.S. capital markets. The credibility of the accounting profession itself as well as of corporate America was called into question. Public outrage over accounting scandals at high-profile companies like **WorldCom, Xerox, Merck, Adelphia Communications,** and others increased the pressure on lawmakers to pass measures that would restore credibility and investor confidence in the financial reporting process.

Driven by these pressures, Congress acted swiftly and passed the *Public Company Accounting Reform and Investor Protection Act of 2002,* commonly referred to as the *Sarbanes-Oxley Act* for the two congressmen who sponsored the bill. The legislation is comprehensive in its inclusion of the key players in the financial reporting process. The law provides for the regulation of auditors and the types of services they furnish to clients, increases accountability of corporate executives, addresses conflicts of interest for securities analysts, and provides for stiff criminal penalties for violators. Graphic 1–5 outlines the key provisions of the act.

The changes imposed by the legislation are dramatic in scope and pose a significant challenge for the public accounting profession. At the same time, many maintain the changes were necessary to lessen the likelihood of corporate and accounting fraud and to restore investor confidence in the U.S. capital markets.

Section 404 is perhaps the most controversial provision of the 2002 act. No one argues the importance of adequate internal controls. However, the costs of implementing this section of the act have been substantial. Not only are companies required to document internal controls and assess their adequacy, but their auditors, too, must provide an

> **PAUL SARBANES— U.S. SENATOR**
> We confront an increasing crisis of confidence with the public's trust in our markets. If this continues, I think it poses a real threat to our economic health.[21]

> **WILLIAM J. MCDONOUGH—PCAOB CHAIRMAN**
> This standard (*Auditing Standard No. 2*) is one of the most important and far-reaching auditing standards the board will ever adopt. In the past, internal controls were merely considered by auditors; now they will have to be tested and examined in detail. (As quoted in *PCAOBUS.org*, June 18, 2004.)

---

[21]James Kuhnhenn, "Bush Vows to Punish Corporate Lawbreakers," *San Jose Mercury News* (July 9, 2002), p. 8A.

GRAPHIC 1–5

Public Company
Accounting Reform
and Investor Protection
Act of 2002
(Sarbanes-Oxley)

Key Provisions of the Act:

- **Oversight board.** The five-member (two accountants) Public Company Accounting Oversight Board has the authority to establish standards dealing with auditing, quality control, ethics, independence and other activities relating to the preparation of audit reports, or can choose to delegate these responsibilities to the AICPA. Prior to the act, the AICPA set auditing standards. The SEC has oversight and enforcement authority.
- **Corporate executive accountability.** Corporate executives must personally certify the financial statements and company disclosures with severe financial penalties and the possibility of imprisonment for fraudulent misstatement.
- **Nonaudit services.** The law makes it unlawful for the auditors of public companies to perform a variety of nonaudit services for audit clients. Prohibited services include bookkeeping, internal audit outsourcing, appraisal or valuation services, and various other consulting services. Other nonaudit services, including tax services, require pre-approval by the audit committee of the company being audited.
- **Retention of work papers.** Auditors of public companies must retain all audit or review work papers for seven years or face the threat of a prison term for willful violations.
- **Auditor rotation.** Lead audit partners are required to rotate every five years. Mandatory rotation of audit firms came under consideration.
- **Conflicts of interest.** Audit firms are not allowed to audit public companies whose chief executives worked for the audit firm and participated in that company's audit during the preceding year.
- **Hiring of auditor.** Audit firms are hired by the audit committee of the board of directors of the company, not by company management.
- **Internal control.** Section 404 of the act requires that company management document and assess the effectiveness of all internal control processes that could affect financial reporting. Company auditors express an opinion on whether management's assessment of the effectiveness of internal control is fairly stated. The PCAOB's *Auditing Standard No. 2* (since replaced by *Auditing Standard No. 5*) also requires that the company auditors express a second opinion on whether the company has maintained effective internal control over financial reporting.

opinion on management's assessment. The Public Company Accounting Oversight Board's (PCAOB) *Auditing Standard No. 2* added an additional requirement that auditors express a second opinion on whether the company has maintained effective internal control over financial reporting.[22]

Are the benefits of Section 404 greater than the compliance costs? The benefits of 404 are difficult to assess. How many business failures like Enron are avoided as a result of the added attention given to the implementation and maintenance of adequate internal controls? The costs of compliance, on the other hand, are easier to see. For example, the four large, international public accounting firms recently employed a consulting company to survey a sample of the firms' Fortune 1,000 clients to determine the costs for the first two years of Section 404 compliance. The survey determined that the average cost of compliance for firms with a market capitalization of over $700 million, including internal costs and auditor fees, was approximately $8.5 million and $4.77 million in years 1 and 2, respectively.[23] The costs dropped significantly in year 2 as expected, but they still were substantial.

In response to the high cost of 404 compliance, the PCAOB issued *Auditing Standard No. 5* to replace its *Auditing Standard No. 2*.[24] The new standard emphasizes audit efficiency with a more focused, risk-based testing approach for material areas. These guidelines should reduce the total costs of 404 compliance.

We revisit Section 404 in Chapter 7 in the context of an introduction to internal controls.

> Complying with Section 404 of SOX costs companies millions of dollars annually.

---

[22]"An Audit of Internal Control over Financial Reporting Performed in Conjunction with an Audit of Financial Statements," *Auditing Standard No. 2* (Washington, D.C.: PCAOB, 2004).

[23]"Sarbanes-Oxley 404 Costs and Implementation Issues: Spring 2006 Survey Update," CRA International (April 17, 2006).

[24]"An Audit of Internal Control Over Financial Reporting That is Integrated with an Audit of Financial Statements," *Auditing Standard No. 5* (Washington, D.C.: PCAOB, 2007).

A Move Away from Rules-Based Standards?

A principles-based, or objectives-oriented, approach to standard setting stresses professional judgment, as opposed to following a list of rules.

The accounting scandals at Enron and other companies also rekindled the debate over principles-based, or more recently termed objectives-oriented, versus rules-based accounting standards. In fact, a provision of the Sarbanes-Oxley Act required the SEC to study the issue and provide a report to Congress on its findings. That report, issued in July 2003, recommended that accounting standards be developed using an objectives-oriented approach.[25] The FASB also issued a proposal addressing this issue.[26]

An objectives-oriented approach to standard setting stresses using professional judgment, as opposed to following a list of rules when choosing the appropriate accounting treatment for a transaction. Lease accounting provides a useful example for comparing the two approaches. In Chapter 15 you will learn that a company records a long-term lease of an asset as either a *capital lease* or an *operating lease*. If a leasing arrangement is "in substance" the purchase of an asset with the lease payments effectively serving as payments for that purchase, we should account for the transaction that way. A capital lease requires that the property being leased be recorded as an asset and a liability to pay for the asset. No asset or liability is recorded for an operating lease. Therein lies the problem. Because company managers are aware that analysts view debt as indicative of financial risk, those managers often try to avoid reporting more debt than absolutely necessary. As a result, firms frequently stretch the limits of the rules to structure lease agreements so that they technically sidestep the FASB's detailed rules, principally four criteria provided in *SFAS No. 13,* for identifying capital leases that require recording a liability.

In contrast, the IASB employs an objectives-oriented approach to lease accounting in its *IAS 17.* In that standard, the focus is on professional judgment rather than specific rules to determine whether the leasing arrangement effectively transfers the "risk and rewards" of ownership. Professional judgment is then applied to determine if the risk and rewards have been transferred.

Which approach is more likely to capture the economic substance of the lease, rather than its form? The FASB's criteria were designed to aid the accountant in determining whether the risk and rewards of ownership have been transferred. Many would argue, though, that the result has been the opposite. Rather than use the criteria to enhance judgment, management and its accountants can use the rules as an excuse to avoid using professional judgment altogether and instead focus on the rules alone. Proponents of an objectives-oriented approach argue that its focus is squarely on professional judgment, there are few rules to sidestep, and we more likely will arrive at an appropriate accounting treatment. Detractors, on the other hand, argue that the absence of detailed rules opens the door to even more abuse. Even in the absence of intentional misuse, reliance on professional judgment could result in different interpretations for similar transactions, raising concerns about comparability.

The FASB is actively considering whether to move toward objectives-oriented standard setting. That the IASB primarily follows an objectives-oriented approach, coupled with the FASB's recent moves toward convergence of U.S. and international standards, hints at a leaning in that direction. Opposition, though, is ardent. The debate has by no means ended.

In a previous section we covered the financial reporting reform in the United States that followed high-profile frauds such as **Enron** and **WorldCom.** The ethical values of key executives in these corporations were tested and found lacking. We now turn to a discussion of ethics in the accounting profession.

> **ROBERT HERZ—FASB CHAIRMAN**
> Under a principles-based approach, one starts with laying out the key objectives of good reporting in the subject area and then provides guidance explaining the objective and relating it to some common examples. While rules are sometimes unavoidable, the intent is not to try to provide specific guidance or rules for every possible situation. Rather, if in doubt, the reader is directed back to the principles. (From his presentation to the FEI in 2002.)

---

[25]"Study Pursuant to Section 108 (d) of the Sarbanes-Oxley Act of 2002 on the Adoption by the United States Financial Reporting System of a Principles-Based Accounting System," Securities and Exchange Commission (July 2003).
[26]"Principles-Based Approach to U.S. Standard Setting," *A Financial Accounting Standards Board Proposal* (Norwalk, Conn.: FASB, 2002).

Ethics in Accounting

Ethics is a term that refers to a code or moral system that provides criteria for evaluating right and wrong. An ethical dilemma is a situation in which an individual or group is faced with a decision that tests this code. Many of these dilemmas are simple to recognize and resolve. For example, have you ever been tempted to call your professor and ask for an extension on the due date of an assignment by claiming a fictitious illness? Temptation like this will test your personal ethics.

Ethics deals with the ability to distinguish right from wrong.

Accountants, like others operating in the business world, are faced with many ethical dilemmas, some of which are complex and difficult to resolve. For instance, the capital markets' focus on periodic profits may tempt a company's management to bend or even break accounting rules to inflate reported net income. In these situations, technical competence is not enough to resolve the dilemma.

Ethics and Professionalism

One of the elements that many believe distinguishes a profession from other occupations is the acceptance by its members of a responsibility for the interests of those it serves. A high standard of ethical behavior is expected of those engaged in a profession. These standards often are articulated in a code of ethics. For example, law and medicine are professions that have their own codes of professional ethics. These codes provide guidance and rules to members in the performance of their professional responsibilities.

Public accounting has achieved widespread recognition as a profession. The AICPA, the national organization of certified public accountants, has its own Code of Professional Conduct which prescribes the ethical conduct members should strive to achieve. Similarly, the Institute of Management Accountants (IMA)—the primary national organization of accountants working in industry and government—has its own code of ethics, as does the Institute of Internal Auditors—the national organization of accountants providing internal auditing services for their own organizations.

Analytical Model for Ethical Decisions

Ethical codes are informative and helpful. However, the motivation to behave ethically must come from within oneself and not just from the fear of penalties for violating professional codes. Presented below is a sequence of steps that provide a framework for analyzing ethical issues. These steps can help you apply your own sense of right and wrong to ethical dilemmas:[27]

Step 1. Determine the facts of the situation. This involves determining the who, what, where, when, and how.

Step 2. Identify the ethical issue and the stakeholders. Stakeholders may include shareholders, creditors, management, employees, and the community.

Step 3. Identify the values related to the situation. For example, in some situations confidentiality may be an important value that may conflict with the right to know.

Step 4. Specify the alternative courses of action.

Step 5. Evaluate the courses of action specified in step 4 in terms of their consistency with the values identified in step 3. This step may or may not lead to a suggested course of action.

Step 6. Identify the consequences of each possible course of action. If step 5 does not provide a course of action, assess the consequences of each possible course of action for all of the stakeholders involved.

Step 7. Make your decision and take any indicated action.

---

[27]Adapted from Harold Q. Langenderfer and Joanne W. Rockness, "Integrating Ethics into the Accounting Curriculum: Issues, Problems, and Solutions," *Issues in Accounting Education* (Spring 1989). These steps are consistent with those provided by the American Accounting Association's Advisory Committee on Professionalism and Ethics in their publication *Ethics in the Accounting Curriculum: Cases and Readings, 1990.*

ETHICAL DILEMMA

You have recently been employed by a large retail chain that sells sporting goods. One of your tasks is to help prepare periodic financial statements for external distribution. The chain's largest creditor, National Savings & Loan, requires quarterly financial statements, and you are currently working on the statements for the three-month period ending June 30, 2009.

During the months of May and June, the company spent $1,200,000 on a large radio and TV advertising campaign. The $1,200,000 included the costs of producing the commercials as well as the radio and TV time purchased to run the commercials. All of the costs were charged to advertising expense. The company's chief financial officer (CFO) has asked you to prepare a June 30 adjusting entry to remove the costs from advertising expense and to set up an asset called *prepaid advertising* that will be expensed in July. The CFO explained that "This advertising campaign has produced significant sales in May and June and I think it will continue to bring in customers through the month of July. By recording the ad costs as an asset, we can match the cost of the advertising with the additional July sales. Besides, if we expense the advertising in May and June, we will show an operating loss on our income statement for the quarter. The bank requires that we continue to show quarterly profits in order to maintain our loan in good standing."

Ethical dilemmas are presented throughout the text. These dilemmas are designed to raise your consciousness on accounting issues with ethical ramifications. The analytical steps outlined above provide a framework with which to evaluate these situations. In addition, your instructor may assign end-of-chapter ethics cases for further discussion and application.

<table>
<tr><td>

PART B

FINANCIAL Reporting Case

Q4, p. 3

● **LO5**

The conceptual framework does not prescribe GAAP. It provides an underlying foundation for accounting standards.

</td><td>

THE CONCEPTUAL FRAMEWORK

The increasing complexity of our business world creates growing pressure on the FASB to delicately balance the many constituents of the accounting standard-setting process. The task of the FASB is made less complex if there exists a set of cohesive objectives and fundamental concepts on which financial accounting and reporting can be based. A number of years after coming into existence in 1973, the FASB's efforts resulted in the establishment of these objectives and concepts.

</td></tr>
</table>

The conceptual framework has been described as a constitution, a coherent system of interrelated objectives and fundamentals that can lead to consistent standards and that prescribe the nature, function, and limits of financial accounting and reporting. The fundamentals are the underlying concepts of accounting, concepts that guide the selection of events to be accounted for, the measurement of those events, and the means of summarizing and communicating them to interested parties.[28]

> **FASB**
> The *Concepts Statements* will guide the board in developing accounting standards by providing the board with a common foundation and basic reasoning on which to consider merits of alternatives.[29]

The FASB has disseminated this framework through seven Statements of Financial Accounting Concepts. *SFAC 4* deals with the objectives of financial reporting for nonprofit organizations, and *SFAC 3* was superseded by *SFAC 6*, which, with the other four statements, is discussed below. It is important to realize that the conceptual framework provides structure and direction to financial accounting and reporting and does not directly prescribe GAAP.

---

[28]"Conceptual Framework for Financial Accounting and Reporting: Elements of Financial Statements and Their Measurement," *Discussion Memorandum* (Stamford, Conn.: FASB, 1976), p. 2.
[29]Introduction to "Objectives of Financial Reporting by Nonbusiness Organizations," *Statement of Financial Accounting Concepts No. 4* (Stamford, Conn.: FASB, 1980).

The financial statements and their elements are most informative when they possess specific qualitative characteristics, subject to the constraints of materiality, cost effectiveness, and conservatism. Proper recognition and measurement of financial information rely on several assumptions and principles that underlie the financial reporting process.

The remainder of this chapter is devoted to discussions of the components of the conceptual framework that bear on financial statements as depicted in Graphic 1–6, beginning with the objectives of financial reporting. The financial statements themselves are discussed and illustrated in subsequent chapters.

GRAPHIC 1–6

The Conceptual Framework

INTERNATIONAL FINANCIAL REPORTING STANDARDS

Conceptual Framework. In the United States, the FASB's conceptual framework serves primarily to guide standard setters, while internationally the IASB's conceptual framework also serves to indicate GAAP when more specific standards are not available. The FASB and the IASB presently are working together to develop a common conceptual framework that might eventually underlie a uniform set of standards internationally.

Objectives of Financial Reporting

● LO6

In specifying the overriding objectives of financial reporting, the board considered the economic, legal, political, and social environment in the United States. The objectives would be quite different in a socialist economy where the majority of productive resources are government owned.

Implicit in the objectives is an overall societal goal of serving the public interest by providing evenhanded financial and other information that, together with information from other sources, facilitates efficient functioning of capital markets and otherwise assists in promoting efficient capital allocation of scarce resources in the economy.[30]

SFAC 1 **establishes the objectives of financial reporting.**

The importance to our economy of providing capital market participants with information was discussed previously, as were the specific cash flow information needs of investors and creditors. *SFAC 1* articulates this importance and investor and creditor needs through three basic financial reporting objectives listed in Graphic 1–7.

GRAPHIC 1–7

Financial Reporting Objectives

The primary objective of financial reporting is to provide useful information for decision making.

1. Financial reporting should provide information that is useful to present and potential investors and creditors and other users in making rational investment, credit, and similar decisions.
   The information should be comprehensible to those who have a reasonable understanding of business and economic activities and are willing to study the information with reasonable diligence.
2. Financial reporting should provide information to help present and potential investors and creditors and other users to assess the amounts, timing, and uncertainty of prospective cash receipts.
   Since investors' and creditors' cash flows are related to enterprise cash flows, financial reporting should provide information to help assess the amounts, timing, and uncertainty of prospective net cash inflows to the related enterprise.
3. Financial reporting should provide information about the economic resources of an enterprise; the claims to those resources (obligations); and the effects of transactions, events, and circumstances that cause changes in resources and claims to those resources.
   These are sources, direct or indirect, of future cash inflows and cash outflows.

The first objective specifies a focus on investors and creditors. In addition to the importance of investors and creditors as key users, information to meet their needs is likely to have general utility to other groups of external users who are interested in essentially the same financial aspects of a business as are investors and creditors.

SFAC 1 **affirms that investors and creditors are the primary external users of financial information.**

The second objective refers to the specific cash flow information needs of investors and creditors. The third objective emphasizes the need for information about economic resources and claims to those resources. This information would include not only the amount of resources and claims at a particular point in time but also changes in resources and claims that occur over periods of time. This information is key to predicting future cash flows.

Qualitative Characteristics of Accounting Information

● LO6

To satisfy the stated objectives, information should possess certain characteristics. The purpose of *SFAC 2* is to outline the desired qualitative characteristics of accounting information.

To be useful, information must make a difference in the decision process.

Graphic 1–8 indicates these qualitative characteristics, presented in the form of a hierarchy of their perceived importance. Notice that the main focus, as stated in the first concept statement is on decision usefulness—the ability to be useful in decision making. Understandability means that users must understand the information within the context of the decision being made. This is a user-specific quality because users will differ in their ability

---

[30]Introduction to "Objectives of Financial Reporting for Business Enterprises," *Statement of Financial Accounting Concepts No. 1* (Stamford, Conn.: FASB, 1978).

GRAPHIC 1–8   Hierarchy of Desirable Characteristics of Accounting Information

to comprehend any set of information. The first stated financial reporting objective of *SFAC 1* is to provide comprehensible information to those who have a reasonable understanding of business and economic activities and are willing to study the information.

Primary Qualitative Characteristics

The primary decision-specific qualities that make accounting information useful are relevance and reliability. Both are critical. No matter how reliable, if information is not relevant to the decision at hand, it is useless. Conversely, relevant information is of little value if it cannot be relied on. Let's look closer at each of these two characteristics, including the components that make those qualities desirable. We also consider two secondary qualities—comparability and consistency.

> To be useful for decision making, accounting information should be *relevant* and *reliable.*

RELEVANCE.   To make a difference in the decision process, information must possess predictive value and/or feedback value. Generally, useful information will possess both qualities. For example, if net income and its components confirm investor expectations about future cash-generating ability, then net income has feedback value for investors. This confirmation can also be useful in predicting future cash-generating ability as expectations are revised.

This predictive ability is central to the concept of "earnings quality," the ability of reported earnings (income) to predict a company's future earnings. This is a concept we revisit frequently throughout this textbook in order to explore the impact on earnings quality of various topics under discussion. For instance, in Chapter 4 we discuss the contents of the income statement and certain classifications used in the statement from the perspective of helping analysts separate a company's transitory earnings from its permanent earnings. This separation is critical to a meaningful prediction of future earnings. In later chapters, we look at how various financial reporting decisions affect earnings quality.

Timeliness also is an important component of relevance. Information is timely when it is available to users early enough to allow its use in the decision process. The need for timely information requires that companies provide information to external users on a periodic basis. The SEC requires its registrants to submit financial statement information not only on an annual basis, but also quarterly for the first three quarters of each fiscal year.

> Information is *timely* if it is available to users before a decision is made.

RELIABILITY.   Reliability is the extent to which information is *verifiable, representationally faithful,* and *neutral.* Verifiability implies a consensus among different measurers. For example, the historical cost of a piece of land to be reported in the balance sheet of a company is usually highly verifiable. The cost can be traced to an exchange transaction, the purchase of the land. However, the fair value of that land is much more difficult to verify. Appraisers could differ in their assessment of fair value. The term *objectivity* often is linked to verifiability. The historical cost of the land is objective but the land's fair value is subjective, influenced by the measurer's past experience and prejudices. A measurement that is subjective is difficult to verify, which makes it more difficult for users to rely on.

Representational faithfulness exists when there is agreement between a measure or description and the phenomenon it purports to represent. For example, assume that the term *inventory* in a balance sheet of a retail company is understood by external users to represent items that are intended for sale in the ordinary course of business. If inventory includes, say, machines used to produce inventory, then it lacks representational faithfulness.

Several years ago, accountants used the term *reserve for doubtful accounts* to describe anticipated bad debts related to accounts receivable. For many, the term *reserve* means that a sum of money has been set aside for future bad debts. Because this was not the case, this term lacked representational faithfulness. The description "reserve. . ." has been changed to "allowance for uncollectible accounts" or "allowance for doubtful accounts."

Reliability assumes the information being relied on is neutral with respect to parties potentially affected. In that regard, neutrality is highly related to the establishment of accounting standards. You learned earlier that changes in accounting standards can lead to adverse economic consequences to certain companies, their investors and creditors, and other interest groups. Accounting standards should be established with overall societal goals and specific objectives in mind and should try not to favor particular groups or companies.

The FASB faces a difficult task in balancing neutrality and the consideration of economic consequences. A new accounting standard may favor one group of companies over others, but the FASB must convince the financial community that this was a consequence of the standard and not an objective used to set the standard. Donald Kirk, one of the members of the first group to serve on the FASB, stressed the importance of neutrality in the standard-setting process.

The qualities of relevance and reliability often clash. For example, a net income forecast provided by the management of a company may possess a high degree of relevance to investors and creditors trying to predict future cash flows. However, a forecast necessarily contains subjectivity in the estimation of future events. GAAP presently do not require companies to provide forecasts of any financial variables.

> **DONALD KIRK**
> If financial reporting is to be credible, there must be public confidence that the standard-setting system is credible, that selection of board members is based on merit and not the influence of special interests, and that standards are developed neutrally with the objective of relevant and reliable information, not purposeful manipulation.[31]

Secondary Qualitative Characteristics

Graphic 1–8 identifies two secondary qualitative characteristics important to decision usefulness—comparability and consistency. Comparability is the ability to help users see similarities and differences between events and conditions. We already have discussed the importance of the ability of investors and creditors to compare information across companies to make their resource allocation decisions. Closely related to comparability is the notion that consistency of accounting practices over time permits valid comparisons between different periods. The predictive and feedback value of information is enhanced if users can compare the performance of a company over time.[32] In the **Google** financial statements and disclosure notes, notice that disclosure Note 1 includes a summary of significant accounting policies. A change in one of these policies would require disclosure in the financial statements and notes to restore comparability between periods.

Margin notes:

Representational faithfulness means agreement between a measure and a real-world phenomenon that the measure is supposed to represent.

Accounting standards should not favor any particular groups or companies nor influence behavior in any specific way.

A trade-off often is required between various degrees of relevance and reliability.

Accounting information should be *comparable* across different companies and over different time periods.

---

[31]Donald J. Kirk, chairman of the FASB, quoted in *Status Report,* December 23, 1986.

[32]Companies occasionally do change their accounting practices, which makes it difficult for users to make comparisons among different reporting periods. Chapter 4 and Chapter 20 describe the disclosures that a company makes in this situation to restore consistency among periods.

Practical Boundaries (Constraints) to Achieving Desired Qualitative Characteristics

Most of us learn early in life that we can't get everything we desire. The latest electronic gadget may have all the qualitative characteristics that current technology can provide, but limited resources may lead us to purchase a fully functional model with fewer bells and whistles. Cost effectiveness also constrains the accounting choices we make. Specifically, it's important that the benefits of endowing accounting information with all the qualitative characteristics we've discussed exceed the costs of doing so.

A related constraint on the type of information we provide is the concept of materiality. For an additional $20 you can add the latest enhancement to that electronic gadget you're considering. However, despite the higher specs, if you feel it will provide no discernible improvement in the performance of the product as you will use it, why pay the extra $20? In an accounting context, if a more costly way of providing information is not expected to have a material effect on decisions made by those using the information, the less costly method may be acceptable.

Cost effectiveness and materiality impart practical constraints on each of the qualitative characteristics of accounting information. Both suggest that a certain accounting treatment might be different from that dictated solely by consideration of desired qualities of information.

Cost Effectiveness

The costs of providing accounting information include those of gathering, processing, and disseminating information. There also are costs to users when interpreting information. In addition, costs include possible adverse economic consequences of implementing accounting standards. These costs in particular are difficult, if not impossible, to quantify.

An example of this is the standard that requires companies operating in more than one operating segment to disclose certain disaggregated financial information.[33] In addition to information gathering, processing, and dissemination costs, many companies feel that this reporting requirement imposes what could be called *competitive disadvantage costs.* These companies do not want their competitors to have the disaggregated data.

The perceived benefit from this or any accounting standard is increased *decision usefulness* of the information provided, which, hopefully, improves the resource allocation process. It is inherently impossible to quantify this benefit. The elaborate information-gathering process undertaken by the FASB in setting accounting standards is an attempt to assess both costs and benefits of a proposed accounting standard, even if in a subjective, nonquantifiable manner. In the case of reporting disaggregated information, the FASB decided that the perceived benefits of disclosing this information exceeded the costs of providing it.

> The costs of providing accounting information include any possible adverse economic consequences of accounting standards.

> Information is *cost effective* only if the perceived benefit of increased *decision usefulness* exceeds the anticipated costs of providing that information.

Materiality

Materiality is another pervasive constraint. Information is material if it can have an effect on a decision made by users. One consequence of considering materiality is that GAAP need not be followed if an item is immaterial. For example, GAAP requires that receivables be measured at their net realizable value. If bad debts are anticipated, they should be estimated and subtracted from the face amount of receivables for balance sheet measurement. This is called the *allowance method* of accounting for bad debts. However, if the amount of anticipated bad debts is not considered to be large enough to affect decisions made by users, the *direct write-off method* of accounting for bad debts can be used even though it is not a generally accepted technique. This method does not require estimation of bad debts for existing receivables.

The threshold for materiality will depend principally on the *relative* dollar amount of the transaction. For example, $10,000 in total anticipated bad debts for a multibillion dollar

> Information is *material* if it has an effect on decisions.

---

[33]"Disclosures about Segments of an Enterprise and Related Information," *Statement of Financial Accounting Standards No. 131* (Norwalk, Conn.: FASB, 1997). The contents of this standard are described in the appendix to Chapter 3.

company like Google would not be considered material. The method used to account for these anticipated bad debts will not affect the decisions made by Google's financial statement users. This same $10,000 amount, however, could easily be material for a neighborhood pizza parlor. The FASB has been reluctant to establish any quantitative materiality guidelines. The threshold for materiality has been left to the subjective judgment of the company preparing the financial statements and its auditors.

Materiality is concerned not only with the dollar amount of an item but with the nature of the item as well. In 1999, the SEC issued *Staff Accounting Bulletin No. 99*.[34] The bulletin expresses the SEC's view that exclusive reliance on quantitative benchmarks to assess materiality in preparing financial statements is inappropriate. A number of other factors, including whether the item in question involves an unlawful transaction, should also be considered when determining materiality. For example, an activity such as the illegal payment of $10,000 to an official of a foreign government to secure a valuable contract would probably be considered material even if the amount is small relative to the size of the company.

> **Professional judgment determines what amount is material in each situation.**

Conservatism

> **Conservatism is a justification for some accounting practices, *not* a desired qualitative characteristic of accounting information.**

Conservatism is a practice followed in an attempt to ensure that uncertainties and risks inherent in business situations are adequately considered. It is a frequently cited characteristic of accounting information. Conservatism is not, however, a desired qualitative characteristic but a practical justification for some accounting choices. In that sense, conservatism serves as a third constraint on the achievement of various qualitative characteristics.[35]

The need for conservatism often is discussed in conjunction with the estimates required to comply with GAAP. For example, assume that a company estimated that its anticipated bad debts on existing receivables could be any number between $20,000 and $30,000, with the most likely amount being $25,000, and that these amounts are material. A conservative estimate would be $30,000, thus showing the lowest amount (of a range of possible values) in the balance sheet for net receivables and the highest expense (and therefore the lowest net income) in the income statement.

However, financial accounting information users could just as easily be misled by a conservative estimate as by an optimistic one. If $25,000 is the best estimate of anticipated bad debts, then that is the number that should be used. Conservatism is *not* a desirable characteristic nor is it an accounting principle. Nevertheless, there seem to be some accounting practices, such as the lower-of-cost-or-market method for measuring inventory (Chapter 9), that appear to be generated by a desire to be conservative. However, these practices are motivated by other accounting principles such as the realization principle as discussed later in this chapter. They also are influenced by practical realities of our legal system. Investors and creditors who lose money from stock purchases or loans are less likely to sue when bad news is exaggerated and good news is underestimated. While recognizing the role that conservatism plays in how information is reported, we also need to emphasize that it is not a desired characteristic from a qualitative standpoint. Instead, conservatism is a practical constraint on the extent to which other qualitative characteristics are instilled in accounting information.

Now that we've discussed the qualities that the elements of financial statements should possess, let's look more closely at the elements themselves.

Elements of Financial Statements

● LO6

SFAC 6 defines 10 elements of financial statements. These elements are "the building blocks with which financial statements are constructed—the classes of items that financial statements comprise."[36] They focus directly on items related to measuring performance and to reporting financial position. The definitions of these elements operationalize the resources,

---

[34]"Materiality," *Staff Accounting Bulletin No. 99* (Washington, D.C.: SEC, August 1999).

[35]The FASB's hierarchy of qualitative characteristics does not specifically identify conservatism as a constraint. Most theorists include conservatism as one of the underlying accounting principles that guide accounting practice. Our classification recognizes its very real role in accounting choices as well as the practical motivation for those choices.

[36]"Elements of Financial Statements," *Statement of Financial Accounting Concepts No. 6* (Stamford, Conn.: FASB, 1985), par. 5.

claims, and changes identified in the third objective of financial reporting of *SFAC 1* (see Graphic 1–7). The *accrual accounting* model actually is embodied in the element definitions. The FASB recognized that accrual accounting produces information that is more successful in predicting future cash flows than is cash flow accounting.

For now, we list and define the elements in Graphic 1–9. You will learn much more about these in subsequent chapters.

The 10 elements of financial statements defined in *SFAC 6* describe financial position and periodic performance.

GRAPHIC 1–9

Elements of Financial Statements

Elements of Financial Statements	
Assets	Probable future economic benefits obtained or controlled by a particular entity as a result of past transactions or events.
Liabilities	Probable future sacrifices of economic benefits arising from present obligations of a particular entity to transfer assets or provide services to other entities in the future as a result of past transactions or events.
Equity (or net assets)	Called shareholders' equity or stockholders' equity for a corporation, it is the residual interest in the assets of an entity that remains after deducting its liabilities.
Investments by owners	Increases in equity of a particular business enterprise resulting from transfers to it from other entities of something of value to obtain or increase ownership interests in it.
Distributions to owners	Decreases in equity of a particular enterprise resulting from transfers to owners.
Comprehensive income	The change in equity of a business enterprise during a period from transactions and other events and circumstances from nonowner sources. It includes all changes in equity during a period except those resulting from investments by owners and distributions to owners.
Revenues	Inflows or other enhancements of assets of an entity or settlements of its liabilities during a period from delivering or producing goods, rendering services, or other activities that constitute the entity's ongoing major or central operations.
Expenses	Outflows or other using up of assets or incurrences of liabilities during a period from delivering or producing goods, rendering services, or other activities that constitute the entity's ongoing major or central operations.
Gains	Increases in equity from peripheral or incidental transactions of an entity.
Losses	Represent decreases in equity arising from peripheral or incidental transactions of an entity.

Recognition and Measurement Concepts

Now that the various elements of financial statements have been identified, we discuss when they should be recognized (recorded) and how they should be measured. *SFAC 5* addresses these issues. Recognition refers to the process of admitting information into the basic financial statements. Measurement is the process of associating numerical amounts to the elements. For example, a revenue was previously defined as an inflow of assets from selling a good or providing a service. But, *when* should the revenue event be recorded, and at *what* amount?

Recognition

According to *SFAC 5,* an item should be recognized in the basic financial statements when it meets the following four criteria, subject to a cost effectiveness constraint and materiality threshold:

1. *Definition.* The item meets the definition of an element of financial statements.
2. *Measurability.* The item has a relevant attribute measurable with sufficient reliability.

Recognition criteria.

3. *Relevance.* The information about it is capable of making a difference in user decisions.
4. *Reliability.* The information is representationally faithful, verifiable, and neutral.[37]

These obviously are very general guidelines. The concept statement does not address *specific* recognition issues.

Measurement

The question of measurement involves two choices: (1) the choice of a unit of measurement, and (2) the choice of an attribute to be measured. *SFAC 5* essentially confirmed existing practice in both of these areas. The monetary unit or measurement scale used in financial statements is nominal units of money without any adjustment for changes in purchasing power. In addition, the board acknowledged that different attributes such as historical cost, net realizable value, and present value of future cash flows are presently used to measure different financial statement elements, and that they expect that practice to continue. For example, property, plant, and equipment are measured at historical cost; accounts receivable are measured at their net realizable value; and most long-term liabilities, such as bonds, are measured at the present value of future cash payments.

SFAC No. 7 provides a framework for using future cash flows in accounting measurements.

Present value measurements have long been associated with accounting valuation. However, because of its increased prominence, present value is the focus of a recent FASB concept statement that provides a framework for using future cash flows as the basis for accounting measurement and also asserts that the objective in valuing an asset or liability using present value is to approximate the fair value of that asset or liability.[38] We explore this objective in more depth in Chapter 6.

Answers to the recognition and measurement questions are imbedded in generally accepted accounting principles. *SFAC 5* confirmed some of the more important of these principles used in present practice. GAAP consist of broad principles and specific standards. The accrual accounting model is an example of a broad principle. Before addressing additional key broad principles, we look at some important assumptions that underlie those fundamental principles.

Underlying Assumptions

● LO7

The four basic assumptions underlying GAAP are (1) the economic entity assumption, (2) the going concern assumption, (3) the periodicity assumption, and (4) the monetary unit assumption.

The *economic entity assumption* presumes that economic events can be identified specifically with an economic entity.

ECONOMIC ENTITY ASSUMPTION. An essential assumption is that all economic events can be identified with a particular economic entity. Investors desire information about an economic entity that corresponds to their ownership interest. For example, if you were considering buying some ownership stock in Google, you would want information on the various operating units that constitute Google. You would need information not only about their United States operations but also about their European and other international operations. Also, you would not want the information about Google combined with that of **Yahoo! Inc.,** another Internet information provider. These would be two separate *economic entities.* The financial information for the various companies (subsidiaries) in which Google owns a controlling interest (greater than 50% ownership of voting stock) should be combined with that of Google (the parent). The parent and its subsidiaries are separate *legal* entities but one *accounting* entity.

Another key aspect of this assumption is the distinction between the economic activities of owners and those of the company. For example, the economic activities of a sole proprietorship, Uncle Jim's Restaurant, should be separated from the activities of its owner, Uncle Jim. Uncle Jim's personal residence, for instance, is not an asset of the business.

GOING CONCERN ASSUMPTION. Another necessary assumption is that, in the absence of information to the contrary, it is anticipated that a business entity will continue

---

[37]"Recognition and Measurement in Financial Statements," *Statement of Financial Accounting Concepts No. 5* (Stamford, Conn.: FASB, 1984), par. 63.

[38]"Using Cash Flow Information and Present Value in Accounting Measurements," *Statement of Financial Accounting Concepts No. 7* (Norwalk, Conn.: FASB, 2000).

to operate indefinitely. Accountants realize that the going concern assumption does not always hold since there certainly are many business failures. However, companies are begun with the hope of a long life, and many achieve that goal.

This assumption is critical to many broad and specific accounting principles. For example, the assumption provides justification for measuring many assets based on their historical costs. If it were known that an enterprise was going to cease operations in the near future, assets and liabilities would not be measured at their historical costs but at their current liquidation values. Similarly, depreciation of a building over an estimated life of 40 years presumes the business will operate that long.

Financial statements of a company presume the business is a *going concern*.

PERIODICITY ASSUMPTION.   The periodicity assumption relates to the qualitative characteristic of *timeliness*. External users need *periodic* information to make decisions. This need for periodic information requires that the economic life of an enterprise (presumed to be indefinite) be divided into artificial time periods for financial reporting. Corporations whose securities are publicly traded are required to provide financial information to the SEC on a quarterly and annual basis.[39] Financial statements often are prepared on a monthly basis for banks and others that might need more timely information.

For many companies, the annual time period (the fiscal year) used to report to external users is the calendar year. However, other companies have chosen a fiscal year that does not correspond to the calendar year. The accounting profession and the Securities and Exchange Commission advocate that companies adopt a fiscal year that corresponds to their natural business year. A natural business year is the 12-month period that ends when the business activities of a company reach their lowest point in the annual cycle. For example, many retailers, **Wal-Mart** for example, have adopted a fiscal year ending on January 31. Business activity in January generally is quite slow following the very busy Christmas period. We can see from the Google financial statements that the company's fiscal year ends on December 31. The **Campbell Soup Company**'s fiscal year ends in July; **Clorox**'s in June; and **Monsanto**'s in August.

The *periodicity assumption* allows the life of a company to be divided into artificial time periods to provide timely information.

Google

MONETARY UNIT ASSUMPTION.   Recall that to *measure* financial statement elements, a unit or scale of measurement must be chosen. Information would be difficult to use if, for example, assets were listed as "three machines, two trucks, and a building." A common denominator is needed to measure all elements. The dollar in the United States is the most appropriate common denominator to express information about financial statement elements and changes in those elements.

One problem with this assumption is that the monetary unit is presumed to be stable over time. That is, the value of the dollar, in terms of its ability to purchase certain goods and services, is constant over time. This obviously does not strictly hold. The U.S. economy has experienced periods of rapidly changing prices. To the extent that prices are unstable, and those machines, trucks and building were purchased at different times, the monetary unit used to measure them is not the same. The effect of changing prices on financial information generally is discussed elsewhere in your accounting curriculum, often in an advanced accounting course.

The *monetary unit assumption* states that financial statement elements should be measured in terms of the United States dollar.

Accounting Principles

There are four important broad accounting principles that provide significant guidance for accounting practice: (1) the historical cost principle, (2) the realization principle (also known as the *revenue recognition principle*), (3) the matching principle, and (4) the full-disclosure principle. These principles deal with the critical issues of recognition and measurement. The accrual accounting model is embodied in each of the principles.

● LO8

HISTORICAL COST PRINCIPLE.   The FASB recognized in *SFAC 5* that elements in financial statements currently are measured by different attributes. In general, however, GAAP measure assets and liabilities based on their *original transaction value*, that is, their historical costs. For an asset, this is the fair value of what is given in exchange (usually

The *historical cost principle* states that asset and liability measurements should be based on the amount given or received in the exchange transaction.

---

[39]The report that must be filed for the first three quarters of each fiscal year is Form 10-Q and the annual report is Form 10-K.

cash) for the asset at its initial acquisition. For liabilities, it is the current cash equivalent received in exchange for assuming the liability. For example, if a company borrowed $1 million cash and signed an interest-bearing note promising to repay the cash in the future, the liability would be valued at $1 million, the cash received in exchange.[40]

Why base measurement on historical costs? After all, the current value of a company's manufacturing plant might seem more relevant than its original cost. First, historical cost provides important cash flow information as it represents the cash or cash equivalent paid for an asset or received in exchange for the assumption of a liability. Second, because historical cost valuation is the result of an exchange transaction between two independent parties, the agreed on exchange value is objective and highly *verifiable*. Alternatives such as measuring an asset at its current fair value involve *estimating* a selling price. An example given earlier in the chapter concerned the valuation of a parcel of land. Appraisers could easily differ in their assessment of current fair value.

There are occasions where a departure from measuring an asset based on its historical cost is warranted. Some assets, for instance, are measured at their *net realizable value*. For example, if customers purchased goods or services on account for $10,000, the asset, accounts receivable, would initially be valued at $10,000, the original transaction value. Subsequently, if $2,000 in bad debts were anticipated, net receivables should be valued at $8,000, the net realizable value. Departures from historical cost measurement such as this provide more appropriate information in terms of the overall objective of providing information to aid in the prediction of future cash flows.

REALIZATION PRINCIPLE. Determining accounting income by the accrual accounting model is a challenging task. When to recognize revenue is critical to this determination. Revenues are inflows of assets resulting from providing a product or service to a customer. At what point is this event recognized by an increase in assets? The realization principle requires that two criteria be satisfied before revenue can be recognized:

1. The earnings process is judged to be complete or virtually complete.
2. There is reasonable certainty as to the collectibility of the asset to be received (usually cash).

These criteria help ensure that a revenue event is not recorded until an enterprise has performed all or most of its earnings activities for a financially capable buyer. The primary earnings activity that triggers the recognition of revenue is known as the *critical event*. The critical event for many businesses occurs at the point-of-sale. This usually takes place when the goods or services sold to the buyer are *delivered* (i.e., title is transferred).

The *timing* of revenue recognition is a key element of earnings measurement. An income statement should report the results of all operating activities for the time period specified in the financial statements. A one-year income statement should report the company's accomplishments only for that one-year period. Revenue recognition criteria help ensure that a proper cut-off is made each reporting period and that exactly one year's activity is reported in that income statement. Not adhering to revenue recognition criteria could result in overstating revenue and hence net income in one reporting period and, consequently, understating revenue and net income in a subsequent period. Notice that revenue recognition criteria allow for the implementation of the accrual accounting model. Revenue should be recognized in the period it is earned, *not necessarily in the period in which cash is received*.

Some revenue-producing activities call for revenue recognition over time, rather than at one particular point in time. For example, revenue recognition could take place *during* the earnings process for long-term construction contracts. We discuss revenue recognition in considerable depth in Chapter 5. That chapter also describes in more detail the concept of an earnings process and how it relates to performance measurement.

MATCHING PRINCIPLE. When are expenses recognized? The matching principle states that expenses are recognized in the same period as the related revenues. There is a cause-and-effect relationship between revenue and expense recognition implicit in this definition. In a given

Historical cost measurement provides relevant cash flow information and also is highly verifiable.

A departure from historical cost valuation sometimes is appropriate.

Revenue should be recognized when the earnings process is virtually complete and collection is reasonably assured.

Both revenue recognition criteria usually are met at the *point-of-sale*.

Revenue is recognized when *earned*, regardless of when cash actually is received.

Expenses are recognized in the same reporting period as the related revenues.

---

[40]This current cash equivalent for many liabilities also will equal the present value of future cash payments. This is illustrated in a subsequent chapter.

period, revenue is recognized according to the realization principle. The matching principle then requires that all expenses incurred in generating that same revenue also be recognized. The net result is a measure—net income—that matches current period accomplishments and sacrifices. This accrual-based measure provides a good indicator of future cash-generating ability.

Although the concept is straightforward, its implementation can be difficult. The difficulty arises in trying to identify cause-and-effect relationships. Many expenses are not incurred *directly* because of a revenue event. Instead, the expense is incurred to generate the revenue, but the association is indirect.

The matching principle is implemented by one of four different approaches, depending on the nature of the specific expense. Only the first approach involves an actual cause-and-effect relationship between revenue and expense. In the other three approaches, the relationship is indirect.

An expense can be recognized:

1. Based on an exact cause-and-effect relationship between a revenue and expense event.
2. By associating an expense with the revenues recognized in a specific time period.
3. By a systematic and rational allocation to specific time periods.
4. In the period incurred, without regard to related revenues.

The first approach is appropriate for *cost of goods sold.* There is a definite cause-and-effect relationship between **Dell Inc.**'s revenue from the sale of personal computers and the costs to produce those computers. Commissions paid to salespersons for obtaining revenues also is an example of an expense recognized based on this approach.

> There is a direct relationship between some expenses and revenues.

Unfortunately, for most expenses there is no obvious cause-and-effect relationship between a revenue and expense event. In other words, the revenue event does not directly *cause* expenses to be incurred. Many expenses, however, can be related to periods of time during which revenue is earned. For example, the monthly salary paid to an office worker is not directly related to any specific revenue event. The employee provides services during the month. The asset used to pay the employee, cash, provides benefits to the company only for that one month and *indirectly* relates to the revenue recognized in that same period.

> Some expenses are associated indirectly with revenues of a particular period.

Some costs are incurred to acquire assets that provide benefits to the company for more than one reporting period. Refer again to the Carter Company example in Illustration 1–1 on page 7. At the beginning of year 1, $60,000 in rent was paid covering a three-year period. This asset, prepaid rent, helps generate revenues for more than one reporting period. In that example, we chose to "systematically and rationally" allocate rent expense equally to each of the three one-year periods rather than to charge the expense to year 1.

> Some expenses are allocated to specific time periods.

The fourth approach to expense recognition is called for in situations when costs are incurred but it is impossible to determine in which period or periods, if any, revenues will occur. For example, consider the cost of advertising. Advertising expenditures are made with the presumption that incurring that expense will generate incremental revenues. Let's say Google spends $1 million for a series of television commercials. It's difficult to determine when, how much, or even whether additional revenues occur as a result of that particular series of ads. Because of this difficulty, advertising expenditures are recognized as expense in the period incurred, with no attempt made to match them with revenues.

> Some expenses are recognized in the period incurred, without regard to related revenues.

THE FULL-DISCLOSURE PRINCIPLE.   Remember, the purpose of accounting is to provide information that is useful to decision makers. So, naturally, if there is accounting information not included in the primary financial statements that would benefit users, that information should be provided too. The full-disclosure principle means that the financial reports should include any information that could affect the decisions made by external users. Of course, the benefits of that information, as noted earlier, should exceed the costs of providing the information. Supplemental information is disclosed in a variety of ways, including:

> Any information useful to decision makers should be provided in the financial statements, subject to the cost effectiveness constraint.

1. Parenthetical comments or modifying comments placed on the face of the financial statements.
2. Disclosure notes conveying additional insights about company operations, accounting principles, contractual agreements, and pending litigation.
3. Supplemental financial statements that report more detailed information than is shown in the primary financial statements.

We find examples of these disclosures in the **Google** financial statements included with all new copies of the text. A parenthetical or modifying comment is provided in the stockholders' equity section of the balance sheet with disclosure of the number of shares of stock authorized, issued, and outstanding, and the statements include several notes. We discuss and illustrate disclosure requirements as they relate to specific financial statement elements in later chapters as those elements are discussed.

Graphic 1–10 provides a summary of the accounting assumptions and principles that guide the recognition and measurement of accounting information.

GRAPHIC 1–10

Summary of Recognition and Measurement Concepts

Assumptions	Description
Economic entity	All economic events can be identified with a particular economic entity.
Going concern	In the absence of information to the contrary, it is anticipated that a business entity will continue to operate indefinitely.
Periodicity	The life of a company can be divided into artificial time periods to provide timely information to external users.
Monetary unit	In the United States, financial statement elements should be measured in terms of the U.S. dollar.
Principles	
Historical cost	Asset and liability measurements should be based on the amount given or received in an exchange transaction.
Realization	Revenue should be recognized only after the earnings process is virtually complete and there is reasonable certainty of collecting the asset to be received from the customer.
Matching	Expenses should be recognized in the same reporting period as the related revenues.
Full disclosure	Any information that could change the decisions made by external users should be provided in the financial statements, subject to the cost effectiveness constraint.

Evolution of Accounting Principles

Earlier in the chapter you learned that the convergence of accounting standards with international standards is having a profound effect on financial reporting in the United States. An approach to recognizing revenues and expenses that has become known as the "asset/liability" approach and an apparent progression toward fair value accounting have influenced several recent IASB and FASB standards and signify fundamental changes in accounting principles. We discuss these two concepts next.

The Asset/Liability Approach

You know from introductory accounting that the balance sheet and income statement are intertwined and must reconcile with each other. For example, the revenues listed in the income statement depict inflows of assets whose balances at a particular point in time are shown in the balance sheet. But which comes first, identifying revenues and expenses, or identifying assets and liabilities?

The realization and matching principles sometimes are described as "income-statement focused," because they focus on determining when we recognize revenues and expenses in the income statement. From this perspective, sometimes referred to as the revenue/expense approach, principles for recognizing revenues and expenses are emphasized, with assets and liabilities recognized as necessary to make the balance sheet reconcile with the income statement. For example, when accounting for a sales transaction our focus would be on whether revenue has been earned, and if we determined that it has, we would record an asset (accounts receivable) that is associated with the revenue. In subsequent chapters you will see that much of our accounting for revenues and expenses follows this revenue/expense approach.

Under the alternative asset/liability approach we first measure the assets and liabilities that exist at a balance-sheet date and then recognize the revenues, expenses, gains and losses needed to account for the changes in these assets and liabilities from the previous measurement date. Under this approach, principles for asset and liability measurement are emphasized, and revenues, expenses, gains and losses are recognized as necessary to make the balance sheet reconcile with the income statement. For example, when accounting for a sales transaction, our focus would be on whether a potential accounts receivable meets the definition of an asset, and if it does, we would record that asset and recognize whatever amount of revenue is implied by the inflow of that asset. In subsequent chapters you will see that recent standards involving accounting for investments and income taxes follow this asset/liability approach.

> With the *asset/liability approach*, the measurement of assets and liabilities drives revenue and expense recognition.

It may seem like it shouldn't matter whether standard setters use the revenue/expense or asset/liability approach, given that both approaches affect both the income statement and balance sheet. However, the particular approach used by a standard setter can affect the amounts and timing of recognition on both statements. In particular, the asset/liability approach encourages standard setters to focus on accurately measuring assets and liabilities. It perhaps is not surprising, then, that a focus on assets and liabilities has led standard setters to lean more and more toward fair value measurement, our next topic.

The Move toward Fair Value

In your study of accounting you've learned that the historical cost principle is the basis of measurement for most assets and liabilities. Often overlooked, though, is that there are over 40 instances in GAAP in which assets or liabilities are required or permitted to be measured at fair value. The FASB recently issued two Standards related to using fair value in financial statements. The first of these, *SFAS No. 157*, establishes a framework for measuring fair value whenever fair value is called for in applying generally accepted accounting principles.[41] The second, *SFAS No. 159*, gives a company the option to report some or all of its *financial* assets and liabilities at fair value.[42] Let's look closer at the content of these two important Standards.

FAIR VALUE DEFINED.   *SFAS No. 157* doesn't change the number of situations in which fair value is used, but defines fair value and provides improved guidance for how to measure it. Here's how *SFAS No. 157* defines fair value:

The price that would be received to sell assets or paid to transfer a liability in an orderly transaction between market participants at the measurement date.

> Fair value definition

A key aspect of this definition is its focus on the perspective of *market participants.* For instance, if a company buys a competitor's patent, not intending to use it but merely to keep the competitor from using it, the company still will have to assign a value to the asset because a market participant would find value in using the patent.

> *SFAS No. 157* provides improved guidance to companies when measuring fair value.

SFAS No. 157 indicates three types of valuation techniques that can be used to measure fair value. *Market approaches* base valuation on market information. For example, the value of a share of a company's stock that's not traded actively could be estimated by multiplying the earnings of that company by the P/E (price of shares/earnings) multiples of similar companies. *Income approaches* estimate value by first estimating future amounts (for example, earnings or cash flows) and then mathematically converting those amounts to a single present value. You will see how to apply such techniques in Chapter 6 when you study time value of money concepts. *Cost approaches* determine value by estimating the amount that would be required to buy or construct an asset of similar quality and condition. The firm can use one or more of these valuation approaches, depending on availability of the data, and should try to use them consistently unless changes in circumstances require a change in approach.

> Fair value can be measured using:
> 1. Market approaches
> 2. Income approaches
> 3. Cost approaches

To increase consistency and comparability in applying this definition, the Standard provides a hierarchy that prioritizes the inputs companies should use when determining fair

---

[41]"Fair Value Measurements," *Statement of Financial Accounting Standards No. 157* (Norwalk, Conn.: FASB, 2006).
[42]"The Fair Value Option for Financial Assets and Financial Liabilities," *Statement of Financial Accounting Standards No. 159* (Norwalk, Conn.: FASB, 2007).

GRAPHIC 1–11   Fair Value Hierarchy

Fair Value Hierarchy		
Level	**Inputs**	**Example**
1 **Most Desirable**	Quoted market prices in active markets for identical assets or liabilities.	In Chapter 12 you will learn that certain investments in marketable securities are reported at their *fair values*. Fair value in this case would be measured using the quoted market price from the NYSE, NASDAQ, or other exchange on which the security is traded.
2	Inputs other than quoted prices that are *observable* for the asset or liability. These inputs include quoted prices for *similar* assets or liabilities in active or inactive markets and inputs that are derived principally from or corroborated by observable related market data.	In Chapter 10 we discuss how companies sometimes acquire assets with consideration other than cash. In any noncash transaction, the controlling valuation principle is that each element of the transaction is recorded at its *fair value*. If one of the assets in the exchange is a building, for instance, then quoted market prices for similar buildings recently sold could be used to value the building or, if there were no similar buildings recently exchanged from which to obtain a comparable market price, valuation could be based on the price per square foot derived from observable market data.
3 **Least Desirable**	*Unobservable* inputs that reflect the entity's own assumptions about the assumptions market participants would use in pricing the asset or liability developed based on the best information available in the circumstances.	Asset retirement obligations (AROs), discussed in Chapter 10, are measured at *fair value*. Neither Level 1 nor Level 2 inputs would be possible in most ARO valuation situations. Fair value would be estimated using Level 3 inputs to include the expected cash flows estimated using the entity's own data if there is no information that indicates that market participants would use different assumptions. This Level 3 input would be used in a present value calculation together with other inputs such as the credit-adjusted risk-free interest rate.

value. The priority is based on three broad preference levels. The higher the level (Level 1 is the highest), the more preferable the input. The Standard encourages companies to strive to obtain the highest level input available for each situation. Graphic 1–11 describes the type of inputs and provides an example for each level.

The Standard also expands the amount of information companies must disclose about the use of fair value to measure assets and liabilities. The additional disclosures include a description of the inputs used to measure fair value. For recurring fair value measurements that rely on significant *unobservable* inputs (within Level 3 of the fair value hierarchy), companies should disclose the effect of the measurements on earnings (or changes in net assets) for the period.

You are not yet familiar with some of the examples mentioned in Graphic 1–11, but as you progress through the book, you will encounter many instances in which we use fair value for valuation purposes. Refer back frequently to this discussion and speculate on the level of input that would be available to a company in these situations. When a company has the option to measure financial assets or liabilities at fair value (discussed next), we address the choices available to the company in those situations.

SFAS No. 159 gives a company the option to value financial assets and liabilities at fair value rather than at historical cost.

SFAS No. 159 doesn't require a company to change the way it currently values any of its assets or liabilities. It does, however, give them the *option* to value some or all of its financial assets and liabilities at fair value. If a company chooses to value a financial asset or financial liability at fair value, then future changes in fair value are reported as gains and losses in the income statement.

What differentiates financial assets and liabilities from, say, buildings or land? Financial assets and liabilities are cash and other assets and liabilities that convert directly into known amounts of cash. Included are investments in stocks and bonds of other entities, notes receivable and payable, bonds payable, and derivative securities.[43] Some of these financial assets and liabilities currently are *required* under GAAP to be reported at fair value. For example, in

---

[43]The standard does not apply to certain specified financial instruments, including pension obligations and assets or liabilities arising from leases.

Chapter 12 you will learn that investments in the stock of other corporations that are designated as either "trading securities" or "securities available for sale" must be valued at fair value.

Now, under *SFAS No. 159,* a company can *choose* to report its other financial instruments at fair value as well. If the fair value option is chosen, changes in fair value of the instrument would be reported as gains and losses in the income statement. Liabilities, too, can be reported at fair value. For instance, a company can choose to report bonds payable at fair value rather than at amortized original issue price as described in Chapter 14.

If a company elects the fair value option, it's not necessary that the company elect the option to report all of its financial instruments at fair value or even all instruments of a particular type at fair value. Companies can "mix and match" on an instrument-by-instrument basis. However, a company is not allowed to switch methods once a method is chosen.

The FASB's objective for issuing this Standard is to improve financial reporting by providing companies a way to reduce volatility in reported earnings without having to comply with complex hedge accounting standards. It also helps in the convergence with international accounting standards we discussed earlier in the chapter as the IASB also has adopted a fair value option for financial instruments.

> There is a strong contingent who believe that fair value is the best measure to use in financial reporting. The FASB and IASB have agreed to long-term objectives for accounting for financial instruments that include a requirement that they be measured at fair value. The recent run of elective fair value standards will provide investors with an important training ground for understanding how fair value accounting is going to change the results we see.[44]

It is not expected that many companies will employ the fair value option. In a 2007 survey of CFOs and controllers, only 14 percent said they plan to make use of the option.[45] However, many believe that this is just the first step in the FASB's fair value agenda that could lead to future standards requiring fair value measurement not only for financial assets and liabilities, but for certain nonfinancial assets as well.

The move toward fair value is controversial. Proponents of fair value cite its relevance and are concerned that historical cost information may not be useful for many types of decisions. Opponents of fair value are concerned that estimates of fair value are not sufficiently reliable, particularly when based on inputs from Level 3 in the fair value hierarchy (see Graphic 1–11), and that managers may exploit the unverifiability of such inputs to bias earnings. They argue that accounting should emphasize the conservatism principle, only recognizing gains and other increases in fair value that have been realized in transactions or are virtually certain to exist.[46]

We will revisit the fair value option in subsequent chapters that address the key financial assets and liabilities that can now be measured at fair value. You'll find it easier to understand the concepts introduced in this chapter in the context of financial assets and liabilities affected: investments (Chapter 12), and bonds payable (Chapter 14).

FINANCIAL REPORTING CASE **SOLUTION**

1. **What should you tell your friend about the presence of accounting standards in the United States? Who has the authority for standard setting? Who has the responsibility?** *(p. 9)*   In the United States we have a set of standards known as generally accepted accounting principles (GAAP). GAAP are a dynamic set of both broad and specific guidelines that companies should follow when measuring and reporting the information in their financial statements and related notes. The Securities and Exchange Commission has the authority to set accounting standards for companies whose securities are publicly traded but always has delegated the responsibility to the accounting profession. At present, the Financial Accounting Standards Board is the private sector body responsible for standard setting.

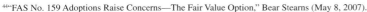

[44]"FAS No. 159 Adoptions Raise Concerns—The Fair Value Option," Bear Stearns (May 8, 2007).
[45]"Few CFOs Will Use Fair Value Option," SmartPros.com (April 20, 2007).
[46]Watts, R. L., "Conservatism in Accounting Part I: Explanations and Implications," *Accounting Horizons* (September 2003), pp. 207–221

2. **What is the economic and political environment in which standard setting occurs?** *(p. 12)* The setting of accounting and reporting standards often has been characterized as a *political process.* Standards, particularly changes in standards, can have significant differential effects on companies, investors and creditors, and other interest groups. A change in an accounting standard or the introduction of a new standard can result in a substantial redistribution of wealth within our economy. The FASB must consider potential economic consequences of a change in an accounting standard or the introduction of a new standard.

3. **What is the relationship among management, auditors, investors, and creditors that tends to preclude the "What would you like it to be?" attitude?** *(p. 15)* It is the responsibility of management to apply accounting standards when communicating with investors and creditors through financial statements. Auditors serve as independent intermediaries to help ensure that the management-prepared statements are presented fairly in accordance with GAAP. In providing this assurance, the auditor precludes the "What would you like it to be?" attitude.

4. **In general, what is the conceptual framework that underlies accounting principles?** *(p. 20)* The conceptual framework is a coherent system of interrelated objectives and fundamentals that can lead to consistent standards and that prescribe the nature, function, and limits of financial accounting and reporting. The fundamentals are the underlying concepts of accounting, concepts that guide the selection of events to be accounted for, the measurement of those events, and the means of summarizing and communicating them to interested parties. ●

THE BOTTOM LINE

● **LO1** Financial accounting is concerned with providing relevant financial information to various external users. However, the primary focus is on the financial information provided by profit-oriented companies to their present and potential investors and creditors. (p. 4)

● **LO2** Cash basis accounting provides a measure of periodic performance called *net operating cash flow,* which is the difference between cash receipts and cash disbursements from transactions related to providing goods and services to customers. Accrual accounting provides a measure of performance called *net income,* which is the difference between revenues and expenses. Periodic net income is considered a better indicator of future operating cash flows than is current net operating cash flows. (p. 7)

● **LO3** Generally accepted accounting principles (GAAP) comprise a dynamic set of both broad and specific guidelines that companies follow when measuring and reporting the information in their financial statements and related notes. The Securities and Exchange Commission (SEC) has the authority to set accounting standards in the United States. However, the SEC has always delegated the task to a private sector body, at this time the Financial Accounting Standards Board (FASB). The International Accounting Standards Board (IASB) sets global accounting standards and works with national accounting standard-setters to achieve convergence in accounting standards around the world. (p. 9)

● **LO4** Accounting standards can have significant differential effects on companies, investors, creditors, and other interest groups. For this reason, the setting of accounting standards often has been characterized as a political process. (p. 12)

● **LO5** The FASB's conceptual framework is a set of cohesive objectives and fundamental concepts on which financial accounting and reporting standards can be based. (p. 20)

● **LO6** The objectives of financial reporting are concerned with providing information to help investors and creditors predict future cash flows. The primary decision-specific qualities that make accounting information useful are relevance and reliability. To be relevant, information must possess predictive value and/or feedback value and must be provided in a timely manner. The characteristics of reliable information are verifiability, representational faithfulness, and neutrality. The 10 elements of financial statements are assets, liabilities, equity, investments by owners, distributions to owners, revenues, expenses, gains, losses, and comprehensive income. (p. 22)

● **LO7** The four basic assumptions underlying GAAP are (1) the economic entity assumption, (2) the going concern assumption, (3) the periodicity assumption, and (4) the monetary unit assumption. (p. 28)

● **LO8**   The four broad accounting principles that guide accounting practice are (1) the historical cost principle, (2) the realization principle, (3) the matching principle, and (4) the full-disclosure principle. (p. 29) ●

QUESTIONS FOR REVIEW OF **KEY TOPICS**

Q 1–1   What is the function and primary focus of financial accounting?

Q 1–2   What is meant by the phrase *efficient allocation of resources?* What mechanism fosters the efficient allocation of resources in the United States?

Q 1–3   Identify two important variables to be considered when making an investment decision.

Q 1–4   What must a company do in the long run to be able to provide a return to investors and creditors?

Q 1–5   What is the primary objective of financial accounting?

Q 1–6   Define net operating cash flows. Briefly explain why periodic net operating cash flows may not be a good indicator of future operating cash flows.

Q 1–7   What is meant by GAAP? Why should all companies follow GAAP in reporting to external users?

Q 1–8   Explain the roles of the SEC and the FASB in the setting of accounting standards.

Q 1–9   Explain the role of the auditor in the financial reporting process.

Q 1–10   List three key provisions of the Sarbanes-Oxley Act of 2002. Order your list from most important to least important in terms of the likely long-term impact on the accounting profession and financial reporting.

Q 1–11   Explain what is meant by *adverse economic consequences* of new or changed accounting standards.

Q 1–12   Why does the FASB undertake a series of elaborate information-gathering steps before issuing a substantive accounting standard?

Q 1–13   What is the purpose of the FASB's conceptual framework project?

Q 1–14   Discuss the terms *relevance* and *reliability* as they relate to financial accounting information.

Q 1–15   What are the components of relevant information? What are the components of reliable information?

Q 1–16   Explain what is meant by: The benefits of accounting information must exceed the costs.

Q 1–17   What is meant by the term *materiality* in financial reporting?

Q 1–18   Briefly define the financial accounting elements: (1) assets, (2) liabilities, (3) equity, (4) investments by owners, (5) distributions to owners, (6) revenues, (7) expenses, (8) gains, (9) losses, and (10) comprehensive income.

Q 1–19   What are the four basic assumptions underlying GAAP?

Q 1–20   What is the going concern assumption?

Q 1–21   Explain the periodicity assumption.

Q 1–22   What are the four key broad accounting principles that guide accounting practice?

Q 1–23   What are two important reasons to base the valuation of assets and liabilities on their historical cost?

Q 1–24   Describe the two criteria that must be satisfied before revenue can be recognized.

Q 1–25   What are the four different approaches to implementing the matching principle? Give an example of an expense that is recognized under each approach.

Q 1–26   In addition to the financial statement elements arrayed in the basic financial statements, what are some other ways to disclose financial information to external users?

Q 1–27   Briefly describe the inputs that companies should use when determining fair value. Organize your answer according to preference levels, from highest to lowest priority.

BRIEF **EXERCISES**

BE 1–1
Accrual accounting

● **LO2**

Cash flows during the first year of operations for the Harman-Kardon Consulting Company were as follows: Cash collected from customers, $340,000; Cash paid for rent, $40,000; Cash paid to employees for services rendered during the year, $120,000; Cash paid for utilities, $50,000.

In addition, you determine that customers owed the company $60,000 at the end of the year and no bad debts were anticipated. Also, the company owed the gas and electric company $2,000 at year-end, and the rent payment was for a two-year period. Calculate accrual net income for the year.

BE 1–2
Sources of GAAP

● **LO3**

Identify the issuing organization for each of the following types of pronouncements: (a) Financial Reporting Releases, (b) Industry Accounting Guides, and (c) Statements of Financial Accounting Standards.

BE 1–3
Financial statement elements

● LO6

For each of the following items, identify the appropriate financial statement element or elements: (1) probable future sacrifices of economic benefits; (2) probable future economic benefits owned by the company; (3) inflows of assets from ongoing, major activities; (4) decrease in equity from peripheral or incidental transactions.

BE 1–4
Basic assumptions and principles

● LO6 through LO8

Listed below are several statements that relate to financial accounting and reporting. Identify the basic assumption, broad accounting principle, or pervasive constraint that applies to each statement.
1. **Sirius Satellite Radio Inc.** files its annual and quarterly financial statements with the SEC.
2. The president of **Applebee's International, Inc.** travels on the corporate jet for business purposes only and does not use the jet for personal use.
3. Jackson Manufacturing does not recognize revenue for unshipped merchandise even though the merchandise has been manufactured according to customer specifications.
4. Lady Jane Cosmetics depreciates the cost of equipment over their useful lives.

BE 1–5
Basic assumptions and principles

● LO6 through LO8

Identify the basic assumption or broad accounting principle that was violated in each of the following situations.
1. Astro Turf Company recognizes an expense, cost of goods sold, in the period the product is manufactured.
2. McCloud Drug Company owns a patent that it purchased three years ago for $2 million. The controller recently revalued the patent to its approximate market value of $8 million.
3. Philips Company pays the monthly mortgage on the home of its president, Larry Crosswhite, and charges the expenditure to miscellaneous expense.

BE 1–6
Basic assumptions and principles

● LO6 through LO8

For each of the following situations, (1) indicate whether you agree or disagree with the financial reporting practice employed and (2) state the basic assumption, pervasive constraint, or accounting principle that is applied (if you agree), or violated (if you disagree).
1. Winderl Corporation did not disclose that it was the defendant in a material lawsuit because the trial was still in progress.
2. Alliant Semiconductor Corporation files quarterly and annual financial statements with the SEC.
3. Reliant Pharmaceutical paid rent on its office building for the next two years and charged the entire expenditure to rent expense.
4. Rockville Engineering records revenue only after products have been shipped, even though customers pay Rockville 50% of the sales price in advance.

EXERCISES

available with McGraw-Hill's Homework Manager www.mhhe.com/spiceland5e

An alternate exercise and problem set is available on the text website: www.mhhe.com/spiceland5e

E 1–1
Accrual accounting

● LO2

Listed below are several transactions that took place during the first two years of operations for the law firm of Pete, Pete, and Roy.

	Year 1	Year 2
Amounts billed to customers for services rendered	$170,000	$220,000
Cash collected from customers	160,000	190,000
Cash disbursements:...		
Salaries paid to employees for services rendered during the year	90,000	100,000
Utilities	30,000	40,000
Purchase of insurance policy	60,000	–0–

In addition, you learn that the company incurred utility costs of $35,000 in year one, that there were no liabilities at the end of year two, no anticipated bad debts on receivables, and that the insurance policy covers a three-year period.

Required:
1. Calculate the net operating cash flow for years 1 and 2.
2. Prepare an income statement for each year similar to Illustration 1–2 on page 8 according to the accrual accounting model.
3. Determine the amount of receivables from customers that the company would show in its year 1 and year 2 balance sheets prepared according to the accrual accounting model.

E 1–2
Accrual accounting

● LO2

Listed below are several transactions that took place during the second two years of operations for RPG Consulting.

	Year 2	Year 3
Amounts billed to customers for services rendered	$350,000	$450,000
Cash collected from credit customers	260,000	400,000
Cash disbursements:		
Payment of rent	80,000	–0–
Salaries paid to employees for services rendered during the year	140,000	160,000
Travel and entertainment	30,000	40,000
Advertising	15,000	35,000

In addition, you learn that the company incurred advertising costs of $25,000 in year 2, owed the advertising agency $5,000 at the end of year 1, and there were no liabilities at the end of year 3. Also, there were no anticipated bad debts on receivables, and the rent payment was for a two-year period, year 2 and year 3.

Required:
1. Calculate accrual net income for both years.
2. Determine the amount due the advertising agency that would be shown as a liability on the RPG's balance sheet at the end of year 2.

E 1–3
Sources of GAAP

● LO3

Different organizations historically and currently have issued various pronouncements that constitute the body of generally accepted accounting principles. Presented below are some of these organizations as well as various authoritative pronouncements. Match each organization with the one or more pronouncement(s) with which it is associated.

Organization	Pronouncements
1. Accounting Principles Board	a. *Statements of Financial Accounting Concepts*
2. Financial Accounting Standards Board	b. *Financial Reporting Releases*
3. Securities and Exchange Commission	c. *Accounting Research Bulletins*
4. Committee on Accounting Procedure	d. *Statements of Financial Accounting Standards*
5. AICPA	e. *APBOs*
	f. *Industry Accounting Guides*
	g. *Technical Bulletins*

E 1–4
Sources of GAAP

● LO3

Generally accepted accounting principles in the United States and abroad include pronouncements issued by several authoritative bodies. Match each pronouncement below with its brief description.

Pronouncemems	Description
1. EITF Issues	a. Issued by the IASB.
2. Statements of Financial Accounting Concepts	b. Issued by the AICPA.
3. Statements of Financial Accounting Standards	c. Rulings on emerging issues that do not require FASB action.
4. International Financial Reporting Standards	d. Provide guidelines for developing accounting standards.
5. Industry Accounting Guides	e. Issued by the FASB's predecessor.
6. Accounting Principles Board Opinions	f. Primary pronouncements issued by the FASB.

E 1–5
Participants in establishing GAAP

● LO3

Three groups that participate in the process of establishing GAAP are users, preparers, and auditors. These groups are represented by various organizations. For each organization listed below, indicate which of these groups it primarily represents.
1. Securities and Exchange Commission
2. Financial Executives International
3. American Institute of Certified Public Accountants
4. Institute of Management Accountants
5. Association of Investment Management and Research

E 1–6
Financial statement elements

● LO6

For each of the items listed below, identify the appropriate financial statement element or elements.
1. Obligation to transfer cash or other resources as a result of a past transaction.
2. Dividends paid by a corporation to its shareholders.
3. Inflow of an asset from providing a good or service.
4. The financial position of a company.
5. Increase in equity during a period from nonowner transactions.
6. Increase in equity from peripheral or incidental transaction.

7. Sale of an asset used in the operations of a business for less than the asset's book value.
8. The owners' residual interest in the assets of a company.
9. An item owned by the company representing probable future benefits.
10. Revenues plus gains less expenses and losses.
11. An owner's contribution of cash to a corporation in exchange for ownership shares of stock.
12. Outflow of an asset related to the production of revenue.

E 1–7
Concepts;
terminology;
conceptual
framework

● LO6

Listed below are several terms and phrases associated with the FASB's conceptual framework. Pair each item from List A (by letter) with the item from List B that is most appropriately associated with it.

List A	List B
____ 1. Predictive value	a. Decreases in equity resulting from transfers to owners.
____ 2. Relevance	b. Requires consideration of the costs and value of information.
____ 3. Timeliness	c. Important for making interfirm comparisons.
____ 4. Distribution to owners	d. Applying the same accounting practices over time.
____ 5. Feedback value	e. Along with relevance, a primary decision-specific quality.
____ 6. Reliability	f. Agreement between a measure and the phenomenon it purports to represent.
____ 7. Gain	g. Information is available prior to the decision.
____ 8. Representational faithfulness	h. Pertinent to the decision at hand.
____ 9. Comprehensive income	i. Implies consensus among different measurers.
____ 10. Materiality	j. Information confirms expectations.
____ 11. Comparability	k. The change in equity from nonowner transactions.
____ 12. Neutrality	l. The process of admitting information into financial statements.
____ 13. Recognition	m. Accounting information should not favor a particular group.
____ 14. Consistency	n. Results if an asset is sold for more than its book value.
____ 15. Cost effectiveness	o. Information is useful in predicting the future.
____ 16. Verifiability	p. Concerns the relative size of an item and its effect on decisions.

E 1–8
Qualitative
characteristics

● LO6

SFAC No. 2 stipulates the desired primary and secondary qualitative characteristics of accounting information. Several constraints impede achieving these desired characteristics. Answer each of the following questions related to these characteristics and constraints.

1. Which constraint would allow a company to record the purchase of a $120 printer as an expense rather than capitalizing the printer as an asset?
2. Donald Kirk, former chairman of the FASB, once noted that " . . . there must be public confidence that the standard-setting system is credible, that selection of board members is based on merit and not the influence of special interests . . ." Which characteristic is implicit in Mr. Kirk's statement?
3. Allied Appliances, Inc., changed its revenue recognition policies. Which characteristic is jeopardized by this change?
4. National Bancorp, a publicly traded company, files quarterly and annual financial statements with the SEC. Which characteristic is relevant to the timing of these periodic filings?
5. In general, relevant information possesses which three qualities?
6. When there is agreement between a measure or description and the phenomenon it purports to represent, information possesses which characteristic?
7. Jeff Brown is evaluating two companies for future investment potential. Jeff's task is made easier because both companies use the same accounting methods when preparing their financial statements. Which characteristic does the information Jeff will be using possess?
8. A company should disclose information only if the perceived benefits of the disclosure exceed the costs of providing the information. Which constraint does this statement describe?

E 1–9
Basic assumptions,
principles, and
constraints

● LO6 through
LO8

Listed below are several terms and phrases associated with basic assumptions, underlying principles, and constraints. Pair each item from List A (by letter) with the item from List B that is most appropriately associated with it.

List A	List B
____ 1. Matching principle	a. The enterprise is separate from its owners and other entities.
____ 2. Periodicity	b. A common denominator is the dollar.
____ 3. Historical cost principle	c. The entity will continue indefinitely.
____ 4. Materiality	d. Record expenses in the period the related revenue is recognized.
____ 5. Realization principle	e. The original transaction value upon acquisition.
____ 6. Going concern assumption	f. All information that could affect decisions should be reported.
____ 7. Monetary unit assumption	g. The life of an enterprise can be divided into artificial time periods.
____ 8. Economic entity assumption	h. Criteria usually satisfied at point of sale.
____ 9. Full-disclosure principle	i. Concerns the relative size of an item and its effect on decisions.

E 1–10

Basic assumptions and principles

● **LO6 through LO8**

Listed below are several statements that relate to financial accounting and reporting. Identify the basic assumption, broad accounting principle, or pervasive constraint that applies to each statement.

1. Jim Marley is the sole owner of Marley's Appliances. Jim borrowed $100,000 to buy a new home to be used as his personal residence. This liability was not recorded in the records of Marley's Appliances.
2. **Apple Computer, Inc.,** distributes an annual report to its shareholders.
3. **Hewlett-Packard Corporation** depreciates machinery and equipment over their useful lives.
4. Crosby Company lists land on its balance sheet at $120,000, its original purchase price, even though the land has a current market value of $200,000.
5. **Honeywell Corporation** records revenue when products are delivered to customers, even though the cash has not yet been received.
6. Liquidation values are not normally reported in financial statements even though many companies do go out of business.
7. **IBM Corporation,** a multibillion dollar company, purchased some small tools at a cost of $800. Even though the tools will be used for a number of years, the company recorded the purchase as an expense.

E 1–11

Basic assumptions and principles

● **LO7 LO8**

Identify the basic assumption or broad accounting principle that was violated in each of the following situations.

1. Pastel Paint Company purchased land two years ago at a price of $250,000. Because the value of the land has appreciated to $400,000, the company has valued the land at $400,000 in its most recent balance sheet.
2. Atwell Corporation has not prepared financial statements for external users for over three years.
3. The Klingon Company sells farm machinery. Revenue from a large order of machinery from a new buyer was recorded the day the order was received.
4. Don Smith is the sole owner of a company called Hardware City. The company recently paid a $150 utility bill for Smith's personal residence and recorded a $150 expense.
5. Golden Book Company purchased a large printing machine for $1,000,000 (a material amount) and recorded the purchase as an expense.
6. Ace Appliance Company is involved in a major lawsuit involving injuries sustained by some of its employees in the manufacturing plant. The company is being sued for $2,000,000, a material amount, and is not insured. The suit was not disclosed in the most recent financial statements because no settlement had been reached.

E 1–12

Basic assumptions and principles

● **LO6 through LO8**

For each of the following situations, indicate whether you agree or disagree with the financial reporting practice employed and state the basic assumption, pervasive constraint, or accounting principle that is applied (if you agree) or violated (if you disagree).

1. Wagner Corporation adjusted the valuation of all assets and liabilities to reflect changes in the purchasing power of the dollar.
2. Spooner Oil Company changed its method of accounting for oil and gas exploration costs from successful efforts to full cost. No mention of the change was included in the financial statements. The change had a material effect on Spooner's financial statements.
3. Cypress Manufacturing Company purchased machinery having a five-year life. The cost of the machinery is being expensed over the life of the machinery.
4. Rudeen Corporation purchased equipment for $180,000 at a liquidation sale of a competitor. Because the equipment was worth $230,000, Rudeen valued the equipment in its subsequent balance sheet at $230,000.
5. Davis Bicycle Company received a large order for the sale of 1,000 bicycles at $100 each. The customer paid Davis the entire amount of $100,000 on March 15. However, Davis did not record any revenue until April 17, the date the bicycles were delivered to the customer.
6. Gigantic Corporation purchased two small calculators at a cost of $32.00. The cost of the calculators was expensed even though they had a three-year estimated useful life.
7. Esquire Company provides financial statements to external users every three years.

E 1–13

Basic assumptions, principles, and constraints

● **LO6 through LO8**

For each of the following situations, state whether you agree or disagree with the financial reporting practice employed, and briefly explain the reason for your answer.

1. The controller of the Dumars Corporation increased the carrying value of land from its original cost of $2 million to its recently appraised value of $3.5 million.
2. The president of Vosburgh Industries asked the company controller to charge miscellaneous expense for the purchase of an automobile to be used solely for personal use.
3. At the end of its 2009 fiscal year, Dower, Inc., received an order from a customer for $45,350. The merchandise will ship early in 2010. Because the sale was made to a long-time customer, the controller recorded the sale in 2009.
4. At the beginning of its 2009 fiscal year, Rossi Imports paid $48,000 for a two-year lease on warehouse space. Rossi recorded the expenditure as an asset to be expensed equally over the two-year period of the lease.

5. The Reliable Tire Company included a note in its financial statements that described a pending lawsuit against the company.
6. The Hughes Corporation, a company whose securities are publicly traded, prepares monthly, quarterly, and annual financial statement for internal use but disseminates to external users only the annual financial statements.

E 1–14
Basic assumptions, principles, and constraints

● **LO6 through LO8**

Listed below are the basic assumptions, underlying principles, and constraints discussed in this chapter.

a. Economic entity assumption
b. Going concern assumption
c. Periodicity assumption
d. Monetary unit assumption
e. Historical cost principle
f. Realization principle
g. Matching principle
h. Full-disclosure principle
i. Cost effectiveness
j. Materiality
k. Conservatism

Identify by letter the assumption, principle, or constraint that relates to each statement or phrase below.

_____ 1. Revenue is recognized only after certain criteria are satisfied.
_____ 2. Information that could affect decision making should be reported.
_____ 3. Cause-and-effect relationship between revenues and expenses.
_____ 4. The basis for measurement of many assets and liabilities.
_____ 5. Relates to the qualitative characteristic of timeliness.
_____ 6. All economic events can be identified with a particular entity.
_____ 7. The benefits of providing accounting information should exceed the cost of doing so.
_____ 8. A consequence is that GAAP need not be followed in all situations.
_____ 9. Not a qualitative characteristic, but a practical justification for some accounting choices.
_____10. Assumes the entity will continue indefinitely.
_____11. Inflation causes a violation of this assumption.

E 1–15
Multiple choice; concept statements, basic assumptions, principles

● **LO5 through LO8**

Determine the response that best completes the following statements or questions.

1. The primary objective of financial reporting is to provide information
   a. About a firm's economic resources and obligations.
   b. Useful in predicting future cash flows.
   c. Concerning the changes in financial position resulting from the income-producing efforts of the entity.
   d. About a firm's financing and investing activities.
2. *Statements of Financial Accounting Concepts* issued by the FASB
   a. Represent GAAP.
   b. Have been superseded by *SFAS*s.
   c. Are subject to approval of the SEC.
   d. Identify the conceptual framework within which accounting standards are developed.
3. In general, revenue is recognized as earned when the earning process is virtually complete and
   a. The sales price has been collected.
   b. A purchase order has been received.
   c. There is reasonable certainty as to the collectibility of the asset to be received.
   d. A contract has been signed.
4. In depreciating the cost of an asset, accountants are most concerned with
   a. Conservatism.
   b. The realization principle.
   c. Full disclosure.
   d. The matching principle.
5. The primary objective of the matching principle is to
   a. Provide full disclosure.
   b. Record expenses in the period that related revenues are recognized.
   c. Provide timely information to decision makers.
   d. Promote comparability between financial statements of different periods.
6. The separate entity assumption states that, in the absence of contrary evidence, all entities will survive indefinitely.
   a. True
   b. False

CPA AND CMA EXAM QUESTIONS

CPA Exam
Questions

SCHWESER

The following questions are used in the Kaplan CPA Review Course to study the environment and theoretical structure of financial accounting while preparing for the CPA examination. Determine the response that best completes the statements or questions.

● LO6   1. Which of the following is *not* an essential qualitative characteristic of accounting information according to the FASB's conceptual framework?
   a. Auditor independence.
   b. Neutrality.
   c. Timeliness.
   d. Predictive value.

● LO6   2. According to FASB's conceptual framework, timeliness is a characteristic of
   a. Understandability.
   b. Reliability.
   c. Relevance.
   d. Both relevance and reliability.

● LO3   3. The Financial Accounting Standards Board (FASB)
   a. Is a division of the Securities and Exchange Commission (SEC).
   b. Is a private body that helps set accounting standards in the United States.
   c. Is responsible for setting auditing standards that all auditors must follow.
   d. Consists entirely of members of the American Institute of Certified Public Accountants.

● LO6   4. Under *Statement of Financial Accounting Concepts No. 2*, feedback value is an ingredient of the primary quality of

	Relevance	Reliability
a.	Yes	No
b.	No	Yes
c.	Yes	Yes
d.	No	No

● LO6   5. According to the FASB's conceptual framework, predictive value is an ingredient of

	Reliability	Relevance
a.	Yes	No
b.	No	No
c.	Yes	Yes
d.	No	Yes

● LO6   6. According to *Statement of Financial Accounting Concepts No. 2*, timeliness is an ingredient of the primary quality of
   a. Verifiability.
   b. Reliability.
   c. Relevance.
   d. Representational faithfulness.

● LO6   7. According to the FASB's conceptual framework, the objectives of financial reporting for business enterprises are based on
   a. Generally accepted accounting principles.
   b. The needs of the users of the information.
   c. The need for conservatism.
   d. None of above.

● LO6   8. According to the FASB's conceptual framework, comprehensive income includes which of the following?

	Operating Income	Investments by Owners
a.	No	Yes
b.	No	No
c.	Yes	Yes
d.	Yes	No

CMA Exam Questions

The following questions dealing with the environment and theoretical structure of financial accounting are adapted from questions that previously appeared on Certified Management Accountant (CMA) examinations. The CMA designation sponsored by the Institute of Management Accountants (**www.imanet.org**) provides members with an objective measure of knowledge and competence in the field of management accounting. Determine the response that best completes the statements or questions.

● **LO3**

1. Accounting standard setting in the United States is
   a. Done primarily by the Securities and Exchange Commission.
   b. Done primarily by the private sector.
   c. The responsibility of the public sector.
   d. Done primarily by the International Accounting Standards Committee.

● **LO6**

2. Reliability as used in accounting includes
   a. Determining the revenue first, then determining the costs incurred in earning that revenue.
   b. The entity's giving the same treatment to comparable transactions from period to period.
   c. Similar results being obtained by both the accountant and an independent party using the same measurement methods.
   d. The disclosure of all facts that may influence the judgment of an informed reader.

● **LO6**

3. Recognition is the process of formally recording and reporting an item in the financial statements. In order for a revenue item to be recognized, it must be all of the following except
   a. Measurable.
   b. Relevant.
   c. Material.
   d. Realized or realizable.

BROADEN YOUR PERSPECTIVE

Apply your critical-thinking ability to the knowledge you've gained. These cases will provide you an opportunity to develop your research, analysis, judgment, and communication skills. You will also work with other students, integrate what you've learned, apply it in real-world situations, and consider its global and ethical ramifications. This practice will broaden your knowledge and further develop your decision-making abilities.

Judgment Case 1–1
The development of accounting standards

● **LO3**

In 1934, Congress created the Securities and Exchange Commission (SEC) and gave the commission both the power and responsibility for setting accounting and reporting standards in the United States.

Required:
1. Explain the relationship between the SEC and the various private sector standard-setting bodies that have, over time, been delegated the responsibility for setting accounting standards.
2. Can you think of any reasons why the SEC has delegated this responsibility rather than set standards directly?

Research Case 1–2
Accessing SEC information through the Internet

● **LO3**

Internet access to the World Wide Web has provided a wealth of information accessible with our personal computers. Many chapters in this text contain Real World Cases that require you to access the web to research an accounting issue. The purpose of this case is to introduce you to the Internet home page of the Securities and Exchange Commission (SEC) and its EDGAR database.

Required:
1. Access the SEC home page on the Internet. The web address is **www.sec.gov**.
2. Choose the subaddress "About the SEC." What are the two basic objectives of the 1933 Securities Act?
3. Return to the SEC home page and access EDGAR. Describe the contents of the database.

Research Case 1–3
Accessing FASB information through the Internet

● **LO4**

The purpose of this case is to introduce you to the information available on the website of the Financial Accounting Standards Board (FASB).

Required:
Access the FASB home page on the Internet. The web address is **www.fasb.org**. Answer the following questions.
1. Describe the mission of the FASB.
2. Who are the current Board members? Briefly describe their backgrounds.

3. How are topics added to the FASB's technical agenda?
4. How many standards have been issued by the FASB? What topic is addressed in the most recently issued standard?
5. How many Exposure Drafts are currently outstanding? What topics do they address?

Research Case 1–4
Accessing IASB information through the Internet

● **LO3**

The purpose of this case is to introduce you to the information available on the website of the International Accounting Standards Board (IASB).

Required:
Access the IASB home page on the Internet. The web address is **www.iasb.co.uk**. Answer the following questions.
1. Describe the mission of the IASB.
2. The IASB has how many board members?
3. Who is the current chairman of the IASB?
4. Where is the IASB located?

Research Case 1–5
Accounting standards in China

● **LO3 LO4**

Economic reforms in the People's Republic of China are moving that nation toward a market-driven economy. China's accounting practices must also change to accommodate the needs of potential investors. In an article entitled "Institutional Factors Influencing China's Accounting Reforms and Standards," Professor Bing Xiang analyzes the changes in the accounting environment of China during the recent economic reforms and their implications for the development of accounting reforms.

Required:
1. In your library or from some other source, locate the indicated article in *Accounting Horizons,* June 1998.
2. Briefly describe the economic reforms that led to the need for increased external financial reporting in China.
3. Conformity with International Accounting Standards was specified as an overriding objective in formulating China's accounting standards. What is the author's opinion of this objective?

Communication Case 1–6
Relevance and reliability

● **LO6**

Some theorists contend that companies that create pollution should report the social cost of that pollution in income statements. They argue that such companies are indirectly subsidized as the cost of pollution is borne by society while only production costs (and perhaps minimal pollution fines) are shown in the income statement. Thus, the product sells for less than would be necessary if all costs were included.

Assume that the FASB is considering a standard to include the social costs of pollution in the income statement. The process would require considering both relevance and reliability of the information produced by the new standard. Your instructor will divide the class into two to six groups depending on the size of the class. The mission of your group is to explain how the concepts of relevance and reliability relate to this issue.

Required:
Each group member should consider the question independently and draft a tentative answer prior to the class session for which the case is assigned.

In class, each group will meet for 10 to 15 minutes in different areas of the classroom. During that meeting, group members will take turns sharing their suggestions for the purpose of arriving at a single group treatment.

After the allotted time, a spokesperson for each group (selected during the group meetings) will share the group's solution with the class. The goal of the class is to incorporate the views of each group into a consensus answer to the question.

Communication Case 1–7
Accounting standard setting

● **LO4**

One of your friends is a financial analyst for a major stock brokerage firm. Recently she indicated to you that she had read an article in a weekly business magazine that alluded to the political process of establishing accounting standards. She had always assumed that accounting standards were established by determining the approach that conceptually best reflected the economics of a transaction.

Required:
Write a one to two-page article for a business journal explaining what is meant by the political process for establishing accounting standards. Be sure to include in your article a discussion of the need for the FASB to balance accounting considerations and economic consequences.

Ethics Case 1–8
The auditors' responsibility

● **LO4**

It is the responsibility of management to apply accounting standards when communicating with investors and creditors through financial statements. Another group, auditors, serves as an independent intermediary to help ensure that management has in fact appropriately applied GAAP in preparing the company's financial statements. Auditors examine (audit) financial statements to express a professional, independent opinion. The opinion reflects the auditors' assessment of the statements' fairness, which is determined by the extent to which they are prepared in compliance with GAAP.

Some feel that it is impossible for an auditor to give an independent opinion on a company's financial statements because the auditors' fees for performing the audit are paid by the company. In addition to the audit fee, quite often the auditor performs other services for the company such as preparing the company's income tax returns.

Required:
How might an auditor's ethics be challenged while performing an audit?

**Judgment
Case 1–9**
Qualitative
characteristics

● LO6

Generally accepted accounting principles do not require companies to disclose forecasts of any financial variables to external users. A friend, who is a finance major, is puzzled by this and asks you to explain why such relevant information is not provided to investors and creditors to help them predict future cash flows.

Required:
Explain to your friend why this information is not routinely provided to investors and creditors.

**Judgment
Case 1–10**
GAAP,
comparability,
and the role of the
auditor

● LO4 LO6

Mary McQuire is trying to decide how to invest her money. A friend recommended that she buy the stock of one of two corporations and suggested that she should compare the financial statements of the two companies before making a decision.

Required:
1. Do you agree that Mary will be able to compare the financial statements of the two companies?
2. What role does the auditor play in ensuring comparability of financial statements between companies?

**Judgment
Case 1–11**
Cost effectiveness

● LO6

Statement of Financial Accounting Concepts No. 2, "Qualitative Characteristics of Accounting Information," includes a discussion of the pervasive constraint cost effectiveness. Assume that the FASB is considering revising an important accounting standard.

Required:
1. What is the desired benefit from revising an accounting standard?
2. What are some of the possible costs that could result from a revision of an accounting standard?
3. What does the FASB do in order to assess possible benefits and costs of a proposed revision of an accounting standard?

**Judgment
Case 1–12**
The realization
principle

● LO8

A new client, the Wolf Company, asks your advice concerning the point in time that the company should recognize revenue from the rental of its office buildings. Renters usually pay rent on a quarterly basis at the beginning of the quarter. The owners contend that the critical event that motivates revenue recognition should be the date the cash is received from renters. After all, the money is in hand and is very seldom returned.

Required:
1. Describe the two criteria that must be satisfied before revenue can be recognized.
2. Do you agree or disagree with the position of the owners of Wolf Company? Support your answer.

**Analysis
Case 1–13**
The matching
principle

● LO8

Revenues measure the accomplishments of a company during the period. Expenses are then matched with revenues to produce a periodic measure of performance called *net income*.

Required:
1. Explain what is meant by the phrase *matched with revenues*.
2. Describe the four approaches used to implement the matching principle and label them 1 through 4.
3. For each of the following, identify which matching approach should be used to recognize the cost as expense.
   a. The cost of producing a product.
   b. The cost of advertising.
   c. The cost of monthly rent on the office building.
   d. The salary of an office employee.
   e. Depreciation on an office building.

**Judgment
Case 1–14**
Capitalize or
expense?

● LO8

When a company makes an expenditure that is neither a payment to a creditor nor a distribution to an owner, management must decide if the expenditure should be capitalized (recorded as an increase in an asset) or expensed (recorded as an expense thereby decreasing owners' equity).

Required:
1. Which factor or factors should the company consider when making this decision?
2. Which key accounting principle is involved?
3. Are there any constraints that could cause the company to alter its decision?

**Real World
Case 1–15**
Elements;
disclosures;
Hewlett-Packard
Company

● LO6 LO8

Real World Financials

Selected financial statements from a recent annual report of **Hewlett-Packard Company (HP)** follow. Use these statements to answer the following questions.

Required:
1. The company's fiscal year ends on what date?
2. What amounts did HP report for the following items for the fiscal year ended October 31, 2007?
   a. Total net revenues
   b. Total operating expenses
   c. Net income (earnings)
   d. Total assets
   e. Total stockholders' equity

3. How many shares of common stock did the company have issued on October 31, 2007?
4. Why do you think HP reports more than one year of data in its financial statements?

HEWLETT-PACKARD COMPANY AND SUBSIDIARIES
Consolidated Balance Sheets

	October 31	
	2007	**2006**
	In millions, except par value	
Assets		
Current assets:		
Cash and cash equivalents	$11,293	$16,400
Short-term investments	152	22
Accounts receivable	13,420	10,873
Financing receivables	2,507	2,440
Inventory	8,033	7,750
Other current assets	11,997	10,779
Total current assets	47,402	48,264
Property, plant and equipment	7,798	6,863
Long-term financing receivables and other assets	7,647	6,649
Goodwill	21,773	16,853
Purchased intangible assets	4,079	3,352
Total assets	$88,699	$81,981
Liabilities and Stockholders' Equity		
Current liabilities:		
Notes payable and short-term borrowings	$ 3,186	$ 2,705
Accounts payable	11,787	12,102
Employee compensation and benefits	3,465	3,148
Taxes on earnings	1,891	1,905
Deferred revenue	5,025	4,309
Accrued restructuring	123	547
Other accrued liabilities	13,783	11,134
Total current liabilities	39,260	35,850
Long-term debt	4,997	2,490
Other liabilities	5,916	5,497
Commitments and contingencies		
Stockholders' equity:		
Preferred stock, $0.01 par value (300 shares authorized; none issued)	—	—
Common stock, $0.01 par value (9,600 shares authorized; 2,580 and 2,732 shares issued and outstanding, respectively)	26	27
Additional paid-in capital	16,381	17,966
Prepaid stock repurchase	—	(596)
Retained earnings	21,560	20,729
Accumulated other comprehensive income	559	18
Total stockholders' equity	38,526	38,144
Total liabilities and stockholders' equity	$88,699	$81,981

HEWLETT-PACKARD COMPANY AND SUBSIDIARIES
Consolidated Statements of Earnings

	For the fiscal years ended October 31		
	2007	2006	2005
	In millions, except per share amounts		
Net revenue:			
Products	$84,229	$73,557	$68,945
Services	19,699	17,773	17,380
Financing income	358	328	371
Total net revenue	104,286	91,658	86,696
Costs and expenses:			
Cost of products	63,435	55,248	52,550
Cost of services	15,163	13,930	13,674
Financing interest	289	249	216
Research and development	3,611	3,591	3,490
Selling, general and administrative	12,226	11,266	11,184
Amortization of purchased intangible assets	783	604	622
In-process research and development charges	190	52	2
Restructuring charges	387	158	1,684
Pension curtailments and pension settlements, net	(517)	—	(199)
Total operating expenses	95,567	85,098	83,223
Earnings from operations	8,719	6,560	3,473
Interest and other, net	444	606	83
Gains (losses) on investments	14	25	(13)
Earnings before taxes	9,177	7,191	3,543
Provision for taxes	1,913	993	1,145
Net earnings	$ 7,264	$ 6,198	$ 2,398
Net earnings per share:			
Basic	$ 2.76	$ 2.23	$ 0.83
Diluted	$ 2.68	$ 2.18	$ 0.82
Weighted-average shares used to compute net earnings per share:			
Basic	2,630	2,782	2,879
Diluted	2,716	2,852	2,909

Review of the Accounting Process

/// OVERVIEW

Chapter 1 explained that the primary means of conveying financial information to investors, creditors, and other external users is through financial statements and related notes. The purpose of this chapter is to review the fundamental accounting process used to produce the financial statements. This review establishes a framework for the study of the concepts covered in intermediate accounting.

Actual accounting systems differ significantly from company to company. This chapter focuses on the many features that tend to be common to any accounting system.

LEARNING OBJECTIVES

After studying this chapter, you should be able to:

- **LO1** Analyze routine economic events—transactions—and record their effects on a company's financial position using the accounting equation format.
- **LO2** Record transactions using the general journal format.
- **LO3** Post the effects of journal entries to T-accounts and prepare an unadjusted trial balance.
- **LO4** Identify and describe the different types of adjusting journal entries.
- **LO5** Determine the required adjustments, record adjusting journal entries in general journal format, and prepare an adjusted trial balance.
- **LO6** Describe the four basic financial statements.
- **LO7** Explain the closing process.
- **LO8** Convert from cash basis net income to accrual basis net income.

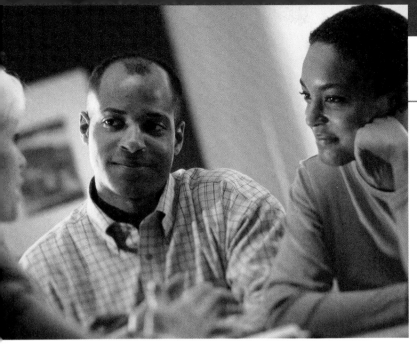

FINANCIAL REPORTING CASE

Engineering Profits

After graduating from college last year, two of your engineering-major friends started an Internet consulting practice. They began operations on July 1 and felt they did quite well during their first year. Now they would like to borrow $20,000 from a local bank to buy new computing equipment and office furniture. To support their loan application, the friends presented the bank with the following income statement for their first year of operations ending June 30:

Consulting revenue		$96,000
Operating expenses:		
Salaries	$32,000	
Rent	9,000	
Supplies	4,800	
Utilities	3,000	
Advertising	1,200	(50,000)
Net income		$46,000

The bank officer noticed that there was no depreciation expense in the income statement and has asked your friends to revise the statement after making year-end adjustments. After agreeing to help, you discover the following information:

a. The friends paid $80,000 for equipment when they began operations. They think the equipment will be useful for five years.

b. They pay $500 a month to rent office space. In January, they paid a full year's rent in advance. This is included in the $9,000 rent expense.

c. Included in consulting revenue is $13,000 they received from a customer in June as a deposit for work to be performed in August.

By the time you finish this chapter, you should be able to respond appropriately to the questions posed in this case. Compare your response to the solution provided at the end of the chapter.

QUESTIONS ///

1. What purpose do adjusting entries serve? (page 67)

2. What year-end adjustments are needed to revise the income statement? Did your friends do as well their first year as they thought? (page 67)

A solid foundation is vital to a sound understanding of intermediate accounting. So, we review the fundamental accounting process here to serve as a framework for the new concepts you will learn in this course.

Chapter 1 introduced the theoretical structure of financial accounting and the environment within which it operates. The primary function of financial accounting—to provide relevant and reliable financial information to external users—is accomplished by periodically disseminating financial statements and related notes. In this chapter we review the *process* used to identify, analyze, record, summarize, and then report the economic events affecting a company's financial position.

Keep in mind as you study this chapter that the accounting information systems businesses actually use are quite different from company to company. Larger companies generally use more complex systems than smaller companies use. The types of economic events affecting companies also cause differences in systems. We focus on the many features that tend to be common to all accounting systems.

It is important to understand that this chapter and its appendixes are not intended to describe actual accounting systems. In most business enterprises, the sheer volume of data that must be processed precludes a manual accounting system. Fortunately, the computer provides a solution. *We describe and illustrate a manual accounting information system to provide an overview of the basic model that underlies the computer software programs actually used to process accounting information.*

Electronic data processing is fast, accurate, and affordable. Many large and medium-sized companies own or rent their own mainframe computers and company-specific data processing systems. Smaller companies can take advantage of technology with relatively inexpensive micro- and minicomputers and generalized data software packages such as QuickBooks and Peachtree Accounting Software. Enterprise Resource Planning (ERP) systems are now being installed in companies of all sizes. The objective of ERP is to create a customized software program that integrates all departments and functions across a company onto a single computer system that can serve the information needs of those different departments, including the accounting department.

> **Computers are used to process accounting information. In this chapter we provide an overview of the basic model that underlies computer software programs.**

The Basic Model

> *Economic events* cause changes in the financial position of the company.

The first objective of any accounting system is to identify the economic events that can be expressed in financial terms by the system.[1] An economic event is any event that *directly* affects the financial position of the company. Recall from Chapter 1 that financial position comprises assets, liabilities, and owners' equity. Broad and specific accounting principles determine which events should be recorded, when the events should be recorded, and the dollar amount at which they should be measured.

> *External events* involve an exchange between the company and another entity.

Economic events can be classified as either external events or internal events. External events involve an exchange between the company and a separate economic entity. Examples are purchasing merchandise inventory for cash, borrowing cash from a bank, and paying salaries to employees. In each instance, the company receives something (merchandise, cash, and services) in exchange for something else (cash, assumption of a liability, and cash).

> *Internal events* do not involve an exchange transaction but do affect the company's financial position.

On the other hand, internal events directly affect the financial position of the company but don't involve an exchange transaction with another entity. Examples are the depreciation of machinery and the use of supplies. As we will see later in the chapter, these events must be recorded to properly reflect a company's financial position and results of operations in accordance with the accrual accounting model.

The Accounting Equation

> ● **LO1**

The accounting equation underlies the process used to capture the effect of economic events.

$$\text{Assets} = \text{Liabilities} + \text{Owners' Equity}$$

The elements of the equation were defined in Chapter 1.

This general expression portrays the equality between the total economic resources of an entity (its assets)—shown on the left side of the equation—and the total claims to those

---

[1]There are many economic events that affect a company *indirectly* and are not recorded. For example, when the Federal Reserve changes its discount rate, it is an important economic event that can affect the company in many ways, but it is not recorded by the company.

resources (liabilities and equity)—shown on the right side. In other words, the resources of an enterprise are provided by creditors or owners.

The equation also implies that each economic event affecting this equation will have a dual effect because resources always must equal claims to those resources. For illustration, consider the events (we refer to these throughout the text as transactions) in Illustration 2–1.

---

1. An attorney invested $50,000 to open a law office.
An investment by the owner causes both assets and owners' equity to increase.

Assets	=	Liabilities	+	Owners' Equity
+$50,000 (cash)				+$50,000 (investment by owner)

2. $40,000 was borrowed from a bank and a note payable was signed.
This transaction causes assets and liabilities to increase. A bank loan increases cash and creates an obligation to repay it.

Assets	=	Liabilities	+	Owners' Equity
+$40,000 (cash)		+$40,000 (note payable)		

3. Supplies costing $3,000 were purchased on account.
Buying supplies on credit also increases both assets and liabilities.

Assets	=	Liabilities	+	Owners' Equity
+$3,000 (supplies)		+$3,000 (accounts payable)		

4. Services were performed on account for $10,000.
Transactions 4, 5, and 6 are revenue and expense transactions. Revenues and expenses (and gains and losses) are events that cause owners' equity to change. Revenues and gains describe inflows of assets, causing owners' equity to increase. Expenses and losses describe outflows of assets (or increases in liabilities), causing owners' equity to decrease.

Assets	=	Liabilities	+	Owners' Equity
+$10,000 (receivables)				+$10,000 (revenue)

5. Salaries of $5,000 were paid to employees.

Assets	=	Liabilities	+	Owners' Equity
−$5,000 (cash)				−$5,000 (expense)

6. $500 of supplies were used.

Assets	=	Liabilities	+	Owners' Equity
−$500 (supplies)				−$500 (expense)

7. $1,000 was paid on account to the supplies vendor.
This transaction causes assets and liabilities to decrease.

Assets	=	Liabilities	+	Owners' Equity
−$1,000 (cash)		−$1,000 (accounts payable)		

ILLUSTRATION 2–1
Transaction Analysis

Each transaction is analyzed to determine its effect on the equation and on the specific financial position elements.

The accounting equation can be expanded to include a column for each type of asset and liability and for each type of change in owners' equity.

As discussed in Chapter 1, owners of a corporation are its shareholders, so owners' equity for a corporation is referred to as shareholders' equity. Shareholders' equity for a corporation arises primarily from two sources: (1) amounts *invested* by shareholders in the corporation and (2) amounts *earned* by the corporation (on behalf of its shareholders). These are reported as (1) paid-in capital and (2) retained earnings. Retained earnings equals net income less distributions to shareholders (primarily dividends) since the inception of the corporation. Graphic 2–1 shows the basic accounting equation for a corporation with shareholders' equity expanded to highlight its composition. We use the corporate format throughout the remainder of the chapter.

Each event, or transaction, has a dual effect on the accounting equation.

Owners' equity for a corporation, called shareholders' equity, is classified by source as either paid-in capital or retained earnings.

Account Relationships

All transactions could be recorded in columnar fashion as increases or decreases to elements of the accounting equation. However, even for a very small company with few transactions, this would become cumbersome. So, most companies use a process called the double-entry system. The term *double-entry* refers to the dual effect that each transaction has on the accounting equation.

The double-entry system is used to process transactions.

GRAPHIC 2–1 Accounting Equation for a Corporation

A general ledger is a collection of storage areas, called *accounts,* used to keep track of increases and decreases in financial position elements.

In the double-entry system, *debit* means *left* side of an account and *credit* means *right* side of an account.

Asset *increases* are entered on the *debit* side of accounts and *decreases* are entered on the *credit* side. Liability and equity account *increases* are *credits* and *decreases* are *debits.*

Elements of the accounting equation are represented by accounts which are contained in a general ledger. Increases and decreases in each element of a company's financial position are recorded in these accounts. A separate account is maintained for individual assets and liabilities, retained earnings, and paid-in capital. Also, to accumulate information needed for the income statement, we use separate accounts to keep track of the changes in retained earnings caused by revenues, expenses, gains, and losses. The number of accounts depends on the complexity of the company's operations.

An account includes the account title, an account number to aid the processing task, and columns or fields for increases, decreases, the cumulative balance, and the date. For instructional purposes we use T-accounts instead of formal ledger accounts. A T-account has space at the top for the account title and two sides for recording increases and decreases.

Account Title

For centuries, accountants have effectively used a system of debits and credits to increase and decrease account balances in the ledger. Debits merely represent the *left* side of the account and credits the *right* side, as shown below.

Account Title	
debit side	credit side

Whether a debit or a credit represents an increase or a decrease depends on the type of account. Accounts on the left side of the accounting equation (assets) are *increased* (+) by *debit* entries and *decreased* (-) by *credit* entries. Accounts on the right side of the accounting equation (liabilities and shareholders' equity) are *increased* (+) by *credit* entries and *decreased* (-) by *debit* entries. This arbitrary, but effective, procedure ensures that for each transaction the net impact on the left sides of accounts always equals the net impact on the right sides of accounts.

For example, consider the bank loan in our earlier illustration. An asset, cash, increased by $40,000. Increases in assets are *debits.* Liabilities also increased by $40,000. Increases in liabilities are *credits.*

Assets		=	**Liabilities**		+	**Owners' Equity**
Cash			**Note Payable**			
debit	credit		debit	credit		
40,000				40,000		
+				+		

The debits equal the credits in every transaction (dual effect), so both before and after a transaction the accounting equation is in balance.

Prior exposure to the terms debit and credit probably comes from your experience with a bank account. For example, when a bank debits your checking account for service charges, it decreases your account balance. When you make a deposit, the bank credits your account, increasing your account balance. You must remember that from the bank's perspective, your bank account balance is a liability—it represents the amount that the bank owes you. Therefore, when the bank debits your account, it is decreasing its liability. When the bank credits your account, its liability increases.

Graphic 2–2 illustrates the relationship among the accounting equation, debits and credits, and the increases and decreases in financial position elements.

Notice that increases and decreases in retained earnings are recorded *indirectly.* For example, an expense represents a decrease in retained earnings, which requires a debit. That

GRAPHIC 2–2   Accounting Equation, Debits and Credits, Increases and Decreases

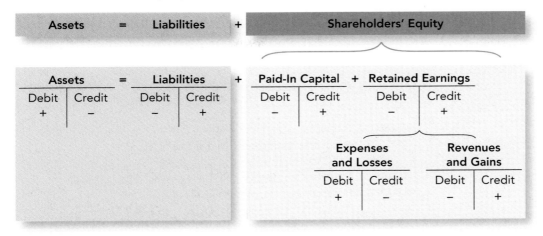

debit, however, is recorded in an appropriate expense account rather than in retained earnings itself. This allows the company to maintain a separate record of expenses incurred during an accounting period. The debit to retained earnings for the expense is recorded in a closing entry (reviewed later) at the end of the period, only after the expense total is reflected in the income statement. Similarly, an increase in retained earnings due to a revenue is recorded indirectly with a credit to a revenue account, which is later reflected as a credit to retained earnings.

The general ledger accounts serve as control accounts. Subsidiary accounts associated with a particular general ledger control account are maintained in separate subsidiary ledgers. For example, a subsidiary ledger for accounts receivable contains individual account receivable accounts for each of the company's credit customers. Subsidiary ledgers are discussed in more detail in Appendix 2C.

Each general ledger account can be classified as either *permanent* or *temporary*. Permanent accounts represent assets, liabilities, and shareholders' equity at a point in time. Temporary accounts represent changes in the retained earnings component of shareholders' equity for a corporation caused by revenue, expense, gain, and loss transactions. It would be cumbersome to record each revenue/expense, gain/loss transaction directly into the retained earnings account. The different types of events affecting retained earnings should be kept separate to facilitate the preparation of the financial statements. The balances in these temporary accounts are periodically, usually once a year, closed or zeroed out, and the net effect is recorded in the permanent retained earnings account. The temporary accounts need to be zeroed out to measure income on an annual basis. This closing process is discussed in a later section of this chapter.

Permanent accounts represent the basic financial position elements of the accounting equation.

Temporary accounts keep track of the changes in the retained earnings component of shareholders' equity.

The Accounting Processing Cycle

Now that we've reviewed the basics of the double-entry system, let's look closer at the process used to identify, analyze, record, and summarize transactions and prepare financial statements. This section deals only with *external transactions,* those that involve an exchange transaction with another entity. Internal transactions are discussed in a later section.

The 10 steps in the accounting processing cycle are listed in Graphic 2–3. Steps 1–4 take place during the accounting period while steps 5–8 occur at the end of the accounting period. Steps 9 and 10 are required only at the end of the year.

We now discuss these steps in order.

The first step in the process is to *identify* external transactions affecting the accounting equation. An accountant usually does not directly witness business transactions. A mechanism is needed to relay the essential information about each transaction to the accountant. Source documents such as sales invoices, bills from suppliers, and cash register tapes serve this need.

STEP 1

Obtain information about transactions from *source documents.*

GRAPHIC 2–3
The Accounting
Processing Cycle

The Steps of the Accounting Processing Cycle

During the accounting period
- Step 1 Obtain information about external transactions from **source documents.**
- Step 2 **Analyze the transaction.**
- Step 3 Record the transaction in a **journal.**
- Step 4 **Post** from the journal to the general ledger accounts.

At the end of the accounting period
- Step 5 Prepare an **unadjusted trial balance.**
- Step 6 Record **adjusting entries** and post to the general ledger accounts.
- Step 7 Prepare an **adjusted trial balance.**
- Step 8 Prepare **financial statements.**

At the end of the year
- Step 9 **Close** the temporary accounts to retained earnings.
- Step 10 Prepare a **post-closing trial balance.**

These source documents usually identify the date and nature of each transaction, the participating parties, and the monetary terms. For example, a sales invoice identifies the date of sale, the customer, the specific goods sold, the dollar amount of the sale, and the payment terms. With this information, the second step in the processing cycle, transaction analysis, can be accomplished. Transaction analysis is the process of reviewing the source documents to determine the dual effect on the accounting equation and the specific elements involved.

This process is summarized in Illustration 2–2 for the seven transactions described previously in Illustration 2–1.

The third step in the process is to record the transaction in a journal. Journals provide a chronological record of all economic events affecting a firm. Each journal entry is expressed in terms of equal debits and credits to accounts affected by the transaction being recorded. Debits and credits represent increases or decreases to specific accounts, depending on the type of account, as explained earlier. For example, for credit sales, a debit to accounts receivable and a credit to sales revenue is recorded in a sales journal.

A sales journal is an example of a special journal used to record a repetitive type of transaction. Appendix 2C discusses the use of special journals in more depth. In this chapter and throughout the text, we use the general journal format to record all transactions.

Any type of transaction can be recorded in a general journal. It has a place for the date of the transaction, a place for account titles, account numbers, and supporting explanations, a place for debit entries, and a place for credit entries. A simplified journal entry is used throughout the text that lists the account titles to be debited and credited and the dollar amounts. A common convention is to list the debited accounts first, indent the credited accounts, and use the first of two columns for the debit amounts and the second column for the credit amounts. For example, the journal entry for the bank loan in Illustration 2–1, which requires a debit to cash and a credit to note payable, is recorded as follows:

STEP 2
Analyze the transaction.

STEP 3
Record the transaction in a *journal.*

● LO2

To record the borrowing of cash and the signing of a note payable.

Cash	40,000	
Note payable		40,000

Step 4 is to periodically transfer or *post* the debit and credit information from the journal to individual ledger accounts. Recall that a ledger is simply a collection of all of the company's various accounts. Each account provides a summary of the effects of all events and transactions on that individual account. This process is called posting. Posting involves transferring debits and credits recorded in individual journal entries to the specific accounts affected. As discussed earlier in the chapter, most accounting systems today are computerized, with the

STEP 4
Post from the journal to the general ledger accounts.

ILLUSTRATION 2-2 Transaction Analysis, the Accounting Equation, and Debits and Credits

Accounting Equation

Transaction	Transaction Analysis	Assets	=	Liabilities	+	Owners' Equity	Account Entry
1. An attorney invested $50,000 to open a law office.	Assets (cash) and owners' equity each increased by $50,000.	+50,000	=		+	+50,000	**Cash** 50,000 **Owners' Equity** 50,000
	Cumulative balances	50,000	=		+	50,000	
2. $40,000 was borrowed from a bank and a note payable was signed.	Assets (cash) and liabilities (note payable) each increased by $40,000.	+40,000	=	+40,000	+		**Cash** 50,000 / 40,000 **Note Payable** 40,000
	Cumulative balances	90,000	=	40,000	+	50,000	
3. Supplies costing $3,000 were purchased on account.	Assets (supplies) and liabilities (accounts payable) each increased by $3,000.	+3,000	=	+3,000	+		**Supplies** 3,000 **Accounts Payable** 3,000
	Cumulative balances	93,000	=	43,000	+	50,000	
4. Services were performed on account for $10,000.	Assets (accounts receivable) and owners' equity (revenue) each increased by $10,000.	+10,000	=		+	+10,000	**Accounts Receivable** 10,000 **Owners' Equity (Revenue)** 10,000
	Cumulative balances	103,000	=	43,000	+	60,000	
5. Salaries of $5,000 were paid to employees.	Assets (cash) decreased and owners' equity decreased (salaries expense increased) by $5,000.	−5,000	=		+	−5,000	**Cash** 50,000 / 5,000 40,000 **Owners' Equity (Salaries Expense)** 5,000
	Cumulative balances	98,000	=	43,000	+	55,000	
6. $500 of supplies were used.	Assets (supplies) decreased and owners' equity decreased (supplies expense increased) by $500.	−500	=		+	−500	**Supplies** 3,000 / 500 **Owners' Equity (Supplies Expense)** 500
	Cumulative balances	97,500	=	43,000	+	54,500	
7. $1,000 was paid on account to the supplies vendor.	Assets (cash) and liabilities (accounts payable) each decreased by $1,000.	−1,000	=	−1,000	+		**Cash** 50,000 / 5,000 40,000 / 1,000 **Accounts Payable** 1,000 / 3,000
	Cumulative balances	96,500	=	42,000	+	54,500	

journal and ledger kept on disk. For these systems, the journal input information is automatically and instantly posted to the ledger accounts.

These first four steps in the processing cycle are illustrated using the external transactions in Illustration 2–3 which occurred during the month of July 2009, the first month of operations for Dress Right Clothing Corporation. The company operates a retail store that sells men's and women's clothing. Dress Right is organized as a corporation so owners' equity is classified by source as either paid-in capital or retained earnings.

ILLUSTRATION 2–3	July	1	Two individuals each invested $30,000 in the corporation. Each investor was issued 3,000 shares of common stock.
External Transactions for July 2009		1	Borrowed $40,000 from a local bank and signed two notes. The first note for $10,000 requires payment of principal and 10% interest in six months. The second note for $30,000 requires the payment of principal in two years. Interest at 10% is payable each year on July 1, 2010, and July 1, 2011.
		1	Paid $24,000 in advance for one year's rent on the store building.
		1	Purchased furniture and fixtures from Acme Furniture for $12,000 cash.
		3	Purchased $60,000 of clothing inventory on account from the Birdwell Wholesale Clothing Company.
		6	Purchased $2,000 of supplies for cash.
		4–31	During the month sold merchandise costing $20,000 for $35,000 cash.
		9	Sold clothing on account to St. Jude's School for Girls for $3,500. The clothing cost $2,000.
		16	Subleased a portion of the building to a jewelry store. Received $1,000 in advance for the first two months' rent beginning on July 16.
		20	Paid Birdwell Wholesale Clothing $25,000 on account.
		20	Paid salaries to employees for the first half of the month, $5,000.
		25	Received $1,500 on account from St. Jude's.
		30	The corporation paid its shareholders a cash dividend of $1,000.

The local bank requires that Dress Right furnish financial statements on a monthly basis. The transactions listed in the illustration are used to demonstrate the accounting processing cycle for the month of July 2009.

For each transaction, a source document provides the necessary information to complete steps two and three in the processing cycle, transaction analysis and recording the appropriate journal entry. Each transaction listed in Illustration 2–3 is analyzed below, preceded by the necessary journal entry.

To record the issuance of common stock.

July 1
Cash 60,000
    Common stock   60,000

This first transaction is an investment by owners that increases an asset, cash, and also increases shareholders' equity. Increases in assets are recorded as debits and increases in shareholders' equity are recorded as credits. We use the paid-in capital account called common stock because stock was issued in exchange for cash paid in.[2]

To record the borrowing of cash and the signing of notes payable.

July 1
Cash 40,000
    Notes payable   40,000

This transaction causes increases in both cash and the liability, notes payable. Increases in assets are debits and increases in liabilities are credits. The notes require payment of $40,000 in principal and $6,500 ([$10,000 × 10% × 6/12 = $500] + [$30,000 × 10% × 2 years = $6,000]) in interest. However, at this point we are concerned only with the external transaction that

---

[2]The different types of stock are discussed in Chapter 18.

occurs when the cash is borrowed and the notes are signed. Later we discuss how the interest is recorded.

July 1			*To record the payment*
Prepaid rent	24,000		*of one year's rent in*
Cash		24,000	*advance.*

This transaction decreased cash (a credit) and increased an asset called prepaid rent, which is debited. Dress Right acquired the right to use the building for one full year. This is an asset because it represents a future benefit to the company. As we will see later, this asset expires over the one-year rental period.

July 1			*To record the purchase*
Furniture and fixtures	12,000		*of furniture and*
Cash		12,000	*fixtures.*

This transaction increases one asset, furniture and fixtures, and decreases another, cash.

July 3			*To record the purchase*
Inventory	60,000		*of merchandise*
Accounts payable		60,000	*inventory.*

This purchase of merchandise on account is recorded by a debit to inventory, an asset, and a credit to accounts payable, a liability. Increases in assets are debits, and increases in liabilities are credits.

The Dress Right Clothing Company uses the *perpetual inventory system* to keep track of its merchandise inventory. This system requires that the cost of merchandise purchased be recorded in inventory, an asset account. When inventory is sold, the inventory account is decreased by the cost of the item sold. The alternative method, the periodic system, is briefly discussed on the next page, and Chapters 8 and 9 cover the topic of inventory in depth.

July 6			*To record the purchase*
Supplies	2,000		*of supplies.*
Cash		2,000	

The acquisition of supplies is recorded as a debit to the asset account supplies (an increase) and a credit to the asset cash (a decrease). Supplies are recorded as an asset because they represent future benefits.

July 4–31			*To record the month's*
Cash	35,000		*cash sales and the cost*
Sales revenue		35,000	*of those sales.*
Cost of goods sold (expense)..	20,000		
Inventory		20,000	

During the month of July, cash sales to customers totaled $35,000. The company's assets (cash) increase by this amount as does shareholders' equity. This increase in equity is recorded by a credit to the temporary account sales revenue.

At the same time, an asset, inventory, decreases and retained earnings decreases. Recall that expenses are outflows or using up of assets from providing goods and services. Dress

Right incurred an expense equal to the cost of the inventory sold. The temporary account cost of goods sold increases. However, this increase in an expense represents a *decrease* in shareholders' equity—retained earnings—and accordingly the account is debited. Both of these transactions are *summary* transactions. Each sale made during the month requires a separate and similar entry.

To record a credit sale and the cost of that sale.

July 9

Accounts receivable	3,500	
Sales revenue		3,500
Cost of goods sold	2,000	
Inventory		2,000

This transaction is similar to the cash sale above. The only difference is that the asset acquired in exchange for merchandise is accounts receivable rather than cash.

ADDITIONAL CONSIDERATION

Periodic Inventory System

The principal alternative to the perpetual inventory system is the periodic system. This system requires that the cost of merchandise purchased be recorded in a temporary account called *purchases*. When inventory is sold, the inventory account is not decreased and cost of goods sold is not recorded. Cost of goods sold for a period is determined and the inventory account is adjusted only at the end of a reporting period.

For example, the purchase of $60,000 of merchandise on account by Dress Right Clothing is recorded as follows:

Purchases	60,000	
Accounts payable		60,000

No cost of goods sold entry is recorded when sales are made in the periodic system.

At the end of July, the amount of ending inventory is determined (either by means of a physical count of goods on hand or by estimation) to be $38,000 and cost of goods sold for the month is determined as follows:

Beginning inventory	–0–
Plus: Purchases	60,000
Less: Ending inventory	(38,000)
Cost of goods sold	22,000

The following journal entry records cost of goods sold for the period and adjusts the inventory account to the actual amount on hand (in this case from zero to $38,000):

Cost of goods sold	22,000	
Inventory	38,000	
Purchases		60,000

Inventory is discussed in depth in Chapters 8 and 9.

To record the receipt of rent in advance.

July 16

Cash	1,000	
Unearned rent revenue (liability)		1,000

Cash increases by $1,000 so the cash account is debited. At this point, Dress Right does not recognize revenue even though cash has been received. Recall that the first criterion required for revenue recognition as stated in the realization principle is that the "earnings process is judged to be complete or virtually complete." Dress Right does not earn the revenue until it has provided the jewelry store with the use of facilities; that is, the revenue is earned as the rental period expires. On receipt of the cash, a liability called *unearned rent revenue* increases and is credited. This liability represents Dress Right's obligation to provide the use of facilities to the jewelry store.

July 20
Accounts payable 25,000
   Cash 25,000

To record the payment of accounts payable.

This transaction decreases both an asset (cash) and a liability (accounts payable). Decreases in assets are credits, and decreases in liabilities are debits.

July 20
Salaries expense 5,000
   Cash 5,000

To record the payment of salaries for the first half of the month.

Employees were paid for services rendered during the first half of the month. The cash expenditure did not create an asset since no future benefits result. Cash decreases and is credited; shareholders' equity decreases and is debited. The debit is recorded in the temporary account salaries expense.

July 25
Cash 1,500
   Accounts receivable 1,500

To record receipt of cash on account.

This transaction is an exchange of one asset, accounts receivable, for another asset, cash.

July 30
Retained earnings 1,000
   Cash 1,000

To record the payment of a cash dividend.

The payment of a cash dividend is a distribution to owners as that reduces both cash and retained earnings.

ADDITIONAL CONSIDERATION

An alternative method of recording a cash dividend is to debit a temporary account called dividends. In that case, the dividends account is later closed (transferred) to retained earnings along with the other temporary accounts at the end of the fiscal year. The journal entry to record the dividend using this approach is

Dividends 1,000
   Cash 1,000

We discuss and illustrate the closing process later in the chapter.

Illustration 2–4 summarizes each of the transactions just discussed as they would appear in a general journal. In addition to the date, account titles, debit and credit columns, the journal also has a column titled Post Ref. (Posting Reference). This usually is a number assigned to the general ledger account that is being debited or credited. For purposes of this illustration, all asset accounts have been assigned numbers in the 100s, all liabilities are 200s, permanent shareholders' equity accounts are 300s, revenues are 400s, and expenses are 500s.

ILLUSTRATION 2–4

The General Journal

General Journal				Page 1
Date 2009	**Account Title and Explanation**	**Post Ref.**	**Debit**	**Credit**
July 1	Cash	100	60,000	
	Common stock	300		60,000
	To record the issuance of common stock.			
1	Cash	100	40,000	
	Notes payable	220		40,000
	To record the borrowing of cash and the *signing of notes payable.*			
1	Prepaid rent	130	24,000	
	Cash	100		24,000
	To record the payment of one year's rent *in advance.*			
1	Furniture and fixtures	150	12,000	
	Cash	100		12,000
	To record the purchase of furniture and fixtures.			
3	Inventory	140	60,000	
	Accounts payable	210		60,000
	To record the purchase of merchandise inventory.			
6	Supplies	125	2,000	
	Cash	100		2,000
	To record the purchase of supplies.			
4–31	Cash	100	35,000	
	Sales revenue	400		35,000
	To record cash sales for the month.			
4–31	Cost of goods sold	500	20,000	
	Inventory	140		20,000
	To record the cost of cash sales.			
9	Accounts receivable	110	3,500	
	Sales revenue	400		3,500
	To record credit sale.			
9	Cost of goods sold	500	2,000	
	Inventory	140		2,000
	To record the cost of a credit sale.			
16	Cash	100	1,000	
	Unearned rent revenue	230		1,000
	To record the receipt of rent in advance.			
20	Accounts payable	210	25,000	
	Cash	100		25,000
	To record the payment of accounts payable.			
20	Salaries expense	510	5,000	
	Cash	100		5,000
	To record the payment of salaries for the first *half of the month.*			
25	Cash	100	1,500	
	Accounts receivable	110		1,500
	To record the receipt of cash on account.			
30	Retained earnings	310	1,000	
	Cash	100		1,000
	To record the payment of a cash dividend.			

The ledger accounts also contain a posting reference, usually the page number of the journal in which the journal entry was recorded. This allows for easy cross-referencing between the journal and the ledger. Page 1 is used for Illustration 2–4.

Step 4 in the processing cycle is to transfer (post) the debit/credit information from the journal to the general ledger accounts. Illustration 2–5 contains the ledger accounts (in T-account form) for Dress Right *after* all of the general journal transactions have been posted. The reference GJ1 next to each of the posted amounts indicates that the source of the entry is page 1 of the general journal.

● LO3

ILLUSTRATION 2–5

General Ledger Accounts

Balance Sheet Accounts

	Cash			100		Prepaid Rent		130
July 1 GJ1	60,000	24,000	July 1 GJ1		July 1 GJ1	24,000		
1 GJ1	40,000	12,000	1 GJ1					
4–31GJ1	35,000	2,000	6 GJ1					
16 GJ1	1,000	25,000	20 GJ1					
25 GJ1	1,500	5,000	20 GJ1					
		1,000	30 GJ1					
July 31 Bal.	68,500				July 31 Bal.	24,000		

	Accounts Receivable			110		Inventory		140
July 9 GJ1	3,500	1,500	July 25 GJ1		July 3 GJ1	60,000	20,000	July 4–31
							2,000	9 GJ1
July 31 Bal.	2,000				July 31 Bal.	38,000		

	Supplies		125		Furniture and Fixtures		150
July 6 GJ1	2,000			July 1 GJ1	12,000		
July 31 Bal.	2,000			July 31 Bal.	12,000		

	Accounts Payable			210		Notes Payable		220
July 20 GJ1	25,000	60,000	July 3 GJ1				40,000	July 1 GJ1
		35,000	July 31 Bal.				40,000	July 31 Bal.

	Unearned Rent Revenue		230
		1,000	July 16 GJ1
		1,000	July 31 Bal.

	Common Stock		300		Retained Earnings		310
		60,000	July 1 GJ1	July 30 GJ1	1,000		
		60,000	July 31 Bal.	July 31 Bal.	1,000		

Income Statement Accounts

	Sales Revenue		400		Cost of Goods Sold		500
		35,000	July 4–31 GJ1	July 4–31 GJ1	20,000		
		3,500	9 GJ1	July 9 GJ1	2,000		
		38,500	July 31 Bal.	July 31 Bal.	22,000		

	Salaries Expense		510
July 20 GJ1	5,000		
July 31 Bal.	5,000		

STEP 5

Prepare an *unadjusted trial balance.*

Before financial statements are prepared and before adjusting entries are recorded (internal transactions) at the end of an accounting period, an unadjusted trial balance usually is prepared—step 5. A trial balance is simply a list of the general ledger accounts and their balances at a particular date. Its purpose is to check for completeness and to prove that the sum of the accounts with debit balances equals the sum of the accounts with credit balances, that is, the accounting equation is in balance. The fact that the debits and credits are equal does not necessarily mean that the equal balances are correct. The trial balance could contain offsetting errors. As we will see later in the chapter, this trial balance also facilitates the preparation of adjusting entries.

The unadjusted trial balance at July 31, 2009, for the Dress Right Clothing Corporation appears in Illustration 2–6. Notice that retained earnings has a debit balance of $1,000. This reflects the payment of the cash dividend to shareholders. The increases and decreases in retained earnings from revenue, expense, gain and loss transactions are recorded indirectly in temporary accounts. Before the start of the next year, these increases and decreases are transferred to the retained earnings account.

ILLUSTRATION 2–6

Unadjusted Trial Balance

DRESS RIGHT CLOTHING CORPORATION
Unadjusted Trial Balance
July 31, 2009

Account Title	Debits	Credits
Cash	68,500	
Accounts receivable	2,000	
Supplies	2,000	
Prepaid rent	24,000	
Inventory	38,000	
Furniture and fixtures	12,000	
Accounts payable		35,000
Notes payable		40,000
Unearned rent revenue		1,000
Common stock		60,000
Retained earnings	1,000	
Sales revenue		38,500
Cost of goods sold	22,000	
Salaries expense	5,000	
Totals	174,500	174,500

At any time, the total of all debit balances should equal the total of all credit balances.

CONCEPT REVIEW EXERCISE

JOURNAL ENTRIES FOR EXTERNAL TRANSACTIONS

The Wyndham Wholesale Company began operations on August 1, 2009. The following transactions took place during the month of August.

a. Owners invested $50,000 cash in the corporation in exchange for 5,000 shares of common stock.
b. Equipment is purchased for $20,000 cash.
c. On the first day of August, $6,000 rent on a building is paid for the months of August and September.
d. Merchandise inventory costing $38,000 is purchased on account. The company uses the perpetual inventory system.
e. $30,000 is borrowed from a local bank, and a note payable is signed.
f. Credit sales for the month are $40,000. The cost of merchandise sold is $22,000.
g. $15,000 is collected on account from customers.
h. $20,000 is paid on account to suppliers of merchandise.
i. Salaries of $7,000 are paid to employees for August.

j. A bill for $2,000 is received from the local utility company for the month of August.

k. $20,000 cash was loaned to another company, evidenced by a note receivable.

l. The corporation paid its shareholders a cash dividend of $1,000.

Required:

1. Prepare a journal entry for each transaction.

2. Prepare an unadjusted trial balance as of August 31, 2009.

1. Prepare a journal entry for each transaction.   **SOLUTION**

  a. The issuance of common stock for cash increases both cash and shareholders' equity (common stock).

Cash	50,000	
Common Stock		50,000

  b. The purchase of equipment increases equipment and decreases cash.

Equipment	20,000	
Cash		20,000

  c. The payment of rent in advance increases prepaid rent and decreases cash.

Prepaid rent	6,000	
Cash		6,000

  d. The purchase of merchandise on account increases both inventory and accounts payable.

Inventory	38,000	
Accounts payable		38,000

  e. Borrowing cash and signing a note increases both cash and note payable.

Cash	30,000	
Note payable		30,000

  f. The sale of merchandise on account increases both accounts receivable and sales revenue. Also, cost of goods sold increases and inventory decreases.

Accounts receivable	40,000	
Sales revenue		40,000
Cost of Goods sold	22,000	
Inventory		22,000

  g. The collection of cash on account increases cash and decreases accounts receivable.

Cash	15,000	
Accounts receivable		15,000

  h. The payment of suppliers on account decreases both accounts payable and cash.

Accounts payable	20,000	
Cash		20,000

i. The payments of salaries for the period increases salaries expense (decreases retained earnings) and decreases cash.

Salaries expense	7,000	
Cash		7,000

j. The receipt of a bill for services rendered increases both an expense (utilities expense) and accounts payable. The expense decreases retained earnings.

Utilities expense	2,000	
Accounts payable		2,000

k. The lending of cash to another entity and the signing of a note increases note receivable and decreases cash.

Note receivable	20,000	
Cash		20,000

l. Cash dividends paid to shareholders reduce both retained earnings and cash.

Retained earnings[3]	1,000	
Cash		1,000

2. Prepare an unadjusted trial balance as of August 31, 2009.

Account Title	Debits	Credits
Cash	21,000	
Accounts receivable	25,000	
Prepaid rent	6,000	
Inventory	16,000	
Note receivable	20,000	
Equipment	20,000	
Accounts payable		20,000
Note payable		30,000
Common stock		50,000
Retained earnings	1,000	
Sales revenue		40,000
Cost of goods sold	22,000	
Salaries expense	7,000	
Utilities expense	2,000	
Totals	140,000	140,000

Adjusting Entries

STEP 6

Record *adjusting entries* and post to the ledger accounts.

Step 6 in the processing cycle is to record in the general journal and post to the ledger accounts the effect of *internal events* on the accounting equation. These transactions do not involve an exchange transaction with another entity and, therefore, are not initiated by a source document. They are recorded *at the end of any period when financial statements are prepared.* These transactions are commonly referred to as adjusting entries.

Even when all transactions and events are analyzed, corrected, journalized, and posted to appropriate ledger accounts, some account balances will require updating. Adjusting entries

---

[3]An alternative is to debit a temporary account—dividends—that is closed to retained earnings at the end of the fiscal year along with the other temporary accounts.

are required to implement the *accrual accounting model.* More specifically, these entries are required to satisfy the *realization principle* and the *matching principle.* Adjusting entries help ensure that all revenues earned in a period are recognized in that period, regardless of when the cash is received. Also, they enable a company to recognize all expenses incurred during a period, regardless of when cash payment is made. As a result, a period's income statement provides a more complete measure of a company's operating performance and a better measure for predicting future operating cash flows. The balance sheet also provides a more complete assessment of assets and liabilities as sources of future cash receipts and disbursements. You might think of adjusting entries as a method of bringing the company's financial information up to date before preparing the financial statements.

Adjusting entries are necessary for three situations:

1. Prepayments, sometimes referred to as *deferrals.*
2. Accruals.
3. Estimates.

Prepayments

Prepayments occur when the cash flow *precedes* either expense or revenue recognition. For example, a company may buy supplies in one period but use them in a later period. The cash outflow creates an asset (supplies) which then must be expensed in a future period as the asset is used up. Similarly, a company may receive cash from a customer in one period but provide the customer with a good or service in a future period. For instance, magazine publishers usually receive cash in advance for magazine subscriptions. The cash inflow creates a liability (unearned revenue) that is recognized as revenue in a future period when it is earned.

PREPAID EXPENSES.   Prepaid expenses are the costs of assets acquired in one period and expensed in a future period. Whenever cash is paid, and it is not to (1) satisfy a liability or (2) pay a dividend or return capital to owners, it must be determined whether or not the payment creates future benefits or whether the payment benefits only the current period. The purchase of machinery, equipment, or supplies or the payment of rent in advance are examples of payments that create future benefits and should be recorded as assets. The benefits provided by these assets expire in future periods and their cost is expensed in future periods as related revenues are recognized.

To illustrate this concept, assume that a company paid a radio station $2,000 in July for advertising. If that $2,000 were for advertising provided by the radio station during the month of July, the entire $2,000 would be expensed in the same period as the cash disbursement. If, however, the $2,000 was a payment for advertising to be provided in a future period, say the month of August, then the cash disbursement creates an asset called *prepaid advertising.* An adjusting entry is required at the end of August to increase advertising expense (decrease shareholders' equity) and to decrease the asset prepaid advertising by $2,000. Assuming that the cash disbursement records a debit to an asset, as in this example, the adjusting entry for a prepaid expense is, therefore, a *debit to an expense* and a *credit to an asset.*

The unadjusted trial balance can provide a starting point for determining which adjusting entries are required for a period, particularly for prepayments. Review the July 31, 2009, unadjusted trial balance for the Dress Right Clothing Corporation in Illustration 2–6 on page 64 and try to anticipate the required adjusting entries for prepaid expenses.

The first asset that requires adjustment is supplies, $2,000 of which were purchased during July. This transaction created an asset as the supplies will be used in future periods. The company could either track the supplies used or simply count the supplies at the end of the period and determine the dollar amount of supplies remaining. Assume that Dress Right determines that at the end of July, $1,200 of supplies remain. The following adjusting journal entry is required.

FINANCIAL
Reporting Case

Q1, p. 51

● **LO4**

FINANCIAL
Reporting Case

Q2, p. 51

Prepayments are transactions in which the cash flow *precedes* expense or revenue recognition.

Prepaid expenses represent assets recorded when a cash disbursement creates benefits beyond the current reporting period.

The adjusting entry required for a prepaid expense is a *debit to an expense* and a *credit to an asset.*

● **LO5**

To record the cost of supplies used during the month of July.

July 31		
Supplies expense	800	
Supplies		800

Supplies		
Beg. bal.	0	
	2,000	800
End bal.	1,200	

Supplies Expense		
Beg. bal.	0	
	800	
End bal.	800	

After this entry is recorded and posted to the ledger accounts, the supplies (asset) account is reduced to a $1,200 debit balance, and the supplies expense account will have an $800 debit balance.

The next prepaid expense requiring adjustment is rent. Recall that at the beginning of July, the company paid $24,000 to its landlord representing one year's rent in advance. As it is reasonable to assume that the rent services provided each period are equal, the monthly rent is $2,000. At the end of July 2009, one month's prepaid rent has expired and must be recognized as expense.

To record the cost of expired rent for the month of July.

July 31
Rent expense ($24,000 ÷ 12) 2,000
    Prepaid rent 2,000

Prepaid Rent		
Beg. bal.	0	
	24,000	2,000
End bal.	22,000	

Rent Expense		
Beg. bal.	0	
	2,000	
End bal.	2,000	

After this entry is recorded and posted to the ledger accounts, the prepaid rent account will have a debit balance of $22,000, representing 11 remaining months at $2,000 a month, and the rent expense account will have a $2,000 debit balance.

The final prepayment involves the asset represented by furniture and fixtures that was purchased for $12,000. This asset has a long life but nevertheless will expire over time. For the previous two adjusting entries, it was fairly straightforward to determine the amount of the asset that expired during the period.

However, it is difficult, if not impossible, to determine how much of the benefits from using the furniture and fixtures expired during any particular period. Recall from Chapter 1 that one approach to implementing the matching principle is to "recognize an expense by a systematic and rational allocation to specific time periods."

Assume that the furniture and fixtures have a useful life of five years or 60 months and will be worthless at the end of that period, and that we choose to allocate the cost equally over the period of use. The amount of monthly expense, called *depreciation expense,* is $200 ($12,000 ÷ 60 months = $200), and the following adjusting entry is recorded.

To record depreciation of furniture and fixtures for the month of July.

July 31
Depreciation expense 200
    Accumulated depreciation—furniture and fixtures 200

The entry reduces an asset, furniture and fixtures, by $200. However, the asset account is not reduced directly. Instead, the credit is to an account called *accumulated depreciation.* This is a contra account to furniture and fixtures. The normal balance in a contra asset account will be a credit, that is, "contra," or opposite, to the normal debit balance in an asset account. The purpose of the contra account is to keep the original cost of the asset intact while reducing it indirectly. In the balance sheet, furniture and fixtures is reported net of accumulated depreciation. This topic is covered in depth in Chapter 11.

After this entry is recorded and posted to the ledger accounts, the accumulated depreciation account will have a credit balance of $200 and the depreciation expense account will have a $200 debit balance. If a required adjusting entry for a prepaid expense is not recorded, net income, assets, and shareholders' equity (retained earnings) will be overstated.

Unearned revenues represent liabilities recorded when cash is received from customers in advance of providing a good or service.

UNEARNED REVENUES. Unearned revenues are created when a company receives cash from a customer in one period for goods or services that are to be provided in a future period. The cash receipt, an external transaction, is recorded as a debit to cash and a credit to a liability. This liability reflects the company's obligation to provide goods or services in the future.

To illustrate an unearned revenue transaction, assume that during the month of June a magazine publisher received $24 in cash for a 24-month subscription to a monthly magazine. The subscription begins in July. On receipt of the cash, the publisher records a liability, unearned subscription revenue, of $24. Subsequently, revenue of $1 is earned as each monthly magazine is published and mailed to the customer. An adjusting entry is required each month to increase shareholders' equity (revenue) to recognize the $1 in revenue earned and to decrease the liability. Assuming that the cash receipt records a credit to a liability, the adjusting entry for unearned revenues, therefore, is a *debit to a liability,* in this case unearned subscription revenue, and a *credit to revenue.*

Once again, the unadjusted trial balance provides information concerning unearned revenues. For Dress Right Clothing Corporation, the only unearned revenue in the trial balance is unearned rent revenue. Recall that the company subleased a portion of its building to a jewelry store for $500 per month. On July 16, the jewelry store paid Dress Right $1,000 in advance for the first two months' rent. The transaction was recorded as a debit to cash and a credit to unearned rent revenue.

At the end of July, how much of the $1,000 has been earned? Approximately one-half of one month's rent has been earned, or $250, requiring the following adjusting journal entry.

The adjusting entry required when unearned revenues are earned is a *debit to a liability* and a *credit to revenue.*

July 31		
Unearned rent revenue	250	
Rent revenue		250

To record the amount of unearned rent revenue earned during July.

Unearned Rent Revenue

	0 Beg. bal.
250	1,000
	750 End bal.

Rent Revenue

	0 Beg. bal.
	250
	250 End bal.

After this entry is recorded and posted to the ledger accounts, the unearned rent revenue account is reduced to a credit balance of $750 for the remaining one and one-half months' rent, and the rent revenue account will have a $250 credit balance. If this entry is not recorded, net income and shareholders' equity (retained earnings) will be understated, and liabilities will be overstated.

ALTERNATIVE APPROACH TO RECORD PREPAYMENTS.

The same end result can be achieved for prepayments by recording the external transaction directly into an expense or revenue account. In fact, many companies prefer this approach. For simplicity, bookkeeping instructions may require all cash payments for expenses to be debited to the appropriate expense account and all cash receipts for revenues to be credited to the appropriate revenue account. The adjusting entry then records the *unexpired* prepaid expense (asset) or *unearned* revenue (liability) as of the end of the period.

For example, on July 1, 2009, Dress Right paid $24,000 in cash for one year's rent on its building. The entry included a debit to prepaid rent. The company could have debited rent expense instead.

Rent Expense

Beg. bal.	0	
	24,000	22,000
End bal.	2,000	

Alternative Approach

July 1		
Rent expense	24,000	
Cash		24,000

The adjusting entry then records the amount of prepaid rent as of the end of July, $22,000, and reduces rent expense to $2,000, the cost of rent for the month of July.

Prepaid Rent

Beg. bal.	0	
	22,000	
End bal.	22,000	

Alternative Approach

July 31		
Prepaid rent	22,000	
Rent expense		22,000

The net effect of handling the transactions in this manner is the same as the previous treatment. Either way, the prepaid rent account will have a debit balance at the end of July of $22,000, and the rent expense account will have a debit balance of $2,000. What's important is that an adjusting entry is recorded to ensure the appropriate amounts are reflected in both the expense and asset *before financial statements are to be prepared.*

Similarly, the July 16 cash receipt from the jewelry store representing an advance for two months' rent could have been recorded by Dress Right as a credit to rent revenue instead of unearned rent revenue (a liability).

Rent Revenue		
	0	Beg. bal.
750	1,000	
	250	End bal.

Alternative Approach

July 16

Cash	1,000	
Rent revenue		1,000

If Dress Right records the entire $1,000 as rent revenue in this way, it would then use the adjusting entry to record the amount of unearned revenue as of the end of July, $750, and reduce rent revenue to $250, the amount of revenue earned during the month of July.

Unearned Rent Revenue		
	0	Beg. bal.
	750	
	750	End bal.

Alternative Approach

July 31

Rent revenue	750	
Unearned rent revenue		750

Accruals

Accruals involve transactions where the cash outflow or inflow takes place in a period subsequent to expense or revenue recognition.

Accruals occur when the cash flow comes *after* either expense or revenue recognition. For example, a company often uses the services of another entity in one period and pays for them in a subsequent period. An expense must be recognized in the period incurred and an accrued liability recorded. Also, goods and services often are provided to customers on credit. In such instances, a revenue is recognized in the period earned and an asset, a receivable, is recorded.

Many accruals involve external transactions that automatically are recorded from a source document. For example, a sales invoice for a credit sale provides all the information necessary to record the debit to accounts receivable and the credit to sales revenue. However, there are some accruals that involve internal transactions and thus require adjusting entries. Because accruals involve recognition of expense or revenue before cash flow, the unadjusted trial balance will not be as helpful in identifying required adjusting entries as with prepayments.

Accrued liabilities represent liabilities recorded when an expense has been incurred prior to cash payment.

ACCRUED LIABILITIES. For accrued liabilities, we are concerned with expenses incurred but not yet paid. Dress Right Clothing Corporation requires two adjusting entries for accrued liabilities at July 31, 2009.

The first entry is for employee salaries for the second half of July. Recall that on July 20 the company paid employees $5,000 for salaries for the first half of the month. Salaries for the second half of July will probably be paid in early August. Nevertheless, the company incurred an expense in July for services provided to it by its employees. Also, there exists an obligation at the end of July to pay the salaries earned by employees. An adjusting entry is required to increase salaries expense (decrease shareholders' equity) and to increase liabilities for the salaries payable. The adjusting entry for an accrued liability always includes a *debit to an expense,* and a *credit to a liability.* Assuming that salaries for the second half of July are $5,500, the following adjusting entry is recorded.

The adjusting entry required to record an accrued liability is a debit to an expense and a credit to a liability.

To record accrued salaries at the end of July.

July 31

Salaries expense..	5,500	
Salaries payable...		5,500

After this entry is recorded and posted to the general ledger, the salaries expense account will have a debit balance of $10,500 ($5,000 + 5,500), and the salaries payable account will have a credit balance of $5,500.

The unadjusted trial balance does provide information about the second required accrued liability entry. In the trial balance we can see a balance in the notes payable account of $40,000. The company borrowed this amount on July 1, 2009. Both notes require the payment of 10% interest. Whenever the trial balance reveals interest-bearing debt, and interest is not paid on the last day of the period, an adjusting entry is required for the amount of interest that has built up (accrued) since the last payment date or the last date interest was accrued. In this case, we calculate interest as follows:

$$\text{Principal} \times \text{Interest rate} \times \text{Time} = \text{Interest}$$
$$\$40,000 \times 10\% \times \tfrac{1}{12} = \$333 \text{ (rounded)}$$

Interest rates always are stated as the annual rate. Therefore, the above calculation uses this annual rate multiplied by the principal amount multiplied by the amount of time outstanding, in this case one month or one-twelfth of a year.

Salaries Payable

	0	Beg. bal.
	5,500	
	5,500	End bal.

Salaries Expense

Beg. bal.	0	
July 20	5,000	
	5,500	
End bal.	10,500	

To accrue interest expense for July on notes payable.

July 31

| Interest expense .... | 333 | |
| Interest payable .... | | 333 |

After this entry is recorded and posted to the ledger accounts, the interest expense account will have a debit balance of $333, and the interest payable account will have a credit balance of $333. Failure to record a required adjusting entry for an accrued liability will cause net income and shareholders' equity (retained earnings) to be overstated, and liabilities to be understated.[4]

ACCRUED RECEIVABLES.   Accrued receivables involve the recognition of revenue earned before cash is received. An example of an internal accrued revenue event is the recognition of interest earned on a loan to another entity. For example, assume that Dress Right loaned another corporation $30,000 at the beginning of August, evidenced by a note receivable. Terms of the note call for the payment of principal, $30,000, and interest at 8% in three months. An external transaction records the cash disbursement—a debit to note receivable and a credit to cash of $30,000.

What adjusting entry would be required at the end of August? Dress Right needs to record the interest revenue earned but not yet received and the corresponding receivable. Interest receivable increases and interest revenue (shareholders' equity) also increases. The adjusting entry for accrued receivables always includes a *debit to an asset,* a receivable, and a *credit to revenue.* In this case, at the end of August Dress Right recognizes $200 in interest revenue ($30,000 × 8% × $\tfrac{1}{12}$) and makes the following adjusting entry. If this entry is not recorded, net income, assets, and shareholders' equity (retained earnings) will be understated.

Accrued receivables involve situations when the revenue is earned in a period prior to the cash receipt.

The adjusting entry required to record an accrued revenue is a debit to an asset, a receivable, and a credit to revenue.

To accrue interest revenue earned in August on note receivable.

August 31

| Interest receivable .... | 200 | |
| Interest revenue .... | | 200 |

---

[4]Dress Right Clothing is a corporation. Corporations are income-tax-paying entities. Income taxes—federal, state, and local—are assessed on an annual basis and payments are made throughout the year. An additional adjusting entry would be required for Dress Right to accrue the amount of estimated income taxes payable that are applicable to the month of July. Accounting for income taxes is introduced in Chapter 4 and covered in depth in Chapter 16.

There are no accrued revenue adjusting entries required for Dress Right at the end of July.

The required adjusting entries for prepayments and accruals are recapped with the aid of T-accounts in Graphic 2–4. In each case an expense or revenue is recognized in a period that differs from the period in which cash was paid or received. These entries are necessary to properly measure operating performance and financial position on an accrual basis.

GRAPHIC 2–4
Adjusting Entries

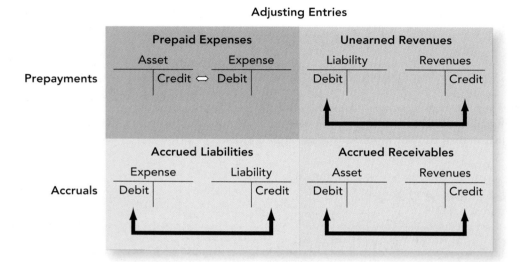

Adjusting Entries

Estimates

Accountants often must make estimates *in order to comply with the accrual accounting model.*

A third classification of adjusting entries is estimates. Accountants often must make estimates of future events to comply with the accrual accounting model. For example, the calculation of depreciation expense requires an estimate of expected useful life of the asset being depreciated as well as its expected residual value. We discussed the adjusting entries for depreciation expense in the context of its being a prepayment, but it also could be thought of as an estimate.

One situation involving an estimate that does not fit neatly into either the prepayment or accrual classification is bad debt expense. Chapter 1 introduced briefly the allowance method of accounting for bad debts. This method requires an estimate of the amount of accounts receivable that will ultimately prove to be uncollectible. This estimate is required to properly match the bad debt expense with the revenue it helps generate as well as reflect the collectible portion of the receivable on the balance sheet.

The July 31, 2009, unadjusted trial balance for Dress Right shows a balance in accounts receivable of $2,000. Assume that the company's management felt that of this amount, only $1,500 would ultimately be collected. An adjusting entry is required to decrease accounts receivable and increase bad debt expense (decrease shareholders' equity) by $500. The adjusting entry is:

To record bad debt expense for July.

July 31

Bad debt expense	500	
Allowance for uncollectible accounts		500

Notice that the accounts receivable account is not reduced directly. A contra account, called *allowance for uncollectible accounts,* is credited. After this entry is recorded and posted to the ledger accounts, bad debt expense will have a debit balance of $500 and the allowance for uncollectible accounts account will have a credit balance of $500.[5]

The contra account is used to keep intact in the accounts receivable account the total amount of receivables that are still outstanding. The allowance account will always have a credit balance equal to estimated bad debts on existing accounts receivable. Only when a specific customer's account is actually written off as uncollectible would accounts receivable be reduced. At this point, the $500 is just an estimate. In the balance sheet, accounts receivable is shown net of the allowance account, in this case $1,500. Chapter 7 addresses the topics of accounts receivable and bad debts in more depth.

Illustration 2–7 recaps the July 31, 2009, adjusting entries for Dress Right Clothing Corporation as they would appear in a general journal.

DRESS RIGHT CLOTHING CORPORATION

General Journal — Page 2

Date 2009		Account Title and Explanation	Post. Ref.	Debit	Credit
July	31	Supplies expense	520	800	
		Supplies	125		800
		To record the cost of supplies used during the month of July.			
	31	Rent expense	530	2,000	
		Prepaid rent	130		2,000
		To record the cost of expired rent for the month of July.			
	31	Depreciation expense	540	200	
		Accumulated depreciation—furniture and fixtures	155		200
		To record depreciation for furniture and fixtures for the month of July.			
	31	Unearned rent revenue	230	250	
		Rent revenue	410		250
		To record the amount of unearned rent revenue earned during July.			
	31	Salaries expense	510	5,500	
		Salaries payable	230		5,500
		To record accrued salaries at the end of July.			
	31	Interest expense	550	333	
		Interest payable	240		333
		To accrue interest expense for July on notes payable.			
	31	Bad debt expense	560	500	
		Allowance for uncollectible accounts	115		500
		To record bad debt expense for July.			

ILLUSTRATION 2–7

The General Journal—Adjusting Entries

● LO5

After the adjusting entries are posted to the general ledger accounts, the next step—step 7—in the processing cycle is to prepare an *adjusted trial balance.* The term adjusted refers to the fact that adjusting entries have now been posted to the accounts. Recall that the column titled Post Ref. (Posting Reference) is the number assigned to the general ledger account that is being debited or credited. Illustration 2–8 shows the July 31, 2009, adjusted trial balance for Dress Right Clothing Corporation.

[5]If the allowance for uncollectible accounts had a credit balance before the adjusting entry, say $150, then the adjusting entry would have required only a $350 debit to bad debt expense and credit to the allowance account.

ILLUSTRATION 2–8	DRESS RIGHT CLOTHING CORPORATION Adjusted Trial Balance July 31, 2009		
Adjusted Trial Balance	**Account Title**	**Debits**	**Credits**

Account Title	Debits	Credits
Cash	68,500	
Accounts receivable	2,000	
Allowance for uncollectible accounts		500
Supplies	1,200	
Prepaid rent	22,000	
Inventory	38,000	
Furniture and fixtures	12,000	
Accumulated depreciation—furniture and fixtures		200
Accounts payable		35,000
Notes payable		40,000
Unearned rent revenue		750
Salaries payable		5,500
Interest payable		333
Common stock		60,000
Retained earnings	1,000	
Sales revenue		38,500
Rent revenue		250
Cost of goods sold	22,000	
Salaries expense	10,500	
Supplies expense	800	
Rent expense	2,000	
Depreciation expense	200	
Interest expense	333	
Bad debt expense	500	
Totals	181,033	181,033

STEP 7

Prepare an *adjusted trial balance.*

CONCEPT REVIEW EXERCISE

ADJUSTING ENTRIES

The Wyndham Wholesale Company needs to prepare financial statements at the end of August 2009 for presentation to its bank. An unadjusted trial balance as of August 31, 2009, was presented in a previous concept review exercise on page 66.

The following information also is available:

a. The company anticipates that of the $25,000 in accounts receivable from customers, $2,500 will *not* be collected.

b. The note payable requires the entire $30,000 in principal plus interest at 10% to be paid on July 31, 2010. The date of the loan is August 1, 2009.

c. Depreciation on the equipment for the month of August is $500.

d. The note receivable is dated August 16, 2009. The note requires the entire $20,000 in principal plus interest at 12% to be repaid in four months (the loan was outstanding for one-half month during August).

e. The prepaid rent of $6,000 represents rent for the months of August and September.

Required:

1. Prepare any necessary adjusting entries at August 31, 2009.
2. Prepare an adjusted trial balance as of August 31, 2009.
3. What is the total net effect on income (overstated or understated) if the adjusting entries are not made?

SOLUTION

1. Prepare any necessary adjusting entries at August 31, 2009.

   a. An adjusting entry is required to adjust allowance for uncollectible accounts to $2,500. Because there is no balance in the allowance account before adjustment, the adjusting entry must record a bad debt expense of $2,500.

Bad debt expense	2,500	
Allowance for uncollectible accounts		2,500

b. An adjusting entry is required to accrue the interest expense on the note payable for the month of August. Accrued interest is calculated as follows:

$$\$30,000 \times 10\% \times \tfrac{1}{12} = \$250$$

Interest expense	250	
Interest payable		250

c. Depreciation expense on the equipment must be recorded.

Depreciation expense	500	
Accumulated depreciation—equipment		500

d. An adjusting entry is required for the one-half month of accrued interest revenue earned on the note receivable. Accrued interest is calculated as follows:

$$\$20,000 \times 12\% \times \tfrac{1}{12} \times \tfrac{1}{2} = \$100$$

Interest receivable	100	
Interest revenue		100

e. An adjusting entry is required to recognize the amount of prepaid rent that expired during August.

Rent expense	3,000	
Prepaid rent		3,000

2. Prepare an adjusted trial balance as of August 31, 2009.

Account Title	Debits	Credits
Cash	21,000	
Accounts receivable	25,000	
Allowance for uncollectible accounts		2,500
Prepaid rent	3,000	
Inventory	16,000	
Interest receivable	100	
Note receivable	20,000	
Equipment	20,000	
Accumulated depreciation—equipment		500
Accounts payable		20,000
Interest payable		250
Note payable		30,000
Common stock		50,000
Retained earnings	1,000	
Sales revenue		40,000
Interest revenue		100
Cost of goods sold	22,000	
Salaries expense	7,000	
Utilities expense	2,000	
Bad debt expense	2,500	
Interest expense	250	
Depreciation expense	500	
Rent expense	3,000	
Totals	143,350	143,350

3. What is the effect on income (overstated or understated), if the adjusting entries are not made?

Adjusting Entry	Income Overstated (understated)
Bad debt expense	$2,500
Interest expense	250
Depreciation expense	500
Interest revenue	(100)
Rent expense	3,000
Net effect, income overstated by	$6,150

We now turn our attention to the preparation of financial statements. ●

Preparing the Financial Statements

● LO6

STEP 8

Preparation of *financial statements.*

The purpose of each of the steps in the processing cycle to this point is to provide information for step 8—preparation of the financial statements. The adjusted trial balance contains the necessary information. After all, the financial statements are the primary means of communicating financial information to external parties.

The Income Statement

The *income statement* is a *change* statement that summarizes the profit-generating transactions that caused shareholders' equity (retained earnings) to change during the period.

The purpose of the income statement is to summarize the profit-generating activities of a company that occurred during a particular period of time. It is a *change* statement in that it reports the changes in shareholders' equity (retained earnings) that occurred during the period as a result of revenues, expenses, gains, and losses. Illustration 2–9 shows the income statement for Dress Right Clothing Corporation for the month of July 2009.

The income statement indicates a profit for the month of July of $2,417. During the month, the company was able to increase its net assets (equity) from activities related to selling its product. Dress Right is a corporation and subject to the payment of income tax on its profits. We ignore this required accrual here and address income taxes in a later chapter.

The components of the income statement usually are classified, that is, grouped according to common characteristics. A common classification scheme is to separate operating items from nonoperating items, as we do in Dress Right's income statement. Operating items include revenues and expenses directly related to the principal revenue-generating activities of the company.

ILLUSTRATION 2–9 Income Statement	**DRESS RIGHT CLOTHING CORPORATION** **Income Statement** **For the Month of July 2009**		
	Sales revenue		$38,500
	Cost of goods sold		22,000
	Gross profit		16,500
	Operating expenses:		
	Salaries	$10,500	
	Supplies	800	
	Rent	2,000	
	Depreciation	200	
	Bad debt	500	
	Total operating expenses		14,000
	Operating income		2,500
	Other income (expense):		
	Rent revenue	250	
	Interest expense	(333)	(83)
	Net income		$ 2,417

For example, operating items for a manufacturing company include sales revenues from the sale of products and all expenses related to this activity. Companies that sell products like Dress Right often report a subtotal within operating income, sales less cost of goods sold, called *gross profit*. Nonoperating items include gains and losses and revenues and expenses from peripheral activities. For Dress Right Clothing, rent revenue and interest expense are nonoperating items because they do not relate to the principal revenue-generating activity of the company, selling clothes. In Chapter 4 we discuss the format and content of the income statement in more depth.

The Balance Sheet

The purpose of the balance sheet is to present the financial position of the company on a particular date. Unlike the income statement, which is a change statement reporting events that occurred *during a period of time,* the balance sheet is a statement that presents an organized list of assets, liabilities, and shareholders' equity *at a point in time.* To provide a quick overview, Illustration 2–10 shows the balance sheet for Dress Right Clothing at July 31, 2009.

The *balance sheet* is a position statement that presents an organized list of assets, liabilities and equity at a particular point in time.

DRESS RIGHT CLOTHING CORPORATION			ILLUSTRATION 2–10
Balance Sheet			Balance Sheet
At July 31, 2009			
Assets			
Current assets:			
Cash		$ 68,500	
Accounts receivable	$ 2,000		
Less: Allowance for uncollectible accounts	500	1,500	
Supplies		1,200	
Inventory		38,000	
Prepaid rent		22,000	
Total current assets		131,200	
Property and equipment:			
Furniture and fixtures	12,000		
Less: Accumulated depreciation	200	11,800	
Total assets		$143,000	
Liabilities and Shareholders' Equity			
Current liabilities:			
Accounts payable		$ 35,000	
Salaries payable		5,500	
Unearned rent revenue		750	
Interest payable		333	
Note payable		10,000	
Total current liabilities		51,583	
Long-term liabilities:			
Note payable		30,000	
Shareholders' equity:			
Common stock, 6,000 shares issued and outstanding	$60,000		
Retained earnings	1,417*		
Total shareholders' equity		61,417	
Total liabilities and shareholders' equity		$143,000	

*Beginning retained earnings + Net income − Dividends
        0   + $2,417   −   1,000   = $1,417

As we do in the income statement, we group the balance sheet elements into meaningful categories. For example, most balance sheets include the classifications of current assets and current liabilities. Current assets are those assets that are cash, will be converted into cash, or will be used up within one year or the operating cycle, whichever is longer. Current liabilities are those liabilities that will be satisfied within one year or the operating cycle, whichever is longer. For a manufacturing company, the operating cycle refers to the period of time necessary to convert cash to raw materials, raw materials to a finished product, the

Balance sheet items usually are classified (grouped) according to common characteristics.

finished product to receivables, and then finally receivables back to cash. For most companies, this period is less than a year.

Examples of assets not classified as current include property and equipment and long-term receivables and investments. The only noncurrent asset that Dress Right has at July 31, 2009, is furniture and fixtures, which is classified under the property and equipment category.

All liabilities not classified as current are listed as long term. Dress Right's liabilities at July 31, 2009, include the $30,000 note payable due to be paid in 23 months. This liability is classified as long term.

Shareholders' equity lists the *paid-in capital* portion of equity—common stock—and *retained earnings*. Notice that the income statement we looked at in Illustration 2–9 ties in to the balance sheet through retained earnings. Specifically, the revenue, expense, gain, and loss transactions that make up net income in the income statement ($2,417) become the major components of retained earnings. Later in the chapter we discuss the closing process we use to transfer, or close, these *temporary* income statement accounts to the *permanent* retained earnings account.

During the month, retained earnings, which increased by the amount of net income, also decreased by the amount of the cash dividend paid to shareholders, $1,000. The net effect of these two changes is an increase in retained earnings from zero at the beginning of the period to $1,417 ($2,417 − 1,000) at the end of the period and is also reported in the statement of shareholders' equity in Illustration 2–12 on page 79.

The Statement of Cash Flows

The purpose of the statement of cash flows is to summarize the transactions that caused cash to change during the period.

Similar to the income statement, the statement of cash flows also is a change statement, disclosing the events that caused cash to change during the period. The statement classifies all transactions affecting cash into one of three categories: (1) operating activities, (2) investing activities, and (3) financing activities. Operating activities are inflows and outflows of cash related to transactions entering into the determination of net income. Investing activities involve the acquisition and sale of (1) long-term assets used in the business and (2) nonoperating investment assets. Financing activities involve cash inflows and outflows from transactions with creditors and owners.

The statement of cash flows for Dress Right for the month of July 2009 is shown in Illustration 2–11. As this is the first period of operations for Dress Right, the cash balance at the

ILLUSTRATION 2–11	**DRESS RIGHT CLOTHING CORPORATION**
Statement of Cash Flows	**Statement of Cash Flows** **For the Month of July 2009**

DRESS RIGHT CLOTHING CORPORATION
Statement of Cash Flows
For the Month of July 2009

Cash Flows from Operating Activities		
Cash inflows:		
From customers	$36,500	
From rent	1,000	
Cash outflows:		
For rent	(24,000)	
For supplies	(2,000)	
To suppliers of merchandise	(25,000)	
To employees	(5,000)	
Net cash flows from operating activities		$(18,500)
Cash Flows from Investing Activities		
Purchase of furniture and fixtures		(12,000)
Cash Flows from Financing Activities		
Issue of common stock	$60,000	
Increase in notes payable	40,000	
Payment of cash dividend	(1,000)	
Net cash flows from financing activities		99,000
Net increase in cash		$ 68,500

beginning of the period is zero. The net increase in cash of $68,500, therefore, equals the ending balance of cash disclosed in the balance sheet.

There are two generally accepted formats that can be used to report operating activities, the direct method and the indirect method. In Illustration 2–11 we use the direct method. These two methods are discussed and illustrated in subsequent chapters.

The Statement of Shareholders' Equity

The final statement, the statement of shareholders' equity, also is a change statement. It discloses the sources of the changes in the various permanent shareholders' equity accounts that occurred during the period. Illustration 2–12 shows the statement of shareholders' equity for Dress Right for the month of July 2009.[6]

The individual profit-generating transactions causing retained earnings to change are summarized in the income statement. Therefore, the statement of shareholders' equity only shows the net effect of these transactions on retained earnings, in this case an increase of $2,417. In addition, the company paid its shareholders a cash dividend that reduced retained earnings.

> The *statement of shareholders' equity* discloses the sources of changes in the permanent shareholders' equity accounts.

DRESS RIGHT CLOTHING CORPORATION Statement of Shareholders' Equity For the Month of July 2009			
	Common Stock	Retained Earnings	Total Shareholders' Equity
Balance at July 1, 2009	–0–	–0–	–0–
Issue of common stock	$60,000		$60,000
Net income for July 2009		$2,417	2,417
Less: Dividends		(1,000)	(1,000)
Balance at July 31, 2009	$60,000	$1,417	$61,417

> **ILLUSTRATION 2–12**
> Statement of Shareholders' Equity

The Closing Process

At the end of any interim reporting period, the accounting processing cycle is now complete. An interim reporting period is any period when financial statements are produced other than at the end of the fiscal year. However, at the end of the fiscal year, two final steps are necessary, closing the temporary accounts—step 9—and preparing a post-closing trial balance—step 10.

The closing process serves a *dual purpose:* (1) the temporary accounts (revenues, expenses, gains and losses) are reduced to *zero balances,* ready to measure activity in the upcoming accounting period, and (2) these temporary account balances are *closed (transferred) to retained earnings* to reflect the changes that have occurred in that account during the period. Often, an intermediate step is to close revenues and expenses to income summary; then income summary is closed to retained earnings. The use of the income summary account is just a bookkeeping convenience that provides a check that all temporary accounts have been properly closed (that is, the balance equals net income or loss).

To illustrate the closing process, assume that the fiscal year-end for Dress Right Clothing Corporation is July 31. Using the adjusted trial balance in Illustration 2–8, we can prepare the following general journal entries.

> **STEP 9**
> *Close* the temporary accounts to retained earnings (at year-end only).
> ● LO7

> To close the revenue accounts to income summary.

July 31		
Sales revenue	38,500	
Rent revenue	250	
Income summary		38,750

---

[6]Some companies choose to disclose the changes in the retained earnings component of shareholders' equity in a separate statement or in a combined statement of income and retained earnings.

The first closing entry transfers the revenue account balances to income summary. Because revenue accounts have credit balances, they are debited to bring them to zero. After this entry is posted to the accounts, both revenue accounts have a zero balance.

To close the expense accounts to income summary.

July 31

Income summary	36,333	
Cost of goods sold		22,000
Salaries expense		10,500
Supplies expense		800
Rent expense		2,000
Depreciation expense		200
Interest expense		333
Bad debt expense		500

The second closing entry transfers the expense account balances to income summary. As expense accounts have debit balances, they are credited to bring them to zero. After this entry is posted to the accounts, the expense accounts have a zero balance and the income summary account has a credit balance equal to net income for the period, in this case $2,417.

Income Summary			
Expenses	36,333	38,750	Revenues
		2,417	Net income

To close the income summary account to retained earnings.

July 31

Income summary	2,417	
Retained earnings		2,417

After this entry is posted to the accounts, the temporary accounts have zero balances and retained earnings has increased by the amount of the net income. It is important to remember that the temporary accounts are closed only at year-end and not at the end of any interim period. Closing the temporary accounts during the year would make it difficult to prepare the annual income statement.

ADDITIONAL CONSIDERATION

A previous additional consideration indicated that an alternative method of recording a cash dividend is to debit a temporary account called dividends, rather than debiting retained earnings. If this approach is used, an additional closing entry is required to close the dividend account to retained earnings, as follows:

Retained earnings	1,000	
Dividends		1,000

As you can see, the net result of a cash dividend is the same — a reduction in retained earnings and a reduction in cash.

STEP 10

Prepare a *post-closing trial balance* (at year-end only).

After the closing entries are posted to the ledger accounts, a post-closing trial balance is prepared. The purpose of this trial balance is to verify that the closing entries were prepared and posted correctly and that the accounts are now ready for next year's transactions. Illustration 2–13 shows the post-closing trial balance for Dress Right at July 31, 2009, assuming a July 31 fiscal year-end.

ILLUSTRATION 2–13

Post-Closing Trial Balance

DRESS RIGHT CLOTHING CORPORATION
Post-Closing Trial Balance
July 31, 2009

Account Title	Debits	Credits
Cash	68,500	
Accounts receivable	2,000	
Allowance for uncollectible accounts		500
Supplies	1,200	
Prepaid rent	22,000	
Inventory	38,000	
Furniture and fixtures	12,000	
Accumulated depreciation—furniture and fixtures		200
Accounts payable		35,000
Notes payable		40,000
Unearned rent revenue		750
Salaries payable		5,500
Interest payable		333
Common stock		60,000
Retained earnings		1,417
Totals	143,700	143,700

CONCEPT REVIEW EXERCISE

Refer to the August 31, 2009, adjusted trial balance of the Wyndham Wholesale Company presented in a previous concept review exercise on page 75.

FINANCIAL STATEMENT PREPARATION AND CLOSING

Required:

1. Prepare an income statement and a statement of shareholders' equity for the month ended August 31, 2009, and a classified balance sheet as of August 31, 2009.
2. Assume that August 31 is the company's fiscal year-end. Prepare the necessary closing entries and a post-closing trial balance.

1. Prepare an income statement and a statement of shareholders' equity for the month ended August 31, 2009, and a classified balance sheet as of August 31, 2009.

SOLUTION

WYNDHAM WHOLESALE COMPANY
Income Statement
For the Month of August 2009

Sales revenue		$40,000
Cost of goods sold		22,000
Gross profit		18,000
Operating expenses:		
Salaries	$7,000	
Utilities	2,000	
Bad debt	2,500	
Depreciation	500	
Rent	3,000	
Total operating expenses		15,000
Operating income		3,000
Other income (expense):		
Interest revenue	100	
Interest expense	(250)	(150)
Net income		$ 2,850

WYNDHAM WHOLESALE COMPANY
Statement of Shareholders' Equity
For the Month of August 2009

	Common Stock	Retained Earnings	Total Shareholders' Equity
Balance at August 1, 2009	–0–	–0–	–0–
Issue of common stock	$50,000		$50,000
Net income for August 2009		$2,850	2,850
Less: Dividends		(1,000)	(1,000)
Balance at August 31, 2009	$50,000	$1,850	$51,850

WYNDHAM WHOLESALE COMPANY
Balance Sheet
At August 31, 2009
Assets

Current assets:		
Cash		$ 21,000
Accounts receivable	$25,000	
Less: Allowance for uncollectible accounts	2,500	22,500
Inventory		16,000
Interest receivable		100
Note receivable		20,000
Prepaid rent		3,000
Total current assets		82,600
Property and equipment:		
Equipment	20,000	
Less: Accumulated depreciation	500	19,500
Total assets		$102,100

Liabilities and Shareholders' Equity

Current liabilities:		
Accounts payable		$ 20,000
Interest payable		250
Note payable		30,000
Total current liabilities		50,250
Shareholders' equity:		
Common stock, 5,000 shares issued and outstanding	$50,000	
Retained earnings	1,850	
Total shareholders' equity		51,850
Total liabilities and shareholders' equity		$102,100

2. Assume that August 31 is the company's fiscal year-end. Prepare the necessary closing entries and a post-closing trial balance.

To close the revenue accounts to income summary.	**August 31**		
	Sales revenue	40,000	
	Interest revenue	100	
	Income summary		40,100
To close the expense accounts to income summary.	**August 31**		
	Income summary	37,250	
	Cost of goods sold		22,000
	Salaries expense		7,000
	Utilities expense		2,000
	Bad debt expense		2,500
	Depreciation expense		500
	Rent expense		3,000
	Interest expense		250

(continued)

August 31

Income summary	2,850		To close the income
Retained earnings		2,850	summary account to
			retained earnings.

Post-Closing Trial Balance

Account Title	Debits	Credits
Cash	21,000	
Accounts receivable	25,000	
Allowance for uncollectible accounts		2,500
Prepaid rent	3,000	
Inventory	16,000	
Interest receivable	100	
Note receivable	20,000	
Equipment	20,000	
Accumulated depreciation—equipment		500
Accounts payable		20,000
Interest payable		250
Note payable		30,000
Common stock		50,000
Retained earnings		1,850
Totals	105,100	105,100

Conversion from Cash Basis to Accrual Basis

 ● LO8

In Chapter 1, we discussed and illustrated the differences between cash and accrual accounting. Cash basis accounting produces a measure called *net operating cash flow*. This measure is the difference between cash receipts and cash disbursements during a reporting period from transactions related to providing goods and services to customers. On the other hand, the accrual accounting model measures an entity's accomplishments and resource sacrifices during the period, regardless of when cash is received or paid. At this point, you might wish to review the material in Chapter 1 on pages 7 and 8 to reinforce your understanding of the motivation for using the accrual accounting model.

Adjusting entries, for the most part, are conversions from cash basis to accrual basis. Prepayments and accruals occur when cash flow precedes or follows expense or revenue recognition.

Accountants sometimes are called upon to convert cash basis financial statements to accrual basis financial statements, particularly for small businesses. You now have all of the tools you need to make this conversion. For example, if a company paid $20,000 cash for insurance during the fiscal year and you determine that there was $5,000 in prepaid insurance at the beginning of the year and $3,000 at the end of the year, then you can determine (accrual basis) *insurance expense* for the year. Prepaid insurance decreased by $2,000 during the year, so insurance expense must be $22,000 ($20,000 in cash paid *plus* the decrease in prepaid insurance). You can visualize as follows:

	Prepaid Insurance
Balance, beginning of year	$ 5,000
Plus: Cash paid	20,000
Less: Insurance expense	?
Balance, end of year	$ 3,000

Insurance expense of $22,000 completes the explanation of the change in the balance of prepaid insurance. Prepaid insurance of $3,000 is reported as an asset in an accrual basis balance sheet.

Suppose a company paid $150,000 for salaries to employees during the year and you determine that there were $12,000 and $18,000 in salaries payable at the beginning and end of the year, respectively. What was salaries expense?

	Salaries Payable
Balance, beginning of year	$ 12,000
Plus: Salaries expense	?
Less: Cash paid	150,000
Balance, end of year	$ 18,000

Salaries payable increased by $6,000 during the year, so *salaries expense* must be $156,000 ($150,000 in cash paid *plus* the increase in salaries payable). Salaries payable of $18,000 is reported as a liability in an accrual basis balance sheet.

Using T-accounts is a convenient approach for converting from cash to accrual accounting.

Salaries Payable			Salaries Expense	
	12,000 Beg.balance			
Cash paid 150,000				
	? Salaries expense		?	
	18,000 End balance			

The debit to salaries expense and credit to salaries payable must have been $156,000 to balance the salaries payable account.

For another example using T-accounts., assume that the amount of cash collected from customers during the year was $220,000, and you know that accounts receivable at the beginning of the year was $45,000 and $33,000 at the end of the year. You can use T-accounts to determine that *sales revenue* for the year must have been $208,000, the necessary debit to accounts receivable and credit to sales revenue to balance the accounts receivable account.

Accounts Receivable			Sales Revenue	
Beg. balance 45,000				
Credit sales ?			? Credit sales	
	220,000 Cash collections			
End balance 33,000				

Now suppose that, on occasion, customers pay in advance of receiving a product or service. Recall from our previous discussion of adjusting entries that this event creates a liability called unearned revenue. Assume the same facts in the previous example except you also determine that unearned revenues were $10,000 and $7,000 at the beginning and end of the year, respectively. A $3,000 decrease in unearned revenues means that the company earned an additional $3,000 in sales revenue for which the cash had been collected in a previous year. So, *sales revenue* for the year must have been $211,000, the $208,000 determined in the previous example *plus* the $3,000 decrease in unearned revenue.

Illustration 2–14 provides another example of converting from cash basis net income to accrual basis net income.

Notice a pattern in the adjustments to cash net income. When converting from cash to accrual income, we add increases and deduct decreases in assets. For example, an increase in accounts receivable means that the company earned more revenue than cash collected, requiring the addition to cash basis income. Conversely, we add decreases and deduct increases in accrued liabilities. For example, a decrease in interest payable means that the company incurred less interest expense than the cash interest it paid, requiring the addition to cash basis income.

The Krinard Cleaning Services Company maintains its records on the cash basis, with one exception. The company reports equipment as an asset and records depreciation expense on the equipment. During 2009, Krinard collected $165,000 from customers, paid $92,000 in operating expenses, and recorded $10,000 in depreciation expense, resulting in net income of $63,000. The owner has asked you to convert this $63,000 in net income to full accrual net income. You are able to determine the following information about accounts receivable, prepaid expenses, accrued liabilities, and unearned revenues:

ILLUSTRATION 2–14

Cash to Accrual

	January 1, 2009	December 31, 2009
Accounts receivable	$16,000	$25,000
Prepaid expenses	7,000	4,000
Accrued liabilities		
(for operating expenses)	2,100	1,400
Unearned revenues	3,000	4,200

Accrual net income is $68,500, determined as follows:

Cash basis net income		$63,000
Add:	Increase in accounts receivable	9,000
Deduct:	Decrease in prepaid expenses	(3,000)
Add:	Decrease in accrued liabilities	700
Deduct:	Increase in unearned revenues	(1,200)
Accrual basis net income		$68,500

FINANCIAL REPORTING CASE SOLUTION

1. **What purpose do adjusting entries serve?** *(p. 67)* Adjusting entries help ensure that only revenues actually earned in a period are recognized in that period, regardless of when cash is received. In this instance, for example, $13,000 cash has been received for services that haven't yet been performed. Also, adjusting entries enable a company to recognize all expenses incurred during a period, regardless of when cash is paid. Without depreciation, the friends' cost of using the equipment is not taken into account. Conversely, without adjustment, the cost of rent is overstated by $3,000 paid in advance for part of next year's rent.

   With adjustments, we get an accrual income statement that provides a more complete measure of a company's operating performance and a better measure for predicting future operating cash flows. Similarly, the balance sheet provides a more complete assessment of assets and liabilities as sources of future cash receipts and disbursements.

2. **What year-end adjustments are needed to revise the income statement? Did your friends do as well their first year as they thought?** *(p. 67)* Three year-end adjusting entries are needed:

1. Depreciation expense ($80,000 ÷ 5 years)	16,000	
Accumulated depreciation—equipment		16,000
2. Prepaid rent ($500 × 6 months [July–Dec.])	3,000	
Rent expense		3,000
3. Consulting revenue	13,000	
Unearned consulting revenue		13,000

No, your friends did not fare as well as their cash based statement would have indicated. With appropriate adjustments, their net income is actually only $20,000:

Consulting revenue ($96,000 − 13,000)		$83,000
Operating expenses:		
Salaries	$32,000	
Rent ($9,000 − 3,000)	6,000	
Supplies	4,800	
Utilities	3,000	
Advertising	1,200	
Depreciation	16,000	63,000
Net income		$20,000

THE BOTTOM LINE

● **LO1** The accounting equation underlies the process used to capture the effect of economic events. The equation (Assets = Liabilities + Owners' Equity) implies an equality between the total economic resources of an entity (its assets) and the total claims to those resources (liabilities and equity). It also implies that each economic event affecting this equation will have a dual effect because resources always must equal claims to those resources. (p. 52)

● **LO2** After determining the dual effect of external events on the accounting equation, the transaction is recorded in a journal. A journal is a chronological list of transactions in debit/credit form. (p. 56)

● **LO3** The next step in the processing cycle is to periodically transfer, or *post,* the debit and credit information from the journal to individual general ledger accounts. A general ledger is simply a collection of all of the company's various accounts. Each account provides a summary of the effects of all events and transactions on that individual account. This process is called *posting.* An unadjusted trial balance is then prepared. (p. 63)

● **LO4** The next step in the processing cycle is to record the effect of *internal events* on the accounting equation. These transactions are commonly referred to as *adjusting entries.* Adjusting entries can be classified into three types: (1) prepayments, (2) accruals, and (3) estimates. Prepayments are transactions in which the cash flow *precedes* expense or revenue recognition. Accruals involve transactions where the cash outflow or inflow takes place in a period *subsequent* to expense or revenue recognition. Estimates for items such as future bad debts on receivables often are required to comply with the accrual accounting model. (p. 67)

● **LO5** Adjusting entries are recorded in the general journal and posted to the ledger accounts at the end of any period when financial statements must be prepared for external use. After these entries are posted to the general ledger accounts, an adjusted trial balance is prepared. (p. 67)

● **LO6** The adjusted trial balance is used to prepare the financial statements. The four basic financial statements are: (1) the income statement, (2) the balance sheet, (3) the statement of cash flows, and (4) the statement of shareholders' equity. The purpose of the income statement is to summarize the profit-generating activities of the company that occurred during a particular period of time. The balance sheet presents the financial position of the company on a particular date. The statement of cash flows discloses the events that caused cash to change during the reporting period. The statement of shareholders' equity discloses the sources of the changes in the various permanent shareholders' equity accounts that occurred during the period. (p. 76)

● **LO7** At the end of the fiscal year, a final step in the accounting processing cycle, closing, is required. The closing process serves a *dual purpose:* (1) the temporary accounts (revenues and expenses) are reduced to *zero balances,* ready to measure activity in the upcoming accounting period, and (2) these temporary account balances are *closed (transferred) to retained earnings* to reflect the changes that have occurred in that account during the period. Often, an intermediate step is to close revenues and expenses to *income summary;* then *income summary* is closed to *retained earnings.* (p. 79)

● **LO8** Cash basis accounting produces a measure called *net operating cash flow.* This measure is the difference between cash receipts and cash disbursements during a reporting period from transactions related to providing goods and services to customers. On the other hand, the accrual accounting model measures an entity's accomplishments and resource sacrifices during the period, regardless of when cash is received or paid. Accountants sometimes are called upon to convert cash basis financial statements to accrual basis financial statements, particularly for small businesses. (p. 83) ●

USE OF A WORKSHEET

A worksheet often is used to organize the accounting information needed to prepare adjusting and closing entries and the financial statements. It is an informal tool only and is not part of the accounting system. There are many different ways to design and use worksheets. We will illustrate a representative method using the financial information for the Dress Right Clothing Corporation presented in the chapter. Computerized programs such as Lotus 1-2-3 and Excel facilitate the use of worksheets.

Illustration 2A–1 presents the completed worksheet. The worksheet is utilized after and instead of step 5 in the processing cycle, preparation of an unadjusted trial balance.

Step 1. The account titles as they appear in the general ledger are entered in column 1 and the balances of these accounts are copied onto columns 2 and 3, entitled Unadjusted Trial Balance. The accounts are copied in the same order as they appear in the general ledger, which usually is assets, liabilities, shareholders' equity permanent accounts, revenues, and expenses. The debit and credit columns are totaled to make sure that they balance. This procedure is repeated for each set of columns in the worksheet to check for accuracy.

Step 2. The end-of-period adjusting entries are determined and entered directly on the worksheet in columns 4 and 5, entitled Adjusting Entries. The adjusting entries for Dress Right Clothing Corporation were discussed in detail in the chapter and exhibited in general journal form in Illustration 2–7 on page 73. You should refer back to this illustration and trace each of the entries to the worksheet. For worksheet purposes, the entries have been numbered from (1) to (7) for easy referencing.

A worksheet can be used as a tool to facilitate the preparation of adjusting and closing entries and the financial statements.

The first step is to enter account titles in column 1 and the unadjusted account balances in columns 2 and 3.

The second step is to determine end-of-period adjusting entries and enter them in columns 4 and 5.

ILLUSTRATION 2A–1   Worksheet, Dress Right Clothing Corporation, July 2009

Account Title	Unadjusted Trial Balance Dr.	Cr.	Adjusting Entries Dr.	Cr.	Adjusted Trial Balance Dr.	Cr.	Income Statement Dr.	Cr.	Balance Sheet Dr.	Cr.
Cash	68,500				68,500				68,500	
Accounts receivable	2,000				2,000				2,000	
Allowance for uncollectible accounts		0		(7) 500		500				500
Supplies	2,000			(1) 800	1,200				1,200	
Prepaid rent	24,000			(2) 2,000	22,000				22,000	
Inventory	38,000				38,000				38,000	
Furniture & fixtures	12,000				12,000				12,000	
Accumulated depreciation—furniture & fixtures		0		(3) 200		200				200
Accounts payable		35,000				35,000				35,000
Note payable		40,000				40,000				40,000
Unearned rent revenue		1,000	(4) 250			750				750
Salaries payable		0		(5) 5,500		5,500				5,500
Interest payable		0		(6) 333		333				333
Common stock		60,000				60,000				60,000
Retained earnings	1,000					1,000				1,000
Sales revenue		38,500				38,500		38,500		
Rent revenue		0		(4) 250		250		250		
Cost of goods sold	22,000				22,000		22,000			
Salaries expense	5,000		(5) 5,500		10,500		10,500			
Supplies expense	0		(1) 800		800		800			
Rent expense	0		(2) 2,000		2,000		2,000			
Depreciation expense	0		(3) 200		200		200			
Interest expense	0		(6) 333		333		333			
Bad debt expense	0		(7) 500		500		500			
Totals	174,500	174,500	9,583	9,583	181,033	181,033				
Net Income							2,417			2,417
Totals							38,750	38,750	144,700	144,700

For example, entry (1) records the cost of supplies used during the month of July with a debit to supplies expense and a credit to supplies for $800. A (1) is placed next to the $800 in the debit column in the supplies expense row as well as next to the $800 in the credit column in the supplies row. This allows us to more easily reconstruct the entry for general journal purposes and locate errors if the debit and credit columns do not balance.

Step 3. The effects of the adjusting entries are added to or deducted from the account balances listed in the Unadjusted Trial Balance columns and copied across to columns 6 and 7, entitled Adjusted Trial Balance. For example, supplies had an unadjusted balance of $2,000. Adjusting entry (1) credited this account by $800, reducing the balance to $1,200.

Step 4. The balances in the temporary retained earnings accounts, revenues and expenses, are transferred to columns 8 and 9, entitled Income Statement. The difference between the total debits and credits in these columns is equal to net income or net loss. In this case, because credits (revenues) exceed debits (expenses), a net income of $2,417 results. To balance the debits and credits in this set of columns, a $2,417 debit entry is made in the line labeled Net income.

Step 5. The balances in the permanent accounts are transferred to columns 10 and 11, entitled Balance Sheet. To keep the debits and credits equal in the worksheet, a $2,417 credit must be recorded to offset the $2,417 debit recorded in step 4 and labeled as net income. This credit represents the fact that when the temporary accounts are closed out to retained earnings, a $2,417 credit to retained earnings will result. The credit in column 11, therefore, represents an increase in retained earnings for the period, that is, net income.

After the worksheet is completed, the financial statements can be prepared directly from columns 8–11. The financial statements for Dress Right Clothing Corporation are shown in Illustrations 2–9 through 2–12. The accountant must remember to then record the adjusting entries in the general journal and post them to the general ledger accounts. An adjusted trial balance should then be prepared which should be identical to the one in the worksheet. At fiscal year-end, the income statement columns can then be used to prepare closing entries. ●

APPENDIX 2B REVERSING ENTRIES

Accountants sometimes use reversing entries at the beginning of a reporting period. These optional entries remove the effects of some of the adjusting entries made at the end of the previous reporting period for the sole purpose of simplifying journal entries made during the new period. If the accountant does use reversing entries, these entries are recorded in the general journal and posted to the general ledger accounts on the first day of the new period.

Reversing entries are used most often with accruals. For example, the following adjusting entry for accrued salaries was recorded at the end of July 2009 for the Dress Right Clothing Corporation in the chapter:

July 31		
Salaries expense	5,500	
Salaries payable		5,500

If reversing entries are not used, when the salaries actually are paid in August, the accountant needs to remember to debit salaries payable and not salaries expense.

The account balances before and after salary payment can be seen below with the use of T-accounts.

Salaries Expense			Salaries Payable		
Bal. July 31 10,500				5,500	Bal. July 31
		(Cash Payment) 5,500			
				–0–	Balance

If the accountant for Dress Right employs reversing entries, the following entry is made on August 1, 2009:

August 1		
Salaries payable	5,500	
Salaries expense		5,500

To reverse accrued salaries expense recorded at the end of July.

This entry reduces the salaries payable account to zero and reduces the salary expense account by $5,500. When salaries actually are paid in August, the debit is to salaries expense, thus increasing the account by $5,500.

Salaries Expense					Salaries Payable	
Bal. July 31	10,500				5,500	Bal. July 31
		5,500	(Reversing entry)	5,500		
(Cash payment)	5,500					
Balance	10,500				–0–	Balance

We can see that balances in the accounts after cash payment is made are identical. The use of reversing entries for accruals, which is optional, simply allows cash payments or cash receipts to be entered directly into the temporary expense or revenue accounts without regard to the accruals made at the end of the previous period. ●

SUBSIDIARY LEDGERS AND SPECIAL JOURNALS

APPENDIX **2C**

Subsidiary Ledgers

The general ledger contains what are referred to as *control accounts.* In addition to the general ledger, a subsidiary ledger contains a group of subsidiary accounts associated with a particular general ledger control account. For example, there will be a subsidiary ledger for accounts receivable that keeps track of the increases and decreases in the account receivable balance for each of the company's customers purchasing goods or services on credit. After all of the postings are made from the appropriate journals, the balance in the accounts receivable control account should equal the sum of the balances in the accounts receivable subsidiary ledger accounts. Subsidiary ledgers also are used for accounts payable, plant and equipment, investments, and other accounts.

Accounting systems employ a *subsidiary ledger* which contains a group of subsidiary accounts associated with particular general ledger control accounts.

Special Journals

An actual accounting system employs many different types of journals. The purpose of each journal is to record, in chronological order, the dual effect of a transaction in debit/credit form. The chapter used the general journal format to record each transaction. However, even for small companies with relatively few transactions, the general journal is used to record only a few types of transactions.[7]

For most external transactions, *special journals* are used to capture the dual effect of the transaction in debit/credit form.

The majority of transactions are recorded in special journals. These journals capture the dual effect of *repetitive* types of transactions. For example, cash receipts are recorded in a cash receipts journal, cash disbursements in a cash disbursements journal, credit sales in a sales journal, and the purchase of merchandise on account in a purchases journal.

Special journals simplify the recording process in the following ways:

1. Journalizing the effects of a particular transaction is made more efficient through the use of specifically designed formats.
2. Individual transactions are not posted to the general ledger accounts but are accumulated in the special journals and a summary posting is made on a periodic basis.
3. The responsibility for recording journal entries for the repetitive types of transactions is placed on individuals who have specialized training in handling them.

---

[7]For example, end-of-period adjusting entries would be recorded in the general journal.

The concepts of subsidiary ledgers and special journals are illustrated using the *sales journal* and the *cash receipts journal*.

Sales Journal

All credit sales are recorded in the *sales journal*.

The purpose of the sales journal is to record all credit sales. Cash sales are recorded in the cash receipts journal. Every entry in the sales journal has exactly the same effect on the accounts; the sales revenue account is credited and the accounts receivable control account is debited. Therefore, there is only one column needed to record the debit/credit effect of these transactions. Other columns are needed to capture information for updating the accounts receivable subsidiary ledger. Illustration 2C–1 presents the sales journal for Dress Right Clothing Corporation for the month of August 2009.

During the month of August, the company made five credit sales, totaling $3,295. This amount is posted as a debit to the accounts receivable control account, account number 110, and a credit to the sales revenue account, account number 400. The T-accounts for accounts receivable and sales revenue appear below. The reference SJ1 refers to page 1 of the sales journal.

General Ledger

Accounts Receivable	110		Sales Revenue	400
July 31 Balance 2,000				3,295 Aug. 31 SJ1
Aug. 31 SJ1 3,295				

In a computerized accounting system, as each transaction is recorded in the sales journal, the subsidiary ledger accounts for the customer involved will automatically be updated. For example, the first credit sale of the month is to Leland High School for $1,500. The sales invoice number for this sale is 10-221 and the customer's subsidiary account number is 801. As this transaction is entered, the subsidiary account 801 for Leland High School is debited for $1,500.

Accounts Receivable Subsidiary Ledger

Leland High School	801
August 5 SJ1 1,500	

As cash is collected from this customer, the cash receipts journal records the transaction with a credit to the accounts receivable control account and a debit to cash. At the same time, the accounts receivable subsidiary ledger account number 801 also is credited. After the postings are made from the special journals, the balance in the accounts receivable control account should equal the sum of the balances in the accounts receivable subsidiary ledger accounts.

ILLUSTRATION 2C–1

Sales Journal, Dress Right Clothing Corporation, August 2009

Page 1

Date	Accounts Receivable Subsidiary Account No.	Customer Name	Sales Invoice No.	Cr. Sales Revenue (400) Dr. Accounts Receivable (110)
2009				
Aug. 5	801	Leland High School	10-221	1,500
9	812	Mr. John Smith	10-222	200
18	813	Greystone School	10-223	825
22	803	Ms. Barbara Jones	10-224	120
29	805	Hart Middle School	10-225	650
				3,295

Date	Explanation or Account Name	Dr. Cash (100)	Cr. Accounts Receivable (110)	Cr. Sales Revenue (400)	Cr. Other	Other Accounts
2009						
Aug. 7	Cash sale	500		500		
11	Borrowed cash	10,000			10,000	Note payable (220)
17	Leland High School	750	750			
20	Cash sale	300		300		
25	Mr. John Smith	200	200			
		11,750	950	800	10,000	

Page 1

ILLUSTRATION 2C–2

Cash Receipts Journal, Dress Right Clothing Corporation, August 2009

Cash Receipts Journal

The purpose of the cash receipts journal is to record all cash receipts, regardless of the source. Every transaction recorded in this journal produces a debit entry to the cash account with the credit to various other accounts. Illustration 2C–2 shows a cash receipts journal using transactions of the Dress Right Clothing Corporation for the month of August 2009.

All cash receipts are recorded in the *cash receipts journal.*

Because every transaction results in a debit to the cash account, No. 100, a column is provided for that account. At the end of August, an $11,750 debit is posted to the general ledger cash account with the source labeled CR1, cash receipts journal, page 1.

Because cash and credit sales are common, separate columns are provided for these accounts. At the end of August, a $950 credit is posted to the accounts receivable general ledger account, No. 110, and an $800 credit is posted to the sales revenue account, No. 400. Two additional credit columns are provided for uncommon cash receipt transactions, one for the credit amount and one for the account being credited. We can see that in August, Dress Right borrowed $10,000 requiring a credit to the note payable account, No. 220.

In addition to the postings to the general ledger control accounts, each time an entry is recorded in the accounts receivable column, a credit is posted to the accounts receivable subsidiary ledger account for the customer making the payment. For example, on August 17, Leland High School paid $750 on account. The subsidiary ledger account for Leland High School is credited for $750. ●

Accounts Receivable Subsidiary Ledger

Leland High School			801
August 5 SJ1	1,500		
		750	August 17 CR1

QUESTIONS FOR REVIEW OF KEY TOPICS

Q 2–1   Explain the difference between external events and internal events. Give an example of each type of event.

Q 2–2   Each economic event or transaction will have a dual effect on financial position. Explain what is meant by this dual effect.

Q 2–3   What is the purpose of a journal? What is the purpose of a general ledger?

Q 2–4   Explain the difference between permanent accounts and temporary accounts. Why does an accounting system include both types of accounts?

Q 2–5   Describe how debits and credits affect assets, liabilities, and permanent owners' equity accounts.

Q 2–6   Describe how debits and credits affect temporary owners' equity accounts.

Q 2–7   What is the first step in the accounting processing cycle? What role do source documents fulfill in this step?

Q 2–8   Describe what is meant by transaction analysis.

Q 2–9   Describe what is meant by posting, the fourth step in the processing cycle.

Q 2–10   Describe the events that correspond to the following two journal entries:

1. Inventory	20,000	
Accounts payable		20,000
2. Accounts receivable	30,000	
Sales revenue		30,000
Cost of goods sold	18,000	
Inventory		18,000

Q 2–11   What is an unadjusted trial balance? An adjusted trial balance?

Q 2–12   Define adjusting entries and discuss their purpose.

Q 2–13   Define closing entries and their purpose.

Q 2–14   Define prepaid expenses and provide at least two examples.

Q 2–15   Unearned revenues represent liabilities recorded when cash is received from customers in advance of providing a good or service. What adjusting journal entry is required at the end of a period to recognize the amount of unearned revenues that were earned during the period?

Q 2–16   Define accrued liabilities. What adjusting journal entry is required to record accrued liabilities?

Q 2–17   Describe the purpose of each of the four primary financial statements.

Q 2–18   [Based on Appendix 2A] What is the purpose of a worksheet? In an 11-column worksheet similar to Illustration 2A–1, what would be the result of incorrectly transferring the balance in a liability account to column 9, the credit column under income statement?

Q 2–19   [Based on Appendix 2B] Define reversing entries and discuss their purpose.

Q 2–20   [Based on Appendix 2C] What is the purpose of special journals? In what ways do they simplify the recording process?

Q 2–21   [Based on Appendix 2C] Explain the difference between the general ledger and a subsidiary ledger.

BRIEF EXERCISES

BE 2–1
Transaction analysis

● LO1

The Marchetti Soup Company entered into the following transactions during the month of June: (1) purchased inventory on account for $165,000 (assume Marchetti uses a perpetual inventory system); (2) paid $40,000 in salaries to employees for work performed during the month; (3) sold merchandise that cost $120,000 to credit customers for $200,000; (4) collected $180.000 in cash from credit customers; and (5) paid suppliers of inventory $145,000. Analyze each transaction and show the effect of each on the accounting equation for a corporation.

BE 2–2
Journal entries

● LO2

Prepare journal entries for each of the transactions listed in BE 2–1.

BE 2–3
T-accounts

● LO3

Post the journal entries prepared in BE 2–2 to T-accounts. Assume that the opening balances in each of the accounts is zero except for cash, accounts receivable, and accounts payable that had opening balances of $65,000, $43,000, and $22,000 respectively.

BE 2–4
Journal entries

● LO2

Prepare journal entries for each of the following transactions for a company that has a fiscal year-end of December 31: (1) on October 1, $12,000 was paid for a one-year fire insurance policy; (2) on June 30 the company lent its chief financial officer $10,000; principal and interest at 6% are due in one year; and (3) equipment costing $60,000 was purchased at the beginning of the year for cash.

BE 2–5
Adjusting entries

● LO4 LO5

Prepare the necessary adjusting entries at December 31 for each of the items listed in BE 2–4. Depreciation on the equipment is $12,000 per year.

BE 2–6
Adjusting entries; income determination

● LO5

If the adjusting journal entries prepared in BE 2–5 were not made, would net income be higher or lower and by how much?

BE 2–7
Adjusting entries

● LO4 LO5

Prepare the necessary adjusting entries at its year-end of December 31, 2009, for the Jamesway Corporation for each of the following situations. No adjusting entries were made during the year.
1. On December 20, 2009, Jamesway received a $4,000 payment from a customer for services to be rendered early in 2010. Service revenue was credited.
2. On December 1, 2009, the company paid a local radio station $2,000 for 40 radio ads that were to be aired, 20 per month, throughout December and January. Prepaid advertising was debited.
3. Employee salaries for the month of December totaling $16,000 will be paid on January 7, 2010.
4. On August 31, 2009, Jamesway borrowed $60,000 from a local bank. A note was signed with principal and 8% interest to be paid on August 31, 2010.

BE 2–8
Income determination

● LO5

If none of the adjusting journal entries prepared in BE 2–7 were made, would assets, liabilities, and shareholders' equity on the 12/31/09 balance sheet be higher or lower and by how much?

BE 2–9
Financial statements

● LO6

The following account balances were taken from the 2009 adjusted trial balance of the Bowler Corporation: sales revenue, $325,000; cost of goods sold, $168,000; salaries expense; $45,000; rent expense, $20,000; depreciation expense, $30,000; and miscellaneous expense, $12,000. Prepare an income statement for 2009.

BE 2–10
Financial statements

● LO6

The following account balances were taken from the 2009 post-closing trial balance of the Bowler Corporation: cash, $5,000; accounts receivable, $10,000; inventory, $16,000; machinery and equipment, $100,000; accumulated depreciation—machinery and equipment, $40,000; accounts payable, $20,000; salaries payable, $12,000; retained earnings, $9,000; and common stock, $50,000. Prepare a 12/31/09 balance sheet.

BE 2–11
Closing entries

● LO7

The year-end adjusted trial balance of the Timmons Tool and Die Corporation included the following account balances: retained earnings, $220,000; sales revenue, $850,000; cost of goods sold, $580,000; salaries expense, $180,000; rent expense, $40,000; and interest expense, $15,000. Prepare the necessary closing entries.

BE 2–12
Cash versus accrual accounting

● LO8

Newman Consulting Company maintains its records on a cash basis. During 2009 the following cash flows were recorded: cash received from customers, $420,000; and cash paid for salaries, utilities, and advertising, $240,000, $35,000, and $12,000, respectively. You also determine that customers owed the company $52,000 and $60,000 at the beginning and end of the year, respectively, and that the company owed the utility company $6,000 and $4,000 at the beginning and end of the year, respectively. Determine accrual net income for the year.

EXERCISES   available with McGraw-Hill's Homework Manager www.mhhe.com/spiceland5e

An alternate exercise and problem set is available on the text website: www.mhhe.com/spiceland5e

E 2–1
Transaction analysis

● LO1

The following transactions occurred during March 2009 for the Wainwright Corporation. The company owns and operates a wholesale warehouse.
1. Issued 30,000 shares of common stock in exchange for $300,000 in cash.
2. Purchased equipment at a cost of $40,000. $10,000 cash was paid and a note payable was signed for the balance owed.
3. Purchased inventory on account at a cost of $90,000. The company uses the perpetual inventory system.
4. Credit sales for the month totaled $120,000. The cost of the goods sold was $70,000.
5. Paid $5,000 in rent on the warehouse building for the month of March.
6. Paid $6,000 to an insurance company for fire and liability insurance for a one-year period beginning April 1, 2009.
7. Paid $70,000 on account for the merchandise purchased in 3.
8. Collected $55,000 from customers on account.
9. Recorded depreciation expense of $1,000 for the month on the equipment.

Required:
Analyze each transaction and show the effect of each on the accounting equation for a corporation.
Example:

    Assets   = Liabilities + Paid-In Capital + Retained Earnings
1. +300,000 (cash)   + 300,000 (common stock)

E 2–2
Journal entries

● LO2

Prepare journal entries to record each of the transactions listed in Exercise 2–1.

E 2–3
T-accounts and trial balance

● LO3

Post the journal entries prepared in Exercise 2–2 to T-accounts. Assume that the opening balances in each of the accounts is zero. Prepare a trial balance from the ending account balances.

E 2–4
Journal entries

● LO2

The following transactions occurred during the month of June 2009 for the Stridewell Corporation. The company owns and operates a retail shoe store.
1. Issued 100,000 shares of common stock in exchange for $500,000 cash.
2. Purchased furniture and fixtures at a cost of $100,000. $40,000 was paid in cash and a note payable was signed for the balance owed.
3. Purchased inventory on account at a cost of $200,000. The company uses the perpetual inventory system.
4. Credit sales for the month totaled $280,000. The cost of the goods sold was $140,000.
5. Paid $6,000 in rent on the store building for the month of June.
6. Paid $3,000 to an insurance company for fire and liability insurance for a one-year period beginning June 1, 2009.
7. Paid $120,000 on account for the merchandise purchased in 3.
8. Collected $55,000 from customers on account.
9. Paid shareholders a cash dividend of $5,000.
10. Recorded depreciation expense of $2,000 for the month on the furniture and fixtures.
11. Recorded the amount of prepaid insurance that expired for the month.

Required:
Prepare journal entries to record each of the transactions and events listed above.

E 2–5
The accounting processing cycle

● LO2 through LO7

Listed below are several terms and phrases associated with the accounting processing cycle. Pair each item from List A (by letter) with the item from List B that is most appropriately associated with it.

List A	List B
_____ 1. Source documents	a. Record of the dual effect of a transaction in debit/credit form.
_____ 2. Transaction analysis	b. Internal events recorded at the end of a reporting period.
_____ 3. Journal	c. Primary means of disseminating information to external decision makers.
_____ 4. Posting	d. To zero out the owners' equity temporary accounts.
_____ 5. Unadjusted trial balance	e. Determine the dual effect on the accounting equation.
_____ 6. Adjusting entries	f. List of accounts and their balances before recording adjusting entries.
_____ 7. Adjusted trial balance	g. List of accounts and their balances after recording closing entries.
_____ 8. Financial statements	h. List of accounts and their balances after recording adjusting entries.
_____ 9. Closing entries	i. A means of organizing information: not part of the formal accounting system.
_____ 10. Post-closing trial balance	j. Transferring balances from the journal to the ledger.
_____ 11. Worksheet	k. Used to identify and process external transactions.

E 2–6
Debits and credits

● LO1

Indicate whether a debit will increase (I) or decrease (D) each of the following accounts listed in items 1 through 16:

Increase (I) or Decrease (D)	Account
1. _____	Inventory
2. _____	Depreciation expense
3. _____	Accounts payable
4. _____	Prepaid rent
5. _____	Sales revenue
6. _____	Common stock
7. _____	Wages payable
8. _____	Cost of goods sold
9. _____	Utility expense
10. _____	Equipment

(continued)

11. ____ Accounts receivable
12. ____ Allowance for uncollectible accounts
13. ____ Bad debt expense
14. ____ Interest expense
15. ____ Interest revenue
16. ____ Gain on sale of equipment

E 2–7
Transaction analysis;
debits and credits

● **LO1**

Some of the ledger accounts for the Sanderson Hardware Company are numbered and listed below. For each of the October 2009 transactions numbered 1 through 12 below, indicate by account number which accounts should be debited and credited. The company uses the perpetual inventory system. Assume that appropriate adjusting entries were made at the end of September.

(1) Accounts payable	(2) Equipment	(3) Inventory
(4) Accounts receivable	(5) Cash	(6) Supplies
(7) Supplies expense	(8) Prepaid rent	(9) Sales revenue
(10) Retained earnings	(11) Note payable	(12) Common stock
(13) Unearned revenue	(14) Rent expense	(15) Wages payable
(16) Cost of goods sold	(17) Wage expense	(18) Interest expense

	Account(s) Debited	Account(s) Credited
Example: Purchased inventory for cash	3	5

1. Paid a cash dividend.
2. Paid rent for the next three months.
3. Sold goods to customers on account.
4. Purchased inventory on account.
5. Purchased supplies for cash.
6. Paid employees wages for September.
7. Issued common stock in exchange for cash.
8. Collected cash from customers for goods sold in 3.
9. Borrowed cash from a bank and signed a note.
10. At the end of October, recorded the amount of supplies that had been used during the month.
11. Received cash for advance payment from customer.
12. Accrued employee wages for October.

E 2–8
Adjusting entries

● **LO4 LO5**

Prepare the necessary adjusting entries at December 31, 2009, for the Falwell Company for each of the following situations. Assume that no financial statements were prepared during the year and no adjusting entries were recorded.
1. A three-year fire insurance policy was purchased on July 1, 2009, for $12,000. The company debited insurance expense for the entire amount.
2. Depreciation on equipment totaled $15,000 for the year.
3. The company determined that accounts receivable in the amount of $6,500 will probably not be collected. The allowance for uncollectible accounts account has a credit balance of $2,000 before any adjustment.
4. Employee salaries of $18,000 for the month of December will be paid in early January 2010.
5. On November 1, 2009, the company borrowed $200,000 from a bank. The note requires principal and interest at 12% to be paid on April 30, 2010.
6. On December 1, 2009, the company received $3,000 in cash from another company that is renting office space in Falwell's building. The payment, representing rent for December and January, was credited to unearned rent revenue.

E 2–9
Adjusting entries

● **LO4 LO5**

Prepare the necessary adjusting entries at December 31, 2009, for the Microchip Company for each of the following situations. Assume that no financial statements were prepared during the year and no adjusting entries were recorded.
1. On October 1, 2009, Microchip lent $90,000 to another company. A note was signed with principal and 8% interest to be paid on September 30, 2010.
2. On November 1, 2009, the company paid its landlord $6,000 representing rent for the months of November through January. Prepaid rent was debited.
3. On August 1, 2009, collected $12,000 in advance rent from another company that is renting a portion of Microchip's factory. The $12,000 represents one year's rent and the entire amount was credited to rent revenue.
4. Depreciation on machinery is $4,500 for the year.
5. Vacation pay for the year that had been earned by employees but not paid to them or recorded is $8,000.
6. Microchip began the year with $2,000 in its asset account, supplies. During the year, $6,500 in supplies were purchased and debited to supplies. At year-end, supplies costing $3,250 remain on hand.

E 2–10
Adjusting entries;
solving for unknowns

● LO4 LO5

The Eldorado Corporation's controller prepares adjusting entries only at the end of the fiscal year. The following adjusting entries were prepared on December 31, 2009:

	Debit	Credit
Interest expense	7,200	
Interest payable		7,200
Rent expense	35,000	
Prepaid rent		35,000
Interest receivable	500	
Interest revenue		500

Additional information:
1. The company borrowed $120,000 on March 31, 2009. Principal and interest are due on March 31, 2010. This note is the company's only interest-bearing debt.
2. Rent for the year on the company's office space is $60,000. The rent is paid in advance.
3. On October 31, 2009, Eldorado lent money to a customer. The customer signed a note with principal and interest at 6% due in one year.

Required:
Determine the following:
1. What is the interest rate on the company's note payable?
2. The 2009 rent payment was made at the beginning of which month?
3. How much did Eldorado lend its customer on October 31?

E 2–11
Financial statements
and closing entries

● LO6 LO7

The December 31, 2009, adjusted trial balance for the Blueboy Cheese Corporation is presented below.

Account Title	Debits	Credits
Cash	21,000	
Accounts receivable	300,000	
Allowance for uncollectible accounts		20,000
Prepaid rent	10,000	
Inventory	50,000	
Equipment	600,000	
Accumulated depreciation—equipment		250,000
Accounts payable		40,000
Note payable (due in six months)		60,000
Salaries payable		8,000
Interest payable		2,000
Common stock		400,000
Retained earnings		100,000
Sales revenue		800,000
Cost of goods sold	480,000	
Salaries expense	120,000	
Rent expense	30,000	
Depreciation expense	60,000	
Interest expense	4,000	
Bad debt expense	5,000	
Totals	1,680,000	1,680,000

Required:
1. Prepare an income statement for the year ended December 31, 2009, and a classified balance sheet as of December 31, 2009.
2. Prepare the necessary closing entries at December 31, 2009.

E 2–12
Closing entries

● LO7

American Chip Corporation's fiscal year-end is December 31. The following is a partial adjusted trial balance as of December 31, 2009.

Account Title	Debits	Credits
Retained earnings		80,000
Sales revenue		750,000
Interest revenue		3,000
Cost of goods sold	420,000	
Salaries expense	100,000	
Rent expense	15,000	
Depreciation expense	30,000	
Interest expense	5,000	
Insurance expense	6,000	

Required:
Prepare the necessary closing entries at December 31, 2009.

E 2–13
Closing entries

● **LO7**

Presented below is income statement information of the Schefter Corporation for the year ended December 31, 2009.

Sales revenue	$492,000	Cost of goods sold	$284,000
Salaries expense	80,000	Insurance expense	12,000
Interest revenue	6,000	Interest expense	4,000
Advertising expense	10,000	Income tax expense	30,000
Gain on sale of investments	8,000	Depreciation expense	20,000

Required:
Prepare the necessary closing entries at December 31, 2009.

E 2–14
Cash versus accrual accounting; adjusting entries

● **LO4 LO5 LO8**

The Righter Shoe Store Company prepares monthly financial statements for its bank. The November 30 and December 31, 2009, trial balances contained the following account information:

	Nov. 30		Dec. 31	
	Dr.	**Cr.**	**Dr.**	**Cr.**
Supplies	1,500		3,000	
Prepaid insurance	6,000		4,500	
Wages payable		10,000		15,000
Unearned rent revenue		2,000		1,000

The following information also is known:
a. The December income statement reported $2,000 in supplies expense.
b. No insurance payments were made in December.
c. $10,000 was paid to employees during December for wages.
d. On November 1, 2009, a tenant paid Righter $3,000 in advance rent for the period November through January. Unearned rent revenue was credited.

Required:
1. What was the cost of supplies purchased during December?
2. What was the adjusting entry recorded at the end of December for prepaid insurance?
3. What was the adjusting entry recorded at the end of December for accrued wages?
4. What was the amount of rent revenue earned in December? What adjusting entry was recorded at the end of December for unearned rent?

E 2–15
External transactions and adjusting entries

● **LO2 LO4 LO5**

The following transactions occurred during 2009 for the Beehive Honey Corporation:

Feb. 1	Borrowed $12,000 from a bank and signed a note. Principal and interest at 10% will be paid on January 31, 2010.
Apr. 1	Paid $3,600 to an insurance company for a two-year fire insurance policy.
July 17	Purchased supplies costing $2,800 on account. The company records supplies purchased in an asset account. At the December 31, 2009, year-end, supplies costing $1,250 remained on hand.
Nov. 1	A customer borrowed $6,000 and signed a note requiring the customer to pay principal and 8% interest on April 30, 2010.

Required:
1. Record each transaction in general journal form. Omit explanations.
2. Prepare any necessary adjusting entries at the December 31, 2009, year-end. No adjusting entries were made during the year for any item.

E 2–16
Accrual accounting income determination

● **LO4 LO8**

During the course of your examination of the financial statements of the Hales Corporation for the year ended December 31, 2009, you discover the following:
a. An insurance policy covering three years was purchased on January 1, 2009, for $6,000. The entire amount was debited to insurance expense and no adjusting entry was made for this item.
b. During 2009, the company received a $1,000 cash advance from a customer for merchandise to be manufactured and shipped in 2010. The $1,000 was credited to sales revenue. No entry was made for the cost of merchandise.
c. There were no supplies listed in the balance sheet under assets. However, you discover that supplies costing $750 were on hand at December 31.

    d. Hales borrowed $20,000 from a local bank on October 1, 2009. Principal and interest at 12% will be paid on September 30, 2010. No accrual was made for interest.

    e. Net income reported in the 2009 income statement is $30,000 before reflecting any of the above items.

Required:
Determine the proper amount of net income for 2009.

E 2–17
Cash versus accrual accounting

● LO8

Stanley and Jones Lawn Service Company (S&J) maintains its books on a cash basis. However, the company recently borrowed $100,000 from a local bank and the bank requires S&J to provide annual financial statements prepared on an accrual basis. During 2009, the following cash flows were recorded:

Cash collected from customers		$320,000
Cash paid for:		
Salaries	$180,000	
Supplies	25,000	
Rent	12,000	
Insurance	6,000	
Miscellaneous	20,000	243,000
Net operating cash flow		$ 77,000

You are able to determine the following information about accounts receivable, prepaid expenses, and accrued liabilities:

	January 1, 2009	December 31, 2009
Accounts receivable	$32,000	$27,000
Prepaid insurance	–0–	2,000
Supplies	1,000	1,500
Accrued liabilities		
(for miscellaneous expenses)	2,400	3,400

In addition, you learn that the bank loan was dated September 30, 2009, with principal and interest at 6% due in one year. Depreciation on the company's equipment is $10,000 for the year.

Required:
Prepare an accrual basis income statement for 2009. (Ignore income taxes)

E 2–18
Worksheet

● Appendix A

The December 31, 2009, unadjusted trial balance for the Wolkstein Drug Company is presented below. December 31 is the company's fiscal year-end.

Account Title	Debits	Credits
Cash	20,000	
Accounts receivable	35,000	
Allowance for uncollectible accounts		2,000
Prepaid rent	5,000	
Inventory	50,000	
Equipment	100,000	
Accumulated depreciation—equipment		30,000
Accounts payable		23,000
Wages payable		–0–
Common stock		100,000
Retained earnings		29,000
Sales revenue		323,000
Cost of goods sold	180,000	
Wage expense	71,000	
Rent expense	30,000	
Depreciation expense	–0–	
Utility expense	12,000	
Bad debt expense	4,000	
Totals	507,000	507,000

The following year-end adjusting entries are required:

    a. Depreciation expense for the year on the equipment is $10,000.

    b. The company has determined that the allowance for uncollectible accounts should be $5,000.

    c. Accrued wages payable at year-end should be $4,000.

Required:
1. Prepare and complete a worksheet similar to Illustration 2A–1.
2. Prepare an income statement for 2009 and a balance sheet as of December 31, 2009.

E 2–19
Reversing entries

● **Appendix B**

The employees of Xitrex, Inc., are paid each Friday. The company's fiscal year-end is June 30, which falls on a Wednesday for the current year. Wages are earned evenly throughout the five-day workweek, and $10,000 will be paid on Friday, July 2.

Required:
1. Prepare an adjusting entry to record the accrued wages as of June 30, a reversing entry on July 1, and an entry to record the payment of wages on July 2.
2. Prepare journal entries to record the accrued wages as of June 30 and the payment of wages on July 2 assuming a reversing entry is not made.

E 2–20
Reversing entries

● **Appendix B**

Refer to Exercise 2–9 and respond to the following requirements.

Required:
1. If Microchip's accountant employed reversing entries, which adjusting entries would she likely reverse at the beginning of the following year?
2. Prepare the adjusting entries at the end of 2009 for the adjustments you identified in requirement 1.
3. Prepare the appropriate reversing entries at the beginning of 2010.

E 2–21
Special journals

● **Appendix C**

The White Company's accounting system consists of a general journal (GJ), a cash receipts journal (CR), a cash disbursements journal (CD), a sales journal (SJ), and a purchases journal (PJ). For each of the following, indicate which journal should be used to record the transaction.

Transaction	Journal
1. Purchased merchandise on account.	_____
2. Collected an account receivable.	_____
3. Borrowed $20,000 and signed a note.	_____
4. Recorded depreciation expense.	_____
5. Purchased equipment for cash.	_____
6. Sold merchandise for cash (the sale only, not the cost of the merchandise).	_____
7. Sold merchandise on credit (the sale only, not the cost of the merchandise).	_____
8. Recorded accrued wages payable.	_____
9. Paid employee wages.	_____
10. Sold equipment for cash.	_____
11. Sold equipment on credit.	_____
12. Paid a cash dividend to shareholders.	_____
13. Issued common stock in exchange for cash.	_____
14. Paid accounts payable.	_____

CPA REVIEW QUESTIONS

CPA Exam Questions

SCHWESER

● **LO8**

1. Compared to the accrual basis of accounting, the cash basis of accounting produces a lower amount of income by the net decrease during the accounting period of

	Accounts Receivable	Accrued Liabilities
a.	Yes	No
b.	No	Yes
c.	Yes	Yes
d.	No	No

LO8

2. On April 1 Ivy Corp. began operating a service company with an initial cash investment by shareholders of $1,000,000. The company provided $3,200,000 of services in April and received full payment in May. Ivy also incurred expenses of $1,500,000 in April that were paid in June. During May, Ivy paid its shareholders cash dividends of $500,000. What was the company's income before income taxes for the two months ended May 31 under the following methods of accounting?

	Cash Basis	Accrual Basis
a.	$3,200,000	$1,700,000
b.	$2,700,000	$1,200,000
c.	$1,700,000	$1,700,000
d.	$3,200,000	$1,200,000

LO5

3. Fay Corp. pays its outside salespersons fixed monthly salaries as well as commissions on net sales. Sales commissions are paid in the month following the month of sale, while the fixed salaries are expensed but considered advances against commissions. However, if salespersons' fixed salaries exceed their sales commissions earned for a month, such excess is not returned to the company. Pertinent data for the month of March for the three salespersons are as follows:

Salesperson	Fixed Salary	Net Sales	Commission Rate
A	$10,000	$ 200,000	4%
B	14,000	400,000	6%
C	18,000	600,000	6%
Totals	$42,000	$1,200,000	

What amount should Fay accrue as a debit to sales commissions expense and a credit to sales commissions payable at March 31?

a. $26,000
b. $28,000
c. $68,000
d. $70,000

LO8

4. Under East Co.'s accounting system, all insurance premiums paid are debited to prepaid insurance. During the year, East records monthly estimated charges to insurance expense with credits to prepaid insurance. Additional information for the year ended December 31 is as follows:

Prepaid insurance at January 1	$105,000
Insurance expense recognized during the year	437,500
Prepaid insurance at December 31	122,500

What was the total amount of cash paid by East for insurance premiums during the year?

a. $332,500
b. $420,000
c. $437,500
d. $455,000

LO1

5. JME Corporation bills its customers when services are rendered and recognizes revenue at the same time. This event causes an

a. Increase in assets.
b. Increase in net income.
c. Increase in retained earnings.
d. All of the above.

An alternate exercise and problem set is available on the text website: www.mhhe.com/spiceland5e

P 2–1
Accounting cycle
through unadjusted
trial balance

● LO2 LO3

Halogen Laminated Products Company began business on January 1, 2009. During January, the following transactions occurred:

Jan. 1 Issued common stock in exchange for $100,000 cash.
2 Purchased inventory on account for $35,000 (the perpetual inventory system is used).
4 Paid an insurance company $2,400 for a one-year insurance policy.
10 Sold merchandise on account for $12,000. The cost of the merchandise was $7,000.
15 Borrowed $30,000 from a local bank and signed a note. Principal and interest at 10% is to be repaid in six months.
20 Paid employees $6,000 wages for the first half of the month.
22 Sold merchandise for $10,000 cash. The cost of the merchandise was $6,000.
24 Paid $15,000 to suppliers for the merchandise purchased on January 2.
26 Collected $6,000 on account from customers.
28 Paid $1,000 to the local utility company for January gas and electricity.
30 Paid $4,000 rent for the building. $2,000 was for January rent, and $2,000 for February rent.

Required:
1. Prepare general journal entries to record each transaction. Omit explanations.
2. Post the entries to T-accounts.
3. Prepare an unadjusted trial balance as of January 30, 2009.

P 2–2
Accounting cycle
through unadjusted
trial balance

● LO2 LO3

The following is the post-closing trial balance for the Whitlow Manufacturing Corporation as of December 31, 2008.

Account Title	Debits	Credits
Cash	5,000	
Accounts receivable	2,000	
Inventory	5,000	
Equipment	11,000	
Accumulated depreciation—equipment		3,500
Accounts payable		3,000
Common stock		10,000
Retained earnings		6,500
Sales revenue		–0–
Cost of goods sold	–0–	
Wage expense	–0–	
Rent expense	–0–	
Advertising expense	–0–	
Totals	23,000	23,000

The following transactions occurred during January 2009:

Jan. 1 Sold merchandise for cash, $3,500. The cost of the merchandise was $2,000. The company uses the perpetual inventory system.
2 Purchased equipment on account for $5,500 from the Strong Company.
4 Received a $150 bill from the local newspaper for an advertisement that appeared in the paper on January 2.
8 Sold merchandise on account for $5,000. The cost of the merchandise was $2,800.
10 Purchased merchandise on account for $9,500.
13 Purchased equipment for cash, $800.
16 Paid the entire amount due to the Strong Company.
18 Received $4,000 from customers on account.
20 Paid $800 to the owner of the building for January's rent.
30 Paid employees $3,000 for salaries for the month of January.
31 Paid a cash dividend of $1,000 to shareholders.

Required:
1. Set up T-accounts and enter the beginning balances as of January 1, 2009.
2. Prepare general journal entries to record each transaction. Omit explanations.
3. Post the entries to T-accounts.
4. Prepare an unadjusted trial balance as of January 31, 2009.

P 2–3
Adjusting entries

● LO4 LO5

Pastina Company manufactures and sells various types of pasta to grocery chains as private label brands. The company's fiscal year-end is December 31. The unadjusted trial balance as of December 31, 2009, appears below.

Account Title	Debits	Credits
Cash	30,000	
Accounts receivable	40,000	
Allowance for uncollectible accounts		3,000
Supplies	1,500	
Inventory	60,000	
Note receivable	20,000	
Interest receivable	–0–	
Prepaid rent	2,000	
Prepaid insurance	–0–	
Equipment	80,000	
Accumulated depreciation—equipment		30,000
Accounts payable		28,000
Wages payable		–0–
Note payable		50,000
Interest payable		–0–
Unearned revenue		–0–
Common stock		60,000
Retained earnings		24,500
Sales revenue		148,000
Interest revenue		–0–
Cost of goods sold	70,000	
Wage expense	18,900	
Rent expense	11,000	
Depreciation expense	–0–	
Interest expense	–0–	
Supplies expense	1,100	
Insurance expense	6,000	
Bad debt expense	3,000	
Totals	343,500	343,500

Information necessary to prepare the year-end adjusting entries appears below.
1. Depreciation on the equipment for the year is $10,000.
2. The company estimates that of the $40,000 in accounts receivable outstanding at year-end, $5,500 probably will not be collected.
3. Employee wages are paid twice a month, on the 22nd for wages earned from the 1st through the 15th, and on the 7th of the following month for wages earned from the 16th through the end of the month. Wages earned from December 16 through December 31, 2009, were $1,500.
4. On October 1, 2009, Pastina borrowed $50,000 from a local bank and signed a note. The note requires interest to be paid annually on September 30 at 12%. The principal is due in 10 years.
5. On March 1, 2009, the company lent a supplier $20,000 and a note was signed requiring principal and interest at 8% to be paid on February 28, 2010.
6. On April 1, 2009, the company paid an insurance company $6,000 for a two-year fire insurance policy. The entire $6,000 was debited to insurance expense.
7. $800 of supplies remained on hand at December 31, 2009.
8. A customer paid Pastina $2,000 in December for 1,500 pounds of spaghetti to be manufactured and delivered in January 2010. Pastina credited sales revenue.
9. On December 1, 2009, $2,000 rent was paid to the owner of the building. The payment represented rent for December and January 2010, at $1,000 per month.

Required:
Prepare the necessary December 31, 2009, adjusting journal entries.

P 2–4

Accounting cycle; adjusting entries through post-closing trial balance

● LO3 LO5 through LO7

P 2–5

Adjusting entries

● LO5

Refer to Problem 2–3 and complete the following steps:
1. Enter the unadjusted balances from the trial balance into T-accounts.
2. Post the adjusting entries prepared in Problem 2–3 to the accounts.
3. Prepare an adjusted trial balance.
4. Prepare an income statement and a statement of shareholders' equity for the year ended December 31, 2009, and a classified balance sheet as of December 31, 2009. Assume that no common stock was issued during the year and that $4,000 in cash dividends were paid to shareholders during the year.
5. Prepare closing entries and post to the accounts.
6. Prepare a post-closing trial balance.

Howarth Company's fiscal year-end is December 31. Below are the unadjusted and adjusted trial balances for December 31, 2009.

	Unadjusted		Adjusted	
Account Title	Debits	Credits	Debits	Credits
Cash	50,000		50,000	
Accounts receivable	35,000		35,000	
Allowance for uncollectible accounts		2,000		3,500
Prepaid rent	2,000		1,200	
Supplies	1,500		800	
Inventory	60,000		60,000	
Note receivable	30,000		30,000	
Interest receivable	–0–		1,500	
Equipment	45,000		45,000	
Accumulated depreciation—equipment		15,000		20,000
Accounts payable		32,000		32,000
Wages payable		–0–		6,200
Note payable		50,000		50,000
Interest payable		–0–		2,500
Unearned rent revenue		–0–		2,000
Common stock		46,000		46,000
Retained earnings		20,000		20,000
Sales revenue		244,000		244,000
Rent revenue		6,000		4,000
Interest revenue		–0–		1,500
Cost of goods sold	126,000		126,000	
Wage expense	45,000		51,200	
Rent expense	11,000		11,800	
Depreciation expense	–0–		5,000	
Supplies expense	1,100		1,800	
Interest expense	5,400		7,900	
Bad debt expense	3,000		4,500	
Totals	415,000	415,000	431,700	431,700

Required:
Prepare the adjusting journal entries that were made at December 31, 2009.

P 2–6

Accounting cycle

● LO2 through LO7

The general ledger of the Karlin Company, a consulting company, at January 1, 2009, contained the following account balances:

Account Title	Debits	Credits
Cash	30,000	
Accounts receivable	15,000	
Allowance for uncollectible accounts		500
Equipment	20,000	
Accumulated depreciation		6,000
Salaries payable		9,000
Common stock		40,000
Retained earnings		9,500
Total	65,000	65,000

The following is a summary of the transactions for the year:
a. Sales of services, $100,000, of which $30,000 was on credit.
b. Collected on accounts receivable, $27,300.

c. Issued shares of common stock in exchange for $10,000 in cash.

d. Paid salaries, $50,000 (of which $9,000 was for salaries payable).

e. Paid miscellaneous expenses, $24,000.

f. Purchased equipment for $15,000 in cash.

g. Paid $2,500 in cash dividends to shareholders.

Required:

1. Set up the necessary T-accounts and enter the beginning balances from the trial balance.

2. Prepare a general journal entry for each of the summary transactions listed above.

3. Post the journal entries to the accounts.

4. Prepare an unadjusted trial balance.

5. Prepare and post adjusting journal entries. Accrued salaries at year-end amounted to $1,000. Depreciation for the year on the equipment is $2,000. The allowance for uncollectible accounts is estimated to be $1,500.

6. Prepare an adjusted trial balance.

7. Prepare an income statement for 2009 and a balance sheet as of December 31, 2009.

8. Prepare and post closing entries.

9. Prepare a post-closing trial balance.

P 2–7
Adjusting entries and income effects

● LO4 LO5

The information necessary for preparing the 2009 year-end adjusting entries for Vito's Pizza Parlor appears below. Vito's fiscal year-end is December 31.

a. On July 1, 2009, purchased $10,000 of **IBM Corporation** bonds at face value. The bonds pay interest twice a year on January 1 and July 1. The annual interest rate is 12%.

b. Vito's depreciable equipment has a cost of $30,000, a five-year life, and no salvage value. The equipment was purchased in 2007. The straight-line depreciation method is used.

c. On November 1, 2009, the bar area was leased to Jack Donaldson for one year. Vito's received $6,000 representing the first six months' rent and credited unearned rent revenue.

d. On April 1, 2009, the company paid $2,400 for a two-year fire and liability insurance policy and debited insurance expense.

e. On October 1, 2009, the company borrowed $20,000 from a local bank and signed a note. Principal and interest at 12% will be paid on September 30, 2010.

f. At year-end there is a $1,800 debit balance in the supplies (asset) account. Only $700 of supplies remain on hand.

Required:

1. Prepare the necessary adjusting journal entries at December 31, 2009.

2. Determine the amount by which net income would be misstated if Vito's failed to make these adjusting entries. (Ignore income tax expense.)

P 2–8
Adjusting entries

● LO4 LO5

Excalibur Corporation manufactures and sells video games for personal computers. The unadjusted trial balance as of December 31, 2009, appears below. December 31 is the company's fiscal year-end. The company uses the perpetual inventory system.

Account Title	Debits	Credits
Cash	23,300	
Accounts receivable	32,500	
Allowance for uncollectible accounts		100
Supplies	–0–	
Prepaid rent	–0–	
Inventory	65,000	
Equipment	75,000	
Accumulated depreciation—equipment		10,000
Accounts payable		26,000
Wages payable		3,000
Note payable		30,000
Common stock		80,000
Retained earnings		16,050
Sales revenue		180,000
Cost of goods sold	95,000	
Interest expense	–0–	
Wage expense	32,350	
Rent expense	14,000	
Supplies expense	2,000	
Utility expense	6,000	
Bad debt expense	–0–	
Totals	345,150	345,150

Information necessary to prepare the year-end adjusting entries appears below.

1. The equipment was purchased in 2007 and is being depreciated using the straight-line method over an eight-year useful life with no salvage value.

2. Accrued wages at year-end should be $4,500.

3. The company estimates that 2% of all year-end accounts receivable will probably not be collected.

4. The company borrowed $30,000 on September 1, 2009. The principal is due to be repaid in 10 years. Interest is payable twice a year on each August 31 and February 28 at an annual rate of 10%.

5. The company debits supplies expense when supplies are purchased. Supplies on hand at year-end cost $500.

6. Prepaid rent at year-end should be $1,000.

Required:
Prepare the necessary December 31, 2009, adjusting entries.

P 2–9
Cash versus accrual accounting

● LO8

Selected balance sheet information for the Wolf Company at November 30, and December 31, 2009, is presented below. The company uses the perpetual inventory system and all sales to customers are made on credit.

	Nov. 30		Dec. 31	
	Dr.	Cr.	Dr.	Cr.
Accounts receivable	10,000		3,000	
Prepaid insurance	5,000		7,500	
Inventory	7,000		6,000	
Accounts payable		12,000		15,000
Wages payable		5,000		3,000

The following cash flow information also is available:
a. Cash collected from credit customers—$80,000.
b. Cash paid for insurance—$5,000.
c. Cash paid to suppliers of inventory—$60,000 (the entire accounts payable amounts relate to inventory purchases).
d. Cash paid to employees for wages—$10,000.

Required:
1. Determine the following for the month of December:
   a. Sales revenue
   b. Cost of goods sold
   c. Insurance expense
   d. Wage expense
2. Prepare a summary journal entry to record the month's sales and cost of those sales.

P 2–10
Accounting cycle; unadjusted trial balance through closing

● LO3 LO4 LO5
   LO7

The unadjusted trial balance as of December 31, 2009, for the Bagley Consulting Company appears below. December 31 is the company's fiscal year-end.

Account Title	Debits	Credits
Cash	8,000	
Accounts receivable	9,000	
Allowance for uncollectible accounts		50
Prepaid insurance	3,000	
Land	200,000	
Buildings	50,000	
Accumulated depreciation—buildings		20,000
Equipment	100,000	
Accumulated depreciation—equipment		40,000
Accounts payable		35,000
Salaries payable		–0–
Unearned rent revenue		–0–
Common stock		200,000
Retained earnings		56,450
Sales revenue		90,000
Interest revenue		3,000
Rent revenue		7,500
Salaries expense	37,000	
Bad debt expense	–0–	
Depreciation expense	–0–	
Insurance expense	–0–	
Utility expense	30,000	
Maintenance expense	15,000	
Totals	452,000	452,000

Required:

1. Enter the account balances in T-accounts.
2. From the trial balance and information given, prepare adjusting entries and post to the accounts.
   a. The buildings have an estimated useful life of 50 years with no salvage value. The company uses the straight-line depreciation method.
   b. The equipment is depreciated at 10 percent of original cost per year.
   c. Prepaid insurance expired during the year, $1,500.
   d. It is estimated that 10% of the accounts receivable balance will be uncollectible.
   e. Accrued salaries at year-end, $1,500.
   f. Unearned rent revenue at year-end should be $1,200.
3. Prepare an adjusted trial balance.
4. Prepare closing entries.
5. Prepare a post-closing trial balance.

P 2–11
Accrual accounting; financial statements

● LO4 LO6 LO8

McGuire Corporation began operations in 2009. The company purchases computer equipment from manufacturers and then sells to retail stores. During 2009, the bookkeeper used a check register to record all cash receipts and cash disbursements. No other journals were used. The following is a recap of the cash receipts and disbursements made during the year.

Cash receipts:	
Sale of common stock	$ 50,000
Collections from customers	320,000
Borrowed from local bank on April 1, note signed requiring principal and interest at 12% to be paid on March 31, 2010	40,000
Total cash receipts	$410,000
Cash disbursements:	
Purchase of merchandise	$220,000
Payment of salaries	80,000
Purchase of equipment	30,000
Payment of rent on building	14,000
Miscellaneous expenses	10,000
Total cash disbursements	$354,000

You are called in to prepare financial statements at December 31, 2009. The following additional information was provided to you:

1. Customers owed the company $22,000 at year-end. Of this amount, it was anticipated that $3,000 would probably not be collected. There were no actual bad debt write-offs in 2009.
2. At year-end, $30,000 was still due to suppliers of merchandise purchased on credit.
3. At year-end, merchandise inventory costing $50,000 still remained on hand.
4. Salaries owed to employees at year-end amounted to $5,000.
5. On December 1, $3,000 in rent was paid to the owner of the building used by McGuire. This represented rent for the months of December through February.
6. The equipment, which has a 10-year life and no salvage value, was purchased on January 1, 2009. Straight-line depreciation is used.

Required:
Prepare an income statement for 2009 and a balance sheet as of December 31, 2009.

P 2–12
Cash versus accrual accounting

● LO8

Zambrano Wholesale Corporation maintains its records on a cash basis. At the end of each year the company's accountant obtains the necessary information to prepare accrual basis financial statements. The following cash flows occurred during the year ended December 31, 2009:

Cash receipts:	
From customers	$675,000
Interest on note	4,000
Loan from a local bank	100,000
Total cash receipts	$779,000
Cash disbursements:	
Purchase of merchandise	$390,000
Annual insurance payment	6,000
Payment of salaries	210,000
Dividends paid to shareholders	10,000
Annual rent payment	24,000
Total cash disbursements	$640,000

Selected balance sheet information:

	12/31/08	12/31/09
Cash	$25,000	$164,000
Accounts receivable	62,000	92,000
Inventory	80,000	62,000
Prepaid insurance	2,500	?
Prepaid rent	11,000	?
Interest receivable	3,000	?
Note receivable	50,000	50,000
Equipment	100,000	100,000
Accumulated depreciation—equipment	(40,000)	(50,000)
Accounts payable (for merchandise)	110,000	122,000
Salaries payable	20,000	24,000
Note payable	–0–	100,000
Interest payable	–0–	?

Additional information:

1. On March 31, 2008, Zambrano lent a customer $50,000. Interest at 8% is payable annually on each March 31. Principal is due in 2012.

2. The annual insurance payment is made in advance on April 30.

3. On October 31, 2009, Zambrano borrowed $100,000 from a local bank. Principal and interest at 6% are due on October 31, 2010.

4. Annual rent on the company's facilities is paid in advance on June 30.

Required:

1. Prepare an accrual basis income statement for 2009 (ignore income taxes).

2. Determine the following balance sheet amounts on December 31, 2009:

   a. Prepaid insurance

   b. Prepaid rent

   c. Interest receivable

   d. Interest payable

P 2–13
Worksheet

● **Appendix A**

Using the information from Problem 2–8, prepare and complete a worksheet similar to Illustration 2A–1. Use the information in the worksheet to prepare an income statement and a statement of shareholders' equity for 2009 and a balance sheet as of December 31, 2009. Cash dividends paid to shareholders during the year amounted to $6,000. Also prepare the necessary closing entries assuming that adjusting entries have been correctly posted to the accounts.

BROADEN YOUR PERSPECTIVE

Apply your critical-thinking ability to the knowledge you've gained. These cases will provide you an opportunity to develop your research, analysis, judgment, and communication skills. You also will work with other students, integrate what you've learned, apply it in real world situations, and consider its global and ethical ramifications. This practice will broaden your knowledge and further develop your decision-making abilities.

**Judgment
Case 2–1**
Cash versus
accrual accounting;
adjusting entries;
Chapters 1 and 2

● **LO4 LO8**

You have recently been hired by Davis & Company, a small public accounting firm. One of the firm's partners, Alice Davis, has asked you to deal with a disgruntled client, Mr. Sean Pitt, owner of the city's largest hardware store. Mr. Pitt is applying to a local bank for a substantial loan to remodel his store. The bank requires accrual based financial statements but Mr. Pitt has always kept the company's records on a cash basis. He does not see the purpose of accrual based statements. His most recent outburst went something like this: "After all, I collect cash from customers, pay my bills in cash, and I am going to pay the bank loan with cash. And, I already show my building and equipment as assets and depreciate them. I just don't understand the problem."

Required:

1. Explain the difference between a cash basis and an accrual basis measure of performance.

2. Why, in most cases, does accrual basis net income provide a better measure of performance than net operating cash flow.

3. Explain the purpose of adjusting entries as they relate to the difference between cash and accrual accounting.

Judgment
Case 2–2
Cash versus accrual
accounting

● LO8

Refer to Case 2–1 above. Mr. Pitt has relented and agrees to provide you with the information necessary to convert his cash basis financial statements to accrual basis statements. He provides you with the following transaction information for the fiscal year ending December 31, 2009:

1. A comprehensive insurance policy requires a payment every year for the upcoming year. The last payment of $12,000 was made on September 1, 2009.

2. Mr. Pitt allows customers to pay using a credit card. At the end of the current year, various credit card companies owed Mr. Pitt $6,500. At the end of last year, customer credit card charges outstanding were $5,000.

3. Employees are paid once a month, on the 10th of the month following the work period. Cash disbursements to employees were $8,200 and $7,200 for January 10, 2010, and January 10, 2009, respectively.

4. Utility bills outstanding totaled $1,200 at the end of 2009 and $900 at the end of 2008.

5. A physical count of inventory is always taken at the end of the fiscal year. The merchandise on hand at the end of 2009 cost $35,000. At the end of 2008, inventory on hand cost $32,000.

6. At the end of 2008, Mr. Pitt did not have any bills outstanding to suppliers of merchandise. However, at the end of 2009, he owed suppliers $4,000.

Required:

1. Mr. Pitt's 2009 cash basis net income (including depreciation expense) is $26,000. Determine net income applying the accrual accounting model.

2. Explain the effect on Mr. Pitt's balance sheet of converting from cash to accrual. That is, would assets, liabilities, and owner's equity be higher or lower and by what amounts?

Communication
Case 2–3
Adjusting entries

● LO4

"I don't understand," complained Chris, who responded to your bulletin board posting in your responsibilities as a tutor. The complaint was in response to your statements that recording adjusting entries is a critical step in the accounting processing cycle, and the two major classifications of adjusting entries are prepayments and accruals.

Required:

Respond to Chris.

1. When do prepayments occur? Accruals?

2. Describe the appropriate adjusting entry for prepaid expenses and for unearned revenues. What is the effect on net income, assets, liabilities, and shareholders' equity of not recording a required adjusting entry for prepayments?

3. Describe the required adjusting entry for accrued liabilities and for accrued receivables. What is the effect on net income, assets, liabilities, and shareholders' equity of not recording a required adjusting entry for accruals?

The Balance Sheet and Financial Disclosures

/// OVERVIEW

Chapter 1 stressed the importance of the financial statements in helping investors and creditors predict future cash flows. The balance sheet, along with accompanying disclosures, provides relevant information useful in helping investors and creditors not only to predict future cash flows, but also to make the related assessments of liquidity and long-term solvency.

The purpose of this chapter is to provide an overview of the balance sheet and financial disclosures and to explore how this information is used by decision makers.

LEARNING OBJECTIVES

After studying this chapter, you should be able to:

- **LO1** Describe the purpose of the balance sheet and understand its usefulness and limitations.
- **LO2** Distinguish among current and noncurrent assets and liabilities.
- **LO3** Identify and describe the various balance sheet asset classifications.
- **LO4** Identify and describe the two balance sheet liability classifications.
- **LO5** Explain the purpose of financial statement disclosures.
- **LO6** Explain the purpose of the management discussion and analysis disclosure.
- **LO7** Explain the purpose of an audit and describe the content of the audit report.
- **LO8** Describe the techniques used by financial analysts to transform financial information into forms more useful for analysis.
- **LO9** Identify and calculate the common liquidity and financing ratios used to assess risk.

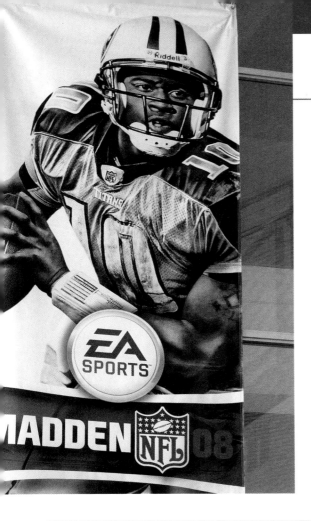

FINANCIAL REPORTING CASE

What's It Worth?

"I can't believe it. Why don't you accountants prepare financial statements that are relevant?" Your friend Jerry is a finance major and is constantly badgering you about what he perceives to be a lack of relevance of financial statements prepared according to generally accepted accounting principles. "For example, take a look at this balance sheet for **Electronic Arts** that I just downloaded off the Internet. Electronic Arts is the company in California that produces all those cool video games like Battlefield 2, NBA Live, and Madden NFL. Anyway, the shareholders' equity of the company according to the 2007 balance sheet is about $4 billion. But if you multiply the number of outstanding shares by the most recent stock price per share, the company's market value is four times that amount. I thought financial statements were supposed to help investors and creditors value a company." You decide to look at the company's balance sheet and try to set Jerry straight.

By the time you finish this chapter, you should be able to respond appropriately to the questions posed in this case. Compare your response to the solution provided at the end of the chapter.

QUESTIONS ///

1. Respond to Jerry's criticism that shareholders' equity does not represent the market value of the company. What information does the balance sheet provide? (page 113)

2. The usefulness of the balance sheet is enhanced by classifying assets and liabilities according to common characteristics. What are the classifications used in Electronic Arts' balance sheet and what elements do those categories include? (page 114)

ELECTRONIC ARTS, INC
Consolidated Balance Sheets
As of March 31
($ in 000s except share data)

Assets	2007	2006
Current assets:		
Cash and cash equivalents	$1,371	$1,242
Short-term investments	1,264	1,030
Marketable equity securities	341	160
Receivables, net of allowances of $214 and $232, respectively	256	199
Inventories	62	61
Deferred income taxes, net	84	86
Other current assets	219	234
Total current assets	3,597	3,012
Property and equipment, net	484	392
Investments in affiliates	6	11
Goodwill	734	647
Other intangibles, net	210	232
Deferred income taxes, net	25	—
Other assets	90	92
Total Assets	$5,146	$4,386
Liabilities, Minority Interest and Stockholders' Equity		
Current liabilities:		
Accounts payable	$ 180	$ 163
Accrued and other current liabilities	823	697
Deferred net revenue—packaged goods and digital content	23	9
Total current liabilities	1,026	869
Deferred income taxes, net	8	29
Other liabilities	80	68
Total liabilities	1,114	966
Commitments and contingencies (See Note 9)		
Minority interest	—	12
Stockholders' equity:		
Preferred stock, $0.01 par value. 10 shares authorized	—	—
Common stock, $0.01 par value. 1,000 shares authorized; 311 and 305 shares issued and outstanding, respectively	3	3
Paid-in capital	1,412	1,081
Retained earnings	2,323	2,241
Accumulated other comprehensive income	294	83
Total stockholders' equity	4,032	3,408
Total Liabilities, Minority Interest and Stockholders' Equity	$5,146	$4,386

The balance sheet, along with accompanying disclosures, provides a wealth of information to external decision makers. The information provided is useful not only in the prediction of future cash flows but also in the related assessments of liquidity and long-term solvency.

This chapter begins our discussion of the financial statements by providing an overview of the balance sheet and the financial disclosures that accompany the financial statements. The first part of the chapter describes the usefulness and limitations of the balance sheet and illustrates the content of the statement. The second part illustrates financial statement disclosures presented to external users in addition to the basic financial statements. In the third part we discuss how this information can be used by decision makers to assess business risk. That discussion introduces some common financial ratios used to assess liquidity and long-term solvency.

Chapter 4 continues this discussion of the financial statements with its coverage of the income statement and the statement of cash flows.

THE BALANCE SHEET

The purpose of the balance sheet is to report a company's financial position on a particular date. Unlike the income statement, which is a change statement reporting events that occurred *during a period of time,* the balance sheet presents an organized array of assets, liabilities, and shareholders' equity *at a point in time.* It is a freeze frame or snapshot of financial position at the end of a particular day marking the end of an accounting period.

● LO1

Usefulness and Limitations

Carter Hawley Hale Stores (CHHS), Inc., was one of the largest department store retailers in the United States. In 1991, the company operated over 100 stores in the sunbelt regions of the country. The company's divisions included The Broadway and Emporium. During the 1980s, the company struggled financially and in February of 1991 declared bankruptcy. CHHS's February 2, 1991, quarterly balance sheet, filed with the SEC and made publicly available, disclosed the information in Graphic 3–1.

The negative shareholders' equity includes negative retained earnings of nearly $1 billion resulting from operating losses incurred over a number of years.

By the summer of 1991, the company's stock price had dropped to $1 per share from a 1989 high of $8. In June 1991, the following (condensed) balance sheet information was reported to the bankruptcy court:

GRAPHIC 3–1   Quarterly Balance Sheet—Carter Hawley Hale Stores, Inc.

Balance Sheet (condensed) At February 2, 1991 ($ in 000s)	
Assets	
Current assets	$1,154,064
Property and equipment, net	511,690
Other assets	89,667
Total assets	$1,755,421
Liabilities	
Current liabilities	$ 175,982
Long-term liabilities	1,852,066
Total liabilities	2,028,048
Shareholders' Equity	(272,627)
Total liabilities and shareholders' equity	$1,755,421

	($ in 000s)
Property	$1,596,312
Debts	1,112,989
Excess of property over debts	$ 483,323

Has the financial position changed this dramatically from February to June? No. Differences in reporting requirements by the SEC and the bankruptcy court cause the apparent discrepancy. First, the property (assets) disclosed to the bankruptcy court does not include accounts receivable and debts do not include the related liabilities for which the receivables had been pledged as collateral. This accounts for the smaller asset and debt figures as compared to those disclosed in the February statement provided to the SEC.

But the striking difference is that the *negative equity* of $272,627,000 disclosed in the SEC report becomes a *positive equity* (excess of assets over liabilities) of $483,323,000 in the information disclosed to the bankruptcy court. This positive equity, divided by the number of common shares outstanding, results in a per share value of nearly $16. Why the discrepancy? The answer relates to the valuation of property. In the balance sheet submitted to the SEC, these assets are valued based on their original cost. However, the bankruptcy court requires assets to be reported at fair value.[1] The market value of CHHS's property, which includes some valuable land in locations like San Francisco, was significantly higher than its original cost.

This example illustrates an important limitation of the balance sheet. *The balance sheet does not portray the market value of the entity* as a going concern, nor, as in the CHHS example, its liquidation value. Many assets, like land and buildings for example, are measured

FINANCIAL Reporting Case

Q1, p. 111

Assets minus liabilities, measured according to GAAP, is not likely to be representative of the market value of the entity.

---

[1]The bankruptcy court requires market value information in order to assess, among other things, the ability of the company to pay its creditors if assets were liquidated.

at their historical costs rather than their fair values. Relatedly, many company resources including its trained employees, its experienced management team, and its reputation are not recorded as assets at all. Also, many items and amounts reported in the balance sheet are heavily reliant on estimates rather than determinable amounts. For example, companies estimate the amount of receivables they will be able to actually collect and the amount of warranty costs they will eventually incur for products already sold. For these and other reasons, a company's book value, its assets minus its liabilities as shown in the balance sheet, usually will not directly measure the company's market value (number of shares of common stock outstanding multiplied by the price per share).

Consider for example that in 2007, the 30 companies constituting the Dow Jones Industrial Average had an average ratio of market value to book value of approximately 4.46. The ratio for **Merck,** one of the world's largest pharmaceutical companies, was approximately 6.0. Can you think of an important reason why Merck's market value would be six times higher than its book value? One reason is that Merck spends significant amounts, over $4.9 billion in 2007 alone, on research and development of new products. Many of the drugs, for example, that the company has developed have been successful, and yet the costs to discover and develop them are not represented in the balance sheet. Research and development costs are expensed in the period incurred, and not capitalized as an asset.

Despite these limitations, the balance sheet does have significant value. An important feature of the statement is that it describes many of the resources a company has available for generating future cash flows. Another way the statement's content is informative is in combination with income statement items. For example, the relation between net income and assets provides a measure of return that is useful in predicting future profitability. In fact, many of the amounts reported in either of the two statements are more informative when viewed relative to an amount from the other statement.[2]

> The balance sheet provides information useful for assessing future cash flows, liquidity, and long-term solvency.

The balance sheet does not simply list assets and liabilities. Instead, assets and liabilities are classified (grouped) according to common characteristics. These classifications, which we explore in the next section, along with related disclosure notes, help the balance sheet to provide additional important information about liquidity and long-term solvency. Liquidity refers to the period of time before an asset is converted to cash or until a liability is paid. This information is useful in assessing a company's ability to pay its *current* obligations. Long-term solvency refers to the riskiness of a company with regard to the amount of liabilities in its capital structure. Other things being equal, the risk to an investor or creditor increases as the percentage of liabilities, relative to equity, increases.

Solvency also provides information about *financial flexibility*—the ability of a company to alter cash flows in order to take advantage of unexpected investment opportunities and needs. For example, the higher the percentage of a company's liabilities to its equity, the more difficult it typically will be to borrow additional funds either to take advantage of a promising investment opportunity or to meet obligations. In general, the lower the financial flexibility, the higher the risk is that the enterprise will fail. In a subsequent section of this chapter, we introduce some common ratios used to assess liquidity and long-term solvency.

In summary, even though the balance sheet does not *directly measure* the market value of the entity, it provides valuable information that can be used to help *judge* market value.

Classifications

FINANCIAL
Reporting Case

Q2, p. 111

The usefulness of the balance sheet is enhanced when assets and liabilities are grouped according to common characteristics. *The broad distinction made in the balance sheet is the current versus noncurrent classification of both assets and liabilities.* The remainder of Part A provides an overview of the balance sheet. We discuss each of the three primary elements of the balance sheet (assets, liabilities, and shareholders' equity) in the order they are

---

[2]We explore some of these relationships in Chapter 5.

reported in the statement as well as the classifications typically made within the elements. The balance sheet elements were defined in Chapter 1 as follows:

> **Assets** are probable future economic benefits obtained or controlled by a particular entity as a result of past transactions or events.

> **Liabilities** are probable future sacrifices of economic benefits arising from present obligations of a particular entity to transfer assets or provide services to other entities in the future as a result of past transactions or events.

> **Equity** (or net assets), called **shareholders' equity** or **stockholders' equity** for a corporation, is the residual interest in the assets of an entity that remains after deducting liabilities.

The key classification of assets and liabilities in the balance sheet is the current versus noncurrent distinction.

Graphic 3–2 lists the balance sheet elements along with their sub-classifications.

We intentionally avoid detailed discussion of the question of valuation in order to focus on an overview of the balance sheet. In later chapters we look closer at the nature and valuation of the specific assets and liabilities.

GRAPHIC 3–2   Classification of Elements within a Balance Sheet

Assets
Current assets
Investments
Property, plant, and equipment
Intangible assets
Other assets
Liabilities
Current liabilities
Long-term liabilities
Shareholders' Equity
Paid-in capital
Retained earnings

Assets

CURRENT ASSETS.   Current assets include cash and other assets that are reasonably expected to be converted to cash or consumed within the coming year, or within the normal operating cycle of the business if that's longer than one year. The operating cycle for a typical manufacturing company refers to the period of time necessary to convert cash to raw materials, raw materials to a finished product, the finished product to receivables, and then finally receivables back to cash. This concept is illustrated in Graphic 3–3.

● **LO2**

Current assets include cash and all other assets expected to become cash or be consumed within one year or the operating cycle, whichever is longer.

In some businesses, such as shipbuilding or distilleries, the operating cycle extends far beyond one year. For example, if it takes two years to build an oil-carrying supertanker, then the shipbuilder will classify as current those assets that will be converted to cash or consumed within two years. But for most businesses the operating cycle will be shorter than one year. In these situations the one-year convention is used to classify both assets and liabilities. Where a company has no clearly defined operating cycle, the one-year convention is used.

Graphic 3–4 presents the current asset sections of **Google Inc.**'s 2006 and 2007 balance sheets that also can be located in the company's financial statements included with all new copies of the text. In keeping with common practice, the individual current assets are listed in the order of their liquidity (nearness to cash).

● **LO3**

GRAPHIC 3–3   Operating Cycle of a Typical Manufacturing Company

Cash and cash equivalents.   The most liquid asset, cash, is listed first. Cash includes cash on hand and in banks that is available for use in the operations of the business and such items as bank drafts, cashier's checks, and money orders. Cash equivalents frequently include certain negotiable items such as commercial paper, money market funds, and U.S. treasury bills. These are highly liquid investments that can be quickly converted into cash. Most companies draw a distinction between investments classified as cash equivalents and the next category of current assets, short-term investments, according to the scheduled maturity of the investment. It is common practice to classify investments that have a maturity date of three months or less from the date of purchase as cash equivalents. **Google Inc.**'s policy follows this practice and is disclosed in the summary of significant accounting policies disclosure note. The portion of the note from the company's 2007 financial statements is shown in Graphic 3–5.

GRAPHIC 3–4
Current Assets—
Google Inc.

Real World Financials

	December 31	
	2006	**2007**
(In thousands)		
Assets		
Current assets:		
Cash and cash equivalents	$3,544,671	$6,081,593
Marketable securities	7,699,243	8,137,020
Accounts receivable, net of allowance of		
$16,914 and $32,887	1,322,340	2,162,521
Deferred income taxes, net	29,713	68,538
Income taxes receivable	—	145,253
Prepaid revenue share, expenses and other assets	443,880	694,213
Total current assets	13,039,847	17,289,138

GRAPHIC 3–5

Disclosure of Cash
Equivalents—Google
Inc.

Real World Financials

Summary of Significant Accounting Policies

Cash and Cash Equivalents and Marketable Securities (in part)
All highly liquid investments with stated maturities of three months or less from date of purchase are classified as cash equivalents.

Investments are
classified as current
if management has
the ability and intent
to liquidate the
investment in the near
term.

Cash that is restricted for a special purpose and not available for current operations should not be classified as a current asset. For example, if cash is being accumulated to repay a debt due in five years, the cash is classified as investments, a noncurrent asset.[3]

Short-term investments. Liquid investments not classified as cash equivalents are reported as either short-term investments, sometimes called *temporary investments* or *short-term marketable securities,* or investments, a noncurrent asset. Investments in stock and debt securities of other corporations are included as short-term investments *if* the company has the ability and intent to sell those securities within the next 12 months or operating cycle, whichever is longer. If, for example, a company owns 1,000 shares of **IBM Corporation** stock and intends to hold those shares for several years, the stock is a long-term investment and should be classified as investments.

For reporting purposes, investments in debt and equity securities are classified in one of three categories: (1) held to maturity, (2) trading securities, or (3) securities available for sale. We discuss these different categories and their accounting treatment in Chapter 12.

Accounts receivable. Accounts receivable result from the sale of goods or services on credit. Notice in Graphic 3–4 that the Google receivables are valued net of allowance, that is, less the amount not expected to be collected. Accounts receivable often are referred to as *trade receivables* because they arise in the course of a company's normal trade. *Nontrade receivables* result from loans or advances by the company to individuals and other entities. When receivables are supported by a formal agreement or note that specifies payment terms they are called notes receivable.

Accounts receivable usually are due in 30 to 60 days, depending on the terms offered to customers and are, therefore, classified as current assets. Any receivable, regardless of the source, not expected to be collected within one year or the operating cycle, whichever is longer, is classified as investments, a noncurrent asset.

Inventories consist
of assets that a
retail or wholesale
company acquires for
resale or goods that
manufacturers produce
for sale.

Inventories. Inventories include goods awaiting sale (finished goods), goods in the course of production (work in process), and goods to be consumed directly or indirectly in production (raw materials). Inventory for a wholesale or retail company consists only of finished goods, but the inventory of a manufacturer will include all three types of goods. Occasionally, a manufacturing company will report all three types of inventory directly in the balance sheet. More often, only the total amount of inventories is shown in the balance sheet and the balances of each type are shown in a disclosure note. For example, the note shown in Graphic 3–6 appears in the 2007 financial statements of **IBM Corporation.**

---

[3]If the debt is due in the next year and classified as a current liability, then the cash also would be classified as current.

GRAPHIC 3–6

Inventories Disclosure—IBM Corporation

Real World Financials

E. Inventories
($ in millions)

	At Dec. 31	
	2007	**2006**
Finished goods	$ 668	$ 506
Work in process and raw materials	1,996	2,304
	$2,664	$2,810

Inventories are reported as current assets because they normally are sold within the operating cycle.

Google Inc. earns revenue by providing services to its customers rather than by selling goods. That is why there are no merchandise inventories listed in the company's balance sheet.

Prepaid expenses.   Recall from Chapter 2 that a prepaid expense represents an asset recorded when an expense is paid in advance, creating benefits beyond the current period. Examples are prepaid rent and prepaid insurance. Even though these assets are not converted to cash, they would involve an outlay of cash if not prepaid.

Whether a prepaid expense is current or noncurrent depends on when its benefits will be realized. For example, if rent on an office building were prepaid for one year, then the entire prepayment is classified as a current asset. However, if rent were prepaid for a period extending beyond the coming year, a portion of the prepayment is classified as an other asset, a noncurrent asset.[4] **Google Inc.** combines prepaid expenses with "prepaid revenue share" and "other assets." Prepaid revenue share represents payments made in advance to Google Network members generally based on the number of search queries or advertisements displayed on the member's website. Other current assets include assets—such as nontrade receivables—that, because their amounts are not material, did not warrant separate disclosure.

Google lists two other current assets in its balance sheet, "Deferred income taxes" and "Income taxes receivable". These assets are discussed in Chapter 16.

When assets are expected to provide economic benefits beyond the next year, or operating cycle, they are reported as *noncurrent assets.* Typical classifications of noncurrent assets are (1) investments, (2) property, plant, and equipment, and (3) intangible assets.

INVESTMENTS.   Most companies occasionally acquire assets that are not used directly in the operations of the business. These "nonoperating" assets include investments in equity and debt securities of other corporations, land held for speculation, noncurrent receivables, and cash set aside for special purposes (such as for future plant expansion). These assets are classified as noncurrent because management does not intend to convert the assets into cash in the next year (or the operating cycle if that's longer).

Investments are nonoperating assets not used directly in operations.

PROPERTY, PLANT, AND EQUIPMENT.   Virtually all companies own assets classified as property, plant, and equipment. The common characteristics these assets share are that they are *tangible, long-lived, and used in the operations of the business.* Property, plant, and equipment, along with intangible assets, generally are referred to as operational assets. They often are the primary revenue-generating assets of the business.

Tangible, long-lived assets used in the operations of the business are classified as *property, plant, and equipment.*

Property, plant, and equipment includes land, buildings, equipment, machinery, and furniture, as well as natural resources, such as mineral mines, timber tracts, and oil wells. These various assets usually are reported as a single amount in the balance sheet, with details provided in a note. They are reported at original cost less accumulated depreciation (or depletion for natural resources) to date. Quite often, a company will present only the net amount of property, plant, and equipment in the balance sheet and provide details in a disclosure note. Land often is listed as a separate item in this classification because it has an unlimited useful life and thus is not depreciated.

---

[4]Companies often include prepayments for benefits extending beyond one year as current assets when the amounts are not material.

Intangible assets generally represent exclusive rights that a company can use to generate future revenues.

INTANGIBLE ASSETS. Some assets used in the operations of a business have no physical substance. These are appropriately called intangible assets. Generally, these represent the ownership of an exclusive right to something such as a product, a process, or a name. This right can be a valuable resource in generating future revenues. Patents, copyrights, and franchises are examples. They are reported in the balance sheet net of accumulated amortization. Some companies include intangible assets as part of property, plant, and equipment, while others report them either in a separate intangible asset classification or as other noncurrent assets.

Quite often, much of the value of intangibles is not reported in the balance sheet. For example, it would not be unusual for the historical cost of a patent to be significantly lower than its market value. As we discuss in Chapter 10, for internally developed intangibles, the costs that are included as part of historical cost are limited. Specifically, none of the research and development costs incurred in developing the intangible are included in cost.

OTHER ASSETS. Balance sheets often include a catch-all classification of noncurrent assets called other assets. This classification includes long-term prepaid expenses, called *deferred charges,* and any noncurrent asset not falling in one of the other classifications. For instance, if a company's noncurrent investments are not material in amount, they might be reported in the other asset classification rather than in a separate investments category.

Graphic 3–7 reproduces the noncurrent asset section of **Google Inc.**'s 2006 and 2007 balance sheets. For Google, noncurrent assets include noncurrent prepaid revenue share, expenses and other, deferred income taxes, noncurrent marketable securities, property and equipment, intangible assets, and the intangible asset goodwill.

GRAPHIC 3–7

Noncurrent Assets— Google Inc.

Real World Financials

Google

	December 31	
	2006	**2007**
(In thousands)		
Assets		
Prepaid revenue share, expenses and other assets, noncurrent	114,455	168,530
Deferred income taxes, net, noncurrent	—	33,219
Nonmarketable equity securities	1,031,850	1,059,694
Property and equipment, net	2,395,239	4,039,261
Intangible assets, net	346,841	446,596
Goodwill	1,545,119	2,299,368

We've seen how assets are grouped into current and noncurrent categories and that noncurrent assets always are subclassified further. Let's now turn our attention to liabilities. These, too, are separated into current and noncurrent (long-term) categories.

Liabilities

● LO4

Liabilities represent obligations to other entities. The information value of reporting these amounts is enhanced by classifying them as current liabilities and long-term liabilities. Graphic 3–8 shows the liability section of Google Inc.'s 2006 and 2007 balance sheets.

Current liabilities are expected to be satisfied within one year or the operating cycle, whichever is longer.

CURRENT LIABILITIES. Current liabilities are those obligations that are expected to be satisfied through the use of current assets or the creation of other current liabilities. So, this classification includes all liabilities that are expected to be satisfied within one year or the operating cycle, whichever is longer. An exception is a liability that management intends to refinance on a long-term basis. For example, if management intends to refinance a six-month note payable by substituting a two-year note payable and has the ability to do so, then the liability would not be classified as current even though it's due within the coming year. This exception is discussed in more detail in Chapter 13.

The most common current liabilities are accounts payable, notes payable (short-term borrowings), unearned revenues, accrued liabilities, and the currently maturing portion of long-term debt. Accounts payable are obligations to suppliers of merchandise or of services purchased

(In millions)	December 31 2006	December 31 2007
Liabilities		
Current liabilities		
Accounts payable	$ 211,169	$ 282,106
Accrued compensation and benefits	351,671	588,390
Accrued expense and other current liabilities	266,247	465,032
Accrued revenue share	370,364	522,001
Deferred revenue	105,136	178,073
Total current liabilities	1,304,587	2,035,602
Deferred revenue, long-term	20,006	30,249
Deferred income taxes, net	40,421	—
Income taxes payable, long-term	—	478,372
Other long-term liabilities	68,497	101,904

on open account, with payment usually due in 30 to 60 days. Notes payable are written promises to pay cash at some future date (I.O.U.s). Unlike accounts payable, notes usually require the payment of explicit interest in addition to the original obligation amount. Notes maturing in the next year or operating cycle, whichever is longer, will be classified as current liabilities. Unearned revenues, sometimes called deferred revenues as in Google's balance sheet, represent cash received from a customer for goods or services to be provided in a future period.

Accrued liabilities represent obligations created when expenses have been incurred but will not be paid until a subsequent reporting period. Examples are accrued salaries payable, accrued interest payable, and accrued taxes payable. **Google Inc.** reported accrued liabilities at the end of 2007 in four categories: (1) accrued compensation and benefits, (2) accrued expenses and other current liabilities, (3) accrued revenue share, and (4) taxes payable.

Long-term notes, loans, mortgages, and bonds payable usually are reclassified and reported as current liabilities as they become payable within the next year (or operating cycle if that's longer).[5] Likewise, when long-term debt is payable in installments, the installment payable currently is reported as a current liability. For example, a $1,000,000 note payable requiring $100,000 in principal payments to be made in each of the next 10 years is classified as a $100,000 current liability—current maturities of long-term debt—and a $900,000 long-term liability.

Chapter 13 provides a more detailed analysis of current liabilities.

LONG-TERM LIABILITIES. Long-term liabilities are obligations that will *not* be satisfied in the next year or operating cycle, whichever is longer. They do not require the use of current assets or the creation of current liabilities for payment. Examples are long-term notes, bonds, pension obligations, and lease obligations.

But simply classifying a liability as long-term doesn't provide complete information to external users. For instance, long-term could mean anything from 2 to 20, 30, or 40 years. Payment terms, interest rates, and other details needed to assess the impact of these obligations on future cash flows and long-term solvency are reported in a disclosure note.

At the end of its 2007 fiscal year, **Google Inc.** reported long-term deferred revenue, deferred income taxes, income taxes payable, and other long-term liabilities. A disclosure note indicated that other long-term liabilities included deferred rental obligations and royalty payments related to licensing agreements. Long-term liabilities are discussed in subsequent chapters.

Shareholders' Equity

Recall from our discussions in Chapters 1 and 2 that owners' equity is simply a residual amount derived by subtracting liabilities from assets. For that reason, it's also sometimes called net assets. Also recall that owners of a corporation are its shareholders, so owners' equity for a corporation is referred to as shareholders' equity or stockholders' equity. Shareholders' equity for a corporation arises primarily from two sources: (1) amounts *invested* by shareholders in the corporation, and (2) amounts *earned* by the corporation (on behalf

Current liabilities usually include *accounts* and *notes payable, unearned revenues, accrued liabilities,* and the *current maturities of long-term debt.*

Current liabilities include the *current maturities of long-term debt.*

Noncurrent, or long-term liabilities, usually are those payable beyond the current year.

Shareholders' equity is composed of *paid-in capital* (invested capital) and *retained earnings* (earned capital).

---

[5]Payment can be with current assets or the creation of other current liabilities.

of its shareholders). These are reported as (1) paid-in capital and (2) retained earnings. Retained earnings represents the accumulated net income earned since the inception of the corporation and not (yet) paid to shareholders as dividends.

Graphic 3–9 presents the shareholders' equity section of **Google Inc.**'s 2006 and 2007 balance sheets.

GRAPHIC 3–9

Shareholders' Equity—Google Inc.

Real World Financials

Google

(In thousands, except par value per share)	December 31 2006	December 31 2007
Stockholders' equity:		
Class A and Class B common stock, $0.001 par value Per share: 9,000,000 shares authorized; 293,027 (Class A 201,268, Class B 91,759) and par value of $293 (Class A $201, Class B $92) and 308,997 (Class A 277,670, Class B 81,327) and par value of $309 (Class A $228, Class B $81) shares issued and outstanding	309	313
Additional paid-in capital	11,882,906	13,241,221
Accumulated other comprehensive income	23,311	113,373
Retained earnings	5,133,314	9,334,772
Total stockholders' equity	17,039,840	22,689,679

From the inception of the corporation through December 31, 2007, Google has accumulated net income, less dividends, of $9,334,772 thousand, which is reported as *retained earnings.* The company's *paid-in capital* is represented by common stock and additional paid-in capital which collectively represent cash invested by shareholders in exchange for ownership interests. Information about the number of shares the company has authorized and how many shares have been issued also must be disclosed.

In addition to paid-in capital and retained earnings, shareholders' equity may include a few other equity components. For example, Google lists accumulated other comprehensive income. Accumulated other comprehensive income is discussed in Chapters 4, 12, and 18. Other equity components are addressed in later chapters, Chapter 18 in particular. We also discuss the concept of par value in Chapter 18.

CONCEPT REVIEW EXERCISE

BALANCE SHEET CLASSIFICATION

The following is a post-closing trial balance for the Sepia Paint Corporation at December 31, 2009, the end of the company's fiscal year:

Account Title	Debits	Credits
Cash	80,000	
Accounts receivable	200,000	
Allowance for uncollectible accounts		20,000
Inventories	300,000	
Prepaid expenses	30,000	
Note receivable (due in one month)	60,000	
Investments	50,000	
Land	120,000	
Buildings	550,000	
Machinery	500,000	
Accumulated depreciation—buildings and machinery		450,000
Patent (net of amortization)	50,000	
Accounts payable		170,000
Salaries payable		40,000
Interest payable		10,000
Note payable		100,000
Bonds payable (due in 10 years)		500,000
Common stock, no par		400,000
Retained earnings		250,000
Totals	1,940,000	1,940,000

The $50,000 balance in the investment account consists of marketable equity securities of other corporations. The company's intention is to hold the securities for at least three years. The $100,000 note payable is an installment loan. $10,000 of the principal, plus interest, is due on each July 1 for the next 10 years. At the end of the year, 100,000 shares of common stock were issued and outstanding. The company has 500,000 shares of common stock authorized.

Required:
Prepare a classified balance sheet for the Sepia Paint Corporation at December 31, 2009.

SOLUTION

SEPIA PAINT CORPORATION
Balance Sheet
At December 31, 2009

Assets

Current assets:		
Cash		$ 80,000
Accounts receivable	$ 200,000	
Less: Allowance for uncollectible amounts	(20,000)	180,000
Note receivable		60,000
Inventories		300,000
Prepaid expenses		30,000
Total current assets		650,000
Investments		50,000
Property, plant, and equipment:		
Land	120,000	
Buildings	550,000	
Machinery	500,000	
	1,170,000	
Less: Accumulated depreciation	(450,000)	
Net property, plant, and equipment		720,000
Intangibles:		
Patent		50,000
Total assets		$1,470,000

Liabilities and Shareholders' Equity

Current liabilities:		
Accounts payable		$ 170,000
Salaries payable		40,000
Interest payable		10,000
Current maturities of long-term debt		10,000
Total current liabilities		230,000
Long-term liabilities:		
Note payable	$ 90,000	
Bonds payable	500,000	
Total long-term liabilities		590,000
Shareholders' equity:		
Common stock, no par, 500,000 shares authorized, 100,000 shares issued and outstanding	400,000	
Retained earnings	250,000	
Total shareholders' equity		650,000
Total liabilities and shareholders' equity		$1,470,000

The usefulness of the balance sheet, as well as the other financial statements, is significantly enhanced by financial statement disclosures. We now turn our attention to these disclosures.

FINANCIAL DISCLOSURES

Financial statements are included in the annual report a company mails to its shareholders. They are, though, only part of the information provided. Critical to understanding the financial statements and to evaluating a firm's performance and financial health are additional disclosures included in the annual report.

Financial statement disclosures are provided (1) by including additional information, often parenthetically, on the face of the statement following a financial statement item and (2) in disclosure notes that often include supporting schedules. Common examples of disclosures included on the face of the balance sheet are the allowance for uncollectible accounts and information about common stock. Disclosure notes, discussed and illustrated in the next section, are the most common means of providing these additional disclosures. The specific format of disclosure is not important, only that the information is, in fact, disclosed.

> The full-disclosure principle requires that financial statements provide all material, relevant information concerning the reporting entity.

Disclosure Notes

Disclosure notes typically span several pages and either explain or elaborate upon the data presented in the financial statements themselves, or provide information not directly related to any specific item in the statements. Throughout this text you will encounter examples of items that usually are disclosed this way. For instance, the fair values of financial instruments and "off-balance-sheet" risk associated with financial instruments are disclosed in notes. Information providing details of many financial statement items is provided using disclosure notes. Some examples include:

- Pension plans
- Leases
- Long-term debt
- Investments
- Income taxes
- Property, plant and equipment
- Employee benefit plans

Disclosure notes must include certain specific notes such as a summary of significant accounting policies, descriptions of subsequent events, and related third-party transactions, but many notes are fashioned to suit the disclosure needs of the particular reporting enterprise. Actually, any explanation that contributes to investors' and creditors' understanding of the results of operations, financial position, or cash flows of the company should be included. Let's take a look at just a few disclosure notes.

> The *summary of significant accounting policies* conveys valuable information about the company's choices from among various alternative accounting methods.

Summary of Significant Accounting Policies

There are many areas where management chooses from among equally acceptable alternative accounting methods. For example, management chooses whether to use accelerated or straight-line depreciation, whether to use FIFO, LIFO, or average cost to measure inventories, and whether the completed contract or percentage-of-completion method best reflects the performance of construction operations. It also defines which securities it considers to be cash equivalents and its policies regarding the timing of recognizing revenues. Typically, the first disclosure note consists of a summary of significant accounting policies that discloses the choices the company makes.[6] Graphic 3–10 shows you a portion of a typical summary note from a recent annual report of the **Starbucks Corporation.**

---

[6]"Disclosure of Accounting Policies," *Accounting Principles Board Opinion No. 22* (New York: AICPA, 1972).

GRAPHIC 3–10   Summary of Significant Accounting Policies—Starbucks Corporation

Note 1: Summary of Accounting Policies (in part)

Principles of Consolidation
The consolidated financial statements reflect the financial position and operating results of Starbucks, which includes wholly owned subsidiaries and investees controlled by the Company.

Cash Equivalents
The Company considers all highly liquid instruments with a maturity of three months or less at the time of purchase to be cash equivalents.

Inventories
Inventories are stated at the lower of cost (primarily moving average cost) or market. The Company records inventory reserves for obsolete and slow-moving items and for estimated shrinkage between physical inventory counts.

Property, Plant, and Equipment
Property, plant, and equipment are carried at cost less accumulated depreciation. Depreciation of property,

plant, and equipment which includes assets under capital leases, is provided on the straight-line method over estimated useful lives, generally ranging from two to seven years for equipment and 30 to 40 years for buildings. Leasehold improvements are amortized over the shorter of their estimated useful lives or the related lease life, generally 10 years.

Revenue Recognition
Company-operated retail store revenues are recognized when payment is tendered at the point of sale. Revenues from the Company's store value cards, such as the Starbucks Card, are recognized when tendered for payment, or upon redemption. Outstanding customer balances are included in Deferred revenue on the consolidated balance sheets.

Real World Financials

Studying this note is an essential step in analyzing financial statements. Obviously, knowing which methods were used to derive certain accounting numbers is critical to assessing the adequacy of those amounts.

Subsequent Events

When an event that has a material effect on the company's financial position occurs after the fiscal year-end but before the financial statements actually are issued, the event is disclosed in a subsequent event disclosure note. Examples include the issuance of debt or equity securities, a business combination or the sale of a business, the sale of assets, an event that sheds light on the outcome of a loss contingency, or any other event having a material effect on operations. Graphic 3–11 illustrates the required disclosure by showing a note that **Wal-Mart Stores, Inc.** included in its January 31, 2007, financial statements, announcing both an increase in the company's annual dividend and the purchase of a 35% interest in a company that operates hypermarkets in China.

We cover subsequent events in more depth in Chapter 13.

A subsequent event is a significant development that takes place after the company's fiscal year-end but before the financial statements are issued.

GRAPHIC 3–11

Subsequent Event— Wal-Mart Stores, Inc.

Real World Financials

14 Subsequent Events (in part)

On March 8, 2007, the Company's Board of Directors approved an increase in the Company's annual dividend to $0.88 per share. The annual dividend will be paid in four quarterly installments on April 2, 2007, June 4, 2007, September 4, 2007, and January 2, 2008 to holders of record on March 16, May 18, August 17 and December 14, 2007, respectively.

In February 2007, the Company announced the purchase of a 35% interest in Bounteous Company Ltd. (BCL). BCL operates 101 hypermarkets in 34 cities in China under the Trust-Mart banner. The purchase price for the 35% interest was $264 million.

Noteworthy Events and Transactions

Some transactions and events occur only occasionally, but when they do occur are potentially important to evaluating a company's financial statements. In this category are related-party transactions, errors and irregularities, and illegal acts. The more frequent of these is related-party transactions.

Sometimes a company will engage in transactions with owners, management, families of owners or management, affiliated companies, and other parties that can significantly influence or be influenced by the company. The potential problem with related-party transactions is that their economic substance may differ from their legal form. For instance, borrowing or lending money at an interest rate that differs significantly from the market interest rate is an example of a transaction that could result from a related-party involvement. As a result of the potential for misrepresentation, financial statement users are particularly interested in more details about these transactions.

When related-party transactions occur, companies must disclose the nature of the relationship, provide a description of the transactions, and report the dollar amounts of transactions and any amounts due from or to related parties.[7] Graphic 3–12 shows a disclosure note from a recent annual report of **GAP Inc.** The note describes the company's relationship with Fisher Development, Inc., a general contractor wholly owned by the brother of GAP's chairman and his immediate family.

The economic substance of *related-party* transactions should be disclosed, including dollar amounts involved.

GRAPHIC 3–12

Related-Party Transactions Disclosure—GAP Inc.

Real World Financials

> **Note 12. Related Party Transactions (in part)**
>
> We generally use a competitive bidding process for construction of new stores, expansions, relocations and major remodels (major store projects). In addition, we utilize a construction industry standard stipulated sum, non-exclusive agreement with our general contractors. Fisher Development, Inc. (FDI), a company that is wholly owned by the brother of Donald G. Fisher, Founder and Chairman Emeritus, and the brother's immediate family, is one of our qualified general contractors. The stipulated sum agreement sets forth the terms under which our general contractors, including FDI, may act in connection with our construction activities. We paid to FDI approximately $2 million, $21 million, and $8 million in fiscal 2006, 2005, and 2004, respectively. There were no amounts due to FDI at February 3, 2007, and at January 28, 2006 the amounts due to FDI were approximately $1 million on our Consolidated Balance Sheets. The Audit and Finance Committee of the Board reviews this relationship periodically.

More infrequent are errors, irregularities, and illegal acts; however, when they do occur, their disclosure is important. The distinction between errors and irregularities is that errors are unintentional while irregularities are *intentional* distortions of financial statements.[8] Obviously, management fraud might cause a user to approach financial analysis from an entirely different and more cautious viewpoint.

Closely related to irregularities are illegal acts such as bribes, kickbacks, illegal contributions to political candidates, and other violations of the law. Accounting for illegal practices has been influenced by the Foreign Corrupt Practices Act passed by Congress in 1977. The Act is intended to discourage illegal business practices through tighter controls and also encourage better disclosure of those practices when encountered. The nature of such disclosures should be influenced by the materiality of the impact of illegal acts on amounts disclosed in the financial statements.[9] However, the SEC in *Staff Accounting Bulletin No. 99*,[10] expressed its view that exclusive reliance on quantitative benchmarks to assess materiality in preparing financial statements is inappropriate. A number of other factors, including whether the item in question involves an unlawful transaction, should also be considered when determining materiality.

As you might expect, any disclosures of related-party transactions, irregularities, and illegal acts can be quite sensitive. Although auditors must be considerate of the privacy of the parties involved, that consideration cannot be subordinate to users' needs for full disclosure.

We've discussed only a few of the disclosure notes most frequently included in annual reports. Other common disclosures include details concerning earnings per share calculations,

Disclosure notes for some financial statement elements are required. Others are provided when required by specific situations in the interest of full disclosure.

---

[7]"Related Party Disclosures," *Statement of Financial Accounting Standards No. 57* (Stamford, Conn.: FASB, 1982).

[8]"The Auditor's Responsibility to Detect and Report Errors and Irregularities," *Statement on Auditing Standards No. 53* (New York: AICPA, 1988).

[9]"Illegal Acts by Clients," *Statement on Auditing Standards No. 54* (New York: AICPA, 1988).

[10]"Materiality," *Staff Accounting Bulletin No. 99* (Washington, D.C.: SEC, August 1999).

income taxes, property and equipment, contingencies, long-term debt, leases, pensions, stock options, changes in accounting methods, fair values of financial instruments, and exposure to market risk and credit risk. We discuss and illustrate these in later chapters in the context of related financial statement elements.

Management Discussion and Analysis

Each annual report of a public company requires a fairly lengthy discussion and analysis provided by the company's management. In this section, management provides its views on significant events, trends, and uncertainties pertaining to the company's (a) operations, (b) liquidity, and (c) capital resources. Although the management discussion and analysis (MDA) section may embody management's biased perspective, it can offer an informed insight that might not be available elsewhere. Graphic 3–13 contains part of the liquidity and capital resources portion of **The Walt Disney Company**'s MDA that followed a discussion of operations in its 2006 annual report.

● **LO6**

The management discussion and analysis provides a biased but informed perspective of a company's (a) operations, (b) liquidity, and (c) capital resources.

GRAPHIC 3–13

Management Discussion and Analysis—Walt Disney Company

Real World Financials

Management Discussion and Analysis of Financial Condition and Results of Operations
(In part: Liquidity and Capital Resources only)

Cash and cash equivalents increased by $688 million during the year ended September 30, 2006.

Capital expenditures for the Parks and Resorts segment are principally for theme park and resort expansion, new rides and attractions and recurring capital and capital improvements. The decrease in capital expenditures was primarily due to lower investment at Hong Kong Disneyland resulting from substantial completion of the park prior to its opening in September 2005, as well as lower expenditures at the domestic theme parks due to increased investment in the prior year in preparation for the Disneyland 50th anniversary celebration.

During fiscal 2006, the Company repurchased 243 million shares of Disney common stock for approximately $6.9 billion. During fiscal 2005, the Company repurchased 91 million shares of Disney common stock for $2.4 billion. During fiscal 2004, the Company repurchased 15 million shares of Disney common stock for approximately $335 million. As of September 30, 2006, the Company had authorization in place to repurchase approximately 206 million additional shares. The repurchase program does not have an expiration date.

We believe that the Company's financial condition is strong and that its cash balances, other liquid assets, operating cash flows, access to debt and equity capital markets and borrowing capacity, taken together, provide adequate resources to fund ongoing operating requirements and future capital expenditures related to the expansion of existing businesses and development of new projects.

Management's Responsibilities

Management prepares and is responsible for the financial statements and other information in the annual report. To enhance the awareness of the users of financial statements concerning the relative roles of management and the auditor, annual reports of public companies include a management's responsibilities section that asserts the responsibility of management for the information contained in the annual report as well as an assessment of the company's internal control procedures.

Graphic 3–14 contains the statement of responsibility disclosure for **Cisco Systems, Inc.** included with the company's financial statements for the year ended July 31, 2007. Recall from our discussion of financial reporting reform in Chapter 1, that the *Sarbanes-Oxley Act of 2002* requires corporate executives to personally certify the financial statements. Submission of false statements carries a penalty of up to 20 years in jail. The graphic also contains Management's Report on Internal Control Over Financial Reporting. John Chambers, Cisco's president and chief executive officer, and Dennis Powell, the company's senior vice president and chief financial officer, signed the required certifications as well as these statements of responsibility.

GRAPHIC 3–14

Management's
Responsibilities—Cisco
Systems, Inc.

Real World Financials

The *management's*
responsibilities
section avows the
responsibility of
management for the
company's *financial*
statements and internal
control system.

Statement of Management's Responsibility

Cisco's management has always assumed full accountability for maintaining compliance with our established financial accounting policies and for reporting our results with objectivity and the highest degree of integrity. It is critical for investors and other users of the Consolidated Financial Statements to have confidence that the financial information that we provide is timely, complete, relevant, and accurate. Management is responsible for the fair presentation of Cisco's Consolidated Financial Statements, prepared in accordance with generally accepted accounting principles (GAAP), and has full responsibility for their integrity and accuracy.

Management, with oversight by Cisco's Board of Directors, has established and maintains a strong ethical climate so that our affairs are conducted to the highest standards of personal and corporate conduct. Management also has established an effective system of internal controls. Cisco's policies and practices reflect corporate governance initiatives that are compliant with the listing requirements of NASDAQ and the corporate governance requirements of the Sarbanes-Oxley Act of 2002.

We are committed to enhancing shareholder value and fully understand and embrace our fiduciary oversight responsibilities. We are dedicated to ensuring that our high standards of financial accounting and reporting, as well as our underlying system of internal controls, are maintained. Our culture demands integrity and we have the highest confidence in our processes, our internal controls and our people, who are objective in their responsibilities and who operate under the highest level of ethical standards.

Management's Report on Internal Control Over Financial Reporting

Management is responsible for establishing and maintaining adequate internal control over financial reporting for Cisco. Internal control over financial reporting is a process designed to provide reasonable assurance regarding the reliability of financial reporting and the preparation of financial statements for external purposes in accordance with generally accepted accounting principles. Internal control over financial reporting includes those policies and procedures that: (i) pertain to the maintenance of records that in reasonable detail accurately and fairly reflect the transactions and dispositions of the assets of the company; (ii) provide reasonable assurance that transactions are recorded as necessary to permit preparation of financial statements in accordance with generally accepted accounting principles, and that receipts and expenditures of the company are being made only in accordance with authorizations of management and directors of the company; and (iii) provide reasonable assurance regarding prevention or timely detection of unauthorized acquisition, use, or disposition of the company's assets that could have a material effect on the financial statements.

Because of its inherent limitations, internal control over financial reporting may not prevent or detect misstatements. Also, projections of any evaluation of effectiveness to future periods are subject to the risk that controls may become inadequate because of changes in conditions, or that the degree of compliance with the policies or procedures may deteriorate.

Management (with the participation of the principal executive officer and principal financial officer) conducted an evaluation of the effectiveness of Cisco's internal control over financial reporting based on the framework in *Internal Control—Integrated Framework* issued by the Committee of Sponsoring Organizations of the Treadway Commission. Based on this evaluation, management concluded that Cisco's internal control over financial reporting was effective as of July 28, 2007. Management's assessment of the effectiveness of Cisco's internal control over financial reporting as of July 28, 2007 has been audited by PricewaterhouseCoopers LLP, an independent registered public accounting firm, as stated in their report which is included herein.

John T. Chambers   Dennis D. Powell
Chairman and Chief Executive Officer   Executive Vice President and Chief Financial Officer

Auditors' Report

● LO7

Auditors examine financial statements and the internal control procedures designed to support the content of those statements. Their role is to attest to the fairness of the financial statements based on that examination. The auditors' attest function results in an opinion stated in the auditors' report.

One step in financial analysis should be an examination of the auditors' report, which is issued by the CPAs who audit the financial statements and informs users of the audit findings.

GRAPHIC 3–15

Auditors' Report—
Microsoft Corporation

Real World Financials

Report of Independent Registered Public Accounting Firm

To the Board of Directors and Stockholders of Microsoft Corporation:

We have audited the accompanying consolidated balance sheets of Microsoft Corporation and subsidiaries (the "Company") as of June 30, 2007 and 2006, and the related consolidated statements of income, cash flows, and stockholders' equity for each of the three years in the period ended June 30, 2007. These financial statements are the responsibility of the Company's management. Our responsibility is to express an opinion on these financial statements based on our audits.

   We conducted our audits in accordance with the standards of the Public Company Accounting Oversight Board (United States). Those standards require that we plan and perform the audit to obtain reasonable assurance about whether the financial statements are free of material misstatement. An audit includes examining, on a test basis, evidence supporting the amounts and disclosures in the financial statements. An audit also includes assessing the accounting principles used and significant estimates made by management, as well as evaluating the overall financial statement presentation. We believe that our audits provide a reasonable basis for our opinion.

   In our opinion, such consolidated financial statements present fairly, in all material respects, the financial position of Microsoft Corporation and subsidiaries as of June 30, 2007 and 2006, and the results of their operations and their cash flows for each of the three years in the period ended June 30, 2007, in conformity with accounting principles generally accepted in the United States of America.

   We have also audited, in accordance with the standards of the Public Company Accounting Oversight Board (United States), the effectiveness of the Company's internal control over financial reporting as of June 30, 2007, based on the criteria established in *Internal Control—Integrated Framework* issued by the Committee of Sponsoring Organizations of the Treadway Commission and our report dated August 3, 2007, expressed an unqualified opinion on management's assessment of the effectiveness of the Company's internal control over financial reporting and an unqualified opinion on the effectiveness of the Company's internal control over financial reporting.

Deloitte & Touche LLP
Seattle, Washington
August 3, 2007

Every audit report looks similar to the one prepared by **Deloitte & Touche LLP** for the financial statements of **Microsoft Corporation,** as shown in Graphic 3–15 (above).

   The reason for the similarities is that auditors' reports must be in exact compliance with the specifications of the AICPA and the PCAOB.[11] In most cases, including the report for Microsoft, the auditors will be satisfied that the financial statements "present fairly" the financial position, results of operations, and cash flows and are "in conformity with accounting principles generally accepted in the United States of America." These situations prompt an unqualified opinion. Notice that the fourth paragraph in the report provides the auditors' opinion on the effectiveness of the company's internal control over financial reporting.

   Sometimes, circumstances cause the auditors' report to include an explanatory paragraph in addition to the standard wording, even though the report is unqualified. Most notably, these include:

* *Lack of consistency* due to a change in accounting principle such that comparability is affected even though the auditor concurs with the desirability of the change.
* *Uncertainty* as to the ultimate resolution of a contingency for which a loss is material in amount but not necessarily probable or probable but not estimable.
* *Emphasis* of a matter concerning the financial statements that does not affect the existence of an unqualified opinion but relates to a significant event such as a related-party transaction.

   Some audits result in the need to issue other than an unqualified opinion due to exceptions such as (a) nonconformity with generally accepted accounting principles, (b) inadequate

> The auditors' report provides the analyst with an independent and professional opinion about the fairness of the representations in the financial statements and about the effectiveness of internal controls.

---

[11]"Reports on Audited Financial Statements," *Statements on Auditing Standards No. 58* (New York: AICPA, 1988), as amended by "Omnibus Statement on Auditing Standards—2000," *Statements on Auditing Standards No. 93* (New York: AICPA, 2000), and "References in Auditors' Reports to the Standards of the Public Company Accounting Oversight Board," *Auditing Standard No. 1* (Washington, D.C.: PCAOB, 2004).

The auditors' report
calls attention to
problems that might
exist in the financial
statements.

disclosures, and (c) a limitation or restriction of the scope of the examination. In these situations the auditor will issue a (an):

- *Qualified opinion* This contains an exception to the standard unqualified opinion but not of sufficient seriousness to invalidate the financial statements as a whole.
- *Adverse opinion* This is necessary when the exceptions (a) and (b) above are so serious that a qualified opinion is not justified. Adverse opinions are rare because auditors usually are able to persuade management to rectify problems to avoid this undesirable report.
- *Disclaimer* An auditor will disclaim an opinion for item (c) above such that insufficient information has been gathered to express an opinion.

The auditor should
assess the firm's ability
to continue as a going
concern.

During the course of each audit, the auditor is required to evaluate the company's ability to continue as a going concern for a reasonable time. If the auditor determines there is significant doubt, an explanation of the potential problem must be included in the auditors' report.[12]

Obviously, the auditors' report is most informative when any of these deviations from the standard unqualified opinion are present. These departures from the norm should raise a red flag to a financial analyst and prompt additional search for information.

The auditors' report of **Silicon Graphics, Inc.,** exhibited in Graphic 3–16, included a fourth paragraph after the standard first three paragraphs.

GRAPHIC 3–16

Going Concern
Paragraph—Silicon
Graphics, Inc.

Real World Financials

The accompanying consolidated financial statements and financial statement schedule have been prepared assuming that the Company will continue as a going concern. As more fully described in Note 1, the Company has incurred recurring operating losses and negative cash flows, has a stockholders' deficit and has filed a voluntary petition seeking to reorganize under Chapter 11 of the United States Bankruptcy Code, all of which raise substantial doubt about its ability to continue as a going concern. Management's plans in regard to these matters are also described in Note 1. The accompanying financial statements and financial statement schedule do not include any adjustments that might result from the outcome of this uncertainty.

Compensation of Directors and Top Executives

In the early 1990s, the compensation large U.S. corporations pay their top executives became an issue of considerable public debate and controversy. Shareholders, employees, politicians, and the public in general began to question the huge pay packages received by company officials at the same time that more and more rank and file employees were being laid off as a result of company cutbacks. Contributing to the debate was the realization that the compensation gap between executives and lower level employees was much wider than in Japan and most other industrial countries. During this time, it also became apparent that discovering exactly how much compensation corporations paid their top people was nearly impossible.

Part of the problem stemmed from the fact that disclosures of these amounts were meager; but a large part of the problem was that a substantial portion of executive pay often is in the form of stock options. Executive stock options give their holders the right to buy stock at a specified price, usually equal to the market price when the options are granted. When stock prices rise, executives can exercise their options and realize a profit. In some cases, options have made executive compensation seem extremely high. Stock options are discussed in depth in Chapter 19.

To help shareholders and others sort out the content of executive pay packages and better understand the commitments of the company in this regard, SEC requirements provide for more disclosures on compensation to directors and executives, and in particular, concerning stock options. The proxy statement that must be sent each year to all shareholders, usually in the same mailing with the annual report, invites shareholders to the meeting to elect board members and to vote on issues before the shareholders or to vote using an enclosed proxy card. The proxy statement also includes compensation and stock option information

The *proxy statement*
contains disclosures
on compensation
to directors and
executives.

---

[12]"The Auditor's Consideration of an Entity's Ability to Continue as a Going Concern," *Statement on Auditing Standards No. 59* (New York: AICPA, 1988).

Summary Compensation Table (in part)

Name and Position	Year	Salary	Bonus(1)	Stock Awards(2)	All Other Compensation	Total (3)
Steven A. Balmer Chief Executive Officer	2007	$620,000	$650,000	N/A	$9,821	$1,279,821
Christopher P. Liddell Senior Vice President Chief Financial Officer	2007	520,833	420,000	$1,726,575	2,065,854	4,733,262
Kevin R. Johnson Co-President, Platforms And Services Division	2007	600,000	600,000	4,684,671	1,141,855	7,026,526
Jeffrey S. Raikes President, Microsoft Business Division	2007	600,000	600,000	4,974,405	8,162	6,182,567
Brian Kevin Turner Chief Operating Officer	2007	595,000	715,000	6,870,236	270,514	8,450,750

(1) The amounts disclosed in the Bonus column were awarded under Microsoft's executive bonus program.
(2) The amounts shown in the Stock Awards column represent the approximate amount we recognized for financial statement reporting purposes in fiscal year 2007 for the fair value of equity awards granted to the named executive officers in fiscal year 2007 and prior years . . .
(3) Includes:
- matching Company contributions under our 401 (k) plan,
- the value of cash and benefits and imputed income received under our broad-based benefits program,
- payments under our options transfer program, and
- other perquisites including home relocation assistance.

GRAPHIC 3–17

Summary Compensation Table— Microsoft Corporation

Real World Financials

for directors and top executives. Graphic 3–17 (above) shows a portion of **Microsoft Corporation**'s 2007 summary compensation table included in a recent proxy statement.

RISK ANALYSIS

Using Financial Statement Information

PART C

● LO8

The overriding objective of financial reporting is providing information that investors and creditors can use to make decisions. Nevertheless, it's sometimes easy to lose sight of that objective while dealing with the intricacies that specific concepts and procedures can involve. In this part of the chapter we provide an overview of financial statement analysis and then demonstrate the use of ratios, a popular financial statement analysis technique, to analyze risk.

Investors, creditors, and others use information that companies provide in corporate financial reports to make decisions. Although the financial reports focus primarily on the past performance and the present financial condition of the reporting company, information users are most interested in the outlook for the future. Trying to gain a glimpse of the future from past and present data entails using various tools and techniques to formulate predictions. This is the goal of financial statement analysis.

Financial statements are not presented in isolation. Every financial statement issued is accompanied by the corresponding financial statement of the preceding year, and often the previous two years. These are called comparative financial statements. They enable investors, creditors, and other users to compare year-to-year financial position, results of operations, and cash flows. These comparative data help an analyst detect and predict trends. Because operations often expand and contract in a cyclical fashion, analysis of any one year's data may not provide an accurate picture of a company.

Some analysts enhance their comparison by expressing each item as a percentage of that same item in the financial statements of another year (base amount) in order to more easily

Comparative financial statements allow financial statement users to compare year-to-year financial position, results of operations, and cash flows.

see year-to-year changes. This is referred to as horizontal analysis. Similarly, vertical analysis involves expressing each item in the financial statements as a percentage of an appropriate corresponding total, or base amount, but within the same year. For example, cash, inventory, and other assets can be restated as a percentage of total assets; net income and each expense can be restated as a percentage of revenues.

> **No accounting numbers are meaningful in and of themselves.**

Regardless of the specific technique used, the essential point is that accounting numbers are virtually meaningless in isolation. Their value derives from comparison with other numbers. The most common way of comparing accounting numbers to evaluate the performance and risk of a firm is ratio analysis.

We use ratios every day. Batting averages indicate how well our favorite baseball players are performing. We evaluate basketball players by field goal percentage and rebounds per game. Speedometers measure the speed of our cars in terms of miles per hour. We compare grocery costs on the basis of price per pound or ounce. In each of these cases, the ratio is more meaningful than a single number by itself. Do 45 hits indicate satisfactory performance? It depends on the number of at-bats. Is $2 a good price for cheese? It depends on how many ounces the $2 buys. Ratios make these measurements meaningful.

> **Evaluating information in ratio form allows analysts to control for size differences over time and among firms.**

Likewise, we can use ratios to help evaluate a firm's performance and financial position. Is net income of $4 million a cause for shareholders to celebrate? Probably not if shareholders' equity is $10 billion. But if shareholders equity is $10 million, that's a 40% return on equity! Although ratios provide more meaningful information than absolute numbers alone, the ratios are most useful when analyzed relative to some standard of comparison. That standard of comparison may be previous performance of the same company, the performance of a competitor company, or an industry average for the particular ratio.

Accountants should be conversant with ratio analysis for at least three reasons. First, when preparing financial statements, accountants should be familiar with the ways users will use the information provided to make better decisions concerning what and how to report. Second, when accountants participate in company decisions concerning operating and financing alternatives, they may find ratio analysis helpful in evaluating available choices. Third, during the planning stages of an audit, independent auditors often use ratio analysis to identify potential audit problems and determine the specific audit procedures that should be performed.

We introduce ratios related to risk analysis in this chapter and ratios related to profitability analysis in Chapter 5. You will also employ ratios in Decision Makers' Perspective sections of many of the chapters in this text. Analysis cases that benefit from ratio analysis are included in many of these chapters as well.

Investors and creditors use financial information to assess the future risk and return of their investments in business enterprises. The balance sheet provides information useful to this assessment. A key element of risk analysis is investigating a company's ability to pay its obligations when they come due. This type of risk often is referred to as default risk. Another aspect of risk is operational risk which relates more to how adept a company is at withstanding various events and circumstances that might impair its ability to earn profits. Obviously, these two types of risk are not completely independent of one another. Inability to earn profits certainly increases a company's chances of defaulting on its obligations. Conversely, regardless of a company's long-run prospects for generating profits, if it can't meet its obligations, the company's operations are at risk.

Assessing risk necessarily involves consideration of a variety of economywide risk factors such as inflation, interest rates, and the general business climate. Industrywide influences including competition, labor conditions, and technological forces also affect a company's risk profile. Still other risk factors are specific to the company itself. Financial ratios often are used in risk analysis to investigate a company's liquidity and long-term solvency. As we discuss some of the more common ratios in the following paragraphs, keep in mind the inherent relationship between risk and return and thus between our risk analysis in this chapter and our profitability analysis in Chapter 5.

Liquidity Ratios

● LO9

Liquidity refers to the readiness of assets to be converted to cash. By comparing a company's liquid assets with its short-term obligations, we can obtain a general idea of the firm's ability to pay its short-term debts as they come due. Usually, current assets are thought of as the most liquid of a company's assets. Obviously, though, some are more liquid than others, so it's important also to evaluate the specific makeup of current assets. Two common measures of liquidity are (1) the current ratio and (2) the acid-test ratio (or quick ratio) calculated as follows:

$$\text{Current ratio} = \frac{\text{Current assets}}{\text{Current liabilities}}$$

$$\text{Acid-test ratio (or quick ratio)} = \frac{\text{Quick assets}}{\text{Current liabilities}}$$

CURRENT RATIO.   Implicit in the definition of a current liability is the relationship between current assets and current liabilities. The difference between current assets and current liabilities is called working capital. By comparing a company's obligations that will shortly become due with the company's cash and other assets that, by definition, are expected to shortly be converted to cash, the ratio offers some indication as to ability to pay those debts. Although used in a variety of decisions, it is particularly useful to those considering whether to extend short-term credit. The current ratio is computed by dividing current assets by current liabilities. A current ratio of 2 indicates that the company has twice as many current assets available as current liabilities.

Working capital, **the difference between current assets and current liabilities, is a popular measure of a company's ability to satisfy its short-term obligations.**

Google Inc.'s working capital (in thousands) at the end of its 2007 fiscal year is $15,253,536 consisting of current assets of $17,289,138 (Graphic 3–4 on page 116) minus current liabilities of $2,035,602 (Graphic 3–8 on page 119). The current ratio can be computed as follows:

$$\text{Current ratio} = \frac{\$17,289,138}{\$2,035,602} = 8.49$$

Care should be taken, however, in assessing liquidity based solely on working capital. Liabilities usually are paid with cash, not other components of working capital. A company could have difficulty paying its liabilities even with a current ratio significantly greater than 1.0. For example, if a significant portion of current assets consisted of inventories, and inventories usually are not converted to cash for several months, there could be a problem in paying accounts payable due in 30 days. On the other hand, a current ratio of less than 1.0 doesn't necessarily mean the company will have difficulty meeting its current obligations. A line of credit, for instance, which the company can use to borrow funds, provides financial flexibility. That also must be considered in assessing liquidity.

Working capital may not present an accurate or complete picture of a company's liquidity.

ETHICAL DILEMMA

The Raintree Cosmetic Company has several loans outstanding with a local bank. The debt agreements all contain a covenant stipulating that Raintree must maintain a current ratio of at least .9. Jackson Phillips, company controller, estimates that the 2009 year-end current assets and current liabilities will be $2,100,000 and $2,400,000, respectively. These estimates provide a current ratio of only .875. Violation of the debt agreement will increase Raintree's borrowing costs as the loans are renegotiated at higher rates.

Jackson proposes to the company president that Raintree purchase inventory of $600,000 on credit before year-end. This will cause both current assets and current liabilities to increase by the same amount, but the current ratio will increase to .9. The extra $600,000 in inventory will be used over the later part of 2010. However, the purchase will cause warehousing costs and financing costs to increase.

Jackson is concerned about the ethics of his proposal. What do you think?

ACID-TEST RATIO (OR QUICK RATIO).   Some analysts like to modify the current ratio to consider only current assets that are readily available to pay current liabilities. One such variation in common use is the acid-test ratio. This ratio excludes inventories and prepaid items from current assets before dividing by current liabilities. The numerator, then, consists of cash, short-term investments, and accounts receivable, the "quick assets." By eliminating

The *acid-test ratio* provides a more stringent indication of a company's ability to pay its current obligations.

current assets less readily convertible into cash, the acid-test ratio provides a more rigorous indication of liquidity than does the current ratio.

Google

Google Inc.'s quick assets at the end of its 2007 fiscal year (in thousands) total $16,381,134 ($6,081,593 + 8,137,020 + 2,162,521). The acid-test ratio can be computed as follows:

$$\text{Acid-test ratio} = \frac{\$16,381,134}{\$2,035,602} = 8.05$$

Are these liquidity ratios adequate? They certainly appear to be, but it's generally difficult to say without some point of comparison. As indicated previously, common standards for such comparisons are industry averages for similar ratios or ratios of the same company in prior years. Industry averages for the above two ratios are as follows:

Industry Average
Current ratio   =   6.22
Acid-test ratio   =   5.82

Google's ratios are significantly higher than the industry average. A close look at the contents of the numerator for both ratios reveals a large balance in marketable securities. Google has been a very profitable company during its brief history and a portion of the cash generated by these profits has been invested in securities that provide a rate of return.

What if the company's ratios were lower than the industry average? Would that indicate a liquidity problem? Not necessarily, but it would raise a red flag that calls for caution in analyzing other areas. Remember that each ratio is but one piece of the entire puzzle. For instance, profitability is perhaps the best indication of liquidity in the long run. We discuss ratios that measure profitability in Chapter 5.

Liquidity ratios should be assessed in the context of both profitability and efficiency of managing assets.

Also, management may be very efficient in managing current assets so that, for example, receivables are collected faster than normal or inventory is sold faster than normal, making those assets more liquid than they otherwise would be. Higher turnover ratios, relative to that of a competitor or the industry, generally indicate a more liquid position for a given level of the current ratio. We discuss these turnover ratios in Chapter 5.

Financing Ratios

● **LO9**

Investors and creditors, particularly long-term creditors, are vitally interested in a company's long-term solvency and stability. Financing ratios provide some indication of the riskiness of a company with regard to its ability to pay its long-term debts. Two common financing ratios are (1) the debt to equity ratio and (2) the times interest earned ratio. These ratios are calculated as follows:

$$\text{Debt to equity ratio} = \frac{\text{Total liabilities}}{\text{Shareholder's equity}}$$

$$\text{Times interest earned ratio} = \frac{\text{Net income} + \text{Interest expense} + \text{Taxes}}{\text{Interest expense}}$$

The debt to equity ratio indicates the extent of reliance on creditors, rather than owners, in providing resources.

DEBT TO EQUITY RATIO.   The debt to equity ratio compares resources provided by creditors with resources provided by owners. It is calculated by dividing total liabilities (current and noncurrent) by total shareholders' equity (including retained earnings).[13]

The ratio provides a measure of creditors' protection in the event of insolvency. Other things being equal, the higher the ratio, the higher the risk. The higher the ratio, the greater the creditor claims on assets, so the higher the likelihood an individual creditor would not be paid in full if the company is unable to meet its obligations. Relatedly, a high ratio indicates not only more fixed interest obligations, but probably a higher *rate* of interest as well because lenders tend to charge higher rates as the level of debt increases.

Google

Google Inc.'s liabilities at the end of its 2007 fiscal year (in thousands) total $2,646,127 (current liabilities, $2,035,602 + deferred revenue, $30,249 + income taxes payable, $478,372 + other long-term liabilities, $101,904—Graphic 3–8 on page 119), and shareholders' equity

---

[13]A commonly used variation of the debt to equity ratio is found by dividing total liabilities by *total assets* (or total equities), rather than by shareholders' equity only. Of course, in this configuration the ratio measures precisely the same attribute of the firm's capital structure but can be interpreted as the percentage of a company's total assets provided by funds from creditors, rather than by owners.

totals $22,689,679. (Graphic 3–9 on page 120). The debt to equity ratio can be computed as follows:

$$\text{Debt to equity ratio} = \frac{\$2,646,127}{\$22,689,679} = .117$$

As with all ratios, the debt to equity ratio is more meaningful if compared to some standard such as an industry or a competitor. For example, the debt to equity ratio for **Yahoo! Inc.,** a major competitor, is .28, significantly higher than Google's ratio, indicating that Yahoo has more debt in its capital structure than does Google. Does this mean that Yahoo's default risk is more than that of Google? Other things equal—yes. Is that good? Not necessarily. As discussed in the next section, it may be that debt is being underutilized by Google. More debt might increase the potential for return to shareholders, but the price would be higher risk. This is a fundamental tradeoff faced by virtually all firms when trying to settle on the optimal capital structure. It should be noted that the ratio for both companies is quite low, relative to, for example, the average liabilities to equity ratio of .78 for the S&P 500 companies. Both Google and Yahoo are primarily financed with equity capital, rather than with borrowed funds.

Relationship between risk and profitability.   The proportion of debt in the capital structure also is of interest to shareholders. After all, shareholders receive no return on their investments until after all creditor claims are paid. Therefore, the higher the debt to equity ratio, the higher the risk to shareholders. On the other hand, by earning a return on borrowed funds that exceeds the cost of borrowing the funds, a company can provide its shareholders with a total return higher than it could achieve by employing equity funds alone. This is referred to as favorable financial leverage.

> The debt to equity ratio indicates the extent of trading on the equity or *financial leverage.*

For illustration, consider a newly formed corporation attempting to determine the appropriate mix of debt and equity. The initial capitalization goal is $50 million. The capitalization mix alternatives have been narrowed to two: (1) $10 million in debt and $40 million in equity and (2) $30 million in debt and $20 million in equity.

Also assume that regardless of the capitalization mix chosen, the corporation will be able to generate a 16% annual return, *before payment of interest and income taxes,* on the $50 million in assets acquired. In other words, income before interest and taxes will be $8 million (16% × $50 million). If the interest rate on debt is 8% and the income tax rate is 40%, comparative net income for the first year of operations for the two capitalization alternatives can be calculated as follows:

	Alternative 1	Alternative 2
Income before interest and taxes	$8,000,000	$8,000,000
Less: Interest expense	(800,000)[a]	(2,400,000)[b]
Income before taxes	$7,200,000	$5,600,000
Less: Income tax expense (40%)	(2,880,000)	(2,240,000)
Net income	$4,320,000	$3,360,000

[a]8% × $10,000,000
[b]8% × $30,000,000

Choose Alternative 1? Probably not. Although alternative 1 provides a higher net income, the return on the shareholders' equity (net income divided by shareholders' equity) is higher for alternative 2. Here's why:

	Alternative 1	Alternative 2
Return on shareholders' equity[14] =	$\dfrac{\$4,320,000}{\$40,000,000}$	$\dfrac{\$3,360,000}{\$20,000,000}$
=	10.8%	16.8%

> Favorable financial leverage means earning a return on borrowed funds that exceeds the cost of borrowing the funds.

---

[14]If return is calculated on *average* shareholders' equity, we're technically assuming that all income is paid to shareholders in cash dividends, so that beginning, ending, and average shareholders' equity are the same. If we assume *no* dividends are paid, rates of return would be:

	Alternative 1	Alternative 2
Return on shareholders' equity =	$\dfrac{\$4,320,000}{(\$44,320,000 + 40,000,000)/2}$	$\dfrac{\$3,360,000}{(\$20,000,000 + 23,360,000)/2}$
=	10.25%	15.50%

In any case our conclusions are the same.

Alternative 2 generated a higher return for each dollar invested by shareholders. This is because the company leveraged its $20 million equity investment with additional debt. Because the cost of the additional debt (8%) is less than the return on assets invested (16%), the return to shareholders is higher. This is the essence of favorable financial leverage.

Be aware, though, leverage is not always favorable; the cost of borrowing the funds might exceed the returns they provide. If the return on assets invested turned out to be less than expected, the additional debt could result in a lower return on equity for alternative 2. If, for example, the return on assets invested (before interest and taxes) had been 6%, rather than 16%, alternative 1 would have provided the better return on equity:

	Alternative 1	Alternative 2
Income before interest and taxes	$3,000,000	$3,000,000
Less: Interest expense	(800,000)[a]	(2,400,000)[b]
Income before taxes	$2,200,000	$ 600,000
Less: Income tax expense (40%)	(880,000)	(240,000)
Net income	$1,320,000	$ 360,000

[a]8% × $10,000,000
[b]8% × $30,000,000

$$\text{Return on shareholders' equity}^{15} = \frac{\$1,320,000}{\$40,000,000} \quad \frac{\$360,000}{\$20,000,000}$$

$$= \quad 3.3\% \quad\quad 1.8\%$$

So, shareholders typically are faced with a tradeoff between the risk that high debt denotes and the potential for a higher return from having the higher debt. In any event, the debt to equity ratio offers a basis for making the choice.

TIMES INTEREST EARNED RATIO.   Another way to gauge the ability of a company to satisfy its fixed debt obligations is by comparing interest charges with the income available to pay those charges. The times interest earned ratio is designed to do this. It is calculated by dividing income before subtracting interest expense and income taxes by interest expense.

> The *times interest earned ratio* indicates the margin of safety provided to creditors.

Bondholders, noteholders, and other creditors can measure the margin of safety they are accorded by a company's earnings. If income is many times greater than interest expense, creditors' interests are more protected than if income just barely covers this expense. For this purpose, income should be the amount available to pay interest which is income before subtracting interest and income taxes, calculated by adding back to net income the interest and taxes that were deducted.

As an example, **Google, Inc.**'s 2007 financial statements report the following items:

	($ in thousands)
Net income	$4,203,720
Interest expense	1,336
Income taxes	1,470,260
Income before interest and taxes	$5,675,316

The times interest earned ratio can be computed as follows:

$$\text{Times interest earned ratio} = \frac{\$5,675,316}{\$1,336} = 4,248 \text{ times}$$

---

[15]If we assume *no* dividends are paid, rates of return would be:

	Alternative 1	Alternative 2
Return on shareholders' equity =	$\frac{\$1,320,000}{(\$41,320,000 + 40,000,000)/2}$	$\frac{\$360,000}{(\$20,000,000 + 20,360,000)/2}$
=	3.25%	1.78%

In any case our conclusions are the same.

The ratio of 15,608 times indicates a considerable margin of safety for creditors. Income could decrease many times and the company would still be able to meet its interest payment obligations.[16] Google is a highly profitable company with very little interest-bearing debt. In comparison, the average times interest earned ratio for the S&P 500 companies is approximately 14 times.

Especially when viewed alongside the debt-equity ratio, the coverage ratio seems to indicate a comfortable safety cushion for creditors. It also indicates a degree of financial mobility if the company were to decide to raise new debt funds to "trade on the equity" and attempt to increase the return to shareholders through favorable financial leverage.

FINANCIAL REPORTING CASE SOLUTION

1. **Respond to Jerry's criticism that shareholders' equity does not represent the market value of the company. What information does the balance sheet provide?** *(p. 113)*   Jerry is correct. The financial statements are supposed to help investors and creditors value a company. However, the balance sheet is not intended to portray the market value of the entity. The assets of a company minus its liabilities as shown in the balance sheet (shareholders' equity) usually will not equal the company's market value for several reasons. For example, many assets are measured at their historical costs rather than their fair values. Also, many company resources including its trained employees, its experienced management team, and its reputation are not recorded as assets at all. The balance sheet must be used in conjunction with other financial statements, disclosure notes, and other publicly available information.

   The balance sheet does, however, provide valuable information that can be used by investors and creditors to help determine market value. After all, it is the balance sheet that describes many of the resources a company has available for generating future cash flows. The balance sheet also provides important information about liquidity and long-term solvency.

2. **The usefulness of the balance sheet is enhanced by classifying assets and liabilities according to common characteristics. What are the classifications used in Electronic Arts' balance sheet and what elements do those categories include?** *(p. 114)*

Electronic Arts' balance sheet contains the following classifications:

Assets:
- *Current assets* include cash and several other assets that are reasonably expected to be converted to cash or consumed within the coming year, or within the normal operating cycle of the business if that's longer than one year.
- *Property and equipment* are the tangible long-lived assets used in the operations of the business. This category includes land, buildings, equipment, machinery, and furniture, as well as natural resources.
- *Investments in affiliates* are investments in debt and equity securities of affiliated companies.
- *Goodwill* is a unique intangible asset in that its cost can't be directly associated with any specifically identifiable right and is not separable from the company as a whole. It represents the unique value of the company as a whole over and above all identifiable tangible and intangible assets.
- *Other intangibles* are assets that represent exclusive rights to something such as a product, a process, or a name. Patents, copyrights, and franchises are examples.
- *Deferred income taxes* result from temporary differences between taxable income and accounting income.

---

[16]Of course, interest is paid with cash, not with "income." The times interest earned ratio often is calculated by using cash flow from operations before subtracting either interest payments or tax payments as the numerator and interest payments as the denominator.

- *Other assets* is a "catch-all" classification of noncurrent assets and could include long-term prepaid expenses and any noncurrent asset not included in one of the other categories.

Liabilities:

Current liabilities are those obligations that are expected to be satisfied through the use of current assets or the creation of other current liabilities. Usually, this means liabilities that are expected to be paid within one year or the operating cycle, whichever is longer. *Other liabilities* could include various long-term liabilities such as pension and lease obligations.

Shareholders' equity:

- *Common stock* and *paid-in capital* collectively equal the amounts invested by shareholders in the corporation.
- *Retained earnings* represents the accumulated net income earned since inception of the corporation and not yet paid out to shareholders as dividends.
- *Accumulated other comprehensive income* is the cumulative amount of other comprehensive income items. This topic is addressed in subsequent chapters. ●

THE BOTTOM LINE

● **LO1** The balance sheet is a position statement that presents an organized array of assets, liabilities, and shareholders' equity at a particular point in time. The statement does not portray the market value of the entity. However, the information in the statement can be useful in assessing market value, as well as in providing important information about liquidity and long-term solvency. (p. 113)

● **LO2** Current assets include cash and other assets that are reasonably expected to be converted to cash or consumed during one year, or within the normal operating cycle of the business if the operating cycle is longer than one year. All other assets are classified as various types of noncurrent assets. Current liabilities are those obligations that are expected to be satisfied through the use of current assets or the creation of other current liabilities. All other liabilities are classified as long term. (p. 115)

● **LO3** In addition to cash and cash equivalents, current assets include short-term investments, accounts receivable, inventories, and prepaid expenses. Other asset classifications include investments; property, plant, and equipment; intangible assets; and other assets. (p. 115)

● **LO4** Current liabilities include notes and accounts payable, unearned revenues, accrued liabilities, and the current maturities of long-term debt. Long-term liabilities include long-term notes, loans, mortgages, bonds, pension and lease obligations, as well as deferred income taxes. (p. 118)

● **LO5** Financial disclosures are used to convey additional information about the account balances in the basic financial statements as well as to provide supplemental information. This information is disclosed, often parenthetically, in the basic financial statements or in disclosure notes that often include supporting schedules. (p. 122)

● **LO6** Annual financial statements of public companies will include management's discussion and analysis of key aspects of the company's business. The purpose of this disclosure is to provide external parties with management's insight into certain transactions, events, and circumstances that affect the enterprise, including their financial impact. (p. 125)

● **LO7** The purpose of an audit is to provide a professional, independent opinion as to whether or not the financial statements are prepared in conformity with generally accepted accounting principles. The audit report contains four paragraphs; the first two deal with the scope of the audit and the third paragraph states the auditors' opinion. The fourth paragraph provides the auditors' opinion on the effectiveness of the company's internal control. (p. 126)

● **LO8** Financial analysts use various techniques to transform financial information into forms more useful for analysis. Horizontal analysis and vertical analysis provide a useful way of analyzing year-to-year changes. Ratio analysis allows analysts to control for size differences over time and among firms while investigating important relationships among financial variables. (p. 129)

● **LO9** The balance sheet provides information that can be useful in assessing risk. A key element of risk analysis is investigating a company's ability to pay its obligations when they come due. Liquidity ratios and financing ratios provide information about a company's ability to pay its obligations. (p. 130) ●

REPORTING SEGMENT INFORMATION

Financial analysis of diversified companies is especially difficult. Consider, for example, a company that operates in several distinct business segments including computer peripherals, home health care systems, textiles, and consumer food products. The results of these distinctly different activities will be aggregated into a single set of financial statements, making difficult an informed projection of future performance. It may well be that the five-year outlook differs greatly among the areas of the economy represented by the different segments. To make matters worse for an analyst, the integrated financial statements do not reveal the relative investments in each of the business segments nor the success the company has had within each area. Given the fact that so many companies these days have chosen to balance their operating risks through diversification, aggregated financial statements pose a widespread problem for analysts, lending and credit officers, and other financial forecasters.

> Many companies operate in several business segments as a strategy to achieve growth and to reduce operating risk through diversification.

Reporting by Operating Segment

To address the problem, the accounting profession requires companies engaged in more than one significant line of business to provide supplemental information concerning individual operating segments. The supplemental disaggregated data do not include complete financial statements for each reportable segment, only certain specified items.

> Segment reporting facilitates the financial statement analysis of diversified companies.

WHAT IS A REPORTABLE OPERATING SEGMENT? *SFAS No. 131* employs a *management approach* in determining which segments of a company are reportable. This approach is based on the way that management organizes the segments within the enterprise for making operating decisions and assessing performance. The segments are, therefore, evident from the structure of the enterprise's internal organization.

More formally, the following characteristics define an operating segment:[17]

An operating segment is a component of an enterprise:

- That engages in business activities from which it may earn revenues and incur expenses (including revenues and expenses relating to transactions with other components of the same enterprise).
- Whose operating results are regularly reviewed by the enterprise's chief operating decision maker to make decisions about resources to be allocated to the segment and assess its performance.
- For which discrete financial information is available.

The FASB hopes that this approach provides insights into the risk and opportunities management sees in the various areas of company operations. Also, reporting information based on the enterprise's internal organization should reduce the incremental cost to companies of providing the data. In addition, there are quantitative thresholds for the definition of an operating segment to limit the number of reportable segments. Only segments of certain size (10% or more of total company revenues, assets, or net income) must be disclosed. However, a company must account for at least 75% of consolidated revenue through segment disclosures.

WHAT AMOUNTS ARE REPORTED BY AN OPERATING SEGMENT? For areas determined to be reportable operating segments, the following disclosures are required:

a. General information about the operating segment.
b. Information about reported segment profit or loss, including certain revenues and expenses included in reported segment profit or loss, segment assets, and the basis of measurement.

---

[17]"Disclosures about Segments of an Enterprise and Related Information," *Statement of Financial Accounting Standards No. 131* (Norwalk, Conn.: FASB, 1997), par. 10.

c. Reconciliations of the totals of segment revenues, reported profit or loss, assets, and other significant items to corresponding enterprise amounts.

d. Interim period information.[18]

Graphic 3A–1 shows the business segment information reported by **3M Co.** in its 2006 annual report.

GRAPHIC 3A–1

Business Segment Information Disclosure—3M Co.

Real World Financials

Business Segment Information
($ in millions)

		Net Sales	Operating Income	Assets	Depr. and Amort.	Capital Expendit.
Industrial and Transportation	2006	$ 6,754	$1,343	$ 5,487	$ 286	$ 283
	2005	6,144	1,211	5,125	274	257
	2004	5,711	1,050	3,626	283	249
Health Care	2006	4,011	1,845	2,477	162	159
	2005	3,760	1,114	2,166	131	138
	2004	3,596	973	2,289	128	117
Display and Graphics	2006	3,765	1,062	3,015	230	326
	2005	3,511	1,162	2,713	186	232
	2004	3,346	1,115	2,552	174	249
Consumer and Office	2006	3,238	579	1,614	91	105
	2005	3,033	561	1,520	107	97
	2004	2,901	514	1,471	116	117
Safety, Security and Protection Services	2006	2,621	575	1,901	112	149
	2005	2,292	537	1,351	113	99
	2004	2,125	465	1,317	101	99
Electro and Communications	2006	2,483	438	1,819	167	112
	2005	2,333	447	1,799	145	102
	2004	2,224	316	1,857	163	95
Corporate and Unallocated	2006	51	(146)	4,981	31	34
	2005	94	(178)	5,867	30	18
	2004	108	(107)	7,611	34	11
Total Company	2006	$22,923	$5,696	$21,294	$1,079	$1,168
	2005	21,167	4,854	20,541	986	943
	2004	20,011	4,326	20,723	999	937

INTERNATIONAL FINANCIAL REPORTING STANDARDS

Segment Reporting. U.S. GAAP, *SFAS No. 131*, requires companies to report information about reported segment profit or loss, including certain revenues and expenses included in reported segment profit or loss, segment assets, and the basis of measurement. The international standard on segment reporting, *IFRS No. 8*, requires that companies also disclose total *liabilities* of its reportable segments.

---

[18]Ibid., par. 25.

REPORTING BY GEOGRAPHIC AREA   In today's global economy it is sometimes difficult to distinguish domestic and foreign companies. Most large U.S. firms conduct significant operations in other countries in addition to having substantial export sales from this country. Differing political and economic environments from country to country means risks and associated rewards sometimes vary greatly among the various operations of a single company. For instance, manufacturing facilities in a South American country embroiled in political unrest pose different risks from having a plant in Vermont, or even Canada. Without disaggregated financial information, these differences cause problems for analysts.

SFAS 131 requires an enterprise to report certain geographic information unless it is impracticable to do so. This information includes:

a. Revenues from external customers (1) attributed to the enterprise's country of domicile and (2) attributed to all foreign countries in total from which the enterprise derives revenues, and
b. Long-lived assets other than financial instruments, long-term customer relationships of a financial institution, mortgage and other servicing rights, deferred policy acquisition costs, and deferred tax assets (1) located in the enterprise's country of domicile and (2) located in all foreign countries in total in which the enterprise holds assets.[19]

3M reported its geographic area information separately in a table reproduced in Graphic 3A–2. Notice that both the business segment (Graphic 3A–1) and geographic information disclosures include a reconciliation to company totals. For example, in both graphics, year 2006 net sales of both the segments and the geographic areas are reconciled to the company's total net sales of $22,923 ($ in millions).

GRAPHIC 3A–2   Geographic Area Information Disclosure—3M Company   **Real World Financials**

Geographic Area Information
($ in millions)

		United States	Asia Pacific	Europe Middle East and Africa	Latin America and Canada	Other Unallocated	Total Company
Net sales to customers	2006	$8,853	$6,251	$5,726	$2,080	$ 13	$22,923
	2005	8,267	5,744	5,219	1,881	56	21,167
	2004	7,878	5,168	5,183	1,731	51	20,011
Operating income	2006	$1,908	$2,097	$1,092	$ 629	$(30)	$ 5,696
	2005	1,200	2,085	1,057	512	0	4,854
	2004	998	1,860	988	473	7	4,326
Property, plant and equipment—net	2006	$3,382	$ 959	$1,162	$ 404	$ —	$ 5,907
	2005	3,291	865	1,076	361	—	5,593
	2004	3,290	810	1,288	323	—	5,711

INFORMATION ABOUT MAJOR CUSTOMERS   Some companies in the defense industry derive substantial portions of their revenues from contracts with the Defense Department. When cutbacks occur in national defense or in specific defense systems, the impact on a company's operations can be considerable. Obviously, financial analysts are extremely interested in information concerning the extent to which a company's prosperity depends on one or more major customers such as in the situation described here. For this reason, if 10% or more of the revenue of an enterprise is derived from transactions with a single customer, the enterprise must disclose that fact, the total amount of revenue from each such customer, and the identity of the operating segment or segments earning the revenue. The identity of the major customer or customers need not be disclosed, although companies routinely provide that information. In its 2006 annual report, 3M did not report any major

Revenues from major customers must be disclosed.

---
[19]Ibid., par. 38.

GRAPHIC 3A–3

Major Customer Disclosure—Procter & Gamble Company

Real World Financials

Note 12. Segment Information (in part)
The Company's largest customer, Wal-Mart Stores, Inc. and its affiliates, accounted for 15% of consolidated net sales in both 2007 and 2006, and 16% of consolidated net sales in 2005.

customer information. As an example of this type of disclosure, **Procter & Gamble Company**'s business segment disclosure included information on its largest customer, **Wal-Mart,** as shown in Graphic 3A–3 (above). ●

QUESTIONS FOR REVIEW OF KEY TOPICS

Q 3–1 Describe the purpose of the balance sheet.

Q 3–2 Explain why the balance sheet does not portray the market value of the entity.

Q 3–3 Define current assets and list the typical asset categories included in this classification.

Q 3–4 Define current liabilities and list the typical liability categories included in this classification.

Q 3–5 Describe what is meant by an operating cycle for a typical manufacturing company.

Q 3–6 Explain the difference(s) between investments in equity securities classified as current assets versus those classified as noncurrent assets.

Q 3–7 Describe the common characteristics of assets classified as property, plant, and equipment and identify some assets included in this classification.

Q 3–8 Distinguish between property, plant, and equipment and intangible assets.

Q 3–9 Explain how each of the following liabilities would be classified in the balance sheet:
  • A note payable of $100,000 due in five years.
  • A note payable of $100,000 payable in annual installments of $20,000 each, with the first installment due next year.

Q 3–10 Define the terms *paid-in-capital* and *retained earnings.*

Q 3–11 Disclosure notes are an integral part of the information provided in financial statements. In what ways are the notes critical to understanding the financial statements and to evaluating the firm's performance and financial health?

Q 3–12 A summary of the company's significant accounting policies is a required disclosure. Why is this disclosure important to external financial statement users?

Q 3–13 Define a subsequent event.

Q 3–14 Every annual report of a public company includes an extensive discussion and analysis provided by the company's management. Specifically, which aspects of the company must this discussion address? Isn't management's perspective too biased to be of use to investors and creditors?

Q 3–15 The auditors' report provides the analyst with an independent and professional opinion about the fairness of the representations in the financial statements. What are the four main types of opinion an auditor might issue? Describe each.

Q 3–16 What is a proxy statement? What information does it provide?

Q 3–17 Define the terms *working capital, current ratio,* and *acid-test ratio* (or *quick ratio*).

Q 3–18 Show the calculation of the following financing ratios: (1) the debt to equity ratio, and (2) the times interest earned ratio.

Q 3–19 (Based on Appendix 3) Segment reporting facilitates the financial statement analysis of diversified companies. What determines whether an operating segment is a reportable segment for this purpose?

Q 3–20 (Based on Appendix 3) For segment reporting purposes, what amounts are reported by each operating segment?

BRIEF EXERCISES

BE 3–1

Current versus noncurrent classification

● LO2

Indicate whether each of the following assets and liabilities should be classified as current or noncurrent: (a) accounts receivable; (b) prepaid rent for the next six months; (c) note receivable due in two years; (d) note payable due in 90 days; (e) note payable due in five years; and (f) patent.

BE 3–2
Balance sheet
classification

● LO3 LO4

The trial balance for K and J Nursery, Inc. listed the following account balances at December, 31, 2009, the end of its fiscal year: cash, $16,000; accounts receivable, $11,000; inventories, $25,000; equipment (net), $80,000; accounts payable, $14,000; wages payable, $9,000; interest payable, $1,000; note payable (due in 18 months), $30,000; common stock, $50,000. Calculate total current assets and total current liabilities that would appear in the company's year-end balance sheet.

BE 3–3
Balance sheet
classification

● LO3 LO4

Refer to the situation described in BE 3–2. Determine the year-end balance in retained earnings for K and J Nursery, Inc.

BE 3–4
Balance sheet
preparation

● LO2 through LO4

Refer to the situation described in BE 3–2. Prepare a classified balance sheet for K and J Nursery, Inc. The equipment originally cost $140,000.

BE 3–5
Balance sheet
preparation

● LO2 through LO4

The following is a December 31, 2009, post-closing trial balance for Culver City Lighting, Inc. Prepare a classified balance sheet for the company.

Account Title	Debits	Credits
Cash	55,000	
Accounts receivable	39,000	
Inventories	45,000	
Prepaid insurance	15,000	
Equipment	100,000	
Accumulated depreciation—equipment		34,000
Patent, net	40,000	
Accounts payable		12,000
Interest payable		2,000
Note payable (due in 10, equal annual installments)		100,000
Common stock		70,000
Retained earnings		76,000
Totals	294,000	294,000

BE 3–6
Balance sheet
classification

● LO2 through LO4

You have been asked to review the December 31, 2009, balance sheet for Champion Cleaning. After completing your review, you list the following three items for discussion with your superior:
1. An investment of $30,000 is included in current assets. Management has indicated that it has no intention of liquidating the investment in 2010.
2. A $100,000 note payable is listed as a long-term liability, but you have determined that the note is due in 10, equal annual installments with the first installment due on March 31, 2010.
3. Unearned revenue of $60,000 is included as a current liability even though only two-thirds will be earned in 2010.
Determine the appropriate classification of each of these items.

BE 3–7
Balance sheet
preparation;
missing elements

● LO2 through LO4

The following information is taken from the balance sheet of Raineer Plumbing: cash and cash equivalents, $40,000; accounts receivable, $120,000; inventories, ?; total current assets, $235,000; property, plant, and equipment (net), ?; total assets, $400,000; accounts payable, $32,000; note payable (due in two years), $50,000; common stock; $100,000; and retained earnings, ?. Determine the missing amounts.

BE 3–8
Financial
disclosures

● LO5

For each of the following note disclosures, indicate whether the disclosure would likely appear in (A) the summary of significant accounts policies or (B) a separate note: (1) depreciation method; (2) contingency information; (3) significant issuance of common stock after the fiscal year-end; (4) cash equivalent designation; (5) long-term debt information; and (6) inventory costing method.

BE 3–9
Calculating ratios

● LO9

Refer to the trial balance information in BE 3–5. Calculate the (a) current ratio, (b) acid-test ratio, and (c) debt to equity ratio.

BE 3–10
Effect of decisions
on ratios

● LO9

At the end of 2009, Barker Corporation's preliminary trial balance indicated a current ratio of 1.2. Management is contemplating paying some of its accounts payable balance before the end of the fiscal year. Explain the effect this transaction would have on the current ratio. Would your answer be the same if the preliminary trial balance indicated a current ratio of .8?

BE 3–11
Calculating
ratios; solving for
unknowns

● LO9

The current asset section of Stibbe Pharmaceutical Company's balance sheet included cash of $20,000 and accounts receivable of $40,000. The only other current asset is inventories. The company's current ratio is 2.0 and its acid-test ratio is 1.5. Determine the ending balance in inventories and total current liabilities.

EXERCISES available with McGraw–Hill's Homework Manager www.mhhe.com/spiceland5e

An alternate exercise and problem set is available on the text website: www.mhhe.com/spiceland5e

E 3–1
Balance sheet;
missing elements

● LO3 LO4 LO8

The following December 31, 2009, fiscal year-end account balance information is available for the Stonebridge Corporation:

Cash and cash equivalents	$ 5,000
Accounts receivable (net)	20,000
Inventories	60,000
Property, plant, and equipment (net)	120,000
Accounts payable	44,000
Wages payable	15,000
Paid-in-capital	100,000

The only asset not listed is short-term investments. The only liabilities not listed are a $30,000 note payable due in two years and related accrued interest of $1,000 due in four months. The current ratio at year-end is 1.5:1.

Required:
Determine the following at December 31, 2009:
1. Total current assets
2. Short-term investments
3. Retained earnings

E 3–2
Balance sheet
classification

● LO3 LO4

The following are the typical classifications used in a balance sheet:

a. Current assets   f. Current liabilities
b. Investments and funds   g. Long-term liabilities
c. Property, plant, and equipment   h. Paid-in-capital
d. Intangible assets   i. Retained earnings
e. Other assets

Required:
For each of the following balance sheet items, use the letters above to indicate the appropriate classification category. If the item is a contra account, place a minus sign before the chosen letter.

1. _____ Equipment   10. _____ Inventories
2. _____ Accounts payable   11. _____ Patent
3. _____ Allowance for uncollectible accounts   12. _____ Land, in use
4. _____ Land, held for investment   13. _____ Accrued liabilities
5. _____ Note payable, due in 5 years   14. _____ Prepaid rent
6. _____ Unearned rent revenue   15. _____ Common stock
7. _____ Note payable, due in 6 months   16. _____ Building, in use
8. _____ Income less dividends, accumulated   17. _____ Cash
9. _____ Investment in XYZ Corp., long-term   18. _____ Taxes payable

E 3–3
Balance sheet
classification

● LO3 LO4

The following are the typical classifications used in a balance sheet:

a. Current assets   f. Current liabilities
b. Investments and funds   g. Long-term liabilities
c. Property, plant, and equipment   h. Paid-in-capital
d. Intangible assets   i. Retained earnings
e. Other assets

Required:

For each of the following 2009 balance sheet items, use the letters above to indicate the appropriate classification category. If the item is a contra account, place a minus sign before the chosen letter.

1. _____ Accrued interest payable

2. _____ Franchise

3. _____ Accumulated depreciation

4. _____ Prepaid insurance, for 2011

5. _____ Bonds payable, due in 10 years

6. _____ Current maturities of long-term debt

7. _____ Note payable, due in three months

8. _____ Long-term receivables

9. _____ Bond sinking fund, will be used to retire bonds in 10 years

10. _____ Supplies

11. _____ Machinery

12. _____ Land, in use

13. _____ Unearned revenue

14. _____ Copyrights

15. _____ Preferred stock

16. _____ Land, held for speculation

17. _____ Cash equivalents

18. _____ Wages payable

E 3–4
Balance sheet preparation

● LO2 through LO4

The following is a December 31, 2009, post-closing trial balance for the Jackson Corporation.

Account Title	Debits	Credits
Cash	40,000	
Accounts receivable	34,000	
Inventories	75,000	
Prepaid rent	16,000	
Marketable securities (short term)	10,000	
Machinery	145,000	
Accumulated depreciation—machinery		11,000
Patent (net of amortization)	83,000	
Accounts payable		8,000
Wages payable		4,000
Taxes payable		32,000
Bonds payable (due in 10 years)		200,000
Common stock		100,000
Retained earnings		48,000
Totals	403,000	403,000

Required:

Prepare a classified balance sheet for Jackson Corporation at December 31, 2009.

E 3–5
Balance sheet preparation

● LO2 through LO4

The following is a December 31, 2009, post-closing trial balance for the Valley Pump Corporation.

Account Title	Debits	Credits
Cash	25,000	
Accounts receivable	56,000	
Inventories	81,000	
Interest payable		10,000
Marketable securities	44,000	
Land	120,000	
Buildings	300,000	
Accumulated depreciation—buildings		100,000
Equipment	75,000	
Accumulated depreciation—equipment		25,000
Copyright (net of amortization)	12,000	
Prepaid expenses	32,000	
Accounts payable		65,000
Unearned revenues		20,000
Notes payable		250,000
Allowance for uncollectible accounts		5,000
Common stock		200,000
Retained earnings		70,000
Totals	745,000	745,000

Additional information:

1. The $120,000 balance in the land account consists of $100,000 for the cost of land where the plant and office buildings are located. The remaining $20,000 represents the cost of land being held for speculation.

2. The $44,000 in the marketable securities account represents an investment in the common stock of another corporation. Valley intends to sell one-half of the stock within the next year.

3. The notes payable account consists of a $100,000 note due in six months and a $150,000 note due in three annual installments of $50,000 each, with the first payment due in August of 2010.

Required:
Prepare a classified balance sheet for the Valley Pump Corporation at December 31, 2009.

E 3–6
Balance sheet; current versus noncurrent classification

● LO2 through LO4

Presented below is a partial trial balance for the Kansas Instruments Corporation at December 31, 2009.

Account Title	Debits	Credits
Cash	20,000	
Accounts receivable	130,000	
Raw materials	24,000	
Note receivable	100,000	
Interest receivable	3,000	
Interest payable		5,000
Marketable securities	32,000	
Land	50,000	
Buildings	1,300,000	
Accumulated depreciation—buildings		620,000
Work in process	42,000	
Finished goods	89,000	
Equipment	300,000	
Accumulated depreciation—equipment		130,000
Patent (net of amortization)	120,000	
Prepaid rent (for the next two years)	60,000	
Unearned revenue		36,000
Accounts payable		180,000
Note payable		400,000
Cash restricted for payment of note payable	80,000	
Allowance for uncollectible accounts		13,000
Sales revenue		800,000
Cost of goods sold	450,000	
Rent expense	28,000	

Additional information:
1. The note receivable, along with any accrued interest, is due on November 22, 2010.
2. The note payable is due in 2013. Interest is payable annually.
3. The marketable securities consist of treasury bills, all of which mature in the next year.
4. Unearned revenue will be earned equally over the next two years.

Required:
Determine the company's working capital (current assets minus current liabilities) at December 31, 2009.

E 3–7
Balance sheet preparation; errors

● LO2 through LO4

The following balance sheet for the Los Gatos Corporation was prepared by a recently hired accountant. In reviewing the statement you notice several errors.

LOS GATOS CORPORATION
Balance Sheet
At December 31, 2009

Assets

Cash	$ 40,000
Accounts receivable	80,000
Inventories	55,000
Machinery (net)	120,000
Franchise (net)	30,000
Total assets	$325,000

Liabilities and Shareholders' Equity

Accounts payable	$ 50,000
Allowance for uncollectible accounts	5,000
Note payable	55,000
Bonds payable	110,000
Shareholders' equity	105,000
Total liabilities and shareholders' equity	$325,000

Additional information:
1. Cash includes a $20,000 bond sinking fund to be used for repayment of the bonds payable in 2013.
2. The cost of the machinery is $190,000.
3. Accounts receivable includes a $20,000 note receivable from a customer due in 2012.
4. The note payable includes accrued interest of $5,000. Principal and interest are both due on February 1, 2010.
5. The company began operations in 2004. Income less dividends since inception of the company totals $35,000.
6. 50,000 shares of no par common stock were issued in 2004. 100,000 shares are authorized.

Required:
Prepare a corrected, classified balance sheet.

E 3–8
Balance sheet;
current versus
noncurrent
classification

● **LO2 through LO4**

Cone Corporation is in the process of preparing its December 31, 2009, balance sheet. There are some questions as to the proper classification of the following items:
a. $50,000 in cash set aside in a savings account to pay bonds payable. The bonds mature in 2013.
b. Prepaid rent of $24,000, covering the period January 1, 2010, through December 31, 2011.
c. Note payable of $200,000. The note is payable in annual installments of $20,000 each, with the first installment payable on March 1, 2010.
d. Accrued interest payable of $12,000 related to the note payable.
e. Investment in marketable securities of other corporations, $80,000. Cone intends to sell one-half of the securities in 2010.

Required:
Prepare a partial classified balance sheet to show how each of the above items should be reported.

E 3–9
Balance sheet
preparation; cash
versus accrual
accounting;
Chapters 2 and 3

● **LO2 through LO4**

The following is the balance sheet of Korver Supply Company at December 31, 2008.

KORVER SUPPLY COMPANY
Balance Sheet
At December 31, 2008

Assets

Cash	$120,000
Accounts receivable	300,000
Inventories	200,000
Furniture and fixtures, net	150,000
Total assets	$770,000

Liabilities and Shareholders' Equity

Accounts payable (for merchandise)	$190,000
Note payable	200,000
Interest payable	6,000
Common stock	100,000
Retained earnings	274,000
Total liabilities and shareholders' equity	$770,000

Transactions during 2009 were as follows:

1. Sales to customers on account	$800,000
2. Cash collected from customers	780,000
3. Purchase of merchandise on account	550,000
4. Cash payment to suppliers	560,000
5. Cost of merchandise sold	500,000
6. Cash paid for operating expenses	160,000
7. Cash paid for interest on note	12,000

The note payable is dated June 30, 2008 and is due on June 30, 2010. Interest at 6% is payable annually on June 30. Depreciation on the furniture and fixtures for the year is $20,000. The furniture and fixtures originally cost $300,000.

Required:
Prepare a classified balance sheet at December 21, 2009 (ignore income taxes).

E 3–10
Financial
disclosures

● **LO5**

The following are typical disclosures that would appear in the notes accompanying financial statements. For each of the items listed, indicate where the disclosure would likely appear—either in (A) the significant accounting policies note or (B) a separate note.

1. Inventory costing method   <u>A</u>
2. Information on related party transactions   ____
3. Composition of property, plant, and equipment   ____
4. Depreciation method   ____
5. Subsequent event information   ____
6. Basis of revenue recognition on long-term contracts   ____
7. Important merger occurring after year-end   ____
8. Composition of receivables   ____

E 3–11
Disclosure notes

● **LO5**

Hallergan Company produces car and truck batteries that it sells primarily to auto manufacturers. Dorothy Hawkins, the company's controller, is preparing the financial statements for the year ended December 31, 2009. Hawkins asks for your advice concerning the following information that has not yet been included in the statements. The statements will be issued on February 28, 2010.

1. Hallergan leases its facilities from the brother of the chief executive officer.
2. On January 8, 2010, Hallergan entered into an agreement to sell a tract of land that it had been holding as an investment. The sale, which resulted in a material gain, was completed on February 2, 2010.
3. Hallergan uses the straight-line method to determine depreciation on all of the company's depreciable assets.
4. On February 8, 2010, Hallergan completed negotiations with its bank for a $10,000,000 line of credit.
5. Hallergan uses the first-in, first-out (FIFO) method to value inventory.

Required:
For each of the above items, discuss any additional disclosures that Hawkins should include in Hallergan's financial statements.

E 3–12
Concepts;
terminology

● **LO2 through LO5**
LO7

Listed below are several terms and phrases associated with the balance sheet and financial disclosures. Pair each item from List A (by letter) with the item from List B that is most appropriately associated with it.

List A	List B
____ 1. Balance sheet	a. Will be satisfied through the use of current assets.
____ 2. Liquidity	b. Items expected to be converted to cash or consumed within one year or the operating cycle.
____ 3. Current assets	c. The statements are presented fairly in conformity with GAAP.
____ 4. Operating cycle	d. An organized array of assets, liabilities and equity.
____ 5. Current liabilities	e. Important to a user in comparing financial information across companies.
____ 6. Cash equivalent	f. Scope limitation or a departure from GAAP.
____ 7. Intangible asset	g. Recorded when an expense is incurred but not yet paid.
____ 8. Working capital	h. Relates to the amount of time before an asset is converted to cash or a liability is paid.
____ 9. Accrued liabilities	i. Occurs after the fiscal year-end but before the statements are issued.
____ 10. Summary of significant accounting policies	j. Cash to cash.
____ 11. Subsequent events	k. One-month U.S. Treasury bill.
____ 12. Unqualified opinion	l. Current assets minus current liabilities.
____ 13. Qualified opinion	m. Lacks physical substance.

E 3–13
Calculating ratios

● **LO9**

The 2009 balance sheet for Hallbrook Industries, Inc. is shown below.

HALLBROOK INDUSTRIES, INC.
Balance Sheet
December 31, 2009
($ in 000s)
Assets

Cash	$ 200
Short-term investments	150
Accounts receivable	200
Inventories	350
Property, plant, and equipment (net)	1,000
Total assets	$1,900

(continued)

(concluded)

Liabilities and Shareholders' Equity

Current liabilities	$ 400
Long-term liabilities	350
Paid-in capital	750
Retained earnings	400
Total liabilities and shareholders' equity	$1,900

The company's 2009 income statement reported the following amounts ($ in 000s):

Net sales	$4,600
Interest expense	40
Income tax expense	100
Net income	160

Required:
Determine the following ratios for 2009:
1. Current ratio
2. Acid-test ratio
3. Debt to equity ratio
4. Times interest earned ratio

E 3–14
Calculating ratios

● **LO9**

Real World Financials

Activision Inc. is a leading publisher of interactive entertainment software. A condensed income statement and balance sheet for the fiscal year ended March 31, 2007, are shown below.

Activision Inc.
Balance Sheet At March 31, 2007
($ in 000s)

Assets

Current assets:	
Cash	$ 384,409
Short-term investments	570,440
Accounts receivable, net	148,694
Inventories	91,231
Deferred income taxes	51,564
Other current assets	154,895
Total current assets	1,401,233
Noncurrent assets	392,714
Total assets	$1,793,947

Liabilities and Shareholders' Equity

Current liabilities:	
Accounts payable	$ 136,517
Accrued expenses	204,652
Total current liabilities	341,169
Long-term liabilities	41,246
Shareholders' equity	1,411,532
Total liabilities and shareholders' equity	$1,793,947

Activision Inc.
Income Statement
For the Year Ended March 31, 2007
($ in 000s)

Revenues	$1,513,012
Costs and expenses	1,439,865
Income from operations	73,147
Investment income, net*	36,678
Income before income taxes	109,825
Income tax expense	24,038
Net income	$ 85,787

*Includes $97 of interest expense.

Liquidity and financing ratios for the game software industry are as follows:

	Industry Average
Current ratio	2.04
Acid-test ratio	1.79
Debt to equity	.16
Times interest earned	15.24 times

Required:

1. Determine the following ratios for the fiscal year ended March 31, 2007:
   a. Current ratio
   b. Acid-test ratio
   c. Debt to equity ratio
   d. Times interest earned ratio
2. Using the ratios from requirement 1, assess Activision's liquidity and solvency relative to its industry.

E 3–15
Calculating ratios;
solve for unknowns

● LO9

The current asset section of the Excalibur Tire Company's balance sheet consists of cash, marketable securities, accounts receivable, and inventories. The December 31, 2009, balance sheet revealed the following:

Inventories	$ 840,000
Total assets	$2,800,000
Current ratio	2.25
Acid-test ratio	1.2
Debt to equity ratio	1.8

Required:

Determine the following 2009 balance sheet items:

1. Current assets
2. Shareholders' equity
3. Noncurrent assets
4. Long-term liabilities

E 3–16
Effect of
management
decisions on ratios

● LO9

Most decisions made by management impact the ratios analysts use to evaluate performance. Indicate (by letter) whether each of the actions listed below will immediately increase (I), decrease (D), or have no effect (N) on the ratios shown. Assume each ratio is less than 1.0 before the action is taken.

Action	Current Ratio	Acid-Test Ratio	Debt to Equity Ratio
1. Issuance of long-term bonds	_____	_____	_____
2. Issuance of short-term notes	_____	_____	_____
3. Payment of accounts payable	_____	_____	_____
4. Purchase of inventory on account	_____	_____	_____
5. Purchase of inventory for cash	_____	_____	_____
6. Purchase of equipment with a 4-year note	_____	_____	_____
7. Retirement of bonds	_____	_____	_____
8. Sale of common stock	_____	_____	_____
9. Write-off of obsolete inventory	_____	_____	_____
10. Purchase of short-term investment for cash	_____	_____	_____
11. Decision to refinance on a long-term basis some currently maturing debt	_____	_____	_____

E 3–17
Segment reporting

● Appendix

The Canton Corporation operates in four distinct business segments. The segments, along with 2009 information on revenues, assets and net income, are listed below ($ in millions):

Segment	Revenues	Assets	Net Income
Pharmaceuticals	$2,000	$1,000	$200
Plastics	3,000	1,500	270
Farm equipment	2,500	1,250	320
Electronics	500	250	40
Total company	$8,000	$4,000	$830

Required:

1. For which segments must Canton report supplementary information according to *SFAS No. 131?*
2. What amounts must be reported for the segments you identified in requirement 1?

E 3–18
Segment reporting

● Appendix

Refer to Exercise 3–17.

Required:

How might your answers differ if Canton Corporation prepares its segment disclosure according to International Accounting Standards?

CPA AND CMA REVIEW QUESTIONS

CPA Exam Questions

KAPLAN

SCHWESER

The following questions are used in the Kaplan CPA Review Course to study balance sheet presentation, financial disclosures, and liquidity ratios while preparing for the CPA examination. Determine the response that best completes the statements or questions.

● LO2   1. In Merf's April 30, 2009, balance sheet, a note receivable was reported as a noncurrent asset and the related accrued interest for eight months was reported as a current asset. Which of the following descriptions would fit Merf's receivable classification?

   a. Both principal and interest amounts are due on August 31, 2009, and August 31, 2010.
   b. Principal is due August 31, 2010, and interest is due August 31, 2009, and August 31, 2010.
   c. Principal and interest are due December 31, 2009.
   d. Both principal and interest amounts are due on December 31, 2009, and December 31, 2010.

● LO2   2. Mill Co.'s trial balance included the following account balances at December 31, 2009:

Accounts payable	$15,000
Bond payable, due 2010	22,000
Dividends payable 1/31/10	8,000
Notes payable, due 2011	20,000

   What amount should be included in the current liability section of Mill's December 31, 2009, balance sheet?

   a. $45,000
   b. $51,000
   c. $65,000
   d. $78,000

● LO5   3. Which of the following would be disclosed in the summary of significant accounting policies disclosure note?

	Composition of Plant Assets	Inventory Pricing
a.	No	Yes
b.	Yes	No
c.	Yes	Yes
d.	No	No

● LO9   4. At December 30, Vida Co. had cash of $200,000, a current ratio of 1.5:1, and a quick ratio of .5:1. On December 31, all the cash was used to reduce accounts payable. How did this cash payment affect the ratios?

	Current Ratio	Quick Ratio
a.	Increased	No effect
b.	Increased	Decreased
c.	Decreased	Increased
d.	Decreased	No effect

● LO7   5. How are management's responsibility and the auditor's report represented in the standard auditor's report?

	Management's Responsibility	Auditor's Responsibility
a.	Implicitly	Explicitly
b.	Implicitly	Implicitly
c.	Explicitly	Explicitly
d.	Explicitly	Implicitly

● LO9   6. Zenk Co. wrote off obsolete inventory of $100,000 during 2009. What was the effect of this write-off on Zenk's ratio analysis?

   a. Decrease in the current ratio but not the quick ratio.
   b. Decrease in the quick ratio but not in the current ratio.
   c. Increase in the current ratio but not in the quick ratio.
   d. Increase in the quick ratio but not in the current ratio.

CMA Exam Questions

The following questions dealing with balance sheet presentation, financial disclosures, and liquidity ratios are adapted from questions that previously appeared on Certified Management Accountant (CMA) examinations. The CMA designation sponsored by the Institute of Management Accountants (**www.imanet.org**) provides members with an objective measure of knowledge and competence in the field of management accounting. Determine the response that best completes the statements or questions.

● LO5   1. The Financial Accounting Standards Board has provided guidance on disclosures of transactions between related parties, for example, transactions between subsidiaries of a common parent. SFAS 57, *Related Party Disclosures,* requires all of the following disclosures except

   a. The nature of the relationship involved.
   b. A description of the transactions for each period an income statement is presented.
   c. The dollar amounts of transactions for each period an income statement is presented.

d. The effect on the cash flow statement for each period a cash flow statement is presented.

● LO6

2. The Management's Discussion and Analysis (MD&A) section of an annual report
   a. Includes the company president's letter.
   b. Covers three financial aspects of a firm's business: liquidity, capital resources, and results of operations.
   c. Is a technical analysis of past results and a defense of those results by management.
   d. Covers marketing and product line issues.

● LO9

3. Windham Company has current assets of $400,000 and current liabilities of $500,000. Windham Company's current ratio would be increased by
   a. The purchase of $100,000 of inventory on account.
   b. The payment of $100,000 of accounts payable.
   c. The collection of $100,000 of accounts receivable.
   d. Refinancing a $100,000 long-term loan with short-term debt.

PROBLEMS
available with McGraw–Hill's Homework Manager www.mhhe.com/spiceland5e

An alternate exercise and problem set is available on the text website: www.mhhe.com/spiceland5e

P 3–1
Balance sheet
preparation

● LO2 through LO4

Presented below is a list of balance sheet accounts presented in alphabetical order.

Accounts payable	Inventories
Accounts receivable	Land (in use)
Accumulated depreciation—buildings	Long-term investments
Accumulated depreciation—equipment	Notes payable (due in 6 months)
Allowance for uncollectible accounts	Notes receivable (due in 2 years)
Bond sinking fund	Patent
Bonds payable (due in 10 years)	Preferred stock
Buildings	Prepaid expenses
Cash	Rent payable (current)
Common stock	Retained earnings
Copyright	Short-term investments
Equipment	Taxes payable
Interest receivable (due in three months)	Wages payable

Required:
Prepare a classified balance sheet ignoring monetary amounts.

P 3–2
Balance sheet
preparation;
missing elements

● LO2 through LO4

Real World Financials

The data listed below are taken from a recent balance sheet of **Amdahl Corporation.** Some amounts, indicated by question marks, have been intentionally omitted.

	($ in 000s)
Cash and cash equivalents	$ 239,186
Short-term investments	353,700
Accounts receivable (net of allowance)	504,944
Inventories	?
Prepaid expenses (current)	83,259
Total current assets	1,594,927
Long-term receivables	110,800
Property and equipment (net)	?
Total assets	?
Notes payable and short-term debt	31,116
Accounts payable	?
Accrued liabilities	421,772
Other current liabilities	181,604
Total current liabilities	693,564
Long-term debt and deferred taxes	?
Total liabilities	956,140
Shareholders' equity	1,370,627

Required:
1. Determine the missing amounts.
2. Prepare Amdahl's classified balance sheet.

P 3–3
Balance sheet
preparation

● **LO2 through LO4**

The following is a December 31, 2009, post-closing trial balance for Almway Corporation.

Account Title	Debits	Credits
Cash	45,000	
Investments	110,000	
Accounts receivable	60,000	
Inventories	200,000	
Prepaid insurance	9,000	
Land	90,000	
Buildings	420,000	
Accumulated depreciation—buildings		100,000
Equipment	110,000	
Accumulated depreciation—equipment		60,000
Patents (net of amortization)	10,000	
Accounts payable		75,000
Notes payable		130,000
Interest payable		20,000
Bonds payable		240,000
Common stock		300,000
Retained earnings		129,000
Totals	1,054,000	1,054,000

Additional information:
1. The investment account includes an investment in common stock of another corporation of $30,000 which management intends to hold for at least three years. The balance of these investments are intended to be sold in the coming year.
2. The land account includes land which cost $25,000 that the company has not used and is currently listed for sale.
3. The cash account includes $15,000 set aside in a fund to pay bonds payable that mature in 2012 and $23,000 set aside in a three-month Treasury bill.
4. The notes payable account consists of the following:
   a. a $30,000 note due in six months.
   b. a $50,000 note due in six years.
   c. a $50,000 note due in five annual installments of $10,000 each, with the next installment due February 15, 2010.
5. The $60,000 balance in accounts receivable is net of an allowance for uncollectible accounts of $8,000.
6. The common stock account represents 100,000 shares of no par value common stock issued and outstanding. The corporation has 500,000 shares authorized.

Required:
Prepare a classified balance sheet for the Almway Corporation at December 31, 2009.

P 3–4
Balance sheet
preparation

● **LO2 through LO4**

The following is a December 31, 2009, post-closing trial balance for the Weismuller Publishing Company.

Account Title	Debits	Credits
Cash	65,000	
Accounts receivable	160,000	
Inventories	285,000	
Prepaid expenses	148,000	
Machinery and equipment	320,000	
Accumulated depreciation—equipment		110,000
Investments	140,000	
Accounts payable		60,000
Interest payable		20,000
Unearned revenue		80,000
Taxes payable		30,000
Notes payable		200,000
Allowance for uncollectible accounts		16,000
Common stock		400,000
Retained earnings		202,000
Totals	1,118,000	1,118,000

Additional information:

1. Prepaid expenses include $120,000 paid on December 31, 2009, for a two-year lease on the building that houses both the administrative offices and the manufacturing facility.

2. Investments include $30,000 in Treasury bills purchased on November 30, 2009. The bills mature on January 30, 2010. The remaining $110,000 includes investments in marketable equity securities that the company intends to sell in the next year.

3. Unearned revenue represents customer prepayments for magazine subscriptions. Subscriptions are for periods of one year or less.

4. The notes payable account consists of the following:

    a. a $40,000 note due in six months.

    b. a $100,000 note due in six years.

    c. a $60,000 note due in three annual installments of $20,000 each, with the next installment due August 31, 2010.

5. The common stock account represents 400,000 shares of no par value common stock issued and outstanding. The corporation has 800,000 shares authorized.

Required:
Prepare a classified balanced sheet for the Weismuller Publishing Company at December 31, 2009.

P 3–5
Balance sheet preparation

● LO2 through LO4

The following is a June 30, 2009, post-closing trial balance for Excell Company.

Account Title	Debits	Credits
Cash	83,000	
Short-term investments	65,000	
Accounts receivable	280,000	
Prepaid expenses	32,000	
Land	75,000	
Buildings	320,000	
Accumulated depreciation—buildings		160,000
Equipment	265,000	
Accumulated depreciation—equipment		120,000
Accounts payable		173,000
Accrued expenses		45,000
Notes payable		100,000
Mortgage payable		250,000
Common stock		100,000
Retained earnings		172,000
Totals	1,120,000	1,120,000

Additional information:

1. The short-term investments account includes $18,000 in U.S. treasury bills purchased in May. The bills mature in July.

2. The accounts receivable account consists of the following:

a. Amounts owed by customers	$225,000
b. Allowance for uncollectible accounts—trade customers	(15,000)
c. Nontrade note receivable (due in three years)	65,000
d. Interest receivable on note (due in four months)	5,000
Total	$280,000

3. The notes payable account consists of two notes of $50,000 each. One note is due on September 30, 2009, and the other is due on November 30, 2010.

4. The mortgage payable is payable in *semiannual* installments of $5,000 each plus interest. The next payment is due on October 31, 2009. Interest has been properly accrued and is included in accrued expenses.

5. Five hundred thousand shares of no par common stock are authorized, of which 200,000 shares have been issued and are outstanding.

6. The land account includes $50,000 representing the cost of the land on which the company's office building resides. The remaining $25,000 is the cost of land that the company is holding for investment purposes.

Required:
Prepare a classified balance sheet for the Excell Company at June 30, 2009.

P 3–6
Balance sheet
preparation;
disclosures

● **LO2 through LO5**

The following is a December 31, 2009, post-closing trial balance for the Vosburgh Electronics Corporation.

Account Title	Debits	Credits
Cash	67,000	
Short-term investments	182,000	
Accounts receivable	123,000	
Long-term investments	35,000	
Inventories	215,000	
Loans to employees	40,000	
Prepaid expenses (for 2010)	16,000	
Land	280,000	
Building	1,550,000	
Machinery and equipment	637,000	
Patent	152,000	
Franchise	40,000	
Note receivable	250,000	
Interest receivable	12,000	
Accumulated depreciation — building		620,000
Accumulated depreciation — equipment		210,000
Accounts payable		189,000
Dividends payable (payable on 1/16/10)		10,000
Interest payable		16,000
Taxes payable		40,000
Unearned revenue		60,000
Notes payable		300,000
Allowance for uncollectible accounts		8,000
Common stock		2,000,000
Retained earnings		146,000
Totals	3,599,000	3,599,000

Additional information:

1. The common stock represents 1 million shares of no par stock authorized, 500,000 shares issued and outstanding.

2. The loans to employees are due on June 30, 2010.

3. The note receivable is due in installments of $50,000, payable on each September 30. Interest is payable annually.

4. Short-term investments consist of marketable equity securities that the company plans to sell in 2010 and $50,000 in treasury bills purchased on December 15 of the current year that mature on February 15, 2010. Long-term investments consist of marketable equity securities that the company does not plan to sell in the next year.

5. Unearned revenue represents customer payments for extended service contracts. Eighty percent of these contracts expire in 2010, the remainder in 2011.

6. Notes payable consists of two notes, one for $100,000 due on January 15, 2011, and another for $200,000 due on June 30, 2012.

Required:

1. Prepare a classified balance sheet for Vosburgh at December 31, 2009.

2. Identify the items that would require additional disclosure, either on the face of the balance sheet or in a disclosure note.

P 3–7
Balance sheet
preparation; errors

● **LO2 through LO4**

The following balance sheet for the Hubbard Corporation was prepared by the company:

HUBBARD CORPORATION
Balance Sheet
At December 31, 2009

Assets

Buildings	$ 750,000
Land	250,000
Cash	60,000
Accounts receivable (net)	120,000
Inventories	240,000
Machinery	280,000
Patent (net)	100,000
Investment in marketable equity securities	60,000
Total assets	$1,860,000

(continued)

(concluded)

Liabilities and Shareholders' Equity

Accounts payable	$ 215,000
Accumulated depreciation	255,000
Notes payable	500,000
Appreciation of inventories	80,000
Common stock, authorized and issued 100,000 shares of no par stock	430,000
Retained earnings	380,000
Total liabilities and shareholders' equity	$1,860,000

Additional information:

1. The buildings, land, and machinery are all stated at cost except for a parcel of land that the company is holding for future sale. The land originally cost $50,000 but, due to a significant increase in market value, is listed at $120,000. The increase in the land account was credited to retained earnings.

2. Marketable equity securities consist of stocks of other corporations and are recorded at cost, $20,000 of which will be sold in the coming year. The remainder will be held indefinitely.

3. Notes payable are all long-term. However, a $100,000 note requires an installment payment of $25,000 due in the coming year.

4. Inventories are recorded at current resale value. The original cost of the inventories is $160,000.

Required:
Prepare a corrected classified balance sheet for the Hubbard Corporation at December 31, 2009.

P 3–8
Balance sheet; errors; missing amounts

● LO2 through LO4

The following incomplete balance sheet for the Sanderson Manufacturing Company was prepared by the company's controller. As accounting manager for Sanderson, you are attempting to reconstruct and revise the balance sheet.

Sanderson Manufacturing Company
Balance Sheet
At December 31, 2009
($ in 000s)

Assets

Current assets:		
Cash		$ 1,250
Accounts receivable		3,500
Allowance for uncollectible accounts		(400)
Finished goods inventory		6,000
Prepaid expenses		1,200
Total current assets		11,550
Noncurrent assets:		
Investments		3,000
Raw materials and work in process inventory		2,250
Equipment		15,000
Accumulated depreciation—equipment		(4,200)
Patent		?
Total assets		$?

Liabilities and Shareholders' Equity

Current liabilities:		
Accounts payable		$ 5,200
Note payable		4,000
Interest payable — note		100
Unearned revenue		3,000
Total current liabilities		12,300
Long-term liabilities:		
Bonds payable		5,500
Interest payable—bonds		200
Shareholders' equity:		
Common stock	$?	
Retained earnings	?	?
Total liabilities and shareholders' equity		?

Additional information ($ in 000s):

1. Certain records that included the account balances for the patent and shareholders' equity items were lost. However, the controller told you that a complete, preliminary balance sheet prepared before the records were lost showed a debt to equity ratio of 1.2. That is, total liabilities are 120% of total shareholders' equity. Retained earnings at the beginning of the year was $4,000. Net income for 2009 was $1,560 and $560 in cash dividends were declared and paid to shareholders.

2. Management intends to sell the investments in the next six months.

3. Interest on both the note and the bonds is payable annually.

4. The note payable is due in annual installments of $1,000 each.

5. Unearned revenue will be earned equally over the next two fiscal years.

6. The common stock represents 400,000 shares of no par stock authorized, 250,000 shares issued and outstanding.

Required:
Prepare a complete, corrected, classified balance sheet.

P 3–9
Balance sheet preparation

● LO2 through LO4

Presented below is the balance sheet for HHD, Inc., at December 31, 2009.

Current assets	$ 600,000	Current liabilities	$ 400,000
Investments	500,000	Long-term liabilities	1,100,000
Property, plant, and equipment	2,000,000	Shareholders' equity	1,800,000
Intangible assets	200,000		
Total assets	$3,300,000	Total liabilities and shareholders' equity	$3,300,000

The captions shown in the summarized statement above include the following:

a. Current assets: cash, $150,000; accounts receivable, $200,000; inventories, $225,000; and prepaid insurance, $25,000.

b. Investments: investments in common stock, short term, $90,000, and long term, $160,000; and bond sinking fund, $250,000.

c. Property, plant, and equipment: buildings, $1,500,000 less accumulated depreciation, $600,000; equipment, $500,000 less accumulated depreciation, $200,000; and land, $800,000.

d. Intangible assets: patent, $110,000; and copyright, $90,000.

e. Current liabilities: accounts payable, $100,000; notes payable, short term, $150,000, and long term, $90,000; and taxes payable, $60,000.

f. Long-term liabilities: bonds payable due 2014.

g. Shareholders' equity: common stock, $1,000,000; retained earnings, $800,000. Five hundred thousand shares of no par common stock are authorized, of which 200,000 shares were issued and are outstanding.

Required:
Prepare a corrected classified balance sheet for HHD, Inc., at December 31, 2009.

P 3–10
Balance sheet preparation

● LO2 through LO4

Melody Lane Music Company was started by John Ross early in 2009. Initial capital was acquired by issuing shares of common stock to various investors and by obtaining a bank loan. The company operates a retail store that sells records, tapes, and compact discs. Business was so good during the first year of operations that John is considering opening a second store on the other side of town. The funds necessary for expansion will come from a new bank loan. In order to approve the loan, the bank requires financial statements.

John asks for your help in preparing the balance sheet and presents you with the following information for the year ending December 31, 2009:

a. Cash receipts consisted of the following:

From customers	$360,000
From issue of common stock	100,000
From bank loan	100,000

b. Cash disbursements were as follows:

Purchase of inventory	$300,000
Rent	15,000
Salaries	30,000
Utilities	5,000
Insurance	3,000
Purchase of equipment and furniture	40,000

c. The bank loan was made on March 31, 2009. A note was signed requiring payment of interest and principal on March 31, 2010. The interest rate is 12%.

d. The equipment and furniture were purchased on January 3, 2009, and have an estimated useful life of 10 years with no anticipated salvage value. Depreciation per year is $4,000.

e. Inventories on hand at the end of the year cost $100,000.

f. Amounts owed at December 31, 2009, were as follows:

To suppliers of inventory	$20,000
To the utility company	1,000

g. Rent on the store building is $1,000 per month. On December 1, 2009, four months' rent was paid in advance.

h. Net income for the year was $76,000. Assume that the company is not subject to federal, state, or local income tax.

i. One hundred thousand shares of no par common stock are authorized, of which 20,000 shares were issued and are outstanding.

Required:
Prepare a balance sheet at December 31, 2009.

BROADEN YOUR **PERSPECTIVE**

Apply your critical-thinking ability to the knowledge you've gained. These cases will provide you an opportunity to develop your research, analysis, judgment, and communication skills. You also will work with other students, integrate what you've learned, apply it in real world situations, and consider its global and ethical ramifications. This practice will broaden your knowledge and further develop your decision-making abilities.

Communication Case 3–1
Current versus noncurrent classification

● LO2

A first-year accounting student is confused by a statement made in a recent class. Her instructor stated that the assets listed in the balance sheet of the **IBM Corporation** include computers that are classified as current assets as well as computers that are classified as noncurrent assets. In addition, the instructor stated that investments in marketable securities of other corporations could be classified in the balance sheet as either current or noncurrent assets.

Required:
Explain to the student the distinction between current and noncurrent assets pertaining to the IBM computers and the investments in marketable securities.

Analysis Case 3–2
Current versus noncurrent classification

● LO2

The usefulness of the balance sheet is enhanced when assets and liabilities are grouped according to common characteristics. The broad distinction made in the balance sheet is the current versus noncurrent classification of both assets and liabilities.

Required:
1. Discuss the factors that determine whether an asset or liability should be classified as current or noncurrent in a balance sheet.
2. Identify six items that under different circumstances could be classified as either current or noncurrent. Indicate the factors that would determine the correct classification.

Communication Case 3–3
Inventory or property, plant, and equipment

● LO2 LO3

The Red Hen Company produces, processes, and sells fresh eggs. The company is in the process of preparing financial statements at the end of its first year of operations and has asked for your help in determining the appropriate treatment of the cost of its egg-laying flock. The estimated life of a laying hen is approximately two years, after which they are sold to soup companies.

The controller considers the company's operating cycle to be two years and wants to present the cost of the egg-producing flock as inventory in the current asset section of the balance sheet. He feels that the hens are "goods awaiting sale." The chief financial officer does not agree with this treatment. He thinks that the cost of the flock should be classified as property, plant, and equipment because the hens are used in the production of product—the eggs.

The focus of this case is the balance sheet presentation of the cost of the egg-producing flock. Your instructor will divide the class into two to six groups depending on the size of the class. The mission of your group is to reach consensus on the appropriate presentation.

Required:
1. Each group member should deliberate the situation independently and draft a tentative argument prior to the class session for which the case is assigned.
2. In class, each group will meet for 10 to 15 minutes in different areas of the classroom. During that meeting, group members will take turns sharing their suggestions for the purpose of arriving at a single group treatment.
3. After the allotted time, a spokesperson for each group (selected during the group meetings) will share the group's solution with the class. The goal of the class is to incorporate the views of each group into a consensus approach to the situation.

**Judgment Case
3–4**
Balance sheet;
errors

● **LO2 through LO5**

You recently joined the internal auditing department of Marcus Clothing Corporation. As one of your first assign-ments, you are examining a balance sheet prepared by a staff accountant.

MARCUS CLOTHING CORPORATION
Balance Sheet
At December 31, 2009

Assets

Current assets:		
Cash		$ 137,000
Accounts receivable, net		80,000
Note receivable		53,000
Inventories		240,000
Investments		66,000
Total current assets		576,000
Other assets:		
Land	$200,000	
Equipment, net	320,000	
Prepaid expenses	27,000	
Patent	22,000	
Total other assets		569,000
Total assets		$1,145,000

Liabilities and Shareholders' Equity

Current liabilities:		
Accounts payable		$ 125,000
Salaries payable		32,000
Total current liabilities		157,000
Long-term liabilities:		
Note payable	$100,000	
Bonds payable	300,000	
Interest payable	20,000	
Total long-term liabilities		420,000
Shareholders' equity:		
Common stock	500,000	
Retained earnings	68,000	
Total shareholders' equity		568,000
Total liabilities and shareholders' equity		$1,145,000

In the course of your examination you uncover the following information pertaining to the balance sheet:
1. The company rents its facilities. The land that appears in the statement is being held for future sale.
2. The note receivable is due in 2011. The balance of $53,000 includes $3,000 of accrued interest. The next interest payment is due in July 2010.
3. The note payable is due in installments of $20,000 per year. Interest on both the notes and bonds is payable annually.
4. The company's investments consist of marketable equity securities of other corporations. Management does not intend to liquidate any investments in the coming year.

Required:
Identify and explain the deficiencies in the statement prepared by the company's accountant. Include in your answer items that require additional disclosure, either on the face of the statement or in a note.

**Judgment Case
3–5**
Financial
disclosures

● **LO5**

You recently joined the auditing staff of Best, Best, and Krug, CPAs. You have been assigned to the audit of Clearview, Inc., and have been asked by the audit senior to examine the balance sheet prepared by Clearview's accountant.

CLEARVIEW, INC.
Balance Sheet
At December 31, 2009
($ in millions)

Assets

Current assets:	
Cash	$ 10.5
Accounts receivable	112.1

(continued)

(concluded)

Inventories		220.6
Prepaid expenses		5.5
Total current assets		348.7
Investments		22.0
Property, plant, and equipment, net		486.9
Total assets		$857.6

Liabilities and Shareholders' Equity

Current liabilities:		
Accounts payable		$ 83.5
Accrued taxes and interest		25.5
Current maturities of long-term debt		20.0
Total current liabilities		129.0
Long-term liabilities:		420.0
Total liabilities		549.0
Shareholders' equity:		
Common stock	$100.0	
Retained earnings	208.6	
Total shareholders' equity		308.6
Total liabilities and shareholders' equity		$857.6

Required:
Identify the items in the statement that most likely would require further disclosure either on the face of the statement or in a note. Further identify those items that would require disclosure in the significant accounting policies note.

Real World Case 3–6
Balance sheet and significant accounting policies disclosure

● **LO3 through LO5 LO9**

Real World Financials

The balance sheet and disclosure of significant accounting policies taken from the 2006 annual report of **International Business Machines Corporation (IBM)** appear below. Use this information to answer the following questions:

1. What are the asset classifications contained in IBM's balance sheet?
2. What amounts did IBM report for the following items for 2006:
   a. Total assets
   b. Current assets
   c. Current liabilities
   d. Total shareholders' equity
   e. Retained earnings
   f. Inventories
3. What is the par value of IBM's common stock? How many shares of common stock are authorized and issued at the end of 2006?
4. Compute IBM's current ratio for 2006.
5. Identify the following items:
   a. The company's inventory valuation method.
   b. The company's depreciation method.
   c. The definition of cash equivalents.

CONSOLIDATED STATEMENT OF FINANCIAL POSITION
INTERNATIONAL BUSINESS MACHINES CORPORATION
and Subsidiary Companies
($ in millions)

	Notes	2006	2005
Assets			
Current assets:			
Cash and cash equivalents		$ 8,022	$ 12,568
Marketable securities	D	2,634	1,118
Notes and accounts receivable—trade (net of allowances of $221 in 2006 and $267 in 2005)		10,789	9,540
Short-term financing receivables (net of allowances of $307 in 2006 and $422 in 2005)	F	15,095	13,750

(continued)

(concluded)

Other accounts receivable (net of allowances of $15 in 2006 and $7 in 2005)		964	1,138
Inventories	E	2,810	2,841
Deferred taxes	P	1,806	1,765
Prepaid expenses and other current assets		2,539	2,941
Total current assets		44,660	45,661
Plant, rental machines and other property	G	36,521	34,261
Less: Accumulated depreciation	G	22,082	20,505
Plant, rental machines and other property—net	G	14,440	13,756
Long-term financing receivables	F	10,068	9,628
Prepaid pension assets	V	10,629	20,625
Goodwill	I	12,854	9,441
Intangible assets—net	I	2,202	1,663
Investments and sundry assets	H	8,381	4,974
Total Assets		$103,234	$105,748
Liabilities and Stockholders' Equity			
Current liabilities:			
Taxes	P	$ 4,670	$ 4,710
Short-term debt	K & L	8,902	7,216
Accounts payable		7,964	7,349
Compensation and benefits		4,595	3,325
Deferred income		8,587	7,319
Other accrued expenses and liabilities		5,372	5,233
Total current liabilities		40,091	35,152
Long-term debt	K & L	13,780	15,425
Retirement and nonpension postretirement benefit obligations	V	13,553	13,779
Other liabilities	M	7,304	8,294
Total Liabilities		74,728	72,650
Contingencies and Commitments	O		
Stockholders' equity:	N		
Common stock, par value $.20 per share and additional paid-in capital		31,271	28,926
Shares authorized: 4,687,500,000			
Shares issued (2006—2,008,470,383; 2005—1,981,259,104)			
Retained earnings		52,432	44,734
Treasury stock, at cost (shares: 2006—501,987,771; 2005—407,279,343)		(46,296)	(38,546)
Accumulated gains and (losses) not affecting retained earnings	N	(8,901)	(2,016)
Total Stockholders' Equity		28,506	33,098
Total Liabilities and Stockholders' Equity		$103,234	$105,748

The accompanying notes are an integral part of the financial statements.

NOTES TO CONSOLIDATED FINANCIAL STATEMENTS
INTERNATIONAL BUSINESS MACHINES CORPORATION
AND SUBSIDIARY COMPANIES

A. Significant accounting policies (in part)

Revenue
The company recognizes revenue when it is realized or realizable and earned. The company considers revenue realized or realizable and earned when it has persuasive evidence of an arrangement, delivery has occurred, the sales price is fixed or determinable and collectibility is reasonably assured. The company reduces revenue for estimated client returns, stock rotation, price protection, rebates, and other similar allowances.

Cash Equivalents
All highly liquid investments with a maturity of three months or less at date of purchase are carried at fair value and considered to be cash equivalents.

Inventories
Raw materials, work in process, and finished goods are stated at the lower of average cost or market.

Depreciation
Plant, rental machines and other property are carried at cost, and depreciated over their estimated useful lives using the straight-line method.

Judgment Case 3–7

Post fiscal year-end events

● LO5

The fiscal year-end for the Northwest Distribution Corporation is December 31. The company's 2009 financial statements were issued on March 15, 2010. The following events occurred between December 31, 2009, and March 15, 2010.

1. On January 22, 2010, the company negotiated a major merger with Blandon Industries. The merger will be completed by the middle of 2010.
2. On February 3, 2010, Northwest negotiated a $10 million long-term note with the Credit Bank of Ohio. The amount of the note is material.
3. On February 25, 2010, a flood destroyed one of the company's manufacturing plants causing $600,000 of uninsured damage.

Required:
Determine the appropriate treatment of each of these events in the 2009 financial statements of Northwest Distribution Corporation.

Research Case 3–8

Related party disclosures; locate and extract relevant information and authoritative support for a financial reporting issue; Enron Corporation

● LO5

Real World Financials

Enron Corporation was a darling in the energy-provider arena and in January of 2001 its stock price rose above $100 per share. A collapse of investor confidence in 2001 and revelations of accounting irregularities led to one of the largest bankruptcies in U.S. history. By the end of the year, its stock price had plummeted to less than $1 per share. Investigations and lawsuits followed. One problem area concerned transactions with related parties that were not adequately disclosed in the company's financial statements. Critics stated that the lack of information about these transactions made it difficult for analysts following Enron to identify problems the company was experiencing.

Required:
1. Consult the Summaries of FASB pronouncements at **www.fasb.org** or access the pronouncements from some other source. What authoritative pronouncement requires the disclosure of related-party transactions? When did the requirement become effective?
2. Describe the disclosures required for related-party transactions.
3. Use EDGAR (**www.sec.gov**) or another method to locate the December 31, 2000, financial statements of Enron. Search for the related-party disclosure. Briefly describe the relationship central to the numerous transactions described.
4. Why is it important that companies disclose related-party transactions? Use the Enron disclosure of the sale of dark fiber inventory in your answer.

Real World Case 3–9

Disclosures; proxy statement

● LO5 LO7

Real World Financials

EDGAR, the Electronic Data Gathering, Analysis, and Retrieval system, performs automated collection, validation, indexing, and forwarding of submissions by companies and others who are required by law to file forms with the SEC. All publicly traded domestic companies use EDGAR to make the majority of their filings. (Some foreign companies file voluntarily.) Form 10-K or 10-KSB, which includes the annual report, is required to be filed on EDGAR. The SEC makes this information available on the Internet.

Required:
1. Access EDGAR on the Internet. The web address is **www.sec.gov**.
2. Search for **Activision Inc.,** a leading publisher of interactive entertainment software. Access the 10-K filing for the fiscal year ended March 31, 2007. Search or scroll to find the disclosure notes and audit report.
3. Answer the following questions:
   a. Describe the subsequent events disclosed by the company.
   b. Which firm is the company's auditor? What type of audit opinion did the auditor render? Does the audit report contain any explanatory paragraphs?
4. Access the proxy statement filed with the SEC on July 30, 2007 (the proxy statement designation is Def 14A) and answer the following questions:
   a. What is the principal position of Robert A. Kotick?
   b. What was the annual salary paid to Mr. Kotick?

Judgment Case 3–10

Debt versus equity

● LO8

A common problem facing any business entity is the debt versus equity decision. When funds are required to obtain assets, should debt or equity financing be used? This decision also is faced when a company is initially formed. What will be the mix of debt versus equity in the initial capital structure? The characteristics of debt are very different from those of equity as are the financial implications of using one method of financing as opposed to the other.

Cherokee Plastics Corporation is formed by a group of investors to manufacture household plastic products. Their initial capitalization goal is $50,000,000. That is, the incorporators have decided to raise $50,000,000 to acquire the initial operating assets of the company. They have narrowed down the financing mix alternatives to two:

1. All equity financing.
2. $20,000,000 in debt financing and $30,000,000 in equity financing.

No matter which financing alternative is chosen, the corporation expects to be able to generate a 10% annual return, before payment of interest and income taxes, on the $50,000,000 in assets acquired. The interest rate on debt would be 8%. The effective income tax rate will be approximately 50%.

Alternative 2 will require specified interest and principal payments to be made to the creditors at specific dates. The interest portion of these payments (interest expense) will reduce the taxable income of the corporation and hence the amount of income tax the corporation will pay. The all-equity alternative requires no specified payments to be made to suppliers of capital. The corporation is not legally liable to make distributions to its owners. If the board of directors does decide to make a distribution, it is not an expense of the corporation and does not reduce taxable income and hence the taxes the corporation pays.

Required:
1. Prepare abbreviated income statements that compare first-year profitability for each of the two alternatives.
2. Which alternative would be expected to achieve the highest first-year profits? Why?
3. Which alternative would provide the highest rate of return on shareholders' equity? Why?
4. What other related implications of the decision should be considered?

Analysis Case 3–11
Obtain and critically evaluate an actual annual report

● **LO5 LO7 through LO9**

Real World Financials

Financial reports are the primary means by which corporations report their performance and financial condition. Financial statements are one component of the annual report mailed to their shareholders and to interested others.

Required:
Obtain an annual report from a corporation with which you are familiar. Using techniques you learned in this chapter and any analysis you consider useful, respond to the following questions:
1. Do the firm's auditors provide a clean opinion on the financial statements?
2. Has the company made changes in any accounting methods it uses?
3. Have there been any subsequent events, errors and irregularities, illegal acts, or related-party transactions that have a material effect on the company's financial position?
4. What are two trends in the company's operations or capital resources that management considers significant to the company's future?
5. Is the company engaged in more than one significant line of business? If so, compare the relative profitability of the different segments.
6. How stable are the company's operations?
7. Has the company's situation deteriorated or improved with respect to liquidity, solvency, asset management, and profitability?

Note: You can obtain a copy of an annual report from a local company, from a friend who is a shareholder, from the investor relations department of the corporation, from a friendly stockbroker, or from EDGAR (Electronic Data Gathering, Analysis, and Retrieval) on the Internet (**www.sec.gov**).

Analysis Case 3–12
Obtain and compare annual reports from companies in the same industry

● **LO5 LO8 LO9**

Real World Financials

Insight concerning the performance and financial condition of a company often comes from evaluating its financial data in comparison with other firms in the same industry.

Required:
Obtain annual reports from three corporations in the same primary industry. Using techniques you learned in this chapter and any analysis you consider useful, respond to the following questions:
1. Are there differences in accounting methods that should be taken into account when making comparisons?
2. How do earnings trends compare in terms of both the direction and stability of income?
3. Which of the three firms had the greatest earnings relative to resources available?
4. Which corporation has made most effective use of financial leverage?
5. Of the three firms, which seems riskiest in terms of its ability to pay short-term obligations? Long-term obligations?

Note: You can obtain copies of annual reports from friends who are shareholders, from the investor relations department of the corporations, from a friendly stockbroker, or from EDGAR (Electronic Data Gathering, Analysis, and Retrieval) on the Internet (**www.sec.gov**).

Analysis Case 3–13
Balance sheet information

● **LO3 through LO5**

Google

Refer to the financial statements and related disclosure notes of **Google Inc.** included with all new copies of the text.

Required:
1. What categories does the company use to classify its assets? Its liabilities?
2. Why are marketable securities shown as a current asset?
3. Explain the current liability "deferred revenue."
4. What purpose do the disclosure notes serve?
5. What method does the company use to depreciate its property and equipment?
6. Does the company report any subsequent events or related party transactions in its disclosure notes?

Analysis Case 3–14
Segment reporting concepts

● Appendix

Levens Co. operates in several distinct business segments. The company does not have any reportable foreign operations or major customers.

Required:
1. What is the purpose of operating segment disclosures?
2. Define an operating segment.
3. List the amounts to be reported by operating segment.

Ethics Case 3–15
Segment reporting

● Appendix

You are in your third year as an accountant with McCarver-Lynn Industries, a multidivisional company involved in the manufacturing, marketing, and sales of surgical prosthetic devices. After the fiscal year-end, you are working with the controller of the firm to prepare supplemental business segment disclosures. Yesterday you presented her with the following summary information:

		($ in millions)				
	Domestic	Union of South Africa	Egypt	France	Denmark	Total
Revenues	$ 845	$222	$265	$343	$311	$1,986
Capital expenditures	145	76	88	21	42	372
Assets	1,005	301	290	38	285	1,919

Upon returning to your office after lunch, you find the following memo:
Nice work. Let's combine the data this way

	($ in millions)			
	Domestic	Africa	Europe	Total
Revenues	$ 845	$487	$654	$1,986
Capital expenditures	145	164	63	372
Assets	1,005	591	323	1,919

Some of our shareholders might react unfavorably to our recent focus on South African operations.

Required:
Do you perceive an ethical dilemma? What would be the likely impact of following the controller's suggestions? Who would benefit? Who would be injured?

4

The Income Statement and Statement of Cash Flows

/// **OVERVIEW**

The purpose of the income statement is to summarize the profit-generating activities that occurred during a particular reporting period. The purpose of the statement of cash flows is to provide information about the cash receipts and cash disbursements of an enterprise that occurred during the period.

This chapter has a twofold purpose: (1) to consider important issues dealing with income statement content, presentation, and disclosure and (2) to provide an *overview* of the statement of cash flows, which is covered in depth in Chapter 21.

LEARNING OBJECTIVES

After studying this chapter, you should be able to:

- **LO1** Discuss the importance of income from continuing operations and describe its components.
- **LO2** Describe earnings quality and how it is impacted by management practices to manipulate earnings.
- **LO3** Discuss the components of operating and nonoperating income and their relationship to earnings quality.
- **LO4** Define what constitutes discontinued operations and describe the appropriate income statement presentation for these transactions.
- **LO5** Define extraordinary items and describe the appropriate income statement presentation for these transactions.
- **LO6** Describe the measurement and reporting requirements for a change in accounting principle.
- **LO7** Explain the accounting treatments of changes in estimates and correction of errors.
- **LO8** Define earnings per share (EPS) and explain required disclosures of EPS for certain income statement components.
- **LO9** Explain the difference between net income and comprehensive income and how we report components of the difference.
- **LO10** Describe the purpose of the statement of cash flows.
- **LO11** Identify and describe the various classifications of cash flows presented in a statement of cash flows.

FINANCIAL REPORTING CASE

Alberto-Culver Company

Your friend, Becky Morgan, just received a generous gift from her grandfather. Accompanying a warm letter were 200 shares of stock of the Alberto-Culver Company, a global manufacturer of beauty and health care products, along with the most recent quarterly financial statements of the company. Becky knows that you are an accounting major and pleads with you to explain some items in the company's income statement. "I remember studying the income statement in my introductory accounting course," says Becky, "but I am still confused. What is this item *discontinued operations?* And how about *restructuring costs?* These don't sound good. Are they something I should worry about? We studied earnings per share briefly, but what does *diluted earnings per share* mean?" You agree to try to help.

ALBERTO-CULVER COMPANY
Income Statements
Three Months Ended March 31
($ in thousands, except per share data)

	2007	2006
Sales	$383,412	$365,677
Cost of products sold	183,575	165,910
Gross profit	199,837	199,767
Advertising, marketing, selling and administrative expenses	166,682	176,479
Restructuring costs	593	—
Operating income	32,562	23,288
Interest expense (income)	(697)	1,197
Income from continuing operations before income taxes	33,259	22,091
Provision for income taxes	11,498	7,322
Income from continuing operations	21,761	14,769
Income from discontinued operations, net of income taxes	797	42,082
Net income	$ 22,558	$ 56,851

(continued)

By the time you finish this chapter, you should be able to respond appropriately to the questions posed in this case. Compare your response to the solution provided at the end of the chapter.

QUESTIONS ///

1. How would you explain restructuring costs to Becky? Are they necessarily a negative? (page 172)

2. In addition to discontinued operations, what other events sometimes are reported separately in the income statement that you might tell Becky about? Why are these items reported separately? (page 176)

3. Explain to Becky what is meant by discontinued operations and describe to her how one is reported in an income statement. (page 179)

4. Describe to Becky the difference between basic and diluted earnings per share. (page 189)

(concluded)

Basic earnings per share:				
Continuing operations	$	.23	$	.16
Discontinued operations		—		.46
Net income	$	.23	$	.62
Diluted earnings per share:				
Continuing operations	$	.22	$	.16
Discontinued operations		.01		.45
Net income	$	.23	$	.61

In Chapter 1 we discussed the critical role of financial accounting information in allocating resources within our economy. Ideally, resources should be allocated to private enterprises that will (1) provide the goods and services our society desires and (2) at the same time provide a fair rate of return to those who supply the resources. A company will be able to achieve these goals only if it can use the resources society provides to generate revenues from selling products and services that exceed the expenses necessary to provide those products and services (that is, generate a profit).

The purpose of the income statement, sometimes called the statement of operations or statement of earnings, is to summarize the profit-generating activities that occurred during a particular reporting period. Many investors and creditors perceive it as the statement most useful for predicting future profitability (future cash-generating ability).

The purpose of the statement of cash flows is to provide information about the cash receipts and cash disbursements of an enterprise that occurred during a period. In describing cash flows, the statement provides valuable information about the operating, investing, and financing activities that occurred during the period.

Unlike the balance sheet, which is a position statement, the income statement and the statement of cash flows are *change* statements. The income statement reports the changes in shareholders' equity (retained earnings) that occurred during the reporting period as a result of revenues, expenses, gains, and losses. The statement of cash flows also is a change statement, disclosing the events that caused cash to change during the period.

This chapter is divided into two parts. The first part describes the content and presentation of the income statement and related disclosure issues. The second part provides an overview of the statement of cash flows.

PART A THE INCOME STATEMENT AND COMPREHENSIVE INCOME

Before we discuss the specific components of an income statement in much depth, let's take a quick look at the general makeup of the statement. Graphic 4–1 offers a statement for a hypothetical manufacturing company that you can refer to as we proceed through the chapter. At this point, our objective is only to gain a general perspective of the items reported and classifications contained in corporate income statements.

Let's first look closer at the components of net income. At the end of this part, we'll see how net income fits within the concept of comprehensive income.

Income from Continuing Operations

● LO1

The need to provide information to help analysts predict future cash flows emphasizes the importance of properly reporting the amount of income from the entity's continuing operations. Clearly, it is the operating transactions that probably will continue into the future that

Income Statements
(In millions, except earnings per share)

	Years Ended June 30	
	2009	**2008**
Sales revenue	$1,450.6	$1,380.0
Cost of goods sold	832.6	800.4
Gross profit	618.0	579.6
Operating expenses:		
Selling	123.5	110.5
General and administrative	147.8	139.1
Research and development	55.0	65.0
Restructuring costs	125.0	—
Total operating expenses	451.3	314.6
Operating income	166.7	265.0
Other income (expense):		
Interest income	12.4	11.1
Interest expense	(25.9)	(24.8)
Gain on sale of investments	18.0	19.0
Income from continuing operations before income taxes and extraordinary item	171.2	270.3
Income tax expense	59.9	94.6
Income from continuing operations before extraordinary item	111.3	175.7
Discontinued operations:		
Loss from operations of discontinued component (including gain on disposal in 2009 of $47)	(7.6)	(45.7)
Income tax benefit	2.0	13.0
Loss on discontinued operations	(5.6)	(32.7)
Income before extraordinary item	105.7	143.0
Extraordinary gain, net of $11 in tax expense	—	22.0
Net income	$ 105.7	$ 165.0
Earnings per common share—basic:		
Income from continuing operations before extraordinary item	$ 2.14	$ 3.38
Discontinued operations	(.11)	(.62)
Extraordinary gain	—	.42
Net income	$ 2.03	$ 3.18
Earnings per common share—diluted:		
Income from continuing operations before extraordinary item	$ 2.06	$ 3.25
Discontinued operations	(.11)	(.62)
Extraordinary gain	—	.42
Net income	$ 1.95	$ 3.05

Left margin brackets: Income from Continuing Operations · Separately Reported Items · Earnings per Share

are the best predictors of future cash flows. The components of income from continuing operations are revenues, expenses (including income taxes), gains, and losses, excluding those related to discontinued operations and extraordinary items.[1]

Income from continuing operations includes the revenues, expenses, gains and losses that will probably continue in future periods.

---

[1]These two separately reported items are addressed in a subsequent section.

Revenues, Expenses, Gains, and Losses

Revenues are inflows of resources resulting from providing goods or services to customers. For merchandising companies like **Wal-Mart,** the main source of revenue is sales revenue derived from selling merchandise. Service firms such as **FedEx** and **State Farm Insurance** generate revenue by providing services.

Expenses are outflows of resources incurred while generating revenue. They represent the costs of providing goods and services. The *matching principle* is a key player in the way we measure expenses. We attempt to establish a causal relationship between revenues and expenses. If causality can be determined, expenses are reported in the same period that the related revenue is recognized. If a causal relationship cannot be established, we either relate the expense to a particular period, allocate it over several periods, or expense it as incurred.

Gains and losses are increases or decreases in equity from peripheral or incidental transactions of an entity. In general, these gains and losses are those changes in equity that do not result directly from operations but nonetheless are related to those activities. For example, gains and losses from the routine sale of equipment, buildings, or other operating assets and from the sale of investment assets normally would be included in income from continuing operations. Later in the chapter we discuss certain gains and losses that are excluded from continuing operations.

Income Tax Expense

Income tax expense is shown as a separate expense in the income statement.

Income taxes represent a major expense to a corporation, and accordingly, income tax expense is given special treatment in the income statement. Income taxes are levied on taxpayers in proportion to the amount of taxable income that is reported to taxing authorities. Like individuals, corporations are income-tax-paying entities.[2] Because of the importance and size of income tax expense (sometimes called *provision for income taxes*), it always is reported as a separate expense in corporate income statements.

Federal, state, and sometimes local taxes are assessed annually and usually are determined by first applying a designated percentage (or percentages), the tax rate (or rates), to taxable income. Taxable income comprises revenues, expenses, gains, and losses as measured according to the regulations of the appropriate taxing authority.

While the actual measurement of income tax expense can be complex, at this point we can consider income tax expense to be a simple percentage of income before taxes.

Many of the components of taxable income and income reported in the income statement coincide. But sometimes tax rules and GAAP differ with respect to when and even whether a particular revenue or expense is included in income. When tax rules and GAAP differ regarding the timing of revenue or expense recognition, the actual payment of taxes may occur in a period different from when income tax expense is reported in the income statement. A common example is when a corporation takes advantage of tax laws by legally deducting more depreciation in the early years of an asset's life in its federal income tax return than it reports in its income statement. The amount of tax actually paid in the early years is less than the amount that is found by applying the tax rate to the reported GAAP income before taxes. We discuss this and other issues related to accounting for income taxes in Chapter 16. At this point, consider income tax expense to be simply a percentage of income before taxes.

Operating versus Nonoperating Income

A distinction often is made between *operating* and *nonoperating* income.

Many corporate income statements distinguish between operating income and nonoperating income within continuing operations. Operating income includes revenues and expenses directly related to the principal revenue-generating activities of the company. For example, operating income for a manufacturing company includes sales revenues from the sale of products and all expenses related to this activity. Nonoperating income includes gains and losses and revenues and expenses related to peripheral or incidental activities of the company. For example, income from investments, gains and losses from the sale of operating assets and from investments, interest and dividend revenue, and interest expense are included in nonoperating income.[3] *Other income (expense)* often is used in income statements as the

---

[2]Partnerships are not tax-paying entities. Their taxable income or loss is included in the taxable income of the individual partners.
[3]Even though these activities are nonoperating, they are still included in continuing operations because they *generally* are expected to continue in future periods.

classification heading for nonoperating items. A financial institution like a bank considers interest revenue and interest expense to be a part of operating income because they relate to the principal revenue-generating activities for that type of business.

Graphic 4–2 presents the 2005, 2006, and 2007 income statements for **Google Inc.** Notice that Google distinguishes between operating income and nonoperating income (labeled Interest income and other). Nonoperating revenues, expenses, gains and losses, and income tax expense (called provision for income taxes) are added to or subtracted from operating income to arrive at net income. As Google has no separately reported items, *income from continuing operations equals net income.*[4]

Now let's consider the formats used to report the components of net income.

GRAPHIC 4–2

Income Statements—
Google Inc.

Google

Real World Financials

Statements of Income
(In thousands, except per share amounts)

	Year Ended December 31		
	2005	**2006**	**2007**
Revenues	$6,138,560	$10,604,917	$16,593,986
Costs and expenses:			
Cost of revenues	2,577,088	4,225,027	6,649,085
Research and development	599,510	1,228,589	2,119,985
Sales and marketing	468,152	849,518	1,461,266
General and administrative	386,532	751,787	1,279,250
Contribution to Google Foundation	90,000	—	—
Total costs and expenses	4,121,282	7,054,921	11,509,586
Income from operations	2,017,278	3,549,996	5,084,400
Interest income and other, net	124,399	461,044	589,580
Income before income taxes	2,141,677	4,011,040	5,673,980
Provision for income taxes	676,280	933,594	1,470,260
Net income	$1,465,397	$ 3,077,446	$ 4,203,720
Net income per share of Class A and Class B common stock:			
Basic	$ 5.31	$ 10.21	$ 13.53
Diluted	$ 5.02	$ 9.94	$ 13.29

Income Statement Formats

No specific standards dictate how income from continuing operations must be displayed, so companies have considerable latitude in how they present the components of income from continuing operations. This flexibility has resulted in a variety of income statement presentations. However, we can identify two general approaches, the single-step and the multiple-step formats, that might be considered the two extremes, with the income statements of most companies falling somewhere in between.

The single-step format first lists all the revenues and gains included in income from continuing operations. Then, expenses and losses are grouped, subtotaled, and subtracted—in a single step—from revenues and gains to derive income from continuing operations. Operating and nonoperating items are not separately classified. Illustration 4–1 shows an example of a single-step income statement for a hypothetical manufacturing company, Maxwell Gear Corporation.

The multiple-step format reports a series of intermediate subtotals such as gross profit, operating income, and income before taxes. The overview income statements presented in Graphic 4–1 and the **Google Inc.** income statements in Graphic 4–2 are variations of the multiple-step format. Illustration 4–2 presents a multiple-step income statement for the Maxwell Gear Corporation.

A *single-step* income statement format groups all revenues and gains together and all expenses and losses together.

A *multiple-step* income statement format includes a number of intermediate subtotals before arriving at income from continuing operations.

---

[4]In a later section we discuss items that are reported separately from continuing operations.

ILLUSTRATION 4–1	
Single-Step Income Statement	**MAXWELL GEAR CORPORATION** **Income Statement** **For the Year Ended December 31, 2009**

Revenues and gains:		
Sales		$573,522
Interest and dividends		26,400
Gain on sale of operating assets		5,500
Total revenues and gains		605,422
Expenses and losses:		
Cost of goods sold	$302,371	
Selling	47,341	
General and administrative	24,888	
Research and development	16,300	
Interest	6,200	
Loss on sale of investments	8,322	
Income taxes	80,000	
Total expenses and losses		485,422
Net income		$120,000

In addition to net income, the components of the income statement and their presentation also are important to financial statement users in their assessment of earnings quality.

An advantage of the single-step format is its simplicity. Revenues and expenses are not classified or prioritized. A primary advantage of the multiple-step format is that, by separately classifying operating and nonoperating items, it provides information that might be useful in analyzing trends. Similarly, the classification of expenses by function also provides useful information. For example, reporting gross profit for merchandising companies highlights the important relationship between sales revenue and cost of goods sold. It is important to note that this issue is one of presentation. The bottom line, net income, is the same regardless of the format used. A recent survey of income statements of 600 large public

ILLUSTRATION 4–2	
Multiple-Step Income Statement	**MAXWELL GEAR CORPORATION** **Income Statement** **For the Year Ended December 31, 2009**

Sales revenue		$573,522
Cost of goods sold		302,371
Gross profit		271,151
Operating expenses:		
Selling	$47,341	
General and administrative	24,888	
Research and development	16,300	
Total operating expenses		88,529
Operating income		182,622
Other income (expense):		
Interest and dividend revenue	26,400	
Gain on sale of operating assets	5,500	
Interest expense	(6,200)	
Loss on sale of investments	(8,322)	
Total other income, net		17,378
Income before income taxes		200,000
Income tax expense		80,000
Net income		$120,000

companies indicates that the multiple-step format is used more than six times as often as the single-step format.[5] We use the multiple-step format for illustration purposes throughout the remainder of this chapter.

Before we investigate separately reported items, let's take a closer look at the components of both operating and nonoperating income and their relationship to earnings quality.

Earnings Quality

Financial analysts are concerned with more than just the bottom line of the income statement— net income. The presentation of the components of net income and the related supplemental disclosures provide clues to the user of the statement in an assessment of *earnings quality*. Earnings quality is used as a framework for more in-depth discussions of operating and nonoperating income.

● **LO2**

The term earnings quality refers to the ability of reported earnings (income) to predict a company's future earnings. After all, an income statement simply reports on events that already have occurred. The relevance of any historical-based financial statement hinges on its predictive value. To enhance predictive value, analysts try to separate a company's *transitory earnings* effects from its *permanent earnings*. Transitory earnings effects result from transactions or events that are not likely to occur again in the foreseeable future, or that are likely to have a different impact on earnings in the future. Later in the chapter we address two items that, because of their transitory nature, are required to be reported separately at the bottom of the income statement. Analysts begin their assessment of permanent earnings with income before these two items, that is, income from continuing operations.

Earnings quality refers to the ability of reported earnings (income) to predict a company's future earnings.

It would be a mistake, though, to assume income from continuing operations reflects permanent earnings entirely. In other words, there may be transitory earnings effects included in income from continuing operations. In a sense, the phrase *continuing* may be misleading.

Manipulating Income and Income Smoothing

A *Fortune* magazine article "Hocus-Pocus: How IBM Grew 27% a Year" contained a subtitle "Do you want to believe in the IBM miracle? Then don't look too closely at the numbers."[7] The article is highly critical of IBM's earnings management practices that allowed the company to report earnings per share growth of 27% per year from 1994 through 1999 with only minimal growth in revenues. The article's author attributes the increase in earnings per share to share buybacks, the sale of assets, and gains in pension fund assets, not a growth in permanent earnings.

KEN SCHAPIRO—CONDOR CAPITAL MANAGEMENT IBM has run out of easy things to do to generate earnings growth. Now they have to do the hard stuff.[6]

An often-debated contention is that, within GAAP, managers have the power, to a limited degree, to manipulate reported company income. And the manipulation is not always in the direction of higher income. One author states that "Most executives prefer to report earnings that follow a smooth, regular, upward path. They hate to report declines, but they also want to avoid increases that vary wildly from year to year; it's better to have two years of 15% earnings increases than a 30% gain one year and none the next. As a result, some companies 'bank' earnings by understating

ARTHUR LEVITT, JR. While the problem of earnings management is not new, it has swelled in a market that is unforgiving of companies that miss their estimates. I recently read of one major U.S. company that failed to meet its so-called numbers by one penny and lost more than six percent of its stock value in one day.[9]

them in particularly good years and use the banked profits to polish results in bad years."[8]

Many believe that manipulating income reduces earnings quality because it can mask permanent earnings. A 1998 *BusinessWeek* issue was devoted entirely to the topic of earnings management. The issue, entitled "Corporate Earnings: Who Can You Trust," contains

Many believe that corporate earnings management practices reduce the quality of reported earnings.

---

[5]*Accounting Trends and Techniques-2007* (New York: AICPA, 2007), p. 281.
[6]Bethany McLean, "Hocus-Pocus: How IBM Grew 27% a Year," *Fortune,* June 26, 2000, p. 168.
[7]Ibid.
[8]Ford S. Worthy, "Manipulating Profits: How It's Done," *Fortune,* June 25, 1984, p. 50.
[9]Arthur Levitt, Jr., "The Numbers Game," *The CPA Journal,* December 1998, p. 16.

articles that are highly critical of corporate America's earnings manipulation practices. Arthur Levitt, Jr., former Chairman of the Securities and Exchange Commission, has been outspoken in his criticism of corporate earnings management practices and their effect on earnings quality. In an article appearing in the *CPA Journal,* he states,

Increasingly, I have become concerned that the motivation to meet Wall Street earnings expectations may be overriding commonsense business practices. Too many corporate managers, auditors, and analysts are participants in a game of nods and winks. In the zeal to satisfy consensus earnings estimates and project a smooth earnings path, wishful thinking may be winning the day over faithful representation. As a result, I fear that we are witnessing an erosion in the *quality of earnings,* and therefore, the quality of financial reporting. Managing may be giving way to manipulation; integrity may be losing out to illusion. (emphasis added)[10]

How do managers manipulate income? Two major methods are (1) income shifting and (2) income statement classification. Income shifting is achieved by accelerating or delaying the recognition of revenues or expenses. For example, a practice called "channel stuffing" accelerates revenue recognition by persuading distributors to purchase more of your product than necessary near the end of a reporting period. The most common income statement classification manipulation involves the inclusion of recurring operating expenses in "special charge" categories such as restructuring costs (discussed below). This practice sometimes is referred to as "big bath" accounting, a reference to cleaning up company balance sheets. Asset reductions, or the incurrence of liabilities, for these restructuring costs result in large reductions in income that might otherwise appear as normal operating expenses either in the current or future years.

Mr. Levitt called for changes by standard setters to improve the transparency of financial statements. He did not want to eliminate necessary flexibility in financial reporting, but wanted to make it easier for financial statement users to "see through the numbers" to the future. A key to a meaningful assessment of a company's future profitability is to understand the events reported in the income statement and their relationship with future earnings. Let's now revisit the components of operating income.

Operating Income and Earnings Quality

● **LO3**

Should all items of revenue and expense included in operating income be considered indicative of a company's permanent earnings? No, not necessarily. Sometimes, for example, operating expenses include some unusual items that may or may not continue in the future. Look closely at the 2006 and 2005 partial income statements of **Ciena Corporation,** a supplier of application-focused communications networking equipment, software and services, presented in Graphic 4–3. What items appear unusual? Certainly "Restructuring costs," "Goodwill impairment," and "Long-lived asset impairment" require further investigation. We discuss restructuring costs first.

FINANCIAL Reporting Case

Q1, p. 165

Restructuring costs include costs associated with shutdown or relocation of facilities or downsizing of operations.

RESTRUCTURING COSTS. When a company reorganizes its operations to attain greater efficiency, it often incurs significant associated costs. Facility closings and related employee layoffs translate into costs incurred for severance pay and relocation costs. These restructuring costs appear regularly on corporate income statements. In fact, a recent survey reports that in 2006, of the 600 companies surveyed, 40% included restructuring costs in their income statements.[11] For instance, let's consider our Ciena Corporation example. A disclosure note accompanying the company's financial statements indicates a 2006 closure of its Shrewsbury, New Jersey, facility. Workforce reduction costs were the primary expenses incurred. Graphic 4–4 reports a portion of the disclosure note related to the restructuring costs incurred during the second quarter of 2006.

Prior to 2003, when a company restructured its operations, it estimated the future costs associated with the restructuring and expensed the costs in the period in which the decision to restructure was made. An offsetting liability was recorded. Later expenditures were

---

[10]Ibid., p. 14.
[11]*Accounting Trends and Techniques—2007* (New York: AICPA, 2007), p. 296.

GRAPHIC 4–3

Partial Income Statements—Ciena Corporation

Real World Financials

Income Statements (in part)
($ in thousands)

	Year Ended October 31	
	2006	**2005**
Total revenue	$564,056	$427,257
Cost of goods sold	306,275	291,067
Gross profit	257,781	136,190
Operating expenses:		
Research and development	111,069	137,245
Selling and marketing	89,755	117,624
General and administrative	47,476	33,715
Amortization of intangible assets	25,181	38,782
Restructuring costs	15,671	18,018
Goodwill impairment	—	176,600
Long-lived asset impairment	—	45,862
Total operating expenses	289,152	567,846
Operating loss	(31,371)	(431,656)

GRAPHIC 4–4

Disclosure of Restructuring Costs—Ciena Corporation

Real World Financials

Restructuring Costs (in part)
During the second quarter of fiscal 2006, Ciena recorded a charge of $0.7 million related to the closure of its Shrewsbury, NJ, facility and a charge of $2.5 million related to a workforce reduction of 86 employees.

charged against this liability as they occurred. The rationale for expensing an estimate of future expenditures was to match the restructuring costs with the decision to restructure and not with the period or periods in which the actual activities take place or when the benefits (if any) are realized.

What if the estimates turned out to be incorrect?

Levi Strauss & Co., the famous jeans manufacturer, reported the following item as part of operating expenses in its 2000 and 1999 income statements ($ in thousands):

Prior to 2003, restructuring costs were recognized (expensed) in the period the decision to restructure was made, not in the period or periods in which the actual activities took place.

	2000	1999
Restructuring costs	$(33,144)	$497,683

Why the negative expense in 2000? A review of the company's disclosure note reveals that in 1998 and 1999 it recorded restructuring costs that included estimated employee-related expenses and estimated facilities expenses associated with a plan to reduce capacity. However, in 2000, Levi lowered its estimate of the total costs associated with the restructuring and recorded an adjustment that increased income. As we discuss later in this chapter and throughout the text, when an estimate is changed in a reporting period after the period the estimate was made, the company should record the effect of the change in the current period rather than restate prior years' financial statements to correct the estimate.

The appearance of restructuring costs in corporate income statements increased significantly in the 1980s and 1990s. Many U.S. companies reacted to increased competition by streamlining their operations. The popular term heard often is *downsizing.* The SEC became concerned about the frequency with which companies were accruing restructuring costs in the manner described above. One of the chief concerns was that some companies purposely expensed large costs currently in an effort to manipulate future income. For example, employee relocation costs incurred in conjunction with a restructuring may produce future benefits to a company through greater operating efficiency. If so, accrual prior to any action may result in premature expense recognition of these costs.

GAAP now requires that restructuring costs be recognized only in the period incurred.

The FASB responded to the SEC's concern in June 2002 with *SFAS No. 146.*[12] The Standard prohibits management from recognizing a liability for a cost associated with an exit or disposal activity unless and until a liability actually *has been incurred.* No longer can a company accrue restructuring costs in the period the company commits to an exit plan, unless the costs actually have been incurred. As an example, suppose terminated employees are to receive termination benefits, but only after they remain with the employer beyond a minimum retention period. In that case, a liability for termination benefits, and corresponding expense, should be accrued in the period(s) the employees render their service. On the other hand, if future service beyond a minimum retention period is not required, the benefits are recognized at the time the company communicates the arrangement to employees. In either case, the liability and expense are recorded at the point they are deemed incurred. Similarly, costs associated with closing facilities and relocating employees are recognized when goods or services associated with those activities are received and are no longer accrued at the commitment date.

Fair value is the objective for the initial measurement of a liability associated with restructuring costs.

Should restructuring costs be considered part of a company's permanent earnings stream?

The Standard also establishes that fair value is the objective for initial measurement of the liability, and that a liability's fair value often will be measured by determining the present value of future estimated cash outflows. We discuss such present value calculations at length in later chapters, particularly in Chapters 6 and 14.

A major benefit of the new requirements is that liabilities accrued as a result of restructuring activities now comply with the definition of a liability in *Statement of Financial Concepts No. 6* and therefore are accounted for consistent with other liabilities. *SFAS No. 146* also significantly reduces the possibility that restructuring costs can be used as a method to manipulate earnings.

Now that we understand the nature of restructuring costs, we can address the important question: Should financial statement users consider these costs part of a company's permanent earnings stream, or are they transitory in nature? There is no easy answer. Ciena incurred restructuring costs in both 2006 and 2005. Will the company incur these costs again in the near future? Consider the following facts. During the 10-year period from 1997 through 2006, the Dow Jones Industrial 30 companies reported 91 restructuring charges in their collective income statements. That is an average of approximately 3 per company. But the average is deceiving. Four of the 30 companies reported no restructuring charges during that period. However, **Pfizer** incurred restructuring charges in 7 of the 10 years, and **Honeywell** reported restructuring charges in all 10 of its income statements. An analyst must interpret restructuring charges in light of a company's past history in this area. Information in disclosure notes describing the restructuring and management plans related to the business involved also can be helpful.

> **BUSINESSWEEK**
> Of course, companies have always taken write-offs and restructuring charges. But nervous regulators and investors fear that such multiyear write-offs are increasingly distorting corporate earnings—so much so, in fact, that some question whether the underlying meaning of profit numbers and their value as a true reflection of corporate performance is getting trampled.[13]

Two other expenses in Ciena's income statements that warrant additional scrutiny are *goodwill impairment* and *long-lived asset impairment.* These items involve what is referred to as *asset impairment* losses or charges. Any operational asset, whether tangible or intangible, should be written down if there has been a significant impairment of value. We explore operational assets in Chapters 10 and 11. After discussing this topic in more depth in those chapters, we revisit the concept of earnings quality as it relates to asset impairment.

Is it possible that financial analysts might look favorably at a company in the year it incurs a substantial restructuring charge or other unusual expense such as an asset impairment loss? Perhaps so, if they view management as creating higher profits in future years through operating efficiencies. Would analysts then reward that company again in future years when those operating efficiencies materialize? Certainly, this double halo effect might provide an attractive temptation to the management of some companies.

---

[12]"Accounting for Costs Associated with Exit or Disposal Activities," *Statement of Financial Accounting Standards No. 146* (Norwalk, Conn.: FASB, 2002).

[13]Nanette Byrnes, Richard A. Melcher, and Debra Sparks, "Earnings Hocus-Pocus: How Companies Come Up with the Numbers They Want," *BusinessWeek,* October 5, 1998, p. 135.

There are other items that could be included in operating expenses that also call into question this issue of earnings quality. For example, in Chapter 9 we discuss the write-down of inventory to comply with the lower-of-cost-or-market rule. Earnings quality also is influenced by the way income from investments is recorded (Chapter 12) and in the manner companies account for their pension plans (Chapter 17). In each case, after discussing these issues, we revisit this concept of earnings quality.

> **ARTHUR LEVITT, JR.**
> When a company decides to restructure, management and employees, investors and creditors, customers and suppliers all want to understand the expected effects. We need, of course, to ensure that financial reporting provides this information. But this should not lead to flushing all the associated costs—and maybe a little extra—through the financial statements.[14]

Earnings quality is affected by revenue issues as well as the expense issues we discussed. As an example, suppose that toward the end of its fiscal year, a company loses a major customer that can't be replaced. That would mean the current year's revenue figures contain a transitory component equal to the revenue generated from sales to that customer. Of course, in addition to its effect on revenues, losing the customer would have implications for the transitory/permanent nature of expenses and the bottom line net income. And, the pressure on companies to meet their earnings numbers often has led to premature revenue recognition, reducing the quality of the current period's earnings.

Accelerating revenue recognition has caused problems for many companies. For example, **Lucent Technologies'** revenue recognition practices attracted the attention of the SEC. Nine current and former employees were charged with securities fraud for improperly recognizing sales of $1.15 billion in fiscal 2000. The SEC accused the former employees of falsely inflating revenues through aggressive sales practices, including the filing of false documents on sales to **Winstar Communications,** which later went bankrupt. The SEC also pressed civil charges and a federal grand jury indicted **McKesson Corporation**'s former CFO for backdating a $20 million software sale by one month to meet the quarterly earnings target.[15]

We save these issues for Chapter 5 in which we discuss revenue recognition in considerable depth. Now, though, let's discuss earnings quality issues related to *nonoperating* items.

Nonoperating Income and Earnings Quality

Most of the components of earnings in an income statement relate directly to the ordinary, continuing operations of the company. Some, though, such as interest and gains or losses are only tangentially related to normal operations. These we refer to as nonoperating items. Some nonoperating items have generated considerable discussion with respect to earnings quality, notably gains and losses generated either from the sale of operational assets or from the sale of investments. For example, as the stock market boom reached its height late in the year 2000, many companies recorded large gains from sale of investments that had appreciated significantly in value. How should those gains be interpreted in terms of their relationship to future earnings? Are they transitory or permanent? Let's consider an example.

> Gains and losses from the sale of operational assets and investments often can significantly inflate or deflate current earnings.

Intel Corporation is the world's largest manufacturer of semiconductors. Graphic 4–5 shows the nonoperating section of Intel's income statements for the 2000 and 1999 fiscal years. In 2000, income before taxes increased by approximately 35% from the prior year. But notice that the *gains on investments, net* (net means net of losses) increased from

Income Statements (in part) (in millions)		
	Years Ended December 30	
	2000	**1999**
Operating income	10,395	9,767
Gains on investments, net	3,759	883
Interest and other, net	987	578
Income before taxes	15,141	11,228

GRAPHIC 4–5

Income Statements (in part)—Intel Corporation

Real World Financials

---

[14]Arthur Levitt, Jr., "The Numbers Game," *The CPA Journal,* December 1998, p. 16.
[15]Jeffrey Marshall, "The Perils of Revenue Recognition," *Financial Executive,* July–August 2004.

$883 million to over $3.7 billion, accounting for a large portion of the increase in income. Some analysts questioned the quality of Intel's 2000 earnings because of these large gains.

Consider **Hecla Mining,** a precious metals company. For its 2006 fiscal year, the company reported income before income taxes of $61.8 million. Included in this amount was a $36.4 million gain on the sale of investments, representing 59% of total before-tax income. Can Hecla sustain these gains? Should they be considered part of permanent earnings or are they transitory? It's interesting to note that in the prior two years Hecla reported no investment gains. **Coca-Cola Company** has been criticized for manipulating its profits through the timely sale of bottling companies. The company often invests in weaker bottlers, enhances their operations, and then sells them for a profit. Are these gains an integral part of the soft-drink business or are they transitory blips in earnings? There are no easy answers to these questions.

Many companies voluntarily provide *pro forma earnings—* management's assessment of permanent earnings.

Companies often voluntarily provide a pro forma earnings number when they announce annual or quarterly earnings. These pro forma earnings numbers are management's view of permanent earnings. For example, **Sun Microsystems, Inc.,** a leading provider of hardware, software, and services that power enterprises and network computing, announced on April 24, 2007, that its income for the quarter ended April 1, 2007, was $67 million. The company also announced that its *pro forma net income* (which excludes stock-based compensation, restructuring and impairment charges, intangible asset amortization charges, gains from the sale of equity investments, and litigation settlement income) for the quarter was more than twice its GAAP income. These pro forma earnings numbers are controversial as they represent management's view of permanent earnings and should be interpreted in that light. Nevertheless, these disclosures do provide additional information to the financial community.

The Sarbanes-Oxley Act requires a reconciliation between pro forma earnings and earnings determined according to GAAP.

The Sarbanes-Oxley Act addressed pro forma earnings in its Section 401. One of the act's important provisions requires that if pro forma earnings are included in any periodic or other report filed with the SEC or in any public disclosure or press release, the company also must provide a reconciliation with earnings determined according to generally accepted accounting principles.[16]

We now turn our attention to two income statement items—discontinued operations and extraordinary items—that, because of their nature, are more obviously not part of a company's permanent earnings and, appropriately, are excluded from continuing operations.

FINANCIAL Reporting Case

Q2, p. 165

GAAP require that certain transactions be reported separately in the income statement, below income from continuing operations.

Separately Reported Items

The information in the income statement is useful if it can help users predict the future. Toward this end, users should be made aware of events reported in the income statement that are not likely to occur again in the foreseeable future.

There are two types of events that, if they have a material effect[17] on the income statement, require separate reporting below income from continuing operations as well as separate disclosure: (1) discontinued operations, and (2) extraordinary items.[18] Although a company has considerable flexibility in reporting income from *continuing operations,* the presentation order of these items is mandated as follows:[19]

Income from continuing operations before income taxes and extraordinary items	$xxx
Income tax expense	xx
Income from continuing operations before extraordinary items	xxx
Discontinued operations, net of $xx in tax	xx
Extraordinary items, net of $xx in tax[20]	xx
Net income	**$xxx**

---

[16]The Congress of the United States of America, *The Sarbanes-Oxley Act of 2002,* Section 401 (b) (2), Washington, D.C., 2004.
[17]The concept of materiality was discussed in Chapter 1. If the effect on the income statement is not material, these items are included in income from continuing operations.
[18]"Reporting Results of Operations," *Accounting Principles Board Opinion No. 30* (New York: AICPA, 1973).
[19]The presentation of these separately reported items is the same for single-step and multiple-step income statement formats. The single-step versus multiple-step distinction applies to items included in income from continuing operations.
[20]Companies that report discontinued operations and one of the other separately reported items often show a subtotal after discontinued operations. This is not required. However, due to its frequency of use, we use this convention in examples and illustrations in the remainder of this chapter.

The objective is to separately report all of the income effects of these items. That's why we include the income tax effect of each item in this separate presentation rather than report them as part of income tax expense. The process of associating income tax effects with the income statement components that create them is referred to as *intraperiod tax allocation.* We address this process in the next section.

A third separately reported item, the *cumulative effect of a change in accounting principle,* might be included for certain mandated changes in accounting principles. Before 2005, most voluntary changes in accounting principles also were treated this way, by including the cumulative effect on the income of previous years from having used the old method rather than the new method in the income statement of the year of change as a separately reported item below extraordinary items. Now, most voluntary changes in accounting principles require retrospective treatment. We no longer report the entire effect in the year of the change. Instead, we retrospectively recast prior years' financial statements when we report those statements again (in comparative statements, for example) so that they appear as if the newly adopted accounting method had been used in those years presented. We discuss the retrospective approach later in this chapter and in subsequent chapters. A subsequent section in this chapter also addresses the distinction between voluntary and mandated changes in accounting principles.

Intraperiod Income Tax Allocation

Intraperiod tax allocation associates (allocates) income tax expense (or income tax benefit if there is a loss) with each major component of income that causes it.[21] More specifically, income tax is allocated to income from continuing operations and each of the two separately reported items. For example, assume a company experienced an extraordinary gain during the year.[22] The amount of income tax expense deducted from income from continuing operations is the amount of income tax expense that the company would have incurred *if there were no extraordinary gain.* The effect on income taxes caused by the extraordinary item is deducted from the extraordinary gain itself in the income statement. Illustration 4–3 demonstrates this concept.

The Maxwell Gear Corporation had income from continuing operations before income tax expense of $200,000 and an extraordinary gain of $60,000 in 2009. The income tax rate is 40% on all items of income or loss. Therefore, the company's total income tax expense is $104,000 (40% × $260,000).	**ILLUSTRATION 4–3** Intraperiod Tax Allocation

How should the company allocate the tax expense between income from continuing operations and the extraordinary gain? A partial income statement, beginning with income from continuing operations before income tax expense, *ignoring* intraperiod tax allocation, is shown in Illustration 4–3A.

Income before income taxes and extraordinary item	$200,000	**ILLUSTRATION 4–3A**
Income tax expense	(104,000)	Income Statement
Income before extraordinary item	96,000	Presented
Extraordinary gain (gross)	60,000	*Incorrectly*—No
		Intraperiod
Net income	$156,000	Tax Allocation
		(extraordinary gain)

The deficiency of this presentation is that the apparent contribution to net income of (a) income before the extraordinary gain (that is, income from continuing operations) and (b) the extraordinary gain, is misleading. If the extraordinary gain had not occurred, income

---

[21]*Intraperiod* tax allocation concerns the association of income tax with income statement components. *Interperiod* tax allocation, covered in Chapter 16, addresses the problem created when taxable income does not equal income before taxes as determined by GAAP because of differences in the timing of revenue or expense recognition.

[22]The criteria for classifying gains and losses as extraordinary are discussed in a later section of this chapter.

tax expense would not have been $104,000 but rather $80,000 (40% × $200,000). Similarly, the net benefit of the extraordinary gain is not $60,000, but rather $36,000 ($60,000 minus 40% × $60,000). The total tax expense of $104,000 must be *allocated*, $80,000 to continuing operations and $24,000 (40% × $60,000) to the extraordinary gain. The appropriate income statement presentation appears in Illustration 4–3B.

ILLUSTRATION 4–3B Income Statement Presented *Correctly*— Intraperiod Tax Allocation (extraordinary gain)		
Income before income taxes and extraordinary item		$200,000
Income tax expense		(80,000)
Income before extraordinary item		120,000
Extraordinary gain, net of $24,000 tax expense		36,000
Net income		$156,000

The two items reported separately below income from continuing operations are presented net of the related income tax effect.

Net income is $156,000 either way. Intraperiod tax allocation is not an issue of measurement but an issue of presentation. The $120,000 income before extraordinary gain properly reflects income from continuing operations *including* the appropriate tax effects. Also, notice that income tax expense represents taxes that relate to the total of all of the revenue, expense, gain, and loss items included in continuing operations. Each of the items following continuing operations (discontinued operations and extraordinary items) are presented *net of their tax effect*. No individual items included in the computation of income from continuing operations are reported net of tax.

In the illustration, the extraordinary gain caused additional income tax expense to be incurred. What if the company had experienced an extraordinary loss of $60,000 instead of an extraordinary gain? In that case, rather than creating additional tax, the loss actually decreases tax due to its reducing taxable income by $60,000. The company's total income tax expense would be $56,000 [40% × ($200,000 − 60,000)].

The extraordinary loss *decreased* the amount of tax the company otherwise would have had to pay by $24,000. This is commonly referred to as a *tax benefit*. A partial income statement, beginning with income from continuing operations before income tax expense, *ignoring* intraperiod tax allocation is shown in Illustration 4–3C.

ILLUSTRATION 4–3C Income Statement Presented *Incorrectly*—No Intraperiod Tax Allocation (extraordinary loss)		
Income before income taxes and extraordinary item		$200,000
Income tax expense		(56,000)
Income before extraordinary item		144,000
Extraordinary loss (gross)		(60,000)
Net income		$ 84,000

Once again, income before the extraordinary loss (that is, income from continuing operations) is misleading. If the extraordinary loss had not occurred, income tax expense would not have been $56,000 but rather $80,000 (40% × $200,000). The total tax expense of $56,000 must be *allocated*, $80,000 tax expense to continuing operations and $24,000 tax benefit to the extraordinary loss. The appropriate income statement presentation appears in Illustration 4–3D.

ILLUSTRATION 4–3D Income Statement Presented *Correctly*— Intraperiod Tax Allocation (extraordinary loss)		
Income before income taxes and extraordinary item		$200,000
Income tax expense		(80,000)
Income before extraordinary item		120,000
Extraordinary loss, net of $24,000 tax benefit		(36,000)
Net income		$ 84,000

Now that we have seen how to report items net of their related tax effects, let's look closer at the two items reported net of tax below income from continuing operations: discontinued operations and extraordinary items.

Discontinued Operations

H&R Block, Inc., is perhaps best known for providing a variety financial services to customers, principally income tax preparation and consulting services. Prior to 2008, the company also operated a mortgage services segment that specialized in mortgage loans. Near the end of its fiscal year ending April 30, 2007, H&R Block entered into an agreement to sell its mortgage services segment. The company also agreed to sell its income tax operations in the United Kingdom. These transactions are examples of discontinued operations.

● **LO4**

FINANCIAL
Reporting Case

Q3, p. 165

WHAT CONSTITUTES AN OPERATION?   For many years *APBO No. 30*[24] provided authoritative guidance for accounting and reporting of discontinued operations. This Opinion defined an operation for this purpose as a "segment of a business." A segment could be either a separate line of business or a separate class of customer. *SFAS No. 144,* issued in 2001, replaced the term segment of a business with *component of an entity.* A component of an entity comprises operations and cash flows that can be clearly distinguished, operationally and for financial reporting purposes, from the rest of the entity.

> **SFAS NO. 144**
> . . . a component of an entity comprises operations and cash flows that can be clearly distinguished, operationally and for financial reporting purposes, from the rest of the entity.[23]

If a component of an entity has either been disposed of or classified as held for sale, we report the results of its operations separately in discontinued operations if two conditions are met:

1. The operations and cash flows of the component have been (or will be) eliminated from the ongoing operations.
2. The entity will not have any significant continuing involvement in the operations of the component after the disposal transaction.

Notice that the definition of an operation is significantly broadened with *SFAS No. 144.* A component of an entity may be a reportable segment or operating segment, a reporting unit, a subsidiary, or an asset group. For example, suppose Chadwick Industries operates a chain of 12 restaurants in the Southeast and also has a division that engages in the production of bottled sauces and salad dressings sold to retailers. Previously, either the restaurant chain or the canned goods division would qualify as an operation for purposes of reporting discontinued operations, but an individual restaurant within the chain or a manufacturing plant in the canned goods division would not qualify. Now, though, under *SFAS No. 144,* either of those could qualify if it represents a component of the company with "operations and cash flows that can be clearly distinguished, operationally and for financial reporting purposes," from the rest of the restaurants or plants.

Remember, too, that the second condition for being reported separately as a discontinued operation is that the entity will not have any significant continuing involvement in the operations of the component after the disposal transaction. As an example, let's say Scooter's Barbecue franchises restaurants to independent owners but also has several company-owned restaurants. If Scooter's commits to a plan to sell its company-owned restaurants to an existing franchisee, the way it reports the transaction would depend on the terms of the agreement. If the franchise agreement requires Scooter's to maintain significant continuing involvement in the operations of the restaurants after they are sold, Scooter's will not report this transaction as a discontinued operation. On the other hand, if no continuing involvement is indicated, Scooter's will report the transaction separate from its franchising operations as a discontinued operation.[25] We see how in the next section.

---

[23]"Accounting for the Impairment or Disposal of Long-Lived Assets," *Statement of Financial Accounting Standards No. 144* (Norwalk, Conn.: FASB, 2001), par. 41.
[24]"Reporting Results of Operations," *Opinions of the Accounting Principles Board No. 30* (New York: AICPA, 1973).
[25]Ibid., par. A25 and A27.

INTERNATIONAL FINANCIAL REPORTING STANDARDS

Real World Financials

Discontinued Operations. U.S. GAAP, *SFAS No. 144,* considers a discontinued operation to be a component of an entity whose operations and cash flows can be clearly distinguished from the rest of the entity that has either been disposed of or classified as held for sale. *IFRS No. 5* also defines a discontinued operation as a component of an entity that has been disposed of or is classified as held for sale. What constitutes a component of an entity, however, differs considerably between the international standard and *SFAS No. 144. IFRS No. 5* considers a component to be primarily either a major line of business or geographical area of operations. The U.S. definition is much broader than its international counterpart.

To better understand the effects of the different definitions on financial reporting, consider the case of **Gottschalks, Inc.,** a department and specialty store chain operating in six Western states. During the fiscal year ended February 3, 2007, the company reported a discontinued operation in its income statement and disclosed the following in a note:

Discontinued Operations (in part)
The Company closed one underperforming store in the Seattle metro-area during the third quarter of fiscal 2006 and one underperforming store in the Seattle/Tacoma market during the first quarter of fiscal 2006. During fiscal 2005, the Company closed two underperforming stores in the Seattle/Tacoma market. These stores . . . are considered discontinued operations.

Because these closures qualified as discontinued operations under *SFAS No. 144,* Gottschalks reported the discontinued operations as a separate item in the income statement. However, because Gottschalks continued to operate eight stores in the state of Washington, the company's closing of a few stores does not constitute the discontinuance of either a major line of business or geographical area, so would not be treated as a discontinued operation under *IFRS No. 5.* Instead, the income effects of operating the stores during the year and their sale would have been reported in various locations throughout the income statement.

REPORTING DISCONTINUED OPERATIONS. By definition, the income or loss stream from an identifiable discontinued operation no longer will continue. If H&R Block had not separately reported the results of discontinuing its businesses, its 2007 and 2006 comparative income statements (in condensed form) would have appeared as in Illustration 4–4A.

ILLUSTRATION 4–4A

Income Statements Presented Incorrectly *without* Separate Reporting of Discontinued Operations

H&R BLOCK, INC.
Income Statements
Years Ended April 30

	($ in millions)	
	2007	**2006**
Revenues	$4,095.8	$4,872.8
Costs and expenses	4,693.1	4,045.4
Income (loss) before income taxes	(597.3)	827.4
Income tax expense (benefit)	(163.6)	337.0
Net income (loss)	$ (433.7)	$ 490.4

The company generated a net loss of $433.7 million in 2007 and net income of $490.4 million in 2006. However, an analyst concerned with H&R's future profitability is more interested in the 2007 and 2006 results after separating the effects of the discontinued operations from the results of operations that will continue. This information might have a significant impact on the analyst's assessment of future profitability.

Now let's compare these with the actual income statements H&R Block reported and reproduced (in condensed form) in Illustration 4–4B.

Compare the two income statements for their ability to predict future profitability. The income statements in Illustration 4–4B separately report the net-of-tax income effects of the discontinued operation. The revenues, expenses, gains, losses, and income tax related to

The net-of-tax income effects of a discontinued operation are reported separately in the income statement, below income from continuing operations.

H&R BLOCK, INC. Income Statements Years Ended April 30	2007	2006
	($ in millions)	
Revenues	$4,021.3	$3,574.7
Costs and expenses	3,385.5	3,064.3
Income from continuing operations before income taxes	635.8	510.4
Income tax expense	261.5	212.9
Income from continuing operations	374.3	297.5
Discontinued operations:		
Income (loss) from discontinued operations (including impairment loss of $350.9 in 2007), net of tax*	(808.0)	192.9
Net income	$ (433.7)	$ 490.4

ILLUSTRATION 4–4B

Income Statements *with* Separate Reporting of Discontinued Operations

Real World Financials

*The company disclosed the tax effects in a disclosure note; a $425.1 tax benefit in 2007 and a $124.1 tax expense in 2006.

the *discontinued* operation have been removed from *continuing* operations and reported separately for both 2007 and 2006.[26] Otherwise, as in Illustration 4–4A, it would appear that the company's profitability decreased from $490.4 million in income in 2006 to a $433.7 million loss in 2007, and that its revenue decreased by 16%, from $4,872.8 million to $4,095.8 million. However, a key in the assessment of profitability is the comparison of the company's performance from *continuing* operations. That comparison reveals an increase in revenue of 12% from $3,574.7 million to $4,021.3 million and an increase in profit of $76.8 million ($297.5 to $374.3). This provides a different picture of H&R's future profitability.

Sometimes a discontinued component actually has been sold by the end of a reporting period. Often, though, as in the H&R Block example, the component is being held for sale but the disposal transaction has not been completed as of the end of the reporting period. We consider these two possibilities next.

When the component has been sold. When the discontinued component is sold before the end of the reporting period, the reported income effects of a discontinued operation will include two elements:

1. Operating income or loss (revenues, expenses, gains, and losses) of the component from the beginning of the reporting period to the disposal date.
2. Gain or loss on disposal of the component's assets.

These two elements can be combined or reported separately, net of their tax effects. If combined, the gain or loss component must be indicated. In our illustrations to follow, we combine the income effects. Illustration 4–5 describes a situation in which the discontinued component is sold before the end of the reporting period.

Notice that a tax *benefit* occurs because a *loss* reduces taxable income, saving the company $880,000. On the other hand, had there been *income* from operations of $2,200,000, the $880,000 income tax effect would have represented additional income tax expense.

For comparison purposes, the net of tax operating income or loss of the discontinued component for any prior years included in the comparative income statements also are separately reported as discontinued operations.

When the component is considered held for sale. What if a company has decided to discontinue a component but, when the reporting period ends, the component has not yet been sold? If the situation indicates that the component is likely to be sold within a year, the

[26]Even though the agreement to sell the sement was reached in 2007, it is important for comparative purposes to separate the effects for any prior years presented. This allows an apples-to-apples comparison of income from *continuing* operations. So, in comparative income statements reporting three years, the 2006 and 2005 income statements would be reclassified and the income from discontinued operations presented as a separately reported item.

ILLUSTRATION 4–5 Discontinued Operations—Gain on Disposal	The Duluth Holding Company has several operating divisions. In October 2009, management decided to sell one of its divisions that qualifies as a separate component according to *SFAS No. 144*. The division was sold on December 18, 2009, for a net selling price of $14,000,000. On that date, the assets of the division had a book value of $12,000,000. For the period January 1 through disposal, the division reported a pretax operating loss of $4,200,000. The company's income tax rate is 40% on all items of income or loss. Duluth generated after-tax profits of $22,350,000 from its continuing operations. Duluth's income statement for the year 2009, beginning with income from continuing operations, would be reported as follows:

Income from continuing operations		$22,350,000
Discontinued operations:		
Loss from operations of discontinued component (including gain on disposal of $2,000,000*)	$(2,200,000)†	
Income tax benefit	880,000‡	
Loss on discontinued operations		(1,320,000)
Net income		$21,030,000

*Net selling price of $14 million less book value of $12 million
†Operating loss of $4.2 million less gain on disposal of $2 million
‡$2,200,000 × 40%

component is considered "held for sale."[27] In that case, the income effects of the discontinued operation still are reported, but the two components of the reported amount are modified as follows:

1. Operating income or loss (revenues, expenses, gains and losses) of the component from the beginning of the reporting period *to the end of the reporting period.*
2. An "impairment loss" if the carrying value of the assets of the component is more than fair value minus cost to sell.

The balance sheet is affected, too. The assets of the component considered held for sale are reported at the lower of their carrying amount (book value) or fair value minus cost to sell. And, because it's not in use, an operational asset classified as held for sale is no longer reported as part of property, plant and equipment and is not depreciated or amortized.

The two income elements can be combined or reported separately, net of their tax effects. In addition, if the amounts are combined and there is an impairment loss, the loss must be disclosed, either parenthetically on the face of the statement or in a disclosure note. Consider the example in Illustration 4–6.

ILLUSTRATION 4–6 Discontinued Operations— Impairment Loss	The Duluth Holding Company has several operating divisions. In October 2009, management decided to sell one of its divisions that qualifies as a separate component according to *SFAS No. 144*. On December 31, 2009, the end of the company's fiscal year, the division had not yet been sold. On that date, the assets of the division had a book value of $12,000,000 and a fair value, minus anticipated costs to sell, of $9,000,000. For the year, the division reported a pre-tax operating loss of $4,200,000. The company's income tax rate is 40% on all items of income or loss. Duluth generated after-tax profits of $22,350,000 from its continuing operations. Duluth's income statement for 2009, beginning with income from continuing operations, would be reported as follows:

Income from continuing operations		$22,350,000
Discontinued operations:		
Loss from operations of discontinued component (including impairment loss of $3,000,000)	$(7,200,000)*	
Income tax benefit	2,880,000†	
Loss on discontinued operations		(4,320,000)
Net income		$18,030,000

*Operating loss of $4.2 million plus impairment loss of $3 million
†$7,200,000 × 40%

---

[27]There are six criteria designed to determine whether the component is likely to be sold and therefore considered "held for sale." You can find these criteria in "Accounting for the Impairment or Disposal of Long-Lived Assets," *Statement of Financial Accounting Standards No. 144* (Norwalk, Conn.: FASB, 2001).

A disclosure note would provide additional details about the discontinued component, including the identity of the component, the major classes of assets and liabilities of the component, the reason for the discontinuance, and the expected manner of disposition. Also, the net-of-tax operating income or loss of the component being discontinued is also reported separate from continuing operations for any prior year that is presented for comparison purposes along with the 2009 income statement.

In Illustration 4–6, if the fair value of the division's assets minus cost to sell exceeded the book value of $12,000,000, there is no impairment loss and the income effects of the discontinued operation would include only the operating loss of $4,200,000, less the income tax benefit.[28]

Interim reporting.   Remember that companies whose ownership shares are publicly traded in the United States must file quarterly reports with the Securities and Exchange Commission. If a component of an entity is considered held for sale at the end of a quarter, the income effects of the discontinued component must be separately reported in the quarterly income statement. These effects would include the operating income or loss for the quarter as well as an impairment loss if the component's assets have a book value more than fair value minus cost to sell. If the assets are impaired and written down, any gain or loss on disposal in a subsequent quarter is determined relative to the new, written-down book value.

Let's now turn our attention to the second separately reported item, extraordinary gains and losses.

Extraordinary Items

Occasionally, an unusual event may occur that materially affects the current year's income but is highly unlikely to occur again in the foreseeable future. If such an item is allowed to simply alter net income without pointing out its extraordinary nature, earnings quality is seriously compromised and investors and creditors may be misled into basing predictions of future income on current income that includes the nonrecurring event. For that reason, extraordinary items are "red flagged" in an income statement by being reported separately, net of tax, and appropriately labeled. Extraordinary items are material events and transactions that are both:

● LO5

1. Unusual in nature
2. Infrequent in occurrence[29]

These criteria must be considered in light of the environment in which the entity operates. There obviously is a considerable degree of subjectivity involved in the determination. The concepts of unusual and infrequent require judgment. In making these judgments, an accountant should keep in mind the overall objective of the income statement. The key question is how the event relates to a firm's future profitability. If it is judged that the event, because of its unusual nature and infrequency of occurrence, *is not likely to occur again,* separate reporting is warranted.

Companies often experience *unexpected* events that are not considered extraordinary items. The loss of a major customer or the death of the company president are unexpected events that likely will affect a company's future but are both normal risks of operating a business that could recur in the future. Other gains and losses from unexpected events that are *not* considered extraordinary include the effects of a strike, including those against competitors and major suppliers, and the adjustment of accruals on long-term contracts.[30]

A key point in the definition of an extraordinary item is that determining whether an event satisfies *both* criteria depends on the environment in which the firm operates. The environment includes factors such as the type of products or services sold and the geographical location of the firm's operations. What is extraordinary for one firm may not be extraordinary for another firm. For example, a loss caused by a hurricane in Florida may not be

*Extraordinary items are material gains and losses that are both *unusual in nature* and *infrequent in occurrence.**

The determination of whether an item is unusual and infrequent should consider the environment in which the company operates.

---

[28]In the following year when the component is sold, the income effects must also be reported as a discontinued operation. Prior to *SFAS No. 144,* operating results for the subsequent period were estimated and considered in determining the income effect for the year the segment was deemed held for sale. This is no longer the case.
[29]"Reporting Results of Operations," *Accounting Principles Board Opinions No. 30* (New York: AICPA, 1973), par. 20.
[30]Ibid, par. 23.

judged to be extraordinary. However, hurricane damage in New York may indeed be unusual and infrequent.

Companies frequently sell subsidiary companies or their partial ownership interest in companies. Generally, the gain or loss is reported as a nonoperating item in the income statement or as a discontinued operation if the subsidiary is considered a component of the entity according to *SFAS No. 144*. In contrast, though, consider the disclosure note from a recent quarterly financial statement of **Verizon Communications, Inc.,** shown in Graphic 4–6.

GRAPHIC 4–6

Extraordinary Loss Disclosure—Verizon Communications, Inc.

Real World Financials

> **Extraordinary Item (in part)**
>
> In January 2007, the Bolivarian Republic of Venezuela declared its intent to nationalize certain companies, including CANTV. On February 12, 2007, we entered into a Memorandum of Understanding (MOU) with the Republic. The MOU provides that the Republic will offer to purchase all of the equity securities of CANTV, including our 28.5% interest . . . at a price equivalent to $17.85 . . . Based upon the terms of the MOU and our current investment balance in CANTV, we recorded an extraordinary loss on our investment of $131 million, net of tax, or $.05 per diluted shares, in the first quarter of 2007.

Why was the loss on sale of the company's 28.5% interest in a Venezuelan company considered an extraordinary item? The unusual nature of the forced sale, the nationalization (expropriation) of CANTV by a foreign government, resulted in the conclusion by Verizon that such a loss was unlikely to occur again in the foreseeable future.

Logic and reasoning must be applied to the determination of whether or not an event is extraordinary. Keep in mind that the income statement should be a guide to predicting the future. If it is extremely unlikely that a material gain or loss will occur again in the future, the quality of earnings is improved and the usefulness of the income statement in predicting the future is enhanced if the income effects of that gain or loss are reported separately.

Extraordinary gains and losses are presented, net of tax, in the income statement below discontinued operations.

As shown previously on page 176, the net-of-tax effects of extraordinary gains and losses are presented in the income statement below discontinued operations. In addition, a disclosure note is necessary to describe the nature of the event and the tax effects, if they are not indicated on the face of the income statement.[31]

INTERNATIONAL FINANCIAL REPORTING STANDARDS

Extraordinary Items. U.S. GAAP provides for the separate reporting, as an extraordinary item, of a material gain or loss that is unusual in nature and infrequent in occurrence. In 2003, the IASB revised *IAS No. 1*, "Presentation of Financial Statements." The revision states that neither the income statement nor any notes may contain any items called "extraordinary."

Very few extraordinary gains and losses are reported in corporate income statements.

The extraordinary item classification could soon be eliminated.

A recent survey of 600 large public companies reported that only four of the companies disclosed an extraordinary gain or loss in their 2006 income statements.[32] Losses from two 21st century "extraordinary" events, the September 11, 2001, terrorist attacks and Hurricane Katrina in 2005, did not qualify for extraordinary treatment. The treatment of these two events, the scarcity of extraordinary gains and losses reported in corporate income statements, and the desire to converge U.S. and international accounting standards could guide the FASB to the elimination of the extraordinary item classification.[33]

---

[31]For several years the FASB required companies to report material gains and losses from the early extinguishment of debt as extraordinary items. This is no longer the case and now these gains and losses are subject to the same criteria as other gains and losses for such treatment; namely, that they be both (a) unusual in nature and (b) infrequent in occurrence.

[32]*Accounting Trends and Techniques,* 2007 (New York: AICPA, 2007), p. 385.

[33]For a thorough discussion of this topic, see Massoud, Raiborn and Humphrey, "Extraordinary Items: Time to Eliminate the Classification," *The CPA Journal* (February 2007).

Unusual or Infrequent Items

If the income effect of an event is material and the event is either unusual or infrequent—but not both—the item should be *included in continuing operations* but reported as a separate income statement component. Recall the Ciena Corporation example in Graphic 4–3 on page 173. Restructuring costs and the impairment of goodwill and long-lived assets included in that company's continuing operations are examples of this type of event. The events may be unusual or infrequent, but, by their nature, they could occur again in the foreseeable future. However, rather than include these items with other gains and losses or with other expenses, they are reported as a separate line item in the income statement.[34] This method of reporting, including note disclosure, enhances earnings quality by providing information to the statement user to help assess the events' relationship with future profitability.

> The income effect of an event that is either unusual or infrequent should be reported as a separate component of continuing operations.

As we discussed earlier, the cumulative effect of a voluntary change in accounting principle no longer is reported as a separate item in the income statement. A recent standard requires that we retrospectively adjust prior financial statements instead. As a result, the income statement and other financial statements are affected by these changes differently than before. In the next section, we explore the way various types of accounting changes are reported.

Accounting Changes

Accounting changes fall into one of three categories: (1) a change in an accounting principle, (2) a change in estimate, or (3) a change in reporting entity. The correction of an error is another adjustment that is accounted for in the same way as certain accounting changes. A brief overview of each is provided here. We cover accounting changes in detail in Chapter 20.

Change in Accounting Principle

A change in accounting principle refers to a change from one acceptable accounting method to another. There are many situations that allow alternative treatments for similar transactions. Common examples of these situations include the choice among FIFO, LIFO, and average cost for the measurement of inventory and among alternative revenue recognition methods. New standards issued by the FASB also require companies to change their accounting methods.

> ● LO6

VOLUNTARY CHANGES IN ACCOUNTING PRINCIPLES.   Occasionally, a company will change from one generally accepted treatment to another. When these changes in accounting principles occur, information lacks consistency, hampering the ability of external users to compare financial information among reporting periods. If, for example, inventory and cost of goods sold are measured in one reporting period using LIFO and using the FIFO method in a subsequent period, inventory, cost of goods sold, and hence net income for the two periods are not comparable. Difficulties created by inconsistency and lack of comparability are alleviated by the way we report voluntary accounting changes.

SFAS No. 154 requires that voluntary accounting changes be accounted for retrospectively.[35] Prior to this standard, the cumulative effect on the income of previous years from having used the old method rather than the new method was included in the income statement of the year of change as a separately reported item. We no longer report the cumulative effect in the year of the change. Instead, we retrospectively recast prior years' financial statements when we report those statements again (in comparative statements, for example). For each year in the comparative statements reported, we revise the balance of each account affected to make those statements appear as if the newly adopted accounting method had been applied all along. Then, a journal entry is created to adjust all account balances affected to what those amounts would have been. An adjustment is made to the beginning balance of retained earnings for the earliest period reported in the comparative statements of

> Voluntary changes in accounting principles are accounted for retrospectively by revising prior years' financial statements.

---

[34]These items are *not* reported net of tax. Only the two separately reported items—discontinued operations and extraordinary items—are reported net of tax.

[35]Accounting Changes and Error Corrections—a replacement of APB Opinion No. 20 and FASB Statement No. 3," *Statement of Financial Accounting Standard No.154,* (Norwalk, Conn.: FASB, 2005).

shareholders' equity to account for the cumulative income effect of changing to the new principle in periods prior to those reported.[36]

Let's suppose that in 2009 the Dearborn Corporation switched from the LIFO inventory method to FIFO. In addition to the 2009 statements, Dearborn presents two additional years of income statements and statements of shareholders' equity (2008 and 2007) as well as a 2008 balance sheet for comparative purposes. Here are the steps Dearborn would follow to account for the change.

1. The comparative financial statements are revised. For all three years—2007, 2008, and 2009—income statements will appear as if FIFO had been applied all along. Dearborn uses its new method, FIFO, to determine cost of goods sold, income tax expense, and net income in 2009 and recalculates the 2007 and 2008 numbers using FIFO rather than LIFO. Similarly, inventory and retained earnings in each year's balance sheet are reported using the newly adopted FIFO method. In its statements of shareholders' equity, Dearborn reports retained earnings each year as if it had used FIFO all along, and because 2007 is the earliest year reported, beginning retained earnings that year is revised to reflect the cumulative income effect of the difference in inventory methods for all years prior to 2007.
2. The appropriate accounts are adjusted. Dearborn will create a journal entry to adjust the book balances from their current LIFO amounts to what those balances would have been using FIFO. Since differences in cost of goods sold and income are reflected in retained earnings, as are the income tax effects, the journal entry updates these accounts.
3. A disclosure note provides additional information. Dearborn must provide clear justification that the change to FIFO is appropriate in a disclosure note. The note also indicates the effects of the change on items not reported on the face of the primary statements, as well as any per share amounts affected for the current period and all prior periods presented.

We will see these steps demonstrated in Chapter 9 in the context of our discussion of inventory methods. Later, we'll revisit accounting changes in depth in Chapter 20.

MANDATED CHANGES IN ACCOUNTING PRINCIPLES. When a new FASB standard mandates a change in accounting principle, the board often allows companies to choose among multiple ways of accounting for the changes. One approach generally allowed is to account for the change retrospectively, exactly as we account for voluntary changes in principles. A second approach is to allow companies to report the cumulative effect on the income of previous years from having used the old method rather than the new method in the income statement of the year of change as a separately reported item below extraordinary items.

As an example of accounting for a mandated change with a cumulative adjustment, consider **Circuit City Stores, Inc.,** a leading specialty retailer of consumer electronics. Circuit City adopted *SFAS No. 123R* for its fiscal year ended February 28, 2007. This standard, discussed in detail in Chapter 19, requires all companies to expense the estimated cost of employee stock options. *SFAS No. 123R* also requires the estimation of stock option forfeitures, not required under *SFAS No. 123*. Circuit City accounted for the adoption of *SFAS No. 123R* by including the $1.8 million, net of tax, cumulative effect of the change in its 2007 income statement as a separately reported item. Graphic 4–7 shows a portion of the disclosure note that explained the change.

Change in Depreciation, Amortization, or Depletion Method

Changes in depreciation, amortization, or depletion methods are accounted for the same way as a change in accounting estimate.

A change in depreciation, amortization, or depletion method is considered to be a change in accounting estimate that is achieved by a change in accounting principle. We account for these changes prospectively, exactly as we would any other change in estimate. We discuss and illustrate this approach in the next section.

---

[36]Sometimes a lack of information makes it impracticable to report a change retrospectively so the new method is simply applied prospectively, that is, we simply use the new method from now on. Also, if a new standard specifically requires prospective accounting, that requirement is followed.

14. Stock-Based Incentive Plans (in part)

SFAS No. 123R requires companies to estimate the number of equity awards granted that are expected to be forfeited, recognize compensation expense based on the number of awards that are expected to vest, and subsequently adjust estimated forfeitures to reflect actual forfeitures. Under *SFAS No. 123*, the company recognized forfeitures when they occurred. During the first quarter of fiscal 2007, the company recorded an after-tax benefit of $1.8 million, $2.8 million pre-tax, as a cumulative effect of a change in accounting principle to adjust for awards granted prior to March 1, 2006, that were not expected to vest.

GRAPHIC 4–7

Disclosure of Change in Accounting Principle—Circuit City Stores, Inc.

Real World Financials

Change in Accounting Estimate

Estimates are a necessary aspect of accounting. A few of the more common accounting estimates are the amount of future bad debts on existing accounts receivable, the useful life and residual value of a depreciable asset, and future warranty expenses.

● **LO7**

Because estimates require the prediction of future events, it's not unusual for them to turn out to be wrong. When an estimate is modified as new information comes to light, accounting for the change in estimate is quite straightforward. We do not revise prior years' financial statements to reflect the new estimate. Instead, we merely incorporate the new estimate in any related accounting determinations from that point on, that is, prospectively.[37]

Consider the example in Illustration 4–7.

A *change in accounting estimate* is reflected in the financial statements of the current period and future periods.

The Maxwell Gear Corporation purchased machinery in 2006 for $2 million. The useful life of the machinery was estimated to be 10 years with no residual value. The straight-line depreciation method was used in 2006 through 2008, with a full year of depreciation taken in 2006. In 2009, the company revised the useful life of the machinery to eight years.

Neither depreciation expense nor accumulated depreciation reported in prior years is restated. No account balances are adjusted. Rather, in 2009 and later years, the adjusting entry to record depreciation expense simply will reflect the new useful life. In 2009, the entry is:

Depreciation expense (below)   280,000
    Accumulated depreciation   280,000

	$2,000,000	Cost
$200,000		Previous annual depreciation ($2,000,000 ÷ 10 years)
× 3 years	600,000	Depreciation to date (2006–2008)
	$1,400,000	Book value as of 1/1/09
	÷ 5 yrs.	Estimated remaining life (8 years − 3 years)
	$ 280,000	New annual depreciation

ILLUSTRATION 4–7

Change in Accounting Estimate

When a company makes a change in an estimate that affects several future periods, such as revising its estimate of an asset's useful life, the company reports in a disclosure note the effect of that change on the current year's income before extraordinary items, net income, and earnings per share. That disclosure isn't necessary for more routine changes such as revising estimates regarding uncollectible accounts, unless the effect of the change is material.

A recent quarterly report of **Time Warner Telecom, Inc.,** provides us an example. The company is a leading national provider of managed network solutions to business customers. Graphic 4–8 reproduces the disclosure note that described a change in the useful life for certain of its depreciable fiber assets.

As we discussed in a previous section, a change in depreciation, amortization, or depletion method is considered a change in estimate resulting from a change in principle. For that reason, we account for such a change prospectively, similar to the way we account for other changes in estimate. One difference is that most changes in estimate do not require a company to justify the change. However, this change in estimate is a result of changing an

---

[37]If the original estimate had been based on erroneous information or calculations or had not been made in good faith, the revision of that estimate would constitute the correction of an error.

GRAPHIC 4-8

Change in Estimate—
Time Warner Telecom,
Inc.

Real World Financials

Change in Accounting Estimate

During the first quarter of 2007, the Company evaluated the depreciable life used for fiber assets and determined that to better reflect the economic utilization of those fiber assets the lives were extended from 15 to 20 years, or the lease term, if shorter, for leased fiber assets. This change in estimate, effective as of January 1, 2007, was accounted for prospectively, in accordance with Financial Accounting Standards Board (FASB) Statement No. 154, Accounting Changes and Error Corrections (SFAS 154). This change lowered depreciation expense and reduced net loss by $4.9 million, or approximately $0.03 per share, for the three months ended March 31, 2007.

accounting principle and therefore requires a clear justification as to why the new method is preferable. Illustration 4–8 provides an example.

ILLUSTRATION 4-8

Change in
Depreciation
Method

The Maxwell Gear Corporation uses the double-declining balance (DDB) depreciation method for most of its equipment. In 2009, for consistency with other firms in the industry, the company switched from the DDB method to straight-line depreciation for a large group of equipment purchased at the beginning of 2007. Maxwell purchased this equipment at a cost of $50 million. The machinery has an expected useful life of five years and no estimated residual value.

When the change occurs, the company does not revise either depreciation expense or accumulated depreciation reported in prior years. No account balances are adjusted. Rather, in 2009 and later years, its adjusting entry to record depreciation expense simply will reflect the new depreciation method (straight-line). In 2009, the adjusting entry is ($ in millions):

Depreciation expense (below)	6	
Accumulated depreciation		6

DDB depreciation:

2007	$20 ($50 × 40%*)
2008	12 ([$50 − 20] × 40%*)
Total	$32

*Double the straight-line rate for five years [(1/5 = 20%) × 2 = 40%]

$50	Cost
32	Depreciation to date, DDB (2007–2008)
$18	Undepreciated cost as of 1/1/09
÷ 3 yrs.	Remaining life (5 years − 2 years)
$ 6	New annual depreciation

A disclosure note reports the effect on net income and earnings per share along with clear justification for changing depreciation methods.

Change in Reporting Entity

A third type of change—the change in reporting entity—involves the preparation of financial statements for an accounting entity other than the entity that existed in the previous period.[38]

Some changes in reporting entity are a result of changes in accounting rules. For example, *SFAS No. 94* requires companies like Ford, General Motors and General Electric to consolidate their manufacturing operations with their financial subsidiaries, creating a new entity that includes them both.[39] For those changes in entity, *SFAS No. 154* requires that the prior-period financial statements that are presented for comparative purposes be restated to appear as if the new entity existed in those periods.

However, the more frequent change in entity occurs when one company acquires another one. In those circumstances, the financial statements of the acquirer include the acquiree

---

[38]In Chapter 20 we discuss the different types of situations that result in a change in accounting entity.

[39]The issuance of *SFAS No. 94*, "Consolidation of All Majority-Owned Subsidiaries," resulted in hundreds of entities consolidating previously unconsolidated finance subsidiaries.

as of the date of acquisition, and the acquirer's prior-period financial statements that are presented for comparative purposes are *not* restated. This makes it difficult to make year-to-year comparisons for a company that frequently acquires other companies. Acquiring companies are required to provide a disclosure note that presents key financial statement information as if the acquisition had occurred before the beginning of the previous year. At a minimum, the supplemental pro forma information should display revenue, income before extraordinary items, net income, and earnings per share.

Correction of Accounting Errors

Errors occur when transactions are either recorded incorrectly or not recorded at all. We briefly discuss the correction of errors here as an overview and in later chapters in the context of the effect of errors on specific chapter topics. In addition, Chapter 20 provides comprehensive coverage of the correction of errors.

● LO7

Accountants employ various control mechanisms to ensure that transactions are accounted for correctly. In spite of this, errors occur. When errors do occur, they can affect any one or several of the financial statement elements on any of the financial statements a company prepares. In fact, many kinds of errors simultaneously affect more than one financial statement. When errors are discovered, they should be corrected.

Most errors are discovered in the same year that they are made. These errors are simple to correct. The original erroneous journal entry is reversed and the appropriate entry is recorded. If an error is discovered in a year subsequent to the year the error is made, accounting treatment depends on whether or not the error is material with respect to its effect on the financial statements. In practice, the vast majority of errors are not material and are, therefore, simply corrected in the year discovered.

Prior Period Adjustments

After its financial statements are published and distributed to shareholders, Roush Distribution Company discovers a material error in the statements. What does it do? The correction of material errors is considered to be a prior period adjustment.[40] A prior period adjustment refers to an addition to or reduction in the beginning retained earnings balance in a statement of shareholders' equity (or statement of retained earnings if that's presented instead).

When it's discovered that the ending balance of retained earnings in the period prior to the discovery of an error was incorrect as a result of that error, the balance is corrected. However, simply reporting a corrected amount might cause misunderstanding for someone familiar with the previously reported amount. Explicitly reporting a prior period adjustment on the statement of shareholders' equity (or statement of retained earnings) avoids this confusion.

In addition to reporting the prior period adjustment to retained earnings, previous years' financial statements that are incorrect as a result of the error are retrospectively restated to reflect the correction. Also, a disclosure note communicates the impact of the error on income.

Earnings per Share Disclosures

As we discussed in Chapter 3, financial statement users often use summary indicators, called *ratios,* to more efficiently make comparisons among different companies and over time for the same company. Besides highlighting important relationships among financial statement variables, ratios also accommodate differences in company size.

● LO8

One of the most widely used ratios is earnings per share (EPS), which shows the amount of income earned by a company expressed on a per share basis. Public companies report basic EPS and, if there are certain potentially dilutive securities, diluted EPS, generally on the face of the income statement. Basic EPS is computed by dividing income available to common shareholders (net income less any preferred stock dividends) by the weighted-average

FINANCIAL
Reporting Case

Q4, p. 165

---

[40]"Prior Period Adjustments," *Statement of Financial Accounting Standards No. 16* (Stamford, Conn.: FASB, 1977).

All corporations whose common stock is publicly traded must disclose EPS.

number of common shares outstanding (weighted by time outstanding) for the period. For example, suppose the Fetzer Corporation reported net income of $600,000 for its fiscal year ended December 31, 2009. Preferred stock dividends of $75,000 were declared during the year. Fetzer had one million shares of common stock outstanding at the beginning of the year and issued an additional one million shares on March 31, 2009. Basic EPS of $.30 per share for 2009 is computed as follows:

$$\frac{\$600,000 - 75,000}{\underset{\substack{\text{Shares} \\ \text{at Jan. 1}}}{1,000,000} + \underset{\text{New shares}}{1,000,000\ (9/12)}} = \frac{\$525,000}{1,750,000} = \$0.30$$

Diluted EPS reflects the potential dilution that could occur for companies that have certain securities outstanding that are convertible into common shares or stock options that could create additional common shares if the options were exercised. These items could cause EPS to decrease (become diluted). Because of the complexity of the calculation and the importance of EPS to investors, we devote a substantial portion of Chapter 19 to this topic. At this point, we focus on the financial statement presentation of EPS. In Graphic 4–2 on page 169, **Google Inc.** discloses both basic and diluted EPS in its income statements for all years presented.

Google

Companies must disclose per share amounts for (1) income before any separately reported items, (2) each separately reported item, and (3) net income.

When the income statement includes one or more of the separately reported items, we report per share amounts for both income from continuing operations and net income, as well as for each separately reported item. We see this demonstrated in income statements of **Newport Corporation,** a global supplier of advanced technology lasers, partially reproduced in Graphic 4–9.

GRAPHIC 4–9

EPS Disclosures—
Newport Corporation

Real World Financials

NEWPORT CORPORATION Consolidated Statements of Income (in part) For the Years Ended December 31		
($ in thousands, except per share data)	**2006**	**2005**
Income from continuing operations before extraordinary gain	$38,502	$ 25,714
Loss from discontinued operations, net of tax	(1,075)	(16,973)
Extraordinary gain on settlement of litigation, net of tax	—	2,891
Net income	$37,427	$ 11,632
Basic earnings (loss) per share:		
Income from continuing operations before extraordinary gain	$ 0.95	$ 0.62
Loss from discontinued operations	(0.03)	(0.41)
Extraordinary gain	—	0.07
Net income	$ 0.92	$ 0.28
Diluted earnings (loss) per share:		
Income from continuing operations before extraordinary gain	$ 0.91	$ 0.60
Loss from discontinued operations	(0.02)	(0.40)
Extraordinary gain	—	0.07
Net income	$ 0.89	$ 0.27

Comprehensive Income

● LO9   Accounting professionals have engaged in an ongoing debate concerning which transactions should be included as components of periodic income. For instance, some argue that certain changes in shareholders' equity besides those attributable to traditional net income should be included in the determination of income. In what might be viewed as a compromise, the

FASB decided to maintain the traditional view of net income, but to require companies also to report an expanded version of income called comprehensive income to include four types of gains and losses that traditionally hadn't been included in income statements. Let's consider what that means.

Other Comprehensive Income

The calculation of net income omits certain types of gains and losses that are included in comprehensive income. As one example, in Chapter 12 you will learn that certain investments are reported in the balance sheet at their fair values, but that the gains and losses resulting from adjusting those investments to fair value might not be included in net income. Instead, they are reported as a separate component of shareholders' equity, other comprehensive income (loss).

Companies must report both net income and comprehensive income and reconcile the difference between the two.[41] Be sure to remember that net income actually is a part of comprehensive income. The reconciliation simply extends net income to include other comprehensive income items, reported net of tax, as shown in Illustration 4–9.

Comprehensive income is the total change in equity for a reporting period other than from transactions with owners.

	($ in millions)	
Net income		$xxx
Other comprehensive income:		
Net unrealized holding gains (losses) on investments (net of tax)*	$x	
Gains (losses) from and amendments to postretirement benefit plans (net of tax)†	(x)	
Deferred gains (losses) from derivatives (net of tax)‡	(x)	
Gains (losses) from foreign currency translation (net of tax)§	x	xx
Comprehensive income		$xxx

ILLUSTRATION 4–9
Comprehensive Income

*Changes in the market value of securities available for sale (described in Chapter 12).
†Gains and losses due to revising assumptions or market returns differing from expectations and prior service cost from amending the plan (described in Chapter 17).
‡When a derivative designated as a cash flow hedge is adjusted to fair value, the gain or loss is deferred as a component of comprehensive income and included in earnings later, at the same time as earnings are affected by the hedged transaction (described in the Derivatives Appendix to the text).
§Gains or losses from changes in foreign currency exchange rates. The amount could be an addition to or reduction in shareholders' equity. (This item is discussed elsewhere in your accounting curriculum.)

The actual terminology used by companies for the four other comprehensive income items varies considerably. For instance, deferred gains (losses) from derivatives are sometimes called *derivative mark-to-market adjustments* or *changes in fair value of derivatives,* and gains (losses) from foreign currency translation are often identified as *foreign currency translation adjustments.*

Comprehensive income includes net income as well as other gains and losses that change shareholders' equity but are not included in traditional net income.

Flexibility in Reporting

The presentation shown in Illustration 4–9 can be (a) included as an extension to the income statement, (b) reported (exactly the same way) as a separate statement of comprehensive income, usually as part of a disclosure note, or (c) included in the statement of changes in shareholders' equity (Chapter 18). Each component of other comprehensive income can be displayed net of tax, as in Illustration 4–9, or alternatively, before tax with one amount shown for the aggregate income tax expense (or benefit).[42] A recent survey of reporting practices of 600 large public companies indicates that, of those companies that had other comprehensive income items, 83% chose to include the presentation of comprehensive income in their statements of changes in shareholders' equity.[43]

Many, though, such as **BMC Software, Inc.,** and **Foster Wheeler Ltd.,** choose to present comprehensive income as an extension to their income statements. The **Google Inc.** statements of stockholders' equity located in the company's annual report included with all new copies of the text, provides an example of a presentation of comprehensive income in that

Reporting comprehensive income can be accomplished with a separate statement or by including the information in either the income statement or the statement of changes in shareholders' equity.

Google

[41]"Reporting Comprehensive Income," *Statement of Financial Accounting Standards No. 130* (Norwalk, Conn.: FASB, 1997).
[42]The standard does not require the reporting of comprehensive earnings per share.
[43]*Accounting Trends and Techniques—2007* (New York: AICPA, 2007), p. 393.

statement. Chapter 18 also illustrates the presentation of comprehensive income in the statement of changes in shareholders' equity. On the other hand, in its 2007 financial statements, **Jabil Circuits Inc.**, a leading contract manufacturer of circuit boards and other electronic products, chose to use the separate statement approach, as shown in Graphic 4–10.

GRAPHIC 4–10
Comprehensive Income Presented as a Separate Statement —Jabil Circuits Inc.

Real World Financials

JABIL CIRCUITS INC. Consolidated Statements of Comprehensive Income For the Year Ended August 31 (In thousands of dollars)	2007	2006	2005
Net income	$73,236	$164,518	$203,875
Other comprehensive income (loss):			
Foreign currency translation adjustment, net of tax	70,350	41,940	37,377
Change in fair value of derivative instruments, net of tax	(7,190)	—	(274)
Losses from pension adjustment, net of tax	(2,098)	(8,939)	(10,057)
Other comprehensive income	61,062	33,001	27,046
Comprehensive income	$134,298	$197,519	$230,921

 INTERNATIONAL FINANCIAL REPORTING STANDARDS

Comprehensive Income. As part of a joint project with the FASB, the International Accounting Standards Board (IASB) in 2007 issued a revised version of *IAS No.1*, "Presentation of Financial Statements," that revised the standard to bring international reporting of comprehensive income largely in line with U.S. standards. It provides the option of presenting revenue and expense items and components of other comprehensive income either in (a) a single statement of comprehensive income or (b) in a separate income statement followed by a statement of comprehensive income. U.S. GAAP also allows reporting other comprehensive income in the statement of shareholders' equity.

Accumulated Other Comprehensive Income

The cumulative total of other comprehensive income (or comprehensive loss) is reported as *accumulated other comprehensive income* (or *loss*), an additional component of shareholders' equity that is displayed separately.

In addition to reporting comprehensive income that occurs in the current reporting period, we must also report these amounts on a cumulative basis in the balance sheet. This is consistent with the way we report net income that occurs in the current reporting period in the income statement and also report accumulated net income (that hasn't been distributed as dividends) in the balance sheet as retained earnings. Similarly, we report other comprehensive income as it occurs in the current reporting period and also report accumulated other comprehensive income (or loss) in the balance sheet. This is demonstrated in Graphic 4–10A for Jabil Circuits Inc.

Referring to the numbers reported in Graphic 4–10, we can reconcile the changes in both retained earnings and accumulated other comprehensive income:

Accumulated other comprehensive income increased by $61,062,000, from $109,898,000 to $170,960,000.

($ in thousands)	Retained Earnings	Accumulated Other Comprehensive Income
Balance, 8/31/06	$1,116,035	$109,898
Add: Net income	73,236	
Deduct: Dividends	(57,868)	
Other comprehensive income		61,062
Balance, 8/31/07	$1,131,403	$170,960

GRAPHIC 4–10A

Shareholders' Equity—
Jabil Circuits Inc.

Real World Financials

JABIL CIRCUITS INC.
Consolidated Balance Sheets (in part)
Years ended August 31

(In thousands of dollars)	2007	2006
Shareholders' equity:		
Common stock	212	211
Additional paid-in capital	1,340,687	1,265,382
Retained earnings	1,131,403	1,116,035
Accumulated other comprehensive income	170,960	109,898*
Treasury stock	(200,251)	(200,251)
Total shareholders' equity	$2,443,011	$2,291,275

*After net-of-tax adjustment of $3,206 thousand to initially adopt *SFAS No. 158.*

To further understand the relationship between net income and other comprehensive income, consider another example. Suppose Philips Corporation began 2009 with retained earnings of $600 million and accumulated other comprehensive income of $34 million. Let's also assume that net income for 2009, before considering the gain discussed below, is $100 million, of which $40 million was distributed to shareholders as dividends. Now assume that Philips purchased shares of IBM stock for $90 million during the year and sold them at year-end for $100 million. In that case, Philips would include the realized gain of $10 million in determining net income, If the income tax rate is 40%, net income includes a $6 million net-of-tax gain from the sale. This means that shareholders' equity, specifically retained earnings, also will include the $6 million.

($ in millions)	Retained Earnings	Accumulated Other Comprehensive Income
Balance, 12/31/08	$600	$34
Net income ($100 + 6)	106	
Dividends	(40)	
Other comprehensive income		–0–
Balance, 12/31/09	$666	$34

On the other hand, what if the shares are not sold before the end of the fiscal year but the year-end fair value is $100 million and Philips accounts for the shares as securities available-for-sale? In that case, the *unrealized* gain of $10 million is not included in net income. Instead, $6 million net-of-tax gain is considered a component of *other comprehensive income (loss)* for 2009 and results in an increase in *accumulated other comprehensive income (loss)*, rather than retained earnings, in the 2009 balance sheet. The total of retained earnings and accumulated other comprehensive income is $700 million either way, as demonstrated below.

($ in millions)	Retained Earnings	Accumulated Other Comprehensive Income
Balance, 12/31/08	$600	$34
Net income	100	
Dividends	(40)	
Other comprehensive income		6
Balance, 12/31/09	$660	$40

If the shares are not sold, the *unrealized* gain is part of other comprehensive income.

Net income and comprehensive income are identical for an enterprise that has no other comprehensive income items. Components of other comprehensive income are described in subsequent chapters.

CONCEPT REVIEW **EXERCISE**

INCOME STATEMENT PRESENTATION

The Barrington Construction Company builds office buildings. It also owns and operates a chain of motels throughout the Northwest. On September 30, 2009, the company decided to sell the entire motel business for $40 million. The sale was completed on December 15, 2009. Income statement information for 2009 is provided below for the two components of the company.

| | ($ in millions) | |
	Construction Component	Motel Component
Sales revenue	$450.0	$200.0
Operating expenses	226.0	210.0
Other income (loss)*	16.0	(30.0)
Income (loss) before income taxes	$240.0	$ (40.0)
Income tax expense (benefit)†	96.0	(16.0)
Net income (loss)	$144.0	$ (24.0)

*For the motel component, the entire Other income (loss) amount represents the loss on sale of assets of the component for $40 million when their book value was $70 million.
†A 40% tax rate applies to all items of income or loss.

In addition to the revenues and expenses of the construction and motel components, Barrington experienced a before-tax loss of $20 million to its construction business from damage to buildings and equipment caused by volcanic activity at Mount St. Helens. The event was considered unusual and infrequent.

Required:
Prepare a 2009 income statement for the Barrington Construction Company including EPS disclosures. There were 100 million shares of common stock outstanding throughout 2009. The company had no potential common shares outstanding.

BARRINGTON CONSTRUCTION COMPANY
Income Statement
For the Year Ended December 31, 2009
($ in millions, except per share amounts)

Sales revenue		$450.0
Operating expenses		226.0
Operating income		224.0
Other income		16.0
Income from continuing operations before income taxes and extraordinary item		240.0
Income tax expense		96.0
Income from continuing operations before extraordinary item		144.0
Discontinued operations:		
Loss from operations of discontinued motel component (including loss on disposal of $30)	$(40)	
Income tax benefit	16	
Loss on discontinued operations		(24.0)
Income before extraordinary item		120.0
Extraordinary loss from volcano damage, net of $8.0 tax benefit		(12.0)
Net income		$108.0
Earnings per share:		
Income from continuing operations before extraordinary item		$ 1.44
Discontinued operations		(.24)
Extraordinary loss		(.12)
Net income		$ 1.08

Now that we have discussed the presentation and content of the income statement, we turn our attention to the statement of cash flows.

THE STATEMENT OF CASH FLOWS

● LO10

In addition to the income statement and the balance sheet, a statement of cash flows (SCF) is an essential component within the set of basic financial statements.[44] Specifically, when a balance sheet and an income statement are presented, a statement of cash flows is required for each income statement period. The purpose of the SCF is to provide information about the cash receipts and cash disbursements of an enterprise that occurred during a period. Similar to the income statement, it is a *change* statement, summarizing the transactions that caused cash to change during a reporting period. The term *cash* refers to *cash plus cash equivalents*. Cash equivalents, discussed in Chapter 3, include highly liquid (easily converted to cash) investments such as Treasury bills. Chapter 21 is devoted exclusively to the SCF. A brief overview is provided here.

A statement of cash flows is presented for each period for which results of operations are provided.

Usefulness of the Statement of Cash Flows

We discussed the difference between cash and accrual accounting in Chapter 1. It was pointed out and illustrated that over short periods of time, operating cash flows may not be indicative of the company's long-run cash-generating ability, and that accrual-based net income provides a more accurate prediction of future operating cash flows. Nevertheless, information about cash flows from operating activities, when combined with information about cash flows from other activities, can provide information helpful in assessing future profitability, liquidity, and long-term solvency. After all, a company must pay its debts with cash, not with income.

Of particular importance is the amount of cash generated from operating activities. In the long run, a company must be able to generate positive cash flow from activities related to selling its product or service. These activities must provide the necessary cash to pay debts, provide dividends to shareholders, and provide for future growth.

Classifying Cash Flows

A list of cash flows is more meaningful to investors and creditors if they can determine the type of transaction that gave rise to each cash flow. Toward this end, the statement of cash flows classifies all transactions affecting cash into one of three categories: (1) operating activities, (2) investing activities, and (3) financing activities.

● LO11

Operating Activities

The inflows and outflows of cash that result from activities reported in the income statement are classified as cash flows from operating activities. In other words, this classification of cash flows includes the elements of net income reported on a cash basis rather than an accrual basis.[45]

Cash inflows include cash received from:

1. Customers from the sale of goods or services.
2. Interest and dividends from investments.

Operating activities are inflows and outflows of cash related to the transactions entering into the determination of net operating income.

These amounts may differ from sales and investment income reported in the income statement. For example, sales revenue measured on the accrual basis reflects revenue earned during the period, not necessarily the cash actually collected. Revenue will not equal cash collected from customers if receivables from customers or unearned revenue changed during the period.

---

[44]"Statement of Cash Flows," *Statement of Financial Accounting Standards No. 95* (Stamford, Conn.: FASB, 1987).

[45]Cash flows related to gains and losses from the sale of assets shown in the income statement are reported as investing activities in the SCF.

Cash outflows include cash paid for:

1. The purchase of inventory.
2. Salaries, wages, and other operating expenses.
3. Interest on debt.
4. Income taxes.

Likewise, these amounts may differ from the corresponding accrual expenses reported in the income statement. Expenses are reported when incurred, not necessarily when cash is actually paid for those expenses. Also, some revenues and expenses, like depreciation expense, don't affect cash at all and aren't included as cash outflows from operating activities.

The difference between the inflows and outflows is called *net cash flows from operating activities*. This is equivalent to net income if the income statement had been prepared on a cash basis rather than an accrual basis.

INTERNATIONAL FINANCIAL REPORTING STANDARDS

Statement of Cash Flows. Like U.S. GAAP, international standards also require a statement of cash flows. Consistent with U.S. GAAP, cash flows are classified as operating, investing, or financing. However, the U.S. standard designates cash outflows for interest payments and cash inflows from interest and dividends received as operating cash flows. *IAS No. 7* allows companies to report cash outflows from interest payments as either an operating *or* financing cash flows and cash inflows from interest and dividends as either an operating *or* investing cash flows. U.S. GAAP classifies dividends paid to shareholders as financing cash flows. The international standard allows companies to report dividends paid as either financing *or* operating cash flows.

DIRECT AND INDIRECT METHODS OF REPORTING. Two generally accepted formats can be used to report operating activities, the direct method and the indirect method. Under the direct method, the cash effect of each operating activity is reported directly in the statement. For example, *cash received from customers* is reported as the cash effect of sales activities. Income statement transactions that have no cash flow effect, such as depreciation, are simply not reported.

> By the *direct method*, the cash effect of each operating activity is reported directly in the SCF.

> By the *indirect method*, cash flow from operating activities is derived indirectly by starting with reported net income and adding or subtracting items to convert that amount to a cash basis.

By the indirect method, on the other hand, we arrive at net cash flow from operating activities indirectly by starting with reported net income and working backwards to convert that amount to a cash basis. Two types of adjustments to net income are needed. First, components of net income that do not affect cash are reversed. That means that noncash revenues and gains are subtracted, while noncash expenses and losses are added. For example, depreciation expense does not reduce cash, but it is subtracted in the income statement. To reverse this, then, we add back depreciation expense to net income to arrive at the amount that we would have had if depreciation had not been subtracted.

Second, we make adjustments for changes in operating assets and liabilities during the period that indicate that amounts included as components of net income are not the same as cash flows for those components. For instance, suppose accounts receivable increases during the period because cash collected from customers is less than sales revenue. This increase in accounts receivable would then be subtracted from net income to arrive at *cash flow from operating activities*. In the indirect method, positive adjustments to net income are made for decreases in related assets and increases in related liabilities, while negative adjustments are made for increases in those assets and decreases in those liabilities.

To contrast the direct and indirect methods further, consider the example in Illustration 4–10.

DIRECT METHOD. Let's begin with the direct method of presentation. We illustrated this method previously in Chapter 2. In that chapter, specific cash transactions were provided

Arlington Lawn Care (ALC) began operations at the beginning of 2009. ALC's 2009 income statement and its year-end balance sheet are shown below ($ in thousands).

ARLINGTON LAWN CARE
Income Statement
For the Year Ended December 31, 2009

Service revenue		$90
Operating expenses:		
General and administrative	$32*	
Depreciation	8	
Total operating expenses		40
Income before income taxes		50
Income tax expense		15
Net income		$35

*Includes $6 in insurance expense

ARLINGTON LAWN CARE
Balance Sheet
At December 31, 2009

Assets			Liabilities and Shareholders' Equity		
Current assets:			Current liabilities:		
Cash	$ 54		Accounts payable**	$ 7	
Accounts receivable	12		Income taxes payable	15	
Prepaid insurance	4		Total current liabilities	22	
Total current assets	70		Shareholders' equity:		
Equipment	40		Common stock	50	
Less: Accumulated depreciation	(8)		Retained earnings	30***	
Total assets	$102		Total liabilities and shareholders' equity	$102	

**For general and administrative expenses
***Net income of $35 less $5 in cash dividends paid

ILLUSTRATION 4–10

Contrasting the Direct and Indirect Methods of Presenting Cash Flows from Operating Activities

Net income is $35,000, but cash flow from these same activities is not necessarily the same amount.

Changes in assets and liabilities can indicate that cash inflows are different from revenues and cash outflows are different from expenses.

and we simply included them in the appropriate cash flow category in the SCF. Here, we start with account balances, so the direct method requires a bit more reasoning.

From the income statement, we see that ALC's net income has four components. Three of those—service revenue, general and administrative expenses, and income tax expense—affect cash flows, but not by the accrual amounts reported in the income statement. One component—depreciation—reduces net income but not cash; it's simply an allocation over time of a prior year's expenditure for a depreciable asset. So, to report these operating activities on a cash basis, rather than an accrual basis, we take the three items that affect cash and adjust the amounts to reflect cash inflow rather than revenue earned and cash outflows rather than expenses incurred. Let's start with service revenue.

Service revenue is $90,000, but ALC did not collect that much cash from its customers. We know that because accounts receivable increased from $0 to $12,000, so ALC must have collected to date only $78,000 of the amount earned.

Similarly, general and administrative expenses of $32,000 were incurred, but $7,000 of that hasn't yet been paid. We know that because accounts payable increased by $7,000. Also, prepaid insurance increased by $4,000 so ALC must have paid $4,000 more cash for insurance coverage than the amount that expired and was reported as insurance expense. That means cash paid thus far for general and administrative expenses was only $29,000 ($32,000 less the $7,000 increase in accounts payable plus the $4,000 increase in prepaid insurance). The other expense, income tax, was $15,000, but that's the amount by which income taxes payable increased so no cash has yet been paid for income taxes.

We can report ALC's cash flows from operating activities using the direct method as shown in Illustration 4–10A.

Accounts receivable			
Beg. bal.	0		
Revenue	90		
		78	Cash
End bal.	12		

ILLUSTRATION 4–10A	**ARLINGTON LAWN CARE**
Direct Method of Presenting Cash Flows from Operating Activities	**Statement of Cash Flows** **For the Year Ended December 31, 2009**

	($ in thousands)
Cash Flows from Operating Activities	
Cash received from customers*	$78
Cash paid for general and administrative expenses**	(29)
Net cash flows from operating activities	$49

By the direct method, we report the components of net income on a cash basis.

*Service revenue of $90 thousand, less increase of $12 thousand in accounts receivable.

**General and administrative expenses of $32 thousand, less increase of $7 thousand in accounts payable, plus increase of $4 thousand in prepaid insurance.

Depreciation expense does not reduce cash, but is subtracted in the income statement. So, we add back depreciation expense to net income to eliminate it.

INDIRECT METHOD. To report operating cash flows using the indirect method, we take a different approach. We start with ALC's net income but realize that the $35,000 includes both cash and noncash components. We need to adjust net income, then, to eliminate the noncash effects so that we're left with only the cash flows. We start by eliminating the only noncash component of net income in our illustration—depreciation expense. Depreciation of $8,000 was subtracted in the income statement, so we simply add it back in to eliminate it.

We make adjustments for changes in assets and liabilities that indicate that components of net income are not the same as cash flows.

That leaves us with the three components that do affect cash but not by the amounts reported. For those, we need to make adjustments to net income to cause it to reflect cash flows rather than accrual amounts. For instance, we saw earlier that only $78,000 cash was received from customers even though $90,000 in revenue is reflected in net income. That means we need to include an adjustment to reduce net income by $12,000, the increase in accounts receivable. In a similar manner, we include adjustments for the changes in accounts payable, income taxes payable, and prepaid insurance to cause net income to reflect cash payments rather than expenses incurred. For accounts payable and taxes payable, because more was subtracted in the income statement than cash paid for the expenses related to these two liabilities, we need to add back the differences. Note that if these liabilities had decreased, we would have subtracted, rather than added, the changes. For prepaid insurance, because less was subtracted in the income statement than cash paid, we need to subtract the difference—the increase in prepaid insurance. If this asset had decreased, we would have added, rather than subtracted, the change.

Cash flows from operating activities using the indirect method are shown in Illustration 4–10B.

ILLUSTRATION 4–10B	**ARLINGTON LAWN CARE**
Indirect Method of Presenting Cash Flows from Operating Activities	**Statement of Cash Flows** **For the Year Ended December 31, 2009**

		($ in thousands)
Cash Flows from Operating Activities		
Net income		$35
Adjustments for noncash effects:		
Depreciation expense	$ 8	
Changes in operating assets and liabilities:		
Increase in prepaid insurance	(4)	
Increase in accounts receivable	(12)	
Increase in accounts payable	7	
Increase in income taxes payable	15	14
Net cash flows from operating activities		$49

By the indirect method, we start with net income and work backwards to convert that amount to a cash basis.

Both the direct and the indirect methods produce the same net cash flows from operating activities ($49 thousand in our illustration); they are merely alternative approaches to reporting the cash flows. The FASB, in *SFAS No. 95,* stated its preference for the direct method. However, while both methods are used in practice, the direct method is infrequently used.

The choice of presentation method for cash flow from operating activities has no effect on how investing activities and financing activities are reported. We now look at how cash flows are classified into those two categories.

Investing Activities

Cash flows from investing activities include inflows and outflows of cash related to the acquisition and disposition of long-term assets used in the operations of the business (such as property, plant, and equipment) and investment assets (except those classified as cash equivalents). The purchase and sale of inventories are not considered investing activities. Inventories are purchased for the purpose of being sold as part of the company's operations, so their purchase and sale are included with operating activities rather than investing activities.

Investing activities involve the acquisition and sale of (1) long-term assets used in the business and (2) nonoperating investment assets.

Cash outflows from investing activities include cash paid for:

1. The purchase of long-term assets used in the business.
2. The purchase of investment securities like stocks and bonds of other entities (other than those classified as cash equivalents).
3. Loans to other entities.

Later, when the assets are disposed of, cash inflow from the sale of the assets (or collection of loans and notes) also is reported as cash flows from investing activities. As a result, cash inflows from these transactions are considered investing activities:

1. The sale of long-term assets used in the business.
2. The sale of investment securities (other than cash equivalents).
3. The collection of a nontrade receivable (excluding the collection of interest, which is an operating activity).

Net cash flows from investing activities represents the difference between the inflows and outflows. The only investing activity indicated in Illustration 4–10 is ALC's investment of $40,000 cash for equipment.

Financing Activities

Financing activities relate to the external financing of the company. Cash inflows occur when cash is borrowed from creditors or invested by owners. Cash outflows occur when cash is paid back to creditors or distributed to owners. The payment of interest to a creditor, however, is classified as an operating activity.

Financing activities involve cash inflows and outflows from transactions with creditors (excluding trade creditors) and owners.

Cash inflows include cash received from:

1. Owners when shares are sold to them.
2. Creditors when cash is borrowed through notes, loans, mortgages, and bonds.

Cash outflows include cash paid to:

1. Owners in the form of dividends or other distributions.
2. Owners for the reacquisition of shares previously sold.
3. Creditors as repayment of the principal amounts of debt (excluding trade payables that relate to operating activities).

Net cash flows from financing activities is the difference between the inflows and outflows. The only financing activity indicated in Illustration 4–10 is ALC's receipt of $50,000 cash from issuing common stock.

Noncash Investing and Financing Activities

As we just discussed, the statement of cash flows provides useful information about the investing and financing activities in which a company is engaged. Even though these primarily result in cash inflows and cash outflows, there may be significant investing and financing activities occurring during the period that do not involve cash flows at all. In order to provide complete information about these activities, any significant *noncash* investing and financing activities (that is, noncash exchanges) are reported either on the face of the SCF or in a disclosure note. An example of a significant noncash investing and financing activity is

Significant investing and financing transactions not involving cash also are reported.

the acquisition of equipment (an investing activity) by issuing either a long-term note payable or equity securities (a financing activity).

The 2009 statement of cash flows for ALC, beginning with net cash flows from operating activities, is shown in Illustration 4–11.

ILLUSTRATION 4–11 Statement of Cash Flows (beginning with net cash flows from operating activities)	**ARLINGTON LAWN CARE** **Statement of Cash Flows (in part)** **For the Year Ended December 31, 2009**

<table>
<tr><td></td><td></td><td>($ in thousands)</td></tr>
<tr><td>Net cash flows from operating activities</td><td></td><td>$49</td></tr>
<tr><td>**Cash flows from investing activities:**</td><td></td><td></td></tr>
<tr><td>Purchase of equipment</td><td></td><td>(40)</td></tr>
<tr><td>**Cash flows from financing activities:**</td><td></td><td></td></tr>
<tr><td>Sale of common stock</td><td>$50</td><td></td></tr>
<tr><td>Payment of cash dividends</td><td>(5)</td><td></td></tr>
<tr><td>Net cash flows from financing activities</td><td></td><td>45</td></tr>
<tr><td>Net increase in cash</td><td></td><td>54</td></tr>
<tr><td>Cash balance, January 1</td><td></td><td>0</td></tr>
<tr><td>Cash balance, December 31</td><td></td><td>$54</td></tr>
</table>

We know $40 thousand was paid to buy equipment because that balance sheet account increased from no balance to $40 thousand. Likewise, because common stock increased from zero to $50 thousand, we include that amount as a cash inflow from financing activities. Finally, Illustration 4–10 told us that $5 thousand was paid as a cash dividend, also a financing activity.

CONCEPT REVIEW EXERCISE

STATEMENT OF CASH FLOWS

Dublin Enterprises, Inc. (DEI) owns a chain of retail electronics stores located in shopping malls. The following are the company's 2009 income statement and comparative balance sheets ($ in millions):

Income Statement
For the Year Ended December 31, 2009

Revenue		$2,100
Cost of goods sold		1,400
Gross profit		700
Operating expenses:		
Selling and administrative	$ 355	
Depreciation	85	
Total operating expenses		440
Income before income taxes		260
Income tax expense		78
Net income		$ 182

Comparative Balance Sheets	12/31/09	12/31/08
Assets:		
Cash	$ 300	$ 220
Accounts receivable (net)	227	240
Inventory	160	120
Property, plant & equipment	960	800
Less: Accumulated depreciation	(405)	(320)
Total assets	$1,242	$1,060

(continued)

(concluded)

Liabilities and shareholders' equity:

Accounts payable	$ 145	$ 130
Payables for selling and admin. expenses	147	170
Income taxes payable	95	50
Long-term debt	–0–	100
Common stock	463	400
Retained earnings	392	210
Total liabilities and shareholders' equity	$1,242	$1,060

Required:
1. Prepare DEI's 2009 statement of cash flows using the direct method.
2. Prepare the cash flows from operating activities section of DEI's 2009 statement of cash flows using the indirect method.

1. Prepare DEI's 2009 statement of cash flows using the direct method.   **SOLUTION**

DUBLIN ENTERPRISES, INC.
Statement of Cash Flows
For the Year Ended December 31, 2009
($ in millions)

Cash Flows from Operating Activities		
Collections from customers[1]	$2,113	
Purchase of inventory[2]	(1,425)	
Payment of selling and administrative expenses[3]	(378)	
Payment of income taxes[4]	(33)	
Net cash flows from operating activities		$277
Cash Flows from Investing Activities		
Purchase of property, plant, and equipment		(160)
Cash Flows from Financing Activities		
Issuance of common stock	63	
Payment on long-term debt	(100)	
Net cash flows from financing activities		(37)
Net increase in cash		80
Cash, January 1		220
Cash, December 31		$300

[1]Sales revenue of $2,100 million, plus $13 million decrease in accounts receivable (net).
[2]Cost of goods sold of $1,400 million, plus $40 million increase in inventory, less $15 million increase in accounts payable.
[3]Selling and administrative expenses of $355 million, plus $23 million decrease in payables for selling and administrative expenses.
[4]Income tax expense of $78 million, less $45 million increase in income taxes payable.

2. Prepare the cash flows from operating activities section of DEI's 2009 statement of cash flows using the indirect method.

DUBLIN ENTERPRISES, INC.
Statement of Cash Flows
For the Year Ended December 31, 2009
($ in millions)

Cash Flows from Operating Activities	
Net Income	$182
Adjustments for noncash effects:	
Depreciation expense	85

(continued)

(concluded)

Changes in operating assets and liabilities:	
Decrease in accounts receivable (net)	13
Increase in inventory	(40)
Increase in accounts payable	15
Increase in income taxes payable	45
Decrease in payables for selling and administrative expenses	(23)
Net cash flows from operating activities	$277

FINANCIAL REPORTING CASE **SOLUTION**

1. **How would you explain restructuring costs to Becky? Are they necessarily a negative?** *(p. 172)* Restructuring costs include employee severance and termination benefits plus other costs associated with the shutdown or relocation of facilities or downsizing of operations. It's not necessarily bad. In fact, the objective is to make operations more efficient. The costs are incurred now in hopes of better earnings later. Prior to 2003, when a company restructured its operations, it estimated the future costs associated with the restructuring and expensed the costs in the period in which the decision to restructure was made. An offsetting liability was recorded. Later expenditures were charged against this liability as they occurred.

2. **In addition to discontinued operations, what other events sometimes are reported separately in the income statement that you might tell Becky about? Why are these items reported separately?** *(p. 176)* In addition to discontinued operations, extraordinary items also are reported separately in the income statement when they are present. The predictive ability of an income statement is significantly enhanced if normal and recurrent transactions are separated from unusual and nonrecurrent items. The income statement is a historical report, summarizing the most recent profit-generating activities of a company. The information in the statement is useful if it can help users predict the future. Toward this end, users should be made aware of events reported in the income statement that are not likely to occur again in the foreseeable future.

3. **Explain to Becky what is meant by discontinued operations and describe to her how one is reported in an income statement.** *(p. 179)* A discontinued operation occurs when a company decides to discontinue a separate component. A component of an entity comprises operations and cash flows that can be clearly distinguished, operationally and for financial reporting purposes, from the rest of the entity. The net-of-tax effect of discontinued operations is separately reported below income from continuing operations. If the component has been disposed of by the end of the reporting period, the income effects include: (1) income or loss from operations of the discontinued component from the beginning of the reporting period through the disposal date and (2) gain or loss on disposal of the component's assets. If the component has not been disposed of by the end of the reporting period, the income effects include: (1) income or loss from operations of the discontinued component from the beginning of the reporting period through the end of the reporting period, and (2) an impairment loss if the fair value minus cost to sell of the component's assets is less than their carrying amount (book value).

4. **Describe to Becky the difference between basic and diluted earnings per share.** *(p. 189)* Basic earnings per share is computed by dividing income available to common shareholders (net income less any preferred stock dividends) by the weighted-average number of common shares outstanding for the period. Diluted earnings per share reflects the potential dilution that could occur for companies that have certain securities outstanding that are convertible into common shares or stock options that could create additional common shares if the options were exercised. These items could cause

earnings per share to decrease (become diluted). Because of the complexity of the calculation and the importance of earnings per share to investors, the text devotes a substantial portion of Chapter 19 to this topic. ●

THE BOTTOM LINE

● **LO1**   The components of income from continuing operations are revenues, expenses (including income taxes), gains, and losses, excluding those related to discontinued operations and extraordinary items. Companies often distinguish between operating and nonoperating income within continuing operations. (p. 166)

● **LO2**   The term *earnings quality* refers to the ability of reported earnings (income) to predict a company's future earnings. The relevance of any historical-based financial statement hinges on its predictive value. To enhance predictive value, analysts try to separate a company's *transitory earnings* effects from its *permanent earnings.* Many believe that manipulating income reduces earnings quality because it can mask permanent earnings. Two major methods used by managers to manipulate earnings are (1) income shifting and (2) income statement classification. (p. 171)

● **LO3**   Analysts begin their assessment of permanent earnings with income from continuing operations. It would be a mistake to assume income from continuing operations reflects permanent earnings entirely. In other words, there may be transitory earnings effects included in both operating and nonoperating income. (p. 172)

● **LO4**   A discontinued operation refers to the disposal or a planned disposal of a component of the entity. A component of an entity comprises operations and cash flows that can be clearly distinguished, operationally and for financial reporting purposes, from the rest of the company. The net-of-tax effects of discontinued operations are separately reported below income from continuing operations. (p. 179)

● **LO5**   Extraordinary items are material gains and losses that are both unusual in nature and infrequent in occurrence. The net-of-tax effects of extraordinary items are presented in the income statement below discontinued operations, if any. (p. 183)

● **LO6**   Most voluntary changes in accounting principles are reported retrospectively. This means revising all previous periods' financial statements to appear as if the newly adopted accounting method had been applied all along. Some changes are reported prospectively. These include: (a) changes in the method of depreciation, amortization, or depletion, (b) some changes in principle for which retrospective application is impracticable, and (c) a few changes for which an authoritative pronouncement requires or allows prospective application. (p. 185)

● **LO7**   A change in accounting estimate is treated currently and prospectively, rather than by recasting prior years' financial statements to correct the estimate. In other words, the new estimate merely is used from that point on. Most errors are discovered in the same year that they are made. These errors are simple to correct. However, material errors discovered in a year subsequent to the year the error was made are considered prior period adjustments. The correction of the error is accounted for by restating prior years' financial statements, causing an adjustment to retained earnings at the beginning of the period. (p. 187)

● **LO8**   Earnings per share (EPS) is the amount of income achieved during a period expressed per share of common stock outstanding. The EPS must be disclosed for income from continuing operations and for each item below continuing operations. (p. 189)

● **LO9**   The FASB's Concept Statement 6 defines the term *comprehensive income* as the change in equity from nonowner transactions. The calculation of net income, however, excludes certain transactions that are included in comprehensive income. To convey the relationship between the two measures, companies must report both net income and comprehensive income and reconcile the difference between the two. The presentation can be (a) included as an extension to the income statement, (b) reported (exactly the same way) as a separate statement of comprehensive income, or (c) included in the statement of changes in shareholders' equity. (p. 190)

● **LO10**   When a company provides a set of financial statements that reports both financial position and results of operations, a statement of cash flows is reported for each period for which results of operations are provided. The purpose of the statement is to provide information about the cash receipts and cash disbursements that occurred during the period. (p. 195)

● **LO11**   To enhance the usefulness of the information, the statement of cash flows classifies all transactions affecting cash into one of three categories: (1) operating activities, (2) investing activities, or (3) financing activities. (p. 195) ●

QUESTIONS FOR REVIEW OF KEY TOPICS

Q 4–1 The income statement is a change statement. Explain what is meant by this.

Q 4–2 What transactions are included in income from continuing operations? Briefly explain why it is important to segregate income from continuing operations from other transactions affecting net income.

Q 4–3 Distinguish between operating and nonoperating income in relation to the income statement.

Q 4–4 Briefly explain the difference between the single-step and multiple-step income statement formats.

Q 4–5 Explain what is meant by the term earnings quality.

Q 4–6 What are restructuring costs and where are they reported in the income statement?

Q 4–7 Define intraperiod tax allocation. Why is the process necessary?

Q 4–8 Define what is meant by a component of an entity in the context of reporting the results of discontinued operations. How are discontinued operations reported in the income statement?

Q 4–9 Define extraordinary items.

Q 4–10 How should extraordinary gains and losses be reported in the income statement?

Q 4–11 What is meant by a change in accounting principle? Describe the accounting treatment for a voluntary change in accounting principle.

Q 4–12 Accountants very often are required to make estimates, and very often those estimates prove incorrect. In what period(s) is the effect of a change in an accounting estimate reported?

Q 4–13 The correction of a material error discovered in a year subsequent to the year the error was made is considered a prior period adjustment. Briefly describe the accounting treatment for prior period adjustments.

Q 4–14 Define earnings per share (EPS). For which income statement items must EPS be disclosed?

Q 4–15 Define comprehensive income. What are the three ways companies can present the reconciliation between net income and comprehensive income?

Q 4–16 Describe the purpose of the statement of cash flows.

Q 4–17 Identify and briefly describe the three categories of cash flows reported in the statement of cash flows.

Q 4–18 Explain what is meant by noncash investing and financing activities pertaining to the statement of cash flows. Give an example of one of these activities.

Q 4–19 Distinguish between the direct method and the indirect method for reporting the results of operating activities in the statement of cash flows.

BRIEF EXERCISES

BE 4–1
Single-step
income statement

● LO1

The adjusted trial balance of Pacific Scientific Corporation on December 31, 2009, the end of the company's fiscal year, contained the following income statement items ($ in millions): sales revenue, $2,106; cost of goods sold, $1,240; selling expenses, $126; general and administrative expenses, $105; interest expense, $35; and gain on sale of investments, $45. Income tax expense has not yet been accrued. The income tax rate is 40%. Prepare a single-step income statement for 2009. Ignore EPS disclosures.

BE 4–2
Multiple-step
income statement

● LO1 LO3

Refer to the situation described in BE 4–1. If the company's accountant prepared a multiple-step income statement, what amount would appear in that statement for (a) operating income and (b) nonoperating income?

BE 4–3
Multiple-step
income statement

● LO1 LO3

Refer to the situation described in BE 4–1. Prepare a multiple-step income statement for 2009. Ignore EPS disclosures.

BE 4–4
Multiple-step
income statement

● LO1 LO3

The following is a partial year-end adjusted trial balance.

Account Title	Debits	Credits
Sales revenue		300,000
Loss on sale of investments	22,000	
Interest revenue		4,000
Loss from flood damage (unusual and infrequent)	50,000	
Cost of goods sold	160,000	
General and administrative expenses	40,000	
Restructuring costs	50,000	
Selling expenses	25,000	
Income tax expense	0	

Income tax expense has not yet been accrued. The income tax rate is 40%. Determine the following: (a) operating income (loss), (b) income (loss) before any separately reported items, and (c) net income (loss).

BE 4–5
Separately reported items

● LO3 LO5 LO8

The following are partial income statement account balances taken from the December 31, 2009, year-end trial balance of White and Sons, Inc.: restructuring costs, $300,000; interest revenue, $40,000; loss from earthquake (unusual and infrequent), $400,000; and loss on sale of investments, $50,000. Income tax expense has not yet been accrued. The income tax rate is 40%. Prepare the lower portion of the 2009 income statement beginning with $850,000 income before income taxes and extraordinary item. Include appropriate basic EPS disclosures. The company had 100,000 shares of common stock outstanding throughout the year.

BE 4–6
Discontinued operations

● LO4

On December 31, 2009, the end of the fiscal year, California Microtech Corporation completed the sale of its semiconductor business for $10 million. The business segment qualifies as a component of the entity according to *SFAS No. 144.* The book value of the assets of the segment was $8 million. The operating loss of the segment during 2009 was $3.6 million. Pretax income from continuing operations for the year totaled $5.8 million. The income tax rate is 30%. Prepare the lower portion of the 2009 income statement beginning with pretax income from continuing operations. Ignore EPS disclosures.

BE 4–7
Discontinued operations

● LO4

Refer to the situation described in BE 4–6. Assume that the semiconductor segment was not sold during 2009 but was held for sale at year-end. The estimated fair value of the segment's assets, less costs to sell, on December 31 was $10 million. Prepare the lower portion of the 2009 income statement beginning with pretax income from continuing operations. Ignore EPS disclosures.

BE 4–8
Discontinued operations

● LO4

Refer to the situation described in BE 4–7. Assume instead that the estimated fair value of the segment's assets, less costs to sell, on December 31 was $7 million rather than $10 million. Prepare the lower portion of the 2009 income statement beginning with pretax income from continuing operations. Ignore EPS disclosures.

BE 4–9
Accounting change

● LO6

The Korver Company decided to change its inventory costing method from average to FIFO. The depreciation method also was changed from double-declining balance to straight line. Identify the type of accounting change for these two changes and briefly describe the difference in accounting treatment between the two, if any.

BE 4–10
Accounting change

● LO7

Powell Manufacturing purchased machinery for $300,000 at the beginning of 2007. A six-year life was estimated and no residual value was anticipated. Straight-line depreciation is used. At the beginning of 2009, the estimated useful life was revised to 10 years in total. What type of accounting change is this? Determine depreciation for 2009.

BE 4–11
Comprehensive income

● LO9

O'Reilly Beverage Company reported net income of $650,000 for 2009. In addition, the company deferred a $60,000 pretax loss on derivatives and had pretax net unrealized holding gains on investment securities of $40,000. Prepare a statement of comprehensive income for 2009. The company's income tax rate is 40%.

BE 4–12
Statement of cash flows; direct method

● LO11

The following are summary cash transactions that occurred during the year for Hilliard Healthcare Co. (HHC):

Cash received from:	
Customers	$660,000
Interest on note receivable	12,000
Collection of note payable	100,000
Sale of land	40,000
Issuance of common stock	200,000
Cash paid for:	
Interest on note payable	18,000
Purchase of equipment	120,000
Operating expenses	440,000
Dividends to shareholders	30,000

Prepare the cash flows from operating activities section of HHC's statement of cash flows using the direct method.

BE 4–13
Statement of cash flows; investing and financing activities

● LO11

Refer to the situation described in BE 4–12. Prepare the cash flows from investing and financing activities sections of HHC's statement of cash flows.

BE 4–14
Statement of cash
flows; indirect
method

● LO11

Net income of Mansfield Company was $45,000. The accounting records reveal depreciation expense of $80,000 as well as increases in prepaid rent, salaries payable, and income taxes payable of $60,000, $15,000, and $12,000, respectively. Prepare the cash flows from operating activities section of Mansfield's statement of cash flows using the indirect method.

EXERCISES

available with McGraw-Hill's Homework Manager www.mhhe.com/spiceland5e

An alternate exercise and problem set is available on the text website: www.mhhe.com/spiceland5e

E 4–1
Income statement
format; single step
and multiple step

● LO1 LO8

The following is a partial trial balance for the Green Star Corporation as of December 31, 2009:

Account Title	Debits	Credits
Sales revenue		1,300,000
Interest revenue		30,000
Gain on sale of equipment		50,000
Cost of goods sold	720,000	
Salaries expense	160,000	
Depreciation expense	50,000	
Interest expense	40,000	
Rent expense	25,000	
Income tax expense	130,000	

100,000 shares of common stock were outstanding throughout 2009.

Required:
1. Prepare a single-step income statement for 2009, including EPS disclosures.
2. Prepare a multiple-step income statement for 2009, including EPS disclosures.

E 4–2
Income statement
format; single step
and multiple step

● LO1 LO3 LO5
LO8

The following is a partial trial balance for General Lighting Corporation as of December 31, 2009:

Account Title	Debits	Credits
Sales revenue		2,350,000
Rental revenue		80,000
Loss on sale of equipment	22,500	
Loss from flood damage (event is both unusual and infrequent)	120,000	
Cost of goods sold	1,200,300	
Loss from write-down of inventory due to obsolescence	200,000	
Salaries expense	300,000	
Depreciation expense	100,000	
Interest expense	90,000	
Rent expense	50,000	

300,000 shares of common stock were outstanding throughout 2009. Income tax expense has not yet been accrued, The income tax rate is 40%.

Required:
1. Prepare a single-step income statement for 2009, including EPS disclosures.
2. Prepare a multiple-step income statement for 2009, including EPS disclosures.

E 4–3
Multiple-step
statement of
income and
comprehensive
income

● LO1 LO5 LO8
LO9

The trial balance for Lindor Corporation, a manufacturing company, for the year ended December 31, 2009, included the following income accounts:

Account Title	Debits	Credits
Sales revenue		2,300,000
Gain on litigation settlement (unusual and infrequent)		400,000
Cost of goods sold	1,400,000	
Selling and administrative expenses	420,000	
Interest expense	40,000	
Unrealized holding gains on investment securities		80,000

The trial balance does not include the accrual for income taxes. Lindor's income tax rate is 30%. One million shares of common stock were outstanding throughout 2009.

Required:
Prepare a combined multiple-step statement of income and comprehensive income for 2009, including appropriate EPS disclosures.

E 4–4
Income statement
presentation;
intraperiod tax
allocation

● LO1 LO5 LO8

The following *incorrect* income statement was prepared by the accountant of the Axel Corporation:

AXEL CORPORATION
Income Statement
For the Year Ended December 31, 2009

Revenues and gains:		
Sales		$592,000
Interest and dividends		32,000
Gain from litigation settlement		86,000
Total revenues and gains		710,000
Expenses and losses:		
Cost of goods sold	$325,000	
Selling expenses	67,000	
Administrative expenses	87,000	
Interest	26,000	
Restructuring costs	55,000	
Income taxes	60,000	
Total expenses and losses		620,000
Net Income		$ 90,000
Earnings per share		$ 0.90

Required:
Prepare a multiple-step income statement for 2009 applying generally accepted accounting principles. The income tax rate is 40%. The gain from litigation settlement is considered an unusual and infrequent event.

E 4–5
Discontinued
operations

● LO4 LO8

Chance Company had two operating divisions, one manufacturing farm equipment and the other office supplies. Both divisions are considered separate components as defined by *SFAS No. 144*. The farm equipment component had been unprofitable, and on September 1, 2009, the company adopted a plan to sell the assets of the division. The actual sale was effected on December 15, 2009, at a price of $600,000. The book value of the division's assets was $1,000,000, resulting in a before-tax loss of $400,000 on the sale.

The division incurred before-tax operating losses of $130,000 from the beginning of the year through December 15. The income tax rate is 40%. Chance's after-tax income from its continuing operations is $350,000.

Required:
Prepare an income statement for 2009 beginning with income from continuing operations. Include appropriate EPS disclosures assuming that 100,000 shares of common stock were outstanding throughout the year.

E 4–6
Income statement
presentation;
discontinued
operations;
restructuring
charges

● LO1 LO3 LO4

Esquire Comic Book Company had income before tax of $1,000,000 in 2009 *before* considering the following material items:
1. Esquire sold one of its operating divisions, which qualified as a separate component according to *SFAS No. 144*. The before-tax loss on disposal was $350,000. The division generated before-tax operating income from the beginning of the year through disposal of $500,000. Neither the loss on disposal nor the operating income is included in the $1,000,000 before-tax income the company generated from its other divisions.
2. The company incurred restructuring costs of $80,000 during the year.

Required:
Prepare a 2009 income statement for Esquire beginning with income from continuing operations. Assume an income tax rate of 40%. Ignore EPS disclosures.

E 4–7
Discontinued
operations; disposal
in subsequent year

● LO4

Kandon Enterprises, Inc. has two operating divisions, one manufactures machinery and the other breeds and sells horses. Both divisions are considered separate components as defined by *SFAS No. 144*. The horse division has been unprofitable, and on November 15, 2009, Kandon adopted a formal plan to sell the division. The sale was completed on April 30, 2010. At December 31, 2009, the component was considered held for sale.

On December 31, 2009, the company's fiscal year-end, the book value of the assets of the horse division was $250,000. On that date, the fair value of the assets, less costs to sell, was $200,000. The before-tax operating loss of the division for the year was $140,000. The company's effective tax rate is 40%. The after-tax income from continuing operations for 2009 was $400,000.

Required:
1. Prepare a partial income statement for 2009 beginning with income from continuing operations. Ignore EPS disclosures.
2. Repeat requirement 1 assuming that the estimated net sales price of the horse division's assets was $400,000, instead of $200,000.

E 4–8
Discontinued
operations; disposal
in subsequent
year; solving for
unknown

● LO4

On September 17, 2009, Ziltech, Inc. entered into an agreement to sell one of its divisions that qualifies as a component of the entity according to *SFAS No. 144*. By December 31, 2009, the company's fiscal year-end, the division had not yet been sold, but was being held for sale. The net fair value (fair value minus costs to sell) of the division's assets at the end of the year was $11 million. The pretax operating income of the division during 2009 was $4 million. Pretax income from continuing operations for the year totaled $14 million. The income tax rate is 40%. Ziltech reported net income for the year of $7.2 million.

Required:
Determine the book value of the division's assets on December 31, 2009.

E 4–9
Accounting change

● LO7

Canliss Milling Company purchased machinery on January 2, 2007, for $800,000. A five-year life was estimated and no residual value was anticipated. Canliss decided to use the straight-line depreciation method and recorded $160,000 in depreciation in 2007 and 2008. Early in 2009, the company revised the *total* estimated life of the machinery to eight years.

Required:
1. What type of accounting change is this?
2. Briefly describe the accounting treatment for this change.
3. Determine depreciation for 2009.

E 4–10
Accounting change

● LO6

[This is a variation of the previous exercise]

   Canliss Milling Company purchased machinery on January 2, 2007, for $800,000. A five-year life was estimated and no residual value was anticipated. Canliss decided to use the double-declining balance method and recorded depreciation of $320,000 in 2007 and $192,000 in 2008. Early in 2009, the company changed its depreciation method to the straight-line method.

Required:
1. Briefly describe the way Canliss should report this accounting change in the 2008–2009 comparative financial statements.
2. Prepare any 2009 journal entry related to the change.

E 4–11
Earnings per share

● LO8

The Esposito Import Company had 1 million shares of common stock outstanding during 2009. Its income statement reported the following items: income from continuing operations, $5 million; loss from discontinued operations, $1.6 million; extraordinary gain, $2.2 million. All of these amounts are net of tax.

Required:
Prepare the 2009 EPS presentation for the Esposito Import Company.

E 4–12
Comprehensive
income

● LO9

The Massoud Consulting Group reported net income of $1,354,000 for its fiscal year ended December 31, 2009. In addition, during the year the company experienced a foreign currency translation adjustment gain of $240,000 and had unrealized losses on investment securities of $80,000. The company's effective tax rate on all items affecting comprehensive income is 30%. Each component of other comprehensive income is displayed net of tax.

Required:
1. Prepare a combined statement of income and comprehensive income for 2009, beginning with net income.
2. Prepare a separate statement of comprehensive income for 2009.

E 4–13
IFRS; reporting
comprehensive
income

● LO9

Exercise 4–12 requires the presentation of other comprehensive income items in (1) a combined statement of income and comprehensive income and (2) in a separate statement of comprehensive income.

Required:
1. What other option(s) are available for the presentation of other comprehensive income items according to U.S. GAAP?
2. What options for the presentation of other comprehensive income items are available to companies complying with International Accounting Standards?

E 4–14
Statement of
cash flows;
classifications

● LO11

The statement of cash flows classifies all cash inflows and outflows into one of the three categories shown below and lettered from a through c. In addition, certain transactions that do not involve cash are reported in the statement as noncash investing and financing activities, labeled d.

a. Operating activities
b. Investing activities
c. Financing activities
d. Noncash investing and financing activities

Required:
For each of the following transactions, use the letters above to indicate the appropriate classification category.

1. ____Purchase of equipment for cash.
2. ____Payment of employee salaries.
3. ____Collection of cash from customers.
4. ____Cash proceeds from a note payable.
5. ____Purchase of common stock of another corporation for cash.
6. ____Issuance of common stock for cash.
7. ____Sale of machinery for cash.
8. ____Payment of interest on note payable.
9. ____Issuance of bonds payable in exchange for land and building.
10. ____Payment of cash dividends to shareholders.
11. ____Payment of principal on note payable.

E 4–15
Statement of cash
flows preparation

● LO11

The following summary transactions occurred during 2009 for Bluebonnet Bakers:

Cash Received from:	
Customers	$380,000
Interest on note receivable	6,000
Principal on note receivable	50,000
Sale of investments	30,000
Proceeds from note payable	100,000
Cash Paid for:	
Purchase of inventory	160,000
Interest on note payable	5,000
Purchase of equipment	85,000
Salaries to employees	90,000
Principal on note payable	25,000
Payment of dividends to shareholders	20,000

The balance of cash and cash equivalents at the beginning of 2009 was $17,000.

Required:
Prepare a statement of cash flows for 2009 for Bluebonnet Bakers. Use the direct method for reporting operating activities.

E 4–16
IFRS; statement of
cash flows

● LO11

Refer to the situation described in Exercise 4–15.

Required:
How might your solution differ if Bluebonnet Bakers prepares the statement of cash flows according to International Accounting Standards?

E 4–17
Indirect method;
reconciliation of
net income to net
cash flows from
operating activities

● LO11

The accounting records of Hampton Company provided the data below ($ in 000s).

Net income	$17,300
Depreciation expense	7,800
Increase in accounts receivable	4,000
Decrease in inventory	5,500
Decrease in prepaid insurance	1,200
Decrease in salaries payable	2,700
Increase in interest payable	800

Required:
Prepare a reconciliation of net income to net cash flows from operating activities.

E 4–18
Statement of cash
flows directly from
transactions

● LO11

The following transactions occurred during March 2009 for the Wainwright Corporation. The company owns and operates a wholesale warehouse. [These are the same transactions analyzed in Exercise 2–1, when we determined their effect on elements of the accounting equation.]
1. Issued 30,000 shares of capital stock in exchange for $300,000 in cash.
2. Purchased equipment at a cost of $40,000. $10,000 cash was paid and a note payable was signed for the balance owed.
3. Purchased inventory on account at a cost of $90,000. The company uses the perpetual inventory system.
4. Credit sales for the month totaled $120,000. The cost of the goods sold was $70,000.
5. Paid $5,000 in rent on the warehouse building for the month of March.

6. Paid $6,000 to an insurance company for fire and liability insurance for a one-year period beginning April 1, 2009.
7. Paid $70,000 on account for the merchandise purchased in 3.
8. Collected $55,000 from customers on account.
9. Recorded depreciation expense of $1,000 for the month on the equipment.

Required:
1. Analyze each transaction and classify each as a financing, investing and/or operating activity (a transaction can represent more than one type of activity). In doing so, also indicate the cash effect of each, if any. If there is no cash effect, simply place a check mark (√) in the appropriate column(s).

Example:

Financing	Investing	Operating
1. $300,000		

2. Prepare a statement of cash flows, using the direct method to present cash flows from operating activities. Assume the cash balance at the beginning of the month was $40,000.

E 4–19
Statement of cash flows; indirect method

● LO11

Presented below is the 2009 income statement and comparative balance sheet information for Tiger Enterprises.

TIGER ENTERPRISES
Income Statement
For the Year Ended December 31, 2009

($ in thousands)

Sales revenue		$7,000
Operating expenses:		
Cost of goods sold	$3,360	
Depreciation	240	
Insurance	100	
Administrative and other	1,800	
Total operating expenses		5,500
Income before income taxes		1,500
Income tax expense		600
Net income		$ 900

Balance Sheet Information ($ in thousands)	Dec. 31, 2009	Dec. 31, 2008
Assets:		
Cash	$ 300	$ 200
Accounts receivable	750	830
Inventory	640	600
Prepaid insurance	50	20
Plant and equipment	2,100	1,800
Less: Accumulated depreciation	(840)	(600)
Total assets	$3,000	$2,850
Liabilities and Shareholders' Equity:		
Accounts payable	$ 300	$ 360
Payables for administrative and other expenses	300	400
Income taxes payable	200	150
Note payable (due 12/31/2010)	800	600
Common stock	900	800
Retained earnings	500	540
Total liabilities and shareholders' equity	$3,000	$2,850

Required:
Prepare Tiger's statement of cash flows, using the indirect method to present cash flows from operating activities. (Hint: You will have to calculate dividend payments.)

E 4–20
Statement of cash flows; direct method

● LO11

Refer to the situation described in Exercise 4–19.

Required:
Prepare the cash flows from operating activities section of Tiger's 2009 statement of cash flows using the direct method. Assume that all purchases and sales of inventory are on account, and that there are no anticipated bad

debts for accounts receivable. (Hint: Use T-accounts for the pertinent items to isolate the information needed for the statement.)

E 4–21
Concepts;
terminology
● LO1 through
LO11

Listed below are several terms and phrases associated with income statement presentation and the statement of cash flows. Pair each item from List A (by letter) with the item from List B that is most appropriately associated with it.

List A	List B
_____ 1. Intraperiod tax allocation	a. Unusual, infrequent, and material gains and losses.
_____ 2. Comprehensive income	b. Starts with net income and works backwards to convert to cash.
_____ 3. Extraordinary items	c. Reports the cash effects of each operating activity directly on the statement.
_____ 4. Operating income	d. Correction of a material error of a prior period.
_____ 5. An operation (according to *SFAS 144*)	e. Related to the external financing of the company.
_____ 6. Earnings per share	f. Associates tax with income statement item.
_____ 7. Prior period adjustment	g. Total nonowner change in equity.
_____ 8. Financing activities	h. Related to the transactions entering into the determination of net income.
_____ 9. Operating activities (SCF)	i. Related to the acquisition and disposition of long-term assets.
_____10. Investing activities	j. Required disclosure for publicly traded corporation.
_____11. Direct method	k. A component of an entity.
_____12. Indirect method	l. Directly related to principal revenue-generating activities.

CPA AND CMA REVIEW QUESTIONS

CPA Exam Questions

The following questions are used in the Kaplan CPA Review Course to study the income statement and statement of cash flows while preparing for the CPA examination. Determine the response that best completes the statements or questions.

● LO4

1. Roco Company manufactures both industrial and consumer electronics. Due to a change in its strategic focus, the company decided to exit the consumer electronics business, and in 2009 sold the division to Sunny Corporation. The consumer electronics division qualifies as a component of the entity according to *SFAS No. 144.* How should Roco report the sale in its 2009 income statement?

   a. Include in income from continuing operations as a nonoperating gain or loss.
   b. As an extraordinary item.
   c. As a discontinued operation, reported below income from continuing operations.
   d. None of the above.

● LO3 LO4 LO5
LO7

2. Bridge Company's results for the year ended December 31, 2009, include the following material items:

Sales revenue	$5,000,000
Cost of goods sold	3,000,000
Administrative expenses	1,000,000
Gain on sale of equipment	200,000
Loss on discontinued operations	400,000
Loss from earthquake damage (unusual and infrequent event)	500,000
Understatement of depreciation expense in 2008 caused by mathematical error	250,000

Bridge Company's income from continuing operations before income taxes for 2009 is:

   a. $700,000
   b. $950,000
   c. $1,000,000
   d. $1,200,000

● LO4 LO5

3. In Baer Food Co.'s 2009 single-step income statement, the section titled "Revenues" consisted of the following:

Net sales revenue	$187,000
Income on discontinued operations including gain on disposal of $21,000 and net taxes of $6,000	12,000
Interest revenue	10,200
Gain on sale of equipment	4,700
Extraordinary gain net of $750 tax effect	1,500
Total revenues	$215,400

In the revenues section of the 2009 income statement, Baer Food should have reported total revenues of
a. $201,900
b. $203,700
c. $215,400
d. $216,300

● LO4

4. On November 30, 2009, Pearman Company committed to a plan to sell a division that qualified as a component of the entity according to *SFAS No. 144,* and was properly classified as held for sale on December 31, 2009, the end of the company's fiscal year. The division was tested for impairment and a $400,000 loss was indicated. The division's loss from operations for 2009 was $1,000,000. The final sale was expected to occur on February 15, 2010. What before-tax amount(s) should Pearman report as loss on discontinued operations in its 2009 income statement?
a. $1,400,000 loss.
b. $400,000 loss.
c. None.
d. $400,000 impairment loss included in continuing operations and a $1,000,000 loss from discontinued operations.

● LO7

5. For 2008, Pac Co. estimated its two-year equipment warranty costs based on $100 per unit sold. Experience during 2009 indicated that the estimate should have been based on $110 per unit. The effect of this $10 difference from the change in estimate is reported
a. As an accounting change below 2009 income from continuing operations.
b. As an accounting change requiring the 2009 financial statements to be restated.
c. As a correction of an error requiring 2009 financial statements to be restated.
d. In 2009 income from continuing operations.

● LO11

6. Which of the following items is *not* considered an operating cash flow in the statement of cash flows?
a. Dividends paid to stockholders.
b. Cash received from customers.
c. Interest paid to creditors.
d. Cash paid for salaries.

● LO11

7. Which of the following items is *not* considered an investing cash flow in the statement of cash flows?
a. Purchase of equipment.
b. Purchase of securities.
c. Issuing common stock for cash.
d. Sale of land.

CMA Exam
Questions

The following questions dealing with the income statement are adapted from questions that previously appeared on Certified Management Accountant (CMA) examinations. The CMA designation sponsored by the Institute of Management Accountants (**www.imanet.org**) provides members with an objective measure of knowledge and competence in the field of management accounting. Determine the response that best completes the statements or questions.

● LO3

1. In a multiple-step income statement for a retail company, all of the following are included in the operating section except
a. Sales.
b. Cost of goods sold.
c. Dividend revenue.
d. Administrative and selling expenses.

● LO1

2. Which one of the following items is included in the determination of income from continuing operations?
a. Discontinued operations.
b. Extraordinary loss.

c. Cumulative effect of a change in an accounting principle.

d. Unusual loss from a write-down of inventory.

● LO5

3. When reporting extraordinary items,

a. Each item (net of tax) is presented on the face of the income statement separately as a component of net income for the period.

b. Each item is presented exclusive of any related income tax.

c. Each item is presented as an unusual item within income from continuing operations.

d. All extraordinary gains or losses that occur in a period are summarized as total gains and total losses, then offset to present the net extraordinary gain or loss.

PROBLEMS

available with McGraw-Hill's Homework Manager www.mhhe.com/spiceland5e

An alternate exercise and problem set is available on the text website: www.mhhe.com/spiceland5e

P 4–1
Comparative
income statements;
multiple-step
format

● LO1 LO3 through
LO5 LO8

Selected information about income statement accounts for the Reed Company are presented below (the company's fiscal year ends on December 31):

	2009	2008
Sales	$4,400,000	$3,500,000
Cost of goods sold	2,860,000	2,000,000
Administrative expenses	800,000	675,000
Selling expenses	360,000	312,000
Interest revenue	150,000	140,000
Interest expense	200,000	200,000
Loss on sale of assets of discontinued component	50,000	—

On July 1, 2009, the company adopted a plan to discontinue a division that qualifies as a component of an entity as defined in *SFAS No. 144*. The assets of the component were sold on September 30, 2009 for $50,000 less than their book value. Results of operations for the component (*included* in the above account balances) were as follows:

	1/1/09–9/30/09	2008
Sales	$400,000	$500,000
Cost of goods sold	(290,000)	(320,000)
Administrative expenses	(50,000)	(40,000)
Selling expenses	(20,000)	(30,000)
Operating income before taxes	$ 40,000	$110,000

In addition to the account balances above, several events occurred during 2009 that have *not* yet been reflected in the above accounts:

1. A fire caused $50,000 in uninsured damages to the main office building. The fire was considered to be an infrequent but not unusual event.

2. An earthquake caused $100,000 in property damage to one of Reed's factories. The amount of the loss is material and the event is considered unusual and infrequent.

3. Inventory that had cost $40,000 had become obsolete because a competitor introduced a better product. The inventory was sold as scrap for $5,000.

4. Income taxes have not yet been accrued.

Required:
Prepare a multiple-step income statement for the Reed Company for 2009, showing 2008 information in comparative format, including income taxes computed at 40% and EPS disclosures assuming 300,000 shares of common stock.

P 4–2
Discontinued
operations

● LO4

The following condensed income statements of the Jackson Holding Company are presented for the two years ended December 31, 2009 and 2008:

	2009	2008
Sales	$15,000,000	$9,600,000
Cost of goods sold	9,200,000	6,000,000
Gross profit	5,800,000	3,600,000
Operating expenses	3,200,000	2,600,000
Operating income	2,600,000	1,000,000
Gain on sale of division	600,000	—

(continued)

(concluded)

	3,200,000	1,000,000
Income tax expense	1,280,000	400,000
Net income	$ 1,920,000	$ 600,000

On October 15, 2009, Jackson entered into a tentative agreement to sell the assets of one of its divisions. The division comprises operations and cash flows that can be clearly distinguished, operationally and for financial reporting purposes, from the rest of the company. The division was sold on December 31, 2009, for $5,000,000. Book value of the division's assets was $4,400,000. The division's contribution to Jackson's operating income before-tax for each year was as follows:

2009	$400,000 loss
2008	$300,000 loss

Assume an income tax rate of 40%.

Required:

1. Prepare revised income statements according to generally accepted accounting principles, beginning with income from continuing operations before income taxes. Ignore EPS disclosures.

2. Assume that by December 31, 2009, the division had not yet been sold but was considered held for sale. The fair value of the division's assets on December 31 was $5,000,000. How would the presentation of discontinued operations be different from your answer to requirement 1?

3. Assume that by December 31, 2009, the division had not yet been sold but was considered held for sale. The fair value of the division's assets on December 31 was $3,900,000. How would the presentation of discontinued operations be different from your answer to requirement 1?

P 4–3
Income statement presentation

● LO4 LO5 LO7

For the year ending December 31, 2009, Micron Corporation had income from continuing operations before taxes of $1,200,000 before considering the following transactions and events. All of the items described below are before taxes and the amounts should be considered material.

1. During 2009, one of Micron's factories was damaged in an earthquake. As a result, the firm recognized a loss of $800,000. The event is considered unusual and infrequent.

2. In November of 2009, Micron sold its Waffle House restaurant chain that qualified as a component of an entity. The company had adopted a plan to sell the chain in May of 2009. The operating income of the chain from January 1, 2009, through November was $160,000 and the loss on sale of the chain's assets was $300,000.

3. In 2009, Micron sold one of its six factories for $1,200,000. At the time of the sale, the factory had a carrying value of $1,100,000. The factory was not considered a component of the entity.

4. In 2007, Micron's accountant omitted the annual adjustment for patent amortization expense of $120,000. The error was not discovered until December, 2009.

Required:

1. Prepare Micron's income statement, beginning with income from continuing operations before taxes, for the year ended December 31, 2009. Assume an income tax rate of 30%. Ignore EPS disclosures.

2. Briefly explain the motivation for segregating certain income statement events from income from continuing operations.

P 4–4
Income statement presentation; unusual items

● LO3 LO5 LO7

The preliminary 2009 income statement of Alexian Systems, Inc., is presented below:

ALEXIAN SYSTEMS, INC.
Income Statement
For the Year Ended December 31, 2009
($ in millions, except earnings per share)

Revenues and gains:	
Net sales	$ 425
Interest	3
Other income	126
Total revenues and gains	554
Expenses:	
Cost of goods sold	270
Selling and administrative	154
Income taxes	52
Total expenses	476
Net Income	$ 78
Earnings per share	$3.90

Additional information:

1. Selling and administrative expenses include $26 million in restructuring costs.
2. Included in other income is an extraordinary gain of $120 million. The remaining $6 million is from the gain on sale of operating assets.
3. Cost of goods sold was increased by $5 million to correct an error in the calculation of 2008's ending inventory. The amount is material.

Required:
For each of the three additional facts listed above, discuss the appropriate presentation of the item described. Do not prepare a revised statement.

P 4–5
Income statement
presentation;
unusual items
● LO1 LO3 LO5
LO7 LO8

[This is a variation of the previous problem focusing on income statement presentation.]

Required:
Refer to the information presented in Problem 4–4. Prepare a revised income statement for 2009 reflecting the additional facts. Use a multiple-step format. Assume that an income tax rate of 40% applies to all income statement items, and that 20 million shares of common stock were outstanding throughout the year.

P 4–6
Income statement
presentation
● LO1 LO3 through
LO5 LO8

Rembrandt Paint Company had the following income statement items for the year ended December 31, 2009 ($ in 000s):

Net sales	$18,000	Cost of goods sold	$10,500
Interest income	200	Selling and administrative expenses	2,500
Interest expense	350	Restructuring costs	800
Extraordinary gain	3,000		

In addition, during the year the company completed the disposal of its plastics business and incurred a loss from operations of $1.6 million and a gain on disposal of the component's assets of $2 million. 500,000 shares of common stock were outstanding throughout 2009. Income tax expense has not yet been accrued. The income tax rate is 30% on all items of income (loss).

Required:
Prepare a multiple-step income statement for 2009, including EPS disclosures.

P 4–7
Income statement
presentation;
unusual items
● LO1 LO3 LO4
LO5 LO7 LO8
LO9

The following income statement items appeared on the adjusted trial balance of Schembri Manufacturing Corporation for the year ended December 31, 2009 ($ in 000s): sales revenue, $15,300; cost of goods sold, $6,200; selling expenses, $1,300; general and administrative expenses, $800; interest revenue, $85; interest expense, $180. Income taxes have not yet been accrued. The company's income tax rate is 40% on all items of income or loss. These revenue and expense items appear in the company's income statement every year. The company's controller, however, has asked for your help in determining the appropriate treatment of the following nonrecurring transactions that also occurred during 2009 ($ in 000s). All transactions are material in amount.

1. Investments were sold during the year at a loss of $220. Schembri also had unrealized gains of $320 for the year on investments accounted for as securities available for sale.
2. One of the company's factories was closed during the year. Restructuring costs incurred were $1,200.
3. An earthquake destroyed a warehouse causing $2,000 in damages. The event is considered to be unusual and infrequent.
4. During the year, Schembri completed the sale of one of its operating divisions that qualifies as a component of the entity according to *SFAS No. 144*. The division had incurred an operating loss of $560 in 2009 prior to the sale, and its assets were sold at a gain of $1,400.
5. In 2009, the company's accountant discovered that depreciation expense in 2008 for the office building was understated by $200.
6. Foreign currency translation losses for the year totaled $240.

Required:
Prepare Schembri's combined statement of income and comprehensive income for 2009, including basic earnings per share disclosures. One million shares of common stock were outstanding at the beginning of the year and an additional 400,000 shares were issued on July 1, 2009.

P 4–8
Multiple-step
statement of income
and comprehensive
income
● LO1 LO3 LO5
LO7 LO9

Duke Company's records show the following account balances at December 31, 2009:

Sales	$15,000,000
Cost of goods sold	9,000,000
General and administrative expenses	1,000,000
Selling expenses	500,000
Interest expense	700,000

Income tax expense has not yet been determined. The following events also occurred during 2009:

1. $300,000 in restructuring costs were incurred in connection with plant closings.

2. The company operates a factory in South America. During the year, the foreign government took over (expropriated) the factory and paid Duke $1,000,000, which was one-fourth of the book value of the assets involved.

3. Inventory costing $400,000 was written off as obsolete. Material losses of this type are not considered to be unusual.

4. It was discovered that depreciation expense for 2008 was understated by $50,000 due to a mathematical error.

5. The company experienced a foreign currency translation adjustment loss of $200,000 and had unrealized gains on investment securities of $180,000.

Required:

Prepare a combined multiple-step statement of income and comprehensive income for 2009. The company's effective tax rate on all items affecting comprehensive income is 40%. Each component of other comprehensive income should be displayed net of tax. Ignore EPS disclosures.

P 4–9
Statement of cash flows
● LO11

The Diversified Portfolio Corporation provides investment advice to customers. A condensed income statement for the year ended December 31, 2009, appears below:

Service revenue	$900,000
Operating expenses	700,000
Income before income taxes	200,000
Income tax expense	80,000
Net income	$120,000

The following balance sheet information also is available:

	12/31/09	12/31/08
Cash	$275,000	$ 70,000
Accounts receivable	120,000	100,000
Accounts payable (operating expenses)	70,000	60,000
Income taxes payable	10,000	15,000

In addition, the following transactions took place during the year:

1. Common stock was issued for $100,000 in cash.

2. Long-term investments were sold for $50,000 in cash. The original cost of the investments also was $50,000.

3. $80,000 in cash dividends was paid to shareholders.

4. The company has no outstanding debt, other than those payables listed above.

5. Operating expenses include $30,000 in depreciation expense.

Required:

1. Prepare a statement of cash flows for 2009 for the Diversified Portfolio Corporation. Use the direct method for reporting operating activities.

2. Prepare the cash flows from operating activities section of Diversified's 2009 statement of cash flows using the indirect method.

P 4–10
Integration of financial statements;
Chapters 3 and 4
● LO11

The chief accountant for Grandview Corporation provides you with the company's 2009 statement of cash flows and income statement. The accountant has asked for your help with some missing figures in the company's comparative balance sheets. These financial statements are shown next ($ in millions).

GRANDVIEW CORPORATION
Statement of Cash Flows
For the Year Ended December 31, 2009

Cash Flows from Operating Activities:		
Collections from customers	$71	
Payment to suppliers	(30)	
Payment of general & administrative expenses	(18)	
Payment of income taxes	(9)	
Net cash flows from operating activities		$14
Cash Flows from Investing Activities:		
Sale of equipment		40

(continued)

(concluded)

Cash Flows from Financing Activities:

Issuance of common stock	10	
Payment of dividends	(3)	
Net cash flows from financing activities		7
Net increase in cash		$61

GRANDVIEW CORPORATION
Income Statement
For the Year Ended December 31, 2009

Sales revenue		$80
Cost of goods sold		32
Gross profit		48
Operating expenses:		
General and administrative	$18	
Depreciation	10	
Total operating expenses		28
Operating income		20
Other income:		
Gain on sale of equipment		15
Income before income taxes		35
Income tax expense		7
Net income		$28

GRANDVIEW CORPORATION
Balance Sheets
At December 31

	2009	2008
Assets:		
Cash	$120	$?
Accounts receivable	?	84
Inventory	60	?
Property, plant & equipment	150	200
Less: Accumulated depreciation	(40)	?
Total assets	?	?
Liabilities and Shareholders' Equity:		
Accounts payable to suppliers	$ 40	$30
Payables for selling & admin. expenses	9	9
Income taxes payable	22	?
Common stock	240	230
Retained earnings	?	47
Total liabilities and shareholders' equity	?	?

Required:
1. Calculate the missing amounts.
2. Prepare the operating activities section of Grandview's 2009 statement of cash flows using the indirect method.

P 4–11
Statement of cash flows; indirect method

● LO11

Presented below are the 2009 income statement and comparative balance sheets for Santana Industries.

Santana Industries
Income Statement
For the Year Ended December 31, 2009
($ in thousands)

Sales revenue	$14,250	
Service revenue	3,400	
Total revenue		$17,650
Operating expenses:		
Cost of goods sold	7,200	

(continued)

(concluded)

Selling	2,400	
General and administrative	1,500	
Total operating expenses		11,100
Operating income		6,550
Interest expense		200
Income before income taxes		6,350
Income tax expense		2,500
Net income		$ 3,850

Balance Sheet Information ($ in thousands)	Dec. 31, 2009	Dec. 31, 2008
Assets:		
Cash	$ 7,350	$ 2,200
Accounts receivable	2,500	2,200
Inventory	4,000	3,000
Prepaid rent	150	300
Plant and equipment	14,500	12,000
Less: Accumulated depreciation	(5,100)	(4,500)
Total assets	$23,400	$15,200
Liabilities and Shareholders' Equity:		
Accounts payable	$ 1,400	$ 1,100
Interest payable	100	0
Unearned service revenue	800	600
Income taxes payable	550	800
Loan payable (due 12/31/2012)	5,000	0
Common stock	10,000	10,000
Retained earnings	5,550	2,700
Total liabilities and shareholders' equity	$23,400	$15,200

Additional information for the 2009 fiscal year ($ in thousands):

1. Cash dividends of $1,000 were declared and paid.
2. Equipment costing $4,000 was purchased with cash.
3. Equipment with a book value of $500 (cost of $1,500 less accumulated depreciation of $1,000) was sold for $500.
4. Depreciation of $1,600 is included in operating expenses.

Required:
Prepare Santana Industries' 2009 statement of cash flows, using the indirect method to present cash flows from operating activities.

BROADEN YOUR PERSPECTIVE

Apply your critical-thinking ability to the knowledge you've gained. These cases will provide you an opportunity to develop your research, analysis, judgment, and communication skills. You also will work with other students, integrate what you've learned, apply it in real world situations, and consider its global and ethical ramifications. This practice will broaden your knowledge and further develop your decision-making abilities.

Judgment
Case 4–1
Earnings quality

● LO2 LO3

The financial community in the United States has become increasingly concerned with the quality of reported company earnings.

Required:
1. Define the term *earnings quality.*
2. Explain the distinction between permanent and transitory earnings as it relates to the concept of earnings quality.
3. How do earnings management practices affect the quality of earnings?
4. Assume that a manufacturing company's annual income statement included a large gain from the sale of investment securities. What factors would you consider in determining whether or not this gain should be included in an assessment of the company's permanent earnings?

Judgment
Case 4–2
Restructuring costs

● LO3

The appearance of restructuring costs in corporate income statements increased significantly in the 1980s and 1990s.

Required:

1. What types of costs are included in restructuring costs?
2. When are restructuring costs recognized?
3. How would you classify restructuring costs in a multi-step income statement?
4. What factors would you consider in determining whether or not restructuring costs should be included in an assessment of a company's permanent earnings?

Judgment Case 4–3
Earnings management
● LO2 LO3

Companies often are under pressure to meet or beat Wall Street earnings projections in order to increase stock prices and also to increase the value of stock options. Some resort to earnings management practices to artificially create desired results.

Required:

Is *earnings management* always intended to produce higher income? Explain.

Real World Case 4–4
Earnings quality and pro forma earnings
● LO3
Real World Financials

[The solution to this case requires access to company data via the Internet.]

Cisco Systems, Inc., the world's largest networking products company, announced on May 8, 2001, that its *pro forma earnings* for the quarter ended April 28, 2001, were $230 million. They also disclosed that actual earnings for the quarter, determined according to generally accepted accounting principles, were a *loss* of $2.69 billion.

Required:

1. What is meant by the term *pro forma earnings* in this context?
2. How do pro forma earnings relate to the concept of earnings quality?
3. Access the company's 10-Q (quarterly report) for the quarter ended April 28, 2001. You can go to the company's Internet site, or EDGAR (**www.sec.gov**). Using the company's income statement for the quarter and disclosure notes, reconcile the GAAP loss of $2.69 billion to the pro forma earnings figure of $230 million. Remember that both of these earnings (loss) figures are net of tax.

Communication Case 4–5
Income statement presentation of gain
● LO5

McMinville Corporation manufactures paper products. In 2005, the company purchased several large tracts of timber for $22 million with the intention of harvesting the timber rather than buying this critical raw material from outside suppliers. However, in 2009, McMinville abandoned the idea and all of the timber tracts were sold for $31 million. Net income for 2009, before considering this event, is $17.5 million and the company's effective tax rate is 30%.

The focus of this case is the income statement presentation of the gain on the sale of the timber tracts. Your instructor will divide the class into two to six groups depending on the size of the class. The mission of your group is to reach consensus on the appropriate income statement presentation of the gain.

Required:

Each group member should deliberate the situation independently and draft a tentative argument prior to the class session for which the case is assigned.

In class, each group will meet for 10 to 15 minutes in different areas of the classroom. During that meeting, group members will take turns sharing their suggestions for the purpose of arriving at a single group treatment.

After the allotted time, a spokesperson for each group (selected during the group meetings) will share the group's solution with the class. The goal of the class is to incorporate the views of each group into a consensus approach to the situation.

Communication Case 4–6
Income statement presentation
● LO5

Carter Hawley Hale Stores (CHHS), Inc. was one of the largest department store retailers in the United States. At the end of fiscal 1989, the company operated 113 stores in the sunbelt regions of the country. The company's divisions included The Broadway, with 43 stores in Southern California and 11 stores in the southwest, and Emporium, with 22 stores in the greater San Francisco Bay Area.

On October 17, 1989, a 7.1 Richter scale earthquake caused significant amounts of monetary damage to the San Francisco Bay Area. This was the largest earthquake to hit the Bay Area since the quake of 1906 destroyed much of San Francisco. California is lined with many active earthquake faults. Hundreds of small earthquakes occur each year throughout the state.

The Emporium division of CHHS suffered extensive damage as a result of the October 17 earthquake. Twelve of the twenty-two stores were closed for varying periods of time, with the Oakland store hardest hit. In total, uninsured damage was $27.5 million ($16.5 million after tax benefits).

For the fiscal year ending August 4, 1990, CHHS reported an after-tax loss of $9.47 million *before* considering the earthquake loss. Total revenues for the year were $2.857 billion.

Required:

Assume that you are the CHHS controller. The chief financial officer of CHHS has asked you to prepare a short report (1–2 pages) in memo form giving your recommendation as to the proper reporting of the earthquake damage costs in the income statement for the year ending August 4, 1990. Explain why your recommendation is appropriate. Be sure to include in your report any references to authoritative pronouncements that support your recommendation.

Ethics Case 4–7
Income statement presentation of unusual loss

● **LO3**

After a decade of consistent income growth, the Cranor Corporation sustained a before-tax loss of $8.4 million in 2009. The loss was primarily due to $10 million in expenses related to a product recall. Cranor manufactures medical equipment, including x-ray machines. The recall was attributable to a design flaw in the manufacture of the company's new line of machines.

The company controller, Jim Dietz, has suggested that the loss should be included in the 2009 income statement as an extraordinary item. "If we report it as an extraordinary item, our income from continuing operations will actually show an increase from the prior year. The stock market will appreciate the continued growth in ongoing profitability and will discount the one-time loss. And our bonuses are tied to income from continuing operations, not net income."

The chief executive officer asked Jim to justify this treatment. "I know we have had product recalls before and, of course, they do occur in our industry," Jim replied, "but we have never had a recall of this magnitude, and we fixed the design flaw and upgraded our quality control procedures."

Required:
Discuss the ethical dilemma faced by Jim Dietz and the company's chief executive officer.

Research Case 4–8
Locate and extract relevant information and authoritative support for a financial reporting issue; treatment of losses from terrorist attacks

● **LO5**

Yesterday you watched a TV special on the terrorist attacks of September 11, 2001. Those attacks resulted in a tragic loss of life and property. Today in your intermediate accounting class, your professor discussed the measurement and reporting of separately reported items, including extraordinary gains and losses. A classmate asked her if companies that sustained significant losses as a result of the attacks reported those losses as extraordinary items in their income statements. She asked the class to think about it and to formulate an answer for the next class period. She also mentioned that there is an Emerging Issues Task Force Issue that addresses this question and suggested you do some research.

Required:
1. Do you think that the terrorist attacks of September 11 constitute an "extraordinary" event?
2. Obtain the EITF Issue on accounting for the impact of the terrorist attacks. You might gain access at the FASB website (www.fasb.org), from your school library, or some other source.
3. Why did the EITF address this issue and not the FASB itself?
4. What did your research reveal? What reasons did the EITF provide for its conclusion?

Judgment Case 4–9
Income statement presentation

● **LO3 through LO6**

Each of the following situations occurred during 2009 for one of your audit clients:
1. The write-off of inventory due to obsolescence.
2. Discovery that depreciation expenses were omitted by accident from 2008's income statement.
3. The useful lives of all machinery were changed from eight to five years.
4. The depreciation method used for all equipment was changed from the declining-balance to the straight-line method.
5. Ten million dollars face value of bonds payable were repurchased (paid off) prior to maturity resulting in a material loss of $500,000. The company considers the event unusual and infrequent.
6. Restructuring costs were incurred.
7. The Stridewell Company, a manufacturer of shoes, sold all of its retail outlets. It will continue to manufacture and sell its shoes to other retailers. A loss was incurred in the disposition of the retail stores. The retail stores are considered components of the entity.
8. The inventory costing method was changed from FIFO to average cost.

Required:
1. For each situation, identify the appropriate reporting treatment from the list below (consider each event to be material):
   a. As an extraordinary item.
   b. As an unusual or infrequent gain or loss.
   c. As a prior period adjustment.
   d. As a change in accounting principle.
   e. As a discontinued operation.
   f. As a change in accounting estimate.
   g. As a change in accounting estimate achieved by a change in accounting principle.
2. Indicate whether each situation would be included in the income statement in continuing operations (CO) or below continuing operations (BC), or if it would appear as an adjustment to retained earnings (RE). Use the format shown below to answer requirements 1 and 2.

Situation	Treatment (a–g)	**Financial Statement Presentation (CO, BC, or RE)**
1.		
2.		
3.		
4.		
5.		
6.		
7.		
8.		

Judgment Case 4–10
Income statement presentation

● LO3 through LO7

The following events occurred during 2009 for various audit clients of your firm. Consider each event to be independent and the effect of each event to be material.

1. A manufacturing company recognized a loss on the sale of equipment used in its manufacturing operations.
2. An automobile manufacturer sold all of the assets related to its financing component. The operations of the financing business can be clearly distinguished from the rest of the entity.
3. A company changed its depreciation method from the double-declining-balance method to the straight-line method.
4. Due to obsolescence, a company engaged in the manufacture of high-technology products incurred a loss on the write-down of inventory.
5. One of your clients discovered that 2008's depreciation expense was overstated. The error occurred because of a miscalculation of depreciation for the office building.
6. A cosmetics company decided to discontinue the manufacture of a line of women's lipstick. Other cosmetic lines will be continued. A loss was incurred on the sale of assets related to the lipstick product line. The operations of the discontinued line cannot be distinguished from the rest of the cosmetics business.

Required:
Discuss the 2009 financial statement presentation of each of the above events. Do not consider earnings per share disclosures.

IFRS Case 4–11
Income statement presentation

● LO4 LO8

Refer to the financial statements of Cadbury Schweppes, PLC, a major global manufacturer of beverages and confectionery located in Great Britain, for the period ended December 31, 2006. You can locate the company's annual report at **www.cadburyschweppes.com/EN/InvestorCentre.** The company's disclosure notes state that "The financial statements have been prepared in accordance with International Financial Reporting Standards. . ."

Required:
1. Locate the company's income statement. Notice that the statement reports a discontinued operation. Briefly describe the difference between U.S. GAAP and IFRS related to the determination of what constitutes a component of the entity requiring disclosure as a discontinued operation.
2. Access the disclosure note on discontinued operations. Briefly describe the segment of the company that was discontinued in 2006. Do you think this segment would qualify as a component of the entity according to U.S. GAAP?

Judgment Case 4–12
Income statement presentation; unusual items; comprehensive income

● LO3 through LO5 LO7 LO9

Norse Manufacturing, Inc., prepares an annual combined statement of income and comprehensive income. The following situations occurred during the company's 2009 fiscal year:

1. Restructuring costs were incurred due to the closing of a factory.
2. Machinery used in the manufacturing process was sold, and a loss was recognized.
3. Gains from foreign currency translation were recognized.
4. Interest expense was incurred.
5. A division was sold that qualifies as a separate component according to *SFAS No. 144.*
6. Obsolete inventory was written off.
7. The controller discovered an error in the calculation of 2008's patent amortization expense.
8. A volcano destroyed a storage facility on a South Sea island. The event is considered to be unusual and infrequent in occurrence.

Required:
1. For each situation, identify the appropriate reporting treatment from the list below (consider each event to be material).
   a. As a component of operating income.
   b. As a nonoperating income item (other income or expense).
   c. As a separately reported item.

    d. As an other comprehensive income item.

    e. As an adjustment to retained earnings.

2. Identify the situations that would be reported net-of-tax.

Judgment Case 4–13
Management incentives for change
● LO6

It has been suggested that not all accounting choices are made by management in the best interest of fair and consistent financial reporting.

Required:

What motivations can you think of for management's choice of accounting methods?

Research Case 4–14
Pro forma earnings
● LO3

Companies often voluntarily provide a pro forma earnings number when they announce annual or quarterly earnings. These pro forma earnings numbers are controversial as they represent management's view of permanent earnings. The Sarbanes-Oxley Act (SOX), issued in 2002, requires that if pro forma earnings are included in any periodic or other report filed with the SEC or in any public disclosure or press release, the company also must provide a reconciliation with earnings determined according to GAAP.

    Professors Entwistle, Feltham, and Mbagwu in "Financial Reporting Regulation and the Reporting of Pro Forma Earnings," examine whether firms changed their reporting practice in response to the pro forma regulations included in SOX.

Required:

1. In your library or from some other source, locate the indicated article in *Accounting Horizons,* March 2006.
2. What sample of firms did the authors use in their examination?
3. What percent of firms reported pro forma earnings in 2001? In 2003?
4. What percent of firms had pro forma earnings greater than GAAP earnings in 2001? In 2003?
5. What was the most frequently reported adjusting item in 2001? In 2003?
6. What are the authors' main conclusions of the impact of SOX on pro forma reporting?

Integrating Case 4–15
Balance sheet and income statement; Chapters 3 and 4
● LO3 LO5

Rice Corporation is negotiating a loan for expansion purposes and the bank requires financial statements. Before closing the accounting records for the year ended December 31, 2009, Rice's controller prepared the following financial statements:

RICE CORPORATION
Balance Sheet
At December 31, 2009
($ in 000s)

Assets	
Cash	$ 275
Marketable securities	78
Accounts receivable	487
Inventories	425
Allowance for uncollectible accounts	(50)
Property and equipment, net	160
Total assets	$1,375

Liabilities and Shareholders' Equity	
Accounts payable and accrued liabilities	$ 420
Notes payable	200
Common stock	260
Retained earnings	495
Total liabilities and shareholders' equity	$1,375

RICE CORPORATION
Income Statement
For the Year Ended December 31, 2009
($ in 000s)

Net sales		$1,580
Expenses:		
Cost of goods sold	$755	
Selling and administrative	385	
Miscellaneous	129	
Income taxes	100	
Total expenses		1,369
Net income		$ 211

Additional information:

1. The company's common stock is traded on an organized stock exchange.

2. The investment portfolio consists of short-term investments valued at $57,000. The remaining investments will not be sold until the year 2011.

3. Miscellaneous expense represents the before-tax loss from damages caused by an earthquake. The event is considered to be both unusual and infrequent.

4. Notes payable consist of two notes:

    Note 1: $80,000 face value dated September 30, 2009. Principal and interest at 10% are due on September 30, 2010.

    Note 2: $120,000 face value dated April 30, 2009. Principal is due in two equal installments of $60,000 plus interest on the unpaid balance. The two payments are scheduled for April 30, 2010, and April 30, 2011.

    Interest on both loans has been correctly accrued and is included in accrued liabilities on the balance sheet and selling and administrative expenses on the income statement.

5. Selling and administrative expenses include a $90,000 charge incurred by the company in restructuring some of its operations. The amount of the charge is material.

Required:

Identify and explain the deficiencies in the presentation of the statements prepared by the company's controller. Do not prepare corrected statements. Include in your answer a list of items which require additional disclosure, either on the face of the statement or in a note.

Analysis **Case 4–16** Income statement information ● LO1 **Google**	Refer to the income statements of **Google Inc.** located in the company's financial statements included with all new copies of the text. **Required:** 1. What was the percentage increase or decrease in the company's net income from 2006 to 2007? From 2005 to 2006? 2. Using 2007 data, what is the company's approximate income tax rate? 3. Using 2007 data, what is the percentage of net income relative to revenue dollars?

Real World Case
4–17
Income statement
information
 	
● LO1 LO3
  through LO5
 	
Real World Financials
	EDGAR, the Electronic Data Gathering, Analysis, and Retrieval system, performs automated collection, validation, indexing, and forwarding of submissions by companies and others who are required by law to file forms with the U.S. Securities and Exchange Commission (SEC). All publicly traded domestic companies use EDGAR to make the majority of their filings. (Some foreign companies file voluntarily.) Form 10-K or 10-KSB, which includes the annual report, is required to be filed on EDGAR. The SEC makes this information available on the Internet.
	
	Required:
	
	1. Access EDGAR on the Internet. The web address is **www.sec.gov.**
	
	2. Search for a public company with which you are familiar. Access the most recent 10-K filing. Search or scroll to find the financial statements and related notes.
	
	3. Answer the following questions related to the company's income statement:
	
	    a. Does the company use the single-step or multiple-step format, or a variation?
	
	    b. Does the income statement contain any separately reported items in any year presented (discontinued operation or extraordinary item)? If it does, describe the event that caused the item. (Hint: there should be a related disclosure note.)
	
	    c. Describe the trend in net income over the years presented.
	
	4. Repeat requirements 2 and 3 for two additional companies.

Trueblood **Accounting Case** **4–18** Restructuring costs ● LO3	The following Trueblood case is recommended for use with this chapter. The case provides an excellent opportunity for class discussion, group projects, and writing assignments. The case, along with Professor's Discussion Material, can be obtained from the Deloitte Foundation at its website: **www.deloitte.com/us/truebloodcases.** **Case 04-5: *Alchemist, Inc.*** This case concerns the amount and timing of restructuring costs.

CPA SIMULATION 4–1

Best Consultants
Financial
Statements

SCHWESER
CPA Review

Test your knowledge of the concepts discussed in this chapter, practice critical professional skills necessary for career success, and prepare for the computer-based CPA exam by accessing our CPA simulations at the text website: **www.mhhe.com/spiceland5e.**

The Best Consultants simulation tests your knowledge of (a) the content and structure of the income statement, (b) the reporting of discontinued operations and comprehensive income, (c) the difference between cash and accrual income statement items addressed in Chapters 1 and 2, and (d) the transactions that cause a change in retained earnings discussed in Chapters 2 and 18.

As on the CPA exam itself, you will be asked to use tools including a spreadsheet, a calculator, and professional accounting standards, to conduct research, derive solutions, and communicate conclusions related to these issues in a simulated environment headed by the following interactive tabs:

Specific tasks in the simulation include:

- Converting income statement items from a cash to accrual basis.
- Demonstrating your knowledge of the content and structure of the income statement.
- Understanding the transactions that affect retained earnings.
- Communicating various aspects of the reporting requirements for discontinued operations.
- Researching the disclosure requirements for the presentation of comprehensive income.

Income Measurement and Profitability Analysis

/// OVERVIEW

The focus of this chapter is revenue recognition. We first discuss situations in which completion of the earnings process occurs within a *single* reporting period. Then, we consider situations in which the earnings process is completed over *multiple* reporting periods. We also continue our discussion of financial statement analysis.

| | | | LEARNING OBJECTIVES | | | | | | | | | |

After studying this chapter, you should be able to:

● **LO1** Discuss the general objective of the timing of revenue recognition, list the two general criteria that must be satisfied before revenue can be recognized, and explain why these criteria usually are satisfied at a specific point in time.

● **LO2** Describe the installment sales and cost recovery methods of recognizing revenue for some types of installment sales and explain the unusual conditions under which these methods might be used.

● **LO3** Discuss the implications for revenue recognition of allowing customers the right of return.

● **LO4** Identify situations that call for the recognition of revenue over time and distinguish between the percentage-of-completion and completed contract methods of recognizing revenue for long-term contracts.

● **LO5** Discuss the revenue recognition issues involving multiple-deliverable contracts, software, and franchise sales.

● **LO6** Identify and calculate the common ratios used to assess profitability.

You Don't Have to Be a Rocket Scientist

"Good news! I got the job," she said, closing the door behind her.

Your sister, an aerospace engineer, goes on to explain that she accepted a position at **Lockheed Martin Corporation**, a world leader in the design, development, manufacture, and servicing of aircraft, spacecraft and launch vehicles, missiles, electronics, and information and telecommunication systems. She will supervise a long-term government contract beginning Tuesday.

"I got the salary I was asking for too," she continued. "Mr. Watson, my supervisor, also said I'll be getting a bonus tied to the gross profit on the project. It didn't hit me until I left his office, though, that this project will take two and a half years to complete. I hope I don't have to wait that long to get my bonus." Pointing to a page where she's circled part of a disclosure note, your sister hands you Lockheed's annual report. "I can't believe they wait that long to record income on all these multiyear projects. You're the accountant in the family; is that what this note is telling us?"

Sales and earnings (in part)
We record sales and anticipated profits under long-term fixed-price design, development, and production contracts on a percentage of completion basis . . .

By the time you finish this chapter, you should be able to respond appropriately to the questions posed in this case. Compare your response to the solution provided at the end of the chapter.

QUESTIONS ///

1. Does your sister have to wait two and a half years to get her bonus? Explain. (page 240)

2. How are gross profits recognized using the percentage-of-completion method? (page 243)

3. Are there other situations in which revenue is recognized at times other than when a product is delivered? (page 233)

Revenue recognition
criteria help ensure
that an income
statement reflects the
actual accomplishments
of a company for the
period.

REVENUE RECOGNITION

In Chapter 4 we discussed the *nature of income* and its presentation in the income statement. In this chapter we turn our attention to the *measurement* of periodic accounting income. Of primary interest here is the timing of revenue recognition. This is an important issue not only in its own right but also because the matching principle states that expenses should be recognized in the period in which the related revenues are recognized.

Why is the timing of revenue recognition so important? An income statement should report the results of operations only for the time period specified in the report. That is, a one-year income statement should report the company's accomplishments and sacrifices (revenues and expenses) only for that one-year period.[1] Revenue recognition criteria help ensure that a proper cutoff is made each period and that no more than one year's activity is reported in the annual income statement. Revenues reflect positive inflows from activities, activities that generate cash flows. By comparing these activity levels period to period, a user can better assess future activities and thus future cash flows.

Our objective, then, is to recognize revenue in the period or periods that the revenue-generating activities of the company are performed. But we also must consider that recognizing revenue presumes that an asset (usually cash) has been received or will be received in exchange for the goods or services sold. Our judgment as to the collectibility of the cash from the sale of a product or service will, therefore, impact the timing of revenue recognition. These two concepts of performance and collectibility are captured by the general guidelines for revenue recognition in the realization principle.

● LO1

The realization principle requires that two criteria be satisfied before revenue can be recognized (recorded):[2]

1. The earnings process is judged to be complete or virtually complete (the earnings process refers to the activity or activities performed by the company to generate revenue).
2. There is reasonable certainty as to the collectibility of the asset to be received (usually cash).

The first criterion indicates that revenue is recognized at a point in time at or near the end of the earnings process. We sometimes encounter situations when strictly adhering to this criterion would violate our overriding objective of recognizing revenue in the period or periods that the revenue-generating activities of the company are performed. Later in this chapter we discuss situations when revenue is recognized over time, rather than at one particular point in time.

Even with this guideline, revenue recognition continues to be a controversial issue. For instance, former SEC chairman Arthur Levitt identified revenue recognition as a popular way for companies to manage their earnings, primarily prematurely.

Premature revenue
recognition reduces
the quality of reported
earnings and can cause
serious problems for
the reporting company.

Premature revenue recognition reduces the quality of reported earnings, particularly if those revenues never materialize. Many sad stories have surfaced involving companies forced to revise earnings numbers due to a restatement of revenues. The case of **Krispy Kreme Doughnuts** offers a prime example. In January 2005, the company announced that it would be restating its earnings for the last three quarters of fiscal 2004. Investors were already alarmed by the recent filing of a lawsuit that alleged the company routinely padded sales by doubling shipments to wholesale customers at the end

> **CBS MARKETWATCH**
> If corporate information is no longer reliable, investors are left twisting in the wind. Suddenly, the financial assumptions you've used to calculate a stock's value become bogus.[3]

---

[1]In addition to reporting on an annual basis, companies often provide information quarterly and, on occasion, monthly. The SEC requires its registrants to provide information on a quarterly and annual basis. This information, referred to as *interim financial statements,* pertains to any financial report covering a period of less than one year. The key accounting issues related to the presentation of interim statements are discussed in Appendix 5.

[2]These criteria are addressed in SFAC 5, "Recognition and Measurement in Financial Statements," *Statement of Financial Accounting Concepts No. 5* (Stamford, Conn.: FASB, 1984).

[3]Deborah Adamson, "What investors should fear the most," *CBS.MarketWatch.com,* April 30, 2001.

ARTHUR LEVITT, JR.
Lastly, companies try to boost earnings by manipulating the recognition of revenue. Think about a bottle of fine wine. You wouldn't pop the cork on that bottle before it was ready. But some companies are doing this with their revenue . . . [4]

of the quarter. In the two-day period following the announced restatement, the company's stock price dropped over 20% in value!

As part of its crackdown on earnings management, the SEC issued *Staff Accounting Bulletin (SAB) No. 101*,[5] summarizing the SEC's views on revenue. The Bulletin provides additional criteria for judging whether or not the realization principle is satisfied:

1. Persuasive evidence of an arrangement exists.
2. Delivery has occurred or services have been rendered.
3. The seller's price to the buyer is fixed or determinable.
4. Collectibility is reasonably assured.

In addition to these four criteria, *SAB 101* also poses a number of revenue recognition questions relating to each of the criteria. The questions provide the facts of the scenario and then the SEC offers its interpretive response. These responses and supporting explanations provide guidance to companies with similar revenue recognition issues. For example, the following question relates to the delivery and performance criteria necessary to recognize revenue on a transaction commonly referred to as a "Bill and Hold" sale:

SEC Staff Accounting Bulletin (SAB) No. 101 provides general and specific guidelines for revenue recognition.

Facts: Company A receives purchase orders for products it manufactures. At the end of its fiscal quarters, customers may not yet be ready to take delivery of the products for various reasons. These reasons may include, but are not limited to, a lack of available space for inventory, having more than sufficient inventory in their distribution channel, or delays in customers' production schedules.
Questions: May Company A recognize revenue for the sale of its products once it has completed manufacturing if it segregates the inventory of the products in its own warehouse from its own products? May Company A recognize revenue for the sale if it ships the products to a third-party warehouse but (1) Company A retains title to the product and (2) payment by the customer is dependent upon ultimate delivery to a customer-specified site?

How would you answer these questions? The SEC's response is generally, no. It believes that delivery generally is not considered to have occurred unless the customer has taken title and assumes the risk and rewards of ownership of the specific products in the customer's purchase order or sales agreement. Typically this occurs when a product is delivered to the customer's delivery site and accepted by the customer.[6]

Soon after *SAB No. 101* was issued, many companies changed their revenue recognition methods. In most cases, the changes resulted in a deferral of revenue recognition. As a case in point, consider the change made by **Brown & Sharpe Manufacturing Company,** a multinational manufacturer of metrology products, described in a disclosure note, displayed in Graphic 5–1.

2. Accounting Change (in part)
In 2000, the Company adopted *SEC Staff Accounting Bulletin No. 101 (SAB 101)*. As a result of adopting *SAB 101*, the Company changed the way it recognizes revenue for machines sold to customers. Prior to the adoption of *SAB 101*, the Company recognized revenue when the machines were shipped and title passed to the customer. Effective as of January 1, 2001, the Company recognizes revenue for machines sold to customers once the performance of machines is accepted by the customers.

GRAPHIC 5–1
Disclosure of Change in Revenue Recognition Policy—Brown & Sharpe Manufacturing Company

Real World Financials

[4]Arthur Levitt, Jr., "The Numbers Game," *The CPA Journal*, December 1998, p. 18.
[5]"Revenue Recognition in Financial Statements," *Staff Accounting Bulletin No. 101* (Washington, D.C.: SEC, December 1999). For additional guidance see *Staff Accounting Bulletin No. 104* (Washington, D.C.: SEC, December 2003).
[6]Ibid., p. 5.

ETHICAL DILEMMA

The Precision Parts Corporation manufactures automobile parts. The company has reported a profit every year since the company's inception in 1980. Management prides itself on this accomplishment and believes one important contributing factor is the company's incentive plan that rewards top management a bonus equal to a percentage of operating income *if the operating income goal for the year is achieved.* However, 2009 has been a tough year, and prospects for attaining the income goal for the year are bleak.

Tony Smith, the company's chief financial officer, has determined a way to increase December sales by an amount sufficient to boost operating income over the goal for the year and earn bonuses for all top management. A reputable customer ordered $120,000 of parts to be shipped on January 15, 2010. Tony told the rest of top management "I know we can get that order ready by December 31 even though it will require some production line overtime. We can then just leave the order on the loading dock until shipment. I see nothing wrong with recognizing the sale in 2009, since the parts will have been manufactured and we do have a firm order from a reputable customer." The company's normal procedure is to ship goods f.o.b. destination and to recognize sales revenue when the customer receives the parts.

In requiring customer acceptance as part of the agreement, revenue recognition is delayed until this part of the earnings process is completed. Although the Brown and Sharpe example relates to product delivery, many of the changes in revenue recognition companies made in response to *SAB No. 101* are related to service revenue. We discuss some of these later in the chapter.

Graphic 5–2 relates various revenue-recognition methods to critical steps in the earnings process, and Graphic 5–3 provides an overview of the methods used in current practice, Recall that the realization principle indicates that the central issues for recognizing revenue are (a) judging when the earnings process is substantially complete and (b) whether there is reasonable certainty as to the collectibility of the cash to be received. Often this decision is straightforward and tied to delivery of the product from the seller to the buyer. At delivery, the earnings process is virtually complete and the seller receives either cash or a receivable.

GRAPHIC 5–2

Relation between Earnings Process and Revenue Recognition Methods

At other times, though, recognizing revenue upon delivery may be inappropriate. It may be that revenue should be deferred to a point *after* delivery because the seller is unable to estimate whether the buyer will return the product or pay the receivable. Or, sometimes revenue should be recognized at a point *prior* to delivery because the earnings process occurs over multiple years and the company can better inform financial statement users by making

GRAPHIC 5–3
Revenue Recognition
Methods

Nature of the Revenue	Usually Recognize Revenue for:	
	Sale of a Product	**Sale of a Service**
Substantive completion of the earnings process at a specific point in time within a single reporting period:		
Collectibility of cash is reasonably certain.	When product is delivered and title transfers	When the key activity is performed
Collectibility of cash is *not* reasonably certain:		
• Because payments are significantly uncertain	When cash is collected (**installment sales or cost recovery method**)	When cash is collected (**installment sales or cost recovery method**)
• Because reliable estimates of product returns are unavailable	When critical event occurs that reduces product return uncertainty	Not applicable
• Because the product sold is out on consignment	When the consignee sells the product to the ultimate consumer	Not applicable
Substantive completion of the earnings process occurs over more than one reporting period:		
Reasonably dependable estimates of progress are available.	Each period during the earnings process (e.g., long-term construction contract) in proportion to its percentage of completion (**percentage-of-completion method**)	Each period during the earnings process (e.g., rental period) in proportion to its percentage of performance (**percentage-of-completion method**)
Dependable estimates of progress are not available.	At the completion of the project (**completed contract method**)	Not applicable
Industry-specific revenue:		
Franchise sales:		
• Initial franchise fee	Not applicable	When initial services are "substantially performed"
• Continuing franchise fees	Not applicable	As services are performed
Computer software sales	As each product component (e.g., initial product; upgrade) is delivered	As each service component (e.g., customer support) is delivered

We usually recognize revenue at or near the completion of the earnings process unless collectibility is an issue.

Sometimes, it is more meaningful to recognize revenue over time in proportion to the performance of the activity.

reliable estimates of revenue and cost prior to delivery. Now let's consider the effect these variations have on the timing of revenue recognition.[7]

Completion of the Earnings Process within a Single Reporting Period
When Collectibility is Reasonably Certain

Consider the timing of revenue recognition for a typical manufacturing company that sells its products on credit. Graphic 5–2 shows three alternative points in time during the earnings process that could be considered the critical event for revenue recognition. It should

While revenue usually is earned during a period of time, revenue often is recognized at one specific point in time when both revenue recognition criteria are satisfied.

[7]"Revenue Recognition," *Proposal for a New Agenda Project,* Norwalk, Conn.: FASB, 2002. In January 2002, the FASB disseminated a proposal for a new project addressing revenue recognition. The FASB is partnering with the International Accounting Standards Board to develop a comprehensive statement on revenue recognition that is conceptually based and framed in terms of principles. At the time this text was published, no new pronouncements had yet resulted from the project. Updates are available at the FASB website (FASB.org).

be pointed out that revenue actually is earned *throughout* the earnings process. The critical event is the point in time when the realization principle is satisfied.[8]

Let's first consider the date production ends. At that point, it might be said that the earnings process is virtually complete. After all, the majority of the costs that must be expended to generate revenue have been incurred. The product has been produced and the remaining tasks are to sell the product and collect the asset to be exchanged for the product, which is usually cash.

However, at this point there usually exists significant uncertainty as to the collectibility of the asset to be received. We don't know if the product will be sold, the selling price, the buyer, or the collectibility of the asset to be received. Because of these uncertainties, revenue recognition usually is delayed until the point of sale, at product delivery. The product delivery date occurs when legal title to the goods passes from seller to buyer. This occurs either on the date the product is shipped from the seller's facility or when the goods actually are received by the buyer, depending on the terms of the sales agreement. If the goods are shipped *f.o.b. (free on board) shipping point,* then legal title to the goods changes hands at the point of shipment, when the seller delivers the goods to the common carrier (for example, a trucking company), and the purchaser is responsible for shipping costs and transit insurance. On the other hand, if the goods are shipped *f.o.b. destination,* the seller is responsible for shipping, and legal title does not pass until the goods arrive at the customer's location.[9]

The basic journal entries to record revenue upon delivery should look familiar. As an example, assume that Taft Company sells a supercomputer for $5,000,000 that cost $4,100,000 to produce. The journal entries to record the sale, assuming that Taft uses the perpetual inventory method, would be

Accounts receivable	5,000,000	
Revenue		5,000,000
Cost of goods sold	4,100,000	
Inventory		4,100,000

This sale yields gross profit of $900,000 ($5,000,000 − 4,100,000).

At the product delivery date we know the product has been sold, the price, and the buyer. However, usually the buyer is given a length of time, say 30 days, to pay for the goods after they have been delivered. Therefore, the only remaining uncertainty at the time of delivery involves the ultimate cash collection, which usually can be accounted for by estimating and recording allowances for possible return of the product and for uncollectibility of the cash, that is, bad debts. Both of these estimates are discussed in Chapter 7. As we discuss in the next section, significant uncertainty at point of product delivery related to either collectibility or product return causes a delay in revenue recognition.

Service revenue, too, often is recognized at a point in time if there is one final activity that is deemed critical to the earnings process. In this case, all revenue and costs are deferred until this final activity has been performed. For example, a moving company will pack, load, transport, and deliver household goods for a fixed fee. Although packing, loading, and transporting all are important to the earning process, delivery is the culminating event of the earnings process. So, the entire service fee is recognized as revenue after the goods have been delivered. **FedEx** recognizes revenue in this manner. The Company's Summary of Significant Accounting Policies disclosure note indicates that "Revenue is recognized upon delivery of shipments." As with the sale of product, estimates of uncollectible amounts must be made for service revenue provided to customers on a credit basis.

Revenue from the sale of products usually is recognized at the point of product delivery.

The point of delivery refers to the date legal title to the product passes from seller to buyer.

For service revenue, if there is one final service that is critical to the earnings process, revenues and costs are deferred and recognized after this service has been performed.

---

[8]As you will learn later in this chapter, revenue often is not only earned throughout an earnings process, but also is recognized during the process rather than at one particular point in time.

[9]We discuss this aspect of title transfer in Chapter 7.

Significant Uncertainty of Collectibility

Recognizing revenue at a specific point in time as described in the previous section assumes we are able to make reasonable estimates of amounts due from customers that potentially might be uncollectible. For product sales, this also includes amounts not collectible due to customers returning the products they purchased. Otherwise, we would violate one of the requirements of the revenue realization principle we discussed earlier that there must be reasonable certainty as to the collectibility of cash from the customer. Now, in this section, we address a few situations when uncertainties could cause a delay in recognizing revenue from a sale of a product or service. For each of these situations, notice that the accounting is essentially the same—deferring recognition of the gross profit arising from a sale of a product or service until uncertainties have been resolved.

Q3, p. 227

INSTALLMENT SALES.   Customers sometimes are allowed to pay for purchases in installments over a long period of time. Many large retail stores, such as **Sears** and **J.C. Penney,** sell products on an installment plan. Increasing the length of time allowed for payment usually increases the uncertainty about whether the store actually will collect a receivable. Is the uncertainty sufficient in an installment sale to cause these companies to delay recognizing revenue and related expenses beyond the point of sale? Usually, it's not.

● **LO2**

At times, revenue recognition is delayed due to a high degree of uncertainty related to ultimate cash collection.

In most situations, the increased uncertainty concerning the collection of cash from installment sales can be accommodated satisfactorily by estimating uncollectible amounts. If, however, the installment sale creates significant uncertainty concerning cash collection, making impossible a reasonable assessment of future bad debts, then revenue and expense recognition should be delayed. For example, real estate sales often are made on an installment basis with relatively small down payments and long payment periods, perhaps 25 years or more. These payment characteristics, combined with the general speculative nature of many of these transactions, may translate into extreme uncertainty concerning the collectibility of the installment receivable.[10] In fact, *SFAS No. 66* requires that the installment sales method (discussed below) be applied to a retail land sale that meets certain criteria.[11]

When extreme uncertainty exists regarding the ultimate collectibility of cash, we delay recognizing revenue and related expenses using one of two accounting techniques, the installment sales method or the cost recovery method. *We emphasize that these methods should be used only in situations involving exceptional uncertainty.* As an example, **Rouse Company** acquires, develops, and manages income-producing properties throughout the United States and develops and sells land for residential, commercial, and other uses. Graphic 5–4 shows the company's revenue recognition disclosure note included with recent annual financial statements. The note indicates that the preferred method is to recognize revenue upon delivery (full accrual method), but that in certain circumstances, one of these two alternative methods could be used.

The installment sales and cost recovery methods are only used in unusual circumstances.

Installment sales method.   To deal with the uncertainty of collection, the installment sales method recognizes revenue and costs only when cash payments are received. Each payment is assumed to be composed of two components: (1) a partial recovery of the cost of the item sold and (2) a gross profit component. These components are determined by the gross profit percentage applicable to the sale. For example, if the gross profit percentage

The *installment sales method* recognizes the gross profit by applying the gross profit percentage on the sale to the amount of cash actually received.

GRAPHIC 5–4

Disclosure of Revenue Recognition Policy— Rouse Company

Real World Financials

Revenue Recognition and Related Matters (in part)
Revenues from land sales are recognized using the full accrual method provided that various criteria relating to the terms of the transactions and any subsequent involvement by us with the land sold are met. Revenues relating to transactions that do not meet the established criteria are deferred and recognized when the criteria are met or using the installment or cost recovery methods, as appropriate in the circumstances.

---

[10]For income tax purposes, the installment sales method applies only to gains from the sale of certain types of properties. The tax law requires the use of the installment sales method for these transactions unless a taxpayer elects not to use the method.
[11]"Accounting for Sales of Real Estate," *Statement of Financial Accounting Standards No. 66* (Stamford, Conn.: FASB, 1982).

ILLUSTRATION 5–1 Installment Sales Method	On November 1, 2009, the Belmont Corporation, a real estate developer, sold a tract of land for $800,000. The sales agreement requires the customer to make four equal annual payments of $200,000 plus interest on each November 1, beginning November 1, 2009. The land cost $560,000 to develop. The company's fiscal year ends on December 31.

Gross profit recognition, installment sales method.

(gross profit ÷ sales price) is 40%, then 60% of each dollar collected represents cost recovery and the remaining 40% is gross profit. Consider the example in Illustration 5–1.

The gross profit of $240,000 ($800,000 − 560,000) represents 30% of the sales price ($240,000 ÷ $800,000). The collection of cash and the recognition of gross profit under the installment method are summarized below. In this example, we ignore the collection of interest charges and the recognition of interest revenue to concentrate on the collection of the $800,000 sales price and the recognition of gross profit on the sale.

Date	Cash Collected	Cost Recovery (70%)	Gross Profit (30%)
Nov. 1, 2009	$200,000	$140,000	$ 60,000
Nov. 1, 2010	200,000	140,000	60,000
Nov. 1, 2011	200,000	140,000	60,000
Nov. 1, 2012	200,000	140,000	60,000
Totals	$800,000	$560,000	$240,000

This illustrates that the gross profit recognized in a period will be equal to the gross profit percentage multiplied by the period's cash collection. The following journal entries are recorded (interest charges ignored):

Inventory is credited for the portion of the receivable that represents the cost of the land sold. The difference is deferred gross profit.

Make Installment Sale:
November 1, 2009

Installment receivables	800,000	
Inventory		560,000
Deferred gross profit		240,000
To record installment sale.		

The first entry records the installment receivable and the reduction of inventory. The difference between the $800,000 selling price and the $560,000 cost of sales represents the gross profit on the sale of $240,000. As it will be recognized in net income only as collections are made, it is recorded in an account called *deferred gross profit*. This is a contra account to the installment receivable. It will be reduced to zero as the payments are received.[12]

When payments are received, gross profit is recognized, calculated by applying the gross profit percentage to the cash collected (30% × $200,000).

Collect Cash:
November 1, 2009

Cash	200,000	
Installment receivables		200,000
To record cash collection from installment sale.		
Deferred gross profit	60,000	
Realized gross profit		60,000
To recognize gross profit from installment sale.		

---

[12]Accountants sometimes record installment sales in the following manner:

Installment receivables	800,000	
Installment sales		800,000
To record installment sales.		
Cost of installment sales	560,000	
Inventory		560,000
To record the cost of installment sales.		

Then at the end of the period, the following adjusting/closing entry is recorded:

Installment sales	800,000	
Cost of installment sales		560,000
Deferred gross profit on installment sales		240,000

The text entries concentrate on the effect of the transactions and avoid this unnecessary procedural complexity.

The second set of entries records the collection of the first installment and recognizes the gross profit component of the payment, $60,000. Journal entries to record the remaining three payments on November 1, 2010, 2011, and 2012, are identical.

At the end of 2009, the balance sheet would report the following:

Installment receivables ($800,000 − $200,000)	$600,000
Less: Deferred gross profit ($240,000 − $60,000)	(180,000)
Installment receivables (net)	$420,000

The net amount of the receivable reflects the portion of the remaining payments that represents cost recovery (70% × $600,000). The installment receivables are classified as current assets if they will be collected within one year (or within the company's operating cycle, if longer); otherwise, they are classified as noncurrent assets.

The income statement for 2009 would report a gross profit from installment sales of $60,000. Sales and cost of goods sold usually are not reported in the income statement under the installment method, just the resulting gross profit. But if installment sales are significant, the 2009 income statement in this illustration would report sales of $200,000 and cost of goods sold of $140,000.

ADDITIONAL CONSIDERATION

We discuss in significant depth in Chapter 7 the problem of accounting for bad debts. However, bad debts related to receivables on sales accounted for using the installment method create a unique problem. The reason a company uses the installment method is that it can't reliably estimate bad debts. Therefore, the company doesn't explicitly recognize bad debt expense or create an allowance for uncollectible accounts in the installment method. Rather, bad debts are dealt with implicitly by deferring gross profit until cash is collected; if the cash never is collected, the related deferred gross profit never gets included in net income. To illustrate, assume that in the example described in Illustration 5–1, the Belmont Corporation collected the first payment but the customer was unable to make the remaining payments. Typically, the seller would repossess the item sold and make the following journal entry:

Repossessed inventory	420,000	
Deferred gross profit	180,000	
Installment receivable		600,000

This entry removes the receivable and the remaining deferred gross profit and records the repossessed land in an inventory account. The entry assumes that the land's current fair value is equal to the net receivable of $420,000. If the land's fair value at the date of repossession is less than $420,000, a loss on repossession is recorded (debited).

Cost recovery method. In situations where there is an extremely high degree of uncertainty regarding the ultimate cash collection on an installment sale, an even more conservative approach, the cost recovery method, can be used. This method defers all gross profit recognition until the cost of the item sold has been recovered. The gross profit recognition pattern applying the cost recovery method to the Belmont Corporation situation used in Illustration 5–1 is shown below.

The *cost recovery method* defers all gross profit recognition until cash equal to the cost of the item sold has been received.

Date	Cash Collected	Cost Recovery	Gross Profit
Nov. 1, 2009	$200,000	$200,000	$ –0–
Nov. 1, 2010	200,000	200,000	–0–
Nov. 1, 2011	200,000	160,000	40,000
Nov. 1, 2012	200,000	–0–	200,000
Totals	$800,000	$560,000	$240,000

Gross profit recognition, cost recovery method.

The journal entries using this method are similar to those by the installment sales method except that $40,000 in gross profit is recognized in 2011 and $200,000 in 2012.

The cost recovery initial journal entry is identical to the installment sales method.

Make Installment Sale:
November 1, 2009

Installment receivables	800,000	
Inventory		560,000
Deferred gross profit		240,000
To record installment sale.		

Collect Cash:
November 1, 2009, 2010, 2011, and 2012

Cash	200,000	
Installment receivables		200,000
To record cash collection from installment sale.		

When payments are received, gross profit is recognized only after cost has been fully recovered.

November 1, 2009 and 2010
No entry for gross profit.

November 1, 2011

Deferred gross profit	40,000	
Realized gross profit		40,000
To recognize gross profit from installment sale.		

November 1, 2012

Deferred gross profit	200,000	
Realized gross profit		200,000
To recognize gross profit from installment sale.		

Why not use the installment sales method or cost recovery method for all installment sales? Because doing so would violate the realization principle and be inconsistent with accrual accounting. If bad debts can be reasonably estimated, there is no reason to delay revenue recognition.

CONCEPT REVIEW **EXERCISE**

INSTALLMENT SALES

Boatwright Implements, Inc., manufactures and sells farm machinery. For most of its sales, revenue and cost of sales are recognized at the delivery date. In 2009, it sold a cotton baler to a new customer for $100,000. The cost of the machinery was $60,000. Payment will be made in five annual installments of $20,000 each, with the first payment due in 2009. Boatwright usually does not allow its customers to pay in installments. Due to the unusual nature of the payment terms and the uncertainty of collection of the installment payments, Boatwright is considering alternative methods of recognizing profit on this sale.

Required:
Ignoring interest charges, prepare a table showing the gross profit to be recognized from 2009 through 2013 on the sale using the following three methods:

1. Point of delivery revenue recognition.
2. The installment sales method.
3. The cost recovery method.

SOLUTION

	Point of Delivery	Installment Sales Method (40% × cash collection)	Cost Recovery Method
2009	$40,000	$ 8,000	$ –0–
2010	–0–	8,000	–0–
2011	–0–	8,000	–0–
2012	–0–	8,000	20,000
2013	–0–	8,000	20,000
Totals	$40,000	$40,000	$40,000

RIGHT OF RETURN.   Retailers usually give their customers the right to return merchandise if they are not satisfied. In most situations, even though the right to return merchandise exists, revenues and expenses can be appropriately recognized at point of delivery. Based on past experience, a company usually can estimate the returns that will result for a given volume of sales. These estimates are used to reduce both sales and cost of goods sold in anticipation of returns. The purpose of the estimates is to avoid overstating gross profit in the period of sale and understating gross profit in the period of return. The specific accounting treatment for sales returns is illustrated in Chapter 7 in conjunction with discussing the valuation of accounts receivable.

● LO3

Because the return of merchandise can retroactively negate the benefits of having made a sale, the seller must meet certain criteria before revenue is recognized in situations when the right of return exists. The most critical of these criteria is that the seller must be able to make reliable estimates of future returns.[13] In certain situations, these criteria are not satisfied at the point of delivery of the product. For example, manufacturers of semiconductors like **Intel Corporation** and **Motorola Corporation** usually sell their products through independent distributor companies. Economic factors, competition among manufacturers, and rapid obsolescence of the product motivate these manufacturers to grant the distributors the right of return if they are unable to sell the semiconductors. So, revenue recognition often is deferred beyond the delivery point to the date the products actually are sold by the distributor to an end user. Alternatively, the right of return could be specified contractually as expiring on some future date, and revenue recognition could be deferred to that date. Regardless, the accounting treatment in these situations would be similar to that used for the installment sales and cost recovery methods. The difference is that the journal entries we use to move deferred gross profit to realized gross profit would be recorded in whatever period returns can be estimated reliably or the right of return no longer exists. The disclosure note shown in Graphic 5–5 appeared in a recent annual report of Intel Corporation.

GRAPHIC 5–5

Disclosure of Revenue Recognition Policy— Intel Corporation

Real World Financials

Revenue Recognition

The company recognizes net revenue when the earnings process is complete, as evidenced by an agreement with the customer, transfer of title and acceptance, if applicable, as well as fixed pricing and probable collectibility. . . . Because of frequent sales price reductions and rapid technology obsolescence in the industry, sales made to distributors under agreements allowing price protection and/or right of return are deferred until the distributors sell the merchandise.

For Intel, the event critical to revenue recognition is *not* the delivery of the product to the buyer but the ultimate sale of the product by the buyer (the distributor company) to an end user.

Similarly, sometimes, a sales agreement requires additional, important performance steps to be performed by the seller. In this case, the earnings process is not virtually complete until those steps are performed, but as in the case of significant uncertainty about cash collection, revenue recognition must be deferred. Graphic 5–1 on page 229 illustrates a situation where the seller, Brown & Sharpe, delays revenue recognition beyond delivery of machines until the performance of the machines has been accepted by the buyer. Customer acceptance is an important part of the agreement between buyer and seller.

Any time a company recognizes revenue at a point other than the point of delivery, the revenue recognition method used is disclosed in the summary of significant accounting policies. Intel's disclosure note is an example. Graphic 5–6, a disclosure note from a recent financial statement of **Pitney Bowes, Inc.,** who manufactures postage meters and offers other information processing services, provides another example.

GRAPHIC 5–6

Disclosure of Revenue Recognition Policy— Pitney Bowes, Inc.

Real World Financials

Sales Revenue (in part)

We sell equipment to our customers, as well as to distributors and dealers (resellers) throughout the world. We recognize revenue from these sales upon the transfer of title, which is generally at the point of shipment. . . . Our sales revenue from customized equipment, mail creation equipment, and shipping products is generally recognized when installed.

[13]Other, less critical criteria are listed in "Revenue Recognition When Right of Return Exists," *Statement of Financial Accounting Standards No. 48* (Stamford, Conn.: FASB, 1981).

As the note indicates, some of Pitney Bowes' revenue is delayed beyond the point of product delivery. Pitney Bowes waits until customized equipment has been properly installed. Why does Pitney Bowes delay revenue recognition? Until the product has been installed, there is a high degree of uncertainty concerning the possibility the product might be returned. Also, installation is an important part of the agreement between Pitney Bowes and its customers.

CONSIGNMENT SALES. Sometimes a company arranges for another company to sell its product under consignment. The "consignor" physically transfers the goods to the other company (the consignee), but the consignor retains legal title. If the consignee can't find a buyer within an agreed-upon time, the consignee returns the goods to the consignor. However, if a buyer is found, the consignee remits the selling price (less commission and approved expenses) to the consignor.

Because the consignor retains the risks and rewards of ownership of the product and title does not pass to the consignee, the consignor does not record a sale (revenue and related expenses) until the consignee sells the goods and title passes to the eventual customer. Of course, that means goods on consignment are still part of the consignor's inventory. As an example, **Intuit, Inc.** provides business and financial management software solutions for small businesses, accounting professionals and consumers. Its flagship products include QuickBooks and TurboTax. Some of the company's product is sold using consignment arrangements. Graphic 5–7 shows a portion of the revenue recognition disclosure note that Intuit included in a recent annual report.

GRAPHIC 5–7

Disclosure of Revenue Recognition Policy— Intuit, Inc.

Real World Financials

> **Product Revenue (in part)**
>
> We recognize revenue from the sale of our packaged software products and supplies when legal title transfers, which is generally when our customers download products from the Web, when we ship the products or, in the case of certain agreements, when products are delivered to retailers. We sell some of our QuickBooks, Consumer Tax and Quicken products on consignment to certain retailers. We recognize revenue for these consignment transactions only when the end-user sale has occurred.

Up until now, we've focused on revenue-generating activities in which some specific event (e.g., delivery, collection, product performance, and resale) indicates that the earnings process is substantially completed and significant uncertainties have been alleviated, prompting us to recognize revenue and related expenses. We now turn our attention to situations in which it's desirable to recognize revenue over more than one reporting period— before a specific event indicates the earnings process is substantially completed.

● **LO4**

Completion of the Earnings Process over Multiple Reporting Periods

Revenue recognition at a single point in time, when an earnings process is virtually complete, is inappropriate for certain types of service revenue activities and also, usually, for long-term contracts.

Service Revenue Earned Over Time

Service revenue often is recognized over time, in proportion to the amount of service performed.

In a previous section we saw that many service activities encompass some final activity that is deemed critical to the earnings process. In these cases, we recognize revenue when that activity occurs. However, in many instances, service revenue activities occur over extended periods and recognizing revenue at any single date within that period would be inappropriate. Instead, it's more meaningful to recognize revenue over time in proportion to the performance of the activity.

As an example, consider the revenue a property owner earns when renting office space. If a landlord charges a tenant $12,000 in rent for the upcoming year, it would seem logical to recognize $1,000 of rent revenue each month over the one-year period (i.e., straight-line method) since services performed are similar over the period. The landlord recognizes rent revenue in proportion to the passage of time. Likewise, **Gold's Gym** will recognize revenue from a two-year membership ratably over the 24-month membership period. If the customer pays in advance in such cases, the seller debits cash and credits a liability, unearned revenue, because the seller is holding the customer's cash and has the obligation now to earn it. The seller only reduces that liability and credits revenue when the service has been provided.

A similar situation occurs if you buy a season pass to Disney World. When would **Walt Disney Co.** recognize revenue for the cash it collects for the sale of a 365-day pass? Rationalizing that a pass can be used any number of times during the season, thus making it difficult to determine when service is provided, many companies once recognized all revenue from the sale of season passes on the date of sale. However, the SEC's *Staff Accounting Bulletin No. 101*, discussed earlier in the chapter, motivated most of these companies to change their revenue recognition policy. For example, Graphic 5–8 provides a disclosure note **Walt Disney Co.** included in a recent annual report. Notice that the company recognizes revenue *over time,* based on the anticipated usage of the season pass over the operating season.

GRAPHIC 5–8

Disclosure of Revenue Recognition Policy— Walt Disney Co.

Real World Financials

Revenue Recognition (in part)

Revenues from advance theme park ticket sales are recognized when the tickets are used. For nonexpiring, multi-day tickets, we recognize revenue over a three-year time period based on estimated usage patterns that are derived from historical usage patterns. Revenues from corporate sponsors at the theme parks are generally recognized over the period of the applicable agreements commencing with the opening of the related attraction.

Long-Term Contracts

Another activity in which it is desirable to recognize revenue over time is one involving a long-term contract. The types of companies that make use of long-term contracts are many and varied. A recent survey of reporting practices of 600 large public companies indicates that one in every five companies engages in long-term contracts.[14] And they are not just construction companies. In fact, even services such as research, installation, and consulting often are contracted for on a long-term basis. Graphic 5–9 lists just a sampling of companies that use long-term contracts, many of which you might recognize.

GRAPHIC 5–9

Companies Engaged in Long-Term Contracts

Company	Type of Industry or Product
Oracle Corp.	Computer software, license and consulting fees
Lockheed Martin Corporation	Aircraft, missiles, and spacecraft
EDS	Information technology and outsourcing
Northrop Grumman Newport News	Shipbuilding
Nortel Networks Corp.	Networking solutions and services to support the Internet
SBA Communications Corp.	Telecommunications
Layne Christensen Company	Water supply services and geotechnical construction
Kaufman & Broad Home Corp.	Commercial and residential construction
Raytheon Company	Defense electronics
Foster Wheeler Corp.	Construction, petroleum and chemical facilities
Halliburton	Construction, energy services
Allied Construction Products Corp.	Large metal stamping presses

The *completed contract method* recognizes revenue at a point in time when the earnings process is complete.

The general revenue recognition criteria described in the realization principle suggest that revenue should be recognized when a long-term project is finished (that is, when the earnings process is virtually complete). This is known as the completed contract method of

---

[14]*Accounting Trends and Techniques—2007* (New York: AICPA, 2007), p. 376.

revenue recognition. The problem with this method is that all revenues, expenses, and resulting income from the project are recognized in the period in which the project is completed; no revenues or expenses are reported in the income statements of earlier reporting periods in which much of the work may have been performed. Net income should provide a measure of periodic accomplishment to help predict future accomplishments. Clearly, income statements prepared using the completed contract method do not fairly report each period's accomplishments when a project spans more than one reporting period. Much of the earnings process is far removed from the point of delivery.

The percentage-of-completion method of revenue recognition for long-term construction and other projects is designed to help address this problem. By this approach, we recognize revenues (and expenses) over time by allocating a share of the project's expected revenues and expenses to each period in which the earnings process occurs, that is, the contract period. Although the contract usually specifies total revenues, the project's expenses are not known until completion. Consequently, it's necessary for a company to estimate the project's future costs at the end of each reporting period in order to estimate total gross profit to be earned on the project.

Because the percentage-of-completion method does a better job of recognizing revenue in the periods in which revenue is earned, U.S. and International GAAP require the use of that method unless it's not possible to make reliable estimates of revenues, expenses, and progress toward completion.[15] Companies prefer the percentage-of-completion method as well because it allows earlier revenue and profit recognition than does the completed contract method. For both reasons, the percentage-of-completion method is more prevalent in practice. However, much of the accounting is the same under either method, so we start by discussing the similarities between the two methods, and then the differences. You'll see that we recognize the same total amounts or revenue and profit over the life of the contract under either method. Only the timing of recognition differs.

Illustration 5–2 provides information to compare accounting for long-term contracts using the completed contract and percentage-of-completion methods.

FINANCIAL
Reporting Case

Q1, p. 227

Using the *percentage-of-completion method* we allocate a share of a project's revenues and expenses to each reporting period during construction.

ILLUSTRATION 5–2

Completed Contract and Percentage-of-Completion Methods Compared

At the beginning of 2009, the Harding Construction Company received a contract to build an office building for $5 million. The project is estimated to take three years to complete. According to the contract, Harding will bill the buyer in installments over the construction period according to a prearranged schedule. Information related to the contract is as follows:

	2009	2010	2011
Construction costs incurred during the year	$1,500,000	$1,000,000	$1,600,000
Construction costs incurred in prior years	–0–	1,500,000	2,500,000
Cumulative construction costs	1,500,000	2,500,000	4,100,000
Estimated costs to complete at end of year	2,250,000	1,500,000	–0–
Total estimated and actual construction costs	$3,750,000	$4,000,000	$4,100,000
Billings made during the year	$1,200,000	$2,000,000	$1,800,000
Cash collections during year	1,000,000	1,400,000	2,600,000

Construction costs include the labor, materials, and overhead costs directly related to the construction of the building. Notice how the total of estimated and actual construction costs changes from period to period. Cost revisions are typical in long-term contracts in which costs are estimated over long periods of time.

---

[15]Specifically, U.S. GAAP requires that the percentage-of-completion method be used whenever (1) reasonable estimates can be made of revenues and costs, (2) the contract specifies the parties' rights, consideration to be paid, and payment terms, and (3) both the purchaser and seller have the ability and expectation to fulfill their obligations under the contract ["Accounting for Performance of Construction-Type and Certain Production-Type Contracts," *Statement of Position 81-1* (New York: AICPA, 1981)].

ACCOUNTING FOR THE COST OF CONSTRUCTION AND ACCOUNTS RECEIVABLE.
Summary journal entries for both the percentage-of-completion and completed contract methods are shown in Illustration 5–2A for construction costs, billings, and cash receipts.

ILLUSTRATION 5–2A   Journal Entries—Costs, Billings, and Cash Receipts

	2009		2010		2011	
Construction in progress	1,500,000		1,000,000		1,600,000	
Cash, materials, etc.		1,500,000		1,000,000		1,600,000
To record construction costs.						
Accounts receivable	1,200,000		2,000,000		1,800,000	
Billings on construction contract		1,200,000		2,000,000		1,800,000
To record progress billings.						
Cash...	1,000,000		1,400,000		2,600,000	
Accounts receivable...........................		1,000,000		1,400,000		2,600,000
To record cash collections.						

With both the completed contract and percentage-of-completion methods, all costs of construction are recorded in an asset account called construction in progress. This account is equivalent to the asset work-in-process inventory in a manufacturing company. This is logical since the construction project is essentially an inventory item in process for the contractor.

Notice that periodic billings are credited to billings on construction contract. This account is a contra account to the construction in progress asset. At the end of each period, the balances in these two accounts are compared. If the net amount is a debit, it is reported in the balance sheet as an asset. Conversely, if the net amount is a credit, it is reported as a liability.[16]

To understand why we use the billings on construction contract account, consider a key difference between accounting for a long-term contract and accounting for a typical sale in which revenue is recognized upon delivery. Recall our earlier example on p. 232 in which Taft Company gives up its physical asset (inventory, in their case a supercomputer) and recognizes cost of goods sold at the same time it gets a financial asset (an accounts receivable) and recognizes revenue. So, first a physical asset is in the balance sheet, and then a financial asset, but the two are not in the balance sheet at the same time.

Now consider our Harding Construction example. Harding is creating a physical asset (construction in progress) in the same periods it recognizes a financial asset (first recognizing accounts receivable when the customer is billed and then recognizing cash when the receivable is collected). Having both the physical asset and the financial asset in the balance sheet at the same time constitutes double counting the same arrangement. The billings on construction contract account solves this problem. Whenever an accounts receivable is recognized, the other side of the journal entry increases the billings on construction contract account, which is contra to (and thus reduces) construction in progress. As a result, the financial asset (accounts receivable) increases and the physical asset (the net of construction in progress and billings) decreases.

> Accounting for costs, billings, and cash receipts are the same for both the percentage-of-completion and completed contract methods.
>
> *Construction in progress* is the contractor's work-in-process inventory.
>
> The billings on construction contract account prevents "double counting" assets by reducing construction in progress whenever an accounts receivable is recognized.

GROSS PROFIT RECOGNITION—GENERAL APPROACH.
Now let's consider recognition of gross profit. The top portion of Illustration 5–2B shows the journal entry to recognize revenue, cost of construction (think of this as cost of goods sold), and gross profit under the completed contract method, while the bottom portion shows the journal entries that achieve this for the percentage-of-completion method. It's important to understand two key aspects of the illustration.

---

[16]If the company is engaged in more than one long-term contract, all contracts for which construction in progress exceeds billings are grouped together and all contracts for which billings exceed construction in progress also are grouped together. This would result in the presentation of both an asset and a liability in the balance sheet.

ILLUSTRATION 5–2B   Journal Entries—Profit Recognition

	2009	2010	2011
Completed Contract			
Construction in progress (gross profit)			900,000
Cost of construction			4,100,000
Revenue from long-term contracts			5,000,000
To record gross profit.			
Percentage-of-Completion			
Construction in progress (gross profit)	500,000	125,000	275,000
Cost of construction	1,500,000	1,000,000	1,600,000
Revenue from long-term contracts	2,000,000	1,125,000	1,875,000
To record gross profit.			

The same total amount of profit or loss is recognized under both the completed contract and the percentage-of-completion methods, but the timing of recognition differs.

First, the same amounts of revenue, cost, and gross profit are recognized under both the completed contract and percentage-of-completion methods. The only difference is timing. To check this, sum all of the revenue recognized for both methods over the three years:

	Percentage-of-Completion	Completed Contract
Revenue recognized:		
2009	$2,000,000	–0–
2010	1,125,000	–0–
2011	1,875,000	$5,000,000
Total revenue	$5,000,000	$5,000,000

Construction in progress includes profits and losses on the contract that have been recognized to date.

Second, notice that in both methods we add gross profit (the difference between revenue and cost) to the construction in progress asset. That seems odd—why add *profit* to what is essentially an *inventory* account? The key here is that, when Harding recognizes gross profit, they are acting like they have sold some portion of the asset to their customer, but Harding keeps the asset in their own balance sheet (in the construction in progress account) until they deliver it to the customer. Putting recognized gross profit into the construction in progress account just updates that account to reflect the total value (cost + gross profit = sales price) of their customer's asset. However, don't forget that the billings on construction contract account is contra to the construction in progress account. Over the life of the construction project, Harding will bill their customer for the entire sales price of the asset. Therefore, at the end of the contract, the construction in progress account (containing total cost and gross profit) and the billings on construction contract account (containing all amounts billed to the customer) will have equal balances that exactly offset to create a net value of zero.

The same journal entry is recorded to close out the billings and construction in progress accounts under the completed contract and percentage-of-completion methods.

When title officially passes to the customer, Harding will prepare a journal entry that removes the contract from their balance sheet by debiting billings on construction contract and crediting construction in progress for the entire value of the contract. As shown in Illustration 5–2C, the same journal entry is recorded to close out the billings on construction contract and construction in progress accounts under the completed contract and percentage-of-completion methods.

ILLUSTRATION 5–2C		2009	2010	2011
Journal Entry to Close Billings and Construction in Progress Accounts	Billings on construction contract		5,000,000	
	Construction in progress			5,000,000
	To close accounts.			

Now that we've seen how gross profit is recognized for long-term contracts, let's consider how the timing of that recognition differs between the completed contract and percentage-of-completion methods.

TIMING OF GROSS PROFIT RECOGNITION UNDER THE COMPLETED CONTRACT METHOD. The timing of gross profit recognition under the completed contract method is simple. As the name implies, all revenues and expenses related to the project are recognized when the contract is completed. As shown in Illustration 5–2B and in the T-accounts below, completion occurs in 2011 for our Harding example. Prior to then, construction in progress includes only costs, showing a balance of $1,500,000 and $2,500,000 of cost at the end of 2009 and 2010, respectively, and including $4,100,000 of cost when the project is completed in 2011. Harding includes an additional $900,000 of gross profit in construction in progress when the project is completed in 2011 because the asset is viewed as "sold" on that date. The company records revenue of $5,000,000, cost of construction (similar to cost of goods sold) of $4,100,000, and the resulting $900,000 gross profit on that date.

Under the completed contract method, profit is not recognized until the project is completed.

FINANCIAL Reporting Case

Q2, p. 227

Completed Contract

	Construction in Progress		Billings on Construction Contract	
2009 construction costs	1,500,000		1,200,000	2009 billings
End balance, 2009	1,500,000		2,000,000	2010 billings
2010 construction costs	1,000,000		1,800,000	2011 billings
End balance, 2010	2,500,000		5,000,000	Balance, before closing
2011 construction costs	1,600,000			
2011 gross profit	900,000			
Balance, before closing	5,000,000			

TIMING OF GROSS PROFIT RECOGNITION UNDER THE PERCENTAGE-OF-COMPLETION METHOD. Using the percentage-of-completion method we recognize a portion of the estimated gross profit each period based on progress to date. How should progress to date be estimated?

One approach is to use *output* measures like units of production. For example, with a multi-year contract to deliver airplanes we might recognize progress according to the number of planes delivered. Another example of an output measure is recognizing portions of revenue associated with achieving particular milestones specified in a sales contract. Accounting guidance[17] states a preference for output measures when they can be established, arguing that they are more directly and reliably related to assessing progress than are input measures.

Another approach is to use an *input* measure like the "cost-to-cost ratio," by which progress to date is estimated by calculating the percentage of estimated total cost that has been incurred to date. Similar input measures might be used instead, like the number of labor hours incurred to date compared to estimated total hours. One advantage of input measures is that they capture progress on long-term contracts that may not translate easily into simple output measures. For example, a natural output measure for highway construction might be finished miles of road, but that measure could be deceptive if not all miles of road require the same effort. A highway contract for the state of Arizona would likely pay the contractor more for miles of road blasted through the mountains than for miles paved across flat dessert, and a cost-to-cost approach reflects that difference. Recent research suggests that the cost-to-cost input measure is most common in practice.[18]

Under the percentage-of-completion method, profit is recognized over the life of the project as the project is completed.

Progress to date can be estimated as the proportion of the project's cost incurred to date divided by total estimated costs, or by relying on an engineer's or architect's estimate.

Regardless of the specific approach used to estimate progress to date, under the percentage-of-completion method we determine the amount of gross profit recognized in each period using the following logic:

$$\text{Total estimated gross profit} = \text{total estimated revenue} - \text{total estimated cost.}$$

$$\begin{matrix}\text{Gross profit} \\ \text{recognized this} \\ \text{period}\end{matrix} = \left(\begin{matrix}\text{total estimated} \\ \text{gross profit}\end{matrix} \times \begin{matrix}\text{percentage completed} \\ \text{to date}\end{matrix}\right) - \begin{matrix}\text{gross profit} \\ \text{recognized in} \\ \text{prior periods}\end{matrix}$$

[17]American Institute of Certified Public Accountants (AICPA), 1981. *Accounting for Performance of Construction-Type and Certain Production-Type Contracts.* Statement of Position No. 81-1. New York, NY: AICPA.
[18]R. K. Larson and K. L. Brown, 2004. "Where are we with long-term contract accounting?" *Accounting Horizons* (September): 207–219.

Illustration 5–2D shows the calculation of gross profit for each of the years for our Harding Construction Company example, with progress to date estimated using the cost-to-cost ratio. Refer to the bottom part of Illustration 5–2B to see the journal entries used to recognize gross profit in each period, and the T-accounts below Illustration 5-2D to see that the gross profit recognized in each period is added to the construction in progress account.

ILLUSTRATION 5–2D		2009	2010	2011
Percentage-of-Completion Method—Allocation of Gross Profit to Each Period	**Contract price**	$5,000,000	$5,000,000	$5,000,000
	Construction costs:			
	Construction costs incurred during the year	$1,500,000	$1,000,000	$1,600,000
	Construction costs incurred in prior years	–0–	1,500,000	2,500,000
	Cumulative construction costs	$1,500,000	$2,500,000	$4,100,000
	Estimated costs to complete at end of year	2,250,000	1,500,000	–0–
	Total estimated and actual construction costs	$3,750,000	$4,000,000	$4,100,000
	Total gross profit (estimated for 2009 & 2010, actual in 2011): Contract price minus total costs	$1,250,000	$1,000,000	$ 900,000
	Multiplied by:	×	×	×
	Percentage-of-completion: Actual costs to date divided by the estimated total project cost	$\left(\frac{\$1,500,000}{\$3,750,000}\right)$ = 40%	$\left(\frac{\$2,500,000}{\$4,000,000}\right)$ = 62.5%	$\left(\frac{\$4,100,000}{\$4,100,000}\right)$ = 100%
	Equals:			
	Gross profit earned to date	$ 500,000	$ 625,000	$ 900,000
	Less:			
	Gross profit recognized in prior periods	–0–	(500,000)	(625,000)
	Equals:			
	Gross profit recognized currently	$ 500,000	$ 125,000	$ 275,000

Construction in progress includes periodic profit by the percentage-of-completion method.

Percentage-of-Completion

	Construction in Progress		Billings on Construction Contract	
2009 construction costs	1,500,000		1,200,000	2009 billings
2009 gross profit	500,000		2,000,000	2010 billings
End balance, 2009	2,000,000		1,800,000	2011 billings
2010 construction costs	1,000,000		5,000,000	Balance, before closing
2010 gross profit	125,000			
End balance, 2010	3,125,000			
2011 construction costs	1,600,000			
2011 gross profit	275,000			
Balance, before closing	5,000,000			

In the income statement, we separate the gross profit into its two components: revenue and construction in progress.

Income statements are more informative if the sales revenue and cost components of gross profit are reported rather than the net figure alone. So, the income statement for each year will report the appropriate revenue and cost of construction amounts. For example, in 2009, the gross profit of $500,000 consists of revenue of $2,000,000 (40% of the $5,000,000 contract price) less the $1,500,000 cost of construction. In subsequent periods, we calculate revenue by multiplying the percentage of completion by the contract price and then subtracting revenue recognized in prior periods, similar to the way we calculate gross profit each period. The cost of construction, then, is the difference between revenue and gross profit. In most cases, cost of construction also equals the construction costs incurred during the period.[19] The table in Illustration 5–2E shows the revenue and cost of construction

[19]Cost of construction does not equal the construction costs incurred during the year when a loss is projected on the entire project. This situation is illustrated later in the chapter.

recognized in each of the three years of our example. Of course, as you can see in this illustration, we could have initially determined the gross profit by first calculating revenue and then subtracting cost of construction.[20]

2009			ILLUSTRATION 5–2E
Revenue recognized ($5,000,000 × 40%)		$2,000,000	Percentage-of-Completion Method—Allocation of Revenue and Cost of Construction to Each Period
Cost of construction		(1,500,000)	
Gross profit		$ 500,000	
2010			
Revenue recognized to date ($5,000,000 × 62.5%)	$3,125,000		
Less: revenue recognized in 2009	2,000,000		
Revenue recognized		$1,125,000	
Cost of construction		(1,000,000)	
Gross profit		$ 125,000	
2011			
Revenue recognized to date ($5,000,000 × 100%)	$5,000,000		
Less: revenue recognized in 2009 and 2010	3,125,000		
Revenue recognized		$1,875,000	
Cost of construction		(1,600,000)	
Gross profit		$ 275,000	

INTERNATIONAL FINANCIAL REPORTING STANDARDS

Long-Term Construction Contracts *IAS No. 11* governs revenue recognition for long-term construction contracts. Like U.S. GAAP, that standard requires the use of percentage-of-completion accounting when estimates can be made precisely. However, unlike U.S. GAAP, IAS No. 11 requires the use of the cost recovery method rather than the completed contract method when estimates cannot be made precisely enough to allow percentage-of-completion accounting. Under the cost recovery method, contract costs are expensed as incurred, and an exactly offsetting amount of contract revenue is recognized, such that no gross profit is recognized until all costs have been incurred. Under both methods, no gross profit is recognized until the contract is essentially completed, but revenue and construction costs will be recognized earlier under the cost recovery method than under the completed contract method.

A Comparison of the Two Methods

INCOME RECOGNITION. Comparing the gross profit patterns produced by each method of revenue recognition demonstrates the essential difference between them:

	Percentage-of-Completion	**Completed Contract**
Gross profit recognized:		
2009	$500,000	–0–
2010	125,000	–0–
2011	275,000	$900,000
Total gross profit	$900,000	$900,000

---

[20]As a practical matter, if the percentage of completion figure is rounded we may calculate different amounts of revenue by (a) directly calculating revenue using the percentage of completion, and (b) indirectly calculating revenue by first calculating gross profit using the percentage of completion and then calculating revenue by adding gross profit to cost of construction. In that case, given that gross profit is defined as revenue minus cost, it is best to use approach (a) and first calculate revenue directly, solving for gross profit by subtracting cost of construction from revenue.

Although both methods yield identical gross profit of $900,000 for the entire 3-year period, the timing differs. The completed contract method defers all gross profit to 2011, when the project is completed. Obviously, the percentage-of-completion method provides a better measure of the company's economic activity and progress over the three-year period. That's why the percentage-of-completion method is preferred, and, as mentioned previously, the completed contract method should be used only when the company is unable to make dependable estimates of future costs necessary to apply the percentage-of-completion method.[21]

BALANCE SHEET RECOGNITION. The balance sheet presentation for the construction-related accounts by both methods is shown in Illustration 5–2F. The balance in the construction in progress account differs between methods because of the earlier gross profit recognition that occurs under the percentage-of-completion method.

ILLUSTRATION 5–2F Balance Sheet Presentation	Balance Sheet (End of Year)		
		2009	**2010**
	Percentage-of-Completion:		
	Current assets:		
	Accounts receivable	$200,000	$800,000
	Costs and profit ($2,000,000) in excess of billings ($1,200,000)	800,000	
	Current liabilities:		
	Billings ($3,200,000) in excess of costs and profit ($3,125,000)		$75,000
	Completed Contract:		
	Current assets:		
	Accounts receivable	$200,000	$800,000
	Costs ($1,500,000) in excess of billings ($1,200,000)	$300,000	
	Current liabilities:		
	Billings ($3,200,000) in excess of costs ($2,500,000)		$700,000

In the balance sheet, the construction in progress (CIP) account (containing costs and profit) is offset against the billings on construction contract account, with CIP > Billings shown as an asset and Billings > CIP shown as a liability. Because a company may have some contracts that have a net asset position and others that have a net liability position, we usually will see both net assets and net liabilities shown in a balance sheet at the same time.

Construction in progress in excess of billings essentially represents an unbilled receivable. The construction company is incurring construction costs (and recognizing gross profit using the percentage-of-completion method) for which it will be paid by the buyer. If the construction company bills the buyer an amount exactly equal to these costs (and profits recognized) then the accounts receivable balance properly reflects the claims of the construction company. If, however, the amount billed is less than the costs incurred (plus profits recognized) the difference represents the remaining claim to cash—an asset.

On the other hand, *Billings in excess of construction in progress* essentially indicates that the overbilled accounts receivable overstates the amount of the claim to cash earned to that date and must be reported as a liability. This is similar to the unearned revenue liability that is recorded when a customer pays for a product or service in advance. The advance is properly shown as a liability representing the obligation to provide the good or service in the future.

The first disclosure note to any set of financial statements usually is a summary of significant accounting policies. This note discloses the method the company uses to account for

---

[21]For income tax purposes, the completed contract method may be used for home construction contracts and certain other real estate construction contracts. All other contracts must use the percentage-of-completion method.

Notes: **Engineering and Construction Contracts (in part)**

The company recognizes engineering and construction contract revenues using the percentage-of-completion method, based primarily on contract costs incurred to date compared with total estimated contract costs. . . . Changes to total estimated contract costs or losses, if any, are recognized in the period in which they are determined. Revenue recognized in excess of amounts billed is classified as current assets under contract work in progress. Amounts billed to clients in excess of revenues recognized to date are classified as current liabilities under advance billings on contracts.

its long-term contracts. As an example of this, Graphic 5–10 shows the disclosure note that appeared in a recent annual report of **Fluor Corporation.**

LONG-TERM CONTRACT LOSSES. The Harding Construction Company example above involves a situation in which a profit was realized on the construction contract. Unfortunately, losses sometimes occur on long-term contracts. As a prelude to the following discussion, notice in Graphic 5–10 that Fluor Corporation recognizes losses "in the period in which they are determined."

Periodic loss occurs for profitable project. When using the percentage-of-completion method, a loss sometimes must be recognized in at least one period over the life of the project even though the project as a whole is expected to be profitable. We determine the loss in precisely the same way we determined the profit in profitable years. For example, assume the same $5 million contract for Harding Construction Company described in Illustration 5–2 but with the following cost information:

	2009	2010	2011
Construction costs incurred during the year	$1,500,000	$1,260,000	$1,840,000
Construction costs incurred in prior years	–0–	1,500,000	2,760,000
Cumulative construction costs	1,500,000	2,760,000	4,600,000
Estimated costs to complete at end of year	2,250,000	1,840,000	–0–
Total estimated and actual construction costs	$3,750,000	$4,600,000	$4,600,000

At the end of 2009, gross profit of $500,000 (revenue of $2,000,000 less cost of construction of $1,500,000) is recognized as previously determined.

At the end of 2010, the company now forecasts a total profit of $400,000 ($5,000,000 − $4,600,000) on the project and, at that time, the project is estimated to be 60% complete ($2,760,000 ÷ $4,600,000). Applying this percentage to the anticipated gross profit of $400,000 results in a gross profit *to date* of $240,000. But remember, a gross profit of $500,000 was recognized in 2009.

This situation is treated as a *change in accounting estimate* because it resulted from a change in the estimation of costs to complete at the end of 2009. Costs to complete—$4,600,000—were much higher than the 2009 year-end estimate of $3,750,000. Recall from our discussion of changes in accounting estimates in Chapter 4 that we don't go back and restate the prior year's gross profit. Instead, the 2010 income statement would report *a loss of $260,000* ($500,000 − 240,000) so that the cumulative amount recognized to date totals $240,000 of gross profit. The loss consists of revenue of $1,000,000 ($5,000,000 × 60% = $3,000,000 less 2009 revenue of $2,000,000) less cost of construction of $1,260,000 (cost incurred in 2010). The following journal entry records the loss:

Cost of construction	1,260,000	
Revenue from long-term contracts		1,000,000
Construction in progress (loss)		260,000

Recognized losses on long-term contracts reduce the construction in progress account.

The 2011 income statement would report a gross profit of $160,000 determined as follows:

Project gross profit	$400,000
Less: Gross profit recognized in prior periods ($500,000 − 260,000)	(240,000)
2011 gross profit	$160,000

The 2011 gross profit comprises $2,000,000 in revenue ($5,000,000 less revenue of $3,000,000 recognized in 2006 and 2007) and $1,840,000 in cost of construction (cost incurred in 2011).

Of course, when using the completed contract method, no profit or loss is recorded in 2009 or 2010. Instead, a $400,000 gross profit (revenue of $5,000,000 and cost of construction of $4,600,000) is recognized in 2011.

Loss is projected on the entire project. When using either the percentage-of-completion or completed contract methods, a more conservative approach is indicated when an overall loss is projected on the entire contract. Again consider the Harding Construction Company example but with the following cost information:

	2009	2010	2011
Construction costs incurred during the year	$1,500,000	$1,260,000	$2,440,000
Construction costs incurred in prior years	–0–	1,500,000	2,760,000
Cumulative construction costs	1,500,000	2,760,000	5,200,000
Estimated costs to complete at end of year	2,250,000	2,340,000	–0–
Total estimated and actual construction costs	$3,750,000	$5,100,000	$5,200,000

An estimated loss on a long-term contract is fully recognized in the first period the loss is anticipated, regardless of the revenue recognition method used.

At the end of 2010, revised costs indicate a loss of $100,000 for the entire project ($5,000,000 − 5,100,000). In this situation, the *total* anticipated loss must be recognized in 2010 for both the percentage-of-completion method and the completed contract method. As a gross profit of $500,000 was recognized in 2009 using the percentage-of-completion method, *a $600,000 loss is recognized in 2010* so that the cumulative amount recognized to date totals a $100,000 loss. Once again, this situation is treated as a change in accounting estimate with no restatement of 2009 income. If the completed contract method is used, because no gross profit is recognized in 2009 the $100,000 loss for the project is recognized in 2010 by debiting loss from long-term contracts and crediting construction in progress for $100,000.

If the loss was not recognized in 2010, construction in progress would be valued at an amount greater than the company expects to realize from the contract. The construction in progress account is reduced to $2,660,000 ($2,760,000 in costs to date less $100,000 loss recognized to date). This amount combined with the estimated costs to complete of $2,340,000 equals the realizable contract price of $5,000,000. Recognizing losses on long-term projects in the period the losses become known is equivalent to measuring inventory at the lower of cost or market.

The pattern of gross profit (loss) over the contract period for the two methods is summarized in the following table. Notice that an unanticipated increase in costs of $100,000 causes a further loss of $100,000 to be recognized in 2011.

	Percentage-of-Completion	Completed Contract
Gross profit (loss) recognized:		
2009	$ 500,000	–0–
2010	(600,000)	$(100,000)
2011	(100,000)	(100,000)
Total project loss	$(200,000)	$(200,000)

2009		
Revenue recognized ($5,000,000 × 40%)		$2,000,000
Costs of construction		(1,500,000)
Gross profit		$ 500,000
2010		
Revenue recognized to date ($5,000,000 × 54.12%)*	$2,706,000	
Less: Revenue recognized in 2009	(2,000,000)	
Revenue recognized		$ 706,000
Cost of construction†		(1,306,000)
Loss		$ (600,000)
2011		
Revenue recognized to date ($5,000,000 × 100%)	$5,000,000	
Less: Revenue recognized in 2009 and 2010	(2,706,000)	
Revenue recognized		$2,294,000
Cost of construction†		(2,394,000)
Loss		$ (100,000)

ILLUSTRATION 5–2G

Percentage-of-Completion Method: Allocation of Revenue and Cost of Construction to Each Period—Loss on Entire Project

*$2,760,000 ÷ $5,100,000 = 54.12%
†The difference between revenue and loss

The table in Illustration 5–2G shows the revenue and cost of construction recognized in each of the three years using the percentage-of-completion method.

Revenue is recognized in the usual way by multiplying a percentage of completion by the total contract price. In situations where a loss is expected on the entire project, cost of construction for the period will no longer be equal to cost incurred during the period. The easiest way to compute cost of construction is to add the amount of the recognized loss to the amount of revenue recognized. For example, in 2010 revenue recognized of $706,000 is added to the loss of $600,000 to arrive at the cost of construction of $1,306,000.[22]

The journal entries to record the losses in 2010 and 2011 are as follows:

2010

Cost of construction	1,306,000	
Revenue from long-term contracts		706,000
Construction in progress (loss)		600,000

2011

Cost of construction	2,394,000	
Revenue from long-term contracts		2,294,000
Construction in progress (loss)		100,000

Recognized losses on long-term contracts reduce the construction in progress account.

---

[22]The cost of construction also can be determined as follows:

Loss to date (100% recognized)		$ 100,000
Add:		
Remaining total project cost, not including the loss ($5,100,000 − 100,000)	$5,000,000	
Multiplied by the percentage of completion	× .5412*	2,706,000
Total		2,806,000
Less: Cost of construction recognized in 2009		(1,500,000)
Cost of construction recognized in 2010		$1,306,000

*$2,760,000 ÷ $5,100,000

Using the completed contract method, no revenue or cost of construction is recognized until the contract is complete. In 2010, a loss on long-term contracts (an income statement account) of $100,000 is recognized. In 2011, the income statement will report revenue of $5,000,000 and cost of construction of $5,100,000, thus reporting the additional loss of $100,000. The journal entries to record the losses in 2010 and 2011 are as follows:

2010

Loss on long-term contracts	100,000	
Construction in progress (loss)		100,000

2011

Cost of construction	5,100,000	
Revenue from long-term contracts		5,000,000
Construction in progress (loss)		100,000

You can see from this example that use of the percentage-of-completion method in this case produces a large overstatement of income in 2009 and a large understatement in 2010 caused by a change in the estimation of future costs. Recall that if management believes they are unable to make dependable forecasts of future costs, the completed contract method should be used.

CONCEPT REVIEW EXERCISE

LONG-TERM CONSTRUCTION CONTRACTS

During 2009, the Samuelson Construction Company began construction on an office building for the City of Gernon. The contract price is $8,000,000 and the building will take approximately 18 months to complete. Completion is scheduled for early in 2011. The company's fiscal year ends on December 31.

The following is a year-by-year recap of construction costs incurred and the estimated costs to complete the project as of the end of each year. Progress billings and cash collections also are indicated.

	2009	2010	2011
Construction costs incurred during the year	$1,500,000	$4,500,000	$1,550,000
Construction costs incurred in prior years	–0–	1,500,000	6,000,000
Cumulative construction costs	1,500,000	6,000,000	7,550,000
Estimated costs to complete at end of year	4,500,000	1,500,000	–0–
Total estimated and actual construction costs	$6,000,000	$7,500,000	$7,550,000
Billings made during the year	$1,400,000	$5,200,000	$1,400,000
Cash collections during year	1,000,000	4,000,000	3,000,000

Required:

1. Determine the amount of gross profit or loss to be recognized in each of the three years applying both the percentage-of-completion and completed contract methods.
2. Prepare the necessary summary journal entries for each of the three years to account for construction costs incurred, recognized revenue and cost of construction, contract billings, and cash collections and to close the construction accounts in 2011 using the percentage-of-completion method only.
3. Prepare a partial balance sheet for 2009 and 2010 to include all construction-related accounts using the percentage-of-completion method.

SOLUTION   1. Determine the amount of gross profit or loss to be recognized in each of the three years applying both the percentage-of-completion and completed contract methods.

Percentage-of-Completion Method

	2009	2010	2011
Contract price	$8,000,000	$8,000,000	$8,000,000
Less: total cost*	6,000,000	$7,500,000	7,550,000
Total estimated gross profit to date	2,000,000	500,000	450,000
Multiplied by % of completion**	25%	80%	100%
Gross profit recognized to date	500,000	400,000	450,000
Less gross profit recognized in prior years	–0–	(500,000)	(400,000)
Gross profit (loss) recognized	$ 500,000	$ (100,000)	$ 50,000

*Estimated in 2009 & 2010; Actual in 2011.
**Estimates of percentage-of-completion:

2009	2010	2011
$\frac{1,500,000}{6,000,000} = 25\%$	$\frac{6,000,000}{7,500,000} = 80\%$	Project complete

Completed Contract Method

	2009	2010	2011
Gross profit recognized	–0–	–0–	$450,000

2. Prepare the necessary summary journal entries for each of the three years to account for construction costs incurred, recognized revenue and cost of construction, contract billings, and cash collections and to close the construction accounts in 2011 using the percentage-of-completion method only.

	2009		2010		2011	
Construction in progress	1,500,000		4,500,000		1,550,000	
Cash, materials, etc.		1,500,000		4,500,000		1,550,000
To record construction costs.						
Construction in progress (gross profit)	500,000				50,000	
Cost of construction	1,500,000				1,550,000	
Revenue from long-term						
contracts (below)		2,000,000				1,600,000
To record gross profit.						
Cost of construction			4,500,000			
Revenue from long-term						
contracts (below)				4,400,000		
Construction in progress (loss)				100,000		
To record loss.						
Accounts receivable	1,400,000		5,200,000		1,400,000	
Billings on construction contract		1,400,000		5,200,000		1,400,000
To record progress billings.						
Cash	1,000,000		4,000,000		3,000,000	
Accounts receivable		1,000,000		4,000,000		3,000,000
To record cash collections.						
Billings on construction contract					8,000,000	
Construction in progress						8,000,000
To close accounts.						

Revenue recognized:

2009:	$8,000,000 × 25% =	$2,000,000
2010:	$8,000,000 × 80% =	$6,400,000
	Less: Revenue recognized in 2009	(2,000,000)
	Revenue recognized in 2010	$4,400,000
2011:	$8,000,000 × 100% =	$8,000,000
	Less: Revenue recognized in 2009 and 2010	(6,400,000)
	Revenue recognized in 2011	$1,600,000

3. Prepare a partial balance sheet for 2009 and 2010 to include all construction related accounts using the percentage-of-completion method.

**Balance Sheet
(End of Year)**

	2009	2010
Current assets:		
Accounts receivable	$400,000	$1,600,000
Costs and profit ($2,000,000) in excess of billings ($1,400,000)	600,000	
Current liabilities:		
Billings ($6,600,000) in excess of costs and profit ($6,400,000)		200,000

Industry-Specific Revenue Issues

● LO5

The previous sections addressed situations when revenue is recognized either at a point in time after the earnings process is virtually complete or over time during the earnings process. We now look at situations that require revenue recognition using a combination of the two approaches.

Software and Other Multiple-Deliverable Arrangements

We all know how important personal computers and the software to run them have become in our daily lives. The software industry is a key economic component of our economy. **Microsoft** alone reported revenues in excess of $51 billion for its 2007 fiscal year.

The recognition of software revenues was a controversial issue throughout the 1990s. The controversy stemmed from the way software vendors typically package their products. It is not unusual for these companies to sell multiple software deliverables in a bundle for a lump-sum contract price. The bundle often includes product, upgrades, postcontract customer support, and other services. The critical accounting question concerns the timing of revenue recognition.

The American Institute of Certified Public Accountants (AICPA) issued a Statement of Position (*SOP 97-2*) providing guidance in this area. *SOP 97-2* indicates that if an arrangement includes multiple elements, the revenue from the arrangement should be allocated to the various elements based on the relative fair values of the individual elements, "regardless of any separate prices stated within the contract for each element."[23]

For example, suppose that a vendor sold software to a customer for $100,000. As part of the contract, the vendor promises to provide technical support over the next six months. Prior to the issuance of *SOP 97-2,* some vendors were recognizing the entire $100,000 as revenue when the initial software was delivered. Now, the $100,000 contract price must be allocated based on fair values. So, the seller might recognize $80,000 in revenue initially and defer the remaining $20,000 and recognize it ratably over the next six months. In its 2007 balance sheet, Microsoft reported a liability for unearned (deferred) software revenue of $12,646 million.

More recently, the FASB's Emerging Issues Task Force (EITF) issued *EITF 00-21* to broaden the application of this basic perspective to other arrangements that involve "multiple deliverables."[24] Examples of such arrangements include sales of appliances with maintenance contracts, cellular phone contracts that have service contracts, computer hardware systems with multiple components, and even painting services that include sales of paint as well as labor. In such arrangements, sellers must separately record revenue for a part of an arrangement if, for example, the part has value to the customer on a stand-alone basis

> Generally, a portion of the proceeds received from the sale of software is deferred and recognized as revenue in future periods.

---

[23]"Software Revenue Recognition," *Statement of Position 97-2* (New York: AICPA, 1997), p. 14.
[24]*EITF 00-21: Revenue Arrangements with Multiple Deliverables* (Stamford, Conn.: FASB, 5/15/2003). For discussion of critical differences between *SOP 97-2* and *EITF 00-21,* see S. T. Petra and N. S. Slavin, "Revenue Recognition for Software Products with Multiple Deliverables," *The CPA Journal Online,* New York State Society of CPAs, April 2005.

and there is objective and reliable evidence of the fair value of the undelivered parts. The amount allocable to any part is limited to the amount that is not contingent upon the delivery of other parts or meeting other performance criteria. Importantly, if part of an arrangement does not qualify for separate accounting, recognition of the revenue from that part is delayed until revenue associated with the other parts is recognized. This results in deferring revenue recognition unless parts of an arrangement clearly qualify for separate revenue recognition. As an example, consider the disclosure by **Affiliated Computer Services** in its 2007 annual report shown in Graphic 5–11.

1. Business and Summary of Significant Accounting Policies (in part)

Where an implementation or development project is contracted with a client, and we will also provide services or operate the system over a period of time, EITF 00-21 provides the methodology for separating the contract elements and allocating total arrangement consideration to the contract elements . . . In certain instances where revenue cannot be allocated to a contract element delivered earlier than other elements, costs of delivery are deferred and recognized as the subsequent elements are delivered.

GRAPHIC 5–11
Disclosure of Revenue Recognition Policy for Multiple Deliverables— Affiliated Computer Services

Real World Financials

INTERNATIONAL FINANCIAL REPORTING STANDARDS

Multiple-Deliverable Arrangements. *IAS No. 18* governs most revenue recognition under IFRS. The general revenue recognition principles in this standard are consistent with U.S. GAAP, but there is less specific guidance for multiple-deliverable arrangements and industry-specific concerns like software revenue recognition.

Franchise Sales

The use of franchise arrangements has become increasingly popular in the United States over the past 30 years. Many retail outlets for fast food, restaurants, motels, and auto rental agencies are operated as franchises. In the franchise arrangements, the franchisor, for example **McDonald's Corporation,** grants to the franchisee, quite often an individual, the right to sell the franchisor's products and use its name for a specified period of time. The restaurant where you ate your last Big Mac was probably owned and operated by an individual under a franchise agreement, not by McDonald's Corporation.

The fees to be paid by the franchisee to the franchisor usually comprise (1) the *initial franchise fee* and (2) *continuing franchise fees.* The services to be performed by the franchisor in exchange for the initial franchise fee, in addition to the right to use its name and sell its products, might include assistance in finding a location, constructing the facilities, and training employees. The initial franchise fee usually is a fixed amount, but it may be payable in installments.

FASB
Franchise fee revenue from an individual franchise sale ordinarily shall be recognized, with an appropriate provision for estimated uncollectible amounts, when all material services or conditions relating to the sale have been substantially performed or satisfied by the franchisor.[25]

The continuing franchise fees are paid to the franchisor for continuing rights as well as for advertising and promotion and other services provided over the life of the franchise agreement. These fees sometimes are a fixed annual or monthly amount, a percentage of the volume of business done by the franchise, or a combination of both.

The continuing franchise fees usually do not present any accounting difficulty and are recognized by the franchisor as revenue *over time* in the periods the services are performed by the franchisor, which generally corresponds to the periods they are received. The challenging revenue recognition

Continuing franchise fees are recognized over time as the services are performed.

[25]"Accounting for Franchise Fee Revenue," *Statement of Financial Accounting Standards No. 45* (Stamford, Conn.: FASB, 1981).

issue pertains to the initial franchise fee. In the early 1960s and 1970s, many franchisors recognized the entire initial franchise fee as revenue in the period in which the contract was signed. In many cases, there were significant services to be performed and the fee was collectible in installments over an extended period of time creating uncertainty as to cash collection.

Initial franchise fees generally are recognized at a point in time when the earnings process is virtually complete.

Specific guidelines for revenue recognition of the initial franchise fee are provided by *SFAS 45*. You should notice the similarity of these specific guidelines with those of the general revenue recognition guidelines we've discussed previously. A key to these conditions is the concept of *substantial performance*. It requires that substantially all of the initial services of the franchisor required by the franchise agreement be performed before the initial franchise fee can be recognized as revenue. The term *substantial* requires professional judgment on the part of the accountant. In situations when the initial franchise fee is collectible in installments, even after substantial performance has occurred, the installment sales or cost recovery methods should be used for profit recognition, if a reasonable estimate of uncollectibility cannot be made.

Consider the example in Illustration 5–3.

ILLUSTRATION 5–3 Franchise Sales	On March 31, 2009, the Red Hot Chicken Wing Corporation entered into a franchise agreement with Thomas Keller. In exchange for an initial franchise fee of $50,000, Red Hot will provide initial services to include the selection of a location, construction of the building, training of employees, and consulting services over several years. $10,000 is payable on March 31, 2009, with the remaining $40,000 payable in annual installments which include interest at an appropriate rate. In addition, the franchisee will pay continuing franchise fees of $1,000 per month for advertising and promotion provided by Red Hot, beginning immediately after the franchise begins operations. Thomas Keller opened his Red Hot franchise for business on September 30, 2009.

INITIAL FRANCHISE FEE. Assuming that the initial services to be performed by Red Hot subsequent to the contract signing are substantial but that collectibility of the installment receivable is reasonably certain, the following journal entry is recorded:

Revenue from initial franchise services is deferred until the services are rendered.

March 31, 2009
Cash	10,000	
Note receivable	40,000	
Unearned franchise fee revenue		50,000

To record franchise agreement and down payment.

Unearned franchise fee revenue is a liability. It would be reduced to zero and revenue would be recognized when the initial services have been performed. This could occur in increments or at one point in time, depending on the circumstances.[26] For example, in our illustration, if substantial performance was deemed to have occurred when the franchise began operations, the following entry would be recorded:

Sept. 30, 2009
Unearned franchise fee revenue	50,000	
Franchise fee revenue		50,000

To recognize franchise fee revenue.

If collectibility of the installment receivable is uncertain and there is no basis for estimating uncollectible amounts, the initial entry would record a credit to deferred franchise fee revenue which is then recognized as being earned using either the installment sales or cost recovery methods.

---

[26]Franchise agreements sometimes require that any payments made to the franchisor will be refunded if the franchise fails to open. If this condition is present, it would be an important factor in deciding whether to recognize revenue before the franchise opens.

CONTINUING FRANCHISE FEES. Continuing franchise fee revenue is recognized on a monthly basis as follows:

Cash (or accounts receivable)	1,000	
Service revenue		1,000

To recognize continuing franchise fee revenue.

Expenses incurred by the franchisor in providing these continuing franchise services should be recognized in the same periods as the service revenue.

Other unique industry-specific revenue recognition situations exist besides those we have discussed. The FASB and AICPA have issued detailed revenue recognition standards for such industries as insurance, record and music, cable television, and motion pictures.[27] These industry standards are beyond the scope of this text. However, in each case, the objective is the same: to recognize revenue in the period or periods that the revenue-generating activities of the company are performed.

ADDITIONAL CONSIDERATION

In certain circumstances, revenue is recognized at the completion of the production process (before delivery). This approach generally is used by companies that deal in precious metals, and "... agricultural, mineral, and other products, units of which are interchangeable and have an immediate marketability at quoted prices. ..."[28] This is called the *production basis* of recognizing revenue and is accomplished by writing inventory up from cost to market value.

Recall that in a typical manufacturing situation, revenue is not recognized at the completion of the production process due to significant uncertainty as to the collectibility of the asset to be received. We don't know if the product will be sold, nor the selling price, nor the buyer if eventually sold. These uncertainties are not significant when there is immediate marketability at quoted market prices for products like precious metals.

In cases when the production basis of recognizing revenue is used, full disclosure of the fact is required.

PROFITABILITY ANALYSIS

PART B

Chapter 3 provided an overview of financial statement analysis and introduced some of the common ratios used in risk analysis to investigate a company's liquidity and long-term solvency. We now introduce ratios related to profitability analysis.

Activity Ratios

One key to profitability is how well a company manages and utilizes its assets. Some ratios are designed to evaluate a company's effectiveness in managing assets. Of particular interest are the activity, or turnover ratios, of certain assets. The greater the number of times an asset turns over—the higher the ratio—the fewer assets are required to maintain a given level of activity (revenue). Given that a company incurs costs to finance its assets with debt (paying interest) or equity (paying dividends), high turnovers are usually attractive.

Although, in concept, the activity or turnover can be measured for any asset, activity ratios are most frequently calculated for total assets, accounts receivable, and inventory. These ratios are calculated as follows:

● **LO6**

Activity ratios measure a company's efficiency in managing its assets.

$$\text{Asset turnover ratio} = \frac{\text{Net sales}}{\text{Average total assets}}$$

---

[27]"Accounting and Reporting by Insurance Enterprises," *Statement of Financial Accounting Standards No. 60* (Stamford, Conn.: FASB, 1982), "Financial Reporting in the Record and Music Industry," *Statement of Financial Accounting Standards No. 50* (Stamford, Conn.: FASB, 1981), "Financial Reporting by Cable Television Companies," *Statement of Financial Accounting Standards No. 51* (Stamford, Conn.: FASB, 1981), "Accounting by Producers or Distributors of Films," *Statement of Position 00-2* (New York: AICPA, 2000).
[28]"Restatement and Revision of Accounting Research Bulletins," *Accounting Research Bulletin No. 43* (New York: AICPA, 1953), Chapter 4, par. 16.

$$\text{Receivables turnover ratio} = \frac{\text{Net sales}}{\text{Average accounts receivable (net)}}$$

$$\text{Inventory turnover ratio} = \frac{\text{Cost of goods sold}}{\text{Average inventory}}$$

The *asset turnover ratio* measures a company's efficiency in using assets to generate revenue.

ASSET TURNOVER. A broad measure of asset efficiency is the asset turnover ratio. The ratio is computed by dividing a company's net sales or revenues by the average total assets available for use during a period. The denominator, average assets, is determined by adding beginning and ending total assets and dividing by two. The asset turnover ratio provides an indication of how efficiently a company utilizes all of its assets to generate revenue.

The *receivables turnover ratio* offers an indication of how quickly a company is able to collect its accounts receivable.

RECEIVABLES TURNOVER. The receivables turnover ratio is calculated by dividing a period's net credit sales by the average net accounts receivable. Because income statements seldom distinguish between cash sales and credit sales, this ratio usually is computed using total net sales as the numerator. The denominator, average accounts receivable, is determined by adding beginning and ending net accounts receivable (gross accounts receivable less allowance for uncollectible accounts) and dividing by two.[29]

The receivables turnover ratio provides an indication of a company's efficiency in collecting receivables. The ratio shows the number of times during a period that the average accounts receivable balance is collected. The higher the ratio, the shorter the average time between credit sales and cash collection.

The *average collection period* indicates the average age of accounts receivable.

A convenient extension is the average collection period. This measure is computed simply by dividing 365 days by the receivables turnover ratio. The result is an approximation of the number of days the average accounts receivable balance is outstanding.

$$\text{Average collection period} = \frac{365}{\text{Receivables turnover ratio}}$$

Monitoring the receivables turnover ratio (and average collection period) over time can provide useful information about a company's future prospects. For example, a decline in the receivables turnover ratio (an increase in the average collection period) could be an indication that sales are declining because of customer dissatisfaction with the company's products. Another possible explanation is that the company has changed its credit policy and is granting extended credit terms in order to maintain customers. Either explanation could signal a future increase in bad debts. Ratio analysis does not explain what is wrong. It does provide information that highlights areas for further investigation.

The *inventory turnover ratio* measures a company's efficiency in managing its investment in inventory.

INVENTORY TURNOVER. An important activity measure for a merchandising company (a retail, wholesale, or manufacturing company) is the inventory turnover ratio. The ratio shows the number of times the average inventory balance is sold during a reporting period. It indicates how quickly inventory is sold. The more frequently a business is able to sell, or turn over, its inventory, the lower its investment in inventory must be for a given level of sales. The ratio is computed by dividing the period's cost of goods sold by the average inventory balance. The denominator, average inventory, is determined by adding beginning and ending inventory and dividing by two.[30]

A relatively high ratio, say compared to a competitor, usually is desirable. A high ratio indicates comparative strength, perhaps caused by a company's superior sales force or maybe a successful advertising campaign. However, it might also be caused by a relatively low inventory level, which could mean either very efficient inventory management or stockouts and lost sales in the future.

---

[29]Although *net* accounts receivable typically is used in practice for the denominator of receivables turnover, some prefer to use *gross* accounts receivable. Why? As the allowance for bad debts increases, net accounts receivable decreases, so if net accounts receivable is in the denominator, more bad debts have the effect of decreasing the denominator and therefore increasing receivables turnover. All else equal, an analyst would rather see receivables turnover improve because of more sales or less gross receivables, and not because of an increase in the allowance for bad debts.

[30]Notice the consistency in the measure used for the numerator and denominator of the two turnover ratios. For the receivables turnover ratio, both numerator and denominator are based on sales dollars, whereas they are both based on cost for the inventory turnover ratio.

On the other hand, a relatively low ratio, or a decrease in the ratio over time, usually is perceived to be unfavorable. Too much capital may be tied up in inventory. A relatively low ratio may result from overstocking, the presence of obsolete items, or poor marketing and sales efforts.

Similar to the receivables turnover, we can divide the inventory turnover ratio into 365 days to compute the average days in inventory. This measure indicates the number of days it normally takes to sell inventory.

$$\text{Average days in inventory} = \frac{365}{\text{Inventory turnover ratio}}$$

Profitability Ratios

● LO6

A fundamental element of an analyst's task is to develop an understanding of a firm's profitability. Profitability ratios attempt to measure a company's ability to earn an adequate return relative to sales or resources devoted to operations. Resources devoted to operations can be defined as total assets or only those assets provided by owners, depending on the evaluation objective.

Three common profitability measures are (1) the profit margin on sales, (2) the return on assets, and (3) the return on shareholders' equity. These ratios are calculated as follows:

$$\text{Profit margin on sales} = \frac{\text{Net income}}{\text{Net sales}}$$

$$\text{Return on assets} = \frac{\text{Net income}}{\text{Average total assets}}$$

$$\text{Return on shareholders' equity} = \frac{\text{Net income}}{\text{Average shareholders' equity}}$$

Profitability ratios assist in evaluating various aspects of a company's profit-making activities.

Notice that for all of the profitability ratios, our numerator is net income. Recall our discussion in Chapter 4 on earnings quality. The relevance of any historical-based financial statement hinges on its predictive value. To enhance predictive value, analysts often adjust net income in these ratios to separate a company's *transitory earnings* effects from its *permanent earnings*. Analysts begin their assessment of permanent earnings with income from continuing operations. Then, adjustments are made for any unusual, one-time gains or losses included in income from continuing operations. It is this adjusted number that they use as the numerator in these ratios.

When calculating profitability ratios, analysts often adjust net income for any transitory income effects.

PROFIT MARGIN ON SALES. The profit margin on sales is simply net income divided by net sales. The ratio measures an important dimension of a company's profitability. It indicates the portion of each dollar of revenue that is available to cover expenses. It offers a measure of the company's ability to withstand either higher expenses or lower revenues.

What is considered to be a desirable profit margin is highly sensitive to the nature of the business activity. For instance, you would expect a specialty shop to have a higher profit margin than, say, **Wal-Mart.** A low profit margin can be compensated for by a high asset turnover rate, and vice versa, which brings us to considering the tradeoffs inherent in generating return on assets.

The profit margin on sales measures the amount of net income achieved per sales dollar.

RETURN ON ASSETS. The return on assets (ROA) ratio expresses income as a percentage of the average total assets available to generate that income. Because total assets are partially financed with debt and partially by equity funds, this is an inclusive way of measuring earning power that ignores specific sources of financing.

A company's return on assets is related to both profit margin and asset turnover. Specifically, profitability can be achieved by either a high profit margin, high turnover, or a combination of the two. In fact, the return on assets can be calculated by multiplying the profit margin and the asset turnover.

$$\text{Return on assets} = \text{Profit margin} \times \text{Asset turnover}$$

$$\frac{\text{Net income}}{\text{Average total assets}} = \frac{\text{Net income}}{\text{Net sales}} \times \frac{\text{Net sales}}{\text{Average total assets}}$$

Industry standards are particularly important when evaluating asset turnover and profit margin. Some industries are characterized by low turnover but typically make up for it with higher profit margins. Others have low profit margins but compensate with high turnover. Grocery stores typically have relatively low profit margins but relatively high asset turnover. In comparison, a manufacturer of specialized equipment will have a higher profit margin but a lower asset turnover ratio.

ADDITIONAL CONSIDERATION

The return on assets ratio often is computed as follows:

$$\text{Return on assets} = \frac{\text{Net income} + \text{Interest expense (1 − Tax rate)}}{\text{Average total assets}}$$

The reason for adding back interest expense (net of tax) is that interest represents a return to suppliers of debt capital and should not be deducted in the computation of net income when computing the return on total assets. In other words, the numerator is the total amount of income available to both debt and equity capital.

The *return on shareholders' equity* measures the return to suppliers of equity capital.

The DuPont framework shows that return on equity depends on profitability, activity, and financial leverage.

RETURN ON SHAREHOLDERS' EQUITY. Equity investors typically are concerned about the amount of profit that management can generate from the resources that owners provide. A closely watched measure that captures this concern is return on equity (ROE), calculated by dividing net income by average shareholders' equity.

In addition to monitoring return on equity, investors want to understand how that return can be improved. The DuPont framework provides a convenient basis for analysis that breaks return on equity into three key components:[31]

- **Profitability,** measured by the profit margin (Net income ÷ Sales). As discussed already, a higher profit margin indicates that a company is generating more profit from each dollar of sales.
- **Activity,** measured by asset turnover (Sales ÷ Average total assets). As discussed already, higher asset turnover indicates that a company is using their assets efficiently to generate more sales from each dollar of assets.
- **Financial Leverage,** measured by the equity multiplier (Average total assets ÷ Average total equity). A high equity multiplier indicates that relatively more of the company's assets have been financed with debt. As indicated in Chapter 3, leverage can provide additional return to the company's equity holders.

In equation form, the DuPont framework looks like this:

Return on equity = Profit margin × Asset turnover × Equity multiplier

$$\frac{\text{Net income}}{\text{Avg. total equity}} = \frac{\text{Net income}}{\text{Total sales}} \times \frac{\text{Total sales}}{\text{Avg. total assets}} \times \frac{\text{Avg. total assets}}{\text{Avg. total equity}}$$

Notice that total sales and average total assets appear in the numerator of one ratio and the denominator of another, so they cancel to yield net income ÷ average total equity, or ROE.

Because profit margin and asset turnover combine to create return on assets, the DuPont framework can also be viewed as indicating that return on equity depends on return on assets and financial leverage.

We have already seen that ROA is determined by profit margin and asset turnover, so another way to compute ROE is by multiplying ROA by the equity multiplier:

Return on equity = Return on assets × Equity multiplier

$$\frac{\text{Net income}}{\text{Avg. total equity}} = \frac{\text{Net income}}{\text{Avg. total assets}} \times \frac{\text{Avg. total assets}}{\text{Avg. total equity}}$$

We can see from this equation that an equity multiplier of greater than 1 will produce a return on equity that is higher than the return on assets. However, as with all ratio analysis, there are tradeoffs. If leverage is too high, creditors become concerned about the potential

---

[31]DuPont analysis is so named because the basic model was developed by F. Donaldson Brown, an electrical engineer who worked for DuPont in the early part of the 20th century.

for default on the company's debt and require higher interest rates. Because interest is recognized as an expense, net income is reduced, so at some point the benefits of a higher equity multiplier are offset by a lower profit margin. Part of the challenge of managing a company is to identify the combination of profitability, activity, and leverage that produces the highest return for equity holders.

ADDITIONAL CONSIDERATION

Sometimes when return on equity is calculated, shareholders' equity is viewed more narrowly to include only common shareholders. In that case, preferred stock is excluded from the denominator, and preferred dividends are deducted from net income in the numerator. The resulting rate of return on common shareholders' equity focuses on profits generated on resources provided by common shareholders.

Graphic 5–12 provides a recap of the ratios we have discussed.

GRAPHIC 5–12

Summary of Profitability Analysis Ratios

Activity ratios

$$\text{Asset turnover} = \frac{\text{Net sales}}{\text{Average total assets}}$$

$$\text{Receivables turnover} = \frac{\text{Net sales}}{\text{Average accounts receivable (net)}}$$

$$\text{Average collection period} = \frac{365}{\text{Receivables turnover ratio}}$$

$$\text{Inventory turnover} = \frac{\text{Cost of goods sold}}{\text{Average inventory}}$$

$$\text{Average days in inventory} = \frac{365}{\text{Inventory turnover ratio}}$$

Profitability ratios

$$\text{Profit margin on sales} = \frac{\text{Net income}}{\text{Net sales}}$$

$$\text{Return on assets} = \frac{\text{Net income}}{\text{Average total assets}}$$

$$\text{Return on shareholders' equity} = \frac{\text{Net income}}{\text{Average shareholders' equity}}$$

Leverage ratio

$$\text{Equity multiplier} = \frac{\text{Average total assets}}{\text{Average total equity}}$$

Profitability Analysis—An Illustration

To illustrate the application of the DuPont framework and the computation of the activity and profitability ratios, we analyze two well-known pharmaceutical companies, **Pfizer, Inc.** and **Merck & Co., Inc.** The operations of these two companies are similar in terms of their involvement in pharmaceutical and other health care products. Illustration 5–4A presents selected financial statement information for the two companies.

On the surface it appears that Pfizer is more profitable than Merck. As shown in Illustration 5–4A, Pfizer's 2006 net income was $11.024 billion, compared to Merck's $4.434 billion. But that's not the whole story. Even though both are very large companies, Pfizer is almost three times the size of Merck in terms of total assets, so how can they be compared?[32]

---

[32]Consistent with financial statement analysis being concerned with prediction, our illustration analyzes continuing operations. For Merck this focus required no adjustment, but for Pfizer we excluded its Consumer Healthcare business, which was sold on 12/20/06 and therefore treated as a discontinued operation in Pfizer's 2006 annual report.

ILLUSTRATION 5–4A		Pfizer		Merck	
		2006	**2005**	**2006**	**2005**
Selected Financial Information for Pfizer, Inc. and Merck & Co., Inc.	Accounts receivable (net)	$ 9,392	$ 9,103	$ 3,315	$ 2,927
	Inventories	$ 6,111	$ 5,478	$ 1,769	$ 1,658
	Total assets	$114,775	$110,311	$44,570	$44,846
Real World Financials	Total liabilities	$ 43,477	$ 49,979	$27,010	$26,868
	Total shareholders' equity	$ 71,298	$ 60,332	$17,560	$17,978
	Two-year averages:				
	Accounts receivable (net)		$ 9,248		$ 3,121
	Inventories		$ 5,795		$ 1,714
	Total assets		$112,543		$44,708
	Total shareholders' equity		$ 65,815		$17,769
	Income Statement-2006				
	Net sales		$ 48,371		$22,636
	Cost of goods sold		$ 7,640		$ 6,001
	Net Income (income from continuing operations for Pfizer)		$ 11,024		$ 4,434

Focusing on financial ratios helps adjust for size differences, and the DuPont framework helps identify the determinants of profitability from the perspective of shareholders.

Illustration 5–4B includes the DuPont analysis for Pfizer and Merck, as well as some additional activity ratios that we have discussed. Notice that both companies have the same

ILLUSTRATION 5–4B		Pfizer		Merck		Industry Average*
DuPont Framework and Activity Ratios— Pfizer, Inc. and Merck & Co, Inc.	**DuPont analysis:**					
	Profit margin on sales	$\dfrac{\$11,024}{\$48,371}$ =	0.23	$\dfrac{\$4,434}{\$22,636}$ =	0.20	0.18
	×		×		×	
	Asset turnover	$\dfrac{\$48,371}{\$112,543}$ =	0.43	$\dfrac{\$22,636}{\$44,708}$ =	0.51	0.59
	=		=		=	
	Return on assets	$\dfrac{\$11,024}{\$112,543}$ =	0.10	$\dfrac{\$4,434}{\$44,708}$ =	0.10	0.11
	×		×		×	
	Equity Multiplier	$\dfrac{\$112,543}{\$65,815}$ =	1.71	$\dfrac{\$44,708}{\$17,769}$ =	2.52	1.82
	=		=		=	
	Return on shareholders' equity	$\dfrac{\$11,024}{\$65,815}$ =	0.17	$\dfrac{\$4,434}{\$17,769}$ =	0.25	0.20
	Other activity ratios:					
	Receivables turnover	$\dfrac{\$48,371}{\$9,248}$ =	5.23	$\dfrac{\$22,636}{\$3,121}$ =	7.25	5.36
	Average collection period	$\dfrac{365}{5.23}$ =	70 days	$\dfrac{365}{7.25}$ =	50 days	68 days
	Inventory turnover	$\dfrac{\$7,640}{\$5,795}$ =	1.32	$\dfrac{\$6,001}{\$1,714}$ =	3.50	2.37
	Average days in inventory	$\dfrac{365}{1.32}$ =	277 days	$\dfrac{365}{3.50}$ =	104 days	154 days

*Industry average based on sample of twelve large pharmaceutical companies

return on assets (ROA) of 10%, but each obtains that ROA differently, with Pfizer having a relatively higher profit margin and lower asset turnover and Merck having a lower profit margin and higher asset turnover. The other activity ratios provide insights into Merck's higher asset turnover. Merck turns over its accounts receivable and its inventory much faster than does Pfizer.

Still, if both companies are producing the same ROA, are their shareholders equally happy? Not necessarily. Merck's return on equity (ROE) of 25% is significantly higher than Pfizer's ROE of 17%. Why? Merck is more highly leveraged, as indicated by its relatively higher equity multiplier of 2.52. The company is better able to use assets funded by debt to increase the income available for shareholders. This is an example of the favorable effects of financial leverage to which we referred earlier.

The essential point of our discussion here, and in Part C of Chapter 3, is that raw accounting numbers alone mean little to decision makers. The numbers gain value when viewed in relation to other numbers. Similarly, the financial ratios formed by those relationships provide even greater perspective when compared with similar ratios of other companies, or relatedly, with averages for several companies in the same industry. Accounting information is useful in making decisions. Financial analysis that includes comparisons of financial ratios enhances the value of that information.

FINANCIAL REPORTING CASE SOLUTION

1. **Does your sister have to wait two and a half years to get her bonus? Explain.** *(p. 240)* No. The *general* revenue recognition criteria would suggest that revenue and costs should be recognized when a project is finished. The difficulty this would create is that all revenues, expenses, and resulting profit from the project are recognized when the project is completed; no revenues or expenses would be reported in the income statements of earlier reporting periods in which much of the work may have been performed. The percentage-of-completion method of revenue recognition for long-term projects addresses this problem. A share of the project's profit is allocated to each period in which the earnings process occurs. This is two and a half years in this instance.

2. **How are gross profits recognized using the percentage-of-completion method?** *(p. 243)* The percentage-of-completion method recognizes part of the estimated gross profit each period. The amount recognized is based on progress to date which is estimated as the fraction of the project's cost incurred to date divided by total estimated costs. The estimated percentage of completion is multiplied by the revised project gross profit estimate. This yields the estimated gross profit earned from the beginning of the project. The gross profit recognized is calculated by subtracting from this amount the gross profit recognized in previous periods.

3. **Are there other situations in which revenue is recognized at times other than when a product is delivered?** *(p. 233)* Yes, revenue recognition sometimes is delayed until after the product is delivered. These situations involve either the possibility of product returns or bad debts. In most cases, product returns and bad debt are estimated and revenues are recognized when a product is delivered. However, in situations involving an abnormal degree of uncertainty about cash collection caused by potential returns or bad debts, revenue recognition *after* delivery sometimes is appropriate. ●

THE BOTTOM LINE

● **LO1**   The objective of revenue recognition is to recognize revenue in the period or periods that the revenue-generating activities of the company are performed. Also, judgment as to the collectibility of the cash from the sale of a product or service will impact the timing of revenue recognition. These two concepts of performance and collectibility are captured by the general guidelines for revenue recognition in the realization principle which requires that revenue should be recognized only after (1) the earnings process is virtually complete and (2) there is reasonable certainty of collecting the asset to be received (usually cash) from the customer. For the sale of product, these criteria usually are satisfied at the point of product delivery. At that point, the majority of the productive activities have taken place and any remaining uncertainty concerning asset collection can be accounted for by estimating possible returns and bad debts. Also, service revenue often is recognized at a point in time if there is one final activity that is deemed critical to the earnings process. (p. 228)

● **LO2** The installment sales method recognizes gross profit in collection periods by applying the gross profit percentage on the sale to the amount of cash actually received. The cost recovery method defers all gross profit recognition until cash has been received equal to the cost of the item sold. These methods of recognizing revenue should only be used in situations where there is an unusually high degree of uncertainty regarding the ultimate cash collection on an installment sale. (p. 233)

● **LO3** In most situations, even though the right to return merchandise exists, revenues and expenses can be appropriately recognized at point of delivery. Based on past experience, a company usually can estimate the returns that will result for a given volume of sales. These estimates reduce both sales and cost of goods sold in anticipation of returns. Revenue cannot be recognized at the point of delivery unless the seller is able to make reliable estimates of future returns. Otherwise, revenue recognition is deferred beyond the delivery point. (p. 236)

● **LO4** Revenue recognition at a single point in time when the earnings process is virtually complete is inappropriate for certain types of service revenue activities and also, usually, for long-term contracts. The completed contract method recognizes revenues and expenses on long-term construction and other long-term contracts at a point in time when the project is complete. This method is only used in unusual situations. The preferable method for recognizing revenues and expenses for long-term contracts is the percentage-of-completion method, which recognizes revenues over time by assigning a share of the project's revenues and costs to each reporting period during the project. (p. 238)

● **LO5** Industry guidelines require that the lump-sum contract price for software be allocated to the various elements of the package based on the relative fair values of the individual elements. Generally, this results in a deferral of a portion of the proceeds that are then recognized as revenue in future periods. Other multiple-deliverable arrangements are accounted for in a similar manner. The use of franchise arrangements has become increasingly popular. The fees to be paid by the franchisee to the franchisor usually are composed of (1) the initial franchise fee and (2) continuing franchise fees. *SFAS 45* requires that the franchisor has substantially performed the services promised in the franchise agreement and that the collectibility of the initial franchise fee is reasonably assured before the initial fee can be recognized as revenue. The continuing franchise fees are recognized by the franchisor as revenue over time in the periods the services are performed by the franchisor. (p. 252)

● **LO6** Activity and profitability ratios provide information about a company's profitability. Activity ratios include the receivables turnover ratio, the inventory turnover ratio, and the asset turnover ratio. Profitability ratios include the profit margin on sales, the return on assets, and the return on shareholders' equity. DuPont analysis explains return on stockholders' equity as determined by profit margin, asset turnover, and the extent to which assets are financed with equity versus debt. (p. 255) ●

APPENDIX 5 | INTERIM REPORTING

Interim reports are issued for periods of less than a year, typically as quarterly financial statements.

Interim reporting serves to enhance the timeliness of financial information.

Financial statements covering periods of less than a year are called *interim reports*. Companies registered with the SEC, which includes most public companies, must submit quarterly reports.[33] Though there is no requirement to do so, most also send quarterly reports to their shareholders and typically include abbreviated, unaudited interim reports as supplemental information within their annual reports. For instance, Graphic 5A–1 shows the quarterly information disclosed in the 2007 annual report of **Microsoft Corporation.**

For accounting information to be useful to decision makers, it must be available on a timely basis. One of the objectives of interim reporting is to enhance the timeliness of financial information. In addition, quarterly reports provide investors and creditors with additional insight on the seasonality of business operations that might otherwise get lost in annual reports.

---

[33]Quarterly reports are filed with the SEC on form 10-Q. Annual reports to the SEC are on form 10-K.

GRAPHIC 5A–1

Interim Data in Annual Report—Microsoft Corporation

Real World Financials

Quarterly Information

(In millions, except per share amounts) (Unaudited)

Quarter Ended	Sep. 30	Dec. 31	Mar. 31	June 30	Total
Fiscal year 2007					
Revenue	$10,811	$12,542[(1)]	$14,398[(2)]	$13,371	$51,122
Gross profit	9,115	8,922	12,258	10,134	40,429
Net income	3,478	2,626	4,926	3,035[(3)]	14,065
Basic earnings per share	0.35	0.27	0.51	0.32	1.44
Diluted earnings per share	0.35	0.26	0.50	0.31	1.42
Fiscal year 2006					
Revenue	$9,741	$11,837	$10,900	$11,804	$44,282
Gross profit	8,488	9,598	8,872	9,674	36,632
Net income	3,141[(4)]	3,653	2,977[(5)]	2,828[(6)]	12,599
Basic earnings per share	0.29	0.35	0.29	0.28	1.21
Diluted earnings per share	0.29	0.34	0.29	0.28	1.20

[(1)] Reflects $1.64 billion of revenue deferred to the third quarter of fiscal year 2007 for the Express Upgrade to Windows Vista and Microsoft Office Technology guarantee programs and pre-shipments of Windows Vista and the 2007 Microsoft Office system.
[(2)] Includes $1.64 billion of revenue discussed above and charges totaling $296 million (pre-tax) related to various legal matters.
[(3)] Includes $1.06 billion charge related to the Xbox 360 warranty policy, inventory write-downs, and product returns.
[(4)] Includes charge of $361 million (pre-tax) related to the settlement with RealNetworks, Inc.
[(5)] Includes charges of $397 million (pre-tax) related to various legal matters.
[(6)] Includes charge of € 281 million ($351 million) as a result of the fine imposed by the European Commission in July 2006.

However, the downside to these benefits is the relative unreliability of interim reporting. With a shorter reporting period, questions associated with estimation and allocation are magnified. For example, certain expenses often benefit an entire year's operations and yet are incurred primarily within a single interim period. Similarly, should smaller companies use lower tax rates in the earlier quarters and higher rates in later quarters as higher tax brackets are reached? Another result of shorter reporting periods is the intensified effect of major events such as discontinued operations or extraordinary items. A second quarter casualty loss, for instance, that would reduce annual profits by 10% might reduce second quarter profits by 40% or more. Is it more realistic to allocate such a loss over the entire year? These and similar questions tend to hinge on the way we view an interim period in relation to the fiscal year. More specifically, should each interim period be viewed as a *discrete* reporting period or as an *integral part* of the annual period?

> The fundamental debate regarding interim reporting centers on the choice between the *discrete* and *integral part* approaches.

Reporting Revenues and Expenses

Existing practice and current reporting requirements for interim reporting generally follow the viewpoint that interim reports are an integral part of annual statements, although the discrete approach is applied to some items. Most revenues and expenses are recognized using the same accounting principles applicable to annual reporting. Some modifications are necessary to help cause interim statements to relate better to annual statements. This is most evident in the way costs and expenses are recognized. Most are recognized in interim periods as incurred. But when an expenditure clearly benefits more than just the period in which it is incurred, the expense should be allocated among the periods benefited on an allocation basis consistent with the company's annual allocation procedures. For example, annual repair expenses, property tax expense, and advertising expenses incurred in the first quarter that clearly benefit later quarters are assigned to each quarter through the use of accruals and deferrals. Costs and expenses subject to year-end adjustments, such as depreciation and bad debt expense, are estimated and allocated to interim periods in a systematic way. Similarly, income tax expense at each interim date should be based on estimates of the effective tax rate for the whole year. This would mean, for example, that if the estimated effective rate has changed since the previous interim period(s), the tax expense that period would be

> With only a few exceptions, the same accounting principles applicable to annual reporting are used for interim reporting.

determined as the new rate times the cumulative pretax income to date, less the total tax expense reported in previous interim periods.

Reporting Unusual Items

Discontinued operations, extraordinary items, and unusual items are reported entirely within the interim period in which they occur.

On the other hand, major events such as discontinued operations or extraordinary items should be reported separately in the interim period in which they occur. That is, these amounts should not be allocated among individual quarters within the fiscal year. The same is true for items that are unusual or infrequent but not both. For example, Microsoft's 2007 interim data in Graphic 5A–1 includes several footnotes designed to help readers understand the effects of unusual items on Microsoft's quarterly performance. Treatment of these items is more consistent with the discrete view than the integral part view.

Earnings Per Share

Quarterly EPS calculations follow the same procedures as annual calculations.

A second item that is treated in a manner consistent with the discrete view is earnings per share. EPS calculations for interim reports follow the same procedures as annual calculations that you will study in Chapter 19. The calculations are based on conditions actually existing during the particular interim period rather than on conditions estimated to exist at the end of the fiscal year.

Reporting Accounting Changes

Accounting changes made in an interim period are reported by retrospectively applying the changes to prior financial statements.

Recall from Chapter 4 that we account for a change in accounting principle retrospectively, meaning we recast prior years' financial statements when we report those statements again in comparative form. In other words, we make those statements appear as if the newly adopted accounting method had been used in those prior years. It's the same with interim reporting. We retrospectively report a change made during an interim period in similar fashion. Then in financial reports of subsequent interim periods of the same fiscal year, we disclose how that change affected (a) income from continuing operations, (b) net income, and (c) related per share amounts for the postchange interim period.

Minimum Disclosures

Complete financial statements are not required for interim period reporting, but certain minimum disclosures are required as follows:[34]

- Sales, income taxes, extraordinary items, and net income.
- Earnings per share.
- Seasonal revenues, costs, and expenses.
- Significant changes in estimates for income taxes.
- Discontinued operations, extraordinary items, and unusual or infrequent items.
- Contingencies.
- Changes in accounting principles or estimates.
- Significant changes in financial position.

When fourth quarter results are not separately reported, material fourth quarter events, including year-end adjustments, should be reported in disclosure notes to annual statements. ●

QUESTIONS FOR REVIEW OF KEY TOPICS

Q 5–1 What are the two general criteria that must be satisfied before a company can recognize revenue?

Q 5–2 Explain why, in most cases, a seller recognizes revenue when it delivers its product rather than when it produces the product.

Q 5–3 Revenue recognition for most installment sales occurs at the point of delivery of the product or service. Under what circumstances would a seller delay revenue recognition for installment sales beyond the delivery date?

Q 5–4 Distinguish between the installment sales method and the cost recovery method of accounting for certain installment sales.

---

[34]"Interim Financial Reporting," *Accounting Principles Board Opinion No 28* (New York: AICPA, 1973).

Q 5–5   How does a company report deferred gross profit resulting from the use of the installment sales method in its balance sheet?

Q 5–6   Revenue recognition for most product sales that allow the right of return occurs at the point of product delivery. Under what circumstances would revenue recognition be delayed?

Q 5–7   Describe a consignment sale. When does a consignor recognize revenue for a consignment sale?

Q 5–8   Service revenue is recognized either at one point in time or over extended periods. Explain the rationale for recognizing revenue using these two approaches.

Q 5–9   Distinguish between the percentage-of-completion and completed contract methods of accounting for long-term contracts with respect to income recognition. Under what circumstances should a company use the completed contract method?

Q 5–10   When percentage-of-completion accounting is not appropriate, U.S. GAAP requires the use of the completed contract method, while IFRS requires the use of the cost recovery method. Explain how the two methods affect recognition of revenue, cost of construction, and gross profit over the life of a profitable contract.

Q 5–11   Periodic billings to the customer for a long-term construction contract are recorded as billings on construction contract. How is this account reported in the balance sheet?

Q 5–12   When is an estimated loss on a long-term contract recognized using the percentage-of-completion method? The completed contract method?

Q 5–13   Briefly describe the guidelines for recognizing revenue from the sale of software and other multiple-deliverable arrangements.

Q 5–14   Briefly describe the guidelines provided by SFAS 45 for the recognition of revenue by a franchisor for an initial franchise fee.

Q 5–15   Show the calculation of the following activity ratios: (1) the receivables turnover ratio, (2) the inventory turnover ratio, and (3) the asset turnover ratio. What information about a company do these ratios offer?

Q 5–16   Show the calculation of the following profitability ratios: (1) the profit margin on sales, (2) the return on assets, and (3) the return on shareholders' equity. What information about a company do these ratios offer?

Q 5–17   Show the DuPont framework's calculation of the three components of return on shareholders' equity. What information about a company do these ratios offer?

Q 5–18   [Based on Appendix 5] Interim reports are issued for periods of less than a year, typically as quarterly financial statements. Should these interim periods be viewed as separate periods or integral parts of the annual period?

BRIEF **EXERCISES**

BE 5–1
Point of delivery recognition

● LO1

On July 1, 2009, Apache Company sold a parcel of undeveloped land to a construction company for $3,000,000. The book value of the land on Apache's books was $1,200,000. Terms of the sale required a down payment of $150,000 and 19 annual payments of $150,000 plus interest at an appropriate interest rate due on each July 1 beginning in 2010. Apache has no significant obligations to perform services after the sale. How much gross profit will Apache recognize in both 2009 and 2010 assuming point of delivery profit recognition?

BE 5–2
Installment sales method

● LO2

Refer to the situation described in BE 5–1. How much gross profit will Apache recognize in both 2009 and 2010 applying the installment sales method?

BE 5–3
Cost recovery method

● LO2

Refer to the situation described in BE 5–1. How much gross profit will Apache recognize in both 2009 and 2010 applying the cost recovery method?

BE 5–4
Installment sales method

● LO2

Refer to the situation described in BE 5–1. What should be the balance in the deferred gross profit account at the end of 2010 applying the installment sales method?

BE 5–5
Right of return

● LO3

Meyer Furniture sells office furniture mainly to corporate clients. Customers who return merchandise within 90 days for any reason receive a full refund. Discuss the issues Meyer must consider in determining its revenue recognition policy.

BE 5–6
Percentage-of-completion method; profit recognition

● LO4

A construction company entered into a fixed-price contract to build an office building for $20 million. Construction costs incurred during the first year were $6 million and estimated costs to complete at the end of the year were $9 million. How much gross profit will the company recognize in the first year using the percentage-of-completion method? How much revenue will appear in the company's income statement?

BE 5–7
Percentage-of-completion method; balance sheet

● LO4

Refer to the situation described in BE 5–6. During the first year the company billed its customer $7 million of which $5 million was collected before year-end. What would appear in the year-end balance sheet related to this contract?

BE 5–8
Completed contract method

● LO4

Refer to the situation described in BE 5–6. The building was completed during the second year. Construction costs incurred during the second year were $10 million. How much gross profit will the company recognize in the first year and in the second year applying the completed contract method?

BE 5–9
Cost recovery method

● LO4

Refer to the situation described in BE 5–8. How much revenue, cost, and gross profit will the company recognize in the first and second year of the contract applying the cost recovery method that is required by IFRS?

BE 5–10
Percentage-of-completion and completed contract methods; loss on entire project

● LO4

Franklin Construction entered into a fixed-price contract to build a freeway-connecting ramp for $30 million. Construction costs incurred in the first year were $16 million and estimated costs to complete at the end of the year were $17 million. How much gross profit or loss will Franklin recognize the first year applying the percentage-of-completion method? Applying the completed contract method?

BE 5–11
Revenue recognition; franchise sales

● LO5

Collins, Inc., entered into a 10-year franchise agreement with an individual. For an initial franchise fee of $40,000, Collins agrees to assist in design and construction of the franchise location and in all other necessary start-up activities. Also, in exchange for advertising and promotional services, the franchisee agrees to pay continuing franchise fees equal to 5% of revenue generated by the franchise. When should Collins recognize revenue for the initial and continuing franchise fees?

BE 5–12
Receivables and inventory turnover ratios

● LO6

Universal Calendar Company began the year with accounts receivable and inventory balances of $100,000 and $80,000, respectively. Year-end balances for these accounts were $120,000 and $60,000, respectively. Sales for the year of $600,000 generated a gross profit of $200,000. Calculate the receivables and inventory turnover ratios for the year.

BE 5–13
Profitability ratios

● LO6

The 2009 income statement for Anderson TV and Appliance reported sales revenue of $420,000 and net income of $65,000. Average total assets for 2009 was $800,000. Shareholders' equity at the beginning of the year was $500,000 and $20,000 was paid to shareholders as dividends. There were no other shareholders' equity transactions that occurred during the year. Calculate the profit margin on sales, return on assets, and return on shareholders' equity for 2009.

BE 5–14
Profitability ratios

● LO6

Refer to the facts described in BE 5–13. Show the DuPont framework's calculation of the three components of the 2009 return on shareholders' equity for Anderson TV and Appliance.

BE 5–15
Inventory turnover ratio

● LO6

During 2009, Rogue Corporation reported sales revenue of $600,000. Inventory at both the beginning and end of the year totaled $75,000. The inventory turnover ratio for the year was 6.0. What amount of gross profit did the company report in its income statement for 2009?

EXERCISES   available with McGraw-Hill's Homework Manager www.mhhe.com/spiceland5e

An alternative exercise and problem set is available on the text website: www.mhhe.com/spiceland5e

E 5–1
Service revenue

● **LO1**

Alpine West, Inc., operates a downhill ski area near Lake Tahoe, California. An all-day, adult ticket can be purchased for $55. Adult customers also can purchase a season pass that entitles the pass holder to ski any day during the season, which typically runs from December 1 through April 30. The season pass is nontransferable, and the $450 price is nonrefundable. Alpine expects its season pass holders to use their passes equally throughout the season. The company's fiscal year ends on December 31.

On November 6, 2009, Jake Lawson purchased a season ticket.

Required:
1. When should Alpine West recognize revenue from the sale of its season passes?
2. Prepare the appropriate journal entries that Alpine would record on November 6 and December 31.
3. What will be included in the 2009 income statement and 2009 balance sheet related to the sale of the season pass to Jake Lawson?

E 5–2
Installment sales method

● **LO2**

Charter Corporation, which began business in 2009, appropriately uses the installment sales method of accounting for its installment sales. The following data were obtained for sales made during 2009 and 2010:

	2009	2010
Installment sales	$360,000	$350,000
Cost of installment sales	234,000	245,000
Cash collections on installment sales during:		
2009	150,000	100,000
2010	—	120,000

Required:
1. How much gross profit should Charter recognize in 2009 and 2010 from installment sales?
2. What should be the balance in the deferred gross profit account at the end of 2009 and 2010?

E 5–3
Installment sales method; journal entries

● **LO2**

[This is a variation of the previous exercise focusing on journal entries.]

Charter Corporation, which began business in 2009, appropriately uses the installment sales method of accounting for its installment sales. The following data were obtained for sales during 2009 and 2010:

	2009	2010
Installment sales	$360,000	$350,000
Cost of installment sales	234,000	245,000
Cash collections on installment sales during:		
2009	150,000	100,000
2010	—	120,000

Required:
Prepare summary journal entries for 2009 and 2010 to account for the installment sales and cash collections. The company uses the perpetual inventory system.

E 5–4
Installment sales; alternative recognition methods

● **LO2**

On July 1, 2009, the Foster Company sold inventory to the Slate Corporation for $300,000. Terms of the sale called for a down payment of $75,000 and three annual installments of $75,000 due on each July 1, beginning July 1, 2010. Each installment also will include interest on the unpaid balance applying an appropriate interest rate. The inventory cost Foster $120,000. The company uses the perpetual inventory system.

Required:
1. Compute the amount of gross profit to be recognized from the installment sale in 2009, 2010, 2011, and 2012 using point of delivery revenue recognition. Ignore interest charges.
2. Repeat requirement 1 applying the installment sales method.
3. Repeat requirement 1 applying the cost recovery method.

E 5–5
Journal entries; point of delivery, installment sales, and cost recovery methods

● **LO1 LO2**

[This is a variation of the previous exercise focusing on journal entries.]

On July 1, 2009, the Foster Company sold inventory to the Slate Corporation for $300,000. Terms of the sale called for a down payment of $75,000 and three annual installments of $75,000 due on each July 1, beginning July 1, 2010. Each installment also will include interest on the unpaid balance applying an appropriate interest rate. The inventory cost Foster $120,000. The company uses the perpetual inventory system.

Required:

1. Prepare the necessary journal entries for 2009 and 2010 using point of delivery revenue recognition. Ignore interest charges.
2. Repeat requirement 1 applying the installment sales method.
3. Repeat requirement 1 applying the cost recovery method.

E 5–6
Installment sales and cost recovery methods; solve for unknowns
● LO2

Wolf Computer Company began operations in 2009. The company allows customers to pay in installments for many of its products. Installment sales for 2009 were $1,000,000. If revenue is recognized at the point of delivery, $600,000 in gross profit would be recognized in 2009. If the company instead uses the cost recovery method, $100,000 in gross profit would be recognized in 2009.

Required:

1. What was the amount of cash collected on installment sales in 2009?
2. What amount of gross profit would be recognized if the company uses the installment sales method?

E 5–7
Installment sales; default and repossession
● LO2

Sanchez Development Company uses the installment sales method to account for some of its installment sales. On October 1, 2009, Sanchez sold a parcel of land to the Kreuze Corporation for $4 million. This amount was not considered significant relative to Sanchez's other sales during 2009. The land had cost Sanchez $1.8 million to acquire and develop. Terms of the sale required a down payment of $800,000 and four annual payments of $800,000 plus interest at an appropriate interest rate, with payments due on each October 1 beginning in 2010.

Kreuze paid the down payment, but on October 1, 2010, defaulted on the remainder of the contract. Sanchez repossessed the land. On the date of repossession the land had a fair value of $1.3 million.

Required:

Prepare the necessary entries for Sanchez to record the sale, receipt of the down payment, and the default and repossession applying the installment sales method. Ignore interest charges.

E 5–8
Real estate sales; gain recognition
● LO1 LO2

On April 1, 2009, the Apex Corporation sold a parcel of underdeveloped land to the Applegate Construction Company for $2,400,000. The book value of the land on Apex's books was $480,000. Terms of the sale required a down payment of $120,000 and 19 annual payments of $120,000 plus interest at an appropriate interest rate due on each April 1 beginning in 2010. Apex has no significant obligations to perform services after the sale.

Required:

1. Prepare the necessary entries for Apex to record the sale, receipt of the down payment, and receipt of the first installment assuming that Apex is able to make a reliable estimate of possible uncollectible amounts (that is, point of delivery profit recognition is used). Ignore interest charges.
2. Repeat requirement 1 assuming that Apex cannot make a reliable estimate of possible uncollectible amounts and decides to use the installment sales method for profit recognition.

E 5–9
Long-term contract; percentage-of-completion and completed contract methods
● LO4

Assume **Nortel Networks** contracted to provide a customer with Internet infrastructure for $2,000,000. The project began in 2009 and was completed in 2010. Data relating to the contract are summarized below:

	2009	2010
Costs incurred during the year	$ 300,000	$1,575,000
Estimated costs to complete as of 12/31	1,200,000	–0–
Billings during the year	380,000	1,620,000
Cash collections during the year	250,000	1,750,000

Required:

1. Compute the amount of gross profit or loss to be recognized in 2009 and 2010 using the percentage-of-completion method.
2. Compute the amount of gross profit or loss to be recognized in 2009 and 2010 using the completed contract method.
3. Prepare a partial balance sheet to show how the information related to this contract would be presented at the end of 2009 using the percentage-of-completion method.
4. Prepare a partial balance sheet to show how the information related to this contract would be presented at the end of 2009 using the completed contract method.

E 5–10
Long-term contract; percentage of completion and completed contract methods
● LO4

On June 15, 2009, Sanderson Construction entered into a long-term construction contract to build a baseball stadium in Washington D.C. for $220 million. The expected completion date is April 1 of 2011, just in time for the 2011 baseball season. Costs incurred and estimated costs to complete at year-end for the life of the contract are as follows ($ in millions):

	2009	2010	2011
Costs incurred during the year	$ 40	$80	$50
Estimated costs to complete as of 12/31	120	60	—

Required:

1. Determine the amount of gross profit or loss to be recognized in each of the three years using the percentage-of-completion method.
2. How much revenue will Sanderson report in its 2009 and 2010 income statements related to this contract using the percentage-of-completion method?
3. Determine the amount of gross profit or loss to be recognized in each of the three years using the completed contract method.
4. Determine the amount of revenue, cost, and gross profit or loss to be recognized in each of the three years using the cost recovery method that is required by IFRS.
5. Suppose the estimated costs to complete at the end of 2010 are $80 million instead of $60 million. Determine the amount of gross profit or loss to be recognized in 2010 using the percentage-of-completion method.

E 5–11
Percentage-of-completion method; loss projected on entire project

● LO4

On February 1, 2009, Arrow Construction Company entered into a three-year construction contract to build a bridge for a price of $8,000,000. During 2009, costs of $2,000,000 were incurred with estimated costs of $4,000,000 yet to be incurred. Billings of $2,500,000 were sent and cash collected was $2,250,000.

In 2010, costs incurred were $2,500,000 with remaining costs estimated to be $3,600,000. 2010 billings were $2,750,000 and $2,475,000 cash was collected. The project was completed in 2011 after additional costs of $3,800,000 were incurred. The company's fiscal year-end is December 31. Arrow uses the *percentage-of-completion* method.

Required:

1. Calculate the amount of gross profit or loss to be recognized in each of the three years.
2. Prepare journal entries for 2009 and 2010 to record the transactions described (credit various accounts for construction costs incurred).
3. Prepare a partial balance sheet to show the presentation of the project as of December 31, 2009 and 2010.

E 5–12
Completed contract method; loss projected on entire project

● LO4

[This is a variation of the previous exercise focusing on the completed contract method.]

On February 1, 2009, Arrow Construction Company entered into a three-year construction contract to build a bridge for a price of $8,000,000. During 2009, costs of $2,000,000 were incurred with estimated costs of $4,000,000 yet to be incurred. Billings of $2,500,000 were sent and cash collected was $2,250,000.

In 2010, costs incurred were $2,500,000 with remaining costs estimated to be $3,600,000. 2010 billings were $2,750,000 and $2,475,000 cash was collected. The project was completed in 2011 after additional costs of $3,800,000 were incurred. The company's fiscal year-end is December 31. Arrow uses the *completed contract* method.

Required:

1. Calculate the amount of gross profit or loss to be recognized in each of the three years.
2. Prepare journal entries for 2009 and 2010 to record the transactions described (credit various accounts for construction costs incurred).
3. Prepare a partial balance sheet to show the presentation of the project as of December 31, 2009 and 2010.

E 5–13
Income (loss) recognition; percentage-of-completion and completed contract methods compared

● LO4

Brady Construction Company contracted to build an apartment complex for a price of $5,000,000. Construction began in 2009 and was completed in 2011. The following are a series of independent situations, numbered 1 through 6, involving differing costs for the project. All costs are stated in thousands of dollars.

Situation	Costs Incurred During Year			Estimated Costs to Complete (As of the End of the Year)		
	2009	2010	2011	2009	2010	2011
1	1,500	2,100	900	3,000	900	—
2	1,500	900	2,400	3,000	2,400	—
3	1,500	2,100	1,600	3,000	1,500	—
4	500	3,000	1,000	3,500	875	—
5	500	3,000	1,300	3,500	1,500	—
6	500	3,000	1,800	4,600	1,700	—

Required:
Copy and complete the following table.

	Gross Profit (Loss) Recognized					
	Percentage-of-Completion			Completed Contract		
Situation	2009	2010	2011	2009	2010	2011
1						
2						
3						
4						
5						
6						

E 5–14
Percentage-of-
completion method;
solve for unknowns

● LO4

In 2009, Long Construction Corporation began construction work under a three-year contract. The contract price is $1,600,000. Long uses the percentage-of-completion method for financial reporting purposes. The financial statement presentation relating to this contract at December 31, 2009, is as follows:

Balance Sheet

Accounts receivable (from construction progress billings)		$30,000
Construction in progress	$100,000	
Less: Billings on construction contract	(94,000)	
Cost of uncompleted contracts in excess of billings		6,000

Income Statement

Income (before tax) on the contract recognized in 2009	$20,000

Required:
1. What was the cost of construction actually incurred in 2009?
2. How much cash was collected in 2009 on this contract?
3. What was the estimated cost to complete as of the end of 2009?
4. What was the estimated percentage of completion used to calculate income in 2009?

(AICPA adapted)

E 5–15
Revenue
recognition;
software

● LO5

Easywrite Software Company shipped software to a customer on July 1, 2009. The arrangement with the customer also requires the company to provide technical support over the next 12 months and to ship an expected software upgrade on January 1, 2010. The total contract price is $243,000, and Easywrite estimates that the individual fair values of the components of the arrangement if sold separately would be:

Software	$210,000
Technical support	30,000
Upgrade	30,000

Required:
1. Determine the timing of revenue recognition for the $243,000.
2. Assume that the $243,000 contract price was paid in advance on July 1, 2009. Prepare a journal entry to record the cash receipt. Do not worry about the cost of the items sold.

E 5–16
Multiple-
deliverable
arrangements

● LO5

Richardson Systems sells integrated bottling manufacturing systems that involve a conveyer, a labeler, a filler, and a capper. All of this equipment is sold separately by other vendors, and the fair values of the separate equipment are as follows:

Conveyer	$20,000
Labeler	10,000
Filler	15,000
Capper	5,000
Total	$50,000

Richardson sells the integrated system for $45,000. Each of the components are shipped separately to the customer for the customer to install.

Required:
1. Assume that each of the components can be used independently, even though Richardson sells them as an integrated system. How much revenue should be allocated to each component?
2. Now assume that the labeler, filler, and capper can't be used in production without the conveyer, and that the conveyer is the last component installed. How much revenue should be recognized at the time the conveyer is installed?

E 5–17
Revenue
recognition;
franchise sales

● LO5

On October 1, 2009, the Submarine Sandwich Company entered into a franchise agreement with an individual. In exchange for an initial franchise fee of $300,000, Submarine will provide initial services to the franchisee to include assistance in design and construction of the building, help in training employees, and help in obtaining financing.

10% of the initial franchise fee is payable on October 1, 2009, with the remaining $270,000 payable in nine equal annual installments beginning on October 1, 2010. These installments will include interest at an appropriate rate. The franchise opened for business on January 15, 2010.

Required:
Assume that the initial services to be performed by Submarine Sandwich subsequent to October 1, 2009, are substantial and that collectibility of the installment receivable is reasonably certain. Substantial performance of

the initial services is deemed to have occurred when the franchise opened. Prepare the necessary journal entries for the following dates (ignoring interest charges):

1. October 1, 2009
2. January 15, 2010

E 5–18
Concepts;
terminology

● LO2 through LO6

Listed below are several terms and phrases associated with revenue recognition and profitability analysis. Pair each item from List A (by letter) with the item from List B that is most appropriately associated with it.

List A	List B
_____ 1. Inventory turnover	a. Net income divided by net sales.
_____ 2. Return on assets	b. Defers recognition until cash collected equals cost.
_____ 3. Return on shareholders' equity	c. Defers recognition until project is complete.
_____ 4. Profit margin on sales	d. Net income divided by assets.
_____ 5. Cost recovery method	e. Risks and rewards of ownership retained by seller.
_____ 6. Percentage-of-completion method	f. Contra account to construction in progress.
_____ 7. Completed contract method	g. Net income divided by shareholders' equity.
_____ 8. Asset turnover	h. Cost of goods sold divided by inventory.
_____ 9. Receivables turnover	i. Recognition is in proportion to work completed.
_____ 10. Right of return	j. Recognition is in proportion to cash received.
_____ 11. Billings on construction contract	k. Net sales divided by assets.
_____ 12. Installment sales method	l. Net sales divided by accounts receivable.
_____ 13. Consignment sales	m. Could cause the deferral of revenue recognition beyond delivery point.

E 5–19
Inventory turnover;
calculation and
evaluation

● LO6

The following is a portion of the condensed income statement for Rowan, Inc., a manufacturer of plastic containers:

Net sales		$2,460,000
Less: Cost of goods sold:		
Inventory, January 1	$ 630,000	
Net purchases	1,900,000	
Inventory, December 31	(690,000)	1,840,000
Gross profit		$ 620,000

Required:

1. Determine Rowan's inventory turnover.
2. What information does this ratio provide?

E 5–20
Evaluating
efficiency of asset
management

● LO6

The 2009 income statement of Anderson Medical Supply Company reported net sales of $8 million, cost of goods sold of $4.8 million, and net income of $800,000. The following table shows the company's comparative balance sheets for 2009 and 2008:

	($ in 000s)	
	2009	**2008**
Assets		
Cash	$ 300	$ 380
Accounts receivable	700	500
Inventory	900	700
Property, plant, and equipment (net)	2,400	2,120
Total assets	$4,300	$3,700
Liabilities and Shareholders' Equity		
Current liabilities	$ 960	$ 830
Bonds payable	1,200	1,200
Paid-in capital	1,000	1,000
Retained earnings	1,140	670
Total liabilities and shareholders' equity	$4,300	$3,700

Some industry averages for Anderson's line of business are

Inventory turnover	5 times
Average collection period	25 days
Asset turnover	1.8 times

Required:
Assess Anderson's asset management relative to its industry.

E 5–21
Profitability ratios

● LO6

The following condensed information was reported by Peabody Toys, Inc., for 2009 and 2008:

	($ in 000s)	
	2009	**2008**
Income statement information		
Net sales	$5,200	$4,200
Net income	180	124
Balance sheet information		
Current assets	$ 800	$ 750
Property, plant, and equipment (net)	1,100	950
Total assets	$1,900	$1,700
Current liabilities	$ 600	$ 450
Long-term liabilities	750	750
Paid-in capital	400	400
Retained earnings	150	100
Liabilities and shareholders' equity	$1,900	$1,700

Required:
1. Determine the following ratios for 2009:
   a. Profit margin on sales
   b. Return on assets
   c. Return on shareholders' equity
2. Determine the amount of dividends paid to shareholders during 2009.

E 5–22
DuPont analysis

● LO6

This exercise is based on the Peabody Toys, Inc., data from Exercise 5–21.

Required:
1. Determine the following components of the DuPont framework for 2009:
   a. Profit margin on sales.
   b. Asset turnover.
   c. Equity multiplier.
   d. Return on shareholders' equity.
2. Write an equation that relates these components in calculating ROE. Use the Peabody Toys data to show that the equation is correct.

E 5–23
Interim financial statements; income tax expense [Based on Appendix 5]

● LO1

Joplin Laminating Corporation reported income before income taxes during the first three quarters and management's estimates of the annual effective tax rate at the end of each quarter as shown below:

	Quarter		
	First	**Second**	**Third**
Income before income taxes	$50,000	$40,000	$100,000
Estimated annual effective tax rate	34%	30%	36%

Required:
Determine the income tax expense to be reported in the income statement in each of the three quarterly reports.

E 5–24
Interim reporting; recognizing expenses [Based on Appendix 5]

● LO1

Security-Rand Corporation determines executive incentive compensation at the end of its fiscal year. At the end of the first quarter, management estimated that the amount will be $300 million. Depreciation expense for the year is expected to be $60 million. Also during the quarter, the company realized a gain of $23 million from selling two of its manufacturing plants.

Required:
What amounts for these items should be reported in the first quarter's income statement?

E 5–25
Interim financial statements; reporting expenses [Based on Appendix 5]

● LO1

Shields Company is preparing its interim report for the second quarter ending June 30. The following payments were made during the first two quarters:

Expenditure	Date	Amount
Annual advertising	January	$800,000
Property tax for the fiscal year	February	350,000
Annual equipment repairs	March	260,000
Extraordinary casualty loss	April	185,000
Research and development	May	96,000

Required:

For each expenditure indicate the amount that would be reported in the quarterly income statements for the periods ending March 31, June 30, September 30, and December 31.

CPA AND CMA EXAM QUESTIONS

CPA Exam Questions

The following questions are used in the Kaplan CPA Review Course to study revenue recognition while preparing for the CPA examination. Determine the response that best completes the statements or questions.

SCHWESER

● **LO1**

1. On October 1, 2009, Acme Fuel Co. sold 100,000 gallons of heating oil to Karn Co. at $3 per gallon. Fifty thousand gallons were delivered on December 15, 2009, and the remaining 50,000 gallons were delivered on January 15, 2010. Payment terms were 50% due on October 1, 2010, 25% due on first delivery, and the remaining 25% due on second delivery. What amount of revenue should Acme recognize from this sale during 2010?

    a. $ 75,000
    b. $150,000
    c. $225,000
    d. $300,000

2. Since there is no reasonable basis for estimating the degree of collectibility, Astor Co. uses the installment sales method of revenue recognition for the following sales:

	2009	2010
Sales	$600,000	$900,000
Collections from:		
2009 sales	200,000	100,000
2010 sales	-	300,000
Accounts written off:		
2009 sales	50,000	150,000
2010 sales	-	50,000
Gross profit percentage	30%	40%

● **LO2**

    What amount should Astor report as deferred gross profit in its December 31, 2010, balance sheet for the 2009 and 2010 sales?

    a. $225,000
    b. $150,000
    c. $160,000
    d. $250,000

3. Dolce Co., which began operations on January 1, 2009, appropriately uses the installment sales method of accounting to record revenues. The following information is available for the years ended December 31, 2009 and 2010:

	2009	2010
Sales	$1,000,000	$2,000,000
Gross profit realized on sales made in:		
2009	150,000	90,000
2010	-	200,000
Gross profit percentages	30%	40%

● **LO2**

    What amount of installment accounts receivable should Dolce report in its December 31, 2010, balance sheet?

    a. $1,700,000
    b. $1,225,000
    c. $1,300,000
    d. $1,775,000

4. Which of the following statements regarding the percentage-of-completion method of accounting is FALSE? The construction-in-progress account:

● **LO4**

    a. is shown net of advance billings as a liability if the amount is less than the amount of advance billings.
    b. is an asset.

   c. is shown net of advance billings on the balance sheet.
   d. does not include the cumulative effect of gross profit recognition.

5. The following data relates to a construction job started by Syl Co. during 2009:

● LO4

Total contract price	$100,000
Actual costs during 2009	20,000
Estimated remaining costs	40,000
Billed to customer during 2009	30,000
Received from customer during 2009	10,000

   Under the percentage-of-completion method, how much should Syl recognize as gross profit for 2009?
   a. $26,667
   b. $0
   c. $13,333
   d. $33,333

6. Hansen Construction, Inc., has consistently used the percentage-of-completion method of recognizing income. During 2009, Hansen started work on a $3,000,000 fixed-price construction contract. The accounting records disclosed the following data for the year ended December 31,2009:

● LO4

Costs incurred	$ 930,000
Estimated cost to complete	2,170,000
Progress billings	1,100,000
Collections	700,000

   How much loss should Hansen have recognized in 2009?
   a. $180,000
   b. $230,000
   c. $30,000
   d. $100,000

CMA Exam Questions

The following questions dealing with income measurement are adapted from questions that previously appeared on Certified Management Accountant (CMA) examinations. The CMA designation sponsored by the Institute of Management Accountants (www.imanet.org) provides members with an objective measure of knowledge and competence in the field of management accounting. Determine the response that best completes the statements or questions.

● LO1

1. On May 28, Markal Company purchased a tooling machine from Arens and Associates for $1,000,000 payable as follows: 50 percent at the transaction closing date and 50 percent due June 28. The cost of the machine to Arens is $800,000. Markal paid Arens $500,000 at the transaction closing date and took possession of the machine. On June 10, Arens determined that a change in the business environment has created a great deal of uncertainty regarding the collection of the balance due from Markal, and the amount is probably uncollectible. Arens and Markal have a fiscal year-end of May 31. The revenue recognized by Arens and Associates on May 28 is
   a. $200,000.
   b. $800,000.
   c. $1,000,000.
   d. $0.

2. The percentage-of-completion method of accounting for long-term construction contracts is an exception to the

● LO4

   a. Matching principle.
   b. Going-concern assumption.
   c. Economic-entity assumption.
   d. Revenue recognition principle.

● LO4

3. Roebling Construction signed a $24 million contract on August 1, 2008 with the city of Candu to construct a bridge over the Vine River. Roebling's estimated cost of the bridge on that date was $18 million. The bridge was to be completed by April 2011. Roebling uses the percentage-of-completion method for income recognition. Roebling's fiscal year ends May 31. Data regarding the bridge contract are presented in the schedule below.

	At May 31 ($000 omitted)	
	2009	**2010**
Actual costs to date	$ 6,000	$15,000
Estimated costs to complete	12,000	5,000
Progress billings to date	5,000	14,000
Cash collected to date	4,000	12,000

The gross profit or loss recognized in the fiscal year ended May 31, 2009 from this bridge contract is

a. $6,000,000 gross profit.
b. $2,000,000 gross profit.
c. $3,000,000 gross profit.
d. $1,000,000 gross profit.

PROBLEMS
available with McGraw-Hill's Homework Manager www.mhhe.com/spiceland5e

An alternative exercise and problem set is available on the text website: www.mhhe.com/spiceland5e

P 5–1
Income statement presentation; installment sales method (Chapters 4 and 5)

● LO2

Reagan Corporation computed income from continuing operations before income taxes of $4,200,000 for 2009. The following material items have not yet been considered in the computation of income:

1. The company sold equipment and recognized a gain of $50,000. The equipment had been used in the manufacturing process and was replaced by new equipment.

2. In December, the company received a settlement of $1,000,000 for a lawsuit it had filed based on antitrust violations of a competitor. The settlement was considered to be an unusual and infrequent event.

3. Inventory costing $400,000 was written off as obsolete. Material losses of this type were incurred twice in the last eight years.

4. It was discovered that depreciation expense on the office building of $50,000 per year was not recorded in either 2008 or 2009.

In addition, you learn that *included* in revenues is $400,000 from installment sales made during the year. The cost of these sales is $240,000. At year-end, $100,000 in cash had been collected on the related installment receivables. Because of considerable uncertainty regarding the collectibility of receivables from these sales, the company's accountant should have used the installment sales method to recognize revenue and gross profit on these sales.

Also, the company's income tax rate is 40% and there were 1 million shares of common stock outstanding throughout the year.

Required:
Prepare an income statement for 2009 beginning with income from continuing operations before income taxes. Include appropriate EPS disclosures.

P 5–2
Installment sales and cost recovery methods

● LO2

Ajax Company appropriately accounts for certain sales using the installment sales method. The perpetual inventory system is used. Information related to installment sales for 2009 and 2010 is as follows:

	2009	2010
Sales	$300,000	$400,000
Cost of sales	180,000	280,000
Customer collections on:		
2009 sales	120,000	100,000
2010 sales		150,000

Required:
1. Calculate the amount of gross profit that would be recognized each year from installment sales.
2. Prepare all necessary journal entries for each year.
3. Repeat requirements 1 and 2 assuming that Ajax uses the cost recovery method to account for its installment sales.

P 5–3
Installment sales; alternative recognition methods

● LO2

On August 31, 2009, the Silva Company sold merchandise to the Bendix Corporation for $500,000. Terms of the sale called for a down payment of $100,000 and four annual installments of $100,000 due on each August 31, beginning August 31, 2010. Each installment also will include interest on the unpaid balance applying an appropriate interest rate. The book value of the merchandise on Silva's books on the date of sale was $300,000. The perpetual inventory system is used. The company's fiscal year-end is December 31.

Required:
1. Prepare a table showing the amount of gross profit to be recognized in each of the five years of the installment sale applying each of the following methods:

a. Point of delivery revenue recognition.
b. Installment sales method.
c. Cost recovery method.

2. Prepare journal entries for each of the five years applying the three revenue recognition methods listed in requirement 1. Ignore interest charges.

3. Prepare a partial balance sheet as of the end of 2009 and 2010 listing the items related to the installment sale applying each of the three methods listed in requirement 1.

P 5–4
Installment sales and cost recovery methods

● LO2

Mulcahey Builders (MB) remodels office buildings in low-income urban areas that are undergoing economic revitalization. MB typically accepts a 25% down payment when they complete a job and a note which requires that the remainder be paid in three equal installments over the next three years, plus interest. Because of the inherent uncertainty associated with receiving these payments, MB has historically used the cost recovery method to recognize revenue.

As of January 1, 2009, MB's outstanding gross installment accounts receivable (not net of deferred gross profit) consist of the following:

1. $400,000 due from the Bluebird Motel. MB completed the Bluebird job in 2007, and estimated gross profit on that job is 25%.

2. $150,000 due from the PitStop Gas and MiniMart. MB completed the PitStop job in 2006, and estimated gross profit on that job is 35%.

Dan Mulcahey has been considering switching from the cost recovery method to the installment sales method, because he wants to show the highest possible gross profit in 2009 and he understands that the installment sales method recognizes gross profit sooner than does the cost recovery method.

Required:

1. Calculate how much gross profit is expected to be earned on these jobs in 2009 under the cost recovery method, and how much would be earned if MB instead used the installment sales method. Ignore interest.

2. If Dan is primarily concerned about 2009, do you think he would be happy with a switch to the installment sales method? Explain.

P 5–5
Percentage-of-completion method

● LO4

In 2009, the Westgate Construction Company entered into a contract to construct a road for Santa Clara County for $10,000,000. The road was completed in 2011. Information related to the contract is as follows:

	2009	2010	2011
Cost incurred during the year	$2,400,000	$3,600,000	$2,200,000
Estimated costs to complete as of year-end	5,600,000	2,000,000	–0–
Billings during the year	2,000,000	4,000,000	4,000,000
Cash collections during the year	1,800,000	3,600,000	4,600,000

Westgate uses the percentage-of-completion method of accounting for long-term construction contracts.

Required:

1. Calculate the amount of gross profit to be recognized in each of the three years.

2. Prepare all necessary journal entries for each of the years (credit *various accounts* for construction costs incurred).

3. Prepare a partial balance sheet for 2009 and 2010 showing any items related to the contract.

4. Calculate the amount of gross profit to be recognized in each of the three years assuming the following costs incurred and costs to complete information:

	2009	2010	2011
Costs incurred during the year	$2,400,000	$3,800,000	$3,200,000
Estimated costs to complete as of year-end	5,600,000	3,100,000	–0–

5. Calculate the amount of gross profit to be recognized in each of the three years assuming the following costs incurred and costs to complete information:

	2009	2010	2011
Costs incurred during the year	$2,400,000	$3,800,000	$3,900,000
Estimated costs to complete as of year-end	5,600,000	4,100,000	–0–

P 5–6
Completed contract method

● LO4

[This is a variation of the previous problem modified to focus on the completed contract method.]

Required:

Complete the requirements of Problem 5–5 assuming that Westgate Construction uses the completed contract method.

P 5–7
Construction
accounting; loss
projected on entire
project

● LO4

Curtiss Construction Company, Inc. entered into a fixed-price contract with Axelrod Associates on July 1, 2009, to construct a four-story office building. At that time, Curtiss estimated that it would take between two and three years to complete the project. The total contract price for construction of the building is $4,000,000. Curtiss appropriately accounts for this contract under the completed contract method in its financial statements. The building was completed on December 31, 2011. Estimated percentage of completion, *accumulated* contract costs incurred, estimated costs to complete the contract, and *accumulated* billings to Axelrod under the contract were as follows:

	At 12-31-09	At 12-31-10	At 12-31-11
Percentage of completion	10%	60%	100%
Costs incurred to date	$ 350,000	$2,500,000	$4,250,000
Estimated costs to complete	3,150,000	1,700,000	–0–
Billings to Axelrod, to date	720,000	2,170,000	3,600,000

Required:
1. Prepare schedules to compute gross profit or loss to be recognized as a result of this contract for each of the three years.
2. Assuming Curtiss uses the percentage-of-completion method of accounting for long-term construction contracts, compute gross profit or loss to be recognized in each of the three years.
3. Assuming the percentage-of-completion method, compute the amount to be shown in the balance sheet at the end of 2009 and 2010 as either cost in excess of billings or billings in excess of costs.

(AICPA adapted)

P 5–8
Long-term contract;
percentage-of-
completion and
completed contract
methods

● LO1 LO4

Citation Builders, Inc., builds office buildings and single-family homes. The office buildings are constructed under contract with reputable buyers. The homes are constructed in developments ranging from 10–20 homes and are typically sold during construction or soon after. To secure the home upon completion, buyers must pay a deposit of 10% of the price of the home with the remaining balance due upon completion of the house and transfer of title. Failure to pay the full amount results in forfeiture of the down payment. Occasionally, homes remain unsold for as long as three months after construction. In these situations, sales price reductions are used to promote the sale.

During 2009, Citation began construction of an office building for Altamont Corporation. The total contract price is $20 million. Costs incurred, estimated costs to complete at year-end, billings, and cash collections for the life of the contract are as follows:

	2009	2010	2011
Costs incurred during the year	$4,000,000	$9,500,000	$4,500,000
Estimated costs to complete as of year-end	12,000,000	4,500,000	-
Billings during the year	2,000,000	10,000,000	8,000,000
Cash collections during the year	1,800,000	8,600,000	9,600,000

Also during 2009, Citation began a development consisting of 12 identical homes. Citation estimated that each home will sell for $600,000, but individual sales prices are negotiated with buyers. Deposits were received for eight of the homes, three of which were completed during 2009 and paid for in full for $600,000 each by the buyers. The completed homes cost $450,000 each to construct. The construction costs incurred during 2009 for the nine uncompleted homes totaled $2,700,000.

Required:
1. Briefly explain the difference between the percentage-of-completion and the completed contract methods of accounting for long-term construction contracts.
2. Answer the following questions assuming that Citation uses the completed contract method for its office building contracts:
   a. What is the amount of gross profit or loss to be recognized for the Altamont contract during 2009 and 2010?
   b. How much revenue related to this contract will Citation report in its 2009 and 2010 income statements?
   c. What will Citation report in its December 31, 2009 balance sheet related to this contract (ignore cash)?
3. Answer 2a–2c assuming that Citation uses the percentage-of-completion method for its office building contracts.
4. Assume that as of year end 2010 the estimated cost to complete the office building is $9,000,000 and that Citation uses the percentage-of-completion method.
   a. What is the amount of gross profit or loss to be recognized for the Altamont contract during 2010?
   b. How much revenue related to this contract will Citation report in the 2010 income statement?
   c. What will Citation report in its 2010 balance sheet related to this contract (ignore cash)?

5. When should Citation recognize revenue for the sale of its single-family homes?
6. What will Citation report in its 2009 income statement and 2009 balance sheet related to the single-family home business (ignore cash in the balance sheet)?

P 5–9
Franchise sales;
installment sales
method

● **LO2 LO5**

Olive Branch Restaurant Corporation sells franchises throughout the western states. On January 30, 2009, the company entered into the following franchise agreement with Jim and Tammy Masters:

1. The initial franchise fee is $1.2 million. $200,000 is payable immediately and the remainder is due in 10, $100,000 installments plus 10% interest on the unpaid balance each January 30, beginning January 30, 2010. The 10% interest rate is an appropriate market rate.
2. In addition to allowing the franchisee to use the franchise name for the 10-year term of the agreement, in exchange for the initial fee Olive Branch agrees to assist the franchisee in selecting a location, obtaining financing, designing and constructing the restaurant building, and training employees.
3. Examine your answer to requirement 2a of this problem (the January 1, 2009 journal entry under the installment sales method). Focusing on only that journal entry, and assuming that initial services are significant and substantial performance has *not* occurred, what will Olive Branch report on its December 31, 2009 balance sheet (ignore cash)? Briefly explain your answer.
4. In addition to the initial franchise fee, the franchisee is required to pay a monthly fee of 3% of franchise sales for advertising, promotion, menu planning, and other continuing services to be provided by Olive Branch over the life of the agreement. This fee is payable on the 10th of the following month.

Substantial performance of the initial services provided by Olive Branch, which are significant, is deemed to have occurred when the franchise opened on September 1, 2009. Franchise sales for the month of September 2009 were $40,000.

Required:
1. Assuming that collectibility of the installment receivable is reasonably certain, prepare the necessary journal entries for Olive Branch on the following dates (ignore interest charges on the installment receivable and the costs of providing franchise services):
   a. January 30, 2009
   b. September 1, 2009
   c. September 30, 2009
   d. January 30, 2010
2. Assume that significant uncertainty exists as to the collection of the installment receivable and that Olive Branch elects to recognize initial franchise fee revenue using the installment sales method. Prepare the necessary journal entries for the dates listed in requirement 1 (ignore interest charges on the installment receivable and the costs of providing franchise services).
3. Examine your answer to requirement 2a of this problem (the January 1, 2009, journal entry under the installment sales method). Focusing on only that journal entry, what will Olive Branch report on its December 31, 2009, balance sheet (ignore cash)? Briefly explain your answer.

P 5–10
Calculating activity
and profitability
ratios

● **LO6**

Financial statements for Askew Industries for 2009 are shown below:

2009 Income Statement

	($ in 000s)
Sales	$ 9,000
Cost of goods sold	(6,300)
Gross profit	2,700
Operating expenses	(2,000)
Interest expense	(200)
Tax expense	(200)
Net income	$ 300

Comparative Balance Sheets

	Dec. 31	
	2009	2008
Assets		
Cash	$ 600	$ 500
Accounts receivable	600	400
Inventory	800	600
Property, plant, and equipment (net)	2,000	2,100
	$4,000	$3,600
Liabilities and Shareholders' Equity		
Current liabilities	$1,100	$ 850
Bonds payable	1,400	1,400
Paid-in capital	600	600
Retained earnings	900	750
	$4,000	$3,600

Required:
Calculate the following ratios for 2009.
1. Inventory turnover ratio
2. Average days in inventory
3. Receivables turnover ratio
4. Average collection period
5. Asset turnover ratio
6. Profit margin on sales
7. Return on assets
8. Return on shareholders' equity
9. Equity multiplier
10. Return on shareholders' equity (using the DuPont framework)

P 5–11
Use of ratios to
compare two
companies in the
same industry

● LO6

Presented below are condensed financial statements adapted from those of two actual companies competing in the pharmaceutical industry—**Johnson and Johnson (J&J)** and **Pfizer, Inc.** ($ in millions, except per share amounts).

Required:
Evaluate and compare the two companies by responding to the following questions.
   Note: Because two-year comparative statements are not provided, you should use year-end balances in place of average balances as appropriate.
1. Which of the two companies appears more efficient in collecting its accounts receivable and managing its inventory?
2. Which of the two firms had greater earnings relative to resources available?
3. Have the two companies achieved their respective rates of return on assets with similar combinations of profit margin and turnover?
4. From the perspective of a common shareholder, which of the two firms provided a greater rate of return?
5. From the perspective of a common shareholder, which of the two firms appears to be using leverage more effectively to provide a return to shareholders above the rate of return on assets?

Balance Sheets
($ in millions, except per share data)

	J&J	Pfizer
Assets:		
Cash	$ 5,377	$ 1,520
Short-term investments	4,146	10,432
Accounts receivable (net)	6,574	8,775
Inventories	3,588	5,837
Other current assets	3,310	3,177
Current assets	22,995	29,741
Property, plant, and equipment (net)	9,846	18,287
Intangibles and other assets	15,422	68,747
Total assets	$48,263	$116,775
Liabilities and Shareholders' Equity:		
Accounts payable	$ 4,966	$ 2,601
Short-term notes	1,139	8,818
Other current liabilities	7,343	12,238
Current liabilities	13,448	23,657
Long-term debt	2,955	5,755
Other long-term liabilities	4,991	21,986
Total liabilities	21,394	51,398
Capital stock (par and additional paid-in capital)	3,120	67,050
Retained earnings	30,503	29,382
Accumulated other comprehensive income (loss)	(590)	195
Less: treasury stock and other equity adjustments	(6,164)	(31,250)
Total shareholders' equity	26,869	65,377
Total liabilities and shareholders' equity	$48,263	$116,775

Income Statements

Net sales	$41,862	$ 45,188
Cost of goods sold	12,176	9,832
Gross profit	29,686	35,356
Operating expenses	19,763	28,486
Other (income) expense—net	(385)	3,610
Income before taxes	10,308	3,260
Tax expense	3,111	1,621
Net income	$ 7,197	$ 1,639*
Basic net income per share	$ 2.42	$ .22

*This is before income from discontinued operations.

P 5–12
Creating a balance
sheet from ratios;
Chapters 3 and 5

● LO6

Cadux Candy Company's income statement for the year ended December 31, 2009, reported interest expense of $2 million and income tax expense of $12 million. Current assets listed in its balance sheet include cash, accounts receivable, and inventories. Property, plant, and equipment is the company's only noncurrent asset. Financial ratios for 2009 are listed below. Profitability and turnover ratios with balance sheet items in the denominator were calculated using year-end balances rather than averages.

Debt to equity ratio	1.0
Current ratio	2.0
Acid-test ratio	1.0
Times interest earned ratio	17 times
Return on assets	10%
Return on shareholders' equity	20%
Profit margin on sales	5%
Gross profit margin (gross profit divided by net sales)	40%
Inventory turnover	8 times
Receivables turnover	20 times

Required:
Prepare a December 31, 2009, balance sheet for the Cadux Candy Company.

P 5–13
Compare two
companies in the
same industry;
Chapters 3 and 5

● LO6

Presented below are condensed financial statements adapted from those of two actual companies competing as the primary players in a specialty area of the food manufacturing and distribution industry. ($ in millions, except per share amounts.)

Balance Sheets

Assets	Metropolitan	Republic
Cash	$ 179.3	$ 37.1
Accounts receivable (net)	422.7	325.0
Short-term investments	—	4.7
Inventories	466.4	635.2
Prepaid expenses and other current assets	134.6	476.7
Current assets	$1,203.0	$1,478.7
Property, plant, and equipment (net)	2,608.2	2,064.6
Intangibles and other assets	210.3	464.7
Total assets	$4,021.5	$4,008.0
Liabilities and Shareholders' Equity		
Accounts payable	$ 467.9	$ 691.2
Short-term notes	227.1	557.4
Accruals and other current liabilities	585.2	538.5
Current liabilities	$1,280.2	$1,787.1
Long-term debt	535.6	542.3
Deferred tax liability	384.6	610.7
Other long-term liabilities	104.0	95.1
Total liabilities	$2,304.4	$3,035.2
Common stock (par and additional paid-in capital)	144.9	335.0
Retained earnings	2,476.9	1,601.9
Less: treasury stock	(904.7)	(964.1)
Total liabilities and shareholders' equity	$4,021.5	$4,008.0

Income Statements

Net sales	$5,698.0	$7,768.2
Cost of goods sold	(2,909.0)	(4,481.7)
Gross profit	$2,789.0	$3,286.5
Operating expenses	(1,743.7)	(2,539.2)
Interest expense	(56.8)	(46.6)
Income before taxes	$ 988.5	$ 700.7
Tax expense	(394.7)	(276.1)
Net income	$ 593.8	$ 424.6
Net income per share	$ 2.40	$ 6.50

Required:
Evaluate and compare the two companies by responding to the following questions.
Note: Because comparative statements are not provided you should use year-end balances in place of average balances as appropriate.
1. Which of the two firms had greater earnings relative to resources available?
2. Have the two companies achieved their respective rates of return on assets with similar combinations of profit margin and turnover?
3. From the perspective of a common shareholder, which of the two firms provided a greater rate of return?
4. Which company is most highly leveraged and which has made most effective use of financial leverage?
5. Of the two companies, which appears riskier in terms of its ability to pay short-term obligations?
6. How efficiently are current assets managed?
7. From the perspective of a creditor, which company offers the most comfortable margin of safety in terms of its ability to pay fixed interest charges?

P 5–14
Interim financial reporting (Based on Appendix 5)

● LO1

Branson Electronics Company is a small, publicly traded company preparing its first quarter interim report to be mailed to shareholders. The following information for the quarter has been compiled:

Revenues		$180,000
Cost of goods sold		35,000
Operating expenses:		
Fixed	$59,000	
Variable	48,000	107,000

Fixed operating expenses include payments of $50,000 to an advertising firm to promote the firm through various media throughout the year. The income tax rate for the firm's level of operations in the first quarter is 30%, but management estimates the effective rate for the entire year will be 36%.

Required:
Prepare the income statement to be included in Branson's first quarter interim report.

BROADEN YOUR PERSPECTIVE

Apply your critical-thinking ability to the knowledge you've gained. These cases will provide you an opportunity to develop your research, analysis, judgment, and communication skills. You also will work with other students, integrate what you've learned, apply it in real world situations, and consider its global and ethical ramifications. This practice will broaden your knowledge and further develop your decision-making abilities.

Real World Case 5–1
Chainsaw Al; revenue recognition and earnings management

● LO1

In May 2001, the Securities and Exchange Commission sued the former top executives at Sunbeam, charging the group with financial reporting fraud that allegedly cost investors billions in losses. **Sunbeam Corporation** is a recognized designer, manufacturer, and marketer of household and leisure products, including Coleman, Eastpak, First Alert, Grillmaster, Mixmaster, Mr. Coffee, Oster, Powermate, and Campingaz. In the mid-1990s, Sunbeam needed help: its profits had declined by over 80% percent, and in 1996, its stock price was down over 50% from its high. To the rescue: Albert Dunlap, also known as "Chainsaw Al" based on his reputation as a ruthless executive known for his ability to restructure and turn around troubled companies, largely by eliminating jobs.

The strategy appeared to work. In 1997, Sunbeam's revenues had risen by 18 percent. However, in April 1998, the brokerage firm of **Paine Webber** downgraded Sunbeam's stock recommendation. Why the downgrade? Paine Webber had noticed unusually high accounts receivable, massive increases in sales of electric blankets in the third quarter 1997, which usually sell best in the fourth quarter, as well as unusually high sales of barbeque grills for the fourth quarter. Soon after, Sunbeam announced a first quarter loss of $44.6 million, and Sunbeam's stock price fell 25 percent.

It eventually came to light that Dunlap and Sunbeam had been using a "bill and hold" strategy with retail buyers. This involved selling products at large discounts to retailers before they normally would buy and then holding the products in third-party warehouses, with delivery at a later date.

Many felt Sunbeam had deceived shareholders by artificially inflating earnings and the company's stock price. A class-action lawsuit followed, alleging that Sunbeam and Dunlap violated federal securities laws, suggesting the motivation to inflate the earnings and stock price was to allow Sunbeam to complete hundreds of millions of dollars of debt financing in order to complete some ongoing mergers. Shareholders alleged damages when Sunbeam's subsequent earnings decline caused a huge drop in the stock price.

Required:
1. How might Sunbeam's 1997 "bill and hold" strategy have contributed to artificially high earnings in 1997?
2. How would the strategy have led to the unusually high accounts receivable Paine Webber noticed?
3. How might Sunbeam's 1997 "bill and hold" strategy have contributed to a 1998 earnings decline?
4. How does earnings management of this type affect earnings quality?

Judgment Case 5–2
Revenue recognition
● LO1

Revenue earned by a business enterprise is recognized for accounting purposes at different times, according to the circumstances. In some situations revenue is recognized approximately as it is earned in the economic sense. In other situations revenue is recognized at point of delivery.

Required:
1. Explain and justify why revenue often is recognized as earned at point of delivery.
2. Explain in what situations it would be useful to recognize revenue as the productive activity takes place.
3. At what times, other than those included in (1) and (2) above, may it be appropriate to recognize revenue?

Judgment Case 5–3
Service revenue
● LO1

Mega Fitness, Inc., operates fitness centers throughout the Western states. Members pay a nonrefundable, initial fee of $100, as well as a monthly fee of $40. As an option, a member could reduce the monthly fee to $30 by increasing the initial fee to $300. The monthly fee is billed to the member near the end of each month and is due by the 15th of the following month. The only cost incurred by Mega when a new member joins a center is the cost of issuing a laminated identification card with the member's picture. The card costs $3 to produce.

Required:
When should Mega Fitness recognize revenue for the initial fee and for the monthly fee?

Judgment Case 5–4
Revenue recognition; trade-ins
● LO1

Apex Computer Company manufactures and sells large, mainframe computers. The computers range in price from $1 to $3 million and gross profit averages 40% of sales price. The company has a liberal trade-in policy. Customers are allowed to trade in their computers for a new generation machine anytime within three years of sale. The trade-in allowance granted will vary depending on the number of years between original sale and trade-in. However, in all cases, the allowance is expected to be approximately 25% higher than the prevailing market price of the computer.

As an example, in 2009 a customer who purchased a computer in 2007 for $2 million (the computer cost Apex $1,200,000 to manufacture) decided to trade it in for a new computer. The sales price of the new computer was $2.5 million and a trade-in allowance of $600,000 was granted on the old machine. As a result of the trade-in allowance, the customer had to pay only $1.9 million ($2.5 million less $600,000) for the new computer. The old computer taken back by Apex had a resale value of $480,000. The new computer cost $1.5 million to manufacture. The company accounted for the trade-in by recognizing revenue of $2,380,000 ($1.9 million received in cash + $480,000 value of old computer).

Required:
Does the company's revenue recognition policy for trade-ins seem appropriate? If not, describe the problem created by the liberal trade-in policy.

Communication Case 5–5
Revenue recognition
● LO1

Jerry's Ice Cream Parlor is considering a marketing plan to increase sales of ice cream cones. The plan will give customers a free ice cream cone if they buy 10 ice cream cones at regular prices. Customers will be issued a card that will be punched each time an ice cream cone is purchased. After 10 punches, the card can be turned in for a free cone.

Jerry Donovan, the company's owner, is not sure how the new plan will affect accounting procedures. He realizes that the company will be incurring costs each time a free ice cream cone is awarded, but there will be no corresponding revenue or cash inflow.

The focus of this case is the matching of revenues and expenses related to the free ice cream cones that will be awarded if the new plan is adopted. Your instructor will divide the class into two to six groups depending on the size of the class. The mission of your group is to reach consensus on the appropriate accounting treatment for the new plan.

Required:

1. Each group member should deliberate the situation independently and draft a tentative argument prior to the class session for which the case is assigned.

2. In class, each group will meet for 10–15 minutes in different areas of the classroom. During that meeting, group members will take turns sharing their suggestions for the purpose of arriving at a single group treatment.

3. After the allotted time, a spokesperson for each group (selected during the group meetings) will share the group's solution with the class. The goal of the class is to incorporate the views of each group into a consensus approach to the situation.

Research Case 5–6
Long-term contract accounting

● **LO4**

An article published in *Accounting Horizons* describes the current accounting practices and disclosures for long-term contracts for the Fortune 500 companies.

Required:

In your library or from some other source, locate the indicated article in *Accounting Horizons,* September, 2004, and answer the following questions:

1. How many firms reported the use of one of the two long-term contract accounting methods?

2. Approximately half of the firms are in which industry?

3. How many firms reported the use of the percentage-of-completion method? The completed contract method?

4. What is the most frequently used approach to estimating a percentage-of-completion?

Research Case 5–7
Earnings management with respect to revenues

● **LO1**

An article published in *Accounting Horizons* describes various techniques that companies use to manage their earnings.

Required:

In your library or from some other source, locate the article "How Are Earnings Managed? Evidence from Auditors" in *Accounting Horizons,* 2003 (Supplement) and answer the following questions:

1. What are the four most common revenue-recognition abuses identified by auditors in that article? From the examples provided in the article, briefly explain each abuse.

2. What is the revenue-recognition abuse identified in the article related to the percentage-of-completion method?

3. Did revenue-recognition abuses tend to increase or decrease net income in the year they occurred?

4. Did auditors tend to require their clients to make adjustments that reduced the revenue-recognition abuses they detected?

Ethics Case 5–8
Revenue recognition

● **LO1**

Horizon Corporation manufactures personal computers. The company began operations in 2002 and reported profits for the years 2004 through 2007. Due primarily to increased competition and price slashing in the industry, 2008's income statement reported a loss of $20 million. Just before the end of the 2009 fiscal year, a memo from the company's chief financial officer to Jim Fielding, the company controller, included the following comments:

If we don't do something about the large amount of unsold computers already manufactured, our auditors will require us to write them off. The resulting loss for 2009 will cause a violation of our debt covenants and force the company into bankruptcy. I suggest that you ship half of our inventory to J.B. Sales, Inc., in Oklahoma City. I know the company's president and he will accept the merchandise and acknowledge the shipment as a purchase. We can record the sale in 2009 which will boost profits to an acceptable level. Then J.B. Sales will simply return the merchandise in 2010 after the financial statements have been issued.

Required:
Discuss the ethical dilemma faced by Jim Fielding.

Judgment Case 5–9
Revenue recognition; installment sale

● **LO1 LO2**

On October 1, 2009, the Marshall Company sold a large piece of machinery to the Hammond Construction Company for $80,000. The cost of the machine was $40,000. Hammond made a down payment of $10,000 and agreed to pay the remaining balance in seven equal monthly installments of $10,000, plus interest at 12% on the unpaid balance, beginning November 1.

Required:

1. Identify three alternative methods for recognizing revenue and costs for the situation described and compute the amount of gross profit that would be recognized in 2009 using each method.

2. Discuss the circumstances under which each of the three methods would be used.

Judgment Case 5–10
Revenue recognition; *SAB 101* questions

● **LO1**

As part of its crackdown on earnings management, the SEC issued *Staff Accounting Bulletin No. 101* to provide additional guidance on when revenue should be recognized. Consider the following situations posed by the SEC and, for each, discuss whether or not you believe it is appropriate to recognize revenue.

1. **Facts:** Company M is a discount retailer. It generates revenue from annual membership fees it charges customers to shop at its stores and from the sale of products at a discount price to those customers. The membership arrangements with retail customers require the customer to pay the entire membership fee (e.g., $35) at the outset of the arrangement. However, the customer has the unilateral right to cancel the

arrangement at any time during its term and receive a full refund of the initial fee. Based on historical data collected over time for a large number of homogeneous transactions, Company M estimates that approximately 40% of the customers will request a refund before the end of the membership contract term. Company M's data for the past five years indicates that significant variations between actual and estimated cancellations have not occurred, and Company M does not expect significant variations to occur in the foreseeable future.

Question: May Company M recognize revenue for the membership fees and accrue the costs to provide membership services at the outset of the arrangement?

2. **Facts:** Company Z enters into an arrangement with Customer A to deliver Company Z's products to Customer A on a consignment basis. Pursuant to the terms of the arrangement, Customer A is a consignee, and title to the products does not pass from Company Z to Customer A until Customer A consumes the products in its operations. Company Z delivers product to Customer A under the terms of their arrangement.

Question: May Company Z recognize revenue upon delivery of its product to Customer A?

3. **Facts:** Company R is a retailer that offers "layaway" sales to its customers. Company R retains the merchandise, sets it aside in its inventory, and collects a cash deposit from the customer. Although Company R may set a time period within which the customer must finalize the purchase, Company R does not require the customer to enter into an installment note or other fixed payment commitment or agreement when the initial deposit is received. The merchandise generally is not released to the customer until the customer pays the full purchase price. In the event that the customer fails to pay the remaining purchase price, the customer forfeits its cash deposit. In the event the merchandise is lost, damaged, or destroyed, Company R either must refund the cash deposit to the customer or provide replacement merchandise.

Question: When may Company R recognize revenue for merchandise sold under its layaway program?

Research Case 5–11
Locate and extract relevant information and authoritative support for a financial reporting issue; revenue recognition; right of return

● LO3

Many companies sell products allowing their customers the right to return merchandise if they are not satisfied. Because the return of merchandise can retroactively negate the benefits of having made a sale, the seller must meet certain criteria before revenue is recognized in situations when the right of return exists. *SFAS No. 48,* "Revenue Recognition When Right of Return Exists," lists the criteria, the most critical of which is that the seller must be able to make reliable estimates of future returns.

Required:

1. Obtain the original *SFAS No. 48*. You might gain access through FARS, the FASB Financial Accounting Research System, from your school library, or some other source.

2. What factors does the standard discuss that may impair the ability to make a reasonable estimate of returns?

3. List all six criteria that must be met before revenue can be recognized when the right of return exists.

4. Using EDGAR (**www.sec.gov**) access the 10-K reports for the most recent fiscal year for **Hewlett Packard Company** and for **Advanced Micro Devices, Inc.** Search for the revenue recognition policy to determine when these two companies recognize revenue for product sales allowing customers the right of return.

5. Using your answers to requirements 2 and 3, speculate as to why the two revenue recognition policies differ.

Research Case 5–12
Locate and extract relevant information and authoritative support for a financial reporting issue; reporting revenue as a principal or as an agent

● LO1

The birth of the Internet in the 1990s led to the creation of a new industry of online retailers such as Amazon, Overstock.com, and PC Mall, Inc. Many of these companies often act as intermediaries between the manufacturer and the customer without ever taking possession of the merchandise sold. Revenue recognition for this type of transaction has been controversial.

Assume that Overstock.com sold you a product for $200 that cost $150. The company's profit on the transaction clearly is $50. Should Overstock recognize $200 in revenue and $150 in cost of goods sold (the gross method), or should it recognize only the $50 in gross profit (the net method) as commission revenue?

Required:

1. Obtain the original FASB standard or EITF issue that addresses this topic. You might gain access through FARS, the FASB Financial Accounting Research System, from the FASB website (**www.fasb.org**), from your school library, or some other source. What standard or EITF issue addresses this topic?

2. What factors does the pronouncement discuss that will influence the choice of method used by these companies?

3. Using EDGAR (**www.sec.gov**), access the 10-K report for Overstock.com for the period ending December 31, 2005. Locate the disclosure note that discusses the company's revenue recognition policy.

4. In 2003, the company switched from using the net method to the gross method for recording its fulfillment partner revenue. What prompted this switch?

Google

5. Now turn to the financial statements of Google. Inc. included with all new copies of the text. Do they discuss determining whether they should report revenue on a gross versus net basis with respect to any of their products or services? What is the reason Google provides for its choices? Do you agree with Google's reasoning?

**Judgment
Case 5–13**
Revenue
recognition; service
sales

● LO1 LO4

Each of the following situations concerns revenue recognition for services.
1. **Delta Airlines** books a reservation for a roundtrip flight to Orlando for Ming Tsai on April 12. Delta charges the $425 to Tsai's Visa card on April 13 and receives the cash from Visa on May 1. The roundtrip flight commences on May 15. The ticket is nonrefundable.
2. Highlife Ski Resort in Colorado sells a season pass to Larry Werner on October 15. Highlife usually opens its season just after Thanksgiving and stays open until approximately April 30.
3. Dixon Management requires tenants to sign a three-year lease and charges $5,000 per month for one floor in its midtown high-rise. In addition to the monthly fee, payable at the beginning of each month, tenants pay a nonrefundable fee of $12,000 to secure the lease.
4. Janora Hawkins, attorney, agrees to accept an accident victim's case. Hawkins will be paid on a contingency basis. That is, if she wins the case, she will receive 30% of the total settlement. The case commences on July 15 and is settled successfully on August 28. On September 15 Hawkins receives her contingency payment of $60,000.

Required:
For each of the above situations, determine the appropriate timing of revenue recognition.

**Judgment
Case 5–14**
Revenue
recognition; long-
term construction
contracts

● LO4

Two accounting students were discussing the alternative methods of accounting for long-term construction contracts. The discussion focused on which method was most like the typical revenue recognition method of recognizing revenue at point of product delivery. Bill argued that the completed contract method was preferable because it was analogous to recognizing revenue at the point of delivery. John disagreed and supported the percentage-of-completion method, stating that it was analogous to accruing revenue during the earnings process, that is, as the work was performed.

Required:
Discuss the arguments made by both students. Which argument do you support? Why?

**Communication
Case 5–15**
Percentage-of-
completion and
completed contract
methods

● LO4

Willingham Construction is in the business of building high-priced, custom, single-family homes. The company, headquartered in Anaheim, California, operates throughout the Southern California area. The construction period for the average home built by Willingham is six months, although some homes have taken as long as nine months.

You have just been hired by Willingham as the assistant controller and one of your first tasks is to evaluate the company's revenue recognition policy. The company presently uses the completed contract method for all of its projects and management is now considering a switch to the percentage-of-completion method.

Required:
Write a 1- to 2-page memo to Virginia Reynolds, company controller, describing the differences between the percentage-of-completion and completed contract methods. Be sure to include references to GAAP as they pertain to the choice of method. Do not address the differential effects on income taxes nor the effect on the financial statements of switching between methods.

**International
Case 5–16**
Comparison of
revenue recognition
in Sweden and the
United States

● LO1 LO4

Electrolux, headquartered in Sweden, is the European leader in food-service equipment and the second largest producer in the world. The revenue recognition disclosure included in a recent financial statement is reproduced below.

Note 1: Accounting and valuation principles

Revenue recognition

Sales are recorded net of value-added tax, specific sales taxes, returns, and trade discounts. Revenues arise from sales of finished products and services. Sales are recognized when the significant risks and rewards connected with ownership of the goods have been transferred to the buyer and the Group retains neither a continuing right to dispose of the goods, nor effective control of those goods and when the amount of revenue can be measured reliably. This means that sales are recorded when goods have been put at the disposal of the customers in accordance with agreed terms of delivery. Revenues from services are recorded when the service, such as installation or repair of products, has been performed.

Required:
On the basis of the information the disclosures provide, compare revenue recognition under IFRS (as applied by Electrolux) with that in the United States.

**Trueblood
Accounting
Case 5–17**
Revenue
recognition; license
agreement

● LO1

The following Trueblood case is recommended for use with this chapter. The case provides an excellent opportunity for class discussion, group projects, and writing assignments. The case, along with Professor's Discussion Material, can be obtained from the Deloitte Foundation at its website: **www.deloitte.com/us/truebloodcases.**

Case 04-7: *Lighthouse*

This case concerns the appropriate timing of revenue recognition for a bundled product and service.

Trueblood Accounting Case 5–18
Revenue recognition for multiple-deliverable contracts.

● LO5

The following Trueblood case is recommended for use with this chapter. The case provides an excellent opportunity for class discussion, group projects, and writing assignments. The case, along with Professor's Discussion Material, can be obtained from the Deloitte Foundation at its website **www.deloitte.com/us/truebloodcases.**

Case 07-3 Part 1: *Columbia On-Line Networks*

This case concerns recognizing revenue of arrangements that have multiple elements.

Real World Case 5–19
Revenue recognition; franchise sales

● LO5

EDGAR, the Electronic Data Gathering, Analysis, and Retrieval system, performs automated collection, validation, indexing, and forwarding of submissions by companies and others who are required by law to file forms with the U.S. Securities and Exchange Commission (SEC). All publicly traded domestic companies use EDGAR to make the majority of their filings. (Some foreign companies file voluntarily.) Form 10-K or 10-KSB, which include the annual report, is required to be filed on EDGAR. The SEC makes this information available on the Internet.

Required:

1. Access EDGAR on the Internet. The web address is **www.sec.gov.**
2. Search for **Jack in the Box, Inc.** Access the most recent 10-K filing. Search or scroll to find the financial statements and related notes.
3. Answer the following questions related to the company's revenue recognition policies:
   a. When does the company recognize initial franchise license fee revenue?
   b. How are continuing fees determined?
4. Repeat requirements 2 and 3 for two additional companies that you suspect also earn revenues through the sale of franchise rights. Compare their revenue recognition policies with the policies of Jack in the Box.

Analysis Case 5–20
Evaluating profitability and asset management; obtain and compare annual reports from companies in the same industry

● LO6

Performance and profitability of a company often are evaluated using the financial information provided by a firm's annual report in comparison with other firms in the same industry. Ratios are useful in this assessment.

Required:

Obtain annual reports from two corporations in the same primary industry. Using techniques you learned in this chapter and any analysis you consider useful, respond to the following questions:

1. How do earnings trends compare in terms of both the direction and stability of income?
2. Which of the two firms had greater earnings relative to resources available?
3. How efficiently are current assets managed?
4. Has each of the companies achieved its respective rate of return on assets with similar combinations of profit margin and turnover?
5. Are there differences in accounting methods that should be taken into account when making comparisons?

Note: You can obtain copies of annual reports from friends who are shareholders, the investor relations department of the corporations, from a friendly stockbroker, or from EDGAR (Electronic Data Gathering, Analysis, and Retrieval) on the Internet (**www.sec.gov**).

Judgment Case 5–21
Relationships among ratios; Chapters 3 and 5

● LO6

You are a part-time financial advisor. A client is considering an investment in common stock of a waste recycling firm. One motivation is a rumor the client heard that the company made huge investments in a new fuel creation process. Unable to confirm the rumor, your client asks you to determine whether the firm's assets had recently increased significantly.

Because the firm is small, information is sparse. Last quarter's interim report showed total assets of $324 million, approximately the same as last year's annual report. The only information more current than that is a press release last week in which the company's management reported "record net income for the year of $21 million, representing a 14.0% return on shareholders' equity. Performance was enhanced by the Company's judicious use of financial leverage on a debt/equity ratio of 2 to 1."

Required:

Use the information available to provide your client with an opinion as to whether the waste recycling firm invested in the new fuel creation process during the last quarter of the year.

Integrating Case 5–22
Using ratios to test reasonableness of data; Chapters 3 and 5

● LO6

You are a new staff accountant with a large regional CPA firm, participating in your first audit. You recall from your auditing class that CPAs often use ratios to test the reasonableness of accounting numbers provided by the client. Since ratios reflect the relationships among various account balances, if it is assumed that prior relationships still hold, prior years' ratios can be used to estimate what current balances should approximate. However, you never actually performed this kind of analysis until now. The CPA in charge of the audit of Covington Pike

Corporation brings you the list of ratios shown below and tells you these reflect the relationships maintained by Covington Pike in recent years.

> Profit margin on sales = 5%
> Return on assets = 7.5%
> Gross profit margin = 40%
> Inventory turnover ratio = 6 times
> Receivables turnover ratio = 25
> Acid-test ratio = .9
> Current ratio = 2 to 1
> Return on shareholders' equity = 10%
> Debt to equity ratio = 1/3
> Times interest earned ratio = 12 times

Jotted in the margins are the following notes:
- Net income $15,000
- Only one short-term note ($5,000); all other current liabilities are trade accounts
- Property, plant, and equipment are the only noncurrent assets
- Bonds payable are the only noncurrent liabilities
- The effective interest rate on short-term notes and bonds is 8%
- No investment securities
- Cash balance totals $15,000

Required:
You are requested to approximate the current year's balances in the form of a balance sheet and income statement, to the extent the information allows. Accompany those financial statements with the calculations you use to estimate each amount reported.

CPA SIMULATION 5–1

Leonard Brothers
Revenue Recognition

SCHWESER

CPA Review

Test your knowledge of the concepts discussed in this chapter, practice critical professional skills necessary for career success, and prepare for the computer-based CPA exam by accessing our CPA simulations at the text website: **www.mhhe.com/spiceland5e.**

The Leonard Brothers simulation tests your knowledge of various revenue recognition issues and methods, including (a) the installment sales method, (b) revenue recognition for long-term contracts, and (c) accounting for franchise sales.

As on the CPA exam itself, you will be asked to use tools including a spreadsheet, a calculator, and professional accounting standards, to conduct research, derive solutions, and communicate conclusions related to these issues in a simulated environment headed by the following interactive tabs:

Specific tasks in the simulation address:
- Applying judgment in determining the revenue recognition method appropriate in various situations.
- Demonstrating an understanding of the installment sales method.
- Determining the appropriate journal entries for a long-term contract accounted for using the percentage-of-completion method.
- Analyzing the effect on the income statement and balance sheet of applying the percentage-of-completion method.
- Communicating the financial statement effects of using the percentage-of-completion method.
- Researching the accounting treatment and disclosure requirements for franchise sales.

Time Value of Money Concepts

/// **OVERVIEW**

Time value of money concepts, specifically future value and present value, are essential in a variety of accounting situations. These concepts and the related computational procedures are the subjects of this chapter. Present values and future values of *single amounts* and present values and future values of *annuities* (series of equal periodic payments) are described separately but shown to be interrelated.

||||| **LEARNING OBJECTIVES** | | | | | | | | | | | | | | |

After studying this chapter, you should be able to:

- **LO1** Explain the difference between simple and compound interest.
- **LO2** Compute the future value of a single amount.
- **LO3** Compute the present value of a single amount.
- **LO4** Solve for either the interest rate or the number of compounding periods when present value and future value of a single amount are known.
- **LO5** Explain the difference between an ordinary annuity and an annuity due situation.
- **LO6** Compute the future value of both an ordinary annuity and an annuity due.
- **LO7** Compute the present value of an ordinary annuity, an annuity due, and a deferred annuity.
- **LO8** Solve for unknown values in annuity situations involving present value.
- **LO9** Briefly describe how the concept of the time value of money is incorporated into the valuation of bonds, long-term leases, and pension obligations.

The Winning Ticket

Al Castellano had been buying California State lottery tickets for 15 years at his neighborhood grocery store. On Sunday, June 24, 2008, his world changed. When he awoke, opened the local newspaper, and compared his lottery ticket numbers with Saturday night's winning numbers, he couldn't believe his eyes. All of the numbers on his ticket matched the winning numbers. He went outside for a walk, came back into the kitchen and checked the numbers again. He woke his wife Carmen, told her what had happened, and they danced through their apartment. Al, a 66-year-old retired supermarket clerk, and Carmen, a 62-year-old semiretired secretary, had won the richest lottery in California's history, $141 million!

On Monday when Al and Carmen claimed their prize, their ecstasy was waned slightly when they were informed that they would soon be receiving a check for approximately $43 million. When the Castellanos purchased the lottery ticket, they indicated that they would like to receive any lottery winnings in one lump payment rather than in 26 equal annual installments beginning now. They knew beforehand that the State of California is required to withhold 31% of lottery winnings for federal income tax purposes, but this reduction was way more than 31%.

Source: This case is adapted from an actual situation.

By the time you finish this chapter, you should be able to respond appropriately to the questions posed in this case. Compare your response to the solution provided at the end of the chapter.

QUESTIONS ///

1. Why were the Castellanos to receive $43 million rather than the $141 million lottery prize? (page 302)
2. What interest rate did the State of California use to calculate the $43 million lump-sum payment? (page 308)
3. What are some of the accounting applications that incorporate the time value of money into valuation? (page 310)

PART A

BASIC CONCEPTS

Time Value of Money

The key to solving the problem described in the financial reporting case is an understanding of the concept commonly referred to as the time value of money. This concept means that money invested today will grow to a larger dollar amount in the future. For example, $100 invested in a savings account at your local bank yielding 6% annually will grow to $106 in one year. The difference between the $100 invested now—the present value of the investment— and its $106 future value represents the time value of money.

This concept has nothing to do with the worth or buying power of those dollars. Prices in our economy can change. If the inflation rate were higher than 6%, then the $106 you would have in the savings account actually would be worth less than the $100 you had a year earlier. The time value of money concept concerns only the growth in the dollar amounts of money.

The concepts you will learn in this chapter are useful in solving many business decisions such as, for example, the determination of the lottery award presented in the financial reporting case. More important, the concepts also are necessary when valuing assets and liabilities for financial reporting purposes. As you will see in this and subsequent chapters, most accounting applications that incorporate the time value of money involve the concept of present value. The valuation of leases, bonds, pension obligations, and certain notes receivable and payable are a few prominent examples. It is important that you master the concepts and tools we review here. This knowledge is essential to the remainder of your accounting education.

Simple versus Compound Interest

● LO1

Interest is the "rent" paid for the use of money for some period of time. In dollar terms, it is the amount of money paid or received in excess of the amount of money borrowed or lent. If you lent the bank $100 today and "received" $106 a year from now, your interest earned would be $6. Interest also can be expressed as a rate at which money will grow. In this case, that rate is 6%. It is this interest that gives money its time value.

Simple interest is computed by multiplying an initial investment times both the applicable interest rate and the period of time for which the money is used. For example, simple interest earned each year on a $1,000 investment paying 10% is $100 ($1,000 × 10%).

Compound interest results in increasingly larger interest amounts for each period of the investment. The reason is that interest is now being earned not only on the initial investment amount but also on the accumulated interest earned in previous periods.

For example, Cindy Johnson invested $1,000 in a savings account paying 10% interest *compounded* annually. How much interest will she earn each year, and what will be her investment balance after three years?

Date	Interest (Interest rate × Outstanding balance = Interest)	Balance
Initial deposit		$1,000
End of year 1	10% × $1,000 = $100	$1,100
End of year 2	10% × $1,100 = $110	$1,210
End of year 3	10% × $1,210 = $121	$1,331

With compound interest at 10% annually, the $1,000 investment would grow to $1,331 at the end of the three-year period. Of course, if Cindy withdrew the interest earned each year, she would earn only $100 in interest each year, that is, the amount of simple interest. If the investment period had been 20 years, 20 individual calculations would be needed. However, calculators, computer programs, and compound interest tables make these calculations much easier.

Most banks compound interest more frequently than once a year. Daily compounding is common for savings accounts. More rapid compounding has the effect of increasing the actual rate, which is called the effective rate, at which money grows per year. It is important to note that interest is typically stated as an annual rate regardless of the length of the compounding period involved. In situations when the compounding period is less than a year, the interest rate per compounding period is determined by dividing the annual rate by the number of periods. Assuming an annual rate of 12%:

Compounded	Interest Rate Per Compounding Period
Semiannually	12% ÷ 2 = 6%
Quarterly	12% ÷ 4 = 3%
Monthly	12% ÷ 12 = 1%

As an example, now let's assume Cindy Johnson invested $1,000 in a savings account paying 10% interest *compounded* twice a year. There are two six-month periods paying interest at 5% (the annual rate divided by two periods). How much interest will she earn the first year, and what will be her investment balance at the end of the year?

Date	Interest (Interest rate × Outstanding balance = Interest)	Balance
Initial deposit		$1,000.00
After six months	5% × $1,000 = $50.00	$1,050.00
End of year 1	5% × $1,050 = $52.50	$1,102.50

The $1,000 would grow by $102.50, the interest earned, to $1,102.50, $2.50 more than if interest were compounded only once a year. The effective annual interest rate, often referred to as the annual *yield,* is 10.25% ($102.50 ÷ $1,000).

Valuing a Single Cash Flow Amount
Future Value of a Single Amount

In the first Cindy example, in which $1,000 was invested for three years at 10% compounded annually, the $1,331 is referred to as the future value (FV). A time diagram is a useful way to visualize this relationship, with 0 indicating the date of the initial investment.

● **LO2**

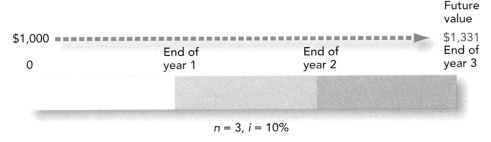

$$n = 3, i = 10\%$$

The future value after one year can be calculated as $1,000 × 1.10 (1.00 + .10) = $1,100. After three years, the future value is $1,000 × 1.10 × 1.10 × 1.10 = $1,331. In fact, the future value of any invested amount can be determined as follows:

$$FV = I (1 + i)^n$$

where: FV = Future value of the invested amount
          I = Amount invested at the beginning of the period
          i = Interest rate
          n = Number of compounding periods

The future value can be determined by using Table 1, Future Value of $1, located at the end of this textbook. The table contains the future value of $1 invested for various periods of time, *n,* and at various rates, *i.*

With this table, it's easy to determine the future value of any invested amount simply by multiplying it by the table value at the *intersection* of the column for the desired rate and the row for the number of compounding periods. Graphic 6–1 contains an excerpt from Table 1.

GRAPHIC 6–1

Future Value of $1 (excerpt from Table 1)

Periods (n)	Interest Rates (i)					
	7%	**8%**	**9%**	**10%**	**11%**	**12%**
1	1.07000	1.08000	1.09000	1.10000	1.11000	1.12000
2	1.14490	1.16640	1.18810	1.21000	1.23210	1.25440
3	1.22504	1.25971	1.29503	1.33100	1.36763	1.40493
4	1.31080	1.36049	1.41158	1.46410	1.51807	1.57352
5	1.40255	1.46933	1.53862	1.61051	1.68506	1.76234
6	1.50073	1.58687	1.67710	1.77156	1.87041	1.97382
7	1.60578	1.71382	1.82804	1.94872	2.07616	2.21068
8	1.71819	1.85093	1.99256	2.14359	2.30454	2.47596

The table shows various values of $(1 + i)^n$ for different combinations of i and n. From the table you can find the future value factor for three periods at 10% to be 1.331. This means that $1 invested at 10% compounded annually will grow to approximately $1.33 in three years. So, the future value of $1,000 invested for three years at 10% is $1,331:

$$FV = I \times FV \text{ factor}$$
$$FV = \$1,000 \times 1.331^* = \$1,331$$
*Future value of $1; n = 3, i = 10%

The future value function in financial calculators or in computer spreadsheet programs calculates future values in the same way. Determining future values (and present values) electronically avoids the need for tables such as those in the chapter appendix. It's important to remember that the n in the future value formula refers to the number of compounding periods, not necessarily the number of years. For example, suppose you wanted to know the future value *two* years from today of $1,000 invested at 12% with *quarterly* compounding. The number of periods is therefore eight and the compounding rate is 3% (12% annual rate divided by four, the number of quarters in a year). The future value factor from Table 1 is 1.26677, so the future value is $1,266.77 ($1,000 × 1.26677).[1]

Present Value of a Single Amount

● LO3

The *present value* of a single amount is today's equivalent to a particular amount in the future.

The example used to illustrate future value reveals that $1,000 invested today is equivalent to $1,100 received after one year, $1,210 after two years, or $1,331 after three years, assuming 10% interest compounded annually. Thus, the $1,000 investment (I) is the present value (PV) of the single sum of $1,331 to be received at the end of three years. It is also the present value of $1,210 to be received in two years and $1,100 in one year.

Remember that the future value of a present amount is the present amount *times* $(1 + i)^n$. Logically, then, that computation can be reversed to find the *present value* of a future amount to be the future amount *divided* by $(1 + i)^n$. We substitute PV for I (invested amount) in the future value formula above.

$$FV = PV (1 + i)^n$$

$$PV = \frac{FV}{(1 + i)^n}$$

---

[1]When interest is compounded more frequently than once a year, the effective annual interest rate, or yield, can be determined using the following equation:

$$\text{Yield} = (1 + \frac{i}{p})^p - 1$$

with i being the annual interest rate and p the number of compounding periods per year. In this example, the annual yield would be 12.55%, calculated as follows:

$$\text{Yield} = (1 + \frac{.12}{4})^4 - 1 = 1.1255 - 1 = .1255$$

Determining the yield is useful when comparing returns on investment instruments with different compounding period length.

In our example,

$$PV = \frac{\$1,331}{(1 + .10)^3} = \frac{\$1,331}{1.331} = \$1,000$$

Of course, dividing by $(1 + i)^n$ is the same as multiplying by its reciprocal, $1/(1 + i)^n$.

$$PV = \$1,331 \times \frac{1}{(1 + .10)^3} = \$1,331 \times .75131 = \$1,000$$

As with future value, these computations are simplified by using calculators, computer programs, or present value tables. Table 2, Present Value of $1, located at the end of this textbook provides the solutions of $1/(1 + i)^n$ for various interest rates (i) and compounding periods (n). These amounts represent the present value of $1 to be received at the *end* of the different periods. The table can be used to find the present value of any single amount to be received in the future by *multiplying* that amount by the value in the table that lies at the *intersection* of the column for the appropriate rate and the row for the number of compounding periods.[2] Graphic 6–2 contains an excerpt from Table 2.

			Interest Rates (*i*)			
Periods (*n*)	**7%**	**8%**	**9%**	**10%**	**11%**	**12%**
1	.93458	.92593	.91743	.90909	.90090	.89286
2	.87344	.85734	.84168	.82645	.81162	.79719
3	.81630	.79383	.77218	.75131	.73119	.71178
4	.76290	.73503	.70843	.68301	.65873	.63552
5	.71299	.68058	.64993	.62092	.59345	.56743
6	.66634	.63017	.59627	.56447	.53464	.50663
7	.62275	.58349	.54703	.51316	.48166	.45235
8	.58201	.54027	.50187	.46651	.43393	.40388

GRAPHIC 6–2

Present Value of $1 (excerpt from Table 2)

Notice that the farther into the future the $1 is to be received, the less valuable it is now. This is the essence of the concept of the time value of money. Given a choice between $1,000 now and $1,000 three years from now, you would choose to have the money now. If you have it now, you could put it to use. But the choice between, say, $740 now and $1,000 three years from now would depend on your time value of money. If your time value of money is 10%, you would choose the $1,000 in three years, because the $740 invested at 10% for three years would grow to only $984.94 [$740 × 1.331 (FV of $1, $i = 10\%$, $n = 3$)]. On the other hand, if your time value of money is 11% or higher, you would prefer the $740 now. Presumably, you would invest the $740 now and have it grow to $1,012.05 ($740 × 1.36763) in three years.

Using the present value table above, the present value of $1,000 to be received in three years assuming a time value of money of 10% is $751.31 [$1,000 × .75131 (PV of $1, $i = 10\%$ and $n = 3$)]. Because the present value of the future amount, $1,000, is higher than $740 we could have today, we again determine that with a time value of money of 10%, the $1,000 in three years is preferred to the $740 now.

In our earlier example, $1,000 now is equivalent to $1,331 in three years, assuming the time value of money is 10%. Graphically, the relation between the present value and the future value can be viewed this way:

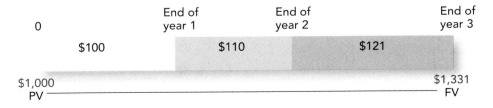

[2]The factors in Table 2 are the reciprocals of those in Table 1. For example, the future value factor for 10%, three periods is 1.331, while the present value factor is .75131. $1 ÷ 1.331 = $.75131, and $1 ÷ .75131 = $1.331.

The calculation of future value requires the addition of interest, while the calculation of present value requires the removal of interest.

While the calculation of future value of a single sum invested today requires the *inclusion* of compound interest, present value problems require the *removal* of compound interest. The process of computing present value *removes* the $331 of interest earned over the three-year period from the future value of $1,331, just as the process of computing future value *adds* $331 of interest to the present value of $1,000 to arrive at the future value of $1,331.

As we demonstrate later in this chapter and in subsequent chapters, present value calculations are incorporated into accounting valuation much more frequently than future value.

Accountants use PV calculations much more frequently than FV.

Solving for Other Values When FV and PV are Known

● **LO4**

There are four variables in the process of adjusting single cash flow amounts for the time value of money: the present value (PV), the future value (FV), the number of compounding periods (*n*), and the interest rate (*i*). If you know any three of these, the fourth can be determined. Illustration 6–1 solves for an unknown interest rate and Illustration 6–2 determines an unknown number of periods.

DETERMINING THE UNKNOWN INTEREST RATE

ILLUSTRATION 6–1 Determining *i* When PV, FV, and *n* are Known	Suppose a friend asks to borrow $500 today and promises to repay you $605 two years from now. What is the annual interest rate you would be agreeing to?

The following time diagram illustrates the situation:

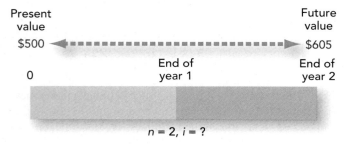

$$n = 2, i = ?$$

The interest rate is the discount rate that will provide a present value of $500 when discounting $605 to be received in two years:

The unknown variable is the interest rate.

$500 (present value) = $605 (future value) × ?*
*Present value of $1: n = 2, i = ?

Rearranging algebraically, we find that the present value table factor is .82645.

$500 (present value) ÷ $605 (future value) = .82645*
*Present value of $1: n = 2, i = ?

When you consult the present value table, Table 2, you search row two (*n* = 2) for this value and find it in the 10% column. So the effective interest rate is 10%. Notice that the computed factor value exactly equals the table factor value.[3]

---

[3]If the calculated factor lies between two table factors, interpolation is useful in finding the unknown value. For example, if the future value in our example is $600, instead of $605, the calculated PV factor is .83333 ($500 ÷ $600). This factor lies between the 9% factor of .84168 and the 10% factor of .82645. The total difference between these factors is .01523 (.84168 − .82645). The difference between the calculated factor of .83333 and the 10% factor of .82645 is .00688. This is 45% of the difference between the 9% and 10% factors:

$$\frac{.00688}{.01523} = .45$$

Therefore, the interpolated interest rate is 9.55% (10 − .45).

DETERMINING THE UNKNOWN NUMBER OF PERIODS

You want to invest $10,000 today to accumulate $16,000 for graduate school. If you can invest at an interest rate of 10% compounded annually, how many years will it take to accumulate the required amount?	**ILLUSTRATION 6–2** Determining *n* When PV, FV, and *i* are Known

The following time diagram illustrates the situation:

The number of years is the value of *n* that will provide a present value of $10,000 when discounting $16,000 at a rate of 10%:

$$\$10,000 \text{ (present value)} = \$16,000 \text{ (future value)} \times ?*$$
*Present value of $1; n = ?, i = 10%

> The unknown variable is the number of periods.

Rearranging algebraically, we find that the present value table factor is .625.

$$\$10,000 \text{ (present value)} \div \$16,000 \text{ (future value)} = .625*$$
*Present value of $1: n = ?, i = 10%

When you consult the present value table, Table 2, you search the 10% column ($i = 10\%$) for this value and find .62092 in row five. So it would take approximately five years to accumulate $16,000 in the situation described.

ADDITIONAL CONSIDERATION

Solving for the unknown factor in either of these examples could just as easily be done using the future value tables. The number of years is the value of *n* that will provide a present value of $10,000 when discounting $16,000 at a discount rate of 10%.

$$\$16,000 \text{ (future value)} = \$10,000 \text{ (present value)} \times ?*$$
*Future value of $1: n = ?, i = 10%

Rearranging algebraically, the future value table factor is 1.6.

$$\$16,000 \text{ (future value)} \div \$10,000 \text{ (present value)} = 1.6*$$
*Future value of $1: n = ?, i = 10%

When you consult the future value table, Table 1, you search the 10% column ($i = 10\%$) for this value and find 1.61051 in row five. So it would take approximately five years to accumulate $16,000 in the situation described.

CONCEPT REVIEW **EXERCISE**

Using the appropriate table, answer each of the following independent questions.

> **VALUING A SINGLE CASH FLOW AMOUNT**

1. What is the future value of $5,000 at the end of six periods at 8% compound interest?
2. What is the present value of $8,000 to be received eight periods from today assuming a compound interest rate of 12%?
3. What is the present value of $10,000 to be received two *years* from today assuming an annual interest rate of 24% and *monthly* compounding?

4. If an investment of $2,000 grew to $2,520 in three periods, what is the interest rate at which the investment grew? Solve using both present and future value tables.

5. Approximately how many years would it take for an investment of $5,250 to accumulate to $15,000, assuming interest is compounded at 10% annually? Solve using both present and future value tables.

SOLUTION

1. FV = $5,000 × 1.58687* = $7,937
   *Future value of $1: $n = 6$, $i = 8\%$ (from Table 1)

2. FV = $8,000 × .40388* = $3,231
   *Present value of $1: $n = 8$, $i = 12\%$ (from Table 2)

3. FV = $10,000 × .62172* = $6,217
   *Present value of $1: $n = 24$, $i = 2\%$ (from Table 2)

4. Using present value table,

   $$\frac{\$2,000}{\$2,520} = .7937*$$

   *Present value of $1: $n = 3$, $i = ?$ (from Table 2, i approximately **8%**)

   Using future value table,

   $$\frac{\$2,520}{\$2,000} = 1.260*$$

   *Future value of $1: $n = 3$, $i = ?$ (from Table 1, i approximately **8%**)

5. Using present value table,

   $$\frac{\$5,250}{\$15,000} = .35*$$

   *Present value of $1: $n = ?$, $i = 10\%$ (from Table 2, n approximately **11 years**)

   Using future value table,

   $$\frac{\$15,000}{\$5,250} = 2.857*$$

   *Future value of $1: $n = ?$. $i = 10\%$ (from Table 1, n approximately **11 years**) ●

Preview of Accounting Applications of Present Value Techniques—Single Cash Amount

Kile Petersen switched off his television set immediately after watching the Super Bowl game and swore to himself that this would be the last year he would watch the game on his 10-year-old 20-inch TV set. "Next year, a big screen TV," he promised himself. Soon after, he saw an advertisement in the local newspaper from Slim Jim's TV and Appliance offering a Philips 60-inch large screen television on sale for $1,800. And the best part of the deal was that Kile could take delivery immediately but would not have to pay the $1,800 for one whole year! "In a year, I can easily save the $1,800," he thought.

In the above scenario, the seller, Slim Jim's TV and Appliance, records a sale when the TV is delivered to Kile. How should the company value its receivable and corresponding sales revenue? We provide a solution to this question at the end of this section on page xxx. The following discussion will help you to understand that solution.

Monetary assets and monetary liabilities are valued at the present value of future cash flows.

Many assets and most liabilities are monetary in nature. Monetary assets include money and claims to receive money, the amount of which is fixed or determinable. Examples include cash and most receivables. Monetary liabilities are obligations to pay amounts of cash, the amount of which is fixed or determinable. Most liabilities are monetary. For example, if you borrow money from a bank and sign a note payable, the amount of cash to be repaid to the bank is fixed. Monetary receivables and payables are valued based on the fixed amount of cash to be received or paid in the future with proper reflection of the time value of money. In other words, we value most receivables and payables at the present value of future cash flows, reflecting an appropriate time value of money.[4]

The example in Illustration 6–3 demonstrates this concept.

---

[4] "Interest on Receivables and Payables," *Accounting Principles Board Opinion No. 21* (New York: AICPA, 1971).

Explicit Interest	**ILLUSTRATION 6–3**
The Stridewell Wholesale Shoe Company manufactures athletic shoes for sale to retailers. The company recently sold a large order of shoes to Harmon Sporting Goods for $50,000. Stridewell agreed to accept a note in payment for the shoes requiring payment of $50,000 in one year plus interest at 10%.	Valuing a Note: One Payment, Explicit Interest

How should Stridewell value the note receivable and corresponding sales revenue earned? How should Harmon value the note payable and corresponding inventory purchased? As long as the interest rate explicitly stated in the agreement properly reflects the time value of money, the answer is $50,000, the face value of the note. It's important to realize that this amount also equals the present value of future cash flows at 10%. Future cash flows equal $55,000, $50,000 in note principal plus $5,000 in interest ($50,000 × 10%). Using a time diagram:

Present value   Future value
? $55,000
End of
0   year 1

n = 1, i = 10%

In equation form, we can solve for present value as follows:

$55,000 (future value) × .90909* = $50,000 (present value)
*Present value of $1: n = 1, i = 10%

By calculating the present value of $55,000 to be received in one year, the interest of $5,000 is removed from the future value, resulting in a proper note receivable/sales revenue value of $50,000 for Stridewell and a $50,000 note payable/inventory value for Harmon.

While most notes, loans, and mortgages explicitly state an interest rate that will properly reflect the time value of money, there can be exceptions. Consider the example in Illustration 6–4.

No Explicit Interest	**ILLUSTRATION 6–4**
The Stridewell Wholesale Shoe Company recently sold a large order of shoes to Harmon Sporting Goods. Terms of the sale require Harmon to sign a noninterest-bearing note of $60,500 with payment due in two years.	Valuing a Note: One Payment, No Explicit Interest

How should Stridewell and Harmon value the note receivable/payable and corresponding sales revenue/inventory? Even though the agreement states a noninterest-bearing note, the $60,500 does, in fact, include interest for the two-year period of the loan. We need to remove the interest portion of the $60,500 to determine the portion that represents the sales price of the shoes. We do this by computing the present value. The following time diagram illustrates the situation assuming that a rate of 10% reflects the appropriate interest rate for a loan of this type:

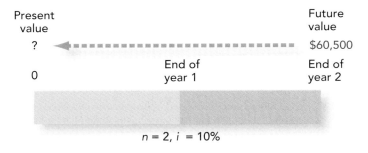

Present value   Future value
? $60,500
End of   End of
0   year 1   year 2

n = 2, i = 10%

Again, using the present value of $1 table,

$$\$60,500 \text{ (future value)} \times .82645^* = \$50,000 \text{ (present value)}$$
*Present value of $1: $n = 2$, $i = 10\%$

Both the note receivable for Stridewell and the note payable for Harmon initially will be valued at $50,000. The difference of $10,500 ($60,500 − 50,000) represents interest revenue/expense to be recognized over the life of the note. The appropriate journal entries are illustrated in later chapters.

Now can you answer the question posed in the scenario at the beginning of this section? Assuming that a rate of 10% reflects the appropriate interest rate in this situation, Slim Jim's TV and Appliance records a receivable and sales revenue of $1,636 which is the present value of the $1,800 to be received from Kile Petersen one year from the date of sale.

$$\$1,800 \text{ (future value)} \times .90909^* = \$1,636 \text{ (present value)}$$
*Present value of $1: $n = 1$, $i = 10\%$ (from Table 2)

Expected Cash Flow Approach

Present value measurement has long been integrated with accounting valuation and is specifically addressed in several accounting standards. Because of its increased importance, the FASB in 2000 issued *Statement of Financial Accounting Concepts No. 7*, "Using Cash Flow Information and Present Value in Accounting Measurements."[5] This statement provides a framework for using future cash flows as the basis for accounting measurement and asserts that the objective in valuing an asset or liability using present value is to approximate the fair value of that asset or liability. Key to that objective is determining the present value of future cash flows associated with the asset or liability, *taking into account any uncertainty concerning the amounts and timing of the cash flows.* Although future cash flows in many instances are contractual and certain, the amounts and timing of cash flows are less certain in other situations.

For example, lease payments are provided in the contract between lessor and lessee. On the other hand, the future cash flows to be paid to settle a pending lawsuit may be highly uncertain. Traditionally, the way uncertainty has been considered in present value calculations has been by discounting the "best estimate" of future cash flows applying a discount rate that has been adjusted to reflect the uncertainty or risk of those cash flows. With the approach described by *SFAC No. 7*, though, the adjustment for uncertainty or risk of cash flows is applied to the cash flows, not the discount rate. This new *expected cash flow approach* incorporates specific probabilities of cash flows into the analysis. Consider Illustration 6–5.

Compare the approach described in Illustration 6–5 to the traditional approach that uses the present value of the most likely estimate of $200 million and ignores information about cash flow probabilities.

The discount rate used to determine present value when applying the expected cash flow approach should be the company's *credit-adjusted risk-free rate of interest.* Other elements of uncertainty are incorporated into the determination of the probability-weighted expected cash flows. In the traditional approach, elements of uncertainty are incorporated into a risk-adjusted discount rate.

> **SFAC NO. 7**
> "While many accountants do not routinely use the expected cash flow approach, expected cash flows are inherent in the techniques used in some accounting measurements, like pensions, other postretirement benefits, and some insurance obligations."[6]

The FASB expects that the traditional approach to calculating present value will continue to be used in many situations, particularly those where future cash flows are contractual. The Board also believes that the expected cash flow approach is more appropriate in more complex situations. In fact, the board has incorporated

---

[5]"Using Cash Flow Information and Present Value in Accounting Measurements," *Statement of Financial Accounting Concepts No. 7* (Norwalk, Conn.: FASB, 2000). Recall that Concept Statements do not directly prescribe GAAP, but instead provide structure and direction to financial accounting.
[6]Ibid., para. 48.

> LDD Corporation faces the likelihood of having to pay an uncertain amount in five years in connection with an environmental cleanup. The future cash flow estimate is in the range of $100 million to $300 million with the following estimated probabilities:
>
> | Loss Amount | Probability |
> |---|---|
> | $100 million | 10% |
> | $200 million | 60% |
> | $300 million | 30% |
>
> The expected cash flow, then, is $220 million:
>
> $$\$100 \times 10\% = \$\ \ 10 \text{ million}$$
> $$200 \times 60\% = \ \ 120 \text{ million}$$
> $$300 \times 30\% = \ \ \ \ \underline{90} \text{ million}$$
> $$\$220 \text{ million}$$
>
> If the company's credit-adjusted risk-free rate of interest is 5%, LDD will report a liability of $172,376,600, the present value of the expected cash outflow:
>
> $$\$220,000,000$$
> $$\underline{\times\ .78353^*}$$
> $$\$172,376,600$$
> *Present value of $1, $n = 5$, $i = 5\%$ (from Table 2)

ILLUSTRATION 6–5

Expected Cash Flow Approach

the concepts developed in *SFAC No. 7* into recent standards on asset retirement obligations, impairment losses, and business combinations. In Chapter 10 we illustrate the use of the expected cash flow approach as it would be applied to the measurement of an asset retirement obligation. In Chapter 13, we use the approach to measure the liability associated with a loss contingency.

BASIC ANNUITIES

PART **B**

● LO5

The previous examples involved the receipt or payment of a single future amount. Financial instruments frequently involve multiple receipts or payments of cash. If the same amount is to be received or paid each period, the cash flows are referred to as an annuity. A common annuity encountered in practice is a loan on which periodic interest is paid in equal amounts. For example, bonds typically pay interest semiannually in an amount determined by multiplying a stated rate by a fixed principal amount. Some loans and most leases are paid in equal installments during a specified period of time.

In an *ordinary annuity* cash flows occur at the end of each period.

An agreement that creates an annuity can produce either an ordinary annuity or an annuity due (sometimes referred to as an annuity in advance) situation. The first cash flow (receipt or payment) of an ordinary annuity is made one compounding period *after* the date on which the agreement begins. The final cash flow takes place on the *last* day covered by the agreement. For example, an installment note payable dated December 31, 2009, might require the debtor to make three equal annual payments, with the first payment due on December 31, 2010, and the last one on December 31, 2012. The following time diagram illustrates an ordinary annuity:

Ordinary annuity.

12/31/09	12/31/10	12/31/11	12/31/12
	1st payment	2nd payment	3rd payment

In an *annuity due* cash flows occur at the *beginning* of each period.

The first payment of an annuity due is made on the *first* day of the agreement, and the last payment is made one period *before* the end of the agreement. For example, a three-year lease of a building that begins on December 31, 2009, and ends on December 31, 2012, may require the first year's lease payment in advance on December 31, 2009. The third and last payment would take place on December 31, 2011, the beginning of the third year of the lease. The following time diagram illustrates this situation:

Annuity due.

Future Value of an Annuity
Future Value of an Ordinary Annuity

Let's first consider the future value of an ordinary annuity in Illustration 6–6.

ILLUSTRATION 6–6	Sally Rogers wants to accumulate a sum of money to pay for graduate school. Rather than investing a single amount today that will grow to a future value, she decides to invest $10,000 a year over the next three years in a savings account paying 10% interest compounded annually. She decides to make the first payment to the bank one year from today.
Future Value of an Ordinary Annuity	

The following time diagram illustrates this ordinary annuity situation. Time 0 is the start of the first period.

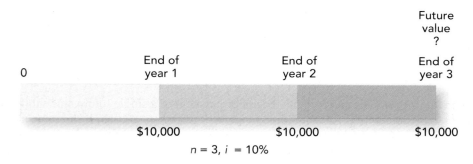

Using the FV of $1 factors from Table 1, we can calculate the future value of this annuity by calculating the future value of each of the individual payments as follows:

	Payment		FV of $1 i = 10%		Future Value (at the end of year 3)	n
First payment	$10,000	×	1.21	=	$12,100	2
Second payment	10,000	×	1.10	=	11,000	1
Third payment	10,000	×	1.00	=	10,000	0
Total			3.31		$33,100	

In the future value of an ordinary annuity, the last cash payment will not earn any interest.

● LO6

From the time diagram, we can see that the first payment has two compounding periods to earn interest. The factor used, 1.21, is the FV of $1 invested for two periods at 10%. The second payment has one compounding period and the last payment does not earn any interest because it is invested on the last day of the three-year annuity period. Therefore, the factor used is 1.00.

This illustration shows that it's possible to calculate the future value of the annuity by separately calculating the FV of each payment and then adding these amounts together. Fortunately, that's not necessary. Table 3, Future Value of an Ordinary Annuity, located at the

GRAPHIC 6–3

Future Value of an
Ordinary Annuity of $1
(excerpt from Table 3)

	Interest Rates (i)					
Periods (n)	**7%**	**8%**	**9%**	**10%**	**11%**	**12%**
1	1.0000	1.0000	1.0000	1.0000	1.0000	1.0000
2	2.0700	2.0800	2.0900	2.1000	2.1100	2.1200
3	3.2149	3.2464	3.2781	3.3100	3.3421	3.3744
4	4.4399	4.5061	4.5731	4.6410	4.7097	4.7793
5	5.7507	5.8666	5.9847	6.1051	6.2278	6.3528
6	7.1533	7.3359	7.5233	7.7156	7.9129	8.1152
7	8.6540	8.9228	9.2004	9.4872	9.7833	10.0890
8	10.2598	10.6366	11.0285	11.4359	11.8594	12.2997

end of this textbook simplifies the computation by summing the individual FV of $1 factors for various factors of n and i. Graphic 6–3 contains an excerpt from Table 3.

The future value of $1 at the end of each of three periods invested at 10% is shown in Table 3 to be $3.31. We can simply multiply this factor by $10,000 to derive the FV of our ordinary annuity (FVA):

$$FVA = \$10,000 \text{ (annuity amount)} \times 3.31^* = \$33,100$$
*Future value of an ordinary annuity of $1: $n = 3$, $i = 10\%$

Future Value of an Annuity Due

Let's modify the previous illustration to create an annuity due in Illustration 6–7.

Sally Rogers wants to accumulate a sum of money to pay for graduate school. Rather than investing a single amount today that will grow to a future value, she decides to invest $10,000 a year over the next three years in a savings account paying 10% interest compounded annually. She decides to make the first payment to the bank immediately. How much will Sally have available in her account at the end of three years?	**ILLUSTRATION 6–7** Future Value of an Annuity Due

The following time diagram depicts the situation. Again, note that 0 is the start of the first period.

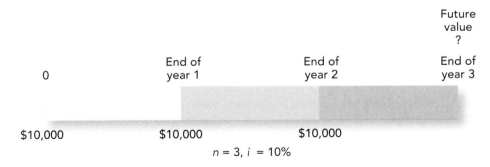

The future value can be found by separately calculating the FV of each of the three payments and then summing those individual future values:

	Payment		FV of $1 $i = 10\%$		Future Value (at the end of year 3)	n
First payment	$10,000	×	1.331	=	$13,310	3
Second payment	10,000	×	1.210	=	12,100	2
Third payment	10,000	×	1.100	=	11,000	1
Total			3.641		$36,410	

In the future value of
an annuity due, the last
cash payment will earn
interest.

And, again, this same future value can be found by using the future value of an annuity due (FVAD) factor from Table 5, Future Value of an Annuity Due, located at the end of this textbook, as follows:

$$\text{FVAD} = \$10,000 \text{ (annuity amount)} \times 3.641^* = \$36,410$$
*Future value of an annuity due of \$1: $n = 3$, $i = 10\%$

Of course, if *unequal* amounts are invested each year, we can't solve the problem by using the annuity tables. The future value of each payment would have to be calculated separately.

Present Value of an Annuity

Present Value of an Ordinary Annuity

● LO7

You will learn in later chapters that liabilities and receivables, with the exception of certain trade receivables and payables, are reported in financial statements at their present values. Most of these financial instruments specify equal periodic interest payments or installment payments. As a result, the most common accounting applications of the time value of money involve determining present value of annuities. As in the future value applications we discussed above, an annuity can be either an ordinary annuity or an annuity due. Let's look at an ordinary annuity first.

In Illustration 6–6 on page 300, we determined that Sally Rogers could accumulate $33,100 for graduate school by investing $10,000 at the end of each of three years at 10%. The $33,100 is the future value of the ordinary annuity described. Another alternative is to invest one single amount at the beginning of the three-year period. (See Illustration 6–8.) This single amount will equal the present value at the beginning of the three-year period of the $33,100 future value. It will also equal the present value of the $10,000 three-year annuity.

ILLUSTRATION 6–8 Present Value of an Ordinary Annuity	Sally Rogers wants to accumulate a sum of money to pay for graduate school. She wants to invest a single amount today in a savings account earning 10% interest compounded annually that is equivalent to investing $10,000 at the end of each of the next three years.

The present value can be found by separately calculating the PV of each of the three payments and then summing those individual present values:

	Payment		PV of $1 $i = 10\%$		Present Value (at the beginning of year 1)	n
First payment	$10,000	×	.90909	=	$ 9,091	1
Second payment	10,000	×	.82645	=	8,264	2
Third payment	10,000	×	.75131	=	7,513	3
Total			2.48685		$24,868	

A more efficient method of calculating present value is to use Table 4, Present Value of an Ordinary Annuity, located at the end of this textbook. Graphic 6–4 contains an excerpt from Table 4.

GRAPHIC 6–4

Present Value of an Ordinary Annuity of $1 (excerpt from Table 4)

Periods (n)	Interest Rates (i)					
	7%	8%	9%	10%	11%	12%
1	0.93458	0.92593	0.91743	0.90909	0.90090	0.89286
2	1.80802	1.78326	1.75911	1.73554	1.71252	1.69005
3	2.62432	2.57710	2.53129	2.48685	2.44371	2.40183
4	3.38721	3.31213	3.23972	3.16987	3.10245	3.03735
5	4.10020	3.99271	3.88965	3.79079	3.69590	3.60478
6	4.76654	4.62288	4.48592	4.35526	4.23054	4.11141
7	5.38929	5.20637	5.03295	4.86842	4.71220	4.56376
8	5.97130	5.74664	5.53482	5.33493	5.14612	4.96764

Using Table 4, we calculate the PV of the ordinary annuity (PVA) as follows:

$$PVA = \$10,000 \text{ (annuity amount)} \times 2.48685^* = \$24,868$$
*Present value of an ordinary annuity of $1: n = 3, i = 10%

The relationship between the present value and the future value of the annuity can be depicted graphically as follows:

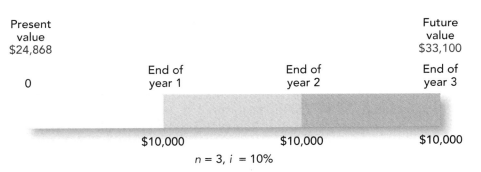

Relationship between present value and future value—ordinary annuit.

This can be interpreted in several ways:

1. $10,000 invested at 10% at the end of each of the next three years will accumulate to $33,100 at the end of the third year.
2. $24,868 invested at 10% now will grow to $33,100 after three years.
3. Someone whose time value of money is 10% would be willing to pay $24,868 now to receive $10,000 at the end of each of the next three years.
4. If your time value of money is 10%, you should be indifferent with respect to paying/receiving (a) $24,868 now, (b) $33,100 three years from now, or (c) $10,000 at the end of each of the next three years.

ADDITIONAL CONSIDERATION

We also can verify that these are the present value and future value of the same annuity by calculating the present value of a single cash amount of $33,100 three years hence:

$$PV = \$33,100 \text{ (future value)} \times .75131^* = \$24,868$$
*Present value of $1: n = 3, i = 10%

Present Value of an Annuity Due

In the previous illustration, suppose that the three equal payments of $10,000 are to be made at the *beginning* of each of the three years. Recall from Illustration 6–7 on page 301 that the future value of this annuity is $36,410. What is the present value?

ILLUSTRATION 6–9

Present Value of an Annuity Due

The following time diagram depicts this situation:

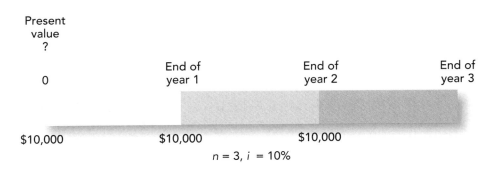

Present value of an annuity due.

Once again, using individual PV factors of $1 from Table 2, the PV of the annuity due can be calculated as follows:

	Payment		PV of $1 $i = 10\%$		Present Value (at the beginning of year 1)	n
First payment	$10,000	×	1.00000	=	$10,000	0
Second payment	10,000	×	.90909	=	9,091	1
Third payment	10,000	×	.82645	=	8,264	2
Total			2.73554		$27,355	

In the present value of an annuity due, no interest needs to be removed from the first cash payment.

The first payment does not contain any interest since it is made on the first day of the three-year annuity period. Therefore, the factor used is 1.00. The second payment has one compounding period and the factor used of .90909 is the PV factor of $1 for one period and 10%, and we need to remove two compounding periods of interest from the third payment. The factor used of .82645 is the PV factor of $1 for two periods and 10%.

The relationship between the present value and the future value of the annuity can be depicted graphically as follows:

Relationship between present value and future value—annuity due.

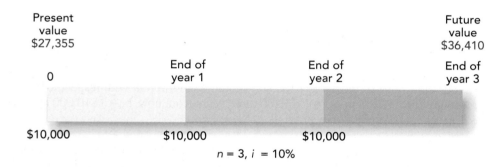

Present value $27,355 ... Future value $36,410

| 0 | End of year 1 | End of year 2 | End of year 3 |

$10,000 $10,000 $10,000

$n = 3, i = 10\%$

Using Table 6, Present Value of an Annuity Due, located at the end of this book, we can more efficiently calculate the PV of the annuity due (PVAD):

$$\text{PVAD} = \$10,000 \text{ (annuity amount)} \times 2.73554^* = \$27,355$$
*Present value of an annuity due of $1: $n = 3, i = 10\%$

To better understand the relationship between Tables 4 and 6, notice that the PVAD factor for three periods, 10%, from Table 6 is 2.73554. This is simply the PVA factor for two periods, 10%, of 1.73554, plus 1.0. The addition of 1.0 reflects the fact that the first payment does not require the removal of any interest.

Present Value of a Deferred Annuity

A *deferred annuity* exists when the first cash flow occurs more than one period after the date the agreement begins.

Accounting valuations often involve the present value of annuities in which the first cash flow is expected to occur more than one time period after the date of the agreement. As the inception of the annuity is deferred beyond a single period, this type of annuity is referred to as a *deferred annuity*.[7]

---

[7]The future value of a deferred annuity is the same as the future amount of an annuity not deferred. That is because there are no interest compounding periods prior to the beginning of the annuity period.

At January 1, 2009, you are considering acquiring an investment that will provide three equal payments of $10,000 each to be received at the end of three consecutive years. However, the first payment is not expected until *December 31, 2011*. The time value of money is 10%. How much would you be willing to pay for this investment?	**ILLUSTRATION 6–10** Deferred Annuity

The following time diagram depicts this situation:

Cash flows for a deferred annuity.

The present value of the annuity can be calculated by summing the present values of the three individual cash flows, each discounted to today's PV:

	Payment		PV of $1 i = 10%		Present Value	n
First payment	$10,000	×	.75131	=	$ 7,513	3
Second payment	10,000	×	.68301	=	6,830	4
Third payment	10,000	×	.62092	=	6,209	5
					$20,552	

A more efficient way of calculating the present value of a deferred annuity involves a two-step process:

1. Calculate the PV of the annuity as of the beginning of the annuity period.
2. Discount the single amount calculated in (1) to its present value *as of today*.

In this case, we compute the present value of the annuity as of December 31, 2010, by multiplying the annuity amount by the three-period ordinary annuity factor:

$$\text{PVA} = \$10,000 \text{ (annuity amount)} \times 2.48685^* = \$24,868$$
*Present value of an ordinary annuity of $1: n = 3, i = 10%

This is the present value as of December 31, 2010. This single amount is then reduced to present value as of January 1, 2009, by making the following calculation:

$$\text{PV} = \$24,868 \text{ (future amount)} \times .82645^* = \$20,552$$
*Present value of $1: n = 2, i = 10%

The following time diagram illustrates this two-step process:

Present value of a deferred annuity— two-step process.

Present value		Present value (at beginning of the annuity period)		i = 10%		
$20,552		$24,868				
1/1/09	12/31/09	12/31/10	12/31/11	12/31/12	12/31/13	
			$10,000	$10,000	$10,000	
	n = 2			n = 3		

If you recall the concepts you learned in this chapter, you might think of other ways the present value of a deferred annuity can be determined. Among them:

1. Calculate the PV of an annuity due, rather than an ordinary annuity, and then discount that amount three periods rather than two:

$$PVAD = \$10,000 \text{ (annuity amount)} \times 2.73554^* = \$27,355$$
*Present value of an annuity due of $1: n = 3, i = 10%

This is the present value as of December 31, 2011. This single amount is then reduced to present value as of January 1, 2009 by making the following calculation:

$$PV = \$27,355 \times .75131^* = \$20,552$$
*Present value of $1: n = 3, i = 10%

2. From Table 4, subtract the two-period PVA factor (1.73554) from the five-period PVA factor (3.79079) and multiply the difference (2.05525) by $10,000 to get $20,552.

Financial Calculators and Excel

As previously mentioned, financial calculators can be used to solve future and present value problems. For example, a Texas Instruments model BA-35 has the following pertinent keys:

$$\boxed{\text{N}} \quad \boxed{\text{\%I}} \quad \boxed{\text{PV}} \quad \boxed{\text{FV}} \quad \boxed{\text{PMT}} \quad \boxed{\text{CPT}}$$

These keys are defined as follows:

$$N = \text{number of periods}$$
$$\%I = \text{interest rate}$$
$$PV = \text{present value}$$
$$FV = \text{future value}$$
$$PMT = \text{annuity payments}$$
$$CPT = \text{compute button}$$

Using a calculator:
Enter: $\boxed{\text{N}}$ 10 $\boxed{\text{I}}$ 10
$\boxed{\text{PMT}}$-200
Output: $\boxed{\text{PV}}$ 1,229

Using Excel, enter:
= PV(.10,10,200)
Output: 1,229

To illustrate its use, assume that you need to determine the present value of a 10-period ordinary annuity of $200 using a 10% interest rate. You would enter $\boxed{\text{N}}$ 10, $\boxed{\text{\%I}}$ 10, $\boxed{\text{PMT}}$ 200 , then press $\boxed{\text{CPT}}$ and $\boxed{\text{PV}}$ to obtain the answer of $1,229.

Many professionals choose to use spreadsheet software, such as Excel, to solve time value of money problems. These spreadsheets can be used in a variety of ways. A template can be created using the formulas shown in Graphic 6–5 on page 313. An alternative is to use the software's built-in financial functions. For example, Excel has a function called PV that calculates the present value of an ordinary annuity. To use the function, you would select the pull-down menu for "Insert," click on "Function" and choose the category called "Financial." Scroll down to PV and double-click. You will then be asked to input the necessary variables—interest rate, the number of periods, and the payment amount.

In subsequent chapters we illustrate the use of both a calculator and Excel in addition to present value tables to solve present value calculations for selected examples and illustrations.

Solving for Unknown Values in Present Value Situations

● LO8

In present value problems involving annuities, there are four variables: (1) present value of an ordinary annuity (PVA) or present value of an annuity due (PVAD), (2) the amount of each annuity payment, (3) the number of periods, *n,* and (4) the interest rate, *i.* If you know any three of these, the fourth can be determined.

Assume that you borrow $700 from a friend and intend to repay the amount in four equal annual installments beginning one year from today. Your friend wishes to be reimbursed for the time value of money at an 8% annual rate. What is the required annual payment that must be made (the annuity amount), to repay the loan in four years?	**ILLUSTRATION 6–11** Determining the Annuity Amount When Other Variables Are Known

The following time diagram illustrates the situation:

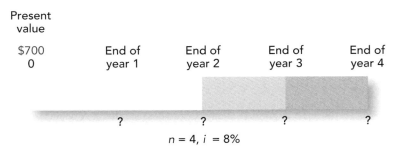

Determining the unknown annuity amount—ordinary annuit.

The required payment is the annuity amount that will provide a present value of $700 when discounting that amount at a discount rate of 8%:

$$\$700 \text{ (present value)} = 3.31213^* \times \text{annuity amount}$$

The unknown variable is the annuity amount.

Rearranging algebraically, we find that the annuity amount is $211.34.

$$\$700 \text{ (present value)} \div 3.31213^* = \$211.34 \text{ (annuity amount)}$$
*Present value of an ordinary annuity of $1: $n = 4$, $i = 8\%$

You would have to make four annual payments of $211.34 to repay the loan. Total payments of $845.36 (4 × $211.34) would include $145.36 in interest ($845.36 − 700.00).

Assume that you borrow $700 from a friend and intend to repay the amount in equal installments of $100 per year over a period of years. The payments will be made at the end of each year beginning one year from now. Your friend wishes to be reimbursed for the time value of money at a 7% annual rate. How many years would it take before you repaid the loan?	**ILLUSTRATION 6–12** Determining n When Other Variables Are Known

Once again, this is an ordinary annuity situation because the first payment takes place one year from now. The following time diagram illustrates the situation:

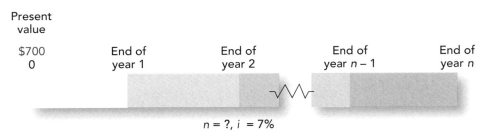

Determining the unknown number of periods—ordinary annuit.

The number of years is the value of n that will provide a present value of $700 when discounting $100 at a discount rate of 7%:

$$\$700 \text{ (present value)} = \$100 \text{ (annuity amount)} \times ?^*$$
*Present value of an ordinary annuity of $1: $n = ?$, $i = 7\%$

The unknown variable is the number of periods.

Rearranging algebraically, we find that the PVA table factor is 7.0.

$$\$700 \text{ (present value)} \div \$100 \text{ (annuity amount)} = 7.0^*$$
*Present value of an ordinary annuity of $1: $n = ?$, $i = 7\%$

When you consult the PVA table, Table 4, you search the 7% column ($i = 7\%$) for this value and find 7.02358 in row 10. So it would take approximately 10 years to repay the loan in the situation described.

ILLUSTRATION 6–13	Suppose that a friend asked to borrow $331 today (present value) and promised to repay you $100 (the annuity amount) at the end of each of the next four years. What is the annual interest rate implicit in this agreement?
Determining *i* When Other Variables Are Known	

FINANCIAL
Reporting Case

Q2, p. 289

Determining the unknown interest rate—ordinary annuity.

First of all, we are dealing with an ordinary annuity situation as the payments are at the end of each period. The following time diagram illustrates the situation:

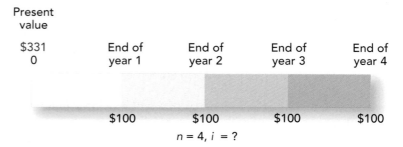

The interest rate is the discount rate that will provide a present value of $331 when discounting the $100 four-year ordinary annuity:

The unknown variable is the interest rate.

$$\$331 \text{ (present value)} = \$100 \text{ (annuity amount)} \times ?^*$$
*Present value of an ordinary annuity of $1: $n = 4$, $i = ?$

Rearranging algebraically, we find that the PVA table factor is 3.31.

$$\$331 \text{ (present value)} \div \$100 \text{ (annuity amount)} = 3.31^*$$
*Present value of an ordinary annuity of $1: $n = 4$, $i = ?$

When you consult the PVA table, Table 4, you search row four ($n = 4$) for this value and find it in the 8% column. So the effective interest rate is 8%.

ILLUSTRATION 6–14	Suppose that you borrowed $400 from a friend and promised to repay the loan by making three annual payments of $100 at the end of each of the next three years plus a final payment of $200 at the end of year four. What is the interest rate implicit in this agreement?
Determining *i* When Other Variables Are Known—Unequal Cash Flows	

The following time diagram illustrates the situation:

Determining the unknown interest rate—unequal cash flow.

The interest rate is the discount rate that will provide a present value of $400 when discounting the $100 three-year ordinary annuity plus the $200 to be received in four years:

The unknown variable is the interest rate.

$$\$400 \text{ (present value)} = \$100 \text{ (annuity amount)} \times ?^* + \$200 \text{ (single payment)} \times ?^\dagger$$
*Present value of an ordinary annuity of $1: $n = 3$, $i = ?$
†Present value of $1: $n = 4$, $i = ?$

This equation involves two unknowns and is not as easily solved as the two previous examples. One way to solve the problem is to trial-and-error the answer. For example, if we assumed i to be 9%, the total PV of the payments would be calculated as follows:

$$PV = \$100\ (2.53129^*) + \$200\ (.70843^\dagger) = \$395$$
*Present value of an ordinary annuity of $1: $n = 3$, $i = 9\%$
†Present value of $1: $n = 4$, $i = 9\%$

Because the present value computed is less than the $400 borrowed, using 9% removes too much interest. Recalculating PV with $i = 8\%$ results in a PV of $405. This indicates that the interest rate implicit in the agreement is between 8% and 9%.

CONCEPT REVIEW **EXERCISE**

Using the appropriate table, answer each of the following independent questions.

ANNUITIES

1. What is the future value of an annuity of $2,000 invested at the *end* of each of the next six periods at 8% interest?
2. What is the future value of an annuity of $2,000 invested at the *beginning* of each of the next six periods at 8% interest?
3. What is the present value of an annuity of $6,000 to be received at the *end* of each of the next eight periods assuming an interest rate of 10%?
4. What is the present value of an annuity of $6,000 to be received at the *beginning* of each of the next eight periods assuming an interest rate of 10%?
5. Jane bought a $3,000 audio system and agreed to pay for the purchase in 10 equal annual installments of $408 beginning one year from today. What is the interest rate implicit in this agreement?
6. Jane bought a $3,000 audio system and agreed to pay for the purchase in 10 equal annual installments beginning one year from today. The interest rate is 12%. What is the amount of the annual installment?
7. Jane bought a $3,000 audio system and agreed to pay for the purchase by making nine equal annual installments beginning one year from today plus a lump-sum payment of $1,000 at the end of 10 periods. The interest rate is 10%. What is the required annual installment?
8. Jane bought an audio system and agreed to pay for the purchase by making four equal annual installments of $800 beginning one year from today plus a lump-sum payment of $1,000 at the end of five years. The interest rate is 12%. What was the cost of the audio system? (Hint: What is the present value of the cash payments?)
9. Jane bought an audio system and agreed to pay for the purchase by making five equal annual installments of $1,100 beginning four years from today. The interest rate is 12%. What was the cost of the audio system? (Hint: What is the present value of the cash payments?)

1. FVA = $2,000 × 7.3359* = $14,672

SOLUTION

*Future value of an ordinary annuity of $1: $n = 6$, $i = 8\%$ (from Table 3)
2. FVAD = $2,000 × 7.9228* = $15,846
*Future value of an annuity due of $1: $n = 6$, $i = 8\%$ (from Table 5)
3. PVA = $6,000 × 5.33493* = $32,010
*Present value of ordinary annuity of $1: $n = 8$, $i = 10\%$ (from Table 4)
4. PVAD = $6,000 × 5.86842* = $35,211
*Present value of an annuity due of $1: $n = 8$, $i = 10\%$ (from Table 6)
5. $\dfrac{\$3,000}{\$408} = 7.35^*$

*Present value of an ordinary annuity of $1: $n = 10$, $i = ?$ (from Table 4, i approximately 6%)

6. Each annuity payment $= \dfrac{\$3,000}{5.65022^*} = \$531$

*Present value of an ordinary annuity of $1: $n = 10$, $i = 12\%$ (from Table 4)

7. $\text{Each annuity payment} = \dfrac{\$3,000 - [\text{PV of }\$1,000\ (n = 10,\ i = 10\%)]}{5.75902*}$

$\text{Each annuity payment} = \dfrac{\$3,000 - (\$1,000 \times .38554^{\dagger})}{5.75902*}$

$\text{Each annuity payment} = \dfrac{\$2,614}{5.75902*} = \$454$

*Present value of an ordinary annuity of $1: $n = 9$, $i = 10\%$ (from Table 4)
†Present value of $1: $n = 10$, $i = 10\%$ (from Table 2)

8. $\text{PV} = \$800 \times 3.03735* + \$1,000 \times .56743^{\dagger} = \$2,997$

*Present value of an ordinary annuity of $1: $n = 4$, $i = 12\%$ (from Table 4)
†Present value of $1: $n = 5$, $i = 12\%$ (from Table 2)

9. $\text{PVA} = \$1,100 \times 3.60478* = \$3,965$

*Present value of an ordinary annuity of $1: $n = 5$, $i = 12\%$ (from Table 4)

This is the present value three years from today (the beginning of the five-year ordinary annuity). This single amount is then reduced to present value as of today by making the following calculation:

$\text{PV} = \$3,965 \times .71178^{\dagger} = \$2,822$

†Present value of $1: $n = 3$, $i = 12\%$, (from Table 2) ●

Preview of Accounting Applications of Present Value Techniques—Annuities

● LO9

The time value of money has many applications in accounting. Most of these applications involve the concept of present value. Because financial instruments typically specify equal periodic payments, these applications quite often involve annuity situations. For example, let's consider one accounting situation using both an ordinary annuity and the present value of a single amount (long-term bonds), one using an annuity due (long-term leases), and a third using a deferred annuity (pension obligations).

Valuation of Long-Term Bonds

**FINANCIAL
Reporting Case**

Q3, p. 289

You will learn in Chapter 14 that a long-term bond usually requires the issuing (borrowing) company to repay a specified amount at maturity and make periodic stated interest payments over the life of the bond. The *stated* interest payments are equal to the contractual stated rate multiplied by the face value of the bonds. At the date the bonds are issued (sold), the market-place will determine the price of the bonds based on the *market* rate of interest for investments with similar characteristics. The market rate at date of issuance may not equal the bonds' stated rate in which case the price of the bonds (the amount the issuing company actually is borrowing) will not equal the bonds' face value. Bonds issued at more than face value are said to be issued at a premium, while bonds issued at less than face value are said to be issued at a discount. Consider the example in Illustration 6–15.

ILLUSTRATION 6–15 Valuing a Long-Term Bond Liability	On June 30, 2009, Fumatsu Electric issued 10% stated rate bonds with a face amount of $200 million. The bonds mature on June 30, 2029 (20 years). The market rate of interest for similar issues was 12%. Interest is paid semiannually (5%) on June 30 and December 31, beginning December 31, 2009. The interest payment is $10 million (5% × $200 million). What was the price of the bond issue?

To determine the price of the bonds, we calculate the present value of the 40-period annuity (40 semiannual interest payments of $10 million) and the lump-sum payment of $200 million paid at maturity using the semiannual market rate of interest of 6%. In equation form,

$$PVA = \$10 \text{ million (annuity amount)} \times 15.04630^* = \$150,463,000$$
$$PV = \$200 \text{ million (lump sum)} \times .09722^\dagger = \underline{19,444,000}$$
$$\text{Price of the bond issue} = \underline{\underline{\$169,907,000}}$$

*Present value of an ordinary annuity of $1: $n = 40$, $i = 6\%$
†Present value of $1: $n = 40$, $i = 6\%$

The bonds will sell for $169,907,000, which represents a discount of $30,093,000 ($200,000,000 − 169,907,000). The discount results from the difference between the semi-annual stated rate of 5% and the market rate of 6%. Fumatsu records a $169,907,000 increase in cash and a corresponding liability for bonds payable. We discuss and illustrate the specific accounts used to record this transaction in Chapter 14.

Valuation of Long-Term Leases

Companies frequently acquire the use of assets by leasing rather than purchasing them. Leases usually require the payment of fixed amounts at regular intervals over the life of the lease. You will learn in Chapter 15 that certain long-term, noncancelable leases are treated in a manner similar to an installment sale by the lessor and an installment purchase by the lessee. In other words, the lessor records a receivable and the lessee records a liability for the several installment payments. For the lessee, this requires that the leased asset and corresponding lease liability be valued at the present value of the lease payments. Consider the example in Illustration 6–16.

On January 1, 2009, the Stridewell Wholesale Shoe Company signed a 25-year non-cancelable lease agreement for an office building. Terms of the lease call for Stridewell to make annual lease payments of $10,000 at the beginning of each year, with the first payment due on January 1, 2009. Assuming an interest rate of 10% properly reflects the time value of money in this situation, how should Stridewell value the asset acquired and the corresponding lease liability if it is to be treated in a manner similar to an installment purchase?

ILLUSTRATION 6–16

Valuing a Long-Term Lease Liability

Once again, by computing the present value of the lease payments, we remove the portion of the payments that represents interest, leaving the portion that represents payment for the asset itself. Because the first payment is due immediately, as is common for leases, this is an annuity due situation. In equation form:

$$PVAD = \$10,000 \text{ (annuity amount)} \times 9.98474^* = \$99,847$$
*Present value of an annuity due of $1: $n = 25$, $i = 10\%$

Certain long-term leases require the recording of an asset and corresponding liability at the present value of future lease payments.

Stridewell initially will value the leased asset and corresponding lease liability at $99,847.

Leased office building	99,847	
Lease payable		99,847

Journal entry at the inception of a lease.

The difference between this amount and total future cash payments of $250,000 ($10,000 × 25) represents the interest that is implicit in this agreement. That difference is recorded as interest over the life of the lease.

Valuation of Pension Obligations

Pension plans are important compensation vehicles used by many U.S. companies. These plans are essentially forms of deferred compensation as the pension benefits are paid to employees after they retire. You will learn in Chapter 17 that some pension plans create obligations during employees' service periods that must be paid during their retirement periods. These obligations are funded during the employment period. This means companies contribute cash to pension funds annually with the intention of accumulating sufficient funds to pay employees the retirement benefits they have earned. The amounts contributed are determined using estimates of retirement benefits. The actual amounts paid to employees during retirement depend on many factors including future compensation levels and length of life. Consider Illustration 6–17.

ILLUSTRATION 6–17 Valuing a Pension Obligation	On January 1, 2009, the Stridewell Wholesale Shoe Company hired Sammy Sossa. Sammy is expected to work for 25 years before retirement on December 31, 2033. Annual retirement payments will be paid at the end of each year during his retirement period, expected to be 20 years. The first payment will be on December 31, 2034. During 2009 Sammy earned an annual retirement benefit estimated to be $2,000 per year. The company plans to contribute cash to a pension fund that will accumulate to an amount sufficient to pay Sammy this benefit. Assuming that Stridewell anticipates earning 6% on all funds invested in the pension plan, how much would the company have to contribute at the end of 2009 to pay for pension benefits earned in 2009?

To determine the required contribution, we calculate the present value on December 31, 2009, of the deferred annuity of $2,000 that begins on December 31, 2034, and is expected to end on December 31, 2053.

The following time diagram depicts this situation:

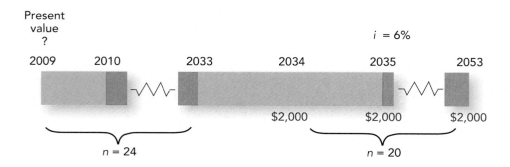

We can calculate the present value of the annuity using a two-step process. The first step computes the present value of the annuity as of December 31, 2033, by multiplying the annuity amount by the 20-period ordinary annuity factor:

$$PVA = \$2,000 \text{ (annuity amount)} \times 11.46992^* = \$22,940$$
*Present value of an ordinary annuity of $1: $n = 20$, $i = 6\%$

This is the present value as of December 31, 2033. This single amount is then reduced to present value as of December 31, 2009, by a second calculation:

$$PV = \$22,940 \text{ (future amount)} \times .24698^* = \$5,666$$
*Present value of $1: $n = 24$, $i = 6\%$

Stridewell would have to contribute $5,666 at the end of 2009 to fund the estimated pension benefits earned by its employee in 2009. Viewed in reverse, $5,666 invested now at 6% will accumulate a fund balance of $22,940 at December 31, 2033. If the fund balance remains invested at 6%, $2,000 can be withdrawn each year for 20 years before the fund is depleted.

Among the other situations you'll encounter using present value techniques are valuing notes (Chapters 10 and 14) and other postretirement benefits (Chapter 17).

Summary of Time Value of Money Concepts

Graphic 6–5 summarizes the time value of money concepts discussed in this chapter.

Concept	Summary	Formula	Table
Future value (FV) of $1	The amount of money that a dollar will grow to at some point in the future.	$FV = \$1\,(1 + i)^n$	1
Present value (PV) of $1	The amount of money today that is equivalent to a given amount to be received or paid in the future.	$PV = \dfrac{\$1}{(1 + i)^n}$	2
Future value of an ordinary annuity (FVA) of $1	The future value of a series of equal-sized cash flows with the first payment taking place at the end of the first compounding period.	$FVA = \dfrac{(1 + i)^n - 1}{i}$	3
Present value of an ordinary annuity (PVA) of $1	The present value of a series of equal-sized cash flows with the first payment taking place at the end of the first compounding period.	$PVA = \dfrac{1 - \dfrac{1}{(1 + i)^n}}{i}$	4
Future value of an annuity due (FVAD) of $1	The future value of a series of equal-sized cash flows with the first payment taking place at the beginning of the annuity period.	$FVAD = \left[\dfrac{(1 + i)^n - 1}{i}\right] \times (1 + i)$	5
Present value of an annuity due (PVAD) of $1	The present value of a series of equal-sized cash flows with the first payment taking place at the beginning of the annuity period.	$PVAD = \left[\dfrac{1 - \dfrac{1}{(1 + i)^n}}{i}\right] \times (1 + i)$	6

GRAPHIC 6–5

Summary of Time Value of Money Concepts

FINANCIAL REPORTING CASE SOLUTION

1. **Why were the Castellanos to receive $43 million rather than the $141 million lottery prize?** *(p. 302)* The Castellanos chose to receive their lottery winnings in one lump payment immediately rather than in 26 equal annual installments beginning immediately. The state calculates the present value of the 26 equal payments, withholds the necessary federal income tax, and pays the Castellanos the remainder.

2. **What interest rate did the State of California use to calculate the $43 million lump-sum payment?** *(p. 308)* The equal payment is determined by dividing $141 million by 26 periods:

$141 million ÷ 26 =	$5,423,077
Less: 31% federal income tax	(1,681,154)
Net-of-tax payment	$3,741,923

Since the first payment is made immediately, this is an annuity due situation. We must find the interest rate that provides a present value of $43 million. There is no 26 period row in Table 6. We can subtract the first payment from the $43 million since it is paid immediately and solve using the 25-period ordinary annuity table (that is, the 25 remaining annual payments beginning in one year):

$$\text{PVA factor} = \frac{\$43,000,000 - 3,741,923}{\$3,741,923} = 10.4914^*$$

*Present value of an ordinary annuity of $1: $n = 25$, $i = ?$ (from Table 4, i = approximately 8%)

So, the interest rate used by the state was approximately 8%.

3. **What are some of the accounting applications that incorporate the time value of money into valuation?** *(p. 310)* Accounting applications that incorporate the time value of money techniques into valuation include the valuation of long-term notes receivable and various long-term liabilities that include bonds, notes, leases, pension obligations, and postretirement benefits other than pensions. We study these in detail in later chapters. ●

THE BOTTOM LINE

● **LO1** A dollar today is worth more than a dollar to be received in the future. The difference between the present value of cash flows and their future value represents the time value of money. Interest is the rent paid for the use of money over time. (p. 290)

● **LO2** The future value of a single amount is the amount of money that a dollar will grow to at some point in the future. It is computed by *multiplying* the single amount by $(1 + i)^n$, where i is the interest rate and n the number of compounding periods. The Future Value of $1 table allows for the calculation of future value for any single amount by providing the factors for various combinations of i and n. (p. 291)

● **LO3** The present value of a single amount is the amount of money today that is equivalent to a given amount to be received or paid in the future. It is computed by *dividing* the future amount by $(1 + i)^n$. The Present Value of $1 table simplifies the calculation of the present value of any future amount. (p. 292)

● **LO4** There are four variables in the process of adjusting single cash flow amounts for the time value of money: present value (PV), future value (FV), i and n. If you know any three of these, the fourth can be computed easily. (p. 294)

● **LO5** An annuity is a series of equal-sized cash flows occurring over equal intervals of time. An ordinary annuity exists when the cash flows occur at the end of each period. An annuity due exists when the cash flows occur at the beginning of each period. (p. 299)

● **LO6** The future value of an ordinary annuity (FVA) is the future value of a series of equalsized cash flows with the first payment taking place at the end of the first compounding period. The last payment will not earn any interest since it is made at the end of the annuity period. The future value of an annuity due (FVAD) is the future value of a series of equal-sized cash flows with the first payment taking place at the beginning of the annuity period (the beginning of the first compounding period). (p. 300)

● **LO7** The present value of an ordinary annuity (PVA) is the present value of a series of equalsized cash flows with the first payment taking place at the end of the first compounding period. The present value of an annuity due (PVAD) is the present value of a series of equal-sized cash flows with the first payment taking place at the beginning of the annuity period. The present value of a deferred annuity is the present value of a series of equal-sized cash flows with the first payment taking place more than one time period after the date of the agreement. (p. 302)

● **LO8** In present value problems involving annuities, there are four variables: PVA or PVAD, the annuity amount, the number of compounding periods (n) and the interest rate (i). If you know any three of these, you can determine the fourth. (p. 306)

● **LO9** Most accounting applications of the time value of money involve the present values of annuities. The initial valuation of long-term bonds is determined by calculating the present value of the periodic stated interest payments and the present value of the lump-sum payment made at maturity. Certain long-term leases require the lessee to compute the present value of future lease payments to value the leased asset and corresponding lease obligation. Also, pension plans require the payment of deferred annuities to retirees. (p. 310) ●

QUESTIONS FOR REVIEW OF KEY TOPICS

Q 6–1 Define interest.
Q 6–2 Explain compound interest.
Q 6–3 What would cause the annual interest rate to be different from the annual effective rate or yield?
Q 6–4 Identify the three items of information necessary to calculate the future value of a single amount.
Q 6–5 Define the present value of a single amount.

Q 6–6   Explain the difference between monetary and nonmonetary assets and liabilities.

Q 6–7   What is an annuity?

Q 6–8   Explain the difference between an ordinary annuity and an annuity due.

Q 6–9   Explain the relationship between Table 2, Present Value of $1, and Table 4, Present Value of an Ordinary Annuity.

Q 6–10   Prepare a time diagram for the present value of a four-year ordinary annuity of $200. Assume an interest rate of 10% per year.

Q 6–11   Prepare a time diagram for the present value of a four-year annuity due of $200. Assume an interest rate of 10% per year.

Q 6–12   What is a deferred annuity?

Q 6–13   Assume that you borrowed $500 from a friend and promised to repay the loan in five equal annual installments beginning one year from today. Your friend wants to be reimbursed for the time value of money at an 8% annual rate. Explain how you would compute the required annual payment.

Q 6–14   Compute the required annual payment in Question 6–13.

Q 6–15   Explain how the time value of money concept is incorporated into the valuation of long-term leases.

BRIEF **EXERCISES**

BE 6–1
Simple versus
compound interest

● LO1

Fran Smith has two investment opportunities. The interest rate for both investments is 8%. Interest on the first investment will compound annually while interest on the second will compound quarterly. Which investment opportunity should Fran choose? Why?

BE 6–2
Future value; single
amount

● LO2

Bill O'Brien would like to take his wife, Mary, on a trip three years from now to Europe to celebrate their 40th anniversary. He has just received a $20,000 inheritance from an uncle and intends to invest it for the trip. Bill estimates the trip will cost $23,500 and he believes he can earn 5% interest, compounded annually, on his investment. Will he be able to pay for the trip with the accumulated investment amount?

BE 6–3
Future value; solving
for unknown; single
amount

● LO4

Refer to the situation described in BE 6–2. Assume that the trip will cost $26,600. What interest rate, compounded annually, must Bill earn to accumulate enough to pay for the trip?

BE 6–4
Present value;
single amount

● LO3

John has an investment opportunity that promises to pay him $16,000 in four years. He could earn a 6% annual return investing his money elsewhere. What is the maximum amount he would be willing to invest in this opportunity?

BE 6–5
Present value;
solving for
unknown; single
amount

● LO4

Refer to the situation described in BE 6–4. Suppose the opportunity requires John to invest $13,200 today. What is the interest rate John would earn on this investment?

BE 6–6
Future value;
ordinary annuity

● LO6

Leslie McCormack is in the spring quarter of her freshman year of college. She and her friends already are planning a trip to Europe after graduation in a little over three years. Mary would like to contribute to a savings account over the next three years in order to accumulate enough money to take the trip. Assuming an interest rate of 4%, compounded quarterly, how much will she accumulate in three years by depositing $500 at the *end* of each of the next 12 quarters, beginning three months from now?

BE 6–7
Future value;
annuity due

● LO6

Refer to the situation described in BE 6–6. How much will Leslie accumulate in three years by depositing $500 at the *beginning* of each of the next 12 quarters?

BE 6–8
Present value;
ordinary annuity

● LO7

Canliss Mining Company borrowed money from a local bank. The note the company signed requires five annual installment payments of $10,000 beginning one year from today. The interest rate on the note is 7%. What amount did Canliss borrow?

BE 6–9
Present value;
annuity due

● LO7

Refer to the situation described in BE 6–8. What amount did Canliss borrow assuming that the first $10,000 payment was due immediately?

BE 6–10
Deferred annuity

● LO7

Refer to the situation described in BE 6–8. What amount did Canliss borrow assuming that the first of the five annual $10,000 payments was not due for three years?

BE 6–11
Solve for unknown;
annuity

● LO8

Kingsley Toyota borrowed $100,000 from a local bank. The loan requires Kingsley to pay 10 equal annual installments beginning one year from today. Assuming an interest rate of 8%, what is the amount of each annual installment payment?

BE 6–12
Price of a bond

● LO9

On December 31, 2009, Interlink Communications issued 6% stated rate bonds with a face amount of $100 million. The bonds mature on December 31, 2039. Interest is payable annually on each December 31, beginning in 2010. Determine the price of the bonds on December 31, 2009, assuming that the market rate of interest for similar bonds was 7%.

BE 6–13
Lease payment

● LO9

On September 30, 2009, Ferguson Imports leased a warehouse. Terms of the lease require Ferguson to make 10 annual lease payments of $55,000 with the first payment due immediately. Accounting standards require the company to record a lease liability when recording this type of lease. Assuming an 8% interest rate, at what amount should Ferguson record the lease liability on September 30, 2009, before the first payment is made?

EXERCISES

available with McGraw–Hill's Homework Manager www.mhhe.com/spiceland5e

An alternate exercise and problem set is available on the text website: www.mhhe.com/spiceland5e

E 6–1
Future value; single
amount

● LO2

Determine the future value of the following single amounts:

	Invested Amount	Interest Rate	No. of Periods
1.	$15,000	6%	12
2.	20,000	8	10
3.	30,000	12	20
4.	50,000	4	12

E 6–2
Present value;
single amount

● LO3

Determine the present value of the following single amounts:

	Future Amount	Interest Rate	No. of Periods
1.	$20,000	7%	10
2.	14,000	8	12
3.	25,000	12	20
4.	40,000	10	8

E 6–3
Present value;
multiple, unequal
amounts

● LO3

Determine the combined present value as of December 31, 2009, of the following four payments to be received at the *end* of each of the designated years, assuming an annual interest rate of 8%.

Payment	Year Received
$5,000	2010
6,000	2011
8,000	2013
9,000	2015

E 6–4
Future value; single amounts

● LO2

Determine the future value of $10,000 under each of the following sets of assumptions:

	Annual Rate	Period Invested	Interest Compounded
1.	10%	10 years	Semiannually
2.	12	5 years	Quarterly
3.	24	30 months	Monthly

E 6–5
Future value; annuities

● LO6

Wiseman Video plans to make four annual deposits of $2,000 each to a special building fund. The fund's assets will be invested in mortgage instruments expected to pay interest at 12% on the fund's balance. Using the appropriate annuity table, determine how much will be accumulated in the fund on December 31, 2012, under each of the following situations:
1. The first deposit is made on December 31, 2009, and interest is compounded annually.
2. The first deposit is made on December 31, 2008, and interest is compounded annually.
3. The first deposit is made on December 31, 2008, and interest is compounded quarterly.
4. The first deposit is made on December 31, 2008, interest is compounded annually, *and* interest earned is withdrawn at the end of each year.

E 6–6
Present value; annuities

● LO7

Using the appropriate present value table and assuming a 12% annual interest rate, determine the present value on December 31, 2009, of a five-period annual annuity of $5,000 under each of the following situations:
1. The first payment is received on December 31, 2010, and interest is compounded annually.
2. The first payment is received on December 31, 2009, and interest is compounded annually.
3. The first payment is received on December 31, 2010, and interest is compounded quarterly.

E 6–7
Solving for unknowns; single amounts

● LO4

For each of the following situations involving single amounts, solve for the unknown (?). Assume that interest is compounded annually. (i = interest rate, and n = number of years)

	Present Value	Future Value	i	n
1.	?	$ 40,000	10%	5
2.	$36,289	65,000	?	10
3.	15,884	40,000	8	?
4.	46,651	100,000	?	8
5.	15,376	?	7	20

E 6–8
Solving for unknowns; single amounts

● LO8

For each of the following situations involving annuities, solve for the unknown (?). Assume that interest is compounded annually and that all annuity amounts are received at the *end* of each period. (i = interest rate, and n = number of years)

	Present Value	Annuity Amount	i	n
1.	?	$ 3,000	8%	5
2.	$242,980	75,000	?	4
3.	161,214	20,000	9	?
4.	500,000	80,518	?	8
5.	250,000	?	10	4

E 6–9
Future value; solving for annuities and single amount

● LO4 LO8

John Rider wants to accumulate $100,000 to be used for his daughter's college education. He would like to have the amount available on December 31, 2014. Assume that the funds will accumulate in a certificate of deposit paying 8% interest compounded annually.

Required:
Answer each of the following independent questions.
1. If John were to deposit a single amount, how much would he have to invest on December 31, 2009?
2. If John were to make five equal deposits on each December 31, beginning on December 31, 2010, what is the required deposit?
3. If John were to make five equal deposits on each December 31, beginning on December 31, 2009, what is the required deposit?

E 6–10
Future and present value

● LO3 LO6 LO7

Answer each of the following independent questions.
1. Alex Meir recently won a lottery and has the option of receiving one of the following three prizes: (1) $64,000 cash immediately, (2) $20,000 cash immediately and a six-period annuity of $8,000 beginning one year from today, or (3) a six-period annuity of $13,000 beginning one year from today. Assuming an interest rate of 6%, which option should Alex choose?
2. The Weimer Corporation wants to accumulate a sum of money to repay certain debts due on December 31, 2018. Weimer will make annual deposits of $100,000 into a special bank account at the end of each of 10 years

beginning December 31, 2009. Assuming that the bank account pays 7% interest compounded annually, what will be the fund balance after the last payment is made on December 31, 2018?

E 6–11
Noninterest-bearing note; single payment
● LO3

The Field Detergent Company sold merchandise to the Abel Company on June 30, 2009. Payment was made in the form of a noninterest-bearing note requiring Abel to pay $85,000 on June 30, 2011. Assume that a 10% interest rate properly reflects the time value of money in this situation.

Required:
Calculate the amount at which Field should record the note receivable and corresponding sales revenue on June 30, 2009.

E 6–12
Solving for unknown annuity payment
● LO8

Don James purchased a new automobile for $20,000. Don made a cash down payment of $5,000 and agreed to pay the remaining balance in 30 monthly installments, beginning one month from the date of purchase. Financing is available at a 24% *annual* interest rate.

Required:
Calculate the amount of the required monthly payment.

E 6–13
Solving for unknown interest rate
● LO8

Lang Warehouses borrowed $100,000 from a bank and signed a note requiring 20 annual payments of $13,388 beginning one year from the date of the agreement.

Required:
Determine the interest rate implicit in this agreement.

E 6–14
Solving for unknown annuity amount
● LO8

Sandy Kupchack just graduated from State University with a bachelors degree in history. During her four years at the U, Sandy accumulated $12,000 in student loans. She asks for your help in determining the amount of the *quarterly* loan payment. She tells you that the loan must be paid back in five years and that the annual interest rate is 8%. Payments begin in three months.

Required:
Determine Sandy's quarterly loan payment.

E 6–15
Price of a bond
● LO9

On September 30, 2009, the San Fillipo Corporation issued 8% stated rate bonds with a face amount of $300 million. The bonds mature on September 30, 2029 (20 years). The market rate of interest for similar bonds was 10%. Interest is paid semiannually on March 31 and September 30.

Required:
Determine the price of the bonds on September 30, 2009.

E 6–16
Deferred annuities
● LO7

Lincoln Company purchased merchandise from Grandville Corp. on September 30, 2009. Payment was made in the form of a noninterest-bearing note requiring Lincoln to make six annual payments of $5,000 on each September 30, beginning on September 30, 2012.

Required:
Calculate the amount at which Lincoln should record the note payable and corresponding purchases on September 30, 2009, assuming that an interest rate of 10% properly reflects the time value of money in this situation.

E 6–17
Deferred annuities; solving for annuity amount
● LO7 LO8

On April 1, 2009, John Vaughn purchased appliances from the Acme Appliance Company for $1,200. In order to increase sales, Acme allows customers to pay in installments and will defer any payments for six months. John will make 18 equal monthly payments, beginning October 1, 2009. The annual interest rate implicit in this agreement is 24%.

Required:
Calculate the monthly payment necessary for John to pay for his purchases.

E 6–18
Lease payments
● LO9

On June 30, 2009, Fly-By-Night Airlines leased a jumbo jet from **Boeing Corporation.** The terms of the lease require Fly-By-Night to make 20 annual payments of $400,000 on each June 30. Accounting standards require this lease to be recorded as a liability for the present value of scheduled payments. Assume that a 7% interest rate properly reflects the time value of money in this situation.

Required:
1. At what amount should Fly-By-Night record the lease liability on June 30, 2009, assuming that the first payment will be made on June 30, 2010?
2. At what amount should Fly-By-Night record the lease liability on June 30, 2009, *before* any payments are made, assuming that the first payment will be made on June 30, 2009?

E 6–19
Concepts; terminology

Listed below are several terms and phrases associated with concepts discussed in the chapter. Pair each item from List A (by letter) with the item from List B that is most appropriately associated with it.

● LO1 through
  LO3 LO5

List A	List B
___ 1. Interest	a. First cash flow occurs one period after agreement begins.
___ 2. Monetary asset	b. The rate at which money will actually grow during a year.
___ 3. Compound interest	c. First cash flow occurs on the first day of the agreement.
___ 4. Simple interest	d. The amount of money that a dollar will grow to.
___ 5. Annuity	e. Amount of money paid/received in excess of amount
___ 6. Present value of a single amount	borrowed/lent.
___ 7. Annuity due	f. Obligation to pay a sum of cash, the amount of which is fixed.
___ 8. Future value of a single amount	g. Money can be invested today and grow to a larger amount.
___ 9. Ordinary annuity	h. No fixed dollar amount attached.
___10. Effective rate or yield	i. Computed by multiplying an invested amount by the interest rate.
___11. Nonmonetary asset	j. Interest calculated on invested amount plus accumulated interest.
___12. Time value of money	k. A series of equal-sized cash flows.
___13. Monetary liability	l. Amount of money required today that is equivalent to a given future amount.
	m. Claim to receive a fixed amount of money.

CPA AND CMA REVIEW QUESTIONS

CPA Exam
Questions

SCHWESER

The following questions are used in the Kaplan CPA Review Course to study the time value of money while preparing for the CPA examination. Determine the response that best completes the statements or questions.

● LO7

1. On January 1, 2009, Ott Company sold goods to Fox Company. Fox signed a noninterest-bearing note requiring payment of $60,000 annually for seven years. The first payment was made on January 1, 2009. The prevailing rate of interest for this type of note at date of issuance was 10%. Information on present value factors is as follows:

Periods	Present Value of 1 at 10%	Present Value of Ordinary Annuity of 1 at 10%
6	.56	4.36
7	.51	4.87

Ott should record sales revenue in January 2009 of
a. $214,200
b. $261,600
c. $292,600
d. $321,600

● LO3

2. An investment product promises to pay $25,458 at the end of nine years. If an investor feels this investment should produce a rate of return of 14 percent, compounded annually, what's the most the investor should be willing to pay for the investment?

n	PV of $1 @ 14%
8	0.3506
9	0.3075
10	0.2697

a. $6,866
b. $7,828
c. $8,926
d. $9,426

● LO7

3. An annuity will pay eight annual payments of $100, with the first payment to be received one year from now. If the interest rate is 12 percent per year, what is the present value of this annuity? Use the appropriate table located at the end of the textbook to solve this problem.
a. $497
b. $556
c. $801
d. $897

● LO7

4. An annuity will pay four annual payments of $100, with the first payment to be received three years from now. If the interest rate is 12 percent per year, what is the present value of this annuity? Use the appropriate table located at the end of the textbook to solve this problem.

    a. $181
    b. $242
    c. $304
    d. $400

● LO7

5. Justin Banks just won the lottery and is trying to decide between the annual cash flow payment option of $100,000 per year for 15 years beginning today, or the lump sum option. Justin can earn 8 percent investing his money. At what lump-sum payment amount would he be indifferent between the two alternatives? Use the appropriate table located at the end of the textbook to solve this problem.

    a. $824,424
    b. $855,948
    c. $890,378
    d. $924,424

● LO3 LO7 LO9

6. An investor purchases a 10-year, $1,000 par value bond that pays *annual* interest of $100. If the market rate of interest is 12 percent, what is the current market value of the bond?

    a. $ 887
    b. $ 950
    c. $1,000
    d. $1,100

● LO8

7. You borrow $15,000 to buy a car. The loan is to be paid off in monthly installments over five years at 12 percent interest annually. The first payment is due one month from today. If the present value of an ordinary annuity of $1 for 5 years @12% with monthly compounding is $44.955, what is the amount of each monthly payment?

    a. $334
    b. $456
    c. $546
    d. $680

CMA Exam
Questions

The following questions dealing with the time value of money are adapted from questions that previously appeared on Certified Management Accountant (CMA) examinations. The CMA designation sponsored by the Institute of Management Accountants (**www.imanet.org**) provides members with an objective measure of knowledge and competence in the field of management accounting. Determine the response that best completes the statements or questions.

● LO7 LO9

1. Essex Corporation is evaluating a lease that takes effect on March 1. The company must make eight equal payments, with the first payment due on March 1. The concept most relevant to the evaluation of the lease is

    a. The present value of an annuity due.
    b. The present value of an ordinary annuity.
    c. The future value of an annuity due.
    d. The future value of an ordinary annuity.

● LO2

2. Janet Taylor Casual Wear has $75,000 in a bank account as of December 31, 2007. If the company plans on depositing $4,000 in the account at the end of each of the next 3 years (2008, 2009, and 2010) and all amounts in the account earn 8% per year, what will the account balance be at December 31, 2010? Ignore the effect of income taxes.

	8% Interest Rate Factors	
Period	Future Value of an Amount of $1	Future Value of an Ordinary Annuity of $1
1	1.08	1.00
2	1.17	2.08
3	1.26	3.25
4	1.36	4.51

    a. $ 87,000
    b. $ 88,000
    c. $ 96,070
    d. $107,500

PROBLEMS   available with McGraw–Hill's Homework Manager www.mhhe.com/spiceland5e

An alternate exercise and problem set is available on the text website: www.mhhe.com/spiceland5e

P 6–1
Analysis of
alternatives

● LO3 LO7

Esquire Company needs to acquire a molding machine to be used in its manufacturing process. Two types of machines that would be appropriate are presently on the market. The company has determined the following:

Machine A could be purchased for $48,000. It will last 10 years with annual maintenance costs of $1,000 per year. After 10 years the machine can be sold for $5,000.

Machine B could be purchased for $40,000. It also will last 10 years and will require maintenance costs of $4,000 in year three, $5,000 in year six, and $6,000 in year eight. After 10 years, the machine will have no salvage value.

Required:
Determine which machine Esquire should purchase. Assume an interest rate of 8% properly reflects the time value of money in this situation and that maintenance costs are paid at the end of each year. Ignore income tax considerations.

P 6–2
Present and future
value

● LO6 LO7 LO9

Johnstone Company is facing several decisions regarding investing and financing activities. Address each decision independently.

1. On June 30, 2009, the Johnstone Company purchased equipment from Genovese Corp. Johnstone agreed to pay Genovese $10,000 on the purchase date and the balance in five annual installments of $8,000 on each June 30 beginning June 30, 2010. Assuming that an interest rate of 10% properly reflects the time value of money in this situation, at what amount should Johnstone value the equipment?

2. Johnstone needs to accumulate sufficient funds to pay a $400,000 debt that comes due on December 31, 2014. The company will accumulate the funds by making five equal annual deposits to an account paying 6% interest compounded annually. Determine the required annual deposit if the first deposit is made on December 31, 2009.

3. On January 1, 2009, Johnstone leased an office building. Terms of the lease require Johnstone to make 20 annual lease payments of $120,000 beginning on January 1, 2009. A 10% interest rate is implicit in the lease agreement. At what amount should Johnstone record the lease liability on January 1, 2009, *before* any lease payments are made?

P 6–3
Analysis of
alternatives

● LO3 LO7

Harding Company is in the process of purchasing several large pieces of equipment from Danning Machine Corporation. Several financing alternatives have been offered by Danning:
1. Pay $1,000,000 in cash immediately.
2. Pay $420,000 immediately and the remainder in 10 annual installments of $80,000, with the first installment due in one year.
3. Make 10 annual installments of $135,000 with the first payment due immediately.
4. Make one lump-sum payment of $1,500,000 five years from date of purchase.

Required:
Determine the best alternative for Harding, assuming that Harding can borrow funds at an 8% interest rate.

P 6–4
Investment analysis

● LO3 LO7

John Wiggins is contemplating the purchase of a small restaurant. The purchase price listed by the seller is $800,000. John has used past financial information to estimate that the net cash flows (cash inflows less cash outflows) generated by the restaurant would be as follows:

Years	Amount
1–6	$80,000
7	70,000
8	60,000
9	50,000
10	40,000

If purchased, the restaurant would be held for 10 years and then sold for an estimated $700,000.

Required:
Assuming that John desires a 10% rate of return on this investment, should the restaurant be purchased? (Assume that all cash flows occur at the end of the year.)

P 6–5
Investment decision;
varying rates

John and Sally Claussen are contemplating the purchase of a hardware store from John Duggan. The Claussens anticipate that the store will generate cash flows of $70,000 per year for 20 years. At the end of 20 years, they intend to sell the store for an estimated $400,000. The Claussens will finance the investment with a variable rate

● LO3 LO7

mortgage. Interest rates will increase twice during the 20-year life of the mortgage. Accordingly, the Claussens' desired rate of return on this investment varies as follows:

Years 1–5	8%
Years 6–10	10%
Years 11–20	12%

Required:
What is the maximum amount the Claussens should pay John Duggan for the hardware store? (Assume that all cash flows occur at the end of the year.)

P 6–6
Solving for unknowns

● LO8

The following situations should be considered independently.
1. John Jamison wants to accumulate $60,000 for a down payment on a small business. He will invest $30,000 today in a bank account paying 8% interest compounded annually. Approximately how long will it take John to reach his goal?
2. The Jasmine Tea Company purchased merchandise from a supplier for $28,700. Payment was a noninterest-bearing note requiring Jasmine to make five annual payments of $7,000 beginning one year from the date of purchase. What is the interest rate implicit in this agreement?
3. Sam Robinson borrowed $10,000 from a friend and promised to pay the loan in 10 equal annual installments beginning one year from the date of the loan. Sam's friend would like to be reimbursed for the time value of money at a 9% annual rate. What is the annual payment Sam must make to pay back his friend?

P 6–7
Solving for unknowns

● LO8

Lowlife Company defaulted on a $250,000 loan that was due on December 31, 2009. The bank has agreed to allow Lowlife to repay the $250,000 by making a series of equal annual payments beginning on December 31, 2010.
Required:
1. Calculate the required annual payment if the bank's interest rate is 10% and four payments are to be made.
2. Calculate the required annual payment if the bank's interest rate is 8% and five payments are to be made.
3. If the bank's interest rate is 10%, how many annual payments of $51,351 would be required to repay the debt?
4. If three payments of $104,087 are to be made, what interest rate is the bank charging Lowlife?

P 6–8
Deferred annuities

● LO7

On January 1, 2009, the Montgomery company agreed to purchase a building by making six payments. The first three are to be $25,000 each, and will be paid on December 31, 2009, 2010, and 2011. The last three are to be $40,000 each and will be paid on December 31, 2012, 2013, and 2014. Montgomery borrowed other money at a 10% annual rate.
Required:
1. At what amount should Montgomery record the note payable and corresponding cost of the building on January 1, 2009?
2. How much interest expense on this note will Montgomery recognize in 2009?

P 6–9
Deferred annuities

● LO7

John Roberts is 55 years old and has been asked to accept early retirement from his company. The company has offered John three alternative compensation packages to induce John to retire:
1. $180,000 cash payment to be paid immediately.
2. A 20-year annuity of $16,000 beginning immediately.
3. A 10-year annuity of $50,000 beginning at age 65.

Required:
Which alternative should John choose assuming that he is able to invest funds at a 7% rate?

P 6–10
Noninterest-bearing note; annuity and lump-sum payment

● LO3 LO7

On January 1, 2009, The Barrett Company purchased merchandise from a supplier. Payment was a noninterest-bearing note requiring five annual payments of $20,000 on each December 31 beginning on December 31, 2009, and a lump-sum payment of $100,000 on December 31, 2013. A 10% interest rate properly reflects the time value of money in this situation.
Required:
Calculate the amount at which Barrett should record the note payable and corresponding merchandise purchased on January 1, 2009.

P 6–11
Solving for unknown lease payment

● LO8 LO9

Benning Manufacturing Company is negotiating with a customer for the lease of a large machine manufactured by Benning. The machine has a cash price of $800,000. Benning wants to be reimbursed for financing the machine at an 8% annual interest rate.
Required:
1. Determine the required lease payment if the lease agreement calls for 10 equal annual payments beginning immediately.

2. Determine the required lease payment if the first of 10 annual payments will be made one year from the date of the agreement.

3. Determine the required lease payment if the first of 10 annual payments will be made immediately and Benning will be able to sell the machine to another customer for $50,000 at the end of the 10-year lease.

P 6–12
Solving for
unknown lease
payment;
compounding
periods of varying
length

● LO9

(This is a variation of the previous problem focusing on compounding periods of varying length.)

Benning Manufacturing Company is negotiating with a customer for the lease of a large machine manufactured by Benning. The machine has a cash price of $800,000. Benning wants to be reimbursed for financing the machine at a 12% annual interest rate over the five-year lease term.

Required:

1. Determine the required lease payment if the lease agreement calls for 10 equal semiannual payments beginning six months from the date of the agreement.

2. Determine the required lease payment if the lease agreement calls for 20 equal quarterly payments beginning immediately.

3. Determine the required lease payment if the lease agreement calls for 60 equal monthly payments beginning one month from the date of the agreement. The present value of an ordinary annuity factor for $n = 60$ and $i = 1\%$ is 44.9550.

P 6–13
Lease vs. buy
alternatives

● LO3 LO7 LO9

Kiddy Toy Corporation needs to acquire the use of a machine to be used in its manufacturing process. The machine needed is manufactured by Lollie Corp. The machine can be used for 10 years and then sold for $10,000 at the end of its useful life. Lollie has presented Kiddy with the following options:

1. *Buy machine.* The machine could be purchased for $160,000 in cash. All maintenance and insurance costs, which approximate $5,000 per year, would be paid by Kiddy.

2. *Lease machine.* The machine could be leased for a 10-year period for an annual lease payment of $25,000 with the first payment due immediately. All maintenance and insurance costs will be paid for by the Lollie Corp. and the machine will revert back to Lollie at the end of the 10-year period.

Required:

Assuming that a 12% interest rate properly reflects the time value of money in this situation and that all maintenance and insurance costs are paid at the end of each year, determine which option Kiddy should choose. Ignore income tax considerations.

P 6–14
Deferred annuities;
pension obligation

● LO7 LO9

Three employees of the Horizon Distributing Company will receive annual pension payments from the company when they retire. The employees will receive their annual payments for as long as they live. Life expectancy for each employee is 15 years beyond retirement. Their names, the amount of their annual pension payments, and the date they will receive their first payment are shown below:

Employee	Annual Payment	Date of First Payment
Tinkers	$20,000	12/31/12
Evers	25,000	12/31/13
Chance	30,000	12/31/14

Required:

1. Compute the present value of the pension obligation to these three employees as of December 31, 2009. Assume an 11% interest rate.

2. The company wants to have enough cash invested at December 31, 2012, to provide for all three employees. To accumulate enough cash, they will make three equal annual contributions to a fund that will earn 11% interest compounded annually. The first contribution will be made on December 31, 2009. Compute the amount of this required annual contribution.

P 6–15
Bonds and leases;
deferred annuities

● LO3 LO7 LO9

On the last day of its fiscal year ending December 31, 2009, the Sedgwick & Reams (S&R) Glass Company completed two financing arrangements. The funds provided by these initiatives will allow the company to expand its operations.

1. S&R issued 8% stated rate bonds with a face amount of $100 million. The bonds mature on December 31, 2029 (20 years). The market rate of interest for similar bond issues was 9% (4.5% semiannual rate). Interest is paid semiannually (4%) on June 30 and December 31, beginning on June 30, 2010.

2. The company leased two manufacturing facilities. Lease A requires 20 annual lease payments of $200,000 beginning on January 1, 2010. Lease B also is for 20 years, beginning January 1, 2010. Terms of the lease require 17 annual lease payments of $220,000 beginning on January 1, 2013. Accounting standards require both leases to be recorded as liabilities for the present value of the scheduled payments. Assume that a 10% interest rate properly reflects the time value of money for the lease obligations.

Required:

What amounts will appear in S&R's December 31, 2009, balance sheet for the bonds and for the leases?

BROADEN YOUR PERSPECTIVE

Apply your critical-thinking ability to the knowledge you've gained. These cases will provide you an opportunity to develop your research, analysis, judgment, and communication skills. You also will work with other students, integrate what you've learned, apply it in real world situations, and consider its global and ethical ramifications. This practice will broaden your knowledge and further develop your decision-making abilities.

Analysis
Case 6–1
Present value of an annuity

● LO7

On a rainy afternoon two years ago, John Smiley left work early to attend a family birthday party. Eleven minutes later, a careening truck slammed into his SUV on the freeway causing John to spend two months in a coma. Now he can't hold a job or make everyday decisions and is in need of constant care. Last week, the 40-year old Smiley won an out-of-court settlement from the truck driver's company. He was awarded payment for all medical costs and attorney fees, plus a lump-sum settlement of $2,330,716. At the time of the accident, John was president of his family's business and earned approximately $200,000 per year. He had anticipated working 25 more years before retirement.[8]

John's sister, an acquaintance of yours from college, has asked you to explain to her how the attorneys came up with the settlement amount. "They said it was based on his lost future income and a 7% rate of some kind," she explained. "But it was all 'legal-speak' to me."

Required:
How was the amount of the lump-sum settlement determined? Create a calculation that might help John's sister understand.

Analysis
Case 6–2
Bonus alternatives; present value analysis

● LO3 LO7

Sally Hamilton has performed well as the chief financial officer of the Maxtech Computer Company and has earned a bonus. She has a choice among the following three bonus plans:
1. A $50,000 cash bonus paid now.
2. A $10,000 annual cash bonus to be paid each year over the next six years, with the first $10,000 paid now.
3. A three-year $22,000 annual cash bonus with the first payment due three years from now.

Required:
Evaluate the three alternative bonus plans. Sally can earn a 6% annual return on her investments.

Communication
Case 6–3
Present value of annuities

● LO7

Harvey Alexander, an all-league professional football player, has just declared free agency. Two teams, the San Francisco 49ers and the Dallas Cowboys, have made Harvey the following offers to obtain his services:

49ers: $1 million signing bonus payable immediately and an annual salary of $1.5 million for the five-year term of the contract.

Cowboys: $2.5 million signing bonus payable immediately and an annual salary of $1 million for the five-year term of the contract.

With both contracts, the annual salary will be paid in one lump-sum at the end of the football season.

Required:
You have been hired as a consultant to Harvey's agent, Phil Marks, to evaluate the two contracts. Write a short letter to Phil with your recommendation including the method you used to reach your conclusion. Assume that Harvey has no preference between the two teams and that the decision will be based entirely on monetary considerations. Also assume that Harvey can invest his money and earn an 8% annual return.

Ethics Case 6–4
Rate of return

● LO1

The Damon Investment Company manages a mutual fund composed mostly of speculative stocks. You recently saw an ad claiming that investments in the funds have been earning a rate of return of 21%. This rate seemed quite high so you called a friend who works for one of Damon's competitors. The friend told you that the 21% return figure was determined by dividing the two-year appreciation on investments in the fund by the average investment. In other words, $100 invested in the fund two years ago would have grown to $121 ($21 ÷ $100 = 21%).

Required:
Discuss the ethics of the 21% return claim made by the Damon Investment Company.

Judgment
Case 6–5
Replacement decision

● LO3 LO7

Hughes Corporation is considering replacing a machine used in the manufacturing process with a new, more efficient model. The purchase price of the new machine is $150,000 and the old machine can be sold for $100,000. Output for the two machines is identical; they will both be used to produce the same amount of product for five years. However, the annual operating costs of the old machine are $18,000 compared to $10,000 for the new machine. Also, the new machine has a salvage value of $25,000, but the old machine will be worthless at the end of the five years.

Required:
Should the company sell the old machine and purchase the new model? Assume that an 8% rate properly reflects the time value of money in this situation and that all operating costs are paid at the end of the year. Ignore the effect of the decision on income taxes.

---

[8]This case is based on actual events.

Real World
Case 6–6
Zero-coupon bonds

● LO3 LO9

Real World Financials

Johnson & Johnson is one of the world's largest manufacturers of health care products. The company's 2007 financial statements included the following information in the long-term debt disclosure note:

	($ in millions) 2007
Zero-coupon convertible subordinated debentures, due 2020	$178

The disclosure note stated that the debenture bonds were issued early in 2000 and have a maturity value of $272.5 million. The maturity value indicates the amount that Johnson & Johnson will pay bondholders in 2020. Each individual bond has a maturity value (face amount) of $1,000. Zero-coupon bonds pay no cash interest during the term to maturity. The company is "accreting" (gradually increasing) the issue price to maturity value using the bonds' effective interest rate computed on a semiannual basis.

Required:
1. Determine the effective interest rate on the bonds.
2. Determine the issue price in early 2000 of a single, $1,000 maturity-value bond.

Real World
Case 6–7
Leases

● LO3 LO9

Real World Financials

Southwest Airlines provides scheduled air transportation services in the United States. Like many airlines, Southwest leases many of its planes from **Boeing Company.** In its long-term debt disclosure note included in the financial statements for the year ended December 31, 2007, the company listed $52 million in lease obligations. The note also disclosed that existing leases had a five-year remaining life and that future lease payments averaged approximately $13 million per year.

Required:
1. Determine the effective interest rate the company used to determine the lease liability assuming that lease payments are made at the end of each fiscal year.
2. Repeat requirement 1 assuming that lease payments are made at the beginning of each fiscal year.

7

Cash and Receivables

/// OVERVIEW

We begin our study of assets by looking at cash and receivables—
the two assets typically listed first in a balance sheet. Internal
control and classification in the balance sheet are key issues we
address in consideration of cash. For receivables, the key issues
are valuation and the related income statement effects of
transactions involving accounts receivable and notes receivable.

|||||| LEARNING OBJECTIVES ||||||||||||||||

After studying this chapter, you should be able to:

- **LO1** Define what is meant by internal control and describe some key elements of an internal control system for cash receipts and disbursements.
- **LO2** Explain the possible restrictions on cash and their implications for classification in the balance sheet.
- **LO3** Distinguish between the gross and net methods of accounting for cash discounts.
- **LO4** Describe the accounting treatment for merchandise returns.
- **LO5** Describe the accounting treatment of anticipated uncollectible accounts receivable.
- **LO6** Describe the two approaches to estimating bad debts.
- **LO7** Describe the accounting treatment of short-term notes receivable.
- **LO8** Differentiate between the use of receivables in financing arrangements accounted for as a secured borrowing and those accounted for as a sale.
- **LO9** Describe the variables that influence a company's investment in receivables and calculate the key ratios used by analysts to monitor that investment.

FINANCIAL REPORTING CASE

What Does It All Mean?

Your roommate, Todd Buckley, was surfing the net looking for information about his future employer, Cisco Systems. Todd, an engineering major, recently accepted a position with Cisco, the world's largest provider of hardware, software, and services that drive the Internet. He noticed an article on TheStreet.com entitled "Cisco Triples Bad-Account Provision." "This doesn't look good," Todd grumbled. "The article says that my new employer's deadbeat account column has more than tripled in the span of a year. I guess all those dot-com companies are not paying their bills. But this sentence is confusing. 'For the fiscal first quarter Cisco moved $275 million from operating cash to cover potential nonpayments from failed customers.' Did they actually move cash and if so, where did they move it and why?"

You studied accounting for bad debts in your intermediate accounting class and are confident you can help. After reading the article, you comfort Todd. "First of all, the term *provision* just means expense, and no, Cisco didn't move any cash. The company uses what is called the *allowance method* to account for its bad debts, and it looks like it simply recorded $275 million in expense for the quarter and increased the allowance for uncollectible accounts." Todd was not happy with your answer. "Provisions! allowance method! uncollectible accounts! I want you to help me understand, not make things worse." "Okay," you offer, "let's start at the beginning."

By the time you finish this chapter, you should be able to respond appropriately to the questions posed in this case. Compare your response to the solution provided at the end of the chapter.

QUESTIONS ///

1. Explain the allowance method of accounting for bad debts. (page 336)
2. What approaches might Cisco have used to arrive at the $275 million bad debt provision? (page 337)
3. Are there any alternatives to the allowance method? (page 340)

In the earlier chapters of this text, we studied the underlying measurement and reporting concepts for the basic financial statements presented to external decision makers. Now we turn our attention to the elements of those financial statements. Specifically, we further explore the elements of the balance sheet including the income statement effects of transactions involving these elements. We first address assets, then liabilities, and finally shareholders' equity. This chapter focuses on the current assets cash and cash equivalents and receivables.

CASH AND CASH EQUIVALENTS

Cash includes currency and coins, balances in checking accounts, and items acceptable for deposit in these accounts, such as checks and money orders received from customers. These forms of cash represent amounts readily available to pay off debt or to use in operations without any legal or contractual restriction.

Managers typically invest temporarily idle cash to earn interest on those funds rather than keep an unnecessarily large checking account. These amounts are essentially equivalent to cash because they can quickly become available for use as cash. So, short-term, highly liquid investments that can be readily converted to cash with little risk of loss are viewed as cash equivalents. For financial reporting we make no distinction between cash in the form of currency or bank account balances and amounts held in cash equivalent investments.

> A company's policy concerning which short-term, highly liquid investments it classifies as cash equivalents should be described in a disclosure note.

Cash equivalents include such things as certain money market funds, treasury bills, and commercial paper. To be classified as cash equivalents, these investments must have a maturity date no longer than three months *from the date of purchase*. Companies are permitted flexibility in designating cash equivalents and must establish individual policies regarding which short-term, highly liquid investments are classified as cash equivalents. A company's policy should be consistent with the usual motivation for acquiring certain types of investments. The policy should be disclosed in the notes to the financial statements. Graphic 7–1 shows a note from a recent annual report of the **Walgreen Co.** that provides a description of the company's cash equivalents.

GRAPHIC 7–1

Disclosure of Cash Equivalents—Walgreen Co.

Real World Financials

Summary of Significant Accounting Policies (in part)
Cash and Cash Equivalents

Cash and cash equivalents include cash on hand and all highly liquid investments with a maturity of three months or less. Included in cash and cash equivalents are credit card and debit card receivables from banks, which settle within two business days.

> Credit and debit card receivables often are included in cash equivalents.

Notice in the disclosure note that Walgreen includes credit card and debit card receivables from banks as cash equivalents. These receivables typically are converted to cash within a few business days.

The measurement and reporting of cash and cash equivalents are largely straightforward because cash generally presents no measurement problems. It is the standard medium of exchange and the basis for measuring assets and liabilities. Cash and cash equivalents usually are combined and reported as a single amount in the balance sheet. However, cash that is not available for use in current operations because it is restricted for a special purpose usually is classified in one of the noncurrent asset categories. Restricted cash is discussed later in this chapter.

All assets must be safeguarded against possible misuse. However, cash is the most liquid asset and the asset most easily expropriated. As a result, a system of internal control of cash is a key accounting issue.

Internal Control

● LO1

The success of any business enterprise depends on an effective system of internal control. Internal control refers to a company's plan to (a) encourage adherence to company policies and procedures, (b) promote operational efficiency, (c) minimize errors and theft, and (d) enhance the reliability and accuracy of accounting data. From a financial accounting perspective, the focus is on controls intended to improve the accuracy and reliability of accounting information and to safeguard the company's assets.

> The Sarbanes-Oxley Act requires a company to document and assess its internal controls. Auditors express an opinion on management's assessment.

Recall from our discussion in Chapter 1 that Section 404 of the *Sarbanes-Oxley Act of 2002* requires that companies not only document their internal controls and assess their adequacy, but that their auditors must provide an opinion on management's assessment. The Public Company Accounting Oversight Board's *Auditing Standard No. 2* further requires the auditor to express its own opinion on whether the company has maintained effective internal control over financial reporting.

Many companies have incurred significant costs in an effort to comply with the require-ments of Section 404.[1] A cottage industry of consulting firms and software products has arisen to help these companies. A framework for designing an internal control system is provided by the Committee of Sponsoring Organizations (COSO) of the Treadway Com-mission.[2] Formed in 1985, the organization is dedicated to improving the quality of financial reporting through, among other things, effective internal controls.

COSO defines internal control as a process, effected by an entity's board of directors, management and other personnel, designed to provide reasonable assurance regarding the achievement of objectives in the following categories:

- Effectiveness and efficiency of operations.
- Reliability of financial reporting.
- Compliance with applicable laws and regulations.[3]

A critical aspect of an internal control system is the *separation of duties*. Individuals that have physical responsibility for assets should not also have access to accounting records. For example, if the same individual has control of both the supplies inventory and the account-ing records, the theft of supplies could be concealed by a reduction of the supplies account.

Employees involved in recordkeeping should not also have physical access to the assets.

As cash is the most liquid of all assets, a well-designed and functioning system of inter-nal control must surround all cash transactions. Separation of duties is critical. Ideally, those who handle cash should not be involved in or have access to accounting records nor be involved in the reconciliation of cash book balances to bank balances.

Internal Control Procedures—Cash Receipts

Consider the cash receipt process. Most nonretail businesses receive payment for goods by checks received through the mail. An approach to internal control over cash receipts might include the following steps:

1. Employee A opens the mail each day and prepares a multicopy listing of all checks including the amount and payor's name.
2. Employee B takes the checks, along with one copy of the listing, to the person responsible for depositing the checks in the company's bank account.
3. A second copy of the check listing is sent to the accounting department where the receipts are entered into the records.

The amount received should equal the amount deposited as verified by comparison with the bank-generated deposit slip and the amount recorded in the accounting records. This helps ensure accuracy as well as safeguard cash against theft.

Internal Control Procedures—Cash Disbursements

Proper controls for cash disbursements should be designed to prevent any unauthorized pay-ments and ensure that disbursements are recorded in the proper general ledger and subsid-iary ledger accounts. Important elements of a cash disbursement control system include:

1. All disbursements, other than very small disbursements from petty cash, should be made by check. This provides a permanent record of all disbursements.
2. All expenditures should be *authorized* before a check is prepared. For example, a vendor invoice for the purchase of inventory should be compared with the purchase order and receiving report to ensure the accuracy of quantity, price, part numbers, and so on. This process should include verification of the proper ledger accounts to be debited.
3. Checks should be signed only by authorized individuals.

---

[1]In response to the high cost of 404 compliance, the PCAOB issued a second standard, *Auditing Standard No. 5*, to replace its Standard No. 2. The new standard emphasizes audit efficiency with a more focused, risk-based testing approach for material areas. These guide-lines should reduce the total costs of 404 compliance.

[2]The sponsoring organizations include the AICPA, the Financial Executives International, the Institute of Internal Auditors, the American Accounting Association, and the Institute of Management Accountants.

[3]www.coso.org.

Responsibilities for check signing, check writing, check mailing, cash disbursement documentation, and recordkeeping ideally should be separated whenever possible.

An important part of any system of internal control of cash is the periodic reconciliation of book balances and bank balances to the correct balance. In addition, a petty cash system is employed by many business enterprises. We cover these two topics in Appendix 7 beginning on page 354.

Restricted Cash and Compensating Balances

● LO2

We discussed the classification of assets and liabilities in Chapter 3. You should recall that only cash available for current operations or to satisfy current liabilities is classified as a current asset. Cash that is restricted in some way and not available for current use usually is reported as *investments and funds* or *other assets.*

Restrictions on cash can be informal, arising from management's intent to use a certain amount of cash for a specific purpose. For example, a company may set aside funds for future plant expansion. This cash, if material, should be classified as investments and funds or other assets. Sometimes restrictions are contractually imposed. Debt instruments, for instance, frequently require the borrower to set aside funds (often referred to as a sinking fund) for the future payment of a debt. In these instances, the restricted cash is classified as investments and funds or other assets if the debt is classified as noncurrent. On the other hand, if the liability is current, the restricted cash also is classified as current. Disclosure notes should describe any material restrictions of cash.

The effect of a *compensating balance* is a higher effective interest rate on the debt.

Banks frequently require cash restrictions in connection with loans or loan commitments (lines of credit). Typically, the borrower is asked to maintain a specified balance in a low-interest or noninterest-bearing account at the bank (creditor). The required balance usually is some percentage of the committed amount (say 2% to 5%). These are known as compensating balances because they compensate the bank for granting the loan or extending the line of credit.

A compensating balance results in the borrower's paying an effective interest rate higher than the stated rate on the debt. For example, suppose that a company borrows $10,000,000 from a bank at an interest rate of 12%. If the bank requires a compensating balance of $2,000,000 to be held in a noninterest-bearing checking account, the company really is borrowing only $8,000,000 (the loan less the compensating balance). This means an effective interest rate of 15% ($1,200,000 interest divided by $8,000,000 cash available for use).

A material compensating balance must be disclosed regardless of the classification of the cash.

The classification and disclosure of a compensating balance depends on the nature of the restriction and the classification of the related debt.[4] If the restriction is legally binding, the cash is classified as either current or noncurrent (investments and funds or other assets) depending on the classification of the related debt. In either case, note disclosure is appropriate.

If the compensating balance arrangement is informal with no contractual agreement that restricts the use of cash, the compensating balance can be reported as part of cash and cash equivalents, with note disclosure of the arrangement. Graphic 7–2 provides an example of a note disclosure of a compensating balance for **CNB Financial Services, Inc.,** a bank holding company incorporated in West Virginia.

GRAPHIC 7–2

Disclosure of Compensating Balances—CNB Financial Services, Inc.

Real World Financials

> **Note 10—Lines of Credit (in part)**
>
> The Bank entered into an open-ended unsecured line of credit with Mercantile Safe Deposit and Trust Company for $3,000,000 for federal fund purchases. Funds issued under this agreement are at the Mercantile Safe Deposit and Trust Company federal funds rate effective at the time of borrowing. The line . . . has a compensating balance requirement of $250,000.

---

[4]"Amendments to Regulations S-X and Related Interpretations and Guidelines Regarding the Disclosure of Compensating Balances and Short-Term Borrowing Arrangements," *Accounting Series Release No. 148,* Securities and Exchange Commission (November 13, 1973).

DECISION MAKERS' PERSPECTIVE

Cash often is referred to as a *nonearning* asset because it earns no interest. For this reason, managers invest idle cash in either cash equivalents or short-term investments, both of which provide a return. Management's goal is to hold the minimum amount of cash necessary to conduct normal business operations, meet its obligations, and take advantage of opportunities. Too much cash reduces profits through lost returns, while too little cash increases risk. This tradeoff between risk and return is an ongoing choice made by internal decision makers. Whether the choice made is appropriate is an ongoing assessment made by investors and creditors.

A company must have cash available for the compensating balances we discussed in the previous section as well as for planned disbursements related to normal operating, investing, and financing cash flows. However, because cash inflows and outflows can vary from planned amounts, a company needs an additional cash cushion as a precaution against that contingency. The size of the cushion depends on the company's ability to convert cash equivalents and short-term investments into cash quickly, along with its short-term borrowing capacity.

Liquidity is a measure of a company's cash position and overall ability to obtain cash in the normal course of business. A company is assumed to be liquid if it has sufficient cash or is capable of converting its other assets to cash in a relatively short period of time so that current needs can be met. Frequently, liquidity is measured with respect to the ability to pay currently maturing debt. The current ratio is one of the most common ways of measuring liquidity and is calculated by dividing current assets by current liabilities. By comparing liabilities that must be satisfied in the near term with assets that either are cash or will be converted to cash in the near term we have a base measure of a company's liquidity. We can refine the measure by adjusting for the implicit assumption of the current ratio that all current assets are equally liquid. In the acid-test or quick ratio, the numerator consists of "quick assets," which include only cash and cash equivalents, short-term investments, and accounts receivable. By eliminating inventories and prepaid expenses, the current assets that are less readily convertible into cash, we get a more precise indication of a company's short-term solvency than with the current ratio. We discussed and illustrated these liquidity ratios in Chapter 3.

We should evaluate the adequacy of any ratio in the context of the industry in which the company operates and other specific circumstances. Bear in mind, though, that industry averages are only one indication of acceptability and any ratio is but one indication of liquidity. Profitability, for instance, is perhaps the best long-run indication of liquidity. And a company may be very efficient in managing its current assets so that, say, receivables are more liquid than they otherwise would be. The receivables turnover ratio we discuss in Part B of this chapter offers a measure of management's efficiency in this regard.

There are many techniques that a company can use to manage cash balances. A discussion of these techniques is beyond the scope of this text. However, it is sufficient here to understand that management must make important decisions related to cash that have a direct impact on a company's profitability and risk. Because the lack of prudent cash management can lead to the failure of an otherwise sound company, it is essential that managers as well as outside investors and creditors maintain close vigil over this facet of a company's health. ●

> Companies hold cash to pay for planned and unplanned transactions and to satisfy compensating balance requirements.

> A liquidity ratio is but one indication of a company's liquidity.

> A manager should actively monitor the company's cash position.

CURRENT RECEIVABLES

PART B

Receivables represent a company's claims to the future collection of cash, other assets, or services. Receivables resulting from the sale of goods or services on account are called accounts receivable and often are referred to as *trade receivables*. Nontrade receivables are those other than trade receivables and include tax refund claims, interest receivable, and loans by the company to other entities including stockholders and employees. When a receivable, trade or nontrade, is accompanied by a formal promissory note, it is referred to as a note receivable. We consider notes receivable after first discussing accounts receivable.

An account receivable
and an account payable
are two sides of the
same coin.

As you study receivables, realize that one company's claim to the future collection of cash corresponds to another company's (or individual's) obligation to pay cash. One company's account receivable will be the mirror image of another company's account payable—the measurement issues are identical. Chapter 13 addresses accounts payable and other current liabilities.

Accounts Receivable

Accounts receivable are
current assets because,
by definition, they
will be converted to
cash within the normal
operating cycle.

Most businesses provide credit to their customers, either because it's not practical to require immediate cash payment or to encourage customers to purchase the company's product or service. Accounts receivable are *informal* credit arrangements supported by an invoice and normally are due in 30 to 60 days after the sale. They almost always are classified as *current* assets because their normal collection period, even if longer than a year, is part of, and therefore less than, the operating cycle.

Typically, revenue
and related accounts
receivable are
recognized at the
point of delivery of the
product or service.

The point at which accounts receivable are recognized depends on the earnings process of the company. We discussed the realization principle in Chapter 5 and the criteria that must be met before revenue can be recognized. Recall that revenue can be recognized only after the earnings process is *virtually complete* and *collection* from the customer is *reasonably assured.* For the typical credit sale, these criteria are satisfied at the point of delivery of the product or service, so revenue and the related receivable are recognized at that time.

Initial Valuation of Accounts Receivable

We know from prior discussions that receivables should be recorded at the present value of future cash receipts using a realistic interest rate. So, a $10,000 sale on credit due in 30 days should result in a receivable valued at the present value of the $10,000. In other words, the interest portion of the $10,000 due in 30 days should be removed and recognized as interest revenue over the 30-day period, not as sales revenue at date of delivery of the product. If the monthly interest rate is 2%, the receivable would be valued at $9,804, calculated by multiplying the future cash payment of $10,000 by the present value of $1 factor for one period at 2% (.98039).

The typical account
receivable is valued at
the amount expected
to be received, not the
present value of that
amount.

However, because the difference between the future and present values of accounts receivable often is immaterial, *APB Opinion 21* specifically excludes accounts receivable from the general rule that receivables be recorded at present value.[5] Therefore, accounts receivable initially are valued at the exchange price agreed on by the buyer and seller. In our example, both the account receivable and sales revenue would be recorded at $10,000. Let's discuss two aspects of accounts receivable related to their initial valuation—trade discounts and cash discounts.

TRADE DISCOUNTS. Companies frequently offer trade discounts to customers, usually a percentage reduction from the list price. Trade discounts can be a way to change prices without publishing a new catalog or to disguise real prices from competitors. They also are used to give quantity discounts to large customers. For example, a manufacturer might list a machine part at $2,500 but sell it to a customer at list less a 10% discount. The trade discount of $250 is not recognized directly when recording the transaction. The discount is recognized indirectly by recording the sale at the net of discount price of $2,250, not at the list price.

Cash discounts reduce
the amount to be paid
if remittance is made
within a specified short
period of time.

CASH DISCOUNTS. Be careful to distinguish a *trade* discount from a *cash* discount. Cash discounts, often called *sales discounts,* represent reductions not in the selling price of a good or service but in the amount to be paid by a credit customer if paid within a specified period of time. It is a discount intended to provide incentive for quick payment.

● LO3

The amount of the discount and the time period within which it's available usually are conveyed by cryptic terms like 2/10, n/30 (meaning a 2% discount if paid within 10 days, otherwise full payment within 30 days). There are two ways to record cash discounts, the

---

[5]"Interest on Receivables and Payables," *Accounting Principles Board Opinion No. 21* (New York: AICPA, 1971).

gross method and the net method. Conceptually, the gross method views a discount not taken by the customer as part of sales of revenue. On the other hand, the net method considers sales revenue to be the net amount, after discount, and any discounts not taken by the customer as interest revenue. The discounts are viewed as compensation to the seller for providing financing to the customer. With both methods, discounts *taken* reduce sales revenue. Consider the example in Illustration 7–1.

The gross method views cash discounts not taken as part of sales revenue.

ILLUSTRATION 7–1
Cash Discounts

The Hawthorne Manufacturing Company offers credit customers a 2% cash discount if the sales price is paid within 10 days. Any amounts not paid within 10 days are due in 30 days. These repayment terms are stated as 2/10, n/30. On October 5, 2009, Hawthorne sold merchandise at a price of $20,000. The customer paid $13,720 ($14,000 less the 2% cash discount) on October 14 and the remaining balance of $6,000 on November 4.

The appropriate journal entries to record the sale and cash collection, comparing the gross and net methods are as follows:

Gross Method			Net Method		
October 5, 2009					
Accounts receivable	20,000		Accounts receivable	19,600	
Sales revenue		20,000	Sales revenue		19,600
October 14, 2009					
Cash	13,720		Cash	13,720	
Sales discounts	280		Accounts receivable		13,720
Accounts receivable		14,000			
November 4, 2009					
Cash	6,000		Cash	6,000	
Accounts receivable		6,000	Accounts receivable		5,880
			Interest revenue		120

By either method, net sales is reduced by discounts taken.

Discounts not taken are included in sales revenue using the gross method and interest revenue using the net method.

Notice that by using the gross method, we record the revenue and related receivable at the full $20,000 price. On remittance within the discount period, the $280 discount is recorded as a debit to an account called *sales discounts.* This is a contra account to sales revenue and is deducted from sales revenue to derive the net sales reported in the income statement. For payments made after the discount period, cash is simply increased and accounts receivable decreased by the gross amount originally recorded.

Under the net method, we record revenue and the related accounts receivable at the agreed on price *less* the 2% discount applied to the entire price. Payments made within the discount period are recorded as debits to cash and credits to accounts receivable for the amount received. If a customer loses a discount by failing to pay within the discount period, the discount not taken is recorded as interest revenue. In this case, $120 in cash (2% × $6,000) is interest.

The net method considers cash discounts not taken as interest revenue.

Total revenue in the 2009 income statement would be the same by either method:

	Gross Method	Net Method
Sales	$20,000	$19,600
Less: Sales discounts	(280)	–0–
Net sales revenue	19,720	19,600
Interest revenue	0	120
Total revenue	$19,720	$19,720

Revenue comparison of the gross method and the net method.

Which is correct? Conceptually, the net method usually reflects the reality of the situation— the real price is $19,600 and $120 is an interest penalty for not paying promptly. The net price usually is the price expected by the seller because the discount usually reflects a hefty interest cost that prudent buyers are unwilling to bear. Consider Illustration 7–1. Although the discount rate is stated as 2%, the effective rate really is 37.23%. In order to save $2, the buyer must pay $98 twenty days earlier than otherwise due, effectively "investing" $98 to "earn" $2, a rate of return of 2.04% ($2/$98) for a 20-day period. To convert this 20-day rate to an annual rate, we multiply by 365/20:

$$2.04\% \times 365/20 = 37.23\% \text{ effective rate}$$

Understandably, most buyers try to take the discount if at all possible.

The difference between the two methods, in terms of the effect of the transactions on income, is in the timing of the recognition of any discounts not taken. The gross method recognizes discounts not taken as revenue when the sale is made. The net method recognizes them as revenue after the discount period has passed and the cash is collected. These two measurement dates could be in different reporting periods.

From a practical standpoint, the effect on the financial statements of the difference between the two methods usually is immaterial. As a result, most companies use the gross method because it's easier and doesn't require adjusting entries for discounts not taken.

Subsequent Valuation of Accounts Receivable

Following the initial valuation of an account receivable, two situations possibly could cause the cash ultimately collected to be less than the initial valuation of the receivable: (1) the customer could return the product, or (2) the customer could default and not pay the agreed upon sales price. When accounting for sales and accounts receivable, we anticipate these possibilities.

● LO4

Recognizing sales returns *when they occur could result in an overstatement of income in the period of the related sale.*

SALES RETURNS.   Customers frequently are given the right to return the merchandise they purchase if they are not satisfied. We discussed how this policy affects revenue recognition in Chapter 5. We now discuss it from the perspective of asset valuation.

When merchandise is returned for a refund or for credit to be applied to other purchases, the situation is called a sales return. When practical, a dissatisfied customer might be given a special price reduction as an incentive to keep the merchandise purchased.[6] Returns are common and often substantial in some industries such as food products, publishing, and retailing. In these cases, recognizing returns and allowances only as they occur could cause profit to be overstated in the period of the sale and understated in the return period. For example, assume merchandise is sold to a customer for $10,000 in December 2009, the last month in the selling company's fiscal year, and that the merchandise cost $6,000. If all of the merchandise is returned in 2010 after financial statements for 2009 are issued, gross profit will be overstated in 2009 and understated in 2010 by $4,000. Assets at the end of 2009 also will be overstated by $4,000 because a $10,000 receivable would be recorded instead of $6,000 in inventory.

To avoid misstating the financial statements, when amounts are material, returns should be anticipated by subtracting an allowance for estimated returns. The allowance for sales returns is a contra account to accounts receivable. When returns actually occur in the following reporting period, the allowance for sales returns is debited. In this way, income is not reduced in the return period but in the period of the sales revenue.[7]

For an example, refer to Illustration 7–2. The perpetual inventory system records increases (debits) and decreases (credits) in the inventory account as they occur. The inventory of $78,000 in the first set of entries represents merchandise actually returned and on hand, while the inventory of $42,000 in the second set of entries represents an estimate of the cost of merchandise expected to be returned. This later amount is included in the period-end inventory in the company's balance sheet even though the actual merchandise belongs to other entities.

Assuming that the estimates of future returns are correct, the following (summary) journal entry would be recorded in 2010:

Allowance for sales returns	70,000	
Accounts receivable		70,000

---

[6]Price reductions sometimes are referred to as *sales allowances* and are distinguished from situations when the products actually are returned for a refund or credit (sales returns).

[7]Of course, if the allowance for sales returns is estimated incorrectly, income in both the period of the sale and the return will be misstated.

ILLUSTRATION 7–2
Sales Returns

During 2009, its first year of operations, the Hawthorne Manufacturing Company sold merchandise on account for $2,000,000. This merchandise cost $1,200,000 (60% of the selling price). Industry experience indicates that 10% of all sales will be returned. Customers returned $130,000 in sales during 2009, prior to making payment.

The entries to record sales and merchandise returned during the year, *assuming that a perpetual inventory system is used,* are as follows:

Sales

Accounts receivable	2,000,000	
Sales revenue		2,000,000
Cost of goods sold (60% × $2,000,000)	1,200,000	
Inventory		1,200,000

Actual Returns

Sales returns (actual returns)	130,000	
Accounts receivable		130,000
Inventory	78,000	
Cost of goods sold (60% × $130,000)		78,000

At the end of 2009, the company would anticipate the remaining estimated returns using the following adjusting entries:

Adjusting Entries

Sales returns ([10% × $2,000,000] – $130,000)	70,000	
Allowance for sales returns		70,000
Inventory—estimated returns	42,000	
Cost of goods sold (60% × $70,000)		42,000

Quite often, a customer will return merchandise because it has been damaged during shipment or is defective. This possibility must be anticipated in a company's estimate of returns. As you will study in Chapter 9, inventory is valued at the lower-of-cost-or-market. Therefore, damaged or defective merchandise returned from a customer must be written down to market value.

What happens if the estimate of future returns turns out to be more or less than $70,000? Remember from previous discussions that when an estimate turns out to be wrong, we don't revise prior years' financial statements to reflect the new estimate. Instead, we merely incorporate the new estimate in any related accounting determinations from that point on. Suppose in our illustration that in 2010 actual returns from 2009 sales are $60,000, instead of $70,000. If that happens, the allowance account will have a $10,000 balance and the inventory account will have a $6,000 balance ($10,000 × 60%) representing inventory that was not returned as anticipated. These balances can be used to offset actual returns in 2010 from 2010 sales. As a result, the 2010 adjusting entry to record estimated returns would be $10,000 ($6,000 in cost of goods sold/inventory) less than if the 2009 estimate had been correct. Similarly, if actual returns are $80,000, the 2010 adjusting entry will be $10,000 ($6,000) higher than if the 2009 estimate had been correct.

How do companies estimate returns? Principally they rely on past history, taking into account any changes that might affect future experience. For example, changes in customer base, payment terms offered to customers, and overall economic conditions might suggest that future returns will differ from past returns. The task of estimating returns is made easier for many large retail companies whose fiscal year-end is the end of January. Since retail companies generate a large portion of their annual sales during the Christmas season, most returns from these sales would already have been accounted for by the end of January.

Activision Inc. is a leading publisher of interactive entertainment software. Graphic 7–3 describes the company's approach to estimating returns.

In some industries, returns typically are small and infrequent. Companies in these industries usually simply record returns in the period they occur because the effect on income

GRAPHIC 7–3

Disclosure of Sales Returns Policy— Activision Inc.

Real World Financials

> **Summary of Significant Accounting Policies (in part)**
> **Allowance for Returns**
>
> Management must make estimates of potential future product returns related to current period product revenue. We estimate the amount of future returns for current period product revenue utilizing historical experience and information regarding inventory levels and the demand and acceptance of our products by the end consumer. The following factors are used to estimate the amount of future returns for a particular title: historical performance of titles in similar genres; historical performance of the hardware platform; historical performance of the brand; console hardware life cycle; Activision sales force and retail customer feedback; industry pricing; weeks of on-hand retail channel inventory; absolute quantity of on-hand retail channel inventory; our warehouse on-hand inventory levels; the title's recent sell-through history (if available); marketing trade programs; and competing titles.

measurement and asset valuation is immaterial. In a few situations, significant uncertainty as to future collection is created by the right of return. In those cases, revenue recognition is deferred until the uncertainty is resolved. We discussed this possibility in Chapter 5.

● LO5

FINANCIAL
Reporting Case

Q1, p. 327

The use of the *allowance method* is an attempt to satisfy the matching principle in accounting for bad debts.

● LO6

UNCOLLECTIBLE ACCOUNTS RECEIVABLE. Companies that extend credit to customers know that it's unlikely that all customers will fully pay their accounts. Bad debt expense is an inherent cost of granting credit. It's an operating expense incurred to boost sales. As a result, even when specific customer accounts haven't been proven uncollectible by the end of the reporting period, the expense properly should be matched with sales revenue in the income statement for that period. Likewise, as it's not expected that all accounts receivable will be collected, the balance sheet should report only the expected net realizable value of the asset, that is, the amount of cash the company expects to actually collect from customers. An estimate is therefore needed to record bad debt expense and the related reduction of accounts receivable. In an adjusting entry, we record bad debt expense and reduce accounts receivable indirectly by crediting a contra account (allowance for uncollectible accounts) to accounts receivable for an estimate of the amount that eventually will prove uncollectible. This approach to accounting for bad debts is known as the allowance method.

There are two ways commonly used to arrive at this estimate of future bad debts—the income statement approach and the balance sheet approach. Illustration 7–3 is used to demonstrate both approaches. As you proceed through the illustration, remember that the two approaches represent alternative ways to estimate the *amount* of future bad debts. Except for the amounts, the accounting entries are identical.

ILLUSTRATION 7–3 Bad Debts	The Hawthorne Manufacturing Company sells its products offering 30 days' credit to its customers. During 2009, its first year of operations, the following events occurred:

Sales on credit	$1,200,000
Cash collections from credit customers	(895,000)
Accounts receivable, end of year	$ 305,000

There were no specific accounts determined to be uncollectible in 2009. The company anticipates that 2% of all credit sales will ultimately become uncollectible.

Bad debt expense is estimated as a percentage of net credit sales.

Income statement approach. Using the income statement approach, we estimate bad debt expense as a percentage of each period's net credit sales. This percentage usually is determined by reviewing the company's recent history of the relationship between credit sales and actual bad debts. For a relatively new company, this percentage may be obtained by referring to other sources such as industry averages.

Under the income statement approach, the Hawthorne Manufacturing Company would make the following adjusting journal entry at the end of 2009:

FINANCIAL
Reporting Case

Q2, p. 327

Bad debt expense (2% × $1,200,000)	24,000	
Allowance for uncollectible accounts		24,000

Allowance for uncollectible accounts is a contra account to accounts receivable. In the current asset section of the 2009 balance sheet, accounts receivable would be reported *net* of the allowance, as follows:

Accounts receivable	$305,000
Less: Allowance for uncollectible accounts	(24,000)
Net accounts receivable	$281,000

Quite often, companies report the allowance for uncollectible accounts (often called *allowance for doubtful accounts*) parenthetically or alongside the accounts receivable account title separated by a dash or a comma. For example, **Google Inc.** reported the following under current assets in its comparative balance sheets for 2006 and 2007:

Google

	($ in thousands)	
	2006	**2007**
Accounts receivables—net of allowance of $16,914 and $32,887	$1,322,340	$2,162,521

The $2,162,521 thousand figure at the end of 2007 is the company's estimate of the net realizable value of accounts receivable. Actual (gross) accounts receivable at the end of 2007 were $2,195,408 thousand ($2,162,521 + $32,887).

It's important to notice that the income statement approach focuses on the current year's credit sales. The effect on the balance sheet—the allowance for uncollectible accounts and hence net accounts receivable—is an incidental result of estimating the expense. An alternative is to focus on the balance sheet amounts instead. We look at this approach next.

Using the income statement approach, the balance sheet amount is an indirect outcome of estimating bad debt expense.

Balance sheet approach.   Using the balance sheet approach to estimate future bad debts, we determine bad debt expense by estimating the net realizable value of accounts receivable to be reported in the balance sheet. In other words, the allowance for uncollectible accounts is determined. Bad debt expense is an indirect outcome of adjusting the allowance account to the desired balance.

For the Hawthorne Manufacturing Company example in Illustration 7–3, the company would estimate the amount of uncollectible accounts that will result from the $305,000 in

Using the balance sheet approach, bad debt expense is an incidental result of estimating the net realizable value of accounts receivable.

ETHICAL DILEMMA

The management of the Auto Parts Division of the Santana Corporation receives a bonus if the division's income achieves a specific target. For 2009 the target will be achieved by a wide margin. Mary Beth Williams, the controller of the division, has been asked by Philip Stanton, the head of the division's management team, to try to reduce this year's income and "bank" some of the profits for future years. Mary Beth suggests that the division's bad debt expense as a percentage of net credit sales for 2009 be increased from 3% to 5%. She believes that 3% is the more accurate estimate but knows that both the corporation's internal auditors as well as the external auditors allow some flexibility when estimates are involved. Does Mary Beth's proposal present an ethical dilemma?

accounts receivable outstanding at the end of 2009. This could be done by analyzing each customer account, by applying a percentage to the entire outstanding receivable balance, or by applying different percentages to accounts receivable balances depending on the length of time outstanding. This latter approach normally employs an accounts receivable aging schedule. For example, the aging schedule for Hawthorne's 2009 year-end accounts receivable is shown in Illustration 7–3A.

ILLUSTRATION 7–3A	Customer	Accounts Receivable 12/31/09	0–60 Days	61–90 Days	91–120 Days	Over 120 Days
Accounts Receivable Aging Schedule	Axel Manufacturing Co.	$ 20,000	$ 14,000	$ 6,000		
	Banner Corporation	33,000		20,000	$10,000	$ 3,000
	Dando Company	60,000	50,000	10,000		
	̃ ̃ ̃ ̃	̃ ̃	̃ ̃	̃ ̃	̃ ̃	̃ ̃
The schedule assumes older accounts are more likely to prove uncollectible.	̃ ̃ ̃ ̃	̃ ̃	̃ ̃	̃ ̃	̃ ̃	̃ ̃
	Xicon Company	18,000	10,000	4,000	3,000	1,000
	Totals	$305,000	$220,000	$50,000	$25,000	$10,000

	Summary		
Age Group	Amount	Estimated Percent Uncollectible	Estimated Allowance
0–60 days	$220,000	5%	$11,000
61–90 days	50,000	10%	5,000
91–120 days	25,000	20%	5,000
Over 120 days	10,000	45%	4,500
Allowance for uncollectible accounts			$25,500

Higher estimated default percentages are applied to groups of older receivables.

The schedule classifies the year-end receivable balances according to their length of time outstanding. Presumably, the longer an account has been outstanding the more likely it will prove uncollectible. Based on past experience or other sources of information, a percentage is applied to age group totals.

The 2009 entry to record bad debts adjusts the balance in the allowance for uncollectible accounts to this required amount of $25,500. Because it is the first year of operations for Hawthorne and the beginning balance in the allowance account is zero, the adjusting entry would *debit* bad debt expense and *credit* allowance for uncollectible accounts for $25,500.

To illustrate the concept further, let's suppose that this was not the first year of operations and the allowance account prior to the adjusting entry had a *credit* balance of $4,000. Then the amount of the entry would be $21,500—the amount necessary to adjust a credit balance of $4,000 to a credit balance of $25,500. Similarly, if the allowance account prior to the adjusting entry had a *debit* balance[8] of $4,000, then the amount of the entry would be $29,500.

Some companies use a combination of approaches in estimating bad debts. For example, Hawthorne could decide to accrue bad debts on a monthly basis using the income statement approach and then employ the balance sheet approach at the end of the year based on an aging of receivables. Each month an adjusting entry would record a debit to bad debt expense and a credit to allowance for uncollectible accounts equal to 2% of credit sales. In our illustration, the monthly accruals for 2009 would result in the following account balances at the end of 2009:

Allowance	
Beg. bal.	4,000
Adj. entry	21,500
Bal.	25,500

---

[8]A debit balance could result if the amount of receivables actually written off (discussed below) during the period exceeds the beginning credit balance in the allowance account.

Accounts Receivable		Bad Debt Expense	
305,000		24,000	

Allowance for Uncollectible Accounts	
	24,000

At the end of the year, if the aging revealed a required allowance of $25,500, the following adjusting entry would be recorded:

Bad debt expense	1,500	
Allowance for uncollectible accounts		1,500

This entry adjusts the allowance account to the required amount.

In the 2009 balance sheet, accounts receivable would be reported net of the allowance, as follows:

Accounts receivable	$305,000
Less: Allowance for uncollectible accounts	(25,500)
Net accounts receivable	$279,500

When accounts are deemed uncollectible. The actual write-off of a receivable occurs when it is determined that all or a portion of the amount due will not be collected. Using the allowance method, the write-off is recorded as a debit to allowance for uncollectible accounts and a credit to accounts receivable. In our illustration, assume that actual bad debts in 2010 were $25,000. These write-offs would be recorded (in a summary journal entry) as follows:

Allowance for uncollectible accounts	25,000	
Accounts receivable		25,000

Net realizable value is not affected directly by the write-offs.

Accounts receivable	$280,000
Less: Allowance for uncollectible accounts	(500)
Net accounts receivable	$279,500

The write-off of an account receivable reduces both receivables and the allowance, thus having no effect on income or financial position.

Of course, actual bad debts will tend to differ from estimates. However, the year in which the estimate is made, 2009 in this case, is unaffected by the incorrect estimate. If the prior year's estimate of bad debts is too low, then, using the balance sheet approach, bad debt expense in the subsequent year will be increased. If the estimate is too high, then bad debt expense in the subsequent year will be decreased. For example, in our illustration, the allowance at the end of 2009 is $25,500. Actual bad debts related to 2009 receivables are $25,000. 2009's financial information cannot be changed. Instead, the $500 credit balance in allowance for uncollectible accounts will cause 2010's bad debt expense to be less than if 2009's estimate of bad debts had been correct.

When previously written-off accounts are collected. Occasionally, a receivable that has been written off will be collected in part or in full. When this happens, the receivable and the allowance should be reinstated. In other words, the entry to write off the account simply is reversed. The collection is then recorded the usual way as a debit to cash and a credit to accounts receivable. This process ensures that the company will have a complete record

Recoveries of accounts receivable previously written off require the reinstatement of both the receivable and the allowance.

of the payment history of the customer. For example, assume that in our illustration, $1,200 that was previously written off is collected. The following journal entries record the event:

To reinstate the receivable previously written off.

To record the cash collection.

Accounts receivable	1,200	
Allowance for uncollectible accounts		1,200
Cash	1,200	
Accounts receivable		1,200

FINANCIAL
Reporting Case

Q3, p. 327

Direct write-off of uncollectible accounts. If uncollectible accounts are not anticipated or are immaterial, or if it's not possible to reliably estimate uncollectible accounts, an allowance for uncollectible accounts is not appropriate. In these few cases, adjusting entries are not recorded and any bad debts that do arise simply are written off as bad debt expense. A $750 uncollectible account would be recorded as follows:

Bad debt expense	750	
Accounts receivable		750

The *direct write-off method* is used only rarely for financial reporting, but it is the required method for income tax purposes.

    This approach is known as the direct write-off method. Of course, if the sale that generated this receivable occurred in a previous reporting period, the matching principle is violated. Operating expenses would have been understated and assets overstated in that period. This is why the direct write-off method of accounting for uncollectible accounts is not permitted by GAAP except in limited circumstances. Specifically, the allowance method must be used if it is probable that a material amount of receivables will not be collected and the amount can be reasonably estimated.[9] For federal income tax purposes, however, the direct write-off method is the required method for most companies and the allowance method is not permitted.

    Graphic 7–4 summarizes the key issues involving measuring and reporting accounts receivable.

GRAPHIC 7–4

Measuring and Reporting Accounts Receivable

Recognition	Depends on the earnings process; for most credit sales, revenue and the related receivables are recognized at the point of delivery.
Initial valuation	Initially recorded at the exchange price agreed upon by the buyer and seller.

Subsequent valuation	Initial valuation reduced to net realizable value by:
	1. Allowance for sales returns
	2. Allowance for uncollectible accounts:
	   —The income statement approach
	   —The balance sheet approach

Classification	Almost always classified as a current asset.

CONCEPT REVIEW EXERCISE

UNCOLLECTIBLE ACCOUNTS RECEIVABLE

The Hawthorne Manufacturing Company sells its products, offering 30 days' credit to its customers. Uncollectible amounts are estimated by accruing a monthly charge to bad debt expense equal to 2% of credit sales. At the end of the year, the allowance for uncollectible accounts is adjusted based on an aging of accounts receivable. The company began 2010 with the following balances in its accounts:

Accounts receivable	$305,000
Allowance for uncollectible accounts	(25,500)

[9]"Accounting for Contingencies," *Statement of Financial Accounting Standards No. 5* (Stamford, Conn.: FASB, 1975), par. 8.

During 2010, sales on credit were $1,300,000, cash collections from customers were $1,250,000, and actual write-offs of accounts were $25,000. An aging of accounts receivable at the end of 2010 indicates a required allowance of $30,000.

Required:

1. Determine the balances in accounts receivable and allowance for uncollectible accounts at the end of 2010.
2. Determine bad debt expense for 2010.
3. Prepare journal entries for the monthly accrual of bad debts (in summary form), the write-off of receivables, and the year-end adjusting entry for bad debts.

1. Determine the balances in accounts receivable and allowance for uncollectible accounts at the end of 2010.   **SOLUTION**

Accounts receivable	
Beginning balance	$ 305,000
Add: Credit sales	1,300,000
Less: Cash collections	(1,250,000)
Write-offs	(25,000)
Ending balance	$ 330,000
Allowance for uncollectible accounts:	
Beginning balance	$ 25,500
Add: Bad debt expense recorded monthly (2% × $1,300,000)	26,000
Less: Write-offs	(25,000)
Balance before year-end adjustment	26,500
Year-end adjustment	3,500*
Ending balance	$ 30,000

*Required allowance of $30,000 less $26,500 already in allowance account.

2. Determine bad debt expense for 2010.

Bad debt expense would be $29,500 (monthly accrual of $26,000 plus year-end adjustment of an additional $3,500).

3. Prepare journal entries for the monthly accrual of bad debts (in summary form), the write-off of receivables, and the year-end adjusting entry for bad debts.

Bad debt expense (2% × $1,300,000)	26,000	
Allowance for uncollectible accounts		26,000
Monthly accrual of 2% of credit sales—summary entry.		
Allowance for uncollectible accounts	25,000	
Accounts receivable		25,000
Write-off of accounts receivable as they are determined uncollectible.		
Bad debt expense	3,500	
Allowance for uncollectible accounts		3,500
Year-end adjusting entry for bad debts.		

Notes Receivable

Notes receivable are formal credit arrangements between a creditor (lender) and a debtor (borrower). Notes arise from loans to other entities including affiliated companies and to stockholders and employees, from the extension of the credit period to trade customers, and occasionally from the sale of merchandise, other assets, or services. Notes receivable are classified as either current or noncurrent depending on the expected payment date(s).

Our examples below illustrate short-term notes. When the term of a note is longer than a year, it is reported as a long-term note. Long-term notes receivable are discussed in conjunction with long-term notes payable in Chapter 14.

● LO7

Interest-Bearing Notes

The typical note receivable requires the payment of a specified face amount, also called *principal,* at a specified maturity date or dates. In addition, interest is paid at a stated percentage of the face amount. Interest on notes is calculated as:

Face amount × Annual rate × Fraction of the annual period

For an example, consider Illustration 7–4.

ILLUSTRATION 7–4 Note Receivable	The Stridewell Wholesale Shoe Company manufactures athletic shoes that it sells to retailers. On May 1, 2009, the company sold shoes to Harmon Sporting Goods. Stridewell agreed to accept a $700,000, 6-month, 12% note in payment for the shoes. Interest is payable at maturity. Stridewell would account for the note as follows:*

May 1, 2009

Note receivable	700,000	
Sales revenue		700,000
To record the sale of goods in exchange for a note receivable.		

November 1, 2009

Cash ($700,000 + $42,000)	742,000	
Interest revenue ($700,000 × 12% × 6/12)		42,000
Note receivable		700,000
To record the collection of the note at maturity.		

*To focus on recording the note we intentionally omit the entry required for the cost of the goods sold if the perpetual inventory system is used.

If the sale in the illustration occurs on August 1, 2009, and the company's fiscal year-end is December 31, a year-end adjusting entry accrues interest earned.

December 31, 2009

| Interest receivable | 35,000 | |
| Interest revenue ($700,000 × 12% × 5/12) | | 35,000 |

The February 1 collection is then recorded as follows:

February 1, 2010

Cash ($700,000 + [$700,000 × 12% × 6/12])	742,000	
Interest revenue ($700,000 × 12% × 1/12)		7,000
Interest receivable (accrued at December 31)		35,000
Note receivable		700,000

Noninterest-Bearing Notes

Sometimes a receivable assumes the form of a so-called noninterest-bearing note. The name is a misnomer, though. Noninterest-bearing notes actually do bear interest, but the interest is deducted (or discounted) from the face amount to determine the cash proceeds made available to the borrower at the outset. For example, the preceding note could be packaged as a $700,000 noninterest-bearing note, with a 12% discount rate. In that case, the

$42,000 interest would be discounted at the outset rather than explicitly stated. As a result, the selling price of the shoes would have been only $658,000. Assuming a May 1, 2009 sale, the transaction is recorded as follows:[10]

May 1, 2009

Note receivable (face amount)	700,000	
Discount on note receivable ($700,000 × 12% × ⁶/₁₂)		42,000
Sales revenue (difference)		658,000

November 1, 2009

Discount on note receivable	42,000	
Interest revenue		42,000
Cash	700,000	
Note receivable (face amount)		700,000

> The discount becomes interest revenue in a noninterest-bearing note.

The discount on note receivable is a contra account to the note receivable account. That is, the note receivable would be reported in the balance sheet net (less) any remaining discount. The discount represents future interest revenue that will be recognized as it is earned over time. The sales revenue under this arrangement is only $658,000, but the interest is calculated as the discount rate times the $700,000 face amount. This causes the *effective* interest rate to be higher than the 12% stated rate.

> When interest is discounted from the face amount of a note, the effective interest rate is higher than the stated discount rate.

$ 42,000	Interest for 6 months
÷ $658,000	Sales price
= 6.383%	Rate for 6 months
× 2*	To annualize the rate
= 12.766%	Effective interest rate

*Two 6-month periods

As we discussed earlier in the chapter, receivables, other than normal trade receivables, should be valued at the present value of future cash receipts. The present value of $700,000 to be received in six months using an effective interest rate of 6.383% is $658,000 ($700,000 ÷ 1.06383 = $658,000). The use of present value techniques for valuation purposes was introduced in Chapter 6, and we'll use these techniques extensively in subsequent chapters to value various long-term liabilities.

In the illustration, if the sale occurs on August 1, the December 31, 2009, adjusting entry and the entry to record the cash collection on February 1, 2010, are recorded as follows:

Using a calculator:
Enter: N 1 I .06383
PMT − 700000
Output: PV 658,000

Using Excel, enter:
= PV(.06383,1,700000)
Output: 658,000

December 31, 2009

Discount on note receivable	35,000	
Interest revenue ($700,000 × 12% × ⁵/₁₂)		35,000

February 1, 2010

Discount on note receivable	7,000	
Interest revenue ($700,000 × 12% × ¹/₁₂)		7,000
Cash	700,000	
Note receivable (face amount)		700,000

---

[10]The entries shown assume the note is recorded by the gross method. By the net method, the interest component is netted against the face amount of the note as follows:

May 1, 2009

Note receivable	658,000	
Sales revenue		658,000

November 1, 2009

Cash	700,000	
Note receivable		658,000
Interest revenue ($700,000 × 12% × ⁶/₁₂)		42,000

In the December 31, 2009, balance sheet, the note receivable is shown at $693,000, face amount ($700,000) less remaining discount ($7,000).

Metro-Goldwyn-Mayer Inc., (MGM) licenses its television programs to networks. The disclosure note shown in Graphic 7–5 describes the company's revenue recognition policy for its license agreements and the use of noninterest-bearing notes.

GRAPHIC 7–5

Disclosure of Revenue Recognition for License Agreements—Metro-Goldwyn-Mayer, Inc.

Real World Financials

Revenue Recognition (in part)

Revenues from television licensing, together with related costs, are recognized when the feature film or television program is available to the licensee for telecast. Long-term, noninterest-bearing receivables arising from licensing agreements are discounted to present value in accordance with *Accounting Principles Board (APB) Opinion No. 21,* "Interest on Receivables and Payables."

> When a noninterest-bearing note is received solely in exchange for cash, the amount of cash exchanged is the basis for valuing the note.

NOTES RECEIVED SOLELY FOR CASH. If a note with an unrealistic interest rate—even a noninterest-bearing note—is received *solely* in exchange for cash, the cash paid to the issuer is considered to be its present value.[11] Even if this means recording interest at a ridiculously low or zero rate, the amount of cash exchanged is the basis for valuing the note. When a non-cash asset is exchanged for a note with a low stated rate, we can argue that its real value is less than it's purported to be, but we can't argue that the present value of a sum of cash currently exchanged is less than that sum. If the noninterest-bearing note in the previous example had been received solely in exchange for $700,000 cash, the transaction would be recorded as follows:

Note receivable (face amount)	700,000	
Cash (given)		700,000

Subsequent Valuation of Notes Receivable

Similar to accounts receivable, if a company anticipates bad debts on short-term notes receivable, it uses an allowance account to reduce the receivable to net realizable value. The process of recording bad debt expense is the same as with accounts receivable.

Long-term notes present a more significant measurement problem. The longer the duration of the note, the more likely are bad debts. One of the more difficult measurement problems facing banks and other lending institutions is the estimation of bad debts on their long-term notes (loans). As an example, **Wells Fargo & Company,** a large bank holding company, reported the following in the asset section of a recent balance sheet:

	December 31 (in millions)	
	2007	**2006**
Loans	$382,195	$319,116
Allowance for loan losses	(5,307)	(3,764)
Net loans	$376,888	$315,352

A disclosure note, reproduced in Graphic 7–6, describes Wells Fargo's loan loss policy.

When it becomes probable that a creditor will be unable to collect all amounts due according to the contractual terms of a note, the receivable is considered impaired. When a creditor's investment in a note receivable becomes impaired for any reason, the receivable

---

[11]This assumes that no other present or future considerations are included in the agreement. For example, a noninterest-bearing note might be given to a vendor in exchange for cash *and* a promise to provide future inventories at prices lower than anticipated market prices. The issuer values the note at the present value of cash payments using a realistic interest rate, and the difference between present value and cash payments is recognized as interest revenue over the life of the note. This difference also increases future inventory purchases to realistic market prices.

Allowance for Credit Losses

The allowance for credit losses, which consists of the allowance for loan losses and the reserve for unfunded credit commitments, is management's estimate of credit losses inherent in the loan portfolio at the balance sheet date. We have an established process, using several analytical tools and benchmarks, to calculate a range of possible outcomes and determine the adequacy of the allowance. No single statistic or measurement determines the adequacy of the allowance. Loan recoveries and the provision for credit losses increase the allowance, while loan charge-offs decrease the allowance.

GRAPHIC 7–6

Disclosure of Allowance for Loan Losses—Wells Fargo & Company

Real World Financials

is remeasured as the discounted present value of currently expected cash flows at the loan's original effective rate. Impairments of receivables are discussed in Appendix 12B.

Financing with Receivables

Receivables, like any other asset, can be sold or used as collateral for debt. In fact, many companies avoid the difficulties of servicing (billing and collecting) receivables by transferring them to financial institutions. This practice also shortens those companies' operating cycles by providing cash to the companies immediately rather than having them wait until credit customers pay the amounts due. Of course, the financial institution will require compensation for providing this service, usually interest and/or a finance charge.

● LO8

Responding to these desires, financial institutions have developed a wide variety of ways for companies to use their receivables to obtain immediate cash. The methods differ with respect to which rights and risks are retained by the *transferor* (the original holder of the receivables) and those passed on to the *transferee* (the new holder, the financial institution). Despite this diversity, any of these methods can be described as either:

1. A secured borrowing.
2. A sale of receivables.

When a company chooses between a borrowing or a sale, the critical element is the extent to which it (the transferor) is willing to *surrender control over the assets transferred.* The distinction for some arrangements is not always obvious. For such situations the FASB has provided guidelines. Specifically, the transferor is determined to have surrendered control over the receivables if and only if all of the following conditions are met:[12]

a. The transferred assets have been isolated from the transferor—put presumptively beyond the reach of the transferor and its creditors, even in bankruptcy or other receivership.
b. Each transferee has the right to pledge or exchange the assets it received.
c. The transferor does not maintain effective control over the transferred assets through either (1) an agreement that the transferor repurchase or redeem them before their maturity or (2) the ability to cause the transferee to return specific assets.

If all of the above conditions are *not* met, the transferor treats the transaction as *a secured borrowing.* In that case the company records a liability with the receivables serving as collateral.

On the other hand, if each of the three conditions is met, the transferor treats the transaction as a *sale* and accounts for it in the same manner as the sale of any other asset. That is, the transferor "derecognizes" (removes) the receivables from its books, records the proceeds received (usually cash), and recognizes the difference as either a gain or loss (usually a loss) on the sale. On the other side of the transaction, the transferee recognizes the receivables obtained and measures them at their fair value. Let's now look in more detail at these two possibilities.

If the transferor is deemed to have surrendered control over the receivables, the arrangement is accounted for as a sale; otherwise as a secured borrowing.

[12]"Accounting for Transfers and Servicing of Financial Assets and Extinguishments of Liabilities," *Statement of Financial Accounting Standards No. 140* (Norwalk, Conn.: FASB, 2000). This standard is amended by *SFAS No. 156.*

Secured Borrowing

As defined in the previous section, companies sometimes use receivables as collateral for loans. You may already be familiar with the concept of assigning or pledging receivables as collateral if you or someone you know has a mortgage on a home. The bank or other financial institution holding the mortgage will require that, if the homeowner defaults on the mortgage payments, the home be sold and the proceeds used to pay off the mortgage debt. Similarly, in the case of an assignment of receivables, nonpayment of a debt will require the proceeds from collecting the assigned receivables to go directly toward repayment of the debt.

Usually, the amount borrowed is less than the amount of receivables assigned. The difference provides some protection for the lender to allow for possible uncollectible accounts. Also, the assignee (transferee) usually charges the assignor an up-front finance charge in addition to stated interest on the collateralized loan. The receivables might be collected either by the assignor or the assignee, depending on the details of the arrangement. Illustration 7–5 provides an example.

ILLUSTRATION 7–5 Assignment of Accounts Receivable	At the end of November 2009, Santa Teresa Glass Company had outstanding accounts receivable of $750,000. On December 1, 2009, the company borrowed $500,000 from Finance Affiliates and signed a promissory note. Interest at 12% is payable monthly. The company assigned $620,000 of its receivables as collateral for the loan. Finance Affiliates charges a finance fee equal to 1.5% of the accounts receivable assigned.

Santa Teresa Glass records the borrowing as follows:

Cash (difference)	490,700	
Finance charge expense* (1.5% × $620,000)	9,300	
Liability—financing arrangement		500,000

Santa Teresa will continue to collect the receivables, record any discounts, sales returns, and bad debt write-offs, but will remit the cash to Finance Affiliates, usually on a monthly basis. When $400,000 of the receivables assigned are collected in December, Santa Teresa Glass records the following entries:

Cash	400,000	
Accounts receivable		400,000
Interest expense ($500,000 × 12% × 1/12)	5,000	
Liability—financing arrangement	400,000	
Cash		405,000

*In theory, this fee should be allocated over the entire period of the loan rather than recorded as an expense in the initial period. However, amounts usually are small and the loan period usually is short. For expediency, then, we expense the entire fee immediately.

In Santa Teresa's December 31, 2009, balance sheet, the company would report the receivables and note payable together as follows:

Current assets:	
Accounts receivable assigned ($620,000 – 400,000)	$220,000
Less: Liability—financing arrangement ($500,000 – 400,000)	(100,000)
Equity in accounts receivable assigned	$120,000

Netting a liability against a related asset usually is not allowed by GAAP. However, in this case, we deduct the note payable from the accounts receivable assigned because, by contractual agreement, the note will be paid with cash collected from the receivables. In Santa Teresa's financial statements, the arrangement also is described in a disclosure note.

A variation of assigning specific receivables occurs when trade receivables in general rather than specific receivables are pledged as collateral. The responsibility for collection of the receivables remains solely with the company. This variation is referred to as a pledging of accounts receivable. No special accounting treatment is needed and the arrangement is simply described in a disclosure note. For example, Graphic 7–7 shows a portion of the long-term debt disclosure note included in recent financial statements of **Lyondell Chemical Company,** a global chemical company.

GRAPHIC 7–7

Disclosure of Receivables Used as Collateral—Lyondell Chemical Company

Real World Financials

> **Long-Term Debt (in part)**
>
> The revolving credit facility is secured by a lien on all inventory and certain personal property, including a pledge of accounts receivable.

Sale of Receivables

Two popular arrangements used for the sale of receivables are *factoring* and securitization.

The sale of accounts receivable has become an increasingly popular method of financing. Traditionally a technique used by companies in a few industries or with poor credit ratings, the sale of receivables is now a common occurrence for many different types of companies. For example, **Delta Air Lines, Chevron, IBM, Sears,** and **Raytheon** all sell receivables. The two most common types of selling arrangements are **factoring** and **securitization.** We'll now discuss each type.

A factor is a financial institution that buys receivables for cash, handles the billing and collection of the receivables, and charges a fee for this service. Actually, credit cards like VISA and Mastercard are forms of factoring arrangements. The seller relinquishes all rights to the future cash receipts in exchange for cash from the buyer (the *factor*).

As an example, Graphic 7–8 shows an excerpt from a recent advertisement of **Bankers Mutual Capital Corporation,** a financial institution that offers factoring as one of its services.

GRAPHIC 7–8

Advertisement of Factoring Service— Bankers Mutual Capital Corporation

> **Accounts Receivable Factoring**
>
> Accounts receivable factoring is the selling of your invoices (accounts receivable) for cash versus waiting 30–60 days to be paid by your customer. Factoring will get you the working capital you need now and improve your cash flow. Bankers will advance 65%–80% against the invoice you generate and pay you the balance less our fee (typically 3%–6%) when the invoice is paid.

Notice that the factor, Bankers Mutual, advances only between 65%–80% of the factored receivables. The remaining balance is retained as security until all of the receivables are collected and then remitted to the transferor, net of the factor's fee. The fee charged by this factor ranges from 3%–6%. The range depends on, among other things, the quality of the receivables and the length of time before payment is required.

Another popular arrangement used to sell receivables is a securitization. In a typical accounts receivable securitization, the company creates a special purpose entity (SPE), usually a trust or a subsidiary. The SPE buys a pool of trade receivables, credit card receivables, or loans from the company, and then sells related securities, for example bonds or commercial paper, that are backed (collateralized) by the receivables.

As an example of a securitization, Graphic 7–9 shows a portion of the disclosure note included in recent financial statements of **Hasbro, Inc.,** a worldwide leader in the manufacture of toys and games, describing the securitization of its trade accounts receivable.

GRAPHIC 7–9

Disclosure of Credit Card Securitizations— Hasbro, Inc.

Real World Financials

> **Securitization (in part)**
>
> . . . the Company is party to a receivable securitization program whereby the Company sells, on an ongoing basis, substantially all of its U.S. trade accounts receivable to a bankruptcy-remote, special-purpose subsidiary, Hasbro Receivables Funding, LLC (HRF), which is wholly owned and consolidated by the Company. . . . The net proceeds of sale will be less than the face amount of accounts receivable sold by an amount that approximates the purchaser's financing costs.

The specific accounting treatment for the sale of receivables using factoring and securitization arrangements depends on the amount of risk the factor assumes, in particular whether it buys the receivables **without recourse** or **with recourse.**

SALE WITHOUT RECOURSE. When a company sells accounts receivable without recourse, the buyer assumes the risk of uncollectibility. This means the buyer has no *recourse* to the seller if customers don't pay the receivables. In that case, the seller simply accounts for the transaction as a sale of an asset. As we discussed above, the buyer charges a fee for providing this service, usually a percentage of the book value of receivables. Because the fee reduces the proceeds the seller receives from selling the asset, the seller records a loss on sale of assets. The typical factoring arrangement is made without recourse. Illustration 7–6 provides an example.

ILLUSTRATION 7–6	At the end of November 2009, the Santa Teresa Glass Company had outstanding accounts receivable of $750,000. In December 2009, the company factored $600,000 of accounts receivable to Finance Affiliates. The transfer was made without recourse. Finance Affiliates remits 90% of the factored receivables to Santa Teresa and retains the remaining 10%. When Finance Affiliates collects the receivables, it remits to Santa Teresa the retained amount, less a 4% fee (4% of the total factored amount).
Accounts Receivable Factored without Recourse	Santa Teresa Glass records the transfer as follows:

The factor's fee is recorded as a loss.	Cash (90% × $600,000)	540,000	
	Loss on sale of receivables (4% × $600,000)	24,000	
	Receivable from factor (10% × $600,000 = $60,000 − 24,000 fee)	36,000	
	Accounts receivable (balance sold)		600,000

SALE WITH RECOURSE. When a company sells accounts receivable with recourse, the seller retains the risk of uncollectibility. In effect, the seller guarantees that the buyer will be paid even if some receivables prove to be uncollectible. In Illustration 7–6, even if the receivables were sold with recourse, as long as the three conditions for sale treatment are met, Santa Teresa Glass would still account for the transfer as a sale. The only difference would be the additional requirement that Santa Teresa record the estimated fair value of the recourse obligation as a liability. The recourse obligation is the estimated amount that Santa Teresa will have to pay Finance Affiliates as a reimbursement for uncollectible receivables. Assuming that this amount is estimated at $5,000, the entry recorded by Santa Teresa appears in Illustration 7–6A.

ILLUSTRATION 7–6A		
Accounts Receivable Factored with Recourse	Cash (90% × $600,000)	540,000	
	Loss on sale of receivables (4% × $600,000 + 5,000)	29,000	
	Receivable from factor (10% × $600,000 = $60,000 − 24,000 fee) ..	36,000	
	Recourse liability		5,000
	Accounts receivable (balance sold)		600,000

Notice that the estimated recourse liability increases the loss on sale. If the factor collects all of the receivables, Santa Teresa eliminates the recourse liability and increases income (reduces the loss).

If the three conditions for sale treatment were not met, the transfer of receivables would be accounted for as a secured borrowing, as demonstrated in Illustration 7–5. Notice in Graphic 7–9A that Hasbro accounts for the securitization of its trade accounts receivable as a sale, indicating that the three conditions for sale treatment have been met.

Summary of Significant Accounting Policies (in part)
Securitization and Transfer of Financial Instruments

Hasbro has an agreement that allows the Company to sell, on an ongoing basis, an undivided interest in certain of its trade accounts receivable through a revolving securitization arrangement. The Company retains servicing responsibilities for, as well as a subordinate interest in, the transferred receivables. Hasbro accounts for the securitization of trade accounts receivable as a sale in accordance with SFAS No. 140, Accounting for Transfers and Servicing of Financial Assets and Extinguishment of Liabilities (SFAS 140). As a result, the related receivables are removed from the consolidated balance sheet.

Discounting a Note

Similar to accounts receivable, a note receivable can be used to obtain immediate cash from a financial institution either by pledging the note as collateral for a loan or by selling the note. The transfer of a note is referred to as discounting. The financial institution accepts the note and gives the seller cash equal to the maturity value of the note reduced by a discount. The discount is computed by applying a discount rate to the maturity value and represents the financing fee the financial institution charges for the transaction. Illustration 7–7 provides an example of the calculation of the proceeds received by the transferor.

The transfer of a note receivable to a financial institution is called *discounting*.

On December 31, 2009, the Stridewell Wholesale Shoe Company sold land in exchange for a nine-month, 10% note. The note requires the payment of $200,000 plus interest on September 30, 2010. The company's fiscal year-end is December 31. The 10% rate properly reflects the time value of money for this type of note. On March 31, 2010, Stridewell discounted the note at the Bank of the East. The bank's discount rate is 12%.

Because the note had been outstanding for three months before it's discounted at the bank, Stridewell first records the interest that has accrued prior to being discounted:

March 31, 2010

Interest receivable	5,000	
Interest revenue ($200,000 × 10% × 3/12)		5,000

Next, the value of the note if held to maturity is calculated. Then the discount for the time remaining to maturity is deducted to determine the cash proceeds from discounting the note:

$200,000	Face amount
15,000	Interest to maturity ($200,000 × 10% × 9/12)
215,000	Maturity value
(12,900)	Discount ($215,000 × 12% × 6/12)
$202,100	Cash proceeds

ILLUSTRATION 7–7
Discounting a Note Receivable

STEP 1: Accrue interest earned on the note receivable prior to its being discounted.

STEP 2: Add interest to maturity to calculate maturity value.

STEP 3: Deduct discount to calculate cash proceeds.

Similar to accounts receivable, if the three conditions for sale treatment are met, Stridewell would account for the transfer as a sale. If the conditions are not met, it is treated as a secured borrowing. For example, if the sale conditions are met, Illustration 7–7A shows the appropriate journal entries.

Cash (proceeds determined above)	202,100	
Loss on sale of note receivable (difference)	2,900	
Note receivable (face amount)		200,000
Interest receivable (accrued interest determined above)		5,000

ILLUSTRATION 7–7A
Discounted Note Treated as a Sale

Record a loss (or gain) for difference between the cash proceeds and the note's book value.

CONCEPT REVIEW **EXERCISE**

The Hollywood Lumber Company obtains financing from the Midwest Finance Company by factoring (or discounting) its receivables. During June 2009, the company factored $1,000,000 of accounts receivable to Midwest. The transfer was made *without* recourse. The factor, Midwest Finance, remits 80% of the factored receivables and retains 20%. When the receivables are collected by Midwest, the retained amount, less a 3% fee (3% of the total factored amount), will be remitted to Hollywood Lumber.

FINANCING WITH RECEIVABLES

In addition, on June 30, 2009, Hollywood discounted a note receivable without recourse. The note, which originated on March 31, 2009, requires the payment of $150,000 *plus* interest at 8% on March 31, 2010. Midwest's discount rate is 10%. The company's fiscal year-end is December 31.

Required:
Prepare journal entries for Hollywood Lumber for the factoring of accounts receivable and the note receivable discounted on June 30. Assume that the required criteria are met and the transfers are accounted for as sales.

SOLUTION

The Factoring of Receivables

Cash (80% × $1,000,000)	800,000	
Loss on sale of receivables (3% × $1,000,000)	30,000	
Receivable from factor (20% × $1,000,000 − 30,000 fee)	170,000	
Accounts receivable (balance sold)		1,000,000

The Note Receivable Discounted

Add interest to maturity to calculate maturity value.

Deduct discount to calculate cash proceeds.

Interest receivable	3,000	
Interest revenue ($150,000 × 8% × 3/12)		3,000
Cash (proceeds determined below)	149,850	
Loss on sale of note receivable (difference)	3,150	
Note receivable (face amount)		150,000
Interest receivable (accrued interest determined above)		3,000

$150,000	Face amount
12,000	Interest to maturity ($150,000 × 8%)
162,000	Maturity value
(12,150)	Discount ($162,000 × 10% × 9/12)
$149,850	Cash proceeds ●

In summary, there are several ways receivables can be used as a method of financing. However, each of these arrangements can be categorized as either a secured borrowing or as an outright sale of the receivables. Graphic 7–10 provides a visual summary of the possibilities.

GRAPHIC 7–10

Accounting for the Financing of Receivables

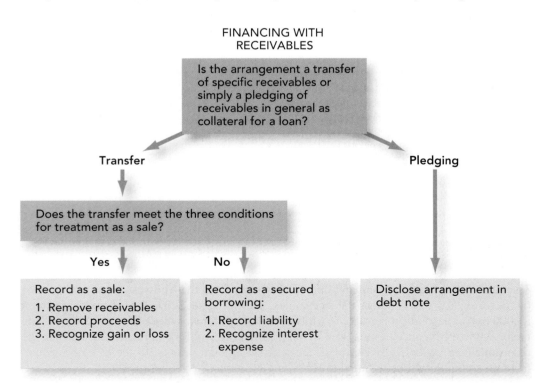

FINANCING WITH RECEIVABLES

DECISION MAKERS' PERSPECTIVE

RECEIVABLES MANAGEMENT   A company's investment in receivables is influenced by several variables, including the level of sales, the nature of the product or service sold, and credit and collection policies. These variables are, of course, related. For example, a change in credit policies could affect sales. In fact, more liberal credit policies—allowing customers a longer time to pay or offering cash discounts for early payment—often are initiated with the specific objective of increasing sales volume.

Management's choice of credit and collection policies often involves trade-offs. For example, offering cash discounts may increase sales volume, accelerate customer payment, and reduce bad debts. These benefits are not without cost. The cash discounts reduce the amount of cash collected from customers who take advantage of the discounts. Extending payment terms also may increase sales volume. However, this creates an increase in the required investment in receivables and may increase bad debts.

The ability to use receivables as a method of financing also offers management alternatives. Assigning, factoring, and discounting receivables are alternative methods of financing operations that must be evaluated relative to other financing methods such as lines of credit or other types of short-term borrowing.

Investors, creditors, and financial analysts can gain important insights by monitoring a company's investment in receivables. Chapter 5 introduced the receivables turnover ratio and the related average collection period, ratios designed to monitor receivables. Recall that these ratios are calculated as follows:

$$\text{Receivables turnover ratio} = \frac{\text{Net sales}}{\text{Average accounts receivable (net)}}$$

$$\text{Average collection period} = \frac{365 \text{ days}}{\text{Receivables turnover ratio}}$$

The turnover ratio shows the number of times during a period that the average accounts receivable balance is collected, and the average collection period is an approximation of the number of days the average accounts receivable balance is outstanding.

As a company's sales grow, receivables also will increase. If the percentage increase in receivables is greater than the percentage increase in sales, the receivables turnover ratio will decline (the average collection period will increase). This could indicate customer dissatisfaction with the product or that the company has extended too generous payment terms in order to attract new customers, which, in turn, could increase sales returns and bad debts.

These ratios also can be used to compare the relative effectiveness of companies in managing the investment in receivables. Of course, it would be meaningless to compare the receivables turnover ratio of a computer products company such as **IBM** with that of, say, a food products company like **Hershey.** A company selling high-priced, low-volume products like mainframe computers generally will grant customers longer payment terms than a company selling lower priced, higher volume food products. Graphic 7–11 lists the 2007 receivables turnover ratio for some well-known companies. The differences are as expected, given the nature of the companies' products.

GRAPHIC 7–11   Receivables Turnover Ratios

Company	2007 Receivables Turnover Ratio
IBM	4.24
Johnson & Johnson	6.48
Merck	6.97
Hershey	9.70
Sara Lee	9.74
Intel	12.60

Let's compute the 2007 receivables turnover ratio and the average collection period for two companies in the same industry, **Electronic Arts** and **Activision.**

($ in millions)	Electronic Arts 2007	Electronic Arts 2006	Activision 2007	Activision 2006
Accounts receivable (net)	$256	$ 199	$149	$29
Two-year averages	$227.5		$ 89	
Net sales—2007	$3,091		$1,513	

● LO9

Management must evaluate the costs and benefits of any change in credit and collection policies.

Balance sheet and income statement information—Electronic Arts and Activision

Real World Financials

Receivables turnover
and average collection
period—Electronic Arts
and Activision

	Electronic Arts	Activision	Industry Average
Receivables turnover	$= \dfrac{\$3{,}091}{\$227.5} = 13.6$	$\dfrac{\$1{,}513}{\$89} = 17.0$	6.3
Average collection period	$= \dfrac{365}{13.6} = 27$ days	$\dfrac{365}{17.0} = 21$ days	58 days

On average, Activision collects its receivables six days sooner than does Electronic Arts. A portion of Activision's sales, electronic downloads and product add-ons, are made directly to consumers online, significantly accelerating payment. This could account for the shorter collection period. Both companies take significantly less time to collect receivables than the industry average.

Academic research also has shown receivables information to be useful in financial statement analysis. Professors Lev and Thiagarajan empirically demonstrated the importance of a set of 12 fundamental variables in valuing companies' common stock. The set of variables included accounts receivable (change in accounts receivable minus change in sales) and allowance for uncollectible accounts (change in accounts receivable minus change in the allowance). Motivation for the receivables variable was that disproportionate increases in accounts receivable (relative to sales increases) can indicate difficulties in selling products, reflected in more lenient credit policies. The allowance variable was expected to indicate inadequate bad debt provisions. Both were found to be significant indicators of stock returns during high inflation years.[13]

EARNINGS QUALITY   In May 2001 the Securities and Exchange Commission sued the former top executives at **Sunbeam,** charging the company with financial reporting fraud that allegedly cost investors billions in losses. In the mid-1990s, Sunbeam needed help: its profits had declined significantly as did its stock price, and in 1996, the company reported a loss from continuing operations of $198 million. To the rescue comes Albert Dunlap, also known as "Chainsaw Al," based on his reputation as a ruthless executive known for his ability to restructure and turn around troubled companies, largely by eliminating jobs.

The strategy appeared to work. In 1997, Sunbeam's revenues had risen by 18% and profits were back in the black with income from continuing operations of $123 million. However, in April 1998, **PaineWebber Inc.** downgraded Sunbeam's stock recommendation. Why the downgrade? PaineWebber had noticed unusually high accounts receivable, massive increases in sales of electric blankets in the third quarter 1997, which usually sell best in the fourth quarter, as well as unusually high sales of barbecue grills for the fourth quarter. Soon after, Sunbeam announced a first quarter loss of $44.6 million, and Sunbeam's stock price fell 25%.

It eventually came to light that Dunlap and Sunbeam had been using a "bill and hold" strategy with retail buyers. This involved selling products at large discounts to retailers before they normally would buy and then holding the products in third-party warehouses, with delivery at a later date. According to an article in *Barron's,* much of the variation in Sunbeam's income from 1996 to 1997 reflected *a discretionary use of accruals* to accelerate expenses to 1996.[14]

Bad debt expense, and the corresponding allowance for uncollectible accounts, is one of several so-called discretionary accruals that directly impact a company's income. Other discretionary accruals include warranty expenses, discretionary compensation expenses such as bonuses, sales returns, and restructuring costs. Each of these accruals requires estimates of future events, thus providing management the opportunity to shift income among reporting periods. For example,

> **ARTHUR LEVITT, JR.**
> A third illusion played by some companies is using unrealistic assumptions to estimate . . . such items as sales returns, loan losses or warranty costs. In doing so, they stash accruals in cookie jars during good times and reach into them when needed in the bad times.[15]

Bad debt expense
is one of a variety
of discretionary
accruals that provide
management with
the opportunity to
manipulate income.

---

[13]B. Lev and S. R. Thiagarajan, "Fundamental Information Analysis," *Journal of Accounting Research 31,* no. 2 (Autumn 1993). The main conclusion of the study was that fundamental variables, not just earnings, are useful in firm valuation, particularly when examined in the context of macroeconomic conditions such as inflation.

[14]Jonathan Laing, "Dangerous Games," *Barron's* (June 8, 1998).

[15]Arthur Levitt, Jr., "The Numbers Game," *The CPA Journal,* December, 1998, p. 16.

if management overestimates bad debt expense in one period, a company will report lower profit that period and higher profit in a later period.

Recall our discussion in Chapter 4 concerning earnings quality. We learned that managers have the ability, to a limited degree, to manipulate reported income and that many observers believe this practice diminishes earnings quality because it can mask permanent earnings. Former SEC Chairman Arthur Levitt listed discretionary accruals, which he called "Miscellaneous Cookie Jar Reserves," as one of the most popular methods companies use to manipulate income.

Financial analysts must be alert to the effect of discretionary accruals on income. Abnormal fluctuations in these items should raise a red flag, motivating further investigation. In the Sunbeam example, for instance, red flags in the 1996 income statement included a variety of unusual expenses and a large increase in general and administrative expenses. The balance sheet reported an increase of 44% in current liabilities from the prior year. This increase was caused by activities that included a significant accrual for restructuring costs and a large increase in the accrued warranty liability. The allowance for uncollectible accounts also increased by 30%. The marketplace was less than vigilant in noting and interpreting these signs.

FINANCIAL REPORTING CASE **SOLUTION**

1. **Explain the allowance method of accounting for bad debts.** *(p. 336)* The allowance method estimates future bad debts in order to (1) match bad debt expense with related revenues and (2) report accounts receivable in the balance sheet at net realizable value. In an adjusting entry, we record bad debt expense and reduce accounts receivable indirectly by crediting a contra account to accounts receivable for an estimate of the amount that eventually will prove uncollectible.

2. **What approaches might Cisco have used to arrive at the $275 million bad debt provision?** *(p. 337)* There are two ways commonly used to arrive at an estimate of future bad debts, the income statement approach and the balance sheet approach. Using the income statement approach, we estimate bad debt expense as a percentage of each period's net credit sales. The balance sheet approach determines bad debt expense by estimating the net realizable value of accounts receivable. In other words, the allowance for uncollectible accounts is determined and bad debt expense is an indirect outcome of adjusting the allowance account to the desired balance.

3. **Are there any alternatives to the allowance method?** *(p. 340)* An alternative to the allowance method is the direct write-off method. Using this method, adjusting entries are not recorded and any bad debt that does arise simply is written off as bad debt expense. Of course, if the sale that generated this receivable occurred in a previous reporting period, this violates the matching principle. Operating expenses would have been understated and assets overstated that period. This is why the direct write-off method is not permitted by GAAP except in limited circumstances.

THE **BOTTOM LINE**

● **LO1**   Internal control refers to the plan designed to encourage adherence to company policies and procedures; promote operational efficiency; minimize irregularities, errors, thefts or fraud; and maximize the reliability and accuracy of accounting data. Key elements of an internal control system for cash receipts and disbursements include separation of record-keeping from control of cash duties and the periodic preparation of a bank reconciliation. (p. 328)

● **LO2**   Cash can be informally restricted by management for a particular purpose. Restrictions also can be contractually imposed. If restricted cash is available for current operations or to pay current liabilities, it's classified as a current asset; otherwise, it's classified as investments and funds or other assets. (p. 330)

● **LO3** The gross method of accounting for cash discounts considers a discount not taken as part of sales revenue. The net method considers a discount not taken as interest revenue. (p. 332)

● **LO4** When merchandise returns are anticipated, an allowance for sales returns should be recorded as a contra account to accounts receivable and sales revenue also should be reduced by the anticipated sales returns. (p. 334)

● **LO5** Uncollectible accounts receivable should be anticipated in order to match bad debt expense with revenues generated. Likewise, accounts receivable should be reduced by an allowance for uncollectible accounts to report accounts receivable at net realizable value. (p. 336)

● **LO6** There are two approaches to estimating future bad debts. The income statement approach estimates bad debt expense based on the notion that a certain percentage of each period's credit sales will prove to be uncollectible. The balance sheet approach to estimating future bad debts indirectly determines bad debt expense by directly estimating the net realizable value of accounts receivable at the end of the period. (p. 336)

● **LO7** Notes receivable are formal credit arrangements between a creditor (lender) and a debtor (borrower). The typical note receivable requires the payment of a specified face amount, also called principal, at a specified maturity date or dates. In addition, interest is paid at a stated percentage of the face amount. Interest on notes is calculated by multiplying the face amount by the annual rate by the fraction of the annual period. (p. 342)

● **LO8** A wide variety of methods exists for companies to use their receivables to obtain immediate cash. These methods can be described as either:
   a. A secured borrowing
   b. A sale of receivables
   If three conditions indicating surrender of control are met, the transferor accounts for the transfer of receivables as a sale; otherwise as a secured borrowing. (p. 345)

● **LO9** A company's investment in receivables is influenced by several related variables, to include the level of sales, the nature of the product or service, and credit and collection policies. Investors, creditors, and financial analysts can gain important insights by monitoring a company's investment in receivables. The receivables turnover and average collection period ratios are designed to monitor receivables. (p. 351) ●

APPENDIX 7 CASH CONTROLS

Bank Reconciliation

One of the most important tools used in the control of cash is the bank reconciliation. Since all cash receipts are deposited into the bank account and cash disbursements are made by check, the bank account provides a separate record of cash. It's desirable to periodically compare the bank balance with the balance in the company's own records and reconcile any differences.

From your own personal experience, you know that the ending balance in your checking account reported on the monthly bank statement you receive rarely equals the balance you have recorded in your checkbook. Differences arise from two types of items: timing differences and errors.

Timing differences occur when the company and the bank record transactions at different times. At any point in time the company may have adjusted the cash balance for items of which the bank is not yet aware. Likewise, the bank may have adjusted its record of that balance by items of which the company is not yet aware. For example, checks written and cash deposits are not all processed by the bank in the same month that they are recorded by the company. Also, the bank may adjust the company's account for items such as service charges that the company is not aware of until the bank statement is received.

Errors can be made either by the company or the bank. For example, a check might be written for $210 but recorded on the company's books as a $120 disbursement; a deposit of $500 might be processed incorrectly by the bank as a $50 deposit. In addition to serving

Differences between the cash book and bank balance occur due to differences in the timing of recognition of certain transactions and errors.

as a safeguard of cash, the bank reconciliation also uncovers errors such as these and helps ensure that the proper cash balance is reported in the balance sheet.

Bank reconciliations include adjustments to the balance per bank for timing differences involving transactions already reflected in the company's accounting records that have not yet been processed by the bank. These adjustments usually include *checks outstanding* and *deposits outstanding*. In addition, the balance per bank would be adjusted for any bank errors discovered. These adjustments produce an adjusted bank balance that represents the corrected cash balance.

The balance per books is similarly adjusted for timing differences involving transactions already reflected by the bank of which the company is unaware until the bank statement is received. These would include service charges, charges for NSF (nonsufficient funds) checks, and collections made by the bank on the company's behalf. In addition, the balance per books is adjusted for any company errors discovered, resulting in an adjusted book balance that will also represent the corrected cash balance. *Each of these adjustments requires a journal entry to correct the book balance.* Only adjustments to the book balance require journal entries. Graphic 7A–1 recaps these reconciling items.

Step 1: Adjustments to Bank Balance:

1. *Add deposits outstanding.* These represent cash amounts received by the company and debited to cash that have not been deposited in the bank by the bank statement cutoff date and cash receipts deposited in the bank near the end of the period that are not recorded by the bank until after the cutoff date.
2. *Deduct checks outstanding.* These represent checks written and recorded by the company as credits to cash that have not yet been processed by the bank before the cutoff date.
3. *Bank errors.* These will either be increases or decreases depending on the nature of the error.

Step 2: Adjustments to Book Balance:

1. *Add collections made by the bank* on the company's behalf and other increases in cash that the company is unaware of until the bank statement is received.
2. *Deduct service and other charges* made by the bank that the company is unaware of until the bank statement is received.
3. *Deduct NSF (nonsufficient funds) checks.* These are checks previously deposited for which the payors do not have sufficient funds in their accounts to cover the amount of the checks. The checks are returned to the company whose responsibility it is to seek payment from payors.
4. *Company errors.* These will either be increases or decreases depending on the nature of the error.

GRAPHIC 7A–1

Bank Reconciliation— Reconciling Items

Bank balance
+ Deposits outstanding
− Checks outstanding
± Errors

Corrected balance

Book balance
+ Collections by bank
− Service charges
− NSF checks
± Errors

Corrected balance

The two corrected balances must equal.

To demonstrate the bank reconciliation process, consider Illustration 7A–1.

The next step is to prepare adjusting journal entries to reflect each of the adjustments to the balance per books. These represent amounts the company was not previously aware of. No adjusting entries are needed for the adjustments to the balance per bank because the company has already recorded these items. However, the bank needs to be notified of any errors discovered.

Cash	1,120	
Notes receivable		1,000
Interest revenue		120

To record the receipt of principal and interest on note collected directly by the bank.

Miscellaneous expense (bank service charges)	80	
Accounts receivable (NSF checks)	2,187	
Accounts payable (error in check to supplier)	1,000	
Cash		3,267

To record credits to cash revealed by the bank reconciliation.

| ILLUSTRATION 7A–1 Bank Reconciliation | The Hawthorne Manufacturing Company maintains a general checking account at the First Pacific Bank. First Pacific provides a bank statement and canceled checks once a month. The cutoff date is the last day of the month. The bank statement for the month of May is summarized as follows: |

Balance, May 1, 2009	$32,120
Deposits	82,140
Checks processed	(78,433)
Service charges	(80)
NSF checks	(2,187)
Note payment collected by bank (includes $120 interest)	1,120
Balance, May 31, 2009	$34,680

The company's general ledger cash account has a balance of $35,276 at the end of May. A review of the company records and the bank statement reveals the following:
1. Cash receipts not yet deposited totaled $2,965.
2. A deposit of $1,020 was made on May 31 that was not credited to the company's account until June.
3. All checks written in April have been processed by the bank. Checks written in May that had not been processed by the bank total $5,536.
4. A check written for $1,790 was incorrectly recorded by the company as a $790 disbursement. The check was for payment to a supplier of raw materials.

The bank reconciliation prepared by the company appears as follows:

Step 1: Bank Balance to Corrected Balance

Balance per bank statement	$34,680
Add: Deposits outstanding	3,985*
Deduct: Checks outstanding	(5,536)
Corrected cash balance	$33,129

Step 2: Book Balance to Corrected Balance

Balance per books	$35,276
Add: Note collected by bank	1,120
Deduct:	
Service charges	(80)
NSF checks	(2,187)
Error—understatement of check	(1,000)
Corrected cash balance	$33,129

*$2,965 + 1,020 = $3,985

After these entries are posted, the general ledger cash account will equal the corrected balance of $33,129.

Petty Cash

Most companies keep a small amount of cash on hand to pay for low-cost items such as postage, office supplies, delivery charges, and entertainment expenses. It would be inconvenient, time consuming, and costly to process a check each time these small payments are made. A petty cash fund provides a more efficient way to handle these payments.

The petty cash fund always should have cash and receipts that together equal the amount of the fund.

A petty cash fund is established by transferring a specified amount of cash from the company's general checking account to an employee designated as the petty cash custodian. The amount of the fund should approximate the expenditures made from the fund during a relatively short period of time (say a week or a month). The custodian disburses cash from the fund when the appropriate documentation is presented, such as a receipt for the purchase of office supplies. At any point in time, the custodian should be in possession of cash and appropriate receipts that sum to the amount of the fund. The receipts serve as the basis for recording appropriate expenses each time the fund is replenished. Consider the example in Illustration 7A–2.

> On May 1, 2009, the Hawthorne Manufacturing Company established a $200 petty cash fund. John Ringo is designated as the petty cash custodian. The fund will be replenished at the end of each month. On May 1, 2009, a check is written for $200 made out to John Ringo, petty cash custodian. During the month of May, John paid bills totaling $160 summarized as follows:
>
> | | |
> |---|---:|
> | Postage | $ 40 |
> | Office supplies | 35 |
> | Delivery charges | 55 |
> | Entertainment | 30 |
> | Total | $160 |

ILLUSTRATION 7A–2

Petty Cash Fund

In journal entry form, the transaction to establish the fund would be recorded as follows:

May 1, 2009

Petty Cash	200	
Cash (checking account)		200

A petty cash fund is established by writing a check to the custodian.

No entries are recorded at the time the actual expenditures are made from the fund. The expenditures are recorded when reimbursement is requested at the end of the month. At that time, a check is written to John Ringo, petty cash custodian, for the total of the fund receipts, $160 in this case. John cashes the check and replenishes the fund to $200. In journal entry form, replenishing the fund would be recorded as follows:

May 31, 2009

Postage expense	40	
Office supplies expense	35	
Delivery expense	55	
Entertainment expense	30	
Cash (checking account)		160

The appropriate expense accounts are debited when the petty cash fund is reimbursed.

The petty cash account is not debited when replenishing the fund. If, however, the size of the fund is increased at time of replenishment, the account is debited for the increase. Similarly, petty cash would be credited if the size of the fund is decreased.

To maintain the control objective of separation of duties, the petty cash custodian should not be involved in the process of writing or approving checks, nor in recordkeeping. In addition, management should arrange for surprise counts of the fund. ●

QUESTIONS FOR REVIEW OF KEY TOPICS

Q 7–1 Define cash equivalents.

Q 7–2 Explain the primary functions of internal controls procedures in the accounting area. What is meant by separation of duties?

Q 7–3 What are the responsibilities of management described in Section 404 of the Sarbanes-Oxley Act? What are the responsibilities of the company's auditor?

Q 7–4 Define a compensating balance. How are compensating balances reported in financial statements?

Q 7–5 Explain the difference between a trade discount and a cash discount.

Q 7–6 Distinguish between the gross and net methods of accounting for cash discounts.

Q 7–7 Briefly explain the accounting treatment for sales returns.

Q 7–8 Explain the typical way companies account for uncollectible accounts receivable (bad debts). When is it permissible to record bad debt expense only at the time when receivables actually prove uncollectible?

Q 7–9 Briefly explain the difference between the income statement approach and the balance sheet approach to estimating bad debts.

Q 7–10   Is any special accounting treatment required for the assigning of accounts receivable in general as collateral for debt?

Q 7–11   Explain any possible differences between accounting for accounts receivable factored without recourse and those factored with recourse.

Q 7–12   What is meant by the discounting of a note receivable? Describe the four-step process used to account for discounted notes.

Q 7–13   What are the key variables that influence a company's investment in receivables? Describe the two ratios used by financial analysts to monitor a company's investment in receivables.

Q 7–14   (Based on Appendix 7) In a two-step bank reconciliation, identify the items that might be necessary to adjust the bank balance to the corrected cash balance. Identify the items that might be necessary to adjust the book balance to the corrected cash balance.

Q 7–15   (Based on Appendix 7) How is a petty cash fund established? How is the fund replenished?

BRIEF EXERCISES

BE 7–1
Internal control

● LO1

Janice Dodds opens the mail for the Ajax Plumbing Company. She lists all customer checks on a spreadsheet that includes the name of the customer and the check amount. The checks, along with the spreadsheet, are then sent to Jim Seymour in the accounting department who records the checks and deposits them daily in the company's checking account. How could the company improve its internal control procedure for the handling of its cash receipts?

BE 7–2
Cash and cash equivalents

● LO2

The following items appeared on the year-end trial balance of Consolidated Freight Corporation: cash in a checking account, U.S. Treasury bills that mature in six months, undeposited customer checks, cash in a savings account, and currency and coins. Which of these items would be included in the company's balance sheet as cash and cash equivalents?

BE 7–3
Cash discounts; gross method

● LO3

On December 28, 2009, Tristar Communications sold 10 units of its new satellite uplink system to various customers for $25,000 each. The terms of each sale were 1/10, n/30. Tristar uses the gross method to account for sales discounts. In what year will income before tax be affected by discounts, assuming that all customers paid the net-of-discount amount on January 6, 2010? By how much?

BE 7–4
Cash discounts; net method

● LO3

Refer to the situation described in BE 7–3. Answer the questions assuming that Tristar uses the net method to account for sales discounts.

BE 7–5
Sales returns

● LO4

During 2009, its first year of operations, Hollis Industries recorded sales of $10,600,000 and experienced returns of $720,000. Cost of goods sold totaled $6,360,000 (60% of sales). The company estimates that 8% of all sales will be returned. Prepare the year-end adjusting journal entries to account for anticipated sales returns.

BE 7–6
Uncollectible accounts; income statement approach

● LO5 LO6

The following information relates to a company's accounts receivable: accounts receivable balance at the beginning of the year, $300,000; allowance for uncollectible accounts at the beginning of the year, $25,000 (credit balance); credit sales during the year, $1,500,000; accounts receivable written off during the year; $16,000, cash collections from customers; $1,450,000. Assuming the company estimates bad debts at an amount equal to 2% of credit sales, calculate (1) bad debt expense for the year and (2) the year-end balance in the allowance for uncollectible accounts.

BE 7–7
Uncollectible accounts; balance sheet approach

● LO5 LO6

Refer to the situation described in BE 7–6. Answer the two questions assuming the company estimates that future bad debts will equal 10% of the year-end balance in accounts receivable.

BE 7–8
Uncollectible accounts; solving for unknown

● LO5 LO6

A company's year-end balance in accounts receivable is $2,000,000. The allowance for uncollectible accounts had a beginning-of-year credit balance of $30,000. An aging of accounts receivable at the end of the year indicates a required allowance of $38,000. If bad debt expense for the year was $40,000, what was the amount of bad debts written off during the year?

BE 7–9
Uncollectible
accounts; solving
for unknown

● LO5 LO6

Refer to the situation described in BE 7–8. If credit sales for the year were $8,200,000 and $7,950,000 was collected from credit customers, what was the beginning-of-year balance in accounts receivable?

BE 7–10
Note receivable

● LO7

On December 1, 2009, Davenport Company sold merchandise to a customer for $20,000. In payment for the merchandise, the customer signed a 6% note requiring the payment of interest and principal on March 1, 2010. How much interest revenue will the company recognize during 2009? In 2010?

BE 7–11
Factoring of
accounts receivable

● LO8

Logitech Corporation transferred $100,000 of accounts receivable to a local bank. The transfer was made without recourse. The local bank remits 85% of the factored amount to Logitech and retains the remaining 15%. When the bank collects the receivables, it will remit to Logitech the retained amount less a fee equal to 3% of the total amount factored. What is the effect of this transaction on the company's assets, liabilities, and income before income taxes?

BE 7–12
Factoring of
accounts receivable

● LO8

Refer to the situation described in BE 7–11. Assuming that the sale criteria are not met, describe how Logitech would account for the transfer.

BE 7–13
Discounting a note

● LO8

On March 31, Dower Publishing discounted a $30,000 note at a local bank. The note was dated February 28 and required the payment of the principal amount and interest at 6% on May 31. The bank's discount rate is 8%. How much cash will Dower receive from the bank on March 31?

BE 7–14
Receivables
turnover

● LO9

Camden Hardware's credit sales for the year were $320,000. Accounts receivable at the beginning and end of the year were $50,000 and $70,000, respectively. Calculate the accounts receivable turnover ratio and the average collection period for the year.

EXERCISES   available with McGraw–Hill's Homework Manager www.mhhe.com/spiceland5e

An alternate exercise and problem set is available on the text website: www.mhhe.com/spiceland5e

E 7–1
Cash and cash
equivalents;
restricted cash

● LO2

The controller of the Red Wing Corporation is in the process of preparing the company's 2009 financial statements. She is trying to determine the correct balance of cash and cash equivalents to be reported as a current asset in the balance sheet. The following items are being considered:

a. Balances in the company's accounts at the First National Bank; checking $13,500, savings $22,100.

b. Undeposited customer checks of $5,200.

c. Currency and coins on hand of $580.

d. Savings account at the East Bay Bank with a balance of $400,000. This account is being used to accumulate cash for future plant expansion (in 2011).

e. $20,000 in a checking account at the East Bay Bank. The balance in the account represents a 20% compensating balance for a $100,000 loan with the bank. Red Wing may not withdraw the funds until the loan is due in 2012.

f. U.S. Treasury bills; 2-month maturity bills totaling $15,000, and 7-month bills totaling $20,000.

Required:
1. Determine the correct balance of cash and cash equivalents to be reported in the current asset section of the 2009 balance sheet.

2. For each of the items not included in your answer to requirement 1, explain the correct classification of the item.

E 7–2
Cash and cash
equivalents

● LO2

Delta Automotive Corporation has the following assets listed in its 12/31/09 trial balance:

Cash in bank—checking account	$22,500
U.S. Treasury bills (mature in 60 days)*	5,000
Cash on hand (currency and coins)	1,350
U.S Treasury bills (mature in six months)*	10,000
Undeposited customer checks	1,840

*Purchased on 11/30/09

Required:

1. Determine the correct balance of cash and cash equivalents to be reported in the current asset section of the 2009 balance sheet.
2. For each of the items not included in your answer to requirement 1, explain the correct classification of the item.

E 7–3
Trade and cash discounts; the gross method and the net method compared

● LO3

Tracy Company, a manufacturer of air conditioners, sold 100 units to Thomas Company on November 17, 2009. The units have a list price of $600 each, but Thomas was given a 30% trade discount. The terms of the sale were 2/10, n/30.

Required:

1. Prepare the journal entries to record the sale on November 17 (ignore cost of goods) and payment on November 26, 2009, assuming that the gross method of accounting for cash discounts is used.
2. Prepare the journal entries to record the sale on November 17 (ignore cost of goods) and payment on December 15, 2009, assuming that the gross method of accounting for cash discounts is used.
3. Repeat requirements 1 and 2 assuming that the net method of accounting for cash discounts is used.

E 7–4
Cash discounts; the gross method

● LO3

Harwell Company manufactures automobile tires. On July 15, 2009, the company sold 1,000 tires to the Nixon Car Company for $50 each. The terms of the sale were 2/10, n/30. Harwell uses the gross method of accounting for cash discounts.

Required:

1. Prepare the journal entries to record the sale on July 15 (ignore cost of goods) and payment on July 23, 2009.
2. Prepare the journal entries to record the sale on July 15 (ignore cost of goods) and payment on August 15, 2009.

E 7–5
Cash discounts; the net method

● LO3

[This is a variation of the previous exercise modified to focus on the net method of accounting for cash discounts.]

Harwell Company manufactures automobile tires. On July 15, 2009, the company sold 1,000 tires to the Nixon Car Company for $50 each. The terms of the sale were 2/10, n/30. Harwell uses the net method of accounting for cash discounts.

Required:

1. Prepare the journal entries to record the sale on July 15 (ignore cost of goods) and payment on July 23, 2009.
2. Prepare the journal entries to record the sale on July 15 (ignore cost of goods) and payment on August 15, 2009.

E 7–6
Sales returns

● LO4

Halifax Manufacturing allows its customers to return merchandise for any reason up to 90 days after delivery and receive a credit to their accounts. The company began 2009 with an allowance for sales returns of $300,000. During 2009, Halifax sold merchandise on account for $11,500,000. This merchandise cost Halifax $7,475,000 (65% of selling prices). Also during the year, customers returned $450,000 in sales for credit. Sales returns, estimated to be 4% of sales, are recorded as an adjusting entry at the end of the year.

Required:

1. Prepare the entry to record the merchandise returns and the year-end adjusting entry for estimated returns.
2. What is the amount of the year-end allowance for sales returns after the adjusting entry is recorded?

E 7–7
Uncollectible accounts; allowance method vs. direct write-off method

● LO5 LO6

Johnson Company uses the allowance method to account for uncollectible accounts receivable. Bad debt expense is established as a percentage of credit sales. For 2009, net credit sales totaled $4,500,000, and the estimated bad debt percentage is 1.5%. The allowance for uncollectible accounts had a credit balance of $42,000 at the beginning of 2009 and $40,000, after adjusting entries, at the end of 2009.

Required:

1. What is bad debt expense for 2009?
2. Determine the amount of accounts receivable written off during 2009.
3. If the company uses the direct write-off method, what would bad debt expense be for 2009?

E 7–8
Uncollectible accounts; allowance method; balance sheet approach

● LO5 LO6

Colorado Rocky Cookie Company offers credit terms to its customers. At the end of 2009, accounts receivable totaled $625,000. The allowance method is used to account for uncollectible accounts. The allowance for uncollectible accounts had a credit balance of $32,000 at the beginning of 2009 and $21,000 in receivables were written off during the year as uncollectible. Also, $1,200 in cash was received in December from a customer whose account previously had been written off. The company estimates bad debts by applying a percentage of 10% to accounts receivable at the end of the year.

Required:

1. Prepare journal entries to record the write-off of receivables, the collection of $1,200 for previously written off receivables, and the year-end adjusting entry for bad debt expense.
2. How would accounts receivable be shown in the 2009 year-end balance sheet?

E 7–9
Uncollectible
accounts; allowance
method and direct
write-off method
compared; solving
for unknown

● **LO6**

Castle Company provides estimates for its uncollectible accounts. The allowance for uncollectible accounts had a credit balance of $17,280 at the beginning of 2009 and a $22,410 credit balance at the end of 2009 (after adjusting entries). If the direct write-off method had been used to account for uncollectible accounts (bad debt expense equals actual write-offs), the income statement for 2009 would have included bad debt expense of $17,100 and revenue of $2,200 from the collection of previously written off bad debts.

Required:
Determine bad debt expense for 2009 according to the allowance method.

E 7–10
Uncollectible
accounts; allowance
method; solving for
unknowns

● **LO5 LO6**

Real World Financials

Cisco Systems reported the following information in its 2007 financial statements ($ in millions):

	2007	2006
Balance Sheet:		
Accounts receivable, net	$ 3,989	$ 3,303
2007 Income statement:		
Sales revenue	$34,922	

A note disclosed that the allowance for uncollectible accounts had a balance of $166 million and $175 million at the end of 2007 and 2006, respectively. Bad debt expense for 2007 was $6 million.

Required:
Determine the amount of cash collected from customers during 2007.

E 7–11
Note receivable

● **LO7**

On June 30, 2009, the Esquire Company sold some merchandise to a customer for $30,000. In payment, Esquire agreed to accept a 6% note requiring the payment of interest and principal on March 31, 2010. The 6% rate is appropriate in this situation.

Required:
1. Prepare journal entries to record the sale of merchandise (omit any entry that might be required for the cost of the goods sold), the December 31, 2009, interest accrual, and the March 31 collection.
2. If the December 31 adjusting entry for the interest accrual is not prepared, by how much will income before income taxes be over- or understated in 2009 and 2010?

E 7–12
Noninterest-bearing
note receivable

● **LO7**

[This is a variation of the previous exercise modified to focus on a noninterest-bearing note.]
    On June 30, 2009, the Esquire Company sold some merchandise to a customer for $30,000 and agreed to accept as payment a noninterest-bearing note with an 8% discount rate requiring the payment of $30,000 on March 31, 2010. The 8% rate is appropriate in this situation.

Required:
1. Prepare journal entries to record the sale of merchandise (omit any entry that might be required for the cost of the goods sold), the December 31, 2009, interest accrual, and the March 31 collection.
2. What is the *effective* interest rate on the note?

E 7–13
Interest-bearing
note receivable;
solving for
unknown rate

● **LO7**

On January 1, 2009, the Apex Company exchanged some shares of common stock it had been holding as an investment for a note receivable. The note principal plus interest is due on January 1, 2010. The 2009 income statement reported $2,200 in interest revenue from this note and a $6,000 gain on sale of investment in stock. The stock's book value was $16,000. The company's fiscal year ends on December 31.

Required:
1. What is the note's effective interest rate?
2. Reconstruct the journal entries to record the sale of the stock on January 1, 2009, and the adjusting entry to record interest revenue at the end of 2009. The company records adjusting entries only at year-end.

E 7–14
Assigning of
specific accounts
receivable

● **LO8**

On June 30, 2009, the High Five Surfboard Company had outstanding accounts receivable of $600,000. On July 1, 2009, the company borrowed $450,000 from the Equitable Finance Corporation and signed a promissory note. Interest at 10% is payable monthly. The company assigned specific receivables totaling $600,000 as collateral for the loan. Equitable Finance charges a finance fee equal to 1.8% of the accounts receivable assigned.

Required:
Prepare the journal entry to record the borrowing on the books of High Five Surfboard.

E 7–15
Factoring of
accounts receivable
without recourse

● **LO8**

Mountain High Ice Cream Company transferred $60,000 of accounts receivable to the Prudential Bank. The transfer was made *without recourse*. Prudential remits 90% of the factored amount to Mountain High and retains 10%. When the bank collects the receivables, it will remit to Mountain High the retained amount less a 2% fee (2% of the total factored amount).

Required:
Prepare the journal entry to record the transfer on the books of Mountain High assuming that the sale criteria are met.

E 7–16
Factoring of accounts receivable with recourse

● LO8

[This is a variation of the previous exercise modified to focus on factoring with recourse.]

Mountain High Ice Cream Company transferred $60,000 of accounts receivable to the Prudential Bank. The transfer was made *with recourse*. Prudential remits 90% of the factored amount to Mountain High and retains 10%. When the bank collects the receivables, it will remit to Mountain High the retained amount less a 2% fee (2% of the total factored amount). Mountain High anticipates a $3,000 recourse obligation.

Required:
Prepare the journal entry to record the transfer on the books of Mountain High assuming that the sale criteria are met.

E 7–17
Discounting a note receivable

● LO8

Selkirk Company obtained a $15,000 note receivable from a customer on January 1, 2009. The note, along with interest at 10%, is due on July 1, 2009. On February 28, 2009, Selkirk discounted the note at Unionville Bank. The bank's discount rate is 12%.

Required:
Prepare the journal entries required on February 28, 2009, to accrue interest and to record the discounting (round all calculations to the nearest dollar) for Selkirk. Assume that the discounting is accounted for as a sale.

E 7–18
Concepts; terminology

● LO1 through LO8

Listed below are several terms and phrases associated with cash and receivables. Pair each item from List A (by letter) with the item from List B that is most appropriately associated with it.

List A	List B
____ 1. Internal control	a. Restriction on cash.
____ 2. Trade discount	b. Cash discount not taken is sales revenue.
____ 3. Cash equivalents	c. Includes separation of duties.
____ 4. Allowance for uncollectibles	d. Bad debt expense a % of credit sales.
____ 5. Cash discount	e. Recognizes bad debts as they occur.
____ 6. Balance sheet approach	f. Sale of receivables to a financial institution.
____ 7. Income statement approach	g. Include highly liquid investments.
____ 8. Net method	h. Estimate of bad debts.
____ 9. Compensating balance	i. Reduction in amount paid by credit customer.
____ 10. Discounting	j. Reduction below list price.
____ 11. Gross method	k. Cash discount not taken is interest revenue.
____ 12. Direct write-off method	l. Bad debt expense determined by estimating realizable value.
____ 13. Factoring	m. Sale of note receivable to a financial institution.

E 7–19
Receivables; transaction analysis

● LO3 LO5 through LO8

Weldon Corporation's fiscal year ends December 31. The following is a list of transactions involving receivables that occurred during 2009:

Mar. 17	Accounts receivable of $1,700 were written off as uncollectible. The company uses the allowance method.
30	Loaned an officer of the company $20,000 and received a note requiring principal and interest at 7% to be paid on March 30, 2010.
May 30	Discounted the $20,000 note at a local bank. The bank's discount rate is 8%. The note was discounted without recourse and the sale criteria are met.
June 30	Sold merchandise to the Blankenship Company for $12,000. Terms of the sale are 2/10, n/30. Weldon uses the gross method to account for cash discounts.
July 8	The Blankenship Company paid its account in full.
Aug. 31	Sold stock in a nonpublic company with a book value of $5,000 and accepted a $6,000 non-interest-bearing note with a discount rate of 8%. The $6,000 payment is due on February 28, 2010. The stock has no ready market value.
Dec. 31	Bad debt expense is estimated to be 2% of credit sales for the year. Credit sales for 2009 were $700,000.

Required:
1. Prepare journal entries for each of the above transactions (round all calculations to the nearest dollar).
2. Prepare any additional year-end adjusting entries indicated.

E 7–20
Ratio analysis

● LO9

Real World Financials

Microsoft Corporation reported the following information in its financial statements for three successive quarters during the 2007 fiscal year ($ in millions):

	Three Months Ended		
	3/31/07 (Q3)	12/31/06 (Q2)	9/30/06 (Q1)
Balance sheets:			
Accounts receivable, net	$ 8,454	$ 9,895	$ 6,879
Income statements:			
Sales revenue	$14,398	$12,542	$10,811

Required:

Compute the receivables turnover ratio and the average collection period for the second and third quarters. Assume that each quarter consists of 91 days.

E 7–21
Ratio analysis;
solve for unknown

● **LO9**

The current asset section of the Moorcroft Outboard Motor Company's balance sheet reported the following amounts:

	12/31/09	12/31/08
Accounts receivable, net	$400,000	$300,000

The average collection period for 2009 is 50 days.

Required:

Determine net sales for 2009.

E 7–22
Petty cash

● **Appendix**

Loucks Company established a $200 petty cash fund on October 2, 2009. The fund is replenished at the end of each month. At the end of October 2009, the fund contained $37 in cash and the following receipts:

Office supplies	$76
Lunch with client	48
Postage	20
Miscellaneous	19

Required:

Prepare the necessary general journal entries to establish the petty cash fund on October 2 and to replenish the fund on October 31.

E 7–23
Petty cash

● **Appendix**

The petty cash fund of Ricco's Automotive contained the following items at the end of September 2009:

Currency and coins		$ 58
Receipts for the following expenditures:		
Delivery charges	$16	
Printer paper	11	
Paper clips and rubber bands	8	35
An I.O.U. from an employee		25
Postage		32
Total		$150

The petty cash fund was established at the beginning of September with a transfer of $150 from cash to the petty cash account.

Required:

Prepare the journal entry to replenish the fund at the end of September.

E 7–24
Bank reconciliation

● **Appendix**

Jansen Company's general ledger showed a checking account balance of $23,820 at the end of May 2009. The May 31 cash receipts of $2,340, included in the general ledger balance, were placed in the night depository at the bank on May 31 and were processed by the bank on June 1. The bank statement dated May 31, 2009, showed bank service charges of $38. All checks written by the company had been processed by the bank by May 31 and were listed on the bank statement except for checks totaling $1,890.

Required:

Prepare a bank reconciliation as of May 31, 2009. [*Hint:* You will need to compute the balance that would appear on the bank statement.]

E 7–25
Bank reconciliation
and adjusting
entries

● **Appendix**

Harrison Company maintains a checking account at the First National City Bank. The bank provides a bank statement along with canceled checks on the last day of each month. The July 2009 bank statement included the following information:

Balance, July 1, 2009	$ 55,678
Deposits	179,500
Checks processed	(192,610)
Service charges	(30)
NSF checks	(1,200)
Monthly loan payment deducted directly by bank from account	
(includes $320 in interest)	(3,320)
Balance, July 31, 2009	$ 38,018

The company's general ledger account had a balance of $38,918 at the end of July. Deposits outstanding totaled $6,300 and all checks written by the company were processed by the bank except for those totaling $8,420. In addition, a $2,000 July deposit from a credit customer was recorded as a $200 debit to cash and credit to accounts receivable, and a check correctly recorded by the company as a $30 disbursement was incorrectly processed by the bank as a $300 disbursement.

Required:

1. Prepare a bank reconciliation for the month of July.
2. Prepare the necessary journal entries at the end of July to adjust the general ledger cash account.

CPA AND CMA REVIEW QUESTIONS

CPA Exam Questions

SCHWESER

The following questions are used in the Kaplan CPA Review Course to study receivables while preparing for the CPA examination. Determine the response that best completes the statements or questions.

● **LO5**

1. At January 1, 2009, Simpson Co. had a credit balance of $260,000 in its allowance for uncollectible accounts. Based on past experience, 2 percent of Simpson's credit sales have been uncollectible. During 2009, Simpson wrote off $325,000 of accounts receivable. Credit sales for 2009 were $9,000,000. In its December 31, 2009, balance sheet, what amount should Simpson report as allowance for uncollectible accounts?

   a. $115,000
   b. $180,000
   c. $245,000
   d. $440,000

● **LO5 LO6**

2. The balance in accounts receivable at the beginning of 2009 was $600. During 2009, $3,200 of credit sales were recorded. If the ending balance in accounts receivable was $500 and $200 in accounts receivable were written off during the year, the amount of cash collected from customers was

   a. $3,100
   b. $3,200
   c. $3,300
   d. $3,800

● **LO5**

3. A company uses the allowance method to account for bad debts. What is the effect on each of the following accounts of the collection of an account previously written off?

	Allowance for Uncollectible Accounts	Bad Debt Expense
a.	Increase	Decrease
b.	No effect	Decrease
c.	Increase	No effect
d.	No effect	No effect

● **LO4 LO5**

4. The following information relates to Jay Co.'s accounts receivable for 2009:

Accounts receivable balance, 1/1/09	$650,000
Credit sales for 2009	2,700,000
Sales returns during 2009	75,000
Accounts receivable written off during 2009	40,000
Collections from customers during 2009	2,150,000
Allowance for uncollectible accounts balance, 12/31/09	110,000

   What amount should Jay report for accounts receivable, before allowances, at December 31, 2009?

   a. $ 925,000
   b. $1,085,000
   c. $1,125,000
   d. $1,200,000

● **LO8**

5. Gar Co. factored its receivables without recourse with Ross Bank. Gar received cash as a result of this transaction, which is best described as a

   a. Loan from Ross collateralized by Gar's accounts receivable.
   b. Loan from Ross to be repaid by the proceeds from Gar's accounts receivables.
   c. Sale of Gar's accounts receivable to Ross, with the risk of uncollectible accounts transferred to Ross.
   d. Sale of Gar's accounts receivable to Ross, with the risk of uncollectible accounts retained by Gar.

● LO5 LO6

6. The following information pertains to Tara Co.'s accounts receivable at December 31, 2009:

Days Outstanding	Amount	Estimated % Uncollectible
0–60	$120,000	1%
61–120	90,000	2%
Over 120	100,000	6%
	$310,000	

During 2009, Tara wrote off $7,000 in receivables and recovered $4,000 that had been written off in prior years. Tara's December 31, 2008, allowance for uncollectible accounts was $22,000. Under the aging method, what amount of allowance for uncollectible accounts should Tara report at December 31, 2009?

a. $ 9,000
b. $10,000
c. $13,000
d. $19,000

● LO5 LO6

7. West Company had the following account balances at December 31, 2009, before recording bad debt expense for the year:

Accounts receivable	$ 900,000
Allowance for uncollectible accounts (credit balance)	16,000
Credit sales for 2009	1,750,000

West is considering the following methods of estimating bad debts for 2009:
● Based on 2% of credit sales
● Based on 5% of year-end accounts receivable

What amount should West charge to bad debt expense at the end of 2009 under each method?

	Percentage of Credit Sales	Percentage of Accounts Receivable
a.	$35,000	$29,000
b.	$35,000	$45,000
c.	$51,000	$29,000
d.	$51,000	$45,000

CMA Exam Questions

The following questions dealing with receivables are adapted from questions that previously appeared on Certified Management Accountant (CMA) examinations. The CMA designation sponsored by the Institute of Management Accountants (**www.imanet.org**) provides members with an objective measure of knowledge and competence in the field of management accounting. Determine the response that best completes the statements or questions.

● LO5 LO6

1. Bad debt expense must be estimated in order to satisfy the matching principle when expenses are recorded in the same periods as the related revenues. In estimating bad debt expense for a period, companies generally accrue

a. Either an amount based on a percentage of total sales or an amount based on a percentage of accounts receivable after adjusting for any balance in the allowance for doubtful accounts.
b. A percentage of total sales.
c. Either an amount based on a percentage of credit sales or an amount based on a percentage of accounts receivable after adjusting for any balance in the allowance for doubtful accounts.
d. An amount equal to last year's bad debt expense.

Questions 2 through 3 are based on the following information:

Madison Corporation uses the allowance method to value its accounts receivable and is making the annual adjustments at fiscal year-end, November 30. The proportion of uncollectible accounts is estimated based on past experience, which indicates 1.5% of net credit sales will be uncollectible. Total sales for the year were $2,000,000, of which $200,000 were cash transactions. Madison has determined that the Norris Corporation accounts receivable balance of $10,000 is uncollectible and will write off this account before year-end adjustments are made. Listed below are Madison's account balances at November 30 prior to any adjustments and the $10,000 write-off.

Sales	$2,000,000
Accounts receivable	750,000
Sales discounts	125,000
Allowance for doubtful accounts	16,500
Sales returns and allowances	175,000
Bad debt expense	0

● LO5

2. The entry to write off Norris Corporation's accounts receivable balance of $10,000 will

   a. Increase total assets and decrease net income.
   b. Decrease total assets and net income.
   c. Have no effect on total assets and decrease net income.
   d. Have no effect on total assets and net income.

● LO5

3. As a result of the November 30 adjusting entry to provide for bad debts, the allowance for doubtful accounts will

   a. Increase by $30,000.
   b. Increase by $25,500.
   c. Increase by $22,500.
   d. Decrease by $22,500.

PROBLEMS

available with McGraw–Hill's Homework Manager www.mhhe.com/spiceland5e

An alternate exercise and problem set is available on the text website: www.mhhe.com/spiceland5e

P 7–1
Uncollectible
accounts;
allowance method;
income statement
and balance sheet
approach

● LO5 LO6

Swathmore Clothing Corporation grants its customers 30 days' credit. The company uses the allowance method for its uncollectible accounts receivable. During the year, a monthly bad debt accrual is made by multiplying 3% times the amount of credit sales for the month. At the fiscal year-end of December 31, an aging of accounts receivable schedule is prepared and the allowance for uncollectible accounts is adjusted accordingly.

At the end of 2008, accounts receivable were $574,000 and the allowance account had a credit balance of $54,000. Accounts receivable activity for 2009 was as follows:

Beginning balance	$ 574,000
Credit sales	2,620,000
Collections	(2,483,000)
Write-offs	(68,000)
Ending balance	$ 643,000

The company's controller prepared the following aging summary of year-end accounts receivable:

	Summary	
Age Group	Amount	Percent Uncollectible
0–60 days	$430,000	4%
61–90 days	98,000	15
91–120 days	60,000	25
Over 120 days	55,000	40
Total	$643,000	

Required:
1. Prepare a summary journal entry to record the monthly bad debt accrual and the write-offs during the year.
2. Prepare the necessary year-end adjusting entry for bad debt expense.
3. What is total bad debt expense for 2009? How would accounts receivable appear in the 2009 balance sheet?

P 7–2
Uncollectible
accounts

● LO5

Real World Financials

Amdahl Corporation manufactures large-scale, high performance computer systems. In a recent annual report, the balance sheet included the following information (dollars in thousands):

	Current Year	Previous Year
Current assets:		
Receivables, net of allowances of $5,042 and $6,590 in the previous year	$504,944	$580,640

In addition, the income statement reported sales revenue of $2,158,755 ($ in thousands) for the current year. All sales are made on a credit basis. The statement of cash flows indicates that cash collected from customers during the current year was $2,230,065 ($ in thousands). There were no recoveries of accounts receivable previously written off.

Required:

1. Compute the following (dollar amounts in thousands):
    a. The amount of uncollectibles written off by Amdahl during the current year.
    b. The amount of bad debt expense that Amdahl would include in its income statement for the current year.
    c. The approximate percentage that Amdahl used to estimate uncollectibles for the current year, assuming that it uses the income statement approach.
2. Suppose that Amdahl had used the direct write-off method to account for uncollectibles. Compute the following (dollars in thousands):
    a. The accounts receivable information that would be included in the year-end balance sheet.
    b. The amount of bad debt expense that Amdahl would include in its income statement for the current year.

P 7–3
Bad debts

● LO5

Real World Financials

Cirrus Logic, Inc. is a leading designer and manufacturer of advanced integrated circuits that integrate algorithms and mixed-signal processing for mass storage, communications, consumer electronics, and industrial markets. The company's 2007 financial statements contained the following information:

	($ in thousands)	
Balance sheets	**2007**	**2006**
Current assets:		
Accounts receivable, net	$ 19,127	$ 20,937
Income statements	**2007**	**2006**
Net sales	$182,304	$193,694

In addition, the statement of cash flows disclosed that accounts receivable decreased during 2007 by $1,810 (in thousands). This indicates that cash received from customers was $1,810 (in thousands) more than accrual sales revenue. Also, a disclosure note reported that the allowance for uncollectible accounts (in thousands) was $105 and $196 at the end of 2007 and 2006, respectively.

Required:

1. What is the amount of accounts receivable due from customers at the end of 2007 and 2006?
2. Assuming that all sales are made on a credit basis, determine the amount of bad debt expense for 2007 and the amount of actual bad debt write-offs made in 2007.

P 7–4
Uncollectible accounts

● LO5 LO6

Raintree Cosmetic Company sells its products to customers on a credit basis. An adjusting entry for bad debt expense is recorded only at December 31, the company's fiscal year-end. The 2008 balance sheet disclosed the following:

Current assets:
  Receivables, net of allowance for uncollectible accounts of $30,000 $432,000

During 2009, credit sales were $1,750,000, cash collections from customers $1,830,000, and $35,000 in accounts receivable were written off. In addition, $3,000 was collected from a customer whose account was written off in 2008. An aging of accounts receivable at December 31, 2009, reveals the following:

Age Group	Percentage of Year-End Receivables in Group	Percent Uncollectible
0–60 days	65%	4%
61–90 days	20	15
91–120 days	10	25
Over 120 days	5	40

Required:

1. Prepare summary journal entries to account for the 2009 write-offs and the collection of the receivable previously written off.
2. Prepare the year-end adjusting entry for bad debts according to each of the following situations:
    a. Bad debt expense is estimated to be 3% of credit sales for the year.
    b. Bad debt expense is estimated by computing net realizable value of the receivables. The allowance for uncollectible accounts is estimated to be 10% of the year-end balance in accounts receivable.
    c. Bad debt expense is estimated by computing net realizable value of the receivables. The allowance for uncollectible accounts is determined by an aging of accounts receivable.
3. For situations (a)–(c) in requirement 2 above, what would be the net amount of accounts receivable reported in the 2009 balance sheet?

P 7–5
Receivables; bad
debts and returns

● LO4 LO5

Real World Financials

National Semiconductor Corporation, located in Santa Clara, California, is one of the world's largest producers of semiconductors. The company's consolidated balance sheets for the 2007 and 2006 fiscal years included the following ($ in millions):

	2007	2006
Current assets:		
Receivables, less allowances of $32.4 in 2007 and $38.8 in 2006	$150.6	$208.6

A disclosure note accompanying the financial statements reported the following ($ in millions):

	2007	2006
Receivables allowances:		
Doubtful accounts	$ 1.2	$ 1.5
Returns	31.2	37.3
Total receivable allowances	$32.4	$38.8

Assume that the company reported bad debt expense in 2007 of $3.5 million and had products returned for credit totaling $30 million (sales price). Net sales for 2007 were $1,929.9 million.

Required:

1. What is the amount of accounts receivable due from customers at the end of 2007 and 2006?
2. What amount of accounts receivable did National write off during 2007?
3. What is the amount of National's gross sales for the 2007 fiscal year?
4. Assuming that all sales are made on a credit basis, what is the amount of cash National collected from customers during the 2007 fiscal year?

P 7–6
Notes receivable;
solving for
unknowns

● LO7

Cypress Oil Company's December 31, 2009, balance sheet listed $645,000 of notes receivable and $16,000 of interest receivable included in current assets. The following notes make up the notes receivable balance:

Note 1   Dated 8/31/09, principal of $300,000 and interest at 10% due on 2/28/10.
Note 2   Dated 6/30/09, principal of $150,000 and interest due 3/31/10.
Note 3 $200,000 face value noninterest-bearing note dated 9/30/09, due 3/31/10. Note was issued in exchange for merchandise.

The company records adjusting entries only at year-end. There were no other notes receivable outstanding during 2009.

Required:

1. Determine the rate used to discount the noninterest-bearing note.
2. Determine the explicit interest rate on Note 2.
3. What is the amount of interest revenue that appears in the company's 2009 income statement related to these notes?

P 7–7
Factoring versus
assigning of
accounts receivable

● LO8

Lonergan Company occasionally uses its accounts receivable to obtain immediate cash. At the end of June 2009, the company had accounts receivable of $780,000. Lonergan needs approximately $500,000 to capitalize on a unique investment opportunity. On July 1, 2009, a local bank offers Lonergan the following two alternatives:

a. Borrow $500,000, sign a note payable, and assign the entire receivable balance as collateral. At the end of each month, a remittance will be made to the bank that equals the amount of receivables collected plus 12% interest on the unpaid balance of the note at the beginning of the period.

b. Transfer $550,000 of specific receivables to the bank without recourse. The bank will charge a 2% finance charge on the amount of receivables transferred. The bank will collect the receivables directly from customers. The sale criteria are met.

Required:

1. Prepare the journal entries that would be recorded on July 1 for each of the alternatives.
2. Assuming that 80% of all June 30 receivables are collected during July, prepare the necessary journal entries to record the collection and the remittance to the bank.
3. For each alternative, explain any required note disclosures that would be included in the July 31, 2009, financial statements.

P 7–8
Factoring
of accounts
receivable; without
recourse

● LO8

Samson Wholesale Beverage Company regularly factors its accounts receivable with the Milpitas Finance Company. On April 30, 2009, the company transferred $800,000 of accounts receivable to Milpitas. The transfer was made without recourse. Milpitas remits 90% of the factored amount and retains 10%. When Milpitas collects the receivables, it remits to Samson the retained amount less a 4% fee (4% of the total factored amount).

Required:
Prepare journal entries for Samson Wholesale Beverage for the transfer of accounts receivable on April 30 assuming the sale criteria are met.

P 7–9
Miscellaneous
receivable
transactions

● LO3 LO4
    LO7 LO8

Evergreen Company sells lawn and garden products to wholesalers. The company's fiscal year-end is December 31. During 2009, the following transactions related to receivables occurred:

Feb. 28	Sold merchandise to Lennox, Inc. for $10,000 and accepted a 10%, 7-month note. 10% is an appropriate rate for this type of note.
Mar. 31	Sold merchandise to Maddox Co. and accepted a noninterest-bearing note with a discount rate of 10%. The $8,000 payment is due on March 31, 2010.
Apr. 3	Sold merchandise to Carr Co. for $7,000 with terms 2/10, n/30. Evergreen uses the gross method to account for cash discounts.
11	Collected the entire amount due from Carr Co.
17	A customer returned merchandise costing $3,200. Evergreen reduced the customer's receivable balance by $5,000, the sales price of the merchandise. Sales returns are recorded by the company as they occur.
30	Transferred receivables of $50,000 to a factor without recourse. The factor charged Evergreen a 1% finance charge on the receivables transferred. The sale criteria are met.
June 30	Discounted the Lennox, Inc., note at the bank. The bank's discount rate is 12%. The note was discounted without recourse.
Aug. 31	Lennox, Inc., paid the note amount plus interest to the bank.

Required:
1. Prepare the necessary journal entries for Evergreen for each of the above dates. For transactions involving the sale of merchandise, ignore the entry for the cost of goods sold (round all calculations to the nearest dollar).
2. Prepare any necessary adjusting entries at December 31, 2009. Adjusting entries are only recorded at year-end (round all calculations to the nearest dollar).
3. Prepare a schedule showing the effect of the journal entries in requirements 1 and 2 on 2009 income before taxes.

P 7–10
Discounting a note
receivable

● LO8

Descriptors are provided below for six situations involving notes receivable being discounted at a bank. In each case, the maturity date of the note is December 31, 2009, and the principal and interest are due at maturity. For each, determine the proceeds received from the bank on discounting the note.

Note	Note Face Value	Date of Note	Interest Rate	Date Discounted	Discount Rate
1	$50,000	3/31/09	8%	6/30/09	10%
2	50,000	3/31/09	8	9/30/09	10
3	50,000	3/31/09	8	9/30/09	12
4	80,000	6/30/09	6	10/31/09	10
5	80,000	6/30/09	6	10/31/09	12
6	80,000	6/30/09	6	11/30/09	10

P 7–11
Accounts and
notes receivable;
discounting a
note receivable;
receivables
turnover ratio

● LO5 LO6 LO7
    LO8 LO9

Chamberlain Enterprises, Inc. reported the following receivables in its December 31, 2009, year-end balance sheet:

Current assets:
Accounts receivable, net of $24,000 in allowance for uncollectible accounts	$218,000
Interest receivable	6,800
Notes receivable	260,000

Additional information:
1. The notes receivable account consists of two notes, a $60,000 note and a $200,000 note. The $60,000 note is dated October 31, 2009, with principal and interest payable on October 31, 2010. The $200,000 note is dated June 30, 2009, with principal and 6% interest payable on June 30, 2010.
2. During 2010, sales revenue totaled $1,340,000, $1,280,000 cash was collected from customers, and $22,000 in accounts receivable were written off. All sales are made on a credit basis. Bad debt expense is recorded at year-end by adjusting the allowance account to an amount equal to 10% of year-end accounts receivable.

3. On March 31, 2010, the $200,000 note receivable was discounted at the Bank of Commerce. The bank's discount rate is 8%. Chamberlain accounts for the discounting as a sale.

Required:
1. In addition to sales revenue, what revenue and expense amounts related to receivables will appear in Chamberlain's 2010 income statement?
2. What amounts will appear in the 2010 year-end balance sheet for accounts receivable?
3. Calculate the receivables turnover ratio for 2010.

P 7–12
Bank reconciliation and adjusting entries; cash and cash equivalents

● Appendix

The bank statement for the checking account of Management Systems, Inc. (MSI) showed a December 31, 2009, balance of $14,632.12. Information that might be useful in preparing a bank reconciliation is as follows:
a. Outstanding checks were $1,320.25.
b. The December 31, 2009, cash receipts of $575 were not deposited in the bank until January 2, 2010.
c. One check written in payment of rent for $246 was correctly recorded by the bank but was recorded by MSI as a $264 disbursement.
d. In accordance with prior authorization, the bank withdrew $450 directly from the checking account as payment on a mortgage note payable. The interest portion of that payment was $350. MSI has made no entry to record the automatic payment.
e. Bank service charges of $14 were listed on the bank statement.
f. A deposit of $875 was recorded by the bank on December 13, but it did not belong to MSI. The deposit should have been made to the checking account of MIS, Inc.
g. The bank statement included a charge of $85 for an NSF check. The check was returned with the bank statement and the company will seek payment from the customer.
h. MSI maintains a $200 petty cash fund that was appropriately reimbursed at the end of December.
i. According to instructions from MSI on December 30, the bank withdrew $10,000 from the account and purchased U.S. Treasury bills for MSI. MSI recorded the transaction in its books on December 31 when it received notice from the bank. Half of the Treasury bills mature in two months and the other half in six months.

Required:
1. Prepare a bank reconciliation for the MSI checking account at December 31, 2009. You will have to compute the balance per books.
2. Prepare any necessary adjusting journal entries indicated.
3. What amount would MSI report as cash and cash equivalents in the current asset section of the December 31, 2009, balance sheet?

P 7–13
Bank reconciliation and adjusting entries

● Appendix

El Gato Painting Company maintains a checking account at American Bank. Bank statements are prepared at the end of each month. The November 30, 2009, reconciliation of the bank balance is as follows:

Balance per bank, November 30		$3,231
Add: Deposits outstanding		1,200
Less: Checks outstanding		
#363	$123	
#365	201	
#380	56	
#381	86	
#382	340	(806)
Adjusted balance per bank, November 30		$3,625

The company's general ledger checking account showed the following for December:

Balance, December 1	$ 3,625
Receipts	42,650
Disbursements	(41,853)
Balance, December 31	$ 4,422

The December bank statement contained the following information:

Balance, December 1	$ 3,231
Deposits	43,000
Checks processed	(41,918)
Service charges	(22)
NSF checks	(440)
Balance, December 31	$ 3,851

The checks that were processed by the bank in December include all of the outstanding checks at the end of November except for check #365. In addition, there are some December checks that had not been processed by the bank by the end of the month. Also, you discover that check #411 for $320 was correctly recorded by the bank but was incorrectly recorded on the books as a $230 disbursement for advertising expense. Included in the bank's deposits is a $1,300 deposit incorrectly credited to the company's account. The deposit should have been posted to the credit of the Los Gatos Company. The NSF checks have not been redeposited and the company will seek payment from the customers involved.

Required:
1. Prepare a bank reconciliation for the El Gato checking account at December 31, 2009.
2. Prepare any necessary adjusting journal entries indicated.

BROADEN YOUR PERSPECTIVE

Apply your critical-thinking ability to the knowledge you've gained. These cases will provide you an opportunity to develop your research, analysis, judgment, and communication skills. You also will work with other students, integrate what you've learned, apply it in real world situations, and consider its global and ethical ramifications. This practice will broaden your knowledge and further develop your decision-making abilities.

**Judgment
Case 7–1**
Accounts and
notes receivable

● **LO5 LO6 LO8**

Magrath Company has an operating cycle of less than one year and provides credit terms for all of its customers. On April 1, 2009, the company factored, without recourse, some of its accounts receivable.

Magrath uses the allowance method to account for uncollectible accounts. During 2009, some accounts were written off as uncollectible and other accounts previously written off as uncollectible were collected.

Required:
1. How should Magrath account for and report the accounts receivable factored on April 1, 2009? Why is this accounting treatment appropriate?
2. How should Magrath account for the collection of the accounts previously written off as uncollectible?
3. What are the two basic approaches to estimating uncollectible accounts under the allowance method? What is the rationale for each approach?

(AICPA adapted)

**Communication
Case 7–2**
Uncollectible
accounts

● **LO5**

You have been hired as a consultant by a parts manufacturing firm to provide advice as to the proper accounting methods the company should use in some key areas. In the area of receivables, the company president does not understand your recommendation to use the allowance method for uncollectible accounts. She stated, "Financial statements should be based on objective data rather than the guesswork required for the allowance method. Besides, since my uncollectibles are fairly constant from period to period, with significant variations occurring infrequently, the direct write-off method is just as good as the allowance method."

Required:
Draft a one-page response in the form of a memo to the president in support of your recommendation for the company to use the allowance method.

**Judgment
Case 7–3**
Accounts
receivable

● **LO3 LO7 LO8**

Hogan Company uses the net method of accounting for sales discounts. Hogan offers trade discounts to various groups of buyers.

On August 1, 2009, Hogan factored some accounts receivable on a without recourse basis. Hogan incurred a finance charge.

Hogan also has some notes receivable bearing an appropriate rate of interest. The principal and total interest are due at maturity. The notes were received on October 1, 2009, and mature on September 30, 2010. Hogan's operating cycle is less than one year.

Required:
1. a. Using the net method, how should Hogan account for the sales discounts at the date of sale? What is the rationale for the amount recorded as sales under the net method?
   b. Using the net method, what is the effect on Hogan's sales revenues and net income when customers do not take the sales discounts?
2. What is the effect of trade discounts on sales revenues and accounts receivable? Why?
3. How should Hogan account for the accounts receivable factored on August 1, 2009? Why?
4. How should Hogan report the effects of the interest-bearing notes receivable in its December 31, 2009, balance sheet and its income statement for the year ended December 31, 2009? Why?

(AICPA adapted)

Ethics Case 7–4
Uncollectible accounts

● LO5

You have recently been hired as the assistant controller for Stanton Industries, a large, publicly held manufacturing company. Your immediate superior is the controller who, in turn, is responsible to the vice president of finance.

The controller has assigned you the task of preparing the year-end adjusting entries. In the receivables area, you have prepared an aging of accounts receivable and have applied historical percentages to the balances of each of the age categories. The analysis indicates that an appropriate balance for the allowance for uncollectible accounts is $180,000. The existing balance in the allowance account prior to any adjusting entry is a $20,000 credit balance.

After showing your analysis to the controller, he tells you to change the aging category of a large account from over 120 days to current status and to prepare a new invoice to the customer with a revised date that agrees with the new aging category. This will change the required allowance for uncollectible accounts from $180,000 to $135,000. Tactfully, you ask the controller for an explanation for the change and he tells you "We need the extra income, the bottom line is too low."

Required:
1. What is the effect on income before taxes of the change requested by the controller?
2. Discuss the ethical dilemma you face. Consider your options and responsibilities along with the possible consequences of any action you might take.

Judgment Case 7–5
Internal control

● LO1

For each of the following independent situations, indicate the apparent internal control weaknesses and suggest alternative procedures to eliminate the weaknesses.
1. John Smith is the petty cash custodian. John approves all requests for payment out of the $200 fund which is replenished at the end of each month. At the end of each month, John submits a list of all accounts and amounts to be charged and a check is written to him for the total amount. John is the only person ever to tally the fund.
2. All of the company's cash disbursements are made by check. Each check must be supported by an approved voucher which is in turn supported by the appropriate invoice and, for purchases, a receiving document. The vouchers are approved by Dean Leiser, the chief accountant, after reviewing the supporting documentation. Betty Hanson prepares the checks for Leiser's signature. Leiser also maintains the company's check register (the cash disbursements journal) and reconciles the bank account at the end of each month.
3. Fran Jones opens the company's mail and makes a listing of all checks and cash received from customers. A copy of the list is sent to Jerry McDonald who maintains the general ledger accounts. Fran prepares and makes the daily deposit at the bank. Fran also maintains the subsidiary ledger for accounts receivable which is used to generate monthly statements to customers.

Real World Case 7–6
Receivables; bad debts

● LO5

Real World Financials

EDGAR, the Electronic Data Gathering, Analysis, and Retrieval system, performs automated collection, validation, indexing, and forwarding of submissions by companies and others who are required by law to file forms with the U.S. Securities and Exchange Commission (SEC). All publicly traded domestic companies use EDGAR to make the majority of their filings. (Some foreign companies file voluntarily.) Form 10-K or 10-KSB, which include the annual report, is required to be filed on EDGAR. The SEC makes this information available on the Internet.

Required:
1. Access EDGAR on the Internet. The web address is **www.sec.gov**.
2. Search for **Avon Products, Inc.** Access the 10-K filing for the most recent fiscal year. Search or scroll to find the financial statements.
3. Answer the following questions related to the company's accounts receivable and bad debts:
   a. What is the amount of gross trade accounts receivable at the end of the year?
   b. What is the amount of bad debt expense for the year? (*Hint:* check the statement of cash flows.)
   c. Determine the amount of actual bad debt write-offs made during the year. Assume that all bad debts relate only to trade accounts receivable.
   d. Using only information from the balance sheets, income statements, and your answer to requirement 3.c., determine the amount of cash collected from customers during the year. Assume that all sales are made on a credit basis, that the company provides no allowances for sales returns, that no previously written-off receivables were collected, and that all sales relate to trade accounts receivable.

Integrating Case 7–7
Change in estimate of bad debts

● LO5

McLaughlin Corporation uses the allowance method to account for bad debts. At the end of the company's fiscal year, accounts receivable are analyzed and the allowance for uncollectible accounts is adjusted. At the end of 2009, the company reported the following amounts:

Accounts receivable	$10,850,000
Less: Allowance for uncollectible accounts	(450,000)
Accounts receivable, net	$10,400,000

In 2010, it was determined that $1,825,000 of year-end 2009 receivables had to be written off as uncollectible. This was due in part to the fact that Hughes Corporation, a long-standing customer that had always paid its bills, unexpectedly declared bankruptcy in 2010. Hughes owed McLaughlin $1,400,000. At the end of 2009, none of the Hughes receivable was considered uncollectible.

Required:

Describe the appropriate accounting treatment and required disclosures for McLaughlin's underestimation of bad debts at the end of 2009.

Analysis Case 7–8
Financing with receivables

● LO8

Financial institutions have developed a wide variety of methods for companies to use their receivables to obtain immediate cash. The methods differ with respect to which rights and risks are retained by the transferor (the original holder of the receivable) and those passed on to the transferee (the new holder, usually a financial institution).

Required:

1. Describe the alternative methods available for companies to use their receivables to obtain immediate cash.
2. Discuss the alternative accounting treatments for these methods.

Research Case 7–9
Locate and extract relevant information and authoritative support for a financial reporting issue; financing with receivables

● LO8

You are spending the summer working for a local wholesale furniture company, Samson Furniture, Inc. The company is considering a proposal from a local financial institution, Old Reliant Financial, to factor Samson's receivables. The company controller is unfamiliar with the most recent FASB pronouncement that deals with accounting for the transfer of financial assets and has asked you to do some research. The controller wants to make sure the arrangement with the financial institution is structured in such a way as to allow the factoring to be accounted for as a sale.

Old Reliant has offered to factor all of the company's receivables on a "without recourse" basis. Old Reliant will remit to Samson 90% of the factored amount, collect the receivables from Samson's customers, and retain the remaining 10% until all of the receivables have been collected. When Old Reliant collects all of the receivables, it will remit to Samson the retained amount, less a 4% fee (4% of the total factored amount).

Required:

1. Explain the meaning of the term *without recourse.*
2. Obtain the FASB standard on accounting for the transfer of financial assets. You might gain access at the FASB Website (**www.fasb.org**), from your school library, or some other source.
3. What conditions must be met for a transfer of receivables to be accounted for as a sale? What is the specific citation that Samson would rely on in applying that accounting treatment?
4. Assuming that the conditions for treatment as a sale are met, prepare Samson's journal entry to record the factoring of $400,000 of receivables.
5. An agreement that both entitles and obligates the transferor, Samson, to repurchase or redeem transferred assets from the transferee, Old Reliant, maintains the transferor's effective control over those assets and the transfer is accounted for as a secured borrowing, not a sale, if and only if what conditions are met?

Analysis Case 7–10
Compare receivables management using ratios

● LO9

Real World Financials

The table below contains selected financial information included in the 2007 financial statements of **Sara Lee Corporation** and **Conagra Foods, Inc.**

	($ in millions)			
	Sara Lee		Conagra Foods	
	2007	2006	2007	2006
Balance sheet:				
Accounts receivable, net	$ 1,307	$ 1,216	$ 1,203	$ 1,178
Income statement:				
Net sales	12,278	11,460	12,028	11,482

Required:

1. Calculate the 2007 receivables turnover ratio and average collection period for both companies. Evaluate the management of each company's investment in receivables.
2. Obtain annual reports from three corporations in the same primary industry and compare the management of each company's investment in receivables.

Note: You can obtain copies of annual reports from your library, from friends who are shareholders, from the investor relations department of the corporations, from a friendly stockbroker, or from EDGAR (Electronic Data Gathering, Analysis, and Retrieval) on the Internet (**www.sec.gov**).

Analysis Case 7–11
Reporting cash and receivables

● LO2 LO5

Refer to the financial statements and related disclosure notes of **Google Inc.** included with all new copies of the text.

Required:

1. What is Google's policy for designating investments as cash equivalents?
2. At the end of the 2007 fiscal year, how much cash was included in cash and cash equivalents?
3. Determine the gross amount of receivables outstanding at December 31, 2007, and December 31, 2006.

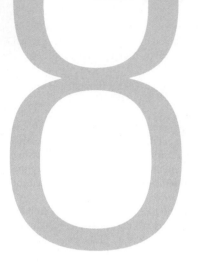

— CHAPTER —

Inventories: Measurement

/// **OVERVIEW**

The next two chapters continue our study of assets by investigating the measurement and reporting issues involving inventories and the related expense—cost of goods sold. Inventory refers to the assets a company (1) intends to sell in the normal course of business, (2) has in production for future sale, or (3) uses currently in the production of goods to be sold.

| | | | | LEARNING OBJECTIVES | | | | | | | | | | | | | | | | |

After studying this chapter, you should be able to:

- **LO1** Explain the difference between a perpetual inventory system and a periodic inventory system.
- **LO2** Explain which physical quantities of goods should be included in inventory.
- **LO3** Determine the expenditures that should be included in the cost of inventory.
- **LO4** Differentiate between the specific identification, FIFO, LIFO, and average cost methods used to determine the cost of ending inventory and cost of goods sold.
- **LO5** Discuss the factors affecting a company's choice of inventory method.
- **LO6** Understand supplemental LIFO disclosures and the effect of LIFO liquidations on net income.
- **LO7** Calculate the key ratios used by analysts to monitor a company's investment in inventories.
- **LO8** Determine ending inventory using the dollar-value LIFO inventory method.

FINANCIAL REPORTING CASE

Inventory Measurement at Ford Motor Company

A recent article in the financial section of your local newspaper reported on the labor negotiations between Ford Motor Company and the United Auto Workers. When you showed the article to a friend, he said, "I'll bet Ford uses LIFO to value its inventories. That way they can report lower profits and give them an edge in the negotiations." This aroused your curiosity and led you to download from the Internet Ford's most recent financial statements, which contained the following disclosure note:

Note 6. Inventories

Inventories at December 31 were as follows (in millions):

	2006	2005
Raw materials, work-in-process, and supplies	$ 4,604	$ 4,056
Finished products	7,989	7,224
Total inventories under first-in, first-out method (FIFO)	12,593	11,280
Less: Last-in, first-out method (LIFO) adjustment	(1,015)	(1,009)
Total inventories	$11,578	$10,271

Inventories are stated at the lower of cost or market. About one-fourth of inventories were determined under the last-in, first-out (LIFO) method. During 2005, inventory quantities were reduced, resulting in a liquidation of LIFO inventory quantities carried at lower costs prevailing in prior years as compared with the cost of 2005 purchases, the effect of which decreased *Automotive cost of sales* by about $12 million.

By the time you finish this chapter, you should be able to respond appropriately to the questions posed in this case. Compare your response to the solution provided at the end of the chapter.

QUESTIONS ///

1. What inventory methods does Ford use to value its inventories? Is this permissible according to GAAP? (page 390)

2. What is the purpose of reporting the entire inventory as if valued on a FIFO basis and then adjusting this amount to reflect the use of LIFO for a portion of the inventory? (page 392)

3. Why would a reduction of LIFO inventory quantities cause a $12 million decrease in 2005 cost of sales? (page 392)

4. Is your friend correct in his assertion that, by using LIFO, Ford was able to report lower profits in 2006? (page 397)

RECORDING AND MEASURING INVENTORY

Inventory refers to the assets a company (1) intends to sell in the normal course of business, (2) has in production for future sale (work in process), or (3) uses currently in the production of goods to be sold (raw materials). The computers produced by **Apple Inc.** that are intended for sale to customers are inventory, as are partially completed components in the assembly lines of Apple's Cupertino facility, and the computer chips and memory modules that will go into computers produced later. The computers *used* by Apple to maintain its accounting system, however, are classified and accounted for as plant and equipment. Similarly, the stocks and bonds a securities dealer holds for sale are inventory, whereas Apple would classify the securities it holds as investments.

Proper accounting for inventories is essential for manufacturing, wholesale, and retail companies (enterprises that earn revenue by selling goods). Inventory usually is one of the most valuable assets listed in the balance sheet for these firms. Cost of goods sold—the expense recorded when inventory is sold—typically is the largest expense in the income statement. For example, a recent balance sheet for **Sara Lee Corporation** reported inventories of $1,050 million, which represented 9% of total assets. The company's income statement reported cost of goods sold of $7,552 million representing 64% of all expenses.

In this and the following chapter we discuss the measurement and reporting issues involving inventory, an asset, and the related expense, cost of goods sold. Inventory represents *quantities* of goods acquired, manufactured, or in the process of being manufactured. The inventory amount in the balance sheet at the end of an accounting period represents the cost of the inventory still on hand, and cost of goods sold in the income statement represents the cost of the inventory sold during the period. The historical cost principle and matching principle offer guidance for measuring inventory and cost of goods sold, but as we will see in this and the next chapter, it's usually difficult to measure inventory (cost of goods sold) at the exact cost of the actual physical quantities on hand (sold). Fortunately, accountants can use one of several techniques to approximate the desired result and satisfy our measurement objectives.

> Inventories consist of assets that a retail or wholesale company acquires for resale or goods that manufacturers produce for sale.

> An important objective in inventory accounting is to match the appropriate cost of goods sold with sales revenue.

Types of Inventory
Merchandising Inventory

Wholesale and retail companies purchase goods that are primarily in finished form. These companies are intermediaries in the process of moving goods from the manufacturer to the end-user. They often are referred to as merchandising companies and their inventory as merchandise inventory. *The cost of merchandise inventory includes the purchase price plus any other costs necessary to get the goods in condition and location for sale.* We discuss the concept of condition and location and the types of costs that typically constitute inventory later in this chapter.

Manufacturing Inventories

Unlike merchandising companies, manufacturing companies actually produce the goods they sell to wholesalers, retailers, or other manufacturers. Inventory for a manufacturer consists of (1) raw materials, (2) work in process, and (3) finished goods. Raw materials represent the cost of components purchased from other manufacturers that will become part of the finished product. For example, Apple's raw materials inventory includes semiconductors, circuit boards, plastic, and glass that go into the production of personal computers.

Work-in-process inventory refers to the products that are not yet complete. The cost of work in process includes the cost of raw materials used in production, the cost of labor that can be directly traced to the goods in process, and an allocated portion of other manufacturing costs, called *manufacturing overhead*. Overhead costs include electricity and other utility costs to operate the manufacturing facility, depreciation of manufacturing equipment, and many other manufacturing costs that cannot be directly linked to the production of specific goods. Once the manufacturing process is completed, these costs that have accumulated in work in process are transferred to finished goods.

> Inventory for a manufacturing company consists of *raw materials, work in process,* and *finished goods.*

> The cost of *work in process* and *finished goods* includes the cost of raw materials, direct labor, and an allocated portion of manufacturing overhead.

Manufacturing companies generally disclose, either in a note or directly in the balance sheet, the dollar amount of each inventory category. For example, **IBM Corporation**'s note disclosure of inventory category was shown on page 117. **Sara Lee Corporation** reports inventory categories directly in the balance sheet, as illustrated in Graphic 8–1.

Balance Sheet

($ in millions)

	2007	2006
Current assets:		
Inventories		
Finished goods	$ 719	$603
Work in process	34	38
Materials and supplies	297	278
Total	$1,050	$919

GRAPHIC 8–1

Inventories Disclosure—Sara Lee Corporation

Real World Financials

The inventory accounts and the cost flows for a typical manufacturing company are shown using T-accounts in Graphic 8–2. The costs of raw materials used, direct labor applied, and manufacturing overhead applied, flow into work in process and then to finished goods. When the goods are sold, the cost of those goods flows to cost of goods sold.

GRAPHIC 8–2
Inventory Components and Cost Flow for a Manufacturing Company

The costs of inventory units follow their physical movement from one stage of activity to another.

We focus here primarily on merchandising companies (wholesalers and retailers). Still, most of the accounting principles and procedures discussed here also apply to manufacturing companies. The unique problems involved with accumulating the direct costs of raw materials and labor and with allocating manufacturing overhead are addressed in managerial and cost accounting textbooks.

Perpetual Inventory System

Two accounting systems are used to record transactions involving inventory: the perpetual inventory system and the periodic inventory system. The perpetual system was introduced in Chapter 2. The system is aptly termed perpetual because the account *inventory* is continually adjusted for each change in inventory, whether it's caused by a purchase, a sale, or a return of merchandise by the company to its supplier (a *purchase return* for the buyer, a *sales return* for the seller).[1] The cost of goods sold account, along with the inventory account, is adjusted each time goods are sold or are returned by a customer. This concept is applied to the Lothridge Wholesale Beverage Company for which inventory information is provided in Illustration 8–1. This hypothetical company also will be used in the next several illustrations.

A *perpetual inventory system* continuously records both changes in inventory quantity and inventory cost.

---

[1]We discussed accounting for sales returns in Chapter 7.

ILLUSTRATION 8–1 Perpetual Inventory System	The Lothridge Wholesale Beverage Company purchases soft drinks from producers and then sells them to retailers. The company begins 2009 with merchandise inventory of $120,000 on hand. During 2009 additional merchandise is purchased on account at a cost of $600,000. Sales for the year, all on account, totaled $820,000. The cost of the soft drinks sold is $540,000. Lothridge uses the perpetual inventory system to keep track of both inventory quantities and inventory costs. The following summary journal entries record the inventory transactions for the Lothridge Company:

2009

Inventory	600,000	
Accounts payable		600,000

To record the purchase of merchandise inventory.

2009

Accounts receivable	820,000	
Sales revenue		820,000

To record sales on account.

Cost of goods sold	540,000	
Inventory		540,000

To record the cost of sales.

An important feature of a perpetual system is that it is designed to track inventory quantities from their acquisition to their sale. If the system is accurate, it allows management to determine how many goods are on hand on any date without having to take a physical count. However, physical counts of inventory usually are made anyway, either at the end of the fiscal year or on a sample basis throughout the year, to verify that the perpetual system is correctly tracking quantities. Differences between the quantity of inventory determined by the physical count and the quantity of inventory according to the perpetual system could be caused by system errors, theft, breakage, or spoilage. In addition to keeping up with inventory, a perpetual system also directly determines how many items are sold during a period.

You are probably familiar with the scanning mechanisms used at grocery store checkout counters. The scanners not only record the sale on the cash register but also can be used to track the sale of merchandise for inventory management purposes. For a company to use the perpetual inventory system to record inventory and cost of goods sold transactions, merchandise cost data also must be included on the system. That is, when merchandise is purchased/sold, the system must be able to record not only the addition/reduction in inventory quantity but also the addition/reduction in the *cost* of inventory.

A perpetual inventory system tracks both inventory quantities and inventory costs.

Periodic Inventory System

A *periodic inventory system* adjusts inventory and records cost of goods sold only at the end of each reporting period.

A periodic inventory system is not designed to track either the quantity or cost of merchandise. The merchandise inventory account balance is not adjusted as purchases and sales are made but only periodically at the end of a reporting period. A physical count of the period's ending inventory is made and costs are assigned to the quantities determined. Merchandise purchases, purchase returns, purchase discounts, and freight-in (purchases plus freight-in less returns and discounts equals net purchases) are recorded in temporary accounts and the period's cost of goods sold is determined at the end of the period by combining the temporary accounts with the inventory account:

Cost of goods sold equation

Beginning inventory + Net purchases − Ending inventory = Cost of goods sold

The cost of goods sold equation assumes that all inventory quantities not on hand at the end of the period were sold. This may not be the case if inventory items were either damaged or stolen. If damaged and stolen inventory are identified, they must be removed from beginning inventory or purchases before calculating cost of goods sold and then classified as a separate expense item.

Illustration 8–2 looks at the periodic system using the Lothridge Wholesale Beverage Company example.

The Lothridge Wholesale Beverage Company purchases soft drinks from producers and then sells them to retailers. The company began 2009 with merchandise inventory of $120,000 on hand. During 2009 additional merchandise was purchased on account at a cost of $600,000. Sales for the year, all on account, totaled $820,000. Lothridge uses a periodic inventory system. A physical count determined the cost of inventory at the end of the year to be $180,000.
 	
The following journal entries summarize the inventory transactions for 2009. Of course, each individual transaction would actually be recorded as incurred:
 	
2009
Purchases 600,000
   Accounts payable 600,000
To record the purchase of merchandise inventory.
 	
2009
Accounts receivable 820,000
   Sales revenue 820,000
To record sales on account.
No entry is recorded for the cost of inventory sold.
	ILLUSTRATION 8–2
	Periodic Inventory System

Because cost of goods sold isn't determined automatically and continually by the periodic system, it must be determined indirectly after a physical inventory count. Cost of goods sold for 2009 is determined as follows:

Beginning inventory	$120,000
Plus: Purchases	600,000
Cost of goods available for sale	720,000
Less: Ending inventory (per physical count)	(180,000)
Cost of goods sold	$540,000

The following journal entry combines the components of cost of goods sold into a single expense account and updates the balance in the inventory account:

December 31, 2009
Cost of goods sold 540,000
Inventory (ending) 180,000
   Inventory (beginning) 120,000
   Purchases 600,000
To adjust inventory, close the purchases account, and record cost of goods sold.

This entry adjusts the inventory account to the correct period-end amount, closes the temporary purchases account, and records the residual as cost of goods sold. Now let's compare the two inventory accounting systems.

A Comparison of the Perpetual and Periodic Inventory Systems

Beginning inventory plus net purchases during the period is the cost of goods available for sale. The main difference between a perpetual and a periodic system is that the periodic system allocates cost of goods available for sale between ending inventory and cost of goods sold (periodically) *at the end of the period*. In contrast, the perpetual system performs this allocation by decreasing inventory and increasing cost of goods sold (perpetually) *each time goods are sold.*

● LO1

The impact on the financial statements of choosing one system over the other generally is not significant. The choice between the two approaches usually is motivated by management control considerations as well as the comparative costs of implementation. Perpetual systems can provide more information about the dollar amounts of inventory levels on a continuous basis. They also facilitate the preparation of interim financial statements by providing fairly accurate information without the necessity of a physical count of inventory.

On the other hand, a perpetual system may be more expensive to implement than a periodic system. This is particularly true for inventories consisting of large numbers of low-cost items. Perpetual systems are more workable with inventories of high-cost items such as construction equipment or automobiles. However, with the help of computers and electronic sales devices such as cash register scanners, the perpetual inventory system is now available to many small businesses that previously could not afford them and is economically feasible for a broader range of inventory items than before.

The periodic system is less costly to implement during the period but requires a physical count before ending inventory and cost of goods sold can be determined. This makes the preparation of interim financial statements more costly unless an inventory estimation technique is used.[2] And, perhaps most importantly, the inventory monitoring features provided by a perpetual system are not available. However, it is important to remember that a perpetual system involves the tracking of both inventory quantities *and* costs. Many companies that determine costs only periodically employ systems to constantly monitor inventory quantities.

What is Included in Inventory?
Physical Quantities Included in Inventory

● **LO2**

Regardless of the system used, the measurement of inventory and cost of goods sold starts with determining the physical quantities of goods. Typically, determining the physical quantity that should be included in inventory is a simple matter because it consists of items in the possession of the company. However, in some situations the identification of items that should be included in inventory is more difficult. Consider, for example, goods in transit, goods on consignment, and sales returns.

GOODS IN TRANSIT. At the end of a reporting period, it's important to ensure a proper inventory cutoff. This means determining the ownership of goods that are in transit between the company and its customers as well as between the company and its suppliers. For example, in December 2009, the Lothridge Wholesale Beverage Company sold goods to the Jabbar Company. The goods were shipped on December 29, 2009, and arrived at Jabbar's warehouse on January 3, 2010. The fiscal year-end for both companies is December 31.

Should the merchandise shipped to Jabbar be recorded as a sale by Lothridge and a purchase by Jabbar in 2009 and thus included in Jabbar's 2009 ending inventory? Should recording the sale/purchase be delayed until 2010 and the merchandise be included in Lothridge's 2009 ending inventory? The answer depends on who owns the goods at December 31. Ownership depends on the terms of the agreement between the two companies. If the goods are shipped f.o.b. (free on board) shipping point, then legal title to the goods changes hands at the point of shipment when the seller delivers the goods to the common carrier (for example, a trucking company), and the purchaser is responsible for shipping costs and transit insurance. In that case, Lothridge records the sale and inventory reduction in 2009 and Jabbar records a 2009 purchase and includes the goods in 2009 ending inventory even though the company is not in physical possession of the goods on the last day of the fiscal year.

On the other hand, if the goods are shipped f.o.b. destination, the seller is responsible for shipping and legal title does not pass until the goods arrive at their destination (the customer's location). In our example, if the goods are shipped f.o.b. destination, Lothridge includes the merchandise in its 2009 ending inventory and the sale is recorded in 2010. Jabbar records the purchase in 2010.

A perpetual system provides more timely information but generally is more costly.

Inventory shipped *f.o.b. shipping point* is included in the purchaser's inventory as soon as the merchandise is shipped.

Inventory shipped *f.o.b. destination* is included in the purchaser's inventory only after it reaches the purchaser's destination.

[2]In Chapter 9 we discuss inventory estimation techniques that avoid the necessity of a physical count to determine ending inventory and cost of goods sold.

GOODS ON CONSIGNMENT.   Sometimes a company arranges for another company to sell its product under consignment. The goods are physically transferred to the other company (the consignee), but the transferor (consignor) retains legal title. If the consignee can't find a buyer, the goods are returned to the consignor. If a buyer is found, the consignee remits the selling price (less commission and approved expenses) to the consignor.

As we discussed in Chapter 5, because risk is retained by the consignor, the sale is not complete (revenue is not recognized) until an eventual sale to a third party occurs. As a result, goods held on consignment generally are not included in the consignee's inventory. While in stock, they belong to the consignor and should be included in inventory of the consignor even though not in the company's physical possession. A sale is recorded by the consignor only when the goods are sold by the consignee and title passes to the customer.

> Goods held on *consignment* are included in the inventory of the consignor until sold by the consignee.

SALES RETURNS.   Recall from our discussions in Chapters 5 and 7 that when the right of return exists, a seller must be able to estimate those returns before revenue can be recognized. The adjusting entry for estimated sales returns reduces sales revenue and accounts receivable. At the same time, cost of goods sold is reduced and inventory is increased (see Illustration 7–2 on page 335). As a result, a company includes in inventory the cost of merchandise it anticipates will be returned.

Now that we've considered which goods are part of inventory, let's examine the types of costs that should be associated with those inventory quantities.

Expenditures Included in Inventory

As mentioned earlier, the cost of inventory includes all necessary expenditures to acquire the inventory and bring it to its desired *condition* and *location* for sale or for use in the manufacturing process. Obviously, the cost includes the purchase price of the goods. But usually the cost of acquiring inventory also includes freight charges on incoming goods borne by the buyer; insurance costs incurred by the buyer while the goods are in transit (if shipped f.o.b. shipping point); and the costs of unloading, unpacking, and preparing merchandise inventory for sale or raw materials inventory for use.[3] The costs included in inventory are called product costs. They are associated with products and *expensed as cost of goods sold only when the related products are sold.*[4]

Shipping charges on outgoing goods are related to the selling activity and are reported as a selling expense when incurred, not as part of inventory cost.

> ● **LO3**
>
> Expenditures necessary to bring inventory to its *condition* and *location* for sale or use are included in its cost.
>
> Shipping charges on outgoing goods are selling expenses, not part of inventory cost.

FREIGHT-IN ON PURCHASES.   Freight-in on purchases is commonly included in the cost of inventory. These costs clearly are necessary to get the inventory in location for sale or use and can generally be associated with particular goods. Freight costs are added to the inventory account in a perpetual system. In a periodic system, freight costs generally are added to a temporary account called freight-in or transportation-in, which is added to purchases in determining net purchases. The account is closed to cost of goods sold along with purchases and other components of cost of goods sold at the end of the reporting period. (See Illustration 8–4 on page 383.) From an accounting system perspective, freight-in also could be added to the purchases account. From a control perspective, by recording freight-in as a separate item, management can more easily track its freight costs. The same perspectives pertain to purchases returns and purchase discounts, which are discussed next.

> The cost of *freight-in* paid by the purchaser generally is part of the cost of inventory.

PURCHASE RETURNS.   In Chapter 7 we discussed merchandise returns from the perspective of the selling company. We now address returns from the buyer's point of view. You may recall that the seller views a return as a reduction of net sales. Likewise,

---

[3]A recent FASB standard clarifies the language in *Accounting Research Bulletin No. 43* by requiring that abnormal amounts of certain costs be recognized as current period expenses rather than being included in the cost of inventory, specifically idle facility costs, freight, handling costs, and waste materials (spoilage). "Inventory Costs—An Amendment of *ARB No. 43,* Chapter 4," *Statement of Financial Accounting Standards No. 151* (Norwalk, Conn.: FASB, 2004).

[4]For practical reasons, though, some of these expenditures often are not included in inventory cost and are treated as **period costs.** They often are immaterial or it is impractical to associate the expenditures with particular units of inventory (for example, unloading and unpacking costs). Period costs are not associated with products and are expensed in the *period* incurred.

a buyer views a return as a reduction of net purchases. When the buyer returns goods to the seller, a purchase return is recorded. In a perpetual inventory system, this means a reduction in both inventory and accounts payable (if the account has not yet been paid) at the time of the return. In a periodic system an account called *purchase returns* temporarily accumulates these amounts. Purchase returns are subtracted from purchases when determining net purchases. The account is closed to cost of goods sold at the end of the reporting period.

A purchase return represents a reduction of net purchases.

PURCHASE DISCOUNTS.

Purchase discounts represent reductions in the amount to be paid if remittance is made within a designated period of time.

Cash discounts also were discussed from the seller's perspective in Chapter 7. These discounts really are quick-payment discounts because they represent reductions in the amount to be paid by the buyer in the event payment is made within a specified period of time. The amount of the discount and the time period within which it's available are conveyed by cryptic terms like 2/10, n/30 (meaning a 2% discount if paid within 10 days, otherwise full payment within 30 days). As with the seller, the purchaser can record these purchase discounts using either the gross method or the net method. Consider Illustration 8–3 which is similar to the cash discount illustration in Chapter 7.

ILLUSTRATION 8–3 Purchase Discounts	On October 5, 2009, the Lothridge Wholesale Beverage Company purchased merchandise at a price of $20,000. The repayment terms are stated as 2/10, n/30. Lothridge paid $13,720 ($14,000 less the 2% cash discount) on October 14 and the remaining balance of $6,000 on November 4. Lothridge employs a periodic inventory system.

The gross and net methods of recording the purchase and cash payment are compared as follows:

	Gross Method			Net Method		
October 5, 2009						
Purchases*.........................	20,000			Purchases*......................	19,600	
Accounts payable		20,000		Accounts payable.......		19,600
October 14, 2009						
Accounts payable	14,000			Accounts payable...........	13,720	
Purchase discounts*.....		280		Cash...........................		13,720
Cash		13,720				
November 4, 2009						
Accounts payable	6,000			Accounts payable...........	5,880	
Cash		6,000		Interest expense.............	120	
				Cash		6,000

By either method, net purchases is reduced by discounts taken.

Discounts not taken are included as purchases using the gross method and as interest expense using the net method.

*The inventory account is used in a perpetual system.

The gross method views discounts not taken as part of inventory cost.

Conceptually, the gross method views a discount not taken as part of the cost of inventory. The net method considers the cost of inventory to include the net, after-discount amount, and any discounts not taken are reported as *interest expense*.[5] The discount is viewed as compensation to the seller for providing financing to the buyer.

The net method considers discounts not taken as interest expense.

Purchase discounts recorded under the gross method are subtracted from purchases when determining net purchases. The account is a temporary account that is closed to cost of goods sold at the end of the reporting period. Under the perpetual inventory system, purchase discounts are treated as a reduction in the inventory account.

The effect on the financial statements of the difference between the two methods usually is immaterial. Net income over time will be the same using either method. There will, however, be a difference in gross profit between the two methods equal to the amount of discounts not taken. In the preceding illustration, $120 in discounts not taken is included as interest expense using the net method and cost of goods sold using the gross method.

Illustration 8–4 compares the perpetual and periodic inventory systems, using the net method.

---

[5]An alternative treatment is to debit an expense account called *purchase discounts lost* rather than interest expense. This enables a company to more easily identify the forgone discounts.

The Lothridge Wholesale Beverage Company purchases soft drinks from producers and then sells them to retailers. The company began 2009 with merchandise inventory of $120,000 on hand. During 2009 additional merchandise is purchased on account at a cost of $600,000. Lothridge's suppliers offer credit terms of 2/10, n/30. All discounts were taken. Lothridge uses the net method to record purchase discounts. All purchases are made f.o.b. shipping point. Freight charges paid by Lothridge totaled $16,000. Merchandise with a net of discount cost of $20,000 was returned to suppliers for credit. Sales for the year, all on account, totaled $830,000. The cost of the soft drinks sold is $550,000. $154,000 of inventory remained on hand at the end of 2009.

The above transactions are recorded in summary form according to both the perpetual and periodic inventory systems as follows:

ILLUSTRATION 8–4

Inventory Transactions— Perpetual and Periodic Systems

($ in 000s)

Perpetual System		Periodic System	
Purchases			
Inventory ($600 × 98%) ...	588	Purchases ($600 × 98%)	588
Accounts payable	588	Accounts payable	588
Freight			
Inventory	16	Freight-in	16
Cash	16	Cash	16
Returns			
Accounts payable	20	Accounts payable	20
Inventory	20	Purchase returns	20
Sales			
Accounts receivable	830	Accounts receivable	830
Sales revenue	830	Sales revenue	830
Cost of goods sold	550	No entry	
Inventory	550		
End of period			
No Entry		Cost of goods sold (below)	550
		Inventory (ending)	154
		Purchase returns	20
		Inventory (beginning)	120
		Purchases	588
		Freight-in	16

Supporting Schedule:

Cost of goods sold:		
Beginning inventory		$120
Purchases	$588	
Less: Returns	(20)	
Plus: Freight-in	16	
Net purchases		584
Cost of goods available		704
Less: Ending inventory		(154)
Cost of goods sold		$550

Inventory Cost Flow Assumptions

● LO4

Regardless of whether the perpetual or periodic system is used, it's necessary to assign dollar amounts to the physical quantities of goods sold and goods remaining in ending inventory. Unless each item of inventory is specifically identified and traced through the system, assigning dollars is accomplished by making an assumption regarding how goods (and their associated costs) flow through the system. We examine the common cost flow assumptions next. In previous illustrations, dollar amounts of the cost of goods sold and the cost of ending inventory were assumed known. However, if various portions of inventory are acquired at different costs, we need a way to decide which units were sold and which remain in inventory. Illustration 8–5 will help explain.

ILLUSTRATION 8–5 Cost Flow	The Browning Company began 2009 with $22,000 of inventory. The cost of beginning inventory (Beg. inv.) is composed of 4,000 units purchased for $5.50 each. Merchandise transactions during 2009 were as follows:

Purchases

Date of Purchase	Units	Unit Cost*	Total Cost
Jan. 17	1,000	$6.00	$ 6,000
Mar. 22	3,000	7.00	21,000
Oct. 15	3,000	7.50	22,500
Totals	7,000		$49,500

Goods available for sale include beginning inventory plus purchases.

Sales

Date of Sale	Units
Jan. 10	2,000
Apr. 15	1,500
Nov. 20	3,000
Total	6,500

*Includes purchase price and cost of freight.

As the data show, 7,000 units were purchased during 2009 at various prices and 6,500 units were sold. What is the cost of the 6,500 units sold? If all units, including beginning inventory, were purchased at the same price, then the answer would be simple. However, that rarely is the case.

The year started with 4,000 units, 7,000 units were purchased, and 6,500 units were sold. This means 4,500 units remain in ending inventory. This allocation of units available for sale is depicted in Graphic 8–3.

GRAPHIC 8–3

Allocation of Units Available

If a periodic system is used, what is the cost of the 4,500 units in ending inventory? In other words, which of the 11,000 (4,000 + 7,000) units available for sale were sold? Are they the more expensive ones bought toward the end of the year, or the less costly ones acquired before prices increased? Using the numbers given, let's consider the question as follows:

Beginning inventory (4,000 units @ $5.50)	$22,000
Plus: Purchases (7,000 units @ various prices)	49,500
Cost of goods available for sale (11,000 units)	$71,500
Less: Ending inventory (4,500 units @ ?)	?
Cost of goods sold (6,500 units @ ?)	?

The $71,500 in cost of goods available for sale must be allocated to ending inventory and cost of goods sold. The allocation decision is depicted in Graphic 8–4.

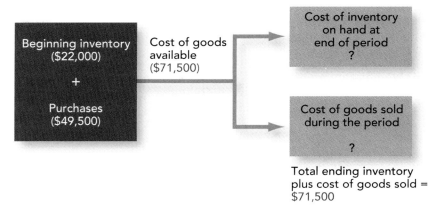

Let's turn our attention now to the various inventory methods that can be used to achieve this allocation.

Specific Identification

It's sometimes possible for each unit sold during the period or each unit on hand at the end of the period to be matched with its actual cost. Actual costs can be determined by reference to the invoice representing the purchase of the item. This method is used frequently by companies selling unique, expensive products with low sales volume which makes it relatively easy and economically feasible to associate each item with its actual cost. For example, automobiles have unique serial numbers that can be used to match a specific auto with the invoice identifying the actual purchase price.

The specific identification method, however, is not feasible for many types of products either because items are not uniquely identifiable or because it is too costly to match a specific purchase price with each item sold or each item remaining in ending inventory. Most companies use cost flow methods to determine cost of goods sold and ending inventory. Cost flow methods are based on assumptions about how inventory might flow in and out of a company. However, it's important to note that the actual flow of a company's inventory does not have to correspond to the cost flow assumed. The various motivating factors that influence management's choice among alternative methods are discussed later in this chapter. We now explore the three most common cost flow methods: average cost, first-in, first-out (FIFO) and last-in, first-out (LIFO).

Average Cost

The average cost method assumes that cost of goods sold and ending inventory consist of a mixture of all the goods available for sale. The average unit cost applied to goods sold or to ending inventory is not simply an average of the various unit costs of purchases during the period but an average unit cost *weighted* by the number of units acquired at the various unit costs.

> The *average cost method* assumes that items sold and items in ending inventory come from a mixture of all the goods available for sale.

PERIODIC AVERAGE COST.   In a periodic inventory system, this weighted average is calculated at the end of the period as follows:

$$\text{Weighted-average unit cost} = \frac{\text{Cost of goods available for sale}}{\text{Quantity available for sale}}$$

The calculation of average cost is demonstrated in Illustration 8–5A using data from Illustration 8–5.

Cost of goods sold also could be determined directly by multiplying the weighted-average unit cost of $6.50 by the number of units sold ($6.50 × 6,500 = $42,250).

> In a perpetual inventory system, the average cost method is applied by computing a moving-average unit cost each time additional inventory is purchased.

PERPETUAL AVERAGE COST.   The weighted-average unit cost in a perpetual inventory system becomes a moving-average unit cost. A new weighted-average unit cost is calculated each time additional units are *purchased.* The new average is determined after each

ILLUSTRATION 8–5A	Beginning inventory (4,000 units @ $5.50)	$22,000
Average Cost— Periodic Inventory System	Plus: Purchases (7,000 units @ various prices)	49,500
	Cost of goods available for sale (11,000 units)	71,500
	Less: Ending inventory (determined below)	(29,250)
	Cost of goods sold (6,500 units)	$42,250

Cost of Ending Inventory:

$$\text{Weighted-average unit cost} = \frac{\$71,500}{11,000 \text{ units}} = \$6.50$$

4,500 units × $6.50 = $29,250

purchase by (1) summing the cost of the previous inventory balance and the cost of the new purchase, and (2) dividing this new total cost (cost of goods available for sale) by the number of units on hand (the inventory units that are available for sale). This average is then used to cost any units sold before the next purchase is made. The moving-average concept is applied in Illustration 8–5B.

ILLUSTRATION 8–5B   Average Cost—Perpetual Inventory System

Date	Purchased	Sold	Balance
Beginning inventory	4,000 @ $5.50 = $22,000		4,000 @ $5.50 = $22,000
Jan. 10		2,000 @ $5.50 = $ 11,000	2,000 @ $5.50 = $11,000
Jan. 17	1,000 @ $6.00 = $6,000		$11,000 + $6,000 = $17,000
			2,000 + 1,000 = 3,000 units
	$\left[\frac{\$17,000}{3,000 \text{ units}}\right] = \$5.667/\text{unit}$		
Mar. 22	3,000 @ $7.00 = $21,000		$17,000 + $21,000 = $38,000
	$\left[\frac{\$38,000}{6,000 \text{ units}}\right] = \$6.333/\text{unit}$		3,000 + 3,000 = 6,000 units
Apr. 15		1,500 @ $6.333 = $ 9,500	4,500 @ $6.333 = $28,500
Oct. 15	3,000 @ $7.50 = $22,500		$28,500 + $22,500 = $51,000
	$\left[\frac{\$51,000}{7,500 \text{ units}}\right] = \$6.80/\text{unit}$		4,500 + 3,000 = 7,500 units
Nov. 20		3,000 @ $6.80 = $ 20,400	4,500 @ $6.80 = **$30,600**
	Total cost of goods sold	= **$40,900**	

On January 17 the new average of $5.667 (rounded) is calculated by dividing the $17,000 cost of goods available ($11,000 from beginning inventory + $6,000 purchased on January 17) by the 3,000 units available (2,000 units from beginning inventory + 1,000 units acquired on January 17). The average is updated to $6.333 (rounded) with the March 22 purchase. The 1,500 units sold on April 15 are then costed at the average cost of $6.333.

Periodic average cost and perpetual average cost generally produce different allocations to cost of goods sold and ending inventory.

First-In, First-Out (FIFO)

The *first-in, first-out (FIFO) method* assumes that items sold are those that were acquired first.

The **first-in, first-out (FIFO) method** assumes that units sold are the first units acquired. Beginning inventory is sold first, followed by purchases during the period in the chronological order of their acquisition. In our illustration, 6,500 units were sold during 2009. Applying FIFO, these would be the 4,000 units in beginning inventory, the 1,000 units purchased on January 17, and 1,500 of the 3,000 units from the March 22 purchase. By default, ending inventory consists of the most recently acquired units. In this case, the 4,500 units in ending inventory consist of the 3,000 units purchased on October 15, and 1,500 of the 3,000 units purchased on March 22. Graphically, the flow is as follows:

Ending inventory applying FIFO consists of the most recently acquired items.

Units Available

Beg. inv.	4,000	
Jan. 17	1,000	6,500 units sold
Mar. 22	1,500	
Mar. 22	1,500	
Oct. 15	3,000	4,500 units in ending inventory
Total	11,000	

FIFO flow

PERIODIC FIFO.   Recall that we determine physical quantities on hand in a periodic inventory system by taking a physical count. Costing the 4,500 units in ending inventory this way automatically gives us the cost of goods sold as well. Using the numbers from our illustration, we determine cost of goods sold to be $38,500 by subtracting the $33,000 ending inventory from $71,500 cost of goods available for sale as shown in Illustration 8–5C.

Beginning inventory (4,000 units @ $5.50)			$22,000	**ILLUSTRATION 8–5C**
Plus: Purchases (7,000 units @ various prices)			49,500	FIFO—Periodic Inventory System
Cost of goods available for sale (11,000 units)			71,500	
Less: Ending inventory (determined below)			(33,000)	
Cost of goods sold (6,500 units)			$38,500	

Cost of Ending Inventory:

Date of Purchase	Units	Unit Cost	Total Cost
Mar. 22	1,500	$7.00	$10,500
Oct. 15	3,000	7.50	22,500
Total	4,500		$33,000

Of course, the 6,500 units sold could be costed directly as follows:

Date of Purchase	Units	Unit Cost	Total Cost
Beg. inv.	4,000	$5.50	$22,000
Jan. 17	1,000	6.00	6,000
Mar. 22	1,500	7.00	10,500
Total	6,500		$38,500

PERPETUAL FIFO.   The same ending inventory and cost of goods sold amounts are always produced in a perpetual inventory system as in a periodic inventory system when FIFO is used. This is because the same units and costs are first in and first out whether cost of goods sold is determined as each sale is made or at the end of the period as a residual amount. The application of FIFO in a perpetual system is shown in Illustration 8–5D.

Last-In, First-Out (LIFO)

The last-in, first-out (LIFO) method assumes that the units sold are the most recent units purchased. In our illustration, the 6,500 units assumed sold would be the 6,500 units acquired most recently: the 3,000 units acquired on October 15, the 3,000 units acquired on March 22,

The last-in, first-out (LIFO) method assumes that items sold are those that were most recently acquired.

ILLUSTRATION 8–5D	Date	Purchased	Sold	Balance
FIFO—Perpetual Inventory System	Beginning inventory	4,000 @ $5.50 = $22,000		4,000 @ $5.50 = $22,000
	Jan. 10		2,000 @ $5.50 = $11,000	2,000 @ $5.50 = $11,000
	Jan. 17	1,000 @ $6.00 = $6,000		2,000 @ $5.50 1,000 @ $6.00 } $17,000
	Mar. 22	3,000 @ $7.00 = $21,000		2,000 @ $5.50 1,000 @ $6.00 3,000 @ $7.00 } $38,000
	Apr. 15		1,500 @ $5.50 = $8,250	500 @ $5.50 1,000 @ $6.00 3,000 @ $7.00 } $29,750
	Oct. 15	3,000 @ $7.50 = $22,500		500 @ $5.50 1,000 @ $6.00 3,000 @ $7.00 3,000 @ $7.50 } $52,250
	Nov. 20		500 @ $5.50 + 1,000 @ $6.00 + 1,500 @ $7.00 = $19,250	1,500 @ $7.00 3,000 @ $7.50 } **$33,000**
		Total cost of goods sold	= **$38,500**	

and 500 of the 1,000 units purchased on January 17. Ending inventory, then, consists of the units acquired first; in this case, the 4,000 units from beginning inventory and 500 of the 1,000 units purchased on January 17. Graphically, the flow is as follows:

Ending inventory applying LIFO consists of the items acquired first.

Units Available

Beg. inv.	4,000 } 4,500 units in ending inventory
Jan. 17	500

LIFO flow

Jan. 17	500
Mar. 22	3,000 } 6,500 units sold
Oct. 15	3,000
Total	11,000

PERIODIC LIFO. The cost of ending inventory determined to be $25,000 (calculated below) by the LIFO assumption and using a periodic system is subtracted from cost of goods available for sale to arrive at the cost of goods sold of $46,500 as shown in Illustration 8–5E.

ILLUSTRATION 8–5E				
LIFO—Periodic Inventory System	Beginning inventory (4,000 units @ $5.50)			$22,000
	Plus: Purchases (7,000 units @ various prices)			49,500
	Cost of goods available for sale (11,000 units)			71,500
	Less: Ending inventory (determined below)			(25,000)
	Cost of goods sold (6,500 units)			$46,500
	Cost of Ending Inventory:			
	Date of Purchase	**Units**	**Unit Cost**	**Total Cost**
	Beginning inventory	4,000	$5.50	$22,000
	Jan. 17	500	6.00	3,000
	Total	4,500		$25,000

The 6,500 sold could be costed directly as follows:

Date of Purchase	Units	Unit Cost	Total Cost
Jan. 17	500	$6.00	$ 3,000
Mar. 22	3,000	7.00	21,000
Oct. 15	3,000	7.50	22,500
Total	6,500		$46,500

PERPETUAL LIFO. The application of LIFO in a perpetual system is shown in Illustration 8–5F. Each time inventory is purchased or sold, the LIFO layers are adjusted. For example, after the March 22 purchase, we have three layers of inventory at different unit costs listed in the chronological order of their purchase. When 1,500 units are sold on April 15, we assume they come from the most recent layer of 3,000 units purchased at $7.00.

Date	Purchased	Sold	Balance
Beginning inventory	4,000 @ $5.50 = $22,000		4,000 @ $5.50 = $22,000
Jan. 10		2,000 @ $5.50 = $11,000	2,000 @ $5.50 = $11,000
Jan. 17	1,000 @ $6.00 = $6,000		2,000 @ $5.50 }$17,000 1,000 @ $6.00
Mar. 22	3,000 @ $7.00 = $21,000		2,000 @ $5.50 1,000 @ $6.00 }$38,000 3,000 @ $7.00
Apr. 15		1,500 @ $7.00 = $10,500	2,000 @ $5.50 1,000 @ $6.00 }$27,500 1,500 @ $7.00
Oct. 15	3,000 @ $7.50 = $22,500		2,000 @ $5.50 1,000 @ $6.00 1,500 @ $7.00 }$50,000 3,000 @ $7.50
Nov. 20		3,000 @ $7.50 = $22,500	2,000 @ $5.50 1,000 @ $6.00 }$27,500 1,500 @ $7.00
	Total cost of goods sold	= $44,000	

ILLUSTRATION 8–5F

LIFO—Perpetual Inventory System

Notice that $44,000 of the cost of goods available for sale is allocated to cost of goods sold by perpetual LIFO and $27,500 to ending inventory (the balance after the last transaction), which is different from the periodic LIFO result of $46,500 and $25,000. Unlike FIFO, applying LIFO in a perpetual inventory system will generally result in an ending inventory and cost of goods sold different from the allocation arrived at applying LIFO in a periodic system. Periodic LIFO applies the last-in, first-out concept to total sales and total purchases only at the conclusion of the reporting period. Perpetual LIFO applies the same concept, but several times during the period—every time a sale is made.

For example, when 2,000 units are sold on January 10, perpetual LIFO costs those units at $5.50, the beginning inventory unit cost. Periodic LIFO, by contrast, would be applied at year-end. By the end of the year, enough purchases have been made that the beginning inventory would be assumed to remain intact, and the January 10 units sold would be costed at a more recent price.

Perpetual LIFO generally results in cost of goods sold and inventory amounts that are different from those obtained by applying periodic LIFO.

Comparison of Cost Flow Methods

The three cost flow methods are compared below assuming a periodic inventory system.

Comparison of cost flow methods

	Average	FIFO	LIFO
Cost of goods sold	$42,250	$38,500	$46,500
Ending inventory	29,250	33,000	25,000
Total	$71,500	$71,500	$71,500

Notice that the average cost method in this example produces amounts that fall in between the FIFO and LIFO amounts for both cost of goods sold and ending inventory. This will usually be the case. Whether it will be FIFO or LIFO that produces the highest or lowest value of cost of goods sold and ending inventory depends on the pattern of the actual unit cost changes during the period.

During periods of generally rising costs, as in our example, FIFO results in a lower cost of goods sold than LIFO because the lower costs of the earliest purchases are assumed sold. LIFO cost of goods sold will include the more recent higher cost purchases. On the other hand, FIFO ending inventory includes the most recent higher cost purchases which results in a higher ending inventory than LIFO. LIFO ending inventory includes the lower costs of the earliest purchases. Conversely, if costs are declining, then FIFO will result in a higher cost of goods sold and lower ending inventory than LIFO.[6]

Each of the three methods is permissible according to generally accepted accounting principles and frequently is used. Also, a company need not use the same method for all of its inventory. For example, International Paper Company uses LIFO for its raw materials and finished pulp and paper products, and both the FIFO and average cost methods for other inventories. Because of the importance of inventories and the possible differential effects of different methods on the financial statements, a company must identify in a disclosure note the method(s) it uses. The chapter's opening case included an example of this disclosure for Ford Motor Company, and you will encounter additional examples later in the chapter.

If unit costs are increasing, LIFO will result in a higher cost of goods sold and lower ending inventory than FIFO.

FINANCIAL
Reporting Case

Q1, p. 375

A company must disclose the inventory method(s) it uses.

GRAPHIC 8–5

Inventory Cost Flow Methods Used in Practice

	2006		1973	
	# of Companies	**% of Companies**	**# of Companies**	**% of Companies**
FIFO	385	48%	394	43%
LIFO	228	28	150	16
Average	159	20	235	25
Other*	30	4	148	16
Total	802	100%	927	100%

*"Other" includes the specific identification method and miscellaneous less popular methods.

Graphic 8–5 shows the results of a survey of inventory methods used by 600 large public companies in 2006 and 1973.[7] FIFO is the most popular method in both periods, but there has been a significant increase in the use of LIFO since the earlier period. Notice that the column total for the number of companies is greater than 600, indicating that many companies included in this sample do use multiple methods.

 INTERNATIONAL FINANCIAL REPORTING STANDARDS

Inventory Cost Flow Assumptions. *IAS NO. 2* does not permit the use of LIFO. Because of this restriction, many U.S. multinational companies employ the use of LIFO only for all or most of their domestic inventories and FIFO or average cost for their foreign subsidiaries. **General Mills** provides an example with a disclosure note included in a recent annual report:

Inventories (in part)

All inventories in the United States other than grain are valued at the lower of cost, using the last-in, first-out (LIFO) method, or market . . . Inventories outside of the United States are valued at the lower of cost, using the first-in, first-out (FIFO) method, or market.

Real World Financials

---

[6]The differences between the various methods also hold when a perpetual inventory system is used.
[7]*Accounting Trends and Techniques—2007* and *1974* (New York, New York: AICPA, 2007 and 1974)

DECISION MAKERS' PERSPECTIVE—Factors Influencing Method Choice

● **LO5**

What factors motivate companies to choose one method over another? What factors have caused the increased popularity of LIFO? Choosing among alternative accounting methods is a complex issue. Often such choices are not made in isolation but in such a way that the combination of inventory cost flow assumptions, depreciation methods, pension assumptions, and other choices meet a particular objective. Also, many believe managers sometimes make these choices to maximize their own personal benefits rather than those of the company or its external constituents. But regardless of the motive, the impact on reported numbers is an important consideration in each choice of method. The inventory choice determines (a) how closely reported costs reflect the actual physical flow of inventory, (b) the timing of reported income and income tax expense, and (c) how well costs are matched with associated revenues.

PHYSICAL FLOW.   If a company wanted to choose a method that most closely approximates specific identification, then the actual physical flow of inventory in and out of the company would motivate the choice of method.

For example, companies often attempt to sell the oldest goods in inventory first for some of their products. This certainly is the case with perishable goods such as many grocery items. The FIFO method best mirrors the physical flow in these situations. The average cost method might be used for liquids such as chemicals where items sold are taken from a mixture of inventory acquired at different times and different prices. There are very few inventories that actually flow in a LIFO manner. It is important for you to understand that there is no requirement that companies choose an inventory method that approximates actual physical flow and few companies make the choice on this basis. In fact, as we discuss next, the effect of inventory method on income and income taxes is the primary motivation that influences method choice.

> A company is not required to choose an inventory method that approximates actual physical flow.

INCOME TAXES AND NET INCOME.   If the unit cost of inventory changes during a period, the inventory method chosen can have a significant effect on the amount of income reported by the company to external parties and also on the amount of income taxes paid to the Internal Revenue Service (IRS) and state and local taxing authorities. Over the entire life of a company, cost of goods sold for all years will equal actual costs of items sold regardless of the inventory method used. However, as we have discussed, different inventory methods can produce significantly different results in each particular year.

When prices rise and inventory quantities are not decreasing, LIFO produces a higher cost of goods sold and therefore lower net income than the other methods. The company's income tax returns will report a lower taxable income using LIFO and lower taxes will be paid currently. Taxes are not reduced permanently, only deferred. The reduced amount will be paid to the taxing authorities when either the unit cost of inventory or the quantity of inventory subsequently declines. However, we know from our discussion of the time value of money that it is advantageous to save a dollar today even if it must be paid back in the future. Recall from the recent survey results exhibited earlier that the popularity of LIFO increased significantly between 1973 and 2006. The main reason for this increased popularity is attributable to high inflation (increasing prices) during the 1970s which motivated many companies to switch to LIFO in order to gain this tax benefit.

> Many companies choose LIFO in order to reduce income taxes in periods when prices are rising.

A corporation's taxable income comprises revenues, expenses (including cost of goods sold), gains, and losses measured according to the regulations of the appropriate taxing authority. Income before tax as reported in the income statement does not always equal taxable income. In some cases, differences are caused by the use of different measurement methods.[8] However, IRS regulations, which determine federal taxable income, require that if a company uses LIFO to measure taxable income, the company also must use LIFO for external financial reporting. This is known as the LIFO conformity rule with respect to inventory methods.

---

[8]For example, a corporation can take advantage of incentives offered by Congress by deducting more depreciation in the early years of an asset's life in its federal income tax return than it reports in its income statement.

If a company uses LIFO to measure its taxable income, IRS regulations require that LIFO also be used to measure income reported to investors and creditors (the *LIFO conformity rule*).

FINANCIAL
Reporting Case

Q2, p. 375

GRAPHIC 8–6

Inventories Disclosure—Alcoa, Inc.

Real World Financials

● LO6

Because of the LIFO conformity rule, to obtain the tax advantages of using LIFO in periods of rising prices, lower net income is reported to shareholders, creditors, and other external parties. The income tax motivation for using LIFO may be offset by a desire to report higher net income. Reported net income could have an effect on a corporation's share price,[9] on bonuses paid to management, or on debt agreements with lenders. For example, research has indicated that the managers of companies with bonus plans tied to income measures are more likely to choose accounting methods that maximize their bonuses (often those that increase net income).[10]

In 1981, the LIFO conformity rule was liberalized to permit LIFO users to present designated supplemental disclosures, allowing a company to report in a note the effect of using another method on inventory valuation rather than LIFO. For example, Graphic 8–6 shows the note provided in a recent annual report by **Alcoa, Inc.,** a leading producer of aluminum, disclosing its use of LIFO for part of its inventories. A second note provides the supplemental LIFO disclosures.[11]

Summary of Significant Accounting Policies
Inventory Valuation

Inventories are carried at the lower of cost or market, with cost for a substantial portion of U.S. and Canadian inventories determined under the last-in, first-out (LIFO) method. The cost of other inventories is principally determined under the average-cost method.

G. Inventories (in part)

Approximately 44% and 48% of total inventories at December 31, 2006 and 2005, respectively, were valued on a LIFO basis. If valued on an average-cost basis, total inventories would have been $1,077 and $836 million higher at the end of 2006 and 2005, respectively.

Proponents of LIFO argue that it results in a better match of revenues and expenses.

LIFO LIQUIDATIONS. Earlier in the text, we demonstrated the importance of matching revenues and expenses in creating an income statement that is useful in predicting future cash flows. If prices change during a period, then LIFO generally will provide a better match of revenues and expenses. Sales reflect the most recent selling prices, and cost of goods sold includes the costs of the most recent purchases.

For the same reason, though, inventory costs in the balance sheet with LIFO generally are out of date because they reflect old purchase transactions. It is not uncommon for a company's LIFO inventory balance to be based on unit costs actually incurred several years earlier.

FINANCIAL
Reporting Case

Q3, p. 375

This distortion sometimes carries over to the income statement as well. When inventory quantities decline during a period, then these out-of-date inventory layers are liquidated and cost of goods sold will partially match noncurrent costs with current selling prices. If costs have been increasing (decreasing), LIFO liquidations produce higher (lower) net income than would have resulted if the liquidated inventory were included in cost of goods sold at current costs. The paper profits (losses) caused by including out of date, low (high) costs in cost of goods sold is referred to as the effect on income of liquidations of LIFO inventory.

To illustrate this problem, consider the example in Illustration 8–6.

ILLUSTRATION 8–6

LIFO Liquidation

National Distributors, Inc., uses the LIFO inventory method. The company began 2009 with inventory of 10,000 units that cost $20 per unit. During 2009, 30,000 units were purchased for $25 each and 35,000 units were sold.

National's LIFO cost of goods sold for 2009 consists of:

30,000 units @ $25 per unit =	$750,000
5,000 units @ $20 per unit =	$100,000
35,000	$850,000

---

[9]The concept of capital market efficiency has been debated for many years. In an efficient capital market, the market is not fooled by differences in accounting method choice that do not translate into real cash flow differences. The only apparent cash flow difference caused by different inventory methods is the amount of income taxes paid currently. In an efficient market, we would expect the share price of a company that switched its method to LIFO and saved tax dollars to increase even though it reported lower net income than if LIFO had not been adopted. Research on this issue is mixed. For example, see William E. Ricks, "Market's Response to the 1974 LIFO Adoptions," *Journal of Accounting Research* (Autumn 1982), and Robert Moren Brown, "Short-Range Market Reaction to Changes to LIFO Using Preliminary Earnings Announcement Dates," *Journal of Accounting Research* (Spring 1980).

[10]For example, see P. M. Healy, "The Effect of Bonus Schemes on Accounting Decisions," *Journal of Accounting and Economics* (April 1985), and D. Dhaliwal, G. Salamon, and E. Smith, "The Effect of Owner Versus Management Control on the Choice of Accounting Methods," *Journal of Accounting and Economics* (July 1982).

[11]Alcoa uses both the LIFO and average cost methods. Earlier in the chapter we pointed out that a company need not use the same inventory method for all of its inventories.

Included in cost of goods sold are 5,000 units from beginning inventory that have now been liquidated. If the company had purchased at least 35,000 units, no liquidation would have occurred. Then cost of goods sold would have been $875,000 (35,000 units × $25 per unit) instead of $850,000. The difference between these two cost of goods sold figures is $25,000 ($875,000 − 850,000). This is the before tax income effect of the LIFO liquidation. Assuming a 40% income tax rate, the net effect of the liquidation is to increase net income by $15,000 [$25,000 × (1 − .40)]. The lower the costs of the units liquidated, the more severe the effect on income.

A company must disclose in a note any material effect of LIFO liquidation on net income. For example, Graphic 8–7 shows the disclosure note that accompanies a recent quarterly financial statement of **Ryerson Inc.,** a large metal products company.

> A material effect on net income of LIFO layer liquidation must be disclosed in a note.

> **GRAPHIC 8–7**
> LIFO Liquidation Disclosure—Ryerson Inc.
> **Real World Financials**

Note 2 Inventories (in part)

During the six months ending June 30, 2007, inventory quantities were reduced. This reduction resulted in a liquidation of LIFO inventory quantities carried at lower costs prevailing in prior years as compared with the cost of 2007 purchases, the effect of which decreased cost of goods sold by approximately $50 million and increased net income by approximately $30 million.

In our illustration, National Distributors, Inc. would disclose that LIFO liquidations increased income by $15,000 in 2009, assuming that this effect on income is considered material.

We've discussed several factors that influence companies in their choice of inventory method. A company could be influenced by the actual physical flow of its inventory, by the effect of inventory method on reported net income and the amount of income taxes payable currently, or by a desire to provide a better match of expenses with revenues. You've seen that the direction of the change in unit costs determines the effect of using different methods on net income and income taxes. While the United States has experienced persistent inflation for many years (increases in the general price-level), the prices of many goods and services have experienced periods of declining prices (for example, personal computers). ●

ADDITIONAL CONSIDERATION

LIFO Reserves

Many companies use LIFO for external reporting and income tax purposes but maintain their internal records using FIFO or average cost. The reasons for doing this might include: (1) the high recordkeeping costs of the LIFO method, (2) the existence of contractual agreements such as bonus or profit sharing plans that prohibit the use of LIFO in the calculation of net income, and (3) the need for FIFO or average cost information for pricing decisions.

Generally, the conversion to LIFO is performed at the end of the period and not entered into the company's records. However, some companies enter the results of the conversion—the difference between the internal method and LIFO—directly into the accounts as a contra account to inventory. This contra account is called either the LIFO reserve or the LIFO allowance.

Occasionally, such companies report ending inventory valued using the internal method less the LIFO reserve or allowance to arrive at LIFO inventory reported in the balance sheet. For example, **General Motors** recently reported the following in a note:

Inventories ($ in millions)	2007	2006
Total inventories at FIFO	$16,362	$15,429
Less LIFO allowance	(1,423)	(1,508)
Total inventories, at LIFO cost	$14,939	$13,921

Real World Financials

Note that this is merely another way of presenting the supplemental non-LIFO disclosures discussed previously.

**INVENTORY COST
FLOW METHODS**

The Rogers Company began 2009 with an inventory of 10 million units of its principal product. These units cost $5 each. The following inventory transactions occurred during the first six months of 2009.

Date	Transaction
Feb. 15	Purchased, on account, 5 million units at a cost of $6.50 each.
Mar. 20	Sold, on account, 8 million units at a selling price of $12 each.
Apr. 30	Purchased, on account, 5 million units at a cost of $7 each.

On June 30, 2009, 12 million units were on hand.

Required:

1. Prepare journal entries to record the above transactions. The company uses a periodic inventory system.
2. Prepare the required adjusting entry on June 30, 2009, applying each of the following inventory methods:

   a. Average
   b. FIFO
   c. LIFO

3. Repeat requirement 1 assuming that the company uses a perpetual inventory system.

SOLUTION

1. Prepare journal entries to record the above transactions. The company uses a periodic inventory system.

February 15	($ in millions)	
Purchases (5 million × $6.50)	32.5	
Accounts payable		32.5
To record the purchase of inventory.		
March 20		
Accounts receivable (8 million × $12)	96	
Sales revenue		96
To record sales on account.		
No entry is recorded for the cost of inventory sold.		
April 30		
Purchases (5 million × $7)	35	
Accounts payable		35
To record the purchase of inventory.		

2. Prepare the required adjusting entry on June 30, 2009, applying each method.

Date	Journal entry	($ in millions)		
		Average	**FIFO**	**LIFO**
June 30	Cost of goods sold (determined below)	47.0	40.0	54.5
	Inventory (ending—determined below)	70.5	77.5	63.0
	Inventory (beginning – [10 million @ $5])	50.0	50.0	50.0
	Purchases ($32.5 million + 35 million)	67.5	67.5	67.5

Calculation of Ending Inventory and Cost of Goods Sold:

a. Average:

	($ in millions)
Beginning inventory (10 million units @ $5.00)	$ 50.0
Plus: Purchases (10 million units @ various prices)	67.5
Cost of goods available for sale (20 million units)	117.5
Less: Ending inventory (determined below)	(70.5)
Cost of goods sold	$ 47.0

Cost of ending inventory:

$$\text{Weighted-average unit cost} = \frac{\$117.5}{20 \text{ million units}} = \$5.875$$

$$12 \text{ million units} \times \$5.875 = \$70.5 \text{ million}$$

b. FIFO:

Cost of goods available for sale (20 million units)	$117.5
Less: Ending inventory (determined below)	(77.5)
Cost of goods sold	$ 40.0

Cost of ending inventory:

Date of Purchase	Units	Unit Cost	Total Cost
Beg. inv.	2 million	$5.00	10.0
Feb. 15	5 million	6.50	32.5
April 30	5 million	7.00	35.0
Total	12 million		$77.5

c. LIFO:

Cost of goods available for sale (20 million units)	$117.5
Less: Ending inventory (determined below)	(63.0)
Cost of goods sold	$ 54.5

Cost of ending inventory:

Date of Purchase	Units	Unit Cost	Total Cost
Beg. inv.	10 million	$5.00	$50.0
Feb. 15	2 million	6.50	13.0
Total	12 million		$63.0

3. Repeat requirement 1 assuming that the company uses a perpetual inventory system.

February 15	($ in millions)	
Inventory (5 million units × $6.50)	32.5	
Accounts payable		32.5

To record the purchase of inventory.

April 30		
Inventory (5 million units × $7.00)	35.0	
Accounts payable		35.0

To record the purchase of inventory.

	($ in millions)		
Journal Entries—March 20	**Average**	**FIFO**	**LIFO**
Accounts receivable (8 million × $12)	96.0	96.0	96.0
Sales revenue	96.0	96.0	96.0
To record sales on account.			
Cost of goods sold (determined below)	44.0	40.0	47.5
Inventory (determined below)	44.0	40.0	47.5
To record cost of goods sold.			

Calculation of Cost of Goods Sold:

a. Average:
   Cost of goods sold:

($, except unit costs, in millions)			
Date	**Purchased**	**Sold**	**Balance**
Beg. inv.	10 million @ $5.00 = $50.0		10 million @ $5.00 = $50.0
Feb. 15	5 million @ $6.50 = $32.5		$50 + $32.5 = $82.5

$$\frac{\$82.5}{15 \text{ million units}} = \$5.50/\text{unit}$$

Date		Sold	
Mar. 20		8 million @ $5.50 = $44.0	

b. FIFO:
   Cost of goods sold:

Units Sold	**Cost of Units Sold**	**Total Cost**
8 million (from Beg. inv.)	$5.00	$40.0

c. LIFO:
   Cost of goods sold:

Units Sold	**Cost of Units Sold**	**Total Cost**
5 million (from Feb. 15 purchase)	$6.50	$32.5
3 million (from Beg. inv.)	5.00	15.0
8 million		$47.5

DECISION MAKERS' PERSPECTIVE

A company should maintain sufficient inventory quantities to meet customer demand while at the same time minimizing inventory ordering and carrying costs.

INVENTORY MANAGEMENT   Managers closely monitor inventory levels to (1) ensure that the inventories needed to sustain operations are available, and (2) hold the cost of ordering and carrying inventories to the lowest possible level.[12] Unfortunately, these objectives often conflict with one another. Companies must maintain sufficient quantities of inventory to meet customer demand. However, maintaining inventory is costly. Fortunately, a variety of tools are available, including computerized inventory control systems and the outsourcing of inventory component production, to help balance these conflicting objectives.[13]

A just-in-time (JIT) system is another valuable technique that many companies have adopted to assist them with inventory management. JIT is a system used by a manufacturer

[12]The cost of carrying inventory includes the possible loss from the write-down of obsolete inventory. We discuss inventory write-downs in Chapter 9. There are analytical models available to determine the appropriate amount of inventory a company should maintain. A discussion of these models is beyond the scope of this text.

[13]Eugene Brigham and Joel Houston, *Fundamentals of Financial Management,* 8th Edition, 1998, The Dryden Press, Orlando, Florida, p. 632.

to coordinate production with suppliers so that raw materials or components arrive just as they are needed in the production process. Have you ever ordered a personal computer from **Dell Inc.**? If so, the PC you received was not manufactured until you placed your order, and many of the components used in the production of your PC were not even acquired by Dell until then as well. This system enables Dell to maintain relatively low inventory balances. At the same time, the company's efficient production techniques, along with its excellent relationships with suppliers ensuring prompt delivery of components, enables Dell to quickly meet customer demand. In its February 2, 2007, fiscal year-end financial statements, Dell reported an inventory balance of $660 million. With this relatively low investment in inventory, Dell was able to generate over $57 billion in sales revenue. To appreciate the advantage this provides, compare these numbers with **Hewlett Packard (HP)**, a company that includes PCs among its wide variety of technology products. For its fiscal year ended October 31, 2007, HP reported product revenue of $84 billion. However, to achieve this level of sales, HP's investment in inventory was over $8 billion.

It is important for a financial analyst to evaluate a company's effectiveness in managing its inventory. As we discussed in Chapter 5, one key to profitability is how well a company utilizes its assets. This evaluation is influenced by the company's inventory method choice. The choice of inventory method is an important and complex management decision. The many factors affecting this decision were discussed in a previous section. The inventory method also affects the analysis of a company's liquidity and profitability by investors, creditors, and financial analysts. Analysts must make adjustments when evaluating companies that use different inventory methods. During periods of rising prices, we would expect a company using FIFO to report higher income than a LIFO or average cost company. If one of the companies being analyzed uses LIFO, precise adjustments can often be made using the supplemental disclosures provided by many LIFO companies. Recall that the LIFO conformity rule was liberalized to permit LIFO users to report in a note the effect of using a method other than LIFO for inventory valuation.

For example, the disclosure note exhibited in Graphic 8–6 on page 392 reveals that **Alcoa Inc.** uses both the LIFO and average-cost inventory methods with 44% of its inventories valued using LIFO. **Alcan, Inc.,** Alcoa's major competitor, values all of its inventory using the average-cost method. Financial statement values for the two companies for 2006 are as follows ($ in millions):

FINANCIAL Reporting Case

Q4, p. 375

	Alcoa, Inc.		Alcan, Inc.	
	2006	**2005**	**2006**	**2005**
Balance sheet:				
Inventories	$ 3,805	$ 3,191	$ 3,186	$ 2,734
Income statement:				
Net sales	30,379	25,568	23,641	20,320
Cost of goods sold	23,318	20,704	17,990	16,135

Real World Financials

We can convert Alcoa's inventory and cost of goods sold to a 100% average cost basis before comparing the two companies by using the information provided in Graphic 8–6. Inventories recorded at LIFO were lower by approximately $1,077 million at December 31, 2006, and $836 million at December 31, 2005, than if they had been valued at average cost:

Supplemental LIFO disclosures can be used to convert LIFO inventory and cost of goods sold amounts.

	2006	2005
Inventories (as reported)	$3,805	$3,191
Add: conversion to average cost	1,077	836
Inventories (100% average cost)	$4,882	$4,027

Cost of goods sold for 2006 would have been $241 million lower had Alcoa used average cost instead of LIFO. While beginning inventory would have been $836 million higher, ending inventory also would have been higher by $1,077 million. An increase in beginning inventory causes an increase in cost of goods sold, but an increase in ending inventory causes a decrease in cost of goods sold. Purchases for 2006 are the same regardless of the inventory valuation method used. Cost of goods sold for 2006 would have been $23,077 million ($23,318 − 241) if average cost had been used for all inventories.

We can now use the 100% average cost amounts to compare the two companies. Since cost of goods sold is lower by $241 million, income taxes and net income require adjustment before calculating any profitability ratio. Also, the converted inventory amounts can be used to compute liquidity ratios.

● LO7

One important profitability indicator using cost of goods sold is gross profit or gross margin, which highlights the important relationship between net sales revenue and cost of goods sold. The gross profit ratio is computed as follows:

$$\text{Gross profit ratio} = \frac{\text{Gross profit}}{\text{Net sales}}$$

The *gross profit ratio* indicates the percentage of each sales dollar available to cover other expenses and provide a profit.

The higher the ratio, the higher is the markup a company is able to achieve on its products. For example, a product that costs $100 that is sold for $150 provides a gross profit of $50 ($150 − 100) and a gross profit ratio of 33% ($50 ÷ $150). If that same product can be sold for $200, the gross profit increases to $100 and the gross profit ratio increases to 50% ($100 ÷ $200) and more dollars are available to cover expenses other than cost of goods sold.

The 2006 gross profit ($ in millions), for Alcoa, using the 100% average cost amounts, is $7,302 ($30,379 − 23,077) and the gross profit ratio is 24% ($7,302 ÷ $30,379). The ratio for Alcan also is 24% [($23,641 − 17,990) = $5,651 ÷ $23,641]. The ratio for both companies is less than the industry average of 45%.

Monitoring this ratio over time can provide valuable insights. For example, a declining ratio could indicate that the company is unable to offset rising costs with corresponding increases in sales price, or that sales prices are declining without a commensurate reduction in costs. In either case, the decline in the ratio has important implications for future profitability.

Chapter 5 introduced an important ratio, the inventory turnover ratio, which is designed to evaluate a company's effectiveness in managing its investment in inventory. The ratio shows the number of times the average inventory balance is sold during a reporting period. The more frequently a business is able to sell or turn over its inventory, the lower its investment in inventory must be for a given level of sales. Usually, the higher the ratio the more profitable a company will be. Monitoring the inventory turnover ratio over time can highlight potential problems. A declining ratio generally is unfavorable and could be caused by the presence of obsolete or slow-moving products, or poor marketing and sales efforts.

Recall that the ratio is computed as follows:

$$\text{Inventory turnover ratio} = \frac{\text{Cost of goods sold}}{\text{Average inventory}}$$

We can divide the inventory turnover ratio into 365 days to compute the average days in inventory, which indicates the average number of days it normally takes to sell inventory.

For Alcoa, the inventory turnover ratio for 2006 is 5.18 ($23,077 ÷ [(4,882 + 4,027) ÷ 2]) and the average days inventory is 70 days (365 ÷ 5.18). This compares to a turnover of 6.08 ($17,990 ÷ [($3,186 + 2,734) ÷ 2]) and an average days inventory of 60 days (365 days ÷ 6.08) for Alcan. It takes 10 more days, on average, for Alcoa to turn over its inventory. The inventory turnover ratio of both companies is higher than the industry average of 4.66.

Inventory increases that outrun increases in cost of goods sold might indicate difficulties in generating sales. These inventory buildups may also indicate that a company has obsolete or slow-moving inventory. This proposition was tested in an important academic research study. Professors Lev and Thiagarajan empirically demonstrated the importance of a set of 12 fundamental variables in valuing companies' common stock. The set of variables included inventory (change in inventory minus change in sales). The inventory variable was found to be a significant indicator of stock returns, particularly during high and medium inflation years.[14]

EARNINGS QUALITY Changes in the ratios we discussed above often provide information about the quality of a company's current period earnings. For example, a slowing turnover ratio combined with higher than normal inventory levels may indicate the potential for decreased production, obsolete inventory, or a need to decrease prices to sell inventory (which will then decrease gross profit ratios and net income).

The choice of which inventory method to use also affects earnings quality, particularly in times of rapidly changing prices. Earlier in this chapter we discussed the effect of a LIFO liquidation on company profits. A LIFO liquidation profit (or loss) reduces the quality of current period earnings. Fortunately for analysts, companies must disclose these profits or losses, if material. In addition, LIFO cost of goods sold determined using a periodic inventory system is more susceptible to manipulation than is FIFO. Year-end purchases can have a dramatic effect on LIFO cost of goods sold in rapid cost-change environments. Recall again our discussion in Chapter 4 concerning earnings quality. Many believe that manipulating income reduces earnings quality because it can mask permanent earnings. Inventory write-downs and changes in inventory method are two additional inventory-related techniques a company could use to manipulate earnings. We discuss these issues in the next chapter.

METHODS OF SIMPLIFYING LIFO

PART B

The LIFO method described and illustrated to this point is called *unit LIFO*[15] because the last-in, first-out concept is applied to individual units of inventory. One problem with unit LIFO is that it can be very costly to implement. It requires records of each unit of inventory. The costs of maintaining these records can be significant, particularly when a company has numerous individual units of inventory and when unit costs change often during a period.

The recordkeeping costs of unit LIFO can be significant.

In the previous section, a second disadvantage of unit LIFO was identified—the possibility that LIFO layers will be liquidated if the quantity of a particular inventory unit declines below its beginning balance. Even if a company's total inventory quantity is stable or increasing, if the quantity of any particular inventory unit declines, unit LIFO will liquidate all or a portion of a LIFO layer of inventory. When inventory quantity declines in a period of rising costs, noncurrent lower costs will be included in cost of goods sold and matched with current selling prices, resulting in LIFO liquidation profit.

Another disadvantage of unit LIFO is the possibility of LIFO liquidation.

This part of the chapter discusses techniques that can be used to significantly reduce the recordkeeping costs of LIFO and to minimize the probability of LIFO inventory layers being liquidated. Specifically, we discuss the use of inventory pools and the dollar-value LIFO method.

LIFO Inventory Pools

The objectives of using LIFO inventory pools are to simplify recordkeeping by grouping inventory units into pools based on physical similarities of the individual units and to reduce the risk of LIFO layer liquidation. For example, a glass company might group its various grades of window glass into a single window pool. Other pools might be auto glass and sliding door glass. A lumber company might pool its inventory into hardwood, framing lumber, paneling, and so on.

A pool consists of inventory units grouped according to natural physical similarities.

This allows a company to account for a few inventory pools rather than every specific type of inventory separately. Within pools, all purchases during a period are considered to have been made at the same time and at the same cost. Individual unit costs are converted to

The average cost for all of the pool purchases during the period is applied to the current year's LIFO layer.

[14]B. Lev and S. R. Thiagarajan, "Fundamental Information Analysis," *Journal of Accounting Research* (Autumn 1993). The main conclusion of the study was that fundamental variables, not just earnings, are useful in firm valuation, particularly when examined in the context of macroeconomic conditions such as inflation.
[15]Unit LIFO sometimes is called *specific goods LIFO*.

an average cost for the pool. If the quantity of ending inventory for the pool increases, then ending inventory will consist of the beginning inventory plus a single layer added during the period at the average acquisition cost for that pool.

Here's an example. Let's say Diamond Lumber Company has a rough-cut lumber inventory pool that includes three types: oak, pine, and maple. The beginning inventory consisted of the following:

	Quantity (Board Feet)	Cost (Per Foot)	Total Cost
Oak	16,000	$2.20	$35,200
Pine	10,000	3.00	30,000
Maple	14,000	2.40	33,600
	40,000		$98,800

The average cost for this pool is $2.47 per board foot ($98,800 ÷ 40,000 board feet). Now assume that during the next reporting period Diamond sold 46,000 board feet of lumber and purchased 50,000 board feet as follows:

	Quantity (Board Feet)	Cost (Per Foot)	Total Cost
Oak	20,000	$2.25	$ 45,000
Pine	14,000	3.00	42,000
Maple	16,000	2.50	40,000
	50,000		$127,000

The average cost for this pool is $2.54 per board foot ($127,000 ÷ 50,000 board feet). Because the quantity of inventory for the pool increased by 4,000 board feet (50,000 purchased less 46,000 sold), ending inventory will include the beginning inventory and a LIFO layer consisting of the 4,000 board feet increase. We would add this LIFO layer at the average cost of purchases made during the period, $2.54. The ending inventory of $108,960 now consists of two layers:

	Quantity (Board Feet)	Cost (Per Foot)	Total Cost
Beginning inventory	40,000	$2.47	$ 98,800
LIFO layer added	4,000	2.54	10,160
Ending inventory	44,000		$108,960

Despite the advantages of LIFO inventory pools, it's easy to imagine situations in which its benefits are not achieved. Suppose, for instance, that a company discontinues a certain product included in one of its pools. The old costs that existed in prior layers of inventory would be recognized as cost of goods sold and produce LIFO liquidation profit. Even if the product is replaced with another product, the replacement may not be similar enough to be included in the same inventory pool. In fact, the process itself of having to periodically redefine pools as changes in product mix occur, can be expensive and time consuming. The dollar-value LIFO approach helps overcome these problems.

Dollar-Value LIFO

● LO8

Dollar-value LIFO (DVL) gained such widespread popularity during the 1960s and 1970s that most LIFO applications are now based on this approach. DVL extends the concept of inventory pools by allowing a company to combine a large variety of goods into one pool. Physical units are not used in calculating ending inventory. Instead, the inventory is viewed as a quantity of value instead of a physical quantity of goods. Instead of layers of units from different purchases, the DVL inventory pool is viewed as comprising layers of dollar value from different years.

Because the physical characteristics of inventory items are not relevant to DVL, an inventory pool is identified in terms of economic similarity rather than physical similarity. Specifically, a pool should consist of those goods that are likely to be subject to the same cost change pressures.

A DVL pool is made up of items that are likely to face the same cost change pressures.

Advantages of DVL

The DVL method has important advantages. First, it simplifies the recordkeeping procedures compared to unit LIFO because no information is needed about unit flows. Second, it minimizes the probability of the liquidation of LIFO inventory layers, even more so than the use of pools alone, through the aggregation of many types of inventory into larger pools. In addition, the method can be used by firms that do not replace units sold with new units of the same kind. For firms whose products are subject to annual model changes, for example, the items in one year's inventory are not the same as the prior year's. Under pooled LIFO, the new replacement items must be substantially identical to previous models to be included in the same pool. Under DVL, no distinction is drawn between the old and new merchandise on the basis of their physical characteristics, so a much broader range of goods can be included in the pool. That is, the acquisition of the new items is viewed as replacement of the dollar value of the old items. Because the old layers are maintained, this approach retains the benefits of LIFO by matching the most recent acquisition cost of goods with sales measured at current selling prices.

Cost Indexes

In either the unit LIFO approach or the pooled LIFO approach, we determine whether a new LIFO layer was added by comparing the ending quantity with the beginning quantity. The focus is on *units* of inventory. Under DVL, we determine whether a new LIFO layer was added by comparing the ending dollar amount with the beginning dollar amount. The focus is on inventory *value*, not units. However, if the price level has changed, we need a way to determine whether an observed increase is a real increase (an increase in the quantity of inventory) or one caused by an increase in prices. So before we compare the beginning and ending inventory amounts, we need to deflate inventory amounts by any increase in prices so that both the beginning and ending amounts are measured in terms of the same price level. We accomplish this by using cost indexes. A cost index for a particular layer year is determined as follows:

$$\text{Cost index in layer year} = \frac{\text{Cost in layer year}}{\text{Cost in base year}}$$

The base year is the year in which the DVL method is adopted and the layer year is any subsequent year in which an inventory layer is created. The cost index for the base year is set at 1.00. Subsequent years' indexes reflect cost changes relative to the base year. For example, if a "basket" of inventory items cost $120 at the end of the current year, and $100 at the end of the base year, the cost index for the current year would be: $120 ÷ $100 = 120%, or 1.20. This index simply tells us that costs in the layer year are 120% of what they were in the base year (i.e., costs increased by 20%).

The cost index for the base year (the year DVL is initially adopted) is set at 1.00.

There are several techniques that can be used to determine an index for a DVL pool. An external index like the Consumer Price Index or the Producer Price Index can be used. However, in most cases these indexes would not properly reflect cost changes for any individual DVL pool. Instead, most companies use an internally generated index. These indexes can be calculated using one of several techniques such as the *double-extension method* or the *link-chain method*. A discussion of these methods is beyond the scope of this text. In our examples and illustrations, we assume cost indexes are given.

The DVL Inventory Estimation Technique

DVL estimation begins with the determination of the current year's ending inventory valued in terms of year-end costs. It's not necessary for a company using DVL to track the item-by-item cost of purchases during the year. All that's needed is to take the physical quantities of goods on hand at the end of the year and apply year-end costs. Let's say the

The starting point in DVL is determining the current year's ending inventory valued at year-end costs.

Hanes Company adopted the dollar-value LIFO method on January 1, 2009, when the inventory value was $400,000. The 2009 ending inventory valued at year-end costs is $441,000, and the cost index for the year is 1.05 (105%).

What is the 2009 ending inventory valued at DVL cost? The first step is to convert the ending inventory from year-end costs to base year costs so we can see if there was a real increase in inventory rather than an illusory one caused by price increases. We divide the ending inventory by the year's cost index to get an amount that can be compared directly with beginning inventory.

STEP 1: Convert ending inventory valued at year-end cost to base year cost.

$$\text{Ending inventory at } \textit{base year } \text{cost} = \frac{\$441,000}{1.05} = \$420,000$$

The $420,000 reflects the 2009 ending inventory deflated to base year cost.

Next we compare the $420,000 ending inventory at base year cost to the beginning inventory, also at base year cost, of $400,000. The $20,000 increase in base-year dollars signifies a real increase in inventory quantity during the year. Applying the LIFO concept, ending inventory at base year cost consists of the beginning inventory layer of $400,000 plus a $20,000 2009 layer. These are the hypothetical costs of the layers as if each was acquired at base year prices.

STEP 2: Identify the layers of ending inventory and the years they were created.

Once the layers are identified, each is restated to prices existing when the layers were acquired. Each layer is multiplied by the cost index for the year it was acquired. The costs are totaled to obtain ending inventory at DVL cost.[16]

STEP 3: Convert each layer's base year cost to layer year cost using the cost index for the year it was acquired.

Date	Ending Inventory at Base Year Cost	×	Cost Index	=	Ending Inventory at DVL Cost
1/1/09	$400,000		1.00		$400,000
2009 layer	20,000		1.05		21,000
Totals	$420,000				$421,000

If we determined that inventory quantity had decreased during the year, then there would have been no 2009 layer added. The most recently added layer, in this case the beginning inventory layer, would be decreased to the inventory valuation determined in step 1. Once a layer of inventory or a portion of a layer is used (that is, sold) it cannot be replaced. In our example, if the base year layer is reduced to $380,000, it will never be increased. Future increases in inventory quantity will result in new layers being added. This situation is illustrated in the concept review exercise that follows.

CONCEPT REVIEW **EXERCISE**

DOLLAR-VALUE LIFO

On January 1, 2009, the Johnson Company adopted the dollar-value LIFO method. The inventory value on this date was $500,000. Inventory data for 2009 through 2012 are as follows:

Date	Ending Inventory at Year-End Costs	Cost Index
12/31/09	$556,500	1.05
12/31/10	596,200	1.10
12/31/11	615,250	1.15
12/31/12	720,000	1.25

Required:
Calculate Johnson's ending inventory for the years 2009 through 2012.

---

[16]It is important to note that the costs of the year's layer are only an approximation of actual acquisition cost. DVL assumes that all inventory quantities added during a particular year were acquired at a single cost.

JOHNSON COMPANY / SOLUTION

Date	Ending Inventory at Year-End Cost	Step 1 Ending Inventory at Base Year Cost	Step 2 Inventory Layers at Base Year Cost	Step 3 Inventory Layers Converted to Acquisition Year Cost	Ending Inventory At DVL Cost
1/1/09	$500,000 (base year)	$\frac{\$500,000}{1.00} = \$500,000$	$500,000 (base)	$500,000 × 1.00 = $500,000	$500,000
12/31/09	556,500	$\frac{\$556,500}{1.05} = \$530,000$	$500,000 (base) 30,000 (2009)	$500,000 × 1.00 = $500,000 30,000 × 1.05 = 31,500	531,500
12/31/10	596,200	$\frac{\$596,200}{1.10} = \$542,000$	$500,000 (base) 30,000 (2009) 12,000 (2010)	$500,000 × 1.00 = $500,000 30,000 × 1.05 = 31,500 12,000 × 1.10 = 13,200	544,700
12/31/11	615,250	$\frac{\$615,250}{1.15} = \$535,000*$	$500,000 (base) 30,000 (2009) 5,000 (2010)	$500,000 × 1.00 = $500,000 30,000 × 1.05 = 31,500 5,000 × 1.10 = 5,500	537,000
12/31/12	720,000	$\frac{\$720,000}{1.25} = \$576,000$	$500,000 (base) 30,000 (2009) 5,000 (2010) 41,000 (2012)	$500,000 × 1.00 = $500,000 30,000 × 1.05 = 31,500 5,000 × 1.10 = 5,500 41,000 × 1.25 = 51,250	588,250

*Since inventory declined during 2011 (from $542,000 to $535,000 at base year costs), no new layer is added. Instead the most recently acquired layer, 2010, is reduced to arrive at the $535,000 ending inventory at base year cost.

FINANCIAL REPORTING CASE SOLUTION

1. **What inventory methods does Ford use to value its inventories? Is this permissible according to GAAP?** *(p. 390)*   Ford uses the LIFO inventory method to value about one-fourth of its inventories. The cost of the remaining inventories is determined primarily by the FIFO method. Yes, both of these methods are permissible according to generally accepted accounting principles.

2. **What is the purpose of reporting the entire inventory as if valued on a FIFO basis and then adjusting this amount to reflect the use of LIFO for a portion of the inventory?** *(p. 392)*   The LIFO conformity rule requires that if a company uses LIFO to measure taxable income, it also must use LIFO for external financial reporting. Ford does this. However, in 1981, the LIFO conformity rule was liberalized to allow LIFO users to provide supplemental disclosure of the effect on inventories of using another method on inventory valuation rather than LIFO. Ford's disclosure note offers this additional information.

3. **Why would a reduction of LIFO inventory quantities cause a $12 million decrease in 2005 cost of sales?** *(p. 392)*   Inventory costs in the balance sheet using LIFO generally are out of date because they reflect old purchase transactions. When inventory quantities decline during a period, these out of date inventory layers are then liquidated, and cost of goods sold will partially match noncurrent costs with current selling prices. If costs have been rising, LIFO liquidations produce lower cost of goods sold and higher net income than would have resulted if the liquidated inventory were included in cost of goods sold at current costs.

4. **Is your friend correct in his assertion that by using LIFO, Ford was able to report lower profits in 2006?** *(p. 397)*   Yes. If Ford had used FIFO instead of LIFO for its LIFO inventories, income before taxes in all prior years, including 2006, would have been higher by $1,015 million (the increase in 2006 ending inventory). In 2006 alone, income before taxes would have been *higher* by $6 million. Here's why. The increase in ending inventory of $1,015 million *decreases* cost of goods sold, but the increase in beginning inventory of $1,009 million *increases* cost of goods sold, resulting in a net decrease in cost of goods sold of $6 million.

THE BOTTOM LINE

● **LO1**   In a perpetual inventory system, inventory is continually adjusted for each change in inventory. Cost of goods sold is adjusted each time goods are sold or returned by a customer. A periodic inventory system adjusts inventory and records cost of goods sold only at the end of a reporting period. (p. 379)

● **LO2**   Generally, determining the physical quantity that should be included in inventory is a simple matter, because it consists of items in the possession of the company. However, at the end of a reporting period it's important to determine the ownership of goods that are in transit between the company and its customers as well as between the company and its suppliers. Also, goods on consignment should be included in inventory of the consignor even though the company doesn't have physical possession of the goods. In addition, a company anticipating sales returns includes in inventory the cost of merchandise it estimates will be returned. (p. 380)

● **LO3**   The cost of inventory includes all expenditures necessary to acquire the inventory and bring it to its desired condition and location for sale or use. Generally, these expenditures include the purchase price of the goods reduced by any returns and purchase discounts, plus freight-in charges. (p. 381)

● **LO4**   Once costs are determined, the cost of goods available for sale must be allocated between cost of goods sold and ending inventory. Unless each item is specifically identified and traced through the system, the allocation requires an assumption regarding the flow of costs. First-in, first-out (FIFO) assumes that units sold are the first units acquired. Last-in, first-out (LIFO) assumes that the units sold are the most recent units purchased. The average cost method assumes that cost of goods sold and ending inventory consist of a mixture of all the goods available for sale. (p. 383)

● **LO5**   A company's choice of inventory method will be influenced by (a) how closely cost flow reflects the actual physical flow of its inventory, (b) the timing of income tax expenses, and (c) how costs are matched with revenues. (p. 391)

● **LO6**   The LIFO conformity rule requires that if a company uses LIFO to measure taxable income, it also must use LIFO for external financial reporting. LIFO users often provide supplemental disclosures describing the effect on inventories of using another method on inventory valuation rather than LIFO. If a company uses LIFO and inventory quantities decline during a period, then out of date inventory layers are liquidated and the cost of goods sold will partially match noncurrent costs with current selling prices. If costs have been increasing (decreasing), LIFO liquidations produce higher (lower) net income than would have resulted if the liquidated inventory were included in cost of goods sold at current costs. The paper profits (losses) caused by including out of date, low (high) costs in cost of goods sold is referred to as the effect on income of liquidations of LIFO inventory. (p. 392)

● **LO7**   Investors, creditors, and financial analysts can gain important insights by monitoring a company's investment in inventories. The gross profit ratio, inventory turnover ratio, and average days in inventory are designed to monitor inventories. (p. 398)

● **LO8**   The dollar-value LIFO method converts ending inventory at year-end cost to base year cost using a cost index. After identifying the layers in ending inventory with the years they were created, each year's base year cost measurement is converted to layer year cost measurement using the layer year's cost index. The layers are then summed to obtain total ending inventory at cost. (p. 400) ●

QUESTIONS FOR REVIEW OF KEY TOPICS

Q 8–1   Describe the three types of inventory of a manufacturing company.

Q 8–2   What is the main difference between a perpetual inventory system and a periodic inventory system?

Q 8–3   The Cloud Company employs a perpetual inventory system and the McKenzie Corporation uses a periodic system. Describe the differences between the two systems in accounting for the following events: (1) purchase of merchandise, (2) sale of merchandise, (3) return of merchandise to supplier, and (4) payment of freight charge on merchandise purchased. Indicate which accounts would be debited and credited for each event.

Q 8–4   The Bockner Company shipped merchandise to Laetner Corporation on December 28, 2009. Laetner received the shipment on January 3, 2010. December 31 is the fiscal year-end for both companies. The merchandise was shipped f.o.b. shipping point. Explain the difference in the accounting treatment of the merchandise if the shipment had instead been designated f.o.b. destination.

Q 8–5   What is a consignment arrangement? Explain the accounting treatment of goods held on consignment.

Q 8–6   Distinguish between the gross and net methods of accounting for purchase discounts.

Q 8–7   The Esquire Company employs a periodic inventory system. Indicate the effect (increase or decrease) of the following items on cost of goods sold:

1. Beginning inventory
2. Purchases
3. Ending inventory
4. Purchase returns
5. Freight-in

Q 8–8   Identify four methods of assigning cost to ending inventory and cost of goods sold and briefly explain the difference in the methods.

Q 8–9   It's common in the electronics industry for unit costs of raw materials inventories to decline over time. In this environment, explain the difference between LIFO and FIFO, in terms of the effect on income and financial position. Assume that inventory quantities remain the same for the period.

Q 8–10   Explain why proponents of LIFO argue that it provides a better match of revenue and expenses. In what situation would it not provide a better match?

Q 8–11   Explain what is meant by the Internal Revenue Service conformity rule with respect to the inventory method choice.

Q 8–12   Describe the ratios used by financial analysts to monitor a company's investment in inventories.

Q 8–13   What is a LIFO inventory pool? How is the cost of ending inventory determined when pools are used?

Q 8–14   Identify two advantages of dollar-value LIFO compared with unit LIFO.

Q 8–15   The Austin Company uses the dollar-value LIFO inventory method with internally developed price indexes. Assume that ending inventory at year-end cost has been determined. Outline the remaining steps used in the dollar-value LIFO computations.

BRIEF **EXERCISES**

BE 8–1
Determining ending inventory; periodic system

● LO1

A company began its fiscal year with inventory of $186,000. Purchases and cost of goods sold for the year were $945,000 and $982,000, respectively. What was the amount of ending inventory?

BE 8–2
Perpetual system; journal entries

● LO1

Litton Industries uses a perpetual inventory system. The company began its fiscal year with inventory of $267,000. Purchases of merchandise on account during the year totaled $845,000. Merchandise costing $902,000 was sold on account for $1,420,000. Prepare the journal entries to record these transactions.

BE 8–3
Goods in transit

● LO2

Kelly Corporation shipped goods to a customer f.o.b. destination on December 29, 2009. The goods arrived at the customer's location in January. In addition, one of Kelly's major suppliers shipped goods to Kelly f.o.b. shipping point on December 30. The merchandise arrived at Kelly's location in January. Which shipments should be included in Kelly's December 31 inventory?

BE 8–4
Purchase discounts; gross method

● LO3

On December 28, 2009, Videotech Corporation (VTC) purchased 10 units of a new satellite uplink system from Tristar Communications for $25,000 each. The terms of each sale were 1/10, n/30. VTC uses the gross method to account for purchase discounts and a perpetual inventory system. VTC paid the net-of-discount amount on January 6, 2010. Prepare the journal entries on December 28 and January 6 to record the purchase and payment.

BE 8–5
Purchase discounts; net method

● LO3

Refer to the situation described in BE 8–4. Prepare the necessary journal entries assuming that VTC uses the net method to account for purchase discounts.

BE 8–6
Inventory cost flow methods; periodic system

● LO4

Samuelson and Messenger (S&M) began 2009 with 200 units of its one product. These units were purchased near the end of 2008 for $25 each. During the month of January, 100 units were purchased on January 8 for $28 each and another 200 units were purchased on January 19 for $30 each. Sales of 125 units and 100 units were made on January 10 and January 25, respectively. There were 275 units on hand at the end of the month. S&M uses a *periodic* inventory system. Calculate ending inventory and cost of goods sold for January using (1) FIFO, and (2) average cost.

BE 8–7

Inventory cost flow methods; perpetual system

● LO4

Refer to the situation described in BE 8–6. S&M uses a *perpetual* inventory system. Calculate ending inventory and cost of goods sold for January using (1) FIFO, and (2) average cost.

BE 8–8

LIFO method

● LO4

Esquire, Inc. uses the LIFO method to value its inventory. Inventory at January 1, 2009, was $500,000 (20,000 units at $25 each). During 2009, 80,000 units were purchased, all at the same price of $30 per unit. 85,000 units were sold during 2009. Esquire uses a periodic inventory system. Calculate the December 31, 2009, ending inventory and cost of goods sold for 2009.

BE 8–9

LIFO method

● LO4

AAA Hardware uses the LIFO method to value its inventory. Inventory at the beginning of the year consisted of 10,000 units of the company's one product. These units cost $15 each. During the year, 60,000 units were purchased at a cost of $18 each and 64,000 units were sold. Near the end of the fiscal year, management is considering the purchase of an additional 5,000 units at $18. What would be the effect of this purchase on income before income taxes? Would your answer be the same if the company used FIFO instead of LIFO?

BE 8–10

LIFO liquidation

● LO6

Refer to the situation described in BE 8–8. Assuming an income tax rate of 40%, what is LIFO liquidation profit or loss that the company would report in a disclosure note accompanying its financial statements?

BE 8–11

Supplemental LIFO disclosures

● LO6

Real World Financials

JC Penney reported inventories of $3,400 million and $3,210 million in its February 3, 2007, and January 28, 2006, balance sheets, respectively. Cost of goods sold for the fiscal year ended February 3, 2007, was $12,078 million. The company uses primarily the LIFO inventory method. A disclosure note reported that if FIFO had been used instead of LIFO, inventory would have been higher by $8 million and $24 million at the end of the February 3, 2007, and January 28, 2006, fiscal years, respectively. Calculate cost of goods sold for the February 3, 2007, fiscal year assuming JC Penney used FIFO instead of LIFO.

BE 8–12

Ratio analysis

● LO7

Selected financial statement data for Schmitzer, Inc. is shown below:

	2009	2008
Balance sheet:		
Inventories	60,000	48,000
Ratios:		
Gross profit ratio for 2009	40%	
Inventory turnover ratio for 2009	5	

What was the amount of net sales for 2009?

BE 8–13

Dollar-value LIFO

● LO8

At the beginning of 2009, a company adopts the dollar-value LIFO inventory method for its one inventory pool. The pool's value on that date was $1,400,000. The 2009 ending inventory valued at year-end costs was $1,664,000 and the year-end cost index was 1.04. Calculate the inventory value at the end of 2009 using the dollar-value LIFO method.

EXERCISES

available with McGraw-Hill's Homework Manager www.mhhe.com/spiceland5e

An alternate exercise and problem set is available on the text website: www.mhhe.com/spiceland5e

E 8–1

Perpetual inventory system; journal entries

● LO1

John's Specialty Store uses a perpetual inventory system. The following are some inventory transactions for the month of May, 2009:

1. John's purchased merchandise on account for $5,000. Freight charges of $300 were paid in cash.
2. John's returned some of the merchandise purchased in (1). The cost of the merchandise was $600 and John's account was credited by the supplier.
3. Merchandise costing $2,800 was sold for $5,200 in cash.

Required:
Prepare the necessary journal entries to record these transactions.

E 8–2

Periodic inventory system; journal entries

● LO1

[This is a variation of the previous exercise modified to focus on the periodic inventory system.]

John's Specialty Store uses a periodic inventory system. The following are some inventory transactions for the month of May, 2009:

1. John's purchased merchandise on account for $5,000. Freight charges of $300 were paid in cash.

2. John's returned some of the merchandise purchased in (1). The cost of the merchandise was $600 and John's account was credited by the supplier.

3. Merchandise costing $2,800 was sold for $5,200 in cash.

Required:
Prepare the necessary journal entries to record these transactions.

E 8–3
Determining cost of goods sold; periodic inventory system

● LO1

Askew Company uses a periodic inventory system. The June 30, 2009, year-end trial balance for the company contained the following information:

Account	Debit	Credit
Merchandise inventory, 7/1/08	32,000	
Sales		380,000
Sales returns	12,000	
Purchases	240,000	
Purchase discounts		6,000
Purchase returns		10,000
Freight-in	17,000	
Freight-out	13,000	

In addition, you determine that the June 30, 2009, inventory balance is $40,000.

Required:
1. Calculate the cost of goods sold for the Askew Company for the year ending June 30, 2009.
2. Prepare the year-end adjusting entry to record cost of goods sold.

E 8–4
Perpetual and periodic inventory systems compared

● LO1

The following information is available for the Johnson Corporation for 2009:

Beginning inventory	$ 25,000
Merchandise purchases (on account)	155,000
Freight charges on purchases (paid in cash)	10,000
Merchandise returned to supplier (for credit)	12,000
Ending inventory	30,000
Sales (on account)	250,000
Cost of merchandise sold	148,000

Required:
Applying both a perpetual and a periodic inventory system, prepare the journal entries that summarize the transactions that created these balances. Include all end-of-period adjusting entries indicated.

E 8–5
Periodic inventory system; missing data

● LO1

The Playa Company uses a periodic inventory system. The following information is taken from Playa's records. Certain data have been intentionally omitted. ($ in thousands)

	2009	2010	2011
Beginning inventory	?	?	225
Cost of goods sold	627	621	?
Ending inventory	?	225	216
Cost of goods available for sale	876	?	800
Purchases (gross)	630	?	585
Purchase discounts	18	15	?
Purchase returns	24	30	14
Freight-in	13	32	16

Required:
Determine the missing numbers. Show computations where appropriate.

E 8–6
Purchase discounts; the gross method

● LO3

On July 15, 2009, the Nixon Car Company purchased 1,000 tires from the Harwell Company for $50 each. The terms of the sale were 2/10, n/30. Nixon uses a periodic inventory system and the *gross* method of accounting for purchase discounts.

Required:
1. Prepare the journal entries to record the purchase on July 15 and payment on July 23, 2009.
2. Prepare the journal entry to record the payment on August 15, 2009.
3. If Nixon instead uses a perpetual inventory system, explain any changes to the journal entries created in requirements 1 and 2.

E 8–7
Purchase discounts;
the net method

● LO3

[This is a variation of the previous exercise modified to focus on the net method of accounting for purchase discounts.]

On July 15, 2009, the Nixon Car Company purchased 1,000 tires from the Harwell Company for $50 each. The terms of the sale were 2/10, n/30. Nixon uses a periodic inventory system and the *net* method of accounting for purchase discounts.

Required:

1. Prepare the journal entries to record the purchase on July 15 and payment on July 23, 2009.
2. Prepare the journal entry to record the payment on August 15, 2009.
3. If Nixon instead uses a perpetual inventory system, explain any changes to the journal entries created in requirements 1 and 2.

E 8–8
Trade and purchase
discounts; the gross
method and the net
method compared

● LO3

Tracy Company, a manufacturer of air conditioners, sold 100 units to Thomas Company on November 17, 2009. The units have a list price of $500 each, but Thomas was given a 30% trade discount. The terms of the sale were 2/10, n/30. Thomas uses a periodic inventory system.

Required:

1. Prepare the journal entries to record the purchase by Thomas on November 17 and payment on November 26, 2009, using the gross method of accounting for purchase discounts.
2. Prepare the journal entry to record the payment on December 15, 2009, using the gross method of accounting for purchase discounts.
3. Repeat requirements 1 and 2 using the net method of accounting for purchase discounts.

E 8–9
Goods in transit

● LO2

The Kwok Company's inventory balance on December 31, 2009, was $165,000 (based on a 12/31/09 physical count) *before* considering the following transactions:

1. Goods shipped to Kwok f.o.b. destination on December 20, 2009, were received on January 4, 2010. The invoice cost was $30,000.
2. Goods shipped to Kwok f.o.b. shipping point on December 28, 2009, were received on January 5, 2010. The invoice cost was $17,000.
3. Goods shipped from Kwok to a customer f.o.b. destination on December 27, 2009, were received by the customer on January 3, 2010. The sales price was $40,000 and the merchandise cost $22,000.
4. Goods shipped from Kwok to a customer f.o.b. destination on December 26, 2009, were received by the customer on December 30, 2009. The sales price was $20,000 and the merchandise cost $13,000.
5. Goods shipped from Kwok to a customer f.o.b. shipping point on December 28, 2009, were received by the customer on January 4, 2010. The sales price was $25,000 and the merchandise cost $12,000.

Required:
Determine the correct inventory amount to be reported in Kwok's 2009 balance sheet.

E 8–10
Goods in transit;
consignment

● LO2

The December 31, 2009, year-end inventory balance of the Raymond Corporation is $210,000. You have been asked to review the following transactions to determine if they have been correctly recorded.

1. Goods shipped to Raymond f.o.b. destination on December 26, 2009, were received on January 2, 2010. The invoice cost of $30,000 *is* included in the preliminary inventory balance.
2. At year-end, Raymond held $14,000 of merchandise on consignment from the Harrison Company. This merchandise *is* included in the preliminary inventory balance.
3. On December 29, merchandise costing $6,000 was shipped to a customer f.o.b. shipping point and arrived at the customer's location on January 3, 2010. The merchandise is *not* included in the preliminary inventory balance.
4. At year-end, Raymond had merchandise costing $15,000 on consignment with the Joclyn Corporation. The merchandise is *not* included in the preliminary inventory balance.

Required:
Determine the correct inventory amount to be reported in Raymond's 2009 balance sheet.

E 8–11
Physical quantities
and costs included
in inventory

● LO2

The Phoenix Corporation's fiscal year ends on December 31. Phoenix determines inventory quantity by a physical count of inventory on hand at the close of business on December 31. The company's controller has asked for your help in deciding if the following items should be included in the year-end inventory count.

1. Merchandise held on consignment for Trout Creek Clothing.
2. Goods shipped f.o.b. destination on December 28 that arrived at the customer's location on January 4.
3. Goods purchased from a vendor shipped f.o.b. shipping point on December 26 that arrived on January 3.
4. Goods shipped f.o.b. shipping point on December 28 that arrived at the customer's location on January 5.
5. Phoenix had merchandise on consignment at Lisa's Markets, Inc.
6. Goods purchased from a vendor shipped f.o.b. destination on December 27 that arrived on January 3.

7. Goods sold to a customer sitting on the loading dock on December 31 waiting to be picked up by the customer.

8. Freight charges on goods purchased in 3.

9. Freight charges on goods sold in 2 and 4.

Required:
Determine if each of the ten items above should be included or excluded from the company's year-end inventory.

E 8–12
Inventory cost flow methods; periodic system

● LO1 LO4

Altira Corporation uses a periodic inventory system. The following information related to its merchandise inventory during the month of August 2009 is available:

Aug. 1	Inventory on hand—2,000 units; cost $6.10 each.
8	Purchased 10,000 units for $5.50 each.
14	Sold 8,000 units for $12.00 each.
18	Purchased 6,000 units for $5.00 each.
25	Sold 7,000 units for $11.00 each.
31	Inventory on hand—3,000 units.

Required:
Determine the inventory balance Altira would report in its August 31, 2009, balance sheet and the cost of goods sold it would report in its August 2009 income statement using each of the following cost flow methods:
1. First-in, first-out (FIFO)
2. Last-in, first-out (LIFO)
3. Average cost

E 8–13
Inventory cost flow methods; perpetual system

● LO1 LO4

[This is a variation of the previous exercise modified to focus on the perpetual inventory system and alternative cost flow methods.]
   Altira Corporation uses a perpetual inventory system. The following transactions affected its merchandise inventory during the month of August 2009:

Aug. 1	Inventory on hand—2,000 units; cost $6.10 each.
8	Purchased 10,000 units for $5.50 each.
14	Sold 8,000 units for $12.00 each.
18	Purchased 6,000 units for $5.00 each.
25	Sold 7,000 units for $11.00 each.
31	Inventory on hand—3,000 units.

Required:
Determine the inventory balance Altira would report in its August 31, 2009, balance sheet and the cost of goods sold it would report in its August 2009 income statement using each of the following cost flow methods:
1. First-in, first-out (FIFO)
2. Last-in, first-out (LIFO)
3. Average cost

E 8–14
Comparison of FIFO and LIFO; periodic system

● LO1 LO4

Alta Ski Company's inventory records contained the following information regarding its latest ski model. The company uses a periodic inventory system.

Beginning inventory, January 1, 2009	600 units @ $80 each
Purchases:	
January 15	1,000 units @ $95 each
January 21	800 units @ $100 each
Sales:	
January 5	400 units @ $120 each
January 22	800 units @ $130 each
January 29	400 units @ $135 each
Ending inventory, January 31, 2009	800 units

Required:
1. Which method, FIFO or LIFO, will result in the highest cost of goods sold figure for January 2009? Why? Which method will result in the highest ending inventory balance? Why?
2. Compute cost of goods sold for January and the ending inventory using both the FIFO and LIFO methods.

E 8–15
Average cost method; periodic and perpetual systems

● LO1 LO4

The following information is taken from the inventory records of the CNB Company:

Beginning inventory, 9/1/09	5,000 units @ $10.00
Purchases:	
9/7	3,000 units @ $10.40
9/25	8,000 units @ $10.75
Sales:	
9/10	4,000 units
9/29	5,000 units

7,000 units were on hand at the end of September.

Required:
1. Assuming that CNB uses a periodic inventory system and employs the average cost method, determine cost of goods sold for September and September's ending inventory.
2. Repeat requirement 1 assuming that the company uses a perpetual inventory system.

E 8–16
FIFO, LIFO, and average cost methods

● LO1 LO4

Causwell Company began 2009 with 10,000 units of inventory on hand. The cost of each unit was $5.00. During 2009 an additional 30,000 units were purchased at a single unit cost, and 20,000 units remained on hand at the end of 2009 (20,000 units therefore were sold during 2009). Causwell uses a periodic inventory system. Cost of goods sold for 2009, applying the average cost method, is $115,000. The company is interested in determining what cost of goods sold would have been if the FIFO or LIFO methods were used.

Required:
1. Determine the cost of goods sold for 2009 using the FIFO method. [*Hint:* Determine the cost per unit of 2009 purchases.]
2. Determine the cost of goods sold for 2009 using the LIFO method.

E 8–17
LIFO liquidation

● LO1 LO6

The Reuschel Company began 2009 with inventory of 10,000 units at a cost of $7 per unit. During 2009, 50,000 units were purchased for $8.50 each. Sales for the year totaled 54,000 units leaving 6,000 units on hand at the end of 2009. Reuschel uses a periodic inventory system and the LIFO inventory cost method.

Required:
1. Calculate cost of goods sold for 2009.
2. From a financial reporting perspective, what problem is created by the use of LIFO in this situation? Describe the disclosure required to report the effects of this problem.

E 8–18
Ratio analysis

● LO7

Real World Financials

The table below contains selected financial information from recent financial statements of **Pathmark Stores, Inc.,** and **The Great Atlantic and Pacific Tea Company, Inc.** (GAPT), two companies in the retail grocery store industry ($ in millions):

	Pathmark		GAPT	
	2/3/07	1/28/06	2/24/07	2/25/06
Net sales	$4,058	$3,977	$6,850	$8,740
Cost of goods sold	2,875	2,846	4,786	6,235
Year-end inventory	180	181	411	405
Industry averages:				
Gross profit ratio		26%		
Inventory turnover ratio		14		
Average days in inventory		26		

Required:
Calculate the gross profit ratio, the inventory turnover ratio, and the average days in inventory for the two companies, and compare those results to the industry, using the most recent fiscal year data.

E 8–19
Dollar-value LIFO

● LO8

On January 1, 2009, the Haskins Company adopted the dollar-value LIFO method for its one inventory pool. The pool's value on this date was $660,000. The 2009 and 2010 ending inventory valued at year-end costs were $690,000 and $760,000, respectively. The appropriate cost indexes are 1.04 for 2009 and 1.08 for 2010.

Required:
Calculate the inventory value at the end of 2009 and 2010 using the dollar-value LIFO method.

E 8–20
Dollar-value LIFO

● LO8

Mercury Company has only one inventory pool. On December 31, 2009, Mercury adopted the dollar-value LIFO inventory method. The inventory on that date using the dollar-value LIFO method was $200,000. Inventory data are as follows:

Year	Ending Inventory at Year-End Costs	Ending Inventory at Base Year Costs
2010	$231,000	$220,000
2011	299,000	260,000
2012	300,000	250,000

Required:
Compute the inventory at December 31, 2010, 2011, and 2012, using the dollar-value LIFO method.

(AICPA adapted)

E 8–21
Concepts;
terminology

● **LO1 through LO5**

Listed below are several terms and phrases associated with inventory measurement. Pair each item from List A (by letter) with the item from List B that is most appropriately associated with it.

List A	List B
_____ 1. Perpetual inventory system	a. Legal title passes when goods are delivered to common carrier.
_____ 2. Periodic inventory system	b. Goods are transferred to another company but title remains with transferor.
_____ 3. F.o.b. shipping point	c. Purchase discounts not taken are included in inventory cost.
_____ 4. Gross method	d. If LIFO is used for taxes, it must be used for financial reporting.
_____ 5. Net method	e. Items sold are those acquired first.
_____ 6. Cost index	f. Items sold are those acquired last.
_____ 7. F.o.b. destination	g. Purchase discounts not taken are considered interest expense.
_____ 8. FIFO	h. Used to convert ending inventory at year-end cost to base year cost.
_____ 9. LIFO	i. Continuously records changes in inventory.
_____ 10. Consignment	j. Items sold come from a mixture of goods acquired during the period.
_____ 11. Average cost	k. Legal title passes when goods arrive at location.
_____ 12. IRS conformity rule	l. Adjusts inventory at the end of the period.

CPA AND CMA REVIEW QUESTIONS

CPA Exam Questions

KAPLAN)

SCHWESER

● **LO4**

The following questions are used in the Kaplan CPA Review Course to study inventory while preparing for the CPA examination. Determine the response that best completes the statements or questions.

Questions 1 through 3 are based on the following information. Esquire Corp. uses the periodic inventory system. During its first year of operations, Esquire made the following purchases (list in chronological order of acquisition):

- 20 units at $50
- 35 units at $40
- 85 units at $30

Sales for the year totaled 135 units, leaving 5 units on hand at the end of the year.

1. Ending inventory using the average cost method is
   a. $ 150
   b. $ 177
   c. $ 250
   d. $1,540

2. Ending inventory using the FIFO method is
   a. $ 150
   b. $ 177
   c. $ 250
   d. $1,540

3. Ending inventory using the LIFO method is
   a. $ 150
   b. $ 177
   c. $ 250
   d. $1,540

● LO4 LO5

4. Jamison Corporation's inventory cost in its balance sheet is lower using the first-in, first-out method than it would have been had it used the last-in, first-out method. Assuming no beginning inventory, what direction did the cost of purchases move during the period?

    a. Up.
    b. Down.
    c. Unchanged.
    d. Can't be determined.

● LO3

5. Dixon Menswear Shop regularly buys shirts from Colt Company. Dixon purchased shirts from Colt on May 27, and received an invoice with a list price amount of $3,600 and payment terms of 2/10, n/30. Dixon uses the net method to record purchases. Dixon should record the purchase at

    a. $3,430
    b. $3,500
    c. $3,528
    d. $3,600

● LO2

6. Herc Co.'s inventory at December 31, 2009, was $1,500,000 based on a physical count priced at cost, and before any necessary adjustment for the following:

    • Merchandise costing $90,000, shipped f.o.b shipping point from a vendor on December 30, 2009, was received and recorded on January 5, 2010.
    • Goods in the shipping area were excluded from inventory although shipment was not made until January 4, 2010. The goods, billed to the customer f.o.b. shipping point on December 30, 2009, had a cost of $120,000.

What amount should Herc report as inventory in its December 31, 2009, balance sheet?

    a. $1,500,000
    b. $1,590,000
    c. $1,700,000
    d. $1,710,000

● LO8

7. Dalton Company adopted the dollar-value LIFO inventory method on January 1, 2009. In applying the LIFO method, Dalton uses internal price indexes and the multiple-pools approach. The following data were available for Inventory Pool No. 1 for the two years following the adoption of LIFO:

| | Ending Inventory | | |
	At Current Year Cost	At Base Year Cost	Cost Index
1/1/09	$100,000	$100,000	1.00
12/31/09	126,000	120,000	1.05
12/31/10	140,800	128,000	1.10

Under the dollar-value LIFO method the inventory at December 31, 2010, should be

    a. $128,000
    b. $129,800
    c. $130,800
    d. $140,800

CMA Exam Questions

The following questions dealing with inventory are adapted from questions that previously appeared on Certified Management Accountant (CMA) examinations. The CMA designation sponsored by the Institute of Management Accountants (www.imanet.org) provides members with an objective measure of knowledge and competence in the field of management accounting. Determine the response that best completes the statements or questions.

● LO1 LO4

Questions 1 through 3 are based on the following information. Thomas Engine Company is a wholesaler of marine engine parts. The activity of carburetor 2642J during the month of March is presented below.

Date	Balance or Transaction	Units	Unit Cost	Unit Sales Price
Mar 1	Inventory	3,200	$64.30	$86.50
4	Purchase	3,400	64.75	87.00
14	Sales	3,600		87.25
25	Purchase	3,500	66.00	87.25
28	Sales	3,450		88.00

1. If Thomas uses a first-in, first-out perpetual inventory system, the total cost of the inventory for carburetor 2642J at March 31 is
   a. $196,115
   b. $197,488
   c. $201,300
   d. $263,825

2. If Thomas uses a last-in, first-out periodic inventory system, the total cost of the inventory for carburetor 2642J at March 31 is
   a. $196,115
   b. $197,488
   c. $201,300
   d. $268,400

3. If Thomas uses a last-in, first-out perpetual inventory system, the total cost of the inventory for carburetor 2642J at March 31 is
   a. $196,200
   b. $197,488
   c. $263,863
   d. $268,400

PROBLEMS   available with McGraw-Hill's Homework Manager www.mhhe.com/spiceland5e

An alternate exercise and problem set is available on the text website: www.mhhe.com/spiceland5e

P 8–1
Various inventory transactions; journal entries

● **LO1 through LO3**

James Company began the month of October with inventory of $15,000. The following inventory transactions occurred during the month:
a. The company purchased merchandise on account for $22,000 on October 12, 2009. Terms of the purchase were 2/10, n/30. James uses the net method to record purchases. The merchandise was shipped f.o.b. shipping point and freight charges of $500 were paid in cash.
b. On October 18 the company returned merchandise costing $3,000. The return reduced the amount owed to the supplier. The merchandise returned came from beginning inventory, not from the October 12 purchase.
c. On October 31, James paid for the merchandise purchased on October 12.
d. During October merchandise costing $18,000 was sold on account for $28,000.
e. It was determined that inventory on hand at the end of October cost $16,060.

Required:
1. Assuming that the James Company uses a periodic inventory system, prepare journal entries for the above transactions including the adjusting entry at the end of October to record cost of goods sold.
2. Assuming that the James Company uses a perpetual inventory system, prepare journal entries for the above transactions.

P 8–2
Items to be included in inventory

● **LO2**

The following inventory transactions took place near December 31, 2009, the end of the Rasul Company's fiscal year-end:
1. On December 27, 2009, merchandise costing $2,000 was shipped to the Myers Company on consignment. The shipment arrived at Myers's location on December 29, but none of the merchandise was sold by the end of the year. The merchandise was *not* included in the 2009 ending inventory.
2. On January 5, 2010, merchandise costing $8,000 was received from a supplier and recorded as a purchase on that date and *not* included in the 2009 ending inventory. The invoice revealed that the shipment was made f.o.b. shipping point on December 28, 2009.
3. On December 29, 2009, the company shipped merchandise costing $12,000 to a customer f.o.b. destination. The goods, which arrived at the customer's location on January 4, 2010, were *not* included in Rasul's 2009 ending inventory. The sale was recorded in 2009.
4. Merchandise costing $4,000 was received on December 28, 2009, on consignment from the Aborn Company. A purchase was *not* recorded and the merchandise was *not* included in 2009 ending inventory.
5. Merchandise costing $6,000 was received and recorded as a purchase on January 8, 2010. The invoice revealed that the merchandise was shipped from the supplier on December 28, 2009, f.o.b. destination. The merchandise was *not* included in 2009 ending inventory.

Required:
State whether Rasul correctly accounted for each of the above transactions. Give the reason for your answer.

P 8–3
Costs included in
inventory

● LO2 LO3

Reagan Corporation is a wholesale distributor of truck replacement parts. Initial amounts taken from Reagan's records are as follows:

Inventory at December 31 (based on a physical count of goods in Reagan's warehouse on December 31)		$1,250,000
Accounts payable at December 31:		

Vendor	Terms	Amount
Baker Company	2%, 10 days, net 30	$ 265,000
Charlie Company	Net 30	210,000
Dolly Company	Net 30	300,000
Eagler Company	Net 30	225,000
Full Company	Net 30	—
Greg Company	Net 30	—
Accounts payable, December 31		$1,000,000
Sales for the year		$9,000,000

Additional information:

1. Parts held by Reagan on consignment from Charlie, amounting to $155,000, were included in the physical count of goods in Reagan's warehouse and in accounts payable at December 31.

2. Parts totaling $22,000, which were purchased from Full and paid for in December, were sold in the last week of the year and appropriately recorded as sales of $28,000. The parts were included in the physical count of goods in Reagan's warehouse on December 31 because the parts were on the loading dock waiting to be picked up by customers.

3. Parts in transit on December 31 to customers, shipped f.o.b. shipping point on December 28, amounted to $34,000. The customers received the parts on January 6 of the following year. Sales of $40,000 to the customers for the parts were recorded by Reagan on January 2.

4. Retailers were holding goods on consignment from Reagan, which had a cost of $210,000 and a retail value of $250,000.

5. Goods were in transit from Greg to Reagan on December 31. The cost of the goods was $25,000, and they were shipped f.o.b. shipping point on December 29.

6. A freight bill in the amount of $2,000 specifically relating to merchandise purchased in December, all of which was still in the inventory at December 31, was received on January 3. The freight bill was not included in either the inventory or in accounts payable at December 31.

7. All the purchases from Baker occurred during the last seven days of the year. These items have been recorded in accounts payable and accounted for in the physical inventory at cost before discount. Reagan's policy is to pay invoices in time to take advantage of all discounts, adjust inventory accordingly, and record accounts payable net of discounts.

Required:

Prepare a schedule of adjustments to the initial amounts using the format shown below. Show the effect, if any, of each of the transactions separately and if the transactions would have no effect on the amount shown, state *none*.

	Inventory	Accounts Payable	Sales
Initial amounts	$1,250,000	$1,000,000	$ 9,000,000
Adjustments—increase (decrease):			
1.			
2.			
3.			
4.			
5.			
6.			
7.			
Total adjustments			
Adjusted amounts	$	$	$

(AICPA adapted)

P 8–4
Various inventory transactions; determining inventory and cost of goods

● **LO1 through LO4**

Johnson Corporation began 2009 with inventory of 10,000 units of its only product. The units cost $8 each. The company uses a periodic inventory system and the LIFO cost method. The following transactions occurred during 2009:

a. Purchased 50,000 additional units at a cost of $10 per unit. Terms of the purchases were 2/10, n/30, and 100% of the purchases were paid for within the 10-day discount period. The company uses the gross method to record purchase discounts. The merchandise was purchased f.o.b. shipping point and freight charges of $.50 per unit were paid by Johnson.

b. 1,000 units purchased during the year were returned to suppliers for credit. Johnson was also given credit for the freight charges of $.50 per unit it had paid on the original purchase. The units were defective and were returned two days after they were received.

c. Sales for the year totaled 45,000 units at $18 per unit.

d. On December 28, 2009, Johnson purchased 5,000 additional units at $10 each. The goods were shipped f.o.b. destination and arrived at Johnson's warehouse on January 4, 2010.

e. 14,000 units were on hand at the end of 2009.

Required:

1. Determine ending inventory and cost of goods sold for 2009.

2. Assuming that operating expenses other than those indicated in the above transactions amounted to $150,000, determine income before income taxes for 2009.

P 8–5
Various inventory costing methods

● **LO1 LO4**

Ferris Company began 2009 with 6,000 units of its principal product. The cost of each unit is $8. Merchandise transactions for the month of January 2009 are as follows:

	Purchases		
Date of Purchase	**Units**	**Unit Cost ***	**Total Cost**
Jan. 10	5,000	$ 9	$ 45,000
Jan. 18	6,000	10	60,000
Totals	11,000		$105,000

*Includes purchase price and cost of freight.

Sales	
Date of Sale	**Units**
Jan. 5	3,000
Jan. 12	2,000
Jan. 20	4,000
Total	9,000

8,000 units were on hand at the end of the month.

Required:
Calculate January's ending inventory and cost of goods sold for the month using each of the following alternatives:

1. FIFO, periodic system
2. LIFO, periodic system
3. LIFO, perpetual system
4. Average cost, periodic system
5. Average cost, perpetual system

P 8–6
Various inventory costing methods; gross profit ratio

● **LO1 LO4 LO7**

Topanga Group began operations early in 2009. Inventory purchase information for the quarter ended March 31, 2009, for Topanga's only product is provided below. The unit costs include the cost of freight. The company uses a periodic inventory system.

Date of Purchase	**Units**	**Unit Cost**	**Total Cost**
Jan. 7	5,000	$4.00	$ 20,000
Feb. 16	12,000	4.50	54,000
March 22	17,000	5.00	85,000
Totals	34,000		$159,000

Sales for the quarter, all at $7.00 per unit, totaled 20,000 units leaving 14,000 units on hand at the end of the quarter.

Required:
1. Calculate the Topanga's gross profit ratio for the first quarter using:
   a. FIFO
   b. LIFO
   c. Average cost
2. Comment on the relative effect of each of the three inventory methods on the gross profit ratio.

P 8–7
Various inventory costing methods

● LO1 LO4

eXcel

Carlson Auto Dealers Inc. sells a handmade automobile as its only product. Each automobile is identical; however, they can be distinguished by their unique ID number. At the beginning of 2009, Carlson had three cars in inventory, as follows:

Car ID	Cost
203	$60,000
207	60,000
210	63,000

During 2009, each of the three autos sold for $90,000. Additional purchases (listed in chronological order) and sales for the year were as follows:

Car ID	Cost	Selling Price
211	$63,000	$ 90,000
212	63,000	93,000
213	64,500	not sold
214	66,000	96,000
215	69,000	100,500
216	70,500	not sold
217	72,000	105,000
218	72,300	106,500
219	75,000	not sold

Required:
1. Calculate 2009 ending inventory and cost of goods sold assuming the company uses the specific identification inventory method.
2. Calculate ending inventory and cost of goods sold assuming FIFO and a periodic inventory system.
3. Calculate ending inventory and cost of goods sold assuming LIFO and a periodic inventory system.
4. Calculate ending inventory and cost of goods sold assuming the average cost method and a periodic inventory system.

P 8–8
Supplemental LIFO disclosures

● LO4 LO6

Real World Financials

Caterpillar, Inc. is one of the world's largest manufacturers of construction, mining, agricultural, and forestry machinery. The following disclosure note is included in the company's 2006 financial statements:

D. Inventories ($ in millions)

Inventories are stated at the lower of cost or market. Cost is principally determined using the last-in, first-out, (LIFO) method. The value of inventories on the LIFO basis represented about 75% of total inventories at December 31, 2006, and about 80% of total inventories at December 31, 2005, and 2004.
   If the FIFO (first-in, first-out) method had been in use, inventories would have been $2,403 million, $2,345 million, and $2,124 million higher than reported at December 31, 2006, 2005, and 2004, respectively.

If inventories valued at LIFO cost had been valued at FIFO cost, net income would have been $41 million higher in 2006 and $157 million lower in 2005.

Required:
1. Approximate the company's effective income tax rate for the year ended December 31, 2006.
2. Why might the information contained in the disclosure note be useful to a financial analyst?
3. Using the income tax rate calculated in 1, how much higher (lower) would retained earnings have been at the end of 2006 if Caterpillar had used the FIFO inventory method for all of its inventory?

P 8–9
LIFO liquidation

● LO4 LO6

Taylor Corporation has used a periodic inventory system and the LIFO cost method since its inception in 2002. The company began 2009 with the following inventory layers (listed in chronological order of acquisition):

10,000 units @ $15	$150,000
15,000 units @ $20	300,000
Beginning inventory	$450,000

During 2009, 30,000 units were purchased for $25 per unit. Due to unexpected demand for the company's product, 2009 sales totaled 40,000 units at various prices, leaving 15,000 units in ending inventory.

Required:

1. Calculate cost of goods sold for 2009.
2. Determine the amount of LIFO liquidation profit that the company must report in a disclosure note to its 2009 financial statements. Assume an income tax rate of 40%.
3. If the company decided to purchase an additional 10,000 units at $25 per unit at the end of the year, how much income tax currently payable would be saved?

P 8–10

Inventory cost flow methods: LIFO liquidation; ratios

● LO4 LO6 LO7

Cast Iron Grills, Inc., manufactures premium gas barbecue grills. The company uses a periodic inventory system and the LIFO cost method for its grill inventory. Cast Iron's December 31, 2009, fiscal year-end inventory consisted of the following (listed in chronological order of acquisition):

Units	Unit Cost
5,000	$700
4,000	800
6,000	900

The replacement cost of the grills throughout 2010 was $1,000. Cast Iron sold 27,000 grills during 2010. The company's selling price is set at 200% of the current replacement cost.

Required:

1. Compute the gross profit (sales minus cost of goods sold) and the gross profit ratio for 2010 assuming that Cast Iron purchased 28,000 units during the year.
2. Repeat requirement 1 assuming that Cast Iron purchased only 15,000 units.
3. Why does the number of units purchased affect your answers to the above requirements?
4. Repeat requirements 1 and 2 assuming that Cast Iron uses the FIFO inventory cost method rather than the LIFO method.
5. Why does the number of units purchased have no effect on your answers to requirements 1 and 2 when the FIFO method is used?

P 8–11

Integrating problem; inventories and accounts receivable; Chapters 7 and 8

● LO4 LO6 LO7

Inverness Steel Corporation is a producer of flat-rolled carbon, stainless and electrical steels, and tubular products. The company's income statement for the 2009 fiscal year reported the following information ($ in millions):

Sales	$6,255
Cost of goods sold	5,190

The company's balance sheets for 2009 and 2008 included the following information ($ in millions):

	2009	2008
Current assets:		
Accounts receivable, net	$703	$583
Inventories	880	808

The statement of cash flows reported bad debt expense for 2009 of $8 million. The summary of significant accounting policies included the following notes ($ in millions):

Accounts Receivable (in part)

The allowance for uncollectible accounts was $10 and $7 at December 31, 2009 and 2008, respectively. All sales are on credit.

Inventories

Inventories are valued at the lower of cost or market. The cost of the majority of inventories is measured using the last in, first out (LIFO) method. Other inventories are measured principally at average cost and consist mostly of foreign inventories and certain raw materials. If the entire inventory had been valued on an average cost basis, inventory would have been higher by $480 and $350 at the end of 2009 and 2008, respectively.

During 2009, 2008, and 2007, liquidation of LIFO layers generated income of $6, $7, and $25, respectively.

Required:

Using the information provided:

1. Determine the amount of accounts receivable Inverness wrote off during 2009.
2. Calculate the amount of cash collected from customers during 2009.
3. Calculate what cost of goods sold would have been for 2009 if the company had used average cost to value its entire inventory.
4. Calculate the following ratios for 2009:
   a. Receivables turnover ratio
   b. Inventory turnover ratio
   c. Gross profit ratio
5. Explain briefly what caused the income generated by the liquidation of LIFO layers. Assuming an income tax rate of 35%, what was the effect of the liquidation of LIFO layers on cost of goods sold in 2009?

P 8–12
Dollar-value LIFO

● LO8

On January 1, 2009, the Taylor Company adopted the dollar-value LIFO method. The inventory value for its one inventory pool on this date was $400,000. Inventory data for 2009 through 2011 are as follows:

Date	Ending Inventory at Year-End Costs	Cost Index
12/31/09	$441,000	1.05
12/31/10	487,200	1.12
12/31/11	510,000	1.20

Required:
Calculate Taylor's ending inventory for 2009, 2010, and 2011.

P 8–13
Dollar-value LIFO

● LO8

Kingston Company uses the dollar-value LIFO method of computing inventory. An external price index is used to convert ending inventory to base year. The company began operations on January 1, 2009, with an inventory of $150,000. Year-end inventories at year-end costs and cost indexes for its one inventory pool were as follows:

Year Ended December 31	Ending Inventory at Year-End Costs	Cost Index (Relative to Base Year)
2009	$200,000	1.08
2010	245,700	1.17
2011	235,980	1.14
2012	228,800	1.10

Required:
Calculate inventory amounts at the end of each year.

P 8–14
Dollar-value LIFO

● LO8

On January 1, 2009, Avondale Lumber adopted the dollar-value LIFO inventory method. The inventory value for its one inventory pool on this date was $260,000. An internally generated cost index is used to convert ending inventory to base year. Year-end inventories at year-end costs and cost indexes for its one inventory pool were as follows:

Year Ended December 31	Inventory Year-End Costs	Cost Index (Relative to Base Year)
2009	$340,000	1.02
2010	350,000	1.06
2011	400,000	1.07
2012	430,000	1.10

Required:
Calculate inventory amounts at the end of each year.

P 8–15
Dollar-value
LIFO; solving for
unknowns

● LO8

At the beginning of 2009, Quentin and Kopps (Q&K) adopted the dollar-value LIFO (DVL) inventory method. On that date the value of its one inventory pool was $84,000. The company uses an internally generated cost index to convert ending inventory to base year. Inventory data for 2009 through 2012 are as follows:

Year Ended December 31	Ending Inventory at Year-End Costs	Ending Inventory at Base-Year Costs	Cost Index	Ending Inventory At DVL cost
2009	$100,800	$ 96,000	1.05	?
2010	136,800	?	1.14	?
2011	150,000	125,000	?	?
2012	?	?	1.25	$133,710

Required:
Determine the missing amounts.

BROADEN YOUR **PERSPECTIVE**

Apply your critical-thinking ability to the knowledge you've gained. These cases will provide you an opportunity to develop your research, analysis, judgment, and communication skills. You also will work with other students, integrate what you've learned, apply it in real world situations, and consider its global and ethical ramifications. This practice will broaden your knowledge and further develop your decision-making abilities.

**Judgment
Case 8–1**
Riding the
Merry-Go-Round

● LO7

Real World Financials

Merry-Go-Round Enterprises, the clothing retailer for dedicated followers of young men's and women's fashion, was looking natty as a company. It was March 1993, and the Joppa, Maryland-based outfit had just announced the acquisition of Chess King, a rival clothing chain, a move that would give it the biggest share of the young men's clothing market. Merry-Go-Round told brokerage firm analysts that the purchase would add $13 million, or 15 cents a share, to profits for the year. So some Wall Street analysts raised their earnings estimates for Merry-Go-Round. The company's stock rose $2.25, or 15 percent, to $17 on the day of the Chess King news. Merry-Go-Round was hot—$100 of its stock in January 1988 was worth $804 five years later. In 1993 the chain owned 1,460 stores in 44 states, mostly under the Cignal, Chess King, and Merry-Go-Round names.

Merry-Go-Round's annual report for the fiscal year ended January 30, 1993, reported a 15% sales growth, to $877.5 million from $761.2 million. A portion of the company's balance sheet is reproduced below:

	Jan. 30, 1993	Feb. 1, 1992
Assets		
Cash and cash equivalents	$40,115,000	$29,781,000
Marketable securities	—	9,703
Receivables	6,466,000	6,195
Merchandise inventories	82,197,000	59,971,000

But Merry-Go-Round spun out. The company lost $544,000 in the first six months of 1993, compared with earnings of $13.5 million in the first half of 1992. In the fall of 1992, Leonard "Boogie" Weinglass, Merry-Go-Round's flamboyant founder and chairman who had started the company in 1968, boarded up his Merry-Go-Ranch in Aspen, Colorado, and returned to management after a 12-year hiatus. But the pony-tailed, shirtsleeved entrepreneur—the inspiration for the character Boogie in the movie *Diner*—couldn't save his company from bankruptcy. In January 1994, the company filed for Chapter 11 protection in Baltimore. Shares crumbled below $3.

Required:
In retrospect, can you identify any advance warning at the date of the financial statements of the company's impending bankruptcy?
[Adapted from Jonathan Burton, "Due Diligence," *Worth,* June 1994, pp. 89–96.]

**Real World
Case 8–2**
Physical quantities
and costs included
in inventory

● LO2

Real World Financials

Determining the physical quantity that should be included in inventory normally is a simple matter because that amount consists of items in the possession of the company. The cost of inventory includes all necessary expenditures to acquire the inventory and bring it to its desired *condition* and *location* for sale or for use in the manufacturing process.

Required:
1. Identify and describe the situations in which physical quantity included in inventory is more difficult than simply determining items in the possession of the company.
2. In addition to the direct acquisition costs such as the price paid and transportation costs to obtain inventory, what other expenditures might be necessary to bring the inventory to its desired condition and location?
3. Access EDGAR on the Internet. The web address is **www.sec.gov.** Search for **Sport Chalet Inc.,** a leading operator of full-service, specialty sporting goods stores in California and Nevada. Access the 10-K filing for the most recent fiscal year. Search or scroll to find the disclosure notes (footnotes). What costs does Sport Chalet include in its inventory?

**Judgment
Case 8–3**
The specific
identification
inventory method;
inventoriable costs

● LO3 LO4

Happlia Co. imports household appliances. Each model has many variations and each unit has an identification number. Happlia pays all costs for getting the goods from the port to its central warehouse in Des Moines. After repackaging, the goods are consigned to retailers. A retailer makes a sale, simultaneously buys the appliance from Happlia, and pays the balance due within one week.

To alleviate the overstocking of refrigerators at a Minneapolis retailer, some were reshipped to a Kansas City retailer where they were still held in inventory at December 31, 2009. Happlia paid the costs of this reshipment. Happlia uses the specific identification inventory costing method.

Required:
1. In regard to the specific identification inventory costing method:
    a. Describe its key elements.
    b. Discuss why it is appropriate for Happlia to use this method.

2. a. What general criteria should Happlia use to determine inventory carrying amounts at December 31, 2009?

   b. Give four examples of costs included in these inventory carrying amounts.

3. What costs should be reported in Happlia's 2009 income statement? Ignore lower of cost or market considerations.

(AICPA adapted)

Communication Case 8–4
LIFO versus FIFO
● **LO4 LO5**

You have just been hired as a consultant to Tangier Industries, a newly formed company. The company president, John Meeks, is seeking your advice as to the appropriate inventory method Tangier should use to value its inventory and cost of goods sold. Mr. Meeks has narrowed the choice to LIFO and FIFO. He has heard that LIFO might be better for tax purposes, but FIFO has certain advantages for financial reporting to investors and creditors. You have been told that the company will be profitable in its first year and for the foreseeable future.

Required:
Prepare a report for the president describing the factors that should be considered by Tangier in choosing between LIFO and FIFO.

Communication Case 8–5
LIFO versus FIFO
● **LO4 LO5**

An accounting intern for a local CPA firm was reviewing the financial statements of a client in the electronics industry. The intern noticed that the client used the FIFO method of determining ending inventory and cost of goods sold. When she asked a colleague why the firm used FIFO instead of LIFO, she was told that the client used FIFO to minimize its income tax liability. This response puzzled the intern because she thought that LIFO would minimize income tax liability.

Required:
What would you tell the intern to resolve the confusion?

Judgment Case 8–6
Goods in transit
● **LO2**

At the end of 2009, the Biggie Company performed its annual physical inventory count. John Lawrence, the manager in charge of the physical count, was told that an additional $22,000 in inventory that had been sold and was in transit to the customer should be included in the ending inventory balance. John was of the opinion that the merchandise shipped should be excluded from the ending inventory since Biggie was not in physical possession of the merchandise.

Required:
Discuss the situation and indicate why John's opinion might be incorrect.

Ethics Case 8–7
Profit manipulation
● **LO4**

In 2008 the Moncrief Company purchased from Jim Lester the right to be the sole distributor in the western states of a product called Zelenex. In payment, Moncrief agreed to pay Lester 20% of the gross profit recognized from the sale of Zelenex in 2009.

Moncrief uses a periodic inventory system and the LIFO inventory method. Late in 2009, the following information is available concerning the inventory of Zelenex:

Beginning inventory, 1/1/09 (10,000 units @ $30)	$ 300,000
Purchases (40,000 units @ $30)	1,200,000
Sales (35,000 units @ $60)	$2,100,000

By the end of the year, the purchase price of Zelenex had risen to $40 per unit. On December 28, 2009, three days before year-end, Moncrief is in a position to purchase 20,000 additional units of Zelenex at the $40 per unit price. Due to the increase in purchase price, Moncrief will increase the selling price in 2010 to $80 per unit. Inventory on hand before the purchase, 15,000 units, is sufficient to meet the next six months' sales and the company does not anticipate any significant changes in purchase price during 2010.

Required:
1. Determine the effect of the purchase of the additional 20,000 units on the 2009 gross profit from the sale of Zelenex and the payment due to Jim Lester.

2. Discuss the ethical dilemma Moncrief faces in determining whether or not the additional units should be purchased.

Real World Case 8–8
Effects of inventory valuation methods; LIFO and FIFO
● **LO4 LO6**

Income statement and balance sheet information abstracted from a recent annual report of **The Kroger Company,** one of the world's largest retailers, appears below:

Balance Sheets
($ in millions)

	February 3, 2007	January 28, 2006
Current assets:		
Inventories	$4,609	$4,486

Income Statements
($ in millions)

	For the Year Ended	
	February 3, 2007	January 28, 2006
Net sales	$66,111	$60,553
Cost of goods sold	50,115	45,565
Gross profit	$15,996	$14,988

The significant accounting policies note disclosure contained the following:

Inventories (in part)

Inventories are stated at the lower of cost (principally on a last-in, first-out "LIFO" basis) or market. In total, approximately 98% of inventories were valued using the LIFO method. Cost for the balance of the inventories, including substantially all fuel inventories, was determined using the first-in, first-out ("FIFO") method. Replacement cost was higher than the carrying amount by $450 million at February 3, 2007 and $400 million at January 28, 2006.

Required:
1. Why is Kroger disclosing the replacement cost of its LIFO inventory?
2. Assuming that year-end replacement cost figures approximate FIFO inventory values, estimate what the beginning and ending inventory balances for the fiscal year ended 2/3/07 would have been if Kroger had used FIFO for all of its inventories.
3. Estimate the effect on cost of goods sold (that is, would it have been greater or less and by how much?) for the fiscal year ended 2/3/07 if Kroger had used FIFO for all of its inventories.

Real World Case 8–9
Effects of inventory valuation methods

● LO4 LO5 LO7

Real World Financials

EDGAR, the Electronic Data Gathering, Analysis, and Retrieval system, performs automated collection, validation, indexing, and forwarding of submission by companies and others who are required by law to file forms with the U.S. Securities and Exchange Commission (SEC). All publicly traded domestic companies use EDGAR to make the majority of their filings. (Some foreign companies file voluntarily.) Form 10-K or 10-KSB, which includes the annual report, is required to be filed on EDGAR. The SEC makes this information available on the Internet.

Required:
1. Access EDGAR on the Internet. The web address is **www.sec.gov**.
2. Search for **Whole Foods Market, Inc.** Access the 10-K filing for the most recent fiscal year. Search or scroll to find the financial statements and related notes.
3. Answer the following questions related to the company's inventories:
   a. What method(s) does the company use to value its inventories?
   b. Calculate what cost of sales would have been for the year if the company had used FIFO to value its inventories.
   c. Calculate inventory turnover for the year using the reported numbers.

Communication Case 8–10
Dollar-value LIFO method

● LO8

Maxi Corporation uses the unit LIFO inventory method. The costs of the company's products have been steadily rising since the company began operations in 1999 and cost increases are expected to continue. The chief financial officer of the company would like to continue using LIFO because of its tax advantages. However, the controller, Sally Hamel, would like to reduce the recordkeeping costs of LIFO that have steadily increased over the years as new products have been added to the company's product line. Sally suggested the use of the dollar-value LIFO method. The chief financial officer has asked Sally to describe the dollar-value LIFO procedure.

Required:
Describe the dollar-value LIFO procedure.

Research Case 8–11
Locate and extract relevant information and authoritative support for a financial reporting issue; product financing arrangement

● LO2 LO3

You were recently hired to work in the controller's office of the Balboa Lumber Company. Your boss, Alfred Eagleton, took you to lunch during your first week and asked a favor. "Things have been a little slow lately, and we need to borrow a little cash to tide us over. Our inventory has been building up and the CFO wants to pledge the inventory as collateral for a short-term loan. But I have a better idea." Mr. Eagleton went on to describe his plan. "On July 1, 2009, the first day of the company's third quarter, we will sell $100,000 of inventory to the Harbaugh Corporation for $160,000. Harbaugh will pay us immediately and then we will agree to repurchase the merchandise in two months for $164,000. The $4,000 is Harbaugh's fee for holding the inventory and for providing financing. I already checked with Harbaugh's controller and he has agreed to the arrangement. Not only will we obtain the financing we need, but the third quarter's before-tax profits will be increased by $56,000, the gross profit on the sale less the $4,000 fee. Go research the issue and make sure we would not be violating any specific accounting standards related to product financing arrangements."

Required:
1. Obtain the original FASB Standard on accounting for product financing arrangements. You might gain access at the FASB website (**www.fasb.org**), from your school library, or some other source. Determine the appropriate treatment of product financing arrangements like the one proposed by Mr. Eagleton.
2. Prepare the journal entry to record the "sale" of the inventory and subsequent repurchase.

Analysis Case 8–12
Compare inventory management using ratios

● LO7

Real World Financials

The table below contains selected financial information included in the 2006 financial statements of **General Motors** and **Ford Motor Company**:

	General Motors		Ford Motor Company	
($ in millions)	2006	2005	2006	2005
Balance sheet:				
Inventories	$13,921	$13,862	$11,578	$10,271
	2006		2006	
Income statement:				
Net sales	$172,927		$143,307	
Cost of goods sold	164,682		148,869	

Disclosure notes reveal that both companies use the LIFO inventory method to value the majority of their inventories.

Required:
1. Calculate the 2006 gross profit ratio, inventory turnover ratio, and average days in inventory for both companies. Evaluate the management of each company's investment in inventory. Industry averages for these ratios are as follows:

Gross profit	14%
Inventory turnover	14.34
Average days in inventory	25

2. Obtain annual reports from three corporations in an industry other than autos and compare the management of each company's investment in inventory.

Note: You can obtain copies of annual reports from your library, from friends who are shareholders, from the investor relations department of the corporations, from a friendly stockbroker, or from EDGAR (Electronic Data Gathering, Analysis, and Retrieval) on the Internet (**www.sec.gov**).

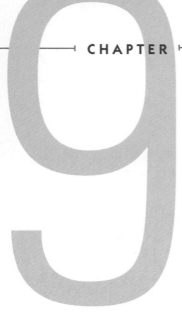

CHAPTER

Inventories: Additional Issues

/// OVERVIEW

We covered most of the principal measurement and reporting issues involving the asset inventory and the corresponding expense cost of goods sold in the previous chapter. In this chapter we complete our discussion of inventory measurement by explaining the lower-of-cost-or-market rule used to value inventories. In addition, we investigate inventory estimation techniques, methods of simplifying LIFO, changes in inventory method, and inventory errors.

||| LEARNING OBJECTIVES

After studying this chapter, you should be able to:

- **LO1** Understand and apply the lower-of-cost-or-market rule used to value inventories.
- **LO2** Estimate ending inventory and cost of goods sold using the gross profit method.
- **LO3** Estimate ending inventory and cost of goods sold using the retail inventory method, applying the various cost flow methods.
- **LO4** Explain how the retail inventory method can be made to approximate the lower-of-cost-or-market rule.
- **LO5** Determine ending inventory using the dollar-value LIFO retail inventory method.
- **LO6** Explain the appropriate accounting treatment required when a change in inventory method is made.
- **LO7** Explain the appropriate accounting treatment required when an inventory error is discovered.

FINANCIAL REPORTING CASE

Does It Count?

Today you drove over to Sears to pick up a few items. Yesterday, your accounting professor had discussed inventory measurement issues and the different methods (FIFO, LIFO, and average) used by companies to determine ending inventory and cost of goods sold. You can't imagine actually counting the inventory in all of the Sears stores around the country. "There must be some way they can avoid counting all of that inventory every time they want to produce financial statements," you tell your dog when you get home. "I think I'll go check their financial statements on the Internet to see what kind of inventory method they use." You find the following in the summary of significant accounting policies included in Sears's most recent financial statements:

Merchandise Inventories (in part):

Merchandise inventories are valued at the lower of cost or market. For Kmart and Sears Domestic, cost is primarily determined using the retail inventory method. Approximately 55% of consolidated merchandise inventories are valued using LIFO. To estimate the effects of inflation on inventories, the Company utilizes external price indices determined by an outside source, the Bureau of Labor Statistics.

By the time you finish this chapter, you should be able to respond appropriately to the questions posed in this case. Compare your response to the solution provided at the end of the chapter.

QUESTIONS ///

1. Sears values its inventory at the lower of cost or market. What does that mean? Under what circumstances might Sears be justified in reporting its inventory at less than cost? (page 426)

2. How does Sears avoid counting all its inventory every time it produces financial statements? What are external price indices used for? (page 443)

REPORTING—LOWER OF COST OR MARKET

In the previous chapter you learned that there are several methods a company could use to determine the cost of inventory at the end of a period and the corresponding cost of goods sold for the period. You also learned that it is important for a company to disclose the inventory method that it uses. Otherwise, investors and creditors would be unable to meaningfully compare accounting information from company to company. This disclosure typically is made in the summary of significant accounting policies accompanying the financial statements. **Coca-Cola Company**'s inventory method disclosure is shown in Graphic 9–1.

GRAPHIC 9–1

Disclosure of Inventory Method—Coca-Cola Company

Real World Financials

● **LO1**

FINANCIAL
Reporting Case

Q1, p. 425

The LCM approach to valuing inventory is required by GAAP.

Inventories

Inventories consists primarily of raw materials and packaging (which includes ingredients and supplies) and finished goods (which includes concentrates and syrups in our concentrate and foodservice operations, and finished beverages in our bottling and canning operations). Inventories are valued at the lower of cost or market. We determine cost on the basis of the average cost or first-in, first-out methods.

The disclosure indicates that Coca-Cola uses both the average cost and FIFO methods to determine the cost of its inventories. Notice that inventories actually are valued at the *lower of cost or market*. Assets are initially valued at their historical costs, but a departure from cost is warranted when the utility of an asset (its probable future economic benefits) is no longer as great as its cost. Accounts receivable, for example, are valued at net realizable value by reducing initial valuation with an allowance for uncollectible accounts.

The utility, or benefits, a company receives from inventory result from the ultimate sale of the goods. So deterioration, obsolescence, changes in price levels, or any situation that might compromise the inventory's salability impairs that utility. The lower-of-cost-or-market (LCM) approach to valuing inventory was developed to avoid reporting inventory at an amount greater than the benefits it can provide. Reporting inventories at LCM causes losses to be recognized in the period the value of inventory declines below its cost rather than in the period in that the goods ultimately are sold. LCM is not an optional approach to valuing inventory; it is required by GAAP.

The tremendous growth of the Internet that took place during the decade of the 90s allowed companies that produced products that support the Internet to become extremely profitable. **Cisco Systems, Inc.,** the world's largest networking products company, is one of those companies. In 1993, Cisco reported $649 million in sales revenue. By 2000, sales had reached nearly $19 billion! Growth rates of 50% year-to-year were commonplace. The company's market capitalization (price per share of common stock multiplied by the number of common shares outstanding) soared to over $500 billion. To keep pace with this growth in sales, inventories swelled from $71 million in 1993 to over $2.5 billion in 2000.

At the end of 2000, corporate spending on Internet infrastructure took a drastic downturn. Many dot-com companies went bankrupt, and companies like Cisco saw their fantastic growth rates nosedive. Early in 2001, the company reported its first-ever quarterly loss and, due to declining demand for its products, recorded an inventory write-down in excess of $2 billion. The company's once lofty market capitalization dropped to just over $100 billion.

CISCO POSTS $5BN LOSS ON HUGE WRITE-DOWNS
Technology giant Cisco Systems posted on Tuesday a third-quarter net loss of $2.69 billion, its first ever, following a write-down of inventory, restructuring costs and a sharp drop-off in corporate spending.

. . . and a write-down of over $2 billion for excess inventory.

Cisco said 80 percent of the inventory charge relates to raw materials, such as semiconductor memories, optical components, . . .

"Most of the excess inventory cannot be sold as it is custom built for Cisco," chief financial officer Mr. Larry Carter said in a conference call.[1]

---

[1]Fiona Buffini, "Cisco Posts $5bn Loss on Huge Writedowns," *Financial Review,* May 9, 2001.

Determining Market Value

From the preceding discussion, you might interpret the term *market* to mean the amount that could be realized if the inventory were sold. However, *Accounting Research Bulletin No. 43* defines market for LCM purposes as the inventory's current replacement cost (by purchase or reproduction) except that market should not:

Replacement cost (RC) generally means the cost to replace the item by purchase or manufacture.

a. Exceed the net realizable value (that is, estimated selling price in the ordinary course of business less reasonably predictable costs of completion and disposal).
b. Be less than net realizable value reduced by an allowance for an approximately normal profit margin.

In effect, we have a ceiling and a floor between which market (that is, replacement cost) must fall. Net realizable value (NRV) represents the upper limit and net realizable value less a normal profit margin (NRV − NP) provides the lower limit. If replacement cost (RC) is within the range, it represents market; if it is above the ceiling or below the floor, the ceiling or the floor becomes market. As a result, the designated market value is the number that falls in the middle of the three possibilities: replacement cost, net realizable value, and net realizable value less a normal profit margin. The designated market value is compared with cost, and the lower of the two is used to value inventory.

Graphic 9–2 portrays the lower-of-cost-or-market approach to inventory valuation.

The ceiling of net realizable value (NRV) and the floor of net realizable value less a normal profit margin (NRV − NP) establish a range within which the market must fall.

Lower-of-cost-or-market Approach to Valuing Inventory

Step 1 – Determine Designated Market

Step 2 – Compare Designated Market with Cost

Ceiling NRV

Not More Than

Replacement Cost

Not Less Than

NRV – NP Floor

Designated Market ← Or → Cost

Lower of Cost Or Market

GRAPHIC 9–2

Lower-of-Cost-or-Market Approach to Valuing Inventory

Let's see how the LCM rule is applied in Illustration 9–1 and then we will discuss its theoretical merit.

Notice that the designated market value is the middle amount of the three market possibilities. This number is then compared to cost and the lower of the two is the final inventory value. For item A, cost is lower than market. For each of the other items, the designated market is lower than cost, requiring an adjustment to the carrying value of inventory. We discuss the adjustment procedure later in the chapter. First though, let's consider the conceptual justification of the LCM rule.

THEORETICAL MERITS. What is the logic for designating replacement cost as the principal meaning of market value in the LCM rule? First, a change in replacement cost usually is a good indicator of the direction of change in selling price. If replacement cost declines, selling price usually will decline, or already has declined. Another reason is that

ILLUSTRATION 9–1

Lower of Cost or Market

The Collins Company has five inventory items on hand at the end of 2009. The year-end unit costs (determined by applying the average cost method), current unit selling prices, and estimated disposal (selling) costs for each of the items are presented below. The gross profit ratio for each of the products is 20% of selling price.

Item	Cost	Replacement Cost	Selling Price	Estimated Disposal Costs
A	$ 50	$55	$100	$15
B	100	90	120	20
C	80	70	85	20
D	90	37	100	24
E	95	92	110	24

The determination of inventory value is a two-step process: first, determine the designated market value and second, compare the designated market value to cost. The lower of the two is the LCM inventory value.

Inventory is valued at the lower of cost or the designated market value.

	(1)	(2)	(3)	(4)	(5)	
				Designated Market Value [Middle Value		Inventory Value [Lower of (4)
Item	RC	NRV	NRV − NP	of (1), (2) and (3)]	Cost	and (5)]
A	$55	$ 85	$65	$65	$ 50	$50
B	90	100	76	90	100	90
C	70	65	48	65	80	65
D	37	76	56	56	90	56
E	92	86	64	86	95	86

RC = Current replacement cost.
NRV = Estimated selling price less estimated disposal costs.
NRV − NP = NRV less a normal profit margin.

Example for item B:

Selling price	$120
Less: Disposal costs	(20)
NRV	100
Less: Normal profit	(24) ($120 selling price × 20%)
NRV − NP	$ 76

if previously acquired inventory is revalued at its replacement cost, then the profit margin realized on its sale will likely approximate the profit margin realizable on the sale of newly acquired items.

The upper limit placed on replacement cost prevents inventory from being valued at an amount above what can be realized from its sale. The lower limit prevents inventory from being valued at an amount below what can be realized from its sale after considering normal profit margin. For example, consider item D in our illustration. If item D is valued at its replacement cost of $37 without considering the ceiling or floor, a loss of $53 ($90 cost less $37) would be recognized. If the item is subsequently sold at its current selling price less usual disposal costs (NRV = $76), then a gross profit of $39 ($76 less $37) would be recognized. This is much higher than its normal profit of $20 (20% × $100) and causes a shifting of income from the period the inventory loss is recognized to the period the item is sold. The ceiling and floor prohibit this kind of profit distortion.

Some accountants complain that LCM promotes conservatism at the expense of consistency.

On the other hand, critics of LCM contend that the method causes losses to be recognized that haven't actually occurred. Others maintain that it introduces needless inconsistency in order to be conservative. Inconsistency is created because LCM recognizes decreases in market value as they occur, but not increases.

The practice of recognizing decreases but not increases is not simply an application motivated by conservatism. Recall our discussions in previous chapters on revenue recognition and the realization principle. Recognizing increases in the value of inventory prior to sale would, in most cases, violate the realization principle. Assume that merchandise costing $100 has a net realizable value of $150. Recognizing the increase in value would increase pretax income by $50. This is equivalent to recognizing revenue of $150, cost of goods sold of $100, and gross profit of $50. Either way, pretax income is increased in a period prior to sale of the product. Prior to sale, there usually exists significant uncertainty as to the collectibility of the asset to be received. We don't know if the product will be sold, nor the selling price, or the buyer if eventually sold.

The LCM rules stated in *ARB No. 43* are intended as a guide rather than a literal rule. In practice, companies frequently define market as net realizable value. This is a number that often is easier to estimate than replacement cost. Also, assuming the NRV does not change, when the item is sold, there will be neither gross profit nor additional loss. The entire effect on income is recognized in the period the realizable value drops below cost.

ETHICAL DILEMMA

The Hartley Paper Company, owned and operated by Bill Hartley, manufactures and sells different types of computer paper. The company has reported profits in the majority of years since the company's inception in 1965 and is projecting a profit in 2009 of $65,000, down from $96,000 in 2008.

Near the end of 2009, the company is in the process of applying for a bank loan. The loan proceeds will be used to replace manufacturing equipment necessary to modernize the manufacturing operation. In preparing the financial statements for the year, the chief accountant, Don Davis, mentioned to Bill Hartley that approximately $40,000 of paper inventory has become obsolete and should be written off as a loss in 2009. Bill is worried that the write-down would lower 2009 income to a level that might cause the bank to refuse the loan. Without the loan, it would be difficult for the company to compete. This could cause decreased future business and employees might have to be laid off. Bill is considering waiting until 2010 to write down the inventory. Don Davis is contemplating his responsibilities in this situation.

ARB NO. 43

The most common practice is to apply the *lower of cost or market rule* separately to each item of the inventory. However, if there is only one end-product category the cost utility of the total stock—the inventory in its entirety—may have the greatest significance for accounting purposes.

Similarly, where more than one major product or operational category exists, the application of the *lower of cost or market, whichever is lower* rule to the total of items included in such major categories may result in the most useful determination of income.[2]

Applying Lower of Cost or Market

Lower of cost or market can be applied to individual inventory items, to logical categories of inventory, or to the entire inventory. A major product line can be considered a logical category of inventory. For income tax purposes, the lower-of-cost-or-market rule must be applied on an individual item basis.

Let's return to our illustration and assume the unit amounts pertain to 1,000 units of each inventory item. Also, let's say items A–B and items C–E are two collections of similar items that can be considered logical categories of inventory. Illustration 9–1A compares the LCM valuation accounting to each of three possible applications.

The final LCM inventory value is different for each of the three applications. The inventory value is $347,000 if LCM is applied to each item, $357,000 if it is applied to product line categories, and $362,000 if applied to the entire inventory. Applying LCM to groups of inventory items will usually cause a higher inventory valuation than if applied on an item-by-item basis because group application permits decreases in the market value of some items to be offset by increases in others. Each approach is acceptable but should be applied consistently from one period to another.

> The LCM rule can be applied to individual inventory items, logical inventory categories, or the entire inventory.

---

[2]"Restatement and Revision of Accounting Research Bulletins," *Accounting Research Bulletin No. 43* (New York: AICPA, 1953), Ch. 4, par. 11.

ILLUSTRATION 9–1A				Lower-of-Cost-or-Market		
LCM Determination— Application at Different Levels of Aggregation	Item	Cost	Designated Market Value	By Individual Items	By Product Line	By Total Inventory
	A	$ 50,000	$ 65,000	$ 50,000		
	B	100,000	90,000	90,000		
	Total A + B	$150,000	$155,000		$150,000	
	C	$ 80,000	$ 65,000	65,000		
	D	90,000	56,000	56,000		
	E	95,000	86,000	86,000		
	Total C, D, & E	$265,000	$207,000		207,000	
	Total	$415,000	$362,000	$347,000	$357,000	$362,000

Adjusting Cost to Market

When a company applies the LCM rule and a material write-down of inventory is required, the company has two choices of how to record the reduction. One way found in practice is to report the loss as a separate item in the income statement. An alternative is to include the loss as part of the cost of goods sold.

Loss on reduction to LCM xx
    Inventory* xx   **or**   Cost of goods sold xx
                                                             Inventory* xx

*Or, inventory can be reduced indirectly with a credit to an allowance account.

> **The preferable way to report a loss from an inventory write-down is as a separate item in the income statement.**

Recording the write-down as a separate item more accurately reports the event that occurred—a loss from holding inventory during a period when inventory value declined. Including this holding loss as part of cost of goods sold has the same effect on reported earnings, but distorts the relationship between sales and cost of goods sold. Conceptually, cost of goods sold should include only the cost of goods actually sold during the period. Even so, many companies do include the "holding loss" in cost of goods sold.

Recall from our introductory discussion to this chapter that **Cisco Systems, Inc.,** recorded an inventory write-down in excess of $2 billion. To understand how the relationship between sales and cost of goods sold can be distorted, let's consider the top part of the company's income statements for the first quarter of 2001 and 2000 shown in Graphic 9–3.

> **GRAPHIC 9–3**
>
> Partial Income Statements—Cisco Systems, Inc.
>
> **Real World Financials**

INCOME STATEMENTS (IN PART) For the Three Months Ended, ($ in millions)		
	April 28, 2001	April 29, 2000
Net sales	$4,728	$4,933
Cost of sales	4,400	1,761
Gross profit	328	3,172

> **Reporting a loss from an inventory write-down as part of cost of goods sold distorts the relationship between sales and cost of goods sold.**

Using the information in the statements, the gross profit ratio dropped from 64% ($3,172 ÷ $4,933) in 2000 to 7% ($328 ÷ $4,728) in 2001. An analyst might conclude that there was a significant deterioration in the markup the company was able to achieve on its products. However, this assessment is premature. A disclosure note included in the financial statements for the first quarter of 2001 reported that during the quarter Cisco recorded "an excess inventory charge of $2.25 billion classified as cost of sales." We get a more accurate portrayal of the company's gross profit ratio if we reduce the cost of goods sold by the inventory charge (write-down):

Sales	$4,728
Adjusted cost of sales ($4,400 − 2,250)	2,150
Adjusted gross profit	2,578
Adjusted gross profit ratio	55%

Cisco's gross profit ratio did decline from the prior year, but not nearly as drastically as the reported financial statement information would lead us to believe.

Regardless of which method we use to record the write-down, the reduced inventory value becomes the new cost basis for subsequent reporting, and if the inventory value later recovers prior to its sale, we do not write it back up.[3]

INTERNATIONAL FINANCIAL REPORTING STANDARDS

Lower of cost or market. International standards also require inventory to be valued at the lower of cost or market. You just learned that in the United States, market is designated as replacement cost with a ceiling of net realizable value (NRV) and a floor of NRV less a normal profit margin. However, the designated market value according to *IAS No. 2* always is net realizable value.

IAS No. 2 also specifies that if circumstances reveal that an inventory write-down is no longer appropriate, it should be reversed. Reversals are not permitted under U.S. GAAP.

Cadbury Schweppes, Plc., a U.K. company, prepares its financial statements according to IFRS. The following disclosure note illustrates the designation of market as net realizable value.

Real World Financials

Inventories (in part)

Inventories are recorded at the lower of average cost and estimated net realizable value.

ADDITIONAL CONSIDERATION

In very limited circumstances, businesses are allowed under GAAP to carry inventory at a market value above cost. *ARB 43* restricted this approach generally to companies that deal in precious metals, and ". . . agricultural, mineral, and other products, units of which are interchangeable and have an immediate marketability at quoted prices . . ."[4] Writing inventory up to market value means recognizing revenue for the increase. This is called the *production basis* of recognizing revenue. In rare cases when the method is appropriate, full disclosure of the fact that inventory is valued at market is required.

CONCEPT REVIEW EXERCISE

The Strand Company sells four products that can be grouped into two major categories. Information necessary to apply the LCM rule at the end of 2009 for each of the four products is presented below. The normal profit margin for each of the products is 25% of selling price. The company records any losses from adjusting cost to market as separate income statement items and reduces inventory directly.

LOWER OF COST OR MARKET

---

[3]The SEC, in its *Staff Accounting Bulletin No. 100,* "Restructuring and Impairment Charges" (Washington, D.C.: SEC, November, 1999), paragraph B.B., reaffirmed the provisions of *Accounting Research Bulletin No. 43* on this issue. For interim reporting purposes, however, recoveries of losses on the same inventory in subsequent interim periods of the same fiscal year through market price recoveries should be recognized as gains in the later interim period, not to exceed the previously recognized losses.

[4]"Restatement and Revision of Accounting Research Bulletins," *Accounting Research Bulletin No. 43* (New York: AICPA, 1953), Ch. 4, par. 16.

Product	Cost	Replacement Cost	Selling Price	Disposal Costs
101	$ 80,000	$ 85,000	$160,000	$30,000
102	175,000	160,000	200,000	25,000
201	160,000	140,000	180,000	50,000
202	45,000	20,000	60,000	22,000

Products 101 and 102 are in category A and products 201 and 202 are in category B.

Required:

1. Determine the designated market value for each of the four products according to the LCM rule.
2. Determine the amount of the loss from write-down of inventory that would be required, applying the LCM rule to:
   a. Individual items
   b. Major categories
   c. The entire inventory

SOLUTION   1. Determine the designated market value for each of the four products according to the LCM rule.

	(1)	(2)	(3)	(4)
Product	RC	NRV (Selling Price Less Disposal Costs)	NRV − NP	Designated Market Value [Middle Value of (1), (2) & (3)]
101	$ 85,000	$130,000	$ 90,000	$ 90,000
102	160,000	175,000	125,000	160,000
201	140,000	130,000	85,000	130,000
202	20,000	38,000	23,000	23,000

Calculation of NRV − NP:

Product	NRV	NP	NRV − NP
101	$ 130,000	$40,000 (25% × $160,000)	$ 90,000
102	175,000	50,000 (25% × $200,000)	125,000
201	130,000	45,000 (25% × $180,000)	85,000
202	38,000	15,000 (25% × $60,000)	23,000

2. Determine the amount of the loss from write-down of inventory that would be required.

			Lower-of-Cost-or-Market		
Product	Cost	Designated Market Value	By Individual Products	By Category	By Total Inventory
101	$ 80,000	$ 90,000	$ 80,000		
102	175,000	160,000	160,000		
Total 101 + 102	$255,000	$250,000		$250,000	
201	$160,000	$130,000	130,000		
202	45,000	23,000	23,000		
Total 201 + 202	$205,000	$153,000		153,000	
Total	$460,000	$403,000	$393,000	$403,000	$403,000

The LCM value for both the category application and the entire inventory application are identical because, in this particular case, market is below cost for both of the categories.

Amount of loss from write-down using individual items:

$$\$460,000 - 393,000 = \textbf{\$67,000}$$

Amount of loss from write-down using categories or the entire inventory:

$$\$460,000 - 403,000 = \textbf{\$57,000} \ \bullet$$

INVENTORY ESTIMATION TECHNIQUES

The Southern Wholesale Company distributes approximately 100 products throughout the state of Mississippi. Southern uses a periodic inventory system and takes a physical count of inventory once a year at its fiscal year-end. A recent fire destroyed the entire inventory in one of Southern's warehouses. How can the company determine the dollar amount of inventory destroyed when submitting an insurance claim to obtain reimbursement for the loss?

Home Improvement Stores, Inc., sells over 1,000 different products to customers in each of its 17 retail stores. The company uses a periodic inventory system and takes a physical count of inventory once a year at its fiscal year-end. Home Improvement's bank has asked for monthly financial statements as a condition attached to a recent loan. Can the company avoid the costly procedure of counting inventory at the end of each month to determine ending inventory and cost of goods sold?

These are just two examples of situations when it is either impossible or infeasible to determine the dollar amount of ending inventory by taking a count of the physical quantity of inventory on hand at the end of a period. Fortunately, companies can estimate inventory in these situations by either the gross profit method or the retail inventory method.

The Gross Profit Method

The gross profit method, also known as the gross margin method, is useful in situations where estimates of inventory are desirable. The technique is valuable in a variety of situations:

● LO2

1. In determining the cost of inventory that has been lost, destroyed, or stolen.
2. In estimating inventory and cost of goods sold for interim reports, avoiding the expense of a physical inventory count.
3. In auditors' testing of the overall reasonableness of inventory amounts reported by clients.
4. In budgeting and forecasting.

However, the gross profit method provides only an approximation of inventory and is not acceptable according to generally accepted accounting principles for annual financial statements.

The *gross profit method* is not acceptable for the preparation of annual financial statements.

The technique relies on a relationship you learned in the previous chapter—ending inventory and cost of goods sold always equal the cost of goods available for sale. Even when inventory is unknown, we can estimate it because accounting records usually indicate the cost of goods available for sale (beginning inventory plus net purchases), and the cost of goods sold can be estimated from available information. So by subtracting the cost of goods sold estimate from the cost of goods available for sale, we obtain an estimate of ending inventory. Let's compare that with the way inventory and cost of goods sold normally are determined.

Usually, in a periodic inventory system, ending inventory is known from a physical count and cost of goods sold is *derived* as follows:

Beginning inventory	(from the accounting records)
Plus: Net purchases	(from the accounting records)
Goods available for sale	
Less: Ending inventory	(from a physical count)
Cost of goods sold	

However, when using the gross profit method, the ending inventory is *not* known. Instead, the amount of sales is known—from which we can estimate the cost of goods sold—and ending inventory is the amount calculated.

Beginning inventory	(from the accounting records)
Plus: Net purchases	(from the accounting records)
Goods available for sale	
Less: Cost of goods sold	(estimated)
Ending inventory	(estimated)

So, a first step in estimating inventory is to estimate cost of goods sold. This estimate relies on the historical relationship among (a) net sales, (b) cost of goods sold, and (c) gross profit. Gross profit, you will recall, is simply net sales minus cost of goods sold. So, if we know what net sales are, and if we know what percentage of net sales the gross profit is, we can fairly accurately estimate cost of goods sold. Companies often sell products that have similar gross profit ratios. As a result, accounting records usually provide the information necessary to estimate the cost of ending inventory, even when a physical count is impractical. Let's use the gross profit method to solve the problem of Southern Wholesale Company introduced earlier in the chapter. Suppose the company began 2009 with inventory of $600,000, and on March 17 a warehouse fire destroyed the entire inventory. Company records indicate net purchases of $1,500,000 and net sales of $2,000,000 prior to the fire. The gross profit ratio in each of the previous three years has been very close to 40%. Illustration 9–2 shows how Southern can estimate the cost of the inventory destroyed for its insurance claim.

ILLUSTRATION 9–2
Gross Profit Method

Beginning inventory (from records)		$ 600,000
Plus: Net purchases (from records)		1,500,000
Goods available for sale		2,100,000
Less: Cost of goods sold:		
Net sales	$2,000,000	
Less: Estimated gross profit of 40%	(800,000)	
Estimated cost of goods sold*		(1,200,000)
Estimated ending inventory		$ 900,000

*Alternatively, cost of goods sold can be calculated as $2,000,000 × (1 − .40) = $1,200,000.

A Word of Caution

The key to obtaining good estimates is the reliability of the gross profit ratio.

The gross profit method provides only an estimate. The key to obtaining good estimates is the reliability of the gross profit ratio. The ratio usually is estimated from relationships between sales and cost of goods sold. However, the current relationship may differ from the past. In that case, all available information should be used to make necessary adjustments. For example, the company may have made changes in the markup percentage of some of its products. Very often different products have different markups. In these situations, a blanket ratio should not be applied across the board. The accuracy of the estimate can be improved by grouping inventory into pools of products that have similar gross profit relationships rather than using one gross profit ratio for the entire inventory.

The company's cost flow assumption should be implicitly considered when estimating the gross profit ratio. For example, if LIFO is used and the relationship between cost and selling price has changed for recent acquisitions, this would suggest a ratio different from one where the average cost method was used. Another difficulty with the gross profit method is that it does not explicitly consider possible theft or spoilage of inventory. The method assumes that if the inventory was not sold, then it must be on hand at the end of the period. Suspected theft or spoilage would require an adjustment to estimates obtained using the gross profit method.

The Retail Inventory Method

The retail inventory method is similar to the gross profit method in that it relies on the relationship between cost and selling price to estimate ending inventory and cost of goods sold.

● LO3

As the name implies, the method is used by many retail companies such as **Target, Wal-Mart, Sears Holding Corporation, Saks, J.C. Penney,** and **Federated Department Stores.** Certain retailers like auto dealers and jewelry stores, whose inventory consists of few, high-priced items, can economically use the specific identification inventory method. However, high-volume retailers selling many different items at low unit prices find the retail inventory method ideal, although with the advent of bar coding on more and more retail merchandise, use of the method is declining. Similar to the gross profit method, its principal benefit is that a physical count of inventory is not required to estimate ending inventory and cost of goods sold.

The retail method tends to provide a more accurate estimate than the gross profit method because it's based on the current cost-to-retail percentage rather than on a historical gross profit ratio.

The retail inventory method uses the cost-to-retail percentage based on a current relationship between cost and selling price.

The increased reliability in the estimate of the cost percentage is achieved by comparing cost of goods available for sale with goods available for sale *at current selling prices.* So, to use the technique, a company must maintain records of inventory and purchases not only at cost, but also at current selling price. We refer to this as *retail information.* In its simplest form, the retail inventory method estimates the amount of ending inventory (at retail) by subtracting sales (at retail) from goods available for sale (at retail). This estimated ending inventory at retail is then converted to cost by multiplying it by the cost-to-retail percentage. This ratio is found by dividing goods available for sale at *cost* by goods available for sale at *retail.*

Let's use the retail inventory method to solve the problem of the Home Improvement Store introduced earlier in the chapter. Suppose the company's bank has asked for monthly financial statements as a condition attached to a loan dated May 31, 2009. To avoid a physical count of inventory, the company intends to use the retail inventory method to estimate ending inventory and cost of goods sold for the month of June. Using data available in its accounting records, Illustration 9–3 shows how Home Improvement can estimate ending inventory and cost of goods sold for June.

	Cost	Retail
ILLUSTRATION 9–3		
Retail Method		
Beginning inventory	$ 60,000	$100,000
Plus: Net purchases	287,200	460,000
Goods available for sale	$347,200	$560,000

Goods available for sale (at retail) minus net sales equals estimated ending inventory (at retail).

Cost-to-retail percentage: $\dfrac{\$347,200}{\$560,000} = 62\%$

	Cost	Retail
Less: Net sales		(400,000)
Estimated ending inventory at retail		$160,000
Estimated ending inventory at cost (62% × $160,000)	(99,200)	
Estimated cost of goods sold—goods available for sale (at cost) minus ending inventory (at cost) equals cost of goods sold	$248,000	

The retail inventory method can be used for financial reporting and income tax purposes.

Unlike the gross profit method, the retail inventory method is acceptable for external financial reporting if the results of applying the method are sufficiently close to what would have been achieved using a more rigorous determination of the cost of ending inventory. Also, it's allowed by the Internal Revenue Service as a method that can be used to determine cost of goods sold for income tax purposes.[5] Another advantage of the method is that different cost flow methods can be explicitly incorporated into the estimation technique. In other words, we can modify the application of the method to estimate ending inventory and cost of goods sold to approximate average cost, lower-of-average-cost-or-market (conventional method) and LIFO. (The FIFO retail method is possible but used less frequently in practice.) We illustrate these variations later in the chapter.

Like the gross profit method, the retail inventory method also can be used to estimate the cost of inventory lost, stolen, or destroyed; for testing the overall reasonableness of physical counts; in budgeting and forecasting as well as in generating information for interim financial statements. Even though the retail method provides fairly accurate estimates, a physical count of inventory usually is performed at least once a year to verify accuracy and detect spoilage, theft, and other irregularities.

Retail Terminology

Changes in the selling prices must be included in the determination of ending inventory at retail.

Our example above is simplified in that we implicitly assumed that the selling prices of beginning inventory and of merchandise purchased did not change from date of acquisition to the end of the period. This frequently is an unrealistic assumption. The terms in Graphic 9–4 are associated with changing retail prices of merchandise inventory.

GRAPHIC 9–4

Terminology Used in Applying the Retail Method

Initial markup	Original amount of markup from cost to selling price.
Additional markup	Increase in selling price subsequent to initial markup.
Markup cancellation	Elimination of an additional markup.
Markdown	Reduction in selling price below the original selling price.
Markdown cancellation	Elimination of a markdown.

To illustrate, assume that a product purchased for $6 is initially marked up $4, from $6 to $10, the original selling price. If the selling price is subsequently increased to $12, the additional markup is $2. If the selling price is then subsequently decreased to $10.50, the markup cancellation is $1.50. We refer to the net effect of the changes ($2.00 − 1.50 = $.50) as the net markup. Graphic 9–5A depicts these events.

---

[5]The retail method is acceptable for external reporting and for tax purposes because it tends to provide a better estimate than the gross profit method. The retail method uses a current cost-to-retail percentage rather than a historical gross profit ratio.

GRAPHIC 9–5A

Retail Inventory
Method Terminology

Now let's say the selling price of the product purchased for $6 and initially marked up to $10, is reduced to $7. The markdown is $3. If the selling price is later increased to $8, the markdown cancellation is $1. The net effect of the change ($3 − 1 = $2) is the net markdown. Graphic 9–5B depicts this possibility.

GRAPHIC 9–5B

Retail Inventory
Method Terminology

When applying the retail inventory method, *net markups and net markdowns must be included in the determination of ending inventory at retail.* We now continue our illustration of the retail inventory method, but expand it to incorporate markups and markdowns as well as to approximate cost by each of the alternative inventory cost flow methods.

Net markups and *net markdowns* are included in the retail column to determine ending inventory at retail.

Cost Flow Methods

Let's continue the Home Improvement Stores example into July with Illustration 9–4 and see how the retail inventory method can be used to approximate different cost flow assumptions. We'll also use the same illustration to see how the retail method can be modified to approximate lower of cost or market.

Home Improvement Stores, Inc., uses a periodic inventory system and the retail inventory method to estimate ending inventory and cost of goods sold. The following data are available from the company's records for the month of July 2009:

	Cost	Retail
Beginning inventory	$ 99,200	$160,000
Net purchases	305,280[1]	470,000[2]
Net markups		10,000
Net markdowns		8,000
Net sales		434,000[3]

ILLUSTRATION 9–4

The Retail Inventory Method—Various Cost Flow Methods

[1]Purchases at cost less returns, plus freight-in.
[2]Original selling price of purchased goods less returns at retail.
[3]Gross sales less returns.

APPROXIMATING AVERAGE COST.   Recall that the average cost method assumes that cost of goods sold and ending inventory each consist of a *mixture* of all the goods available for sale. So when we use the retail method to approximate average cost, the cost-to-retail percentage should be based on the weighted averages of the costs and retail amounts for

To approximate average cost, the cost-to-retail percentage is determined for *all* goods available for sale.

all goods available for sale. This is achieved by calculating the cost-to-retail percentage by dividing the total cost of goods available for sale by total goods available for sale at retail. When this average percentage is applied to ending inventory at retail, we get an estimate of ending inventory at average cost. If you look back to our simplified example for the month of June, you'll notice that we used this approach there. So, our ending inventory and cost of goods sold estimates for June were estimates of average cost.[6]

Now, we use the retail inventory method to approximate average costs for July. Notice in Illustration 9–5 that both markups and markdowns are included in the determination of goods available for sale at retail.

ILLUSTRATION 9–5		Cost	Retail
Retail Method—Average Cost	Beginning inventory	$ 99,200	$160,000
	Plus: Net purchases	305,280	470,000
	Net markups		10,000
	Less: Net markdowns		(8,000)
	Goods available for sale	404,480	632,000
	Cost-to-retail percentage: $\frac{\$404,480}{\$632,000} = 64\%$		
	Less: Net sales		(434,000)
	Estimated ending inventory at retail		$198,000
	Estimated ending inventory at cost (64% × $198,000)	(126,720)	
	Estimated cost of goods sold	$277,760	

● LO4

APPROXIMATING AVERAGE LCM—THE CONVENTIONAL RETAIL METHOD. Recall from our discussion earlier in the chapter that, however costs are determined, inventory should be reported in the balance sheet at LCM. Fortunately, we can apply the retail inventory method in such a way that LCM is approximated. This method often is referred to as the conventional retail method. We apply the method by *excluding markdowns from the calculation of the cost-to-retail percentage.* Markdowns still are subtracted in the retail column but only after the percentage is calculated. To approximate lower of average cost or market, the retail method is modified as shown in Illustration 9–6.

To approximate LCM, markdowns are not included in the calculation of the cost-to-retail percentage.

ILLUSTRATION 9–6		Cost	Retail
Retail Method—Average Cost, LCM	Beginning inventory	$ 99,200	$160,000
	Plus: Net purchases	305,280	470,000
	Net markups		10,000
			640,000
	Cost-to-retail percentage: $\frac{\$404,480}{\$640,000} = 63.2\%$		
	Less: Net markdowns		(8,000)
	Goods available for sale	404,480	632,000
	Less: Net sales		(434,000)
	Estimated ending inventory at retail		$198,000
	Estimated ending inventory at cost (63.2% × $198,000)	(125,136)	
	Estimated cost of goods sold	$279,344	

---

[6]We also implicitly assumed no net markups or markdowns.

Notice that by not subtracting net markdowns from the denominator, the cost-to-retail percentage is lower than it was previously (63.2% versus 64%). This always will be the case when markdowns exist. As a result, the cost approximation of ending inventory always will be less when markdowns exist. To understand why this lower amount approximates LCM, we need to realize that markdowns usually occur when obsolescence, spoilage, overstocking, price declines, or competition has lessened the utility of the merchandise. To recognize this decline in utility in the period it occurs, as LCM does, we exclude net markdowns from the calculation of the cost-to-retail (market) percentage. It should be emphasized that this approach provides only an *approximation* of what ending inventory might be as opposed to applying the LCM rule in the more exact way described earlier in the chapter.

The logic for using this approximation is that a markdown is evidence of a reduction in the utility of inventory.

Also notice that the ending inventory at retail is the same using both approaches ($198,000). This will be the case regardless of the cost flow method used because in all approaches this amount reflects the ending inventory at current retail prices.

The LCM variation is not generally used in combination with LIFO. This does not mean that a company using LIFO ignores the LCM rule. Any obsolete or slow-moving inventory that has not been marked down by year-end can be written down to market after the estimation of inventory using the retail method. This is usually not a significant problem. If prices are rising, LIFO ending inventory includes old lower priced items whose costs are likely to be lower than current market. The LCM variation could be applied to the FIFO method.

THE LIFO RETAIL METHOD.   The last-in, first-out (LIFO) method assumes that units sold are those most recently acquired. When there's a net increase in inventory quantity during a period, the use of LIFO results in ending inventory that includes the beginning inventory as well as one or more additional layers added during the period. When there's a net decrease in inventory quantity, LIFO layer(s) are liquidated. In applying LIFO to the retail method in the simplest way, we assume that the retail prices of goods remained stable during the period. This assumption, which is relaxed later in the chapter, allows us to look at the beginning and ending inventory in dollars to determine if inventory quantity has increased or decreased.

We'll use the numbers from our previous example to illustrate using the retail method to approximate LIFO so we can compare the results with those of the conventional retail method. Recall that beginning inventory at retail is $160,000 and ending inventory at retail is $198,000. If we assume stable retail prices, inventory quantity must have increased during the year. This means ending inventory includes the beginning inventory layer of $160,000 ($99,200 at cost) as well as some additional merchandise purchased during the period. To estimate total ending inventory at LIFO cost, we also need to determine the inventory layer added during the period. When using the LIFO retail method, we assume no more than one inventory layer is added per year if inventory increases.[7] Each layer will carry its own cost-to-retail percentage.

If inventory at retail increases during the year, a new layer is added.

Illustration 9–7 shows how Home Improvement Stores would estimate total ending inventory and cost of goods sold for the period using the LIFO retail method. The beginning inventory layer carries a cost-to-retail percentage of 62% ($99,200 ÷ $160,000). The layer of inventory added during the period is $38,000 at retail, which is determined by subtracting beginning inventory at retail from ending inventory at retail ($198,000 − 160,000). This layer will be converted to cost by multiplying it by its own cost-to-retail percentage reflecting the *current* period's ratio of cost to retail amounts, in this case 64.68%.

The next period's (August's) beginning inventory will include the two distinct layers (June and July), each of which carries its own unique cost-to-retail percentage. Notice in the illustration that both net markups and net markdowns are included in the calculation of the current period's cost-to-retail percentage.

---

[7]Of course, any number of layers at different costs can actually be added through the years. When using the regular LIFO method, rather than LIFO retail, we would keep track of each of those layers.

ILLUSTRATION 9–7		Cost	Retail
LIFO Retail Method	Beginning inventory	$ 99,200	$160,000
	Plus: Net purchases	305,280	470,000
	Net markups		10,000
	Less: Net markdowns		(8,000)
Beginning inventory is excluded from the calculation of the cost-to-retail percentage.	Goods available for sale (excluding beginning inventory)	305,280	472,000
	Goods available for sale (including beginning inventory)	404,480	632,000

Beginning inventory cost-to-retail percentage: $\dfrac{\$99,200}{\$160,000} = 62\%$

July cost-to-retail percentage: $\dfrac{\$305,280}{\$472,000} = 64.68\%$

		Retail
Less: Net sales		(434,000)
Estimated ending inventory at retail		$198,000

Estimated ending inventory at cost:

	Retail	Cost	
Beginning inventory	$160,000 × 62.00% =	$ 99,200	
Current period's layer	38,000 × 64.68% =	24,578	
Total	$198,000	$123,778	(123,778)
Estimated cost of goods sold			$280,702

Each layer has its own cost-to-retail percentage.

Other Issues Pertaining to the Retail Method

To focus on the key elements of the retail method, we've so far ignored some of the details of the retail process. Fundamental elements such as returns and allowances, discounts, freight, spoilage, and shortages can complicate the retail method.

Recall that net purchases is found by adding freight-in to purchases and subtracting both purchase returns and purchase discounts. When these components are considered separately in the retail method, purchase returns are deducted from purchases on both the cost and retail side (at different amounts) and freight-in is added only to the cost side in determining net purchases. If the gross method is used to record purchases, purchase discounts taken also are deducted in determining the cost of net purchases.

If sales are recorded net of employee discounts, the discounts are added to sales.

Likewise, net sales is found by subtracting sales returns from sales. However, sales discounts are *not* subtracted because to do so would cause the inventory to be overstated. Sales discounts do not represent an adjustment in selling price but a financial incentive for customers to pay early. On the other hand, when sales are recorded net of employee discounts, the discounts are *added* to net sales before sales are deducted in the retail column.

For example, suppose an item of merchandise purchased for $6 is initially marked up to $10. Original selling price is therefore $10. When the item is sold, we deduct sales of $10 from the retail column. But if the item is sold to an employee for $7 (a $3 employee discount) and recorded as a $7 sale, the $3 employee discount must be added back to sales so the full $10 is deducted from goods available at retail to arrive at ending inventory at retail.

We also need to consider spoilage, breakage, and theft. So far we've assumed that by subtracting goods sold from goods available for sale, we find ending inventory. It's possible, though, that some of the goods available for sale were lost to such shortages and therefore do not remain in ending inventory.

Normal shortages are deducted in the retail column *after* the calculation of the cost-to-retail percentage.

To take these shortages into account when using the retail method, we deduct the retail value of inventory lost due to spoilage, breakage, or theft in the retail column. These losses are expected for most retail ventures so they are referred to as *normal shortages* (spoilage, breakage, etc.), and are deducted in the retail column *after* the calculation of the cost-to-retail percentage. Because these losses are anticipated, they are included implicitly in the determination of selling prices. Including normal spoilage in the calculation of the percentage would distort the normal relationship between cost and retail. *Abnormal shortages* should be deducted in both the cost and retail columns *before* the calculation of the cost-to-retail percentage. These losses are not anticipated and are not included in the determination of selling prices.

We recap the treatment of special elements in the application of the retail method in Graphic 9–6 and illustrate the use of some of them in the concept review exercise that follows.

GRAPHIC 9–6 Recap of Other Retail Method Elements

Element	Treatment
Before calculating the cost-to-retail percentage:	
Freight-in	*Added* in the cost column.
Purchase returns	*Deducted* in both the cost and retail columns.
Purchase discounts taken (if gross method used to record purchases)	*Deducted* in the cost column.
Abnormal shortages (spoilage, breakage, theft)	*Deducted* in both the cost and retail columns.
After calculating the cost-to-retail percentage:	
Normal shortages (spoilage, breakage, theft)	*Deducted* in the retail column.
Employee discounts (if sales recorded net of discounts)	*Added* to net sales.

CONCEPT REVIEW EXERCISE

The Henderson Company uses the retail inventory method to estimate ending inventory and cost of goods sold. The following data for 2009 are available in Henderson's accounting records:

RETAIL INVENTORY METHOD

	Cost	Retail
Beginning inventory	$ 8,000	$12,000
Purchases	68,000	98,000
Freight-in	3,200	
Purchase returns	3,000	4,200
Net markups		6,000
Net markdowns		2,400
Normal spoilage		1,800
Net sales		92,000

The company records sales net of employee discounts. These discounts for 2009 totaled $2,300.

Required:

1. Estimate Henderson's ending inventory and cost of goods sold for the year using the average cost method.
2. Estimate Henderson's ending inventory and cost of goods sold for the year using the conventional retail method (LCM, average cost).
3. Estimate Henderson's ending inventory and cost of goods sold for the year using the LIFO retail method.

SOLUTION   1. Estimate Henderson's ending inventory and cost of goods sold for the year using the average cost method.

	Cost	Retail
Beginning inventory	$ 8,000	$ 12,000
Plus: Purchases	68,000	98,000
Freight-in	3,200	
Less: Purchase returns	(3,000)	(4,200)
Plus: Net markups		6,000
Less: Net markdowns		(2,400)
Goods available for sale	$76,200	$109,400

Cost-to-retail percentage: $\dfrac{\$76{,}200}{\$109{,}400} = 69.65\%$

Less: Normal spoilage		(1,800)
Sales:		
Net sales	$92,000	
Add back employee discounts	2,300	(94,300)
Estimated ending inventory at retail		$ 13,300
Estimated ending inventory at cost (69.65% × $13,300)	(9,263)	
Estimated cost of goods sold	$66,937	

2. Estimate Henderson's ending inventory and cost of goods sold for the year using the conventional retail method (LCM, average cost).

	Cost	Retail
Beginning inventory	$ 8,000	$ 12,000
Plus: Purchases	68,000	98,000
Freight-in	3,200	
Less: Purchase returns	(3,000)	(4,200)
Plus: net markups		6,000
		111,800

Cost-to-retail percentage: $\dfrac{\$76{,}200}{\$111{,}800} = 68.16\%$

Less: Net markdowns		(2,400)
Goods available for sale	76,200	109,400
Less: Normal spoilage		(1,800)
Sales:		
Net sales	$92,000	
Add back employee discounts	2,300	(94,300)
Estimated ending inventory at retail		$ 13,300
Estimated ending inventory at cost (68.16% × $13,300)	(9,065)	
Estimated cost of goods sold	$67,135	

3. Estimate Henderson's ending inventory and cost of goods sold for the year using the LIFO retail method.

	Cost	Retail
Beginning inventory	$ 8,000	$ 12,000
Plus: Purchases	68,000	98,000
Freight-in	3,200	
Less: Purchase returns	(3,000)	(4,200)
Plus: Net markups		6,000
Less: Net markdowns		(2,400)
Goods available for sale (excluding beginning inventory)	68,200	97,400

(concluded)

Goods available for sale (including beginning inventory)	76,200	109,400

Cost-to-retail percentage: $\dfrac{\$68,200}{\$97,400} = 70.02\%$

Less: Normal spoilage		(1,800)
Sales:		
Net sales	$92,000	
Add back employee discounts	2,300	(94,300)
Estimated ending inventory at retail		$ 13,300
Estimated ending inventory at cost:		

	Retail	Cost	
Beginning inventory	$12,000 × 66.67%*	= $8,000	
Current period's layer	1,300 × 70.02%	= 910	
Total	$13,300	$8,910	(8,910)
Estimated cost of goods sold		$67,290	

*$8,000 ÷ $12,000 = 66.67%

DOLLAR-VALUE LIFO RETAIL

PART **C**

● LO5

FINANCIAL
Reporting Case

Q2, p. 425

In our earlier illustration of the LIFO retail method, we assumed that the retail prices of the inventory remained stable during the period. If you recall, we compared the ending inventory (at retail) with the beginning inventory (at retail) to see if inventory had increased. If the dollar amount of ending inventory exceeded the beginning amount, we assumed a new LIFO layer had been added. But this isn't necessarily true. It may be that the dollar amount of ending inventory exceeded the beginning amount simply because prices increased, without an actual change in the quantity of goods. So, to see if there's been a "real" increase in quantity, we need a way to eliminate the effect of any price changes before we compare the ending inventory with the beginning inventory. Fortunately, we can accomplish this by combining two methods we've already discussed—the LIFO retail method (Part B of this chapter) and dollar-value LIFO (previous chapter). The combination is called the dollar-value LIFO retail method.

To illustrate, we return to the Home Improvement Stores situation (Illustration 9–7) in which we applied LIFO retail. We keep the same inventory data, but change the illustration from the month of July to the fiscal year 2009. This allows us to build into Illustration 9–7A a significant change in retail prices over the year of 10% (an increase in the retail price index from 1 to 1.10). We follow the LIFO retail procedure up to the point of comparing the ending inventory with the beginning inventory. However, because prices have risen, the apparent increase in inventory is only partly due to an additional layer of inventory and partly due to the increase in retail prices. The real increase is found by deflating the ending inventory amount to beginning of the year prices before comparing beginning and ending amounts. We did this with the dollar-value LIFO technique discussed in the previous chapter.[8]

In this illustration, a $20,000 year 2009 layer is added to the base layer. Two adjustments are needed to convert this amount to LIFO cost. Multiplying by the 2009 price index (1.10) converts it from its base year retail to 2009 retail. Multiplying by the 2009 cost-to-retail percentage (.6468) converts it from its 2009 retail to 2009 cost. The two steps are combined in our illustration. The base year inventory also is converted to cost. The two layers are added to derive ending inventory at dollar-value LIFO retail cost.

When additional layers are added in subsequent years, their LIFO amounts are determined the same way. For illustration, let's assume ending inventory in 2010 is $226,200 at current retail prices and the price level has risen to 1.16. Also assume that the cost-to-retail

Using the retail method to approximate LIFO is referred to as the *dollar-value LIFO retail method.*

Each layer year carries its unique retail price index and its unique cost-to-retail percentage.

---

[8]The index used here is analogous to the cost index used in regular DVL except that it reflects the change in retail prices rather than in acquisition costs.

	Cost	Retail
Beginning inventory	$ 99,200	$160,000
Plus: Net purchases	305,280	470,000
Net markups		10,000
Less: Net markdowns		(8,000)
Goods available for sale (excluding beginning inventory)	305,280	472,000
Goods available for sale (including beginning inventory)	404,480	632,000

ILLUSTRATION 9–7A

The Dollar-Value LIFO Retail Method

Base layer cost-to-retail percentage: $\dfrac{\$99,200}{\$160,000} = 62\%$

2009 layer cost-to-retail percentage: $\dfrac{\$305,280}{\$472,000} = 64.68\%$

	Cost	Retail
Less: Net sales		(434,000)
Ending inventory at current year retail prices		$198,000
Estimated ending inventory at cost (calculated below)	(113,430)	
Estimated cost of goods sold	$291,050	

Ending Inventory at Year-End Retail Prices	Step 1 Ending Inventory at Base Year Retail Prices	Step 2 Inventory Layers at Base Year Retail Prices	Step 3 Inventory Layers Converted to Cost
$198,000 (determined above) →	$\dfrac{\$198,000}{1.10}$ = $180,000 →	$180,000	

Base year retail amounts are converted to layer year retail and then to cost.

160,000 (base) × 1.00 × .62 = $ 99,200
$ 20,000 (2009) × 1.10 × .6468 = 14,230

Total ending inventory at dollar-value LIFO retail cost $113,430

percentage for 2010 net purchases is 63%. In Illustration 9–7B, the ending inventory is converted to base year retail (step 1). This amount is apportioned into layers, each at base year retail (step 2). Layers then are converted to layer year costs (step 3).

ILLUSTRATION 9–7B

The Dollar-Value LIFO Retail Inventory Method

Ending Inventory at Year-End Retail Prices	Step 1 Ending Inventory at Base Year Retail Prices	Step 2 Inventory Layers at Base Year Retail Prices	Step 3 Inventory Layers Converted to LIFO Cost
$226,200 (assumed) →	$\dfrac{\$226,200}{1.16}$ = $195,000 →	$195,000	

Base year retail amounts are converted to layer year retail and then to cost.

160,000 (base) × 1.00 × .62 = $ 99,200
20,000 (2009) × 1.10 × .6468 = 14,230
$ 15,000 (2010) × 1.16 × .63 = 10,962

Total ending inventory at dollar-value LIFO retail cost $124,392

Now, let's assume that ending inventory in 2010 is $204,160 at current retail prices (instead of $226,200) and the price level has risen to 1.16. Also assume that the cost-to-retail percentage for 2010 net purchases is 63%. Step 1 converts the ending inventory to a base year price of $176,000 ($204,160 ÷ 1.16). A comparison to the beginning inventory at base year prices of $180,000 ($160,000 base year layer + $20,000 2009 layer) indicates that inventory *decreased* during 2010. In this case, no 2010 layer is added and 2010 ending inventory at dollar-value LIFO retail of $110,584 is determined in Illustration 9–7C.

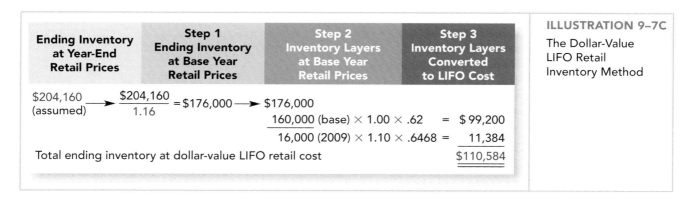

ILLUSTRATION 9-7C

The Dollar-Value
LIFO Retail
Inventory Method

A portion of the 2009 inventory layer has been liquidated—reduced from $20,000 to $16,000 at base year prices—to reduce total inventory at base year prices to $176,000.

As we mentioned earlier in this section, many high-volume retailers selling many different items use the retail method. **J.C. Penney Company, Inc.,** for example, uses the dollar-value LIFO variation of the retail method. Graphic 9–7 shows the inventory disclosure note included in the company's recent financial statements.

GRAPHIC 9-7

Disclosure of Inventory
Method—J.C. Penney
Company, Inc.

Real World Financials

Summary of Significant Accounting Policies (in part) Merchandise Inventories

Inventories are valued primarily at the lower of cost (using the last-in, first-out, or LIFO, method) or market, determined by the retail method for department stores and store distribution centers, and standard cost, representing average vendor cost, for direct and regional warehouses. The lower of cost or market is determined on an aggregate basis for similar types of merchandise. To estimate the effects of inflation/deflation on ending inventory, an internal index measuring price changes from the beginning to the end of the year is calculated using merchandise cost data at the item level.

Notice that J.C. Penney uses an internal index to adjust for changing prices and that the lower-of-cost-or-market rule is determined on an aggregate basis for similar types of merchandise.

CONCEPT REVIEW EXERCISE

On January 1, 2009, the Nicholson Department Store adopted the dollar-value LIFO retail inventory method. Inventory transactions at both cost and retail and cost indexes for 2009 and 2010 are as follows:

DOLLAR-VALUE LIFO
RETAIL METHOD

	2009		2010	
	Cost	Retail	Cost	Retail
Beginning inventory	$16,000	$24,000		
Net purchases	42,000	58,500	45,000	58,700
Net markups		3,000		2,400
Net markdowns		1,500		1,100
Net sales		56,000		57,000
Price index:				
January 1, 2009	1.00			
December 31, 2009	1.08			
December 31, 2010	1.15			

Required:
Estimate the 2009 and 2010 ending inventory and cost of goods sold using the dollar-value LIFO retail inventory method.

SOLUTION

	2009		2010	
	Cost	**Retail**	**Cost**	**Retail**
Beginning inventory	$16,000	$24,000	$17,456	$28,000
Plus: Net purchases	42,000	58,500	45,000	58,700
Net markups		3,000		2,400
Less: Net markdowns		(1,500)		(1,100)
Goods available for sale (excluding beg. inv.)	42,000	60,000	45,000	60,000
Goods available for sale (including beg. inv.)	58,000	84,000	62,456	88,000
Base layer				

Cost-to-retail percentage: $\dfrac{\$16,000}{\$24,000} = 66.67\%$

2009

Cost-to-retail percentage: $\dfrac{\$42,000}{\$60,000} = 70\%$

2010

Cost-to-retail percentage: $\dfrac{\$45,000}{\$60,000} = 75\%$

Less: Net sales		(56,000)		(57,000)
Estimated ending inv. at current year retail prices		$28,000		$31,000
Less: Estimated ending inventory at cost (below)	(17,456)		(18,345)	
Estimated cost of goods sold	$40,544		$44,111	

2009

Ending Inventory at Year-End Retail Prices	Step 1 Ending Inventory at Base Year Retail Prices	Step 2 Inventory Layers at Base Year Retail Prices	Step 3 Inventory Layers Converted to Cost
$28,000 (above)	$\dfrac{\$28,000}{1.08} = 25,926$	$24,000 (base) × 1.00 × 66.67% =	$16,000
		1,926 (2009) × 1.08 × 70.00% =	1,456
Total ending inventory at dollar-value LIFO retail cost			$17,456

2010

Ending Inventory at Year-End Retail Prices	Step 1 Ending Inventory at Base Year Retail Prices	Step 2 Inventory Layers at Base Year Retail Prices	Step 3 Inventory Layers Converted to Cost
$31,000 (above)	$\dfrac{\$31,000}{1.15} = \$26,957$	$24,000 (base) × 1.00 × 66.67% =	$16,000
		1,926 (2009) × 1.08 × 70.00% =	1,456
		1,031 (2010) × 1.15 × 75.00% =	889
Total ending inventory at dollar-value LIFO retail cost			$18,345

PART D

CHANGE IN INVENTORY METHOD AND INVENTORY ERRORS

Change in Inventory Method

● LO6

Accounting principles should be applied consistently from period to period to allow for comparability of operating results. However, changes within a company as well as changes in the external economic environment may require a company to change an accounting method. As we mentioned in Chapter 8, high inflation in the 1970s motivated many companies to switch to the LIFO inventory method.

Specific accounting treatment and disclosures are prescribed for companies that change accounting principles. Chapter 4 introduced the subject of accounting changes and Chapter 20 provides in-depth coverage of the topic. Here we provide an overview of how changes in inventory methods are reported.

Most Inventory Changes

Recall from our discussion in Chapter 4 that most voluntary changes in accounting principles are reported retrospectively. This means reporting all previous periods' financial statements as if the new method had been used in all prior periods. Changes in inventory methods, other than a change to LIFO, are treated this way. We discuss the *to LIFO* exception in the next section. In Chapter 4 we outlined the steps a company undertakes to account for a change in inventory method. We demonstrate those steps using a real world example in Illustrations 9–8 and 9–8A.

> Changes in inventory methods, other than a change to LIFO, are accounted for retrospectively.

McKesson Corporation is a Fortune 100 company producing products and services in the healthcare industry. In a note accompanying its 2007 financial statements, the company disclosed that it uses the LIFO inventory method for 87% of its inventories and FIFO for the remainder. The company's balance sheets reported inventories of $8,153 million and $7,127 million at the end of 2007 and 2006, respectively. The inventory disclosure note reports that if the FIFO method had been used to value the entire inventory, instead of just 13% of it, inventories would have been $8,244 million and $7,283 million at the end of 2007 and 2006, respectively. Partial income statements for 2007 and 2006 are as follows:

McKESSON CORPORATION
Partial Income Statements
For the Years Ended March 31,

	($ in millions)	
	2007	**2006**
Sales revenue	$92,977	$86,983
Cost of goods sold	88,645	83,206
Gross profit	4,332	3,777
Operating expenses	3,068	2,651
Operating income	$ 1,264	$ 1,126

Let's suppose that in 2007 McKesson decided to value all of its inventories using the FIFO method.

> **ILLUSTRATION 9–8**
> Change in Inventory Method
>
> **Real World Financials**

McKESSON CORPORATION
Partial Income Statements
For the Years Ended March 31,

	($ in millions)	
	2007	**2006**
Sales revenue	$92,977	$86,983
Cost of goods sold	88,710	83,237
Gross profit	4,267	3,746
Operating expenses	3,068	2,651
Operating income	$ 1,199	$ 1,095

2007 cost of goods sold of $88,710 million is $65 million higher on a 100% FIFO basis. Here's why. McKesson's note reported that beginning inventory is $156 million higher ($7,283 − 7,127), and ending inventory also is higher by $91 million ($8,244 − 8,153). An increase in beginning inventory causes an increase in cost of goods sold, but an increase in ending inventory causes a decrease in cost of goods sold. The net effect of the two adjustments ($156 − 91) is the $65 million increase in cost of goods sold.

In a similar manner, 2006 cost of goods sold would be adjusted to $83,237 million. A note included in McKesson's 2006 financial statements reports that 2005 ending inventory of $7,495 million would have been $7,682 million on an all FIFO basis. 2006's beginning inventory would have been $187 higher ($7,682 − 7,495) and ending inventory for 2006 would be $156 million higher ($7,283 − 7,127). The net effect of the two adjustments ($187 − 156) is that cost of goods sold would be $31 million higher.

> **ILLUSTRATION 9–8A**
> Income statements—100% FIFO
>
> McKesson would report 2007 cost of goods sold by its newly adopted method, 100% FIFO.
>
> McKesson would increase the amount it reported last year for its cost of goods sold as if 100% FIFO had been used.

Step 1: Revise Comparative Financial Statements

The first step is to revise prior years' financial statements. That is, for each year reported in the comparative statements, McKesson makes those statements appear as if the newly adopted accounting method (100% FIFO) had been applied all along. In its balance sheets, McKesson would report 2007 inventory by its newly adopted method, 100% FIFO, and also would revise the amounts it reported last year for its 2006 inventory. In its income statements, cost of goods sold also would reflect the new method in both 2007 and 2006 as shown in Illustration 9–8A.

In its statements of shareholders' equity, McKesson would report retained earnings each year as if it had used FIFO all along, and for the earliest year reported, it would revise beginning retained earnings that year to reflect the cumulative income effect of the difference in inventory methods for all prior years. We see this step illustrated in Chapter 20 after you have studied the statement of shareholders' equity in more depth.

Step 2: The appropriate accounts are adjusted.

McKesson also would create a journal entry to adjust the book balances from their current amounts to what those balances would have been using 100% FIFO. Since differences in cost of goods sold and income are reflected in retained earnings, as are the income tax effects, the journal entry updates inventory, retained earnings, and the appropriate income tax account. We ignore the income tax effects here and include those effects in an illustration in Chapter 20. The journal entry below, *ignoring income taxes,* adjusts the 2007 beginning inventory to the 100% FIFO basis amount of $7,283 million.

Inventory at the beginning of 2007 would be $156 million higher if FIFO is used to value the entire inventory.

		($ in millions)
Inventory ($7,283 − 7,127)		156
Retained earnings		156

Step 3: A disclosure note provides additional information.

McKesson must provide in a disclosure note clear justification that the change to 100% FIFO is appropriate. The note also would indicate the effects of the change on items not reported on the face of the primary statements, as well as any per share amounts affected for the current period and all prior periods presented.

We see an example of such a note in a recent annual report of **Hormel Foods Corporation,** a leading processor of meat and food products, when it changed its inventory method from LIFO to FIFO. Graphic 9–8 shows the disclosure note that described the change.

GRAPHIC 9–8

Disclosure of Change in Inventory Method—Hormel Foods Corporation

Real World Financials

Change in Accounting Principle (in part)
In the first quarter of 2006, the company changed its method of accounting for the materials portion of turkey products and substantially all inventoriable expenses, packages, and supplies that had previously been accounted for utilizing the Last-In First-Out (LIFO) method to the First-In First-Out (FIFO) method. As a result, all inventories are now stated at the lower of cost, determined on a FIFO basis, or market. The change is preferable because it provides a more meaningful presentation of the company's financial position as it values inventory in a manner which more closely approximates current cost; it provides a consistent and uniform costing method across the company's operations; FIFO inventory values better represent the underlying commercial substance of selling the oldest products first; it is the prevalent method used by other entities within the company's industry; and it enhances the comparability of the financial statements with those of our industry peers.

As required by U.S. generally accepted accounting principles, the change has been reflected in the consolidated statements of financial position, consolidated statements of operations, and consolidated statements of cash flows through retrospective application of the FIFO method. Inventories as of the beginning of fiscal 2005 were increased by $36.7 million . . . Previously reported net earnings for fiscal years 2005 and 2004 were increased by $1.1 million and $1.9 million, respectively.

Change to the LIFO Method

Accounting records usually are inadequate for a company changing to *LIFO* to report the change retrospectively.

When a company changes *to the LIFO inventory method* from any other method, it usually is impossible to calculate the income effect on prior years. To do so would require assumptions as to when specific LIFO inventory layers were created in years prior to the change. As a result, a company changing to LIFO usually does not report the change retrospectively. Instead, the LIFO method simply is used from that point on. The base year inventory for all future LIFO determinations is the beginning inventory in the year the LIFO method is adopted.[9]

A disclosure note is needed to explain (a) the nature of and justification for the change, (b) the effect of the change on current year's income and earnings per share, and (c) why retrospective application was impracticable. When **General Cable Corporation** adopted the LIFO inventory method, it reported the change in the note shown in Graphic 9–9.

Inventories (in part)

As of January 1, General Cable changed its accounting method for its North American non-metal inventories from the FIFO method to the LIFO method. The impact of the change was an increase in operating income of $6.4 million, or $0.12 of earnings per share on both a basic and diluted basis during the year. The cumulative effect of the change on prior years was not determinable. The Company believes that the change to the LIFO accounting method for its North American non-metal inventories more accurately reflects the impact of both volatile raw material prices and ongoing cost productivity initiatives, conforms the accounting for all North American inventories and provides a more comparable basis of accounting with direct competitors in North America who are on LIFO for the majority of their inventories.

GRAPHIC 9–9

Change in Inventory Method Disclosure— General Cable Corporation

Real World Financials

As we discussed in Chapter 8, an important motivation for using LIFO in periods of rising costs is that it produces higher cost of goods sold and lowers income and income taxes. Notice in the disclosure note that the switch to LIFO caused an *increase* in income in the year of the switch indicating an environment of decreasing costs. General Cable had reasons other than an immediate reduction in its tax bill for switching to LIFO.

ADDITIONAL CONSIDERATION

When changing from one generally accepted accounting principle to another, a company must justify that the change results in financial information that more properly portrays operating results and financial position. For income tax purposes, a company generally must obtain consent from the Internal Revenue Service before changing an accounting method. A special form also must be filed with the IRS when a company intends to adopt the LIFO inventory method. When a company changes from LIFO for tax purposes, it can't change back to LIFO until five tax returns have been filed using the non-LIFO method.

Inventory Errors

Accounting errors must be corrected when they are discovered. In Chapter 4 we briefly discussed the correction of accounting errors and Chapter 20 provides in-depth coverage. Here we provide an overview of the accounting treatment and disclosures in the context of inventory errors. Inventory errors include the over- or understatement of ending inventory due to a mistake in physical count or a mistake in pricing inventory quantities. Also, errors include the over- or understatement of purchases which could be caused by the cutoff errors described in Chapter 8.

● LO7

If an inventory error is discovered in the same accounting period it occurred, the original erroneous entry should simply be reversed and the appropriate entry recorded. This situation presents no particular reporting problem.

If a *material* inventory error is discovered in an accounting period subsequent to the period in which the error was made, any previous years' financial statements that were incorrect as a result of the error are retrospectively restated to reflect the correction.[10] And, of course, any account balances that are incorrect as a result of the error are corrected by journal entry. If, due to an error affecting net income, retained earnings is one of the incorrect accounts, the correction is reported as a prior period adjustment to the beginning balance on the statement

For material errors, previous years' financial statements are retrospectively restated.

---

[9]A change to LIFO is handled the same way for income tax purposes.
[10]If the effect of the error is not material, it is simply corrected in the year of discovery.

of shareholders' equity.[11] In addition, a disclosure note is needed to describe the nature of the error and the impact of its correction on net income, income before extraordinary items, and earnings per share.

When analyzing inventory errors, it's helpful to visualize the way cost of goods sold, net income, and retained earnings are determined (see Graphic 9–10). Beginning inventory and net purchases are *added* in the calculation of cost of goods sold. If either of these is overstated (understated) then cost of goods sold would be overstated (understated). On the other hand, ending inventory is *deducted* in the calculation of cost of goods sold, so if ending inventory is overstated (understated) then cost of goods sold is understated (overstated). Of course, errors that affect income also will affect income taxes. In the illustration that follows, we ignore the tax effects of the errors and focus on the errors themselves rather than their tax aspects.

GRAPHIC 9–10

Visualizing the Effect of Inventory Errors

Let's look at an example in Illustration 9–9.

ILLUSTRATION 9–9

Inventory Error Correction

The Barton Company uses a periodic inventory system. At the end of 2008, a mathematical error caused an $800,000 overstatement of ending inventory. Ending inventories for 2009 and 2010 are correctly determined.

The way we correct this error depends on when the error is discovered. Assuming that the error is not discovered until after 2009, the 2008 and 2009 effects of the error, ignoring income tax effects, are shown below. The overstated and understated amounts are $800,000 in each instance.

Analysis: U = Understated   O = Overstated

2008		2009	
Beginning inventory		Beginning inventory	O - 800,000
Plus: Net puchases		Plus: Net puchases	
Less: Ending inventory	O - 800,000	Less: Ending inventory	
Cost of goods sold	U - 800,000	Cost of goods sold	O - 800,000
Revenues		Revenues	
Less: Cost of goods sold	U - 800,000	Less: Cost of goods sold	O - 800,000
Less: Other expenses		Less: Other expenses	
Net income	O - 800,000	Net income	U - 800,000
↓		↓	
Retained earnings	O - 800,000	Retained earnings	*corrected*

When the Inventory Error is Discovered the Following Year

First, let's assume the error is discovered in 2009. The 2008 financial statements that were incorrect as a result of the error are retrospectively restated to reflect the correct inventory amount, cost of goods sold, net income, and retained earnings when those statements are

---

[11]The prior period adjustment is applied to beginning retained earnings for the year following the error, or for the earliest year being reported in the comparative financial statements when the error occurs prior to the earliest year presented. The retained earnings balances in years after the first year also are adjusted to what those balances would be if the error had not occurred, but a company may choose not to explicitly report those adjustments as separate line items.

reported again for comparative purposes in the 2009 annual report. The following journal entry, ignoring income taxes, corrects the error.

Retained earnings	800,000	
Inventory		800,000

A journal entry corrects any incorrect account balance.

Because retained earnings is one of the accounts that is incorrect, when the error is discovered in 2009, the correction to that account is reported as a prior period adjustment to the 2009 beginning retained earnings balance in Barton's statement of shareholders' equity (or statement of retained earnings). Prior period adjustments do not flow through the income statement but directly adjust retained earnings. This adjustment is illustrated in Chapter 20.

When retained earnings requires correction, a prior period adjustment is made on the statement of shareholders' equity.

When the Inventory Error is Discovered Subsequent to the Following Year

If the error isn't discovered until 2010, the 2009 financial statements also are retrospectively restated to reflect the correct cost of goods sold and net income even though no correcting entry would be needed at that point. Inventory and retained earnings would not require adjustment. The error has self-corrected and no prior period adjustment is needed.

Also, a disclosure note in Barton's annual report should describe the nature of the error and the impact of its correction on each year's net income (overstated by $800,000 in 2008; understated by $800,000 in 2009), income before extraordinary items (same as net income in this case), and earnings per share.

A disclosure note describes the nature of the error and the impact of the correction on income.

CONCEPT REVIEW **EXERCISE**

In 2009, the controller of the Fleischman Wholesale Beverage Company discovered the following material errors related to the 2007 and 2008 financial statements:

INVENTORY ERRORS

a. Inventory at the end of 2007 was understated by $50,000.
b. Late in 2008, a $3,000 purchase was incorrectly recorded as a $33,000 purchase. The invoice has not yet been paid.
c. Inventory at the end of 2008 was overstated by $20,000.

    The company uses a periodic inventory system.

Required:
1. Assuming that the errors were discovered after the 2008 financial statements were issued, analyze the effect of the errors on 2007 and 2008 cost of goods sold, net income, and retained earnings. Ignore income taxes.
2. Prepare a journal entry to correct the errors.

1.   **Analysis:**   **U = Understated**   **O = Overstated**

SOLUTION

2007		2008	
Beginning inventory		Beginning inventory	U - 50,000
Plus: Net purchases		Plus: Net purchases	O - 30,000
Less: Ending inventory	U - 50,000	Less: Ending inventory	O - 20,000
Cost of goods sold	O - 50,000	Cost of goods sold	U - 40,000
Revenues		Revenues	
Less: Cost of goods sold	O - 50,000	Less: Cost of goods sold	U - 40,000
Less: Other expenses		Less: Other expenses	
Net income	U - 50,000	Net income	O - 40,000
↓		↓	
Retained earnings	U - 50,000	Retained earnings	U - 10,000

2. Prepare a journal entry to correct the errors.

Accounts payable	30,000	
Inventory		20,000
Retained earnings		10,000

Earnings Quality

A change in the accounting method a company uses to value inventory is one way managers can artificially manipulate income. However, this method of income manipulation is transparent. As we learned in a previous section, the effect on income of switching from one inventory method to another must be disclosed. That disclosure restores comparability between periods and enhances earnings quality.

On the other hand, inventory write-downs are included in the broader category of "big bath" accounting techniques some companies use to manipulate earnings. By overstating the write-down, profits are increased in future periods as the inventory is used or sold. When the demand for many high technology products decreased significantly in late 2000 and early 2001, several companies, including **Sycamore Networks, Lucent Technologies,** and **JDS Uniphase,** recorded large inventory write-offs, some in the billions of dollars. In the introduction to this chapter, we discussed the over $2 billion inventory write-off recorded by **Cisco Systems.** Certainly these write-offs reflected the existing economic environment. However, some analysts questioned the size of some of the write-offs. For example, William Schaff, an investment officer at Bay Isle Financial noted that Cisco's write-off was approximately equal to the balance of inventory on hand at the end of the previous quarter and about equal to the cost of goods actually sold during the quarter.

> **WILLIAM SCHAFF—
> BAY ISLE FINANCIAL**
> I have nothing on which to base these theories other than the fact that writing off a whole quarter's inventory seems a bit much to just shrug off. It's very disturbing.[12]

Inventory write-downs often are cited as a method used to shift income between periods.

A financial analyst must carefully consider the effect of any significant asset write-down on the assessment of a company's permanent earnings.

FINANCIAL REPORTING CASE **SOLUTION**

1. **Sears values its inventory at the lower of cost or market. What does that mean? Under what circumstances might Sears be justified in reporting its inventory at less than cost?** *(p. 426)* A departure from historical cost is warranted when the probable benefits to be received from any asset drop below the asset's cost. The benefits from inventory result from the ultimate sale of the goods. Deterioration, obsolescence, and changes in price levels are situations that might cause the benefits to be received from sale to drop below cost. The lower-of-cost-or-market approach recognizes losses in the period when the value of the inventory declines below its cost rather than in the period in which the goods ultimately are sold.

2. **How does Sears avoid counting all its inventory every time it produces financial statements? What are external price indices used for?** *(p. 443)* Sears uses the dollar-value LIFO retail inventory method. The retail inventory estimation technique avoids the counting of ending inventory by keeping track of goods available for sale not only at cost but also at retail prices. Each period's sales, at sales prices, are deducted from the retail amount of goods available for sale to arrive at ending inventory at retail. This amount is then converted to cost using a cost-to-retail percentage.

   The dollar-value LIFO retail method uses a price index to first convert ending inventory at retail to base year prices. Yearly LIFO layers are then determined and each layer is converted to that year's current year retail prices using the year's price index and then to cost using the layer's cost-to-retail percentage. For the price index, Sears uses an external index rather than an internally generated price index. ●

---

[12]William Schaff, "What Is the Definition of an Earnings Bath," *Information Week Online,* April 24, 2001.

THE **BOTTOM LINE**

● **LO1**   Inventory is valued at the lower of cost or market (LCM). The designated market value in the LCM rule is the middle number of replacement cost (RC), net realizable value (NRV), and net realizable value less a normal profit margin (NRV − NP). (p. 426)

● **LO2**   The gross profit method estimates cost of goods sold which is then subtracted from cost of goods available for sale to estimate ending inventory. The estimate of cost of goods sold is determined by subtracting an estimate of gross profit from net sales. The estimate of gross profit is determined by multiplying the historical gross profit ratio times net sales. (p. 433)

● **LO3**   The retail inventory method determines the amount of ending inventory at retail by subtracting sales for the period from goods available for sale at retail. Ending inventory at retail is then converted to *cost* by multiplying it by the cost-to-retail percentage, which is based on a current relationship between cost and selling price. (p. 435)

● **LO4**   By the conventional retail method, we estimate average cost at lower of cost or market. Average cost is estimated by including beginning inventory in the calculation of the cost-to-retail percentage. LCM is estimated by excluding markdowns from the calculation. Markdowns are subtracted in the retail column after the percentage is calculated. (p. 438)

● **LO5**   By the LIFO retail method, ending inventory includes the beginning inventory plus the current year's layer. To determine layers, we compare ending inventory at retail to beginning inventory at retail and assume that no more than one inventory layer is added if inventory increases. Each layer carries its own cost-to-retail percentage which is used to convert each layer from retail to cost. The dollar-value LIFO retail inventory method combines the LIFO retail method and the dollar-value LIFO method (Chapter 8) to estimate LIFO from retail prices when the price level has changed. (p. 443)

● **LO6**   Most changes in inventory methods are reported retrospectively. This means revising all previous periods' financial statements to appear as if the newly adopted inventory method had been applied all along. An exception is a change to the LIFO method. In this case, it usually is impossible to calculate the income effect on prior years. To do so would require assumptions as to when specific LIFO inventory layers were created in years prior to the change. As a result, a company changing to LIFO usually does not report the change retrospectively. Instead, the LIFO method simply is used from that point on. (p. 446)

● **LO7**   If a material inventory error is discovered in an accounting period subsequent to the period in which the error is made, previous years' financial statements that were incorrect as a result of the error are retrospectively restated to reflect the correction. Account balances are corrected by journal entry. A correction of retained earnings is reported as a prior period adjustment to the beginning balance in the statement of shareholders' equity. In addition, a disclosure note is needed to describe the nature of the error and the impact of its correction on income. (p. 449) ●

PURCHASE COMMITMENTS

APPENDIX 9

Purchase commitments protect the buyer against price increases and provide a supply of product.

Purchase commitments are contracts that obligate a company to purchase a specified amount of merchandise or raw materials at specified prices on or before specified dates. Companies enter into these agreements to make sure they will be able to obtain important inventory as well as to protect against increases in purchase price. However, if the purchase price decreases before the agreement is exercised, the commitment has the disadvantage of requiring the company to purchase inventory at a higher than market price. If this happens, a loss on the purchase commitment is recorded.

Because purchase commitments create the possibility of this kind of loss, the loss occurs when the market price falls below the commitment price rather than when the inventory eventually is sold. This means recording the loss when the product is purchased or, if the commitment is still outstanding, at the end of the reporting period. In other words, purchases are recorded at market price when that price is lower than the contract price, and a loss is recognized for the difference. Also, losses are recognized for any purchase commitments outstanding at the end of a reporting period when market price is less than contract price. In effect, the LCM rule is applied to purchase commitments. This is best understood by the example in Illustration 9A–1.

Purchases made pursuant to a purchase commitment are recorded at the lower of contract price or market price on the date the contract is executed.

ILLUSTRATION 9A–1	In July 2009, the Lassiter Company signed two purchase commitments. The first requires Lassiter to purchase inventory for $500,000 by November 15, 2009. The second requires the company to purchase inventory for $600,000 by February 15, 2010. Lassiter's fiscal year-end is December 31. The company uses a perpetual inventory system.
Purchase Commitments	

Contract Period within Fiscal Year

The contract period for the first commitment is contained within a single fiscal year. Lassiter would record the purchase at the contract price if the market price at date of acquisition is at least *equal to* the contract price of $500,000.[13]

If market price is equal to or greater than the contract price, the purchase is recorded at the contract price.

Inventory (contract price)	500,000	
Cash (or accounts payable)		500,000

If the market price at acquisition is *less* than the contract price, inventory is recorded at the market price and a loss is recognized.[14] For example, if the market price is $425,000, the following entry records the purchase:

If market price is less than the contract price, the purchase is recorded at the market price.

Inventory (market price)	425,000	
Loss on purchase commitment	75,000	
Cash (or accounts payable)		500,000

The objective of this treatment is to associate the loss with the period in which the price declines rather than with the period in which the company eventually sells the inventory. This is the same objective as the LCM rule you studied in the chapter.

Contract Period Extends beyond Fiscal Year

Now let's consider Lassiter's second purchase commitment that is outstanding at the end of the fiscal year 2009 (that is, the purchases have not yet been made). If the market price at the end of the year is at least *equal* to the contract price of $600,000, no entry is recorded. However, if the market price at year-end is *less* than the contract price, a loss must be recognized to satisfy the LCM objective of associating the loss with the period in which the price declines rather than with the period in which the company eventually sells the inventory. Let's say the year-end market price of the inventory for Lassiter's second purchase commitment is $540,000. The following adjusting entry is recorded:

If the market price at year-end is less than the contract price a loss is recorded for the difference.

December 31, 2009

Estimated loss on purchase commitment ($600,000 − 540,000)........	60,000	
Estimated liability on purchase commitment...............................		60,000

At this point, the loss is an *estimated* loss. The actual loss, if any, will not be known until the inventory actually is purchased. The best estimate of the market price on date of purchase is the current market price, in this case $540,000. Because no inventory has been acquired, we can't credit inventory for the LCM loss. Instead, a liability is credited because, in a sense, the loss represents an obligation to the seller of the inventory to purchase inventory above market price.

A liability is credited for estimated losses on purchase commitments.

The entry to record the actual purchase on or before February 15, 2010, will vary depending on the market price of the inventory at date of purchase. If the market price is unchanged or has increased from the year-end price, the following entry is made:

---

[13]In each of the following situations, if a periodic inventory system is used *purchases* is debited instead of *inventory*.
[14]Recall from the LCM discussion in the chapter that the preferred method of recording losses from inventory write-downs is to recognize the loss as a separate item in the income statement, rather than as an increase in cost of goods sold.

Inventory (accounting cost)	540,000	
Estimated liability on purchase commitment	60,000	
Cash (or accounts payable)		600,000

If market price on purchase date has not declined from year-end price, the purchase is recorded at the year-end market price.

Even if the market price of the inventory increases, there is no recovery of the $60,000 loss recognized in 2009. Remember that when the LCM rule is applied, the reduced inventory value, in this case the reduced value of purchases, is considered to be the new cost and any recovery of value is ignored.

If the market price declines even further from year-end levels, an additional loss is recognized. For example, if the market price of the inventory covered by the commitment declines to $510,000, the following entry is recorded:

Inventory (market price)	510,000	
Loss on purchase commitment ($540,000 − 510,000)	30,000	
Estimated liability on purchase commitment	60,000	
Cash (or accounts payable)		600,000

If market price on purchase date declines from year-end price, the purchase is recorded at the market price.

The total loss on this purchase commitment of $90,000 is thus allocated between 2009 and 2010 according to when the decline in value of the inventory covered by the commitment occurred.

If there are material amounts of purchase commitments outstanding at the end of a reporting period, the contract details are disclosed in a note. This disclosure is required even if no loss estimate has been recorded. ●

QUESTIONS FOR REVIEW OF KEY TOPICS

Q 9–1   Explain the lower-of-cost-or-market approach to valuing inventory.

Q 9–2   What is the meaning of market in the lower-of-cost-or-market rule?

Q 9–3   What are the various ways the LCM determination can be made?

Q 9–4   Describe the preferred method of adjusting from cost to market for material inventory write-downs.

Q 9–5   Explain the gross profit method of estimating ending inventory.

Q 9–6   The Rider Company uses the gross profit method to estimate ending inventory and cost of goods sold. The cost percentage is determined based on historical data. What factors could cause the estimate of ending inventory to be overstated?

Q 9–7   Explain the retail inventory method of estimating ending inventory.

Q 9–8   Both the gross profit method and the retail inventory method provide a way to estimate ending inventory. What is the main difference between the two estimation techniques?

Q 9–9   Define each of the following retail terms: initial markup, additional markup, markup cancellation, markdown, markdown cancellation.

Q 9–10   Explain how to estimate the average cost of inventory when using the retail inventory method.

Q 9–11   What is the conventional retail method?

Q 9–12   Explain the LIFO retail inventory method.

Q 9–13   Discuss the treatment of freight-in, net markups, normal spoilage, and employee discounts in the application of the retail inventory method.

Q 9–14   Explain the difference between the retail inventory method using LIFO and the dollar-value LIFO retail method.

Q 9–15   Describe the accounting treatment for a change in inventory method other than to LIFO.

Q 9–16   When a company changes its inventory method to LIFO, an exception is made for the way accounting changes usually are reported. Explain the difference in the accounting treatment of a change *to* the LIFO inventory method from other inventory method changes.

Q 9–17   Explain the accounting treatment of material inventory errors discovered in an accounting period subsequent to the period in which the error is made.

Q 9–18   It is discovered in 2009 that ending inventory in 2007 was understated. What is the effect of the understatement on the following:

2007:   Cost of goods sold
Net income
Ending retained earnings
2008:   Net purchases
Cost of goods sold
Net income
Ending retained earnings

Q 9–19   (Based on Appendix 9) Define purchase commitments. What is the advantage(s) of these agreements to buyers?

Q 9–20   (Based on Appendix 9) Explain how the lower-of-cost-or-market rule is applied to purchase commitments.

BRIEF EXERCISES

BE 9–1
Lower of cost or market

● LO1

Ross Electronics has one product in its ending inventory. Per unit data consist of the following: cost, $20; replacement cost, $18; selling price, $30; disposal costs, $4. The normal profit margin is 30% of selling price. What unit value should Ross use when applying the LCM rule to ending inventory?

BE 9–2
Lower of cost or market

● LO1

SLR Corporation has 1,000 units of each of its two products in its year-end inventory. Per unit data for each of the products are as follows:

	Product 1	Product 2
Cost	$50	$30
Replacement cost	48	26
Selling price	70	36
Disposal costs	6	4
Normal profit margin	10	8

Determine the balance sheet carrying value of SLR's inventory assuming that the LCM rule is applied to individual products. What is the before-tax income effect of the LCM adjustment?

BE 9–3
Gross profit method

● LO2

On February 26 a hurricane destroyed the entire inventory stored in a warehouse owned by the Rockford Corporation. The following information is available from the records of the company's periodic inventory system: beginning inventory, $220,000; purchases and net sales from the beginning of the year through February 26, $400,000 and $600,000, respectively; gross profit ratio, 30%. Estimate the cost of the inventory destroyed by the hurricane using the gross profit method.

BE 9–4
Gross profit method; solving for unknown

● LO2

Adams Corporation estimates that it lost $75,000 in inventory from a recent flood. The following information is available from the records of the company's periodic inventory system: beginning inventory, $150,000; purchases and net sales from the beginning of the year through the date of the flood, $450,000 and $700,000, respectively. What is the company's gross profit ratio?

BE 9–5
Retail inventory method; average cost

● LO3

Kiddie World uses a periodic inventory system and the retail inventory method to estimate ending inventory and cost of goods sold. The following data are available for the quarter ending September 30, 2009:

	Cost	Retail
Beginning inventory	$300,000	$ 450,000
Net purchases	861,000	1,210,000
Freight-in	22,000	
Net markups		48,000
Net markdowns		18,000
Net sales		1,200,000

Estimate ending inventory and cost of goods sold (average cost).

BE 9–6
Retail inventory
method; LIFO

● LO3

Refer to the situation described in BE 9–5. Estimate ending inventory and cost of goods sold (LIFO).

BE 9–7
Conventional retail
method

● LO4

Refer to the situation described in BE 9–5. Estimate ending inventory and cost of goods sold using the conventional method (average cost and the LCM approximation).

BE 9–8
Conventional retail
method

● LO4

Roberson Corporation uses a periodic inventory system and the retail inventory method. Accounting records provided the following information for the 2009 fiscal year:

	Cost	Retail
Beginning inventory	$220,000	$ 400,000
Net purchases	640,000	1,180,000
Freight-in	17,800	
Net markups		16,000
Net markdowns		6,000
Normal spoilage		3,000
Net sales		1,300,000

The company records sales to employees net of discounts. These discounts totaled $15,000 for the year. Estimate ending inventory and cost of goods sold using the conventional method (average cost and the LCM approximation).

BE 9–9
Dollar-value LIFO
retail

● LO5

On January 1, 2009, Sanderson Variety Store adopted the dollar-value LIFO retail inventory method. Accounting records provided the following information:

	Cost	Retail
Beginning inventory	$ 40,800	$ 68,000
Net purchases	155,440	270,000
Net markups		6,000
Net markdowns		8,000
Net sales		250,000
Retail price index, end of year		1.02

Calculate the inventory value at the end of the year using the dollar-value LIFO retail method.

BE 9–10
Dollar-value LIFO
retail

● LO5

This exercise is a continuation of BE 9–9. During 2010, purchases at cost and retail were $168,000 and $301,000, respectively. Net markups, net markdowns, and net sales for the year were $3,000, $4,000, and $280,000, respectively. The retail price index at the end of 2010 was 1.06. Calculate the inventory value at the end of 2010 using the dollar-value LIFO retail method.

BE 9–11
Change in
inventory costing
methods

● LO6

In 2009, Hopyard Lumber changed its inventory method from LIFO to FIFO. Inventory at the end of 2008 of $127,000 would have been $145,000 if FIFO had been used. Inventory at the end of 2009 is $162,000 using the new FIFO method but would have been $151,000 if the company had continued to use LIFO. Describe the steps Hopyard should take to report this change. What is the effect of the change on 2009 cost of goods sold?

BE 9–12
Change in inventory
costing methods

● LO6

In 2009, Wade Window and Glass changed its inventory method from FIFO to LIFO. Inventory at the end of 2008 is $150,000. Describe the steps Wade Window and Glass should take to report this change.

BE 9–13
Inventory error

● LO7

In 2009, Winslow International, Inc.'s controller discovered that ending inventories for 2007 and 2008 were overstated by $200,000 and $500,000, respectively. Determine the effect of the errors on retained earnings at January 1, 2009. (Ignore income taxes.)

BE 9–14
Inventory error

● LO7

Refer to the situation described in BE 9–13. What steps would be taken to report the error in the 2009 financial statements?

An alternate exercise and problem set is available on the text website: www.mhhe.com/spiceland5e

E 9–1
Lower of cost or market

● LO1

Herman Company has three products in its ending inventory. Specific per unit data for each of the products are as follows:

	Product 1	Product 2	Product 3
Cost	$20	$ 90	$50
Replacement cost	18	85	40
Selling price	40	120	70
Disposal costs	6	40	10
Normal profit margin	5	30	12

Required:
What unit values should Herman use for each of its products when applying the LCM rule to ending inventory?

E 9–2
IFRS; Lower of cost or market

● LO1

Refer to the situation described in Exercise 9–1.

Required:
How might your solution differ if Herman Company prepares its financial statements according to International Accounting Standards?

E 9–3
Lower of cost or market

● LO1

Tatum Company has four products in its inventory. Information about the December 31, 2009, inventory is as follows:

Product	Total Cost	Total Replacement Cost	Total Net Realizable Value
101	$120,000	$110,000	$100,000
102	90,000	85,000	110,000
103	60,000	40,000	50,000
104	30,000	28,000	50,000

The normal gross profit percentage is 25% of *cost.*

Required:
1. Determine the balance sheet inventory carrying value at December 31, 2009, assuming the LCM rule is applied to individual products.
2. Assuming that Tatum recognizes an inventory write-down as a separate income statement item, determine the amount of the loss.

E 9–4
Lower of cost or market

● LO1

The inventory of Royal Decking consisted of five products. Information about the December 31, 2009, inventory is as follows:

		Per Unit	
Product	Cost	Replacement Cost	Selling Price
A	$ 40	$35	$ 60
B	80	70	100
C	40	55	80
D	100	70	130
E	20	28	30

Disposal costs consist only of a sales commission equal to 10% of selling price and shipping costs equal to 5% of cost. The normal gross profit percentage is 30% of selling price.

Required:
What unit value should Royal Decking use for each of its products when applying the LCM rule to units of inventory?

E 9–5
Gross profit method

● LO2

On September 22, 2009, a flood destroyed the entire merchandise inventory on hand in a warehouse owned by the Rocklin Sporting Goods Company. The following information is available from the records of the company's periodic inventory system:

Inventory, January 1, 2009	$140,000
Net purchases, January 1 through September 22	370,000
Net sales, January 1 through September 22	550,000
Gross profit ratio	25%

Required:
Estimate the cost of inventory destroyed in the flood using the gross profit method.

E 9–6
Gross profit method

● LO2

On November 21, 2009, a fire at Hodge Company's warehouse caused severe damage to its entire inventory of Product Tex. Hodge estimates that all usable damaged goods can be sold for $12,000. The following information was available from the records of Hodge's periodic inventory system:

Inventory, November 1	$100,000
Net purchases from November 1, to the date of the fire	140,000
Net sales from November 1, to the date of the fire	220,000

Based on recent history, Hodge's gross profit ratio on Product Tex is 35% of net sales.

Required:
Calculate the estimated loss on the inventory from the fire, using the gross profit method.

(AICPA adapted)

E 9–7
Gross profit method

● LO2

A fire destroyed a warehouse of the Goren Group, Inc., on May 4, 2009. Accounting records on that date indicated the following:

Merchandise inventory, January 1, 2009	$1,900,000
Purchases to date	5,800,000
Freight-in	400,000
Sales to date	8,200,000

The gross profit ratio has averaged 20% of sales for the past four years.

Required:
Use the gross profit method to estimate the cost of the inventory destroyed in the fire.

E 9–8
Gross profit method

● LO2

Royal Gorge Company uses the gross profit method to estimate ending inventory and cost of goods sold when preparing monthly financial statements required by its bank. Inventory on hand at the end of October was $58,500. The following information for the month of November was available from company records:

Purchases	$110,000
Freight-in	3,000
Sales	180,000
Sales returns	5,000
Purchases returns	4,000

In addition, the controller is aware of $8,000 of inventory that was stolen during November from one of the company's warehouses.

Required:
1. Calculate the estimated inventory at the end of November, assuming a gross profit ratio of 40%.
2. Calculate the estimated inventory at the end of November, assuming a markup on cost of 100%.

E 9–9
Gross profit method; solving for unknown cost percentage

● LO2

National Distributing Company uses a periodic inventory system to track its merchandise inventory and the gross profit method to estimate ending inventory and cost of goods sold for interim periods. Net purchases for the month of August were $31,000. The July 31 and August 31, 2009, financial statements contained the following information:

Income Statements
For the Months Ending

	August 31, 2009	July 31, 2009
Net sales	$50,000	$40,000

Balance Sheets
At

	August 31, 2009	July 31, 2009
Assets:		
Merchandise inventory	$28,000	$27,000

Required:
Determine the company's cost percentage.

E 9–10
Retail inventory
method; average
cost

● LO3

San Lorenzo General Store uses a periodic inventory system and the retail inventory method to estimate ending inventory and cost of goods sold. The following data are available for the month of October 2009:

	Cost	Retail
Beginning inventory	$35,000	$50,000
Net purchases	19,120	31,600
Net markups		1,200
Net markdowns		800
Net sales		32,000

Required:
Estimate the average cost of ending inventory and cost of goods sold for October. Do not approximate LCM.

E 9–11
Conventional retail
method

● LO4

Campbell Corporation uses the retail method to value its inventory. The following information is available for the year 2009:

	Cost	Retail
Merchandise inventory, January 1, 2009	$190,000	$280,000
Purchases	600,000	840,000
Freight-in	8,000	
Net markups		20,000
Net markdowns		4,000
Net sales		800,000

Required:
Determine the December 31, 2009, inventory that approximates average cost, lower of cost or market.

E 9–12
Retail inventory
method; LIFO

● LO3

Crosby Company owns a chain of hardware stores throughout the state. The company uses a periodic inventory system and the retail inventory method to estimate ending inventory and cost of goods sold. The following data are available for the three months ending March 31, 2009:

	Cost	Retail
Beginning inventory	$160,000	$280,000
Net purchases	607,760	840,000
Net markups		20,000
Net markdowns		4,000
Net sales		800,000

Required:
Estimate the LIFO cost of ending inventory and cost of goods sold for the three months ending March 31, 2009. Assume stable retail prices during the period.

E 9–13
Conventional retail
method; normal
spoilage

● LO4

Almaden Valley Variety Store uses the retail inventory method to estimate ending inventory and cost of goods sold. Data for 2009 are as follows:

	Cost	Retail
Beginning inventory	$ 12,000	$ 20,000
Purchases	102,600	165,000
Freight-in	3,480	
Purchase returns	4,000	7,000
Net markups		6,000
Net markdowns		3,000
Normal spoilage		4,200
Net sales		152,000

Required:
Estimate the ending inventory and cost of goods sold for 2009, applying the conventional retail method (average, LCM).

E 9–14
Conventional
retail method;
employee
discounts

● LO3 LO4

LeMay Department Store uses the retail inventory method to estimate ending inventory for its monthly financial statements. The following data pertain to one of its largest departments for the month of March 2009:

	Cost	Retail
Beginning inventory	$ 40,000	$ 60,000
Purchases	207,000	400,000
Freight-in	14,488	
Purchase returns	4,000	6,000
Net markups		5,800
Net markdowns		3,500
Normal breakage		6,000
Net sales		280,000
Employee discounts		1,800

Sales are recorded net of employee discounts.

Required:
1. Compute estimated ending inventory and cost of goods sold for March applying the conventional retail method (average, LCM).
2. Recompute the cost-to-retail percentage using the average cost method and ignoring LCM considerations.

E 9–15
Retail inventory method; solving for unknowns

● LO3

Adams Corporation uses a periodic inventory system and the retail inventory method to estimate ending inventory and cost of goods sold. The following data are available for the month of September 2009:

	Cost	Retail
Beginning inventory	$21,000	$35,000
Net purchases	10,500	?
Net markups		4,000
Net markdowns		1,000
Net sales		?

The company used the average cost flow method and estimated inventory at the end of September to be $17,437.50. If the company had used the LIFO cost flow method, the cost-to-retail percentage would have been 50%.

Required:
Compute net purchases at retail and net sales for the month of September.

E 9–16
Dollar-value LIFO retail

● LO5

On January 1, 2009, the Brunswick Hat Company adopted the dollar-value LIFO retail method. The following data are available for 2009:

	Cost	Retail
Beginning inventory	$ 71,280	$132,000
Net purchases	112,500	255,000
Net markups		6,000
Net markdowns		11,000
Net sales		232,000
Retail price index, 12/31/09		1.04

Required:
Calculate the estimated ending inventory and cost of goods sold for 2009.

E 9–17
Dollar-value LIFO retail

● LO5

Canova Corporation adopted the dollar-value LIFO retail method on January 1, 2009. On that date, the cost of the inventory on hand was $15,000 and its retail value was $18,750. Information for 2009 and 2010 is as follows:

Date	Ending Inventory at Retail	Retail Price Index	Cost-to-Retail Percentage
12/31/09	$25,000	1.25	82%
12/31/10	28,600	1.30	85

Required:
1. What is the cost-to-retail percentage for the inventory on hand at 1/1/09?
2. Calculate the inventory value at the end of 2009 and 2010 using the dollar-value LIFO retail method.

E 9–18
Dollar-value LIFO retail

● LO5

Lance-Hefner Specialty Shoppes decided to use the dollar-value LIFO retail method to value its inventory. Accounting records provide the following information:

	Cost	Retail
Merchandise inventory, January 1, 2009	$160,000	$250,000
Net purchases	350,200	510,000
Net markups		7,000
Net markdowns		2,000
Net sales		380,000

Pertinent retail price indexes are as follows:

January 1, 2009	1.00
December 31, 2009	1.10

Required:
Determine ending inventory and cost of goods sold.

E 9–19
Dollar-value LIFO retail; solving for unknowns

● **LO5**

Bosco Company adopted the dollar-value LIFO retail method at the beginning of 2009. Information for 2009 and 2010 is as follows, with certain data intentionally omitted:

Date	Inventory Cost	Inventory Retail	Retail Price Index	Cost-to-Retail Percentage
Inventory, 1/1/09	$21,000	$28,000	1.00	?
Inventory, 12/31/09	22,792	33,600	1.12	?
2010 net purchases	60,000	88,400		
2010 net sales		80,000		
Inventory, 12/31/10	?	?	1.20	

Required:
Determine the missing data.

E 9–20
Change in inventory costing methods

● **LO6**

In 2009, CPS Company changed its method of valuing inventory from the FIFO method to the average cost method. At December 31, 2008, CPS's inventories were $32 million (FIFO). CPS's records indicated that the inventories would have totaled $23.8 million at December 31, 2008, if determined on an average cost basis.

Required:
1. Prepare the journal entry to record the adjustment. (Ignore income taxes.)
2. Briefly describe other steps CPS should take to report the change.

E 9–21
Change in inventory costing methods

● **LO6**

Goddard Company has used the FIFO method of inventory valuation since it began operations in 2006. Goddard decided to change to the average cost method for determining inventory costs at the beginning of 2009. The following schedule shows year-end inventory balances under the FIFO and average cost methods:

Year	FIFO	Average Cost
2006	$45,000	$54,000
2007	78,000	71,000
2008	83,000	78,000

Required:
1. Ignoring income taxes, prepare the 2009 journal entry to adjust the accounts to reflect the average cost method.
2. How much higher or lower would cost of goods sold be in the 2008 revised income statement?

E 9–22
Error correction; inventory error

● **LO7**

During 2009, WMC Corporation discovered that its ending inventories reported in its financial statements were misstated by the following amounts:

2007	understated by	$120,000
2008	overstated by	150,000

WMC uses a periodic inventory system and the FIFO cost method.

Required:
1. Determine the effect of these errors on retained earnings at January 1, 2009, before any adjustments. Explain your answer. (Ignore income taxes.)
2. Prepare a journal entry to correct the error.
3. What other step(s) would be taken in connection with the error?

E 9–23
Inventory errors

● **LO7**

For each of the following inventory errors occurring in 2009, determine the effect of the error on 2009's cost of goods sold, net income, and retained earnings. Assume that the error is not discovered until 2010 and that a periodic inventory system is used. Ignore income taxes.

U = understand   O = overstated   NE = no effect

	Cost of Goods Sold	Net Income	Retained Earnings
1. Overstatement of ending inventory	U	O	O
2. Overstatement of purchases			
3. Understatement of beginning inventory			
4. Freight-in charges are understated			
5. Understatement of ending inventory			
6. Understatement of purchases			
7. Overstatement of beginning inventory			
8. Understatement of purchases plus understatement of ending inventory by the same amount			

E 9–24
Inventory error

● **LO7**

In 2009, the internal auditors of Development Technologies, Inc. discovered that a $4 million purchase of merchandise in 2009 was recorded in 2008 instead. The physical inventory count at the end of 2008 was correct.

Required:
Prepare the journal entry needed in 2009 to correct the error. Also, briefly describe any other measures Development Technologies would take in connection with correcting the error. (Ignore income taxes.)

E 9–25
Concepts;
terminology

● **LO1 through LO7**

Listed below are several terms and phrases associated with inventory measurement. Pair each item from List A (by letter) with the item from List B that is most appropriately associated with it.

List A	List B
____ 1. Gross profit ratio	a. Reduction in selling price below the original selling price.
____ 2. Cost-to-retail percentage	b. Beginning inventory is not included in the calculation of the cost-to-retail percentage.
____ 3. Additional markup	c. Deducted in the retail column after the calculation of the cost-to-retail percentage.
____ 4. Markdown	d. Requires base year retail to be converted to layer year retail and then to cost.
____ 5. Net markup	e. Gross profit divided by net sales.
____ 6. Retail method, FIFO and LIFO	f. Material inventory error discovered in a subsequent year.
____ 7. Conventional retail method	g. Must be added to sales if sales are recorded net of discounts.
____ 8. Change from LIFO	h. Deducted in the retail column to arrive at goods available for sale at retail.
____ 9. Dollar-value LIFO retail	i. Divide cost of goods available for sale by goods available at retail.
____ 10. Normal spoilage	j. Average cost, LCM.
____ 11. Requires retrospective restatement	k. Added to the retail column to arrive at goods available for sale.
____ 12. Employee discounts	l. Increase in selling price subsequent to initial markup.
____ 13. Net markdowns	m. Ceiling in the determination of market.
____ 14. Net realizable value	n. Accounting change requiring retrospective treatment.

E 9–26
Purchase
commitments

● **Appendix**

On October 6, 2009, the Elgin Corporation signed a purchase commitment to purchase inventory for $60,000 on or before March 31, 2010. The company's fiscal year-end is December 31. The contract was exercised on March 21, 2010, and the inventory was purchased for cash at the contract price. On the purchase date of March 21, the market price of the inventory was $54,000. The market price of the inventory on December 31, 2009, was $56,000. The company uses a perpetual inventory system.

Required:
1. Prepare the necessary adjusting journal entry (if any is required) on December 31, 2009.
2. Prepare the journal entry to record the purchase on March 21, 2010.

E 9–27
Purchase
commitments

● **Appendix**

In March 2009, the Phillips Tool Company signed two purchase commitments. The first commitment requires Phillips to purchase inventory for $100,000 by June 15, 2009. The second commitment requires the company to purchase inventory for $150,000 by August 20, 2009. The company's fiscal year-end is June 30. Phillips uses a periodic inventory system.

The first commitment is exercised on June 15, 2009, when the market price of the inventory purchased was $85,000. The second commitment was exercised on August 20, 2009, when the market price of the inventory purchased was $120,000.

Required:
Prepare the journal entries required on June 15, June 30, and August 20, 2009, to account for the two purchase commitments. Assume that the market price of the inventory related to the outstanding purchase commitment was $140,000 at June 30.

CPA AND CMA REVIEW QUESTIONS

CPA Exam
Questions

SCHWESER

The following questions are used in the Kaplan CPA Review Course to study inventory while preparing for the CPA examination. Determine the response that best completes the statements or questions.

● LO1

1. Kahn Co., in applying the lower of cost or market method, reports its inventory at replacement cost. Which of the following statements are correct?

	Cost is greater than replacement cost	NRV, less a normal profit margin, is greater than replacement cost
a.	Yes	Yes
b.	No	No
c.	Yes	No
d.	No	Yes

● LO1

2. Moss Co. has determined its year-end inventory on a FIFO basis to be $400,000. Information pertaining to that inventory is as follows:

Estimated selling price	$408,000
Estimated cost of disposal	20,000
Normal profit margin	60,000
Current replacement cost	360,000

What should be the carrying value of Moss's inventory?
a. $328,000
b. $360,000
c. $388,000
d. $400,000

● LO2

3. On May 2, a fire destroyed the entire merchandise inventory on hand of Sanchez Wholesale Corporation. The following information is available:

Sales, January 1 through May 2	$360,000
Inventory, January 1	80,000
Merchandise purchases, January 1 through May 2 (including $40,000 of goods in transit on May 2, shipped f.o.b. shipping point)	330,000
Markup percentage on cost	20%

What is the estimated inventory on May 2 immediately prior to the fire?
a. $ 70,000
b. $ 82,000
c. $110,000
d. $122,000

● LO7

4. Bren Co.'s beginning inventory on January 1 was understated by $26,000, and its ending inventory on December 31 was overstated by $52,000. As a result, Bren's cost of goods sold for the year was
a. Understated by $26,000.
b. Overstated by $78,000.
c. Understated by $78,000.
d. Overstated by $26,000.

● LO4

5. Hutch, Inc., uses the conventional retail inventory method to account for inventory. The following information relates to current year's operations:

	Average	
	Cost	Retail
Beginning inventory and purchases	$600,000	$920,000
Net markups		40,000
Net markdowns		60,000
Sales		780,000

What amount should be reported as cost of sales for the year?

a. $480,000
b. $487,500
c. $500,000
d. $525,000

**CMA Exam
Questions**

The following questions dealing with inventory are adapted from questions that previously appeared on Certified Management Accountant (CMA) examinations. The CMA designation sponsored by the Institute of Management Accountants (**www.imanet.org**) provides members with an objective measure of knowledge and competence in the field of management accounting. Determine the response that best completes the statements or questions.

● LO7

1. All sales and purchases for the year at Ross Corporation are credit transactions. Ross uses a perpetual inventory system. During the year, it shipped certain goods that were correctly excluded from ending inventory although the sale was not recorded. Which one of the following statements is correct?

   a. Accounts receivable was not affected, inventory was not affected, sales were understated, and cost of goods sold was understated.
   b. Accounts receivable was understated, inventory was not affected, sales were understated, and cost of goods sold was understated.
   c. Accounts receivable was understated, inventory was overstated, sales were understated, and cost of goods sold was overstated.
   d. Accounts receivable was understated, inventory was not affected, sales were understated, and cost of goods sold was not affected.

● LO7

2. During the year 1 year-end physical inventory count at Tequesta Corporation, $40,000 worth of inventory was counted twice. Assuming that the year 2 year-end inventory was correct, the result of the year 1 error was that

   a. Year 1 retained earnings was understated, and year 2 ending inventory was correct.
   b. Year 1 cost of goods sold was overstated, and year 2 income was understated.
   c. Year 1 income was overstated, and year 2 ending inventory was overstated.
   d. Year 1 cost of goods sold was understated, and year 2 retained earnings was correct.

3. The following FCL Corporation inventory information is available for the year ended December 31:

	Cost	Retail
Beginning inventory at 1/1	$35,000	$100,000
Net purchases	55,000	110,000
Net markups		15,000
Net markdowns		25,000
Net sales		150,000

The December 31 ending inventory at cost using the conventional (lower of average cost or market) retail inventory method equals

a. $17,500
b. $20,000
c. $27,500
d. $50,000

PROBLEMS   available with McGraw–Hill's Homework Manager www.mhhe.com/spiceland5e   **HM**

An alternate exercise and problem set is available on the text website: www.mhhe.com/spiceland5e

P 9–1
Lower of cost or market

● LO1

Decker Company has five products in its inventory. Information about the December 31, 2009, inventory follows.

Product	Quantity	Unit Cost	Unit Replacement Cost	Unit Selling Price
A	1,000	$10	$12	$16
B	800	15	11	18
C	600	3	2	8
D	200	7	4	6
E	600	14	12	13

The selling cost for each product consists of a 15 percent sales commission. The normal profit percentage for each product is 40 percent of the selling price.

Required:

1. Determine the balance sheet inventory carrying value at December 31, 2009, assuming the LCM rule is applied to individual products.

2. Determine the balance sheet inventory carrying value at December 31, 2009, assuming the LCM rule is applied to the entire inventory. Also, assuming that Decker recognizes an inventory write-down as a separate income statement item, determine the amount of the loss.

P 9–2
Lower of cost or market

● LO1

Almaden Hardware Store sells two distinct types of products, tools and paint products. Information pertaining to its 2009 year-end inventory is as follows:

Inventory, by Product Type	Quantity	Per Unit Cost	Designated Market
Tools:			
Hammers	100	$ 5.00	$5.50
Saws	200	10.00	9.00
Screwdrivers	300	2.00	2.60
Paint products:			
1-gallon cans	500	6.00	5.00
Paint brushes	100	4.00	4.50

Required:

1. Determine the balance sheet inventory carrying value at year-end, assuming the LCM rule is applied to (a) individual products, (b) product type, and (c) total inventory.

2. Assuming that the company recognizes an inventory write-down as a separate income statement item, for each of the LCM applications determine the amount of the loss.

P 9–3
Gross profit method

● LO2

Smith Distributors, Inc., supplies ice cream shops with various toppings for making sundaes. On November 17, 2009, a fire resulted in the loss of all of the toppings stored in one section of the warehouse. The company must provide its insurance company with an estimate of the amount of inventory lost. The following information is available from the company's accounting records:

	Fruit Toppings	Marshmallow Toppings	Chocolate Toppings
Inventory, January 1, 2009	$ 20,000	$ 7,000	$ 3,000
Net purchases through Nov. 17	150,000	36,000	12,000
Net sales through Nov. 17	200,000	55,000	20,000
Historical gross profit ratio	20%	30%	35%

Required:

1. Calculate the estimated cost of each of the toppings lost in the fire.

2. What factors could cause the estimates to be over-or understated?

P 9–4
Retail inventory method; various cost methods

● LO3 LO4

Sparrow Company uses the retail inventory method to estimate ending inventory and cost of goods sold. Data for 2009 are as follows:

	Cost	Retail
Beginning inventory	$ 90,000	$180,000
Purchases	355,000	580,000
Freight-in	9,000	
Purchase returns	7,000	11,000
Net markups		16,000
Net markdowns		12,000
Normal spoilage		3,000
Abnormal spoilage	4,800	8,000
Sales		540,000
Sales returns		10,000

The company records sales net of employee discounts. Discounts for 2009 totaled $4,000.

Required:
Estimate Sparrow's ending inventory and cost of goods sold for the year using the retail inventory method and the following applications:

1. Average cost
2. Conventional (average, LCM)

P 9–5
Retail inventory method; conventional and LIFO

● LO3 LO4

Alquist Company uses the retail method to estimate its ending inventory. Selected information about its year 2009 operations is as follows:

a. January 1, 2009, beginning inventory had a cost of $100,000 and a retail value of $150,000.

b. Purchases during 2009 cost $1,387,500 with an original retail value of $2,000,000.

c. Freight costs were $10,000 for incoming merchandise and $25,000 for outgoing (sold) merchandise.

d. Net additional markups were $300,000 and net markdowns were $150,000.

e. Based on prior experience, shrinkage due to shoplifting was estimated to be $15,000 of retail value.

f. Merchandise is sold to employees at a 20% of selling price discount. Employee sales are recorded in a separate account at the net selling price. The balance in this account at the end of 2009 is $250,000.

g. Sales to customers totaled $1,750,000 for the year.

Required:
1. Estimate ending inventory and cost of goods sold using the conventional retail method (average, LCM).
2. Estimate ending inventory and cost of goods sold using the LIFO retail method. (Assume stable prices.)

P 9–6
Retail inventory method; conventional

● LO4

Grand Department Store, Inc., uses the retail inventory method to estimate ending inventory for its monthly financial statements. The following data pertain to a single department for the month of October 2009:

Inventory, October 1, 2009:	
At cost	$ 20,000
At retail	30,000
Purchases (exclusive of freight and returns):	
At cost	100,151
At retail	146,495
Freight-in	5,100
Purchase returns:	
At cost	2,100
At retail	2,800
Additional markups	2,500
Markup cancellations	265
Markdowns (net)	800
Normal spoilage and breakage	4,500
Sales	135,730

Required:
1. Using the conventional retail method, prepare a schedule computing estimated lower-of-cost-or-market inventory for October 31, 2009.
2. A department store using the conventional retail inventory method estimates the cost of its ending inventory as $29,000. An accurate physical count reveals only $22,000 of inventory at lower of cost or market. List the factors that may have caused the difference between computed inventory and the physical count.

(AICPA adapted)

P 9–7
Retail method— average cost and LCM

● LO3 LO4

Smith-Kline Company maintains inventory records at selling prices as well as at cost. For 2009, the records indicate the following data:

	($ in 000s)	
	Cost	**Retail**
Beginning inventory	$ 80	$ 125
Purchases	671	1,006
Freight-in on purchases	30	
Purchase returns	1	2
Net markups		4
Net markdowns		8
Net sales		916

Required:
Use the retail method to approximate cost of ending inventory in each of the following ways:

1. Average cost
2. Average (LCM) cost

P 9–8
Dollar-value LIFO
retail method

● LO5

[This is a variation of the previous problem, modified to focus on the dollar-value LIFO retail method.]
Smith-Kline Company maintains inventory records at selling prices as well as at cost. For 2009, the records indicate the following data:

	($ in 000s)	
	Cost	**Retail**
Beginning inventory	$ 80	$ 125
Purchases	671	1,006
Freight-in on purchases	30	
Purchase returns	1	2
Net markups		4
Net markdowns		8
Net sales		916

Required:
Assuming the price level increased from 1.00 at January 1 to 1.10 at December 31, 2009, use the dollar-value LIFO retail method to approximate cost of ending inventory and cost of goods sold.

P 9–9
Dollar-value LIFO
retail

● LO5

On January 1, 2009, HGC Camera Store adopted the dollar-value LIFO retail inventory method. Inventory transactions at both cost and retail, and cost indexes for 2009 and 2010 are as follows:

	2009		2010	
	Cost	**Retail**	**Cost**	**Retail**
Beginning inventory	$28,000	$ 40,000		
Net purchases	85,000	108,000	90,000	114,000
Freight-in	2,000		2,500	
Net markups		10,000		8,000
Net markdowns		2,000		2,200
Net sales to customers		100,000		104,000
Sales to employees (net of 20% discount)		2,400		4,000
Price Index:				
January 1, 2009	1.00			
December 31, 2009	1.06			
December 31, 2010	1.10			

Required:
Estimate the 2009 and 2010 ending inventory and cost of goods sold using the dollar-value LIFO retail inventory method.

P 9–10
Retail inventory
method; various
applications

● LO3 through LO5

Raleigh Department Store converted from the conventional retail method to the LIFO retail method on January 1, 2007, and is now considering converting to the dollar-value LIFO retail inventory method. Management requested, during your examination of the financial statements for the year ended December 31, 2009, that you furnish a summary showing certain computations of inventory costs for the past three years. Available information follows:
a. The inventory at January 1, 2007, had a retail value of $45,000 and a cost of $27,500 based on the conventional retail method.
b. Transactions during 2007 were as follows:

	Cost	**Retail**
Gross purchases	$282,000	$490,000
Purchase returns	6,500	10,000
Purchase discounts	5,000	
Gross sales		492,000
Sales returns		5,000
Employee discounts		3,000
Freight-in	26,500	
Net markups		25,000
Net markdowns		10,000

Sales to employees are recorded net of discounts.
c. The retail value of the December 31, 2008, inventory was $56,100, the cost-to-retail percentage for 2008 under the LIFO retail method was 62%, and the appropriate price index was 102% of the January 1, 2008, price level.

d. The retail value of the December 31, 2009, inventory was $48,300, the cost-to-retail percentage for 2009 under the LIFO retail method was 61%, and the appropriate price index was 105% of the January 1, 2008, price level.

Required:
1. Prepare a schedule showing the computation of the cost of inventory at December 31, 2007, based on the conventional retail method.
2. Prepare a similar schedule as in requirement 1 based on the LIFO retail method.
3. Same requirement as (1) for December 31, 2008 and 2009, based on the dollar-value LIFO retail method.

(AICPA adapted)

P 9–11
Retail inventory method; various applications

● LO3 through LO5

On January 1, 2009, Pet Friendly Stores adopted the retail inventory method. Inventory transactions at both cost and retail, and cost indexes for 2009 and 2010 are as follows:

	2009		2010	
	Cost	Retail	Cost	Retail
Beginning inventory	$ 90,000	$150,000		
Purchases	478,000	730,000	511,000	760,000
Purchase returns	2,500	3,500	2,200	4,000
Freight-in	6,960		8,000	
Net markups		8,500		10,000
Net markdowns		4,000		6,000
Net sales to customers		650,000		680,000
Sales to employees (net of 30% discount)		14,000		17,500
Normal spoilage		5,000		6,600
Price Index:				
January 1, 2009	1.00			
December 31, 2009	1.03			
December 31, 2010	1.06			

Required:
1. Estimate the 2009 and 2010 ending inventory and cost of goods sold using the dollar-value LIFO retail method.
2. Estimate the 2009 ending inventory and cost of goods sold using the average cost method.
3. Estimate the 2009 ending inventory and cost of goods sold using the conventional retail method (average, LCM).

P 9–12
Change in methods

● LO6

Rockwell Corporation uses a periodic inventory system and has used the FIFO cost method since inception of the company in 1974. In 2009, the company decided to switch to the average cost method. Data for 2009 are as follows:

Beginning inventory, FIFO (5,000 units @ $30)		$150,000
Purchases:		
5,000 units @ $36	$180,000	
5,000 units @ $40	200,000	380,000
Cost of goods available for sale		$530,000
Sales for 2009 (8,000 units @ $70)		$560,000

Additional Information:
a. The company's effective income tax rate is 40% for all years.
b. If the company had used the average cost method prior to 2009, ending inventory for 2008 would have been $130,000.
c. 7,000 units remained in inventory at the end of 2009.

Required:
1. Ignoring income taxes, prepare the 2009 journal entry to adjust the accounts to reflect the average cost method.
2. What is the effect of the change in methods on 2009 net income?

P 9–13
Inventory errors

● LO7

You have been hired as the new controller for the Ralston Company. Shortly after joining the company in 2009, you discover the following errors related to the 2007 and 2008 financial statements:
a. Inventory at 12/31/07 was understated by $6,000.
b. Inventory at 12/31/08 was overstated by $9,000.
c. On 12/31/08, inventory was purchased for $3,000. The company did not record the purchase until the inventory was paid for early in 2009. At that time, the purchase was recorded by a debit to purchases and a credit to cash.

The company uses a periodic inventory system.

Required:

1. Assuming that the errors were discovered after the 2008 financial statements were issued, analyze the effect of the errors on 2008 and 2007 cost of goods sold, net income, and retained earnings. (Ignore income taxes.)
2. Prepare a journal entry to correct the errors.
3. What other step(s) would be taken in connection with the error?

P 9–14
Inventory errors

● **LO7**

The December 31, 2009, inventory of Tog Company, based on a physical count, was determined to be $450,000. Included in that count was a shipment of goods that cost $50,000 received from a supplier at the end of the month. The purchase was recorded and paid for in 2010. Another supplier shipment costing $20,000 was correctly recorded as a purchase in 2009. However, the merchandise, shipped FOB shipping point, was not received until 2010 and was incorrectly omitted from the physical count. A third purchase, shipped from a supplier FOB shipping point on December 28, 2009, did not arrive until January 3, 2010. The merchandise, which cost $80,000, was not included in the physical count and the purchase has not yet been recorded.

The company uses a periodic inventory system.

Required:

1. Determine the correct December 31, 2009, inventory balance and, assuming that the errors were discovered after the 2009 financial statements were issued, analyze the effect of the errors on 2009 cost of goods sold, net income, and retained earnings. (Ignore income taxes.)
2. Prepare a journal entry to correct the errors.

P 9–15
Integrating
problem; Chapters
8 and 9; inventory
errors

● **LO7**

Capwell Corporation uses a periodic inventory system. The company's ending inventory on December 31, 2009, its fiscal-year end, based on a physical count, was determined to be $326,000. Capwell's unadjusted trial balance also showed the following account balances: Purchases, $620,000; Accounts payable; $210,000; Accounts receivable, $225,000; Sales revenue, $840,000.

The internal audit department discovered the following items:

1. Goods valued at $32,000 held on consignment from Dix Company were included in the physical count but not recorded as a purchase.
2. Purchases from Xavier Corporation were incorrectly recorded at $41,000 instead of the correct amount of $14,000. The correct amount was included in the ending inventory.
3. Goods that cost $25,000 were shipped from a vendor on December 28, 2009, terms f.o.b. destination. The merchandise arrived on January 3, 2010. The purchase and related accounts payable were recorded in 2009.
4. One inventory item was incorrectly included in ending inventory as 100 units, instead of the correct amount of 1,000 units. This item cost $40 per unit.
5. The 2008 balance sheet reported inventory of $352,000. The internal auditors discovered that a mathematical error caused this inventory to be understated by $62,000. This amount is considered to be material.
6. Goods shipped to a customer f.o.b. destination on December 25, 2009, were received by the customer on January 4, 2010. The sales price was $40,000 and the merchandise cost $22,000. The sale and corresponding accounts receivable were recorded in 2009.
7. Goods shipped from a vendor f.o.b. shipping point on December 27, 2009, were received on January 3, 2010. The merchandise cost $18,000. The purchase was not recorded until 2010.

Required:

1. Determine the correct amounts for 2009 ending inventory, purchases, accounts payable, sales revenue, and accounts receivable.
2. Calculate cost of goods sold for 2009.
3. Describe the steps Capwell would undertake to correct the error in the 2008 ending inventory. What was the effect of the error on 2008 before-tax income?

P 9–16
Purchase
commitments

● **Appendix**

In November 2009, the Brunswick Company signed two purchase commitments. The first commitment requires Brunswick to purchase 10,000 units of inventory at $10 per unit by December 15, 2009. The second commitment requires the company to purchase 20,000 units of inventory at $11 per unit by March 15, 2010. Brunswick's fiscal year-end is December 31. The company uses a periodic inventory system. Both contracts were exercised on their expiration date.

Required:

1. Prepare the journal entry to record the December 15 purchase for cash assuming the following alternative unit market prices on that date:
    a. $10.50
    b. $ 9.50

2. Prepare any necessary adjusting entry at December 31, 2009, for the second purchase commitment assuming the following alternative unit market prices on that date:
   a. $12.50
   b. $10.30
3. Assuming that the unit market price on December 31 was $10.30, prepare the journal entry to record the purchase on March 15, 2010, assuming the following alternative unit market prices on that date:
   a. $11.50
   b. $10.00

BROADEN YOUR PERSPECTIVE

Apply your critical-thinking ability to the knowledge you've gained. These cases will provide you an opportunity to develop your research, analysis, judgment, and communication skills. You also will work with other students, integrate what you've learned, apply it in real world situations, and consider its global and ethical ramifications. This practice will broaden your knowledge and further develop your decision-making abilities.

Judgment Case 9–1
Inventoriable costs; lower of cost or market; retail inventory method

● LO1 LO3 LO4

Hudson Company, which is both a wholesaler and a retailer, purchases its inventories from various suppliers. Additional facts for Hudson's wholesale operations are as follows:
a. Hudson incurs substantial warehousing costs.
b. Hudson uses the lower-of-cost-or-market method. The replacement cost of the inventories is below the net realizable value and above the net realizable value less the normal profit margin. The original cost of the inventories is above replacement cost and below the net realizable value.

Additional facts for Hudson's retail operations are as follows:
a. Hudson determines the estimated cost of its ending inventories held for sale at retail using the conventional retail inventory method, which approximates lower of average cost or market.
b. Hudson incurs substantial freight-in costs.
c. Hudson has net markups and net markdowns.

Required:
1. Theoretically, how should Hudson account for the warehousing costs related to its wholesale inventories? Why?
2. a. In general, why is the lower-of-cost-or-market method used to value inventory?
   b. At which amount should Hudson's wholesale inventories be reported in the balance sheet?
      Explain the application of the lower-of-cost-or-market method in this situation.
3. In the calculation of the cost-to-retail percentage used to determine the estimated cost of its ending retail inventories, how should Hudson treat
   a. Freight-in costs?
   b. Net markups?
   c. Net markdowns?
4. Why does Hudson's retail inventory method approximate lower of average cost or market?

(AICPA adapted)

Communication Case 9–2
Lower of cost or market

● LO1

The lower-of-cost-or-market approach to valuing inventory is a departure from the accounting principle of reporting assets at their historical costs. There are those who believe that inventory, as well as other assets, should be valued at market, regardless of whether market is above or below cost.

The focus of this case is the justification for the lower-of-cost-or-market rule for valuing inventories. Your instructor will divide the class into two to six groups depending on the size of the class. The mission of your group is to defend the lower-of-cost-or-market approach against the alternatives of valuing inventory at either historical cost or market value.

Required:
1. Each group member should consider the situation independently and draft a tentative argument prior to the class session for which the case is assigned.
2. In class, each group will meet for 10 to 15 minutes in different areas of the classroom. During that meeting, group members will take turns sharing their suggestions for the purpose of arriving at a single group argument.
3. After the allotted time, a spokesperson for each group (selected during the group meetings) will share the group's solution with the class. The goal of the class is to incorporate the views of each group into a consensus approach to the situation.

**Integrating
Case 9–3
Unit LIFO and
LCM**

● **LO1**

York Co. sells one product, which it purchases from various suppliers. York's trial balance at December 31, 2009, included the following accounts:

Sales (33,000 units @ $16)	$528,000
Sales discounts	7,500
Purchases	368,900
Purchase discounts	18,000
Freight-in	5,000
Freight-out	11,000

York Co.'s inventory purchases during 2009 were as follows:

	Units	Cost per Unit	Total Cost
Beginning inventory	8,000	$8.20	$ 65,600
Purchases, quarter ended March 31	12,000	8.25	99,000
Purchases, quarter ended June 30	15,000	7.90	118,500
Purchases, quarter ended September 30	13,000	7.50	97,500
Purchases, quarter ended December 31	7,000	7.70	53,900
	55,000		$434,500

Additional Information:

a. York's accounting policy is to report inventory in its financial statements at the lower of cost or market, applied to total inventory. Cost is determined under the last-in, first-out (LIFO) method.

b. York has determined that, at December 31, 2009, the replacement cost of its inventory was $8 per unit and the net realizable value was $8.80 per unit. York's normal profit margin is $1.05 per unit.

Required:

1. Prepare York's schedule of cost of goods sold, with a supporting schedule of ending inventory. York uses the direct method of reporting losses from market decline of inventory.

2. Explain the rule of lower of cost or market and its application in this situation.

(AICPA adapted)

**Judgment
Case 9–4
The dollar-value
LIFO method; the
retail inventory
method**

● **LO3 LO4**

Huddell Company, which is both a wholesaler and retailer, purchases merchandise from various suppliers. The dollar-value LIFO method is used for the wholesale inventories.

Huddell determines the estimated cost of its retail ending inventories using the conventional retail inventory method, which approximates lower of average cost or market.

Required:

1. a. What are the advantages of using the dollar-value LIFO method as opposed to the traditional LIFO method?

 b. How does the application of the dollar-value LIFO method differ from the application of the traditional LIFO method?

2. a. In the calculation of the cost-to-retail percentage used to determine the estimated cost of its ending inventories, how should Huddell use

 • Net markups?

 • Net markdowns?

 b. Why does Huddell's retail inventory method approximate lower of average cost or market?

(AICPA adapted)

**Communication
Case 9–5
Retail inventory
method**

● **LO3 LO4**

The Brenly Paint Company, your client, manufactures paint. The company's president, Mr. Brenly, decided to open a retail store to sell paint as well as wallpaper and other items that would be purchased from other suppliers. He has asked you for information about the retail method of estimating inventories at the retail store.

Required:

Prepare a report to the president explaining the retail method of estimating inventories.

**Analysis
Case 9–6
Change in
inventory method**

Generally accepted accounting principles should be applied consistently from period to period. However, changes within a company, as well as changes in the external economic environment, may force a company to change an accounting method. The specific reporting requirements when a company changes from one generally accepted inventory method to another depend on the methods involved.

● LO6

Required:

Explain the accounting treatment for a change in inventory method (a) not involving LIFO, (b) from the LIFO method, and (c) to the LIFO method. Explain the logic underlying those treatments. Also, describe how disclosure requirements are designed to address the departure from consistency and comparability of changes in accounting principle.

Real World Case 9–7
Change in inventory method

● LO6

Real World Financials

Amcon Distributing Company is a wholesale distributor of consumer products in the Great Plains and Rocky Mountain regions. The following disclosure note was included in recent financial statements:

> In the fourth quarter of fiscal 2007, the Company changed its inventory valuation method from the Last-In First-Out (LIFO) method to the First-In First-Out (FIFO) method. The change is preferable as it provides a more meaningful presentation of the Company's financial position as it values inventory in a manner which more closely approximates current cost; better represents the underlying commercial substance of selling the oldest products first; and more accurately reflects the Company's realized periodic income.
>
> As required by U.S. generally accepted accounting principles, this change in accounting principle has been reflected in the consolidated statements of financial position, consolidated statements of operations, and consolidated statements of cash flows through retrospective application of the FIFO method. Accordingly, inventories from continuing operations as of the beginning of fiscal 2005 were increased by $4.0 million. . ., and shareholders' equity was increased by the after-tax effect ($2.5 million). Previously reported net income (loss) available to common shareholders' for the fiscal years 2006 and 2005 were also increased by $0.1 million and $0.5 million after income taxes, respectively.

Required:

1. Why does GAAP require Amcon to retrospectively adjust historical earnings for this type of accounting change?
2. Assuming that the quantity of inventory remained stable during the 2006 fiscal year, did the cost of Amcon's inventory move up or down during the year?

Real World Case 9–8
Various inventory issues; Chapters 8 and 9

● LO5 LO6

Real World Financials

Gottschalks, Inc., is a regional department and specialty store chain operating in six Western states. Using EDGAR (www.sec.gov) access the 10-K report for Gottschalks for the period ending February 3, 2007, and answer the following questions.

1. What approach is used by the company to implement the LIFO inventory method?
2. How does Gottschalks determine its inventory pools?
3. How often are physical inventories taken?
4. A company that uses LIFO is allowed to provide supplemental disclosures reporting the effect of using another inventory method rather than LIFO. What income effect of using LIFO versus another method for the current fiscal year does Gottschalks report in its supplemental LIFO disclosure?
5. Calculate Gottschalks's inventory turnover ratio for the fiscal year ended February 3, 2007.
6. Assume that in the next fiscal year the company decides to switch to the average cost inventory method. Describe the accounting treatment required for the switch.

Communication Case 9–9
Change in inventory method; disclosure note

● LO6

Mayfair Department Stores, Inc., operates over 30 retail stores in the Pacific Northwest. Prior to 2009, the company used the FIFO method to value its inventory. In 2009, Mayfair decided to switch to the dollar value LIFO retail inventory method. One of your responsibilities as assistant controller is to prepare the disclosure note describing the change in method that will be included in the company's 2009 financial statements. Kenneth Meier, the controller, provided the following information:

a. Internally developed retail price indexes are used to adjust for the effects of changing prices.
b. If the change had not been made, cost of goods sold for the year would have been $22 million lower. The company's income tax rate is 40% and there were 100 million shares of common stock outstanding during 2009.
c. The cumulative effect of the change on prior years' income is not determinable.
d. The reasons for the change were (a) to provide a more consistent matching of merchandise costs with sales revenue, and (b) the new method provides a more comparable basis of accounting with competitors that also use the LIFO method.

Required:

1. Prepare for Kenneth Meier the disclosure note that will be included in the 2009 financial statements.
2. Explain why the "cumulative effect of the change on prior years' income is not determinable."

Judgment Case 9–10
Inventory errors
● LO7

Some inventory errors are said to be self-correcting in that the error has the opposite financial statement effect in the period following the error, thereby correcting the original account balance errors.

Required:
Despite this self-correcting feature, discuss why these errors should not be ignored and describe the steps required to account for the error correction.

Ethics Case 9–11
Overstatement of ending inventory
● LO7

Danville Bottlers is a wholesale beverage company. Danville uses the FIFO inventory method to determine the cost of its ending inventory. Ending inventory quantities are determined by a physical count. For the fiscal year-end June 30, 2009, ending inventory was originally determined to be $3,265,000. However, on July 17, 2009, John Howard, the company's controller, discovered an error in the ending inventory count. He determined that the correct ending inventory amount should be $2,600,000.

Danville is a privately owned corporation with significant financing provided by a local bank. The bank requires annual audited financial statements as a condition of the loan. By July 17, the auditors had completed their review of the financial statements which are scheduled to be issued on July 25. They did not discover the inventory error.

John's first reaction was to communicate his finding to the auditors and to revise the financial statements before they are issued. However, he knows that his and his fellow workers' profit-sharing plans are based on annual pretax earnings and that if he revises the statements, everyone's profit-sharing bonus will be significantly reduced.

Required:
1. Why will bonuses be negatively affected? What is the effect on pretax earnings?
2. If the error is not corrected in the current year and is discovered by the auditors during the following year's audit, how will it be reported in the company's financial statements?
3. Discuss the ethical dilemma John Howard faces.

Analysis Case 9–12
Purchase commitments
● Appendix

The management of the Esquire Oil Company believes that the wholesale price of heating oil that they sell to homeowners will increase again as the result of increased political problems in the Middle East. The company is currently paying $.80 a gallon. If they are willing to enter an agreement in November 2009 to purchase a million gallons of heating oil during the winter of 2010, their supplier will guarantee the price at $.80 per gallon. However, if the winter is a mild one, Esquire would not be able to sell a million gallons unless they reduced their retail price and thereby increase the risk of a loss for the year. On the other hand, if the wholesale price did increase substantially, they would be in a favorable position with respect to their competitors. The company's fiscal year-end is December 31.

Required:
Discuss the accounting issues related to the purchase commitment that Esquire is considering.

CPA SIMULATION 9–1

Central Engines
Inventory Costing Methods

SCHWESER
CPA Review

Test your knowledge of the concepts discussed in this chapter, practice critical professional skills necessary for career success, and prepare for the computer-based CPA exam by accessing our CPA simulations at the text website: **www.mhhe.com/spiceland5e.**

The Central Engines simulation tests your knowledge of (a) the differential effects on financial statements of the various inventory costing methods, the difference between the gross and net method of accounting for purchase discounts, and LIFO liquidations that you studied in Chapter 8 and (b) the lower-of-cost or market approach to valuing inventory covered in this chapter.

As on the CPA exam itself, you will be asked to use tools including a spreadsheet, a calculator, and professional accounting standards to conduct research, derive solutions, and communicate conclusions related to these issues in a simulated environment headed by the following interactive tabs:

Specific tasks in the simulation address:
● Demonstrating your knowledge of the effect on inventory and cost of goods sold of using different cost flow assumptions.
● Understanding the implications of using LIFO versus FIFO to value inventory.

- Analyzing the effects of differing cost flow assumptions on numerous financial statement elements.
- Understanding the differences between the gross and net method of accounting for purchase discounts.
- Communicating the effect of a LIFO liquidation on financial statements.
- Researching the application of the lower-of-cost-or market approach to valuing inventory.

CPA SIMULATION 9–2

Ohio Valley Pet Company
Inventory

KAPLAN
SCHWESER

CPA Review

Test your knowledge of the concepts discussed in this chapter, practice critical professional skills necessary for career success, and prepare for the computer-based CPA exam by accessing our CPA simulations at the text website: **www.mhhe.com/spiceland5e.**

The Ohio Valley Pet Company simulation tests your knowledge of (a) the costs to be included in inventory and the inventory turnover ratio addressed in Chapter 8, (b) the application of the lower-of-cost-or-market approach to valuing inventory, inventory estimation techniques, and inventory errors covered in this chapter, and (c) accounting for purchase commitments covered in the Appendix to this chapter.

As on the CPA exam itself, you will be asked to use tools including a spreadsheet, a calculator, and professional accounting standards, to conduct research, derive solutions, and communicate conclusions related to these issues in a simulated environment headed by the following interactive tabs:

Specific tasks in the simulation address:
- Determining whether or not certain costs should be included in inventory.
- Analyzing the effect of various transactions on the inventory turnover ratio.
- Applying the lower-of-cost-or-market approach to valuing inventory.
- Understanding the retail inventory method and the gross profit method used for estimating ending inventory.
- Communicating the effects of inventory errors on financial statement elements.
- Researching how to report an unrealized loss on an outstanding purchase commitment.

10

Operational Assets: Acquisition and Disposition

/// **OVERVIEW**

This chapter and the one that follows address the measurement and reporting issues involving operational assets. Operational assets include tangible and intangible long-term assets that are used in the production of goods and services. This chapter covers the valuation at date of acquisition and the disposition of these assets. In Chapter 11 we discuss the allocation of the cost of operational assets to the periods benefited by their use, the treatment of expenditures made over the life of these assets to maintain and improve them, and the impairment of operational assets.

| | | **LEARNING OBJECTIVES** | | | | | |

After studying this chapter, you should be able to:

- **LO1** Identify the various costs included in the initial cost of property, plant, and equipment, natural resources, and intangible assets.
- **LO2** Determine the initial cost of individual operational assets acquired as a group for a lump-sum purchase price.
- **LO3** Determine the initial cost of an operational asset acquired in exchange for a deferred payment contract.
- **LO4** Determine the initial cost of operational assets acquired in exchange for equity securities or through donation.
- **LO5** Calculate the fixed-asset turnover ratio used by analysts to measure how effectively managers use property, plant, and equipment.
- **LO6** Explain how to account for dispositions and exchanges for other nonmonetary assets.
- **LO7** Identify the items included in the cost of a self-constructed asset and determine the amount of capitalized interest.
- **LO8** Explain the difference in the accounting treatment of costs incurred to purchase intangible assets versus the costs incurred to internally develop intangible assets.

FINANCIAL REPORTING CASE

A Disney Adventure

"Now I'm really confused," confessed Stan, your study partner, staring blankly at the Walt Disney Company balance sheet that your professor handed out last week. "I thought that interest is always expensed in the income statement. Now I see that Disney is capitalizing interest. I'm not even sure what *capitalize* means! And what about this other account called *goodwill?* What's that all about?"

"If you hadn't missed class today, we wouldn't be having this conversation. Let's take a look at the Disney financial statements and the disclosure note on capitalized interest and I'll try to explain it all to you."

Borrowings (in part):
The Company capitalizes interest on assets constructed for its theme parks, resort and other property, and on theatrical and television productions in process. In 2007, 2006, and 2005, total interest capitalized was $37 million, $30 million, and $77 million, respectively.

> By the time you finish this chapter, you should be able to respond appropriately to the questions posed in this case. Compare your response to the solution provided at the end of the chapter.

QUESTIONS ///

1. Describe to Stan what it means to capitalize an expenditure. What is the general rule for determining which costs are capitalized when an operational asset is acquired? (page 480)

2. Which costs might be included in the initial cost of equipment? (page 480)

3. In what situations is interest capitalized rather than expensed? (page 498)

4. What is the three-step process used to determine the amount of interest capitalized? (page 500)

5. What is goodwill and how is it measured? (page 487)

General Motors Corporation has significant investments in the production facilities it uses to manufacture the automobiles it sells. On the other hand, the principal revenue-producing assets of **Microsoft Corporation** are the copyrights on its computer software that permit it the exclusive rights to earn profits from those products. Timber reserves provide major revenues to **International Paper.** From a reporting perspective, we classify GM's production facilities as property, plant, and equipment;[1] Microsoft's copyrights as intangible assets, and International Paper's timber reserves as natural resources. Together, these three noncurrent assets constitute operational assets, a term used to describe the broad category of *long-term, revenue-producing assets.* Unlike manufacturers, many service firms and merchandising

---

[1]These are sometimes called *plant assets* or *fixed assets.*

companies rely primarily on people or investments in inventories rather than on operational assets to generate revenues. Even nonmanufacturing firms, though, typically have at least modest investments in buildings, equipment, and other operational assets.

The measurement and reporting issues pertaining to this group of assets include valuation at date of acquisition, disposition, the treatment of expenditures made over the life of these assets to maintain and improve them, the allocation of cost to reporting periods that benefit from their use, and impairment. The allocation of asset cost over time is called *depreciation* for plant and equipment, *amortization* for intangible assets, and *depletion* for natural resources. We focus on initial valuation and disposition in this chapter, and subsequent expenditures, cost allocation, and impairment in the next chapter.

PART A

VALUATION AT ACQUISITION
Types of Operational Assets

For financial reporting purposes, operational assets typically are classified in two categories:

1. Property, plant, and equipment. Assets in this category include land, buildings, equipment, machinery, autos, and trucks. Natural resources such as oil and gas deposits, timber tracts, and mineral deposits also are included.
2. Intangible assets. Unlike other operational assets, these lack physical substance and the extent and timing of their future benefits typically are highly uncertain. They include patents, copyrights, trademarks, franchises, and goodwill.

Of course, every company maintains its own unique mix of operational assets. The way these assets are classified and combined for reporting purposes also varies from company to company. As an example, a recent **Tyson Foods, Inc.,** balance sheet reported net property, plant, and equipment of $3,693 million and $3,945 million at the end of fiscal 2007 and 2006, respectively. A disclosure note, shown in Graphic 10–1, provided the details.

GRAPHIC 10–1

Property, Plant, and Equipment—Tyson Foods, Inc.

Real World Financials

Property, Plant, and Equipment and Depreciation (in part):

The major categories of property, plant, and equipment and accumulated depreciation, at cost, at September 29, 2007, and September 30, 2006, are as follows:

	($ in millions)	
	2007	**2006**
Land	$ 108	$ 114
Buildings and leasehold improvements	2,465	2,453
Machinery and equipment	4,337	4,270
Land improvements and other	203	202
Buildings and equipment under construction	253	279
	7,366	7,318
Less: accumulated depreciation	3,673	3,373
Net property, plant, and equipment	$3,693	$3,945

In practice, some companies report intangibles as part of property, plant, and equipment. Some include intangible assets in the other asset category in the balance sheet, and others show intangibles as a separate balance sheet category.

For example, **Bristol-Myers Squibb Company,** a leading pharmaceuticals company, reported goodwill of $4,831 million and other intangible assets of $1,632 million in a recent quarterly balance sheet. A disclosure note, shown in Graphic 10–2, provided the details of the other intangible assets. We discuss patents, trademarks and other traditional intangible assets later in this part of the chapter. Technology and capitalized software are addressed in Part C of the chapter.

Before we examine in detail specific operational assets, you should find it helpful to study the overview provided by Graphic 10–3 on page 479.

GRAPHIC 10–2

Intangible Assets—
Bristol-Myers Squibb
Company

Real World Financials

Note 11. Other Intangible Assets (in part)

As of September 30, 2007, and December 31, 2006, other intangible assets (net of
amortization) are as follows (dollars in millions):

	September 30, 2007	December 31, 2006
Patents/trademarks	$ 93	$ 113
Technology	832	951
Capitalized software	247	291
Other	460	497
Other intangible assets, net	$1,632	$1,852

GRAPHIC 10–3   Operational Assets and Their Acquisition Costs

Asset	Description	Typical Acquisition Costs
Property, plant, and equipment	Productive assets that derive their value from long-term use in operations rather than from resale.	All expenditures necessary to get the asset in condition and location for its intended use.
Equipment	Broad term that includes machinery, computers and other office equipment, vehicles, furniture, and fixtures.	Purchase price (less discounts), taxes, transportation, installation, testing, trial runs, reconditioning.
Land	Real property used in operations (land held for speculative investment or future use is reported as investments or other assets).	Purchase price, attorney's fees, title, recording fees, commissions, back taxes, mortgages, liens, clearing, filling, draining, removing old buildings.
Land improvements	Enhancements to property such as parking lots, driveways, private roads, fences, landscaping, and sprinkler systems.	Separately identifiable costs.
Buildings	Structures that include warehouses, plant facilities, and office buildings.	Purchase price, attorney's fees, commissions, reconditioning.
Natural resources	Productive assets that are physically consumed in operations such as timber, mineral deposits, and oil and gas reserves.	Acquisition, exploration, development, and restoration costs.
Intangible Assets	Productive assets that lack physical substance and have long-term but typically uncertain benefits.	All expenditures necessary to get the asset in condition and location for its intended use.
Patents	Exclusive 20-year right to manufacture a product or use a process.	Purchase price, legal fees, filing fees, not including internal R&D.
Copyrights	Exclusive right to benefit from a creative work such as a song, film, painting, photograph, or book.	Purchase price, legal fees, filing fees, not including internal R&D.
Trademarks (tradenames)	Exclusive right to display a word, a slogan, a symbol, or an emblem that distinctively identifies a company, product, or a service.	Purchase price, legal fees, filing fees, not including internal R&D.
Franchises	A contractual arrangement under which a franchisor grants the franchisee the exclusive right to use the franchisor's trademark or tradename and certain product rights.	Franchise fee plus any legal fees.
Goodwill	The unique value of the company as a whole over and above all identifiable assets.	Excess of the purchase price of the company over the fair value of the net assets acquired.

Costs to Be Capitalized

Operational assets can be acquired through purchase, exchange, lease, donation, self-construction, or a business combination. We address acquisitions through leasing in Chapter 15 and acquisitions through business combinations later in this chapter and in Chapter 12.

The initial valuation of operational assets usually is quite simple. We know from prior study that assets are valued on the basis of their original costs. In Chapter 8 we introduced the concept of condition and location in determining the cost of inventory. This concept applies to the valuation of operational assets as well. The initial cost of an operational asset includes the purchase price and all expenditures necessary to bring the asset to its desired condition and location for use.

Our objective in identifying the costs of an asset is to distinguish the expenditures that produce future benefits from those that produce benefits only in the current period. The costs in the second group are recorded as expenses, but those in the first group are *capitalized*. That is, they are recorded as an asset and expensed in future periods.[2]

The distinction is not trivial. This point was unmistakably emphasized in the summer of 2002 when **WorldCom, Inc.,** disclosed that it had improperly capitalized nearly $4 billion in expenditures related to the company's telecom network. This massive fraud resulted in one of the largest financial statement restatements in history and triggered the collapse of the once powerful corporation. Capitalizing rather than expensing these expenditures caused a substantial overstatement of reported income for 2001 and the first quarter of 2002, in fact, producing impressive profits where losses should have been reported. If the deception had not been discovered, not only would income for 2001 and 2002 have been overstated, but income for many years into the future would have been understated as the fraudulent capitalized assets were depreciated. Of course, the balance sheet also would have overstated the assets and equity of the company.

Property, Plant, and Equipment

COST OF EQUIPMENT. Equipment is a broad term that encompasses machinery used in manufacturing, computers and other office equipment, vehicles, furniture, and fixtures. The cost of equipment includes the purchase price plus any sales tax (less any discounts received from the seller), transportation costs paid by the buyer to transport the asset to the location in which it will be used, expenditures for installation, testing, legal fees to establish title, and any other costs of bringing the asset to its condition and location for use. To the extent that these costs can be identified and measured, they should be included in the asset's initial valuation rather than expensed currently.

Although most costs can be identified easily, others are more difficult. For example, the costs of training personnel to operate machinery could be considered a cost necessary to make the asset ready for use. However, because it is difficult to measure the amount of training costs associated with specific assets, these costs usually are expensed. Consider Illustration 10–1.

COST OF LAND. The cost of land also should include each expenditure needed to get the land ready for its intended use. These include the purchase price plus closing costs such as fees for the attorney, real estate agent commissions, title and title search, and recording. If the property is subject to back taxes, liens, mortgages, or other obligations, these amounts are included also. In addition, any expenditures such as clearing, filling, draining, and even removing (razing) old buildings that are needed to prepare the land for its intended use are part of the land's cost. Proceeds from the sale of salvaged materials from old buildings torn down after purchase reduce the cost of land. Illustration 10–2 provides an example.

LAND IMPROVEMENTS. It's important to distinguish between the cost of land and the cost of land improvements because land has an indefinite life and land improvements usually do not. Examples of land improvements include the cost of parking lots, driveways,

---

[2]Exceptions are land and certain intangible assets that have indefinite useful lives. Costs to acquire these assets also produce future benefits and therefore are capitalized, but unlike other operational assets, their costs are not systematically expensed in future periods as depreciation or amortization.

Central Machine Tools purchased an industrial lathe to be used in its manufacturing process. The purchase price was $62,000. Central paid a freight company $1,000 to transport the machine to its plant location plus $300 shipping insurance. In addition, the machine had to be installed and mounted on a special platform built specifically for the machine at a cost of $1,200. After installation, several trial runs were made to ensure proper operation. The cost of these trials including wasted materials was $600. At what amount should Central capitalize the lathe?

Purchase price	$62,000
Freight and handling	1,000
Insurance during shipping	300
Special foundation	1,200
Trial runs	600
	$65,100

Each of the expenditures described was necessary to bring the machine to its condition and location for use and should be capitalized and then expensed in the future periods in which the asset is used.

ILLUSTRATION 10–1

Initial Cost of Equipment

The Byers Structural Metal Company purchased a six-acre tract of land and an existing building for $500,000. The company plans to raze the old building and construct a new office building on the site. In addition to the purchase price, the company made the following expenditures at closing of the purchase:

Title insurance	$ 3,000
Commissions	16,000
Property taxes	6,000

Shortly after closing, the company paid a contractor $10,000 to tear down the old building and remove it from the site. An additional $5,000 was paid to grade the land. The $6,000 in property taxes included $4,000 of delinquent taxes paid by Byers on behalf of the seller and $2,000 attributable to the portion of the current fiscal year after the purchase date. What should be the capitalized cost of the land?

Capitalized cost of land:	
Purchase price of land (and building to be razed)	$500,000
Title insurance	3,000
Commissions	16,000
Delinquent property taxes	4,000
Cost of removing old building	10,000
Cost of grading	5,000
Total cost of land	$538,000

Two thousand dollars of the property taxes relate only to the current period and should be expensed. Other costs were necessary to acquire the land and are capitalized.

ILLUSTRATION 10–2

Initial Cost of Land

---

and private roads and the costs of fences and lawn and garden sprinkler systems. Costs of these assets are separately identified and capitalized. We depreciate their cost over periods benefited by their use.

COST OF BUILDINGS. The cost of acquiring a building usually includes realtor commissions and legal fees in addition to the purchase price. Quite often a building must be refurbished, remodeled, or otherwise modified to suit the needs of the new owner. These reconditioning costs are part of the building's acquisition cost. When a building is constructed rather than purchased, unique accounting issues are raised. We discuss these in the "Self-Constructed Assets" section of this chapter.

INTERNATIONAL FINANCIAL REPORTING STANDARDS

Valuation of Property, Plant and Equipment. *IAS No. 16* allows a company to value property, plant and equipment (PP&E) subsequent to initial valuation at (1) cost less accumulated depreciation or (2) fair value (revaluation). If revaluation is chosen, all assets within a class of PP&E must be revalued on a regular basis. U.S. GAAP prohibits revaluation.

British Airways, Plc., a U.K. company, prepares its financial statements according to IFRS. The following disclosure note illustrates the company's choice to value PP&E at cost:

Property, Plant and Equipment (in part)

Property, plant and equipment is held at cost. The Group has a policy of not revaluing tangible fixed assets.

COST OF NATURAL RESOURCES. Natural resources that provide long-term benefits are reported as property, plant, and equipment. These include timber tracts, mineral deposits, and oil and gas deposits. They can be distinguished from other assets by the fact that their benefits are derived from their physical consumption. For example, mineral deposits are physically diminishing as the minerals are extracted from the ground and either sold or used in the production process.[3] On the contrary, equipment, land, and buildings produce benefits for a company through their *use* in the production of goods and services. Unlike those of natural resources, their physical characteristics usually remain unchanged during their useful lives.

Sometimes a company buys natural resources from another company. In that case, initial valuation is simply the purchase price plus any other costs necessary to bring the asset to condition and location for use. More frequently, though, the company will develop these assets. In this situation, the initial valuation can include (a) acquisition costs, (b) exploration costs, (c) development costs, and (d) restoration costs. Acquisition costs are the amounts paid to acquire the rights to explore for undiscovered natural resources or to extract proven natural resources. Exploration costs are expenditures such as drilling a well, or excavating a mine, or any other costs of searching for natural resources. Development costs are incurred after the resource has been discovered but before production begins. They include a variety of costs such as expenditures for tunnels, wells, and shafts. It is not unusual for the cost of a natural resource, either purchased or developed, also to include estimated restoration costs. These are costs to restore land or other property to its original condition after extraction of the natural resource ends. Because restoration expenditures occur later—after production begins—they initially represent an obligation incurred in conjunction with an asset retirement. Restoration costs are one example of *asset retirement obligations,* the topic of the next subsection.

On the other hand, the costs of heavy equipment and other assets a company uses during drilling or excavation usually are not considered part of the cost of the natural resource itself. Instead, they are considered depreciable plant and equipment. However, if an asset used in the development of a natural resource cannot be moved and has no alternative use, its depreciable life is limited by the useful life of the natural resource.

> The cost of a natural resource includes the *acquisition costs* for the use of land, the *exploration* and *development costs* incurred before production begins, and *restoration costs* incurred during or at the end of extraction.

ASSET RETIREMENT OBLIGATIONS. Sometimes a company incurs obligations associated with the disposition of an operational asset, often as a result of acquiring that asset. For example, an oil and gas exploration company might be required to restore land to its original condition after extraction is completed. Before 2001, there was considerable diversity in the ways companies accounted for these obligations. Some companies recognized these asset retirement obligations (AROs) gradually over the life of the asset while others did not recognize the obligations until the asset was retired or sold.

---

[3]Because of this characteristic, natural resources sometimes are called *wasting assets.*

SFAS No.143, issued in 2001, requires that an existing legal obligation associated with the retirement of a tangible, long-lived asset be recognized as a liability and measured at fair value, if value can be reasonably estimated. When the liability is credited, the offsetting debit is to the related operational asset.[4] These retirement obligations could arise in connection with several types of operational assets. We introduce the topic here because they are most likely with natural resources. Let's consider some of the provisions of this accounting standard.

An asset retirement obligation (ARO) is measured at fair value and is recognized as a liability and corresponding increase in asset valuation.

Scope. AROs arise only from *legal* obligations associated with the retirement of a tangible long-lived asset that result from the acquisition, construction, or development and (or) normal operation of a long-lived asset.

Recognition. A retirement obligation might arise at the inception of an asset's life or during its operating life. For instance, an offshore oil-and-gas production facility typically incurs its removal obligation when it begins operating. On the other hand, a landfill or a mining operation might incur a reclamation obligation gradually over the life of the asset as space is consumed with waste or as the mine is excavated.

Measurement. A company recognizes the fair value of an ARO in the period it's incurred. The liability increases the valuation of the operational asset. Usually, the fair value is estimated by calculating the present value of estimated future cash outflows.

Present value calculations. Traditionally, the way uncertainty has been considered in present value calculations has been by discounting the "best estimate" of future cash flows applying a discount rate that has been adjusted to reflect the uncertainty or risk of those cash flows. That's not the approach we take here. Instead, we follow the approach described in the FASB's Concept Statement No. 7[5] which is to adjust the cash flows, not the discount rate, for the uncertainty or risk of those cash flows. This expected cash flow approach incorporates specific probabilities of cash flows into the analysis. We use a discount rate equal to the *credit-adjusted risk free rate.* The higher a company's credit risk, the higher will be the discount rate. All other uncertainties or risks are incorporated into the cash flow probabilities. We first considered an illustration of this approach in Chapter 6. Illustration 10–3 demonstrates the approach in connection with the acquisition of a natural resource.

As we discuss in Chapter 11, the cost of the coal mine is allocated to future periods as *depletion* using a depletion rate based on the estimated amount of coal discovered. The $600,000 cost of the excavation equipment, less any anticipated residual value, is allocated to future periods as *depreciation.*

The difference between the asset retirement liability of $468,360 and the probability weighted expected cash outflow of $590,000 is recognized as accretion expense, an additional expense that accrues as an operating expense, over the three-year excavation period. This process increases the liability to $590,000 by the end of the excavation period.

Year	Accretion Expense	Increase in Balance	Asset Retirement Obligation
			468,360
1	8% (468,360) = 37,469	37,469	505,829
2	8% (505,829) = 40,466	40,466	546,295
3	8% (546,295) = 43,705*	43,705	590,000

*rounded

If the actual restoration costs are more (less) than the $590,000, a loss (gain) on retirement of the obligation is recognized for the difference.

St. Mary Land & Exploration Company is engaged in the exploration, development, acquisition, and production of natural gas and crude oil. At the end of its 2007 fiscal year,

---

[4]"Accounting for Asset Retirement Obligations," *Statement of Financial Accounting Standards No. 143* (Norwalk, Conn.: FASB, 2001).
[5]"Using Cash Flow Information and Present Value in Accounting Measurements," *Statement of Financial Accounting Concepts No. 7* (Norwalk, Conn.: FASB, 2000).

ILLUSTRATION 10–3
Cost of Natural Resources

The Jackson Mining Company paid $1,000,000 for the right to explore for a coal deposit on 500 acres of land in Pennsylvania. Costs of exploring for the coal deposit totaled $800,000 and intangible development costs incurred in digging and erecting the mine shaft were $500,000. In addition, Jackson purchased new excavation equipment for the project at a cost of $600,000. After the coal is removed from the site, the equipment will be sold.

Jackson is required by its contract to restore the land to a condition suitable for recreational use after it extracts the coal. The company has provided the following three cash flow possibilities (A, B and C) for the restoration costs to be paid in three years, after extraction is completed:

	Cash Outflow	Probability
A	$500,000	30%
B	600,000	50%
C	700,000	20%

The company's credit-adjusted risk free interest rate is 8%.
Total capitalized cost for the coal deposit is:

Purchase of rights to explore	$1,000,000
Exploration costs	800,000
Development costs	500,000
Restoration costs	468,360*
Total cost of coal deposit	$2,768,360

*Present value of expected cash outflow for restoration costs (asset retirement obligation):
$500,000 × 30% = $150,000
600,000 × 50% = 300,000
700,000 × 20% = 140,000
$590,000 × .79383 = $468,360
(.79383 is the present value of $1, $n = 3$, $i = 8\%$)

Journal Entries:

Coal mine (determined above)	2,768,360	
Cash ($1,000,000 + 800,000 + 500,000)		2,300,000
Asset retirement liability (determined above)		468,360
Excavation equipment	600,000	
Cash (cost)		600,000

St. Mary reported $105 million in asset retirement obligations in its balance sheet. Graphic 10–4 describes the company's policy and provides a summary of the requirements of *SFAS No. 143*.

Asset retirement obligations could result from the acquisition of many different types of tangible operational assets, not just natural resources.

It is important to understand that asset retirement obligations could result from the acquisition of many different types of tangible operational assets, not just natural resources. For example, **Dow Chemical Company** reported a $45 million asset retirement liability in its 2007 balance sheet related to anticipated demolition and remediation activities at its manufacturing sites in the United States, Canada, and Europe.

Sometimes, after exploration or development, it becomes apparent that continuing the project is economically infeasible. If that happens, any costs incurred are expensed rather than capitalized. An exception is in the oil and gas industry, where we have two generally accepted accounting alternatives for accounting for projects that prove unsuccessful. We discuss these alternatives in Appendix 10.

Intangible Assets

Intangible assets generally represent exclusive rights that provide benefits to the owner.

Intangible assets include such items as patents, copyrights, trademarks, franchises, and goodwill. Despite their lack of physical substance, these assets can be extremely valuable resources for a company. For example, **Interbrand Sampson**, the world's leading branding consulting company, estimated the value of the **Coca-Cola** trademark to be $67 billion.[6] In

---
[6]This $67 billion represents an estimate of the fair value to the company at the time the estimate was made, not the historical cost valuation that appears in the balance sheet of Coca-Cola.

GRAPHIC 10–4

Disclosure of
Asset Retirement
Obligations—St. Mary
Land & Exploration
Company

Real World Financials

Note 9—Asset Retirement Obligations (in part)

The Company recognizes an estimated liability for future costs associated with the abandonment of its oil and gas properties. A liability for the fair value of an asset retirement obligation and a corresponding increase to the carrying value of the related long-lived asset are recorded at the time a well is completed or acquired. The increase in carrying value is included in proved oil and gas properties in the consolidated balance sheets. The Company depletes the amount added to proved oil and gas property costs and recognizes accretion expense in connection with the discounted liability over the remaining estimated economic lives of the respective oil and gas properties. Cash paid to settle asset retirement obligations is included in the operating section of the Company's consolidated statement of cash flows.

The Company's estimated asset retirement obligation liability is based on historical experience in abandoning wells, estimated economic lives, estimates as to the cost to abandon the wells in the future and federal, and state regulatory requirements. The liability is discounted using a credit-adjusted risk-free rate estimated at the time the liability is incurred or revised. The credit-adjusted risk-free rates used to discount the Company's abandonment liabilities range from 6.5 percent to 7.25 percent. Revisions to the liability are due to increases in estimated abandonment costs and changes in well economic lives, or if federal or state regulators enact new requirements regarding the abandonment of wells.

general, intangible assets refer to the ownership of exclusive rights that provide benefits to the owner in the production of goods and services.

The issues involved in accounting for intangible assets are similar to those of other operational assets. One key difference, though, is that the future benefits that we attribute to intangible assets usually are much less certain than those attributed to tangible operational assets. For example, will the new toy for which a company acquires a patent be accepted by the market? If so, will it be a blockbuster like Beanie Babies or Rubik's Cube, or will it be only a moderate success? Will it have lasting appeal like Barbie dolls, or will it be a short-term fad? In short, it's often very difficult to anticipate the timing, and even the existence, of future benefits attributable to many intangible assets. In fact, this uncertainty is a discriminating characteristic of intangible assets that perhaps better distinguishes them from tangible assets than their lack of physical substance. After all, other assets, too, do not exist physically but are not considered intangible assets. Accounts receivable and prepaid expenses, for example, have no physical substance and yet are reported among tangible assets.

Companies can either (1) *purchase* intangible assets from other entities (existing patent, copyright, trademark, or franchise rights) or (2) *develop* intangible assets internally (say, develop a new product or process that is then patented). In either case, we amortize its cost, unless it has an indefinite useful life.[7] Also, just like other operational assets, intangibles are subject to asset impairment rules. We discuss amortization and impairment in Chapter 11. In this chapter, we consider the acquisition cost of intangible assets.

> Intangible assets with finite useful lives are amortized; intangible assets with indefinite useful lives are not amortized.

The initial valuation of purchased intangible assets usually is quite simple. We value a purchased intangible at its original cost, which includes its purchase price and all other costs necessary to bring it to condition and location for intended use. For example, if a company purchases a patent from another entity, it might pay legal fees and filing fees in addition to the purchase price. We value intangible assets acquired in exchange for stock, or for other nonmonetary assets, or with deferred payment contracts exactly as we do other operational assets. Let's look briefly at the costs of purchasing some of the more common intangible assets.

> Purchased intangible assets are valued at their original cost.

PATENTS.　A patent is an exclusive right to manufacture a product or to use a process. This right is granted by the U.S. Patent Office for a period of 20 years. In essence, the holder of a patent has a monopoly on the use, manufacture, or sale of the product or process. If a patent is purchased from an inventor or another individual or company, the amount paid is its initial valuation. The cost might also include such other costs as legal and filing fees to secure the patent. Holders of patents often need to defend a patent in court against

---

[7]"Goodwill and Other Intangible Assets," *Statement of Financial Accounting Standards No. 142* (Norwalk, Conn.: FASB, 2001).

infringement. Any attorney fees and other costs of successfully defending a patent are added to the patent account.

When a patent is *developed internally,* the research and development costs of doing so are expensed as incurred. We discuss research and development in more detail in a later section. We capitalize legal and filing fees to secure the patent, even if internally developed.

COPYRIGHTS. A copyright is an exclusive right of protection given to a creator of a published work, such as a song, film, painting, photograph, or book. Copyrights are protected by law and give the creator the exclusive right to reproduce and sell the artistic or published work for the life of the creator plus 70 years. Accounting for the costs of copyrights is virtually identical to that of patents.

TRADEMARKS. A trademark, also called tradename, is an exclusive right to display a word, a slogan, a symbol, or an emblem that distinctively identifies a company, a product, or a service. The trademark can be registered with the U.S. Patent Office which protects the trademark from use by others for a period of 10 years. The registration can be renewed for an indefinite number of 10-year periods, so a trademark is an example of an intangible asset whose useful life could be indefinite.

Trademarks or tradenames often are acquired through a business combination. As an example, in 2002, **Hewlett-Packard Company (HP)** acquired all of the outstanding stock of **Compaq Computer Corporation** for $24 billion. Of that amount, $1.4 billion was assigned to the Compaq tradename. HP stated in a disclosure note that this ". . . intangible asset will not be amortized because it has an indefinite remaining useful life based on many factors and considerations, including the length of time that the Compaq name has been in use, the Compaq brand awareness and market position and the plans for continued use of the Compaq brand within a portion of HP's overall product portfolio."

Trademarks can be very valuable. The estimated value of $67 billion for the Coca-Cola trademark mentioned previously is a good example. Note that the cost of the trademark reported in the balance sheet is far less than the estimate of its worth to the company. The Coca-Cola Company's 2007 balance sheet disclosed trademarks at a cost of only $2 billion.

FRANCHISES. A franchise is a contractual arrangement under which the franchisor grants the franchisee the exclusive right to use the franchisor's trademark or tradename and may include product and formula rights, within a geographical area, usually for a specified period of time. Many popular retail businesses such as fast food outlets, automobile dealerships, and motels are franchises. For example, the last time you ordered a hamburger at McDonald's, you were probably dealing with a franchise.

The owner of that McDonald's outlet paid McDonald's Corporation a fee in exchange for the exclusive right to use the McDonald's name and to sell its products within a specified geographical area. In addition, many franchisors provide other benefits to the franchisee, such as participating in the construction of the retail outlet, training of employees, and national advertising.

Payments to the franchisor usually include an initial payment plus periodic payments over the life of the franchise agreement. The franchisee capitalizes as an intangible asset the initial franchise fee plus any legal costs associated with the contract agreement. The franchise asset is then amortized over the life of the franchise agreement. The periodic payments usually relate to services provided by the franchisor on a continuing basis and are expensed as incurred.

Most purchased intangibles are *specifically identifiable.* That is, cost can be directly associated with a specific intangible right. An exception is goodwill, which we discuss next.

GOODWILL. Goodwill is a unique intangible asset in that its cost can't be directly associated with any specifically identifiable right and it is not separable from the company itself. It represents the unique value of a company as a whole over and above its identifiable tangible and intangible assets. Goodwill can emerge from a company's clientele and reputation, its trained employees and management team, its favorable business location, and any other unique features of the company that can't be associated with a specific asset.

Trademarks or tradenames often are considered to have indefinite useful lives.

Franchise operations are among the most common ways of doing business.

Goodwill can only be purchased through the acquisition of another company.

Because goodwill can't be separated from a company, it's not possible for a buyer to acquire it without also acquiring the whole company or a portion of it. Goodwill will appear as an asset in a balance sheet only when it was purchased in connection with the acquisition of control over another company. In that case, the capitalized cost of goodwill equals the fair value of the consideration exchanged (purchase price) for the company less the fair value of the net assets acquired. The fair value of the net assets equals the fair value of all identifiable tangible and intangible assets less the fair value of any liabilities of the selling company assumed by the buyer. Goodwill is a residual asset; it's the amount left after other assets are identified and valued. Consider Illustration 10–4.

FINANCIAL Reporting Case

Q5, p. 477

Goodwill is the excess of the purchase price over the fair value of the net assets acquired.

ILLUSTRATION 10–4
Goodwill

The Smithson Corporation acquired all of the outstanding common stock of the Rider Corporation in exchange for $18 million cash.* Smithson assumed all of Rider's long-term debts which have a fair value of $12 million at the date of acquisition. The fair values of all identifiable assets of Rider are as follows ($ in millions):

Receivables	$ 5
Inventory	7
Property, plant, and equipment	9
Patent	4
Total	$25

The cost of the goodwill resulting from the acquisition is $5 million:

Fair value of consideration exchanged		$18
Less: Fair value of net assets acquired		
Assets	$25	
Less: Fair value of liabilities assumed	(12)	(13)
Goodwill		$ 5

The Smithson Corporation records the acquisition as follows:

Receivables (fair value)	5	
Inventory (fair value)	7	
Property, plant, and equipment (fair value)	9	
Patent (fair value)	4	
Goodwill (difference)	5	
Liabilities (fair value)		12
Cash (purchase price)		18

*Determining the amount a purchaser is willing to pay for a company in excess of the identifiable net assets is a question of determining the value of a company as a whole. This question is addressed in most introductory and advanced finance textbooks.

Of course, a company can develop its own goodwill through advertising, training, and other efforts. In fact, most do. However, a company must expense all such costs incurred in the internal generation of goodwill. By not capitalizing these items, accountants realize that the matching principle is violated because many of these expenditures do result in significant future benefits. Also, it's difficult to compare two companies when one has purchased goodwill and the other has not. But imagine how difficult it would be to associate these expenditures with any objective measure of goodwill. In essence, we have a situation where the characteristic of reliability overshadows relevance.

As we discussed in Chapter 1, accounting standards have significantly changed the way we account for business combinations. Before these standards became effective in 2001, we amortized (expensed over time) goodwill just like any other intangible asset. This no longer is the case. Now, just like for other intangible assets that have indefinite useful lives, *we do not amortize goodwill.* This makes it imperative that companies make every effort to identify specific intangibles other than goodwill that they acquire in a business combination since goodwill is the amount left after other assets are identified.

Goodwill, along with other intangible assets with indefinite useful lives, is not amortized.

ADDITIONAL CONSIDERATION

It's possible for the fair value of net assets to exceed the fair value of the consideration exchanged for those net assets. A "bargain purchase" situation could result from an acquisition involving a "forced sale" in which the seller is acting under duress. *SFAS No. 141* previously required this excess, deemed negative goodwill, to be allocated as a pro rata reduction of the amounts that otherwise would have been assigned to particular assets acquired. This resulted in assets acquired being recorded at amounts less than their fair values. *SFAS No. 141(R),* issued in 2007, makes it mandatory that assets and liabilities acquired in a business combination be valued at their fair values.[8] Any negative goodwill is reported as a gain in the year of the combination. *SFAS No. 141(R)* is effective for acquisitions made during fiscal years beginning on or after December 15, 2008.

INTERNATIONAL FINANCIAL REPORTING STANDARDS

Valuation of Intangible Assets. *IAS No. 38* allows a company to value an intangible asset subsequent to initial valuation at (1) cost less accumulated amortization or (2) fair value if fair value can be determined by reference to an active market. If revaluation is chosen, all assets within that class of intangibles must be revalued on a regular basis. U.S. GAAP prohibits revaluation.

SFAS 141(R) requires that in a business combination an intangible asset must be recognized as an asset apart from goodwill if it arises from contractual or other legal rights or is separable.

In keeping with that goal, *SFAS 141(R)* provides guidelines for determining which intangibles should be separately recognized and valued. Specifically, an intangible should be recognized as an asset apart from goodwill if it arises from contractual or other legal rights or is capable of being separated from the acquired entity. Possibilities are patents, trademarks, copyrights, and franchise agreements, and such items as customer lists, license agreements, order backlogs, employment contracts, and noncompetition agreements.[9] In past years, some of these intangibles, if present in a business combination, often were included in the cost of goodwill.[10]

Lump-Sum Purchases

● LO2

It's not unusual for a group of operational assets to be acquired for a single sum. If these assets are indistinguishable, for example 10 identical delivery trucks purchased for a lump-sum price of $150,000, valuation is obvious. Each of the trucks would be valued at $15,000 ($150,000 ÷ 10). However, if the lump-sum purchase involves different assets, it's necessary to allocate the lump-sum acquisition price among the separate items. The assets acquired may have different characteristics and different useful lives. For example, the acquisition of a factory may include assets that are significantly different such as land, building, and equipment.

The allocation is made in proportion to the individual assets' relative fair values. This process is best explained by an example in Illustration 10–5.

The relative fair value percentages are multiplied by the lump-sum purchase price to determine the initial valuation of each of the separate assets. Notice that the lump-sum purchase includes inventories, which is not an operational asset. The procedure used here to allocate the purchase price in a lump-sum acquisition pertains to any type of asset mix, not just to operational assets.

---

[8]"Business Combinations," *Statement of Financial Accounting Standards No. 141 (revised)* (Norwalk, Conn.: FASB, 2007).

[9]"Business Combinations," *Statement of Financial Accounting Standards No. 141 (revised)* (Norwalk, Conn.: FASB, 2007). *SFAS No. 141(R)* replaced *SFAS No. 141* issued in 2001.

[10]An assembled workforce is an example of an intangible that is not recognized as a separate asset. A workforce does not represent a contractual or legal right, nor is it separable from the company as a whole.

The Smyrna Hand & Edge Tools Company purchased an existing factory for a single sum of $2,000,000. The price included title to the land, the factory building, and the manufacturing equipment in the building, a patent on a process the equipment uses, and inventories of raw materials. An independent appraisal estimated the fair values of the assets (if purchased separately) at $330,000 for the land, $550,000 for the building, $660,000 for the equipment, $440,000 for the patent and $220,000 for the inventories. The lump-sum purchase price of $2,000,000 is allocated to the separate assets as follows:

ILLUSTRATION 10–5

Lump-Sum Purchase

	Fair Values	
Land	$ 330,000	15%
Building	550,000	25
Equipment	660,000	30
Patent	440,000	20
Inventories	220,000	10
Total	$2,200,000	100%

Land	(15% × $2,000,000)...	300,000
Building	(25% × $2,000,000)...	500,000
Equipment	(30% × $2,000,000)...	600,000
Patent	(20% × $2,000,000)...	400,000
Inventories	(10% × $2,000,000)...	200,000
Cash	....	2,000,000

The total purchase price is allocated in proportion to the relative fair values of the assets acquired.

ETHICAL DILEMMA

Grandma's Cookie Company purchased a factory building. The company controller, Don Nelson, is in the process of allocating the lump-sum purchase price between land and building. Don suggests to the company's chief financial officer, Judith Prince, that they fudge a little by allocating a disproportionately higher share of the price to land. Don reasons that this will reduce depreciation expense, boost income, increase their profit-sharing bonus, and hopefully, increase the price of the company's stock. Judith has some reservations about this because the higher reported income will also cause income taxes to be higher than they would be if a correct allocation of the purchase price is made.

What are the ethical issues? What stakeholders' interests are in conflict?

Noncash Acquisitions

Companies sometimes acquire operational assets without paying cash but instead by issuing debt or equity securities, receiving donated assets, or exchanging other assets. *The controlling principle in each of these situations is that in any noncash transaction (not just those dealing with operational assets), the components of the transaction are recorded at their fair values.* The first indicator of fair value is the fair value of the assets, debt, or equity securities given. Sometimes the fair value of the assets received is used when their fair value is more clearly evident than the fair value of the assets given.

Assets acquired in noncash transactions are valued at the fair value of the assets given or the fair value of the assets received, whichever is more clearly evident.

Deferred Payments

A company can acquire an operational asset by giving the seller a promise to pay cash in the future and thus creating a liability, usually a note payable. The initial valuation of the asset is, again, quite simple as long as the note payable explicitly requires the payment of interest at a realistic interest rate. For example, suppose a machine is acquired for $15,000 and the buyer signs a note requiring the payment of $15,000 sometime in the future *plus* interest in

● LO3

the meantime at a realistic interest rate. The machine would be valued at $15,000 and the transaction recorded as follows:

Machine	15,000	
Note payable		15,000

We know from our discussion of the time value of money in Chapter 6 that most liabilities are valued at the present value of future cash payments, reflecting an appropriate time value of money. As long as the note payable explicitly contains a realistic interest rate, the present value will equal the face value of the note, $15,000 in our previous example. This also should be equal to the fair value of the machine purchased. On the other hand, when an interest rate is not specified or is unrealistic, determining the cost of the asset is less straightforward. In that case, the accountant should look beyond the form of the transaction and record its substance. Consider Illustration 10–6.

ILLUSTRATION 10–6 Asset Acquired with Debt—Present Value of Note Indicative of Fair Value	On January 2, 2009, the Midwestern Steam Gas Corporation purchased an industrial furnace. In payment, Midwestern signed a noninterest-bearing note requiring $50,000 to be paid on December 31, 2010. If Midwestern had borrowed cash to buy the furnace, the bank would have required an interest rate of 10%.

Some portion of the payment(s) required by a noninterest-bearing note in reality is interest.

On the surface, it might appear that Midwestern is paying $50,000 for the furnace, the eventual cash payment. However, when you recognize that the agreement specifies no interest even though the payment won't be made for two years, it becomes obvious that a portion of the $50,000 payment is not actually payment for the furnace, but instead is interest on the note. At what amount should Midwestern value the furnace and the related note payable?

Noncash transactions are recorded at the fair value of the items exchanged.

The answer is fair value, as it is for any noncash transaction. This might be the fair value of the furnace or the fair value of the note. Let's say, in this situation, that the furnace is custom-built, so its cash price is unavailable. But Midwestern can determine the fair value of the note payable by computing the present value of the cash payments at the appropriate interest rate of 10%. The amount actually paid for the machine, then, is the present value of the cash flows called for by the loan agreement, discounted at the market rate—10% in this case.

$$PV = \$50,000 \ (.82645^*) = \$41,323$$
*Present value of $1: $n = 2$, $i = 10\%$ (from Table 2)

So the furnace should be recorded at its *real* cost, $41,323, as follows:[11]

The economic essence of a transaction should prevail over its outward appearance.

Furnace (determined above)	41,323	
Discount on note payable (difference)	8,677	
Note payable (face amount)		50,000

Notice that the note also is recorded at $41,323, its present value, but this is accomplished by using a contra account, called *discount on note payable,* for the difference between the face amount of the note ($50,000) and its present value ($41,323). The difference of $8,677 is the portion of the eventual $50,000 payment that represents interest and is recognized as interest expense over the life of the note.

Assuming that Midwestern's fiscal year-end is December 31 and that adjusting entries are recorded only at the end of each year, the company would record the following entries at the end of 2009 and 2010 to accrue interest and the payment of the note:

---

[11]The entry shown assumes the note is recorded using the gross method. By the net method, a discount account is not used and the note is simply recorded at present value.

Machine	41,323	
Note payable		41,323

December 31, 2009

Interest expense ($41,323 × 10%)	4,132	
Discount on note payable		4,132

December 31, 2010

Interest expense ([$41,323 + 4,132]* × 10%)	4,545	
Discount on note payable		4,545
Note payable (face amount)	50,000	
Cash		50,000

*The 2009 unpaid interest increases the amount owed by $4,132.

Note payable	
	Jan. 1, 2009 50,000
50,000	Dec. 31, 2010
Bal. 12/31/10	0

Discount on note payable	
8,677	Jan. 1, 2009
Dec. 31, 2009 4,132	
Dec. 31, 2010 4,545	
0	Bal. 12/31/10

Sometimes, the fair value of an asset acquired in a noncash transaction is readily available from price lists, previous purchases, or otherwise. In that case, this fair value may be more clearly evident than the fair value of the note and it would serve as the best evidence of the exchange value of the transaction. As an example, let's consider Illustration 10–7.

On January 2, 2009, Dennison, Inc. purchased a machine and signed a noninterest-bearing note in payment. The note requires the company to pay $100,000 on December 31, 2011. Dennison is not sure what interest rate appropriately reflects the time value of money. However, price lists indicate the machine could have been purchased for cash at a price of $79,383.

Dennison records both the asset and liability at $79,383 on January 2:

Machine (cash price)	79,383	
Discount on note payable (difference)	20,617	
Note payable (face amount)		100,000

ILLUSTRATION 10–7

Noninterest-Bearing Note—Fair Value of Asset Is Known

In this situation, we infer the present value of the note from the fair value of the asset. Again, the difference between the note's $79,383 present value and the cash payment of $100,000 represents interest. We can determine the interest rate that is implicit in the agreement as follows:

$$\$79,383 \text{ (present value)} = \$100,000 \text{ (face amount)} \times \text{PV factor}$$
$$\$79,383 \div \$100,000 = .79383*$$

*Present value of $1: $n = 3$, $i = ?$ (from Table 2, $i = 8\%$)

We refer to the 8% rate as the *implicit rate of interest*. Dennison records interest each year at 8% in the same manner as demonstrated in Illustration 10–6 and discussed in greater depth in Chapter 14.

We now turn our attention to the acquisition of operational assets acquired in exchange for equity securities or through donation.

Issuance of Equity Securities

● **LO4**

The most common situation in which equity securities are issued for operational assets occurs when small companies incorporate and the owner or owners contribute assets to the new corporation in exchange for ownership securities, usually common stock. Because the common shares are not publicly traded, it's difficult to determine their fair value. In that case, the fair value of the assets received by the corporation is probably the better indicator of the transaction's exchange value. In other situations, particularly those involving corporations whose stock is actively traded, the market value of the shares is the best indication of fair value. Consider Illustration 10–8.

If the market value of the common stock had not been reliably determinable, the value of the land as determined through an independent appraisal would be used as the cost of the land and the value of the common stock.

Assets acquired by issuing common stock are valued at the fair value of the securities or the fair value of the assets, whichever is more clearly evident.

ILLUSTRATION 10–8	On March 31, 2009, the Elcorn Company issued 10,000 shares of its nopar common stock in exchange for land. On the date of the transaction, the fair value of the common stock, evidenced by its market price, was $20 per share. The journal entry to record this transaction is:
Asset Acquired by Issuing Equity Securities	Land .... 200,000 Common stock (10,000 shares × $20) 200,000

Donated Assets

Donated assets are recorded at their fair values.

On occasion, companies acquire operational assets through donation. The donation usually is an enticement to do something that benefits the donor. For example, the developer of an industrial park might pay some of the costs of building a manufacturing facility to entice a company to locate in its park. Companies record assets donated by unrelated parties at their fair values based on either an available market price or an appraisal value. This should not be considered a departure from historical cost valuation. Instead, it is equivalent to the donor contributing cash to the company and the company using the cash to acquire the asset.

Revenue is credited for the amount paid by an unrelated party.

As the recipient records the asset at its fair value, what account receives the offsetting credit? Over the years, there has been disagreement over this question. Should the recipient increase its paid-in capital—the part of shareholders' equity representing investments in the firm? Or, should the donated asset be considered revenue? *SFAS 116* requires that donated assets be recorded as *revenue*.[12] Recall that revenues generally are inflows of assets from delivering or producing goods, rendering services, or from other activities that constitute the entity's ongoing major or central operations. The rationale is that the company receiving the donation is performing a service for the donor in exchange for the asset donated.

Corporations occasionally receive donations from governmental units. A local governmental unit might provide land or pay all or some of the cost of a new office building or manufacturing plant to entice a company to locate within its geographical boundaries. For example, the city of San Jose, California, recently paid a significant portion of the cost of a new office building for **IBM Corporation**. *SFAS 116 does not apply to transfers of assets from governmental units.* However, it is the opinion of the authors that this type of donation also should be accounted for as revenue by the recipient. In the IBM example, the new office building, located in downtown San Jose, brought jobs to a revitalized downtown area and increased revenues to the city. The City of San Jose did not receive an equity interest in IBM through its donation, but significantly benefited nevertheless.

Illustration 10–9 provides an example. In this illustration, we assume that, even though the donation is from a governmental unit, *SFAS 116* guidelines apply.

ILLUSTRATION 10–9	Elcorn Enterprises decided to relocate its office headquarters to the city of Westmont. The city agreed to pay 20% of the $20 million cost of building the headquarters in order to entice Elcorn to relocate. The building was completed on May 3, 2009. Elcorn paid its portion of the cost of the building in cash. Elcorn records the transaction as follows:

Asset Donation	Building 20,000,000
	  Cash 16,000,000
	  Revenue—donation of asset (20% × $20 million) 4,000,000

Operational assets also can be acquired in an exchange. Because an exchange transaction inherently involves a disposition of one operational asset as it is given up in exchange for another, we cover these transactions in Part B, Dispositions and Exchanges.

---

[12]"Accounting for Contributions Received and Contributions Made," *Statement of Financial Accounting Standards No. 116* (Norwalk, Conn.: FASB, 1993).

INTERMEDIATE ACCOUNTING

DECISION MAKERS' PERSPECTIVE

The operational asset acquisition decision is among the most significant decisions that management must make. A decision to acquire a new fleet of airplanes or to build or purchase a new office building or manufacturing plant could influence a company's performance for many years.

These decisions, often referred to as capital budgeting decisions, require management to forecast all future net cash flows (cash inflows minus cash outflows) generated by the operational asset(s). These cash flows are then used in a model to determine if the future cash flows are sufficient to warrant the capital expenditure. One such model, the net present value model, compares the present value of future net cash flows with the required initial acquisition cost of the asset(s). If the present value is higher than the acquisition cost, the asset is acquired. You have studied or will study capital budgeting in considerable depth in a financial management course. The introduction to the time value of money concept in Chapter 6 provided you with important tools necessary to evaluate capital budgeting decisions.

A key to profitability is how well a company manages and utilizes its assets. Financial analysts often use activity, or turnover, ratios to evaluate a company's effectiveness in managing assets. This concept was illustrated with receivables and inventory in previous chapters. Operational assets—particularly property, plant, and equipment (PP&E)—usually are a company's primary revenue-generating assets. Their efficient use is critical to generating a satisfactory return to owners. One ratio analysts often use to measure how effectively managers use PP&E is the fixed-asset turnover ratio. This ratio is calculated as follows:

● **LO5**

The fixed-asset turnover ratio measures a company's effectiveness in managing property, plant, and equipment.

$$\text{Fixed-asset turnover ratio} = \frac{\text{Net sales}}{\text{Average fixed assets}}$$

The ratio indicates the level of sales generated by the company's investment in fixed assets. The denominator usually is the book value (cost less accumulated depreciation and depletion) of property, plant, and equipment.[13]

As with other turnover ratios, we can compare a company's fixed-asset turnover with that of its competitors, with an industry average, or with the same company's ratio over time. Let's compare the fixed-asset turnover ratios for **Dell** and **Apple**.

| | ($ in millions) | | | |
| | **Dell** | | **Apple** | |
	2007	**2006**	**2007**	**2006**
Property, plant, and equipment (net)	$2,409	$1,993	$1,832	$1,281
Net sales—2007		$57,420		$24,006

Real World Financials

The 2007 fixed-asset turnover for Dell is 26 ($57,420 ÷ [($2,409 + 1,993) ÷ 2]) compared to Apple's turnover of 15 ($24,006 ÷ [($1,832 + 1,281) ÷ 2]). Dell is able to generate nearly twice as much as Apple in sales dollars for each dollar invested in fixed assets. ●

DISPOSITIONS AND EXCHANGES

PART B

After using operational assets, companies will sell, retire, or exchange those assets. Accounting for exchanges differs somewhat from accounting for sales and retirements because they involve both an acquisition and a disposition. So let's look first at sales and retirements and then we'll address accounting for exchanges. Be sure to note that in each case, the companies should record depreciation, depletion, or amortization up to the date of disposition or exchange.

● **LO6**

---

[13]If intangible assets are significant, their book value could be added to the denominator to produce a turnover that reflects all operational assets. The use of book value provides an approximation of the company's current investment in these assets.

Dispositions

When selling operational assets for monetary consideration (cash or a receivable), the seller recognizes a gain or loss for the difference between the consideration received and the book value of the asset sold. Illustration 10–10 provides an example.

ILLUSTRATION 10–10 Sale of Operational Asset **A gain or loss is recognized for the difference between the consideration received and the asset's book value.**	The Robosport Company sold for $6,000 machinery that originally cost $20,000. Depreciation of $12,000 had been recorded up to the date of sale. Since the $8,000 book value of the asset ($20,000 − 12,000) exceeds the $6,000 consideration Robosport received, the company recognizes a $2,000 loss. The sale is recorded as follows: Cash (selling price) .... 6,000 Accumulated depreciation (account balance) .... 12,000 Loss on disposal of machinery (difference) .... 2,000 Machinery (account balance) 20,000

Retirements (or abandonments) are treated similarly. The only difference is that there will be no monetary consideration received. A loss is recorded for the remaining book value of the asset.

Operational assets to be disposed of by sale are classified as held for sale and measured at the lower of book value or fair value less cost to sell.

When an operational asset is to be disposed of by *sale*, we classify it as "held for sale" and report it at the lower of its book value or fair value less any cost to sell.[14] If the fair value less cost to sell is below book value, we recognize an impairment loss. Operational assets classified as held for sale are not depreciated or amortized. Recall from your study of discontinued operations in Chapter 4 that this treatment is the same one we employed in accounting for a component of an entity that is held for sale. We cover this topic in more depth in the impairment section of Chapter 11.

ADDITIONAL CONSIDERATION

Involuntary Conversions

Occasionally companies dispose of operational assets unintentionally. These so-called involuntary conversions include destruction by fire, earthquake, flood, or other catastrophe and expropriation by a governmental body.

Usually, the company receives a cash settlement from an insurance company for destroyed assets or from the governmental body for expropriated assets. The company often immediately reinvests this cash in similar assets. Nevertheless, involuntary conversions are treated precisely the same as voluntary conversions. That is, the proceeds are recorded, the book value of the lost assets are removed, and a gain or loss is recognized for the difference.

Exchanges

Sometimes a company will acquire an operational asset in exchange for another operational asset. This frequently involves a trade-in by which a new asset is acquired in exchange for an old asset, and cash is given to equalize the fair values of the assets exchanged. The basic principle followed in these nonmonetary asset[15] exchanges is to value the asset received at fair value. This can be the fair value of the asset(s) given up or the fair value of the asset(s) received plus (or minus) any cash exchanged. We first look to the fair value of the asset given up. However, in a trade-in, quite often the fair value of the new asset is more clearly evident than the second-hand value of the asset traded in. We recognize a gain or loss for the difference between the fair value of the asset given up and its book value. See the example in Illustration 10–11A.

---

[14]"Accounting for the Impairment or Disposal of Long-Lived Assets," *Statement of Financial Accounting Standards No. 144* (Norwalk, Conn.: FASB, 2001)

[15]Monetary items are assets and liabilities whose *amounts are fixed*, by contract or otherwise, in terms of a specific number of dollars. Others are considered nonmonetary.

The Elcorn Company traded its laser equipment for the newer air-cooled ion lasers manufactured by American Laser Corporation. The old equipment had a book value of $100,000 (cost of $500,000 less accumulated depreciation of $400,000) and a fair value of $150,000. To equalize the fair values of the assets exchanged, in addition to the old machinery, Elcorn paid American Laser $430,000 in cash. This means that the fair value of the new laser equipment is $580,000. We know this because American Laser was willing to trade the new lasers in exchange for old lasers worth $150,000 plus $430,000 cash. The following journal entry records the transaction:

Laser equipment—new (fair value: $150,000 + 430,000) ...	580,000	
Accumulated depreciation (account balance)	400,000	
Laser equipment—old (account balance)		500,000
Cash (amount paid)...		430,000
Gain (to balance; also: $150,000 − 100,000)....................		50,000

The new laser equipment is recorded at $580,000, the fair value of the old equipment, $150,000, plus the cash given of $430,000. This also equals the fair value of the new lasers. Elcorn recognizes a gain of $50,000, which is simply the difference between the old equipment's fair value of $150,000 and its $100,000 book value as well as the amount needed to allow the debits to equal credits in the journal entry.

ILLUSTRATION 10–11A

Nonmonetary Asset Exchange

An operational asset received in an exchange of nonmonetary assets generally is valued at fair value.

A gain is recognized when the fair value of an asset given is more than its book value.

Let's modify the illustration slightly by assuming that the fair value of the old equipment is $75,000 instead of $150,000. Illustration 10–11B shows the journal entry to record the transaction.

The Elcorn Company traded its laser equipment for the newer air-cooled ion lasers manufactured by American Laser Corporation. The old equipment had a book value of $100,000 (cost of $500,000 less accumulated depreciation of $400,000) and a fair value of $75,000. To equalize the fair values of the assets exchanged, in addition to the old machinery, Elcorn paid American Laser $430,000 in cash. This means that the fair value of the new laser equipment is $505,000. We know this because American Laser was willing to trade the new lasers in exchange for old lasers worth $75,000 plus $430,000 in cash. The following journal entry records the transaction:

Laser equipment—new (fair value: $75,000 + 430,000)	505,000	
Accumulated depreciation (account balance)	400,000	
Loss (to balance; also: $100,000 − 75,000)	25,000	
Laser equipment—old (account balance)		500,000
Cash (amount paid)		430,000

The $25,000 difference between the equipment's fair value of $75,000 and its book value of $100,000 is recognized as a loss. The new equipment is valued at $505,000, the fair value of the old equipment of $75,000 plus the $430,000 cash given.

ILLUSTRATION 10–11B

Nonmonetary Asset Exchange

A loss is recognized when the fair value of an asset given is less than its book value.

It's important to understand that the gain or loss recognized in these transactions is the difference between the fair value and book value of the asset given. The amount of cash given or received has no effect on the amount of gain or loss recognized. The cash given or received simply serves to equalize the fair value of the assets exchanged.

Until 2005, the accounting treatment of nonmonetary asset exchanges depended on a number of factors including (1) whether the assets exchanged were similar or dissimilar, (2) whether a gain or loss was indicated in the exchange, and (3) whether cash was given or received. A new accounting standard[16] simplified accounting for exchanges of operational assets by requiring the use of fair value except in rare situations in which the fair value can't be determined or the exchange lacks commercial substance.[17]

Let's discuss each of these situations.

Gain or loss is the difference between fair value and book value of the asset given.

---

[16]"Exchanges of Nonmonetary Assets an amendment of APB Opinion No. 29," *Statement of Financial Accounting Standards No. 153,* (Norwalk, Conn.: FASB, 2004).
[17]There is a third situation, not involving operational assets, which precludes the use of fair value in a nonmonetary exchange. The transaction is an exchange of inventories to facilitate sales to customers other than the parties to the exchange.

Fair Value not Determinable

It would be unusual for a company to be unable to reasonably determine fair value of either asset in an exchange. Nevertheless, if the situation does occur, the company would simply use the book value of the asset given up, plus (minus) any cash given (received) to value the asset acquired. For example, if fair value had not been determinable in Illustration 10–11A, Elcorn would have recorded the exchange as follows:

If we can't determine the fair value of either asset in the exchange, the asset received is valued at the book value of the asset given.

Equipment—new (book value + cash: $100,000 + 430,000)	530,000	
Accumulated depreciation (account balance)	400,000	
Equipment—old (account balance)		500,000
Cash (amount paid)		430,000

The new equipment is valued at the book value of the old equipment ($100,000) plus the cash given ($430,000). No gain or loss is recognized.

Exchange Lacks Commercial Substance

If we record an exchange at fair value, we recognize a gain or loss for the difference between the fair value and book value of the asset(s) given up. To preclude the possibility of a company exchanging appreciated assets solely to recognize a gain, fair value can be used only in gain situations that have "commercial substance."

Commercial substance is present when future cash flows change as a result of the exchange.

A nonmonetary exchange is considered to have commercial substance if future cash flows will change as a result of the exchange. Most exchanges are for legitimate business reasons and would not be transacted if there were no anticipated change in future cash flows. The exchange of old laser equipment for the *newer* model in Illustration 10–11A is an example of an exchange transacted for legitimate business reasons.

GAIN SITUATION.   Suppose a company owned a tract of land that had a book value of $1 million and a fair value of $5 million. The only ways to recognize the $4 million appreciation are to either sell the land or to exchange the land for another nonmonetary asset for a legitimate business purpose. For example, if the land were exchanged for a different type of asset, say a building, then future cash flows most likely will change, the exchange has commercial substance, fair value is used and the $4 million gain can be recognized. On the other hand, if the land were exchanged for a tract of land that has the identical characteristics as the land given, then it is unlikely that future cash flows would change. In this case, the exchange lacks commercial substance and the new land is valued at the book value of the old land. Illustration 10–12 provides an example.

ILLUSTRATION 10–12
 	
Nonmonetary Asset Exchange—Exchange Lacks Commercial Substance
	The Elcorn Company traded a tract of land to Sanchez Development for a similar tract of land. The old land had a book value of $2,500,000 and a fair value of $4,500,000. To equalize the fair values of the assets exchanged, in addition to the land, Elcorn paid Sanchez $500,000 in cash. This means that the fair value of the land acquired is $5,000,000. The following journal entry records the transaction, *assuming that the exchange lacks commercial substance:*
	
	Land—new (book value + cash: $2,500,000 + 500,000) 3,000,000
	   Land—old (account balance) 2,500,000
	   Cash (amount paid) 500,000
	
	The new land is recorded at $3,000,000, the book value of the old land, $2,500,000, plus the cash given of $500,000. No gain is recognized.

When the fair value of the asset given is less than its book value, we always use fair value to record the exchange.

LOSS SITUATION.   In Illustration 10–12, what if the fair value of the land given was less than its book value? It's unlikely that a company would enter into this type of transaction unless there was a legitimate business reason. The FASB's intent in including the commercial substance requirement for the use of fair value was to avoid companies' trading *appreciated* property for no legitimate reason other than to recognize the gain. This means that when a loss is indicated in a nonmonetary exchange, it's okay to record the loss and we use fair value to value the asset acquired.

ADDITIONAL CONSIDERATION

In Illustration 10–12, cash was given to equalize the fair values of the assets exchanged. What if cash was received? Suppose that $500,000 cash was *received* instead of given. In that case, part of the transaction is considered monetary and a portion of the $2,000,000 gain ($4,500,000 − 2,500,000) is recognized. The amount of gain recognized is equal to the proportion of cash received relative to total received:

$$\frac{\$500,000}{\$500,000 + 4,500,000} = 10\%$$

Elcorn would recognize a $200,000 gain (10% × $2,000,000) and would value the land received at $2,200,000, the book value of the land given ($2,500,000), plus the gain recognized ($200,000), less the cash received ($500,000). The following journal entry records the transaction:

Land—new ($2,500,000 + 200,000 − 500,000)	2,200,000	
Cash	500,000	
Land—old		2,500,000
Gain		200,000

CONCEPT REVIEW EXERCISE

EXCHANGES

The MD Corporation recently acquired new equipment to be used in its production process. In exchange, the company traded in an existing asset that had an original cost of $60,000 and accumulated depreciation on the date of the exchange of $45,000. In addition, MD paid $40,000 cash to the equipment manufacturer. The fair value of the old equipment is $17,000.

Required:

1. Prepare the journal entry MD would use to record the exchange transaction assuming that the transaction has commercial substance.
2. Prepare the journal entry MD would use to record the exchange transaction assuming that the transaction does *not* have commercial substance.

1. Prepare the journal entry MD would use to record the exchange transaction assuming that the transaction has commercial substance.

SOLUTION

Equipment—new ($17,000 + 40,000)	57,000	
Accumulated depreciation (account balance)	45,000	
Cash (amount paid)		40,000
Equipment—old (account balance)		60,000
Gain ($17,000 fair value − $15,000 book value)		2,000

2. Prepare the journal entry MD would use to record the exchange transaction assuming that the transaction does *not* have commercial substance.

Equipment—new ($15,000 + 40,000)	55,000	
Accumulated depreciation (account balance)	45,000	
Cash (amount paid)		40,000
Equipment—old (account balance)		60,000

PART C

SELF-CONSTRUCTED ASSETS AND RESEARCH AND DEVELOPMENT

Two types of expenditures relating to operational assets whose accounting treatment has generated considerable controversy are interest costs pertaining to self-constructed assets and amounts spent for research and development. We now consider those expenditures and why those controversies have developed.

Self-Constructed Assets

● **LO7**

A company might decide to construct an operational asset for its own use rather than buy an existing one. For example, a retailer like **Nordstrom** might decide to build its own store rather than purchase an existing building. A manufacturing company like **Intel** could construct its own manufacturing facility. In fact, Nordstrom and Intel are just two of the many companies that self-construct assets. Other recognizable examples include **Walt Disney**, **Sears**, and **Caterpillar**. Quite often these companies act as the main contractor and then subcontract most of the actual construction work.

The critical accounting issue in these instances is identifying the cost of the self-constructed asset. The task is more difficult than for purchased assets because there is no external transaction to establish an exchange price. Actually, two difficulties arise in connection with assigning costs to self-constructed assets: (1) determining the amount of the company's indirect manufacturing costs (overhead) to be allocated to the construction and (2) deciding on the proper treatment of interest (actual or implicit) incurred during construction.

Overhead Allocation

The cost of a self-constructed asset includes identifiable materials and labor and a portion of the company's manufacturing overhead costs.

One difficulty of associating costs with self-constructed assets is the same difficulty encountered when determining cost of goods manufactured for sale. The costs of material and direct labor usually are easily identified with a particular construction project and are included in cost. However, the treatment of manufacturing overhead cost and its allocation between construction projects and normal production is a controversial issue.

Some accountants advocate the inclusion of only the *incremental* overhead costs in the total cost of construction. That is, the asset's cost would include only those additional costs that are incurred because of the decision to construct the asset. This would exclude such indirect costs as depreciation and the salaries of supervisors that would be incurred whether or not the construction project is undertaken. If, however, a new construction supervisor was hired specifically to work on the project, then that salary would be included in asset cost.

Others advocate assigning overhead on the same basis that is used for a regular manufacturing process. That is, all overhead costs are allocated both to production and to self-constructed assets based on the relative amount of a chosen cost driver (for example, labor hours) incurred. This is known as the *full-cost approach* and is the generally accepted method used to determine the cost of a self-constructed asset.

Interest Capitalization

FINANCIAL Reporting Case

Q3, p. 477

To reiterate, the cost of an asset includes all costs necessary to get the asset ready for its intended use. Unlike one purchased from another company, a self-constructed asset requires time to create it. During this construction period, the project must be financed in some way. This suggests the question as to whether interest costs during the construction period are one of the costs of acquiring the asset itself or simply costs of financing the asset. On the one hand, we might point to interest charges to finance inventories during their period of manufacture or to finance the purchase of plant assets from others and argue that construction period interest charges are merely costs of financing the asset that should be expensed as incurred like all other interest costs. On the other hand, we might argue that self-constructed assets are different in that during the construction period, they are not yet ready for their intended use for producing revenues. And, so, in keeping with both the historical cost principle and the matching concept, all costs during this period, including interest, should be capitalized and then allocated as depreciation during later periods when the assets are providing benefits.

QUALIFYING ASSETS.   Generally accepted accounting principles are consistent with the second argument. Specifically, interest is capitalized during the construction period for (a) assets built for a company's own use as well as for (b) assets constructed *as discrete projects* for sale or lease (a ship or a real estate development, for example). This excludes from interest capitalization consideration inventories that are routinely manufactured in large quantities on a repetitive basis and assets that already are in use or are ready for their intended use.[18] Interest costs incurred during the productive life of the asset are expensed as incurred.

> Only assets that are constructed as discrete projects qualify for interest capitalization.
>
> Only interest incurred during the construction period is eligible for capitalization.

INTERNATIONAL FINANCIAL REPORTING STANDARDS

Interest Capitalization. *SFAS No. 34* requires a company to capitalize interest during the construction period of a qualified asset. *IAS No. 23*, as originally issued, allowed a company to choose between (1) capitalization and (2) immediate expensing of interest incurred during the construction period.

In 2007, *IAS No. 23* was revised and now requires the capitalization of interest in most situations, effectively eliminating the major difference between U.S. GAAP and international standards in this area. This illustrates one of three ways the IASB and FASB are moving toward convergence: (1) revising international standards to converge with U.S. standards (this instance), (2) revising U.S. standards to converge with international standards, and (3) working jointly to develop common standards.

PERIOD OF CAPITALIZATION.   The capitalization period for a self-constructed asset starts with the first expenditure (materials, labor, or overhead) and ends either when the asset is substantially complete and ready for use or when interest costs no longer are being incurred. Interest costs incurred can pertain to borrowings other than those obtained specifically for the construction project. However, interest costs can't be imputed; actual interest costs must be incurred.

> The interest capitalization period begins when construction begins and the first expenditure is made as long as interest costs are actually being incurred.

AVERAGE ACCUMULATED EXPENDITURES.   Because we consider interest to be a necessary cost of getting a self-constructed asset ready for use, the amount capitalized is only that portion of interest cost incurred during the construction period that *could have been avoided* if expenditures for the asset had not been made. In other words, if construction had not been undertaken, debt incurred for the project would not have been necessary and/or other interest-bearing debt could have been liquidated or employed elsewhere.

> *Average accumulated expenditures* approximates the average debt necessary for construction.

As a result, interest should be determined for only the construction expenditures actually incurred during the capitalization period. And unless all expenditures are made at the outset of the period, it's necessary to determine the *average* amount outstanding during the period. This is the amount of debt that would be required to finance the expenditures and thus the amount on which interest would accrue. For instance, if a company accumulated $1,500,000 of construction expenditures fairly evenly throughout the construction period, the average expenditures would be:

Total accumulated expenditures incurred evenly throughout the period	$1,500,000
	÷ 2
Average accumulated expenditures	$ 750,000

At the beginning of the period, no expenditures have accumulated, so no interest has accrued (on the equivalent amount of debt). But, by the end of the period interest is accruing on the total amount, $1,500,000. On average, then, interest accrues on half the total or $750,000.

If expenditures are not incurred evenly throughout the period, a simple average is insufficient. In that case, a weighted average is determined by time-weighting individual

> Average accumulated expenditures is determined by time-weighting individual expenditures made during the construction period.

---

[18]"Capitalization of Interest Costs," *Statement of Financial Accounting Standards No. 34* (Stamford, Conn.: FASB, 1979).

expenditures or groups of expenditures by the number of months from their incurrence to the end of the construction period. This is demonstrated in Illustration 10–13.

ILLUSTRATION 10–13 Interest Capitalization	On January 1, 2009, the Mills Conveying Equipment Company began construction of a building to be used as its office headquarters. The building was completed on June 30, 2010. Expenditures on the project, mainly payments to subcontractors, were as follows:

January 3, 2009	$ 500,000
March 31, 2009	400,000
September 30, 2009	600,000
Accumulated expenditures at December 31, 2009 (before interest capitalization)	$1,500,000
January 31, 2010	600,000
April 30, 2010	300,000

On January 2, 2009, the company obtained a $1 million construction loan with an 8% interest rate. The loan was outstanding during the entire construction period. The company's other interest-bearing debt included two long-term notes of $2,000,000 and $4,000,000 with interest rates of 6% and 12%, respectively. Both notes were outstanding during the entire construction period.

FINANCIAL Reporting Case

Q4, p. 477

STEP 1: Determine the average accumulated expenditures.

The weighted-average accumulated expenditures by the end of 2009 are:

January 3, 2009	$500,000 × $^{12}/_{12}$ =	$500,000
March 31, 2009	400,000 × $^{9}/_{12}$ =	300,000
September 30, 2009	600,000 × $^{3}/_{12}$ =	150,000
Average accumulated expenditures for 2009	=	$950,000

Again notice that the average accumulated expenditures are less than the total accumulated expenditures of $1,500,000. If Mills had borrowed exactly the amount necessary to finance the project, it would not have incurred interest on a loan of $1,500,000 for the whole year but only on an average loan of $950,000. The next step is to determine the interest to be capitalized for the average accumulated expenditures.

INTEREST RATES. In this situation, debt financing was obtained specifically for the construction project, and the amount borrowed is sufficient to cover the average accumulated expenditures. To determine the interest capitalized, then, we simply multiply the construction loan rate of 8% by the average accumulated expenditures.

STEP 2: Calculate the amount of interest to be capitalized.

$$\text{Interest capitalized for 2009} = \$950,000 \times 8\% = \$76,000$$

The amount of interest capitalized is determined by multiplying an interest rate by the average accumulated expenditures.

Notice that this is the same answer we would get by assuming separate 8% construction loans were made for each expenditure at the time each expenditure was made:

Loans		Annual Rate		Portion of Year Outstanding		Interest
$500,000	×	8%	×	$^{12}/_{12}$	=	$40,000
400,000	×	8%	×	$^{9}/_{12}$	=	24,000
600,000	×	8%	×	$^{3}/_{12}$	=	12,000
Interest capitalized for 2009						$76,000

The interest of $76,000 is added to the cost of the building, bringing accumulated expenditures at December 31, 2009, to $1,576,000 ($1,500,000 + 76,000). The remaining interest cost incurred but not capitalized is expensed.

It should be emphasized that interest capitalization does not require that funds actually be borrowed for this specific purpose, only that the company does have outstanding debt. The presumption is that even if the company doesn't borrow specifically for the project, funds from other borrowings must be diverted to finance the construction. Either way—directly or indirectly—interest costs are incurred. In our illustration, for instance, even without the construction loan, interest would be capitalized because other debt was outstanding. The capitalized interest would be the average accumulated expenditures multiplied by the weighted-average rate on these other loans. The weighted-average interest rate on all debt other than the construction loan would be 10%, calculated as follows:[19]

Loans		Rate		Interest
$2,000,000	×	6%	=	$120,000
4,000,000	×	12%	=	480,000
$6,000,000				$600,000

$$\text{Weighted-average rate: } \frac{\$600,000}{\$6,000,000} = 10\%$$

This is a weighted average because total interest is $600,000 on total debt of $6,000,000.

ADDITIONAL CONSIDERATION

The weighted-average rate isn't used for 2009 in our illustration because the specific construction loan is sufficient to cover the average accumulated expenditures. If the specific construction loan had been insufficient to cover the average accumulated expenditures, its 8% interest rate would be applied to the average accumulated expenditures up to the amount of the specific borrowing, and any remaining average accumulated expenditures in excess of specific borrowings would be multiplied by the weighted-average rate on all other outstanding interest-bearing debt. Suppose, for illustration, that the 8% construction loan had been only $500,000 rather than $1,000,000. We would calculate capitalized interest using both the specific rate and the weighted-average rate:

	Average Accumulated Expenditures		Rate		Interest
Total	$950,000				
Specific borrowing	500,000	×	8%	=	$40,000
Excess	$450,000	×	10%	=	45,000
Capitalized interest					$85,000

In our illustration, it's necessary to use this approach in 2010.

It's possible that the amount of interest calculated to be capitalized exceeds the amount of interest actually incurred. If that's the case, we limit the interest capitalized to the actual interest incurred. In our illustration, total interest cost incurred during 2009 far exceeds the $76,000 of capitalized interest calculated, so it's not necessary to limit the capitalized amount.

Interest capitalized is limited to interest incurred.

Loans		Annual Rate		Actual Interest	Calculated Interest
$1,000,000	×	8%	=	$ 80,000	
2,000,000	×	6%	=	120,000	
4,000,000	×	12%	=	480,000	
				$680,000	$76,000
					↑
					Use lower amount

STEP 3: Compare calculated interest with actual interest incurred.

---

[19]The same result can be obtained simply by multiplying the individual debt interest rates by the relative amount of debt at each rate. In this case, one-third of total debt is at 6% and two-thirds of the total debt is at 12% (1/3 × 6% + 2/3 × 12% = 10%).

Continuing the example based on the information in Illustration 10–13, let's determine the amount of interest capitalized during 2010 for the building. The total accumulated expenditures by the end of the project are:

Accumulated expenditures at the beginning of 2010	
(including interest capitalization)	$1,576,000
January 31, 2010	600,000
April 30, 2010	300,000
Accumulated expenditures at June 30, 2010	
(before 2010 interest capitalization)	$2,476,000

The weighted-average accumulated expenditures by the end of the project are:

STEP 1: Determine the average accumulated expenditures.

January 1, 2010	$1,576,000 × ⁶⁄₆ =	$1,576,000
January 31, 2010	600,000 × ⁵⁄₆ =	500,000
April 30, 2010	300,000 × ²⁄₆ =	100,000
Average accumulated expenditures for 2010		$2,176,000

Notice that the 2010 expenditures are weighted relative to the construction period of six months because the project was finished on June 30, 2010. Interest capitalized for 2010 would be $98,800, calculated as follows:

STEP 2: Calculate the amount of interest to be capitalized.

	Average Accumulated Expenditures		Annual Rate		Fraction of Year		
	$2,176,000						
Specific borrowing	1,000,000	×	8%	×	$\frac{6}{12}$	=	$40,000
Excess	$1,176,000	×	10%	×	$\frac{6}{12}$	=	58,800
Capitalized interest							$98,800

Multiplying by six-twelfths reflects the fact that the interest rates are annual rates (12-month rates) and the construction period is only 6 months.

STEP 3: Compare calculated interest with actual interest incurred.

Loans		Annual Rate	Actual Interest	Calculated Interest
$1,000,000	×	8% × $\frac{6}{12}$ =	$ 40,000	
2,000,000	×	6% × $\frac{6}{12}$ =	60,000	
4,000,000	×	12% × $\frac{6}{12}$ =	240,000	
			$340,000	$98,800
				↑
				Use lower amount

ADDITIONAL CONSIDERATION

To illustrate how the actual interest limitation might come into play, let's assume the nonspecific borrowings in our illustration were $200,000 and $400,000 (instead of $2,000,000 and $4,000,000). Our comparison would change as follows:

Loans		Annual Rate	Actual Interest	Calculated Interest
$1,000,000	×	8% × $\frac{6}{12}$ =	$40,000	
200,000	×	6% × $\frac{6}{12}$ =	6,000	
400,000	×	12% × $\frac{6}{12}$ =	24,000	
			$70,000	$98,800
			↑	
			Use lower amount	

For the first six months of 2010, $98,800 of interest would be capitalized, bringing the total capitalized cost of the building to $2,574,800 ($2,476,000 + 98,800), and $241,200 in interest would be expensed ($340,000 − 98,800).

The method of determining interest to capitalize that we've discussed is called the specific interest method because we use rates from specific construction loans to the extent of specific borrowings before using the average rate of other debt. Sometimes, though, it's difficult to associate specific borrowings with projects. In these situations, it's acceptable to just use the weighted-average rate on all interest-bearing debt, including all construction loans. This is known as the weighted-average method. In our illustration, for example, if the $1,000,000, 8% loan had not been specifically related to construction, we would calculate a single weighted-average rate as shown below.

Loans		Rate		Interest
$1,000,000	×	8%	=	$ 80,000
2,000,000	×	6%	=	120,000
4,000,000	×	12%	=	480,000
$7,000,000				$680,000

$$\text{Weighted-average rate: } \frac{\$680,000}{\$7,000,000} = 9.7\%$$

Weighted-average method

If we were using the weighted-average method rather than the specific interest method, we would simply multiply this single rate times the average accumulated expenditures to determine capitalizable interest.

DISCLOSURE.   For an accounting period in which interest costs are capitalized, both the total amount of interest costs incurred and the amount that has been capitalized should be disclosed. Graphic 10–5 shows an interest capitalization disclosure note that was included in a recent annual report of **Carnival Corporation**, the world's largest cruise company.

If material, the amount of interest capitalized during the period must be disclosed.

GRAPHIC 10–5

Capitalized Interest Disclosure—Carnival Corporation

Real World Financials

Note 4—Property and Equipment (in part)

Capitalized interest, primarily on our ships under construction, amounted to $44 million, $37 million, and $21 million in fiscal 2007, 2006, and 2005, respectively. Amounts related to ships under construction include progress payments for the construction of the ship, as well as design and engineering fees, capitalized interest, construction oversight costs, and various owner supplied items.

Research and Development (R&D)

Prior to *SFAS No. 2,* the practice was to allow companies to either expense or capitalize R&D costs, but *SFAS No. 2* requires all research and development costs to be charged to expense when incurred.[20] This was a controversial standard opposed by many companies who preferred delaying the recognition of these expenses until later years when presumably the expenditures bear fruit.

● LO8

A company undertakes an R&D project because it believes the project will eventually provide benefits that exceed the current expenditures. Unfortunately, though, it's difficult to predict which individual research and development projects will ultimately provide benefits. In fact, only 1 in 10 actually reach commercial production. Moreover, even for those projects that pan out, a direct relationship between research and development costs and specific future revenue is difficult to establish. In other words, even if R&D costs do lead to future benefits, it's difficult to objectively determine the size of the benefits and in which periods the costs should be expensed if they are capitalized. These are the issues that prompted the FASB to require immediate expensing.

Most R&D costs are expensed in the periods incurred.

R&D costs entail a high degree of uncertainty of future benefits and are difficult to match with future revenues.

The FASB's approach is certain in most cases to understate assets and overstate current expense because at least some of the R&D expenditures will likely produce future benefits.

---

[20]"Accounting for Research and Development Costs," *Statement of Financial Accounting Standards No. 2* (Stamford, Conn.: FASB, 1974), par. 12.

DETERMINING R&D COSTS. *SFAS 2* distinguishes research and development as follows:

Research is planned search or critical investigation aimed at discovery of new knowledge with the hope that such knowledge will be useful in developing a new product or service or a new process or technique or in bringing about a significant improvement to an existing product or process.

Development is the translation of research findings or other knowledge into a plan or design for a new product or process or for a significant improvement to an existing product or process whether intended for sale or use.[21]

R&D costs include salaries, wages, and other labor costs of personnel engaged in R&D activities, the costs of materials consumed, equipment, facilities, and intangibles used in R&D projects, the costs of services performed by others in connection with R&D activities, and a reasonable allocation of indirect costs related to those activities. General and administrative costs should not be included unless they are clearly related to the R&D activity.

If an operational asset is purchased specifically for a single R&D project, its cost is considered R&D and expensed immediately even though the asset's useful life extends beyond the current year. However, the cost of an operational asset that has an alternative future use beyond the current R&D project is *not* a current R&D expense. Instead, the depreciation or amortization of these alternative-use assets is included as R&D expenses in the current and future periods the assets are used for R&D activities.

In general, R&D costs pertain to activities that occur prior to the start of commercial production, and costs of starting commercial production and beyond are not R&D costs. Graphic 10–6 captures this concept with a time line beginning with the start of an R&D project and ending with the ultimate sale of a developed product or the use of a developed process. The graphic also provides examples of activities typically included as R&D and examples of activities typically excluded from R&D.[22]

> R&D expense includes the depreciation and amortization of operational assets used in R&D activities.

GRAPHIC 10–6
Research and Development Expenditures

> Costs incurred *before* the start of commercial production are all expensed as R&D.

> Costs incurred *after* commercial production begins would be either expensed or included in the cost of inventory.

Start of R&D Activity | Start of Commercial Production | Sale of Product or Process

Examples of R&D Costs:

- Laboratory research aimed at discovery of new knowledge
- Searching for applications of new research findings or other knowledge
- Design, construction, and testing of preproduction prototypes and models
- Modification of the formulation or design of a product or process

Examples of Non-R&D Costs:

- Engineering follow-through in an early phase of commercial production
- Quality control during commercial production including routine testing of products
- Routine ongoing efforts to refine, enrich, or otherwise improve on the qualities of an existing product
- Adaptation of an existing capability to a particular requirement or customer's need as a part of a continuing commercial activity

---

[21]Ibid., par. 8.
[22]Ibid., par. 9 and 10.

Costs incurred before the start of commercial production are all expensed as R&D. The costs incurred after commercial production begins would be either expensed or treated as manufacturing overhead and included in the cost of inventory. Let's look at an example in Illustration 10–14.

<table>
<tr><td colspan="2">The Askew Company made the following cash expenditures during 2009 related to the development of a new industrial plastic:</td><td>ILLUSTRATION 10–14
Research and
Development Costs</td></tr>
<tr><td>R&D salaries and wages</td><td>$10,000,000</td><td></td></tr>
<tr><td>R&D supplies consumed during 2009</td><td>3,000,000</td><td></td></tr>
<tr><td>Purchase of R&D equipment</td><td>5,000,000</td><td></td></tr>
<tr><td>Patent filing and legal costs</td><td>100,000</td><td></td></tr>
<tr><td>Payments to others for services performed in connection
with R&D activities</td><td>1,200,000</td><td></td></tr>
<tr><td>Total</td><td>$19,300,000</td><td></td></tr>
</table>

The project resulted in a new product to be manufactured in 2010. A patent was filed with the U.S. Patent Office. The equipment purchased will be employed in other projects. Depreciation on the equipment for 2009 was $500,000.

The salaries and wages, supplies consumed, and payments to others for R&D services are expensed in 2009 as R&D. The equipment is capitalized and the 2009 depreciation is expensed as R&D. Even though the costs to develop the patented product are expensed, the filing and legal costs for the patent are capitalized and amortized in future periods just as similar costs are capitalized for purchased intangibles. Amortization of the patent is discussed in Chapter 11.

The various expenditures would be recorded as follows:

R&D expense ($10,000,000 + 3,000,000 + 1,200,000)	14,200,000	
Cash		14,200,000
To record R&D expenses.		
Equipment	5,000,000	
Cash		5,000,000
To record the purchase of equipment.		
R&D expense	500,000	
Accumulated depreciation—equipment		500,000
To record R&D depreciation.		
Patent	100,000	
Cash		100,000
To capitalize the patent filing and legal costs.		

Expenditures reconciliation:

Recorded as R&D	$14,200,000
Capitalized as equipment	5,000,000
Capitalized as patent	100,000
Total expenditures	$19,300,000

GAAP require that total R&D expense incurred must be disclosed either as a line item in the income statement or in a disclosure note. For example, **Microsoft** reported $7,121 billion of R&D expense on the face of its 2007 income statement. In our illustration, total R&D expense disclosed in 2009 would be $14,700,000 ($14,200,000 in expenditures and $500,000 in depreciation). Note that if Askew later sells this patent to another company for, say, $15 million, the buyer would capitalize the entire purchase price rather than only the filing and legal costs. Once again, the reason for the apparent inconsistency in accounting treatment of internally generated intangibles and externally purchased intangibles is the difficulty of associating costs and benefits.

R&D PERFORMED FOR OTHERS. The requirements of *SFAS 2* do not apply to companies that perform R&D for other companies under contract. In these situations, the R&D costs are capitalized as inventory and carried forward into future years until the project is completed. Of course, justification is that the benefits of these expenditures are the contract fees that are determinable and are earned over the term of the project. Income from these contracts can be recognized using either the percentage-of-completion or completed contract method. We discussed these alternatives in Chapter 5.

Another exception pertains to a company that develops computer software. Expenditures made after the software is determined to be technologically feasible but before it is ready for commercial production are capitalized. Costs incurred before technological feasibility is established are expensed as incurred. We discuss software development costs below.

START-UP COSTS. For the nine-month period ending September 29, 2007, **McCormick & Schmick's Seafood Restaurants, Inc.,** opened nine new restaurants. The company incurred a variety of one-time preopening costs for salaries of employees supervising construction, training, travel, and relocation of employees totaling $3 million. In fact, whenever a company introduces a new product or service, or commences business in a new territory or with a new customer, it incurs similar start-up costs. As with R&D expenditures, a company must expense all the costs related to a company's start-up activities in the period incurred, rather than capitalize those costs as an asset. Start-up costs also include organization costs related to organizing a new entity, such as legal fees and state filing fees to incorporate.[23]

> Start-up costs are expensed in the period incurred.

ADDITIONAL CONSIDERATION

Development Stage Enterprises

A development stage enterprise is a new business that has either not commenced its principal operations or has begun its principal operations but has not generated significant revenues. Prior to *SFAS 7*,[24] many of these companies recorded an asset for the normal operating costs incurred during the development stage. This asset was then expensed over a period of time beginning with the commencement of operations.

SFAS 7 requires that these enterprises comply with the same generally accepted accounting principles that apply to established operating companies in determining whether a cost is to be charged to expense when incurred or capitalized and expensed in future periods. Therefore, normal operating costs incurred during the development stage are expensed, not capitalized. *SFAS 7* does allow development stage enterprises to provide items of supplemental information to help financial statement readers more readily assess their future cash flows.

SOFTWARE DEVELOPMENT COSTS. The computer software industry has become a large and important U.S. business over the last two decades. Relative newcomers such as **Microsoft** and **Adobe Systems**, as well as traditional hardware companies like **IBM**, are leaders in this multibillion dollar industry. A significant expenditure for these companies is the cost of developing software. Prior to *SFAS No. 86,* some companies were capitalizing software development costs and expensing them in future periods and others were expensing these costs in the period incurred.

SFAS No. 86 requires all companies to expense costs incurred to develop or purchase computer software to be sold, leased, or otherwise marketed as R&D costs until technological feasibility of the product has been established.[25] The Statement does not address the

> GAAP requires the capitalization of software development costs incurred after *technological feasibility* is established.

[23]"Reporting on the Costs of Start-Up Activities," *Statement of Position 98-5* (New York: AIPA, 1998).
[24]"Accounting and Reporting by Development Stage Enterprises," *Statement of Financial Accounting Standards No. 7* (Stamford, Conn.: FASB, 1975).
[25]"Accounting for the Costs of Computer Software to be Sold, Leased, or Otherwise Marketed," *Statement of Financial Accounting Standards No. 86* (Stamford, Conn.: FASB, 1985).

accounting treatment of costs incurred to develop computer software to be used internally. The authoritative GAAP is an AICPA pronouncement by which we account for these costs in a similar manner. Costs incurred during the preliminary project stage are expensed as R&D. After the application development stage is reached (for example, at the coding stage or installation stage), we capitalize any further costs.[26] We generally capitalize the costs of computer software *purchased* for internal use.

Technological feasibility is established "when the enterprise has completed all planning, designing, coding, and testing activities that are necessary to establish that the product can be produced to meet its design specifications including functions, features, and technical performance requirements."[27] Costs incurred after technological feasibility but before the product is available for general release to customers are capitalized as an intangible asset. These costs include coding and testing costs and the production of product masters. Similar to the treatment of such costs under *SFAS 2,* costs incurred after the product release date usually are not R&D expenditures. Graphic 10–7 shows the R&D time line introduced earlier in the chapter and adds the point of establishment of technological feasibility. Only the costs incurred between technological feasibility and the product release date are capitalized.

GRAPHIC 10–7

Research and Development Expenditures— Computer Software

The amortization of capitalized computer software development costs begins when the product is available for general release to customers. The periodic amortization percentage is the greater of (1) the ratio of current revenues to current and anticipated revenues (percentage-of-revenue method) or (2) the straight-line percentage over the useful life of the asset, as shown in Illustration 10–15.

The Astro Corporation develops computer software graphics programs for sale. A new development project begun in 2008 reached technological feasibility at the end of June 2009, and the product was available for release to customers early in 2010. Development costs incurred in 2009 prior to June 30 were $1,200,000 and costs incurred from June 30 to the product availability date were $800,000. 2010 revenues from the sale of the new product were $3,000,000 and the company anticipates an additional $7,000,000 in revenues. The economic life of the software is estimated at four years.

Astro Corporation would expense the $1,200,000 in costs incurred prior to the establishment of technological feasibility and capitalize the $800,000 in costs incurred between technological feasibility and the product availability date. 2010 amortization of the intangible asset, software development costs, is calculated as follows:

1. Percentage-of-revenue method:

$$\frac{\$3,000,000}{\$3,000,000 + 7,000,000} = 30\% \times \$800,000 = \$240,000$$

2. Straight-line method:

$$\tfrac{1}{4} \text{ or } 25\% \times \$800,000 = \$200,000.$$

The percentage-of-revenue method is used because it produces the greater amortization, $240,000.

ILLUSTRATION 10–15

Software Development Costs

---

[26]"Accounting for the Costs of Computer Software Developed or Obtained for Internal Use," *Statement of Position 98-1* (New York: AICPA, 1998).
[27]"Accounting for the Costs of Computer Software to Be Sold, Leased, or Otherwise Marketed," *Statement of Financial Accounting Standards No. 86* (Stamford, Conn.: FASB, 1985), par. 4.

Graphic 10–8 shows the software disclosure included in a recent annual report of **Computer Associates International, Inc.** The note provides a good summary of the accounting treatment of software development costs.

GRAPHIC 10–8

Software Disclosure— Computer Associates International, Inc.

Real World Financials

Capitalized Software Costs and Other Identified Intangible Assets (in part)

In accordance with *SFAS No. 86*, "Accounting for the Costs of Computer Software to be Sold, Leased, or Otherwise Marketed," internally generated software development costs associated with new products and significant enhancements to existing software products are expensed as incurred until technological feasibility has been established. Internally generated software development costs of $85 million, $84 million, and $70 million were capitalized during fiscal years 2007, 2006, and 2005, respectively. The Company recorded amortization of $54 million, $48 million, and $41 million for the fiscal years ended March 31, 2007, 2006, and 2005, respectively.

Annual amortization of capitalized software costs is the greater of the amount computed using the ratio that current gross revenues for a product bear to the total of current and anticipated future gross revenues for that product or the straight-line method over the remaining estimated economic life of the software product, generally estimated to be five years.

Why do generally accepted accounting principles allow this exception to the general rule of expensing all R&D? We could attribute it to the political process. Software is a very important industry to our economy and perhaps its lobbying efforts resulted in the standard allowing software companies to capitalize certain R&D costs.

We could also attribute the exception to the nature of the software business. Recall that R&D costs in general are expensed in the period incurred for two reasons: (1) they entail a high degree of uncertainty of future benefits, and (2) they are difficult to match with future benefits. With software, there is an important identifiable engineering milestone, technological feasibility. When this milestone is attained, the probability of the software product's success increases significantly. And because the useful life of software is fairly short (one to four years in most cases), it is much easier to determine the periods of increased revenues than for R&D projects in other industries. Compare this situation with, say, the development of a new drug. Even after the drug has been developed, it must go through extensive testing to meet FDA (Food and Drug Administration) approval, which may never be attained. If attained, the useful life of the drug could be anywhere from a few months to many years.

INTERNATIONAL FINANCIAL REPORTING STANDARDS

Research and Development Expenditures. Other than software development costs incurred after technological feasibility has been established, U.S. GAAP requires all research and development expenditures to be expensed in the period incurred. *IAS No. 38* draws a distinction between research activities and development activities. Research expenditures are expensed in the period incurred. However, development expenditures that meet specified criteria are capitalized as an intangible asset.

Heineken, a company based in Amsterdam, prepares its financial statements according to IFRS. The following disclosure note describes the company's adherence to *IAS No. 38*. The note also describes the criteria for capitalizing development expenditures.

Real World Financials

Software, Research and Development and Other Intangible Assets (in part)

Expenditures on research activities, undertaken with the prospect of gaining new technical knowledge and understanding, is recognized in the income statement when incurred.

Development activities involve a plan or design for the production of new or substantially improved products and processes. Development expenditures are capitalized only if development costs can be measured reliably, the product or process is technically and commercially feasible, future economic benefits are probable, and Heineken intends to and has sufficient resources to complete development and to use or sell the asset.

PURCHASED RESEARCH AND DEVELOPMENT.   It's not unusual for one company to buy another company in order to obtain technology that the acquired company has developed or is in the process of developing. Any time a company buys another, it values the tangible and intangible assets acquired at fair value. When technology is involved, we distinguish between *developed technology* and *in-process research and development.* To do that, we borrow a criterion used in accounting for software development costs, and determine whether *technological feasibility* has been achieved. If so, the value of that technology is considered "developed," and we capitalize its fair value (record it as an asset) and amortize that amount over its useful life just like any other finite-life intangible asset.

We treat in-process R&D differently. Before 2009, we expensed the amount allocated to in-process R&D in the period of the acquisition. A new standard now requires the capitalization of the fair value of in-process R&D. But, unlike developed technology, we view it as an *indefinite-life* intangible asset.[28] As you will learn in Chapter 11, we don't amortize indefinite-life intangibles. Instead, we test them for "impairment" at least annually. If the R&D project is completed successfully, we switch to the way we account for developed technology and amortize the capitalized amount over the estimated period the product or process developed will provide benefits. If the project instead is abandoned, we expense the entire balance immediately. Research and development costs incurred after the acquisition to complete the project are expensed as incurred, consistent with the treatment of any other R&D expenditure not acquired in an acquisition.

> For business acquisitions made during fiscal years beginning on or after December 15, 2008, the fair value of in-process research and development is capitalized as an indefinite-life intangible asset.

As an example, **Cisco Systems, Inc.,** acquired 100% of the shares of **WebEx Communications, Inc.,** in 2007 for $3,025 million. Cisco allocated the purchase price (assigned fair values) as follows ($ in millions):

Tangible assets	$ 400
Finite life intangible assets (including developed technology)	541
In-process research and development	66
Goodwill	2,098
	3,105
Less: Fair value of liabilities assumed	(80)
Total	$3,025

> **Real World Financials**

Cisco immediately expensed the $66 million of in-process R&D. For acquisitions made during fiscal years beginning on or after December 15, 2008, that $66 million would be capitalized instead as an indefinite life intangible asset and accounted for subsequently as discussed above.

FINANCIAL REPORTING CASE SOLUTION

1. **Describe to Stan what it means to capitalize an expenditure. What is the general rule for determining which costs are capitalized when an operational asset is acquired?** *(p. 480)*   To capitalize an expenditure simply means to record it as an asset. All expenditures other than payments to shareholders and debt repayments are either expensed as incurred or capitalized. In general, the choice is determined by whether the expenditure benefits more than just the current period. Exceptions to this general principle are discussed in the chapter. The initial cost of an operational asset includes all expenditures necessary to bring the asset to its desired condition and location for use.

2. **Which costs might be included in the initial cost of equipment?** *(p. 480)*   In addition to the purchase price, the cost of equipment might include the cost of transportation, installation, testing, and legal fees to establish title.

3. **In what situations is interest capitalized rather than expensed?** *(p. 498)*   Interest is capitalized only for assets constructed for a company's own use or for assets constructed as discrete products for sale or lease. For example, **Walt Disney** capitalizes

---

[28]"Business Combinations," *Statement of Financial Accounting Standards No. 141 (revised)* (Norwalk, Conn.: FASB, 2007).

interest on assets constructed for its theme parks, resorts and other property, and on theatrical and television productions in process. During the construction period, interest is considered a cost necessary to get the asset ready for its intended use.

4. **What is the three-step process used to determine the amount of interest capitalized?** *(p. 500)* The first step is to determine the average accumulated expenditures for the period. The second step is to multiply the average accumulated expenditures by an appropriate interest rate or rates to determine the amount of interest capitalized. A final step compares the interest determined in step two with actual interest incurred. Interest capitalized is limited to the amount of interest incurred.

5. **What is goodwill and how is it measured?** *(p. 487)* Goodwill represents the unique value of a company as a whole over and above its identifiable tangible and intangible assets. Because goodwill can't be separated from a company, it's not possible for a buyer to acquire it without also acquiring the whole company or a substantial portion of it. Goodwill will appear as an asset in a balance sheet only when it was purchased in connection with the acquisition of another company. In that case, the capitalized cost of goodwill equals the fair value of the consideration exchanged for the company less the fair value of the net assets acquired. Goodwill is a residual asset; it's the amount left after other assets are identified and valued. Prior to standards effective in 2001, we amortized (expensed over time) goodwill just like any other intangible asset. This no longer is the case. Now, just like for other intangible assets that have indefinite useful lives, we do not amortize goodwill. ●

THE BOTTOM LINE

● **LO1** The initial cost of an operational asset acquired in an exchange transaction includes the purchase price and all expenditures necessary to bring the asset to its desired condition and location for use. The cost of a natural resource includes the acquisition costs for the use of land, the exploration and development costs incurred before production begins, and restoration costs incurred during or at the end of extraction. Purchased intangible assets are valued at their original cost to include the purchase price and legal and filing fees. (p. 480)

● **LO2** If a lump-sum purchase involves different assets, it is necessary to allocate the lump-sum acquisition price among the separate items according to some logical allocation method. A widely used allocation method is to divide the lump-sum purchase price according to the individual assets' relative fair values. (p. 488)

● **LO3** Assets acquired in exchange for deferred payment contracts are valued at their fair value or the present value of payments using a realistic interest rate. (p. 489)

● **LO4** Assets acquired through the issuance of equity securities are valued at the fair value of the securities if known; if not known, the fair value of the assets received is used. Donated assets are valued at their fair value. (p. 491)

● **LO5** A key to profitability is how well a company manages and utilizes its assets. Financial analysts often use activity, or turnover, ratios to evaluate a company's effectiveness in managing its assets. Operational assets—particularly property, plant, and equipment (PP&E)—usually are a company's primary revenue-generating assets. Their efficient use is critical to generating a satisfactory return to owners. One ratio that analysts often use to measure how effectively managers use PP&E is the fixed-asset turnover ratio. This ratio is calculated by dividing net sales by average fixed assets. (p. 493)

● **LO6** When an operational asset is sold, a gain or loss is recognized for the difference between the consideration received and the asset's book value. The basic principle used for non-monetary exchanges is to value the asset(s) received based on the fair value of the asset(s) given up. In certain situations, the valuation of the asset(s) received is based on the book value of the asset(s) given up. (p. 493)

● **LO7** The cost of a self-constructed asset includes identifiable materials and labor and a portion of the company's manufacturing overhead costs. In addition, GAAP provide for the capitalization of interest incurred during construction. The amount of interest capitalized is equal to the average accumulated expenditures for the period multiplied by the appropriate interest rates, not to exceed actual interest incurred. (p. 498)

● **LO8** Research and development costs incurred to internally develop an intangible asset are expensed in the period incurred. Filing and legal costs for developed intangibles are capitalized. (p. 503) ●

OIL AND GAS ACCOUNTING

Chapter 1 characterized the establishment of accounting and reporting standards as a political process. Standards, particularly changes in standards, can have significant differential effects on companies, investors and creditors, and other interest groups. The FASB must consider potential economic consequences of a change in an accounting standard or the introduction of a new standard. The history of oil and gas accounting provides a good example of this political process and the effect of possible adverse economic consequences on the standard-setting process.

There are two generally accepted methods that companies can use to account for oil and gas exploration costs. The successful efforts method requires that exploration costs that are known *not* to have resulted in the discovery of oil or gas (sometimes referred to as *dry holes*) be included as expenses in the period the expenditures are made. The alternative, the full-cost method, allows costs incurred in searching for oil and gas within a large geographical area to be capitalized as assets and expensed in the future as oil and gas from the successful wells are removed from that area. Both of these methods are widely used. Illustration 10A–1 compares the two alternatives.

The Shannon Oil Company incurred $2,000,000 in exploration costs for each of 10 oil wells drilled in 2009 in west Texas. Eight of the 10 wells were dry holes.

The accounting treatment of the $20 million in total exploration costs will vary significantly depending on the accounting method used. The summary journal entries using each of the alternative methods are as follows:

ILLUSTRATION 10A–1

Oil and Gas Accounting

Successful Efforts		**Full Cost**	
Oil deposit 4,000,000		Oil deposit 20,000,000	
Exploration expense 16,000,000		Cash	20,000,000
Cash	20,000,000		

Using the full-cost method, Shannon would capitalize the entire $20 million which is expensed as oil from the two successful wells is depleted. On the other hand, using the successful efforts method, the cost of the unsuccessful wells is expensed in 2009, and only the $4 million cost related to the successful wells is capitalized and expensed in future periods as the oil is depleted.

In 1977 the FASB attempted to establish uniformity in the accounting treatment of oil and gas exploration costs. *SFAS 19* was issued requiring all companies to use the successful efforts method.[29]

SFAS 19 met with criticism from the oil and gas companies that were required to switch from full cost to successful efforts accounting. These companies felt that the switch would seriously depress their reported income over time. As a result, they argued, their ability to raise capital in the securities markets would be inhibited, which would result in a cutback of new exploration. The fear that the standard would cause domestic companies to significantly reduce oil and gas exploration and thus increase our dependence on foreign oil was compelling to the U.S. Congress, the SEC, and the Department of Energy.

Many feared that the implementation of *SFAS 19* would cause a significant cutback in the exploration for new oil and gas in the United States.

Extensive pressure from Congress, the SEC, and affected companies forced the FASB to rescind *Standard 19.* Presently, oil and gas companies can use either the successful efforts or full-cost method to account for oil and gas exploration costs. Of course, the method used must be disclosed. For example, Graphic 10A–1 shows how **Chevron Corp.**, disclosed their use of the successful efforts method in a note to recent financial statements. ●

Properties, Plant and Equipment

The successful efforts method is used for crude oil and gas exploration and production activities.

GRAPHIC 10A–1

Oil and Gas Accounting Disclosure—Chevron Corp.

Real World Financials

---

[29]"Financial Accounting and Reporting by Oil and Gas Producing Companies," *Statement of Financial Accounting Standards No. 19* (Stamford, Conn.: FASB, 1977).

Q 10–1   Define operational assets and explain the difference between tangible and intangible operational assets.

Q 10–2   What is included in the original cost of an operational asset acquired in an exchange transaction?

Q 10–3   Identify the costs associated with the initial valuation of a developed natural resource.

Q 10–4   Briefly summarize the accounting treatment for intangible assets, explaining the difference between purchased and internally developed intangible assets.

Q 10–5   What is goodwill and how is it measured?

Q 10–6   Explain the method generally used to allocate the cost of a lump-sum purchase to the individual assets acquired.

Q 10–7   When an operational asset is acquired and a note payable is assumed, explain how acquisition cost of the asset is determined when the interest rate for the note is less than the current market rate for similar notes.

Q 10–8   Explain how operational assets acquired in exchange for equity securities are valued.

Q 10–9   Explain how operational assets acquired through donation are valued.

Q 10–10   When an operational asset is disposed of, how is gain or loss on disposal computed?

Q 10–11   What is the basic principle for valuing operational assets acquired in exchange for other nonmonetary assets?

Q 10–12   Identify the two exceptions to valuing operational assets acquired in nonmonetary exchanges at the fair value of the asset(s) given up.

Q 10–13   In what situations is interest capitalized?

Q 10–14   Define average accumulated expenditures and explain how it is computed.

Q 10–15   Explain the difference between the specific interest method and the weighted-average method in determining the amount of interest to be capitalized.

Q 10–16   Define R&D according to *SFAS 2*.

Q 10–17   Explain the accounting treatment of equipment acquired for use in R&D projects.

Q 10–18   Explain the accounting treatment of costs incurred to develop computer software.

Q 10–19   Explain the difference in the accounting treatment of the cost of developed technology and the cost of in process R&D in an acquisition.

Q 10–20   (Based on Appendix 10) Explain the difference between the successful efforts and the full-cost methods of accounting for oil and gas exploration costs.

BRIEF **EXERCISES**

BE 10–1
Acquisition cost;
machine

● LO1

Beaverton Lumber purchased a milling machine for $35,000. In addition to the purchase price, Beaverton made the following expenditures: freight, $1,500; installation, $3,000; testing, $2,000; personal property tax on the machine for the first year, $500. What is the initial cost of the machine?

BE 10–2
Acquisition cost;
land and building

● LO1

Fullerton Waste Management purchased land and a warehouse for $600,000. In addition to the purchase price, Fullerton made the following expenditures related to the acquisition: broker's commission, $30,000; title insurance, $3,000; miscellaneous closing costs, $6,000. The warehouse was immediately demolished at a cost of $18,000 in anticipation of the building of a new warehouse. Determine the amounts Fullerton should capitalize as the cost of the land and the building.

BE 10–3
Lump-sum
acquisition

● LO2

Refer to the situation described in BE 10–2. Assume that Fullerton decides to use the warehouse rather than demolish it. An independent appraisal estimates the fair values of the land and warehouse at $420,000 and $280,000, respectively. Determine the amounts Fullerton should capitalize as the cost of the land and the building.

BE 10–4
Cost of a natural
resource

● LO1

Smithson Mining operates a silver mine in Nevada. Acquisition, exploration, and development costs totaled $5.6 million. After the silver is extracted in approximately five years, Smithson is obligated to restore the land to its original condition, including constructing a wildlife preserve. The company's controller has provided the following three cash flow possibilities for the restoration costs: (1) $500,000, 20% probability; (2) $550,000, 45% probability; and (3) $650,000, 35% probability. The company's credit-adjusted, risk-free rate of interest is 6%. What is the initial cost of the silver mine?

BE 10–5
Cost of a natural resource

● LO1

Refer to the situation described in BE 10–4. What is the carrying value of the asset retirement liability at the end of one year? Assuming that the actual restoration costs incurred after extraction is completed are $596,000, what amount of gain or loss will Smithson recognize on retirement of the liability?

BE 10–6
Goodwill

● LO1

Pro-tech Software acquired all of the outstanding stock of Reliable Software for $14 million. The book value of Reliable's net assets (assets minus liabilities) was $8.3 million. The fair values of Reliable's assets and liabilities equaled their book values with the exception of certain intangible assets whose fair values exceeded book values by $2.5 million. Calculate the amount paid for goodwill.

BE 10–7
Acquisition cost; noninterest-bearing note

● LO3

On June 30, 2009, Kimberly Farms purchased custom-made harvesting machinery from a local producer. In payment, Kimberly signed a noninterest-bearing note requiring the payment of $60,000 in two years. The fair value of the machinery is not known, but an 8% interest rate properly reflects the time value of money for this type of loan agreement. At what amount will Kimberly initially value the machinery? How much interest expense will Kimberly recognize in its income statement for this note for the year ended December 31, 2009?

BE 10–8
Acquisition cost; issuance of equity securities

● LO4

Shackelford Corporation acquired a patent from its founder, Jim Shackelford, in exchange for 50,000 shares of the company's nopar common stock. On the date of the exchange, the common stock had a fair value of $22 per share. Determine the cost of the patent.

BE 10–9
Fixed-asset turnover ratio; solve for unknown

● LO5

The balance sheets of Pinewood Resorts reported net fixed assets of $740,000 and $940,000 at the end of 2008 and 2009, respectively. The fixed-asset turnover ratio for 2009 was 3.25. Calculate Pinewood's net sales for 2009.

BE 10–10
Disposal of operational assets

● LO6

Lawler Clothing sold manufacturing equipment for $16,000. Lawler originally purchased the equipment for $80,000, and depreciation through the date of sale totaled $71,000. What was the gain or loss on the sale of the equipment?

BE 10–11
Nonmonetary exchange

● LO6

Calaveras Tire exchanged machinery for two pickup trucks. The book value and fair value of the machinery were $20,000 (original cost of $65,000 less accumulated depreciation of $45,000) and $17,000, respectively. To equalize fair values, Calaveras paid $8,000 in cash. At what amount will Calaveras value the pickup trucks? How much gain or loss will the company recognize on the exchange?

BE 10–12
Nonmonetary exchange

● LO6

Refer to the situation described in BE 10–11. Answer the questions assuming that the fair value of the machinery was $24,000, instead of $17,000.

BE 10–13
Nonmonetary exchange

● LO6

Refer to the situation described in BE 10–12. Answer the questions assuming that the exchange lacks commercial substance.

BE 10–14
Interest capitalization

● LO7

A company constructs a building for its own use. Construction began on January 2 and ended on December 28. The expenditures for construction were as follows: January 2, $500,000; March 31, $600,000; June 30, $400,000; October 30, $600,000. To help finance construction, the company arranged a 7% construction loan on January 2 for $700,000. The company's other borrowings, outstanding for the whole year, consisted of a $3 million loan and a $5 million note with interest rates of 8% and 6%, respectively. Assuming the company uses the *specific interest method,* calculate the amount of interest capitalized for the year.

BE 10–15
Interest capitalization

● LO7

Refer to the situation described in BE 10–14. Assuming the company uses the *weighted-average method,* calculate the amount of interest capitalized for the year.

BE 10–16
Research and
development

● LO8

Maxtor Technology incurred the following costs during the year related to the creation of a new type of personal computer monitor:

Salaries	$220,000
Depreciation on R&D facilities and equipment	125,000
Utilities and other direct costs incurred for the R&D facilities	66,000
Patent filing and related legal costs	22,000
Payment to another company for performing a portion of the development work	120,000
Costs of adapting the new monitor for the specific needs of a customer	80,000

What amount should Maxtor report as research and development expense in its income statement?

EXERCISES

available with McGraw–Hill's Homework Manager www.mhhe.com/spiceland5e

An alternate exercise and problem set is available on the text website: www.mhhe.com/spiceland5e

E 10–1
Acquisition costs;
land and building

● LO1

On March 1, 2009, Beldon Corporation purchased land as a factory site for $60,000. An old building on the property was demolished, and construction began on a new building that was completed on December 15, 2009. Costs incurred during this period are listed below:

Demolition of old building	$ 4,000
Architect's fees (for new building)	12,000
Legal fees for title investigation of land	2,000
Property taxes on land (for period beginning March 1, 2009)	3,000
Construction costs	500,000
Interest on construction loan	5,000

Salvaged materials resulting from the demolition of the old building were sold for $2,000.
Required:
Determine the amounts that Beldon should capitalize as the cost of the land and the new building.

E 10–2
Acquisition cost;
machinery

● LO1

Oaktree Company purchased a new machine and made the following expenditures:

Purchase price	$45,000
Sales tax	2,200
Freight charges for shipment of machine	700
Insurance on the machine for the first year	900
Installation of machine	1,000

The machine, including sales tax, was purchased on open account, with payment due in 30 days. The other expenditures listed above were paid in cash.
Required:
Prepare the necessary journal entries to record the above expenditures.

E 10–3
Acquisition
costs; lump-sum
acquisition

● LO1 LO2

Semtech Manufacturing purchased land and building for $4 million. In addition to the purchase price, Semtech made the following expenditures in connection with the purchase of the land and building:

Title insurance	$16,000
Legal fees for drawing the contract	5,000
Pro-rated property taxes for the period after acquisition	36,000
State transfer fees	4,000

An independent appraisal estimated the fair values of the land and building, if purchased separately, at $3.3 and $1.1 million, respectively. Shortly after acquisition, Semtech spent $82,000 to construct a parking lot and $40,000 for landscaping.
Required:
1. Determine the initial valuation of each asset Semtech acquired in these transactions.
2. Repeat requirement 1, assuming that immediately after acquisition, Semtech demolished the building. Demolition costs were $250,000 and the salvaged materials were sold for $6,000. In addition, Semtech spent $86,000 clearing and grading the land in preparation for the construction of a new building.

E 10–4
Cost of a natural
resource

● LO1

Jackpot Mining Company operates a copper mine in central Montana. The company paid $1,000,000 in 2009 for the mining site and spent an additional $600,000 to prepare the mine for extraction of the copper. After the copper is extracted in approximately four years, the company is required to restore the land to its original condition, including repaving of roads and replacing a greenbelt. The company has provided the following three cash flow possibilities for the restoration costs:

	Cash Outflow	Probability
1	$300,000	25%
2	400,000	40%
3	600,000	35%

To aid extraction, Jackpot purchased some new equipment on July 1, 2009, for $120,000. After the copper is removed from this mine, the equipment will be sold. The credit-adjusted, risk-free rate of interest is 10%.

Required:
1. Determine the cost of the copper mine.
2. Prepare the journal entries to record the acquisition costs of the mine and the purchase of equipment.

E 10–5
Intangibles

● LO1

Freitas Corporation was organized early in 2009. The following expenditures were made during the first few months of the year:

Attorneys' fees in connection with the organization of the corporation	$ 12,000
State filing fees and other incorporation costs	3,000
Purchase of a patent	20,000
Legal and other fees for transfer of the patent	2,000
Purchase of furniture	30,000
Pre-opening salaries	40,000
Total	$107,000

Required:
Prepare a summary journal entry to record the $107,000 in cash expenditures.

E 10–6
Goodwill

● LO1

On March 31, 2009, Wolfson Corporation acquired all of the outstanding common stock of Barney Corporation for $17,000,000 in cash. The book values and fair values of Barney's assets and liabilities were as follows:

	Book Value	Fair Value
Current assets	$ 6,000,000	$ 7,500,000
Property, plant, and equipment	11,000,000	14,000,000
Other assets	1,000,000	1,500,000
Current liabilities	4,000,000	4,000,000
Long-term liabilities	6,000,000	5,500,000

Required:
Calculate the amount paid for goodwill.

E 10–7
Goodwill

● LO1

Johnson Corporation purchased all of the outstanding common stock of Smith Corporation for $11,000,000 in cash. The book value of Smith's net assets (assets minus liabilities) was $7,800,000. The fair values of all of Smith's assets and liabilities were equal to their book values with the following exceptions:

	Book Value	Fair Value
Receivables	$1,300,000	$1,100,000
Property, plant, and equipment	8,000,000	9,400,000
Intangible assets	200,000	1,200,000

Required:
Calculate the amount paid for goodwill.

E 10–8
Lump-sum
acquisition

● LO2

Pinewood Company purchased two buildings on four acres of land. The lump-sum purchase price was $900,000. According to independent appraisals, the fair values were $450,000 (building A) and $250,000 (building B) for the buildings and $300,000 for the land.

Required:
Determine the initial valuation of the buildings and the land.

E 10–9
Acquisition cost;
noninterest-bearing
note

● LO3

On January 1, 2009, Byner Company purchased a used tractor. Byner paid $5,000 down and signed a noninterest-bearing note requiring $25,000 to be paid on December 31, 2011. The fair value of the tractor is not determinable. An interest rate of 10% properly reflects the time value of money for this type of loan agreement. The company's fiscal year-end is December 31.

Required:

1. Prepare the journal entry to record the acquisition of the tractor. Round computations to the nearest dollar.

2. How much interest expense will the company include in its 2009 and 2010 income statements for this note?

3. What is the amount of the liability the company will report in its 2009 and 2010 balance sheets for this note?

E 10–10
Acquisition costs;
noninterest-bearing
note

● LO1 LO3

Teradene Corporation purchased land as a factory site and contracted with Maxtor Construction to construct a factory. Teradene made the following expenditures related to the acquisition of the land, building, and machinery to equip the factory:

Purchase price of the land	$1,200,000
Demolition and removal of old building	80,000
Clearing and grading the land before construction	150,000
Various closing costs in connection with acquiring the land	42,000
Architect's fee for the plans for the new building	50,000
Payments to Maxtor for building construction	3,250,000
Machinery purchased	860,000
Freight charges on machinery	32,000
Trees, plants, and other landscaping	45,000
Installation of a sprinkler system for the landscaping	5,000
Cost to build special platforms and install wiring for the machinery	12,000
Cost of trial runs to ensure proper installation of the machinery	7,000
Fire and theft insurance on the factory for the first year of use	24,000

In addition to the above expenditures, Teradene purchased four forklifts from **Caterpillar**. In payment, Teradene paid $16,000 cash and signed a noninterest-bearing note requiring the payment of $70,000 in one year. An interest rate of 7% properly reflects the time value of money for this type of loan.

Required:
Determine the initial valuation of each of the assets Teradene acquired in the above transactions.

E 10–11
Acquisition cost;
issuance of equity
securities and
donation

● LO4

On February 1, 2009, the Xilon Corporation issued 5,000 shares of its nopar common stock in exchange for five acres of land located in the city of Monrovia. On the date of the acquisition, Xilon's common stock had a fair value of $18 per share. An office building was constructed on the site by an independent contractor. The building was completed on November 2, 2009, at a cost of $600,000. Xilon paid $400,000 in cash and the remainder was paid by the city of Monrovia.

Required:
Prepare the journal entries to record the acquisition of the land and the building, assuming that *SFAS 116* guidelines apply.

E 10–12
Fixed-asset
turnover ratio

● LO5

Real World Financials

Cisco Systems, Inc., reported the following information in its 2007 financial statements ($ in millions):

	2007	2006
Balance sheets		
Property, plant, and equipment (net)	$ 3,893	$3,440
Income statement		
Net sales for 2007	$34,922	

Required:

1. Calculate Cisco's 2007 fixed-asset turnover ratio.

2. How would you interpret this ratio?

E 10–13
Disposal of
operational asset

● LO6

Funseth Farms, Inc. purchased a tractor in 2006 at a cost of $30,000. The tractor was sold for $3,000 in 2009. Depreciation recorded through the disposal date totaled $26,000.

Required:

1. Prepare the journal entry to record the sale.

2. Assuming that the tractor was sold for $10,000, prepare the journal entry to record the sale.

E 10–14
Nonmonetary
exchange

● LO6

Cedric Company recently traded in an older model computer for a new model. The old model's book value was $180,000 (original cost of $400,000 less $220,000 in accumulated depreciation) and its fair value was $200,000. Cedric paid $60,000 to complete the exchange which has commercial substance.

Required:
Prepare the journal entry to record the exchange.

E 10–15
Nonmonetary exchange
● LO6

[This is a variation of the previous exercise.]

Required:
Assume the same facts as in Exercise 10–14, except that the fair value of the old equipment is $170,000. Prepare the journal entry to record the exchange.

E 10–16
Nonmonetary exchange
● LO6

The Bronco Corporation exchanged land for equipment. The land had a book value of $120,000 and a fair value of $150,000. Bronco paid the owner of the equipment $10,000 to complete the exchange which has commercial substance.

Required:
1. What is the fair value of the equipment?
2. Prepare the journal entry to record the exchange.

E 10–17
Nonmonetary exchange
● LO6

[This is a variation of the previous exercise.]

Required:
Assume the same facts as in Exercise 10–16 except that Bronco *received* $10,000 from the owner of the equipment to complete the exchange.
1. What is the fair value of the equipment?
2. Prepare the journal entry to record the exchange.

E 10–18
Nonmonetary exchange
● LO6

The Tinsley Company exchanged land that it had been holding for future plant expansion for a more suitable parcel located farther from residential areas. Tinsley carried the land at its original cost of $30,000. According to an independent appraisal, the land currently is worth $72,000. Tinsley gave $14,000 in cash to complete the transaction.

Required:
1. What is the fair value of the new parcel of land received by Tinsley?
2. Prepare the journal entry to record the exchange assuming the exchange has commercial substance.
3. Prepare the journal entry to record the exchange assuming the exchange lacks commercial substance.

E 10–19
Acquisition cost; multiple methods
● LO1 LO3 LO4

Connors Corporation acquired manufacturing equipment for use in its assembly line. Below are four *independent* situations relating to the acquisition of the equipment.
1. The equipment was purchased on account for $25,000. Credit terms were 2/10, n/30. Payment was made within the discount period and the company records the purchases of equipment net of discounts.
2. Connors gave the seller a noninterest-bearing note. The note required payment of $27,000 one year from date of purchase. The fair value of the equipment is not determinable. An interest rate of 10% properly reflects the time value of money in this situation.
3. Connors traded in old equipment that had a book value of $6,000 (original cost of $14,000 and accumulated depreciation of $8,000) and paid cash of $22,000. The old equipment had a fair value of $2,500 on the date of the exchange.
4. Connors issued 1,000 shares of its nopar common stock in exchange for the equipment. The market value of the common stock was not determinable. The equipment could have been purchased for $24,000 in cash.

Required:
For each of the above situations, prepare the journal entry required to record the acquisition of the equipment. Round computations to the nearest dollar.

E 10–20
Interest capitalization
● LO7

On January 1, 2009, the Marjlee Company began construction of an office building to be used as its corporate headquarters. The building was completed early in 2010. Construction expenditures for 2009, which were incurred evenly throughout the year, totaled $6,000,000. Marjlee had the following debt obligations which were outstanding during all of 2009:

Construction loan, 10%	$1,500,000
Long-term note, 9%	2,000,000
Long-term note, 6%	4,000,000

Required:
Calculate the amount of interest capitalized for the building using the specific interest method.

E 10–21
Interest capitalization
● LO7

On January 2, 2009, the Shagri Company began construction on a new manufacturing facility for its own use. The building was completed in 2010. The only interest-bearing debt the company had outstanding during 2009 was long-term bonds with a book value of $10,000,000 and an effective interest rate of 8%. Construction expenditures incurred during 2009 were as follows:

January 2	$500,000
March 1	600,000
July 31	480,000
September 30	600,000
December 31	300,000

Required:
Calculate the amount of interest capitalized for 2009.

E 10–22
Interest capitalization

● **LO7**

On January 2, 2009, the Highlands Company began construction on a new manufacturing facility for its own use. The building was completed in 2010. The company borrowed $1,500,000 at 8% on January 2 to help finance the construction. In addition to the construction loan, Highlands had the following debt outstanding throughout 2009:

$5,000,000, 12% bonds
$3,000,000, 8% long-term note

Construction expenditures incurred during 2009 were as follows:

January 2	$ 600,000
March 31	1,200,000
June 30	800,000
September 30	600,000
December 31	400,000

Required:
Calculate the amount of interest capitalized for 2009 using the specific interest method.

E 10–23
IFRS; Interest capitalization

● **LO7**

Refer to the situation described in Exercise 10–22.

Required:
How might your solution differ if Highlands Company prepares its financial statements according to International Accounting Standards?

E 10–24
Research and development

● **LO8**

In 2009, Space Technology Company modified its model Z2 satellite to incorporate a new communication device. The company made the following expenditures:

Basic research to develop the technology	$2,000,000
Engineering design work	680,000
Development of a prototype device	300,000
Acquisition of equipment	60,000
Testing and modification of the prototype	200,000
Legal and other fees for patent application on the new communication system	40,000
Legal fees for successful defense of the new patent	20,000
Total	$3,300,000

The equipment will be used on this and other research projects. Depreciation on the equipment for 2009 is $10,000.

During your year-end review of the accounts related to intangibles, you discover that the company has capitalized all of the above as costs of the patent. Management contends that the device simply represents an improvement of the existing communication system of the satellite and, therefore, should be capitalized.

Required:
Prepare correcting entries that reflect the appropriate treatment of the expenditures.

E 10–25
Research and development

● **LO8**

Delaware Company incurred the following research and development costs during 2009:

Salaries and wages for lab research	$ 400,000
Materials used in R&D projects	200,000
Purchase of equipment	900,000
Fees paid to outsiders for R&D projects	320,000
Patent filing and legal costs for a developed product	65,000
Salaries, wages, and supplies for R&D work performed for another company under a contract	350,000
Total	$2,235,000

The equipment has a seven-year life and will be used for a number of research projects. Depreciation for 2009 is $120,000.

Required:
Calculate the amount of research and development expense that Delaware should report in its 2009 income statement.

E 10–26
Concepts;
terminology

● LO1 LO4
   LO6 LO7

Listed below are several terms and phrases associated with operational assets. Pair each item from List A (by letter) with the item from List B that is most appropriately associated with it.

List A	List B
____ 1. Depreciation	a. Exclusive right to display a word, a symbol, or an emblem.
____ 2. Depletion	b. Exclusive right to benefit from a creative work.
____ 3. Amortization	c. Operational assets that represent rights.
____ 4. Average accumulated expenditures	d. The allocation of cost for natural resources.
	e. Purchase price less fair value of net identifiable assets.
____ 5. Revenue—donation of asset	f. The allocation of cost for plant and equipment.
____ 6. Nonmonetary exchange	g. Approximation of average amount of debt if all construction funds were borrowed.
____ 7. Natural resources	
____ 8. Intangible assets	h. Account credited when assets are donated to a corporation.
____ 9. Copyright	i. The allocation of cost for intangible assets.
____10. Trademark	j. Basic principle is to value assets acquired using fair value of assets given.
____11. Goodwill	k. Wasting assets.

E 10–27
Software
development costs

● LO8

Early in 2009, the Excalibur Company began developing a new software package to be marketed. The project was completed in December 2009 at a cost of $6 million. Of this amount, $4 million was spent before technological feasibility was established. Excalibur expects a useful life of five years for the new product with total revenues of $10 million. During 2010, revenue of $4 million was recognized.

Required:
1. Prepare a journal entry to record the 2009 development costs.
2. Calculate the required amortization for 2010.
3. At what amount should the computer software costs be reported in the December 31, 2010, balance sheet?

E 10–28
Full-cost and
successful efforts
methods compared.

● Appendix

The Manguino Oil Company incurred exploration costs in 2009 searching and drilling for oil as follows:

Well 101	$ 50,000
Well 102	60,000
Well 103	80,000
Wells 104–108	260,000
Total	$450,000

It was determined that Wells 104–108 were dry holes and were abandoned. Wells 101, 102, and 103 were determined to have sufficient oil reserves to be commercially successful.

Required:
1. Prepare a summary journal entry to record the indicated costs assuming that the company uses the full-cost method of accounting for exploration costs. All of the exploration costs were paid in cash.
2. Prepare a summary journal entry to record the indicated costs assuming that the company uses the successful efforts method of accounting for exploration costs. All of the exploration costs were paid in cash.

CPA AND CMA REVIEW QUESTIONS

CPA Exam Questions

SCHWESER

The following questions are used in the Kaplan CPA Review Course to study operational assets while preparing for the CPA examination. Determine the response that best completes the statements or questions.

● LO1

1. Simons Company purchased land to build a new factory. The following expenditures were made in conjunction with the land purchase:
   • Purchase price of the land, $150,000
   • Real estate commissions of 7% of the purchase price
   • Land survey, $5,000
   • Back taxes, $5,000

What is the initial value of the land?
a. $160,000
b. $160,500
c. $165,500
d. $170,500

● LO1

2. During 2009, Burr. Co. made the following expenditures related to the acquisition of land and the construction of a building:

Purchase price or land	$ 60,000
Legal fees for contracts to purchase land	2,000
Architects' fees	8,000
Demolition of old building on site	5,000
Sale of scrap from old building	3,000
Construction cost of new building (fully completed)	350,000

What amounts should be recorded as the initial values of the land and the building?

	Land	Building
a.	$60,000	$360,000
b.	$62,000	$360,000
c.	$64,000	$358,000
d.	$65,000	$362,000

● LO3

3. On December 31, 2009, Bart Inc. purchased a machine from Fell Corp. in exchange for a noninterest-bearing note requiring eight payments of $20,000. The first payment was made on December 31, 2009, and the remaining seven payments are due annually on each December 31, beginning in 2010. At the date of the transaction, the prevailing rate of interest for this type of note was 11%. Present value factors are as follows:

Period	Present value of ordinary annuity of 1 at 11%	Present value of an annuity due of 1 at 11%
7	4.712	5.231
8	5.146	5.712

The initial value of the machine is
a. $ 94,240
b. $102,920
c. $104,620
d. $114,240

● LO6

4. Amble Inc. exchanged a truck with a book value of $12,000 and a fair value of $20,000 for a truck and $5,000 cash. The exchange has commercial substance. At what amount should Amble record the truck received?
a. $12,000
b. $15,000
c. $20,000
d. $25,000

● LO7

5. Dahl Corporation has just built a machine to produce car doors. Dahl had to build this machine because it couldn't purchase one that met its specifications. The following are the costs related to the machine's construction and the first month of operations:
- Construction materials, $20,000
- Labor, $9,000 (construction, $3,000; testing, $1,000; operations, $5,000)
- Engineering fees, $5,000
- Utilities, $4,000 (construction, $1,000; testing, $1,000; operations, $2,000)

What is the initial value of the machine?
a. $28,000
b. $29,000
c. $31,000
d. $38,000

● LO7

6. Cole Co. began constructing a building for its own use in January 2009. During 2009, Cole incurred interest of $50,000 on specific construction debt, and $20,000 on other borrowings. Interest computed on the weighted-average amount of accumulated expenditures for the building during 2009 was $40,000. What amount of interest should Cole capitalize?

a. $20,000
b. $40,000
c. $50,000
d. $70,000

● LO8

7. On December 31, 2008, Bit Co. had capitalized costs for a new computer software product with an economic life of five years. Sales for 2009 were 30 percent of expected total sales of the software. At December 31, 2009, the software had a fair value equal to 90 percent of the capitalized cost. What percentage of the original capitalized cost should be reported as the net amount in Bit's December 31, 2009, balance sheet?
   a. 70%
   b. 72%
   c. 80%
   d. 90%

● LO8

8. During the current year, Orr Company incurred the following costs:

Research and development services performed by Key Corp. for Orr	$150,000
Design, construction, and testing of preproduction prototypes and models	200,000
Testing in search for new products or process alternatives	175,000

In its income statement for the current year, what amount should Orr report as research and development expense?
   a. $150,000
   b. $200,000
   c. $350,000
   d. $525,000

CMA Exam Questions

The following questions dealing with operational assets are adapted from questions that previously appeared on Certified Management Accountant (CMA) examinations. The CMA designation sponsored by the Institute of Management Accountants (**www.imanet.org**) provides members with an objective measure of knowledge and competence in the field of management accounting. Determine the response that best completes the statements or questions.

● LO1

1. Pearl Corporation acquired manufacturing machinery on January 1 for $9,000. During the year, the machine produced 1,000 units, of which 600 were sold. There was no work-in-process inventory at the beginning or at the end of the year. Installation charges of $300 and delivery charges of $200 were also incurred. The machine is expected to have a useful life of five years with an estimated salvage value of $1,500. Pearl uses the straight-line depreciation method. The original cost of the machinery to be recorded in Pearl's books is
   a. $9,500
   b. $9,300
   c. $9,200
   d. $9,000

● LO6

Questions 2 and 3 are based on the following information. Harper is contemplating exchanging a machine used in its operations for a similar machine on May 31. Harper will exchange machines with either Austin Corporation or Lubin Company. The data relating to the machines are presented below. Assume that the exchanges would have commercial substance.

	Harper	Austin	Lubin
Original cost of the machine	$162,500	$180,000	$150,000
Accumulated depreciation thru May 31	98,500	70,000	65,000
Fair value at May 31	80,000	95,000	60,000

2. If Harper exchanges its used machine and $15,000 cash for Austin's used machine, the gain that Harper should recognize from this transaction for financial reporting purposes would be
   a. $0
   b. $2,526
   c. $15,000
   d. $16,000

3. If Harper exchanges its used machine for Lubin's used machine and also receives $20,000 cash, the gain that Harper should recognize from this transaction for financial reporting purposes would be
   a. $0
   b. $4,000
   c. $16,000
   d. $25,000

PROBLEMS

available with McGraw–Hill's Homework Manager www.mhhe.com/spiceland5e

An alternate exercise and problem set is available on the text website: www.mhhe.com/spiceland5e

P 10–1
Acquisition costs

● **LO1 through LO4**

Tristar Production Company began operations on September 1, 2009. Listed below are a number of transactions that occurred during its first four months of operations.

1. On September 1, the company acquired five acres of land with a building that will be used as a warehouse. Tristar paid $100,000 in cash for the property. According to appraisals, the land had a fair value of $75,000 and the building had a fair value of $45,000.

2. On September 1, Tristar signed a $40,000 noninterest-bearing note to purchase equipment. The $40,000 payment is due on September 1, 2010. Assume that 8% is a reasonable interest rate.

3. On September 15, a truck was donated to the corporation. Similar trucks were selling for $2,500.

4. On September 18, the company paid its lawyer $3,000 for organizing the corporation.

5. On October 10, Tristar purchased machinery for cash. The purchase price was $15,000 and $500 in freight charges also were paid.

6. On December 2, Tristar acquired various items of office equipment. The company was short of cash and could not pay the $5,500 normal cash price. The supplier agreed to accept 200 shares of the company's nopar common stock in exchange for the equipment. The fair value of the stock is not readily determinable.

7. On December 10, the company acquired a tract of land at a cost of $20,000. It paid $2,000 down and signed a 10% note with both principal and interest due in one year. Ten percent is an appropriate rate of interest for this note.

Required:
Prepare journal entries to record each of the above transactions.

P 10–2
Acquisition costs;
land and building

● **LO1 LO2 LO7**

On January 1, 2009, the Blackstone Corporation purchased a tract of land (site number 11) with a building for $600,000. Additionally, Blackstone paid a real estate broker's commission of $36,000, legal fees of $6,000, and title insurance of $18,000. The closing statement indicated that the land value was $500,000 and the building value was $100,000. Shortly after acquisition, the building was razed at a cost of $75,000.

Blackstone entered into a $3,000,000 fixed-price contract with Barnett Builders, Inc., on March 1, 2009, for the construction of an office building on land site 11. The building was completed and occupied on September 30, 2010. Additional construction costs were incurred as follows:

Plans, specifications, and blueprints	$12,000
Architects' fees for design and supervision	95,000

To finance the construction cost, Blackstone borrowed $3,000,000 on March 1, 2009. The loan is payable in 10 annual installments of $300,000 plus interest at the rate of 14%. Blackstone's average amounts of accumulated building construction expenditures were as follows:

For the period March 1 to December 31, 2009	$ 900,000
For the period January 1 to September 30, 2010	2,300,000

Required:
1. Prepare a schedule that discloses the individual costs making up the balance in the land account in respect of land site 11 as of September 30, 2010.

2. Prepare a schedule that discloses the individual costs that should be capitalized in the office building account as of September 30, 2010.

(AICPA adapted)

P 10–3
Acquisition costs

● LO1 LO4 LO6

The plant asset and accumulated depreciation accounts of Pell Corporation had the following balances at December 31, 2008:

	Plant Asset	Accumulated Depreciation
Land	$ 350,000	$ —
Land improvements	180,000	45,000
Building	1,500,000	350,000
Machinery and equipment	1,158,000	405,000
Automobiles	150,000	112,000

Transactions during 2009 were as follows:

a. On January 2, 2009, machinery and equipment were purchased at a total invoice cost of $260,000, which included a $5,500 charge for freight. Installation costs of $27,000 were incurred.

b. On March 31, 2009, a machine purchased for $58,000 in 2005 was sold for $36,500. Depreciation recorded through the date of sale totaled $24,650.

c. On May 1, 2009, expenditures of $50,000 were made to repave parking lots at Pell's plant location. The work was necessitated by damage caused by severe winter weather.

d. On November 1, 2009, Pell acquired a tract of land with an existing building in exchange for 10,000 shares of Pell's common stock that had a market price of $38 per share. Pell paid legal fees and title insurance totaling $23,000. Shortly after acquisition, the building was razed at a cost of $35,000 in anticipation of new building construction in 2010.

e. On December 31, 2009, Pell purchased a new automobile for $15,250 cash and trade-in of an old automobile purchased for $18,000 in 2005. Depreciation on the old automobile recorded through December 31, 2009, totaled $13,500. The fair value of the old automobile was $3,750.

Required:
1. Prepare a schedule analyzing the changes in each of the plant assets during 2009, with detailed supporting computations.
2. Prepare a schedule showing the gain or loss from each asset disposal that would be recognized in Pell's income statement for the year ended December 31, 2009.

(AICPA adapted)

P 10–4
Intangibles

● LO1 LO8

The Horstmeyer Corporation commenced operations early in 2009. A number of expenditures were made during 2009 that were debited to one account called *intangible asset*. A recap of the $644,000 balance in this account at the end of 2009 is as follows:

Date	Transaction	Amount
2/3/09	State incorporation fees and legal costs related to organizing the corporation	$ 7,000
3/1/09	Fire insurance premium for three-year period	6,000
3/15/09	Purchased a copyright	20,000
4/30/09	Research and development costs	40,000
6/15/09	Legal fees for filing a patent on a new product resulting from an R&D project	3,000
9/30/09	Legal fee for successful defense of patent developed above	12,000
10/13/09	Entered into a 10-year franchise agreement with franchisor	40,000
Various	Advertising costs	16,000
11/30/09	Purchase of all of the outstanding common stock of Stiltz Corp.	500,000
	Total	$644,000

The total purchase price of the Stiltz Corp. stock was debited to this account. The fair values of Stiltz Corp.'s assets and liabilities on the date of the purchase were as follows:

Receivables	$ 100,000
Equipment	350,000
Patent	150,000
Total assets	600,000
Note payable assumed	(220,000)
Fair value of net assets	$ 380,000

Required:
Prepare the necessary journal entries to clear the intangible asset account and to set up accounts for separate intangible assets, other types of assets, and expenses indicated by the transactions.

P 10–5
Acquisition costs;
journal entries

● LO1 LO3
   LO6 LO8

Consider each of the transactions below. All of the expenditures were made in cash.
1. The Edison Company spent $12,000 during the year for experimental purposes in connection with the development of a new product.
2. In April, the Marshall Company lost a patent infringement suit and paid the plaintiff $7,500.
3. In March, the Cleanway Laundromat bought equipment. Cleanway paid $6,000 down and signed a noninterest-bearing note requiring the payment of $18,000 in nine months. The cash price for this equipment was $23,000.
4. On June 1, the Jamsen Corporation installed a sprinkler system throughout the building at a cost of $28,000.
5. The Mayer Company, plaintiff, paid $12,000 in legal fees in November, in connection with a successful infringement suit on its patent.
6. The Johnson Company traded its old machine with an original cost of $7,400 and a book value of $3,000 plus cash of $8,000 for a new one that had a fair value of $10,000.

Required:
Prepare journal entries to record each of the above transactions.

P 10–6
Nonmonetary
exchange

● LO6

Southern Company owns a building that it leases. The building's fair value is $1,400,000 and its book value is $800,000 (original cost of $2,000,000 less accumulated depreciation of $1,200,000). Southern exchanges this for another building owned by the Eastern Company. The building's book value on Eastern's books is $950,000 (original cost of $1,600,000 less accumulated depreciation of $650,000). Eastern also gives Southern $140,000 to complete the exchange. The exchange has commercial substance for both companies.

Required:
Prepare the journal entries to record the exchange on the books of both Southern and Eastern.

P 10–7
Nonmonetary
exchange

● LO6

On September 3, 2009, the Robers Company exchanged operational assets with Phifer Corporation. The facts of the exchange are as follows:

	Robers' Asset	**Phifer's Asset**
Original cost	$120,000	$140,000
Accumulated depreciation	55,000	63,000
Fair value	75,000	70,000

To equalize the exchange, Phifer paid Robers $5,000 in cash.

Required:
Record the exchange for both Robers and Phifer. The exchange has commercial substance for both companies.

P 10–8
Nonmonetary
exchange

● LO6

Case A. Kapono Farms exchanged an old tractor for a newer model. The old tractor had a book value of $12,000 (original cost of $28,000 less accumulated depreciation of $16,000) and a fair value of $9,000. Kapono paid $20,000 cash to complete the exchange. The exchange has commercial substance.

Required:
1. What is the amount of gain or loss that Kapono would recognize on the exchange? What is the initial value of the new tractor?
2. Repeat requirement 1 assuming that the fair value of the old tractor is $14,000 instead of $9,000.

Case B. Kapono Farms exchanged 100 acres of farmland for similar land. The farmland given had a book value of $500,000 and a fair value of $700,000. Kapono paid $50,000 cash to complete the exchange. The exchange has commercial substance.

Required:
1. What is the amount of gain or loss that Kapono would recognize on the exchange? What is the initial value of the new land?
2. Repeat requirement 1 assuming that the fair value of the farmland given is $400,000 instead of $700,000.
3. Repeat requirement 1 assuming that the exchange lacked commercial substance.

P 10–9
Interest
capitalization;
specific interest
method

● LO7

On January 1, 2009, the Mason Manufacturing Company began construction of a building to be used as its office headquarters. The building was completed on September 30, 2010.
   Expenditures on the project were as follows:

January 3, 2009	$1,000,000
March 1, 2009	600,000
June 30, 2009	800,000
October 1, 2009	600,000
January 31, 2010	270,000
April 30, 2010	585,000
August 31, 2010	900,000

On January 2, 2009, the company obtained a $3 million construction loan with a 10% interest rate. The loan was outstanding all of 2009 and 2010. The company's other interest-bearing debt included two long-term notes of $4,000,000 and $6,000,000 with interest rates of 6% and 8%, respectively. Both notes were outstanding during all of 2009 and 2010. The company's fiscal year-end is December 31.

Required:
1. Calculate the amount of interest that Mason should capitalize in 2009 and 2010 using the specific interest method.
2. What is the total cost of the building?
3. Calculate the amount of interest expense that will appear in the 2009 and 2010 income statements.

P 10–10
Interest capitalization; weighted-average method

● LO7

[This is a variation of the previous problem, modified to focus on the weighted-average interest method.]

Required:
Refer to the facts in Problem 10–9 and answer the following questions:
1. Calculate the amount of interest that Mason should capitalize in 2009 and 2010 using the weighted-average method.
2. What is the total cost of the building?
3. Calculate the amount of interest expense that will appear in the 2009 and 2010 income statements.

P 10–11
Research and development

● LO8

In 2009, Starsearch Corporation began work on three research and development projects. One of the projects was completed and commercial production of the developed product began in December. The company's fiscal year-end is December 31. All of the following 2009 expenditures were included in the R&D expense account:

Salaries and wages for:	
Lab research	$ 300,000
Design and construction of preproduction prototype	160,000
Quality control during commercial production	20,000
Materials and supplies consumed for:	
Lab research	60,000
Construction of preproduction prototype	30,000
Purchase of equipment	600,000
Patent filing and legal fees for completed project	40,000
Payments to others for research	120,000
Total	$1,330,000

$200,000 of equipment was purchased solely for use in one of the projects. After the project is completed, the equipment will be abandoned. The remaining $400,000 in equipment will be used on future R&D projects. The useful life of equipment is five years. Assume that all of the equipment was acquired at the beginning of the year.

Required:
Prepare journal entries, reclassifying amounts in R&D expense, to reflect the appropriate treatment of the expenditures.

P 10–12
Acquisition costs; lump-sum acquisition; noninterest-bearing note; interest capitalization

● LO1 LO2
  LO3 LO7

Early in its fiscal year ending December 31, 2009, San Antonio Outfitters finalized plans to expand operations. The first stage was completed on March 28 with the purchase of a tract of land on the outskirts of the city. The land and existing building were purchased for $800,000. San Antonio paid $200,000 and signed a noninterest-bearing note requiring the company to pay the remaining $600,000 on March 28, 2011. An interest rate of 8% properly reflects the time value of money for this type of loan agreement. Title search, insurance, and other closing costs totaling $20,000 were paid at closing.

During April, the old building was demolished at a cost of $70,000, and an additional $50,000 was paid to clear and grade the land. Construction of a new building began on May 1 and was completed on October 29. Construction expenditures were as follows:

May 30	$1,200,000
July 30	1,500,000
September 1	900,000
October 1	1,800,000

San Antonio borrowed $3,000,000 at 8% on May 1 to help finance construction. This loan, plus interest, will be paid in 2010. The company also had the following debt outstanding throughout 2009:

$2,000,000, 9% long-term note payable
$4,000,000, 6% long-term bonds payable

In November, the company purchased 10 identical pieces of equipment and office furniture and fixtures for a lump-sum price of $600,000. The fair values of the equipment and the furniture and fixtures were $455,000 and $245,000, respectively. In December, San Antonio paid a contractor $285,000 for the construction of parking lots and for landscaping.

Required:

1. Determine the initial values of the various assets that San Antonio acquired or constructed during 2009. The company uses the specific interest method to determine the amount of interest capitalized on the building construction.

2. How much interest expense will San Antonio report in its 2009 income statement?

BROADEN YOUR PERSPECTIVE

Apply your critical-thinking ability to the knowledge you've gained. These cases will provide you an opportunity to develop your research, analysis, judgment, and communication skills. You also will work with other students, integrate what you've learned, apply it in real world situations, and consider its global and ethical ramifications. This practice will broaden your knowledge and further develop your decision-making abilities.

Judgment Case 10–1
Acquisition costs

● LO1 LO3 LO6

A company may acquire operational assets for cash, in exchange for a deferred payment contract, by ex-changing other operational assets, or by a combination of these methods.

Required:

1. Identify six types of costs that should be capitalized as the cost of a parcel of land. For your answer, assume that the land has an existing building that is to be removed in the immediate future in order that a new building can be constructed on the site.

2. At what amount should a company record an operational asset acquired in exchange for a deferred payment contract?

3. In general, at what amount should operational assets received in exchange for other nonmonetary assets be valued? Specifically, at what amount should a company value a new machine acquired by exchanging an older, similar machine and paying cash?

(AICPA adapted)

Research Case 10–2
Locate and extract relevant information and cite authoritative support for a financial reporting issue; restoration costs; asset retirement obligation

● LO1

Your client, Hazelton Mining, recently entered into an agreement to obtain the rights to operate a coal mine in West Virginia for $15 million. Hazelton incurred development costs of $6 million in preparing the mine for extraction, which began on July 1, 2009. The contract requires Hazelton to restore the land and surrounding area to its original condition after extraction is complete in three years.

The company controller, Alice Cushing, is not sure how to account for the restoration costs and has asked your advice. Alice is aware of a recent accounting pronouncement addressing this issue, but is not sure of its provisions. She has narrowed down the possible cash outflows for the restoration costs to four possibilities:

Cash Outflow	Probability
$3 million	20%
4 million	30%
5 million	25%
6 million	25%

Alice also informs you that the company's credit-adjusted risk-free interest rate is 9%. Before responding to Alice, you need to research the issue.

Required:

1. Obtain the original FASB Standard on accounting for asset retirement obligations. You might gain access at the FASB website (**www.fasb.org**), from your school library, or some other source. Explain the basic treatment of asset retirement obligations.

2. Determine the capitalized cost of the coal mine.

3. Prepare a summary journal entry to record the acquisition costs of the mine.
4. How much accretion expense will the company record in its income statement for the fiscal year 2009, related to this transaction?
5. Explain to Alice how Hazelton would account for the restoration if the restoration costs differed from the recorded liability in three years. By way of explanation, prepare the journal entry to record the payment of the retirement obligation in three years assuming that the actual restoration costs were $4.7 million.
6. Describe to Alice the necessary disclosure requirements for the obligation.

Judgment Case 10–3
Self-constructed assets
● LO7

Chilton Peripherals manufactures printers, scanners, and other computer peripheral equipment. In the past, the company purchased equipment used in manufacturing from an outside vendor. In March 2009, Chilton decided to design and build equipment to replace some obsolete equipment. A section of the manufacturing plant was set aside to develop and produce the equipment. Additional personnel were hired for the project. The equipment was completed and ready for use in September.

Required:
1. In general, what costs should be capitalized for a self-constructed asset?
2. Discuss two alternatives for the inclusion of overhead costs in the cost of the equipment constructed by Chilton. Which alternative is generally accepted for financial reporting purposes?
3. Under what circumstance(s) would interest be included in the cost of the equipment?

Judgment Case 10–4
Interest capitalization
● LO7

SFAS 34 provides guidelines for the inclusion of interest in the initial cost of an operational asset.
Required:
1. What assets qualify for interest capitalization? What assets do not qualify for interest capitalization?
2. Over what period should interest be capitalized?
3. Explain average accumulated expenditures.
4. Explain the two methods that could be used to determine the appropriate interest rate(s) to be used in capitalizing interest.
5. Describe the three steps used to determine the amount of interest capitalized during a reporting period.

Research Case 10–5
Goodwill
● LO1

Accounting for purchased goodwill has been a controversial issue for many years. In the United States, the amount of purchased goodwill is capitalized and not amortized. Globally, the treatment of goodwill varies significantly, with some countries not recognizing goodwill as an asset. Professors Johnson and Petrone, in "Is Goodwill an Asset?" discuss this issue.
Required:
1. In your library or from some other source, locate the indicated article in Accounting Horizons, September 1998.
2. Does goodwill meet the FASB's definition of an asset?
3. What are the key concerns of those that believe goodwill is not an asset?

Real World Case 10–6
Property, plant, and equipment; intangibles
● LO1
Real World Financials

Coca-Cola Company reported the following amounts in the asset section of its balance sheets for the years ended December 31, 2006 and 2005:

	($ in millions)	
	2006	**2005**
Property, plant, and equipment, net	$6,903	$5,831
Intangible assets, net*	1,687	828

*These are the company's finite life intangibles.

In addition, the 2006 statement of cash flows reported the following items ($ in millions):

Depreciation and amortization	$ 938
Additions to property and equipment	2,007
Additions to intangible assets	901
Proceeds from sale of equipment	112

Required:
What was the gain or loss recognized in 2006 from the sale of property, plant, and equipment?

Judgment Case 10–7
Goodwill
● LO1

Athena Paper Corporation acquired for cash 100% of the outstanding common stock of Georgia, Inc., a supplier of wood pulp. The purchase price of $4,500,000 was significantly higher than the book value of Georgia's net assets (assets less liabilities) of $2,800,000. The Athena controller recorded the difference of $1,700,000 as an asset, goodwill.

Required:

1. Discuss the meaning of the term *goodwill*.
2. In what situation would the Athena controller be correct in her valuation of goodwill?

Judgment Case 10–8
Research and development

● LO8

Prior to 1974, accepted practice was for companies to either expense or capitalize R&D costs. In 1974, the FASB issued *SFAS 2* which now requires all research and development costs to be charged to expense when incurred. This was a controversial standard, opposed by many companies who preferred delaying the recognition of these expenses until later years when presumably the expenditures bear fruit.

Several research studies have been conducted to determine if the standard had any impact on the behavior of companies. One interesting finding was that, prior to *SFAS 2*, companies that expensed R&D costs were significantly larger than those companies that capitalized R&D costs.

Required:

1. Explain the FASB's logic in deciding to require all companies to expense R&D costs in the period incurred.
2. Identify possible reasons to explain why, prior to *SFAS 2*, companies that expensed R&D costs were significantly larger than those companies that capitalized R&D costs.

Judgment Case 10–9
Research and development

● LO8

Clonal, Inc., a biotechnology company, developed and patented a diagnostic product called Trouver. Clonal purchased some research equipment to be used exclusively for Trouver and subsequent research projects. Clonal defeated a legal challenge to its Trouver patent, and began production and marketing operations for the project.

Corporate headquarters' costs were allocated to Clonal's research division as a percentage of the division's salaries.

Required:

1. How should the equipment purchased for Trouver be reported in Clonal's income statements and statements of financial position?
2. a. Describe the matching principle.
   b. Describe the accounting treatment of research and development costs and consider whether this is consistent with the matching principle. What is the justification for the accounting treatment of research and development costs?
3. How should corporate headquarters' costs allocated to the research division be classified in Clonal's income statements? Why?
4. How should the legal expenses incurred in defending Trouver's patent be reported in Clonal's financial statements?

(AICPA adapted)

Communication Case 10–10
Research and development

● LO8

The focus of this case is the situation described in Case 10–9. What is the appropriate accounting for R&D costs? Do you believe that (1) capitalization is the correct treatment of R&D costs, (2) expensing is the correct treatment of R&D costs, or (3) that companies should be allowed to choose between expensing and capitalizing R&D costs?

Required:

1. Develop a list of arguments in support of your view prior to the class session for which the case is assigned. Do not be influenced by the method required by the FASB. Base your opinion on the conceptual merit of the options.
2. In class, your instructor will pair you (and everyone else) with a classmate who also has independently developed a position.
   a. You will be given three minutes to argue your view to your partner. Your partner likewise will be given three minutes to argue his or her view to you. During these three-minute presentations, the listening partner is not permitted to speak.
   b. Then after each person has had a turn attempting to convince his or her partner, the two partners will have a three-minute discussion in which they will decide which alternative is more convincing and arguments will be merged into a single view for each pair.
3. After the allotted time, a spokesperson for each of the three alternatives will be selected by the instructor. Each spokesperson will field arguments from the class as to the appropriate alternative. The class will then discuss the merits of the alternatives and attempt to reach a consensus view, though a consensus is not necessary.

Trueblood Accounting Case 10–11
Asset retirement obligations

● LO1

The following Trueblood case is recommended for use with this chapter. The case provides an excellent opportunity for class discussion, group projects, and writing assignments. The case, along with Professor's Discussion Material, can be obtained from the Deloitte Foundation at its website: **www.deloitte.com/us/truebloodcases.**

Case 06–11: *Black Gold Inc.*
This case concerns the accounting treatment for a change in the estimate of an asset retirement obligation.

Communication Case 10–12
Research and development

● LO8

Thomas Plastics is in the process of developing a revolutionary new plastic valve. A new division of the company was formed to develop, manufacture, and market this new product. As of year-end (December 31, 2009), the new product has not been manufactured for sale; however, prototype units were built and are in operation.

Throughout 2009, the new division incurred a variety of costs. These costs included expenses (including salaries of administrative personnel) and market research costs. In addition, approximately $500,000 in equipment (estimated useful life of 10 years) was purchased for use in developing and manufacturing the new valve. Approximately $200,000 of this equipment was built specifically for developing the design of the new product; the remaining $300,000 of the equipment was used to manufacture the preproduction prototypes and will be used to manufacture the new product once it is in commercial production.

The president of the company, Sally Rogers, has been told that research and development costs must be expensed as incurred, but she does not understand this treatment. She believes the research will lead to a profitable product and to increased future revenues. Also, she wonders how to account for the $500,000 of equipment purchased by the new division. "I thought I understood accounting," she growled. "Explain to me why expenditures that benefit our future revenues are expensed rather than capitalized!"

Required:
Write a one-to two-page report to Sally Rogers explaining the generally accepted accounting principles relevant to this issue. The report should also address the treatment of the equipment purchases.

(AICPA adapted)

Ethics Case 10–13
Research and development

● LO8

Mayer Biotechnical, Inc., develops, manufactures, and sells pharmaceuticals. Significant research and development (R&D) expenditures are made for the development of new drugs and the improvement of existing drugs. During 2009, $220 million was spent on R&D. Of this amount, $30 million was spent on the purchase of equipment to be used in a research project involving the development of a new antibiotic.

The controller, Alice Cooper, is considering capitalizing the equipment and depreciating it over the five- year useful life of the equipment at $6 million per year, even though the equipment likely will be used on only one project. The company president has asked Alice to make every effort to increase 2009 earnings because in 2010 the company will be seeking significant new financing from both debt and equity sources. "I guess we might use the equipment in other projects later," Alice wondered to herself.

Required:
1. Assuming that the equipment was purchased at the beginning of 2009, by how much would Alice's treatment of the equipment increase before tax earnings as opposed to expensing the equipment cost?
2. Discuss the ethical dilemma Alice faces in determining the treatment of the $30 million equipment purchase.

IFRS Case 10–14
Operational assets; comparison of U.S. GAAP and IFRS

● LO1 LO8

Cadbury Schweppes, Plc., a U.K. company, is an international confectionery and beverage business that sells its products in almost every country in the world. The company prepares its financial statements according to IFRS.

Required:
Use the Internet to locate Cadbury's most recent annual report. The address is **www.cadburyschweppes.com**. Locate the significant accounting policies disclosure note and answer the following questions:
1. How does Cadbury value its property, plant, and equipment? Does the company have any other options under IFRS for valuing these assets? How do these options differ from U.S. GAAP?
2. How does the company account for research and development expenditures? Does this policy differ from U.S. GAAP?

Analysis Case 10–15
Fixed-asset turnover ratio

● LO5

Real World Financials

National Semiconductor Corporation, headquartered in Santa Clara, California, is a global semiconductor manufacturer. The company's 2007 fixed-asset turnover ratio, using the average book value of property, plant, and equipment (PP&E) as the denominator, was approximately 3.18. Additional information taken from the company's 2007 annual report is as follows:

	($ in millions)
Book value of PP&E—beginning of 2007	$628
Purchases of PP&E during 2007	107
Depreciation of PP&E for 2007	145

Equipment having a book value of $6 million was sold during 2007.

Required:
1. How is the fixed-asset turnover ratio computed? How would you interpret National's ratio of 3.18?
2. Use the data to determine National's net sales for 2007.
3. Obtain annual reports from three corporations in the same primary industry as National (Intel Corporation and Advanced Micro Devices are two well-known competitors) and compare the management of each company's investment in property, plant, and equipment.

Note: You can obtain copies of annual reports from your library, from friends who are shareholders, from the investor relations department of the corporations, from a friendly stockbroker, or from EDGAR (Electronic Data Gathering, Analysis, and Retrieval) on the Internet (**www.sec.gov**).

**Judgment
Case 10–16**
Computer
software costs

● **LO8**

The Elegant Software Company recently completed the development and testing of a new software program that provides the ability to transfer data from among a variety of operating systems. The company believes this product will be quite successful and capitalized all of the costs of designing, developing, coding, and testing the software. These costs will be amortized over the expected useful life of the software on a straight-line basis.

Required:

1. Was Elegant correct in its treatment of the software development costs? Why?
2. Explain the appropriate method for determining the amount of periodic amortization for any capitalized software development costs.

**Real World
Case 10–17**
Operational assets

● **LO1 LO7**

Real World Financials

EDGAR, the Electronic Data Gathering, Analysis, and Retrieval system, performs automated collection, validation, indexing, and forwarding of submissions by companies and others who are required by law to file forms with the U.S. Securities and Exchange Commission (SEC). All publicly traded domestic companies use EDGAR to make the majority of their filings. (Some foreign companies file voluntarily.) Form 10-K or 10-KSB, which includes the annual report, is required to be filed on EDGAR. The SEC makes this information available on the Internet.

Required:

1. Access EDGAR on the Internet. The web address is **www.sec.gov**.
2. Search for **Home Depot, Inc.** Access the 10-K filing for the most recent fiscal year. Search or scroll to find the financial statements and related notes.
3. Answer the following questions related to the company's operational assets:
   a. Name the different types of operational assets the company lists in its balance sheet under property, plant, and equipment.
   b. How much cash was used for the acquisition of property, plant, and equipment during the year?
   c. What was the amount of interest capitalized during the year?
   d. Compute the fixed-asset turnover ratio for the fiscal year.

**Analysis
Case 10–18**
Reporting
operational assets

● **LO1 LO5**

Google

Refer to the financial statements and related disclosure notes of **Google Inc.** included with all new copies of the text.

Required:

1. What categories of operational assets does Google report in its 2007 balance sheet?
2. How much cash was used in 2007 to purchase property and equipment? How does this compare with purchases in previous years?
3. The fixed-asset turnover ratio for **Yahoo! Inc.**, a Google competitor, is 7.14. How does this compare with Google's ratio? What is the ratio intended to measure?

Operational Assets: Utilization and Impairment

/// OVERVIEW

This chapter completes our discussion of accounting for operational assets. We address the allocation of the cost of these assets to the periods benefited by their use.

The usefulness of most operational assets is consumed as the assets are applied to the production of goods or services. Cost allocation corresponding to this consumption of usefulness is known as *depreciation* for plant and equipment, *depletion* for natural resources, and *amortization* for intangibles.

We also consider the treatment of expenditures incurred subsequent to acquisition and the impairment of operational assets.

|||||| LEARNING OBJECTIVES |||||||||||||||||||||||||||||||||||||||

After studying the chapter you should be able to:

- **LO1** Explain the concept of cost allocation as it pertains to operational assets.
- **LO2** Determine periodic depreciation using both time-based and activity-based methods.
- **LO3** Calculate the periodic depletion of a natural resource.
- **LO4** Calculate the periodic amortization of an intangible asset.
- **LO5** Explain the appropriate accounting treatment required when a change is made in the service life or residual value of an operational asset.
- **LO6** Explain the appropriate accounting treatment required when a change in depreciation, amortization, or depletion method is made.
- **LO7** Explain the appropriate treatment required when an error in accounting for an operational asset is discovered.
- **LO8** Identify situations that involve a significant impairment of the value of operational assets and describe the required accounting procedures.
- **LO9** Discuss the accounting treatment of repairs and maintenance, additions, improvements, and rearrangements to operational assets.

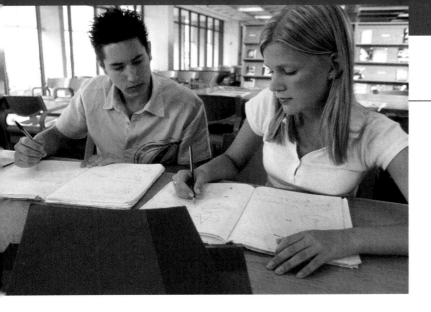

What's in a Name?

"I don't understand this at all," your friend Penny Lane moaned. "Depreciation, depletion, amortization; what's the difference? Aren't they all the same thing?" Penny and you are part of a class team working on a case involving Potlatch Corporation, a large producer of lumber and paper products. Part of the project involves comparing reporting methods over a three-year period. "Look at these disclosure notes from last year's annual report. Besides mentioning those three terms, they also talk about asset impairment. How is that different?" Penny showed you the disclosure notes.

Property and Equipment (in part)

Depreciation of buildings, equipment, and other depreciable assets is determined using the straight-line method of depreciation. Timber, timberlands, and related logging facilities are valued at cost less depletion and amortization. Our depletion is determined based on costs capitalized and the related current estimated recoverable timber volume. Logging roads and related facilities on land not owned by us are amortized as the related timber is removed.

Long-lived Assets (in part)

We account for impairment of long-lived assets in accordance with *SFAS No. 144.* "Accounting for the Impairment or Disposal of Long-Lived Assets." *SFAS No. 144* requires that long-lived assets be reviewed for impairment whenever events or changes in circumstances indicate that the carrying amount of an asset may not be recoverable, as measured by its undiscounted estimated future cash flows.

By the time you finish this chapter, you should be able to respond appropriately to the questions posed in this case. Compare your response to the solution provided at the end of the chapter.

QUESTIONS ///

1. Is Penny correct? Do the terms *depreciation, depletion,* and *amortization* all mean the same thing? (page 534)

2. Potlatch determines depletion based on the "estimated recoverable timber volume." Explain this approach. (page 538)

3. Explain how asset impairment differs from depreciation, depletion, and amortization. How do companies measure impairment losses for tangible operational assets and intangible assets with finite useful lives? (page 553)

DEPRECIATION, DEPLETION, AND AMORTIZATION
Cost Allocation—an Overview

● LO1

Operational assets are purchased with the expectation that they will provide future benefits, usually for several years. Specifically, they are acquired to be used as part of the revenue-generating operations. Logically, then, the costs of acquiring the assets should be allocated to expense during the reporting periods benefited by their use. That is, their costs are matched with the revenues they help generate.

Let's suppose that a company purchases a used delivery truck for $8,200 to be used to deliver product to customers. The company estimates that five years from the acquisition date the truck will be sold for $2,200. The cost of using the truck during the five-year period is $6,000 ($8,200 − 2,200). The situation is portrayed in Graphic 11–1.

GRAPHIC 11–1

Cost Allocation for an Operational Asset

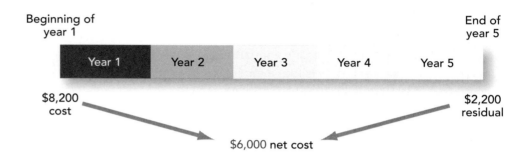

Theoretically, the matching principle requires that the $6,000 be allocated to the five individual years of asset use in direct proportion to the role the asset played in revenue production. However, very seldom is there a clear-cut relationship between the use of operational assets and revenue production. In other words, we can't tell precisely the portion of the total benefits of the asset that was consumed in any particular period. As a consequence, we must resort to arbitrary allocation methods to approximate a matching of expense with revenue. Contrast this situation with the $24,000 prepayment of one year's rent on an office building at $2,000 per month. In that case, we know precisely that the benefits of the asset, prepaid rent, are consumed at a rate of $2,000 per month.

FINANCIAL
Reporting Case

Q1, p. 533

Depreciation, depletion, and amortization are processes that attempt to satisfy the matching principle.

Depreciation, depletion, and amortization for an asset used to manufacture a product is an overhead cost included in the cost of inventory.

Cost allocation for operational assets is known as depreciation for plant and equipment, depletion for natural resources, and amortization for intangibles. The process often is confused with measuring a decline in fair value of an asset. For example, let's say our delivery truck purchased for $8,200 can be sold for $5,000 at the end of one year but we intend to keep it for the full five-year estimated life. It has experienced a decline in value of $3,200 ($8,200 − 5,000). However, *depreciation is a process of cost allocation, not valuation.* We would not record depreciation expense of $3,200 for year one of the truck's life. Instead, we would distribute the cost of the asset, less any anticipated residual value, over the estimated useful life in a systematic and rational manner that attempts to match revenues with the *use* of the asset, not the decline in its value. After all, the truck is purchased to be used in operations, not to be sold.

The specific accounting treatment depends on the intended use of the asset. For assets used in the manufacture of a product, for example, depreciation, depletion, or amortization is considered a product cost to be included as part of the cost of inventory. Eventually, when the product is sold, it becomes part of the cost of goods sold. For assets *not* used in production, primarily plant and equipment and certain intangibles used in the selling and administrative functions of the company, periodic depreciation or amortization is reported as expense in the income statement. You might recognize this distinction as the difference between a product cost and a period cost. When a product cost is reported as an expense (cost of goods sold) depends on when the product is sold; when a period cost is reported as an expense depends on the reporting period in which it is incurred.

Measuring Cost Allocation

The process of cost allocation for operational assets requires that three factors be established at the time the asset is put into use. These factors are:

1. Service life—the estimated use that the company expects to receive from the asset.
2. Allocation base—the value of the usefulness that is expected to be consumed.
3. Allocation method—the pattern in which the usefulness is expected to be consumed.

Let's consider these one at a time.

Service Life

The service life, or useful life, of an operational asset is the amount of use that the company expects to obtain from the asset before disposing of it. This use can be expressed in units of time, or in units of activity. For example, the estimated service life of a delivery truck could be expressed in terms of years or in terms of the number of miles that the company expects the truck to be driven before disposition. We use the terms service life and useful life interchangeably throughout the chapter.

Physical life provides the upper bound for service life of tangible operational assets. Physical life will vary according to the purpose for which the asset is acquired and the environment in which it is operated. For example, a diesel powered electric generator may last for many years if it is used only as an emergency backup or for only a few years if it is used regularly.

The service life of a tangible operational asset may be less than physical life for a variety of reasons. For example, the expected rate of technological change may shorten service life. If suppliers are expected to develop new technologies that are more efficient, the company may keep an asset for a period of time much shorter than physical life. Likewise, if the company sells its product in a market that frequently demands new products, the machinery and equipment used to produce products may be useful only for as long as its output can be sold. Similarly, a mineral deposit might be projected to contain 4 million tons of a mineral, but it may be economically feasible with existing extraction methods to mine only 2 million tons. For intangible assets, legal or contractual life often is a limiting factor. For instance, a patent might be capable of providing enhanced profitability for 50 years, but the legal life of a patent is only 20 years.

Management intent also may shorten the period of an asset's usefulness below its physical, legal, or contractual life. For example, a company may have a policy of using its delivery trucks for a three-year period and then trading the trucks for new models.

Companies quite often disclose the range of service lives for different categories of operational assets. For example, Graphic 11–2 shows how **IBM Corporation** disclosed its service lives in a note accompanying recent financial statements.

> **Depreciation and Amortization (in part)**
> The estimated useful lives of depreciable properties are as follows: buildings, 50 years; building equipment, 10 to 20 years; land improvements, 20 years; plant, laboratory and office equipment, 2 to 15 years; and computer equipment, 1.5 to 5 years.

Allocation Base

The total amount of cost to be allocated over an asset's service life is called its allocation base. The amount is the difference between the initial value of the asset at its acquisition (its cost) and its residual value. Residual or salvage value is the amount the company expects to receive for the asset at the end of its service life less any anticipated disposal costs. In our delivery truck example above, the allocation base is $6,000 ($8,200 cost less $2,200 anticipated residual value).

In certain situations, residual value can be estimated by referring to a company's prior experience or to publicly available information concerning resale values of various types of assets. For example, if a company intends to trade its delivery trucks in three years for the new model, approximations of the three-year residual value for that type of truck can be obtained from used truck blue books.

However, estimating residual value for many operational assets can be very difficult due to the uncertainty about the future. For this reason, along with the fact that residual values often are immaterial, many companies simply assume a residual value of zero. Companies usually do not disclose estimated residual values.

Allocation Method

The allocation method used should be systematic and rational and correspond to the pattern of asset use.

In determining how much cost to allocate to periods of an asset's use, a method should be selected that corresponds to the pattern of the loss of the asset's usefulness. *ARB 43* states that the chosen method should allocate the asset's cost "as equitably as possible to the periods during which services are obtained from [its] use." The bulletin further specifies that the method should produce a cost allocation in a "systematic and rational manner."[1] The objective is to try to allocate cost to the period in an amount that is proportional to the amount of benefits generated by the asset during the period relative to the total benefits provided by the asset during its life.

In practice, there are two general approaches that attempt to obtain this systematic and rational allocation. The first approach allocates the cost base according to the *passage of time*. Methods following this approach are referred to as time-based methods. The second approach allocates an asset's cost base using a measure of the asset's *input* or *output*. This is an activity-based method. We compare these approaches first in the context of depreciation. Later we see that depletion of natural resources typically follows an activity-based approach and the amortization of intangibles typically follows a time-based approach.

Depreciation of Operational Assets

● LO2

To demonstrate and compare the most common depreciation methods, we refer to the situation described in Illustration 11–1.

ILLUSTRATION 11–1 Depreciation Methods	The Hogan Manufacturing Company purchased a machine for $250,000. The company expects the service life of the machine to be five years. During that time, it is expected that the machine will produce 140,000 units. The anticipated residual value is $40,000. The machine was disposed of after five years of use. Actual production during the five years of the asset's life was:

Year	Units Produced
1	24,000
2	36,000
3	46,000
4	8,000
5	16,000
Total	130,000

Time-Based Depreciation Methods

The straight-line depreciation method allocates an equal amount of depreciable base to each year of the asset's service life.

STRAIGHT-LINE METHOD. By far the most easily understood and widely used depreciation method is straight line. By this approach, an equal amount of depreciable base is allocated to each year of the asset's service life. The depreciable base is simply divided by

[1]"Restatement and Revision of Accounting Research Bulletins," *Accounting Research Bulletin No. 43* (New York: AICPA, 1953), Ch. 9.

the number of years in the asset's life to determine annual depreciation. In our illustration, the straightline annual depreciation is $42,000, calculated as follows:

$$\frac{\$250,000 - 40,000}{5 \text{ years}} = \$42,000 \text{ per year}$$

ACCELERATED METHODS.   Using the straight-line method implicitly assumes that the benefits derived from the use of the asset are the same each year. In some situations it might be more appropriate to assume that the asset will provide greater benefits in the early years of its life than in the later years. In these cases, a more appropriate matching of depreciation with revenues is achieved with a declining pattern of depreciation, with higher depreciation in the early years of the asset's life and lower depreciation in later years. An accelerated depreciation method also would be appropriate when benefits derived from the asset are approximately equal over the asset's life, but repair and maintenance costs increase significantly in later years. The early years incur higher depreciation and lower repairs and maintenance expense, while the later years have lower depreciation and higher repairs and maintenance. Two commonly used ways to achieve such a declining pattern are the sum-of-the-years'-digits method and declining balance methods.

Accelerated depreciation methods are appropriate when the asset is more useful in its earlier years.

Sum-of-the-years'-digits method.   The sum-of-the-years'-digits (SYD) method has no logical foundation other than the fact that it accomplishes the objective of accelerating depreciation in a systematic manner. This is achieved by multiplying the depreciable base by a fraction that declines each year and results in depreciation that decreases by the same amount each year. The denominator of the fraction remains constant and is the sum of the digits from one to n, where n is the number of years in the asset's service life. For example, if there are five years in the service life, the denominator is the sum of 1, 2, 3, 4, and 5, which equals 15.[2] The numerator decreases each year; it begins with the value of n in the first year and decreases by one each year until it equals one in the final year of the asset's estimated service life. The annual fractions for an asset with a five-year life are: $\frac{5}{15}$, $\frac{4}{15}$, $\frac{3}{15}$, $\frac{2}{15}$, and $\frac{1}{15}$. We calculate depreciation for the five years of the machine's life using the sum-of-the-years'-digits method in Illustration 11–1A.

The SYD method multiplies depreciable base by a declining fraction.

Year	Depreciable Base	×	Depreciation Rate per Year	=	Depreciation	Book Value End of Year
1	$210,000		$\frac{5}{15}$*		$ 70,000	$180,000
2	210,000		$\frac{4}{15}$		56,000	124,000
3	210,000		$\frac{3}{15}$		42,000	82,000
4	210,000		$\frac{2}{15}$		28,000	54,000
5	210,000		$\frac{1}{15}$		14,000	40,000
Totals			$\frac{15}{15}$		$210,000	

ILLUSTRATION 11–1A

Sum-of-the-Years'-Digits Depreciation

$$*\frac{n(n + 1)}{2} = \frac{5(5 + 1)}{2} = 15$$

Declining balance methods.   As an alternative, an accelerated depreciation pattern can be achieved by various declining balance methods. Rather than multiplying a constant balance by a declining fraction as we do in SYD depreciation, we multiply a constant fraction by a declining balance each year. Specifically, we multiply a constant percentage rate times the decreasing book value (cost less accumulated depreciation) of the asset (*not depreciable base*) at the beginning of the year. Because the rate remains constant while the book value declines, annual depreciation is less each year.

Declining balance depreciation methods multiply beginning-of-year book value, not depreciable base, by an annual rate that is a multiple of the straight-line rate.

The rates used are multiples of the straight-line rate. The straight-line rate is simply one, divided by the number of years in the asset's service life. For example, the straight-line rate for an asset with a five-year life is one-fifth, or 20%. Various multiples used in practice are 125%, 150%, or 200% of the straight-line rate. When 200% is used as the multiplier, the

---

[2]A formula useful when calculating the denominator is $n(n + 1)/2$.

method is known as the double-declining-balance (DDB) method because the rate used is twice the straight-line rate.

In our illustration, the double-declining-balance rate would be 40% (two times the straight-line rate of 20%). Depreciation is calculated in Illustration 11–1B for the five years of the machine's life using the double-declining-balance method.

ILLUSTRATION 11–1B Double-Declining- Balance Depreciation	Year	Book Value Beginning of Year	×	Depreciation Rate per Year	=	Depreciation	Book Value End of Year
	1	$250,000		40%		$100,000	$150,000
	2	150,000		40		60,000	90,000
	3	90,000		40		36,000	54,000
	4	54,000				14,000*	40,000
	5	40,000				—	40,000
	Total					$210,000	

*Amount necessary to reduce book value to residual value.

Notice that in the fourth year depreciation expense is a plug amount that reduces book value to the expected residual value (book value beginning of year, $54,000, minus expected residual value, $40,000, = $14,000). There is no depreciation expense in year 5 since book value has already been reduced to the expected residual value. Declining balance methods often allocate the asset's depreciable base over fewer years than the expected service life.

It is not uncommon for a company to switch from accelerated to straight line approximately halfway through an asset's useful life as part of the company's planned depreciation approach.

SWITCH FROM ACCELERATED TO STRAIGHT LINE. The result of applying the double-declining-balance method in our illustration produces an awkward result in the later years of the asset's life. By using the double-declining-balance method in our illustration, no depreciation expense is recorded in year 5 even though the asset is still producing benefits. In practice, many companies switch to the straight-line method approximately halfway through an asset's useful life.

In our illustration, the company would switch to straight line in either year 3 or year 4. Assuming the switch is made at the beginning of year 4, and the book value at the beginning of that year is $54,000, an additional $14,000 ($54,000 − 40,000 in residual value) of depreciation must be recorded. Applying the straight-line concept, $7,000 ($14,000 divided by two remaining years) in depreciation is recorded in both year 4 and year 5.

It should be noted that this switch to straight line is not a change in depreciation method. The switch is part of the company's planned depreciation approach. However, as you will learn later in the chapter, the accounting treatment is the same as a change in depreciation method.

Activity-Based Depreciation Methods

Activity-based depreciation methods estimate service life in terms of some measure of productivity.

The most logical way to allocate an asset's cost to periods of an asset's use is to measure the usefulness of the asset in terms of its productivity. For example, we could measure the service life of a machine in terms of its *output* (for example, the estimated number of units it will produce) or in terms of its *input* (for example, the number of hours it will operate). We have already mentioned that one way to measure the service life of a vehicle is to estimate the number of miles it will operate. The most common activity-based method is called the units-of-production method.

The measure of output used is the estimated number of units (pounds, items, barrels, etc.) to be produced by the machine. We could also use a measure of input such as the number of hours the machine is expected to operate. By the units-of-production method, we first compute the average depreciation rate per unit by dividing the depreciable base by the number of units expected to be produced. This per unit rate is then multiplied by the

FINANCIAL Reporting Case

Q2, p. 533

number of units produced each period. In our illustration, the depreciation rate per unit is $1.50, computed as follows:

$$\frac{\$250,000 - 40,000}{140,000 \text{ units}} = \$1.50 \text{ per unit}$$

The *units-of-production method* computes a depreciation rate per measure of activity and then multiplies this rate by actual activity to determine periodic depreciation.

Each unit produced will require $1.50 of depreciation to be recorded. As we are estimating service life based on units produced rather than in years, depreciation is not constrained by time. However, total depreciation is constrained by the asset's cost and the anticipated residual value. In our illustration, suppose the company intended to dispose of the asset at the end of five years. Depreciation for year five must be modified. Depreciation expense would be a residual amount necessary to bring the book value of the asset down to residual value. Depreciation for the five years is determined in Illustration 11–1C using the units-of-production method. Notice that the last year's depreciation expense is a plug amount that reduces book value to the expected residual value.

Year	Units Produced	×	Depreciation Rate per Unit	=	Depreciation	Book Value End of Year
1	24,000		$1.50		$ 36,000	$214,000
2	36,000		1.50		54,000	160,000
3	46,000		1.50		69,000	91,000
4	8,000		1.50		12,000	79,000
5	16,000				39,000*	40,000
Totals	130,000				$210,000	

ILLUSTRATION 11–1C

Units-of-Production Depreciation

*Amount necessary to reduce book value to residual value.

DECISION MAKERS' PERSPECTIVE—Selecting a Depreciation Method

Illustration 11–1D compares periodic depreciation calculated using each of the alternatives we discussed and illustrated.

Year	Straight Line	Sum-of-the-Years' Digits	Double-Declining Balance	Units of Production
1	$ 42,000	$ 70,000	$100,000	$ 36,000
2	42,000	56,000	60,000	54,000
3	42,000	42,000	36,000	69,000
4	42,000	28,000	14,000	12,000
5	42,000	14,000	0	39,000
Total	$210,000	$210,000	$210,000	$210,000

ILLUSTRATION 11–1D

Comparison of Various Depreciation Methods

All methods provide the same total depreciation over an asset's life.

Theoretically, using an activity-based depreciation method provides a better matching of revenues and expenses. Clearly, the productivity of a plant asset is more closely associated with the benefits provided by that asset than the mere passage of time. Also, these methods allow for random patterns of depreciation to correspond with the random patterns of asset use.

However, activity-based methods quite often are either infeasible or too costly to use. For example, buildings don't have an identifiable measure of productivity. Even for machinery, there may be an identifiable measure of productivity such as machine hours or units produced, but it frequently is more costly to determine each period than it is to simply measure the passage of time. For these reasons, most companies use time-based depreciation methods.

Activity-based methods are theoretically superior to time-based methods but often are impractical to apply in practice.

Graphic 11–3 shows the results of a recent survey of depreciation methods used by large public companies.[3]

GRAPHIC 11–3

Use of Various
Depreciation Methods

Depreciation Method	Number of Companies
Straight line	592
Declining balance	16
Sum-of-the-years'-digits	5
Accelerated method—not specified	27
Units of production	23
Group/composite	9

Why do so many companies use the straight-line method as opposed to other time-based methods? Many companies perhaps consider the benefits derived from the majority of plant assets to be realized approximately evenly over these assets' useful lives. Certainly a contributing factor is that straight line is the easiest method to understand and apply.

Another motivation is the positive effect on reported income. Straight-line depreciation produces a higher net income than accelerated methods in the early years of an asset's life. In Chapter 8 we pointed out that reported net income can affect bonuses paid to management or debt agreements with lenders.

A company does not have to use the same depreciation method for both financial reporting and income tax purposes.

Conflicting with the desire to report higher profits is the desire to reduce taxes by reducing taxable income. An accelerated method serves this objective by reducing taxable income more in the early years of an asset's life than straight line. You probably recall a similar discussion from Chapter 8 in which the benefits were described of using the LIFO inventory method during periods of increasing costs. However, remember that the LIFO conformity rule requires companies using LIFO for income tax reporting to also use LIFO for financial reporting. *No such conformity rule exists for depreciation methods.* Income tax regulations allow firms to use different approaches to computing depreciation in their tax returns and in their financial statements. The method used for tax purposes is therefore not a constraint in the choice of depreciation methods for financial reporting. As a result, most companies use the straight-line method for financial reporting and the Internal Revenue Service's prescribed accelerated method (discussed in Appendix 11A) for income tax purposes. For example, Graphic 11–4 shows **Merck & Co.**'s depreciation policy as reported in a disclosure note accompanying recent financial statements.

GRAPHIC 11–4

Depreciation Method
Disclosure—Merck &
Co.

Real World Financials

Summary of Accounting Policies (in part):
Depreciation

Depreciation is provided over the estimated useful lives of the assets, principally using the straight-line method. For tax purposes, accelerated methods are used.

It is not unusual for a company to use different depreciation methods for different classes of assets. For example, Graphic 11–5 illustrates the **International Paper Company** depreciation policy disclosure contained in a note accompanying recent financial statements.

GRAPHIC 11–5

Depreciation Method
Disclosure—
International Paper
Company

Real World Financials

Summary of Accounting Policies (in part):
Plants, Properties, and Equipment

Plants, properties, and equipment are stated at cost, less accumulated depreciation. The units-of-production method of depreciation is used for major pulp and paper mills and the straight-line method is used for other plants and equipment.

---

[3]*Accounting Trends and Techniques—2007* (New York: AICPA, 2007), p. 360.

CONCEPT REVIEW **EXERCISE**

The Sprague Company purchased a fabricating machine on January 1, 2009, at a net cost of $130,000. At the end of its four-year useful life, the company estimates that the machine will be worth $30,000. Sprague also estimates that the machine will run for 25,000 hours during its four-year life. The company's fiscal year ends on December 31.

DEPRECIATION METHODS

Required:
Compute depreciation for 2009 through 2012 using each of the following methods:

1. Straight line.
2. Sum-of-the-years'-digits.
3. Double-declining balance.
4. Units of production (using machine hours). Actual production was as follows:

Year	Machine Hours
2009	6,000
2010	8,000
2011	5,000
2012	7,000

1. Straight line.

SOLUTION

$$\frac{\$130,000 - 30,000}{4 \text{ years}} = \$25,000 \text{ per year}$$

2. Sum-of-the-years'-digits.

Year	Depreciable Base	×	Depreciation Rate per Year	=	Depreciation
2009	$100,000		$4/10$		$ 40,000
2010	100,000		$3/10$		30,000
2011	100,000		$2/10$		20,000
2012	100,000		$1/10$		10,000
Total					$100,000

3. Double-declining balance.

Year	Book Value Beginning of Year	×	Depreciation Rate per Year	=	Depreciation	Book Value End of Year
2009	$130,000		50%		$ 65,000	$65,000
2010	65,000		50		32,500	32,500
2011	32,500				2,500*	30,000
2012	30,000				—	30,000
Total					$100,000	

*Amount necessary to reduce book value to residual value.

4. Units of production (using machine hours).

Year	Machine Hours	×	Depreciation Rate per Hour	=	Depreciation	Book Value End of Year
2009	6,000		$4*		$ 24,000	$106,000
2010	8,000		4		32,000	74,000
2011	5,000		4		20,000	54,000
2012	7,000				24,000†	30,000
Total					$100,000	

*($130,000 − 30,000)/25,000 hours = $4 per hour.

†Amount necessary to reduce book value to residual value.

Group and Composite Depreciation Methods

Group and composite depreciation methods aggregate assets to reduce the recordkeeping costs of determining periodic depreciation.

As you might imagine, depreciation records could become quite cumbersome and costly if a company has hundreds, or maybe thousands, of depreciable assets. However, the burden can be lessened if the company uses the group or composite method to depreciate assets collectively rather than individually. The two methods are the same except for the way the collection of assets is aggregated for depreciation. The group depreciation method defines the collection as depreciable assets that share similar service lives and other attributes. For example, group depreciation could be used for fleets of vehicles or collections of machinery. The composite depreciation method is used when assets are physically dissimilar but are aggregated anyway to gain the convenience of group depreciation. For instance, composite depreciation can be used for all of the depreciable assets in one manufacturing plant, even though individual assets in the composite may have widely diverse service lives.

Both approaches are similar in that they involve applying a single straight-line rate based on the average service lives of the assets in the group or composite.[4] The process is demonstrated using Illustration 11–2.

ILLUSTRATION 11–2	The Express Delivery Company began operations in 2009. It will depreciate its fleet of delivery vehicles using the group method. The cost of vehicles purchased early in 2009, along with residual values, estimated lives, and straight-line depreciation per year by type of vehicle, are as follows:				
Group Depreciation					

Asset	Cost	Residual Value	Depreciable Base	Estimated Life (yrs.)	Depreciation per Year (straight line)
Vans	$150,000	$30,000	$120,000	6	$20,000
Trucks	120,000	16,000	104,000	5	20,800
Wagons	60,000	12,000	48,000	4	12,000
Totals	$330,000	$58,000	$272,000		$52,800

The *group depreciation* rate is determined by dividing the depreciation per year by the total cost. The group's *average service* life is calculated by dividing the depreciable base by the depreciation per year:

$$\text{Group depreciation rate} = \frac{\$52,800}{\$330,000} = 16\%$$

$$\text{Average service life} = \frac{\$272,000}{\$52,800} = 5.15 \text{ years (rounded)}$$

The depreciation rate is applied to the total cost of the group or composite for the period.

If there are no changes in the assets contained in the group, depreciation of $52,800 per year (16% × $330,000) will be recorded for 5.15 years. This means the depreciation in the sixth year will be $7,920 (.15 of a full year's depreciation = 15% × $52,800), which depreciates the cost of the group down to its estimated residual value. In other words, the group will be depreciated over the average service life of the assets in the group.

In practice, there very likely will be changes in the assets constituting the group as new assets are added and others are retired or sold. Additions are recorded by increasing the group asset account for the cost of the addition. Depreciation is determined by multiplying the group rate by the total cost of assets in the group for that period. Once the group or composite rate and the average service life are determined, they normally are continued despite the addition and disposition of individual assets. This implicitly assumes that the service lives of new assets approximate those of individual assets they replace.

---

[4]A declining balance method could also be used with either the group or composite method by applying a multiple (e.g., 200%) to the straight-line group or composite rate.

Because depreciation records are not kept on an individual asset basis, dispositions are recorded under the assumption that the book value of the disposed item exactly equals any proceeds received and no gain or loss is recorded. For example, if a delivery truck in the above illustration that cost $15,000 is sold for $3,000 in the year 2012, the following journal entry is recorded:

Cash	3,000	
Accumulated depreciation (difference)	12,000	
Vehicles		15,000

No gain or loss is recorded when a group or composite asset is retired or sold.

Any actual gain or loss is included in the accumulated depreciation account. This practice generally will not distort income as the unrecorded gains tend to offset unrecorded losses.

The group and composite methods simplify the recordkeeping of depreciable assets. This simplification justifies any immaterial errors in income determination. Graphic 11–6 shows a disclosure note accompanying recent financial statements of the **El Paso Natural Gas Company (EPNG)** describing the use of the group depreciation method for its regulated property.

GRAPHIC 11–6

Disclosure of Depreciation Method—El Paso Natural Gas Company

Real World Financials

Property, Plant, and Equipment (in part)

We use the group method to depreciate property, plant, and equipment. Under this method, assets with similar lives and characteristics are grouped and depreciated as one asset. We apply the depreciation rate to the total cost of the group until its net book value equals its salvage value. For certain general plant and rights-of-way, we depreciate the asset to zero. The majority of our property, plant, and equipment is on our EPNG system. In December 2006, we filed a proposed rate case settlement, which included a modification of our depreciation rates resulting in depreciation rates ranging from 1 to 20 percent and the depreciable lives ranging from 5 to 92 years for assets on our EPNG system.

When we retire property, plant, and equipment, we charge accumulated depreciation and amortization for the original cost of the assets in addition to the cost to remove, sell, or dispose of the assets, less their salvage value. We do not recognize a gain or loss unless we sell an entire operating unit.

Additional group-based depreciation methods, the retirement and replacement methods, are discussed in Appendix 11B.

Depletion of Natural Resources

Allocation of the cost of natural resources is called depletion. Because the usefulness of natural resources generally is directly related to the amount of the resources extracted, the activity-based units-of-production method is widely used to calculate periodic depletion. Service life is therefore the estimated amount of natural resource to be extracted (for example, tons of mineral or barrels of oil).

● **LO3**

Depletion base is cost less any anticipated residual value. Residual value could be significant if cost includes land that has a value after the natural resource has been extracted.

The example in Illustration 11–3 was first introduced in Chapter 10.

ILLUSTRATION 11–3

Depletion of Natural Resources

The Jackson Mining Company paid $1,000,000 for the right to explore for a coal deposit on 500 acres of land in Pennsylvania. Costs of exploring for the coal deposit totaled $800,000 and intangible development costs incurred in digging and erecting the mine shaft were $500,000. In addition, Jackson purchased new excavation equipment for the project at a cost of $600,000. After the coal is removed from the site, the equipment will be sold for an anticipated residual value of $60,000.

The company geologist estimates that 1 million tons of coal will be extracted over the three-year period. During 2009, 300,000 tons were extracted. Jackson is required by its contract to restore the land to a condition suitable for recreational use after it extracts the coal.

In Chapter 10 on page 484 we determined that the capitalized cost of the natural resource, coal mine, including the restoration costs, is $2,768,360. Since there is no residual value to the land, the depletion base equals cost and the depletion rate per ton is calculated as follows:

Depletion of the cost of natural resources usually is determined using the units-of-production method.

$$\text{Depletion per ton} = \frac{\text{Depletion base}}{\text{Estimated extractable tons}}$$

$$\text{Depletion per ton} = \frac{\$2,768,360}{1,000,000 \text{ tons}} = \$2.76836 \text{ per ton}$$

For each ton of coal extracted, $2.768360 in depletion is recorded. In 2009, the following journal entry records depletion.

Depletion ($2.76836 × 300,000 tons)	830,508	
Coal mine		830,508

Notice that the credit is to the asset, coal mine, rather than to a contra account, accumulated depletion. Although this approach is traditional, the use of a contra account is acceptable.

Depletion is a product cost and is included in the cost of the inventory of coal, just as the depreciation on manufacturing equipment is included in inventory cost. The depletion is then included in cost of goods sold in the income statement when the coal is sold.

What about depreciation on the $600,000 cost of excavation equipment? If the equipment can be moved from the site and used on future projects, the equipment's depreciable base should be allocated over its useful life. If the asset is not movable, as in our illustration, then it should be depreciated over its useful life or the life of the natural resource, whichever is shorter.

The units-of-production method often is used to determine depreciation and amortization on assets used in the extraction of natural resources.

Quite often, companies use the units-of-production method to calculate depreciation and amortization on assets used in the extraction of natural resources. The activity base used is the same as that used to calculate depletion, the estimated recoverable natural resource. In our illustration, the depreciation rate would be $.54 per ton, calculated as follows.

$$\text{Depreciation per ton} = \frac{\$600,000 - 60,000}{1,000,000 \text{ tons}} = \$.54 \text{ per ton}$$

In 2009, $162,000 in depreciation ($.54 × 300,000 tons) is recorded and also included as part of the cost of the coal inventory.

The summary of significant accounting policies disclosure accompanying recent financial statements of **ConocoPhilips** shown in Graphic 11–7 provides a good summary of depletion, amortization, and depreciation for natural resource properties.

GRAPHIC 11–7

Depletion Method Disclosure— ConocoPhilips

Real World Financials

> **Summary of Significant Accounting Policies (in part)**
>
> Depletion and Amortization—Leasehold costs of producing properties are depleted using the units-of-production method based on estimated proved oil and gas reserves. Amortization of intangible development costs is based on the units-of-production method using estimated proved developed oil and gas reserves.
>
> Depreciation and amortization of properties, plants and equipment on producing oil and gas properties, certain pipeline assets, and on Syncrude mining operations are determined by the units-of-production method.

ADDITIONAL CONSIDERATION

Percentage Depletion

Depletion of cost less residual value required by GAAP should not be confused with percentage depletion (also called *statutory depletion*) allowable for income tax purposes for oil, gas, and most mineral natural resources. Under these tax provisions, a producer is allowed to deduct a fixed percentage of gross income as depletion expense without regard to the cost of the natural resource. Over the life of the asset, percentage depletion could exceed the asset's cost. The percentage allowed varies according to the type of natural resource.

Because percentage depletion usually differs from cost depletion, a difference between taxable income and financial reporting income before tax results. These differences are discussed in Chapter 16.

Amortization of Intangible Assets

Let's turn now to a third type of long-lived asset—intangible assets. As for most other operational assets, we allocate the cost of an intangible asset over its service or useful life. However, for the few intangible assets with indefinite useful lives, amortization is inappropriate.

● LO4

Intangible Assets Subject to Amortization

Allocating the cost of intangible assets is called amortization. For an intangible asset with a finite useful life, we allocate its capitalized cost less any estimated residual value to periods in which the asset is expected to contribute to the company's revenue-generating activities. This requires that we determine the asset's useful life, its amortization base (cost less estimated residual value), and the appropriate allocation method, similar to our depreciating tangible assets.

The cost of an intangible asset with a finite useful life is amortized.

USEFUL LIFE.   Legal, regulatory, or contractual provisions often limit the useful life of an intangible asset. On the other hand, useful life might sometimes be less than the asset's legal or contractual life. For example, the useful life of a patent would be considerably less than its legal life of 20 years if obsolescence were expected to limit the longevity of a protected product.

RESIDUAL VALUE.   We discussed the cost of intangible assets in Chapter 10. The expected residual value of an intangible asset usually is zero. This might not be the case, though, if at the end of its useful life to the reporting entity the asset will benefit another entity. For example, if Quadra Corp. has a commitment from another company to purchase one of Quadra's patents at the end of its useful life at a determinable price, we use that price as the patent's residual value.

ALLOCATION METHOD.   The method of amortization should reflect the pattern of use of the asset in generating benefits. Most companies use the straight-line method. We discussed and illustrated a unique approach to determining the periodic amortization of software development costs in Chapter 10. Recall that the periodic amortization percentage for software development costs is the *greater* of (1) the ratio of current revenues to current and anticipated revenues (percentage of revenue method), or (2) the straight-line percentage over the useful life of the asset.

   Intel Corporation reported several intangible assets in a recent balance sheet. A note, shown in Graphic 11–8, disclosed the range of estimated useful lives and the use of the straight-line method of amortization.

GRAPHIC 11–8

Intangible Asset Useful Life Disclosure—Intel Corporation

Real World Financials

Summary of Significant Accounting Policies (in part)
Identified Intangible Assets

Intellectual property assets primarily represent rights acquired under technology licenses and are generally amortized on a straight-line basis over periods ranging from 2 to 17 years. Acquisition-related developed technology is amortized on a straight-line basis over periods ranging from 4 to 6 years. Other intangible assets include acquisition-related customer lists which are amortized on a straight-line basis, and customer supply agreements, which are amortized based on product volume. Other intangible assets are amortized over periods ranging from 2 to 6 years. All identified intangible assets are classified within other long-term assets on the consolidated balance sheets. In the quarter following the period in which identified intangible assets become fully amortized, the fully amortized balances are removed from the gross asset and accumulated amortization amounts.

   Like depletion, amortization expense traditionally is credited to the asset account itself rather than to accumulated amortization. However, the use of a contra account is acceptable. Notice in Graphic 11–8 that Intel uses an accumulated amortization contra account. Let's look at an example in Illustration 11–4.

ILLUSTRATION 11–4 Amortization of Intangibles	Hollins Corporation began operations in 2009. Early in January, the company purchased a franchise from Ajax Industries for $200,000. The franchise agreement is for a period of 10 years. In addition, Hollins purchased a patent for $50,000. The remaining legal life of the patent is 13 years. However, due to expected technological obsolescence, the company estimates that the useful life of the patent is only 8 years. Hollins uses the straight-line amortization method for all intangible assets. The company's fiscal year-end is December 31. The journal entries to record a full year of amortization for these intangibles are as follows:

Amortization expense ($200,000 ÷ 10 years)	20,000	
Franchise		20,000
To record amortization of franchise.		
Amortization expense ($50,000 ÷ 8 years)	6,250	
Patent		6,250
To record amortization of patent.		

Similar to depreciation, amortization is either a product cost or a period cost depending on the use of the asset. For intangibles used in the manufacture of a product, amortization is a product cost and is included in the cost of inventory (and doesn't become an expense until the inventory is sold). For intangible assets not used in production, such as the franchise cost in our illustration, periodic amortization is expensed in the period incurred.

Intangible Assets Not Subject to Amortization

The cost of an intangible asset with an *indefinite* useful life is not amortized

An intangible asset that is determined to have an indefinite useful life is not subject to periodic amortization. Useful life is considered indefinite if there is no foreseeable limit on the period of time over which the asset is expected to contribute to the cash flows of the entity.[5]

Indefinite does not necessarily mean permanent. For example, suppose Collins Corporation acquired a trademark in conjunction with the acquisition of a tire company. Collins plans to continue to produce the line of tires marketed under the acquired company's trademark. Recall from our discussion in Chapter 10 that trademarks have a legal life of 10 years, but the registration can be renewed for an indefinite number of 10-year periods. The life of the purchased trademark is initially considered to be indefinite and the cost of the trademark is not amortized. However, if after several years management decides to phase out production of the tire line over the next three years, Collins would amortize the remaining book value over a three-year period.

Trademarks or tradenames often are considered to have indefinite useful lives.

Recall the **Hewlett-Packard Company (HP)** acquisition of **Compaq Computer Corporation** discussed in Chapter 10. HP allocated $1.4 million of the purchase price to Compaq's tradename, which is not being amortized. Graphic 11–9 provides another example in a disclosure made by **Staples, Inc.**, in a recent annual report.

GRAPHIC 11–9

Indefinite Life Intangibles Disclosure— Staples, Inc.

Real World Financials

Goodwill and Intangible Assets (in part)
Intangible assets not subject to amortization, which include registered trademarks and tradenames, were $153.0 million at February 2, 2008, and February 3, 2007.

Goodwill is an intangible asset whose cost is *not* expensed through periodic amortization.

Goodwill is the most common intangible asset with an indefinite useful life. Recall that goodwill is measured as the difference between the purchase price of a company and the fair value of all of the identifiable net assets (tangible and intangible assets minus the fair value of liabilities assumed). Does this mean that goodwill and other intangible assets with indefinite useful lives will remain in a company's balance sheet at their original capitalized values indefinitely? Not necessarily. Like other operational assets, intangibles are subject to the impairment of value rules we discuss in a subsequent section of this chapter. In fact, indefinite life intangibles must be tested for impairment annually, or more frequently if events or circumstances indicate that the asset might be impaired.

[5]"Goodwill and Other Intangible Assets," *Statement of Financial Accounting Standards No. 142* (Norwalk, Conn.: FASB, 2001), par. B45.

ADDITIONAL ISSUES

In this part of the chapter, we discuss the following issues related to cost allocation:

1. Partial periods
2. Changes in estimates
3. Change in depreciation method
4. Error correction
5. Impairment of value

Partial Periods

Only in textbooks are operational assets purchased and disposed of at the very beginning or very end of a company's fiscal year. When acquisition and disposal occur at other times, a company theoretically must determine how much depreciation, depletion, and amortization to record for the part of the year that each asset actually is used.

Let's repeat the Hogan Manufacturing Company illustration used earlier in the chapter but modify it in Illustration 11–5 to assume that the asset was acquired *during* the company's fiscal year.

On April 1, 2009, the Hogan Manufacturing Company purchased a machine for $250,000. The company expects the service life of the machine to be five years and the anticipated residual value is $40,000. The machine was disposed of after five years of use. The company's fiscal year-end is December 31. Partial-year depreciation is recorded based on the number of months the asset is in service.	**ILLUSTRATION 11–5** Depreciation Methods—Partial Year

Notice that no information is provided on the estimated output of the machine. Partial-year depreciation presents a problem only when time-based depreciation methods are used. In an activity-based method, the rate per unit of output simply is multiplied by the actual output for the period, regardless of the length of that period.

Depreciation per year of the asset's life calculated earlier in the chapter for the various time-based depreciation methods is shown in Illustration 11–5A.

Year	Straight Line	Sum-of-the-Years'-Digits	Double-Declining Balance	
1	$ 42,000	$ 70,000	$100,000	**ILLUSTRATION 11–5A** Yearly Depreciation
2	42,000	56,000	60,000	
3	42,000	42,000	36,000	
4	42,000	28,000	14,000	
5	42,000	14,000	0	
Total	$210,000	$210,000	$210,000	

Illustration 11–5B shows how Hogan would depreciate the machinery by these three methods assuming an April 1 acquisition date.

Notice that 2009 depreciation is three-quarters of the full year's depreciation for the first year of the asset's life, because the asset was used nine months, or 3/4 of the year. The remaining one-quarter of the first year's depreciation is included in 2010's depreciation along with 3/4 of the depreciation for the second year of the asset's life. This calculation is not necessary for the straight-line method because a full year's depreciation is the same for each year of the asset's life.

Usually, the above procedure is impractical or at least cumbersome. As a result, most companies adopt a simplifying assumption, or convention, for computing partial year's

ILLUSTRATION 11–5B Partial-Year Depreciation

Year	Straight Line	Sum-of-the-Years'-Digits	Double-Declining Balance
2009	$42,000 × 3/4 = **$ 31,500**	$70,000 × 3/4 = **$ 52,500**	$100,000 × 3/4 = **$ 75,000**
2010	**$ 42,000**	$70,000 × 1/4 = $ 17,500	$100,000 × 1/4 = $ 25,000
		+56,000 × 3/4 = 42,000	+60,000 × 3/4 = 45,000
		$ 59,500	**$ 70,000***
2011	**$ 42,000**	$56,000 × 1/4 = $ 14,000	$60,000 × 1/4 = $ 15,000
		+42,000 × 3/4 = 31,500	+36,000 × 3/4 = 27,000
		$ 45,500	**$ 42,000**
2012	**$ 42,000**	$42,000 × 1/4 = $ 10,500	$36,000 × 1/4 = $ 9,000
		+28,000 × 3/4 = 21,000	+14,000 × 3/4 = 10,500
		$ 31,500	**$ 19,500**
2013	**$ 42,000**	$28,000 × 1/4 = $ 7,000	$14,000 × 1/4 = **$ 3,500**
		+14,000 × 3/4 = 10,500	
		$ 17,500	
2014	$42,000 × 1/4 = **$ 10,500**	$14,000 × 1/4 = **$ 3,500**	
	Totals **$210,000**	**$210,000**	**$210,000**

*Could also be determined by multiplying the book value at the beginning of the year by twice the straight-line rate: ($250,000 − 75,000) × 40% = $70,000.

depreciation and use it consistently. A common convention is to record one-half of a full year's depreciation in the year of acquisition and another half year in the year of disposal. This is known as the **half-year convention**.[6]

CONCEPT REVIEW EXERCISE

DEPLETION AND AMORTIZATION

Part A:
On March 29, 2009, the Horizon Energy Corporation purchased the mineral rights to a coal deposit in New Mexico for $2 million. Development costs and the present value of estimated land restoration costs totaled an additional $3.4 million. The company removed 200,000 tons of coal during 2009 and estimated that an additional 1,600,000 tons would be removed over the next 15 months.

Required:
Compute depletion on the mine for 2009.

SOLUTION

Cost of Coal Mine:	($ in millions)
Purchase price of mineral rights	$2.0
Development and restoration costs	3.4
	$5.4

Depletion:

$$\text{Depletion per ton} = \frac{\$5.4 \text{ million}}{1.8 \text{ million tons*}} = \$3 \text{ per ton}$$

*200,000 + 1,600,000

2009 depletion = $3 × 200,000 tons = $600,000

---
[6]Another common method is the modified half-year convention. This method records a full year's depreciation when the asset is acquired in the first half of the year or sold in the second half. No depreciation is recorded if the asset is acquired in the second half of the year or sold in the first half. These half-year conventions are simple and, in most cases, will not result in material differences from a more precise calculation.

Part B:

On October 1, 2009, Advanced Micro Circuits, Inc., completed the purchase of Zotec Corporation for $200 million. Included in the allocation of the purchase price were the following identifiable intangible assets ($ in millions), along with the fair values and estimated useful lives:

Intangible Asset	Fair value	Useful Life (in years)
Patent	$10	5
Developed technology	50	4
Customer list	10	2

In addition, the fair value of acquired tangible assets was $100 million. Goodwill was valued at $30 million. Straight-line amortization is used for all purchased intangibles.

During 2009, Advanced finished work on a software development project. Development costs incurred after technological feasibility was achieved and before the product release date totaled $2 million. The software was available for release to the general public on September 29, 2009. During the last three months of the year, revenue from the sale of the software was $4 million. The company estimates that the software will generate an additional $36 million in revenue over the next 45 months.

Required:

Compute amortization for purchased intangibles and software development costs for 2009.

SOLUTION

Amortization of Purchased Intangibles:

Patent	$10 million / 5 = $2 million × 3/12 year = $.5 million
Developed technology	$50 million / 4 = $12.5 million × 3/12 year = $3.125 million
Customer list	$10 million / 2 = $5 million × 3/12 year = $1.25 million
Goodwill	The cost of goodwill is not amortized.

Amortization of Software Development Costs:

(1) Percentage-of-revenue method:

$$\frac{\$4 \text{ million}}{(\$4 \text{ million} + 36 \text{ million})} = 10\% \times \$2 \text{ million} = \$200,000$$

(2) Straight-line:

$$\frac{3 \text{ months}}{48 \text{ months}} \text{ or } 6.25\% \times \$2 \text{ million} = \$125,000$$

Advanced will use the percentage-of-revenue method since it produces the greater amortization, $200,000. ●

Changes in Estimates

● LO5

The calculation of depreciation, depletion, or amortization requires estimates of both service life and residual value. It's inevitable that at least some estimates will prove incorrect. Chapter 4 introduced the topic of changes in estimates along with coverage of changes in accounting principles and the correction of errors. Here and in subsequent sections of this chapter, we provide overviews of the accounting treatment and disclosures required for these changes and errors when they involve operational assets.

Changes in estimates are accounted for prospectively. When a company revises a previous estimate based on new information, prior financial statements are not restated. Instead, the company merely incorporates the new estimate in any related accounting determinations from then on. So, it usually will affect some aspects of both the balance sheet and the income statement in the current and future periods. And a disclosure note should describe the effect of a change in estimate on income before extraordinary items, net income, and related pershare amounts for the current period.

A change in estimate should be reflected in the financial statements of the current period and future periods.

Consider the example in Illustration 11–6.

ILLUSTRATION 11–6	On January 1, 2007, the Hogan Manufacturing Company purchased a machine for $250,000. The company expects the service life of the machine to be five years and its anticipated residual value to be $40,000. The company's fiscal year-end is December 31 and the straight-line depreciation method is used for all depreciable assets. During 2009, the company revised its estimate of service life from five to eight years and also revised estimated residual value to $22,000.
Change in Accounting Estimate	For 2007 and 2008, depreciation is $42,000 per year [($250,000 − 40,000) ÷ 5 years] or $84,000 for the two years. However, with the revised estimate, depreciation for 2009 and subsequent years is determined by allocating the book value remaining at the beginning of 2009 less the revised residual value equally over the remaining service life of six years (8 − 2). The remaining book value at the beginning of 2009 is $166,000 ($250,000 − 84,000) and depreciation for 2009 and subsequent years is recorded as follows:

Depreciation expense (below) 24,000
    Accumulated depreciation 24,000

	$250,000	Cost
$42,000		Old annual depreciation ($210,000 ÷ 5 years)
× 2 years	84,000	Depreciation to date (2007–2008)
	166,000	Book value as of 1/1/09
	22,000	Less revised residual value
	144,000	Revised depreciable base
	÷ 6	Estimated remaining life (8 years − 2 years)
	$ 24,000	New annual depreciation

The asset's book value is depreciated down to the anticipated residual value of $22,000 at the end of the revised eight-year service life. In addition, a note discloses the effect of the change in estimate on income, if material. The before-tax effect is an increase in income of $18,000 (depreciation of $42,000 if the change had not been made, less $24,000 depreciation after the change). **Goodyear Tire & Rubber Company** recently revised the service lives for its tire mold equipment. Graphic 11–10 shows the note that disclosed the change.

GRAPHIC 11–10

Change in Estimate Disclosure—Goodyear Tire & Rubber Company

Real World Financials

Note 19. Change in Estimate

Effective April 1, 2006, we increased the estimated useful lives of our tire mold equipment for depreciation purposes. The change was due primarily to improved practices related to mold maintenance and handling in our tire manufacturing facilities and the completion of a review, in the second quarter of 2006, of current and forecasted product lives. The change resulted in a benefit to pretax income in 2006 of $28 million ($23 million after-tax or $0.13 per share). Prior periods have not been adjusted for this change

Change in Depreciation, Amortization, or Depletion Method

● LO6

Changes in depreciation, amortization, or depletion methods are accounted for the same way as a change in accounting estimate.

Recall from our discussion in Chapter 4 that generally accepted accounting principles require that a change in depreciation, amortization, or depletion method be considered a change in accounting estimate that is achieved by a change in accounting principle. We account for these changes prospectively, exactly as we would any other change in estimate. One difference is that most changes in estimate do not require a company to justify the change. However, this change in estimate is a result of changing an accounting principle and therefore requires a clear justification as to why the new method is preferable. Consider the example in Illustration 11–7.

Graphic 11–11 provides an example of a disclosure describing a recent change in depreciation method made by **Texas Instruments**.

On January 1, 2007, the Hogan Manufacturing Company purchased a machine for $250,000. The company expects the service life of the machine to be five years and its anticipated residual value to be $30,000. The company's fiscal year-end is December 31 and the double-declining-balance (DDB) depreciation method is used. During 2009, the company switched from the DDB to the straight-line method. In 2009, the adjusting entry is:

Depreciation expense (below) 20,000
    Accumulated depreciation   20,000

> DDB depreciation:
>
> | | | |
> |---|---|---|
> | 2007 | $100,000 | ($250,000 × 40%*) |
> | 2008 | 60,000 | ([$250,000 − 100,000] × 40%*) |
> | Total | $160,000 | |
>
> *Double the straight-line rate for 5 years ([1/5 = 20%] × 2 = 40%)

$250,000	Cost
160,000	Depreciation to date, DDB (2007–2008)
90,000	Undepreciated cost as of 1/1/09
30,000	Less residual value
60,000	Depreciable base
÷ 3 yrs.	Remaining life (5 years − 2 years)
$ 20,000	New annual depreciation

    A disclosure note reports the effect of the change on net income and earnings per share along with clear justification for changing depreciation methods.

Change in Depreciation Method

Effective January 1, 2006, as a result of a study made of the pattern of usage of our long-lived depreciable assets, we adopted the straight-line method of depreciation for all property, plant, and equipment. Under the provisions of *SFAS No. 154,* "Accounting Changes and Error Corrections, a replacement of APB Opinion No. 20 and FASB Statement No. 3," which became effective as of January 1, 2006, a change in depreciation method is treated on a prospective basis as a change in estimate. Prior period results have not been restated. We believe that the change from the 150 percent declining-balance method to the straight-line method better reflects the pattern of consumption of the future benefits to be derived from those assets being depreciated and provides a better matching of costs and revenues over the assets' estimated useful lives. The effect of the change in depreciation method for the year ended December 31, 2006, was to reduce depreciation expense by $156 million and increase both income from continuing operations and net income by $77 million ($ 0.05 per share).

    Frequently, when a company changes depreciation method, the change will be effective only for assets placed in service after that date. Of course, that means depreciation schedules do not require revision because the change does not affect assets depreciated in prior periods. A disclosure note still is required to provide justification for the change and to report the effect of the change in the current year's income.

Error Correction

Errors involving operational assets include computational errors in the calculation of depreciation, depletion, or amortization and mistakes made in determining whether expenditures should be capitalized or expensed. These errors can affect many years. For example, let's say a major addition to an operational asset should be capitalized but incorrectly is expensed. Not only is income in the year of the error understated, but subsequent years' income is overstated because depreciation is omitted.

● LO7

Recall from our discussion of inventory errors in Chapter 9 that if a material error is discovered in an accounting period subsequent to the period in which the error is made, any previous years' financial statements that were incorrect as a result of the error are retrospectively restated to reflect the correction. Any account balances that are incorrect as a result of the error are corrected by journal entry. If retained earnings is one of the incorrect accounts, the correction is reported as a *prior period adjustment* to the beginning balance in the statement of shareholders' equity.[7] In addition, a disclosure note is needed to describe the nature of the error and the impact of its correction on net income, income before extraordinary items, and earnings per share.

Here is a summary of the treatment of material errors occurring in a previous year:

- Previous years' financial statements are retrospectively restated.
- Account balances are corrected.
- If retained earnings requires correction, the correction is reported as a prior period adjustment.
- A note describes the nature of the error and the impact of the correction on income.

Consider Illustration 11–8. The 2007 and 2008 financial statements that were incorrect as a result of the error are *retrospectively restated* to report the addition to the patent and to reflect the correct amount of amortization expense, assuming both statements are reported again for comparative purposes in the 2009 annual report.

ILLUSTRATION 11–8 Error Correction	In 2009, the controller of the Hathaway Corporation discovered an error in recording $300,000 in legal fees to successfully defend a patent infringement suit in 2007. The $300,000 was charged to legal fee expense but should have been capitalized and amortized over the five-year remaining life of the patent. Straight-line amortization is used by Hathaway for all intangibles.

Analysis

($ in thousands)

		Correct **(Should Have Been Recorded)**			**Incorrect** **(As Recorded)**	
2007	Patent	300		Expense	300	
	Cash		300	Cash		300
2007	Expense	60		Amortization entry omitted		
	Patent		60			
2008	Expense	60		Amortization entry omitted		
	Patent		60			

During the two-year period, amortization expense was *understated* by $120 thousand, but other expenses were *overstated* by $300 thousand, so net income during the period was *understated* by $180 thousand (ignoring income taxes). This means retained earnings is currently *understated* by that amount.

Patent is understated by $180 thousand.

($ in thousands)

Patent	180	
Retained earnings		180
To correct incorrect accounts.		

Because retained earnings is one of the accounts incorrect as a result of the error, a correction to that account of $180,000 is reported as a prior period adjustment to the 2009

---

[7]The prior period adjustment is applied to beginning retained earnings for the year following the error, or for the earliest year being reported in the comparative financial statements when the error occurs prior to the earliest year presented. The retained earnings balances in years after the first year also are adjusted to what those balances would be if the error had not occurred, but a company may choose not to explicitly report those adjustments as separate line items.

beginning retained earnings balance in Hathaway's comparative statements of shareholders' equity. Assuming that 2008 is included with 2009 in the comparative statements, a correction would be made to the 2008 beginning retained earnings balance as well. That prior period adjustment, though, would be for the pre-2008 difference: $300,000 − 60,000 = $240,000.

Also, a disclosure note accompanying Hathaway's 2009 financial statements should describe the nature of the error and the impact of its correction on each year's net income (understated by $240,000 in 2007 and overstated by $60,000 in 2008), income before extraordinary items (same as net income), and earnings per share.

Chapter 20 provides in-depth coverage of changes in estimates and methods, and of accounting errors. We cover the tax effect of these changes and errors in that chapter.

Impairment of Value

Depreciation, depletion, and amortization reflect a gradual consumption of the benefits inherent in an operational asset. An implicit assumption in allocating the cost of an asset over its useful life is that there has been no significant reduction in the anticipated total benefits or service potential of the asset. Situations can arise, however, that cause a significant decline or impairment of those benefits or service potentials. An extreme case would be the destruction of a plant asset—say a building destroyed by fire—before the asset is fully depreciated. The remaining carrying value of the asset in that case should be written off as a loss. Sometimes, though, the impairment of future value is more subtle.

The way we recognize and measure an impairment loss differs depending on whether the operational assets are to be held and used or are being held to be sold. Accounting is different, too, for operational assets with finite lives and those with indefinite lives. We consider those differences now.

● **LO8**

FINANCIAL Reporting Case

Q3, p. 533

Operational Assets to Be Held and Used

An increasingly common occurrence in practice is the partial write-down of operational assets that remain in use. For example, in the second quarter of 2001, **American Airlines** reduced the carrying value (book value) of certain aircraft by $685 million. The write-down reflected the significant reduction in demand for air travel that occurred even before the September 11, 2001, terrorist attacks on the World Trade Center and the Pentagon.

Conceptually, there is considerable merit for a policy requiring the write-down of an operational asset when there has been a significant decline in value. A write-down can provide important information about the future cash flows that a company can generate from using the asset. However, in practice, this process is very subjective. Even if it appears certain that significant impairment of value has occurred, it often is difficult to measure the amount of the required write-down.

For example, let's say a company purchased $2,000,000 of equipment to be used in the production of a new type of laser printer. Depreciation is determined using the straight-line method over a useful life of six years and the residual value is estimated at $200,000. At the beginning of year 3, the machine's book value has been reduced by accumulated depreciation to $1,400,000 [$2,000,000 − ($300,000 × 2)]. At that time, new technology is developed causing a significant reduction in the selling price of the new laser printer as well as a reduction in anticipated demand for the product. Management estimates that the equipment will be useful for only two more years and will have no significant residual value.

This situation is not simply a matter of a change in the estimates of useful life and residual value. Management must decide if the events occurring in year 3 warrant a write-down of the asset below $1,400,000. A write-down would be appropriate if the company decided that it would be unable to fully recover this amount through future use.

For operational assets to be held and used, different guidelines apply to (1) tangible operational assets and intangible operational assets with finite useful lives (subject to depreciation, depletion, or amortization) and (2) intangible operational assets with indefinite useful lives (not subject to amortization).

An operational asset held for use should be written down if there has been a significant impairment of value.

Tangible operational
assets and finite
life intangibles are
tested for impairment
only when events
or changes in
circumstances indicate
book value may not be
recoverable.

TANGIBLE OPERATIONAL ASSETS AND FINITE LIFE INTANGIBLES.

SFAS No. 144[8] provides guidelines for when to recognize and how to measure impairment losses of long-lived tangible assets and intangible assets with finite useful lives. For purposes of this recognition and measurement, assets are grouped at the lowest level for which identifiable cash flows are largely independent of the cash flows of other assets.

Recognition. It would be impractical to test all assets or asset groups for impairment at the end of every reporting period. *SFAS No. 144* requires investigation of possible impairment only if events or changes in circumstances indicate that the book value of the asset or asset group may not be recoverable. This might happen from:

- a. A significant decrease in market price.
- b. A significant adverse change in how the asset is being used or in its physical condition.
- c. A significant adverse change in legal factors or in the business climate.
- d. An accumulation of costs significantly higher than the amount originally expected for the acquisition or construction of an asset.
- e. A current-period loss combined with a history of losses or a projection of continuing losses associated with the asset.
- f. A realization that the asset will be disposed of significantly before the end of its estimated useful life.[9]

STEP 1—An impairment
loss is required only
when the undiscounted
sum of future cash
flows is less than book
value.

STEP 2—The
impairment loss is the
excess of book value
over fair value.

Measurement. Determining whether to record an impairment loss and actually recording the loss is a two-step process. The first step is a recoverability test—an impairment loss is required only when the undiscounted sum of estimated future cash flows from an asset is less than the asset's book value. The measurement of impairment loss—step 2—is the difference between the asset's book value and its fair value. If an impairment loss is recognized, the written-down book value becomes the new cost base for future cost allocation. Later recovery of an impairment loss is prohibited.

Let's look closer at the measurement process (step two). Fair value is the amount at which the asset could be bought or sold in a current transaction between willing parties. Quoted market prices could be used if they're available. If fair value is not determinable, it must be estimated.

The present value of
future cash flows often
is used as a measure of
fair value.

The process is best described by an example. Consider Illustration 11–9.

In the entry in Illustration 11–9, we reduce accumulated depreciation to zero and decrease the cost of the assets to their fair value of $135 million ($300 − 165). This adjusted amount serves as the revised basis for subsequent depreciation over the remaining useful life of the assets, just as if the assets had been acquired on the impairment date for their fair values.

Because the fair value of the factory assets was not readily available to Dakota in Illustration 11–9, the $135 million had to be estimated. One method that can be used to estimate fair value is to compute the discounted present value of future cash flows expected from the asset. Keep in mind that we use *undiscounted* estimates of cash flows in step one to determine whether an impairment loss is indicated, but *discounted* estimates of cash flows to determine the amount of the loss. In calculating present value, either a traditional approach or an expected cash flow approach can be used. The traditional approach is to incorporate risk and uncertainty into the discount rate. Recall from discussions in previous chapters that the expected cash flow approach incorporates risk and uncertainty instead into a determination of a probability-weighted cash flow expectation, and then discounts this expected cash flow using a risk-free interest rate. We discussed and illustrated the expected cash flow approach in previous chapters.

A disclosure note is needed to describe the impairment loss. The note should include a description of the impaired asset or asset group, the facts and circumstances leading to the impairment, the amount of the loss if not separately disclosed on the face of the income statement, and the method used to determine fair value.

---

[8]"Accounting for the Impairment of Long-Lived Assets and for Long-Lived Assets to Be Disposed Of," *Statement of Financial Accounting Standards No. 144* (Norwalk, Conn.: FASB, 2001).
[9]Ibid., par. 8.

ILLUSTRATION 11–9

Impairment Loss—
Tangible Operational
Assets

The Dakota Corporation operates several factories that manufacture medical equipment. Near the end of the company's 2009 fiscal year, a change in business climate related to a competitor's innovative products indicated to management that the $170 million book value (original cost of $300 million less accumulated depreciation of $130 million) of the assets of one of Dakota's factories may not be recoverable.

Management is able to identify cash flows from this factory and estimates that future cash flows over the remaining useful life of the factory will be $150 million. The fair value of the factory's assets is not readily available but is estimated to be $135 million.

Change in circumstances. A change in the business climate related to a competitor's innovative products requires Dakota to investigate for possible impairment.

Step 1. Recoverability. Because the book value of $170 million exceeds the $150 million undiscounted future cash flows, an impairment loss is indicated.

Step 2. Measurement of impairment loss. The impairment loss is $35 million, determined as follows:

Book value	$170 million
Fair value	135 million
Impairment loss	$ 35 million

The entry to record the loss is ($ in millions):

Loss on impairment	35	
Accumulated depreciation	130	
Factory assets		165

The loss normally is reported in the income statement as a separate component of operating expenses.

Visteon Corporation is a leading global supplier of automotive systems, modules, and components to global vehicle manufacturers. Lower than anticipated vehicle production volumes was the primary triggering event that led the company to record impairment losses in several recent fiscal years. Graphic 11–12 shows Visteon's disclosure note describing the losses. The note provides a summary of the two-step approach used to identify and measure impairment losses.

GRAPHIC 11–12

Asset Impairment
Disclosure—Visteon
Corporation

Real World Financials

Long-lived Assets and Certain Identifiable Intangibles (in part)

Asset impairment charges are recorded for long-lived assets and intangible assets subject to amortization when events and circumstances indicate that such assets may be impaired and the undiscounted net cash flows estimated to be generated by those assets are less than their carrying amounts. If estimated future undiscounted cash flows are not sufficient to recover the carrying value of the assets, an impairment charge is recorded for the amount by which the carrying value of the assets exceeds its fair value. Fair value is determined using appraisals, management estimates, or discounted cash flow calculations. Asset impairment charges of $22 million, $1,511 million, and $314 million were recorded for the years ended December 31, 2006, 2005, and 2004, respectively.

INDEFINITE LIFE INTANGIBLE ASSETS OTHER THAN GOODWILL.

Intangible assets with indefinite useful lives should be tested for impairment annually, or more frequently if events or changes in circumstances indicate that the asset may be impaired. The measurement of an impairment loss for indefinite life intangibles other than goodwill is a one-step process. We compare the fair value of the asset with its book value. If book value exceeds fair value, an impairment loss is recognized for the difference. Notice that we omit the recoverability test with these assets. Because we anticipate cash flows to continue indefinitely, recoverability is not a good indicator of impairment.

Similar to tangible operational assets and finite life intangibles, if an impairment loss is recognized, the written-down book value becomes the new cost base for future cost allocation. Recovery of the impairment loss is prohibited. Disclosure requirements also are similar.

Intangible assets with indefinite useful lives should be tested for impairment at least annually.

If book value exceeds fair value, an impairment loss is recognized for the difference.

INTERNATIONAL FINANCIAL REPORTING STANDARDS

Impairment of Value. Highlighted below are some important differences in accounting for impairment of value of tangible operational assets and finite life intangibles between *SFAS No. 144* and *IAS No. 36,* "Impairment of Assets."

	U.S. GAAP	**IFRS**
Recognition	An impairment loss is required when an asset's book value exceeds the undiscounted sum of the asset's estimated future cash flows.	An impairment loss is required when an asset's book value exceeds the higher of the asset's value-in-use (present value of estimated future cash flows) and fair value less costs to sell.
Measurement	The impairment loss is the difference between book value and fair value.	The impairment loss is the difference between book value and the recoverable amount (the higher of the asset's value-in-use and fair value less costs to sell).
Subsequent reversal of loss	Prohibited.	Required if the circumstances that caused the impairment are resolved.

Real World Financials

Cadbury Schweppes, Plc., a U.K. company, prepares its financial statements according to IFRS. The following disclosure note describes the company's impairment policy:

Impairment Review (in part)

The Group carries out an impairment review of its tangible assets when a change in circumstances or situation indicates that those assets may have suffered an impairment loss. . . . Impairment is measured by comparing the carrying amount of an asset . . . with the "recoverable amount," that is the higher of its fair value less costs to sell and its "value in use." Value in use is calculated by discounting the expected future cash flows, . . .

GOODWILL. Recall that goodwill is a unique intangible asset. Unlike other assets, its cost (a) can't be directly associated with any specific identifiable right and (b) is not separable from the company as a whole. Because of these unique characteristics, we can't measure the impairment of goodwill the same way as other operational assets. *SFAS No. 142*[10] provides guidelines for impairment, which while similar to general impairment guidelines, are specific to goodwill. Let's compare the two-step process for measuring goodwill impairment with the two-step process for measuring impairment for tangible operational assets and finite-life intangibles.

In Step 1, for all classifications of operational assets, we decide whether a write-down due to impairment is required by determining whether the value of an asset has fallen below its book value. However, in this comparison, the value of assets for tangible operational assets and finite-life intangibles is considered to be value in use as measured by the sum of undiscounted cash flows expected from the asset. But due to its unique characteristics, the value of goodwill is not associated with any specific cash flows and must be measured in a unique way. By its very nature, goodwill is inseparable from a particular *reporting unit*. So, for this step, we compare the value of the reporting unit itself with its book value. If the fair value of the reporting unit is less than its book value, an impairment loss is indicated. A reporting unit is an operating segment of a company or a component of an operating segment for which discrete financial information is available and segment management regularly reviews the operating results of that component.

If goodwill is tested for impairment at the same time as other operational assets of the reporting unit, the other assets must be tested first and any impairment loss and asset write-down recorded prior to testing goodwill.

STEP 1—A goodwill impairment loss is indicated when the fair value of the *reporting* unit is less than its book value.

---

[10]"Goodwill and Other Intangible Assets," *Statement of Financial Accounting Standards No. 142* (Norwalk, Conn.: FASB, 2001).

In Step 2, for all classifications of operational assets, if impairment is indicated from step 1, we measure the amount of impairment as the excess of the book value of the asset over its fair value. However, unlike for most other operational assets, the fair value of goodwill cannot be measured directly (market value, present value of associated cash flows, etc.) and so must be "implied" from the fair value of the reporting unit that acquired the goodwill.

The implied fair value of goodwill is calculated in the same way that goodwill is determined in a business combination. That is, it's a residual amount measured by subtracting the fair value of all identifiable net assets from the purchase price using the unit's previously determined fair value as the purchase price.[11] An example is provided in Illustration 11–10.

STEP 2—A goodwill impairment loss is measured as the excess of the book value of the goodwill over its "implied" fair value.

In 2008, the Upjane Corporation acquired Pharmacopia Corporation for $500 million. Upjane recorded $100 million in goodwill related to this acquisition because the fair value of the net assets of Pharmacopia was $400 million. After the acquisition, Pharmacopia continues to operate as a separate company and is considered a reporting unit.

Upjane performs a goodwill impairment test at the end of every fiscal year. At the end of 2009, the book value of Pharmacopia's net assets is $440 million, including the $100 million in goodwill. On that date, the fair value of Pharmacopia has dropped to $360 million and the fair value of all of its identifiable tangible and intangible assets, excluding goodwill, is $335 million.

Step 1. Recoverability. Because the book value of the net assets of $440 million exceeds the $360 million fair value of the reporting unit, an impairment loss is indicated.

Step 2. Measurement of impairment loss. The impairment loss is $75 million, determined as follows:

Determination of implied goodwill:

Fair value of Pharmacopia	$360 million
Fair value of Pharmacopia's net assets (excluding goodwill)	335 million
Implied value of goodwill	$ 25 million

Measurement of impairment loss:

Book value of goodwill	$100 million
Implied value of goodwill	25 million
Impairment loss	$ 75 million

The entry to record the loss is ($ in millions):

Loss on impairment of goodwill	75	
Goodwill		75

The loss normally is reported in the income statement as a separate component of operating expenses.

ILLUSTRATION 11–10

Impairment Loss—Goodwill

Similar to other intangible assets with indefinite useful lives, goodwill should be tested for impairment on an annual basis and in between annual test dates if events or circumstances indicate that the fair value of the reporting unit is below its book value.

The acquiring company in a business combination often pays for the acquisition using its own stock. In the late 1990s, the stock prices of many companies were unusually high. These often-inflated stock prices meant high purchase prices for many acquisitions and, in many cases, incredibly high values allocated to goodwill. When stock prices retreated in 2000 and 2001, it became obvious that the book value of goodwill for many companies would never be recovered. Some examples of multibillion dollar goodwill impairment losses are shown in Graphic 11–13.

Atari, Inc., the video game company, provides a more recent example. In 2007, Atari recorded a $54 million goodwill impairment loss. Graphic 11–14 describes the impairment.

Goodwill should be tested for impairment at least annually.

---

[11]The impairment loss recognized cannot exceed the book value of goodwill.

GRAPHIC 11–13

Goodwill Impairment Losses

Company	Goodwill Impairment Loss
AOL Time Warner	$54 billion
JDS Uniphase	50 billion
Nortel Networks	12 billion
Lucent Technologies	4 billion
Vivendi Universal SA	15 billion (Euro dollars)

GRAPHIC 11–14

Goodwill Impairment Disclosure—Atari, Inc.

Real World Financials

Goodwill and Acquired Intangible Assets (in part)

A two-step approach is required to test goodwill for impairment for each reporting unit. The first step tests for impairment by applying fair value-based tests (described below) to a reporting unit. The second step, if deemed necessary, measures the impairment by applying fair value-based tests to specific assets and liabilities within the reporting unit. Application of the goodwill impairment tests require judgment, including identification of reporting units, assignment of assets and liabilities to each reporting unit, assignment of goodwill to each reporting unit, and determination of the fair value of each reporting unit.

During the fourth quarter ended March 31, 2007, our market capitalization declined significantly. As this measure is our primary indicator of the fair value of our publishing unit, management considered this decline to be a triggering event, requiring us to perform an impairment analysis. As of March 31, 2007, we completed this analysis and our management, with the concurrence of the Audit Committee of our Board of Directors, has concluded that an impairment charge of $54.1 million should be recognized. This is a non-cash charge and has been recorded in the fourth quarter of fiscal 2007.

 INTERNATIONAL FINANCIAL REPORTING STANDARDS

Impairment of Value—Goodwill. Highlighted below are some important differences in accounting for the impairment of goodwill between U.S. GAAP and *IAS No. 36*.

	U.S. GAAP	**IFRS**
Level of testing	*Reporting unit*—a segment or a component of an operating segment for which discrete financial information is available.	*Cash generating unit* (CGU)—the lowest level at which goodwill is monitored by management. A CGU can't be lower than a segment.
Measurement	A two step process: 1. Compare the fair value of the reporting unit with its book value. A loss is indicated if fair value is less than book value. 2. The impairment loss is the excess of book value over implied fair value.	One step: Compare the recoverable amount of the CGU (the higher of fair value less costs to sell and value in use) to book value. If the recoverable amount is less, reduce goodwill first, then other assets.

U.S. GAAP and *IAS No. 36* both require goodwill to be tested for impairment at least annually, and both prohibit the reversal of goodwill impairment losses.

Operational Assets to Be Sold

We have been discussing the recognition and measurement for the impairment of value of assets to be held and used. We also test for impairment of operational assets held for sale. These are operational assets management has actively committed to immediately sell in their present condition and for which sale is probable.

An operational asset or group of assets classified as held for sale is measured at the lower of its book value or fair value less cost to sell. An impairment loss is recognized for any write-down to fair value less cost to sell.[12] Except for including the cost to sell, notice the similarity to impairment of assets to be held and used. We don't depreciate or amortize these assets while classified as held for sale and we report them separately in the balance sheet. Recall from our discussion of discontinued operations in Chapter 4 that similar rules apply for a component of an entity that is classified as held for sale.[13]

For operational assets held for sale, if book value exceeds fair value less cost to sell, an impairment loss is recognized for the difference.

Graphic 11–15 summarizes the guidelines for the recognition and measurement of impairment losses.

GRAPHIC 11–15

Summary of Operational Asset Impairment Guidelines

Type of Operational Asset	When to Test for Impairment	Impairment Test
To Be Held and Used:		
Tangible and finite-life intangibles	When events or circumstances indicate book value may not be recoverable	Step 1—An impairment loss is required only when book value is not recoverable (undiscounted sum of estimated future cash flows less than book value). Step 2—The impairment loss is the excess of book value over fair value.
Indefinite life intangibles (other than goodwill)	At least annually, or more frequently if indicated	If book value exceeds fair value, an impairment loss is recognized for the difference.
Goodwill	At least annually, or more frequently if indicated	Step 1—A loss is indicated when the fair value of the reporting unit is less than its book value. Step 2—An impairment loss is measured as the excess of book value over implied fair value.
To Be Sold	When considered held for sale	If book value exceeds fair value less cost to sell, an impairment loss is recognized for the difference.

Impairment Losses and Earnings Quality

What do losses from the write-down of inventory and restructuring costs have in common? The presence of these items in a corporate income statement presents a challenge to an analyst trying to determine a company's permanent earnings—those likely to continue in the future. We discussed these issues in prior chapters.

We now can add asset impairment losses to the list of "big bath" accounting techniques some companies use to manipulate earnings. By writing off large amounts of operational assets, companies significantly reduce earnings in the year of the write-off but are able to increase future earnings by lowering future depreciation, depletion, or amortization. Here's how. We measure the impairment loss as the difference between an asset's book value and its fair value. However, in most cases, fair value must be estimated, and the estimation process usually involves a forecast of future net cash flows the company expects to generate from the asset's use. If a company underestimates future net cash flows, fair value is understated. This has two effects: (1) current year's income is unrealistically low due to the impairment loss being overstated and (2) future income is unrealistically high because depreciation, depletion, and amortization are based on understated asset values.

An analyst must decide whether to consider asset impairment losses as transitory in nature or as a part of permanent earnings.

---

[12]If the asset is unsold at the end of a subsequent reporting period, a gain is recognized for any increase in fair value less cost to sell, but not in excess of the loss previously recognized.

[13]A component of an entity comprises operations and cash flows that can be clearly distinguished, operationally and for financial reporting purposes, from the rest of the entity. One objective of *SFAS No. 144* is to establish a single accounting model, based on the framework developed in *SFAS No. 121,* for long-lived assets to be disposed of by sale.

SUBSEQUENT EXPENDITURES

Now that we have acquired and measured operational assets, we can address accounting issues incurred subsequent to their acquisition. This part of the chapter deals with the treatment of expenditures made over the life of these assets to maintain and/or improve them.

Expenditures Subsequent to Acquisition

● LO9

Many operational assets require expenditures to repair, maintain, or improve them. These expenditures can present accounting problems if they are material. In general, a choice must be made between capitalizing the expenditures by either increasing the asset's book value or creating a new asset, or expensing them in the period in which they are incurred. Conceptually, we can refer to the matching principle that requires the capitalization of expenditures that are expected to produce benefits beyond the current fiscal year. Expenditures that simply maintain a given level of benefits are expensed in the period they are incurred.

Expenditures related to operational assets can increase future benefits in the following ways:

1. An extension of the *useful life* of the asset.
2. An increase in the *operating efficiency* of the asset resulting in either an increase in the quantity of goods or services produced or a decrease in future operating costs.
3. An increase in the *quality* of the goods or services produced by the asset.

Theoretically, expenditures that cause any of these results should be capitalized initially and then expensed in future periods through depreciation, depletion, or amortization. This permits the matching of the expenditure with the future benefits. Of course, materiality is an important factor in the practical application of this approach.

Many companies do not capitalize any expenditure unless it exceeds a predetermined amount that is considered material.

For expediency, many companies set materiality thresholds for the capitalization of any expenditure. For example, a company might decide to expense all expenditures under $200 regardless of whether or not future benefits are increased. Judgment is required to determine the appropriate materiality threshold as well as the appropriate treatment of expenditures over $200. There often are practical problems in capitalizing these expenditures. For example, even if future benefits are increased by the expenditure, it may be difficult to determine how long the benefits will last. It's important for a company to establish a policy for treating these expenditures and apply it consistently.

We classify subsequent expenditures as (1) repairs and maintenance, (2) additions, (3) improvements, or (4) rearrangements.

Repairs and Maintenance

Expenditures for *repairs and maintenance* generally are expensed when incurred.

These expenditures are made to *maintain* a given level of benefits provided by the asset and do not *increase* future benefits. For example, the cost of an engine tune-up or the repair of an engine part for a delivery truck allows the truck to continue its productive activity. If the maintenance is not performed, the truck will not provide the benefits originally anticipated. In that sense, future benefits are provided; without the repair, the truck will no longer operate. The key, though, is that future benefits are not provided *beyond those originally anticipated*. Expenditures for these activities should be expensed in the period incurred.

ADDITIONAL CONSIDERATION

If repairs and maintenance costs are seasonal, interim financial statements may be misstated. For example, suppose annual maintenance is performed on a company's fleet of delivery trucks. The annual income statement correctly includes one year's maintenance expense. However, for interim reporting purposes, if the entire expenditure is made in one quarter, should that quarter's income statement include as expense the entire cost of the annual maintenance? If these expenditures can be anticipated, they should be accrued evenly throughout the year by crediting an allowance account. The allowance account is then debited when the maintenance is performed.

Additions

As the term implies, additions involve adding a new major component to an existing asset and should be capitalized because future benefits are increased. For example, adding a refrigeration unit to a delivery truck increases the capability of the truck, thus increasing its future benefits. Other examples include the construction of a new wing on a building and the addition of a security system to an existing building.

The capitalized cost includes all necessary expenditures to bring the addition to a condition and location for use. For a building addition, this might include the costs of tearing down and removing a wall of the existing building. The capitalized cost of additions are depreciated over the remaining useful life of the original asset or its own useful life, whichever is shorter.

The costs of additions usually are capitalized.

Improvements

Expenditures classified as improvements involve the replacement of a major component of an operational asset. The replacement can be a new component with the same characteristics as the old component or a new component with enhanced operating capabilities. For example, an existing refrigeration unit in a delivery truck could be replaced with a new but similar unit or with a new and improved refrigeration unit. In either case, the cost of the improvement usually increases future benefits and should be capitalized by increasing the book value of the related asset (the delivery truck) and depreciated over the useful life of the improved asset. There are three methods used to record the cost of improvements.

The costs of improvements usually are capitalized.

1. *Substitution.* The improvement can be recorded as both (1) a disposition of the old component and (2) the acquisition of the new component. This approach is conceptually appealing but it is practical only if the original cost and accumulated depreciation of the old component can be separately identified.
2. *Capitalization of new cost.* Another way to record an improvement is to include the cost of the improvement (net of any consideration received from the disposition of the old component) as a debit to the related asset account, without removing the original cost and accumulated depreciation of the original component. This approach is acceptable only if the book value of the original component has been reduced to an immaterial amount through prior depreciation.
3. *Reduction of accumulated depreciation.* Another way to increase an asset's book value is to leave the asset account unaltered but decrease its related accumulated depreciation. The argument for this method is that many improvements extend the useful life of an asset and are equivalent to a partial recovery of previously recorded depreciation. This approach produces the same book value as the capitalization of cost to the asset account. However, cost and accumulated depreciation amounts will differ under the two methods.

The three methods are compared in Illustration 11–11.

Rearrangements

Expenditures made to restructure an asset without addition, replacement, or improvement are termed rearrangements. The objective is to create a new capability for the asset and not necessarily to extend its useful life. Examples include the rearrangement of machinery on the production line to increase operational efficiency and the relocation of a company's operating plant or office building. If these expenditures are material and they clearly increase future benefits, they should be capitalized and expensed in the future periods benefited. If the expenditures are not material or if it's not certain that future benefits have increased, they should be expensed in the period incurred.

The costs of material rearrangements should be capitalized if they clearly increase future benefits.

Graphic 11–16 provides a summary of the accounting treatment for the various types of expenditures related to tangible operational assets.

ILLUSTRATION 11–11 Improvements	The Palmer Corporation replaced the air conditioning system in one of its office buildings that it leases to tenants. The cost of the old air conditioning system, $200,000, is included in the cost of the building. However, the company has separately depreciated the air conditioning system. Depreciation recorded up to the date of replacement totaled $160,000. The old system was removed and the new system installed at a cost of $230,000, which was paid in cash. Parts from the old system were sold for $12,000. Accounting for the improvement differs depending on the alternative chosen.		
Substitution (1) Disposition of old component.	Cash .... Accumulated depreciation—buildings .... Loss on disposal (difference) .... Buildings	12,000 160,000 28,000	 200,000
(2) Acquisition of new component.	Buildings .... Cash	230,000	 230,000
Capitalization of new cost	Buildings .... Cash ($230,000 − 12,000)	218,000	 218,000
Reduction of accumulated depreciation	Accumulated depreciation—buildings .... Cash ($230,000 − 12,000)	218,000	 218,000

GRAPHIC 11–16

Expenditures Subsequent to Acquisition

Type of Expenditure	Definition	Usual Accounting Treatment
Repairs and maintenance	Expenditures to maintain a given level of benefits	Expense in the period incurred
Additions	The addition of a new major component to an existing asset	Capitalize and depreciate over the remaining useful life of the *original asset or its own useful life*, whichever is shorter
Improvements	The replacement of a major component	Capitalize and depreciate over the useful life of the improved asset
Rearrangements	Expenditures to restructure an asset without addition, replacement, or improvement	If expenditures are material and clearly increase future benefits, capitalize and depreciate over the future periods benefited

Costs of Defending Intangible Rights

The costs incurred to *successfully* defend an intangible right should be capitalized.

Repairs, additions, improvements, and rearrangements generally relate to tangible operational assets. A possible significant expenditure incurred subsequent to the acquisition of intangible assets is the cost of defending the right that gives the asset its value. If an intangible right is *successfully* defended, the litigation costs should be capitalized and amortized over the remaining useful life of the related intangible. This is the appropriate treatment of these expenditures even if the intangible asset was originally developed internally rather than purchased.

The costs incurred to *unsuccessfully* defend an intangible right should be expensed.

If the defense of an intangible right is *unsuccessful,* then the litigation costs should be expensed as incurred because they provide no future benefit. In addition, the book value of any intangible asset should be reduced to realizable value. For example, if a company is unsuccessful in defending a patent infringement suit, the patent's value may be eliminated. The book value of the patent should be written off as a loss.

1. **Is Penny correct? Do the terms *depreciation, depletion,* and *amortization* all mean the same thing?** *(p. 534)* Penny is correct. Each of these terms refers to the cost allocation of operational assets over their service lives. The term *depreciation* is used for plant and equipment, *depletion* for natural resources, and *amortization* for intangibles.

2. **Potlatch determines depletion based on the "estimated recoverable timber volume." Explain this approach.** *(p. 538)* Potlatch is using the units-of-production method to determine depletion. The units-of-production method is an activity-based method that computes a depletion (or depreciation or amortization) rate per measure of activity and then multiplies this rate by actual activity to determine periodic cost allocation. The method is used by Potlatch to measure depletion of the cost of timber harvested and the amortization of logging roads and facilities. The cost of logging roads and related facilities are intangible assets because the company does not own the roads.

3. **Explain how asset impairment differs from depreciation, depletion, and amortization. How do companies measure impairment losses for tangible operational assets and intangible assets with finite useful lives?** *(p. 553)* Depreciation, depletion, and amortization reflect a gradual consumption of the benefits inherent in an operational asset. An implicit assumption in allocating the cost of an asset over its useful life is that there has been no significant reduction in the anticipated total benefits or service potential of the asset. Situations can arise, however, that cause a significant decline or *impairment* of those benefits or service potentials. Determining whether to record an impairment loss for a tangible operational asset and actually recording the loss is a two-step process. The first step is a recoverability test—an impairment loss is required only when the undiscounted sum of estimated future cash flows from an asset is less than the asset's book value. The measurement of impairment loss—step 2—is the difference between the asset's book value and its fair value. If an impairment loss is recognized, the written-down book value becomes the new cost base for future cost allocation. ●

THE **BOTTOM LINE**

● **LO1** The use of operational assets represents a consumption of benefits, or service potentials, inherent in the assets. The matching principle requires that the cost of these inherent benefits or service potentials that were consumed be recognized as an expense. As there very seldom is a direct relationship between the use of operational assets and revenue production, accounting resorts to arbitrary allocation methods to achieve a matching of expenses with revenues. (p. 534)

● **LO2** The allocation process for plant and equipment is called *depreciation.* Time-based depreciation methods estimate service life in years and then allocate depreciable base, cost less estimated residual value, using either a straight-line or accelerated pattern. Activity-based depreciation methods allocate the depreciable base by estimating service life according to some measure of productivity. (p. 536)

● **LO3** The allocation process for natural resources is called *depletion.* The activity-based method called units-of-production usually is used to determine periodic depletion. (p. 543)

● **LO4** The allocation process for intangible assets is called *amortization.* For an intangible asset with a finite useful life, the capitalized cost less any estimated residual value must be allocated to periods in which the asset is expected to contribute to the company's revenue-generating activities. An intangible asset that is determined to have an indefinite useful life is not subject to periodic amortization. Goodwill is perhaps the most typical intangible asset with an indefinite useful life. (p. 545)

● **LO5** A change in either the service life or residual value of an operational asset should be reflected in the financial statements of the current period and future periods by recalculating periodic depreciation, depletion, or amortization. (p. 549)

● **LO6** A change in depreciation, depletion, or amortization method is considered a change in accounting estimate that is achieved by a change in accounting principle. We account for these changes prospectively, exactly as we would any other change in estimate. One difference is that most changes in estimate do not require a company to justify the change. However, this change in estimate is a result of changing an accounting principle and therefore requires a clear justification as to why the new method is preferable. (p. 550)

● **LO7** A material error in accounting for an operational asset that is discovered in a year subsequent to the year of the error requires that previous years' financial statements that were incorrect as a result of the error are retrospectively restated to reflect the correction. Any account balances that are incorrect as a result of the error are corrected by journal entry. If retained earnings is one of the incorrect accounts, the correction is reported as a prior period adjustment to the beginning balance in the statement of shareholders' equity. In addition, a disclosure note is needed to describe the nature of the error and the impact of its correction on income. (p. 551)

● **LO8** Conceptually, there is considerable merit for a policy requiring the write-down of an operational asset when there has been a *significant* decline in value below carrying value (book value). The write-down provides important information about the future cash flows to be generated from the use of the asset. However, in practice this policy is very subjective. *SFAS No. 144* establishes guidance for when to recognize and how to measure impairment losses of tangible operational assets and intangible operational assets that have finite useful lives. *SFAS No. 142* provides additional guidance for the recognition and measurement of impairment for indefinite life intangibles and goodwill. (p. 553)

● **LO9** Expenditures for repairs and maintenance generally are expensed when incurred. The costs of additions and improvements usually are capitalized. The costs of material rearrangements should be capitalized if they clearly increase future benefits. (p. 560) ●

APPENDIX 11A   COMPARISON WITH MACRS (TAX DEPRECIATION)

Depreciation for financial reporting purposes is an attempt to distribute the cost of the asset, less any anticipated residual value, over the estimated useful life in a systematic and rational manner that attempts to match revenues with the use of the asset. Depreciation for income tax purposes is influenced by the revenue needs of government as well as the desire to influence economic behavior. For example, accelerated depreciation schedules currently allowed are intended to provide incentive for companies to expand and modernize their facilities thus stimulating economic growth.

The federal income tax code allows taxpayers to compute depreciation for their tax returns on assets acquired after 1986 using the modified accelerated cost recovery system (MACRS).[14] Key differences between the calculation of depreciation for financial reporting and the calculation using MACRS are:

1. Estimated useful lives and residual values are not used in MACRS.
2. Firms can't choose among various accelerated methods under MACRS.
3. A half-year convention is used in determining the MACRS depreciation rates.

Under MACRS, each asset is placed within a recovery period category. The six categories for personal property are 3, 5, 7, 10, 15, and 20 years. For example, the 5-year category includes most machinery and equipment, automobiles, and light trucks.

Depending on the category, fixed percentage rates are applied to the original cost of the asset. The rates for the 5-year asset category are as follows:

Year	Rate
1	20.00%
2	32.00
3	19.20
4	11.52
5	11.52
6	5.76
Total	100.00%

[14]For assets acquired between 1981 and 1986, tax depreciation is calculated using the accelerated cost recovery system (ACRS), which is similar to MACRS. For assets acquired before 1981, tax depreciation can be calculated using any of the depreciation methods discussed in the chapter. Residual values are used in the calculation of depreciation for pre-1981 assets.

These rates are equivalent to applying the double-declining-balance method with a switch to straight-line in the year straight line yields an equal or higher deduction than DDB. In most cases, the half-year convention is used regardless of when the asset is placed in service.[15] The first-year rate of 20% for the five-year category is one-half of the DDB rate for an asset with a five-year life (2 × 20%). The sixth year rate of 5.76% is one-half of the straight-line rate established in year 4, the year straight-line depreciation exceeds DDB depreciation.

Companies have the option to use the straight-line method for the entire tax life of the asset, applying the half-year convention, rather than using MACRS depreciation schedules. Because of the differences discussed above, tax depreciation for a given year will likely be different from GAAP depreciation. ●

RETIREMENT AND REPLACEMENT METHODS OF DEPRECIATION

APPENDIX **11B**

Retirement and replacement depreciation methods occasionally are used to depreciate relatively low-valued assets with short service lives. Under either approach, an aggregate asset account that represents a group of similar assets is increased at the time the initial collection is acquired.

Retirement Method

Using the retirement depreciation method, the asset account also is increased for the cost of subsequent expenditures. When an item is disposed of, the asset account is credited for its cost, and depreciation expense is recorded for the difference between cost and proceeds received, if any. No other entries are made for depreciation. As a consequence, one or more periods may pass without any expense recorded. For example, the following entry records the purchase of 100 handheld calculators at $50 acquisition cost each:

The retirement depreciation method records depreciation when assets are disposed of and measures depreciation as the difference between the proceeds received and cost.

Calculators (100 × $50)	5,000	
Cash		5,000
To record the acquisition of calculators.		

If 20 new calculators are acquired at $45 each, the asset account is increased.

Calculators (20 × $45)	900	
Cash		900
To record additional calculator acquisitions.		

Thirty calculators are disposed of (retired) by selling them secondhand to a bookkeeping firm for $5 each. The following entry reflects the retirement method:

Cash (30 × $5)	150	
Depreciation expense (difference)	1,350	
Calculators (30 × $50)		1,500
To record the sale/depreciation of calculators.		

Notice that the retirement system assumes a FIFO cost flow approach in determining the cost of assets, $50 each, that were disposed.

Replacement Method

By the replacement depreciation method, the initial acquisition of assets is recorded the same way as by the retirement method; that is, the aggregate cost is increased. However, depreciation expense is the amount paid for new or replacement assets. Any proceeds

By the replacement method, depreciation is recorded when assets are replaced.

---

[15]In certain situations, mid-quarter and mid-month conventions are used.

received from asset dispositions reduces depreciation expense. For our example, the acquisition of 20 new calculators at $45 each is recorded as depreciation as follows:

Depreciation expense (20 × $45)	900	
Cash		900
To record the replacement/depreciation of calculators.		

The sale of the old calculators is recorded as a reduction of depreciation:

Cash (30 × $5)	150	
Depreciation expense		150
To record the sale of calculators.		

The asset account balance remains the same throughout the life of the aggregate collection of assets.

Because these methods are likely to produce aggregate expense measurements that differ from individual calculations, retirement and replacement methods are acceptable only in situations where the distortion in depreciation expense does not have a material effect on income. These methods occasionally are encountered in regulated industries such as utilities. ●

QUESTIONS FOR REVIEW OF **KEY TOPICS**

Q 11–1 Explain the similarities in and differences among depreciation, depletion, and amortization.

Q 11–2 Depreciation is a process of cost allocation, not valuation. Explain this statement.

Q 11–3 Identify and define the three characteristics of an asset that must be established to determine periodic depreciation, depletion, or amortization.

Q 11–4 Discuss the factors that influence the estimation of service life for a depreciable asset.

Q 11–5 What is meant by depreciable base? How is it determined?

Q 11–6 Briefly differentiate between activity-based and time-based allocation methods.

Q 11–7 Briefly differentiate between the straight-line depreciation method and accelerated depreciation methods.

Q 11–8 Why are time-based depreciation methods used more frequently than activity-based methods?

Q 11–9 What are some factors that could explain the predominant use of the straight-line depreciation method?

Q 11–10 Briefly explain the differences and similarities between the group approach and composite approach to depreciating aggregate assets.

Q 11–11 Define depletion and compare it with depreciation.

Q 11–12 Compare and contrast amortization of intangible assets with depreciation and depletion.

Q 11–13 What are some of the simplifying conventions a company can use to calculate depreciation for partial years?

Q 11–14 Explain the accounting treatment required when a change is made to the estimated service life of a machine.

Q 11–15 Explain the accounting treatment and disclosures required when a change is made in depreciation method.

Q 11–16 Explain the steps required to correct an error in accounting for an operational asset that is discovered in a year subsequent to the year the error was made.

Q 11–17 Explain what is meant by the impairment value of an operational asset. How should these impairments be accounted for?

Q 11–18 Explain the differences in the accounting treatment of repairs and maintenance, additions, improvements, and rearrangements.

BRIEF **EXERCISES**

BE 11–1
Cost allocation

● LO1

At the beginning of its fiscal year, Koeplin Corporation purchased a machine for $50,000. At the end of the year, the machine had a fair value of $32,000. Koeplin's controller recorded depreciation expense of $18,000 for the year, the decline in the machine's value. Why is this an incorrect approach to measuring periodic depreciation?

BE 11–2
Depreciation
methods

● LO2

On January 1, 2009, Canseco Plumbing Fixtures purchased equipment for $30,000. Residual value at the end of an estimated four-year service life is expected to be $2,000. The company expects the machine to operate for 10,000 hours. Calculate depreciation expense for 2009 and 2010 using each of the following depreciation methods: (a) straight line, (b) sum-of-the-years'-digits, (c) double-declining balance, and (d) units-of-production using machine hours. The machine operated for 2,200 and 3,000 hours in 2009 and 2010, respectively.

BE 11–3
Depreciation
methods; partial
years

● LO2

Refer to the situation described in BE 11–2. Assume the machine was purchased on March 31, 2009, instead of January 1. Calculate depreciation expense for 2009 and 2010 using each of the following depreciation methods: (a) straight line, (b) sum-of-the-years'-digits, and (c) double-declining balance.

BE 11–4
Group depreciation

● LO2

Mondale Winery depreciates its equipment using the group method. The cost of equipment purchased in 2009 totaled $425,000. The estimated residual value of the equipment was $40,000 and the group depreciation rate was determined to be 18%. What is the annual depreciation for the group? If equipment that cost $42,000 is sold in 2010 for $35,000, what amount of gain or loss will the company recognize for the sale?

BE 11–5
Depletion

● LO3

Fitzgerald Oil and Gas incurred costs of $8.25 million for the acquisition and development of a natural gas deposit. The company expects to extract 3 million cubic feet of natural gas during a four-year period. Natural gas extracted during year 1 and year 2 were 700,000 and 800,000 cubic feet, respectively. What was the depletion for year 1 and year 2?

BE 11–6
Amortization

● LO4

On June 28 Lexicon Corporation acquired 100% of the common stock of Gulf & Eastern. The purchase price allocation included the following items: $4 million, patent; $3 million, developed technology; $2 million, in-process research and development; $5 million, goodwill. Lexicon's policy is to amortize intangible assets using the straight-line method, no residual value, and a five-year useful life. What is the total amount of expenses (ignoring taxes) that would appear in Lexicon's income statement for the year ended December 31 related to these items?

BE 11–7
Change in estimate;
useful life of
equipment

● LO5

At the beginning of 2007, Robotics, Inc. acquired a manufacturing facility for $12 million. $9 million of the purchase price was allocated to the building. Depreciation for 2007 and 2008 was calculated using the straight-line method, a 25-year useful life, and a $1 million residual value. In 2009, the estimates of useful life and residual value were changed to 20 years and $500,000, respectively. What is depreciation on the building for 2009?

BE 11–8
Change in
principle; change
in depreciation
method

● LO5

Refer to the situation described in BE 11–7. Assume that instead of changing the useful life and residual value, in 2009 the company switched to the double-declining-balance depreciation method. How should Robotics account for the change? What is depreciation on the building for 2009?

BE 11–9
Error correction

● LO7

Refer to the situation described in BE 11–7. Assume that 2007 depreciation was incorrectly recorded as $32,000. This error was discovered in 2009. How should Robotics account for the error? What is depreciation on the building for 2009 assuming no change in estimate of useful life or residual value?

BE 11–10
Impairment;
tangible operational
assets

● LO8

Collison and Ryder Company (C&R) has been experiencing declining market conditions for its sportswear division. Management decided to test the operational assets of the division for possible impairment. The test revealed the following: book value of division's assets, $26.5 million; fair value of division's assets, $21 million; sum of estimated future cash flows generated from the division's assets, $28 million. What amount of impairment loss should C&R recognize?

BE 11–11
Impairment;
tangible operational
assets

● LO8

Refer to the situation described in BE 11–10. Assume that the sum of estimated future cash flows is $24 million instead of $28 million. What amount of impairment loss should C&R recognize?

BE 11–12
Impairment;
goodwill

● LO8

WebHelper, Inc. acquired 100% of the outstanding stock of Silicon Chips Corporation (SCC) for $45 million, of which $15 million was allocated to goodwill. At the end of the current fiscal year, the annual impairment test revealed the following: fair value of SCC, $40 million; fair value of SCC's net assets (excluding goodwill), $31 million; book value of SCC's net assets (including goodwill), $42 million. What amount of impairment loss should WebHelper recognize?

BE 11–13
Impairment;
goodwill

● LO8

Refer to the situation described in BE 11–12. Assume that the fair value of SCC is $44 million instead of $40 million. What amount of impairment loss should WebHelper recognize?

BE 11–14
Subsequent
expenditures

● LO9

Demmert Manufacturing incurred the following expenditures during the current fiscal year: annual maintenance on its machinery, $5,400; remodeling of offices, $22,000; rearrangement of the shipping and receiving area resulting in an increase in productivity, $35,000; addition of a security system to the manufacturing facility, $25,000. How should Demmert account for each of these expenditures?

EXERCISES

available with McGraw-Hill's Homework Manager www.mhhe.com/spiceland5e

An alternate exercise and problem set is available on the text website: www.mhhe.com/spiceland5e

E 11–1
Depreciation
methods

● LO2

On January 1, 2009, the Excel Delivery Company purchased a delivery van for $33,000. At the end of its five-year service life, it is estimated that the van will be worth $3,000. During the five-year period, the company expects to drive the van 100,000 miles.

Required:
Calculate annual depreciation for the five-year life of the van using each of the following methods. Round all computations to the nearest dollar.

1. Straight line.
2. Sum-of-the-years' digits.
3. Double-declining balance.
4. Units of production using miles driven as a measure of output, and the following actual mileage:

Year	Miles
2009	22,000
2010	24,000
2011	15,000
2012	20,000
2013	21,000

E 11–2
Depreciation
methods

● LO2

On January 1, 2009, the Allegheny Corporation purchased machinery for $115,000. The estimated service life of the machinery is 10 years and the estimated residual value is $5,000. The machine is expected to produce 220,000 units during its life.

Required:
Calculate depreciation for 2009 and 2010 using each of the following methods. Round all computations to the nearest dollar.

1. Straight line.
2. Sum-of-the-years' digits.
3. Double-declining balance.
4. One hundred fifty percent declining balance.
5. Units of production (units produced in 2009, 30,000; units produced in 2010, 25,000).

E 11–3
Depreciation
methods; partial
years

● LO2

[This is a variation of the previous exercise modified to focus on depreciation for partial years.]
On October 1, 2009, the Allegheny Corporation purchased machinery for $115,000. The estimated service life of the machinery is 10 years and the estimated residual value is $5,000. The machine is expected to produce 220,000 units during its life.

Required:
Calculate depreciation for 2009 and 2010 using each of the following methods. Partial-year depreciation is calculated based on the number of months the asset is in service. Round all computations to the nearest dollar.

1. Straight line.
2. Sum-of-the-years' digits.
3. Double-declining balance.
4. One hundred fifty percent declining balance.
5. Units of production (units produced in 2009, 10,000; units produced in 2010, 25,000).

E 11–4
Depreciation
methods; asset
addition

● LO2

Funseth Company purchased a five-story office building on January 1, 2007, at a cost of $5,000,000. The building has a residual value of $200,000 and a 30-year life. The straight-line depreciation method is used. On June 30, 2009, construction of a sixth floor was completed at a cost of $1,650,000.

Required:
Calculate the depreciation on the building and building addition for 2009 and 2010 assuming that the addition did not change the life or residual value of the building.

E 11–5
Depreciation
methods; solving
for unknowns

● LO2

For each of the following depreciable assets, determine the missing amount (?). Abbreviations for depreciation methods are SL for straight line, SYD for sum-of-the-years' digits, and DDB for double-declining balance.

Asset	Cost	Residual Value	Service Life (Years)	Depreciation Method	Depreciation (Year 2)
A	?	$ 20,000	5	DDB	$ 24,000
B	$ 40,000	?	8	SYD	7,000
C	65,000	5,000	?	SL	6,000
D	230,000	10,000	10	?	22,000
E	200,000	20,000	8	150%DB	?

E 11–6
Depreciation
methods

● LO2

On April 29, 2009, Quality Appliances purchased equipment for $260,000. The estimated service life of the equipment is six years and the estimated residual value is $20,000. Quality's fiscal year ends on December 31.

Required:
Calculate depreciation for 2009 and 2010 using each of the three methods listed. Quality calculates partial year depreciation based on the number of months the asset is in service. Round all computations to the nearest dollar.
1. Straight-line.
2. Sum-of-the-years' digits.
3. Double-declining balance.

E 11–7
Group depreciation

● LO2

Highsmith Rental Company purchased an apartment building early in 2009. There are 20 apartments in the building and each is furnished with major kitchen appliances. The company has decided to use the group depreciation method for the appliances. The following data are available:

Appliance	Cost	Residual Value	Service Life (in Years)
Stoves	$15,000	$3,000	6
Refrigerators	10,000	1,000	5
Dishwashers	8,000	500	4

In 2012, three new refrigerators costing $2,700 were purchased for cash. The old refrigerators, which originally cost $1,500, were sold for $200.

Required:
1. Calculate the group depreciation rate, group life, and depreciation for 2009.
2. Prepare the journal entries to record the purchase of the new refrigerators and the sale of the old refrigerators.

E 11–8
Double-declining-
balance method;
switch to straight
line

● LO2

On January 2, 2009, the Jackson Company purchased equipment to be used in its manufacturing process. The equipment has an estimated life of eight years and an estimated residual value of $30,625. The expenditures made to acquire the asset were as follows:

Purchase price	$154,000
Freight charges	2,000
Installation charges	4,000

Jackson's policy is to use the double-declining-balance (DDB) method of depreciation in the early years of the equipment's life and then switch to straight line halfway through the equipment's life.

Required:
1. Calculate depreciation for each year of the asset's eight-year life.
2. Discuss the accounting treatment of the depreciation on the equipment.

E 11–9
Depletion

● LO3

On April 17, 2009, the Loadstone Mining Company purchased the rights to a coal mine. The purchase price plus additional costs necessary to prepare the mine for extraction of the coal totaled $4,500,000. The company expects to extract 900,000 tons of coal during a four-year period. During 2009, 240,000 tons were extracted and sold immediately.

Required:
1. Calculate depletion for 2009.
2. Discuss the accounting treatment of the depletion calculated in requirement 1.

E 11–10
Depreciation and depletion

● LO2 LO3

At the beginning of 2009, Terra Lumber Company purchased a timber tract from Boise Cantor for $3,200,000. After the timber is cleared, the land will have a residual value of $600,000. Roads to enable logging operations were constructed and completed on March 30, 2009. The cost of the roads, which have no residual value and no alternative use after the tract is cleared, was $240,000. During 2009, Terra logged 500,000 of the estimated five million board feet of timber.

Required:
Calculate the 2009 depletion of the timber tract and depreciation of the logging roads assuming the units-of-production method is used for both assets.

E 11–11
Cost of a natural resource; depletion and depreciation; Chapters 10 and 11

● LO2 LO3

[This exercise is a continuation of Exercise 10–4 in Chapter 10 focusing on depletion and depreciation.] Jackpot Mining Company operates a copper mine in central Montana. The company paid $1,000,000 in 2009 for the mining site and spent an additional $600,000 to prepare the mine for extraction of the copper. After the copper is extracted in approximately four years, the company is required to restore the land to its original condition, including repaving of roads and replacing a greenbelt. The company has provided the following three cash flow possibilities for the restoration costs:

	Cash Outflow	Probability
1	$300,000	25%
2	400,000	40%
3	600,000	35%

To aid extraction, Jackpot purchased some new equipment on July 1, 2009, for $120,000. After the copper is removed from this mine, the equipment will be sold for an estimated residual amount of $20,000. There will be no residual value for the copper mine. The credit-adjusted risk-free rate of interest is 10%.

The company expects to extract 10 million pounds of copper from the mine. Actual production was 1.6 million pounds in 2009 and 3 million pounds in 2010.

Required:
1. Compute depletion and depreciation on the mine and mining equipment for 2009 and 2010. The units-of-production method is used to calculate depreciation.
2. Discuss the accounting treatment of the depletion and depreciation on the mine and mining equipment.

E 11–12
Amortization

● LO4

Janes Company provided the following information on intangible assets:
a. A patent was purchased from the Lou Company for $700,000 on January 1, 2007. Janes estimated the remaining useful life of the patent to be 10 years. The patent was carried on Lou's accounting records at a net book value of $350,000 when Lou sold it to Janes.
b. During 2009, a franchise was purchased from the Rink Company for $500,000. The contractual life of the franchise is 10 years and Janes records a full year of amortization in the year of purchase.
c. Janes incurred research and development costs in 2009 as follows:

Materials and supplies	$140,000
Personnel	180,000
Indirect costs	60,000
Total	$380,000

d. Effective January 1, 2009, based on new events that have occurred, Janes estimates that the remaining life of the patent purchased from Lou is only five more years.

Required:
1. Prepare the entries necessary in 2007 and 2009 to reflect the above information.
2. Prepare a schedule showing the intangible asset section of Janes's December 31, 2009, balance sheet.

E 11–13
Patent amortization

● LO4

On January 2, 2009, David Corporation purchased a patent for $500,000. The remaining legal life is 12 years, but the company estimated that the patent will be useful only for eight years. In January 2011, the company incurred legal fees of $45,000 in successfully defending a patent infringement suit. The successful defense did not change the company's estimate of useful life.

Required:
Prepare journal entries related to the patent for 2009, 2010, and 2011.

E 11–14
Change in estimate; useful life of patent

● LO4 LO5

Van Frank Telecommunications has a patent on a cellular transmission process. The company has amortized the patent on a straight-line basis since 2005, when it was acquired at a cost of $9 million at the beginning of that year. Due to rapid technological advances in the industry, management decided that the patent would benefit the company over a total of six years rather than the nine-year life being used to amortize its cost. The decision was made at the end of 2009 (before adjusting and closing entries).

Required:
Prepare the appropriate adjusting entry for patent amortization in 2009 to reflect the revised estimate.

E 11–15
Change in estimate; useful life and residual value of equipment

● **LO2 LO5**

Wardell Company purchased a minicomputer on January 1, 2007, at a cost of $40,000. The computer was depreciated using the straight-line method over an estimated five-year life with an estimated residual value of $4,000. On January 1, 2009, the estimate of useful life was changed to a total of 10 years, and the estimate of residual value was changed to $900.

Required:
1. Prepare the appropriate adjusting entry for depreciation in 2009 to reflect the revised estimate.
2. Repeat requirement 1 assuming that the company uses the sum-of-the-years'-digits method instead of the straight-line method.

E 11–16
Change in principle; change in depreciation methods

● **LO2 LO6**

Alteran Corporation purchased a machine for $1.5 million in 2006. The machine is being depreciated over a 10-year life using the sum-of-the-years'-digits method. The residual value is expected to be $300,000. At the beginning of 2009, Alteran decided to change to the straight-line depreciation method for this machine.

Required:
Prepare the 2009 depreciation adjusting entry.

E 11–17
Change in principle; change in depreciation methods

● **LO2 LO6**

For financial reporting, Clinton Poultry Farms has used the declining-balance method of depreciation for conveyor equipment acquired at the beginning of 2006 for $2,560,000. Its useful life was estimated to be six years, with a $160,000 residual value. At the beginning of 2009, Clinton decides to change to the straight-line method. The effect of this change on depreciation for each year is as follows:

		($ in 000s)	
Year	**Straight Line**	**Declining Balance**	**Difference**
2006	$ 400	$ 853	$453
2007	400	569	169
2008	400	379	(21)
	$1,200	$1,801	$601

Required:
1. Briefly describe the way Clinton should report this accounting change in the 2008–2009 comparative financial statements.
2. Prepare any 2009 journal entry related to the change.

E 11–18
Error correction

● **LO2 LO7**

In 2009, internal auditors discovered that PKE Displays, Inc., had debited an expense account for the $350,000 cost of a machine purchased on January 1, 2006. The machine's life was expected to be five years with no residual value. Straight-line depreciation is used by PKE.

Required:
1. Prepare the appropriate correcting entry assuming the error was discovered in 2009 before the adjusting and closing entries. (Ignore income taxes.)
2. Assume the error was discovered in 2011 after the 2010 financial statements are issued. Prepare the appropriate correcting entry.

E 11–19
Impairment; tangible operational assets

● **LO8**

Chadwick Enterprises, Inc., operates several restaurants throughout the Midwest. Three of its restaurants located in the center of a large urban area have experienced declining profits due to declining population. The company's management has decided to test the operational assets of the restaurants for possible impairment. The relevant information for these assets is presented below.

Book value	$6.5 million
Estimated undiscounted sum of future cash flows	4.0 million
Fair value	3.5 million

Required:
1. Determine the amount of the impairment loss, if any.
2. Repeat requirement 1 assuming that the estimated undiscounted sum of future cash flows is $6.8 million and fair value is $5 million.

E 11–20
IFRS; impairment; tangible operational assets

● **LO8**

Refer to the situation described in Exercise 11–19.

Required:
How might your solution differ if Chadwick Enterprises, Inc., prepares its financial statements according to International Accounting Standards? Assume that the fair value amount given in the exercise equals both (a) the fair value less costs to sell and (b) the present value of estimated future cash flows.

E 11–21
Impairment;
tangible operational
assets

● LO8

General Optic Corporation operates a manufacturing plant in Arizona. Due to a significant decline in demand for the product manufactured at the Arizona site, an impairment test is deemed appropriate. Management has acquired the following information for the assets at the plant:

Cost	$32,500,000
Accumulated depreciation	14,200,000
General's estimate of the total cash flows to be generated by selling the products manufactured at its Arizona plant, not discounted to present value	15,000,000

The fair value of the Arizona plant is estimated to be $11,000,000.

Required:

1. Determine the amount of impairment loss, if any.
2. If a loss is indicated, where would it appear in General Optic's multiple-step income statement?
3. If a loss is indicated, prepare the entry to record the loss.
4. Repeat requirement 1 assuming that the estimated undiscounted sum of future cash flows is $12,000,000 instead of $15,000,000.
5. Repeat requirement 1 assuming that the estimated undiscounted sum of future cash flows is $19,000,000 instead of $15,000,000

E 11–22
Impairment;
goodwill

● LO8

In 2007, Alliant Corporation acquired Centerpoint, Inc. for $300 million, of which $50 million was allocated to goodwill. Alliant tests for goodwill impairment at the end of each year. At the end of 2009, management has provided the following information:

Fair value of Centerpoint, Inc.	$220 million
Fair value of Centerpoint's net assets (excluding goodwill)	200 million
Book value of Centerpoint's net assets (including goodwill)	250 million

Required:

1. Determine the amount of the impairment loss.
2. Repeat requirement 1 assuming that the fair value of Centerpoint is $270 million.

E 11–23
Goodwill valuation
and impairment;
Chapters 10 and 11

● LO8

On May 28, 2009, Pesky Corporation acquired all of the outstanding common stock of Harman, Inc., for $420 million. The fair value of Harman's identifiable tangible and intangible assets totaled $512 million, and the fair value of liabilities assumed by Pesky was $150 million.

Pesky performed the required goodwill impairment test at the end of its fiscal year ended December 31, 2009. Management has provided the following information:

Fair value of Harman, Inc.	$400 million
Fair value of Harman's net assets (excluding goodwill)	370 million
Book value of Harman's net assets (including goodwill)	410 million

Required:

1. Determine the amount of goodwill that resulted from the Harman acquisition.
2. Determine the amount of goodwill impairment loss that Pesky should recognize at the end of 2009, if any.
3. If an impairment loss is required, prepare the journal entry to record the loss.

E 11–24
Subsequent
expenditures

● LO9

Belltone Company made the following expenditures related to its 10-year-old manufacturing facility:
1. The heating system was replaced at a cost of $250,000. The cost of the old system was not known. The company accounts for improvements as reductions of accumulated depreciation.
2. A new wing was added at a cost of $750,000. The new wing substantially increases the productive capacity of the plant.
3. Annual building maintenance was performed at a cost of $14,000.
4. All of the machinery on the assembly line in the plant was rearranged at a cost of $50,000. The rearrangement clearly increases the productive capacity of the plant.

Required:
Prepare journal entries to record each of the above expenditures.

E 11–25
Depreciation
methods; disposal
of operational asset;
Chapters 10 and 11

● LO2

Howarth Manufacturing Company purchased a lathe on June 30, 2005, at a cost of $80,000. The residual value of the lathe was estimated to be $5,000 at the end of a five-year life. The lathe was sold on March 31, 2009, for $17,000. Howarth uses the straight-line depreciation method for all of its plant and equipment. Partial-year depreciation is calculated based on the number of months the asset is in service.

Required:

1. Prepare the journal entry to record the sale.
2. Assuming that Howarth had instead used the sum-of-the-years'-digits depreciation method, prepare the journal entry to record the sale.

E 11–26
Concepts;
terminology

● LO1 through
 LO6 LO8

Listed below are several items and phrases associated with depreciation, depletion, and amortization. Pair each item from List A (by letter) with the item from List B that is most appropriately associated with it.

List A	List B
_____ 1. Depreciation	a. Cost allocation for natural resource.
_____ 2. Service life	b. Accounted for prospectively.
_____ 3. Depreciable base	c. When there has been a significant decline in value.
_____ 4. Activity-based methods	d. The amount of use expected from an operational asset.
_____ 5. Time-based methods	e. Estimates service life in units of output.
_____ 6. Double-declining balance	f. Cost less residual value.
_____ 7. Group method	g. Cost allocation for plant and equipment.
_____ 8. Composite method	h. Does not subtract residual value from cost.
_____ 9. Depletion	i. Accounted for in the same way as a change in estimate.
_____ 10. Amortization	j. Aggregates assets that are similar.
_____ 11. Change in useful life	k. Aggregates assets that are physically unified.
_____ 12. Change in depreciation method	l. Cost allocation for an intangible asset.
_____ 13. Write-down of asset	m. Estimates service life in years.

E 11–27
Retirement and
replacement
depreciation

● Appendix

Cadillac Construction Company uses the retirement method to determine depreciation on its small tools. During 2007, the first year of the company's operations, tools were purchased at a cost of $8,000. In 2009, tools originally costing $2,000 were sold for $250 and replaced with new tools costing $2,500.

Required:

1. Prepare journal entries to record each of the above transactions.
2. Repeat requirement 1 assuming that the company uses the replacement depreciation method instead of the retirement method.

CPA AND CMA REVIEW QUESTIONS

**CPA Exam
Questions**

KAPLAN

SCHWESER

The following questions are used in the Kaplan CPA Review Course to study operational assets while preparing for the CPA examination. Determine the response that best completes the statements or questions.

● LO2

1. Slovac Company purchased a machine that has an estimated useful life of eight years for $7,500. Its salvage value is estimated at $500. What is the depreciation for the second year of the asset's life, assuming Slovac uses the double-declining balance method of depreciation?
   a. $1,406
   b. $1,438
   c. $1,875
   d. $3,750

● LO2

2. Calculate depreciation for year 2 based on the following information:

   Historical cost $40,000
   Useful life 5 years
   Salvage value $3,000
   Year 1 depreciation $7,400

   a. $7,000
   b. $7,400
   c. $8,000
   d. $8,600

● LO3

3. A company pays $20,000 for the rights to a well with 5 million gallons of water. If the company extracts 250,000 gallons of water in the first year, what is the total depletion in year 1?
   a. $ 400
   b. $1,000
   c. $1,250
   d. $5,000

● LO4

4. Black, Inc., purchased another company for $5,000,000. The fair value of all identifiable tangible and intangible assets was $4,500,000. Black will amortize any goodwill over the maximum number of years allowed. What is the annual amortization of goodwill for this acquisition?

    a. $12,500
    b. $20,000
    c. $25,000
    d.   0

● LO4

5. On January 2, 2009, Rafa Company purchased a franchise with a useful life of 10 years for $50,000. An additional franchise fee of 3% of franchise operating revenues also must be paid each year to the franchisor. Revenues during 2009 totaled $400,000. In its December 31, 2009, balance sheet, what net amount should Rafa report as an intangible asset-franchise?

    a. $33,000
    b. $43,800
    c. $45,000
    d. $50,000

● LO5

6. JME acquired a depreciable asset on January 1, 2007, for $60,000 cash. At that time JME estimated the asset would last 10 years and have no salvage value. During 2009, JME estimated the remaining life of the asset to be only three more years with a salvage value of $3,000. If JME uses straight-line depreciation, what is the depreciation for 2009?

    a. $ 6,000
    b. $12,000
    c. $15,000
    d. $16,000

● LO8

7. The following information concerns Franklin, Inc.'s stamping machine:

> Acquired: January 1, 2003
> Cost: $22 million
> Depreciation: straight-line method
> Estimated useful life: 12 years
> Salvage value: $4 million

As of December 31, 2009, the stamping machine is expected to generate $1,500,000 per year for five more years and will then be sold for $1,000,000. The stamping machine is

    a. Impaired because expected salvage value has declined.
    b. Not impaired because annual expected revenue exceeds annual depreciation.
    c. Not impaired because it continues to produce revenue.
    d. Impaired because its book value exceeds expected future cash flows.

● LO9

8. During 2008, Yvo Corp. installed a production assembly line to manufacture furniture. In 2009, Yvo purchased a new machine and rearranged the assembly line to install this machine. The rearrangement did not increase the estimated useful life of the assembly line, but it did result in significantly more efficient production. The following expenditures were incurred in connection with this project:

Machine	$75,000
Labor to install machine	14,000
Parts added in rearranging the assembly line to provide future benefits	40,000
Labor and overhead to rearrange the assembly line	18,000

What amount of the above expenditures should be capitalized in 2009?

    a. $ 75,000
    b. $ 89,000
    c. $107,000
    d. $147,000

CMA Exam Questions

The following questions dealing with operational assets are adapted from questions that previously appeared on Certified Management Accountant (CMA) examinations. The CMA designation sponsored by the Institute of Management Accountants (**www.imanet.org**) provides members with an objective measure of knowledge and competence in the field of management accounting. Determine the response that best completes the statements or questions.

● LO3

1. WD Mining Company purchased a section of land for $600,000 in 1998 to develop a zinc mine. The mine began operating in 2000. At that time, management estimated that the mine would produce 200,000 tons of quality ore. A total of 100,000 tons of ore was mined and processed from 2000 through December 31, 2007. During January 2008, a very promising vein was discovered. The revised estimate of ore still to be mined was 250,000 tons. Estimated salvage value for the mine land was $100,000 in both 2000 and 2008. Assuming that 10,000 tons of ore was mined in 2008, the computation WD Mining Company should use to determine the amount of depletion to record in 2008 would be
   a. (($600,000 − $100,000)/450,000 tons) × 10,000 tons.
   b. (($600,000 − $100,000)/350,000 tons) × 10,000 tons.
   c. (($600,000 − $100,000 − $250,000)/350,000 tons) × 10,000 tons.
   d. (($600,000 − $100,000 − $250,000)/250,000 tons) × 10,000 tons.

● LO9

2. Costs that are capitalized with regard to a patent include
   a. Legal fees of obtaining the patent, incidental costs of obtaining the patent, and costs of successful patent infringement suits.
   b. Legal fees of obtaining the patent, incidental costs of obtaining the patent, and research and development costs incurred on the invention that is patented.
   c. Legal fees of obtaining the patent, costs of successful patent infringement suits, and research and development costs incurred on the invention that is patented.
   d. Incidental costs of obtaining the patent, costs of successful and unsuccessful patent infringement suits, and the value of any signed patent licensing agreement.

● LO4

3. On September 1, year 1, for $4,000,000 cash and $2,000,000 notes payable, Norbend Corporation acquired the net assets of Crisholm Company, which had a fair value of $5,496,000 on that date. Norbend's management is of the opinion that the goodwill generated has an indefinite life. During the year-end audit for year 3 after all adjusting entries have been made, the goodwill is determined to be worthless. The amount of the write-off as of December 31, year 3 should be
   a. $504,000.
   b. $478,800.
   c. $466,200.
   d. $474,600.

PROBLEMS   available with McGraw-Hill's Homework Manager www.mhhe.com/spiceland5e

An alternate exercise and problem set is available on the text website: www.mhhe.com/spiceland5e

P 11–1
Depreciation
methods; change in
methods

● LO2 LO6

The fact that generally accepted accounting principles allow companies flexibility in choosing between certain allocation methods can make it difficult for a financial analyst to compare periodic performance from firm to firm.

Suppose you were a financial analyst trying to compare the performance of two companies. Company A uses the double-declining-balance depreciation method. Company B uses the straight-line method. You have the following information taken from the 12/31/09 year-end financial statements for Company B:

Income Statement

Depreciation expense	$ 10,000

Balance Sheet

Assets:	
Plant and equipment, at cost	$200,000
Less: Accumulated depreciation	(40,000)
Net	$160,000

You also determine that all of the assets constituting the plant and equipment of Company B were acquired at the same time, and that all of the $200,000 represents depreciable assets. Also, all of the depreciable assets have the same useful life and residual values are zero.

Required:

1. In order to compare performance with Company A, estimate what B's depreciation expense would have been for 2009 if the double-declining-balance depreciation method had been used by Company B since acquisition of the depreciable assets.
2. If Company B decided to switch depreciation methods in 2009 from the straight line to the double-declining-balance method, prepare the 2009 adjusting journal entry to record depreciation for the year.

P 11–2
Comprehensive problem; Chapters 10 and 11

At December 31, 2008, Cord Company's plant asset and accumulated depreciation and amortization accounts had balances as follows:

Category	Plant Asset	Accumulated Depreciation and Amortization
Land	$ 175,000	$ —
Buildings	1,500,000	328,900
Machinery and equipment	1,125,000	317,500
Automobiles and trucks	172,000	100,325
Leasehold improvements	216,000	108,000
Land improvements	—	—

Depreciation methods and useful lives:
Buildings—150% declining balance; 25 years.
Machinery and equipment—Straight line; 10 years.
Automobiles and trucks—150% declining balance; 5 years, all acquired after 2005.
Leasehold improvements—Straight line.
Land improvements—Straight line.

Depreciation is computed to the nearest month and residual values are immaterial. *Transactions during 2009 and other information:*

a. On January 6, 2009, a plant facility consisting of land and building was acquired from King Corp. in exchange for 25,000 shares of Cord's common stock. On this date, Cord's stock had a fair value of $50 a share. Current assessed values of land and building for property tax purposes are $187,500 and $562,500, respectively.

b. On March 25, 2009, new parking lots, streets, and sidewalks at the acquired plant facility were completed at a total cost of $192,000. These expenditures had an estimated useful life of 12 years.

c. The leasehold improvements were completed on December 31, 2005, and had an estimated useful life of eight years. The related lease, which would terminate on December 31, 2011, was renewable for an additional four-year term. On April 29, 2009, Cord exercised the renewal option.

d. On July 1, 2009, machinery and equipment were purchased at a total invoice cost of $325,000. Additional costs of $10,000 for delivery and $50,000 for installation were incurred.

e. On August 30, 2009, Cord purchased a new automobile for $12,500.

f. On September 30, 2009, a truck with a cost of $24,000 and a carrying amount of $9,100 on date of sale was sold for $11,500. Depreciation for the nine months ended September 30, 2009, was $2,650.

g. On December 20, 2009, a machine with a cost of $17,000 and a book value of $2,975 at date of disposition was scrapped without cash recovery.

Required:

1. Prepare a schedule analyzing the changes in each of the plant asset accounts during 2009. This schedule should include columns for beginning balance, increase, decrease, and ending balance for each of the plant asset accounts. Do not analyze changes in accumulated depreciation and amortization.

2. For each asset category, prepare a schedule showing depreciation or amortization expense for the year ended December 31, 2009. Round computations to the nearest whole dollar.

(AICPA adapted)

P 11–3
Depreciation methods

● LO2

[This problem is a continuation of Problem 10–3 in Chapter 10 focusing on depreciation.]

Required:
For each asset classification, prepare a schedule showing depreciation expense for the year ended December 31, 2009, using the following depreciation methods and useful lives:

Land improvements—Straight line; 15 years.
Building—150% declining balance; 20 years.
Machinery and equipment—Straight line; 10 years.
Automobiles—150% declining balance; 3 years.

Depreciation is computed to the nearest month and no residual values are used.

(AICPA adapted)

P 11–4
Partial-year depreciation; asset addition; increase in useful life

● LO2 LO9

On April 1, 2007, the KB Toy Company purchased equipment to be used in its manufacturing process. The equipment cost $48,000, has an eight-year useful life, and has no residual value. The company uses the straight-line depreciation method for all manufacturing equipment.

On January 4, 2009, $12,350 was spent to repair the equipment and to add a feature that increased its operating efficiency. Of the total expenditure, $2,000 represented ordinary repairs and annual maintenance and $10,350 represented the cost of the new feature. In addition to increasing operating efficiency, the total useful life of the equipment was extended to 10 years.

Required:

Prepare journal entries for the following:
1. Depreciation for 2007 and 2008.
2. The 2009 expenditure.
3. Depreciation for 2009.

P 11–5
Operational assets;
comprehensive

● **LO2**

The Thompson Corporation, a manufacturer of steel products, began operations on October 1, 2007. The accounting department of Thompson has started the fixed-asset and depreciation schedule presented below. You have been asked to assist in completing this schedule. In addition to ascertaining that the data already on the schedule are correct, you have obtained the following information from the company's records and personnel:

a. Depreciation is computed from the first of the month of acquisition to the first of the month of disposition.

b. Land A and Building A were acquired from a predecessor corporation. Thompson paid $812,500 for the land and building together. At the time of acquisition, the land had a fair value of $72,000 and the building had a fair value of $828,000.

c. Land B was acquired on October 2, 2007, in exchange for 3,000 newly issued shares of Thompson's common stock. At the date of acquisition, the stock had a par value of $5 per share and a fair value of $25 per share. During October 2007, Thompson paid $10,400 to demolish an existing building on this land so it could construct a new building.

d. Construction of Building B on the newly acquired land began on October 1, 2008. By September 30, 2009, Thompson had paid $210,000 of the estimated total construction costs of $300,000. Estimated completion and occupancy are July 2010.

e. Certain equipment was donated to the corporation by the city. An independent appraisal of the equipment when donated placed the fair value at $16,000 and the residual value at $2,000.

f. Machine A's total cost of $110,000 includes installation charges of $550 and normal repairs and maintenance of $11,000. Residual value is estimated at $5,500. Machine A was sold on February 1, 2009.

g. On October 1, 2008, Machine B was acquired with a down payment of $4,000 and the remaining payments to be made in 10 annual installments of $4,000 each beginning October 1, 2009. The prevailing interest rate was 8%.

THOMPSON CORPORATION
Fixed Asset and Depreciation Schedule
For Fiscal Years Ended September 30, 2008, and September 30, 2009

Assets	Acquisition Date	Cost	Residual	Depreciation Method	Estimated Life in Years	Depreciation for Year Ended 9/30	
						2008	2009
Land A	10/1/07	$(1)	N/A	N/A	N/A	N/A	N/A
Building A	10/1/07	(2)	$47,500	SL	(3)	$14,000	$(4)
Land B	10/2/07	(5)	N/A	N/A	N/A	N/A	N/A
Building B	Under construction	210,000 to date	—	SL	30	—	(6)
Donated Equipment	10/2/07	(7)	2,000	150% Declining balance	10	(8)	(9)
Machine A	10/2/07	(10)	5,500	Sum-of-the-years'-digits	10	(11)	(12)
Machine B	10/1/08	(13)	—	SL	15	—	(14)

N/A = not applicable

Required:

Supply the correct amount for each numbered item on the schedule. Round each answer to the nearest dollar.

(AICPA adapted)

P 11–6
Depreciation
methods; partial-
year depreciation;
sale of assets

● **LO2**

On March 31, 2009, the Herzog Company purchased a factory complete with machinery and equipment. The allocation of the total purchase price of $1,000,000 to the various types of assets along with estimated useful lives and residual values are as follows:

Asset	Cost	Estimated Residual Value	Estimated Useful Life in Years
Land	$ 100,000	N/A	N/A
Building	500,000	none	25
Machinery	240,000	10% of cost	8
Equipment	160,000	$13,000	6
Total	$1,000,000		

On June 29, 2010, machinery included in the March 31, 2009, purchase that cost $100,000 was sold for $80,000. Herzog uses the straight-line depreciation method for buildings and machinery and the sum-of-the-years'-digits method for equipment. Partial-year depreciation is calculated based on the number of months an asset is in service.

Required:

1. Compute depreciation expense on the building, machinery, and equipment for 2009.

2. Prepare the journal entries to record (1) depreciation on the machinery sold on June 29, 2010, and (2) the sale of machinery.

3. Compute depreciation expense on the building, remaining machinery, and equipment for 2010.

P 11–7
Depletion; change in estimate

● LO3 LO5

e**X**cel

⭐

In 2009, the Marion Company purchased land containing a mineral mine for $1,600,000. Additional costs of $600,000 were incurred to develop the mine. Geologists estimated that 400,000 tons of ore would be extracted. After the ore is removed, the land will have a resale value of $100,000.

To aid in the extraction, Marion built various structures and small storage buildings on the site at a cost of $150,000. These structures have a useful life of 10 years. The structures cannot be moved after the ore has been removed and will be left at the site. In addition, new equipment costing $80,000 was purchased and installed at the site. Marion does not plan to move the equipment to another site, but estimates that it can be sold at auction for $4,000 after the mining project is completed.

In 2009, 50,000 tons of ore were extracted and sold. In 2010, the estimate of total tons of ore in the mine was revised from 400,000 to 487,500. During 2010, 80,000 tons were extracted, of which 60,000 tons were sold.

Required:

1. Compute depletion and depreciation of the mine and the mining facilities and equipment for 2009 and 2010. Marion uses the units-of-production method to determine depreciation on mining facilities and equipment.

2. Compute the book value of the mineral mine, structures, and equipment as of December 31, 2010.

3. Discuss the accounting treatment of the depletion and depreciation on the mine and mining facilities and equipment.

P 11–8
Amortization

● LO4

The following information concerns the intangible assets of Epstein Corporation:

a. On June 30, 2009, Epstein completed the purchase of the Johnstone Corporation for $2,000,000 in cash. The fair value of the net identifiable assets of Johnstone was $1,700,000.

b. Included in the assets purchased from Johnstone was a patent that was valued at $80,000. The remaining legal life of the patent was 13 years, but Epstein believes that the patent will only be useful for another eight years.

c. Epstein acquired a franchise on October 1, 2009, by paying an initial franchise fee of $200,000. The contractual life of the franchise is 10 years.

Required:

1. Prepare year-end adjusting journal entries to record amortization expense on the intangibles at December 31, 2009.

2. Prepare the intangible asset section of the December 31, 2009, balance sheet.

P 11–9
Straight-line depreciation; change in useful life and residual value

● LO2 LO5

The property, plant, and equipment section of the Jasper Company's December 31, 2008, balance sheet contained the following:

Property, plant, and equipment:		
Land		$120,000
Building	$ 840,000	
Less: Accumulated depreciation	(200,000)	640,000
Equipment	180,000	
Less: Accumulated depreciation	?	?
Total property, plant, and equipment		?

The land and building were purchased at the beginning of 2004. Straight-line depreciation is used and a residual value of $40,000 for the building is anticipated.

The equipment is comprised of the following three machines:

Machine	Cost	Date Acquired	Residual Value	Life in Years
101	$70,000	1/1/06	$7,000	10
102	80,000	6/30/07	8,000	8
103	30,000	9/1/08	3,000	9

The straight-line method is used to determine depreciation on the equipment. On March 31, 2009, Machine 102 was sold for $52,500. Early in 2009, the useful life of machine 101 was revised to seven years in total, and the residual value was revised to zero.

Required:
1. Calculate the accumulated depreciation on the equipment at December 31, 2008.
2. Prepare the journal entry to record the sale of machine 102. Also prepare the journal entry to record 2009 depreciation on machine 102 up to the date of sale.
3. Prepare the 2009 year-end adjusting journal entries to record depreciation on the building and equipment.

P 11–10
Accounting changes; three accounting situations

● LO2 LO5 LO6

Described below are three independent and unrelated situations involving accounting changes. Each change occurs during 2009 before any adjusting entries or closing entries are prepared.
a. On December 30, 2005, Rival Industries acquired its office building at a cost of $1,000,000. It has been depreciated on a straight-line basis assuming a useful life of 40 years and no residual value. However, plans were finalized in 2009 to relocate the company headquarters at the end of 2014. The vacated office building will have a residual value at that time of $700,000.
b. At the beginning of 2005, the Hoffman Group purchased office equipment at a cost of $330,000. Its useful life was estimated to be 10 years with no residual value. The equipment has been depreciated by the sum-of-the-years'-digits method. On January 1, 2009, the company changed to the straight-line method.
c. At the beginning of 2009, Jantzen Specialties, which uses the sum-of-the-years'-digits method, changed to the straight-line method for newly acquired buildings and equipment. The change increased current year net income by $445,000.

Required:
For each situation:
1. Identify the type of change.
2. Prepare any journal entry necessary as a direct result of the change as well as any adjusting entry for 2009 related to the situation described. (Ignore income tax effects.)
3. Briefly describe any other steps that should be taken to appropriately report the situation.

P 11–11
Error correction; change in depreciation method

● LO2 LO6 LO7

Collins Corporation purchased office equipment at the beginning of 2007 and capitalized a cost of $2,000,000. This cost figure included the following expenditures:

Purchase price	$1,850,000
Freight charges	30,000
Installation charges	20,000
Annual maintenance charge	100,000
Total	$2,000,000

The company estimated an eight-year useful life for the equipment. No residual value is anticipated. The double-declining-balance method was used to determine depreciation expense for 2007 and 2008.

In 2009, after the 2008 financial statements were issued, the company decided to switch to the straight-line depreciation method for this equipment. At that time, the company's controller discovered that the original cost of the equipment incorrectly included one year of annual maintenance charges for the equipment.

Required:
1. Ignoring income taxes, prepare the appropriate correcting entry for the equipment capitalization error discovered in 2009.
2. Ignoring income taxes, prepare any 2009 journal entry(s) related to the change in depreciation methods.

P 11–12
Depreciation and amortization; impairment of operational assets

● LO2 LO4 LO8

At the beginning of 2007, Metatec, Inc. acquired Ellison Technology Corporation for $600 million. In addition to cash, receivables, and inventory, the following assets and their fair values were also acquired:

Plant and equipment (depreciable assets)	$150 million
Patent	40 million
Goodwill	100 million

The plant and equipment are depreciated over a 10-year useful life on a straight-line basis. There is no estimated residual value. The patent is estimated to have a 5-year useful life, no residual value, and is amortized using the straight-line method.

At the end of 2009, a change in business climate indicated to management that the operational assets of Ellison might be impaired. The following amounts have been determined:

Plant and equipment:	
Undiscounted sum of future cash flows	$ 80 million
Fair value	60 million
Patent:	
Undiscounted sum of future cash flows	$ 20 million
Fair value	13 million

(continued)

(concluded)

Goodwill:

Fair value of Ellison Technology	$450 million
Fair value of Ellison's net assets (excluding goodwill)	390 million
Book value of Ellison's net assets (including goodwill)	470 million*

*After first recording any impairment losses on plant and equipment and the patent.

Required:

1. Compute the book value of the plant and equipment and patent at the end of 2009.
2. When should the plant and equipment and the patent be tested for impairment?
3. When should goodwill be tested for impairment?
4. Determine the amount of any impairment loss to be recorded, if any, for the three assets.

P 11–13

Chapters 10 and 11; depreciation and depletion; change in useful life; asset retirement obligation

● LO2 LO3 LO5

On May 1, 2009, Hecala Mining entered into an agreement with the state of New Mexico to obtain the rights to operate a mineral mine in New Mexico for $10 million. Additional costs and purchases included the following:

Development costs in preparing the mine	$3,200,000
Mining machinery	140,000
Construction of various structures on site	68,000

After the minerals are removed from the mine, the machinery will be sold for an estimated residual value of $10,000. The structures will be torn down.

Geologists estimate that 800,000 tons of ore can be extracted from the mine. After the ore is removed the land will revert back to the state of New Mexico.

The contract with the state requires Hecala to restore the land to its original condition after mining operations are completed in approximately four years. Management has provided the following possible outflows for the restoration costs:

Cash Outflow	Probability
$600,000	30%
700,000	30%
800,000	40%

Hecala's credit-adjusted risk-free interest rate is 8%. During 2009, Hecala extracted 120,000 tons of ore from the mine.

Required:

1. Determine the amount at which Hecala will record the mine.
2. Calculate the depletion of the mine and the depreciation of the mining facilities and equipment for 2009, assuming that Hecala uses the units-of-production method for both depreciation and depletion. Round depletion and depreciation rates to four decimals.
3. Are depletion of the mine and depreciation of the mining facilities and equipment reported as separate expenses in the income statement? Discuss the accounting treatment of these items in the income statement and balance sheet.
4. During 2010, Hecala changed its estimate of the total amount of ore originally in the mine from 800,000 to 1,000,000 tons. Briefly describe the accounting treatment the company will employ to account for the change *and* calculate the depletion of the mine and depreciation of the mining facilities and equipment for 2010 assuming Hecala extracted 150,000 tons of ore in 2010.

BROADEN YOUR PERSPECTIVE

Apply your critical-thinking ability to the knowledge you've gained. These cases will provide you an opportunity to develop your research, analysis, judgment, and communication skills. You also will work with other students, integrate what you've learned, apply it in real world situations, and consider its global and ethical ramifications. This practice will broaden your knowledge and further develop your decision-making abilities.

Analysis Case 11–1

Depreciation, depletion, and amortization

● LO1

The terms depreciation, depletion, and amortization all refer to the process of allocating the cost of an operational asset to the periods the asset is used.

Required:

Discuss the differences between depreciation, depletion, and amortization as the terms are used in accounting for operational assets.

Communication Case 11–2
Depreciation

● LO1

At a recent luncheon, you were seated next to Mr. Hopkins, the president of a local company that manufactures bicycle parts. He heard that you were a CPA and made the following comments to you:

Why is it that I am forced to recognize depreciation expense in my company's income statement when I know that I could sell many of my operational assets for more than I paid for them? I thought that the purpose of the balance sheet was to reflect the value of my business and that the purpose of the income statement was to report the net change in value or wealth of a company. It just doesn't make sense to penalize my profits when there hasn't been any loss in value from using the operational assets.

At the conclusion of the luncheon, you promised to send him a short explanation of the rationale for current depreciation practices.

Required:
Prepare a letter to Mr. Hopkins. Explain the accounting concept of depreciation and include a brief example in your explanation showing that over the life of the asset the change in value approach to depreciation and the allocation of cost approach will result in the same total effect on income.

Judgment Case 11–3
Straight-line method; composite depreciation

● LO1 LO2

Portland Co. uses the straight-line depreciation method for depreciable assets. All assets are depreciated individually except manufacturing machinery, which is depreciated by the composite method.

Required:
1. What factors should have influenced Portland's selection of the straight-line depreciation method?
2. a. What benefits should derive from using the composite method rather than the individual basis for manufacturing machinery?
   b. How should Portland have calculated the manufacturing machinery's annual depreciation in its first year of operation?

(AICPA adapted)

Judgment Case 11–4
Depreciation

● LO1 LO2

At the beginning of the year, Patrick Company acquired a computer to be used in its operations. The computer was delivered by the supplier, installed by Patrick, and placed into operation. The estimated useful life of the computer is five years, and its estimated residual value is significant.

Required:
1. a. What costs should Patrick capitalize for the computer?
   b. What is the objective of depreciation accounting?
2. What is the rationale for using accelerated depreciation methods?

(AICPA adapted)

Judgment Case 11–5
Capitalize or expense; materiality

● LO9

Redline Publishers, Inc., produces various manuals ranging from computer software instructional booklets to manuals explaining the installation and use of large pieces of industrial equipment. At the end of 2009, the company's balance sheet reported total assets of $62 million and total liabilities of $40 million. The income statement for 2009 reported net income of $1.1 million, which represents an approximate 3% increase from the prior year. The company's effective income tax rate is 30%.

Near the end of 2009, a variety of expenditures were made to overhaul the company's manufacturing equipment. None of these expenditures exceeded $750, the materiality threshold the company has set for the capitalization of any such expenditure. Even though the overhauls extended the service life of the equipment, the expenditures were expensed, not capitalized.

John Henderson, the company's controller, is worried about the treatment of the overhaul expenditures. Even though no individual expenditure exceeded the $750 materiality threshold, total expenditures were $70,000.

Required:
Should the overhaul expenditures be capitalized or expensed?

Communication Case 11–6
Capitalize or expense; materiality

● LO9

The focus of the case is the situation described in the previous case. Your instructor will divide the class into two to six groups depending on the size of the class. The mission of your group is to determine the treatment of the overhaul expenditures.

Required:
1. Each group member should deliberate the situation independently and draft a tentative argument prior to the class session for which the case is assigned.
2. In class, each group will meet for 10 to 15 minutes in different areas of the classroom. During the meeting, group members will take turns sharing their suggestions for the purpose of arriving at a single group treatment.
3. After the allotted time, a spokesperson for each group (selected during the group meetings) will share the group's solution with the class. The goal of the class is to incorporate the views of each group into a consensus approach to the situation.

Whaley Distributors is a wholesale distributor of electronic components. Financial statements for the year ended December 31, 2009, reported the following amounts and subtotals ($ in millions):

	Assets	Liabilities	Shareholders' Equity	Net Income	Expenses
2008	$640	$330	$310	$210	$150
2009	$820	$400	$420	$230	$175

In 2010 the following situations occurred or came to light:

a. Internal auditors discovered that ending inventories reported in the financial statements the two previous years were misstated due to faulty internal controls. The errors were in the following amounts:

2008 inventory	Overstated by $12 million
2009 inventory	Understated by $10 million

b. A patent costing $18 million at the beginning of 2008, expected to benefit operations for a total of six years, has not been amortized since acquired.

c. Whaley's conveyer equipment has been depreciated by the sum-of-the-years'-digits (SYD) method since constructed at the beginning of 2008 at a cost of $30 million. It has an expected useful life of five years and no expected residual value. At the beginning of 2010, Whaley decided to switch to straight-line depreciation.

Required:
For each situation:

1. Prepare any journal entry necessary as a direct result of the change or error correction as well as any adjusting entry for 2010 related to the situation described. (Ignore tax effects.)

2. Determine the amounts to be reported for each of the items shown above from the 2008 and 2009 financial statements when those amounts are reported again in the 2010, 2009, and 2008 comparative financial statements.

There are various types of accounting changes, each of which is required to be reported differently.

Required:

1. What type of accounting change is a change from the sum-of-the-years'-digits method of depreciation to the straight-line method for previously recorded assets? Under what circumstances does this type of accounting change occur?

2. What type of accounting change is a change in the expected service life of an asset arising because of more experience with the asset? Under what circumstances does this type of accounting change occur?

(AICPA adapted)

The following Trueblood case is recommended for use with this chapter. The case provides an excellent opportunity for class discussion, group projects, and writing assignments. The case, along with Professor's Discussion Material, can be obtained from the Deloitte & Touche Foundation at its website: **www.deloitte.com/us/truebloodcases.**

Case 04-3: *Home Computer, Inc.*

The objectives of this case are (a) to determine if Home Computer should recognize an impairment loss for operational assets and, if so, (b) to calculate the amount of the loss.

The company controller, Barry Melrose, has asked for your help in interpreting accounting standards for the recognition and measurement of impairment losses for operational assets. "We have a significant amount of goodwill on our books from last year's acquisition of Comcast Corporation. Also, I think we may have a problem with the assets of some of our factories out West. And one of our divisions is currently considering disposing of a large group of depreciable assets."

Your task as assistant controller is to research the issue.

Required:

1. Obtain the original FASB Standards on accounting for the impairment of operational assets. You might gain access at the FASB website (**www.fasb.org**), from your school library, or some other source.
2. When should operational assets be tested for impairment?
3. Explain the processes for measuring an impairment loss for operational assets to be held and used.
4. What are the specific criteria that must be met for an asset or asset group to be classified as held for sale?
5. Explain the processes for measuring an impairment loss for operational assets classified as held for sale.

At the beginning of 2007, the Healthy Life Food Company purchased equipment for $42 million to be used in the manufacture of a new line of gourmet frozen foods. The equipment was estimated to have a 10-year service life and no residual value. The straight-line depreciation method was used to measure depreciation for 2007 and 2008.

Late in 2009, it became apparent that sales of the new frozen food line were significantly below expectations. The company decided to continue production for two more years (2010 and 2011) and then discontinue the line. At that time, the equipment will be sold for minimal scrap values.

The controller, Heather Meyer, was asked by Harvey Dent, the company's chief executive officer (CEO), to determine the appropriate treatment of the change in service life of the equipment. Heather determined that there has been an impairment of value requiring an immediate write-down of the equipment of $12,900,000. The remaining book value would then be depreciated over the equipment's revised service life.

The CEO does not like Heather's conclusion because of the effect it would have on 2009 income. "Looks like a simple revision in service life from 10 years to 5 years to me," Dent concluded. "Let's go with it that way, Heather."

Required:
1. What is the difference in before-tax income between the CEO's and Heather's treatment of the situation?
2. Discuss Heather Meyer's ethical dilemma.

Companies often are under pressure to meet or beat Wall Street earnings projections in order to increase stock prices and also to increase the value of stock options. Some resort to earnings management practices to artificially create desired results.

Required:
1. How can a company manage earnings by changing its depreciation method? Is this an effective technique to manage earnings?
2. How can a company manage earnings by changing the estimated useful lives of depreciable assets? Is this an effective technique to manage earnings?
3. Using a fictitious example and numbers you make up, describe in your own words how asset impairment losses could be used to manage earnings. How might that benefit the company?

The Cummings Company charged various expenditures made during 2009 to an account called repairs and maintenance expense. You have been asked by your supervisor in the company's internal audit department to review the expenditures to determine if they were appropriately recorded. The amount of each of the transactions included in the account is considered material.

1. Engine tune-up and oil change on the company's 12 delivery trucks—$1,300.
2. Rearrangement of machinery on the main production line—$5,500. It is not evident that the rearrangement will increase operational efficiency.
3. Installation of aluminum siding on the manufacturing plant—$32,000.
4. Replacement of the old air conditioning system in the manufacturing plant with a new system— $120,000.
5. Replacement of broken parts on three machines—$1,500.
6. Annual painting of the manufacturing plant—$11,000.
7. Purchase of new forklift to move finished product to the loading dock—$6,000.
8. Patching leaks in the roof of the manufacturing plant—$6,500. The repair work did not extend the useful life of the roof.

Required:
For each of the transactions listed above, indicate whether the expenditure is appropriately charged to the repair and maintenance expense account, and if not, indicate the proper account to be charged.

Caterpillar Inc. (CAT) is a world leader in the manufacture of construction and mining equipment, diesel and natural gas engines, and industrial gas turbines. CAT reported the following in a disclosure note accompanying its 2006 financial statements:

	2006	2005
($ in millions)		
Property, plant and equipment	$17,278	$15,862
Less: Accumulated depreciation	8,427	7,874
Property, plant and equipment - Net	$ 8,851	$ 7,988

Also, Note 10 disclosed that the total cost of property, plant, and equipment included $184 and $154 (dollars in millions) in land at the end of 2006 and 2005, respectively. In addition, the statement of cash flows for the year ended December 31, 2006, reported the following as cash flows from investing activities:

($ in millions)	
Payments for property, plant and equipment	$(2,675)
Proceeds from disposition of property, plant and equipment	572

The statement of cash flows also reported 2006 depreciation of $1,570 million.

Required:

1. Assume that all property, plant, and equipment acquired during 2006 were purchased for cash. Determine the amount of gain or loss from dispositions of property, plant, and equipment that Caterpillar recognized during 2006.
2. Assume that Caterpillar uses the straight-line method to depreciate plant and equipment. What is the approximate average service life of CAT's depreciable assets?

Real World Case 11–15
Depreciation and depletion method; asset impairment; subsequent expenditures

● LO2 LO3 LO8 LO9

Real World Financials

EDGAR, the Electronic Data Gathering, Analysis, and Retrieval system, performs automated collection, validation, indexing, and forwarding of submissions by companies and others who are required by law to file forms with the U.S. Securities and Exchange Commission (SEC). All publicly traded domestic companies use EDGAR to make the majority of their filings. (Some foreign companies file voluntarily.) Form 10-K or 10-KSB, which includes the annual report, is required to be filed on EDGAR. The SEC makes this information available on the Internet.

Required:

1. Access EDGAR on the Internet. The web address is **www.sec.gov**.
2. Search for **Chevron Corporation**. Access the 10-K filing for most recent fiscal year. Search or scroll to find the financial statements and related notes.
3. Answer the following questions related to the company's operational assets:
   a. Describe the company's depreciation and depletion policies.
   b. Describe the company's policy for subsequent expenditures made for operational assets.

Analysis Case 11–16
Depreciation and amortization

● LO2 LO4

Google

Refer to the financial statements and related disclosure notes of **Google** included with all new copies of the text.

Required:

1. What amount of depreciation and amortization did the company report in 2007?
2. What depreciation method is used for financial reporting purposes and what are the service lives of depreciable assets?

CPA SIMULATION 11–1

Yamashita Kyle
Operational Assets

KAPLAN
SCHWESER

CPA Review

Test your knowledge of the concepts discussed in this chapter, practice critical professional skills necessary for career success, and prepare for the computer-based CPA exam by accessing our CPA simulations at the text website: **www.mhhe.com/spiceland5e**.

The Yamashita Kyle simulation tests your knowledge of (a) depreciation methods including group depreciation, and the measurement of impairment of value for tangible, operational assets covered in this chapter, and (b) accounting for the disposal of operational assets, the capitalization of interest, and research and development expenditures discussed in Chapter 10.

As on the CPA exam itself, you will be asked to use tools including a spreadsheet, a calculator, and professional accounting standards, to conduct research, derive solutions, and communicate conclusions related to these issues in a simulated environment headed by the following interactive tabs:

Specific tasks in the simulation address:

- Testing your knowledge of various aspects of accounting for interest capitalization.
- Calculating the appropriate amount of depreciation, applying several depreciation methods.
- Understanding the appropriate steps involved in determining the amount of impairment loss to recognize for a tangible, operational asset.
- Determining the appropriate income statement effect of the disposal of operational assets.
- Communicating your understanding of (1) the treatment of expenditures subsequent to the acquisition of operational assets and (2) the situations that require the capitalization of interest.
- Researching various items related to the measurement and reporting of operational assets, including useful lives, group depreciation, and research and development expenditures.

12

⊢ CHAPTER ⊢

Investments

/// **OVERVIEW**

In this chapter you will learn about various approaches used to account for investments that companies make in the debt and equity of other companies. An investing company always has the option to account for these investments at fair value, with changes in fair values reported on the income statement. However, depending on the nature of an investment, investors can use alternative accounting approaches that ignore most fair value changes (e.g., *held-to-maturity* investments) or that include fair value changes only in other comprehensive income (e.g., *available-for-sale* investments). And, when an equity investor can significantly influence an investee but does not control it, the investor can use the *equity method* of accounting, which ignores fair value changes but includes the investee's income when reporting the investor's income.

‖‖‖ **LEARNING OBJECTIVES** ‖‖‖‖‖‖‖‖‖‖‖‖‖‖‖

After studying this chapter, you should be able to:

- **LO1** Demonstrate how to identify and account for investments classified for reporting purposes as held-to-maturity.
- **LO2** Demonstrate how to identify and account for investments classified for reporting purposes as trading securities.
- **LO3** Demonstrate how to identify and account for investments classified for reporting purposes as available-for-sale securities.
- **LO4** Explain what constitutes significant influence by the investor over the operating and financial policies of the investee.
- **LO5** Demonstrate how to identify and account for investments accounted for under the equity method.
- **LO6** Explain the adjustments made in the equity method when the fair value of the net assets underlying an investment exceeds their book value at acquisition.
- **LO7** Explain how electing the fair value option affects accounting for investments.

FINANCIAL REPORTING CASE

A Case of Coke

You are the lone accounting major in your five-member group in your Business Policy class. A part of the case your group is working on is the analysis of the financial statements of the **Coca-Cola Company.**

The marketing major in the group is confused by the following disclosure note from Coca-Cola's 2006 annual report:

Note 11: Financial Instruments (in part)

Certain Debt and Marketable Equity Securities

Investments in debt and marketable equity securities, other than investments accounted for by the equity method, are categorized as trading, available-for-sale, or held-to-maturity. Our marketable equity investments are categorized as trading or available-for-sale with their cost basis determined by the specific identification method. Trading securities are carried at fair value with realized and unrealized gains and losses included in net income. We record available-for-sale instruments at fair value, with unrealized gains and losses, net of deferred income taxes, reported as a component of AOCI. Debt securities categorized as held-to-maturity are stated at amortized cost.

As of December 31, 2006 and 2005, trading, available-for-sale, and held-to-maturity securities consisted of the following (in millions):

	Cost	Gross Unrealized Gains	Losses	Estimated Fair Value
2006				
Trading securities:				
Equity securities	$ 60	$ 6	$ —	$ 66
Available-for-sale securities:				
Equity securities	$240	$219	$ (1)	$458
Other securities	13	—	—	13
	$253	$219	$ (1)	$471
Held-to-maturity securities:				
Bank and corporate debt	$ 83	$ —	$ —	$ 83

"They say unrealized gains and losses are reported as part of comprehensive income? I don't see these gains and losses on the income statement," he complained. "And held-to-maturity securities—why are they treated differently? And what about equity method investments? On the balance sheet they have over $6 *billion* of other investments accounted for under the equity method, and I found a footnote that says their income from those investments is almost $600 million lower in 2006 than in 2005!"

By the time you finish this chapter, you should be able to respond appropriately to the questions posed in this case. Compare your response to the solution provided at the end of the chapter.

QUESTIONS ///

1. How should you respond? Why are held-to-maturity securities treated differently from other investment securities? (page 593)
2. Why are unrealized gains and losses on trading securities reported in the income statement? (page 593)
3. Why are unrealized gains and losses on available-for-sale securities not reported in the income statement, but instead are in comprehensive income? (page 597)
4. Explain why Coke accounts for some of its investments by the equity method and what that means. (page 611)

To finance its operations, and often the expansion of those operations, a corporation raises funds by selling equity securities (common and preferred stock) and debt securities (bonds and notes). These securities are purchased as investments by individual investors, mutual funds, and also by other corporations. In later chapters we discuss equity and debt securities from the perspective of the issuing company. Our focus in this chapter is on the corporations that invest in securities issued by other corporations as well as those issued by governmental units (bonds, Treasury bills, and Treasury bonds).

Most companies invest in financial instruments issued by other companies. For some investors, these investments represent ongoing affiliations with the companies whose securities are acquired. For instance, in recent years **AT&T** acquired **BellSouth** in a deal valued at $85.6 billion dollars, and **Microsoft** invested $600 million in nationwide wireless phone company **Nextel Communications Inc.**, gaining access to wireless Internet users. Some investments, though, are made not to obtain a favorable business relationship with another firm but simply to earn a return from the dividends or interest the securities pay or from increases in the market prices of the securities—the same prospective rewards that might motivate you to buy stocks, bonds, or other investment securities.

With such diversity in investment objectives, it's not surprising that there is diversity in the approaches used to account for investments. As you'll discover when reading this chapter, investments are accounted for in five primary ways, depending on the nature of the investment relationship and the preferences of the investor. Before we discuss the approaches in detail, see the quick overview in Graphic 12–1.

GRAPHIC 12–1

Reporting Categories for Investments

Control Characteristics of the Investment	Reporting Method Used by the Investor
The investor *lacks significant influence* over the operating and financial policies of the investee:	
Investments in debt securities for which the investor has the "positive intent and ability" to hold to maturity	**Held-to-maturity ("HTM")**—investment reported at amortized cost*
Investments held in an active trading account	**Trading securities ("TS")**—investment reported at fair value (with unrealized holding gains and losses included in net income)
Other	**Securities available-for-sale ("AFS")**—investment reported at fair value (with unrealized holding gains and losses excluded from net income and reported in other comprehensive income)*
The investor *has significant influence* over the operating and financial policies of the investee:	
Typically the investor owns between 20% and 50% of the voting stock of the investee	**Equity method**—investment cost adjusted for subsequent earnings and dividends of the investee*
The investor *controls* the investee:	
The investor owns more than 50% of the investee	**Consolidation**—the financial statements of the investor and investee are combined as if they are a single company

*If the investor elects the *fair value option,* this type of investment also can be accounted for using the same approach that's used for trading securities, with the investment reported at fair value and unrealized holding gains and losses included in net income.

In Part A of this chapter we discuss accounting for investments when the investor lacks significant influence over the operating and financial policies of the investee. In Part B we discuss accounting for "significant influence" investments. In both Parts A and B, we first discuss specific reporting methods and then discuss how the reporting changes if the investor elects the fair value option.

INVESTOR LACKS SIGNIFICANT INFLUENCE

The reporting approaches we use for investments differ according to how the approaches account for one or more of the four critical events that an investor experiences in the life of an investment:

1. Purchasing the investment.
2. Recognizing investment revenue (interest in the case of debt, dividends in the case of equity).
3. Holding the investment during periods in which the investment's fair value changes (and thus incurring *unrealized holding* gains and losses, since the security has not yet been sold).
4. Selling the investment (and thus incurring *realized* gains and losses, since the security has been sold and the gains or losses actually incurred).

As shown in Graphic 12–1, when the investor lacks significant influence over the investee, the investment is classified in one of three categories: held-to-maturity securities (HTM), trading securities (TS), and available-for-sale securities (AFS). Each type of investment has its own reporting method. However, regardless of the investment type, investors can elect the "fair value option" and classify HTM and AFS securities as TS. The key difference among the reporting approaches is how we account for unrealized holding gains and losses (critical event number 3 above), as shown in Graphic 12–2.

Reporting Approach	Treatment of Unrealized Holding Gains and Losses	Investment Reported in the Balance Sheet at
Held-to-maturity (HTM): used for debt that is planned to be held for its entire life	Not recognized	Amortized Cost*
Trading (TS): used for debt or equity that is held in an active trading account for immediate resale	Recognized in net income, and therefore in retained earnings as part of shareholders' equity	Fair Value
Available-for-sale (AFS): used for debt or equity that does not qualify as held-to-maturity or trading	Recognized in other comprehensive income, and therefore in accumulated other comprehensive income in shareholders' equity	Fair Value

GRAPHIC 12–2

Accounting for Unrealized Holding Gains and Losses When Investor Lacks Significant Influence

* SFAS No. 159 refers to this as "amortized initial measurement." We use that terminology in Chapter 14 when discussing the FVO with respect to liabilities.

Graphic 12–3 provides a description from a recent annual report of how the **Bank of America** accounts for its investments in each of the three reporting categories.

Note 1 (in part): Securities
Debt Securities which management has the intent and ability to hold to maturity are classified as held-to-maturity and reported at amortized cost. Debt Securities that are bought and held principally for the purpose of resale in the near term are classified as Trading Account Assets and are stated at fair value with unrealized gains and losses included in Trading Account Profits. All other Debt Securities that management has the intent and ability to hold to recovery unless there is a significant deterioration in credit quality in any individual security are classified as available-for-sale (AFS) and carried at fair value with net unrealized gains and losses included in Accumulated OCI on an after-tax basis.

GRAPHIC 12–3

Disclosure about Investments—Bank of America

Real World Financials

Why treat unrealized gains and losses differently depending on the type of investment? As you know, the primary purpose of accounting is to provide information useful for making decisions. What's most relevant for that purpose is not necessarily the same for each investment a company might make. For example, a company might invest in corporate bonds to provide a steady return until the bonds mature, in which case day-to-day changes in market value may not be viewed as very relevant, so the held-to-maturity approach is preferable. On the other hand, a company might invest in the same bonds because it plans to sell them at a profit in the near future, in which case the day-to-day changes in market value could be viewed as very relevant, and the trading security or available-for-sale approach is preferable.

Let's examine the three reporting classifications, one by one.

Securities to Be Held to Maturity

● LO1

The market value of a fixed-rate investment moves in the opposite direction of market rates of interest.

Unlike a share of stock, a bond or other debt security has a specified date on which it matures. On its maturity date, the principal (also called the "face amount") is paid to investors. In the meantime, interest equal to a specified percentage of the principal is paid to investors on specified interest dates. Think of the principal and interest payments of the bond as a stream of cash flows that an investor will receive in exchange for purchasing the bond. The investor values that stream of cash flows using the prevailing market interest rate for debt of similar risk and maturity. If the interest rate paid by the bond (the "stated rate") is higher than the market rate, the bond can be sold for more than its maturity value (so it is "sold at a premium"). If the stated rate is lower than the market rate, the bond must be sold for less than its maturity value (so it is "sold at a discount"). For an example of valuing a bond, see Illustration 12-1.

ILLUSTRATION 12–1	On July 1, 2009, Masterwear Industries issued $700,000 of 12% bonds, dated July 1. Interest of $42,000 is payable semiannually on June 30 and December 31. The bonds mature in three years, on June 30, 2012. The market interest rate for bonds of similar risk and maturity is 14%. The entire bond issue was purchased by United Intergroup, Inc.*
Bonds Purchased at a Discount	
Because interest is paid semiannually, the present value calculations use:	**Calculation of the Price of the Bonds**

		Present Values
Interest	$ 42,000 × 4.76654** =	$200,195
Principal (face amount)	$700,000 × 0.66634† =	466,438
Present value (price) of the bonds		$666,633

Because interest is paid semiannually, the present value calculations use:

a. one-half the stated rate (6%),

b. one-half the market rate (7%), and

c. 6 (3 × 2) semiannual periods.

* The numbers in this illustration are the same as those in Illustration 14–2 in Chapter 14 (except for some differences in dates between the two chapters). This helps us to better appreciate in Chapter 14 how Masterwear's accounting for its bond liability to United compares to United's accounting for its investment in Masterwear bonds. You can find an explanation of why we calculate the bond price this way on pages 704–711.

** Present value of an ordinary annuity of $1: $n = 6$, $i = 7\%$ (Table 4).

† Present value of $1: $n = 6$, $i = 7\%$ (Table 2).

Note: Present value tables are provided at the end of this textbook. If you need to review the concept of the time value of money, refer to the discussions in Chapter 6.

The fair value of a bond changes when market interest rates change. If market rates of interest *rise* after a fixed-rate security is purchased, the value of the fixed-interest payments declines. So, the fair value of the investment falls. Conversely, if market rates of interest *fall* after a fixed-rate security is purchased, the fixed interest payments become relatively more attractive, so the fair value of the investment rises.

Changes in market value are less relevant to an investor who will hold a security to its maturity regardless of those changes.

Increases and decreases in fair value between time a debt security is acquired and the day it matures to a prearranged maturity value are less important if sale before maturity isn't an alternative. For this reason, if an investor has the "positive intent and ability" to hold the securities to maturity, investments in debt securities can be classified as held-to-maturity ("HTM") and reported at their *amortized cost* in the balance sheet.[1] A debt security can not be classified as held-to-maturity if the investor might sell it in response to changes in market prices or interest rates, to meet the investor's liquidity needs, or similar factors.

Let's use the bond from Illustration 12–1 to see how we account for an investment in held-to-maturity debt securities.

---

[1]"Accounting for Certain Investments in Debt and Equity Securities," *Statement of Financial Accounting Standards No. 115* (Norwalk, Conn.: FASB, 1993), par. 46.

PURCHASE OF INVESTMENT. The journal entry to record the *purchase* of HTM investment securities is:

July 1		
Investment in bonds (face amount).....	700,000	
Discount on bond investment (difference)		33,367
Cash (price paid for the bonds)		666,633

All investment securities are initially recorded at cost.

Discount on bond investment is a contra-asset to investment in bonds that serves to reduce the carrying value of the bond asset to its cost at the date of purchase.

RECOGNIZE INVESTMENT REVENUE. The Masterwear bonds pay cash interest at a rate of 12%, but were issued at a time when the market rate of interest was 14%. As a result, the bonds were sold at a discount that was large enough to provide bond purchasers with the same effective rate of return on their investment (14%) that they could get elsewhere in the market. Think of it this way: a little piece of that initial discount serves each period to make up the difference between the relatively low rate of interest that the bond pays (12%) and the higher rate of interest that the market demands (14%). Recording interest each period as the *effective market rate of interest multiplied by the outstanding balance of the investment* is referred to as the effective interest method. This simply is an application of the accrual concept, consistent with accruing all revenues as they are earned, regardless of when cash is received.

The effective interest on debt is the *market rate of interest multiplied by the outstanding balance of the debt.*

Continuing our example, the initial investment is $666,633. Since the effective interest rate is 14%, interest recorded as *revenue* to the investor for the first six-month interest period is $46,664:

$$\underset{\text{Outstanding balance}}{\$666,633} \quad \times \quad \underset{\text{Effective rate}}{[14\% \div 2]} \quad = \quad \underset{\text{Effective interest}}{\$46,664}$$

However, the bond calls for semiannual interest payments of only $42,000—the *stated* rate (6%) times the *face amount* ($700,000). As always, when only a portion of revenue is received, the remainder becomes an asset—in this case an addition to the existing investment. So the difference, $4,664, increases the investment and is reflected as a reduction in the discount to $28,703 ($33,367 − 4,664). The journal entry to record the interest received for the first six months as *investment revenue* is:

The "unreceived" portion of the effective interest increases the existing investment.

December 31		
Cash (stated rate × face amount)	42,000	
Discount on bond investment (difference)	4,664	
Investment revenue (market rate × outstanding balance)		46,664

The amortized cost of the investment now is $700,000 − $28,703 = $671,297.

Graphic 12–4 demonstrates interest being recorded at the effective rate over the life of this investment. As you can see, the amortization of discount gradually increases the carrying value of the investment, until the investment reaches its face amount of $700,000 at the time when the debt matures.

We discuss accounting for discounts and premiums in much greater detail in Chapter 14.

DO NOT RECOGNIZE UNREALIZED HOLDING GAINS AND LOSSES FOR HTM INVESTMENTS. Suppose that, as of the end of the first reporting period, the market interest rate for similar securities has fallen to 11%. A market participant valuing the Masterwear bonds at that time would do so at the current market interest rate (11%) because that's the rate of return she or he could get from similar bonds. Calculating the present value of the bonds using a lower discount rate results in a higher present value. Let's say that checking market prices in *The Wall Street Journal* indicates that the fair value of the Masterwear bonds on that date is $714,943. How will United account for this increase in fair value? If United views the bonds as HTM investments, that change in fair value will

For HTM securities, unrealized holding gains and losses from fair value changes are ignored.

GRAPHIC 12–4

Amortization Schedule—Discount

Since less cash is received each period than the effective interest, the unpaid difference increases the outstanding balance of the investment.

Date	Cash Interest	Effective Interest	Increase in Balance	Outstanding Balance
	(6% × Face amount)	(7% × Outstanding balance)	(Discount reduction)	
7/1/09				666,633
12/31/09	42,000	.07 (666,633) = 46,664	4,664	671,297
6/30/10	42,000	.07 (671,297) = 46,991	4,991	676,288
12/31/10	42,000	.07 (676,288) = 47,340	5,340	681,628
6/30/11	42,000	.07 (681,628) = 47,714	5,714	687,342
12/31/11	42,000	.07 (687,342) = 48,114	6,114	693,456
6/30/12	42,000	.07 (693,456) = 48,544*	6,544	700,000
	252,000	285,367	33,367	

*Rounded.

be ignored.[2] The investment simply will be recorded at amortized cost (the amounts in the right-hand column of the amortization schedule above). United will *disclose* the fair value of its HTM investments in a footnote, but will not recognize any fair value changes in the income statement or balance sheet.[3]

ADDITIONAL CONSIDERATION

Suppose the bonds are not traded on an active exchange. How would you determine the fair value of the Masterwear bonds on December 31, 2009? Recall from Chapter 1 that *SFAS No. 157* identifies different ways that a firm can determine fair value. If the Masterwear bonds are publicly traded, United can find the fair value by looking up the current market price (this way of obtaining fair value is consistent with "level one" of the fair value hierarchy). On the other hand, if the bonds are not publicly traded, United can calculate the fair value by using the present value techniques shown in Illustration 12–1 (this way of obtaining fair value is consistent with "level two" of the fair value hierarchy). With five interest periods remaining, and a current market rate of 11% (5.5% semi-annually), the present value would be $714,943:

		Present Values
Interest	$ 42,000 × 4.27028* =	$179,352
Principal	$700,000 × 0.76513† =	535,591
Present value of the bonds		$714,943

*Present value of an ordinary annuity of $1: n = 5, i = 5.5%. (Table 4)
†Present value of $1: n = 5, i = 5.5%. (Table 2)

Using Excel, enter:
=PV (.055,5,42000,700000)
Output: 714,946

Using a calculator:
enter: N 5 I 5.5
PMT -42000 FV -700000
Output:= PV 714,946

SELL HTM INVESTMENTS.
Typically, held-to-maturity investments are—you guessed it—held to maturity. However, suppose that due to unforeseen circumstances the company decided to sell its debt investment for $725,000 on January 15, 2010.[4] United would record the sale as follows (for simplicity we ignore any interest earned during 2010):

January 15, 2010

Cash..	725,000	
Discount on bond investment	28,703	
Investment in Masterwear bonds....................................		700,000
Gain on sale of investments (to balance)		53,703

---

[2]An exception occurs when an unrealized loss from holding an HTM investment is viewed as "other than temporary." In that case the company includes in net income an impairment loss equal to the amount necessary to write down the carrying value of the HTM investment to its fair value. We discuss impairments of investments in more detail on p. 602.

[3]If United had chosen the fair value option for this investment, it would classify the investment as a trading security rather than as an HTM security. We'll illustrate the fair value option when we discuss trading securities.

[4]*SFAS No. 115* lists major unforeseen events that could justify sale of an HTM investment. Sale for other reasons could call into question whether the company actually had the intent and ability to hold the investment to maturity. In that case, the company's HTM classification is viewed as "tainted", and the company can be required to reclassify all of its HTM investments as AFS investments.

In other words, United would record this sale just like any other asset sale, with a gain or loss determined by comparing the cash received with the carrying value (in this case, the amortized cost) of the asset given up.

We will revisit our discussion of investments in debt securities to be "held to maturity" in Chapter 14, "Bonds and Long-Term Notes." This way we can more readily see that accounting by the company that issues bonds and by the company that invests in those bonds is opposite but parallel; that is, each side of the transaction is the mirror image of the other.

Obviously, not all investments are intended to be held to maturity. When an investment is acquired to be held for an *unspecified period of time,* we classify the investment as either (a) "trading securities" or (b) "securities available-for-sale." These include investments in *debt* securities that are not classified as held-to-maturity and *equity* securities that have *readily determinable fair values.* You'll notice that, unlike held-to-maturity securities, we report investments in the other two categories at their fair values.

Trading Securities

Some companies—primarily financial institutions—actively and frequently buy and sell securities, expecting to earn profits on short-term differences in price. Investments in debt or equity securities acquired principally for the purpose of selling them in the near term are classified as trading securities. The holding period for trading securities generally is measured in hours and days rather than months or years. These investments typically are reported among the investor's current assets. Keep in mind as you study this section that relatively few investments are classified this way, because usually only banks and other financial operations invest in securities in the manner and for the purpose necessary to be categorized as trading securities. However, the FASB's recent decision to allow the fair value option could increase the prevalence of this classification.

Just like any investment, regardless of how we classify it, trading securities are initially recorded at cost—that is, the total amount paid for the securities including any brokerage fees. But then, when a balance sheet is prepared, this type of investment is written up or down to its fair value, or "marked to market."

Be sure to notice that fair value accounting is a departure from historical costs, which is the way most assets are reported in balance sheets. Why the difference? For these investments, fair value information is more relevant than for other assets intended primarily to be used in company operations, like buildings, land and equipment, or for investments to be *held to maturity.*[5] For instance, consider an investment in debt. As interest rates rise or fall, the fair value of the investment will decrease or increase. Movements in fair values are less relevant if the investment is to be held to maturity; the investor receives the same contracted interest payments and principal at maturity, regardless of changes in fair value. This is similar to changes in the fair values of operational assets, typically intended to be held throughout their productive lives.

On the other hand, if the debt investment is held for active trading changes in market values, and thus market returns, provide an indication of management's success in deciding when to acquire the investment, when to sell it, whether to invest in fixed-rate or variable-rate securities, and whether to invest in long-term or short-term securities. For that reason, it makes sense to report unrealized holding gains and losses on trading securities in net income during a period that fair values change, even though those gains and losses haven't yet been realized through the sale of the securities.

To see how we account for trading securities, let's modify the example we used for HTM securities. We'll assume that those debt investments are held in an active trading portfolio, with United intending to profit from short-term changes in price. In addition, let's add a couple of equity (stock) investments to highlight that, while the HTM approach applies only to debt securities, the TS approach applies to both debt and equity securities. The relevant facts are included in Illustration 12–2. Assuming all investments are classified as trading securities, the accounting would be as follows.

● **LO2**

Trading securities are actively managed in a trading account for the purpose of profiting from short-term price changes.

FINANCIAL Reporting Case

Q1, p. 587

Unrealized holding gains and losses for trading securities are included in net income in the period in which fair value changes.

FINANCIAL Reporting Case

Q2, p. 587

---

[5]Investments to be held to maturity, of course, include only debt securities.

ILLUSTRATION 12–2 Example to Illustrate Accounting for Trading Securities and Securities Available-for-Sale	United Intergroup, Inc., buys and sells both debt and equity securities of other companies as investments. United's fiscal year-end is December 31. The following events during 2009 and 2010 pertain to the investment portfolio.

Purchase Investments July 1, 2009	Purchased Masterwear Industries' 12%, 3-year bonds for $666,633 to yield an effective interest rate of 14%. Purchased $1,500,000 of Arjent, Inc., common stock. Purchased $1,000,000 of Bendac common stock.
Receive Investment Revenue December 31, 2009	Received a semi-annual cash interest payment of $42,000 from Masterwear. Received a cash dividend of $75,000 from Arjent. (Bendac does not pay dividends)
Adjust Investments to Fair Value December 31, 2009	Valued the Masterwear bonds at $714,943. Valued the Arjent stock at $1,450,000. Valued the Bendac stock at $990,000.
Sell Investments January 15, 2010	Sold the Masterwear bonds for $725,000. Sold the Arjent stock for $1,446,000.
Adjust Remaining Investments to Fair Value December 31, 2010	Valued the Bendac stock at $985,000.

PURCHASE INVESTMENTS. The journal entry to record the purchase of the bond investment is the same as it is for HTM securities. The journal entries to record the equity investments are even simpler, just exchanging one asset (cash) for another (investment):

All investment securities are recorded initially at cost.

July 1, 2009		
Investment in Masterwear bonds...	700,000	
Discount on bond investment..		33,367
Cash..		666,633
Investment in Arjent stock	1,500,000	
Cash..		1,500,000
Investment in Bendac stock	1,000,000	
Cash..		1,000,000

RECOGNIZE INVESTMENT REVENUE. The journal entry to record the receipt of bond interest is the same as it is for HTM securities, with the carrying value of the investment increasing due to amortization of $4,664 of discount. The journal entry to record the receipt of dividends related to the Arjent equity investment is straightforward. There is no entry for the Bendac equity investment, because Bendac doesn't pay dividends.

Dividend and interest income is included in net income.

December 31, 2009		
Cash (6% × $700,000)	42,000	
Discount on bond investment..	4,664	
Investment revenue (interest: 7% × $666,633)		46,664
Cash...	75,000	
Investment revenue (dividends received)		75,000

ADJUST TRADING SECURITY INVESTMENTS TO FAIR VALUE (2009). Unlike HTM securities, the carrying value of trading securities in the balance sheet is adjusted to fair value at the end of every reporting period. Rather than increasing or decreasing the investment account itself, we use a valuation allowance, *fair value adjustment,* to increase or decrease the carrying value of the investment. At the same time, we record an unrealized holding gain or loss that is included in net income in the period in which fair value changes (the gain or loss is *unrealized* because the securities haven't actually been sold). The next table summarizes the relevant facts for United's investments.

Trading securities are adjusted to their fair value at each reporting date.

December 31, 2009

Security	Amortized Cost	Fair Value	Fair Value Adjustment
Masterwear	$ 671,297	$ 714,943	$ 43,646
Arjent	1,500,000	1,450,000	(50,000)
Bendac	1,000,000	990,000	(10,000)
Total	$3,171,297	$3,154,943	$(16,354)
	Existing balance in fair value adjustment:		–0–
	Increase (decrease) needed in fair value adjustment:		($16,354)

United has an unrealized loss of $16,354. Note that, to determine the amount of unrealized holding gain or loss on the Masterwear bonds, United first identifies the bonds' *amortized cost* and then determines the amount necessary to adjust them to fair value:

Face amount of the bond	$700,000
Less: Discount on bond investment	
$33,367 initial discount	
(4,664) accumulated amortization	
$28,703 discount at 12/31/09	(28,703)
Amortized cost of the bonds	671,297
+/– Fair value adjustment (plug)	+43,646
Fair value of the bond at 12/31/09	$714,943

There is no discount to amortize for the equity investments, so for the Arjent and Bendac investments, their amortized cost is simply their initial cost. The journal entry to record the unrealized loss in United's fair value adjustment is

December 31, 2009[6]

Net unrealized holding gains and losses—I/S[7]	16,354	
Fair value adjustment.....		16,354

SELL TRADING SECURITY INVESTMENTS.

To record the gain or loss realized on the sale of the Masterwear and Arjent investments, United records the receipt of cash ($725,000 for Masterwear and $1,446,000 for Arjent), removes all balance sheet accounts that are directly associated with the investments, and plugs to determine realized gain or loss.[8]

January 15, 2010

Cash (amount received)	725,000	
Discount on bond investment (account balance)	28,703	
Investment in Masterwear bonds (account balance)		700,000
Gain on sale of investments (to balance)		53,703
Cash (amount received)	1,446,000	
Loss on sale of investments (to balance)	54,000	
Investment in Arjent stock (account balance)		1,500,000

Realized gain or loss for the difference between carrying value and the cash received from selling a trading security is included in net income.

For the Masterwear bonds, this journal entry is identical to what United used when recording the sale of held-to-maturity investments. However, United isn't done yet. Now that those investments are sold, United needs to remove their fair value adjustment from the balance sheet. Also, because United has recognized in this period's net income the entire gain or loss *realized* on sale of the investments, it must back out of this period's net income

---

[6]Sometimes companies don't bother with a separate fair value adjustment account and simply adjust the investment account to fair value. Also, sometimes companies set up separate fair value adjustment accounts for each investment.

[7]We title this account "Net unrealized holding gains and losses—I/S" to highlight that, for trading securities, unrealized holding gains and losses are included in the income statement (I/S) in the period in which they occur.

[8]For purposes of this example, we ignore any unpaid interest associated with the bonds. In practice, that amount would be added to the sales price of the bonds and included in investment revenue.

any *unrealized* gains and losses that were included in net income in prior periods. That way, this period's net income includes only the fair value changes arising since the last period, and United avoids double counting gains and losses (once when unrealized, and again when realized). United can accomplish all of this when it adjusts its investment portfolio to fair value at the end of the reporting period.

ADJUST TRADING SECURITY INVESTMENTS TO FAIR VALUE (2010). The following table summarizes the situation at the end of 2010:

December 31, 2010

Security	Amortized Cost	Fair Value	Fair Value Adjustment
Masterwear	(sold)	–0–	–0–
Arjent	(sold)	–0–	–0–
Bendac	$1,000,000	$985,000	($15,000)
Total	$1,000,000	$985,000	($15,000)
	Existing balance in fair value adjustment:		($16,354)
	Increase (decrease) needed in fair value adjustment:		$ 1,354

The journal entry necessary to show the appropriate balance in the fair value adjustment at the end of 2010 is

December 31, 2010

Fair value adjustment	1,354	
Net unrealized holding gains and losses—I/S		1,354

This journal entry serves two purposes: (a) accounts for changes in the fair value of investments that have not been sold (in this case, Bendac), and (b) removes from the fair value adjustment and net income any unrealized holding gains or losses that were recognized in prior periods and that are associated with investments that now have been sold (in this case, Masterwear and Arjent). We discuss those purposes in more detail when we show how these investments would be accounted for as available-for-sale securities later in this chapter.

FINANCIAL STATEMENT PRESENTATION. We present trading securities in the financial statements as follows:

- **Income Statement and Comprehensive Income Statement:** For trading securities, fair value changes are included on the income statement in the periods in which they occur, regardless of whether they are realized or unrealized. Investments in trading securities do not affect other comprehensive income.
- **Balance Sheet:** Investments in trading securities are reported at fair value, typically as current assets, and do not affect accumulated other comprehensive income in shareholders' equity.
- **Cash Flow Statement:** Cash flows from buying and selling trading securities typically are classified as operating activities, because the financial institutions that routinely hold trading securities consider them as part of their normal operations.

United's 2009 and 2010 financial statements will include the amounts shown in Illustration 12–3.

● LO3

Investments in available-for-sale securities are reported at their fair values.

Securities Available-for-Sale

When you or I buy stock in a corporation, say **Coca-Cola**, we hope the market value will rise before we sell it. We also might look forward to the cash dividends Coca-Cola pays its

> The Board concluded that fair value information is more relevant than amortized cost information, in part because it reflects the effects of a management decision to buy a financial asset at a specific time and then continue to hold it for an unspecified period of time.[9]

[9]"Accounting for Certain Investments in Debt and Equity Securities," *Statement of Financial Accounting Standards No. 115* (Norwalk, Conn.: FASB, 1993), par. 51.

Income Statement	2009	2010
Revenues	$ ◆	$ ◆
Expenses	◆	◆
Other income (expense):		
Interest and dividend income	121,664[a]	–0–
Realized and unrealized gains and losses on investments	(16,354)[b]	$1,057[c]
Tax expense	◆	◆
Net income	◆	◆
Balance Sheet		
Assets:		
Trading securities	3,154,943	985,000
Statement of Cash Flows (direct method)		
Operating Activities:		
Cash from investment revenue	117,000	–0–
Purchase of trading securities	(3,166,633)	–0–
Sale of trading securities	–0–	2,171,000

ILLUSTRATION 12–3

Reporting Trading Securities

For trading securities, fair value changes affect net income in the period in which they occur.

Trading securities are reported at fair value in the balance sheet.

Cash flows from buying and selling trading securities are classified as operating activities

[a]$121,664 is the sum of $46,664 interest revenue from Masterwear and $75,000 dividends from Arjent.
[b]$16,354 is the net unrealized loss from the 2009 fair value adjustment.
[c]$1,057 is the $1,354 net unrealized gain from the 2010 fair value adjustment minus the $297 loss realized on sale of investments during 2010 (the $297 net realized loss results from the $54,000 loss realized on sale of the Arjent stock and the $53,703 gain realized on sale of the Masterwear bonds).

shareholders every three months. We may even have fairly defined criteria for when we plan to sell the stock, or we may intend to wait and see what happens to market prices. In either case, we aren't planning to trade the investment actively, but our investment is available to sell given the right combination of market factors and our own cash situation. So it often is, too, with companies who invest in the securities of other corporations or governmental entities. When a company acquires an investment, not for an active trading account (as a financial institution might) or to be held to maturity (which of course couldn't be stock because it has no maturity date), the company classifies its investment as securities available-for-sale (AFS). Like trading securities, we report investments in AFS securities in the balance sheet at fair value. Unlike trading securities, though, unrealized holding gains and losses on AFS securities are *not* included in net income. Instead, they are reported in the statement of comprehensive income as other comprehensive income (OCI).

Unrealized holding gains and losses on available-for-sale securities affect comprehensive income, but not net income.

COMPREHENSIVE INCOME. You may recall from Chapter 4 that comprehensive income is a more all-encompassing view of changes in shareholders' equity than net income, including not only net income but also all other changes in equity that do not arise from transactions with owners.[10] Comprehensive income therefore includes net income and *other comprehensive income (OCI)*. Both net income and OCI accumulate in shareholders' equity in the balance sheet, but in different accounts. While net income accumulates in retained earnings, OCI accumulates in *accumulated other comprehensive income (AOCI)*.

Comprehensive income includes not only net income, but also other changes in equity that don't arise from transactions with owners.

RATIONALE FOR AFS TREATMENT OF UNREALIZED HOLDING GAINS AND LOSSES. Why use an approach for accounting for AFS securities that differs from that used for trading securities? The big concern is that including in net income unrealized holding gains and losses on AFS investments might make income appear more volatile than it really is. For example, many companies purchase AFS investments for the purpose of having the changes in fair value of those investments offset changes in the fair value of liabilities. This *hedging* insulates the company from risk and ensures that earnings are stable. However, if fair value changes for investments were to be recognized in income (as is the case with trading securities), but the offsetting fair value changes for liabilities were not recognized in income as well, we could end up with income appearing very volatile when in fact the underlying assets and liabilities are hedged effectively.[11]

FINANCIAL Reporting Case

Q3, p. 587

---

[10]Transactions with owners primarily include dividends and the sale or purchase of shares of the company's stock.
[11]The option to report in earnings changes in the fair value of liabilities was not permitted at the time the FASB wrote *SFAS No. 115* to specify this accounting method. As we will see in Chapter 14, that option now is allowed.

More generally, because AFS securities are likely to be held for multiple reporting periods, one could argue that there is sufficient time for unrealized holding gains in some periods to balance out with unrealized holding losses in other periods, so including unrealized holding gains and losses in income would confuse investors by making income appear more volatile than it really is over the long run. Of course, one could counter-argue that these unrealized holding gains and losses still are relevant, given that each period an investor has discretion over whether or not to continue holding the security or sell that security to realize a gain or loss.

To consider accounting for AFS investments, refer to the facts shown in Illustration 12–2. Let's assume now that United classifies its investments as AFS rather than trading securities.

PURCHASE INVESTMENTS. The journal entries to record the purchase of the investments are the same for AFS securities as they are for trading securities:

All investment securities are initially recorded at cost.

July 1, 2009

Investment in Masterwear bonds	700,000	
Discount on bond investment		33,367
Cash		666,633
Investment in Arjent stock	1,500,000	
Cash		1,500,000
Investment in Bendac stock	1,000,000	
Cash		1,000,000

RECOGNIZE INVESTMENT REVENUE. The journal entries to record the receipt of investment revenue also are the same for AFS securities as they are for trading securities.

Interest income and dividends on AFS investments are included in net income.

December 31, 2009

Cash (6% × $700,000)	42,000	
Discount on bond investment (difference)	4,664	
Investment revenue (interest: 7% × $666,633)		46,664
Cash	75,000	
Investment revenue (dividends)		75,000

ADJUST AFS INVESTMENTS TO FAIR VALUE (2009). Let's first recall the facts:

December 31, 2009

Security	Amortized Cost	Fair Value	Fair Value Adjustment
Masterwear	$ 671,297	$ 714,943	$ 43,646
Arjent	1,500,000	1,450,000	(50,000)
Bendac	1,000,000	990,000	(10,000)
Total	$3,171,297	$3,154,943	$(16,354)
		Existing balance in fair value adjustment:	–0–
		Increase (decrease) needed in fair value adjustment:	($ 16,354)

AFS securities are adjusted to their fair value at each reporting date.

For AFS securities, unrealized holding gains and losses from fair value changes are not included in net income, but instead are recorded as OCI.

Like trading securities, AFS securities are adjusted to fair value at the end of each reporting period, which produces an unrealized holding gain or loss due to holding the securities while their fair values change. The journal entry to record United's unrealized holding loss is:

December 31, 2009

Net unrealized holding gains and losses—OCI[12]	16,354	
Fair value adjustment		16,354

---

[12]We title this account "Net unrealized holding gains and losses—OCI" to highlight that, for available-for-sale securities, unrealized holding gains and losses are included in other comprehensive income (OCI) in the period in which they occur.

Notice that the amount of unrealized holding loss is the same as with trading securities. What differs is that the net unrealized holding loss of $16,354 is included in net income for trading securities and in OCI for AFS securities.[13] At the end of the reporting period the net unrealized holding loss ends up being closed to a shareholders' equity account for both approaches. What differs is that it gets closed to retained earnings for trading securities and to AOCI for AFS securities.

ADDITIONAL CONSIDERATION

Don't Shoot the Messenger
Using fair values that are hard to estimate is controversial. For example, problems in the credit markets during 2007 and 2008 made it very difficult to sell some types of debt. As a result, companies like AIG who held these investments had to recognize huge unrealized losses in earnings, and some blamed their losses on SFAS No. 157 for requiring estimates of fair value that were driven by depressed current market prices. Others countered that these companies were using SFAS No. 157 as a "scapegoat" for their bad investment decisions. "Fair value accounting. . . does not create losses but rather reflects a firm's present condition," says Georgene Palacky, director of the CFA's financial reporting group."[14]

SELL AFS INVESTMENTS. AFS investments require the same journal entry on the date of sale as is made to record the sale of trading securities. United simply records the receipt of cash, removes from the balance sheet any accounts that are directly associated with the investment, and plugs to determine realized gain or loss.

January 15, 2010

Cash (amount received)	725,000	
Discount on bond investment (account balance)	28,703	
Investment in Masterwear bonds (account balance)		700,000
Gain on sale of investments (to balance)		53,703
Cash (amount received)	1,446,000	
Loss on sale of investments (to balance)	54,000	
Investment in Arjent stock (account balance)		1,500,000

Realized gain or loss for the difference between carrying value and the cash received from selling an AFS security is included in net income.

United also needs to adjust the fair value adjustment account and AOCI to remove any unrealized gains or losses previously recorded that relate to the sold investments. That is typically done at the end of the accounting period as part of the journal entry that adjusts the AFS investment portfolio to fair value, as we see below.

When AFS securities are sold, *unrealized* gains or losses that were recorded previously are removed from the fair value adjustment and OCI.

ADJUST AFS INVESTMENTS TO FAIR VALUE (2010). The following table summarizes the situation at the end of 2010:

December 31, 2010

Security	Amortized Cost	Fair Value	Unrealized Gain (loss)
Masterwear	(sold)	–0–	–0–
Arjent	(sold)	–0–	–0–
Bendac	1,000,000	985,000	($15,000)
Total	1,000,000	985,000	($15,000)
	Existing balance in fair value adjustment:		($16,354)
	Increase (decrease) needed in fair value adjustment:		$ 1,354

[13]As with trading securities, we could have not used a separate valuation allowance and simply adjusted the AFS investment account itself to fair value, and we also could set up separate valuation allowances and record separate journal entries for each AFS investment.
[14]Johnson, Sarah, "The Fair Value Blame Game", CFO.com, 3/19/2008.

This analysis indicates that United needs to increase the fair value adjustment by $1,354 and record an unrealized gain of the same amount in OCI.

December 31, 2010

Fair value adjustment	1,354	
Net unrealized holding gains and losses—OCI		1,354

This journal entry serves two purposes: it (a) accounts for new changes during 2010 in the fair value of investments that haven't been sold and (b) removes amounts associated with investments that were sold during 2010.

($5,000)	to add 2010 unrealized loss associated with investments not sold
6,354	to remove 2009 net unrealized loss that's no longer unrealized
$1,354	2010 adjustment to OCI

Let's consider the two purposes separately.

New changes in the fair value of investments held. First, the journal entry records in OCI any new unrealized gains or losses associated with investments that have not been sold. For United, that's the Bendac stock.

$1,000,000	initial cost of Bendac stock
(985,000)	fair value at the end of 2010
$ 15,000	total unrealized loss
(10,000)	balance at end of 2009
$ 5,000	new unrealized loss in 2010

If the 2010 journal entry had focused only on this first purpose, the journal entry would have been:

Net unrealized holding gains and losses-OCI	*5,000*	
Fair value adjustment		*5,000*

Reclassification adjustment. Second, the journal entry removes from OCI any amounts associated with *sold* investments. What amounts must United consider? Last year, in 2009, United recorded a net unrealized loss of $6,354 on the Arjent and Masterwear investments as part of the $16,354 fair value adjustment made at the end of that year.

$50,000	unrealized loss for the Arjent stock
43,646	unrealized gain for the Masterwear bonds
$ 6,354	net unrealized loss in 2009

If the *2009* fair value adjustment had only included the net unrealized loss on the Arjent and Masterwear investments, it would have been:

Net unrealized holding gains and losses—OCI	6,354	
Fair value adjustment		6,354

Because those investments have now been sold, United must reverse this entry in 2010 to remove their effects from OCI and the fair value adjustment. If the 2010 journal entry had focused only on this second purpose, it would have been:

Fair value adjustment	*6,354*	
Net unrealized holding gains and losses—OCI		*6,354*

See how the two purposes combine to create the single journal entry we use to increase the fair value adjustment by $1,354 and recognize a net unrealized holding gain of that amount in OCI?

Fair value adjustment ($6,354 – 5,000)	1,354	
Net unrealized holding gains and losses—OCI		1,354

For AFS securities, *unrealized* gains and losses affect OCI and accumulate in AOCI until such time as the investment is sold.

Now, why is this often referred to as a "reclassification adjustment"? Remember that United included a $6,354 unrealized loss in 2009 OCI (and therefore in AOCI). Then, in 2010, it backed out that amount from OCI (and AOCI) as part of the fair value adjustment entry, and included the realized gain or loss in net income (and therefore retained earnings). From the perspective of shareholders' equity, the amount was basically reclassified from AOCI to retained earnings in the period of sale.[15]

Note that we don't separately *record* the reclassification. That happens automatically as part of the fair value adjustment entry. What we do is *report* the reclassification in the statement of comprehensive income, as you will see in the next section.

FINANCIAL STATEMENT PRESENTATION.   We present AFS securities in the financial statements as follows:

- **Income Statement and Comprehensive Income Statement:** *Realized* gains and losses are shown in net income in the period in which securities are sold. *Unrealized* gains and losses are shown in OCI in the periods in which changes in fair value occur, and reclassified out of OCI in the periods in which securities are sold.
- **Balance Sheet:** Investments in AFS securities are reported at fair value. *Unrealized* gains and losses affect AOCI in shareholders' equity, and are reclassified out of AOCI in the periods in which securities are sold.
- **Cash Flow Statement:** Cash flows from buying and selling AFS securities typically are classified as investing activities.

Individual securities available for sale are classified as either current or noncurrent assets, depending on how long they're likely to be held. An example from the 2007 annual report of **Cisco Systems** is shown in Graphic 12–5.

Note 2: Summary of Significant Accounting Policies (in part)

The Company's investments comprise U.S. government notes and bonds; corporate notes, bonds, and asset-backed securities; municipal notes and bonds; and publicly traded equity securities. At July 28, 2007 and July 29, 2006, the Company's investments were classified as available-for-sale. These investments are recorded in the Consolidated Balance Sheets at fair value. Unrealized gains and losses on these investments, to the extent the investments are unhedged, are included as a separate component of accumulated other comprehensive income, net of tax.

Note 6: Investments (in part)

The following tables summarize the Company's investments (in millions):

July 28, 2007	Amortized Cost	Gross Unrealized Gains	Gross Unrealized Losses	Fair Value
Fixed Income Securities				
U.S. government notes and bonds	$ 6,919	$ 29	$ (8)	$ 6,940
Corporate notes, bonds, and asset-backed securities	8,765	7	(57)	8,715
Municipal notes and bonds	1,643	—	(1)	1,642
Total fixed income securities	17,327	36	(66)	17,297
Publicly traded equity securities	901	354	(14)	1,241
Total	$18,228	$390	$(80)	$18,538

[15]Reclassification also avoids double accounting with respect to comprehensive income and equity. If United didn't back out the 2009 unrealized loss from 2010 OCI, it would end up having included it in comprehensive income twice, once in OCI (2009) and once in net income (2010), thereby overstating total shareholders' equity.

United's 2009 and 2010 financial statements will include the amounts shown in Illustration 12–4.

ILLUSTRATION 12–4		**2009**	**2010**
Reporting Available-for-Sale Securities	**Income Statement**		
	Revenues	$ ♦	$ ♦
Only *realized* gains and losses are included in net income.	Expenses	♦	♦
	Other income (expense):		
	Interest and dividend income	121,664	–0–
	Realized net loss on sale of investments	–0–	(297)
Other comprehensive income includes *unrealized* holding gains and losses *that occur during the reporting period.*	Tax Expense	♦	♦
	Net income	♦	♦
	Other comprehensive income (loss) items (OCI):[16]		
	Unrealized holding gains (losses) on investments	(16,354)	(5,000)
	Reclassification adjustment for net gains and losses		
AFS securities are reported at fair value.	included in net income	–0–	6,354
	Total	(16,354)	1,354
	Comprehensive income	♦	♦
AOCI (in shareholders' equity) includes net unrealized holding gains or losses *accumulated over the current and prior periods.*	**Balance Sheet**		
	Assets:		
	Available-for-sale securities	3,154,943	985,000
	Stockholders' equity:		
	Accumulated other comprehensive income (AOCI)	(16,354)	(15,000)
	Statement of Cash Flows (direct method)		
Cash flows from buying and selling AFS securities are classified as investing activities.	Operating Activities:		
	Cash from investment revenue	117,000	–0–
	Investing Activities:		
	Purchase of available-for-sale securities	(3,166,633)	–0–
	Sale of available-for-sale securities	–0–	2,171,000

Impairment of Investments

An "other-than-temporary" impairment loss is recognized in net income even though the security hasn't been sold.

Occasionally, the fair value of a security will decline for a specific reason that's judged to be "other than temporary." In that case, when the investment is written down to its fair value, the amount of the write-down should be treated as though it were a realized loss (meaning it's included in income for the period), regardless of whether the investment is classified as an HTM, TS, or AFS investment. For example, during late 2007 and into 2008, many companies suffered large losses on their investments in residential mortgages and mortgage-backed securities due to problems in the credit markets. Some of these companies were banks that classified their investments as trading securities, so they recognized unrealized losses in income as part of their normal accounting for trading securities. However, other companies classified these investments as AFS or HTM securities and had to recognize "other-than-temporary" impairments in income, even though they believed that the values of their investments would eventually recover. As an example, see Graphic 12-6:

GRAPHIC 12–6

Disclosure of Other-than-Temporary Impairements— American Internaitonal Group, Inc.

Real World Financials

> **Other-Than-Temporary Impairments**
>
> . . . In light of the recent significant disruption in the U.S. residential mortgage and credit markets, **AIG** has recognized an other-than-temporary impairment charge of $2.2 billion. . . Notwithstanding AIG's intent and ability to hold such securities indefinitely, and despite structures which indicate that a substantial amount of the securities should continue to perform in accordance with original terms, AIG concluded that it could not reasonably assert that the recovery period would be temporary.

After the other-than-temporary impairment is recorded, the normal treatment of unrealized gains or losses is resumed; that is, changes in fair value are reported in OCI for AFS investments and not recognized for HTM investments.

---

[16]As we discuss in more detail in Chapter 18, the statement of comprehensive income can be reported as a continuation of the income statement as shown here, or alternatively either in a separate statement or in the statement of shareholders' equity.

ADDITIONAL CONSIDERATION

What if the Fair Value Isn't "Readily Determinable?"

According to *SFAS No. 115,* all debt securities are viewed as having "readily determinable" fair values, but the fair value of an equity security is considered readily determinable only if its selling price is currently available on a securities exchange.[17] If the fair value of an equity security is *not* readily determinable, we use the *cost method* (except when the equity method described in Part B of this chapter is appropriate). The cost method is so named because the investment is carried in the balance sheet at cost, and temporary unrealized holding gains and losses are not recognized in either net income or other comprehensive income. Any dividends received are reported as investment revenue, and any gain or loss realized upon selling the investment is included in income. However, fair values still matter under the cost method, because the investment still is subject to testing for other-than-temporary impairments. Therefore, even if fair value isn't viewed as readily determinable, companies have to determine it if there are indications that a cost-method investment has been impaired.

Comparison of HTM, TS, and AFS Approaches

Illustration 12–5 compares accounting for the Masterwear bonds under the three different approaches used when an investor lacks significant influence.

ILLUSTRATION 12–5 Comparison of HTM, TS, and AFS Approaches

	Held-to-Maturity (HTM)	**Trading (TS)**	**Available-for-Sale (AFS)**
Purchase bonds at a discount	Investments 700,000 　Discount　　33,367 　Cash　　666,633	Same as HTM	Same as HTM
Receive investment revenue	Cash　　42,000 Discount　　4,664 　Invest. income　46,664	Same as HTM	Same as HTM
Adjust to fair value	No entry (unless impaired)	FV adjustment　　43,646 　Net unrealized 　　gain/loss—I/S　　43,646	FV adjustment　43,646 　Net unrealized 　　gain/loss—OCI　　43,646
Sell bonds for a realized gain	Discount　　28,703 Cash　　725,000 　Investments　700,000 　Gain　　53,703	Recognize gain or loss: 　　Same as HTM Reverse out previously recorded unrealized gain or loss that's no longer unrealized (automatically part of next adjustment to fair value): Net unrealized 　gain/loss—I/S　　43,646 　FV adjustment　　43,646	Recognize gain or loss: 　　Same as HTM Reverse out previously recorded unrealized gain or loss that's no longer unrealized (automatically part of next adjustment to fair value): Net unrealized 　gain/loss—OCI　43,646* 　FV adjustment　　43,646

*Reported as a reclassification adjustment in the statement of comprehensive income.

This side-by-side comparison highlights several aspects of these accounting approaches:

- To record the purchase of an investment and the receipt of investment revenue, we use identical entries in all three approaches.
- To record changes in fair value, the entries we use for TS and AFS securities have the same effect on the investment (via the fair value adjustment valuation allowance) and the same eventual effect on shareholders' equity. What differs is whether the unrealized gain or loss is recognized in the income statement and then in retained earnings (TS) or recognized in OCI and then in AOCI (AFS).
- To record the sale of the security, we use identical entries in all three approaches. For TS and AFS securities, the fair value adjustment and unrealized holding gains and

---

[17]"Accounting for Certain Investments in Debt and Equity Securities (as amended)," *Statement of Financial Accounting standards No. 115* (Netwalk, Conn.: FASB 2008), par. 3a.

losses associated with sold securities are dealt with automatically as part of the next adjustment to fair value.
- Regardless of approach, the cash flows are the same, and the same total amount of gain or loss is recognized in the income statement (TS: $43,646 in 2009 + [$53,703 − $43,646] in 2010 = $53,703 total; AFS and HTM: $53,703 in 2010). Thus, the question is not how much total net income is recognized, but *when* that net income is recognized.

ADDITIONAL CONSIDERATION

Available-for-Sale Investments and Income Taxes
When comparing accounting for TS and AFS securities, we saw that total shareholders' equity ends up being the same amount, regardless of whether unrealized gains and losses are included in net income and closed to retained earnings in shareholders' equity (for TS) or included only in OCI and shown in AOCI in shareholders' equity (for AFS securities). But what about taxes? Tax expense affects net income, so retained earnings includes after-tax amounts. For AOCI to be equivalent to retained earnings, it also should include only after-tax amounts. Therefore, adjustments must be made to OCI and AOCI that include tax effects. Typically these adjustments also give rise to deferred tax assets and liabilities, as unrealized holding gains and losses rarely affect the current period's taxes payable.

Transfers between Reporting Categories

> A transfer of a security between reporting categories is accounted for at fair value and in accordance with *the new reporting classification.*

At acquisition, an investor assigns debt and equity securities to one of the three reporting classifications—held-to-maturity, available-for-sale, or trading. At each reporting date, the appropriateness of the classification is reassessed. For instance, if the investor no longer has the ability to hold certain securities to maturity and will now hold them for resale, those securities would be reclassified from HTM to AFS. When a security is reclassified between two reporting categories, the security is transferred at its fair value on the date of transfer. Any unrealized holding gain or loss at reclassification should be accounted for *in a manner consistent with the classification into which the security is being transferred.* A summary is provided in Graphic 12–7.

GRAPHIC 12–7
Transfer between Investment Categories

Transfer from:	To:	Unrealized Gain or Loss from Transfer at Fair Market Value
Either of the other	Trading	Include in current net income
Trading	Either of the other	There is none (already recognized in net income)
Held-to-maturity	Available-for-sale	Report as a separate component of shareholders' equity (in Other Comprehensive Income)
Available-for-sale	Held-to-maturity	Don't write off any existing unrealized holding gain or loss, but amortize it to net income over the remaining life of the security (fair value amount becomes the security's amortized cost basis).

Reclassifications are quite unusual, so when they occur, disclosure notes should describe the circumstances that resulted in the transfers. Other footnote disclosures are described in a later section.

Fair Value Option

> ● LO7
>
> TS already are accounted for at fair value, so there is no need to choose the fair value option for them.

You may recall from Chapter 1 that the FASB recently issued *SFAS No. 159,* which permits companies to elect to account for most financial assets and liabilities at fair value, with unrealized gains and losses recognized in net income in the period in which they occur. That accounting approach should sound familiar—it's the same approach we use to account for trading securities.

Here's how the fair value option works for these investments. When a security that qualifies for HTM or AFS treatment is purchased, the company makes an irrevocable decision about

INTERNATIONAL FINANCIAL REPORTING STANDARDS

Fair Value Option. International accounting standards are more restrictive than U.S. standards for determining when firms are allowed to elect the fair value option. Under *IFRS No. 39*, companies can elect the fair value option only in specific circumstances. For example, a firm could elect the fair value option for an asset or liability in order to avoid the accounting mismatch that occurs when some parts of a fair value risk-hedging arrangement are accounted for at fair value and others are not. Or, a firm could elect the fair value option for a group of financial assets or liabilities that are managed on a fair value basis, as documented by a particular risk-management or investment strategy. Although *SFAS No. 159* indicates that the intent of the fair value option is to address these sorts of circumstances, it does not require that those circumstances exist.

whether to elect the fair value option. The company can elect the fair value option for some securities and not for identical others—it's entirely up to the company, but the company has to explain in the notes why they made a partial election. If the fair value option is elected for a security that would normally be accounted for as HTM or AFS, the company just classifies that security as a trading security, and that's how it appears in the financial statements.[18] Note, though, that electing the fair value option is irrevocable. If a company elects the fair value option and later believes that the fair value of an investment will likely decline, it can't change the election and discontinue use of fair value accounting.

> Choosing the fair value option for HTM and AFS investments just means reclassifying those investments as TS.

Why allow the fair value option? Recall that a primary reason for creating the AFS approach was to allow companies to avoid excess earnings volatility that would result from reporting in earnings the fair value changes of only part of a hedging arrangement. As described in Appendix A of the text, other accounting rules apply to hedging arrangements that involve derivatives, but those rules are very complex and don't cover all forms of hedging arrangements. The fair value option simplifies this process by allowing companies to choose whether to use fair value for most types of financial assets and liabilities. Thus, when a company enters into a hedging arrangement, it just has to make sure to elect the fair value option for each asset and liability in the hedging arrangement, and fair value changes of those assets and liabilities will be included in earnings.

CONCEPT REVIEW **EXERCISE**

Diversified Services, Inc., offers a variety of business services, including financial services through its escrow division. Diversified entered into the following investment activities during the last month of 2009 and the first week of 2010. Diversified's fiscal year ends on December 31. The only securities held by Diversified at December 1 were 12 million common shares of Shelby Laminations, Inc., purchased in November for $48 million and classified as available-for-sale.

> VARIOUS INVESTMENT SECURITIES

2009

Dec. 1	Purchased $30 million of 12% bonds of Vince-Gill Amusement Corporation and $24 million of 10% bonds of Eastern Waste Disposal Corporation, both at face value and both to be held until they mature. Interest on each bond issue is payable semiannually on November 30 and May 31.
9	Sold one-half of the Shelby Laminations common shares for $25 million.
29	Received cash dividends of $1.5 million from the Shelby Laminations common shares.
30	Purchased U.S. Treasury bonds for $5.8 million as trading securities hoping to earn profits on short-term differences in prices.
31	Recorded the necessary adjusting entry(s) relating to the investments.

[18]"The Fair Value Option for Financial Assets and Financial Liabilities," *Statement of Financial Accounting Standards No. 159* (Norwalk, Conn.: FASB, 2007), par. 29.

The year-end market price of the Shelby Laminations common stock was $4.25 per share. The fair values of the bond investments were $32 million for Vince-Gill Amusement Corporation and $20 million for Eastern Waste Disposal Corporation. A sharp rise in short-term interest rates on the last day of the year caused the fair value of the Treasury bonds to fall to $5.7 million.

2010

Jan. 7   Sold the remaining Shelby Laminations common shares for $26 million.

Required:

Prepare the appropriate journal entry for each transaction or event and show the amounts that would be reported in the company's 2009 income statement relative to these investments. Determine the effects of the Shelby Laminations investment on net income, other comprehensive income, and comprehensive income for 2009, 2010, and combined over both years.

SOLUTION   **2009**

Dec. 1   Purchased $30 million of 12% bonds of Vince-Gill Amusement Corporation and $24 million of 10% bonds of Eastern Waste Disposal Corporation, both at face value and both to be held until they mature. Interest on each bond issue is payable semiannually on November 30 and May 31.

	($ in millions)	
Investment in Vince-Gill Amusement bonds	30	
Investment in Eastern Waste Disposal bonds	24	
Cash		54

Dec. 9   Sold one-half of the Shelby Laminations common shares for $25 million.

Sale of one-half of the Shelby Laminations shares results in a $1 million gain ($25 million sales price − [$48 million cost ÷ 2]).

	($ in millions)	
Cash (selling price)	25	
Investment in Shelby Laminations common shares ($48 × ½)		24
Gain on sale of investments (difference)		1

Dec. 29   Received cash dividends of $1.5 million from the Shelby Laminations common shares.

	($ in millions)	
Cash	1.5	
Investment revenue		1.5

Dec. 30   Purchased U.S. Treasury bonds for $5.8 million as trading securities, hoping to earn profits on short-term differences in prices.

	($ in millions)	
Investment in U.S. Treasury bonds	5.8	
Cash		5.8

(continued)

Dec. 31   Recorded the necessary adjusting entry(s) relating to the investments.

Accrued Interest (one month)	($ in millions)	
Investment revenue receivable—Vince-Gill Amusement ($30 million × 12% × ¹⁄₁₂)	0.3	
Investment revenue receivable—Eastern Waste Disposal ($24 million × 10% × ¹⁄₁₂)	0.2	
Investment revenue		0.5
Fair Value Adjustments		
Net unrealized holding gains and losses—I/S ($5.7 − 5.8)	0.1	
Fair value adjustment, TS investments		0.1
Fair value adjustment, AFS investments ([12 million shares × ½ × $4.25] − [$48 million × ½])	1.5	
Net unrealized holding gains and losses—OCI		1.5

Note: Securities held-to-maturity are not adjusted to fair value.

Reported in the 2009 Income Statement:	($ in millions)
Investment revenue ($1.5 dividends + 0.5 interest)	$2.0
Gain on sale of investments (Shelby)	1.0
Unrealized holding loss on investments (trading securities)	(0.1)

Note: The $1.5 million unrealized holding gain for the Shelby Laminations common shares is not included in income because it pertains to securities available-for-sale rather than trading securities.

2010

Jan. 7   Sold the remaining Shelby Laminations common shares for $26 million.

The fair value of the Shelby shares at the time of sale is $26 million. Those shares were purchased for $24 million ($48 million × ½), so the gain realized on the sale is $2 million.

	($ in millions)	
Cash (selling price)	26	
Investment in Shelby Laminations common shares (cost: ½ × $48)		24
Gain on sale of investments (difference)		2

Given that the fair value adjustment for the Shelby shares has a $1.5 million balance (recorded on 12/31/09), we need to remove that amount and eliminate the corresponding unrecognized gain from AOCI. This happens automatically when we next adjust the portfolio to fair value. If we were to make the adjustment separately, the entry would be:

	($ in millions)	
Net unrealized holding gains and losses—OCI	1.5	
Fair value adjustment, AFS investments		1.5

The Shelby investment affected net income, other comprehensive income, and comprehensive income as follows ($ in millions):

2009	
$1.0	realized gain on sale of investments (in net income)
_1.5_	unrealized gain on investments (in OCI)
$2.5	total 2009 effect in comprehensive income

2010	
$2.0	realized gain on sale of investments (in net income)
(1.5)	reclassification out of OCI of previously recognized unrealized gain associated with sold investments
____	
$0.5	total 2010 effect in comprehensive income
$3.0	grand total effect in comprehensive income ($2.5 + 0.5).
$3.0	grand total effect in net income ($1.0 + 2.0).
$0.0	grand total effect in other comprehensive income ($1.5 + (1.5)).

Note that the $3.0 grand total effect of the Shelby shares on comprehensive income and net income reconciles with the difference between their purchase price ($48) and their sales price ($51, which is equal to the sum of $25 for the half sold in 2009 and $26 for the half sold in 2010). The only difference between comprehensive income and net income is timing. ●

Financial Statement Presentation and Disclosure

Trading securities, held-to-maturity securities and available-for-sale securities are either current or noncurrent depending on when they are expected to mature or to be sold. However, it's not necessary that a company report individual amounts for the three categories of investments—held-to-maturity, available-for-sale, or trading—on the face of the balance sheet as long as that information is presented in the disclosure notes.[19]

On the statement of cash flows, inflows and outflows of cash from buying and selling trading securities typically are considered operating activities because, for companies that routinely transact in trading securities (financial institutions), trading in those securities constitutes an appropriate part of the companies' normal operations. But because held-to-maturity and available-for-sale securities are not purchased and held principally to be sold in the near term, cash flows from the purchase, sale, and maturity of these securities are considered investing activities.

Investors should disclose the following in the disclosure notes for each year presented:

- Aggregate fair value.
- Gross realized and unrealized holding gains.
- Gross realized and unrealized holding losses.
- Change in net unrealized holding gains and losses.
- Amortized cost basis by major security type.

The notes also include disclosures designed to help financial statement users understand the quality of the inputs companies use when determining fair values and to identify parts of the financial statements that are affected by those fair value estimates. For example, the notes should include the level of the fair value hierarchy (levels 1, 2, or 3) in which all fair value measurements fall. For fair value measurements that use unobservable inputs (level 3), the notes need to provide information about the effect of fair value measurements on earnings, including a reconciliation of beginning and ending balances of the investment that identifies:

- Total gains or losses for the period (realized and unrealized), unrealized gains and losses associated with assets and liabilities still held at the reporting date, and where those amounts are included in earnings or shareholders' equity.
- Purchases, sales, issuances and settlements.
- Transfers in and out of level 3 of the fair value hierarchy (e.g., because of changes in the observability of inputs used to determine fair values).
- (For instruments accounted for under the fair value option) an estimate of the gains or losses included in earnings that are attributable to changes in instrument-specific credit risk.

For annual financial statements, the disclosures should also describe the valuation techniques used to measure fair value.

Information about maturities should be reported for debt securities by disclosing the fair value and cost for at least four maturity groupings: (a) within 1 year, (b) after 1 year through 5 years, (c) after 5 years through 10 years, and (d) after 10 years. A disclosure note from **Microsoft**'s 2007 annual report (Graphic 12–8) provides an example.

---

[19]*Statement of Financial Accounting Standards No. 115,* "Accounting for Certain Investments in Debt and Equity Securities," (Norwalk, Conn.: FASB, 1993), par. 18.

The maturities of debt securities, including fixed-maturity securities, at June 30, 2007, were as follows:

(In millions)	Cost basis	Estimated fair value
Due in one year or less	$ 5,519	$ 5,518
Due after one year through five years	6,886	6,849
Due after five years through ten years	2,935	2,890
Due after ten years	4,910	4,853
Total	$20,250	$20,110

GRAPHIC 12–8

Disclosures of Investment Securities— Microsoft Corporation

Real World Financials

INVESTOR HAS SIGNIFICANT INFLUENCE

PART B

When a company invests in the equity securities (primarily common stock) of another company, the investing company can benefit either (a) *directly* through dividends and/or market price appreciation or (b) *indirectly* through the creation of desirable operating relationships with the investee. The way we report a company's investment in the stock of another company depends on the nature of the relationship between the investor and the investee.

For reporting purposes, we classify the investment relationship in one of three ways, and account for the investment differently depending on the classification, as shown in Graphic 12–9:

Relationship: How much does the investor influence the operating and financial policies of the investee?	Reporting Method
Lacks significant influence (usually < 20% equity ownership)	Varies by type of investment (see Part A of this chapter)
Has significant influence (usually 20%–50% equity ownership)	Equity method
Has control (usually > 50% equity ownership)	Consolidation

GRAPHIC 12–9

Reporting Classifications for Investment Relationships

We focused on situations in which the investor lacks significant influence in Part A of this chapter. In Part B of this chapter we focus on situations in which the investor has significant influence and discuss the equity method and fair value option that are used to account for those investments.

A detailed discussion of the third classification—consolidated financial statements—is beyond the scope of this book. That discussion often is a major focus of the advanced accounting course or is taught as a separate consolidations course. In this chapter, we'll briefly overview consolidation only to provide perspective to aspects of the equity method that purposely mimic some effects of consolidation. Let's do that now, before addressing the specifics of the equity method.

The equity method can be used when an investor can't control, but can significantly influence, the investee.

How the Equity Method Relates to Consolidated Financial Statements

If a company acquires more than 50% of the voting stock of another company, it's said to have a controlling interest, because by voting those shares, the investor actually can control the company acquired. The investor is referred to as the *parent;* the investee is termed the *subsidiary.* For reporting purposes (although not legally), the parent and subsidiary are considered to be a single reporting entity, and their financial statements are *consolidated.* Both companies continue to operate as separate legal entities and the subsidiary reports separate financial statements. However, because of the controlling interest, the parent company reports consolidated financial statements.

Consolidated financial statements combine the individual elements of the parent and subsidiary statements.

The acquired company's assets are included in consolidated financial statements at their fair values as of the date of the acquisition, and the difference between the acquisition price and the sum of the fair values of the acquired net assets is recorded as goodwill.

Consolidated financial statements combine the separate financial statements of the parent and the subsidiary each period into a single aggregate set of financial statements as if there were only one company. This entails an item-by-item combination of the parent and subsidiary statements (after first eliminating any amounts that are shared by the separate financial statements).[20] For instance, if the parent has $8 million cash and the subsidiary has $3 million cash, the consolidated balance sheet would report $11 million cash.

Two aspects of the consolidation process are of particular interest to us in understanding the equity method. First, in consolidated financial statements, the acquired company's assets are included in the financial statements at their fair values as of the date of the acquisition, rather than their book values on that date. Second, if the acquisition price is more than the sum of the separate fair values of the acquired net assets (assets less liabilities), that difference is recorded as an intangible asset—goodwill.[21] We'll return to the discussion of these two aspects when we reach the point in our discussion of the equity method where their influence is felt. As we'll see, the equity method is in many ways a partial consolidation.

We use the equity method when the investor can't control the investee but can exercise significant influence over the operating and financial policies of an investee.

What Is Significant Influence?

● **LO4**

Usually an investor can exercise significant influence over the investee when it owns between 20% and 50% of the investee's voting shares.

When effective control is absent, the investor still may be able to exercise significant influence over the operating and financial policies of the investee. This would be the case if the investor owns a large percentage of the outstanding shares relative to other shareholders. By voting those shares as a block, decisions often can be swayed in the direction the investor desires. When significant influence exists, the investment should be accounted for by the equity method. It should be presumed, in the absence of evidence to the contrary, that the investor exercises significant influence over the investee when it owns between 20% and 50% of the investee's voting shares.[22]

ADDITIONAL CONSIDERATION

It's possible that a company that owns more than 20% of the voting shares cannot exercise significant influence over the investee. If, for instance, another company or a small group of shareholders owns 51% or more of the shares, they control the investee regardless of how other investors vote their shares. *FASB Interpretation No. 35* provides this and other examples of indications that an investor may be unable to exercise significant influence:

- The investee challenges the investor's ability to exercise significant influence (through litigation or complaints to regulators).
- The investor surrenders significant shareholder rights in a signed agreement.
- The investor is unable to acquire sufficient information about the investee to apply the equity method.
- The investor tries and fails to obtain representation on the board of directors of the investee.[23]

---

[20]This avoids double counting those amounts in the consolidated statements. For example, amounts owed by one company to the other are represented by accounts payable in one set of financial statements and accounts receivable in the other. These amounts are not included in the statements of the consolidated entity because a company can't "owe itself."

[21]This is the usual case because most companies are worth more than the sum of the values of individual components of the company due to reputation, longevity, managerial expertise, customer loyalty, or a host of other possibilities. Accounting for goodwill in acquisitions is discussed in Chapter 10.

[22]Shareholders are the owners of the corporation. By voting their shares, it is they who determine the makeup of the board of directors—who, in turn, appoint officers—who, in turn, manage the company. Common stock usually is the class of shares given voting privileges. However, a corporation can create classes of preferred shares that also have voting rights. This is discussed at greater length in Chapter 18.

[23]"Criteria for Applying the Equity Method of Accounting for Investments in Common Stock," *FASB Interpretation No. 35* (Stamford, Conn.: FASB, 1981).

In such cases, the equity method would be inappropriate.

Conversely, it's also possible that a company that owns less than 20% of the voting shares is able to exercise significant influence over the investee. Ability to exercise significant influence with less than 20% ownership might be indicated, for example, by having an officer of the investor corporation on the board of directors of the investee corporation or by having, say, 18% of the voting shares while no other investor owns more than ½%. In such cases the equity method would be appropriate. Amazon.com provided the following example in a recent disclosure note:

Note 6—Investments

At December 31, 2000, the Company's equity-method investees and the Company's approximate ownership interest in each investee, based on outstanding shares, were as follows:

Company	Percentage Ownership
Basis Technology	11%
Drugstore.com	21
Eziba.com	20
Greenlight.com	5
Kozmo.com	16

Although the Company's ownership percentage for Basis Technology, Greenlight.com and Kozmo.com is below 20%, the Company's representation on the investees' Board of Directors and the impact of commercial arrangements result in the Company having significant influence over the operations of each investee.

A Single Entity Concept

Much like consolidation, the equity method views the investor and investee collectively as a special type of single entity (as if the two companies were one company). However, using the equity method, the investor doesn't include separate financial statement items of the investee on an item-by-item basis as in consolidation. Instead, the investor reports its equity interest in the investee as a single investment account. For that reason, the equity method sometimes is referred to as a "one-line consolidation," because it essentially collapses the consolidation approach into single lines in the balance sheet and income statement, while having the same effect on total income and shareholders' equity.

Under the equity method, the investor recognizes investment income equal to its percentage share (based on stock ownership) of the net income earned by the investee rather than the portion of that net income received as cash dividends. The rationale for this approach is the presumption of the equity method that the fortunes of the investor and investee are sufficiently intertwined that as the investee prospers, the investor prospers proportionately. Stated differently, as the investee earns additional net assets, the investor's share of those net assets increases.

Initially, the investment is recorded at cost. The carrying amount of this investment subsequently is:

- Increased by the investor's percentage share of the investee's net income (or decreased by its share of a loss).
- Decreased by dividends paid.

To see how the equity method works, let's assume that United Intergroup purchased 30% of Arjent, Inc.'s, common stock for $1,500,000 cash. Illustration 12–6 highlights that buying 30% of Arjent can be viewed as buying 30% of all of Arjent's assets and liabilities. Those assets and liabilities likely have book values on Arjent's balance sheet that differ from their separate fair values. We can think of United as paying a price equal to 30% of the sum of the fair values of all of those assets and liabilities, plus an extra amount, goodwill, that captures 30% of the value of other attractive aspects of Arjent (e.g., loyal customers, well-trained workers) that GAAP doesn't capture as separate assets or liabilities. We will see that, under the equity method, all of those amounts are shown in a single investment account, but we still need to track their individual information to account for them correctly.

● LO5

The investor's ownership interest in individual assets and liabilities of the investee is represented by a single investment account.

The investment account is adjusted to reflect the investor's share of both increases and decreases in the investee's net assets.

FINANCIAL
Reporting Case

Q4, p. 587

ILLUSTRATION 12–6 Equity Method	Account	Book Value on Arjent's Financial Statements	Fair Value at Time of United's Investment
	Buildings (10-year remaining useful life, no salvage value)	$1,000,000	$ 2,000,000
	Land	500,000	1,000,000
	Other net assets*	600,000	600,000
	Net assets	2,100,000	3,600,000
	Goodwill		1,400,000 (to balance)
	Total fair value of Arjent		$ 5,000,000
			× 30% purchased
			$1,500,000 purchase price
	Other information:		
	Arjent's 2009 net income:	$500,000	
	Arjent's 2009 dividends:	$250,000	

*Other net assets = other assets – liabilities

The cost principal governs the acquisition of assets.

PURCHASE OF INVESTMENT. Recording United's purchase of 30% of Arjent is straightforward. In fact, it requires the same entry used to record the purchase of the Arjent investment in Part A of this chapter.

Investment in Arjent stock	1,500,000	
Cash		1,500,000

As the investee earns additional net assets, the investor's investment in those net assets increases.

As the investee prospers, the investor prospers proportionately.

RECORDING INVESTMENT REVENUE. Under the equity method, the investor includes in net income its proportionate share of the investee's net income. The reasoning is that, as the investee earns additional net assets, the investor's equity interest in those net assets also increases, so the investor increases its investment by the amount of income recognized. United's entry would be:

Investment in Arjent stock	150,000	
Investment revenue (30% × $500,000)		150,000

Of course, if Argent had recorded a net loss rather than net income, United would *reduce* its investment in Arjent and recognize a *loss* on investment for its share of the loss. Note that you won't always see these amounts called "investment revenue" or "investment loss." Rather, United might call this line "equity in earnings (losses) of affiliate" or some other title that suggests they are using the equity method.

As the investee distributes net assets as dividends, the investor does not recognize revenue. Rather, the investor's investment in the investee's net assets is reduced.

RECEIVING DIVIDENDS. Because investment revenue is recognized as it is earned by the investee, it would be inappropriate to recognize revenue again when earnings are distributed as dividends. That would be double counting. Instead, we view the dividend distribution as a reduction of the investee's net assets. The rationale is that the investee is returning assets back to its investors in the form of a cash payment, so each investor's equity interest in the remaining net assets declines proportionately.

Cash	75,000	
Investment in Arjent stock (30% × $250,000)		75,000

Further Adjustments

● LO6

When the investor's expenditure to acquire an investment exceeds the book value of the underlying net assets acquired, additional adjustments to both the investment account and investment revenue might be needed. The purpose is to approximate the effects of consolidation, without actually consolidating financial statements. More specifically, both the investment account and investment revenue are adjusted for differences between net income reported by the investee and what that amount would have been if consolidation procedures had been followed. This process is often referred to as "amortizing the purchase differential," because it mimics the process of expensing some of the difference between the purchase price and the book value of the investment. Let's look closer at what that means.

As mentioned earlier, consolidated financial statements report (a) the acquired company's assets at their fair market values on the date of acquisition rather than their book values and (b) goodwill for the excess of the acquisition price over the fair value of the identifiable net assets acquired.

The first of these two consequences of the consolidation process usually has an effect on income, and it's the income effect that we're interested in when applying the equity method. Increasing asset balances to their fair values usually will result in higher expenses. For instance, if buildings, equipment, or other depreciable assets are written up to higher values, depreciation expense will be higher during their remaining useful lives. Likewise, if the recorded amount of inventory is increased, cost of goods sold will be higher when the inventory is sold.

However, if it's land that's increased, there is no income effect because we don't depreciate land. Also, recording goodwill will not result in higher expenses. Goodwill is an intangible asset, but one whose cost usually is not charged to earnings.[24] As a consequence, then, of increasing asset balances to fair value but not of recording goodwill, expenses will rise and income will fall. It is this negative effect on income that the equity method seeks to imitate.

In our example, United needs to make adjustments for the fact that, at the time it purchased its investment in Arjent, the fair values of Arjent's assets and liabilities were higher than the book values of those assets and liabilities in Arjent's balance sheet. Graphic 12–10 highlights the portions of United's investment that may require adjustment:

	Investee Net Assets ↓	Net Assets Purchased ↓	($ in thousands) Difference Attributed to: ↓	
Cost	$5,000 × 30% =	$1,500	Goodwill:	$420
Fair value	$3,600 × 30% =	$1,080		
			Undervaluation of:	
			Buildings	$300
			Land	$150
Book value	$2,100 × 30% =	$630		

GRAPHIC 12–10

Source of Differences between the Investment and the Book Value of Net Assets Acquired

Notice in Graphic 12–10 that United paid (in thousands) $1,500 for identifiable net assets that, sold separately, would be worth $1,080 and the $420 difference is attributable to goodwill. The identifiable net assets worth $1,080 have a book value of only $630, and we assumed the $450 difference is attributable to undervalued buildings ($300) and land ($150).

ADJUSTMENTS FOR ADDITIONAL DEPRECIATION.   When Arjent determines its net income, it bases depreciation expense on the book value of its buildings, but United needs to depreciate its share of the *fair value* of those buildings at the time it made its investment. Therefore, United must adjust its investment revenue for additional depreciation expense. Over the life of the buildings, United will need to recognize its 30% share of a total of $1,000,000

---

[24]Beginning in 2002, goodwill was not amortized periodically to expense. Only if the asset's value is subsequently judged to be impaired is all or a portion of the recorded amount charged against earnings. "Goodwill and Other Intangible Assets," *Statement of Financial Accounting Standards No. 141* (Norwalk, Conn.: FASB, 2001). For review, see Chapter 11.

The investor adjusts its share of the investee's net income to reflect revenues and expenses associated with differences between the fair value and book value of the investee's assets and liabilities that existed at the time the investment was made.

of additional depreciation expense ($2,000,000 fair value less $1,000,000 book value), or $300,000. Assuming a 10-year life of the buildings and straight-line depreciation, United must recognize $30,000 of additional depreciation each year. Had Arjent recorded that additional depreciation, United's portion of Arjent's net income would have been lower by $30,000 (ignoring taxes). To act as if Arjent had recorded the additional depreciation, United adjusts the accounts to reduce investment revenue and reduce its investment in Arjent stock by $30,000.

Investment revenue	30,000	
Investment in Arjent stock (30% × [$2,000,000 – 1,000,000] ÷ 10 yrs.)		30,000

NO ADJUSTMENTS FOR LAND OR GOODWILL. United makes no adjustments for land or goodwill. Land, unlike buildings, is not an asset that we depreciate. As a result, the difference between the fair value and book value of the land would not cause higher expenses, and we have no need to adjust investment revenue or the investment in Arjent stock for the land.

Recall from Chapter 11 that goodwill, unlike most other intangible assets, is not amortized. In that sense, goodwill resembles land. Thus, acquiring goodwill will not cause higher expenses, so we have no need to adjust investment revenue or the investment in Arjent stock for goodwill.

ADJUSTMENTS FOR OTHER ASSETS AND LIABILITIES. Also, because in our example there was no difference between the book value and fair value of the remaining net assets, we don't need an adjustment for them either. However, that often will not be the case.

If the fair value of purchased inventory exceeds its book value, we usually assume the inventory is sold in the next year and reduce investment revenue in the next year by the entire difference.

For example, Arjent's inventory could have had a fair value that exceeds its book value at the time United purchased its Arjent investment. To recognize expense associated with that higher fair value, United would need to identify the period in which that inventory is sold (usually the next year) and, in that period, reduce its investment revenue and its investment in Arjent stock by its 30% share of the difference between the fair value and book value of the inventory. If, for instance, the $300,000 difference between fair value and book value had been attributable to inventory rather than buildings, and that inventory was sold by Arjent in the year following United's investment, United would reduce investment revenue by the entire $300,000 in the year following the investment. By so doing, United would be making an adjustment that yielded the same net investment revenue as if Arjent had carried the inventory on its books at fair value at the time the Arjent investment was made and therefore recorded higher cost of goods sold ($300,000) when it was sold in the next year. More generally, an equity method investor needs to make these sorts of adjustments whenever there are revenues or expenses associated with an asset or liability that had a difference between book value and fair value at the time the investment was made.

ADDITIONAL CONSIDERATION

Effect on Deferred Income Taxes

Investment revenue is recorded by the equity method when income is earned by the investee, but that revenue is not taxed until it's actually received as cash dividends. This creates a temporary difference between book income and taxable income. You will learn in Chapter 16 that the investor must report a deferred tax liability for the income tax that ultimately will be paid when the income eventually is received as dividends.

Reporting the Investment

The carrying amount of the investment is its initial cost plus the investor's equity in the undistributed earnings of the investee.

The fair value of the investment shares at the end of the reporting period is not reported when using the equity method. The investment account is reported at its original cost, increased by the investor's share of the investee's net income (adjusted for additional expenses like depreciation), and decreased by the portion of those earnings actually received as dividends. In other words, the investment account represents the investor's share of the investee's net assets initially acquired, adjusted for the investor's share of the subsequent increase in the investee's net assets (net assets earned and not yet distributed as dividends).

The balance of United's 30% investment in Arjent at December 31, 2009, would be calculated as follows:

Investment in Arjent Stock

Cost	1,500,000		
Share of income	150,000		
		30,000	Depreciation adjustment
		75,000	Dividends
	1,545,000		

In the statement of cash flows, the purchase and sale of the investment are reported as outflows and inflows of cash in the investing section, and the receipt of dividends is reported as an inflow of cash in the operating section.[25]

WHEN THE INVESTEE REPORTS A NET LOSS.   Our illustration assumed the investee earned net income. If the investee reports a *net loss* instead, the investment account would be *decreased* by the investor's share of the investee's net loss (adjusted for additional expenses).

ADDITIONAL CONSIDERATION

It's possible that the investor's proportionate share of investee losses could exceed the carrying amount of the investment. If this happens, the investor should discontinue applying the equity method until the investor's share of subsequent investee earnings has equaled losses not recognized during the time the equity method was discontinued. This avoids reducing the investment account below zero.

WHEN THE INVESTMENT IS ACQUIRED IN MID-YEAR.   Obviously, we've simplified the illustration by assuming the investment was acquired at the beginning of 2009, entailing a full year's income, dividends, and adjustments to account for the income effects of any differences between book value and fair value on the date the investment was acquired. In the more likely event that an investment is acquired sometime after the beginning of the year, the application of the equity method is easily modified to include the appropriate fraction of each of those amounts. For example, if United's purchase of 30% of Arjent had occurred on October 1 rather than January 2, we would simply record income, dividends, and adjustments for three months, or $3/12$ of the year. This would result in the following entries to the investment account:

Investment in Arjent Stock

Cost	1,500,000		
Share of income			
($3/12$ × $150,000)	37,500		
			Depreciation adjustment
		7,500	($3/12$ × $30,000)
			Dividends
		18,750	($3/12$ × $75,000)
	1,511,250		

Changes in the investment account the first year are adjusted for the fraction of the year the investor has owned the investment.

---

[25]Some companies prepare a statement of cash flows using the indirect method of reporting operating activities. In that case, the operating section begins with net income and adjustments are made to back out the effects of accrual accounting and calculate cash from operations. For companies with equity method investments, net income will include investment revenue and gains or losses associated with sold investments, but cash from operations should include only cash dividends. As an example, because United's 2009 net income includes $120,000 of investment revenue from Arjent ($150,000 portion of income − $30,000 depreciation adjustment), but United received only $75,000 of dividends from Arjent, an indirect method statement of cash flows would include an adjustment that reduces net income by $45,000 ($75,000 − $120,000) when determining cash from operations.

GRAPHIC 12–11

Equity Method Investments on the Balance Sheet—AT&T

Real World Financials

	December 31	
	2006	**2005**
Total current assets	25,553	14,654
Property, plant, and equipment—Net	94,596	58,727
Goodwill	67,657	14,055
Intangible assets—net	59,740	8,503
Investments in equity affiliates	1,995	2,031
Investments in and advances to AT&T Mobility	—	31,404
Postemployment benefit	14,228	12,666
Other assets	6,865	3,592
Total assets	$270,634	$145,632

AT&T reported its investments in affiliated companies for which it exercised significant influence using the equity method as shown in Graphic 12–11.

What If Conditions Change?

A CHANGE FROM THE EQUITY METHOD TO ANOTHER METHOD. When the investor's level of influence changes, it may be necessary to change from the equity method to another method. This could happen, for instance, if a sale of shares causes the investor's ownership interest to fall from, say, 25% to 15%, resulting in the equity method no longer being appropriate.[26] Another example is provided by **Sprint,** which in February 2001 agreed to end its exclusive alliance with **EarthLink** and relinquished its seats on EarthLink's board of directors. As a result, Sprint discontinued using the equity method for its investment in EarthLink.

When this situation happens, *no adjustment* is made to the remaining carrying amount of the investment. Instead, the equity method is simply discontinued and the new method applied from then on. The balance in the investment account when the equity method is discontinued would serve as the new cost basis for writing the investment up or down to fair value on the next set of financial statements.

A CHANGE FROM ANOTHER METHOD TO THE EQUITY METHOD. Sometimes companies change from another method to the equity method. For example, in 2007 the **Bank of Tokyo-Mitsubishi UFJ** converted its investment in the consumer credit company **Jaccs Co.** into an equity method affiliate by raising its ownership in that company from 4.7% to around 20%. When a change *to* the equity method is appropriate, the investment account should be retroactively adjusted to the balance that would have existed if the equity method always had been used. As income also would have been different, retained earnings would be adjusted as well. For example, assume it's determined that an investor's share of investee net income, reduced by dividends, was $4 million during a period when the equity method was not used, but additional purchases of shares cause the equity method to be appropriate now. The following journal entry would record the change (ignoring taxes):

> **Both the investment and retained earnings would be increased by the investor's share of the undistributed earnings in years prior to a change to the equity method.**

	($ in millions)	
Investment in equity securities	4	
Retained earnings (investment revenue from the equity method)		4

In addition to the adjustment of account balances, financial statements would be restated to the equity method for each year reported in the annual report for comparative purposes.

---

[26]When a portion of an equity method investment is sold, the investor removes from the investment account the appropriate proportion of the carrying value and records a gain or loss for the difference between that amount and the selling price.

Also, the income effect for years prior to those shown in the comparative statements is reported on the statement of retained earnings as an adjustment to beginning retained earnings of the earliest year reported. A disclosure note also should describe the change. Reporting accounting changes is described in more detail in Chapter 20.

If an Equity Method Investment is Sold

When an investment being reported by the equity method is sold, a gain or loss is recognized if the selling price is more or less than the carrying amount (book value) of the investment. For example, let's continue our illustration and assume United sells its investment in Arjent on January 1, 2010, for $1,446,000. A journal entry would record a loss as follows:

> **When an equity method investment is sold, a gain or loss is recognized for the difference between its selling price and its carrying amount.**

Cash	1,446,000	
Loss on sale of investments (to balance)	99,000	
Investment in Arjent stock (account balance)		1,545,000

Comparison of Fair Value and Equity Methods

Illustration 12–7 compares accounting for the Arjent investment at fair value (as trading securities or securities available for sale, discussed in Part A of this chapter) and under the equity method (covered in Part B of this chapter):

ILLUSTRATION 12–7   Comparison of Fair Value and Equity Methods

	Fair Value Method	Equity Method
Purchase equity investment	Investment in Arjent 1,500,000 Cash 1,500,000	Same as Fair Value Method

Recognize proportionate share of investee's net income and any related adjustments	No entry	Investment in Arjent 150,000
		    Investment revenue 150,000
		Investment revenue 30,000
		    Investment in Arjent 30,000

Adjust investment to reflect changes in fair value from $1,500,000 to $1,450,000	Net unrealized gain/loss* 50,000 FV adjustment 50,000	No entry

Receive dividend	Cash 75,000
	    Investment revenue 75,000
		Cash 75,000
		    Investment in Arjent 75,000

Sell equity investment	Recognize gain or loss:
	  Cash 1,446,000
	  Loss (to balance) 54,000
	    Investment in Arjent 1,500,000
	
	Reverse out previously recorded unrealized gain or loss that's no longer unrealized (automatically part of next adjustment to fair value):
	
	  FV adjustment 50,000
	    Net unrealized gain/loss* 50,000
		Cash 1,446,000
		Loss (to balance) 99,000
		    Investment in Arjent 1,545,000

*Net unrealized holding gains and losses are reported in net income for trading securities and in other comprehensive income for available-for-sale securities.

This side-by-side comparison highlights several aspects of these accounting approaches:

- To record the purchase of an investment, we use identical entries for both approaches.
- The two approaches differ in whether we record investment revenue when dividends are received and whether we recognize unrealized holding gains and losses associated with changes in the fair value of the investment.

- The differences in how the two approaches account for unrealized holding gains and losses result in different book values for the investment at the time the investment is sold, and therefore result in different realized gains or losses when the investment is sold.
- Regardless of approach, the same cash flows occur, and the same total amount of net income is recognized over the life of the investment. In the case of Arjent:
  - **Fair value method:** A total of $21,000 of net income is recognized over the life of the investment, equal to $75,000 of dividend revenue minus $54,000 realized loss on sale of investment.
  - **Equity method:** A total of $21,000 of net income is recognized over the life of the investment, equal to $150,000 of United's portion of Arjent's income minus $30,000 depreciation adjustment and minus $99,000 realized loss on sale of investment.
  - Thus, the question is not how much total net income is recognized, but *when* that net income is recognized.

Fair Value Option

● LO7

If the fair value option is chosen for investments otherwise accounted for by the equity method, the amount that is reported at fair value is clearly indicated.

We learned in Part A of this chapter that *SFAS No. 159* allows a fair value option with respect to investments that otherwise would be accounted for using the held-to-maturity or available-for-sale approaches. Electing the fair value option for those investments is simple—the investments are reclassified as trading securities and accounted for in that manner.

SFAS No. 159 also allows the fair value option for "significant influence" investments that otherwise would be accounted for under the equity method. The company makes an irrevocable decision about whether to elect the fair value option, and can make that election for some investments and not for others. As shown for the fair value method in Illustration 12–7, the company carries the investment at fair value in the balance sheet and includes unrealized gains and losses in earnings.

However, investments that otherwise would be accounted for under the equity method but for which the fair value option has been elected are not reclassified as trading securities. Instead, these investments are shown on their own line in the balance sheet or are combined with equity method investments with the amount at fair value shown parenthetically. Still, they are reported at fair value with changes in fair value reported in earnings as if they were trading securities. Also, all of the disclosures that are required when reporting fair values as well as some of those that would be required under the equity method still must be provided.[27]

Exactly how a company does the bookkeeping necessary to comply with these broad requirements is up to the company. One alternative is to account for the investment using entries similar to those that would be used to account for trading securities. A second alternative is to record all of the accounting entries during the period under the equity method, and then record a fair value adjustment at the end of the period to comply with *SFAS No. 159*. Regardless of which alternative the company uses to account for the investment during the

INTERNATIONAL FINANCIAL REPORTING STANDARDS

Equity Method. Like U.S. GAAP, international accounting standards require the equity method for use with significant influence investees (which they call "associates"), but there are a few important differences. *IFRS No. 28* governs application of the equity method and requires that the accounting policies of investees be adjusted to correspond to those of the investor when applying the equity method.[28] U.S. GAAP has no such requirement.

IFRS No. 31 governs accounting for joint ventures, in which two or more investors have joint control. That standard allows investors to account for a joint venture using either the equity method or a method called "proportionate consolidation," whereby the investor combines its proportionate share of the investee's accounts with its own accounts on an item-by-item basis.[29] U.S. GAAP generally requires that the equity method be used to account for joint ventures.

[27]"The Fair Value Option for Financial Assets and Financial Liabilities," *Statement of Financial Accounting Standards No. 159* (Norwalk, Conn.: FASB, 2007), paragraph 18.f.

[28]"Investments in Associates," *International Accounting Standard 28* (London, UK: IASCF, 2003).

[29]"Interests in Joint Ventures," *International Accounting Standard 31* (London, UK: IASCF, 2003).

period, though, the same fair value is reported in the balance sheet at the end of the period, and the same total amount is shown on the income statement (the fair value adjustment amount plus the investment revenue recorded).

CONCEPT REVIEW **EXERCISE**

Delta Apparatus bought 40% of Clay Crating Corp.'s outstanding common shares on January 2, 2009, for $540 million. The carrying amount of Clay Crating's net assets (shareholders' equity) at the purchase date totaled $900 million. Book values and fair values were the same for all financial statement items except for inventory and buildings, for which fair values exceeded book values by $25 million and $225 million, respectively. All inventory on hand at the acquisition date was sold during 2009. The buildings have average remaining useful lives of 18 years. During 2009, Clay Crating reported net income of $220 million and paid an $80 million cash dividend.

THE EQUITY METHOD

Required:
1. Prepare the appropriate journal entries during 2009 for the investment.
2. Determine the amounts relating to the investment that Delta Apparatus should report in the 2009 financial statements:
   a. As an investment in the balance sheet.
   b. As investment revenue in the income statement.
   c. Among investing activities in the statement of cash flows.

1. Prepare the appropriate journal entries during 2009 for the investment.

SOLUTION

	($ in millions)	
Purchase		
Investment in Clay Crating shares	540	
Cash		540
Net income		
Investment in Clay Crating shares (40% × $220 million)	88	
Investment revenue		88
Dividends		
Cash (40% × $80 million)	32	
Investment in Clay Crating shares		32
Inventory		
Investment revenue (higher cost of goods sold during 2009		
if beginning inventory had been adjusted to fair value)	10	
Investment in Clay Crating shares (40% × $25 million)		10
Buildings		
Investment revenue ([$225 million × 40%] ÷ 18 years)	5	
Investment in Clay Crating shares		5

	Investee Net Assets ↓	Net Assets Purchased ↓	Difference Attributed to ↓
Cost		$540 ⎤	
			Goodwill: $80 [difference]
Fair value	$1,150[†] × 40% =	$460 ⎤	
			Undervaluation $10 [$25 × 40%] of inventory
Book value	$ 900 × 40% =	$360 ⎦	
			Undervaluation $90 [$225 × 40%] of buildings

[†]($900 + 25 + 225)

2. Determine the amounts that Delta Apparatus should report in the 2009 financial statements:

a. As an investment in the balance sheet:

Investment in Clay Crating Shares

($ in millions)

Cost	540		
Share of income	88		
		32	Dividends
		10	Cost of goods sold adjustment for inventory
		5	Depreciation adjustment for buildings
Balance	581		

b. As investment revenue in the income statement:

$$\underset{\text{(share of income)}}{\$88 \text{ million}} \quad - \underset{\text{(adjustments)}}{[\$10 + 5] \text{ million}} = \underline{\$73 \text{ million}}$$

c. In the statement of cash flows:

- Among investing activities: $540 million cash outflow
- Among operating activities: $32 million cash inflow

DECISION MAKERS' PERSPECTIVE

The various approaches used to account for investments can have very different effects on an investor's income statement and balance sheet. Consequently, it's critical that both managers and external decision makers clearly understand those effects and make decisions accordingly.

To highlight key considerations, suppose that, on January 1, 2009, BigCo spent $5,000,000 to purchase 20% of TechStart, a small start-up company that is developing products that apply an exciting new technology. The purchase price included $500,000 for BigCo's share of the difference between the fair value and book value of TechStart's inventory, all of which was then sold in 2009. TechStart paid a small dividend of $100,000 in 2009, so BigCo received 20% of it, or $20,000. TechStart incurs and expenses large amounts of research and development costs as it develops new technology, so it had a net loss in 2009 of $1,000,000. Yet, the future income-generating potential of the products that TechStart is developing has made TechStart a hot stock, and the fair value of BigCo's 20% investment increased to $5,500,000 by the end of 2009. Illustration 12–8 shows how BigCo's investment would be accounted for under three alternative approaches.

The accounting method does not affect cash flows, but it has a big effect on net income in current and future periods. Also, because the accounting method affects the book value of the

ILLUSTRATION 12–8		Trading Security	Available-for-Sale	Equity Method
Comparison of Methods Used to Account for Investments	Share of investee net income*	–0–	–0–	($ 700,000)
	Dividend income†	$ 20,000	$ 20,000	–0–
	Increase in investee's fair value#	$ 500,000	–0–	–0–
	Total 2009 effect on net income	$ 520,000	$ 20,000	($ 700,000)
Which reporting method causes net income to be highest?	12/31/09 investment book value&	$5,500,000	$5,500,000	$4,280,000

*Not recognized for trading securities or available-for-sale securities. Under the equity method, investment revenue (loss) is 20% × ($1,000,000 loss) + ($500,000) additional expense for fair value inventory adjustment = ($700,000).

†Not recognized for equity method investments. Instead, dividends reduce book value of the investment.

#Recognized in net income for trading securities, in other comprehensive income for available-for-sale securities, and not recognized for equity method investments.

&Equals fair value for trading securities and available-for-sale securities. For equity method equals initial cost plus income (or minus loss) and minus dividends.

investment, it affects gain or loss on sale of that investment. In our example, if BigCo sold its TechStart investment at the beginning of 2010 for $5,000,000, it would recognize a $720,000 gain on sale if the investment was accounted for under the equity method, but a $500,000 loss if it was accounted for as a trading security or available-for-sale security. All of these income effects are predictable, but only if a user understands the relevant accounting methods and the fact that those methods all end up recognizing the same amount of total gain or loss over the life of an investment. Nevertheless, sometimes even experienced analysts get confused.[30]

One strength of the equity method is that it prevents the income manipulation that would be possible if a company recognized income when it received dividends and could significantly influence an investee to pay dividends whenever the company needed an income boost. Remember, under the equity method dividends aren't income, but rather reduce the book value of the investment. Nevertheless, users still need to realize that managers may choose and apply methods in ways that make their company appear most attractive. For example, research suggests that investments sometimes are structured to avoid crossing the 20 to 25 percent threshold that typically requires using the equity method,[31] presumably to avoid the negative effect on earnings that comes from having to recognize the investor's share of investee losses and other income adjustments. Also, a company might smooth income by timing the sale of available-for-sale or equity method investments to realize gains in otherwise poor periods and realize losses in otherwise good periods. While consistent with GAAP, mixing these sorts of one-time gains and losses with operating income could encourage users to think that operating income is less volatile than it really is.

Of particular concern is the potential for inaccurate fair value estimates. Even if management is trying to provide the most accurate fair value estimate possible, there is much potential for error, particularly when making estimates at level 3 of the fair value hierarchy. Also, a company conceivably could use the discretion inherent in fair value estimation to manage earnings with respect to trading securities or other investments for which they have elected the fair value option. Given this potential for error and bias, it's not surprising that investors are nervous about the accuracy of fair value estimates. For example, in the third quarter of 2007 **E-Trade** recognized $198 million of impairments for overvalued investments accounted for as available-for-sale and trading securities, and saw its share price plunge 59% on analyst warnings of the potential for further impairments.[32] To address these sorts of concerns, the FASB has required extensive footnote disclosure about the quality of inputs associated with estimates of fair value, but financial statement users need to know to look for those disclosures and still must understand that they cannot assess fully the accuracy of fair value estimates. ◉

> The way an investment is accounted for affects net income, investment book value, and the amount of gain or loss recognized in the future when the investment is sold.

> Managers may structure investments to include only the amount of equity that qualifies for their preferred accounting approach.

> If investments are not accounted for at fair value, their sale can be timed to recognize gains or losses in particular accounting periods.

> A concern with fair value accounting is that management has much discretion over fair values, and may not be able to estimate fair values accurately.

Financial Instruments and Investment Derivatives

A financial instrument is defined as:

- Cash,
- Evidence of an *ownership interest* in an entity,[33]
- A contract that (a) imposes on one entity an obligation to *deliver* cash (say accounts payable) or another financial instrument and (b) conveys to the second entity a right to *receive* cash (say accounts receivable) or another financial instrument, or
- A contract that (a) imposes on one entity an obligation to *exchange* financial instruments on potentially unfavorable terms (say the issuer of a stock option) and (b) conveys to a second entity a right to *exchange* other financial instruments on potentially favorable terms (say the holder of a stock option).[34]

---

[30]For example, in 2000, analysts were accustomed to including **Intel**'s investment gains as ordinary income, because those amounts were not particularly large and could be viewed as part of Intel's business. However, in the 2nd quarter of 2000, Intel recorded a net $2.1 billion gain from selling securities in its available-for-sale portfolio. Analysts were surprised and confused, with some eliminating the gain from their earnings estimates but others including them ("Intel Says Net Jumped 79%; Analysts Upset," *The Wall Street Journal*, July 19, 2000, p. A3).

[31]Comiskey, E. E., and C. W. Mulford, "Investment Decisions and the Equity Accounting Standard," *The Accounting Review*, Vol. 61, No. 3 (July 1986), pp. 519–525.

[32]Craig, S. "Mortgage Crisis Extends its Reach: E*Trade Plunges 59% on Analyst's Warnings; Bank Unit Goes Awry," *The Wall Street Journal*, November 13, 2007, p. A.1.

[33]This category includes not just shares of stock, but also partnership agreements and stock options.

[34]"Disclosure of Information about Financial Instruments with Off-Balance-Sheet Risk and Financial Instruments with Concentrations of Credit Risk," *Statement of Financial Accounting Standards No. 105*, (Stamford, Conn.: FASB, 1990), par. 6.

Derivatives are financial instruments that "derive" their values from some other security or index.

A complex class of financial instruments exists in financial markets in response to the desire of firms to manage risks. In fact, these financial instruments would not exist in their own right, but have been created solely to hedge against risks created by other financial instruments or by transactions that have yet to occur but are anticipated. Financial futures, interest rate swaps, forward contracts, and options have become commonplace.[35] These financial instruments often are called derivatives because they "derive" their values or contractually required cash flows from some other security or index. For instance, an option to buy an asset in the future at a preset price has a value that is dependent on, or derived from, the value of the underlying asset. Their rapid acceptance as indispensable components of the corporate capital structure has left the accounting profession scrambling to keep pace.

The urgency to establish accounting standards for financial instruments has been accelerated by headline stories in the financial press reporting multimillion-dollar losses on exotic derivatives by **Enron Corporation, Procter & Gamble, Orange County** (California), **Piper Jaffrey,** and **Gibson Greetings,** to mention a few. The headlines have tended to focus attention on the misuse of these financial instruments rather than their legitimate use in managing risk.

The FASB's ongoing financial instruments project is expected to lead to a consistent framework for accounting for all financial instruments.

Actually, the FASB has been involved since 1986 in a project to provide a consistent framework for resolving financial instrument accounting issues, including those related to derivatives and other "off-balance-sheet" instruments. The financial instruments project has three separate but related parts: disclosure, recognition and measurement, and distinguishing between liabilities and equities. Unfortunately, issues to be resolved are extremely complex and will likely require several years to resolve. To help fill the disclosure gap in the mean-time, the FASB has offered a series of temporary, "patchwork" solutions. These are primarily in the form of additional disclosures for financial instruments. More recently, the FASB has tackled the issues of recognition and measurement. We discuss these requirements in Appendix A after we've spent some time with the measurement issues necessary to understand accounting for derivatives.

FINANCIAL REPORTING CASE **SOLUTION**

1. **How should you respond? Why are held-to-maturity securities treated differently from other investment securities?** *(p. 593)* You should explain that if an investor has the positive intent and ability to hold the securities to maturity, investments in debt securities are classified as held-to-maturity and reported at amortized cost in the balance sheet. Increases and decreases in fair value are not reported in the financial statements. The reasoning is that the changes are not as relevant to an investor who will hold a security to its maturity regardless of those changes. Changes in the fair value between the time a debt security is acquired and the day it matures to a prearranged maturity value aren't as important if sale before maturity isn't an alternative.

2. **Why are unrealized gains and losses on trading securities reported in the income statement?** *(p. 593)* Trading securities are acquired for the purpose of profiting from short-term market price changes, so gains and losses from holding these securities while prices change are often viewed as relevant performance measures that should be included in net income.

3. **Why are unrealized gains and losses on available-for-sale securities not reported in the income statement, but instead are in comprehensive income?** *(p. 597)* Available-for-sale securities are not acquired for the purpose of profiting from short-term market price changes, so gains and losses from holding these securities while prices change are viewed as insufficiently relevant performance measures to be included in net income. Rather, those amounts are shown in other comprehensive income and accumulated in an owners' equity account (AOCI). It's likely that holding gains in some periods will be offset by holding losses in other periods. When the investment is sold, the net amount of gain or loss is removed from AOCI and recognized in net income.

---

[35]Interest rate futures were traded for the first time in 1975 on the Chicago Board of Trade. Interest rate swaps were invented in the early 1980s. They now comprise over 70% of derivatives in use.

4. Explain why Coke accounts for some of its investments by the equity method and what that means. *(p. 609)*   When an investor does not have "control," but still is able to exercise *significant influence* over the operating and financial policies of the investee, the investment should be accounted for by the equity method. Apparently Coke owns between 20% and 50% of the voting shares of some of the companies it invests in. By the equity method, Coke recognizes investment income in an amount equal to its percentage share of the net income earned by those companies, instead of the amount of that net income it receives as cash dividends. The rationale is that as the investee earns additional net assets, Coke's share of those net assets increases. ●

THE **BOTTOM LINE**

● **LO1**   When an investor lacks significant influence over the operating and financial policies of the investee, its investment is classified for reporting purposes as held-to-maturity (HTM), available-for-sale (AFS), or trading securities (TS). If an investor has the positive intent and ability to hold the securities to maturity, investments in debt securities are classified as HTM and reported at amortized cost in the balance sheet. These investments are recorded at cost, and holding gains or losses from fair value changes are ignored. (p. 590)

● **LO2**   Investments in debt or equity securities acquired principally for the purpose of selling them in the near term are classified as trading securities. They are reported at their fair values. Holding gains and losses for trading securities are included in earnings. (p. 593)

● **LO3**   Investments in debt and equity securities that don't fit the definitions of the other reporting categories are classified as available-for-sale. They are reported at their fair values. Holding gains and losses from retaining securities during periods of price change are not included in the determination of income for the period; they are reported as a separate component of shareholders' equity. (p. 596)

● **LO4**   When an investor is able to exercise significant influence over the operating and financial policies of the investee, the investment should be accounted for by the equity method. Usually an investor can exercise significant influence when it owns between 20% and 50% of the investee's voting shares. (p. 610)

● **LO5**   By the equity method, the investor recognizes investment income equal to its percentage share (based on share ownership) of the net income earned by the investee, rather than the portion of that net income received as cash dividends. The investment account is adjusted for the investor's percentage share of net income or loss reported by the investee. When the investor actually receives dividends, the investment account is reduced accordingly. (p. 611)

● **LO6**   When the cost of an investment exceeds the book value of the underlying net assets acquired, both the investment account and investment revenue are adjusted for differences between net income reported by the investee and what that amount would have been if consolidation procedures had been followed. (p. 612)

● **LO7**   The fair value option allows companies to account for most financial assets and liabilities in the same way they account for trading securities, with unrealized holding gains and losses included in net income and the investment carried at fair value in the balance sheet. For HTM and AFS investments, this simply requires reclassifying those investments as trading securities. For equity method investments, this requires clearly identifying the portion of those investments classified in the significant-influence category that is being accounted for at fair value. In all cases, additional disclosures are required that indicate the quality of inputs used to calculate fair values. (pp. 604, 618) ●

OTHER INVESTMENTS (SPECIAL PURPOSE FUNDS, INVESTMENTS IN LIFE INSURANCE POLICIES)   APPENDIX **12A**

Special Purpose Funds

It's often convenient for companies to set aside money to be used for specific purposes. You learned about one such special purpose fund in Chapter 7 when we discussed petty cash funds. Recall that a petty cash fund is money set aside to conveniently make small expenditures using currency rather than having to follow the time-consuming, formal procedures normally used to process checks. Similar funds sometimes are used to pay interest, payroll, or other short-term needs. Like petty cash, these short-term special purpose funds are reported as current assets.

Some special purpose funds—like petty cash—are current assets.

Special purpose funds also are sometimes established to serve longer term needs. It's common, for instance, to periodically set aside cash into a fund designated to repay bonds and other long-term debt. Such funds usually accumulate cash over the debt's term to maturity and are composed of the company's periodic contributions plus interest or dividends from investing the money in various return-generating investments. In fact, some debt contracts require the borrower to establish such a fund to repay the debt. In similar fashion, management might voluntarily choose to establish a fund to accumulate money to expand facilities, provide for unexpected losses, buy back shares of stock, or any other special purpose that might benefit from an accumulation of funds. Of course, funds that won't be used within the upcoming operating cycle are noncurrent assets. They are reported as part of investments and funds. The same criteria for classifying securities into reporting categories that we discussed previously should be used to classify securities in which funds are invested. Any investment revenue from these funds is reported as such on the income statement.

A special purpose fund can be established for virtually any purpose.

Noncurrent special purpose funds are reported within the category investments and funds.

Investments in Life Insurance Policies

Companies frequently buy life insurance policies on the lives of their key officers. Under normal circumstances, the company pays the premium for the policy and, as beneficiary, receives the proceeds when the officer dies. Of course, the objective is to compensate the company for the untimely loss of a valuable resource in the event the officer dies. However, some types of life insurance policies can be surrendered while the insured is still alive in exchange for a determinable amount of money, called the cash surrender value. In effect, a portion of each premium payment is not used by the insurance company to pay for life insurance coverage, but instead is invested on behalf of the insured company in a fixed-income investment. Accordingly, the cash surrender value increases each year by the portion of premiums invested plus interest on the previous amount invested. This is simply a characteristic of whole life insurance, unlike term insurance whose lower premiums provide death benefits only.

Certain life insurance policies can be surrendered while the insured is still alive in exchange for its cash surrender value.

From an accounting standpoint, the periodic insurance premium should not be expensed in its entirety. Rather, part of each premium payment, the investment portion, is recorded as an asset. Illustration 12A–1 provides an example. ●

Part of each insurance premium represents an increase in the cash surrender value.

ILLUSTRATION 12A–1 Cash Surrender Value	Several years ago, American Capital acquired a $1 million insurance policy on the life of its chief executive officer, naming American Capital as beneficiary. Annual premiums are $18,000, payable at the beginning of each year. In 2009, the cash surrender value of the policy increased according to the contract from $5,000 to $7,000. The CEO died at the end of 2009.
Part of the annual premium represents a build-up in the cash surrender value.	Insurance expense (difference) .... 16,000 Cash surrender value of life insurance ($7,000 − 5,000) .... 2,000 Cash (2009 premium) .... 18,000 *To record insurance expense and the increase in the investment.* The cash surrender value is considered to be a noncurrent investment and would be reported in the investments and funds section of the balance sheet. Of course when the insured officer dies, the corporation receives the death benefit of the insurance policy, and the cash surrender value ceases to exist because canceling the policy no longer is an option. The corporation recognizes a gain for the amount of the death benefit less the cash surrender value:

When the death benefit is paid, the cash surrender value becomes null and void.	Cash (death benefit) 1,000,000
	  Cash surrender value of life insurance (balance) 7,000
	  Gain on life insurance settlement (difference) 993,000
	To record the proceeds at death.

IMPAIRMENT OF A RECEIVABLE DUE TO A TROUBLED DEBT RESTRUCTURING

When a company invests in the debt of another company, there is some potential that their investment (the principal receivable) will eventually be impaired. When a creditor's receivable becomes impaired for any reason, the receivable is remeasured based on the discounted present value of currently expected cash flows at the loan's original effective rate (regardless of the extent to which expected cash receipts have been reduced).

When the original terms of a debt agreement are changed as a result of financial difficulties experienced by the debtor (borrower), the new arrangement is referred to as a **troubled debt restructuring.** We discuss troubled debt restructurings in much more detail in Chapter 14. The essential point here is that such an arrangement involves some concessions on the part of the creditor (lender), resulting in the impairment of the creditor's asset: the investment in a receivable.

When the Receivable Is Settled Outright

Sometimes a receivable in a troubled debt restructuring is actually settled at the time of the restructuring with the receipt of cash (or a noncash asset), or even shares of the debtor's stock. In that case, the creditor simply records a loss for the difference between the carrying amount of the receivable and the fair value of the asset(s) or equity securities received. Illustration 12B–1 provides an example.

First Prudent Bank is owed $30 million by Brillard Properties under a 10% note with two years remaining to maturity. Due to financial difficulties of the developer, the previous year's interest ($3 million) was not received. The bank agrees to settle the receivable (and accrued interest receivable) in exchange for property having a fair value of $20 million.		**ILLUSTRATION 12B–1** Debt Settled at the Time of a Restructuring

	($ in millions)	
Land (fair value)	20	
Loss on troubled debt restructuring (to balance)	13	
Accrued interest receivable (10% × $30 million)		3
Note receivable (balance)		30

The carrying amount of the receivable is $33 million.

For most active lenders, a troubled debt restructuring unfortunately is not both unusual and infrequent; so usually the loss is not reported as an extraordinary loss.

When the Receivable Is Continued, but with Modified Terms

In the previous example we assumed that First Prudent Bank agreed to accept property in full settlement of the receivable. In a troubled debt restructuring, it is more likely that the bank would allow the receivable to continue but with the terms of the debt agreement modified to make it easier for the debtor to comply. The lender might agree to reduce or delay the scheduled interest payments. Or, it may agree to reduce or delay the maturity amount. Often a troubled debt restructuring will call for some combination of these concessions.

As one of many possibilities, suppose the bank agrees to (1) forgive the interest accrued from last year, (2) reduce the two remaining interest payments from $3 million each to $2 million each, and (3) reduce the face amount from $30 million to $25 million. Clearly, the bank's investment in the receivable has been impaired. The extent of impairment is the difference between the $33 million carrying amount of the receivable (the present value of the receivable's cash flows prior to the restructuring) and the present value of the revised cash flows discounted at the loan's original effective rate (10%). See Illustration 12B–2 for a demonstration.

After restructuring, the lender still records interest annually at the 10% effective rate. ●

ILLUSTRATION 12B–2	Brillard Properties owes First Prudent Bank $30 million under a 10% note with two years remaining to maturity. Due to financial difficulties of the developer, the previous year's interest ($3 million) was not paid. First Prudent Bank agrees to:
Receivable Impaired by Troubled Debt Restructuring— Terms Modified	1. Forgive the interest accrued from last year. 2. Reduce the remaining two interest payments to $2 million each. 3. Reduce the principal to $25 million.

Analysis

Previous Value

Accrued interest	(10% × $30,000,000)	$ 3,000,000	
Principal		30,000,000	
Carrying amount of the receivable			$33,000,000

The discounted present value of the cash flows prior to the restructuring is the same as the receivable's carrying amount.

New Value

Present value of future interest	$ 2 million × 1.73554* =	$ 3,471,080	
Present value of principal	$25 million × 0.82645† =	20,661,250	
Present value of the receivable			(24,132,330)
Loss			$ 8,867,670

The discounted present value of the cash flows after the restructuring is less.

*Present value of an ordinary annuity of $1: $n = 2$, $i = 10\%$
†Present value of $1: $n = 2$, $i = 10\%$

Journal Entry

The difference is a loss.

Loss on troubled debt restructuring (to balance)	8,867,670	
Accrued interest receivable (10% × $30,000,000)		3,000,000
Note receivable ($30,000,000 − 24,132,330)		5,867,670

QUESTIONS FOR REVIEW OF KEY TOPICS

Q 12–1 All investments in *debt* securities and investments in *equity* securities for which the investor lacks significant influence over the operation and financial policies of the investee are classified for reporting purposes in one of three categories, and can be accounted for differently depending on the classification. What are these three categories?

Q 12–2 When market rates of interest *rise* after a fixed-rate security is purchased, the value of the now-below-market, fixed-interest payments declines, so the market value of the investment falls. On the other hand, if market rates of interest *fall* after a fixed-rate security is purchased, the fixed-interest payments become relatively attractive, and the market value of the investment rises. How are these price changes reflected in the investment account for a security classified as held-to-maturity?

Q 12–3 What accounting standard governs the determination of the fair value of an investment? Does the standard distinguish between fair values that are readily determinable from a securities exchange versus those needing to be calculated based on the company's own assumptions? Explain how a user will know about the reliability of the inputs used to determine fair value.

Q 12–4 When an investment is acquired to be held for an unspecified period of time as opposed to being held to maturity, it is reported at the fair value of the investment securities on the reporting date. Why?

Q 12–5 Reporting an investment at its fair value means adjusting its carrying amount for changes in fair value after its acquisition (or since the last reporting date if it was held at that time). Such changes are called unrealized holding gains and losses because they haven't yet been realized through the sale of the security. If the security is classified as available-for-sale, how are unrealized holding gains and losses reported?

Q 12–6 What is "comprehensive income"? Its composition varies from company to company but may include which investment-related items that are not included in net income?

Q 12–7 Why are holding gains and losses treated differently for trading securities and securities available-for-sale?

Q 12–8 The market value of Helig Forestry and Mining Corporation common stock dropped 6¼ points when the federal government passed new legislation banning one of the company's primary techniques for extracting ore. Harris Corporation owns shares of Helig and classifies its investment as securities available-for-sale. How should the decline in market value be handled by Harris?

Q 12–9 Western Die-Casting Company holds an investment in unsecured bonds of LGB Heating Equipment, Inc. When the investment was acquired, management's intention was to hold the bonds for resale. Now management has the positive intent and ability to hold the bonds to maturity. How should the reclassification of the investment be accounted for?

Q 12–10   Is it necessary for an investor to report individual amounts for the three categories of investments—held-to-maturity, available-for-sale, or trading—in the financial statements? What information should be disclosed about these investments?

Q 12–11   What is the effect of a company electing the fair value option with respect to a held-to-maturity investment or an available-for-sale investment?

Q 12–12   Do U.S. GAAP and IFRS differ in the amount of flexibility that companies have in electing the fair value option? Explain.

Q 12–13   Under what circumstances is the equity method used to account for an investment in stock?

Q 12–14   The equity method has been referred to as a *one-line consolidation*. What might prompt this description?

Q 12–15   In the application of the equity method, how should dividends from the investee be accounted for? Why?

Q 12–16   The fair value of depreciable assets of Penner Packaging Company exceeds their book value by $12 million. The assets' average remaining useful life is 10 years. They are being depreciated by the straight-line method. Finest Foods Industries buys 40% of Penner's common shares. When adjusting investment revenue and the investment by the equity method, how will the situation described affect those two accounts?

Q 12–17   Superior Company owns 40% of the outstanding stock of Bernard Company. During 2009, Bernard paid a $100,000 cash dividend on its common shares. What effect did this dividend have on Superior's 2009 financial statements?

Q 12–18   Sometimes an investor's level of influence changes, making it necessary to change from the equity method to another method. How should the investor account for this change in accounting method?

Q 12–19   How does IFRS differ from U.S. GAAP with respect to using the equity method?

Q 12–20   What is the effect of a company electing the fair value option with respect to an investment that otherwise would be accounted for using the equity method?

Q 12–21   Define a financial instrument. Provide three examples of current liabilities that represent financial instruments.

Q 12–22   Some financial instruments are called derivatives. Why?

Q 12–23   (Based on Appendix 12A) Northwest Carburetor Company established a fund in 2006 to accumulate money for a new plant scheduled for construction in 2009. How should this special purpose fund be reported in Northwest's balance sheet?

Q 12–24   (Based on Appendix 12A) Whole-life insurance policies typically can be surrendered while the insured is still alive in exchange for a determinable amount of money called the *cash surrender value*. When a company buys a life insurance policy on the life of a key officer to protect the company against the untimely loss of a valuable resource in the event the officer dies, how should the company account for the cash surrender value?

Q 12–25   (Based on Appendix 12B) Marshall Companies, Inc., holds a note receivable from a former subsidiary. Due to financial difficulties, the former subsidiary has been unable to pay the previous year's interest on the note. Marshall agreed to restructure the debt by both delaying and reducing remaining cash payments. The concessions impair the creditor's investment in the receivable. How is this impairment recorded?

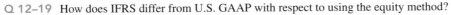

BRIEF EXERCISES

BE 12–1
Securities held-to-maturity; bond investment; effective interest

● LO1

Lance Brothers Enterprises acquired $720,000 of 3% bonds, dated July 1, on July 1, 2009, as a long-term investment. Management has the positive intent and ability to hold the bonds until maturity. The market interest rate (yield) was 4% for bonds of similar risk and maturity. Lance Brothers paid $600,000 for the investment in bonds and will receive interest semiannually on June 30 and December 31. Prepare the journal entries (a) to record Lance Brothers' investment in the bonds on July 1, 2009, and (b) to record interest on December 31, 2009, at the effective (market) rate.

BE 12–2
Trading securities

● LO2

S&L Financial buys and sells securities expecting to earn profits on short-term differences in price. On December 27, 2009, S&L purchased **Coca-Cola** common shares for $875,000 and sold the shares on January 3, 2010, for $880,000. At December 31, the shares had a fair value of $873,000. What pretax amounts did S&L include in its 2009 and 2010 earnings as a result of this investment?

BE 12–3
Available-for-sale securities

● LO3

S&L Financial buys and sells securities which it classifies as available-for-sale. On December 27, 2009, S&L purchased **Coca-Cola** common shares for $875,000 and sold the shares on January 3, 2010, for $880,000. At December 31, the shares had a fair value of $873,000. What pretax amounts did S&L include in its 2009 and 2010 earnings as a result of this investment?

BE 12–4
Securities
available-for-sale;
adjusting entry

● LO3

For several years Fister Links Products has held shares of **Microsoft** common stock, considered by the company to be securities available-for-sale. The shares were acquired at a cost of $500,000. Their fair value last year was $610,000 and is $670,000 this year. At what amount will the investment be reported in this year's balance sheet? What adjusting entry is required to accomplish this objective?

BE 12–5
Classification of
securities;
reporting

● LO3

Adams Industries holds 40,000 shares of **FedEx** common stock. On December 31, 2008, and December 31, 2009, the market value of the stock is $95 and $100 per share, respectively. What is the appropriate reporting category for this investment and at what amount will it be reported in the 2009 balance sheet?

BE 12–6
Fair value option;
available-for-sale
securities

● LO7

S&L Financial buys and sells securities that it typically classifies as available-for-sale. On December 27, 2009, S&L purchased **Coca-Cola** common shares for $875,000 and sold the shares on January 3, 2010, for $880,000. At December 31, the shares had a fair value of $873,000. When it purchased the Coca-Cola shares, S&L Financial decided to elect the fair value option for this investment. What pretax amounts did S&L include in its 2009 and 2010 earnings as a result of this investment?

BE 12–7
Equity method

● LO4 LO5

Turner Company owns 40% of the outstanding stock of ICA Company. During the current year, ICA paid a $5 million cash dividend on its common shares. What effect did this dividend have on Turner's 2009 financial statements? Explain the reasoning for this effect.

BE 12–8
Equity method

● LO2 LO3

Turner Company owns 10% of the outstanding stock of ICA Company. During the current year, ICA paid a $5 million cash dividend on its common shares. What effect did this dividend have on Turner's 2009 financial statements? Explain the reasoning for this effect.

BE 12–9
Fair value
option; equity
method
investments

● LO7

Turner Company purchased 40% of the outstanding stock of ICA Company for $10,000,000 on January 2, 2009. Turner elects the fair value option to account for the investment. During 2009, ICA earns $750,000 of income and on December 30 pays a dividend of $500,000. On December 31, 2009, the fair value of Turner's investment has increased to $11,500,000. What journal entries would Turner make to account for this investment during 2009, assuming Turner will account for the investment similar to how it would account for a trading security?

BE 12–10
Equity method

● LO6

The fair value of Wallis, Inc.'s depreciable assets exceeds their book value by $50 million. The assets have an average remaining useful life of 15 years and are being depreciated by the straight-line method. Park Industries buys 30% of Wallis's common shares. When Park adjusts its investment revenue and the investment by the equity method, how will the situation described affect those two accounts?

BE 12–11
Equity method
investments

● LO6

Refer to the situation described in BE 12–10, but assume that Park Industries buys 50% of Wallis's common shares. Also assume that Park reports under International Financial Reporting Standards, and has elected the "proportionate consolidation" method to account for the Wallis investment. How would the situation described affect Park's depreciable asset accounts?

BE 12–12
Impairment

● LO3

LED Corporation owns 100,000 shares of Branch Pharmaceuticals common stock and classifies its investment as securities available-for-sale. The market price of Branch's stock fell over 30%, by $4.50 per share, when the FDA banned one of the company's principal drugs. What journal entry should LED record to account for the decline in market value? How should the decline be reported?

BE 12–13
Change in
principle; change
to the equity
method

● LO5

At the beginning of 2009, Pioneer Products' ownership interest in the common stock of LLB Co. increased to the point that it became appropriate to begin using the equity method of accounting for the investment. The balance in the investment account was $44 million at the time of the change but would have been $56 million if Pioneer had used the equity method and the account had been adjusted for investee net income and dividends. How should Pioneer report the change? Would your answer be the same if Pioneer is changing *from* the equity method rather than *to* the equity method?

An alternate exercise and problem set is available on the text website: www.mhhe.com/spiceland5e

E 12–1
Securities held-to-maturity;
bond investment;
effective interest

● **LO1**

Tanner-UNF Corporation acquired as a long-term investment $240 million of 6% bonds, dated July 1, on July 1 2009. Company management has the positive intent and ability to hold the bonds until maturity. The market interest rate (yield) was 8% for bonds of similar risk and maturity. Tanner-UNF paid $200 million for the bonds. The company will receive interest semiannually on June 30 and December 31. As a result of changing market conditions, the fair value of the bonds at December 31, 2009, was $210 million.

Required:
1. Prepare the journal entry to record Tanner-UNF's investment in the bonds on July 1, 2009.
2. Prepare the journal entries by Tanner-UNF to record interest on December 31, 2009, at the effective (market) rate.
3. At what amount will Tanner-UNF report its investment in the December 31, 2009, balance sheet? Why?
4. Suppose Moody's bond rating agency downgraded the risk rating of the bonds motivating Tanner-UNF to sell the investment on January 2, 2010, for $190 million. Prepare the journal entry to record the sale.

E 12–2
Securities held-to-maturity

● **LO1**

FF&T Corporation is a confectionery wholesaler that frequently buys and sells securities to meet various investment objectives. The following selected transactions relate to FF&T's investment activities during the last two months of 2009. At November 1, FF&T held $48 million of 20-year, 10% bonds of Convenience, Inc., purchased May 1, 2009, at face value. Management has the positive intent and ability to hold the bonds until maturity. FF&T's fiscal year ends on December 31.

Nov. 1	Received semiannual interest of $2.4 million from the Convenience, Inc., bonds.
Dec. 1	Purchased 12% bonds of Facsimile Enterprises at their $30 million face value, to be held until they mature in 2022. Semiannual interest is payable May 31 and November 30.
31	Purchased U.S. Treasury bills that mature in two months for $8.9 million.
31	Recorded any necessary adjusting entry(s) relating to the investments.

The fair values of the investments at December 31 were:

Convenience bonds	$44.7 million
Facsimile Enterprises bonds	30.9 million
U.S. Treasury bills	8.9 million

Required:
Prepare the appropriate journal entry for each transaction or event.

E 12–3
Purchase and sale
of investment
securities

● **LO2 LO3**

Shott Farm Supplies Corporation purchased 800 shares of **General Motors** stock at $50 per share and paid a brokerage fee of $1,200. Two months later, the shares were sold for $53 per share. The brokerage fee on the sale was $1,300.

Required:
Prepare entries for the purchase and the sale.

E 12–4
Securities
available-for-sale;
adjusting entries

● **LO3**

Loreal-American Corporation purchased several marketable securities during 2009. At December 31, 2009, the company had the investments in common stock listed below. None was held at the last reporting date, December 31, 2008, and all are considered securities available-for-sale.

	Cost	Fair Value	Unrealized Holding Gain (Loss)
Short term:			
Blair, Inc.	$ 480,000	$ 405,000	$(75,000)
ANC Corporation	450,000	480,000	30,000
Totals	$ 930,000	$ 885,000	$(45,000)
Long term:			
Drake Corporation	$ 480,000	$ 560,000	$ 80,000
Aaron Industries	720,000	660,000	(60,000)
Totals	$1,200,000	$1,220,000	$ 20,000

Required:
1. Prepare appropriate adjusting entries at December 31, 2009.
2. What amounts would be reported in the income statement at December 31, 2009, as a result of these adjusting entries?

E 12–5
Classification of securities; adjusting entries

● LO3

On February 18, 2009, Union Corporation purchased 10,000 shares of **IBM** common stock as a long-term investment at $60 per share. On December 31, 2009, and December 31, 2010, the market value of IBM stock is $58 and $61 per share, respectively.

Required:

1. What is the appropriate reporting category for this investment? Why?
2. Prepare the adjusting entry for December 31, 2009.
3. Prepare the adjusting entry for December 31, 2010.

E 12–6
Various transactions related to securities available-for-sale

● LO3

Construction Forms Corporation buys securities to be available for sale when circumstances warrant, not to profit from short-term differences in price and not necessarily to hold debt securities to maturity. The following selected transactions relate to investment activities of Construction Forms whose fiscal year ends on December 31. No investments were held by Construction Forms at the beginning of the year.

2009

Mar. 2	Purchased 1 million Platinum Gauges, Inc., common shares for $31 million, including brokerage fees and commissions.
Apr. 12	Purchased $20 million of 10% bonds at face value from Zenith Wholesale Corporation.
July 18	Received cash dividends of $2 million on the investment in Platinum Gauges, Inc., common shares.
Oct. 15	Received semiannual interest of $1 million on the investment in Zenith bonds.
16	Sold the Zenith bonds for $21 million.
Nov. 1	Purchased 500,000 LTD International preferred shares for $40 million, including brokerage fees and commissions.
Dec. 31	Recorded the necessary adjusting entry(s) relating to the investments. The market prices of the investments are $32 per share for Platinum Gauges, Inc., and $74 per share for LTD International preferred shares.

2010

Jan. 23	Sold half the Platinum Gauges, Inc., shares for $32 per share.
Mar. 1	Sold the LTD International preferred shares for $76 per share.

Required:

1. Prepare the appropriate journal entry for each transaction or event.
2. Show the amounts that would be reported in the company's 2009 income statement relative to these investments.

E 12–7
Securities available-for-sale; journal entries

● LO3

On January 2, 2009, Sanborn Tobacco, Inc. bought 5% of Jackson Industry's capital stock for $90 million as a temporary investment. Sanborn classified the securities acquired as available-for-sale. Jackson Industry's net income for the year ended December 31, 2009, was $120 million. The fair value of the shares held by Sanborn was $98 million at December 31, 2009. During 2009, Jackson declared a dividend of $60 million.

Required:

1. Prepare all appropriate journal entries related to the investment during 2009.
2. Indicate the effect of this investment on 2009 income before taxes.

E 12–8
Various transactions relating to trading securities

● LO2

Rantzow-Lear Company buys and sells securities expecting to earn profits on short-term differences in price. The company's fiscal year ends on December 31. The following selected transactions relating to Rantzow-Lear's trading account occurred during December 2009 and the first week of 2010.

2009

Dec. 17	Purchased 100,000 Grocers' Supply Corporation preferred shares for $350,000.
28	Received cash dividends of $2,000 from the Grocers' Supply Corporation preferred shares.
31	Recorded any necessary adjusting entry relating to the Grocers' Supply Corporation preferred shares. The market price of the stock was $4 per share.

2010

Jan. 5	Sold the Grocers' Supply Corporation preferred shares for $395,000.

Required:

1. Prepare the appropriate journal entry for each transaction.
2. Indicate any amounts that Rantzow-Lear Company would report in its 2009 balance sheet and income statement as a result of this investment.

E 12–9
Various investment securities

● LO1 LO2 LO3

At December 31, 2009, Hull-Meyers Corp. had the following investments that were purchased during 2009, its first year of operations:

	Cost	Fair Value
Trading Securities:		
Security A	$ 900,000	$ 910,000
Security B	105,000	100,000
Totals	$1,005,000	$1,010,000
Securities Available-for-Sale:		
Security C	$ 700,000	$ 780,000
Security D	900,000	915,000
Totals	$1,600,000	$1,695,000
Securities to Be Held-to-Maturity:		
Security E	$ 490,000	$ 500,000
Security F	615,000	610,000
Totals	$1,105,000	$1,110,000

No investments were sold during 2009. All securities except Security D and Security F are considered short-term investments. None of the fair value changes is considered permanent.

Required:
Determine the following amounts at December 31, 2009.
1. Investments reported as current assets.
2. Investments reported as noncurrent assets.
3. Unrealized gain (or loss) component of income before taxes.
4. Unrealized gain (or loss) component of accumulated other comprehensive income in shareholders' equity.

E 12–10
Securities available-for-sale; adjusting entries
● LO3

The accounting records of Jamaican Importers, Inc. at January 1, 2009, included the following:

Assets:	
Investment in IBM common shares	$1,345,000
Less: Fair value adjustment	(145,000)
	$1,200,000
Shareholders' Equity:	
Accumulated unrealized holding gains and losses	$ 145,000

No changes occurred during 2009 in the investment portfolio.

Required:
Prepare appropriate adjusting entry(s) at December 31, 2009, assuming the fair value of the IBM common shares was:
1. $1,175,000
2. $1,275,000
3. $1,375,000

E 12–11
Securities available-for-sale; fair value adjustment
● LO3

The investments of Harlon Enterprises included the following cost and fair value amounts:

($ in millions)		Fair Value, Dec. 31	
Securities Available-for-Sale	Cost	2009	2010
A Corporation shares	$ 20	$14	na
B Corporation bonds	35	35	$ 37
C Corporation shares	15	na	14
D Industries shares	45	46	50
Totals	$115	$95	$101

Harlon Enterprises sold its holdings of A Corporation shares on June 1, 2010, for $15 million. On September 12, it purchased the C Corporation shares.

Required:
1. What is the effect of the sale of the A Corporation shares and the purchase of the C Corporation shares on Harlon's 2010 pretax earnings?
2. At what amount should Harlon's securities available-for-sale portfolio be reported in its 2010 balance sheet? What adjusting entry is needed to accomplish this? What is the effect of the adjustment on Harlon's 2010 pretax earnings?

E 12–12
Investment securities and equity method investments compared

● LO3 LO4

As a long-term investment, Painters' Equipment Company purchased 20% of AMC Supplies, Inc.'s 400,000 shares for $480,000 at the beginning of the fiscal year of both companies. On the purchase date, the fair value and book value of AMC's net assets were equal. During the year, AMC earned net income of $250,000 and distributed cash dividends of 25 cents per share. At year-end, the fair value of the shares is $505,000.

Required:
1. Assume no significant influence was acquired. Prepare the appropriate journal entries from the purchase through the end of the year.
2. Assume significant influence was acquired. Prepare the appropriate journal entries from the purchase through the end of the year.

E 12–13
Equity method; purchase; investee income; dividends

● LO4 LO5

As a long-term investment at the beginning of the fiscal year, Florists International purchased 30% of Nursery Supplies, Inc.'s 8 million shares for $56 million. The fair value and book value of the shares were the same at that time. During the year, Nursery Supplies earned net income of $40 million and distributed cash dividends of $1.25 per share. At the end of the year, the fair value of the shares is $52 million.

Required:
Prepare the appropriate journal entries from the purchase through the end of the year.

E 12–14
Change in principle; change to the equity method

● LO5

The Trump Companies, Inc. has ownership interests in several public companies. At the beginning of 2009, the company's ownership interest in the common stock of Milken Properties increased to the point that it became appropriate to begin using the equity method of accounting for the investment. The balance in the investment account was $31 million at the time of the change. Accountants working with company records determined that the balance would have been $48 million if the account had been adjusted for investee net income and dividends as prescribed by the equity method.

Required:
1. Prepare the journal entry to record the change in principle.
2. Briefly describe other steps Trump should take to report the change.
3. Suppose Trump is changing *from* the equity method rather than *to* the equity method. How would your answers to requirements 1 and 2 differ?

E 12–15
Error corrections; investment

● LO1 LO2 LO3

On December 12, 2009, an investment costing $80,000 was sold for $100,000. The total of the sale proceeds was credited to the investment account.

Required:
1. Prepare the journal entry to correct the error assuming it is discovered before the books are adjusted or closed in 2009. (Ignore income taxes.)
2. Prepare the journal entry to correct the error assuming it is not discovered until early 2010. (Ignore income taxes.)

E 12–16
Equity method; adjustment for depreciation

● LO5 LO6

Fizer Pharmaceutical paid $68 million on January 2, 2009, for 4 million shares of Carne Cosmetics common stock. The investment represents a 25% interest in the net assets of Carne and gave Fizer the ability to exercise significant influence over Carne's operations. Fizer received dividends of $1 per share on December 21, 2009, and Carne reported net income of $40 million for the year ended December 31, 2009. The fair value of Carne's common stock at December 31, 2009, was $18.50 per share.
- The book value of Carne's net assets was $192 million.
- The fair value of Carne's depreciable assets exceeded their book value by $32 million. These assets had an average remaining useful life of eight years.
- The remainder of the excess of the cost of the investment over the book value of net assets purchased was attributable to goodwill.

Required:
Prepare all appropriate journal entries related to the investment during 2009.

E 12–17
Equity method

● LO5 LO6

On January 1, 2009, Cameron, Inc. bought 20% of the outstanding common stock of Lake Construction Company for $300 million cash. At the date of acquisition of the stock, Lake's net assets had a fair value of $900 million. Their book value was $800 million. The difference was attributable to the fair value of Lake's buildings and its land exceeding book value, each accounting for one-half of the difference. Lake's net income for the year ended December 31, 2009, was $150 million. During 2009, Lake declared and paid cash dividends of $30 million. The buildings have a remaining life of 10 years.

Required:
1. Prepare all appropriate journal entries related to the investment during 2009, assuming Cameron accounts for this investment by the equity method.
2. Determine the amounts to be reported by Cameron:
   a. As an investment in Cameron's 2009 balance sheet.
   b. As investment revenue in the income statement.
   c. Among investing activities in the statement of cash flows.

E 12–18
Proportionate
consolidation of
investments under
IFRS

● LO6

[This is a variation of Exercise 12–17 focusing on using proportionate consolidation to account for joint ventures under IFRS.]

Refer to the situation described in Exercise 12–17, but assume that Cameron bought 50% of the outstanding stock of Lake for $750 million cash, that half of the book value and fair value of Lake's individual net assets is attributable to land and the other half to buildings, that Cameron reports under IFRS, and that Cameron has elected the proportionate consolidation method to account for its investment in Lake.

Required:

1. What would be the effect on January 1, 2009, of the Lake investment on the following accounts on Cameron's consolidated balance sheet?
   a. Buildings
   b. Land
   c. Goodwill
   d. Equity method investments

2. What would be the effect on December 31, 2009, of the Lake investment on the following accounts on Cameron's consolidated balance sheet?
   a. Buildings
   b. Land
   c. Goodwill
   d. Equity method investments

3. Would the effect on Cameron's December 31, 2009, retained earnings differ between an equity method and a proportionate consolidation treatment? Explain.

E 12–19
Fair value option;
held-to-maturity
investments

● LO1 LO2 LO7

[This is a variation of Exercise 12–1 focusing on the fair value option.]

Tanner-UNF Corporation acquired as a long-term investment $240 million of 6% bonds, dated July 1, on July 1, 2009. Company management has the positive intent and ability to hold the bonds until maturity, but when the bonds were acquired Tanner-UNF decided to elect the fair value option for accounting for its investment. The market interest rate (yield) was 8% for bonds of similar risk and maturity. Tanner-UNF paid $200 million for the bonds. The company will receive interest semiannually on June 30 and December 31. As a result of changing market conditions, the fair value of the bonds at December 31, 2009, was $210 million.

Required:

1. Would this investment be classified on Tanner-UNF's balance sheet as held-to-maturity securities, trading securities, available-for-sale securities, significant-influence investments, or other? Explain.

2. Prepare the journal entry to record Tanner-UNF's investment in the bonds on July 1, 2009.

3. Prepare the journal entries by Tanner-UNF to record interest on December 31, 2009, at the effective (market) rate.

4. Prepare any journal entry necessary to recognize fair value changes as of December 31, 2009.

5. At what amount will Tanner-UNF report its investment in the December 31, 2009, balance sheet? Why?

6. Suppose Moody's bond rating agency downgraded the risk rating of the bonds motivating Tanner-UNF to sell the investment on January 2, 2010, for $190 million. Prepare the journal entry to record the sale.

E 12–20
Fair value option;
available-for-sale
investments

● LO2 LO3 LO7

[This is a variation of Exercise 12–7 focusing on the fair value option.]

On January 2, 2009, Sanborn Tobacco, Inc., bought 5% of Jackson Industry's capital stock for $90 million as a temporary investment. Sanborn realized that these securities normally would be classified as available-for-sale, but elected the fair value option to account for the investment. Jackson Industry's net income for the year ended December 31, 2009, was $120 million. The fair value of the shares held by Sanborn was $98 million at December 31, 2009. During 2009, Jackson declared a dividend of $60 million.

Required:

1. Would this investment be classified on Sanborn's balance sheet as held-to-maturity securities, trading securities, available-for-sale securities, significant-influence investments, or other? Explain.

2. Prepare all appropriate journal entries related to the investment during 2009.

3. Indicate the effect of this investment on 2009 income before taxes.

E 12–21
Fair value option;
equity method
investments

● LO2 LO5 LO7

[This is a variation of Exercise 12–13 focusing on the fair value option.]

As a long-term investment at the beginning of the fiscal year, Florists International purchased 30% of Nursery Supplies, Inc.'s 8 million shares for $56 million. The fair value and book value of the shares were the same at that time. The company realizes that this investment typically would be accounted for under the equity method, but instead chooses the fair value option. During the year, Nursery Supplies earned net income of $40 million and distributed cash dividends of $1.25 per share. At the end of the year, the fair value of the shares is $52 million.

Required:
1. Would this investment be classified on Florists' balance sheet as held-to-maturity securities, trading securities, available-for-sale securities, significant-influence investments, or other? Explain.
2. Prepare all appropriate journal entries related to the investment during 2009.
3. Indicate the effect of this investment on 2009 income before taxes.

E 12–22
Life insurance policy (Based on Appendix 12A)

Edible Chemicals Corporation owns a $4 million whole life insurance policy on the life of its CEO, naming Edible Chemicals as beneficiary. The annual premiums are $70,000 and are payable at the beginning of each year. The cash surrender value of the policy was $21,000 at the beginning of 2009.

Required:
1. Prepare the appropriate 2009 journal entry to record insurance expense and the increase in the investment assuming the cash surrender value of the policy increased according to the contract to $27,000.
2. The CEO died at the end of 2009. Prepare the appropriate journal entry.

E 12–23
Life insurance policy (Based on Appendix 12A)

Below are two unrelated situations relating to life insurance.

Required:
Prepare the appropriate journal entry for each situation.
1. Ford Corporation owns a whole life insurance policy on the life of its president. Ford Corporation is the beneficiary. The insurance premium is $25,000. The cash surrender value increased during the year from $2,500 to $4,600.
2. Petroleum Corporation received a $250,000 life insurance settlement when its CEO died. At that time, the cash surrender value was $16,000.

E 12–24
Impairment of securities available-for-sale; troubled debt restructuring (Based on Appendix 12B)

● LO3

At January 1, 2009, Clayton Hoists, Inc. owed Third BancCorp $12 million, under a 10% note due December 31, 2010. Interest was paid last on December 31, 2007. Clayton was experiencing severe financial difficulties and asked Third BancCorp to modify the terms of the debt agreement. After negotiation Third BancCorp agreed to:
• Forgive the interest accrued for the year just ended.
• Reduce the remaining two years' interest payments to $1 million each.
• Reduce the principal amount to $11 million.

Required:
Prepare the journal entries by Third BancCorp necessitated by the restructuring of the debt at
1. January 1, 2009.
2. December 31, 2009.
3. December 31, 2010.

E 12–25
Impairment of securities available-for-sale; troubled debt restructuring (Based on Appendix 12B)

● LO3

At January 1, 2009, NCI Industries, Inc. was indebted to First Federal Bank under a $240,000, 10% unsecured note. The note was signed January 1, 2005, and was due December 31, 2010. Annual interest was last paid on December 31, 2007. NCI was experiencing severe financial difficulties and negotiated a restructuring of the terms of the debt agreement. First Federal agreed to reduce last year's interest and the remaining two years' interest payments to $11,555 each and delay all payments until December 31, 2010, the maturity date.

Required:
Prepare the journal entries by First Federal Bank necessitated by the restructuring of the debt at
1. January 1, 2009.
2. December 31, 2009.
3. December 31, 2010.

CPA AND CMA REVIEW QUESTIONS

CPA Exam Questions

The following questions are used in the Kaplan CPA Review Course to study investments while preparing for the CPA examination. Determine the response that best completes the statements or questions.

● LO2

1. During year 4, Wall Co. purchased 2,000 shares of Hemp Corp. common stock for $31,500 as a short-term investment. The investment was appropriately classified as a trading security. The market value of this investment was $29,500 at December 31, year 4. Wall sold all of the Hemp common stock for $14 per share

on January 15, year 5, incurring $1,400 in brokerage commissions and taxes. On the sale, Wall should report a realized loss of:

a. $1,500
b. $2,900
c. $3,500
d. $4,900

● LO3   2. The following information pertains to Lark Corp.'s long-term marketable equity securities portfolio:

	December 31	
	2009	**2008**
Cost	$200,000	$200,000
Fair value	240,000	180,000

Differences between cost and market values are considered to be temporary. The decline in market value was properly accounted for at December 31, 2008. At December 31, 2009, what is the net unrealized holding gain or loss to be reported as:

	Other Comprehensive Income	**Accumulated Other Comprehensive Income**
a.	$60,000 gain	$40,000 gain
b.	$40,000 gain	$60,000 gain
c.	$20,000 loss	$20,000 loss
d.	–0–	–0–

● LO3   3. The following information was extracted from Gil Co.'s December 31, 2009, balance sheet:

Noncurrent assets:
  Long-term investments in marketable
    equity securities (at fair value) $96,450
Stockholders' equity:
  Accumulated other comprehensive
    income**   (25,000)
  **Includes a net unrealized holding loss on long-term investments in marketable equity securities of $19,800.

The historical cost of the long-term investments in marketable equity securities was:

a. $ 63,595
b. $ 76,650
c. $ 96,450
d. $116,250

● LO3   4. On both December 31, 2008, and December 31, 2009, Kopp Co.'s only marketable equity security had the same fair value, which was below cost. Kopp considered the decline in value to be temporary in 2008 but other than temporary in 2009. At the end of both years the security was classified as a noncurrent asset. Kopp could not exercise significant influence over the investee. What should be the effects of the determination that the decline was other than temporary on Kopp's 2009 net noncurrent assets and net income?

a. Decrease in both net noncurrent assets and net income.
b. No effect on both net noncurrent assets and net income.
c. Decrease in net noncurrent assets and no effect on net income.
d. No effect on net noncurrent assets and decrease in net income.

● LO5   5. When the equity method is used to account for investments in common stock, which of the following affect(s) the investor's reported investment income?

	A Change in Fair Value of Investee's Common Stock	**Cash Dividends from Investee**
a.	Yes	Yes
b.	No	Yes
c.	Yes	No
d.	No	No

● LO5   6. A corporation uses the equity method to account for its 40% ownership of another company. The investee earned $20,000 and paid $5,000 in dividends. The investor made the following entries:

Investment in affiliate	$8,000	
Equity in earnings of affiliate		$8,000
Cash	2,000	
Dividend revenue		2,000

What effect will these entries have on the investor's statement of financial position?

a. Investment in affiliate overstated, retained earnings understated.

b. Financial position will be fairly stated.

c. Investment in affiliate overstated, retained earnings overstated.

d. Investment in affiliate understated, retained earnings understated.

● LO6

7. Park Co. uses the equity method to account for its January 1, 2009, purchase of Tun Inc.'s common stock. On January 1, 2009, the fair values of Tun's FIFO inventory and land exceeded their carrying amounts. How do these excesses of fair values over carrying amounts affect Park's reported equity in Tun's 2009 earnings?

	Inventory Excess	Land Excess
a.	Decrease	Decrease
b.	Decrease	No effect
c.	Increase	No effect
d.	Increase	Increase

● LO4

8. On January 2, 2009, Well Co. purchased 10% of Rea, Inc.'s outstanding common shares for $400,000. Well is the largest single shareholder in Rea, and Well's officers are a majority on Rea's board of directors. Rea reported net income of $500,000 for 2009, and paid dividends of $150,000. In its December 31, 2009, balance sheet, what amount should Well report as investment in Rea?

a. $435,000

b. $450,000

c. $400,000

d. $385,000

CMA Exam Questions

The following questions dealing with investments are adapted from questions that previously appeared on Certified Management Accountant (CMA) examinations. The CMA designation sponsored by the Institute of Management Accountants (**www.imanet.org**) provides members with an objective measure of knowledge and competence in the field of management accounting. Determine the response that best completes the statements or questions.

● LO3

1. An investment in available-for-sale securities is valued on the balance sheet at

a. The cost to acquire the asset.

b. Accumulated income minus accumulated dividends since acquisition.

c. Fair value.

d. The par or stated value of the securities.

Questions 2 and 3 are based on the following information concerning Monahan Company's portfolio of debt securities at May 31, year 2 and May 31, year 3. All of the debt securities were purchased by Monahan during June, year 1. Prior to June, year 1, Monahan had no investments in debt or equity securities.

As of May 31, Year 2	Amortized Cost	Fair Value
Cleary Company bonds	$164,526	$168,300
Beauchamp Industry bonds	204,964	205,200
Morrow Inc. bonds	305,785	285,200
Total	$675,275	$658,700

As of May 31, Year 3	Amortized Cost	Fair Value
Cleary Company bonds	$152,565	$147,600
Beauchamp Industry bonds	193,800	204,500
Morrow Inc. bonds	289,130	291,400
Total	$635,495	$643,500

● LO3

2. Assuming that the above securities are properly classified as available-for-sale securities under SFAS 115, *Accounting for Certain Investments in Debt and Equity Securities,* the unrealized holding gain or loss as of May 31, year 3 would be

a. recognized as an $8,005 unrealized holding gain on the income statement.

b. recognized in accumulated other comprehensive income by a year-end credit of $8,005.

c. recognized in accumulated other comprehensive income by a year-end debit of $8,005.

d. not recognized.

● LO1   3. Assuming that the above securities are properly classified as held-to-maturity securities under SFAS 115, *Accounting for Certain Investments in Debt and Equity Securities,* the unrealized holding gain or loss as of May 31, year 3 would be

a. recognized as an $8,005 unrealized holding gain on the income statement.

b. recognized in accumulated other comprehensive income by a year-end credit of $8,005.

c. recognized in accumulated other comprehensive income by a year-end debit of $8,005.

d. not recognized.

PROBLEMS

available with McGraw-Hill's Homework Manager www.mhhe.com/spiceland5e

An alternate exercise and problem set is available on the text website: www.mhhe.com/spiceland5e

P 12–1
Securities held-
to-maturity;
bond investment;
effective interest

● LO1

Fuzzy Monkey Technologies, Inc. purchased as a long-term investment $80 million of 8% bonds, dated January 1, on January 1, 2009. Management has the positive intent and ability to hold the bonds until maturity. For bonds of similar risk and maturity the market yield was 10%. The price paid for the bonds was $66 million. Interest is received semiannually on June 30 and December 31. Due to changing market conditions, the fair value of the bonds at December 31, 2009, was $70 million.

Required:

1. Prepare the journal entry to record Fuzzy Monkey's investment on January 1, 2009.
2. Prepare the journal entry by Fuzzy Monkey to record interest on June 30, 2009 (at the effective rate).
3. Prepare the journal entries by Fuzzy Monkey to record interest on December 31, 2009 (at the effective rate).
4. At what amount will Fuzzy Monkey report its investment in the December 31, 2009, balance sheet? Why?
5. How would Fuzzy Monkey's 2009 statement of cash flows be affected by this investment?

P 12–2
Trading securities;
bond investment;
effective interest

● LO2

[This problem is a variation of the preceding problem, modified to cause the investment to be in trading securities.]

Fuzzy Monkey Technologies, Inc. purchased as a short-term investment $80 million of 8% bonds, dated January 1, on January 1, 2009. Management intends to include the investment in a short-term, active trading portfolio. For bonds of similar risk and maturity the market yield was 10%. The price paid for the bonds was $66 million. Interest is received semiannually on June 30 and December 31. Due to changing market conditions, the fair value of the bonds at December 31, 2009, was $70 million.

Required:

1. Prepare the journal entry to record Fuzzy Monkey's investment on January 1, 2009.
2. Prepare the journal entry by Fuzzy Monkey to record interest on June 30, 2009 (at the effective rate).
3. Prepare the journal entries by Fuzzy Monkey to record interest on December 31, 2009 (at the effective rate).
4. At what amount will Fuzzy Monkey report its investment in the December 31, 2009, balance sheet? Why? Prepare any entry necessary to achieve this reporting objective.
5. How would Fuzzy Monkey's 2009 statement of cash flows be affected by this investment?

P 12–3
Securities
available-for-sale;
bond investment;
effective interestt

● LO3

(Note: This problem is a variation of the preceding problem, modified to cause the investment to be in securities available-for-sale.)

Fuzzy Monkey Technologies, Inc. purchased as a long-term investment $80 million of 8% bonds, dated January 1, on January 1, 2009. Management intends to have the investment available for sale when circumstances warrant. For bonds of similar risk and maturity the market yield was 10%. The price paid for the bonds was $66 million. Interest is received semiannually on June 30 and December 31. Due to changing market conditions, the fair value of the bonds at December 31, 2009, was $70 million.

Required:

1. Prepare the journal entry to record Fuzzy Monkey's investment on January 1, 2009.
2. Prepare the journal entry by Fuzzy Monkey to record interest on June 30, 2009 (at the effective rate).
3. Prepare the journal entries by Fuzzy Monkey to record interest on December 31, 2009 (at the effective rate).
4. At what amount will Fuzzy Monkey report its investment in the December 31, 2009, balance sheet? Why? Prepare any entry necessary to achieve this reporting objective.
5. How would Fuzzy Monkey's 2009 statement of cash flows be affected by this investment?

P 12–4
Fair value option; bond investment; effective interest

● LO1 LO2 LO3 LO7

[This problem is a variation of the preceding problem, modified to cause the investment to be accounted for under the fair value option.]

Fuzzy Monkey Technologies, Inc. purchased as a long-term investment $80 million of 8% bonds, dated January 1, on January 1, 2009. Management intends to have the investment available for sale when circumstances warrant. When the company purchased the bonds, management elected to account for them under the fair value option. For bonds of similar risk and maturity the market yield was 10%. The price paid for the bonds was $66 million. Interest is received semiannually on June 30 and December 31. Due to changing market conditions, the fair value of the bonds at December 31, 2009, was $70 million.

Required:
1. Prepare the journal entry to record Fuzzy Monkey's investment on January 1, 2009.
2. Prepare the journal entry by Fuzzy Monkey to record interest on June 30, 2009 (at the effective rate).
3. Prepare the journal entries by Fuzzy Monkey to record interest on December 31, 2009 (at the effective rate).
4. At what amount will Fuzzy Monkey report its investment in the December 31, 2009, balance sheet? Why? Prepare any entry necessary to achieve this reporting objective.
5. How would Fuzzy Monkey's 2009 statement of cash flows be affected by this investment?
6. How would your answers to requirements 1–5 differ if management had the intent and ability to hold the investments until maturity?

P 12–5
Various transactions related to securities available-for-sale

● LO3

The following selected transactions relate to investment activities of Ornamental Insulation Corporation. The company buys securities, *not* intending to profit from short-term differences in price and *not* necessarily to hold debt securities to maturity, but to have them available for sale when circumstances warrant. Ornamental's fiscal year ends on December 31. No investments were held by Ornamental on December 31, 2008.

2009

Feb. 21	Acquired Distribution Transformers Corporation common shares costing $400,000.
Mar. 18	Received cash dividends of $8,000 on the investment in Distribution Transformers common shares.
Sep. 1	Acquired $900,000 of American Instruments' 10% bonds at face value.
Oct. 20	Sold the Distribution Transformers shares for $425,000.
Nov. 1	Purchased M&D Corporation common shares costing $1,400,000.
Dec. 31	Recorded any necessary adjusting entry(s) relating to the investments. The market prices of the investments are:

American Instruments bonds	$ 850,000
M&D Corporation shares	$1,460,000

(Hint: Interest must be accrued for the American Instruments' bonds.)

2010

Jan. 20	Sold the M&D Corporation shares for $1,485,000.
Mar. 1	Received semiannual interest of $45,000 on the investment in American Instruments bonds.
Aug. 12	Acquired Vast Communication common shares costing $650,000.
Sept. 1	Received semiannual interest of $45,000 on the investment in American Instruments bonds.
Dec. 31	Recorded any necessary adjusting entry(s) relating to the investments. The market prices of the investments are:

Vast Communication shares	$670,000
American Instruments bonds	$830,000

Required:
1. Prepare the appropriate journal entry for each transaction or event during 2009.
2. Indicate any amounts that Ornamental Insulation would report in its 2009 balance sheet and income statement as a result of these investments.
3. Prepare the appropriate journal entry for each transaction or event during 2010.
4. Indicate any amounts that Ornamental Insulation would report in its 2010 balance sheet and income statement as a result of these investments.

P 12–6
Various transactions relating to trading securities

American Surety and Fidelity buys and sells securities expecting to earn profits on short-term differences in price. For the first 11 months of 2009, gains from selling trading securities totaled $8 million, losses were $11 million, and the company had earned $5 million in investment revenue. The following selected transactions relate to American's trading account during December, 2009, and the first week of 2010. The company's fiscal year ends on December 31. No trading securities were held by American on December 1, 2009.

● LO2

2009

Dec. 12   Purchased FF&G Corporation bonds for $12 million.
    13   Purchased 2 million Ferry Intercommunications common shares for $22 million.
    15   Sold the FF&G Corporation bonds for $12.1 million.
    22   Purchased U.S. Treasury bills for $56 million and Treasury bonds for $65 million.
    23   Sold half the Ferry Intercommunications common shares for $10 million.
    26   Sold the U.S. Treasury bills for $57 million.
    27   Sold the Treasury bonds for $63 million.
    28   Received cash dividends of $200,000 from the Ferry Intercommunications common shares.
    31   Recorded any necessary adjusting entry(s) and closing entries relating to the investments. The market price of the Ferry Intercommunications stock was $10 per share.

2010

Jan. 2   Sold the remaining Ferry Intercommunications common shares for $10.2 million.
     5   Purchased Warehouse Designs Corporation bonds for $34 million.

Required:

1. Prepare the appropriate journal entry for each transaction or event during 2009, including the closing entry to income summary for the year.

2. Indicate any amounts that American would report in its 2009 balance sheet and income statement as a result of these investments.

3. Prepare the appropriate journal entry for each transaction or event during 2010.

P 12–7
Securities held-to-maturity, securities available for sale, and trading securities

Amalgamated General Corporation is a consulting firm that also offers financial services through its credit division. From time to time the company buys and sells securities intending to earn profits on short-term differences in price. The following selected transactions relate to Amalgamated's investment activities during the last quarter of 2009 and the first month of 2010. The only securities held by Amalgamated at October 1 were $30 million of 10% bonds of Kansas Abstractors, Inc. purchased on May 1 at face value. The company's fiscal year ends on December 31.

● LO1 LO2 LO3

2009

Oct. 18   Purchased 2 million preferred shares of Millwork Ventures Company for $58 million as a speculative investment to be sold under suitable circumstances.
    31   Received semiannual interest of $1.5 million from the Kansas Abstractors bonds.
Nov. 1   Purchased 10% bonds of Holistic Entertainment Enterprises at their $18 million face value, to be held until they mature in 2016. Semiannual interest is payable April 30 and October 31.
     1   Sold the Kansas Abstractors bonds for $28 million because rising interest rates are expected to cause their fair value to continue to fall.
Dec. 1   Purchased 12% bonds of Household Plastics Corporation at their $60 million face value, to be held until they mature in 2026. Semiannual interest is payable May 31 and November 30.
    20   Purchased U. S. Treasury bonds for $5.6 million as trading securities, hoping to earn profits on short-term differences in prices.
    21   Purchased 4 million common shares of NXS Corporation for $44 million as trading securities, hoping to earn profits on short-term differences in prices.
    23   Sold the Treasury bonds for $5.7 million.
    29   Received cash dividends of $3 million from the Millwork Ventures Company preferred shares.
    31   Recorded any necessary adjusting entry(s) and closing entries relating to the investments. The market price of the Millwork Ventures Company preferred stock was $27.50 per share and $11.50 per share for the NXS Corporation common. The fair values of the bond investments were $58.7 million for Household Plastics Corporation and $16.7 million for Holistic Entertainment Enterprises.

2010

Jan. 7   Sold the NXS Corporation common shares for $43 million.

Required:
Prepare the appropriate journal entry for each transaction or event.

P 12–8
Securities available-for-sale; fair value adjustment; reclassification adjustment

At December 31, 2009, the investments in securities available-for-sale of Beale Developments were reported at $78 million:

Securities available-for-sale	$74	
Plus: Fair value adjustment	4	$78

During 2010, Beale sold its investment in Schwab Pharmaceuticals, which had cost $25 million, for $28 million. Those shares had a fair value at December 31, 2009, of $27 million. No other investments were sold. At

● LO3

December 31, 2010, the investments in securities available-for-sale included the cost and fair value amounts shown below.

($ in millions) Securities Available-for-Sale	Cost	Fair Value	Unrealized Gain (Loss)
Daisy Theaters, Inc. shares	$40	$42	$2
Orpheum Entertainment bonds	9	12	3
Totals	$49	$54	$5

Required:

1. At what amount should Beale report its securities available-for-sale in its December 31, 2010, balance sheet?
2. What journal entry is needed to enable the investment to be reported at this amount?
3. What is the amount of the reclassification adjustment to 2010 other comprehensive income? Show how the reclassification adjustment should be reported.

P 12–9
Investment securities and equity method investments compared

● LO3 LO4 LO5 LO6

On January 4, 2009, Runyan Bakery paid $324 million for 10 million shares of Lavery Labeling Company common stock. The investment represents a 30% interest in the net assets of Lavery and gave Runyan the ability to exercise significant influence over Lavery's operations. Runyan received dividends of $2.00 per share on December 15, 2009, and Lavery reported net income of $160 million for the year ended December 31, 2009. The market value of Lavery's common stock at December 31, 2009, was $31 per share. On the purchase date, the book value of Lavery's net assets was $800 million and:

a. The fair value of Lavery's depreciable assets, with an average remaining useful life of six years, exceeded their book value by $80 million.

b. The remainder of the excess of the cost of the investment over the book value of net assets purchased was attributable to goodwill.

Required:

1. Prepare all appropriate journal entries related to the investment during 2009, assuming Runyan accounts for this investment by the equity method.
2. Prepare the journal entries required by Runyan, assuming that the 10 million shares represents a 10% interest in the net assets of Lavery rather than a 30% interest.

P 12–10
Fair value option; equity method investments

● LO2 LO4 LO7

[This problem is a variation of Problem 12–9 focusing on the fair value option.]

On January 4, 2009, Runyan Bakery paid $324 million for 10 million shares of Lavery Labeling Company common stock. The investment represents a 30% interest in the net assets of Lavery and gave Runyan the ability to exercise significant influence over Lavery's operations. Runyan chose the fair value option to account for this investment. Runyan received dividends of $2.00 per share on December 15, 2009, and Lavery reported net income of $160 million for the year ended December 31, 2009. The market value of Lavery's common stock at December 31, 2009, was $31 per share. On the purchase date, the book value of Lavery's net assets was $800 million and:

a. The fair value of Lavery's depreciable assets, with an average remaining useful life of six years, exceeded their book value by $80 million.

b. The remainder of the excess of the cost of the investment over the book value of net assets purchased was attributable to goodwill.

Required:

1. Prepare all appropriate journal entries related to the investment during 2009, assuming Runyan accounts for this investment under the fair value option and accounts for the Lavery investment in a manner similar to what they would use for trading securities.
2. What would be the effect of this investment on Runyan's 2009 net income?

P 12–11
Fair value option; equity method investments

● LO2 LO4 LO5 LO7

[This problem is an expanded version of Problem 12–10 that considers alternative ways in which a firm might apply the fair value option to account for significant-influence investments that would normally be accounted for under the equity method.]

SFAS No. 159 indicates that companies can choose the fair value option for investments that otherwise would be accounted for under the equity method. If the fair value option is chosen, the investment is shown at fair value on the balance sheet, and unrealized holding gains and losses are recognized in the income statement. However, exactly how a company complies with those broad requirements is up to the company. This problem requires you to consider alternative ways in which a company might apply the fair value option for investments that otherwise would be accounted for under the equity method.

On January 4, 2009, Runyan Bakery paid $324 million for 10 million shares of Lavery Labeling Company common stock. The investment represents a 30% interest in the net assets of Lavery and gave Runyan the ability to exercise significant influence over Lavery's operations. Runyan chose the fair value option to account for this investment. Runyan received dividends of $2.00 per share on December 15, 2009, and Lavery reported net income of $160 million for the year ended December 31, 2009. The market value of Lavery's common stock at December 31, 2009, was $31 per share. On the purchase date, the book value of Lavery's net assets was $800 million and:

a. The fair value of Lavery's depreciable assets, with an average remaining useful life of six years, exceeded their book value by $80 million.

b. The remainder of the excess of the cost of the investment over the book value of net assets purchased was attributable to goodwill.

Required:

1. Prepare all appropriate journal entries related to the investment during 2009, assuming Runyan accounts for this investment under the fair value option, and simply accounts for the Lavery investment in a manner similar to what they would use for trading securities. Indicate the effect of these journal entries on 2009 net income, and show the amount at which the investment is carried in the December 31, 2009, balance sheet.

2. Prepare all appropriate journal entries related to the investment during 2009, assuming Runyan accounts for this investment under the fair value option, but uses equity method accounting to account for Lavery's income and dividends, and then records a fair value adjustment at the end of the year that allows it to comply with *SFAS No. 159*. Indicate the effect of these journal entries on 2009 net income, and show the amount at which the investment is carried in the December 31, 2009, balance sheet. (Note: You should end up with the same total 2009 income effect and same carrying value on the balance sheet for requirements 1 and 2.)

P 12–12
Equity method

● **LO5 LO6**

Northwest Paperboard Company, a paper and allied products manufacturer, was seeking to gain a foothold in Canada. Toward that end, the company bought 40% of the outstanding common shares of Vancouver Timber and Milling, Inc. on January 2, 2009, for $400 million.

At the date of purchase, the book value of Vancouver's net assets was $775 million. The book values and fair values for all balance sheet items were the same except for inventory and plant facilities. The fair value exceeded book value by $5 million for the inventory and by $20 million for the plant facilities.

The estimated useful life of the plant facilities is 16 years. All inventory acquired was sold during 2009.

Vancouver reported net income of $140 million for the year ended December 31, 2009. Vancouver paid a cash dividend of $30 million.

Required:

1. Prepare all appropriate journal entries related to the investment during 2009.

2. What amount should Northwest report as its income from its investment in Vancouver for the year ended December 31, 2009?

3. What amount should Northwest report in its balance sheet as its investment in Vancouver?

4. What should Northwest report in its statement of cash flows regarding its investment in Vancouver?

P 12–13
Equity method

● **LO5 LO6**

On January 2, 2009, Miller Properties paid $19 million for 1 million shares of Marlon Company's 6 million outstanding common shares. Miller's CEO became a member of Marlon's board of directors during the first quarter of 2009.

The carrying amount of Marlon's net assets was $66 million. Miller estimated the fair value of those net assets to be the same except for a patent valued at $24 million over cost. The remaining amortization period for the patent is 10 years.

Marlon reported earnings of $12 million and paid dividends of $6 million during 2009. On December 31, 2009, Marlon's common stock was trading on the NYSE at $18.50 per share.

Required:

1. When considering whether to account for its investment in Marlon under the equity method, what criteria should Miller's management apply?

2. Assume Miller accounts for its investment in Marlon using the equity method. Ignoring income taxes, determine the amounts related to the investment to be reported in its 2009:

    a. Income statement.

    b. Balance sheet.

    c. Statement of cash flows.

P 12–14
Classifying investments

● **LO1 through LO5**

Indicate (by letter) the way each of the investments listed below most likely should be accounted for based on the information provided.

Item	Reporting Category
_____ 1. 35% of the nonvoting preferred stock of American Aircraft Company.	T. Trading securities
_____ 2. Treasury bills to be held to maturity.	M. Securities held-to-maturity
_____ 3. Two-year note receivable from affiliate.	A. Securities available-for-sale
_____ 4. Accounts receivable.	E. Equity method
_____ 5. Treasury bond maturing in one week.	C. Consolidation
_____ 6. Common stock held in trading account for immediate resale.	N. None of these
_____ 7. Bonds acquired to profit from short-term differences in price.	
_____ 8. 35% of the voting common stock of Computer Storage Devices Company.	
_____ 9. 90% of the voting common stock of Affiliated Peripherals, Inc.	
_____ 10. Corporate bonds of Primary Smelting Company to be sold if interest rates fall ½%.	
_____ 11. 25% of the voting common stock of Smith Foundries Corporation: 51% family-owned by Smith family; fair value determinable.	
_____ 12. 17% of the voting common stock of Shipping Barrels Corporation: Investor's CEO on the board of directors of Shipping Barrels Corporation.	

P 12–15

Impairment of securities available-for-sale; troubled debt restructuring (Based on Appendix 12B)

● LO3

At January 1, 2009, Rothschild Chair Company, Inc. was indebted to First Lincoln Bank under a $20 million, 10% unsecured note. The note was signed January 1, 2003, and was due December 31, 2012. Annual interest was last paid on December 31, 2007. Rothschild Chair Company was experiencing severe financial difficulties and negotiated a restructuring of the terms of the debt agreement.

Required:
Prepare all journal entries by First Lincoln Bank to record the restructuring and any remaining transactions relating to the debt under each of the independent circumstances below:

1. First Lincoln Bank agreed to settle the debt in exchange for land having a fair value of $16 million but carried on Rothschild Chair Company's books at $13 million.

2. First Lincoln Bank agreed to (a) forgive the interest accrued from last year, (b) reduce the remaining four interest payments to $1 million each, and (c) reduce the principal to $15 million.

3. First Lincoln Bank agreed to defer all payments (including accrued interest) until the maturity date and accept $27,775,000 at that time in settlement of the debt.

P 12–16

Fair value option; held-to-maturity investments

● LO1 LO7

On January 1, 2009, Ithaca Corp. purchases Cortland Inc. bonds that have a face value of $150,000. The Cortland bonds have a stated interest rate of 6%. Interest is paid semiannually on June 30 and December 31, and the bonds mature in 10 years. For bonds of similar risk and maturity, the market yield on particular dates is as follows:

January 1, 2009	7.0%
June 30, 2009	8.0%
December 31, 2009	9.0%

Required:
1. Calculate the price Ithaca would have paid for the Cortland bonds on January 1, 2009 (ignoring brokerage fees), and prepare a journal entry to record the purchase.

2. Prepare all appropriate journal entries related to the bond investment during 2009 assuming Ithaca accounts for the bonds as a held-to-maturity investment. Ithaca calculates interest revenue at the effective interest rate as of the date they purchased the bonds.

3. Prepare all appropriate journal entries related to the bond investment during 2009, assuming that Ithaca chose the fair value option when the bonds were purchased, and that Ithaca determines fair value of their bonds semiannually. Ithaca calculates interest revenue at the effective interest rate as of the date they purchased the bonds.

BROADEN YOUR **PERSPECTIVE**

Apply your critical-thinking ability to the knowledge you've gained. These cases will provide you an opportunity to develop your research, analysis, judgment, and communication skills. You also will work with other students, integrate what you've learned, apply it in real world situations, and consider its global and ethical ramifications. This practice will broaden your knowledge and further develop your decision-making abilities.

Real World Case 12–1
Intel's investments

● LO3

The following disclosure note appeared in the 2006 annual report of the **Intel Corporation**.

Intel's 2006 annual report includes the following information for available-for-sale investments (in millions):

	2006				2005		
Adjusted Cost	Gross Unrealized Gains	Gross Unrealized Losses	Estimated Fair Value	Adjusted Cost	Gross Unrealized Gains	Gross Unrealized Losses	Estimated Fair Value
$12,794	$178	$(1)	$12,971	$15,228	$164	$(5)	$15,387

The company sold available-for-sale securities for proceeds of approximately $2.0 billion in 2006. The gross realized gains on these sales totaled $135 million, which included a gain of $103 million, with proceeds of $275 million, from the sale of a portion of the company's investment in Micron Technology, Inc. . . . The recognized impairment losses on available-for-sale investments as well as gross realized losses on sales were insignificant during 2006. . . . The company recognized impairment losses on available-for-sale investments of $105 million in 2005. . . . The impairment in 2005 represented an impairment charge of $105 million on the company's investment in Micron reflecting the difference between the cost basis of the investment and the price of Micron's stock at the end of the second quarter of 2005.

Required:

1. What would have been Intel's journal entry to adjust its valuation allowance to recognize net change in gross unrealized gains and losses during 2006?

2. What would have been the journal entry to record the impairment loss associated with the Micron investment during 2005?

3. What would have been the journal entry to record the sale of the Micron investment during 2006?

4. Compare your answers to requirements 2 and 3. Speculate about alternative explanations for this pattern of results.

Research Case 12–2
Reporting securities available-for-sale; obtain and critically evaluate an annual report

● LO3

Investments in common stocks potentially affect each of the various financial statements as well as the disclosure notes that accompany those statements.

Required:

1. Locate a recent annual report of a public company that includes a footnote that describes an investment in securities available-for-sale. You can use EDGAR at **www.sec.gov**.

2. Under what caption are the investments reported in the comparative balance sheets? Are they reported as current or noncurrent assets?

3. Are realized gains or losses reported in the comparative income statements?

4. Are unrealized gains or losses reported in the comparative statements and shareholders' equity?

5. Are unrealized gains or losses identifiable in the comparative balance sheets? If so, under what caption? Why are unrealized gains or losses reported here rather than in the income statements?

6. Are cash flow effects of these investments reflected in the company's comparative statements of cash flows? If so, what information is provided by this disclosure?

7. Does the footnote provide information not available in the financial statements?

Integrating Case 12–3
How was the adoption of *SFAS 115* an exception to the usual method of accounting for changes in accounting principle?

● LO1 LO2 LO3

In Chapter 4 you learned that most changes in accounting principle require retrospective application of the new method in years prior to the change. Some changes mandated by new FASB accounting standards instead require or permit *prospective* application of the new standard. An example of this exception is *SFAS 115,* "Accounting for Certain Investments in Debt and Equity Securities." Recall that the standard requires that certain investments that previously were reported at lower of cost or market were required by the new standard to be reported instead at their fair values.

Required:
Explain how *SFAS 115* is an exception to the general method of accounting for changes in accounting principle.

Trueblood Accounting Case 12–4
Equity method

● LO3

The following Trueblood case is recommended for use with this chapter. The case provides an excellent opportunity for class discussion, group projects, and writing assignments. The case, along with Professor's Discussion Material, can be obtained from the Deloitte Foundation at its website: **www.deloitte.com/us/truebloodcases**.

Case: 03–10: *Painless, Inc.*

This case gives students an opportunity to discuss whether and how the equity method should ever be applied to preferred stock investments.

International Case 12–5
Comparison of equity method between IFRS and U.S. GAAP

● **LO4 LO5 LO6**

The following are excerpts from the 2006 financial statements of **Renault**, a large French automobile manufacturer.

Investment in Nissan: Renault holds 44.3% ownership in Nissan. Renault and Nissan have chosen to develop a unique type of alliance between two distinct companies with common interests, uniting forces to achieve optimum performance. The Alliance is organised so as to preserve individual brand identities and respect each company's corporate culture. Consequently:

● Renault does not hold the majority of Nissan voting rights;
● The terms of the Renault-Nissan agreements do not entitle Renault to appoint the majority of Nissan directors, nor to hold the majority of voting rights at meetings of Nissan's Board of Directors.
● Renault can neither use nor influence the use of Nissan's assets in the same way as its own assets.
● Renault provides no guarantees in respect of Nissan's debt.

In view of this situation, Renault is considered to exercise significant influence in Nissan, and therefore uses the equity method to include its investment in Nissan in the consolidation. . . .

Nissan financial information under IFRS: (When accounting for its investment in Nissan, Renault makes restatements that) include adjustments for harmonisation of accounting standards and the adjustments to fair value of assets and liabilities applied by Renault at the time of acquisitions in 1999 and 2002.

Required:

1. Go to Deloitte's IAS Plus website and examine the summary of the IASB's IAS 28 (at **http://www.iasplus.com/standard/ias28.htm**), which governs application of the equity method. Focus on two areas: Identification of Associates and Applying the Equity Method of Accounting.

2. Evaluate Renault's decision to use the equity method to account for its investment in Nissan. Does Renault have insignificant influence, significant influence, or control?

3. Evaluate the fact that, when accounting for its investment in Nissan under the equity method, Renault makes adjustments that take into account the fair value of assets and liabilities at the time Renault invested in Nissan. Give an example of the sorts of adjustments that might be made. Are such adjustments consistent with IFRS? With U.S. GAAP? Explain.

4. Evaluate the fact that, when accounting for its investment in Nissan under the equity method, Renault makes adjustments for harmonization of accounting standards. Are such adjustments consistent with IFRS? With U.S. GAAP? Explain.

Research Case 12–6
Researching the way investments are reported; retrieving information from the Internet

● **LO1 LO2 LO3**

All publicly traded domestic companies use EDGAR, the Electronic Data Gathering, Analysis, and Retrieval system, to make the majority of their filings with the SEC. You can access EDGAR at **www.sec.gov**.

Required:

1. Search for a public company with which you are familiar. Access its most recent 10-K filing. Search or scroll to find financial statements and related notes.

2. Answer the following questions. (If the chosen company does not report investments in the securities of other companies, choose another company.)

   a. What is the amount and classification of any investment securities reported in the balance sheet? Are unrealized gains or losses reported in the shareholders' equity section?

   b. Are any investments reported by the equity method?

   c. What amounts from these investments are reported in the comparative income statements? Has that income increased or decreased over the years reported?

   d. Are any acquisitions or disposals of investments reported in the statement of cash flows?

Real World Case 12–7
Merck's investments

● **LO3 LO4 LO5**

Corporations frequently invest in securities issued by other corporations. Some investments are acquired to secure a favorable business relationship with another company. On the other hand, others are intended only to earn an investment return from the dividends or interest the securities pay or from increases in the market prices of the securities—the same motivations that might cause you to invest in stocks, bonds, or other securities. This diversity in investment objectives means no single accounting method is adequate to report every investment.

Merck & Co., Inc. invests in securities of other companies. Access Merck's 2006 10-K (which includes financial statements) using EDGAR at **www.sec.gov**.

Required:

1. What is the amount and classification of any investment securities reported on the balance sheet? In which current and noncurrent asset categories are investments reported by Merck? What criteria are used to determine the classifications?

2. How are unrealized gains or losses reported? realized gains and losses?

3. Are any investments reported by the equity method?

4. What amounts from equity method investments are reported in the comparative income statements?

5. Are cash flow effects of these investments reflected in the company's comparative statements of cash flows? If so, what information is provided by this disclosure?

Real World
Case 12–8
Comprehensive
income—Microsoft

● LO3

As required by *SFAS No. 115*, **Microsoft Corporation** reports its investments available-for-sale at the *fair value* of the investment securities. The *net* unrealized holding gain is not reported in the income statement. Instead, it's reported as part of Other comprehensive income in shareholders' equity.

Comprehensive income is a broader view of the change in shareholders' equity than traditional net income, encompassing all changes in equity from nonowner transactions. Microsoft chose to report its Other comprehensive income as a separate statement in a disclosure note in its 2007 annual report.

Note 13 Other Comprehensive Income

The activity in other comprehensive income and related tax effects were as follows:

($in millions)			
Year Ended June 30	**2007**	**2006**	**2005**
Net unrealized gains/(losses) on derivative instruments:			
Unrealized gains, net of tax effect of $66 in 2007, $107 in 2006, and $0 in 2005	$123	$ 199	$ —
Reclassification adjustment for gains included in net income, net of tax effect of $(59) in 2007, $(66) in 2006, and $(31) in 2005	(109)	(123)	(58)
Net unrealized gains/(losses) on derivative instruments	14	76	(58)
Net unrealized gains/(losses) on investments:			
Unrealized gains/(losses), net of tax effect of $393 in 2007, $(105) in 2006, and $469 in 2005	730	(195)	870
Reclassification adjustment for gains included in net income, net of tax effect of $(217) in 2007, $(47) in 2006, and $(269) in 2005	(404)	(87)	(499)
Net unrealized gains/(losses) on investments	326	(282)	371
Translation adjustments and other	85	9	(6)
Other comprehensive income/(loss)	$425	$(197)	$307

Required:
1. The note indicates Unrealized holding gains during 2007 in the amount of $730 million. Is this the amount Microsoft would include as a separate component of shareholders' equity? Explain.
2. What does Microsoft mean by the term, "Reclassification adjustment for gains included in net income"?

CPA SIMULATION 12–1

Barbados Investments
Investments

KAPLAN

SCHWESER

CPA Review

Test your knowledge of the concepts discussed in this chapter, practice critical professional skills necessary for career success, and prepare for the computer-based CPA exam by accessing our CPA simulations at the text website: **www.mhhe.com/spiceland5e**.

The Barbados Investments simulation tests your knowledge of a) the way we classify investment securities among the categories of trading securities, available-for-sale securities, and those held-to-maturity, b) how we account for those investments, c) the way accounting for investments affects comprehensive income, and d) the appropriate use of the equity method.

As on the CPA exam itself, you will be asked to use tools including a spreadsheet, a calculator, and professional accounting standards, to conduct research, derive solutions, and communicate conclusions related to these issues in a simulated environment headed by the following interactive tabs:

Specific tasks in the simulation include:
- Analyzing various transactions involving investment securities and determining their appropriate balance sheet classification.
- Applying judgment in the application of the equity method.
- Determining the amount of interest revenue to be reported from a debt investment.
- Demonstrating an understanding of comprehensive income and how it is affected by investments in securities.
- Communicating the way we account for investments using the equity method.
- Researching the financial reporting ramifications of changing the classification of investment securities.

This page is intentionally blank

This page is intentionally blank

This page is intentionally blank

Derivatives

In today's global economy and evolving financial markets, businesses are increasingly exposed to a variety of risks, which, unmanaged, can have major impacts on earnings or even threaten a company's very existence. Risk management, then, has become critical. Derivative financial instruments have become the key tools of risk management.[1]

Derivatives are financial instruments that "derive" their values or contractually required cash flows from some other security or index. For instance, a contract allowing a company to buy a particular asset (say steel, gold, or flour) at a designated future date, at a predetermined price is a financial instrument that derives its value from expected and actual changes in the price of the underlying asset. Financial futures, forward contracts, options, and interest rate swaps are the most frequently used derivatives. Derivatives are valued as tools to manage or hedge companies' increasing exposures to risk, including interest rate risk, price risk, and foreign exchange risk. The variety, complexity, and magnitude of derivatives have grown rapidly in recent years. Tens of trillions of dollars in derivative contracts are used every year. Accounting standard-setters have scrambled to keep pace.

A persistent stream of headline stories has alerted us to multimillion-dollar losses by **Dell Computer, Procter & Gamble,** and **Orange County** (California), to name a few. Focusing on these headlines, it would be tempting to conclude that derivatives are risky business indeed. Certainly they can be quite risky, if misused, but the fact is, these financial instruments exist to lessen, not increase, risk. Properly used, they serve as a form of "insurance" against risk. In fact, if a company is exposed to a substantial risk and does not hedge that risk, it is taking a gamble. On the other hand, if a derivative is used improperly, it can be a huge gamble itself.

> *Derivatives* are financial instruments that "derive" their values from some other security or *index.*

> Derivatives serve as a form of "insurance" against risk.

Derivatives Used to Hedge Risk

Hedging means taking an action that is expected to produce exposure to a particular type of risk that is precisely the *opposite* of an actual risk to which the company already is exposed. For instance, the volatility of interest rates creates exposure to interest-rate risk for companies that issue debt—which, of course, includes most companies. So, a company that frequently arranges short-term loans from its bank under a floating (variable) interest rate agreement is exposed to the risk that interest rates might increase and adversely affect borrowing costs. Similarly, a company that regularly reissues commercial paper as it matures faces the possibility that new rates will be higher and cut into forecasted income. When borrowings are large, the potential cost can be substantial. So, the firm might choose to hedge its position by entering into a transaction that would produce a *gain* of roughly the same amount as the potential loss if interest rates do, in fact, increase.

Hedging is used to deal with three areas of risk exposure: fair value risk, cash flow risk, and foreign currency risk. Let's look at some of the more common derivatives.

> *Hedging* means taking a risk position that is opposite to an actual position that is exposed to risk.

Financial Futures

A futures contract is an agreement between a seller and a buyer that requires the seller to deliver a particular commodity (say corn, gold, or pork bellies) at a designated future date, at a *predetermined* price. These contracts are actively traded on regulated futures exchanges. When the "commodity" is a *financial instrument,* such as a Treasury bond, Treasury bill,

> A *futures contract* allows a firm to sell (or buy) a financial instrument at a designated future date, at today's price.

---

[1]Almost all financial institutions and over half of all nonfinancial companies use derivatives.

commercial paper, or a certificate of deposit, the agreement is referred to as a *financial futures contract.*[2]

To appreciate the way these hedges work, you need to remember that when interest rates rise, the market price of interest-bearing securities goes down. For instance, if you have an investment in a 10% bond and market interest rates go up to, say, 12%, your 10% bond is less valuable relative to other bonds paying the higher rate. Conversely, when interest rates decline, the market price of interest-bearing securities goes up. This risk that the investment's value might change is referred to as *fair value risk.* The company that issued the securities is faced with fair value risk also. If interest rates decline, the fair value of that company's debt would rise, a risk the borrower may want to hedge against. Later in this section, we'll look at an illustration of how the borrower would account for and report such a hedge.

The seller in a financial futures contract realizes a gain (loss) when interest rates rise (decline).

Now let's look at the effect on a contract to sell or buy securities (or any asset for that matter) at preset prices. One who is contracted to *sell* securities at a *preset* price after their market price has fallen, benefits from the rise in interest rates. Consequently, the value of the *contract* that gives one the right to sell securities at a preset price goes up as the market price declines. The seller in a futures contract derives a gain (loss) when interest rates rise (decline).[3] Conversely, the one obligated to *buy* securities at a preset price experiences a loss. This risk of having to pay more cash or receive less cash is referred to as *cash flow risk.*

Another example of cash flow risk would be borrowing money by issuing a variable (floating) rate note. If market interest rates rise, the borrower would have to pay more interest. Similarly, the lender (investor) in the variable (floating) rate note transaction would face cash flow risk that interest rates would decline, resulting in lower cash interest receipts.

Let's look closer at how a futures contract can mitigate cash flow risk. Consider a company in April that will replace its $10 million of 8.5% bank notes when they mature in June. The company is exposed to the risk that interest rates in June will have risen, increasing borrowing costs. To counteract that possibility, the firm might enter a contract in April to deliver (sell) bonds in June at their *current* price. Since there are no corporate bond futures contracts, the company buys Treasury bond futures, which will accomplish essentially the same purpose. In essence, the firm agrees to sell Treasury bonds in June at a price established now (April). Let's say it's April 6 and the price of Treasury bond futures on the International Monetary Market of the Chicago Mercantile Exchange is quoted as 95.24.[4] Since the trading unit of Treasury bond futures is a 15-year, $100,000, 8% Treasury bond, the company might sell 105 Treasury bond futures to hedge the June issuance of debt. This would effectively provide a hedge of 105 × $100,000 × 95.24% = $10,000,200.[5]

Here's what happens then. If interest rates rise, borrowing costs will go up for our example company because it will have to sell debt securities at a higher interest cost (or lower price). But that loss will be offset (approximately) by the gain produced by being in the opposite position on Treasury bond futures. Take note, though, this works both ways. If interest rates go down causing debt security prices to rise, the potential benefit of being able to issue debt at that lower interest rate (higher price) will be offset by a loss on the futures position.

A very important point about futures contracts is that the seller does not need to have actual possession of the commodity (the Treasury bonds, in this case), nor is the purchaser of the contract required to take possession of the commodity. In fact, virtually all financial futures contracts are "netted out" before the actual transaction is to take place. This is simply a matter of reversing the original position. A seller closes out his transaction with a purchase. Likewise, a purchaser would close out her transaction with a sale. After all, the objective is not to actually buy or sell Treasury bonds (or whatever the commodity might be), but to incur the financial impact of movements in interest rates as reflected in changes in Treasury bond prices. Specifically, it will buy at the lower price (to reverse the original seller position) at the same time it's selling its new bond issue at that same lower price. The

---

[2]Note that a financial futures contract meets the definition of a financial instrument because it entails the exchange of financial instruments (cash for Treasury bonds, for instance). But, a futures contract for the sale or purchase of a nonfinancial commodity like corn or gold does not meet the definition because one of the items to be exchanged is not a financial instrument.

[3]The seller of a futures contract is obligated to sell the bonds at a future date. The buyer of a futures contract is obligated to buy the bonds at a future date. The company in our example, then, is the seller of the futures contract.

[4]Price quotes are expressed as a percentage of par.

[5]This is a simplification of the more sophisticated way financial managers determine the optimal number of futures.

financial futures market is an "artificial" exchange in that its reason for existing is to provide a mechanism to transfer risk from those exposed to it to those willing to accept the risk, not to actually buy and sell the underlying financial instruments.

If the impending debt issue being hedged is a short-term issue, the company may attain a more effective hedge by selling Treasury *bill* futures since Treasury bills are 90-day securities, or maybe certificate of deposit (CD) futures that also are traded in futures markets. The object is to get the closest association between the financial effects of interest rate movements on the actual transaction and the effects on the financial instrument used as a hedge.

> The effectiveness of a hedge is influenced by the closeness of the match between the item being hedged and the financial instrument chosen as a hedge.

Financial Forward Contracts

A forward contract is similar to a futures contract but differs in three ways:

1. A forward contract calls for delivery on a specific date, whereas a futures contract permits the seller to decide later which specific day within the specified month will be the delivery date (if it gets as far as actual delivery before it is closed out).
2. Unlike a futures contract, a forward contract usually is not traded on a market exchange.
3. Unlike a futures contract, a forward contract does not call for a daily cash settlement for price changes in the underlying contract. Gains and losses on forward contracts are paid only when they are closed out.

Options

Options frequently are purchased to hedge exposure to the effects of changing interest rates. Options serve the same purpose as futures in that respect but are fundamentally different. An option on a financial instrument—say a Treasury bill—gives its holder the right either to buy or to sell the Treasury bill at a specified price and within a given time period. Importantly, though, the option holder has no obligation to exercise the option. On the other hand, the holder of a futures contract must buy or sell within a specified period unless the contract is closed out before delivery comes due.

Foreign Currency Futures

Foreign loans frequently are denominated in the currency of the lender (Japanese yen, Swiss franc, Euro, and so on). When loans must be repaid in foreign currencies, a new element of risk is introduced. This is because if exchange rates change, the dollar equivalent of the foreign currency that must be repaid differs from the dollar equivalent of the foreign currency borrowed.

To hedge against "foreign exchange risk" exposure, some firms buy or sell foreign currency futures contracts. These are similar to financial futures except specific foreign currencies are specified in the futures contracts rather than specific debt instruments. They work the same way to protect against foreign exchange risk as financial futures protect against fair value or cash flow risk.

> Foreign exchange risk often is hedged in the same manner as interest rate risk.

Interest Rate Swaps

Over 70% of derivatives are interest rate swaps. These contracts exchange fixed interest payments for floating rate payments, or vice versa, without exchanging the underlying principal amounts. For example, suppose you owe $100,000 on a 10% fixed rate home loan. You envy your neighbor who also is paying 10% on her $100,000 mortgage, but hers is a floating rate loan, so if market rates fall, so will her loan rate. To the contrary, she is envious of your fixed rate, fearful that rates will rise, increasing her payments. A solution would be for the two of you to effectively swap interest payments using an interest rate swap agreement. The way a swap works, you both would continue to actually make your own interest payments, but would exchange the net cash difference between payments at specified intervals. So, in this case, if market rates (and thus floating payments) increase, you would pay your neighbor; if rates fall, she pays you. The net effect is to exchange the consequences of rate changes. In other words, you have effectively converted your fixed-rate debt to floating-rate debt; your neighbor has done the opposite.

> *Interest rate swaps exchange fixed interest payments for floating rate payments, or vice versa, without exchanging the underlying notional amounts.*

Of course, this technique is not dependent on happening into such a fortuitous pairing of two borrowers with opposite philosophies on interest rate risk. Instead, banks or other intermediaries offer, for a fee, one-sided swap agreements to companies desiring to be either fixed-rate payers or variable-rate payers. Intermediaries usually strive to maintain a balanced portfolio of matched, offsetting swap agreements.

Theoretically, the two parties to such a transaction exchange principal amounts, say the $100,000 amount above, in addition to the interest on those amounts. It makes no practical sense, though, for the companies to send each other $100,000. So, instead, the principal amount is not actually exchanged, but serves merely as the computational base for interest calculations and is called the *notional amount*. Similarly, the fixed-rate payer doesn't usually send the entire fixed interest amount (say 10% × $100,000 = $10,000) and receive the entire variable interest amount (say 9% × $100,000 = $9,000). Generally, only the net amount ($1,000 in this case) is exchanged. This is illustrated in Graphic A–1.

GRAPHIC A–1
Interest Rate Swap

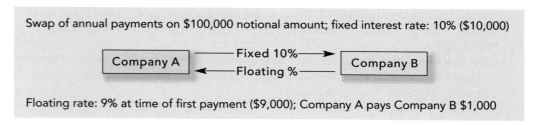

Swap of annual payments on $100,000 notional amount; fixed interest rate: 10% ($10,000)

Company A — Fixed 10% → Company B
← Floating % —

Floating rate: 9% at time of first payment ($9,000); Company A pays Company B $1,000

From an accounting standpoint, the central issue is not the operational differences among various hedge instruments, but their similarities in functioning as hedges against risk.

Accounting for Derivatives

A key to accounting for derivatives is knowing the purpose for which a company holds them and whether the company is effective in serving that purpose. Derivatives, for instance, may be held for risk management (hedging activities). The desired effect, and often the real effect, is a reduction in risk. On the other hand, derivatives sometimes are held for speculative position taking, hoping for large profits. The effect of this activity usually is to increase risk. Perhaps more important, derivatives acquired as hedges and intended to reduce risk may, in fact, unintentionally increase risk instead.

It's important to understand that, serving as investments rather than as hedges, derivatives are extremely speculative. This is due to the high leverage inherent in derivatives. Here's why. The investment outlay usually is negligible, but, the potential gain or loss on the investment usually is quite high. A small change in interest rates or another underlying event can trigger a large change in the fair value of the derivative. Because the initial investment was minimal, the change in value relative to the investment itself represents a huge percentage gain or loss. Accounting for derivatives is designed to treat differently (a) derivatives designated as hedges and those not designated as hedges as well as (b) the effective portion and the ineffective portion of gains and losses from intended hedges.

The basic approach to accounting for derivatives is fairly straightforward, although implementation can be quite cumbersome. All derivatives, no exceptions, are carried on the balance sheet as either assets or liabilities at fair (or market) value.[6] The reasoning is that (a) derivatives create either rights or obligations that meet the definition of assets or liabilities, and (b) fair value is the most meaningful measurement.

Accounting for the gain or loss on a derivative depends on how it is used. Specifically, if the derivative is not designated as a hedging instrument, or doesn't qualify as one, any gain or loss from fair value changes is recognized immediately in earnings. On the other hand, if a derivative is used to hedge against exposure to risk, any gain or loss from fair value changes is either (a) recognized immediately in earnings along with an offsetting loss or gain on the item being hedged or (b) deferred in comprehensive income until it can be recognized in earnings

Derivatives not serving as hedges are extremely speculative due to the high leverage inherent in such investments.

All derivatives are reported on the balance sheet at fair value.

[6]"Accounting for Derivative Instruments and Hedging Activities," *Statement of Financial Accounting Standards No. 133* (Norwalk, Conn.: FASB, 1998).

at the same time as earnings are affected by a hedged transaction. Which way depends on whether the derivative is designated as a (a) fair value hedge, (b) cash flow hedge, or (c) foreign currency hedge. Let's look now at each of the three hedge designations.

Fair Value Hedges

A company can be adversely affected when a change in either prices or interest rates causes a change in the fair value of one of its assets, its liabilities, or a commitment to buy or sell assets or liabilities. If a derivative is used to hedge against the exposure to changes in the fair value of an asset or liability or a firm commitment, it can be designated as a fair value hedge. In that case, when the derivative is adjusted to reflect changes in fair value, the other side of the entry recognizes a gain or loss to be included *currently* in earnings. At the same time, though, the loss or gain from changes in the fair value (due to the risk being hedged)[7] of the item being hedged also is included currently in earnings. This means that, to the extent the hedge is effective in serving its purpose, the gain or loss on the derivative will be offset by the loss or gain on the item being hedged. In fact, this is precisely the concept behind the procedure.

> A gain or loss from a *fair value hedge* is recognized immediately in earnings along with the loss or gain from the item being hedged.

The reasoning is that as interest rates or other underlying events change, a hedge instrument will produce a gain approximately equal to a loss on the item being hedged (or vice versa). These income effects are interrelated and offsetting, so it would be improper to report the income effects in different periods. More critically, the intent and effect of having the hedge instrument is to *lessen* risk. And yet, recognizing gains in one period and counterbalancing losses in another period would tend to cause fluctuations in income that convey an *increase* in risk. However, to the extent that a hedge is ineffective and produces gains or losses different from the losses or gains being hedged, the ineffective portion is recognized in earnings immediately.

> The income effects of the hedge instrument and the income effects of the item being hedged should affect earnings at the same time.

Some of the more common fair value hedges use:

- An interest rate swap to synthetically convert fixed-rate debt (for which interest rate changes could change the fair value of the debt) into floating-rate debt.
- A futures contract to hedge changes in the fair value (due to price changes) of aluminum, sugar, or some other type of inventory.
- A futures contract to hedge the fair value (due to price changes) of a firm commitment to sell natural gas or some other asset.

Illustration

Because interest rate swaps comprise over 70% of derivatives in use, we will use swaps to illustrate accounting for derivatives. Let's look at the example in Illustration A–1 on the next page.

When the floating rate declined from 10% to 9%, the fair values of both the derivative (swap) and the note increased. This created an offsetting gain on the derivative and holding loss on the note. Both are recognized in earnings at the same time (at June 30, 2009).

January 1, 2009

Cash	1,000,000	
Notes payable		1,000,000

To record the issuance of the note.

> The interest rate swap is designated as a fair value hedge on this note at issuance.

June 30, 2009

Interest expense (10% × ½ × $1 million)	50,000	
Cash		50,000

To record interest.

Cash ($50,000 − [9% × ½ × $1 million])	5,000	
Interest expense		5,000

To record the net cash settlement.

> The swap settlement is the difference between the fixed interest (5%) and variable interest (4.5%).

(continued)

[7]The fair value of a hedged item might also change for reasons other than from effects of the risk being hedged. For instance, the hedged risk may be that a change in interest rates will cause the fair value of a bond to change. The bond price might also change, though, if the market perceives that the bond's default risk has changed.

ILLUSTRATION A–1
Interest Rate Swap

Wintel Semiconductors issued $1 million of 18-month, 10% bank notes on January 1, 2009. Wintel is exposed to the risk that general interest rates will decline, causing the fair value of its debt to rise. (If the fair value of Wintel's debt increases, its effective borrowing cost is higher relative to the market.) To hedge against this fair value risk, the firm entered into an 18-month interest rate swap agreement on January 1 and designated the swap as a hedge against changes in the fair value of the note. The swap calls for the company to *receive payment* based on a 10% fixed interest rate on a notional amount of $1 million and to *make payment* based on a floating interest rate tied to changes in general rates.[8] As the Illustration will show, this effectively converts Wintel's fixed-rate debt to floating-rate debt. Cash settlement of the net interest amount is made semiannually at June 30 and December 31 of each year with the net interest being the difference between the $50,000 fixed interest [$1 million × (10% × ½)] and the floating interest rate times $1 million at those dates.

Floating (market) settlement rates were 9% at June 30, 2009, 8% at December 31, 2009, and 9% at June 30, 2010. Net interest receipts can be calculated as shown below. Fair values of both the derivative and the note resulting from those market rate changes are assumed to be quotes obtained from securities dealers.

	1/1/09	6/30/09	12/31/09	6/30/10
Fixed rate	10%	10%	10%	10%
Floating rate	10%	9%	8%	9%
Fixed payments ($1 million × [10% × ½])		$ 50,000	$ 50,000	$ 50,000
Floating payments ($1 million × ½ floating rate)		45,000	40,000	45,000
Net interest receipts		$ 5,000	$ 10,000	$ 5,000
Fair value of interest rate swap	0	$ 9,363	$ 9,615	0
Fair value of note payable	$1,000,000	$1,009,363	$1,009,615	$1,000,000

The fair value of derivatives is recognized in the balance sheet.

June 30, 2009 entries continued from previous page:

Interest rate swap[9] ($9,363 – 0)	9,363	
Holding gain—interest rate swap		9,363
To record change in fair value of the derivative.		

The hedged liability (or asset) is adjusted to fair value as well.

Holding loss—hedged note	9,363	
Note payable ($1,009,363 – 1,000,000)		9,363
To record change in fair value of the note due to interest rate changes.		

The net interest settlement on June 30, 2009, is $5,000 because the fixed rate is 5% (half of the 10% annual rate) and the floating rate is 4.5% (half of the 9% annual rate).

As with any debt, interest expense is the effective rate times the outstanding balance.

December 31, 2009

Interest expense	50,000	
Cash (10% × ½ × $1,000,000)		50,000
To record interest.		

The settlement is the difference between the fixed interest (5%) and variable interest (4%).

Cash ($50,000 – [8% × ½ × $1 million])	10,000	
Interest expense		10,000
To record the net cash settlement.		

The derivative is increased by the change in fair value.

Interest rate swap ($9,615 – 9,363)	252	
Holding gain—interest rate swap		252
To record the change in fair value of the derivative.		

The note is increased by the change in fair value.

Holding loss—hedged note	252	
Note payable ($1,009,615 – 1,009,363)		252
To record the change in fair value of the note due to interest rate changes.		

---

[8]A common measure for benchmarking variable interest rates is LIBOR, the London Interbank Offered Rate, a base rate at which large international banks lend funds to each other.

[9]This would be a liability rather than an investment (asset) if the fair value had declined.

The fair value of the swap increased by $252 (from $9,363 to $9,615). Similarly, we adjust the note's carrying value by the amount necessary to increase it to fair value. This produces a holding loss on the note that exactly offsets the gain on the swap. This result is the hedging effect that motivated Wintel to enter the fair value hedging arrangement in the first place.

At June 30, 2010, Wintel repeats the process of adjusting to fair value both the derivative investment and the note being hedged.

June 30, 2010

Interest expense	50,000	
Cash (10% × ½ × $1,000,000)		50,000
To record interest.		
Cash [$50,000 − (9% × ½ × $1 million)]	5,000	
Interest expense		5,000
To record the net cash settlement.		
Holding loss—interest rate swap	9,615	
Interest rate swap ($0 − 9,615)		9,615
To record the change in fair value of the derivative.		
Note payable ($1,000,000 − 1,009,615)	9,615	
Holding gain—hedged note		9,615
To record the change in fair value of the note due to interest rate changes.		
Note payable	1,000,000	
Cash		1,000,000
To repay the loan.		

*The net interest received is the difference between the fixed interest (**5%**) and floating interest (**4.5%**).*

The swap's fair value now is zero.

The net interest received is the difference between the fixed rate (5%) and floating rate (4.5%) times $1 million. The fair value of the swap decreased by $9,615 (from $9,615 to zero).[10] That decline represents a holding *loss* that we recognize in earnings. Similarly, we record an offsetting holding *gain* on the note for the change in its fair value.

Now let's see how the carrying values changed for the swap account and the note:

	Swap				Note	
Jan. 1, 2009					1,000,000	
June 30, 2009	9,363				9,363	
Dec. 31, 2009	252				252	
June 30, 2010		9,615			9,615	
					1,000,000	
	0				0	

The income statement is affected as follows:

Income Statement + (−)

June 30, 2009	(50,000)	Interest expense—fixed payment
	5,000	Interest expense—net cash settlement
	9,363	Holding gain—interest rate swap
	(9,363)	Holding loss—hedged note
	(45,000)	Net effect—same as floating interest payment
Dec. 31, 2009	(50,000)	Interest expense—fixed payment
	10,000	Interest expense—net cash settlement
	252	Holding gain—interest rate swap
	(252)	Holding loss—hedged note
	(40,000)	Net effect—same as floating interest payment
June 30, 2010	(50,000)	Interest expense—fixed payment
	5,000	Interest expense—net cash settlement
	9,615	Holding gain—interest rate swap
	(9,615)	Holding loss—hedged note
	(45,000)	Net effect—same as floating interest payment

---

[10]Because there are no future cash receipts from the swap arrangement at this point, the fair value of the swap is zero.

As this demonstrates, the swap effectively converts fixed-interest debt to floating-interest debt.

ADDITIONAL CONSIDERATION

Fair Value of the Swap

The fair value of a derivative typically is based on a quote obtained from a derivatives dealer. That fair value will approximate the present value of the expected net interest settlement receipts for the remaining term of the swap. In fact, we can actually calculate the fair value of the swap that we accepted as given in our illustration.

Since the June 30, 2009, floating rate of 9% caused the cash settlement on that date to be $5,000, it's reasonable to look at 9% as the best estimate of future floating rates and therefore assume the remaining two cash settlements also will be $5,000 each. We can then calculate at June 30, 2009, the present value of those expected net interest settlement receipts for the remaining term of the swap:

Fixed interest	10% × ½ × $1 million	$ 50,000
Expected floating interest	9% × ½ × $1 million	45,000
Expected cash receipts for both Dec. 31, 2009 and June 30, 2010		$ 5,000
		× 1.87267*
Present value		$ 9,363

*Present value of an ordinary annuity of $1: $n = 2$, $i = 4.5\%$ (½ of 9%) (from Table 4)

Fair Value of the Notes

The fair value of the note payable will be the present value of principal and remaining interest payments discounted at the *market rate*. The market rate will vary with the designated floating rate but might differ due to changes in default (credit) risk and the term structure of interest rates. Assuming it's 9% at June 30, 2009, we can calculate the fair value (present value) of the notes:

Interest	$50,000* × 1.87267† =	$ 93,633
Principal	$1,000,000 × .91573‡ =	915,730
		$1,009,363

*½ of 10% × $1,000,000
†Present value of an ordinary annuity of $1: $n = 2$, $i = 4.5\%$ (from Table 4)
‡Present value of $1: $n = 2$, $i = 4.5\%$ (from Table 2)

Note: Often the cash settlement rate is "reset" as of each cash settlement date (thus the floating rate actually used at the end of each period to determine the payment is the floating market rate as of the *beginning* of the same period). In our illustration, for instance, there would have been no cash settlement at June 30, 2009, since we would use the beginning floating rate of 10% to determine payment. Similarly, we would have used the 9% floating rate at June 30, 2009, to determine the cash settlement six months later at December 31. In effect, each cash settlement would be delayed six months. Had this arrangement been in effect in the current illustration, there would have been one fewer cash settlement payments (two rather than three), but would not have affected the fair value calculations above because, either way, our expectation would be cash receipts of $5,000 for both Dec. 31, 2009, and June 30, 2010.

Cash Flow Hedges

> A gain or loss from a *cash flow hedge* is deferred as Other comprehensive income until it can be recognized in earnings along with the earnings effect of the item being hedged.

The risk in some transactions or events is the risk of a change in cash flows, rather than a change in fair values. We noted earlier, for instance, that *fixed-rate* debt subjects a company to the risk that interest rate changes could change the fair value of the debt. On the other hand, if the obligation is *floating-rate* debt, the fair value of the debt will not change when interest rates do, but cash flows will. If a derivative is used to hedge against the exposure to changes in cash inflows or cash outflows of an asset or liability or a forecasted transaction (like a future purchase or sale), it can be designated as a cash flow hedge. In that case, when the derivative is adjusted to reflect changes in fair value, the other side of the entry is a gain or loss to be deferred as a component of Other comprehensive income and included in earnings later, at the same time as earnings are affected by the hedged transaction. Once again, the effect is matching the earnings effect of the derivative with the earnings effect of the item being hedged, precisely the concept behind hedge accounting.

To understand the deferral of the gain or loss, we need to revisit the concept of comprehensive income. Comprehensive income, as you may recall from Chapters 4, 12, 17, and 18 is a more expansive view of the change in shareholders' equity than traditional net income. In fact, it encompasses all changes in equity other than from transactions with owners.[11] So, in addition to net income itself, comprehensive income includes up to four other changes in equity that don't (yet) belong in net income, namely, net holding gains (losses) on investments (Chapter 12), gains (losses) from and amendments to postretirement benefit plans (Chapter 17), gains (losses) from foreign currency translation, and deferred gains (losses) from derivatives designated as cash flow hedges.[12]

Some of the more commonly used cash flow hedges are:

- An interest rate swap to synthetically convert floating rate debt (for which interest rate changes could change the cash interest payments) into fixed rate debt.
- A futures contract to hedge a forecasted sale (for which price changes could change the cash receipts) of natural gas, crude oil, or some other asset.

Foreign Currency Hedges

Today's economy is increasingly a global one. The majority of large "U.S." companies are, in truth, multinational companies that may receive only a fraction of their revenues from U.S. operations. Many operations of those companies are located abroad. Foreign operations often are denominated in the currency of the foreign country (the Euro, Japanese yen, Russian rubles, and so on). Even companies without foreign operations sometimes hold investments, issue debt, or conduct other transactions denominated in foreign currencies. As exchange rates change, the dollar equivalent of the foreign currency changes. The possibility of currency rate changes exposes these companies to the risk that some transactions require settlement in a currency other than the entities' functional currency or that foreign operations will require translation adjustments to reported amounts.

A foreign currency hedge can be a hedge of foreign currency exposure of:

> **The possibility that foreign currency exchange rates might change exposes many companies to foreign currency risk.**

- A firm commitment—treated as a fair value hedge.
- An available-for-sale security—treated as a fair value hedge.
- A forecasted transaction—treated as a cash flow hedge.
- A company's net investment in a foreign operation—the gain or loss is reported in *other comprehensive income* as part of unrealized gains and losses from foreign currency translation.[13]

Hedge Effectiveness

When a company elects to apply hedge accounting, it must establish at the inception of the hedge the method it will use to assess the effectiveness of the hedging derivative as well as the measurement approach it will use to determine the ineffective portion of the hedge.[14] The key criterion for qualifying as a hedge is that the hedging relationship must be highly effective in achieving offsetting changes in fair values or cash flows based on the hedging company's specified risk management objective and strategy.

> **To qualify as a hedge, the hedging relationship must be highly effective in achieving offsetting changes in fair values or cash flows.**

An assessment of this effectiveness must be made at least every three months and whenever financial statements are issued. There are no precise guidelines for assessing effectiveness, but it generally means a high correlation between changes in the fair value or cash flows of the derivative and of the item being hedged, not necessarily a specific reduction in risk. Hedge accounting must be terminated for hedging relationships that no longer are highly effective.

Hedge Ineffectiveness

In Illustration A–1, the loss on the hedged note exactly offset the gain on the swap. This is because the swap in this instance was highly effective in hedging the risk due to interest rate

---

[11]Transactions with owners primarily include dividends and the sale or purchase of shares of the company's stock.

[12]"Reporting Comprehensive Income," *Statement of Financial Accounting Standards No. 130* (Norwalk, Conn.: FASB, 1997)

[13]This is the same treatment previously prescribed for these translation adjustments by *Statement of Financial Accounting Standards No. 52.*

[14]Remember, if a derivative is not designated as a hedge, any gains or losses from changes in its fair value are recognized immediately in earnings.

changes. However, the loss and gain would not have exactly offset each other if the hedging arrangement had been ineffective. For instance, suppose the swap's term had been different from that of the note (say a three-year swap term compared with the 18-month term of the note) or if the notional amount of the swap differed from that of the note (say $500,000 rather than $1 million). In that case, changes in the fair value of the swap and changes in the fair value of the note would not be the same. The result would be a greater (or lesser) amount recognized in earnings for the swap than for the note. Because there would not be an exact offset, earnings would be affected, an effect resulting from hedge ineffectiveness. That is a desired effect of hedge accounting; to the extent that a hedge is effective, the earnings effect of a derivative cancels out the earnings effect of the item being hedged. However, even if a hedge is highly effective, all ineffectiveness is recognized currently in earnings.

> Imperfect hedges result in part of the derivative gain or loss being included in current earnings.

Fair Value Changes Unrelated to the Risk Being Hedged

In Illustration A–1, the fair value of the hedged note and the fair value of the swap changed by the same amounts each year because we assumed the fair values changed only due to interest rate changes. It's also possible, though, that the note's fair value would change by an amount different from that of the swap for reasons unrelated to interest rates. Remember from our earlier discussion that the market's perception of a company's creditworthiness, and thus its ability to pay interest and principal when due, also can affect the value of debt, whether interest rates change or not. In hedge accounting, we ignore those changes. We recognize only the fair value changes in the hedged item that we can attribute to the risk being hedged (interest rate risk in this case). For example, if a changing perception of default risk had caused the note's fair value to increase by an additional, say $5,000, our journal entries in Illustration A–1 would have been unaffected. Notice, then, that although we always mark a *derivative* to fair value, the reported amount of the *item being hedged* may not be its fair value. We mark a hedged item to fair value only to the extent that its fair value changed due to the risk being hedged.

> Fair value changes unrelated to the risk being hedged are ignored.

Disclosure of Derivatives and Risk

To be adequately informed about the adequacy of a company's risk management, investors and creditors need information about strategies for holding derivatives and specific hedging activities. Toward that end, extensive disclosure requirements provide information that includes:

- Objectives and strategies for holding and issuing derivatives.
- A description of the items for which risks are being hedged.
- For forecasted transactions: a description, time before the transaction is expected to occur, the gains and losses accumulated in other comprehensive income, and the events that will trigger their recognition in earnings.
- Beginning balance of, changes in, and ending balance of the derivative component of other comprehensive income.
- The net amount of gain or loss reported in earnings (representing aggregate hedge ineffectiveness).
- Qualitative and quantitative information about failed hedges: canceled commitments or previously hedged forecasted transactions no longer expected to occur.

The intent is to provide information about the company's success in reducing risks and consequently about risks not managed successfully. Remember, too, that when derivatives are employed ineffectively, risks can escalate. Ample disclosures about derivatives are essential to maintain awareness of potential opportunities and problems with risk management.

In addition, *SFAS No. 161* requires companies to provide enhanced disclosures indicating (a) how and why the company uses derivative instruments, (b) how the company accounts for derivative instruments and related hedged items, and (c) how derivative instruments and related hedged items affect the company's balance sheet, income statement, and cash flows.[15] The required disclosures includes two tables, one that highlights the location and

---

[15]"Disclosures about Derivative Instruments and Hedging Activities—an amendment of FASB Statement No. 133)," *Statement of Financial Accounting Standards No. 161* (Stamford, Conn.: FASB, 2008)

fair values of derivative instruments in the balance sheet, and another that indicates the location and amounts of gains and losses on derivative instruments in the income statement. The two tables distinguish between derivative instruments that are designated as hedging instruments under *SFAS No. 133* and those that are not. The tables also categorize derivative instruments by each major type—interest rate contracts, foreign exchange contracts, equity contracts, commodity contracts, credit contracts and other types of contracts.

Even for some traditional liabilities, the amounts reported on the face of the financial statements provide inadequate disclosure about the degree to which a company is exposed to risk of loss. To provide adequate disclosure about a company's exposure to risk, additional information must be provided about (a) concentrations of credit risk and (b) the fair value of all financial instruments.[16]

Extended Method for Interest Rate Swap Accounting

A shortcut method for accounting for an interest rate swap is permitted by *SFAS No. 133* when a hedge meets certain criteria. In general, the criteria are designed to see if the hedge supports the assumption of "no ineffectiveness." Illustration A–1 of a fair value hedge met those criteria, in particular, (a) the swap's notional amount matches the note's principal amount, (b) the swap's expiration date matches the note's maturity date, (c) the fair value of the swap is zero at inception, and (d) the floating payment is at the market rate.[17] Because Wintel can conclude that the swap will be highly effective in offsetting changes in the fair value of the debt, it can use the changes in the fair value of the swap to measure the offsetting changes in the fair value of the debt. That's the essence of the shortcut method used in Illustration A–1. The extended method required when the criteria are *not* met for the shortcut method is described in this section (Illustration A–2). It produces the same effect on earnings and in the balance sheet as does the procedure shown in Illustration A–1.

Wintel Semiconductors issued $1 million of 18-month, 10% bank notes on January 1, 2009. Wintel is exposed to the risk that general interest rates will decline, causing the fair value of its debt to rise. (If the fair value of Wintel's debt increases, its effective borrowing cost is higher relative to the market.) To hedge against this fair value risk, the firm entered into an 18-month interest rate swap agreement on January 1 and designated the swap as a hedge against changes in the fair value of the note. The swap calls for the company to *receive payment* based on a 10% fixed interest rate on a notional amount of $1 million and to *make payment* based on a floating interest rate tied to changes in general rates. Cash settlement of the net interest amount is made semiannually at June 30 and December 31 of each year with the net interest being the difference between the $50,000 fixed interest [$1 million × (10% × ½)] and the floating interest rate times $1 million at those dates. Floating (market) settlement rates were 9% at June 30, 2009, 8% at December 31, 2009, and 8% at June 30, 2010. Net interest receipts can be calculated as shown below. Fair values of both the derivative and the note resulting from those market rate changes are assumed to be quotes obtained from securities dealers.	**ILLUSTRATION A–2** Interest Rate Swap—Extended Method	

	1/1/09	6/30/09	12/31/09	6/30/10
Fixed rate	10%	10%	10%	10%
Floating rate	10%	9%	8%	9%
Fixed payments				
[$1 million × (10% × ½)]		$ 50,000	$ 50,000	$ 50,000
Floating payments				
($1 million × ½ floating rate)		45,000	40,000	45,000
Net interest receipts		$ 5,000	$ 10,000	$ 5,000
Fair value of interest rate swap	0	$ 9,363	$ 9,615	0
Fair value of note payable	$1,000,000	$1,009,363	$1,009,615	$1,000,000

---

[16]"Disclosures About Fair Values of Financial Instruments," *Statement of Financial Accounting Standards No. 107* (Norwalk, Conn.: FASB, 1991) as amended by *Statement of Financial Accounting Standards No. 133*, "Accounting for Derivative Instruments and Hedging Activities" (Norwalk, Conn.: FASB, 1998).

[17]There is no precise minimum interval, though it generally is three to six months or less. Other criteria are specified by *SFAS No. 133* (para. 68) in addition to the key conditions listed here.

When the floating rate declined in Illustration A–2 from 10% to 9%, the fair values of both the derivative (swap) and the note increased. This created an offsetting gain on the derivative and holding loss on the note. Both are recognized in earnings the same period (June 30, 2009).

January 1, 2009		
Cash	1,000,000	
Notes payable		1,000,000
To record the issuance of the note.		

The interest rate swap is designated as a fair value hedge on this note at issuance.

June 30, 2009		
Interest expense (10% × ½ × $1 million)	50,000	
Cash		50,000
To record interest.		
Cash ($50,000 – [9% × ½ × × $1 million])	5,000	
Interest rate swap ($9,363 – 0)	9,363	
Interest revenue (10% × ½ × $0)		0
Holding gain—interest rate swap (to balance)		14,363
To record the net cash settlement, accrued interest on the swap, and change in the fair value of the derivative.		
Holding loss—hedged note	9,363	
Notes payable ($1,009,363 – 1,000,000)		9,363
To record change in fair value of the note due to interest rate changes.		

The swap settlement is the difference between the fixed interest (5%) and variable interest (4.5%).

The fair value of derivatives is recognized in the balance sheet.

The hedged liability (or asset) is adjusted to fair value as well.

The net interest settlement on June 30, 2009, is $5,000 because the fixed rate is 5% (half of the 10% annual rate) and the floating rate is 4.5% (half of the 9% annual rate). A holding gain ($14,363) is produced by holding the derivative security during a time when an interest rate decline caused an increase in the value of that asset. A portion ($5,000) of the gain was received in cash and another portion ($9,363) is reflected as an increase in the value of the asset.

We also have holding loss of the same amount. This is because we also held a liability during the same time period, and the interest rate change caused its fair value to increase as well.

December 31, 2009		
Interest expense (9% × ½ × $1,009,363)	45,421	
Notes payable (difference)*	4,579	
Cash (10% × ½ × $1,000,000)		50,000
To record interest.		
Cash [$50,000 – (8% × ½ × $1 million)]	10,000	
Interest rate swap ($9,615 – 9,363)	252	
Interest revenue (9% × ½ × $9,363)		421
Holding gain—interest rate swap (to balance)		9,831
To record the net cash settlement, accrued interest on the swap, and change in the fair value of the derivative.		
Holding loss—hedged note	4,831	
Notes payable ($1,009,615 – 1,009,363 + 4,579)		4,831
To record the change in fair value of the note due to interest rate changes.		

As with any debt, interest expense is the effective rate times the outstanding balance.

The cash settlement is the difference between the fixed interest (5%) and variable interest (4%).

Interest ($421) accrues on the asset.

The note is increased by the change in fair value.

*We could use a premium on the note to adjust its carrying amount.

We determine interest on the note the same way we do for any liability, as you learned earlier—at the effective rate (9% × ½) times the outstanding balance ($1,009,363). This results in reducing the note's carrying amount for the cash interest paid in excess of the interest expense.

The fair value of the swap increased due to the interest rate decline by $252 (from $9,363 to $9,615). The holding gain we recognize in earnings consists of that increase (a) plus the $10,000 cash settlement also created by the interest rate decline and (b) minus the $421 increase that results not from the interest rate decline, but from interest accruing on the asset.[18] Similarly, we adjust the note's carrying value by the amount necessary to increase it to fair value, allowing for the $4,579 reduction in the note in the earlier entry to record interest.

At June 30, 2010, Wintel repeats the process of adjusting to fair value both the derivative investment and the note being hedged.

June 30, 2010

Interest expense (8% × ½ × $1,009,615)	40,385	
Notes payable (difference)	9,615	
Cash (10% × ½ × $1,000,000)		50,000
To record interest.		
Cash [$50,000 − (9% × ½ × $1 million)]	5,000	
Holding loss—interest rate swap (to balance)	5,000	
Interest rate swap ($0 − $9,615)		9,615
Interest revenue (8% × ½ × $9,615)		385
To record the net cash settlement, accrued interest on the swap,		
and change in the fair value of the derivative.		
Notes payable ($1,000,000 − 1,009,615 + 9,615)	0	
Holding gain—hedged note		0
To record the change in fair value of the note due to interest rate changes.		
Note payable	1,000,000	
Cash		1,000,000
To repay the loan		

Interest expense is the effective rate times the outstanding balance.

The net interest received is the difference between the fixed interest (5%) and floating interest (4.5%).

The swap's fair value now is zero.

The net interest received is the difference between the fixed rate (5%) and floating rate (4.5%) times $1 million. The fair value of the swap decreased by $9,615 (from $9,615 to zero).[19] The holding loss we recognize in earnings consists of that decline (a) minus the $5,000 portion of the decline resulting from it being realized in cash settlement and (b) plus the $385 increase that results not from the interest rate change, but from interest accruing on the asset.

Now let's see how the carrying values changed for the swap account and the note:

	Swap		Note	
Jan. 1, 2009				1,000,000
June 30, 2009	9,363			9,363
Dec. 31, 2009	252		4,579	4,831
June 30, 2010		9,615	9,615	
			1,000,000	
	0			0

The income statement is affected as follows:

	Income Statement + (−)	
June 30, 2009	(50,000)	Interest expense
	0	Interest revenue (no time has passed)
	14,363	Holding gain interest rate swap
	(9,363)	Holding loss—hedged note
	(45,000)	Net effect—same as floating interest payment
Dec. 31, 2009	(45,421)	Interest expense
	421	Interest revenue
	9,831	Holding gain—interest rate swap
	(4,831)	Holding loss—hedged note
	(40,000)	Net effect—same as floating interest payment

[18]The investment in the interest rate swap represents the present value of expected future net interest receipts. As with other such assets, interest accrues at the effective rate times the outstanding balance. You also can think of the accrued interest mathematically as the increase in present value of the future cash flows as we get one period nearer to the dates when the cash will be received.

[19]Because there are no future cash receipts or payments from the swap arrangement at this point, the fair value of the swap is zero.

June 30, 2010	(40,385)	Interest expense
	385	Interest revenue
	(5,000)	Holding gain—interest rate swap
	0	Holding loss—hedged note
	(45,000)	Net effect—same as floating interest payment

As this demonstrates, the swap effectively converts Wintel's fixed-interest debt to floating-interest debt.

THE BOTTOM LINE

1. All derivatives are reported in the balance sheet at fair value.

2. *Hedging* means taking a risk position that is opposite to an actual position that is exposed to risk. For a derivative used to hedge against exposure to risk, treatment of any gain or loss from fair value changes depends on whether the derivative is designated as (a) a fair value hedge or (b) a cash flow hedge.

3. We recognize a gain or loss from a *fair value hedge* immediately in earnings along with the loss or gain from the item being hedged. This is so the income effects of the hedge instrument and the income effects of the item being hedged will affect earnings at the same time.

4. We defer a gain or loss from a *cash flow hedge* as part of Other comprehensive income until it can be recognized in earnings along with the earnings effect of the item being hedged.

5. Imperfect hedges result in part of the derivative gain or loss being included in current earnings. We ignore market value changes unrelated to the risk being hedged.

6. Extensive disclosure requirements about derivatives are designed to provide investors and creditors information about the adequacy of a company's risk management and the company's success in reducing risks, including risks not managed successfully. ●

QUESTIONS FOR REVIEW OF KEY TOPICS

Q A–1 Some financial instruments are called derivatives. Why?

Q A–2 Should gains and losses on a fair value hedge be recorded as they occur, or should they be recorded to coincide with losses and gains on the item being hedged?

Q A–3 Hines Moving Company held a fixed-rate debt of $2 million. The company wanted to hedge its fair value exposure with an interest rate swap. However, the only notional available at the time on the type of swap it desired was $2.5 million. What will be the effect of any gain or loss on the $500,000 notional difference?

Q A–4 What is a futures contract?

Q A–5 What is the effect on interest of an interest rate swap?

Q A–6 How are derivatives reported on the balance sheet? Why?

Q A–7 When is a gain or a loss from a cash flow hedge reported in earnings?

EXERCISES

available with McGraw–Hill's Homework Manager www.mhhe.com/spiceland5e

E A–1
Derivatives—hedge classification

Indicate (by abbreviation) the type of hedge each activity described below would represent.

Hedge Type
FV   Fair value hedge
CF   Cash flow hedge
FC   Foreign currency hedge
N   Would not qualify as a hedge

Activity

_____ 1. An options contract to hedge possible future price changes of inventory.

_____ 2. A futures contract to hedge exposure to interest rate changes prior to replacing bank notes when they mature.

_____ 3. An interest rate swap to synthetically convert floating rate debt into fixed rate debt.

_____ 4. An interest rate swap to synthetically convert fixed rate debt into floating rate debt.

_____ 5. A futures contract to hedge possible future price changes of timber covered by a firm commitment to sell.

_____ 6. A futures contract to hedge possible future price changes of a forecasted sale of tin.

_____ 7. ExxonMobil's net investment in a Kuwait oil field.

_____ 8. An interest rate swap to synthetically convert floating rate interest on a stock investment into fixed rate interest.

_____ 9. An interest rate swap to synthetically convert fixed rate interest on a held-to-maturity debt investment into floating rate interest.

_____ 10. An interest rate swap to synthetically convert floating rate interest on a held-to-maturity debt investment into fixed rate interest.

_____ 11. An interest rate swap to synthetically convert fixed rate interest on a stock investment into floating rate interest.

E A–2

Derivatives; interest rate swap; fixed rate debt

On January 1, 2009, LLB Industries borrowed $200,000 from Trust Bank by issuing a two-year, 10% note, with interest payable quarterly. LLB entered into a two-year interest rate swap agreement on January 1, 2009, and designated the swap as a fair value hedge. Its intent was to hedge the risk that general interest rates will decline, causing the fair value of its debt to increase. The agreement called for the company to receive payment based on a 10% fixed interest rate on a notional amount of $200,000 and to pay interest based on a floating interest rate. The contract called for cash settlement of the net interest amount quarterly.

Floating (LIBOR) settlement rates were 10% at January 1, 8% at March 31, and 6% June 30, 2009. The fair values of the swap are quotes obtained from a derivatives dealer. Those quotes and the fair values of the note are as indicated below.

	January 1	March 31	June 30
Fair value of interest rate swap	0	$ 6,472	$ 11,394
Fair value of note payable	$200,000	$206,472	$211,394

Required:

1. Calculate the net cash settlement at March 31 and June 30, 2009.

2. Prepare the journal entries through June 30, 2009, to record the issuance of the note, interest, and necessary adjustments for changes in fair value.

E A–3

Derivatives; interest rate swap; fixed rate investment

(This is a variation of Exercise A–2, modified to consider an investment in debt securities.)

On January 1, 2009, S&S Corporation invested in LLB Industries' negotiable two-year, 10% notes, with interest receivable quarterly. The company classified the investment as available-for-sale. S&S entered into a two-year interest rate swap agreement on January 1, 2009, and designated the swap as a fair value hedge. Its intent was to hedge the risk that general interest rates will decline, causing the fair value of its investment to increase. The agreement called for the company to make payment based on a 10% fixed interest rate on a notional amount of $200,000 and to receive interest based on a floating interest rate. The contract called for cash settlement of the net interest amount quarterly.

Floating (LIBOR) settlement rates were 10% at January 1, 8% at March 31, and 6% June 30, 2009. The fair values of the swap are quotes obtained from a derivatives dealer. Those quotes and the fair values of the investment in notes are as follows:

	January 1	March 31	June 30
Fair value of interest rate swap	0	$ 6,472	$ 11,394
Fair value of the investment in notes	$200,000	$206,472	$211,394

Required:

1. Calculate the net cash settlement at March 31 and June 30, 2009

2. Prepare the journal entries through June 30, 2009, to record the investment in notes, interest, and necessary adjustments for changes in fair value.

E A–4

Derivatives; interest rate swap; fixed rate debt; fair value change unrelated to hedged risk

(This is a variation of Exercise A–2, modified to consider fair value change unrelated to hedged risk.)

LLB Industries borrowed $200,000 from Trust Bank by issuing a two-year, 10% note, with interest payable quarterly. LLB entered into a two-year interest rate swap agreement on January 1, 2009 and designated the swap as a fair value hedge. Its intent was to hedge the risk that general interest rates will decline, causing the fair value of its debt to increase. The agreement called for the company to receive payment based on a 10% fixed interest rate on a notional amount of $200,000 and to pay interest based on a floating interest rate.

Floating (LIBOR) settlement rates were 10% at January 1, 8% at March 31, and 6% at June 30, 2009. The fair values of the swap are quotes obtained from a derivatives dealer. Those quotes and the fair values of the note are as indicated below. The additional rise in the fair value of the note (higher than that of the swap) on June 30 was due to investors' perceptions that the creditworthiness of LLB was improving.

	January 1	March 31	June 30
Fair value of interest rate swap	0	$ 6,472	$ 11,394
Fair value of note payable	$200,000	$206,472	$220,000

Required:

1. Calculate the net cash settlement at June 30, 2009

2. Prepare the journal entries on June 30, 2009, to record the interest and necessary adjustments for changes in fair value.

E A–5

Derivatives; interest rate swap; fixed rate debt; extended method

This is a variation of Exercise A–2, modified to consider the extended method.

On January 1, 2009, LLB Industries borrowed $200,000 from Trust Bank by issuing a two-year, 10% note, with interest payable quarterly. LLB entered into a two-year interest rate swap agreement on January 1, 2009, and designated the swap as a fair value hedge. Its intent was to hedge the risk that general interest rates will decline, causing the fair value of its debt to increase. The agreement called for the company to receive payment based on a 10% fixed interest rate on a notional amount of $200,000 and to pay interest based on a floating interest rate. The contract called for cash settlement of the net interest amount quarterly.

Floating (LIBOR) settlement rates were 10% at January 1, 8% at March 31, and 6% at June 30, 2009. The fair values of the swap are quotes obtained from a derivatives dealer. Those quotes and the fair values of the note are as follows:

	January 1	March 31	June 30
Fair value of interest rate swap	0	$ 6,472	$ 11,394
Fair value of note payable	$200,000	$206,472	$211,394

Required:

Prepare the journal entries through June 30, 2009, to record the issuance of the note, interest, and necessary adjustments for changes in fair value. Use the extended method demonstrated in Illustration A–2.

E A–6

Derivatives; interest rate swap; fixed-rate debt; fair value change unrelated to hedged risk; extended method

(Note: This is a variation of Exercise A–5, modified to consider fair value change unrelated to hedged risk.)

On January 1, 2009, LLB Industries borrowed $200,000 from trust Bank by issuing a two-year, 10% note, with interest payable quarterly. LLB entered into a two-year interest rate swap agreement on January 1, 2009, and designated the swap as a fair value hedge. Its intent was to hedge the risk that general interest rates will decline, causing the fair value of its debt to increase. The agreement called for the company to receive payment based on a 10% fixed interest rate on a notional amount of $200,000 and to pay interest based on a floating interest rate. The contract called for cash settlement of the net interest amount quarterly.

Floating (LIBOR) settlement rates were 10% at January 1, 8% at March 31, and 6% June 30, 2009. The fair values of the swap are quotes obtained from a derivatives dealer. Those quotes and the fair values of the note are as indicated below. The additional rise in the fair value of the note (higher than that of the swap) on June 30 was due to investors' perceptions that the creditworthiness of LLB was improving.

	January 1	March 31	June 30
Fair value of interest rate swap	0	$ 6,472	$ 11,394
Fair value of note payable	$200,000	206,472	220,000

Required:

1. Calculate the net cash settlement at June 30, 2009.

2. Prepare the journal entries on June 30, 2009, to record the interest and necessary adjustments for changes in fair value. Use the extended method demonstrated in Illustration A–2.

PROBLEMS

available with McGraw–Hill's Homework Manager www.mhhe.com/spiceland5e

P A–1

Derivatives— interest rate swap

On January 1, 2009, Labtech Circuits borrowed $100,000 from First Bank by issuing a three-year, 8% note, payable on December 31, 2011. Labtech wanted to hedge the risk that general interest rates will decline, causing the fair value of its debt to increase. Therefore, Labtech entered into a three-year interest rate swap agreement on January 1, 2009, and designated the swap as a fair value hedge. The agreement called for the company to receive payment based on an 8% fixed interest rate on a notional amount of $100,000 and to pay interest based on a floating interest rate tied to LIBOR. The contract called for cash settlement of the net interest amount on December 31 of each year.

Floating (LIBOR) settlement rates were 8% at inception and 9%, 7%, and 7% at the end of 2009, 2010, and 2011, respectively. The fair values of the swap are quotes obtained from a derivatives dealer. These quotes and the fair values of the note are as follows:

	January 1	December 31		
	2009	2009	2010	2011
Fair value of interest rate swap	0	$ (1,759)	$ 935	0
Fair value of note payable	$100,000	$98,241	$100,935	$100,000

Required:

1. Calculate the net cash settlement at the end of 2009, 2010, and 2011.

2. Prepare the journal entries during 2009 to record the issuance of the note, interest, and necessary adjustments for changes in fair value.

3. Prepare the journal entries during 2010 to record interest, net cash interest settlement for the interest rate swap, and necessary adjustments for changes in fair value.

4. Prepare the journal entries during 2011 to record interest, net cash interest settlement for the interest rate swap, necessary adjustments for changes in fair value, and repayment of the debt.

5. Calculate the carrying values of both the swap account and the note in each of the three years.

6. Calculate the net effect on earnings of the hedging arrangement in each of the three years. (Ignore income taxes.)

7. Suppose the fair value of the note at December 31, 2009, had been $97,000 rather than $98,217 with the additional decline in fair value due to investors' perceptions that the creditworthiness of Labtech was worsening. How would that affect your entries to record changes in the fair values?

P A–2
Derivatives;
interest rate swap;
comprehensive

CMOS Chips is hedging a 20-year, $10 million, 7% bond payable with a 20-year interest rate swap and has designated the swap as a fair value hedge. The agreement called for CMOS to receive payment based on a 7% fixed interest rate on a notional amount of $10 million and to pay interest based on a floating interest rate tied to LIBOR. The contract calls for cash settlement of the net interest amount on December 31 of each year.

At December 31, 2009, the fair value of the derivative and of the hedged bonds has increased by $100,000 because interest rates declined during the reporting period.

Required:

1. Does CMOS have an unrealized gain or loss on the derivative for the period? On the bonds? Will earnings increase or decrease due to the hedging arrangement? Why?

2. Suppose interest rates increased, rather than decreased, causing the fair value of both the derivative and of the hedged bonds to decrease by $100,000. Would CMOS have an unrealized gain or loss on the derivative for the period? On the bonds? Would earnings increase or decrease due to the hedging arrangement? Why?

3. Suppose the fair value of the bonds at December 31, 2009, had increased by $110,000 rather than $100,000, with the additional increase in fair value due to investors' perceptions that the creditworthiness of CMOS was improving. Would CMOS have an unrealized gain or loss on the derivative for the period? On the bonds? Would earnings increase or decrease due to the hedging arrangement? Why?

4. Suppose the notional amount of the swap had been $12 million, rather than the $10 million principal amount of the bonds. As a result, at December 31, 2009, the swap's fair value had increased by $120,000 rather than $100,000. Would CMOS have an unrealized gain or loss on the derivative for the period? On the bonds? Would earnings increase or decrease due to the hedging arrangement? Why?

5. Suppose BIOS Corporation is an investor having purchased all $10 million of the bonds issued by CMOS as described in the original situation above. BIOS is hedging its investment, classified as available-for-sale, with a 20-year interest rate swap and has designated the swap as a fair value hedge. The agreement called for BIOS to make *payment* based on a 7% fixed interest rate on a notional amount of $10 million and to *receive* interest based on a floating interest rate tied to LIBOR. Would BIOS have an unrealized gain or loss on the derivative for the period due to interest rates having declined? On the bonds? Would earnings increase or decrease due to the hedging arrangement? Why?

P A–3
Derivatives;
interest rate swap;
fixed rate debt;
extended method

(Note: This is a variation of Problem A–1, modified to consider the extended method demonstrated in Illustration A–2.)

On January 1, 2009, Labtech Circuits borrowed $100,000 from First Bank by issuing a three-year, 8% note, payable on December 31, 2011. Labtech wanted to hedge the risk that general interest rates will decline, causing the fair value of its debt to increase. Therefore, Labtech entered into a three-year interest rate swap agreement on January 1, 2009, and designated the swap as a fair value hedge. The agreement called for the company to receive payment based on an 8% fixed interest rate on a notional amount of $100,000 and to pay interest based on a floating interest rate tied to LIBOR. The contract called for cash settlement of the net interest amount on December 31 of each year.

Floating (LIBOR) settlement rates were 8% at inception and 9%, 7%, and 7% at the end of 2009, 2010, and 2011, respectively. The fair values of the swap are quotes obtained from a derivatives dealer. Those quotes and the fair values of the note are as follows:

	January 1	December 31		
	2009	**2009**	**2010**	**2011**
Fair value of interest rate swap	0	$ (1,759)	$ 935	0
Fair value of note payable	$100,000	$ 98,241	100,935	$100,000

Required:
Use the extended method demonstrated in Illustration A–2.
1. Calculate the net cash settlement at the end of 2009, 2010, and 2011.
2. Prepare the journal entries during 2009 to record the issuance of the note, interest, and necessary adjustments for changes in fair value.
3. Prepare the journal entries during 2010 to record interest, net cash interest settlement for the interest rate swap, and necessary adjustments for changes in fair value.
4. Prepare the journal entries during 2011 to record interest, net cash interest settlement for the interest rate swap, necessary adjustments for changes in fair value, and repayment of the debt.
5. Calculate the carrying values of both the swap account and the note in each of the three years.
6. Calculate the net effect on earnings of the hedging arrangement in each of the three years. (Ignore income taxes.)
7. Suppose the fair value of the note at December 31, 2009, had been $97,000 rather than $98,217 with the additional decline in fair value due to investors' perceptions that the creditworthiness of Labtech was worsening. How would that affect your entries to record changes in the fair values?

BROADEN YOUR **PERSPECTIVE**

Apply your critical-thinking ability to the knowledge you've gained. These cases will provide you an opportunity to develop your research, analysis, judgment, and communication skills. You also will work with other students, integrate what you've learned, apply it in real world situations, and consider its global and ethical ramifications. This practice will broaden your knowledge and further develop your decision-making abilities.

Real World Case A–1
Derivative losses; recognition in earnings

The following is an excerpt from a disclosure note of **Johnson & Johnson:**

15. Financial Instruments (in part)
As of December 31, 2006, the balance of deferred net losses on derivatives included in accumulated other comprehensive income was $9 million after-tax. The Company expects that substantially all of this amount will be reclassified into earnings over the next 12 months as a result of transactions that are expected to occur over that period.

Required:
1. Johnson & Johnson indicates that it expects that substantially all of the balance of deferred net losses on derivatives will be reclassified into earnings over the next 12 months as a result of transactions that are expected to occur over that period. What is meant by "reclassified into earnings"?
2. What type(s) of hedging transaction might be accounted for in this way?

Communication Case A–2
Derivatives; hedge accounting

A conceptual question in accounting for derivatives is: Should gains and losses on a hedge instrument be recorded as they occur, or should they be recorded to coincide (match) with income effects of the item being hedged?

ABI Wholesalers plans to issue long-term notes in May that will replace its $20 million of 9.5% bonds when they mature in July. ABI is exposed to the risk that interest rates in July will have risen, increasing borrowing costs (reducing the selling price of its notes). To hedge that possibility, ABI entered a (Treasury bond) futures contract in May to deliver (sell) bonds in July at their *current* price.

As a result, if interest rates rise, borrowing costs will go up for ABI because it will sell notes at a higher interest cost (or lower price). But that loss will be offset (approximately) by the gain produced by being in the opposite position on Treasury bond futures.

Two opposing viewpoints are:

View 1: Gains and losses on instruments designed to hedge anticipated transactions should be recorded as they occur.

View 2: Gains and losses on instruments designed to hedge anticipated transactions should be recorded to coincide (match) with income effects of the item being hedged.

In considering this question, focus on conceptual issues regarding the practicable and theoretically appropriate treatment, unconstrained by GAAP. Your instructor will divide the class into two to six groups depending on the size of the class. The mission of your group is to reach consensus on the appropriate accounting for the gains and losses on instruments designed to hedge anticipated transactions.

Required:
1. Each group member should deliberate the situation independently and draft a tentative argument prior to the class session for which the case is assigned.

2. In class, each group will meet for 10 to 15 minutes in different areas of the classroom. During that meeting, group members will take turns sharing their suggestions for the purpose of arriving at a single group treatment.

3. After the allotted time, a spokesperson for each group (selected during the group meetings) will share the group's solution with the class. The goal of the class is to incorporate the views of each group into a consensus approach to the situation.

Real World Case A–3
Researching the way interest rate futures prices are quoted on the Chicago Mercantile Exchange; retrieving information from the Internet

The **Chicago Mercantile Exchange,** or Merc, at 30 S. Wacker Drive in Chicago, is the world's largest financial exchange, an international marketplace enabling institutions and businesses to trade futures and options contracts including currencies, interest rates, stock indices, and agricultural commodities.

Required:
1. Access the Merc on the Internet. The web address is **www.cme.com.**
2. Access the daily settlement prices within the site. Scroll to find the 13-week Treasury bill futures.
3. What are the settlement prices for September and December futures contracts?
4. In terms of dollars, how can we interpret the settlement price?

Research Case A–4
Issue related to the derivatives standard; research an article

In an effort to keep up with the rapidly changing global financial markets, the FASB issued a standard—*SFAS No. 133*—on accounting for derivative financial instruments. A *Journal of Accountancy* article that discusses this standard is "The Decision on Derivatives," by Arlette C. Wilson, Gary Waters and Barry J. Bryan, November 1998.

Required:
On the Internet, go to the AICPA site at **www.aicpa.org** and find the article mentioned.

1. What are the primary problems or issues the FASB is attempting to address with the new standard?
2. In considering the issues, the FASB made four fundamental decisions that became the cornerstones of the proposed statement. What are those fundamental decisions? Which do you think is most critical to fair financial reporting?

Glossary

Accounting equation the process used to capture the effect of economic events; Assets = Liabilities + Owner's Equity.

Accounting Principles Board (APB) the second private sector body delegated the task of setting accounting standards.

Accounts storage areas to keep track of the increases and decreases in financial position elements.

Accounts payable obligations to suppliers of merchandise or of services purchased on open account.

Accounts receivable receivables resulting from the sale of goods or services on account.

Accounts receivable aging schedule applying different percentages to accounts receivable balances depending on the length of time outstanding.

Accrual accounting measurement of the entity's accomplishments and resource sacrifices during the period, regardless of when cash is received or paid.

Accruals when the cash flow comes after either expense or revenue recognition.

Accrued interest interest that has accrued since the last interest date.

Accrued liabilities expenses already incurred but not yet paid (accrued expenses).

Accrued receivables the recognition of revenue earned before cash is received.

Accumulated benefit obligation (ABO) the discounted present value of estimated retirement benefits earned so far by employees, applying the plan's pension formula using existing compensation levels.

Accumulated other comprehensive income amount of other comprehensive income (nonowner changes in equity other than net income) accumulated over the current and prior periods.

Accumulated postretirement benefit obligation (APBO) portion of the EPBO attributed to employee service up to a particular date.

Acid-test ratio current assets, excluding inventories and prepaid items, divided by current liabilities.

Acquisition costs the amounts paid to acquire the rights to explore for undiscovered natural resources or to extract proven natural resources.

Activity-based method allocation of an asset's cost base using a measure of the asset's input or output.

Actuary a professional trained in a particular branch of statistics and mathematics to assess the various uncertainties and to estimate the company's obligation to employees in connection with its pension plan.

Additions the adding of a new major component to an existing asset.

Adjusted trial balance trial balance after adjusting entries have been recorded.

Adjusting entries internal transactions recorded at the end of any period when financial statements are prepared.

Allocation base the value of the usefulness that is expected to be consumed.

Allocation method the pattern in which the usefulness is expected to be consumed.

Allowance method recording bad debt expense and reducing accounts receivable indirectly by crediting a contra account (allowance for uncollectible accounts) to accounts receivable for an estimate of the amount that eventually will prove uncollectible.

American Institute of Accountants (AIA)/American Institute of Certified Public Accountants (AICPA) national organization of professional public accountants.

Amortization cost allocation for intangibles.

Amortization schedule schedule that reflects the changes in the debt over its term to maturity.

Annuity cash flows received or paid in the same amount each period.

Annuity due cash flows occurring at the beginning of each period.

Antidilutive securities the effect of the conversion or exercise of potential common shares would be to increase rather than decrease, EPS.

Articles of incorporation statement of the nature of the firm's business activities, the shares to be issued, and the composition of the initial board of directors.

Asset retirement obligations (AROs) obligations associated with the disposition of an operational asset.

Assets probable future economic benefits obtained or controlled by a particular entity as a result of past transactions or events.

Asset turnover ratio measure of a company's efficiency in using assets to generate revenue.

Assigning using receivables as collateral for loans; nonpayment of a debt will require the proceeds from collecting the assigned receivables to go directly toward repayment of the debt.

Attribution process of assigning the cost of benefits to the years during which those benefits are assumed to be earned by employees.

Auditors independent intermediaries who help ensure that management has appropriately applied GAAP in preparing the company's financial statements.

Auditor's report report issued by CPAs who audit the financial statements that informs users of the audit findings.

Average collection period indication of the average age of accounts receivable.

Average cost method assumes cost of goods sold and ending inventory consist of a mixture of all the goods available for sale.

Average days in inventory indicates the average number of days it normally takes to sell inventory.

Bad debt expense an operating expense incurred to boost sales; inherent cost of granting credit.

Balance sheet a position statement that presents an organized list of assets, liabilities, and equity at a particular point in time.

Balance sheet approach determination of bad debt expense by estimating the net realizable value of accounts receivable to be reported in the balance sheet.

Bank reconciliation comparison of the bank balance with the balance in the company's own records.

Bargain purchase option (BPO) provision in the lease contract that gives the lessee the option of purchasing the leased property at a bargain price.

Bargain renewal option gives the lessee the option to renew the lease at a bargain rate.

Basic EPS computed by dividing income available to common stockholders (net income less any preferred stock dividends) by the weighted-average number of common shares outstanding for the period.

Billings of construction contract contra account to the asset construction in progress; subtracted from construction in progress to determine balance sheet presentation.

Board of directors establishes corporate policies and appoints officers who manage the corporation.

Bond indenture document that describes specific promises made to bondholders.

Bonds A form of debt consisting of separable units (bonds) that obligates the issuing corporation to repay a stated amount at a specified maturity date and to pay interest to bondholders between the issue date and maturity.

Book value assets minus liabilities as shown in the balance sheet.

Callable allows the issuing company to buy back, or call, outstanding bonds from the bondholders before their scheduled maturity date.

Capital budgeting The process of evaluating the purchase of operational assets.

Capital leases installment purchases/sales that are formulated outwardly as leases.

Capital markets mechanisms that foster the allocation of resources efficiently.

Cash currency and coins, balances in checking accounts, and items acceptable for deposit in these accounts, such as checks and money orders received from customers.

Cash basis accounting/net operating cash flow difference between cash receipts and cash disbursements during a reporting period from transactions related to providing goods and services to customers.

Cash disbursements journal record of cash disbursements.

Cash discounts sales discounts; represent reductions not in the selling price of a good or service but in the amount to be paid by a credit customer if paid within a specific period of time.

Cash equivalents certain negotiable items such as commercial paper, money market funds, and U.S. Treasury bills that are highly liquid investments quickly convertible to cash.

Cash equivalents short-term, highly liquid investments that can be readily converted to cash with little risk of loss.

Cash flow hedge a derivative used to hedge against the exposure to changes in cash inflows or cash outflows of an asset or liability or a forecasted transaction (like a future purchase or sale).

Cash flows from financing activities both inflows and outflows of cash resulting from the external financing of a business.

Cash flows from investing activities both outflows and inflows of cash caused by the acquisition and disposition of assets.

Cash flows from operating activities both inflows and outflows of cash that result from activities reported on the income statement.

Cash receipts journal record of cash receipts.

Certified Public Accountants (CPAs) licensed individuals who can represent that the financial statements have been audited in accordance with generally accepted auditing standards.

Change in accounting estimate a change in an estimate when new information comes to light.

Change in accounting principle switch by a company from one accounting method to another.

Change in reporting entity presentation of consolidated financial statements in place of statements of individual companies, or a change in the specific companies that constitute the group for which consolidated or combined statements are prepared.

Closing process the temporary accounts are reduced to zero balances, and these temporary account balances are closed (transferred) to retained earnings to reflect the changes that have occurred in that account during the period.

Commercial paper unsecured notes sold in minimum denominations of $25,000 with maturities ranging from 30 to 270 days.

Committee on Accounting Procedure (CAP) the first private sector body that was delegated the task of setting accounting standards.

Comparability the ability to help users see similarities and differences among events and conditions.

Comparative financial statements corresponding financial statements from the previous years accompanying the issued financial statements.

Compensating balance a specified balance (usually some percentage of the committee amount) a borrower of a loan is asked to maintain in a low-interest or noninterest-bearing account at the bank.

Completed contract method recognition of revenue for a long-term contract when the project is complete.

Complex capital structure potential common shares are outstanding.

Composite depreciation method physically dissimilar assets are aggregated to gain the convenience of group depreciation.

Compound interest interest computed not only on the initial investment but also on the accumulated interest in previous periods.

Comprehensive income traditional net income plus other nonowner changes in equity.

Conceptual framework deals with theoretical and conceptual issues and provides an underlying structure for current and future accounting and reporting standards.

Conservatism practice followed in an attempt to ensure that uncertainties and risks inherent in business situations are adequately considered.

Consignment the consignor physically transfers the goods to the other company (the consignee), but the consignor retains legal title.

Consistency permits valid comparisons between different periods.

Consolidated financial statements combination of the separate financial statements of the parent and subsidiary each period into a single aggregate set of financial statements as if there were only one company.

Construction in progress asset account equivalent to the asset work-in-progress inventory in a manufacturing company.

Contingently issuable shares additional shares of common stock to be issued, contingent on the occurrence of some future circumstance.

Conventional retail method applying the retail inventory method in such a way that LCM is approximated.

Convertible bonds bonds for which bondholders have the option to convert the bonds into shares of stock.

Copyright exclusive right of protection given to a creator of a published work, such as a song, painting, photograph, or book.

Corporation the dominant form of business organization that acquires capital from investors in exchange for ownership interest and from creditors by borrowing.

Correction of an error an adjustment a company makes due to an error made.

Cost effectiveness the perceived benefit of increased decision usefulness exceeds the anticipated cost of providing that information.

Cost of goods sold cost of the inventory sold during the period.

Cost recovery method deferral of all gross profit recognition until the cost of the item sold has been recovered.

Cost-to-retail percentage ratio found by dividing goods available for sale at cost by goods available for sale at retail.

Coupons bonds name of the owner was not registered; the holder actually clipped an attached coupon and redeemed it in accordance with instructions on the indenture.

Credits represent the right side of the account.

Cumulative if the specified dividend is not paid in a given year, the unpaid dividends accumulate and must be made up in a later dividend year before any dividends are paid on common shares.

Current assets includes assets that are cash, will be converted into cash, or will be used up within one year or the operating cycle, whichever is longer.

Current liabilities expected to require current assets and usually are payable within one year.

Current maturities of long-term debt the current installment due on long-term debt, reported as a current liability.

Current ratio current assets divided by current liabilities.

Date of record specific date stated as to when the determination will be made of the recipient of the dividend.

Debenture bond secured only by the "full faith and credit" of the issuing corporation.

Debits represent the left side of the account.

Debt issue cost with either publicly or privately sold debt, the issuing company will incur costs in connection with issuing bonds or notes, such as legal and accounting fees and printing costs, in addition to registration and underwriting fees.

Debt to equity ratio compares resources provided by creditors with resources provided by owners.

Decision usefulness the quality of being useful to decision making.

Default risk a company's ability to pay its obligations when they come due.

Deferred annuity the first cash flow occurs more than the one period after the date the agreement begins.

Deferred tax asset taxes to be saved in the future when future deductible amounts reduce taxable income (when the temporary differences reverse).

Deferred tax liability taxes to be paid in the future when future taxable amounts become taxable (when the temporary differences reverse).

Deficit debit balance in retained earnings.

Defined benefit pension plans fixed retirement benefits defined by a designated formula, based on employees' years of service and annual compensation.

Defined contribution pension plans fixed annual contributions to a pension fund; employees choose where funds are invested—usually stocks or fixed-income securities.

Depletion allocation of the cost of natural resources.

Depreciation cost allocation for plant and equipment.

Derivatives financial instruments usually created to hedge against risks created by other financial instruments or by transactions that have yet to occur but are anticipated and that "derive" their values or contractually required cash flows from some other security or index.

Detachable stock purchase warrants the investor has the option to purchase a stated number of shares of common stock at a specified option price, within a given period of time.

Development costs for natural resources, costs incurred after the resource has been discovered but before production begins.

Diluted EPS incorporates the dilutive effect of all potential common shares.

Direct financing lease lease in which the lessor finances the asset for the lessee and earns interest revenue over the lease term.

Direct method the cash effect of each operating activity (i.e., income statement item) is reported directly on the statement of cash flows.

Direct write-off method an allowance for uncollectible accounts is not used; instead bad debts that do arise are written off as bad debt expense.

Disclosure notes additional insights about company operations, accounting principles, contractual agreements, and pending litigation.

Discontinued operations The discontinuance of a component of an entity whose operations and cash flows can be clearly distinguished from the rest of the entity.

Discount Arises when bonds are sold for less than face amount.

Discounting the transfer of a note receivable to a financial institution.

Distributions to owners decreases in equity resulting from transfers to owners.

Dividend distribution to shareholders of a portion of assets earned.

Dollar-value LIFO (DVL) Inventory is viewed as a quantity of value instead of a physical quantity of goods. Instead of layers of units from different purchases, the DVL inventory pool is viewed as comprising layers of dollar value from different years.

Dollar-value LIFO retail method LIFO retail method combined with dollar-value LIFO.

Double-declining-balance (DDB) method 200% of the straight-line rate is multiplied by book value.

Double-entry system dual effect that each transaction has on the accounting equation when recorded.

DuPont framework depict return on equity as determined by profit margin (representing profitability), asset turnover (representing efficiency), and the equity multiplier (representing leverage).

Early extinguishment of debt debt is retired prior to its scheduled maturity date.

Earnings per share (EPS) the amount of income earned by a company expressed on a per share basis.

Earnings quality refers to the ability of reported earnings (income) to predict a company's future earnings.

Economic events any event that directly affects the financial position of the company.

Effective interest method recording interest each period as the effective rate of interest multiplied by the outstanding balance of the debt.

Effective rate the actual rate at which money grows per year.

Emerging Issues Task Force (EITF) responsible for providing more timely responses to emerging financial reporting issues.

Employee share purchase plans permit all employees to buy shares directly from their company, often at favorable terms.

Equity method used when an investor can't control, but can significantly influence, the investee.

Equity multiplier depicts leverage as total assets divided by total equity.

Equity/net assets called shareholders' equity or stockholders' equity for a corporation; the residual interest in the assets of an entity that remains after deducting liabilities.

Estimates prediction of future events.

Ethics a code or moral system that provides criteria for evaluating right and wrong.

Ex-dividend date date usually two business days before the date of the record and is the first day the stock trades without the right to receive the declared dividend.

Executory costs maintenance, insurance, taxes, and any other costs usually associated with ownership.

Expected cash flow approach adjusts the cash flows, not the discount rate, for the uncertainty or risk of those cash flows.

Expected economic life useful life of an asset.

Expected postretirement benefit obligation (EPBO) discounted present value of the total net cost to the employer of postretirement benefits.

Expected return on plan assets estimated long-term return on invested assets.

Expenses outflows or other using up of assets or incurrences of liabilities during a period from delivering or producing good, rendering services, or other activities that constitute the entity's ongoing major, or central, operations.

Exploration costs for natural resources, expenditures such as drilling a well, or excavating a mine, or any other costs of searching for natural resources.

External events exchange between the company and a separate economic entity.

Extraordinary items material events and transactions that are both unusual in nature and infrequent in occurrence.

F.O.B. (free on board) shipping point legal title to the goods changes hands at the point of shipment when the seller delivers the goods to the common carrier, and the purchaser is responsible for shipping costs and transit insurance.

F.O.B. destination the seller is responsible for shipping and the legal title does not pass until the goods arrive at their destination.

Factor financial institution that buys receivables for cash, handles the billing and collection of the receivables, and charges a fee for this service.

Fair value hedge a derivative is used to hedge against the exposure to changes in the fair value of an asset or liability or a firm commitment.

Fair value hierarchy prioritizes the inputs companies should use when determinig fair value.

Fair value option allows companies to report their financial assets and liabilities at fair value.

Financial accounting provides relevant financial information to various external users.

Financial Accounting Foundation (FAF) responsible for selecting the members of the FASB and its Advisory Council, ensuring adequate funding of FASB activities, and exercising general oversight of the FASB's activities.

Financial Accounting Standards Board (FASB) the current private sector body that has been delegated the task of setting accounting standards.

Financial activities cash inflows and outflows from transactions with creditors and owners.

Financial instrument cash; evidence of an ownership interest in an entity; a contract that imposes on one entity an obligation to deliver cash or another financial instrument, and conveys to the second entity a right to receive cash or another financial instrument; and a contract that imposes on one entity an obligation to exchange financial instruments on potentially unfavorable terms and conveys to a second entity a right to exchange other financial instruments on potentially favorable terms.

Financial leverage by earning a return on borrowed funds that exceeds the cost of borrowing the funds, a company can provide its shareholders with a total return higher than it could achieve by employing equity funds alone.

Financial reporting process of providing financial statement information to external users.

Financial statements primary means of communicating financial information to external parties.

Finished goods costs that have accumulated in work in process are transferred to finished goods once the manufacturing process is completed.

Fiscal year the annual time period used to report to external users.

Fixed-asset turnover ratio used to measure how effectively managers used PP&E.

$$\frac{\text{Fixed-asset}}{\text{turnover ratio}} = \frac{\text{Net sales}}{\text{Average-fixed assets}}$$

Foreign currency futures contract agreement that requires the seller to deliver a specific foreign currency at a designated future date at a specific price.

Foreign currency hedge if a derivative is used to hedge the risk that some transactions require settlement in a currency other than the entities' functional currency or that foreign operations will require translation adjustments to reported amounts.

Forward contract calls for delivery on a specific date; is not traded on a market exchange; does not call for a daily cash settlement for price changes in the underlying contract.

Fractional shares a stock dividend or stock split results in some shareholders being entitled to fractions of whole shares.

Franchise contractual arrangement under which the franchisor grants the franchisee the exclusive right to use the franchisor's trademark or tradename within a geographical area, usually for specified period of time.

Franchisee individual or corporation given the right to sell the franchisor's products and use its name for a specified period of time.

Franchisor grants to the franchisee the right to sell the franchisor's products and use its name for a specific period of time.

Freight-in transportation-in; in a periodic system, freight costs generally are added to this temporary account, which is added to purchases in determining net purchases.

Full-cost method allows costs incurred in searching for oil and gas within a large geographical area to be capitalized as assets and expensed in the future as oil and gas from the successful wells are removed from that area.

Full-disclosure principle the financial reports should include any information that could affect the decisions made by external users.

Funded status difference between the employer's obligation (PBO) and the resources available to satisfy that obligation (plan assets).

Future deductible amounts the future tax consequence of a temporary difference will be to decrease taxable income relative to accounting income.

Futures contract agreement that requires the seller to deliver a particular commodity at a designated future date at a specified price.

Future taxable amounts the future tax consequence of temporary difference will be to increase taxable income relative to accounting income.

Future value amount of money that a dollar will grow to at some point in the future.

Gain or loss on the PBO the decrease or increase in the PBO when one or more estimates used in determining the PBO require revision.

Gains increases in equity from peripheral, or incidental, transactions of an entity.

General journal used to record any type of transaction.

General ledger collection of accounts.

Generally Accepted Accounting Principles (GAAP) set of both broad and specific guidelines that companies should follow when measuring and reporting the information in their financial statements and related notes.

Going concern assumption in the absence of information to the contrary, it is anticipated that a business entity will continue to operate indefinitely.

Goodwill unique intangible asset in that its cost can't be directly associated with any specifically identifiable right and it is not separable from the company itself.

Government Accounting Standards Board (GASB) responsible for developing accounting standards for governmental units such as states and cities.

Gross investment in the lease total of periodic rental payments and residual value.

Gross method For the buyer, views a discount not taken as part of the cost of inventory. For the seller, views a discount not taken by the customer as part of sales of revenue.

Gross profit method (gross margin method) estimates cost of goods sold which is then subtracted from cost of goods available for sale to estimate ending inventory.

Gross profit/ratio highlights the important relationship between net sales revenue and cost of goods sold.

$$\text{Gross profit ratio} = \frac{\text{Gross profit}}{\text{Net sales}}$$

Group depreciation method collection of assets defined as depreciable assets that share similar service lives and other attributes.

Half-year convention record one-half of a full year's depreciation in the year of acquisition and another half year in the year of disposal.

Hedging taking an action that is expected to produce exposure to a particular type of risk that is precisely the opposite of an actual risk to which the company already is exposed.

Historical costs original transaction value.

Horizontal analysis comparison by expressing each item as a percentage of that same item in the financial statements of another year (base amount) in order to more easily see year-to-year changes.

Illegal acts violations of the law, such as bribes, kickbacks, and illegal contributions to political candidates.

Impairment of value operational assets should be written down if there has been a significant impairment (fair value less than book value) of value.

Implicit rate of interest rate implicit in the agreement.

Improvements replacement of a major component of an operational asset.

Income from continuing operations revenues, expenses (including income taxes), gain, and losses, excluding those related to discontinued operations and extraordinary items.

Income statement statement of operations or statement of earnings is used to summarize the profit-generating activities that occurred during a particular reporting period.

Income statement approach estimating bad debt expense as a percentage of each period's net credit sales; usually determined by reviewing the company's recent history of the relationship between credit sales and actual bad debts.

Income summary account that is a bookkeeping convenience used in the closing process that provides a check that all temporary accounts have been properly closed.

Income tax expense provision for income taxes; reported as a separate expense in corporate income statements.

Indirect method the net cash increase or decrease from operating activities is derived indirectly by starting with reported net income and working backwards to convert that amount to a cash basis.

Initial direct costs costs incurred by the lessor that are associated directly with originating a lease and are essential to acquire the lease.

In-process research and development the amount of the purchase price in a business acquisition that is allocated to projects that have not yet reached technological feasibility.

Installment notes Notes payable for which equal installment payments include both an amount that represents interest and an amount that represents a reduction of the outstanding balance so that at maturity the note is completely paid.

Installment sales method recognizes revenue and costs only when cash payments are received.

Institute of Internal Auditors national organization of accountants providing internal auditing services for their own organizations.

Institute of Management Accountants (IMA) primary national organization of accountants working in industry and government.

Intangible assets operational assets that lack physical substance; examples include patents, copyrights, franchises, and goodwill.

Interest "rent" paid for the use of money for some period of time.

Interest cost interest accrued on the projected benefit obligation calculated as the discount rate multiplied by the projected benefit obligation at the beginning of the year.

Interest rate swap agreement to exchange fixed interest payments for floating rate payments, or vice versa, without exchanging the underlying principal amounts.

Internal control a company's plan to encourage adherence to company policies and procedures, promote operational efficiency, minimize errors and theft, and enhance the reliability and accuracy of accounting data.

Internal events events that directly affect the financial position of the company but don't involve an exchange transaction with another entity.

International Accounting Standards Board (IASB) objectives are to develop a single set of high-quality, understandable global accounting standards, to promote the use of those standards, and to bring about the convergence of national accounting standards and International Accounting Standards.

International Accounting Standards Committee (IASC) umbrella organization formed to develop global accounting standards.

International Financial Reporting Standards developed by the ISAB and used by more than 100 countries.

Intraperiod tax allocation associates (allocates) income tax expense (or income tax Gross profit Net sales benefit if there is a loss) with each major component of income that causes it.

Intrinsic value the difference between the market price of the shares and the option price at which they can be acquired.

Inventories goods awaiting sale (finished goods), goods in the course of production (work in process), and goods to be consumed directly or indirectly in production (raw materials).

Inventory goods acquired, manufactured, or in the process of being manufactured for sale.

Inventory turnover ratio measures a company's efficiency in managing its investment in inventory.

Investing activities involve the acquisition and sale of long-term assets used in the business and non-operating investment assets.

Investments by owners increases in equity resulting from transfers of resources (usually cash) to a company in exchange for ownership interest.

Irregularities intentional distortions of financial statements.

Journal a chronological record of all economic events affecting financial position.

Journal entry captures the effect of a transaction on financial position in debit/credit form.

Just-in-time (JIT) system a system used by a manufacturer to coordinate production with suppliers so that raw materials or components arrive just as they are needed in the production process.

Land improvements the cost of parking lots, driveways, and private roads and the costs of fences and lawn and garden sprinkler systems.

Last-in, first-out (LIFO) method assumes units sold are the most recent units purchased.

Leasehold improvements account title when a lessee makes improvements to leased property that reverts back to the lessor at the end of the lease.

Lessee user of a leased asset.

Lessor owner of a leased asset.

Leveraged lease a third-party, long-term creditor provides nonrecourse financing for a lease agreement between a lessor and a lessee.

Liabilities probable future sacrifices of economic benefits arising from present obligations of a particular entity to transfer assets or provide services to other entities in the future as a result of past transactions or events.

LIFO conformity rule if a company uses LIFO to measure taxable income, the company also must use LIFO for external financial reporting.

LIFO inventory pools simplifies recordkeeping and reduces the risk of LIFO liquidation by grouping inventory units into pools based on physical similarities of the individual units.

LIFO liquidation the decline in inventory quantity during the period.

Limited liability company owners are not liable for the debts of the business, except to the extent of their investment; all members can be involved with managing the business without losing liability protection; no limitations on the number of owners.

Limited liability partnership similar to a limited liability company, except it doesn't offer all the liability protection available in the limited liability company structure.

Line of credit allows a company to borrow cash without having to follow formal loan procedures and paperwork.

Liquidating dividend when a dividend exceeds the balance in retained earnings.

Liquidity period of time before an asset is converted to cash or until a liability is paid.

Long-term solvency the riskiness of a company with regard to the amount of liabilities in its capital structure.

Loss contingency existing, uncertain situation involving potential loss depending on whether some future event occurs.

Losses decreases in equity arising from peripheral, or incidental, transactions of the entity.

Lower-of-cost-or-market (LCM) recognizes losses in the period that the value of inventory declines below its cost.

Management discussion and analysis (MDA) provides a biased but informed perspective of a company's operations, liquidity, and capital resources.

Managerial accounting deals with the concepts and methods used to provide information to an organization's internal users (i.e., its managers).

Matching principle expenses are recognized in the same period as the related revenues.

Materiality if a more costly way of providing information is not expected to have a material effect on decisions made by those using the information, the less costly method may be acceptable.

Measurement process of associating numerical amounts to the elements.

Minimum lease payments payments the lessee is required to make in connection with the lease.

Minimum pension liability an employer must report a pension liability at least equal to the amount by which its ABO exceeds its plan assets.

Model Business Corporation Act designed to serve as a guide to states in the development of their corporation statutes.

Modified accelerated cost recovery system (MACRS) The federal income tax code allows taxpayers to compute depreciation for their tax returns using this method.

Monetary assets money and claims to receive money, the amount of which is fixed or determinable.

Monetary liabilities obligations to pay amounts of cash, the amount of which is fixed or determinable.

Mortgage bond backed by a lien on specified real estate owned by the issuer.

Multiple-deliverable arrangements require allocation of revenue to multiple elements that qualify for separate revenue recognition.

Multiple-step income statement format that includes a number of intermediate subtotals before arriving at income from continuing operations.

Natural resources oil and gas deposits, timber tracts, and mineral deposits.

Net income/net loss revenue + gains − (expenses and losses for a period) income statement bottom line.

Net markdown net effect of the change in selling price (increase, decrease, increase).

Net markup net effect of the change in selling price (increase, increase, decrease).

Net method For the buyer, considers the cost of inventory to include the net, after-discount amount, and any discounts not taken are reported as interest expense. For the seller, considers sales revenue to be the net amount, after discount, and any discounts not taken by the customer as interest revenue.

Net operating loss negative taxable income because tax-deductible expenses exceed taxable revenues.

Net realizable less a normal profit margin (NRV − NP) lower limit of market.

Net realizable value: the amount of cash the company expects to actually collect from customers.

Net realizable value (NRV) upper limit of market.

Neutrality neutral with respect to parties potentially affected.

Noncash investing and financing activities transactions that do not increase or decrease cash but that result in significant investing and financing activities.

Noninterest-bearing note notes that bear interest, but the interest is deducted (or discounted) from the face amount to determine the cash proceeds made available to the borrower at the outset.

Nonoperating income includes gains and losses and revenues and expenses related to peripheral or incidental activities of the company.

Nontemporary difference difference between pretax accounting income and taxable income and, consequently, between the reported amount of an asset or liability in the financial statements and its tax basis that will not "reverse" resulting from transactions and events that under existing tax law will never affect taxable income or taxes payable.

Note payable A promissory note (essentially an IOU) that obligates the issuing corporation to repay a stated amount at or by a specified maturity date and to pay interest to the lender between the issue date and maturity.

Notes receivable receivables supported by a formal agreement or note that specifies payment terms.

Objectives-oriented/principles-based accounting standards approach to standard setting stresses professional judgment, as opposed to following a list of rules.

Operating activities inflows and outflows of cash related to transactions entering into the determination of net income.

Operating cycle period of time necessary to convert cash to raw materials, raw materials to finished product, the finished product to receivables, and then finally receivables back to cash.

Operating income includes revenues and expenses directly related to the principal revenue-generating activities of the company.

Operating leases fundamental rights and responsibilities of ownership are retained by the lessor and that the lessee merely is using the asset temporarily.

Operating loss carryback reduction of prior (up to two) years' taxable income by a current net operating loss.

Operating loss forward reduction of future (up to 20) years' taxable income by a current net operating loss.

Operating segment a component of an enterprise that engages in business activities from which it may earn revenues and incur expenses (including revenues and expenses relating to transactions with other companies of the same enterprise); whose operating results are regularly reviewed by the enterprise's chief operating decision maker to make decisions about resources to be allocated to the segment and assess its performance; for which discrete financial information is available.

Operational assets property, plant, and equipment, along with intangible assets.

Operational risk how adept a company is at withstanding various events and circumstances that might impair its ability to earn profits.

Option gives the holder the right either to buy or sell a financial instrument at a specified price.

Option pricing models statistical models that incorporate information about a company's stock and the terms of the stock option to estimate the option's fair value.

Ordinary annuity cash flows occur at the end of each period.

Other comprehensive income certain gains and losses that are excluded from the calculation of net income, but included in the calculation of comprehensive income.

Paid-in capital invested capital consisting primarily of amounts invested by shareholders when they purchase shares of stock from the corporation.

Parenthetical comments/modifying comments supplemental information disclosed on the face of financial statements.

Participating preferred shareholders are allowed to receive additional dividends beyond the stated amount.

Patent exclusive right to manufacture a product or to use a process.

Pension plan assets employer contributions and accumulated earnings on the investment of those contributions to be used to pay retirement benefits to retired employees.

Percentage-of-completion method allocation of a share of a project's revenues and expenses to each reporting period during the contract period.

Periodic inventory system the merchandise inventory account balance is not adjusted as purchases and sales are made but only periodically at the end of a reporting period when a physical count of the period's ending inventory is made and costs are assigned to the quantities determined.

Periodicity assumption allows the life of a company to be divided into artificial time periods to provide timely information.

Permanent accounts represent assets, liabilities, and shareholders' equity at a point in time.

Perpetual inventory system account inventory is continually adjusted for each change in inventory, whether it's caused by a purchase, a sale, or a return of merchandise by the company to its supplier.

Pledging trade receivables in general rather than specific receivables are pledged as collateral; the responsibility for collection of the receivables remains solely with the company.

Point-of-sale the goods or services sold to the buyer are delivered (the title is transferred).

Post-closing trial balance verifies that the closing entries were prepared and posted correctly and that the accounts are now ready for next year's transactions.

Posting transferring debits and credits recorded in individual journal entries to the specific accounts affected.

Postretirement benefits all types of retiree benefits; may include medical coverage, dental coverage, life insurance, group legal services, and other benefits.

Potential common shares Securities that, while not being common stock may become common stock through their exercise, conversion, or issuance and therefore dilute (reduce) earnings per share.

Predictive value/feedback value confirmation of investor expectations about future cash-generating ability.

Preferred stock typically has a preference (a) to specified amount of dividends (stated dollar amount per share or percentage of par value per share) and (b) to distribution of assets in the event the corporation is dissolved.

Premium arises when bonds are sold for more than face amount.

Prepaid expense represents an asset recorded when an expense is paid in advance, creating benefits beyond the current period.

Prepayments/deferrals the cash flow precedes either expense or revenue recognition.

Present value today's equivalent to a particular amount in the future.

Prior period adjustment addition to or reduction in the beginning retained earnings balance in a statement of shareholders' equity due to a correction of an error.

Prior service cost the cost of credit given for an amendment to a pension plan to employee service rendered in prior years.

Product costs costs associated with products and expensed as cost of goods sold only when the related products are sold.

Profit margin on sales net income divided by net sales; measures the amount of net income achieved per sales dollar.

Pro forma earnings actual (GAAP) earnings reduced by any expenses the reporting company feels are unusual and should be excluded.

Projected benefit obligation (PBO) the discounted present value of estimated retirement benefits earned so far by employees, applying the plan's pension formula using projected future compensation levels.

Property dividend when a noncash asset is distributed.

Property, plant, and equipment land, buildings, equipment, machinery, autos, and trucks.

Prospective approach the accounting change is implemented in the present, and its effects are reflected in the financial statements of the current and future years only.

Proxy statement contains disclosures on compensation to directors and executives; sent to all shareholders each year.

Purchase commitments contracts that obligate a company to purchase a specified amount of merchandise or raw materials at specified prices on or before specified dates.

Purchase discounts reductions in the amount to be paid if remittance is made within a designated period of time.

Purchase return a reduction in both inventory and accounts payable (if the account has not yet been paid) at the time of the return.

Purchases journal records the purchase of merchandise on account.

Quasi reorganization a firm undergoing financial difficulties, but with favorable future prospects, may use a quasi reorganization to write down inflated asset values and eliminate an accumulated deficit.

Rate of return on stock investment

$$\frac{\text{Dividends + Share price appreciation}}{\text{Initial investment}}$$

Ratio analysis comparison of accounting numbers to evaluate the performance and risk of a firm.

Raw materials cost of components purchased from other manufacturers that will become part of the finished product.

Real estate lease involves land—exclusively or in part.

Realization principle requires that the earnings process is judged to be complete or virtually complete, and there is reasonable certainty as to the collectibility of the asset to be received (usually cash) before revenue can be recognized.

Rearrangements expenditures made to restructure an asset without addition, replacement, or improvement.

Receivables a company's claims to the future collection of cash, other assets, or services.

Receivables turnover ratio indicates how quickly a company is able to collect its accounts receivable.

Recognition process of admitting information into the basic financial statements.

Redemption privilege might allow preferred shareholders the option, under specified conditions, to return their shares for a predetermined redemption price.

Related-party transactions transactions with owners, management, families of owners or management, affiliated companies, and other parties that can significantly influence or be influenced by the company.

Relevance one of the primary decision-specific qualities that make accounting information useful; made up of predictive value and/or feedback value, and timeliness.

Reliability the extent to which information is verifiable, representationally faithful, and neutral.

Rent abatement lease agreements may call for uneven rent payments during the term of the lease, e.g., when the initial payment (or maybe several payments) is waived.

Replacement cost (RC) the cost to replace the item by purchase or manufacture.

Replacement depreciation method depreciation is recorded when assets are replaced.

Representational faithfulness agreement between a measure or description and the phenomenon it purports to represent.

Residual value or salvage value, the amount the company expects to receive for the asset at the end of its service life less any anticipated disposal costs.

Restoration costs costs to restore land or other property to its original condition after extraction of the natural resource ends.

Restricted stock shares subject to forfeiture by the employee if employment is terminated within some specified number of years from the date of grant.

Retail inventory method relies on the relationship between cost and selling price to estimate ending inventory and cost of goods sold; provides a more accurate estimate than the gross profit method.

Retained earnings amounts earned by the corporation on behalf of its shareholders and not (yet) distributed to them as dividends.

Retired stock shares repurchased and not designated as treasury stock.

Retirement depreciation method Records depreciation when assets are disposed of and measures depreciation as the difference between the proceeds received and cost.

Retrospective approach financial statements issued in previous years are revised to reflect the impact of an accounting change whenever those statements are presented again for comparative purpose.

Return on assets (ROA) indicates a company's overall profitability.

Return on shareholders' equity: Amount of profit management can generate from the assets that owners provide.

Revenues inflows or other enhancements of assets or settlements of liabilities from delivering or producing goods, rendering services, or other activities that constitute the entity's ongoing major, or central, operations.

Reverse stock split when a company decreases, rather than increases, its outstanding shares.

Reversing entries optional entries that remove the effects of some of the adjusting entries made at the end of the previous reporting period for the sole purpose of simplifying journal entries made during the new period.

Right of conversion shareholders' right to exchange shares of preferred stock for common stock at specified conversion ratio.

Right of return customers' right to return merchandise to retailers if they are not satisfied.

Rules-based accounting standards a list of rules for choosing the appropriate accounting treatment for a transaction.

S corporation characteristics of both regular corporations and partnerships.

SAB No. 101 *Staff Accounting Bulletin 101* summarizes the SEC's views on revenue recognition.

Sale-leaseback transaction the owner of an asset sells it and immediately leases it back from the new owner.

Sales journal records credit sales.

Sales return the return of merchandise for a refund or for credit to be applied to other purchases.

Sales-type lease in addition to interest revenue earned over the lease term, the lessor receives a manufacturer's or dealer's profit on the sale of the asset.

Sarbanes-Oxley Act law provides for the regulation of the key players in the financial reporting process.

Secondary market transactions provide for the transfer of stocks and bonds among individuals and institutions.

Securities and Exchange Commission (SEC) responsible for setting accounting and reporting standards for companies whose securities are publicly traded.

Securities available-for-sale equity or debt securities the investor acquires, not for an active trading account or to be held to maturity.

Securities to be held-to-maturity debt securities for which the investor has the "positive intent and ability" to hold the securities to maturity.

Securitization the company creates a special purpose entity (SPE), usually a trust or a subsidiary; the SPE buys a pool of trade receivables, credit card receivables, or loans from the company and then sells related securities.

Serial bonds more structured (and less popular) way to retire bonds on a piecemeal basis.

Service cost increase in the projected benefit obligation attributable to employee service performed during the period.

Service life (useful life) the estimated use that the company expects to receive from the asset.

Service method allocation approach that reflects the declining service pattern of the prior service cost.

Share purchase contract shares ordinarily are sold in exchange for a promissory note from the subscriber—in essence, shares are sold on credit.

Short-term investments investments not classified as cash equivalents that will be liquidated in the coming year or operating cycle, whichever is longer.

Significant influence effective control is absent but the investor is able to exercise significant influence over the operating and financial policies of the investee (usually between 20% and 50% of the investee's voting shares are held).

Simple capital structure a firm that has no potential common shares (outstanding securities that could potentially dilute earnings per share).

Simple interest computed by multiplying an initial investment times both the applicable interest rate and the period of time for which the money is used.

Single-step income statement format that groups all revenues and gains together and all expenses and losses together.

Sinking fund debentures bonds that must be redeemed on a prespecified year-by-year basis; administered by a trustee who repurchases bonds in the open market.

Source documents relay essential information about each transaction to the accountant, e.g., sales invoices, bills from suppliers, cash register tapes.

Special journal record of a repetitive type of transaction, e.g., a sales journal.

Specific identification method each unit sold during the period or each unit on hand at the end of the period to be matched with its actual cost.

Specific interest method for interest capitalization, rates from specific construction loans to the extent of specific borrowings are used before using the average rate of other debt.

Start-up costs whenever a company introduces a new product or service, or commences business in a new territory or with a new customer, it incurs one-time costs that are expensed in the period incurred.

Statement of cash flows change statement summarizing the transactions that caused cash to change during the period.

Statement of shareholders' equity statement disclosing the source of changes in the shareholders' equity accounts.

Stock appreciation rights (SARs) awards that enable an employee to benefit by the amount that the market price of the company's stock rises above a specified amount without having to buy shares.

Stock dividend distribution of additional shares of stock to current shareholders of the corporation.

Stock options employees aren't actually awarded shares, but rather are given the option to buy shares at a specified exercise price within some specified number of years from the date of grant.

Stock split stock distribution of 25% or higher, sometimes call a *large* stock dividend.

Straight line an equal amount of depreciable base is allocated to each year of the asset's service life.

Straight-line method recording interest each period at the same dollar amount.

Subordinated debenture the holder is not entitled to receive any liquidation payments until the claims of other specified debt issues are satisfied.

Subsequent event a significant development that takes place after the company's fiscal year-end but before the financial statements are issued.

Subsidiary ledger record of a group of subsidiary accounts associated with a particular general ledger control account.

Successful efforts method requires that exploration costs that are known not to have resulted in the discovery of oil or gas be included as expense in the period the expenditures are made.

Sum-of-the-years'-digits (SYD) method systematic acceleration of depreciation by multiplying the depreciable base by a fraction that declines each year.

Supplemental financial statements reports containing more detailed information than is shown in the primary financial statements.

T-account account with space at the top for the account title and two sides for recording increases and decreases.

Taxable income comprises revenues, expenses, gains, and losses as measured according to the regulations of the appropriate taxing authority.

Technological feasibility established when the enterprise has completed all planning, designing, coding, and testing activities that are necessary to establish that the product can be produced to meet its design specifications including functions, features, and technical performance requirements.

Temporary accounts represent changes in the retained earnings component of shareholders' equity for a corporation caused by revenue, expense, gain, and loss transactions.

Temporary difference difference between pretax accounting income and taxable income and, consequently, between the reported amount of an asset or liability in the financial statements and its tax basis which will "reverse" in later years.

Time-based methods allocates the cost base according to the passage of time.

Timeliness information that is available to users early enough to allow its use in the decision process.

Times interest earned ratio a way to gauge the ability of a company to satisfy its fixed debt obligations by comparing interest charges with the income available to pay those charges.

Time value of money money can be invested today to earn interest and grow to a larger dollar amount in the future.

Trade discounts percentage reduction from the list price.

Trademark (tradename) exclusive right to display a word, a slogan, a symbol, or an emblem that distinctively identifies a company, a product, or a service.

Trade notes payable formally recognized by a written promissory note.

Trading securities equity or debt securities the investor (usually a financial institution) acquires principally for the purpose of selling in the near term.

Transaction analysis process of reviewing the source documents to determine the dual effect on the accounting equation and the specific elements involved.

Transaction obligation the unfunded accumulated postretirement benefit obligation existing when *SFAS 106* was adopted.

Transactions economic events.

Treasury stock shares repurchased and not retired.

Troubled debt restructuring the original terms of a debt agreement are changed as a result of financial difficulties experienced by the debtor (borrower).

Trustee person who accepts employer contributions, invests the contributions, accumulates the earnings on the investments, and pays benefits from the plan assets to retired employees or their beneficiaries.

Unadjusted trial balance a list of the general ledger accounts and their balances at a particular date.

Understandability users must understand the information within the context of the decision being made.

Unearned revenues cash received from a customer in one period for goods or services that are to be provided in a future period.

Units-of-production method computes a depreciation rate per measure of activity and then multiplies this rate by actual activity to determine periodic depreciation.

Unqualified opinion auditors are satisfied that the financial statements present fairly the company's financial position, results of operations, and cash flows and are in conformity with generally accepted accounting principles.

Valuation allowance indirect reduction (contra account) in a deferred tax asset when it is more likely than not that some portion or all of the deferred tax asset will not be realized.

Verifiability implies a consensus among different measurers.

Vertical analysis expression of each item in the financial statements as a percentage of an appropriate corresponding total, or base amount, but within the same year.

Vested benefits benefits that employees have the right to receive even if their employment were to cease today.

Weighted-average interest method for interest capitalization, weighted-average rate on all interest-bearing debt, including all construction loans, is used.

Without recourse the buyer assumes the risk of uncollectibility.

With recourse the seller retains the risk of uncollectibility.

Working capital differences between current assets and current liabilities.

Work-in-process inventory products that are not yet complete.

Worksheet used to organize the accounting information needed to prepare adjusting and closing entries and the financial statements.

Photo Credits

Subject Index

Note: page numbers followed by *n* indicate material in footnotes.

Accounting Standards Index

Note: page numbers followed by *n* indicate material in footnotes.

Present and Future Value Tables

This table shows the future value of $1 at various interest rates (i) and time periods (n). It is used to calculate the future value of any single amount.

TABLE 1 Future Value of $1

$$FV = \$1\,(1 + i)^n$$

n/i	1.0%	1.5%	2.0%	2.5%	3.0%	3.5%	4.0%	4.5%	5.0%	5.5%	6.0%	7.0%	8.0%	9.0%	10.0%	11.0%	12.0%	20.0%
1	1.01000	1.01500	1.02000	1.02500	1.03000	1.03500	1.04000	1.04500	1.05000	1.05500	1.06000	1.07000	1.08000	1.09000	1.10000	1.11000	1.12000	1.20000
2	1.02010	1.03022	1.04040	1.05063	1.06090	1.07123	1.08160	1.09203	1.10250	1.11303	1.12360	1.14490	1.16640	1.18810	1.21000	1.23210	1.25440	1.44000
3	1.03030	1.04568	1.06121	1.07689	1.09273	1.10872	1.12486	1.14117	1.15763	1.17424	1.19102	1.22504	1.25971	1.29503	1.33100	1.36763	1.40493	1.72800
4	1.04060	1.06136	1.08243	1.10381	1.12551	1.14752	1.16986	1.19252	1.21551	1.23882	1.26248	1.31080	1.36049	1.41158	1.46410	1.51807	1.57352	2.07360
5	1.05101	1.07728	1.10408	1.13141	1.15927	1.18769	1.21665	1.24618	1.27628	1.30696	1.33823	1.40255	1.46933	1.53862	1.61051	1.68506	1.76234	2.48832
6	1.06152	1.09344	1.12616	1.15969	1.19405	1.22926	1.26532	1.30226	1.34010	1.37884	1.41852	1.50073	1.58687	1.67710	1.77156	1.87041	1.97382	2.98598
7	1.07214	1.10984	1.14869	1.18869	1.22987	1.27228	1.31593	1.36086	1.40710	1.45468	1.50363	1.60578	1.71382	1.82804	1.94872	2.07616	2.21068	3.58318
8	1.08286	1.12649	1.17166	1.21840	1.26677	1.31681	1.36857	1.42210	1.47746	1.53469	1.59385	1.71819	1.85093	1.99256	2.14359	2.30454	2.47596	4.29982
9	1.09369	1.14339	1.19509	1.24886	1.30477	1.36290	1.42331	1.48610	1.55133	1.61909	1.68948	1.83846	1.99900	2.17189	2.35795	2.55804	2.77308	5.15978
10	1.10462	1.16054	1.21899	1.28008	1.34392	1.41060	1.48024	1.55297	1.62889	1.70814	1.79085	1.96715	2.15892	2.36736	2.59374	2.83942	3.10585	6.19174
11	1.11567	1.17795	1.24337	1.31209	1.38423	1.45997	1.53945	1.62285	1.71034	1.80209	1.89830	2.10485	2.33164	2.58043	2.85312	3.15176	3.47855	7.43008
12	1.12683	1.19562	1.26824	1.34489	1.42576	1.51107	1.60103	1.69588	1.79586	1.90121	2.01220	2.25219	2.51817	2.81266	3.13843	3.49845	3.89598	8.91610
13	1.13809	1.21355	1.29361	1.37851	1.46853	1.56396	1.66507	1.77220	1.88565	2.00577	2.13293	2.40985	2.71962	3.06580	3.45227	3.88328	4.36349	10.69932
14	1.14947	1.23176	1.31948	1.41297	1.51259	1.61869	1.73168	1.85194	1.97993	2.11609	2.26090	2.57853	2.93719	3.34173	3.79750	4.31044	4.88711	12.83918
15	1.16097	1.25023	1.34587	1.44830	1.55797	1.67535	1.80094	1.93528	2.07893	2.23248	2.39656	2.75903	3.17217	3.64248	4.17725	4.78459	5.47357	15.40702
16	1.17258	1.26899	1.37279	1.48451	1.60471	1.73399	1.87298	2.02237	2.18287	2.35526	2.54035	2.95216	3.42594	3.97031	4.59497	5.31089	6.13039	18.48843
17	1.18430	1.28802	1.40024	1.52162	1.65285	1.79468	1.94790	2.11338	2.29202	2.48480	2.69277	3.15882	3.70002	4.32763	5.05447	5.89509	6.86604	22.18611
18	1.19615	1.30734	1.42825	1.55966	1.70243	1.85749	2.02582	2.20848	2.40662	2.62147	2.85434	3.37993	3.99602	4.71712	5.55992	6.54355	7.68997	26.62333
19	1.20811	1.32695	1.45681	1.59865	1.75351	1.92250	2.10685	2.30786	2.52695	2.76565	3.02560	3.61653	4.31570	5.14166	6.11591	7.26334	8.61276	31.94800
20	1.22019	1.34686	1.48595	1.63862	1.80611	1.98979	2.19112	2.41171	2.65330	2.91776	3.20714	3.86968	4.66096	5.60441	6.72750	8.06231	9.64629	38.33760
21	1.23239	1.36706	1.51567	1.67958	1.86029	2.05943	2.27877	2.52024	2.78596	3.07823	3.39956	4.14056	5.03383	6.10881	7.40025	8.94917	10.80385	46.00512
25	1.28243	1.45095	1.64061	1.85394	2.09378	2.36324	2.66584	3.00543	3.38635	3.81339	4.29187	5.42743	6.84848	8.62308	10.83471	13.58546	17.00006	95.39622
30	1.34785	1.56308	1.81136	2.09757	2.42726	2.80679	3.24340	3.74532	4.32194	4.98395	5.74349	7.61226	10.06266	13.26768	17.44940	22.89230	29.95992	237.37631
40	1.48886	1.81402	2.20804	2.68506	3.26204	3.95926	4.80102	5.81636	7.03999	8.51331	10.28572	14.97446	21.72452	31.40942	45.25926	65.00087	93.05097	1469.77160

This table shows the present value of $1 at various interest rates (i) and time periods (n). It is used to calculate the present value of any single amount.

TABLE 2 Present Value of $1

$$PV = \frac{\$1}{(1+i)^n}$$

n/i	1.0%	1.5%	2.0%	2.5%	3.0%	3.5%	4.0%	4.5%	5.0%	5.5%	6.0%	7.0%	8.0%	9.0%	10.0%	11.0%	12.0%	20.0%
1	0.99010	0.98522	0.98039	0.97561	0.97087	0.96618	0.96154	0.95694	0.95238	0.94787	0.94340	0.93458	0.92593	0.91743	0.90909	0.90090	0.89286	0.83333
2	0.98030	0.97066	0.96117	0.95181	0.94260	0.93351	0.92456	0.91573	0.90703	0.89845	0.89000	0.87344	0.85734	0.84168	0.82645	0.81162	0.79719	0.69444
3	0.97059	0.95632	0.94232	0.92860	0.91514	0.90194	0.88900	0.87630	0.86384	0.85161	0.83962	0.81630	0.79383	0.77218	0.75131	0.73119	0.71178	0.57870
4	0.96098	0.94218	0.92385	0.90595	0.88849	0.87144	0.85480	0.83856	0.82270	0.80722	0.79209	0.76290	0.73503	0.70843	0.68301	0.65873	0.63552	0.48225
5	0.95147	0.92826	0.90573	0.88385	0.86261	0.84197	0.82193	0.80245	0.78353	0.76513	0.74726	0.71299	0.68058	0.64993	0.62092	0.59345	0.56743	0.40188
6	0.94205	0.91454	0.88797	0.86230	0.83748	0.81350	0.79031	0.76790	0.74622	0.72525	0.70496	0.66634	0.63017	0.59627	0.56447	0.53464	0.50663	0.33490
7	0.93272	0.90103	0.87056	0.84127	0.81309	0.78599	0.75992	0.73483	0.71068	0.68744	0.66506	0.62275	0.58349	0.54703	0.51316	0.48166	0.45235	0.27908
8	0.92348	0.88771	0.85349	0.82075	0.78941	0.75941	0.73069	0.70319	0.67684	0.65160	0.62741	0.58201	0.54027	0.50187	0.46651	0.43393	0.40388	0.23257
9	0.91434	0.87459	0.83676	0.80073	0.76642	0.73373	0.70259	0.67290	0.64461	0.61763	0.59190	0.54393	0.50025	0.46043	0.42410	0.39092	0.36061	0.19381
10	0.90529	0.86167	0.82035	0.78120	0.74409	0.70892	0.67556	0.64393	0.61391	0.58543	0.55839	0.50835	0.46319	0.42241	0.38554	0.35218	0.32197	0.16151
11	0.89632	0.84893	0.80426	0.76214	0.72242	0.68495	0.64958	0.61620	0.58468	0.55491	0.52679	0.47509	0.42888	0.38753	0.35049	0.31728	0.28748	0.13459
12	0.88745	0.83639	0.78849	0.74356	0.70138	0.66178	0.62460	0.58966	0.55684	0.52598	0.49697	0.44401	0.39711	0.35553	0.31863	0.28584	0.25668	0.11216
13	0.87866	0.82403	0.77303	0.72542	0.68095	0.63940	0.60057	0.56427	0.53032	0.49856	0.46884	0.41496	0.36770	0.32618	0.28966	0.25751	0.22917	0.09346
14	0.86996	0.81185	0.75788	0.70773	0.66112	0.61778	0.57748	0.53997	0.50507	0.47257	0.44230	0.38782	0.34046	0.29925	0.26333	0.23199	0.20462	0.07789
15	0.86135	0.79985	0.74301	0.69047	0.64186	0.59689	0.55526	0.51672	0.48102	0.44793	0.41727	0.36245	0.31524	0.27454	0.23939	0.20900	0.18270	0.06491
16	0.85282	0.78803	0.72845	0.67362	0.62317	0.57671	0.53391	0.49447	0.45811	0.42458	0.39365	0.33873	0.29189	0.25187	0.21763	0.18829	0.16312	0.05409
17	0.84438	0.77639	0.71416	0.65720	0.60502	0.55720	0.51337	0.47318	0.43630	0.40245	0.37136	0.31657	0.27027	0.23107	0.19784	0.16963	0.14564	0.04507
18	0.83602	0.76491	0.70016	0.64117	0.58739	0.53836	0.49363	0.45280	0.41552	0.38147	0.35034	0.29586	0.25025	0.21199	0.17986	0.15282	0.13004	0.03756
19	0.82774	0.75361	0.68643	0.62553	0.57029	0.52016	0.47464	0.43330	0.39573	0.36158	0.33051	0.27651	0.23171	0.19449	0.16351	0.13768	0.11611	0.03130
20	0.81954	0.74247	0.67297	0.61027	0.55368	0.50257	0.45639	0.41464	0.37689	0.34273	0.31180	0.25842	0.21455	0.17843	0.14864	0.12403	0.10367	0.02608
21	0.81143	0.73150	0.65978	0.59539	0.53755	0.48557	0.43883	0.39679	0.35894	0.32486	0.29416	0.24151	0.19866	0.16370	0.13513	0.11174	0.09256	0.02174
24	0.78757	0.69954	0.62172	0.55288	0.49193	0.43796	0.39012	0.34770	0.31007	0.27666	0.24698	0.19715	0.15770	0.12640	0.10153	0.08170	0.06588	0.01258
25	0.77977	0.68921	0.60953	0.53939	0.47761	0.42315	0.37512	0.33273	0.29530	0.26223	0.23300	0.18425	0.14602	0.11597	0.09230	0.07361	0.05882	0.01048
28	0.75684	0.65910	0.57437	0.50088	0.43708	0.38165	0.33348	0.29157	0.25509	0.22332	0.19563	0.15040	0.11591	0.08955	0.06934	0.05382	0.04187	0.00607
29	0.74934	0.64936	0.56311	0.48866	0.42435	0.36875	0.32065	0.27902	0.24295	0.21168	0.18456	0.14056	0.10733	0.08215	0.06304	0.04849	0.03738	0.00506
30	0.74192	0.63976	0.55207	0.47674	0.41199	0.35628	0.30832	0.26700	0.23138	0.20064	0.17411	0.13137	0.09938	0.07537	0.05731	0.04368	0.03338	0.00421
31	0.73458	0.63031	0.54125	0.46511	0.39999	0.34423	0.29646	0.25550	0.22036	0.19018	0.16425	0.12277	0.09202	0.06915	0.05210	0.03935	0.02980	0.00351
40	0.67165	0.55126	0.45289	0.37243	0.30656	0.25257	0.20829	0.17193	0.14205	0.11746	0.09722	0.06678	0.04603	0.03184	0.02209	0.01538	0.01075	0.00068

This table shows the future value of an ordinary annuity of $1 at various interest rates (i) and time periods (n). It is used to calculate the future value of any series of equal payments made at the *end* of each compounding period.

TABLE 3 Future Value of an Ordinary Annuity of $1

$$FVA = \frac{(1+i)^n - 1}{i}$$

n/i	1.0%	1.5%	2.0%	2.5%	3.0%	3.5%	4.0%	4.5%	5.0%	5.5%	6.0%	7.0%	8.0%	9.0%	10.0%	11.0%	12.0%	20.0%
1	1.0000	1.0000	1.0000	1.0000	1.0000	1.0000	1.0000	1.0000	1.0000	1.0000	1.0000	1.0000	1.0000	1.0000	1.0000	1.0000	1.0000	1.0000
2	2.0100	2.0150	2.0200	2.0250	2.0300	2.0350	2.0400	2.0450	2.0500	2.0550	2.0600	2.0700	2.0800	2.0900	2.1000	2.1100	2.1200	2.2000
3	3.0301	3.0452	3.0604	3.0756	3.0909	3.1062	3.1216	3.1370	3.1525	3.1680	3.1836	3.2149	3.2464	3.2781	3.3100	3.3421	3.3744	3.6400
4	4.0604	4.0909	4.1216	4.1525	4.1836	4.2149	4.2465	4.2782	4.3101	4.3423	4.3746	4.4399	4.5061	4.5731	4.6410	4.7097	4.7793	5.3680
5	5.1010	5.1523	5.2040	5.2563	5.3091	5.3625	5.4163	5.4707	5.5256	5.5811	5.6371	5.7507	5.8666	5.9847	6.1051	6.2278	6.3528	7.4416
6	6.1520	6.2296	6.3081	6.3877	6.4684	6.5502	6.6330	6.7169	6.8019	6.8881	6.9753	7.1533	7.3359	7.5233	7.7156	7.9129	8.1152	9.9299
7	7.2135	7.3230	7.4343	7.5474	7.6625	7.7794	7.8983	8.0192	8.1420	8.2669	8.3938	8.6540	8.9228	9.2004	9.4872	9.7833	10.0890	12.9159
8	8.2857	8.4328	8.5830	8.7361	8.8923	9.0517	9.2142	9.3800	9.5491	9.7216	9.8975	10.2598	10.6366	11.0285	11.4359	11.8594	12.2997	16.4991
9	9.3685	9.5593	9.7546	9.9545	10.1591	10.3685	10.5828	10.8021	11.0266	11.2563	11.4913	11.9780	12.4876	13.0210	13.5795	14.1640	14.7757	20.7989
10	10.4622	10.7027	10.9497	11.2034	11.4639	11.7314	12.0061	12.2882	12.5779	12.8754	13.1808	13.8164	14.4866	15.1929	15.9374	16.7220	17.5487	25.9587
11	11.5668	11.8633	12.1687	12.4835	12.8078	13.1420	13.4864	13.8412	14.2068	14.5835	14.9716	15.7836	16.6455	17.5603	18.5312	19.5614	20.6546	32.1504
12	12.6825	13.0412	13.4121	13.7956	14.1920	14.6020	15.0258	15.4640	15.9171	16.3856	16.8699	17.8885	18.9771	20.1407	21.3843	22.7132	24.1331	39.5805
13	13.8093	14.2368	14.6803	15.1404	15.6178	16.1130	16.6268	17.1599	17.7130	18.2868	18.8821	20.1406	21.4953	22.9534	24.5227	26.2116	28.0291	48.4966
14	14.9474	15.4504	15.9739	16.5190	17.0863	17.6770	18.2919	18.9321	19.5986	20.2926	21.0151	22.5505	24.2149	26.0192	27.9750	30.0949	32.3926	59.1959
15	16.0969	16.6821	17.2934	17.9319	18.5989	19.2957	20.0236	20.7841	21.5786	22.4087	23.2760	25.1290	27.1521	29.3609	31.7725	34.4054	37.2797	72.0351
16	17.2579	17.9324	18.6393	19.3802	20.1569	20.9710	21.8245	22.7193	23.6575	24.6411	25.6725	27.8881	30.3243	33.0034	35.9497	39.1899	42.7533	87.4421
17	18.4304	19.2014	20.0121	20.8647	21.7616	22.7050	23.6975	24.7417	25.8404	26.9964	28.2129	30.8402	33.7502	36.9737	40.5447	44.5008	48.8837	105.9306
18	19.6147	20.4894	21.4123	22.3863	23.4144	24.4997	25.6454	26.8551	28.1324	29.4812	30.9057	33.9990	37.4502	41.3013	45.5992	50.3959	55.7497	128.1167
19	20.8109	21.7967	22.8406	23.9460	25.1169	26.3572	27.6712	29.0636	30.5390	32.1027	33.7600	37.3790	41.4463	46.0185	51.1591	56.9395	63.4397	154.7400
20	22.0190	23.1237	24.2974	25.5447	26.8704	28.2797	29.7781	31.3714	33.0660	34.8683	36.7856	40.9955	45.7620	51.1601	57.2750	64.2028	72.0524	186.6880
21	23.2392	24.4705	25.7833	27.1833	28.6765	30.2695	31.9692	33.7831	35.7193	37.7861	39.9927	44.8652	50.4229	56.7645	64.0025	72.2651	81.6987	225.0256
30	34.7849	37.5387	40.5681	43.9027	47.5754	51.6227	56.0849	61.0071	66.4388	72.4355	79.0582	94.4608	113.2832	136.3075	164.4940	199.0209	241.3327	1181.8816
40	48.8864	54.2679	60.4020	67.4026	75.4013	84.5503	95.0255	107.0303	120.7998	136.6056	154.7620	199.6351	259.0565	337.8824	442.5926	581.8261	767.0914	7343.8578

TABLE 4   Present Value of an Ordinary Annuity of $1

$$PVA = \frac{1 - \frac{1}{(1+i)^n}}{i}$$

n/i	1.0%	1.5%	2.0%	2.5%	3.0%	3.5%	4.0%	4.5%	5.0%	5.5%	6.0%	7.0%	8.0%	9.0%	10.0%	11.0%	12.0%	20.0%
1	0.99010	0.98522	0.98039	0.97561	0.97087	0.96618	0.96154	0.95694	0.95238	0.94787	0.94340	0.93458	0.92593	0.91743	0.90909	0.90090	0.89286	0.83333
2	1.97040	1.95588	1.94156	1.92742	1.91347	1.89969	1.88609	1.87267	1.85941	1.84632	1.83339	1.80802	1.78326	1.75911	1.73554	1.71252	1.69005	1.52778
3	2.94099	2.91220	2.88388	2.85602	2.82861	2.80164	2.77509	2.74896	2.72325	2.69793	2.67301	2.62432	2.57710	2.53129	2.48685	2.44371	2.40183	2.10648
4	3.90197	3.85438	3.80773	3.76197	3.71710	3.67308	3.62990	3.58753	3.54595	3.50515	3.46511	3.38721	3.31213	3.23972	3.16987	3.10245	3.03735	2.58873
5	4.85343	4.78264	4.71346	4.64583	4.57971	4.51505	4.45182	4.38998	4.32948	4.27028	4.21236	4.10020	3.99271	3.88965	3.79079	3.69590	3.60478	2.99061
6	5.79548	5.69719	5.60143	5.50813	5.41719	5.32855	5.24214	5.15787	5.07569	4.99553	4.91732	4.76654	4.62288	4.48592	4.35526	4.23054	4.11141	3.32551
7	6.72819	6.59821	6.47199	6.34939	6.23028	6.11454	6.00205	5.89270	5.78637	5.68297	5.58238	5.38929	5.20637	5.03295	4.86842	4.71220	4.56376	3.60459
8	7.65168	7.48593	7.32548	7.17014	7.01969	6.87396	6.73274	6.59589	6.46321	6.33457	6.20979	5.97130	5.74664	5.53482	5.33493	5.14612	4.96764	3.83716
9	8.56602	8.36052	8.16224	7.97087	7.78611	7.60769	7.43533	7.26879	7.10782	6.95220	6.80169	6.51523	6.24689	5.99525	5.75902	5.53705	5.32825	4.03097
10	9.47130	9.22218	8.98259	8.75206	8.53020	8.31661	8.11090	7.91272	7.72173	7.53763	7.36009	7.02358	6.71008	6.41766	6.14457	5.88923	5.65022	4.19247
11	10.36763	10.07112	9.78685	9.51421	9.25262	9.00155	8.76048	8.52892	8.30641	8.09254	7.88687	7.49867	7.13896	6.80519	6.49506	6.20652	5.93770	4.32706
12	11.25508	10.90751	10.57534	10.25776	9.95400	9.66333	9.38507	9.11858	8.86325	8.61852	8.38384	7.94269	7.53608	7.16073	6.81369	6.49236	6.19437	4.43922
13	12.13374	11.73153	11.34837	10.98319	10.63496	10.30274	9.98565	9.68285	9.39357	9.11708	8.85268	8.35765	7.90378	7.48690	7.10336	6.74987	6.42355	4.53268
14	13.00370	12.54338	12.10625	11.69091	11.29607	10.92052	10.56312	10.22283	9.89864	9.58965	9.29498	8.74547	8.24424	7.78615	7.36669	6.98187	6.62817	4.61057
15	13.86505	13.34323	12.84926	12.38138	11.93794	11.51741	11.11839	10.73955	10.37966	10.03758	9.71225	9.10791	8.55948	8.06069	7.60608	7.19087	6.81086	4.67547
16	14.71787	14.13126	13.57771	13.05500	12.56110	12.09412	11.65230	11.23402	10.83777	10.46216	10.10590	9.44665	8.85137	8.31256	7.82371	7.37916	6.97399	4.72956
17	15.56225	14.90765	14.29187	13.71220	13.16612	12.65132	12.16567	11.70719	11.27407	10.86461	10.47726	9.76322	9.12164	8.54363	8.02155	7.54879	7.11963	4.77463
18	16.39827	15.67256	14.99203	14.35336	13.75351	13.18968	12.65930	12.15999	11.68959	11.24607	10.82760	10.05909	9.37189	8.75563	8.20141	7.70162	7.24967	4.81219
19	17.22601	16.42617	15.67846	14.97889	14.32380	13.70984	13.13394	12.59329	12.08532	11.60765	11.15812	10.33560	9.60360	8.95011	8.36492	7.83929	7.36578	4.84350
20	18.04555	17.16864	16.35143	15.58916	14.87747	14.21240	13.59033	13.00794	12.46221	11.95038	11.46992	10.59401	9.81815	9.12855	8.51356	7.96333	7.46944	4.86958
21	18.85698	17.90014	17.01121	16.18455	15.41502	14.69797	14.02916	13.40472	12.82115	12.27524	11.76408	10.83553	10.01680	9.29224	8.64869	8.07507	7.56200	4.89132
25	22.02316	20.71961	19.52346	18.42438	17.41315	16.48151	15.62208	14.82821	14.09394	13.41393	12.78336	11.65358	10.67478	9.82258	9.07704	8.42174	7.84314	4.94759
30	25.80771	24.01584	22.39646	20.93029	19.60044	18.39205	17.29203	16.28889	15.37245	14.53375	13.76483	12.40904	11.25778	10.27365	9.42691	8.69379	8.05518	4.97894
40	32.83469	29.91585	27.35548	25.10278	23.11477	21.35507	19.79277	18.40158	17.15909	16.04612	15.04630	13.33171	11.92461	10.75736	9.77905	8.95105	8.24378	4.99660

This table shows the present value of an ordinary annuity of $1 at various interest rates (*i*) and time periods (*n*). It is used to calculate the present value of any series of equal payments made at the *end* of each compounding period.

This table shows the future value of an annuity due of $1 at various interest rates (i) and time periods (n). It is used to calculate the future value of any series of equal payments made at the *beginning* of each compounding period.

TABLE 5 Future Value of an Annuity Due of $1

$$FVAD = \left[\frac{(1+i)^n - 1}{i}\right] \times (1+i)$$

n/i	1.0%	1.5%	2.0%	2.5%	3.0%	3.5%	4.0%	4.5%	5.0%	5.5%	6.0%	7.0%	8.0%	9.0%	10.0%	11.0%	12.0%	20.0%
1	1.0100	1.0150	1.0200	1.0250	1.0300	1.0350	1.0400	1.0450	1.0500	1.0550	1.0600	1.0700	1.0800	1.0900	1.1000	1.1100	1.1200	1.2000
2	2.0301	2.0452	2.0604	2.0756	2.0909	2.1062	2.1216	2.1370	2.1525	2.1680	2.1836	2.2149	2.2464	2.2781	2.3100	2.3421	2.3744	2.6400
3	3.0604	3.0909	3.1216	3.1525	3.1836	3.2149	3.2465	3.2782	3.3101	3.3423	3.3746	3.4399	3.5061	3.5731	3.6410	3.7097	3.7793	4.3680
4	4.1010	4.1523	4.2040	4.2563	4.3091	4.3625	4.4163	4.4707	4.5256	4.5811	4.6371	4.7507	4.8666	4.9847	5.1051	5.2278	5.3528	6.4416
5	5.1520	5.2296	5.3081	5.3877	5.4684	5.5502	5.6330	5.7169	5.8019	5.8881	5.9753	6.1533	6.3359	6.5233	6.7156	6.9129	7.1152	8.9299
6	6.2135	6.3230	6.4343	6.5474	6.6625	6.7794	6.8983	7.0192	7.1420	7.2669	7.3938	7.6540	7.9228	8.2004	8.4872	8.7833	9.0890	11.9159
7	7.2857	7.4328	7.5830	7.7361	7.8923	8.0517	8.2142	8.3800	8.5491	8.7216	8.8975	9.2598	9.6366	10.0285	10.4359	10.8594	11.2997	15.4991
8	8.3685	8.5593	8.7546	8.9545	9.1591	9.3685	9.5828	9.8021	10.0266	10.2563	10.4913	10.9780	11.4876	12.0210	12.5795	13.1640	13.7757	19.7989
9	9.4622	9.7027	9.9497	10.2034	10.4639	10.7314	11.0061	11.2882	11.5779	11.8754	12.1808	12.8164	13.4866	14.1929	14.9374	15.7220	16.5487	24.9587
10	10.5668	10.8633	11.1687	11.4835	11.8078	12.1420	12.4864	12.8412	13.2068	13.5835	13.9716	14.7836	15.6455	16.5603	17.5312	18.5614	19.6546	31.1504
11	11.6825	12.0412	12.4121	12.7956	13.1920	13.6020	14.0258	14.4640	14.9171	15.3856	15.8699	16.8885	17.9771	19.1407	20.3843	21.7132	23.1331	38.5805
12	12.8093	13.2368	13.6803	14.1404	14.6178	15.1130	15.6268	16.1599	16.7130	17.2868	17.8821	19.1406	20.4953	21.9534	23.5227	25.2116	27.0291	47.4966
13	13.9474	14.4504	14.9739	15.5190	16.0863	16.6770	17.2919	17.9321	18.5986	19.2926	20.0151	21.5505	23.2149	25.0192	26.9750	29.0949	31.3926	58.1959
14	15.0969	15.6821	16.2934	16.9319	17.5989	18.2957	19.0236	19.7841	20.5786	21.4087	22.2760	24.1290	26.1521	28.3609	30.7725	33.4054	36.2797	71.0351
15	16.2579	16.9324	17.6393	18.3802	19.1569	19.9710	20.8245	21.7193	22.6575	23.6411	24.6725	26.8881	29.3243	32.0034	34.9497	38.1899	41.7533	86.4421
16	17.4304	18.2014	19.0121	19.8647	20.7616	21.7050	22.6975	23.7417	24.8404	25.9964	27.2129	29.8402	32.7502	35.9737	39.5447	43.5008	47.8837	104.9306
17	18.6147	19.4894	20.4123	21.3863	22.4144	23.4997	24.6454	25.8551	27.1324	28.4812	29.9057	32.9990	36.4502	40.3013	44.5992	49.3959	54.7497	127.1167
18	19.8109	20.7967	21.8406	22.9460	24.1169	25.3572	26.6712	28.0636	29.5390	31.1027	32.7600	36.3790	40.4463	45.0185	50.1591	55.9395	62.4397	153.7400
19	21.0190	22.1237	23.2974	24.5447	25.8704	27.2797	28.7781	30.3714	32.0660	33.8683	35.7856	39.9955	44.7620	50.1601	56.2750	63.2028	71.0524	185.6880
20	22.2392	23.4705	24.7833	26.1833	27.6765	29.2695	30.9692	32.7831	34.7193	36.7861	38.9927	43.8652	49.4229	55.7645	63.0025	71.2651	80.6987	224.0256
21	23.4716	24.8376	26.2990	27.8629	29.5368	31.3289	33.2480	35.3034	37.5052	39.8643	42.3923	48.0057	54.4568	61.8733	70.4027	80.2143	91.5026	270.0307
25	28.5256	30.5140	32.6709	35.0117	37.5530	40.3131	43.3117	46.5706	50.1135	53.9660	58.1564	67.6765	78.9544	92.3240	108.1818	126.9988	149.3339	566.3773
30	35.1327	38.1018	41.3794	45.0003	49.0027	53.4295	58.3283	63.7524	69.7608	76.4194	83.8017	101.0730	122.3459	148.5752	180.9434	220.9132	270.2926	1418.2579
40	49.3752	55.0819	61.6100	69.0876	77.6633	87.5095	98.8265	111.8467	126.8398	144.1189	164.0477	213.6096	279.7810	368.2919	486.8518	645.8269	859.1424	8812.6294